THE
unofficial GUIDE®
TO Walt Disney World®

2016

COME CHECK US OUT!

Other *Unofficial Guides*

Beyond Disney: The Unofficial Guide to Universal Orlando, SeaWorld, & the Best of Central Florida

The Disneyland Story: The Unofficial Guide to the Evolution of Walt Disney's Dream

Mini-Mickey: The Pocket-Sized Unofficial Guide to Walt Disney World

Universal vs. Disney: The Unofficial Guide to American Theme Parks' Greatest Rivalry

The Unofficial Guide Color Companion to Walt Disney World

The Unofficial Guide to Disney Cruise Line

The Unofficial Guide to Disneyland

The Unofficial Guide to Las Vegas

The Unofficial Guide to Universal Orlando

The Unofficial Guide to Walt Disney World with Kids

The Unofficial Guide to Washington, D.C.

THE *unofficial* GUIDE®
TO Walt Disney World®

2016

BOB SEHLINGER *and* LEN TESTA

(Walt Disney World® is officially known as Walt Disney World® Resort.)

!k
keen
communications

Please note that prices fluctuate in the course of time and that travel information changes under the impact of many factors that influence the travel industry. We therefore suggest that you write or call ahead for confirmation when making your travel plans. Every effort has been made to ensure the accuracy of information throughout this book, and the contents of this publication are believed to be correct at the time of printing. Nevertheless, the publishers cannot accept responsibility for errors or omissions, for changes in details given in this guide, or for the consequences of any reliance on the information provided by the same. Assessments of attractions and so forth are based upon the authors' own experiences; therefore, descriptions given in this guide necessarily contain an element of subjective opinion, which may not reflect the publisher's opinion or dictate a reader's own experience on another occasion. Readers are invited to write the publisher with ideas, comments, and suggestions for future editions.

The Unofficial Guides
An imprint of Keen Communications, LLC
2204 1st Ave. S., Suite 102
Birmingham, AL 35233
theunofficialguides.com, facebook.com/theunofficialguides, twitter.com/theugseries

Cover design by Scott McGrew

Text design by Vertigo Design and Annie Long

For information on our other products and services or to obtain technical support, please contact us from within the United States at 888-604-4537 or by fax at 205-326-1012.

Keen Communications, LLC, also publishes its books in a variety of electronic formats. Some content that appears in print may not be available in electronic formats.

ISBN: 978-1-62809-036-9, eISBN: 978-1-62809-037-6

Distributed by Publishers Group West

Manufactured in the United States of America

5 4 3 2 1

CONTENTS

LIST *of* MAPS *and* DIAGRAMS

INTRODUCTION

■ WHY "UNOFFICIAL"?

DECLARATION OF INDEPENDENCE

THE AUTHORS AND RESEARCHERS of this guide specifically and categorically declare that they are and always have been totally independent of the Walt Disney Company, Inc.; of Disneyland, Inc.; of Walt Disney World, Inc.; and of any and all other members of the Disney corporate family not listed.

The material in this guide originated with the authors and researchers and has not been reviewed, edited, or approved by the Walt Disney Company, Inc.; Disneyland, Inc.; or Walt Disney World, Inc.

This guidebook represents the first comprehensive *critical* appraisal of Walt Disney World. Its purpose is to provide the reader with the information necessary to tour Walt Disney World with the greatest efficiency and economy and with the least hassle.

In this guide, we represent and serve you. If a restaurant serves bad food or a gift item is overpriced or a ride isn't worth the wait, we say so, and in the process we hope to make your visit more fun and rewarding.

DANCE TO THE MUSIC

A DANCE HAS A BEGINNING and an end. But when you're dancing, you're not concerned about getting to the end or where on the dance floor you might wind up. In other words, you're totally in the moment. That's the way you should be on your Walt Disney World vacation.

You may feel a bit of pressure concerning your vacation. Vacations, after all, are very special events—and expensive ones to boot. So you work hard to make your vacation the best that it can be. Planning and organizing are essential to a successful Walt Disney World vacation, but if they become your focus, you won't be able to hear the music and enjoy the dance.

So think of us as your dancing coaches. We'll teach you the steps to the dance in advance so that when you're on vacation and the music plays, you'll dance with effortless grace and ease.

THE IMPORTANCE OF BEING GOOFY

THE DISNEY-CHARACTER PHYSICIAN is having lunch with the director of park operations when the doc's phone rings. . . .

"Excuse me," he says. "It's the fertility clinic—I'd better take it." Getting up, he exits the restaurant and returns a few minutes later looking concerned.

"It's the darndest thing," the doctor says. "But there's not a thing wrong with any of them. . . ."

"Any of whom?" the director asks.

"The Disney princes and princesses. They all checked out fine."

The director can't believe his ears. He stares at the doctor. "Wait a minute—are you telling me that you sent the Disney princes and princesses to a *fertility clinic?*"

"Just the human ones who are married, plus the Beast. I didn't send Mickey and Minnie, Donald and Daisy, Lady and the Tramp, and a bunch of others who've been coupled up for decades."

Still stupefied, the director stammers, "Why? I didn't even know there was a problem."

"Well, the characters have never complained, but most have been married for years and years, and, um . . . haven't you noticed that none of them have any children?"

"I've never given it any thought, but it's fewer high-earning characters on my payroll."

"Well, *I've* given it plenty of thought. We're locked in a blood-feud competition with Universal, and *their* characters are having babies right and left. Shrek and Princess Fiona alone have been popping out little ogres and ogre-ettes like Big Macs."

The director gives the doctor a hard look. "I could have told you there's nothing wrong physically with the princes and princesses."

"If that's the case, why aren't they having children? Don't they know about the birds and the bees?"

"*The birds and the bees shall not be spoken of at Disney!* But that's not why they don't have kids."

"Then why?"

The director leans across the table to keep from being overheard. "Why do you think princes and princesses live 'happily ever after'?"

And so it goes. . . .

What really makes writing about Walt Disney World fun is that the Disney people take everything so seriously. Day to day, they debate momentous decisions with far-ranging consequences: Will Pluto look silly in a silver cape? Have we gone too far with The Little Mermaid's cleavage? With the nation's drug problem a constant concern, should we have a dwarf named Dopey?

Unofficially, we think having a sense of humor is important. This guidebook has one, and it's probably necessary that you do, too—not to use this book, but to have the most fun possible at Walt Disney World. Think of the *Unofficial Guide* as a private trainer to help get your sense of humor in shape. It will help you understand the importance of being Goofy.

HONEY, I BLEW UP THE BOOK!

THE FIRST EDITION OF *The Unofficial Guide to Walt Disney World* was fewer than 200 pages, a mere shadow of its current size. Since that edition, Disney World has grown tremendously. The *Unofficial Guide* has grown to match this expansion.

A mom from Streator, Illinois, is amazed by the size of the *Unofficial Guide,* writing not unsympathetically:

> It had been 10 years since we'd been to WDW, and I was shocked by how the size of your book grew. After going, I'm surprised that it's so small.

The good news is that we're working with leading scientists to put the entire book on a computer chip implanted directly in your brain! In the meantime, we offer a qualified apology for the bulk of this edition. We know it may be too heavy to carry comfortably, but we defend the inclusion of all the information presented. Not every diner uses ketchup, A.1. sauce, or Tabasco, but it's nice to have all three on the table.

Concerning *Unofficial Guide* content, readers have offered these suggestions for new material:

- *I think your guide should have a list of attractions that provide (1) seats, (2) air-conditioning, and (3) at least 15 minutes off your feet.*

- *I feel the* Unofficial Guide *should include a claustrophobia rating for each attraction.*

- *I wish you'd discuss restrooms more in the next edition. I found myself constantly searching for one.*

- *We think you need a rating system regarding water [i.e., how wet you can expect to get on specific attractions]. EW = Extreme Water; SW = Some Water; M = Mist.*

These comments are representative in that many of you would like more detailed coverage of one thing or another. We've debated adding hundreds of things, but we haven't done so. Why? Because we don't have an infinite number of pages to work with, and we felt other information was more important. New ideas for book material are usually tested first at **blog.touringplans.com,** so check there to see what your fellow readers have suggested.

YOUR *UNOFFICIAL* WALT DISNEY WORLD TOOLBOX

WHEN IT COMES TO WALT DISNEY WORLD, a couple with two toddlers in diapers needs different advice than a party of seniors going to the Epcot International Flower & Garden Festival. Likewise, adults touring without children, families with kids of varying ages, and honeymooners all require their own special guidance.

To meet the varying needs of our readers, we've created the very comprehensive guide before you. We call **The Unofficial Guide to Walt Disney World,** at about 850 pages, the "Big Book." It contains the detailed information that anyone traveling to Walt Disney World needs to have a super vacation. It's our cornerstone.

As thorough as we try to make the main guide, there just isn't sufficient space for all the tips and resources that may be useful to certain readers. Therefore, we've developed five additional guides that provide information tailored to specific visitors.

Here's what's in the toolbox:

The Unofficial Guide Color Companion to Walt Disney World, by Bob Sehlinger and Len Testa, proves that a picture is *indeed* worth a thousand words. In the Big Book, for instance, you can learn about the best guest rooms to request at the Wilderness Lodge, but in the *Color Companion* you can *see* the rooms, along with the pool and the magnificent lobby. Full-color photos show how long the lines get at different times of day, how wet riders get on Splash Mountain, and how the parks are decked out for various holidays. Most of all, the *Color Companion* is for fun. For the first time, we're able to use photography to express our zany *Unofficial* sense of humor. Think of it as Monty Python meets Walt Disney . . . in Technicolor.

The Unofficial Guide to Disney Cruise Line, by Len Testa with Laurel Stewart, Erin Foster, and Ritchey Halphen, presents advice for first-time cruisers; money-saving tips for booking your cruise; and detailed profiles for restaurants, shows, and nightclubs, along with deck plans and thorough coverage of the ports visited by DCL.

The Unofficial Guide to Walt Disney World with Kids, by Bob Sehlinger and Liliane J. Opsomer with Len Testa, presents detailed planning and touring tips for a family vacation, along with more than 20 family touring plans that are exclusive to this book.

Mini-Mickey: The Pocket-Sized Unofficial Guide to Walt Disney World, by Bob Sehlinger, Len Testa, and Ritchey Halphen, is a CliffsNotes-style portable version of the Big Book. It distills information to help short-stay or last-minute visitors decide quickly how to plan their limited hours at Disney World.

Beyond Disney: The Unofficial Guide to Universal Orlando, SeaWorld, and the Best of Central Florida, by Bob Sehlinger and Seth Kubersky with Len Testa, is a guide to non-Disney theme parks, attractions, restaurants, outdoor recreation, and nightlife in Orlando and Central Florida.

THE DEATH OF SPONTANEITY

ONE OF OUR ALL-TIME FAVORITE LETTERS came from a man in Chapel Hill, North Carolina:

> *Your book reads like the operations plan for an amphibious landing: Go here, do this, proceed to Step 15. You must think that everyone is a hyperactive, type-A theme park commando. What happened to the satisfaction of self-discovery or the joy of spontaneity? Next you'll be telling us when to empty our bladders.*

(We'd love to hear this reader's thoughts on FastPass+, which lets you reserve spots on popular rides two months in advance.)

As it happens, we *Unofficial Guide* researchers are a pretty existential crew who are big on self-discovery. But Disney World—especially for first-time travelers—probably isn't the place you want to "discover" the spontaneity of needless waits in line or mediocre meals when you could be doing better.

In many ways, Disney's theme parks are the quintessential system, the ultimate in mass-produced entertainment, the most planned and programmed environment anywhere. Lines for rides form in predictable ways at predictable times, for example, and you can either learn here how to avoid them or "discover" them on your own.

We aren't saying that you can't have a great time at Walt Disney World. What we *are* saying is that you should think about what you want to do before you go. The time and money you save by planning will help your family have more fun.

THE BIG HURT

GOOD PLANNING for a Walt Disney World vacation takes time, effort, and creativity. If you're lucky enough to have someone in your group to take on the responsibility of planning, don't throw them under the bus the second you hit the theme parks. Take to heart the experience of this Manassas, Virginia, mom:

> First, if you're allowing one member of your group to plan your days in the park, FOLLOW THEIR PLAN! This is not the time to decide that you know better. Secondly, a Disney vacation is not for being lazy or sleeping in. If that's what you want out of a vacation, then please go to the Caribbean and drink rum for three days. A Disney vacation takes planning, and a lot of it. Once you're there, it's doubtful that you'll do better on your own. This is not the place for "let's see what we feel like when we get there and then we'll make some plans."

DON'T LET THE TAIL WAG THE DOG

SOME FOLKS BECOME SO INVESTED in their plan that it becomes the centerpiece of the vacation. Witness this Columbia, Missouri, mom:

> Getting to the park when it opens is the key to beating the lines. To make that happen: (1) Pack breakfast on the go—you can eat your Pop-Tarts once you're on the shuttle bus, then drink your juice while you wait in line for Dumbo. (2) Send the fastest runner in your party to jump on the bus or boat; the driver will wait if he sees you coming and one of your kids is already hanging on. (3) Showering wastes precious park and rest time; the pool will do. (4) Braid your daughter's hair. Seriously. My 8-year-old never had to brush her hair in the morning. (5) Ball caps for boys also avoid hair brushing.

The stress and doggedness of such an approach would push most of us over the edge. So remember the basics: Know thyself, nothing to excess, and concentrate on having fun.

WE'VE GOT ATTITUDE

SOME READERS DISAGREE with our attitude toward Disney. A woman from Golden, Colorado, lambastes us:

> I read your book cover-to-cover and felt you were way too hard on Disney. It's disappointing when you're all enthused about going to Walt Disney World to be slammed with all these criticisms.

A reader from Little Rock, Arkansas, takes us to task for the opposite prejudice:

Your book was quite complimentary of Disney, perhaps too complimentary. Maybe the free trips you travel writers get at Disney World are chipping away at your objectivity.

And from a Williamsport, Pennsylvania, mother of three:

Reading your book irritated me before we went to Disney World because of all the warnings and cautions. I guess I'm used to having guidebooks pump me up about where I'm going. But once I arrived, I found I was fully prepared and we had a great time. In retrospect, I have to admit you were right on the money. What I regarded as you being negative was just a good dose of reality.

Finally, a reader from Phoenixville, Pennsylvania, prefers no opinions at all, writing:

While each person has the right to his or her own opinion, I didn't purchase the book for an opinion.

For the record, we've always paid our own way at Walt Disney World: hotels, admissions, meals, the works. We don't dislike Disney, and we don't have an ax to grind. Personally, we have enjoyed the Disney parks immensely over the years, both experiencing them and writing about them. Disney, however, as with all corporations (and all people), is better at some things than others. Because our readers shell out big bucks to go to Walt Disney World, we believe they have the right to know in advance what's good and what's not. For those who think we're overly positive, please understand that the *Unofficial Guide* is a guidebook, not an exposé. Our aim is for you to enjoy your visit. To that end, we report fairly and objectively. When readers disagree with our opinions, we, in the interest of fairness, publish their viewpoints alongside ours. To the best of our knowledge, the *Unofficial Guides* are the only travel guides in print that do this.

THE SUM OF ALL FEARS

EVERY WRITER WHO EXPRESSES an opinion is accustomed to readers who strongly agree or disagree: It comes with the territory. Extremely troubling, however, is the possibility that our efforts to be objective have frightened some readers away from Walt Disney World or made others apprehensive.

A mom from Avon, Ohio, was just such a person, writing:

After reading parts of the Unofficial Guide, *I seriously reconsidered going to WDW at all because I felt it required too much planning— too many things that could go wrong, too many horrible outcomes (like waiting for hours in scorching heat with kids), etc. A friend convinced me it wouldn't be that bad, so I kept on with planning the trip.*

We certainly understand the reader's feelings, but the key point was that, though apprehensive, she stayed the course. Here's what she said after returning home:

Let me tell you, your guide and touring plans were dead-on accurate! We didn't wait more than 10 or 15 minutes for almost every attraction in two days!

For the record, if you love theme parks, Disney World is as good as it gets—absolute nirvana. If you arrive without knowing a thing about the place and make every possible mistake, chances are about 90% that you'll have a wonderful vacation anyway. The job of a guidebook is to give you a heads-up regarding opportunities and potential problems. We're certain we can help you turn a great vacation into an absolutely *superb* one.

TOO MANY COOKS IN THE KITCHEN?

WE RECEIVED THIS QUERY from a Manchester, Vermont, reader and feel it deserves a serious response:

> I read a review on the Internet criticizing the Unofficial Guide because it was "written by a team of researchers." The reviewer doesn't say why he thinks the team approach is inferior, but the inference is along the lines of "too many cooks spoil the soup." Why do you use this approach?

There are several reasons. Most guidebooks do a reasonably good job with the what and where; *Unofficial Guides* add the how and why. Describing attractions or hotels or restaurants (the what) at a given destination (the where) is the foundation of other travel guidebooks. We know from our research, though, that our readers like to know how things work.

unofficial TIP
Researching and writing this book as a team results in a more objective guidebook for you.

However, no individual author can possibly be qualified to write about every topic in the vast range of important subjects that make up a good guide to Walt Disney World. Our team approach enables us to provide deeper explanations of Disney's operations and undertake much more sophisticated and extensive research. Creating touring plans (see page 79), for example, requires statisticians who can analyze millions of attraction wait times to predict how and why lines will build throughout any day. Another project, monitoring the Disney transportation system, requires riding and timing every bus, boat, and monorail route, a task that takes four researchers almost a week to complete. Our Walt Disney World with Kids chapter (Part Five) was developed in consultation with three nationally respected child psychologists and an advisory group of parents. Similarly, our professional culinary experts ensure, say, that the *pollo al forno* you order at Epcot's Italy Pavilion is a decent approximation of what you might get in Rome.

We also conduct extensive research on you, the reader. Your tastes, preferences, and opinions—expressed in reader surveys, e-mails, and blog comments—dictate the subjects we research and the content of our books. Other guides are researched and developed by individual authors or coauthors, the content filtered through the lens of their tastes, preferences, and opinions. Publishers of these guides hope the information is compatible with the needs of the reader—but if it is, the compatibility is largely accidental.

Known and respected in both the travel industry and academe, *Unofficial Guide* research has been recognized by the BBC, CNN, the *Dallas Morning News, The New York Times,* the Travel Channel,

USA Today, and Wired.com, plus numerous academic journals. We (Bob and Len) put the fruits of our research into words, but behind us is an organization unequaled in travel publishing.

THE *UNOFFICIAL* TEAM

SO WHO ARE THESE FOLKS? Allow us to introduce them all, except for our dining critic, who shall remain anonymous:

Steve Bloom is the voice of reason in the wilderness that is statistical analysis. Gerelyn Reaves answers e-mail better than we could and generally keeps everyone in line. Seth Kubersky is our Universal Orlando guru, assisted by food *consigliere* Derek Burgan. David Davies is our jack-of-all-trades; Brad Huber assists with software development. Brian McNichols does Disney bar "research" and whatever photographer Tom Bricker tells him. Todd Perlmutter and Bryan Klinck skillfully debugged our touring plan software. Our Lines app was created by Henry Work, who's now trying to perfect soccer-playing animatronics for Disney. Lines' chat is moderated by the fabulous weasus.

We'd like to thank the following folks for their assistance with fact-checking: Lines users bwalker75, Jags, JenWSU, Keithloveswaffles, LoisLane, MissingDisney, mossmacl, and onehappysahm, along with Erin Foster, Melissa Adele Haskin, Marie Hillin, Richard and Lillian Macko, Sara Moore, and Darcie Vance.

BOB SEHLINGER Author and publisher | **LEN TESTA** Coauthor
FRED HAZELTON Statistician | **SARAH KELLETH** touringplans.com webmaster, Lines developer
LARRY OLMSTED Golf expert | **KAREN TURNBOW, PhD** Child psychologist
JIM HILL Entertainment reporter | **PAM BRANDON** Shopping diva
LAUREL STEWART Fact-checking supervisor

DATA COLLECTORS	**CONTRIBUTING WRITERS**	**HOTEL INSPECTORS**
Chantale Brazeau	Rich Bernato	Ritchey Halphen
Guy Garguilo	Liliane J. Opsomer	Kristen Helmstetter
Shane Grizzard	Sue Pisaturo	Lillian Macko
Lillian Macko	Laurel Stewart	Richard Macko
Richard Macko	Darcie Vance	Myra E. Merkle
Kristen Mitchell	Mary Waring	Darcie Vance
Cliff Myers	Deb Wills	
Jeff "Fred" Reisdorf		
Darcie Vance	**EDITORIAL, ART, AND PRODUCTION**	
Rich Vosburgh	**HOLLY CROSS, RITCHEY HALPHEN,**	
Kelly Whitman	**AMBER KAYE HENDERSON** Editors	

EDITORIAL, ART, AND PRODUCTION
HOLLY CROSS, RITCHEY HALPHEN,
  AMBER KAYE HENDERSON Editors
ANNIE LONG Typesetter
CHRIS ELIOPOULOS, TAMI KNIGHT Cartoonists
STEVE JONES, SCOTT McGREW, CASSANDRA POERTNER
  Cartographers
JOHN MICHAEL ARNAUD Proofreader | **ANN CASSAR** Indexer

THIS IS NOT A NOVEL!

THOUGH THIS GUIDE IS FULL OF CHARACTERS—and was created by a few more—it is at heart a reference work, and many readers do not read it cover-to-cover, as they would a piece of fiction. For some this causes problems—witness this angry reader who identified him/herself as "None of Your Business":

> *This e-mail is in regards to* The Unofficial Guide to Walt Disney World, *which I purchased last year for our trip to Disney World this year. I am very disappointed that the book doesn't mention that an*

additional fee is required to access the touring plans and crowd-level information on your website. Here is an excerpt from the book:

If you decide to splurge and burn a pass on a half-day or less, refer to our *Unofficial Guide* Crowd Calendar at **touringplans.com.**

The book refers to this website in other sections as well but does not mention that a fee is involved! I don't mind paying, but I am disgusted that you would not mention it in your book. Shame on me for assuming this information would be free, even though I shelled out $23.99 [Canadian] for the book.

Don't you hate it when people hide their true feelings just to be polite? In any event, None of Your Business's complaint illustrates how readers use the guide in different ways. Here's our reply to NOYB:

Dear None,

Thanks for your letter. Here's the thing:

The Unofficial Guide to Walt Disney World *is used by many readers as a reference work as opposed to a cover-to-cover read. Consequently, a reader might miss something, say, at the beginning of the guide, that provides information necessary for understanding references to the same subject elsewhere. For several editions, we've been explaining in Part One, Gathering Information, specifically what readers can access on our website at no cost and what they can access only with a paid subscription.*

In the last edition, this information read as follows:

Much of our web content, including new research, book updates, resort photos and video, and up-to-date dining menus, is completely free. Access to part of the site, most notably the Crowd Calendar, additional touring plans, and in-park wait times, requires a small subscription fee (current-book owners get a substantial discount). This nominal charge helps keep us online and costs less than a sandwich at Flame Tree Barbecue in Disney's Animal Kingdom. Plus, **touring plans.com** offers a 45-day money-back guarantee—something we don't think the Flame Tree can match.

In an 850-page book, it's unrealistic for us to think everyone will read every word. On the other hand, it's totally impractical to explain things that are mentioned multiple times each time they're referenced. So we don't blame you for being angry—you probably were using the guide as a reference and just missed the explanation.

All the best,
Bob and Len

To sum up: If you use the guide like an encyclopedia or dictionary —for example, you look something up in one of the indexes, then go to the cited page—you may overlook information presented in previous sections that is vital to understanding the subject. Likewise, if you skip or skim over explanatory material in the introductory chapters, that might lead to a misunderstanding later on.

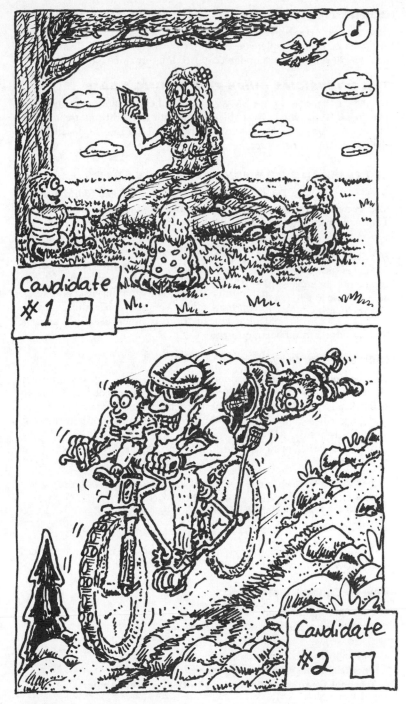

SURVEY: *Which author do you prefer to write your guidebooks? (Guess which ones you got?)*

CORRECTIONS, UPDATES, AND BREAKING NEWS

LOOK FOR THESE at the *Unofficial Guide* website, **touringplans.com.** See page 26 for a complete description of the site. The Kindle and ePub versions of the guide are updated approximately once a month.

THE *UNOFFICIAL GUIDE* PUBLISHING YEAR

WE RECEIVE MANY QUERIES asking when the next edition of the *Unofficial Guide* will be available. Usually our new editions are in stores by late August or early September. Thus, the 2017 edition will be on shelves in August or September 2016.

LETTERS AND COMMENTS FROM READERS

MANY WHO USE *The Unofficial Guide to Walt Disney World* write us to comment or share their own strategies for visiting Disney World. Their comments and observations are frequently incorporated into revised editions of the *Unofficial Guide* and have contributed immeasurably to its improvement. If you write us or complete our reader survey, rest assured that we won't release your name and address to any mailing-list companies, direct-mail advertisers, or other third parties. Unless you instruct us otherwise, we'll assume that you don't mind being quoted.

unofficial **TIP**
If you're up for having your comments quoted in the guide, be sure to tell us where you're from.

Online Reader Survey

Our website hosts a questionnaire you can use to express opinions about your Walt Disney World visit. Access it here: **touringplans.com /walt-disney-world/survey.** The questionnaire lets every member of your party, regardless of age, tell us what he or she thinks about attractions, hotels, restaurants, and more.

If you'd rather print out the survey and snail-mail it to us, send it to this address:

Reader Survey
The Unofficial Guide to Walt Disney World
2204 1st Ave. S., Suite 102
Birmingham, AL 35233

Finally, if you'd like to review this book on Amazon, go to **tinyurl .com/wdw2016reviews.**

How to Contact the Authors

Bob Sehlinger and Len Testa
The Unofficial Guide to Walt Disney World
2204 1st Ave. S., Suite 102
Birmingham, AL 35233
unofficialguides@menasharidge.com,
facebook.com/theunofficialguides, twitter.com/theugseries

When you write, put your address on both your letter and envelope; the two sometimes get separated. It's also a good idea to include your phone number. If you e-mail us, please tell us where you're from. Remember, as travel writers, we're often out of the office for long periods of time, so forgive us if our response is slow. *Unofficial Guide* e-mail isn't forwarded to us when we're traveling, but we'll respond as soon as possible after we return.

WALT DISNEY WORLD:
An OVERVIEW

IF YOU'RE CHOOSING a US tourist destination, the question is not whether to visit Walt Disney World, but how to see its best offerings with some economy of time, effort, and finances.

WHAT WALT DISNEY WORLD ENCOMPASSES

WALT DISNEY WORLD COMPRISES 43 square miles, an area twice as large as Manhattan. Situated strategically in this vast expanse are the **Magic Kingdom, Epcot, Disney's Hollywood Studios,** and **Disney's Animal Kingdom** theme parks; 2 swimming theme parks; a sports complex; 5 golf courses; 41 hotels and a campground; more than 100 restaurants; 4 interconnected lakes; 2 shopping complexes; 8 convention venues; a nature preserve; and a transportation system consisting of four-lane highways, elevated monorails, and a network of canals.

Walt Disney World employs around 62,000 people, or "cast members," making it the largest single-site employer in the United States. Keeping the costumes of those cast members clean requires the equivalent of 16,000 loads of laundry a day and the dry cleaning of 30,000 garments daily. (Mickey Mouse alone has 290 different sets of duds, ranging from a scuba wet suit to a tux; Minnie boasts more than 200 outfits.) Each year, Disney restaurants serve 10 million burgers, 6 million hot dogs, 75 million Cokes, 9 million pounds of French fries, and 150 tons of popcorn. In the state of Florida, only the cities of Miami and Jacksonville have bus systems larger than Disney World's. The Disney monorail trains have logged mileage equal to more than 30 round-trips to the moon.

DISNEY-SPEAK POCKET TRANSLATOR
AND GUIDE TO COMMON ABBREVIATIONS

IT MAY COME AS A SURPRISE to many, but Walt Disney World has its own somewhat peculiar language. The following charts list some terms and abbreviations you're likely to bump into, both in this guide and in the larger Disney (and Universal) community.

THE DISNEY LEXICON IN A NUTSHELL
ADVENTURE Ride | **ATTRACTION** Ride or theater show
ATTRACTION HOST Ride operator | **AUDIENCE** Crowd
BACKSTAGE Behind the scenes, out of view of customers
CAST MEMBER Employee |
CHARACTER Disney character impersonated by an employee

THE DISNEY LEXICON IN A NUTSHELL (CONTINUED)	
COSTUME Work attire or uniform | DARK RIDE Indoor ride	
DAY GUEST Any customer not staying at a Disney resort	
FACE CHARACTER A character who doesn't wear a head-covering costume (Snow White, Cinderella, Jasmine, and the like)	
GENERAL PUBLIC Same as day guest	
GREETER Employee positioned at an attraction entrance | GUEST Customer	
HIDDEN MICKEYS Frontal silhouette of Mickey's head worked subtly into the design of buildings, railings, golf greens, attractions, and just about anything else	
ON STAGE In full view of customers	
PRESHOW Entertainment at an attraction before the feature presentation	
RESORT GUEST A customer staying at a Disney resort	
ROLE A cast member's job	
SOFT OPENING Opening a park or attraction before its stated opening date	
TRANSITIONAL EXPERIENCE An element of the queuing area and/or preshow that provides information essential to understanding the attraction	

COMMON ABBREVIATIONS AND WHAT THEY STAND FOR			
CM	Cast member	FP+/FPP	FastPass+
DCL	Disney Cruise Line	I-DRIVE	International Drive (major Orlando thoroughfare)
DDRA	Downtown Disney Resort Area	IOA	Universal's Islands of Adventure theme park
DDV	Disney Deluxe Villas	TTC	Ticket and Transportation Center
DHS	Disney's Hollywood Studios	USF	Universal Studios Florida theme park
DTS	Disney Transportation System	WDI	Walt Disney Imagineering
DVC	Disney Vacation Club	WDTC	Walt Disney Travel Company
EMH	Extra Magic Hours	WDW	Walt Disney World

THE MAJOR THEME PARKS
The Magic Kingdom

When people think of Walt Disney World, most think of the Magic Kingdom, opened in 1971. It consists of the adventures, rides, and shows featuring the Disney cartoon characters, and Cinderella Castle. It's only one element of Disney World, but it remains the heart.

The Magic Kingdom is divided into six "lands," with five arranged around a central hub. First you come to **Main Street, U.S.A.,** which connects the Magic Kingdom entrance with the hub. Clockwise around the hub are **Adventureland, Frontierland, Liberty Square, Fantasyland,** and **Tomorrowland.** Five hotels (**Bay Lake Tower;** the **Contemporary, Polynesian Village,** and **Grand Floridian Resorts;** and **The Villas at the Grand Floridian**) are connected to the Magic Kingdom by monorail and boat. Three other hotels, **Shades of Green, Wilderness Lodge & Villas,** and **Four Seasons Orlando at Walt Disney World Resort,** are nearby but aren't served by the monorail.

Epcot

Opened in October 1982, Epcot is twice as big as the Magic Kingdom and comparable in scope. It has two major areas: **Future World** consists of pavilions concerning human creativity and technological advancement; **World Showcase,** arranged around a 40-acre lagoon, presents the architectural, social, and cultural heritages of almost a dozen nations, each country represented by replicas of famous landmarks and settings familiar to world travelers.

The Epcot resort hotels—the **BoardWalk Inn & Villas, Caribbean Beach Resort, Dolphin, Swan,** and **Yacht & Beach Club Resorts and Beach Club Villas**—are within a 5- to 15-minute walk of the International Gateway, the World Showcase entrance to the theme park. The hotels are also linked to Epcot and Disney's Hollywood Studios by canal and walkway. Epcot is connected to the Magic Kingdom and its hotels by monorail.

Disney's Hollywood Studios

Opened in 1989 as Disney-MGM Studios and a little larger than the Magic Kingdom, Disney's Hollywood Studios has two areas. One area, occupying about 75% of the Studios, is a theme park focused on the motion picture, music, and television industries. Park highlights include a re-creation of Hollywood and Sunset Boulevards from Hollywood's Golden Age, four high-tech rides, several musical shows, and a movie stunt show.

The second area encompasses soundstages, a back lot of streets and sets, and an outdoor theater for an automobile stunt show. Until 2014, the public could access the soundstages on a tour that took visitors behind the scenes of Disney animation and moviemaking.

Disney's Hollywood Studios is connected to other Walt Disney World areas by highway and canal but not by monorail. Guests can park in the Studios' pay parking lot or commute by bus. Guests at Epcot resort hotels can reach the Studios by boat or on foot.

We wouldn't be surprised to hear a major expansion of the Studios announced soon.

Disney's Animal Kingdom

About five times the size of the Magic Kingdom, Disney's Animal Kingdom combines zoological exhibits with rides, shows, and live entertainment. The park is arranged in a hub-and-spoke configuration somewhat like the Magic Kingdom. A lush tropical rainforest serves as Main Street, funneling visitors to **Discovery Island,** the park's hub. Dominated by the park's central icon, the 14-story-tall, hand-carved **Tree of Life,** Discovery Island offers services, shopping, and dining. From there, guests can access the themed areas: **Africa, Asia,** and **DinoLand U.S.A.** Discovery Island, Africa, and DinoLand U.S.A. opened in 1998, followed by Asia in 1999. Africa, the largest themed area at 100 acres, features free-roaming herds in a re-creation of the Serengeti Plain.

Camp Minnie-Mickey, the park's character-greeting area, also opened in 1998 but closed in 2014 to make way for a new "land" based on James Cameron's *Avatar* films, with construction ongoing until 2017.

What's New at Walt Disney World Since Your Last Visit

If it's been a few years (or more) since your last trip, here's a quick summary of the major developments:

LAST 2 YEARS

• **"New Fantasyland"** opened in the Magic Kingdom, comprising **Seven Dwarfs Mine Train; Under the Sea: Journey of the Little Mermaid; Enchanted Tales with Belle; Be Our Guest** restaurant; and **Princess Fairytale Hall,** which replaced Snow White's Scary Adventures and is home to Princess Anna and Queen Elsa (*Frozen*), among other royalty.

• The **FastPass+** ride-reservation system, with online and mobile apps, replaced the paper-based Fastpass system in use since 1998.

• The Maelstrom attraction in Epcot's Norway Pavilion closed to make way for a *Frozen*-themed ride opening in 2016.

• *For the First Time in Forever: A Frozen Sing-Along Celebration,* opened at Disney's Hollywood Studios.

• Camp Minnie-Mickey closed at Disney's Animal Kingdom to make way for a new "land" called **Pandora: The Land of Avatar.** The *Festival of the Lion King* show was moved to a newly expanded **Harambe Village.**

• **Festival of Fantasy** became the new daytime parade at the Magic Kingdom.

• **The Villas at Disney's Grand Floridian Resort & Spa** opened, adding studios and one- and two-bedroom suites.

• **The Villas at Disney's Polynesian Village Resort** opened, adding studios and two-bedroom rooms as well as a remodeled pool and a new bar, **Trader Sam's Grog Grotto.**

• New restaurants include **Trattoria al Forno** at the BoardWalk, **Spice Road Table** in Epcot's Morocco Pavilion, and **L'Artisan des Glaces,** an ice-cream parlor in Epcot's France Pavilion.

• Downtown Disney—now **Disney Springs**—has doubled in size, adding restaurants, shops, and more.

LAST 5 YEARS

• Mickey's Toontown Fair at the Magic Kingdom was fully renovated and renamed **Storybook Circus** as part of the "New Fantasyland."

• At Disney's Hollywood Studios, the *Disney Junior—Live on Stage!* show was added, and Star Tours became **Star Tours—The Adventures Continue.**

• Interactive games debuted at the Magic Kingdom (**Sorcerers of the Magic Kingdom**), Epcot (**Agent P's World Showcase Adventure**), and Disney's Animal Kingdom (**Wilderness Explorers**).

• **Bay Lake Tower** at Disney's Contemporary Resort opened, adding studios and one-, two-, and three-bedroom suites.

• A new Value resort, **Disney's Art of Animation,** opened with many one-bedroom suites.

LAST 10 YEARS

• New attractions included **Expedition Everest** and *Finding Nemo—The Musical* at Disney's Animal Kingdom, **Gran Fiesta Tour** and **The Seas with Nemo and Friends** at Epcot, **Toy Story Midway Mania!** and **Jedi Training Academy** at Disney's Hollywood Studios, and *Monsters, Inc. Laugh Floor* at the Magic Kingdom.

• **Kidani Village** at Disney's Animal Kingdom Lodge opened, adding studios and one-, two-, and three-bedroom suites.

• New restaurants included **Yak & Yeti** at Disney's Animal Kingdom and **La Cava del Tequila, Via Napoli,** and **Tutto Gusto** at Epcot.

Disney's Animal Kingdom has its own parking lot and is connected to other Walt Disney World destinations by the Disney bus system. Although no hotels lie within Animal Kingdom proper, the **All-Star Resorts, Animal Kingdom Lodge & Villas,** and **Coronado Springs Resort** are all nearby.

THE WATER PARKS

DISNEY WORLD HAS TWO MAJOR water parks: **Typhoon Lagoon** and **Blizzard Beach.** Opened in 1989, Typhoon Lagoon is distinguished by a wave pool capable of making 6-foot waves. Blizzard Beach is newer, having opened in 1995, and it features more slides. Both parks are beautifully landscaped, and great attention is paid to atmosphere and aesthetics. Typhoon Lagoon and Blizzard Beach have their own adjacent parking lots and can be reached by Disney bus.

OTHER WALT DISNEY WORLD VENUES

Disney Springs

Redevelopment of the sprawling shopping, dining, and entertainment complex formerly known as Downtown Disney began in 2013 and is scheduled to be completed in 2016. Themed to evoke a Florida waterfront town, Disney Springs currently encompasses the **Marketplace** on the east, the **West Side** on the west, and **The Landing** on the waterfront. Redevelopment of the old Pleasure Island nightlife district began in late 2014; the reimagined area, called **Town Center,** will feature shops and restaurants and Florida–meets–Spanish Colonial architecture. Two desperately needed multistory parking garages opened in 2015.

The Marketplace contains the world's largest store selling Disney-character merchandise; upscale resort-wear and specialty shops; and numerous restaurants, including **Rainforest Cafe** and **T-REX.** The West Side is a diverse mix of nightlife, shopping, dining, and entertainment, most notably featuring a Disney outpost of **House of Blues** and a permanent showplace for the extraordinary **Cirque du Soleil** *La Nouba.* The Landing, partially open at press time, offers additional shopping and dining options; **The Boathouse,** an upscale waterfront seafood eatery, opened here in spring 2015. Disney Springs is accessed via Disney transportation from Disney resort hotels.

Disney's BoardWalk

Near Epcot, the BoardWalk is an idealized replication of an East Coast 1930s waterfront resort. Open all day, the BoardWalk features upscale restaurants, shops and galleries, a brewpub, and an ESPN sports bar. In the evening, a nightclub with dueling pianos and a DJ dance club join the lineup. Both are for guests age 21 and up only. There's no admission fee for the BoardWalk, but the piano bar levies a cover charge at night. This area is anchored by the **BoardWalk Inn & Villas,** along with its adjacent convention center. The BoardWalk is within walking distance of the Epcot resorts, Epcot's International Gateway, and Disney's Hollywood Studios. Boat transportation is available to and from Epcot and Disney's Hollywood Studios; buses serve other Disney World locations.

ESPN Wide World of Sports Complex

The 220-acre Wide World of Sports is a state-of-the-art competition and training facility consisting of a 9,500-seat ballpark, two field houses, and venues for baseball, softball, tennis, track and field, beach volleyball, and 27 other sports. The spring-training home of the Atlanta Braves, the complex also hosts a mind-boggling calendar of professional and amateur competitions. Walt Disney World guests not participating in events may pay admission to watch any of the scheduled competitions.

Disney Cruise Line: The Mouse at Sea

In 1998, the Walt Disney Company launched (literally) its own cruise line with the 2,400-passenger *Disney Magic.* Its sister ship, the *Disney Wonder,* first sailed in 1999. Most cruises depart from Port Canaveral, Florida (about a 90-minute drive from Walt Disney World), or Miami on three-, four-, and seven-night itineraries. Bahamian and Caribbean cruises include a day at **Castaway Cay,** Disney's 1,000-acre private island. Cruises can be packaged with a stay at Disney World. In 2011 and 2012, respectively, two new ships, the *Disney Dream* and the *Disney Fantasy,* joined the fleet, enabling DCL to expand its sailings in the Caribbean as well as Alaska, California, Hawaii, the Mediterranean, and Northern Europe.

The ships are modern ocean liners with classic lines. Cabins are among the most spacious in the cruise industry, and the staff is attentive and accommodating.

Disney cruises are perfect for families and kids of all ages. Extensive children's programs and elaborate child-care facilities allow grown-ups plenty of opportunities to relax and do adult stuff.

Dining is varied and plentiful. Each night, passengers move to a different family restaurant—each with its own unique theme and menu—and take their table companions and waitstaff with them. The ships also have a range of cafés offering pizza, burgers, sandwiches, and ice cream. Room service is available 24/7. For sophisticated adult dining, there's **Palo** on all four ships, plus **Remy** on the *Dream* and the *Fantasy.*

The pools and water attractions are another draw. The *Dream* and the *Fantasy* feature the first-ever onboard water coaster. At 765 feet long and the height of four decks, **AquaDuck** is a major attraction for kids and grown-ups alike (the *Magic*'s counterpart, similar though not identical, is **AquaDunk**). Following an initial drop, guests glide through a translucent tube in a loop that extends 12 feet over the side of the vessel, allowing them to look down on the ocean 150 feet below. The ride lasts about 90 seconds and comes with climbs and drops, twists and turns. If you can keep your eyes open while riding, the AquaDuck will provide you with a spectacular view of the ship.

Senses Spa & Salon on the *Dream, Magic,* and *Fantasy* is a great place to relax not just for adults but also for teens, who get their own separate area called **Chill Spa.** (**Vista Spa & Salon** on the *Wonder* is adults-only.)

Keys, the piano bar on the *Magic,* and **Cadillac Lounge,** on the *Wonder,* are the most relaxing and beautiful lounges on the Seven Seas. Make a before-or-after dinner drink there part of your routine.

Shore excursions depend on the itinerary, but all Bahamian and Caribbean cruises make at least one call at Castaway Cay. The best way to enjoy the island is to disembark first thing in the morning and secure a prime spot at the beach complete with hammock and shade. **Cookie's BBQ** and **Cookie's Too** serve burgers and such. Programs for kids on Castaway Cay give parents a chance to enjoy **Serenity Bay,** the adults-only beach.

Disney Cruise Line fared better than most of its competitors during the recession and is thriving as of this writing. Sailings enjoy high occupancy, and a number of new itineraries have been added. Fans of Disney's *Frozen,* for example, can experience the country that inspired the icy kingdom of Arendelle on a Norwegian Fjord Cruise of 7, 9, or 11 nights. (Anna and Elsa have also joined the character-greeting lineup on the *Magic, Wonder,* and *Fantasy.*)

DCL offers a free planning DVD that tells you all you need to know about Disney cruises and then some. Get your copy by calling ☎ 888-DCL-2500, or order it online at **tinyurl.com/dcldvdonline.**

Finally, to get the most out of your cruise, check out *The Unofficial Guide to Disney Cruise Line,* by Len Testa with Erin Foster, Laurel Stewart, and Ritchey Halphen.

THE PEOPLE

HOW YOU'RE TREATED BY THE CAST MEMBERS you encounter at Walt Disney World can make or break a vacation. Fortunately, Disney staff often go the extra mile to make your visit special, as the following three readers report. First, from a New York City man:

I lost my glasses during the trip and had to go 24 hours awaiting a spare pair to be sent by overnight mail. Went to Sunshine Seasons for lunch; found a cast member and explained my situation. Said I couldn't read the menu displays and asked for a printed menu. He said they didn't have those but offered to tell me what was available. I said that would be too much bother; his response: "You're why I'm here." He took me to each of the four stations and described every dish. When I had my order, he took me to the dessert station and told me every option. Then he got my drink for me along with napkins, utensils, and a straw, then escorted me to the cashier.

A family from St. Joseph, Michigan, has this to relate:

We had a very unexpected and wonderful surprise waiting in our stroller after the Country Bear Jamboree. Out of nearly 30 strollers, ours had been visited by Santa Mickey while we were in the show. We came out to a stroller decorated with silly bands, Christmas ornaments, and a snowman Mickey plush toy. Our 5-year-old son was delighted, not to mention the rest of our party. Just another way that WDW goes one more step to make a magical experience.

Finally, from a suburban Philadelphia family:

At Expedition Everest, I witnessed expert handling of a group of teenage line-jumpers by Disney staff. Once they reached the loading area, cast members ushered them aside in a very calm and friendly fashion, causing no apparent disruption. I didn't see where they were ushered or what happened next, but I did not see them board the ride. It was as if they were never there.

█ UNIVERSAL ORLANDO

TIME TO TAKE OFF THE BLINDERS

READERS ASK US EVERY YEAR why we cover Universal theme parks in this guide. Simply stated, Universal is a high-quality direct competitor of Walt Disney World, and we think you should have detailed information on both the Disney and Universal parks so you can make an informed decision about where to spend your time. We also get comments from readers who are under the impression that Universal's offerings are inferior to Disney's. By any objective measure, they are not.

In many ways, Universal Orlando will never achieve parity with Walt Disney World. It's minuscule compared with the 27,000-odd acres of the World. But in the areas where it *can* compete—namely, in theme park design and attraction quality—Universal has pulled even, if not ahead.

Universal has been technologically ascendant for several years, introducing revolutionary ride systems and special effects on both rides and in theater performances. While Disney relies conservatively on a combination of highly detailed themed areas, beloved characters, and inspiration from classic animated features (which many young people under age 16 have never seen), Universal takes more technological swings for the fences—the most notable examples being the spectacular **Harry Potter and the Forbidden Journey** at Universal's Islands of Adventure (IOA) and **Harry Potter and the Escape from Gringotts** at Universal Studios Florida (USF).

Granted, the Walt Disney World parks do have their share of high-tech attractions, and not all Universal attractions approach the creative genius of Forbidden Journey or Escape from Gringotts. But while guests at both Disney and Universal report high levels of satisfaction, it's the next-gen technology manifested in Universal's headliners that delivers true "Wow!" moments. Plus, **Port of Entry** and **Jurassic Park** at Islands of Adventure—along with **The Wizarding World of Harry Potter,** now encompassing both **Hogsmeade** at IOA and **Diagon Alley** at USF—clearly demonstrate that Universal can create exquisitely detailed and totally immersive themed areas.

We see the two Universal parks and the four Walt Disney World parks as rough equals—and every one a gem. There's more for little kids at Disney's Magic Kingdom and Hollywood Studios than at the other parks, and more for teens and young adults at the Universal parks. In keeping with that young-adult demographic, Universal offers the **CityWalk** nightclub venue, just outside the park gates, for those with the energy to make a night of it; Disney World has nothing comparable. Both Universal and Disney have splendid on-site hotels, with Universal offering more perks to its guests. Disney parks have the edge in landscaping as well as full-service dining.

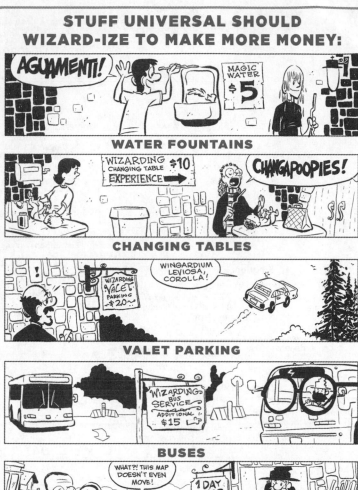

South Orlando & Walt Disney World Area

Orlando

Florida's Turnpike

Windermere

Lake Butler

Universal Studios Florida
Universal's Islands of Adventure

Vineland Rd.

Wet 'n Wild

429

535

Winter Garden–Vineland Rd.

S. Apopka–Vineland Rd.

74-B

75

Universal Blvd.

74-A

Orange County Convention Center

72

1

Magic Kingdom

SeaWorld Orlando

Discovery Cove

71

Aquatica

Fort Wilderness Campground

The Walt Disney World Resort

Downtown Disney (Disney Springs)

Lake Buena Vista

International Dr.

Flamingo Crossings

Western Way

Epcot Center Dr.

World Dr.

Epcot

68

Disney's Hollywood Studios

Buena Vista Dr.

To 27
← & Ocala

Disney's Animal Kingdom

Osceola Pkwy.

67

536

417

W. Irlo Bronson Memorial Hwy.

192

65

535

ESPN Wide World of Sports Complex

3

64

Celebration

2

192

429

Western Beltway (toll road)

4

Poinciana Blvd.

58

532

27

To Busch Gardens & Tampa

17
92

To Davenport

Western Beltway (toll road)

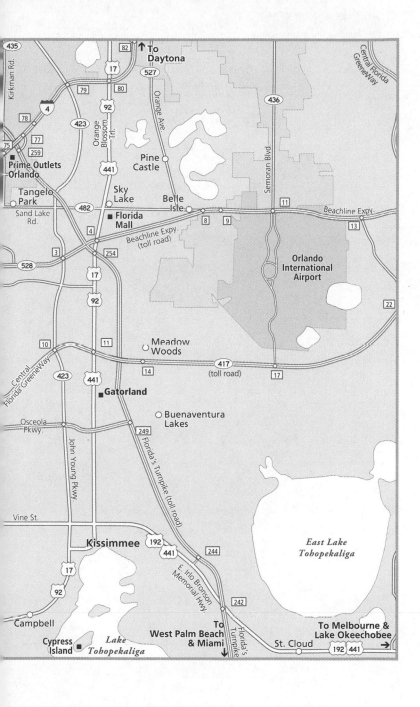

Walt Disney World

Reedy Lake

THE MAGIC KINGDOM

Seven Seas Lagoon

Bay Lake Tower

Contemporary Resort

Bay Lake

Grand Floridian Resort & Spa, Villas

Wilderness Lodge & Villas

Floridian Way

Polynesian Village Resort & Villas

Magnolia Golf Course

Oak Trail Golf Course

7 Seas Dr.

Fort Wilderness Resort & Campground

Shades of Green

World Dr.

Fou at V

Vista Blvd.

Palm Golf Course

World Dr.

Bay Lake

toll road

429

Epcot Center Dr.

Future site of Disney's Flamingo Crossings

Western Way

Western Expy. (toll road)

Yacht & Beach Club Resorts

W. Savannah Cir.

E. Savannah Cir.

Western Way

Coronado Springs Resort

Dolphin

BoardWalk Inn & Villas

Swan

Fantasia Gardens

DISNEY'S ANIMAL KINGDOM

DISNEY'S HOLLYWOOD STUDIOS

Animal Kingdom Lodge & Villas

toll road

Buena Vista Dr.

Vict

Blizzard Beach & Winter Summerland

Osceola Pkwy.

W. Irlo Bronson Memorial Hwy.

192

530

Sherberth Rd.

World Dr.

Formosa Gardens Blvd.

All-Star Resorts

ESPN Wide World of Sports Complex

429

Funie Steed Rd.

530

W. Irlo Bronson Memorial Hwy.

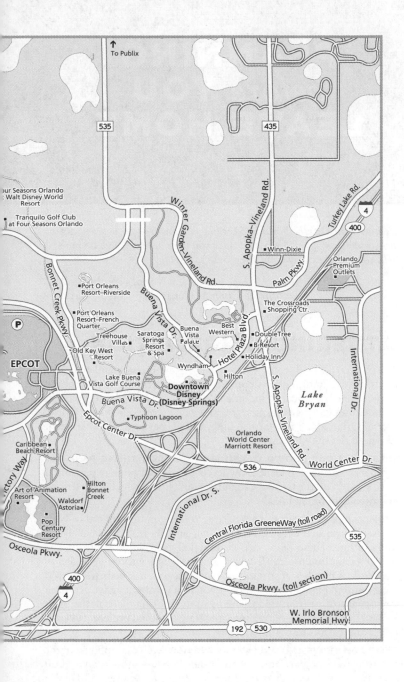

↑ To Publix

535

435

S. Apopka-Vineland Rd.

Turkey Lake Rd.

4
400

our Seasons Orlando
: Walt Disney World
Resort

Tranquilo Golf Club
at Four Seasons Orlando

Winter Garden-Vineland Rd.

Winn-Dixie

Palm Pkwy.

Orlando
Premium
Outlets

Bonnet Creek Pkwy.

Port Orleans
Resort–Riverside

Buena Vista Dr.

The Crossroads
Shopping Ctr.

Port Orleans
Resort–French
Quarter

P

Treehouse
Villas

Saratoga
Springs
Resort
& Spa

Buena
Vista
Palace

Best
Western

Hotel Plaza Blvd.

DoubleTree

B Resort

International Dr.

Old Key West
Resort

EPCOT

Lake Buena
Vista Golf Course

Wyndham

Holiday Inn

Hilton

Downtown
Disney
(Disney Springs)

Buena Vista Dr.

Typhoon Lagoon

Epcot Center Dr.

Lake
Bryan

S. Apopka-Vineland Rd.

Orlando
World Center
Marriott Resort

World Center Dr.

Caribbean
Beach Resort

ctory Way

536

Art of Animation
Resort

Hilton
Bonnet
Creek

International Dr. S.

Waldorf
Astoria

Central Florida GreeneWay (toll road)

535

Pop
Century
Resort

Osceola Pkwy.

400

4

Osceola Pkwy. (toll section)

W. Irlo Bronson
Memorial Hwy.

192   530

PART ONE

PLANNING
before YOU
LEAVE HOME

Visiting Walt Disney World is a bit like childbirth—you never really believe what people tell you, but once you have been through it yourself, you know exactly what they were saying!

—Hilary Wolfe, a mother and
Unofficial Guide reader from Swansea, Wales

GATHERING INFORMATION

IN ADDITION TO USING THIS GUIDE, we recommend that you visit our website, **touringplans.com,** which has interactive trip-planning tools that aren't practical to include in a printed book. The companion blog, **blog.touringplans.com,** posts breaking news for Walt Disney World, Universal Orlando, Disney Cruise Line, and Disneyland. Here's a quick rundown of the site's features:

DETAILED 365-DAY CROWD CALENDAR FOR EACH THEME PARK See which parks will be the least crowded every day of your trip, using a 1-to-10 scale. With the Crowd Calendar, you'll know which park to visit each day to avoid long lines.

CUSTOMIZABLE TOURING PLANS Create touring plans tailored to your family's favorite attractions, restaurants, and more, and save up to 4 hours in line. These plans can be updated even while you're in the parks. *Our best and most effective touring plans are those provided in this guide.* In a number of situations, however, you may be better served by a customized plan—for instance, if you don't want to arrive at a park before opening time (required by many of the touring plans in the print version of the guide) or you want to integrate personal preferences such as meals and breaks into your touring plan.

HOTEL-ROOM VIEWS AND ONLINE FAX SERVICE We've got photos of the views from every hotel room in Walt Disney World—more than 30,000 images in all—and we'll give you the exact wording to use with Disney to request a specific room. We'll even automatically fax your room request to Disney right before you arrive.

TICKET DISCOUNTS A customizable search helps you find the cheapest tickets for your specific needs. The average family can save $20–$80 by purchasing admission from one of our recommended ticket wholesalers.

FASTPASS+ INFORMATION We show every FastPass+ reservation available at every attraction in the parks on a single page of our site.

ANSWERS TO YOUR TRIP-PLANNING QUESTIONS Our online community includes tens of thousands of Disney experts and fans willing to help with your vacation plans. Ask questions and offer your own helpful tips.

Much of our online content, including new research, menus, and updates and changes to this book, is completely free. Access to parts of the site, including the Crowd Calendar, hotel-room views, and custom touring plans, requires a small subscription fee (current-book owners get a substantial discount). This nominal charge—less than a meal at most Disney counter-service restaurants—subsidizes our research and keeps the site up and running day and night.

Our online app, **Lines,** available free to touringplans.com subscribers, is designed to accompany you in the parks. It provides ride and park information that Disney doesn't, including the following:

- **Posted and actual wait times at attractions.** Lines is the only Disney-parks app that displays both posted wait times and the actual times you'll wait in line. The wait time you see posted outside of a ride is often much higher than the real wait time, because Disney wants you to go to another part of the park—it's a simple form of crowd control. With Lines, you can make better decisions about what to see.

- **"Ride now or wait" recommendations.** Lines shows you whether ride wait times are likely to get longer or shorter. If you find a long line at a particular attraction, Lines tells you the best time to come back.

- **Real-time touring plan updates while you're in a park.** Lines automatically updates your custom touring plan to reflect actual crowd conditions at a given moment. You can also restart your plan and add or change attractions, breaks, meals, and more.

- **In-park chat feature with our Lines community.** Have a quick question while you're in the parks? Ask our community of thousands of Liners and get a response within seconds.

The *Unofficial Guide* and touringplans.com, along with the Lines app, were created to work together, providing the most comprehensive planning and touring support possible. This mom from St. Louis shares her experience using all the tools in our toolbox:

> The Unofficial Guide *was the perfect place to start planning our vacation (actually our honeymoon). I loved having the book to read from cover to cover and then easily refer back to. After reading the book, I felt I had a good idea of what hotels I was interested in, and I had "must-do" and "must-eat" places somewhat picked out. I then took the knowledge from the book and switched to the website to personalize our touring plans and use as an easy reference when needed. The book and the website together made our trip INCRED-IBLE. My husband even complimented me on our touring plans— they worked perfectly and were super-easy to use and manipulate.*

Next, we recommend that you obtain the following:

1. **THE WALT DISNEY TRAVEL COMPANY FLORIDA VACATIONS BROCHURE AND DVD** These cover Walt Disney World in its entirety, list rates for all Disney resort hotels and campgrounds, and describe Disney World package vacations. They're available from most travel agents, by calling the Walt Disney Travel Company at ☎ 407-828-8101 or 407-934-7639, or by visiting **disneyworld.com.** Be prepared to hold. When you get a representative, ask for the DVD vacation planner.

2. **DISNEY CRUISE LINE BROCHURE AND DVD** This brochure provides details on vacation packages that combine a cruise on the Disney Cruise Line with a stay at Disney World. Disney Cruise Line also offers a free DVD that tells you all you need to know about Disney cruises and then some. To obtain a copy, call ☎ 800-951-3532 or order at **disneycruise.com,** where you can also view the entire DVD online.

3. **ORLANDO MAGICARD** If you're considering lodging outside Disney World or if you think you might patronize out-of-the-World attractions and restaurants, obtain an Orlando Magicard, a Vacation Planner, and the *Orlando Official Visitors Guide* (all free) from the Visit Orlando Official Visitors Center. The Magicard entitles you to discounts for hotels, restaurants, ground transportation, shopping malls, dinner theaters, and non-Disney theme parks and attractions. Download it at **orlandoinfo.com/magicard.** To order the accommodations guide, call ☎ 800-643-9492. For more information and materials, call ☎ 407-363-5872 weekdays during business hours and 9 a.m.–3 p.m. Eastern time weekends, or go to **visitorlando.com.**

4. *HOTELCOUPONS.COM FLORIDA GUIDE* This is another good source of discounts on lodging, restaurants, and attractions. You can sign up at **hotelcoupons.com** to have a free monthly guide sent to you by e-mail, or you can view the guide online. If you prefer a hard copy over a digital version, you can request one by calling ☎ 800-222-3948 Monday–Friday, 8 a.m.–5 p.m. Eastern time. The guide is free, but you pay $4 for handling ($6 if it's shipped to Canada).

5. *KISSIMMEE VISITOR'S GUIDE* This full-color guide is one of the most complete resources available and is of particular interest to those who intend to lodge outside of Disney World, featuring ads for hotels, rental houses, time-shares, and condominiums, as well as a directory of attractions, restaurants, special events, and other useful info. For a copy, call the Kissimmee Convention and Visitors Bureau at ☎ 800-327-9159 or 407-742-8200, or view it online at **floridakiss.com.**

6. *GUIDEBOOK FOR GUESTS WITH DISABILITIES* Available at Guest Relations when entering the theme/water parks, at resort front desks, and wheelchair-rental areas (listed in each theme park chapter). More-limited information is available at **disneyworld.disney.go.com/plain-text.**

YOUR DISNEY TRIP-PLANNING TIMELINE

AS YOU GO THROUGH THIS BOOK, you'll see many references to date-specific planning milestones for your trip: You can start making Disney dining reservations 180 days before your arrival, for example, and you can make FastPass+ ride reservations at 60 or 30 days before your visit, depending on where you're staying. And that got us thinking about other milestone dates that are important to know for your Disney trip.

Starting on page 32 is a comprehensive timeline that represents the major research, decisions, and tasks that come into play when preparing

Important Walt Disney World Addresses

General Information
Walt Disney World Guest Communications
PO Box 10040
Lake Buena Vista, FL 32830-0040
wdw.guest.communications@disneyworld.com
General online help: **disneyworld.disney.go.com/help/email**

Convention and Banquet Information
Walt Disney World Resort South
PO Box 10000
Lake Buena Vista, FL 32830-1000
☎ 321-939-7129, **disneymeetings.com**

Merchandise Mail Order (Guest Service Mail Order)
PO Box 10070
Lake Buena Vista, FL 32830-0070
☎ 877-560-6477, **merchandise.guest.services@disneyparks.com**

Walt Disney World Central Reservations
PO Box 10100
Lake Buena Vista, FL 32830-0100
☎ 407-W-DISNEY

Walt Disney World Youth Programs
PO Box 10000
Lake Buena Vista, FL 32830-1000
☎ 877-WD-YOUTH, **disneyyouth.com**

Walt Disney World Ticket Mail Order
PO Box 10140
Lake Buena Vista, FL 32830-0140
☎ 407-566-4985, **ticket.inquiries@disneyworld.com**

for a typical Walt Disney World vacation. Next to each milestone, we've put a reference to the section in this book that has the information you need for that milestone, and/or links to our website and blog for additional material like photos or video.

Most Disney trips involve about a dozen important dates to remember. If you've started planning more than 11 months before your trip, you'll have plenty of time to do research ahead of them. If you've just decided to visit Disney World within the next couple of months, you'll have a few more decisions to make a bit quicker.

Do you really need to do this? Absolutely—the demand for good rides and restaurants far exceeds their capacity, and you won't get near them without planning and reservations. Consider that around 52,000 people visit the Magic Kingdom on an *average* day. A hot restaurant such as Be Our Guest, running at full speed, can serve lunch to maybe 1 in 12 of them. A very popular character meet and greet, such as the *Frozen* princesses, may be able to handle 1 in 50 park guests during an entire day of operation. Those are not good odds.

Making dining and attraction reservations as soon as possible is vital if you want to eat at nice restaurants and avoid hours-long waits at popular rides. Other reservations, such as those for spas or recreational activities, can frequently be made when you arrive in Orlando, especially if you're visiting during a slower time of year or you're flexible with the date or time of your appointment. But your best bet is to research early and make reservations as soon as Disney allows.   *(Continued on page 32)*

Walt Disney World Phone Numbers

General Information	☎ 407-824-4321 or 407-824-2222
General Information for the Hearing-Impaired (TTY)	☎ 407-827-5141
Accommodations/Reservations	☎ 407-W-DISNEY (934-7639)
All-Star Movies Resort	☎ 407-939-7000
All-Star Music Resort	☎ 407-939-6000
All-Star Sports Resort	☎ 407-939-5000
AMC Downtown Disney 24 Theatres	☎ 888-262-4386
Animal Kingdom Lodge & Villas (*Jambo House & Kidani Village*)	☎ 407-938-3000
Art of Animation Resort	☎ 407-938-7000
Beach Club Resort	☎ 407-934-8000
Beach Club Villas	☎ 407-934-2175
Blizzard Beach Information	☎ 407-560-3400
BoardWalk Inn	☎ 407-939-5100
Caribbean Beach Resort	☎ 407-934-3400
Centra Care	
Kissimmee	☎ 407-390-1888
Lake Buena Vista	☎ 407-934-2273
Universal–Dr. Phillips	☎ 407-291-8975
Cirque du Soleil	☎ 407-939-7600
Contemporary Resort–Bay Lake Tower	☎ 407-824-1000
Convention Information	☎ 321-939-7129
Coronado Springs Resort	☎ 407-939-1000
Dining Advance Reservations	☎ 407-WDW-DINE (939-3463)
Disabled Guests Special Requests	☎ 407-939-7807
Disney Institute	☎ 407-824-7997 or 321-939-4600
DisneyQuest	☎ 407-828-4600
Disney Springs Information	☎ 407-827-2281
ESPN Wide World of Sports Complex	☎ 407-939-GAME (4263)
Fantasia Gardens Miniature Golf	☎ 407-560-4753
Fort Wilderness Resort & Campground	☎ 407-824-2900
Golf Reservations and Information	☎ 407-WDW-GOLF (939-4653)
Grand Floridian Resort & Spa/Villas	☎ 407-824-3000
Group Camping	☎ 407-939-7807 (press *4*)
Guided-Tour Information	☎ 407-WDW-TOUR (939-8687)

Guided VIP Solo Tours	☎ 407-560-4033
House of Blues Tickets & Information	☎ 407-934-2583
Lost and Found (for articles lost):	
Today at Disney's Animal Kingdom	☎ 407-938-2784
Today at Disney's Hollywood Studios	☎ 407-560-4668
Today at Epcot	☎ 407-560-7500
Today at the Magic Kingdom	☎ 407-824-4521
Today at Universal Orlando (Universal Studios, Islands of Adventure, and CityWalk)	☎ 407-224-4233
Yesterday or before (at all Disney parks)	☎ 407-824-4245
Merchandise Guest Services	☎ 877-560-6477
Old Key West Resort	☎ 407-827-7700
Outdoor Recreation Reservations & Information	☎ 407-WDW-PLAY (939-7529)
Polynesian Village Resort & Villas	☎ 407-824-2000
Pop Century Resort	☎ 407-938-4000
Port Orleans French Quarter Resort	☎ 407-934-5000
Port Orleans Riverside Resort	☎ 407-934-6000
Resort Dining	☎ 407-WDW-DINE (939-3463)
Saratoga Springs Resort & Spa, Treehouse Villas	☎ 407-827-1100
Security	
Routine	☎ 407-560-7959
Urgent	☎ 407-560-1990
Shades of Green Resort	☎ 407-824-3400 ☎ 407-824-3600
Telecommunication for the Deaf Reservations	☎ 407-939-7670
Tennis Reservations & Lessons	☎ 321-228-1146
Walt Disney Travel Company	☎ 407-939-6244
Walt Disney World Dolphin	☎ 407-934-4000
Walt Disney World Swan	☎ 407-934-3000
Walt Disney World Ticket Inquiries	☎ 407-566-4985
Weather Information	☎ 407-827-4545
Wilderness Lodge & Villas	☎ 407-824-3200
Winter Summerland Miniature Golf	☎ 407-560-3000
Wrecker Service (if closed, call Security, above)	☎ 407-824-0976
Yacht Club Resort	☎ 407-934-7000

12–9 Months Before Your Trip

You may already have a general idea of when you want to visit Disney World. What the trip will cost you, however, can be a surprise. Take a couple of evenings to plan out a budget, an approximate time of year to travel, and narrow down your hotel choices.

- **Establish a budget.** See page 54 in Part Two for an idea of how much Disney vacation you can get for $500, $1,000, $1,500, and $2,000, for various family sizes. More information is available at **tinyurl.com /500-disney-vacation.**
- **Figure out when to go and where to stay.** Begin researching resorts (see Part Three) and the best times of year to visit to avoid crowds (see page 39). Our own Erin Foster has devised an excellent method for finding the best vacation dates for your family: See **tinyurl.com /when-to-visit-wdw.**
- **Brush up on discounts.** Disney releases certain discounts around the same time every year. Check **mousesavers.com** for a list of these regular discounts, when they're usually announced, and the travel dates they cover at **tinyurl.com/wdw-historic-discounts.**
- **Create an account at mydisneyexperience.com** (see page 36). You'll need it to make hotel, dining, and ride reservations later.
- **Make a preliminary hotel reservation.** This typically requires a deposit equal to one night's cost, and it guarantees you a room. You can change or cancel your reservation without penalty for several months while you continue your research.
  Disney Vacation Club members can make reservations at their home resorts starting 11 months before their trip. See page 122 for information on how anyone can rent points from a DVC member.
- **Investigate whether trip insurance makes sense for your situation.** If you'll be traveling to Disney World during peak hurricane season (August and September), it might be worthwhile. Third-party policies, such as those from **insuremytrip.com,** are usually cheaper than Disney's trip insurance, and often more comprehensive.
- **If you're not a US citizen, make sure your family's passports and visas are in order.** Passports typically need to be valid for six months beyond your travel dates. An electronic US visa is typically good for two years from the date of issue, if you need one. See **travel.state .gov/content/visas/english.html** for details.

9–7 Months Before Your Trip

Now is the time to start thinking about where you'll be eating and what you want to do in the theme parks.

- **Get familiar with Disney World restaurants** (see Part Four). When Disney's dining system opens at your 180-day mark, you'll be ready to make reservations. Also see our website, **touringplans.com/walt -disney-world/dining,** for current menus and prices at every Disney World restaurant, all searchable.
  Disney Vacation Club members can make reservations outside their home resorts starting seven months before their trip.
- **Also get familiar with the Disney Dining Plan** (see Part Three, page 301). If you're planning to stay at a Disney hotel, you'll want to determine whether the plan will save you money on the restaurants you've identified.

- **Check the best days to visit each park.** Use our Disney World Crowd Calendar to select the parks you'll visit on each day of your trip: **touringplans.com/walt-disney-world/crowd-calendar.**

180 Days Before Your Trip

Now you can start making dining, recreation, and other reservations.

- **Make sit-down dining reservations** beginning at 6 a.m. Eastern time online at **disneyworld.disney.go.com/dining** or at 7 a.m. by phone: ☎ 407-WDW-DINE (see page 302 in Part Four for tips on how to do this). If you're staying at a Disney resort, you'll be able to make reservations for up to 10 days of your trip today.
- **Revisit the economics of the Disney Dining Plan** after you've made dining reservations, to verify it's still worth the money. If not, call Disney to drop it from your reservation.
- **Make reservations for the following:**
  Theme park tours (page 717): ☎ 407-WDW-TOUR
  Recreational activities (such as boating): ☎ 407-WDW-PLAY
  Spa treatments (page 755): ☎ 407-WDW-SPAS
  Bibbidi Bobbidi Boutique (page 731): ☎ 407-WDW-STYLE
  Theme park dessert parties (page 522): ☎ 407-WDW-DINE

6–4 Months Before Your Trip

Become familiar with the rides, shows, and attractions at Disney World's four theme parks, and start planning what you'll see each day. This will help you identify any potential bottlenecks, which you can address using our touring plans and Disney's FastPass+ system. You'll be able to make FastPass+ reservations in a few weeks.

- **Review the attractions and shows** at the Magic Kingdom (page 490), Epcot (page 544), Disney's Animal Kingdom (page 582), and Disney's Hollywood Studios (page 608).
- **Make a list of must-see attractions in each park.** If you're unsure about your children experiencing a particular attraction, preview it for them on YouTube: **tinyurl.com/wdw-ride-videos.**
- **Review our touring plans** (see page 804), and use them to begin putting together a preliminary touring strategy for each park. You can also use our touring plan software online at **touringplans.com/walt -disney-world/touring-plans.** By starting now, you'll be able to see which attractions would benefit from FastPass+ reservations, which you can make 60 or 30 days before your trip. You'll also see whether you'll need the Park Hopper option on your theme park tickets, which you'll purchase later.

120 Days Before Your Trip

As your vacation approaches, it's time to make concrete arrangements for your days in the theme parks.

- **Purchase your park admission** at least this far in advance (see page 60 for ticket details and add-ons). Our online **Least Expensive Ticket Calculator** tool will find you the best discounts on Disney tickets: **touringplans.com/walt-disney-world/ticket-calculator.**
- **Link your tickets to your My Disney Experience account** so you can make FastPass+ reservations at the 30- or 60-day mark.

- **Save money on stroller rentals in the parks** (if needed) by renting from a third-party company. Several will drop off and pick up at your resort or vacation home. See Part Five, page 398, for our recommendations. You can save on **wheelchair and ECV rentals** by using third-party companies, too; see Part Six, page 435, for details and recommendations.

60 Days Before Your Trip

The theme for this week is "the three F's": FastPass+, fitness, and refunds. (If you're a stickler for precision, substitute *funds retrieval* for *refunds*.)

- **Disney resort guests can make FastPass+ reservations** (see page 88) beginning at midnight Eastern time. Once you have your reservations, update your touring plans. If you're using our online touring plans, we'll redo your schedule so that you get to your chosen attractions on time.
- **Start a walking regimen** to prepare for the 7–10 miles per day you may be walking in the parks. See page 386 for more on that.
- **If you decide not to go to Disney World,** you have two weeks to cancel most Disney vacation packages without penalty; room-only reservations can be cancelled without penalty until five days before your trip (six days if you booked online). See page 117 for a review of Disney's cancellation policies. Otherwise, you can start your online check-in at Disney resorts 60 days before you arrive: **disneyworld .disney.go.com/trip/online-check-in.**

45 Days Before Your Trip

- **Final payment is due for Disney vacation packages.** Final payment for room-only reservations is due at check-in.
- **Customize and order your MagicBands** (see page 67) if you're staying on-site.
- **Make Disney's Magical Express reservations** (page 449) if you're flying, or make other transportation arrangements.
- **If you want to switch resorts** or make additional dining reservations, check for availability from people who cancelled their vacations at the 45-day mark.

30 Days Out

- **Off-site guests can make FastPass+ reservations** (see page 88) beginning at midnight Eastern time.
- **Confirm park hours** and finish preliminary touring plans.
- **Download our mobile app, Lines,** to your Apple or Android device, so you can follow your touring plan and get updates while you're in the parks: **touringplans.com/disney-world-app.**
- **Arrange to stop delivery of mail and newspapers.**
- **Check that you have enough prescription medication.**
- **Arrange for pet or house sitters.**

Two Weeks Out

- **Arrange grocery delivery to your resort** (see Part Eight, page 482).
- **If you're flying to the US from another country,** complete the **Advance Passenger Information and Secure Flight** (**APIS**) process at least 72 hours before your flight. You should be able to do this through

your airline's website; otherwise, make sure your travel agent has your information. You'll need to provide the address where you'll be staying in the US, so have that information handy when you complete this form. See **tinyurl.com/ustravel-apis** for details.

Six Days Out

• This is your last chance to cancel Disney room-only reservations booked online without a penalty. Call ☎ 407-W-DISNEY to do so.

Five Days Out

• Fax your room request to Disney. We can do this for you automatically—see **tinyurl.com/wdw-hotel-fax** for details.
• This is your last chance to cancel Disney room-only reservations booked by phone or travel agent without a penalty. Call ☎ 407-W-DISNEY to do so.
• Check the weather forecast for Orlando: **tinyurl.com/wdw-weather**.
• Start packing. See **tinyurl.com/wdw-packing-tips** for our tips.

Four Days Out

• Purchase Disney's Memory Maker photo package (see Part Eight, page 479) at least three days in advance to ensure that all photos are linked as soon as you arrive. You'll also get a $30 discount by purchasing your package ahead of time.

The Day Before

• Check in to your airline online.
• Finish Disney resort online check-in, if you haven't already done so: **disneyworld.disney.go.com/trip/online-check-in**.
• Cancel any unneeded dining or babysitting reservations.
• Do one last check of park hours and weather.

DISNEY ONLINE: OFFICIAL AND OTHERWISE

THE WALT DISNEY COMPANY HAS ROLLED OUT a set of high-tech enhancements to its theme parks and hotels. This collection of initiatives, officially known as **MyMagic+,** includes issuing rubber wristbands (**MagicBands**) with embedded computer chips that function as admission tickets and hotel keys; it also involved major changes to Disney's Fastpass ride-reservation system, restaurants, and attractions. Many of the changes require you to make detailed decisions about every day of your trip, up to two months in advance, if you want to avoid long waits in line. See the previous section for a complete trip-planning timeline.

The changes to Fastpass—now known as **FastPass+**—require that you make reservations months in advance to ride Disney's headliner attractions, if you want any chance of avoiding long waits in line. Other features, such as MagicBands and restaurant reservations, require you to enter detailed information about your traveling party.

The Walt Disney World website (**disneyworld.com**) and mobile app are the "glue" that binds all of this together. Because you've got to plan so much before you leave home, we cover the basics of the website and app in the following section. While we provide navigational instructions here, Disney's web designers change direction faster than hypercaffeinated squirrels in traffic, so you may have to hunt around to find some features. Full coverage of MagicBands starts on page 67; details on the FastPass+ system start on page 87.

My Disney Experience at DisneyWorld.com

A lot of work has gone into the Disney website. You can make hotel, dining, and recreation reservations; buy admission; and get park hours, attraction information, and much more.

The most important of the site's features support My Disney Experience. To make use of some of these, you'll need to register by providing your e-mail address and choosing a password. You'll also need to have reserved a room at a Disney-owned hotel or have in your possession a valid theme park ticket.

GETTING STARTED In the upper-right corner of the home page, click "My Disney Experience" to access a welcome page with links to any existing hotel and dining reservations. Click the "My Family & Friends" link, then enter the names and ages of everyone traveling with you. You'll need this information when you make your FastPass+ and dining reservations.

unofficial **TIP**
Disney's websites work better with Firefox than with Google Chrome.

Back on the "My Disney Experience" page, click "My Itinerary" in the top right corner of the page. A calendar will then appear—if you've got a Disney-hotel reservation, the calendar should display those dates of travel. If not, you'll need to manually enter your reservation number, then select your travel dates using the calendar.

For each day of your trip, the website will display operating hours for the theme and water parks. Select the theme park you'll be visiting on a particular day; if you're visiting more than one, select the one at which you want to make reservations now.

MAKING FASTPASS+ RESERVATIONS Click the "FastPass+" link from the menu on the right side of your screen. Next, select one of your displayed travel dates, then indicate which members of your group will be with you and which park you'll be visiting on that date. At press time, you could use FastPass+ at just one park per day.

Now you'll see a list of your chosen park's participating FastPass+ attractions. Select the ones you'd like to reserve; if an attraction isn't selectable, all of its available FastPass+ reservations are gone.

At this point, the website will give you a "Best Match" set of Fast-Pass+ reservations and return times for your attractions, plus three optional sets of return times. Select the set that most closely fits the rest of your plans for the day, or, if you're using our touring plans, select the set that most closely matches the suggested FastPass+ return times on the plans. After confirming your selections, you can check for alternative return-time windows for each attraction.

You'll need to repeat these steps for every day for which you want to use FastPass+ in the theme parks. Having fun yet?

If you're unsure of the attractions or times of day for which you should use FastPass+, our touring plan software can make recommendations that will minimize your time in line. See page 79 for details.

MAKING DINING RESERVATIONS From the "My Itinerary" page, click the "Reserve Dining" link. (You may have to reenter your travel dates.) A list of every Disney World eatery will be displayed. Use the filtering criteria at the top of the page to narrow the list.

Once you've settled on a restaurant, click the restaurant's name to check availability for your dining time and the number of people in your party. If space is available and you want to make a reservation, you'll need to indicate which members of your party will be joining you. If you want to make other dining reservations, you'll need to repeat this process for every reservation.

Once you've made your initial set of FastPass+ and dining reservations, you'll be able to view and edit them (along with your hotel reservation) in the "My Reservation" section of My Disney Experience.

My Disney Experience Mobile App

Along with the website, Disney offers a companion app for iOS and Android devices. It includes park hours, attraction operating hours and descriptions, restaurant hours and descriptions, the ability to make Fast-Pass+ and dining reservations online, GPS-based directions, and more. My Disney Experience is optimized for the latest phones and tablets, so some features may not be available on all devices.

Early versions of My Disney Experience had many issues, and it was rated iTunes's second-worst app for navigating Disney World (and the very worst on the Google Play Store). But Disney's a big company with lots of money, and the most recent versions of the app are better. You still see only Disney's "official" information, including (we believe) intentionally wrong attraction wait times so you'll go somewhere else in the park. Search for "My Disney Experience" on iTunes, Google Play, or the Amazon Appstore for Android to try the latest version.

Our Recommended Websites

Searching online for Disney information is like navigating an immense maze for a very small piece of cheese: There's a lot of information available, but you may find a lot of dead-ends before getting what you want. Our picks follow.

BEST Q&A SITE Who knew? Walt Disney World has a **Mom's Panel** all chosen from among 10,000-plus applicants. The panelists have a website, **disneyworldmoms.com,** where they offer tips and discuss how to plan a Disney World vacation. Several moms have specialized experience in areas such as Disney Cruise Line, runDisney, and traveling with sports groups; some speak Spanish, too. The parents are unpaid and are free to speak their minds.

BEST GENERAL UNOFFICIAL WALT DISNEY WORLD WEBSITE Besides touringplans.com, Deb Wills's **allears.net** is the first website we recommend to friends who want to make a trip to Disney World. Updated several times a week, the site includes breaking news, tons of photos, Disney restaurant menus, resort and ticket information, tips for guests with special needs, and more. We also check **wdwmagic.com** for news and happenings around Walt Disney World.

BEST MONEY-SAVING SITE MouseSavers (**mousesavers.com**) keeps an updated list of discounts and reservation codes for use at Disney resorts. Codes are separated into categories such as "For the general public" and "For residents of certain states." Anyone who calls or books online can use a current code and get the discounted rate. Savings can be considerable—up to 40% in many cases. MouseSavers also has discount codes for rental cars and non-Disney hotels in the area, along with a calendar showing when Disney sales typically launch.

BEST WALT DISNEY WORLD PREVIEW SITE If you want to see what a particular attraction is like, **touringplans.com** offers free videos or photos of every attraction. Videos of indoor ("dark") rides are sometimes inferior to those of outdoor rides due to poor lighting, but even the videos and photos of indoor rides generally provide a good sense of what the attraction is about. **YouTube** is also an excellent place to find videos of Disney and other Central Florida attractions.

SOCIAL MEDIA **Facebook, Twitter,** and **Instagram** are popular places for Disney fans to gather online and share comments, tips, and photos. Following fellow Disneyphiles as they share their in-park experiences can make you feel like you're there, even as you're stuck in a cubicle at work. For Disney World's official social-media outlets, visit **facebook.com /waltdisneyworld, twitter.com/waltdisneyworld,** and **instagram.com /waltdisneyworld.**

BEST INTERNET RADIO STATION MouseWorld Radio (**mouseworldradio .com**) plays everything from attraction themes and hotel background music to sound clips from old TV ads for Disney resorts. What makes MouseWorld Radio special is that the tracks match what the Disney parks are playing at the time of day you're listening. Also try the **Walt Disney World Today Podcast** on iTunes and at **wdwtoday.com,** cohosted by the *Unofficial Guide*'s Len Testa.

BEST THEME-PARK-INSIDER SITE It's been said that people who eat sausage should never watch it being made. If you have the stomach to learn how theme parks get built, take a look around **jimhillmedia.com.** Jim's got insider accounts of the politics, frantic project management, and pipe dreams that somehow combine to create the attractions that Disney and Universal build.

BEST DISNEY DISCUSSION BOARDS There are tons of these; among the most active are **disboards.com, forums.wdwmagic.com,** our own **forum .touringplans.com,** and, for Brits, **thedibb.co.uk** (*DIBB* stands for "Disney Information Bulletin Board").

BEST SITE FOR GUESTS WITH FOOD ALLERGIES At **allergyeats.com /disney,** you put in your allergies and your park, and it shows you where and what you can eat.

BEST SITES FOR TRAFFIC, ROADWORK, CONSTRUCTION, AND SAFETY INFORMATION Visit **expresswayauthority.com** for the latest information on roadwork in the Orlando and Orange County areas. The site also contains detailed maps, directions, and toll-rate information for the most popular tourist destinations.

A seven-year construction project to improve I-4 was launched in 2015. Information on the northern section between Kirkman Road (near Universal) and downtown Orlando can be found at **i4ultimate .com**. Construction updates on the southern section from Kirkman Road to US 27 in Polk County are available at **i4express.com**.

Check **flhsmv.gov/fhp/cps** to learn about state child-restraint requirements. Finally, we like **maps.google.com** for driving directions.

WHEN *to* GO *to* WALT DISNEY WORLD

Why do they call it tourist season if we can't shoot them?

—Palatka, Florida, outdoorsman

SELECTING THE TIME OF YEAR FOR YOUR VISIT

WALT DISNEY WORLD IS BUSIEST Christmas Day through the first few days of January. Next busiest is the spring-break period from mid-March through the week of Easter, then Thanksgiving week. Following those are the first few weeks of June, when summer vacation starts, and the week of Presidents Day.

unofficial TIP
Though crowds have grown in September and October as a result of promotions aimed at the international market and families without school-age children, these months continue to be good for touring.

The least-busy time is from Labor Day in September through the beginning of October. Next slowest are the weeks in mid-January after the Martin Luther King Jr. holiday weekend up to Presidents Day in February (except when the Walt Disney World Marathon runs after MLK Day). The weeks after Thanksgiving and before Christmas are less crowded than average, as is mid-April–mid-May, after spring break and before Memorial Day.

Late February, March, and early April are dicey. Crowds ebb and flow according to spring-break schedules and the timing of Presidents Day weekend. Besides being asphalt-melting hot, July brings throngs of South American tourists on their winter holiday.

A family who vacationed during the slow period following the Thanksgiving holiday had this to say:

> My family went down when the Christmas decorations were up, and it was AMAZING! The decorations were incredible and put you in just the right mood for the holidays. It leaves you speechless, especially when you see the castle at the Magic Kingdom lit up at night.

The Downside of Off-Season Touring

Though we strongly recommend going to Disney World in the fall, winter, or spring, there are a few trade-offs. The parks often close early during the off-season, either because of low crowds or special events such as the Halloween and Christmas parties at the Magic Kingdom. This drastically reduces touring hours. Even when crowds are small, it's difficult to see big parks such as the Magic Kingdom between 9 a.m. and 7 p.m. Early closing also usually means no evening parades or

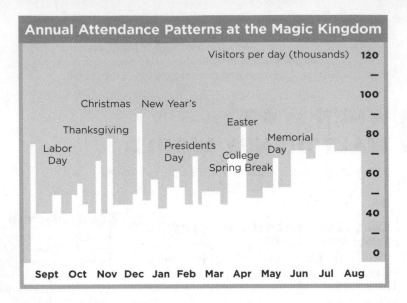

Annual Attendance Patterns at the Magic Kingdom

Visitors per day (thousands)   120

Christmas   New Year's

Thanksgiving

Labor Day   Presidents Day

Easter

Memorial Day

College Spring Break

Sept Oct Nov Dec Jan Feb Mar Apr May Jun Jul Aug

fireworks. And because these are slow times, some rides and attractions may be closed. Finally, Central Florida temperatures fluctuate wildly during late fall, winter, and early spring; daytime highs in the 40s and 50s aren't uncommon.

Given the choice, however, smaller crowds, bargain prices, and stress-free touring are worth risking cold weather or closed attractions. Touring in fall and other "off" periods is so much easier that our research team, at the risk of being blasphemous, would advise taking children out of school for a Disney World visit. For the pros and cons of this approach, see page 384.

BE UNCONVENTIONAL Orlando's Orange County Convention Center hosts some of the largest conventions and trade shows in the world. Hotel rooms anywhere near Walt Disney World are hard to find when there's a big convention—rooms under $75 and over $200 a night (that is, budget and upscale) go fast.

You can check the convention schedule at the Orlando Orange County Convention Center for the next seven months at **occc.net /global/calendar**.

DON'T FORGET AUGUST Kids go back to school pretty early in Florida (and in a lot of other places, too). This makes mid-to-late August a good time to visit Walt Disney World for families who can't vacation during the off-season. A New Jersey mother of two school-age children spells it out:

The end of August is the PERFECT time to go (just watch out for hurricanes; it's the season). There were virtually no wait times, 20 minutes at the most.

A mom from Rapid City, South Dakota, agrees:

School starts very early in Florida, so our mid-August visit was great for crowds, but not for heat.

Walt Disney World Climate

JAN	FEB	MAR	APR	MAY	JUN	JUL	AUG	SEP	OCT	NOV	DEC
AVERAGE DAILY LOW (°F)											
47	50	54	59	65	71	73	73	72	66	58	51
AVERAGE DAILY HIGH (°F)											
71	73	78	83	89	91	92	92	90	84	78	72
AVERAGE DAILY TEMPERATURE (°F)											
60	61	67	71	77	81	82	83	81	75	68	62
AVERAGE DAILY HUMIDITY PERCENTAGE											
62	73	71	70	71	70	74	76	76	75	74	73
AVERAGE RAINFALL PER MONTH (INCHES)											
2.9	2.7	4.0	2.3	3.1	8.3	7.0	7.7	5.1	2.5	2.1	2.9
NUMBER OF DAYS OF RAIN PER MONTH											
6	7	8	6	8	14	17	16	14	9	6	6

And from a family from Roxbury, New Jersey:

I recommend the last two weeks of August for anyone traveling there during the summer. We have visited twice during this time of year and have had great success touring the parks.

HIGH-LOW, HIGH-LOW, IT'S OFF TO DISNEY WE GO Though we recommend off-season touring, we realize that it's not possible for many families. We want to make it clear, therefore, that you can have a wonderful experience regardless of when you go. Our advice, irrespective of season, is to arrive early at the parks and avoid the crowds by using one of our touring plans. If attendance is light, kick back and forget the touring plans.

WE'VE GOT WEATHER! Long before Walt Disney World, tourists visited Florida year-round to enjoy the temperate tropical and subtropical climates. The best weather months generally are October, November, March, and April (see chart above). Fall is usually dry, whereas spring is wetter. December, January, and February vary, with average highs of 72°–73°F intermixed with highs in the 50°–65°F range. May is hot but tolerable. June, July, August, and September are the warmest months. Rain is possible anytime, usually in the form of scattered thunderstorms. An entire day of rain is unusual.

CROWD CONDITIONS AND THE BEST AND WORST PARKS TO VISIT FOR EACH DAY OF THE YEAR We receive thousands of e-mails and letters inquiring about crowd conditions on specific dates throughout the year.

Readers also want to know which park is best to visit on each day of their stay. To make things easier for you (and us!), we provide at **touringplans.com** a calendar covering the next year (click "Crowd Calendar" on the home page). For each date, we offer a crowd-level index based on a scale of 1–10, with 1 being least crowded and 10 being most crowded. Our calendar takes into account all holidays, special events, and more, as described on page 43.

Because Disney is constantly testing resort discounts and tinkering with park hours, it's just not possible to include an accurate calendar in this book. Keeping the online Crowd Calendar updated requires

TOP 10 AMERICAN THEME PARKS

	THEME PARK	2014 ATTENDANCE	CHANGE FROM 2013	DAILY AVERAGE
1.	The Magic Kingdom	19.33 million	+4.0%	52,964
2.	Disneyland	16.77 million	+3.5%	45,942
3.	Epcot	11.45 million	+2.0%	31,381
4.	Disney's Animal Kingdom	10.40 million	+2.0%	28,499
5.	Disney's Hollywood Studios	10.31 million	+2.0%	28,252
6.	Disney California Adventure	8.77 million	+3.0%	24,025
7.	Universal Studios Florida	8.26 million	+17.0%	22,638
8.	Universal's Islands of Adventure	8.14 million	0.0	22,304
9.	Universal Studios Hollywood	6.82 million	+11.0%	18,696
10.	SeaWorld Orlando	4.68 million	-8.0%	12,830

Source: *Themed Entertainment Association/AECOM Global Attractions Attendance Report 2014 (released June 3, 2015)*

year-round work from our statisticians. Thus, we have to charge a modest subscription fee. The same fee also provides access to additional touring plans and other features. Owners of the current edition of the guide are eligible for a substantial discount on the subscription. See the beginning of this chapter for more information about our website.

A Bristol, Tennessee, couple had good luck with the calendar:

The UG Crowd Calendar is 100% accurate. We love it and will continue to use it every trip. We even tested it in heavy-duty crowds just to see if it worked, and you were dead-on correct!

But a Braintree, Massachusetts, woman cautions:

It should be emphasized that parks can still feel really crowded on a low-crowd day, especially the Magic Kingdom. But you will notice the difference when you see the wait times for the rides. Anyone expecting to have room to roam freely in certain parts of the Magic Kingdom on a low attendance day will be disappointed. The same is true for Animal Kingdom: We went there on a "low" attendance day in the afternoon, and it was extremely congested and difficult to walk through some areas of the park.

Even on a slow day, you may find waits of 30–45 minutes or more on popular rides such as Seven Dwarfs Mine Train at the Magic Kingdom and Test Track at Epcot. To save on maintenance costs, Disney doesn't run most rides at 100% of their capacity when crowds are low. Instead, they run fewer mine trains, test cars, and other vehicles and assume that most people simply expect a certain amount of waiting at a theme park. Running fewer vehicles means less wear and tear on the track, cars, and other moving parts—which saves Disney money—without generating many complaints.

HOW WE DETERMINE CROWD LEVELS AND BEST DAYS A number of factors contribute to the models we use to predict both crowd levels and the best days to visit each theme park.

Data we use to predict crowd levels:
- Historical wait times from the same time period in past years
- Historical theme park hours from the same time period in past years
- Future hotel-room bookings in the Orlando area
- Disney's special-events calendar (for example, Mickey's Not-So-Scary Halloween Party)
- Legal holidays in the United States
- Public-school schedules (including spring-break schedules for the 100 largest school districts east of the Mississippi River, plus Massachusetts and Connecticut)

We collect thousands of wait times from every Disney park every day, including posted and actual times. Historical park hours include the actual operating hours for all of the theme parks over the past five years. Special events include everything from official Walt Disney World–sanctioned events to such independent events as Gay Days. Our Central Florida tourism demographics cover everything from where Orlando visitors come from and how long they stay to how many people make up each party and which theme parks they visit.

CROWD-CALENDAR REASONING AND ACCURACY Our online Crowd Calendar explains why we rate the parks a specific way on a specific day, including how we weigh each of the factors listed above. The site also shows you our predictions versus actual crowd levels for past days, so you can see how we fared with our predictions.

EXTRA MAGIC HOURS

EXTRA MAGIC HOURS (EMHS) is a perk for families staying at a Walt Disney World resort, including the Swan, Dolphin, and Shades of Green, and the Hilton in the Downtown Disney Resort Area. On selected days of the week, Disney resort guests will be able to enter a Disney theme park 1 hour earlier or stay in a selected theme park about 2 hours later than the official park-operating hours. Theme park visitors not staying at a Disney resort may stay in the park for Extra Magic Hour evenings, but they can't experience any rides, attractions, or shows. In other words, they can shop and eat. The swimming theme parks, Typhoon Lagoon and Blizzard Beach, rarely offer EMHs. If they do, it's usually during the summer.

WHAT'S REQUIRED? A valid admission ticket or MagicBand wristband is required to enter the park, and you must show your Disney resort ID or have your MagicBand scanned when entering. For evening EMHs, you may be asked to show your Disney resort ID or MagicBand to experience rides or attractions.

WHEN ARE EMHS OFFERED? You can check the Crowd Calendar at **touringplans.com** for the dates of your visit, check the parks calendar at **disneyworld.com,** or call Walt Disney World Information at ☎ 407-824-4321 or 407-939-6244 (press 0 for a live representative).

In addition to these, it's common for Epcot to have evening EMHs on Wednesdays in September and October, and for Animal Kingdom to have morning EMHs on Mondays later in the year.

SAMPLE EXTRA MAGIC HOURS SCHEDULE *(frequently varies)*						
MORNING						
MON	TUES	WED	THUR	FRI	SAT	SUN
—	Epcot	Animal Kingdom	Magic Kingdom	—	DHS	Animal Kingdom
EVENING						
MON	TUES	WED	THUR	FRI	SAT	SUN
DHS	—	—	—	Epcot	Magic Kingdom	—

WHAT DO EXTRA MAGIC HOURS MEAN TO YOU? Disney seems to use EMHs in two ways: to provide Disney resort guests some extra park time on days when those parks are traditionally crowded, and as an incentive to visit one park on days when another park is typically more crowded.

unofficial **TIP**
If you're going to get up early for one morning Extra Magic Hour session during your vacation, make sure that it's for the Magic Kingdom.

Crowds typically range from slightly below average to average at Disney's Animal Kingdom and the Magic Kingdom on days when those parks host Extra Magic Hours. Crowds are higher than average at Disney's Hollywood Studios, and slightly higher than average at Epcot, on days when they have EMHs.

Not many families have the stamina to take advantage of morning and evening EMHs on consecutive days. If you have to choose between morning or evening Extra Magic Hour sessions, consider first whether your family functions better getting up early or staying up late. Also, consider the time at which the parks close to day guests. Evening EMHs are most useful when the crowds are low and the parks close relatively early to the general public, so your family doesn't have to stay up past midnight to take advantage of the perk.

MORNING EXTRA MAGIC HOURS *(a.k.a. Early Entry)*

MORNING EXTRA MAGIC HOURS are offered at all four theme parks throughout the year, and rarely (during summer) at Blizzard Beach and Typhoon Lagoon water parks. Several days of the week, Disney resort guests are invited to enter a designated theme park 1 hour before the general public. During this hour, guests can enjoy selected attractions opened early just for them.

How Early Entry Affects Attendance at the Theme Parks

Morning Extra Magic Hours strongly affect attendance at Disney's Hollywood Studios and Epcot, especially during busier times of year. Crowds at those parks are usually larger than average, as a Winston-Salem, North Carolina, mom discovered:

Disney Hollywood Studios was a MADHOUSE. Do NOT go on Extra Magic Hours days. After spending about 3 hours to ride three rides, I just wanted to trample the people stampeding to the exit.

Magic Kingdom crowds are about average when it has morning EMHs (usually Thursday). Because Disney's Animal Kingdom typically has two morning EMHs but no evening EMHs, crowds are spread out, resulting in lower-than-average waits on both days.

If you're staying at a Disney resort, remember these three things about Extra Magic Hours:

1. The Magic Kingdom has more attractions open for morning EMHs than any other park. Coupled with a good touring plan, we think the Magic Kingdom's morning session is the most worthwhile of any EMHs at any park.

2. Morning EMHs are least useful at Disney's Animal Kingdom because it has fewer rides overall. There's simply not as much benefit for the lost sleep.

3. If you think it unlikely that you'll be at the park offering morning Extra Magic Hours 30 minutes before it opens, visit another park instead.

During holiday periods and summer, when Disney hotels are full, getting in early makes a tremendous difference in crowds at the designated park. The program funnels so many people into the EMH park that it fills by about 10 a.m. and is practically gridlocked by noon. A mother of three from Lee's Summit, Missouri, writes:

Our first full day at WDW, we went to the Magic Kingdom on an early-entry day for resort guests. We were there at 7:30 a.m. and were able to walk onto all the rides in Fantasyland with no wait. At 8:45 a.m. we positioned ourselves at the Adventureland rope and ran toward Splash Mountain when the rope dropped. We were able to ride Splash Mountain with no wait and then Big Thunder with about a 15-minute wait. We then went straight to the Jungle Cruise and the wait was already 30 minutes, so we skipped it. The park became incredibly crowded as the day progressed, and we were all exhausted from getting up so early. We left the park around noon. After that day, I resolved to avoid early-entry days and instead be at a non-early-entry park about a half-hour before official opening time.

Note that during holidays, the Magic Kingdom opens to regular guests at 8 a.m. Morning EMHs begin at 7 a.m., so you'll need to be at the Magic Kingdom entrance at around 6:30 a.m. You won't be alone, but relatively few people are willing to get up that early for a theme park, and your first hour in the parks will be (pardon us) magical.

This note from a North Bend, Washington, dad emphasizes the importance of arriving at the beginning of the early-entry period.

We only used early entry once—to Disney's Hollywood Studios. We got there 20 minutes after early entry opened, and the wait for Tower of Terror was 1½ hours long without FastPass+. We skipped it.

Morning Extra Magic Hours and Park-Hopping

An alternative strategy for Disney resort guests is to take advantage of morning Extra Magic Hours, but only until the designated park gets crowded. At that time, move to another park.

A Dillsburg, Pennsylvania, mom has another tip:

If you have FastPass+ opportunities [see page 87], schedule them for the park you're visiting second.

This works particularly well at the Magic Kingdom for families with young children who love the attractions in Fantasyland.

However, it will take you about an hour to commute to the second park of the day. If, for example, you depart the Magic Kingdom for Disney's Hollywood Studios at 11 a.m., you'll find the Studios pretty crowded when you arrive at about noon, as this Texas mom found:

> We made the mistake of doing a morning at the Magic Kingdom and an afternoon at the Studios. Worst idea ever. By the time we got to the Studios, all the [FastPass+ reservations] were gone for Toy Story Midway Mania!, the Tower of Terror, and Rock 'n' Roller Coaster. And all three rides had at least 90-minute waits.

Keeping these and other considerations in mind, here are some tips:

1. Use the morning–EMH–park-hopping strategy during the less busy times of year when the parks close early. You'll get a jump on the general public and add an hour to what, in the off-season, is an already short touring day.

2. Use the morning–EMH–park-hopping strategy to complete touring a second park that you've already visited on a previous day, or specifically to see live entertainment in the second park.

Don't hop to Disney's Animal Kingdom if it closes before 7 p.m. Crowds generally start leaving between 3 and 4 p.m. If the park closes at 5 or 6, you'll have only 1–3 hours of touring with lower crowds.

On any day except its EMH days, hopping to Epcot is usually good. Epcot is equipped to handle large crowds better than any other Disney park, minimizing the effects of a midday arrival. Also, World Showcase has a large selection of interesting dining options, making it a good choice for evening touring.

Don't hop to the park with morning EMHs. The idea is to avoid crowds, not join them. Finally, limit your hopping to two parks per day. Hopping to a third park in one day would result in more time spent commuting than saved by avoiding crowds.

Evening Extra Magic Hours

The evening Extra Magic Hours program lets Disney resort guests enjoy a different theme park on specified nights for about 2 hours after it closes to the general public. Guests pay no additional charge to participate but must scan their MagicBands (see page 67) at each ride or attraction they wish to experience. You can also show up at the turnstiles at any point after evening Extra Magic Hours have started. Note that if you've been in another park that day, you'll need the Park Hopper feature on your admission ticket to enter. Evening Extra Magic Hours are offered at the Magic Kingdom, Epcot, and Disney's Hollywood Studios, but not at Disney's Animal Kingdom.

Evening sessions are usually more crowded at the Magic Kingdom and the Studios than at Epcot. Those evening EMH crowds can be just as large as those throughout the day. During summer, when the Magic Kingdom's evening EMH session runs until 1 a.m., lines at headliner attractions can still be long at midnight. A mom from Fairhaven, Massachusetts, doesn't mince words:

> I say steer clear of a park that is open late. There are only a few attractions open and tons of people trying to get on them.

More attractions operate during evening EMHs than during morning EMHs. Certain fast-food and full-service restaurants remain open
as well.

SUMMER AND HOLIDAYS

A READER FROM COLUMBUS, OHIO, once observed, "The main
thing I learned from your book is not to go during the summer or at
holiday times. Once you know that, you don't need a guidebook."

While we might argue with the reader's conclusion, we agree that
avoiding summer and holidays is a wise strategy. That said, we also
understand that many folks have no choice concerning the time of year
they visit Disney World. Much of this book, in fact, is dedicated to making sure those readers who visit during busier times enjoy their experience. Sure, off-season touring is preferable, but, armed with knowledge
and some strategy, you can have a great time whenever you visit.

To put things in perspective, early summer (up to about June 15)
and late summer (after August 15) aren't nearly as crowded as the
intervening period. And even midsummer crowds pale in comparison
to the hordes during holiday periods. If you visit in midsummer or
during a holiday, the first thing you need to know is that the theme
parks' guest capacity is not infinite. In fact, once a park reaches capacity, only Disney resort guests arriving via the Disney transportation
system are allowed to enter. If you're not staying in the World, you
may find yourself in a situation similar to this Boise, Idaho, dad's:

> The Magic Kingdom and Hollywood Studios were so full they closed
> the parks. For three days we couldn't enter those parks, so we were
> forced to go to Epcot and use up two days of our four-day pass. We
> paid for another night at our hotel to see if the crowds would let up,
> but no luck. All we could do was drive around Orlando and sightsee.

We hasten to point out that this reader would've had no difficulty
gaining admission to the parks of his choice had he committed to
being at the turnstiles 40–60 minutes before official opening time.

Packed-Parks Compensation Plan

The thought of teeming throngs jockeying for position in endless lines
under the baking Fourth of July sun is enough to wilt the will and ears
of the most ardent Mouseketeer. Disney, however, feeling bad about
those long lines and challenging touring conditions on packed holidays,
compensates patrons with a no-less-than-incredible array of first-rate
live entertainment and events.

Shows, parades, concerts, and pageantry continue throughout the
day. In the evening, so much is going on that you have to make tough
choices. Concerts, parades, light shows, laser shows, fireworks, and
dance productions occur almost continuously. Disney also provides
colorful decorations for most holidays, plus special parades and live
entertainment for Christmas, New Year's, Easter, and the Fourth of July,
among others. (See "The Walt Disney World Calendar," next, for specific holiday advice.) No question about it: You can go to Walt Disney
World on the Fourth of July or any crowded extended-hours day, never
get on a ride, and still have a good time.

If you visit on a nonholiday midsummer day, arrive at the turnstile 40–60 minutes before the stated opening on a non–Extra Magic Hour morning day. If you visit during a major holiday period, arrive 1 hour before. To save time in the morning, buy your admission in advance. Also, consider bringing your own stroller or wheelchair instead of renting one of Disney's.

Hit your favorite rides early using one of our touring plans, then go back to your hotel for lunch, a swim, and perhaps a nap. If you're interested in the special parades and shows, return to the park in late afternoon or early evening. Assume that unless you use FastPass+, early morning will be the only time you can experience the attractions without long waits. Finally, don't wait until the last minute in the evening to leave the park—the exodus at closing is truly mind-boggling. Above all, bring your sense of humor, and pay attention to your group's morale.

THE WALT DISNEY WORLD CALENDAR

DISNEY CELEBRATES SPECIAL EVENTS throughout the year. Some commemorate major holidays, while others are events designed specifically by Disney to boost attendance during otherwise-slow times of year.

JANUARY Usually held the second weekend after New Year's, the **Walt Disney World Marathon** pulls in more runners and their families every year. In 2015, some 50,000 runners participated in the event—enough people to affect crowd conditions and pedestrian traffic throughout Disney World. In the spirit of participatory journalism, *Unofficial Guide* coauthor Len Testa usually runs one of the 5K, 10K, half, or full marathons. (Bob ices Len's tequila.) Following the marathon by a few days is the **Castaway Cay 5K,** but you'll need passage on Disney Cruise Line to run it. Information on all Disney running events can be found at **rundisney.com.** Also check **mickeymilespodcast.com** for in-depth coverage and tips.

FEBRUARY **Black History Month** is celebrated throughout Walt Disney World with displays, artisans, storytellers, and entertainers. The Kinsey Collection at Epcot's United States Pavilion is a highlight.

Mardi Gras is Tuesday, February 9, in 2016, and **Presidents Day** is Monday, February 16. These holidays will bring increases in attendance starting the weekend before. Usually held the second weekend of the month is the **Princess Half-Marathon** event, February 18–21 in 2016. The schedule includes a health expo, kids' races, a family 5K, a 10K, and the big race. The 2015 event drew more than 20,000 runners, enough to increase park attendance and affect vehicular and pedestrian traffic.

MARCH The **Epcot International Flower & Garden Festival** runs annually from mid-March to mid-May. Expert horticulturists showcase exotic floral displays and share gardening tips. The 30 million blooms from some 1,200 species will make your eyes pop, and best of all, the event doesn't seem to affect crowd levels at Epcot. The festival features food and beverage kiosks, making it more like September's Food & Wine event (see next page), only with flowers.

Easter is March 27, so expect most of March and early April to be peak spring-break season.

MAY Disney's Hollywood Studios hosts *Star Wars* Weekends annually beginning this month, with appearances from that franchise's actors and technicians. These events draw mainly local sci-fi fans, but some come from all over the country. While the impact on regular Disney World crowds is low, you'll find long lines if you want to meet the celebrities.

Disney usually announces a **"free" Disney Dining Plan** promotion around the first week of May for travel dates in September. See page 225 for more details.

JUNE Events this month include both *Star Wars* **Weekends** and **Gay Days,** May 31–June 6, 2016. Since 1991, lesbian, gay, bisexual, and transgender (LGBT) people from around the world have been converging on and around the World in early June for a week of events centered around the theme parks. Today, Gay Days attracts more than 160,000 LGBT visitors and their families and friends. For additional information, visit **gaydays.com.**

SEPTEMBER Radio personality Tom Joyner hosts an extremely popular party at Walt Disney World. Held Labor Day weekend (September 3–7 in 2015), the **Allstate Tom Joyner Family Reunion** typically features live musical performances, comedy acts, and family-oriented discussions. For more information, visit **familyreunion.blackamericaweb.com.**

Night of Joy, a Christian-music festival, is staged at the Magic Kingdom the first or second weekend of the month (September 11 and 12 in 2015). About 16 nationally known acts perform concerts on Friday and Saturday evenings after the park has closed. For information or to purchase tickets, call ☎ 407-W-DISNEY (934-7639) or visit **tinyurl .com/wdwnightofjoy.** One-day tickets are $69 per person for adults and children, including tax; two-day tickets are $122.50. Same-day tickets cost $85 per person for adults and children, including tax.

Those who say Christmas is the most wonderful time of year have never been to the **Epcot International Food & Wine Festival.** Held in World Showcase from mid-September through mid-November, the celebration represents 25 nations and cuisines, including demonstrations, wine seminars, tastings, and opportunities to see some of the world's top chefs. Although many activities are included in Epcot admission, some workshops and tastings are by reservation only and cost more than $100. Call ☎ 407-WDW-DINE starting around the beginning of August for more information. We think the culinary demos and the wine-and-beverage seminars (about $15–$20 each) are the best values at the festival. Because most of the food kiosks are set up around World Showcase, it can be difficult to walk through the crowds at some of the popular spots. Wait times at Epcot's attractions, however, are affected only slightly.

From a Dallas/Fort Worth–area reader:

> *The Food & Wine Festival was great, as it always is, but crowded. I think it's important to stress that while it's fun to make a meal out of the festival's offerings, it can take a long time. Some lines, especially in the afternoon and early evening on weekdays, were short or nonexistent. But on weekends, a simple dinner could take well over 2 hours between waiting in line, ordering, getting the food, finding a trash can to balance it on, eating, then deciding the next thing to eat. If you're a little person who eats very little, then only two stops might be good for you. But for big eaters, five or six stops was not uncommon. And*

the lack of tables is really a pain. Just put up some bar tables, Disney—there's space for them! The trash cans feel weird to eat off of.

Held around 22 nights each year from mid-September through October 31 (and occasionally into November), **Mickey's Not-So-Scary Halloween Party** runs from 7 p.m. to midnight at the Magic Kingdom. The event includes trick-or-treating in costume, parades, live music, storytelling, and a fireworks show. Advance tickets for the 2015 events went on sale in early May and cost (including tax) $72–$79 for adults, $67–$73 for kids. Same-day tickets cost $79–$84 for adults, $73–$79 for kids, and Halloween night (October 31) tickets cost $93 for adults, $87 for kids. Discounts are available for members of the US military, Disney Annual Pass holders, and Disney Vacation Club members. The least-crowded events are typically in September and on Tuesdays; tickets for the late-October dates usually sell out one to four days in advance. See **tinyurl.com/mickeysnotsoscary** for more information.

If you're wondering what "really crowded" looks like, here's how an Atlanta reader describes it:

The only time the crowds were unbearable was during the Halloween party. When I say it was sold out—man, was it sold out! Just moving 20 feet took forever. My 72-year-old mom ended up renting a scooter at the end of the day because her hip was bothering her. Anytime we wanted to go somewhere, it was an ordeal. The lines for the characters were off the chain, so we skipped them entirely. We loved the parade and the people in costume, but the intense crowds made it way less fun than we expected. Candy lines stayed long until the end, and we were glad we rode The Haunted Mansion early, as the end of the line was way past the Liberty Belle boat all evening.

Fortunately, the party isn't always jam-packed. A Maryland family of four had a great experience:

Went to Mickey's Not-So-Scary Halloween Party. Had read a lot of mixed reviews both in your book and online, mostly complaining about crowds, and based on these reviews we almost decided to skip it but were talked out of it by a friend. The event was fantastic—plenty of trick-or-treating, a great parade, and no problems with rides. We are very glad we took our 8- and 5-year-olds.

NOVEMBER The **Wine and Dine Half-Marathon** early this month revolves around a 13.1-mile race that ends with a party amid Epcot's International Food & Wine Festival. The number of runners and their "cheer squads"—combined with the guests who descend upon Epcot for the food festival alone—blows up the crowd levels like an agitated pufferfish. Again, vehicular and pedestrian traffic is disturbed by the running courses throughout Disney property.

DECEMBER The **Pop Warner Super Bowl** and **Pop Warner National Cheer & Dance Championships** are held at Disney World's ESPN Wide World of Sports Complex each year in early December. The 2015 championships run December 5–12. The Value resorts, especially All-Star Sports, fill up fast with these participants. Because they're competing, the 20,000 or so participants and their families tend to spend more time at Wide World of Sports than the parks.

The annual **Disney Parks Christmas Day Parade,** televised on December 25, is usually taped at the Magic Kingdom on the weekend that falls nine days after Thanksgiving, roughly the last weekend in November or first week of December. The parade ties up pedestrian traffic on Main Street, U.S.A. all day.

Christmas and New Year's at the Theme Parks

Don't expect to see all the attractions in a single day of touring at any park. That said, Disney's Animal Kingdom is usually the least crowded park during the winter holidays, especially on New Year's Eve, because the park doesn't have fireworks. Epcot is a good choice, too, because it typically has lower crowds and about twice the land of the Magic Kingdom. (It also has fewer attractions, but many of them are high-capacity shows and rides.)

As with summer, your best bet during winter holidays is to arrive early, take a midday break, and head back to the parks around dusk. Touring in the evening will reward you with stunning displays of holiday decorations and slightly smaller crowds than during the day. In particular, Disney's Hollywood Studios is a good choice for evening touring. Crowds will be larger than normal, but the decorations make up for it. One must-see is the **Osborne Family Spectacle of Dancing Lights,** featuring a staggering 5 million Christmas lights. They're typically turned on at 6 p.m., so you'll want to be in line by 5:30 p.m.

A Bridgewater, Massachusetts, mom loves Disney World during the holidays but warns that it's not the best time for everyone:

> *Having just completed our first holiday trip, I would never recommend a Christmas-week vacation for first-time visitors. But for anyone who's visited enough to navigate the parks without a map, the opportunity to experience the beauty and joy of the holiday season outweighs the huge crowds. You must accept that access to rides and shows will be limited and instead concentrate on the unique offerings such as the Osborne lights at the Studios and the parades and fireworks at the Magic Kingdom. Allow yourself time to visit the resorts—the gingerbread house at the Grand Floridian must be seen to be believed. And arrive early: We were in the MK by 7:10 a.m. on New Year's Eve and enjoyed all of the parades, shows, and fireworks, as well as all the major rides (except Splash Mountain—it was too cold).*

The Magic Kingdom stages New Year's Eve fireworks on both December 30 and 31 for those who either wish to see fireworks in multiple parks or who don't wish to be caught in the largest crowds of the year on New Year's Eve.

MICKEY'S VERY MERRY CHRISTMAS PARTY This event is staged 7 p.m.–midnight (after regular hours) on about 20 evenings in November and December. Advance tickets for the 2015 events went on sale in early May and cost (including tax) $79 for adults, $73 for kids. Same-day tickets cost $84 for adults, $79 for kids, and tickets for the final night (December 18) cost $87 for adults, $82 for kids. Tickets for busier dates usually sell out one to four days in advance. Included in the cost is the use of all attractions during party hours, holiday-themed stage shows featuring Disney characters, cookies and hot chocolate, performances of Mickey's

Once Upon a Christmastime Parade, carolers, "a magical snowfall on Main Street," white lights on Cinderella Castle, and fireworks. The least crowded dates are usually the weeks before Thanksgiving week, and the week after. Tuesday (and the rare Wednesday) parties are the slowest, too. See **tinyurl.com/mickeysverymerryxmas** for more details.

A reader from Pineville, Louisiana, tried the Very Merry Christmas Party and found the guest list too large for her liking:

> We went in early December to avoid crowds and were taken by surprise to find wall-to-wall people. They offered some great shows, but we could not get to them. The parade at 9 p.m. and the fireworks at 10 p.m., then fighting our way back to the parking lot, was all we could muster.

A Hoffman Estates, Illinois, reader was likewise overwhelmed:

> Everything was terrific except that our 12/7 experience with Mickey's Very Merry Christmas was awful. Wristbands were not checked, too many people were in the park, things were disorganized, and the Christmas celebration that we waited 1½ hours for lasted only 5 minutes!

But a woman from Buffalo, New York, says that, as with all things Disney, you need a plan:

> I just wanted to note a counterpoint to the comments about Mickey's Very Merry Christmas Party and the crowds. We attended on 12/18/14, the second-to-last party, which was sold out. If you go in with a plan (as you should with any park at any time) and avoid Main Street as much as possible, you'll be fine. We were able to meet the Seven Dwarfs, Aurora and Prince Philip, Snow White and Snow Prince, Winnie the Pooh and friends, Donald, Daisy, and Scrooge McDuck, as well as Santa Goofy and Peppermint Minnie during the party. Additionally, we saw the second parade in Frontierland, watched Celebrate the Magic and Holiday Wishes from the Adventureland bridge, and braved Main Street only for the castle lighting and Celebrate the Season shows. In short, we accomplished everything we set out to do and even squeezed in some dinner, because we had a plan beforehand.

If your schedule permits, we advise visiting in early December, when you can enjoy the decorations and festivities without the crowds.

PART TWO

MAKING *the* MOST *of* YOUR TIME *and* MONEY

▌ ALLOCATING MONEY

CAN YOU AFFORD A DISNEY VACATION?
WE CRUNCH THE NUMBERS

EVERY YEAR, WE GET E-MAILS from tens of thousands of families who are either planning or just back from a Walt Disney World vacation, and we talk with travel agents who hear from thousands more. And the thing that surprises these families the most—the number one thing they're unprepared for—is how expensive their trip turned out to be.

Those families are surprised for a good reason: Excluding transportation, a two-day, one-night night visit to Disney World for four costs more than what 80% of American families spend on vacations *in an entire year.* And that assumes the family stays at a no-frills budget motel in Kissimmee and eats fast food for two days.

So that you know what you're dealing with up front, we've created the chart on pages 54–56. It shows how much Disney vacation you get for $500, $1,000, $1,500, and $2,000, for families of various sizes.

Most cells in the chart contain a list of options, such as the type of hotel at which you stay or the restaurants at which you dine. These options illustrate the trade-offs you should consider when planning your trip (and there *will* be trade-offs). Here's an example for a family of two adults and one child with a $1,500 vacation budget (excluding transportation):

OPTION A Two full days at Disney's theme parks, all counter-service meals both days, and two nights at a Disney Deluxe resort

OPTION B Three full days at Disney's theme parks, counter-service breakfasts and lunches every day, a nice sit-down dinner every evening, and three nights at a budget off-site motel

In this case (and in general), your choice is between (1) a nicer hotel or (2) a longer trip, including more time in the parks plus more nights in a cheaper hotel, plus better meals every day.

If you'd like to try your own numbers, you can download our spreadsheet at **tinyurl.com/wdwyouget**. All hotel prices are quoted for

Continued on page 56

What You Pay and What You Get at WDW

2 ADULTS	2 ADULTS, 1 KID
$500	**$500**

• 1 day theme park admission
• 1 counter-service breakfast, lunch, and dinner
• 1 night at a Disney Moderate resort
  ($511)
	• 1 day theme park admission
	• 1 counter-service breakfast, lunch, and dinner
	• 1 night at a budget off-site motel
	  ($480)

$1,000	**$1,000**
BUDGET OPTION ($1,004): • 3 days theme park admission • 3 counter-service breakfasts, lunches, and dinners • 3 nights at a budget off-site motel **VALUE OPTION ($920):** • 2 days theme park admission • 2 counter-service breakfasts and lunches, 2 sit-down dinners • 2 nights at a Disney Value resort **MODERATE OPTION ($1,000):** Same as Value with 2 nights at a Disney Moderate resort **DELUXE OPTION ($990):** Same as Value with 1 night at a Disney Deluxe resort	**BUDGET OPTION ($1,017):** • 2 days theme park admission • 2 counter-service breakfasts and lunches, • 2 sit-down dinners • 2 nights at a budget off-site motel **VALUE OPTION ($957):** • 2 days theme park admission • 2 counter-service breakfasts, lunches, and dinners • 1 night at a Disney Value resort **MODERATE OPTION ($997):** Same as Value with 1 night at a Disney Moderate resort **DELUXE OPTION ($805):** • 1 day theme park admission • 1 counter-service breakfast and lunch, 1 sit-down dinner • 1 night at a Disney Deluxe resort
$1,500	**$1,500**
BUDGET OPTION ($1,509): • 6 days theme park admission • 6 counter-service breakfasts, lunches, and dinners • 6 nights at a budget off-site motel **VALUE OPTION ($1,506):** • 4 days theme park admission • 4 counter-service breakfasts, lunches, and dinners • 4 nights at a Disney Value resort **MODERATE OPTION ($1,496):** Same as Value with 3 nights at a Disney Moderate resort **DELUXE OPTION ($1,514):** • 3 days of theme park admission • 3 counter-service breakfasts, lunches, and dinners • 2 nights at a Disney Deluxe resort	**BUDGET OPTION ($1,500):** • 3 days theme park admission • 3 counter-service breakfasts and lunches, 3 sit-down dinners • 3 nights at a budget off-site motel **VALUE OPTION ($1,475):** • 3 days theme park admission • 3 counter-service breakfasts, lunches, and dinners • 2 nights at a Disney Value resort **MODERATE OPTION ($1,555):** Same as Value with 2 nights at a Disney Moderate resort **DELUXE OPTION ($1,514):** • 2 days theme park admission • 2 counter-service breakfasts, lunches, and dinners • 2 nights at a Disney Deluxe resort
$2,000	**$2,000**
BUDGET OPTION ($1,993): • 9 days theme park admission • 9 counter-service breakfasts, lunches, and dinners • 9 nights at a budget off-site motel **VALUE OPTION ($1,989):** • 6 days theme park admission • 6 counter-service breakfasts, lunches and dinners • 6 nights at a Disney Value resort **MODERATE OPTION ($1,948):** • 5 days theme park admission • 5 counter-service breakfasts, lunches, and dinners • 5 nights at a Disney Moderate resort **DELUXE OPTION ($1,976):** • 4 days theme park admission • 4 counter-service breakfasts, lunches, and dinners • 3 nights at a Disney Deluxe resort	**BUDGET OPTION ($2,002):** • 6 days theme park admission • 6 counter-service breakfasts, lunches, and dinners • 6 nights at a budget off-site motel **VALUE OPTION ($1,918):** • 4 days theme park admission • 4 counter-service breakfasts, lunches and dinners • 4 nights at a Disney Value resort **MODERATE OPTION ($1,908):** • 4 days theme park admission • 4 counter-service breakfasts, lunches, and dinners • 3 nights at a Disney Moderate resort **DELUXE OPTION ($2,010):** • 3 days theme park admission • 3 counter-service breakfasts, lunches, and dinners • 2 nights at a Disney Deluxe resort

What You Pay and What You Get at WDW

2 ADULTS, 2 KIDS	3 ADULTS
$500	**$500**
Nothing	• 1 day theme park admission • 1 counter-service breakfast, lunch, and dinner • 1 night at a budget off-site motel **($501)**
$1,000	**$1,000**

• 1 day theme park admission
• 1 counter-service breakfast and lunch, 1 sit-down dinner, and (choose one of the following)
  ◆ 1 night at a budget off-site motel ($659)
  ◆ 1 night at a Disney Value resort ($739)
  ◆ 1 night at a Disney Moderate resort ($779)
  ◆ 1 night at a Disney Deluxe resort ($939)
	BUDGET OPTION ($971):
	• 2 days theme park admission
	• 2 counter-service breakfasts, lunches, and dinners
	• 2 nights at a budget off-site motel
	
	VALUE OPTION ($1,011):
	• 2 days theme park admission
	• 2 counter-service breakfasts, lunches, and dinners
	• 1 night at a Disney Value resort
	
	MODERATE OPTION ($1,056):
	Same as Value with 1 night at a Disney Moderate resort
	
	DELUXE OPTION ($866):
	• 1 day theme park admission
	• 1 counter-service breakfast and lunch, 1 sit-down dinner
	• 1 night at a Disney Deluxe resort

$1,500	**$1,500**
BUDGET OPTION ($1,273): • 2 days theme park admission • 2 counter-service breakfasts and lunches, 2 sit-down dinners • 2 nights at a budget off-site motel **VALUE OPTION ($1,433):** • 2 days theme park admission • 2 counter-service breakfasts and lunches, 2 sit-down dinners • 2 nights at a Disney Value resort **MODERATE OPTION ($1,513):** Same as Value with 2 nights at a Disney Moderate resort **DELUXE OPTION ($1,503):** Same as Value with 1 night at a Disney Deluxe resort	**BUDGET OPTION ($1,430):** • 3 days theme park admission • 3 counter-service breakfasts, lunches, and dinners • 3 nights at a budget off-site motel **VALUE OPTION ($1,560):** • 3 days theme park admission • 3 counter-service breakfasts, lunches, and dinners • 2 nights at a Disney Value resort **MODERATE OPTION ($1,361):** • 2 days theme park admission • 2 counter-service breakfasts and lunches, 2 sit-down dinners • 2 nights at a Disney Moderate resort **DELUXE OPTION ($1,581):** • 2 days theme park admission • 2 counter-service breakfasts, lunches, and dinners • 2 nights at a Disney Deluxe resort
$2,000	**$2,000**
BUDGET OPTION ($2,010): • 4 days theme park admission • 4 counter-service breakfasts, lunches, and dinners • 4 nights at a budget off-site motel **VALUE OPTION ($1,967):** • 3 days theme park admission • 3 counter-service breakfasts, lunches, and dinners • 3 nights at a Disney Value resort **MODERATE OPTION ($2,087):** • 3 days theme park admission • 3 counter-service breakfasts, lunches, and dinners • 3 nights at a Disney Moderate resort **DELUXE OPTION ($1,833):** • 2 days theme park admission • 2 counter-service breakfasts and lunches, 2 sit-down dinners • 2 nights at a Disney Deluxe resort	**BUDGET OPTION ($2,063):** • 5 days theme park admission • 5 counter-service breakfasts, lunches, and dinners • 5 nights at a budget off-site motel **VALUE OPTION ($2,039):** • 4 days theme park admission • 4 counter-service breakfasts, lunches and dinners • 4 nights at a Disney Value resort **MODERATE OPTION ($2,034):** • 4 days theme park admission • 4 counter-service breakfasts, lunches, and dinners • 3 nights at a Disney Moderate resort **DELUXE OPTION ($1,990):** • 3 days theme park admission • 3 counter-service breakfasts, lunches, and dinners • 2 nights at a Disney Deluxe resort *(Continued)*

What You Pay and What You Get at WDW

3 ADULTS, 1 KID

$500	$1,000

Nothing	• 1 day theme park admission
	• 1 counter-service breakfast and lunch, 1 sit-down dinner, and (choose one of the following)
	  ♦ 1 night at a budget off-site motel ($695)
	  ♦ 1 night at a Disney Value resort ($785)
	  ♦ 1 night at a Disney Moderate resort ($830)
	  ♦ 1 night at a Disney Deluxe resort ($1,000)

$1,500	$2,000
BUDGET OPTION ($1,347): • 2 days theme park admission • 2 counter-service breakfasts and lunches, 2 sit-down dinners • 2 nights at a budget off-site motel **VALUE OPTION ($1,527):** • 2 days theme park admission • 2 counter-service breakfasts and lunches, 2 sit-down dinners • 2 nights at a Disney Value resort **MODERATE OPTION ($1,487):** • 2 days theme park admission • 2 counter-service breakfasts, lunches, and dinners • 2 nights at a Disney Moderate resort **DELUXE OPTION ($1,472):** • 2 days theme park admission • 2 counter-service breakfasts, lunches, and dinners • 1 night at a Disney Deluxe resort	**BUDGET OPTION ($2,041):** • 4 days theme park admission • 4 counter-service breakfasts, lunches, and dinners • 3 nights at a budget off-site motel **VALUE OPTION ($2,062):** • 3 days theme park admission • 3 counter-service breakfasts, lunches and dinners • 3 nights at a Disney Value resort **MODERATE OPTION ($2,012):** • 3 days theme park admission • 3 counter-service breakfasts, lunches, and dinners • 2 nights at a Disney Moderate resort **DELUXE OPTION ($1,957):** • 3 days theme park admission • 3 counter-service breakfast and lunches, 2 sit-down dinners • 2 nights at a Disney Deluxe resort

Continued from page 53

mid-June nights in 2015 and include tax. Here are the assumptions we made to go along with actual prices from Disney's website:

- Children are ages 3–9; adults are ages 10 and up.
- The cost of base Magic Your Way tickets comes from Disney's website and includes tax.
- One night at our off-site budget hotel (the Magnuson Grand Hotel Maingate West) costs $45 via Expedia.
- One night at Disney's Pop Century Resort (Value) costs $130 with the Spring Value discount on the WDW website.
- One night at Disney's Coronado Springs Resort (Moderate) costs $170 using the same discount.
- One night at Disney's Animal Kingdom Lodge (Deluxe) costs $330 using the same discount.
- A day's worth of counter-service meals, plus one snack, costs $45 for adults and $30 for kids.
- A counter-service breakfast and lunch, a snack, and a table-service meal costs $65 per adult and $45 per child.

In most places in the chart, theme park admission ranges from 30% to 60% of the cost of a trip, regardless of family size. If you're not staying at a Deluxe resort, it's safe to assume that ticket costs will take half of your budget (again, excluding transportation).

In any case, we get lots of comments about the cost of a Walt Disney World vacation. This complaint from a Cincinnati reader is typical:

> We travel to WDW frequently, and we were disgusted by the obvious trend toward "pay more, get less" that we observed in almost every area of our last vacation. Unfortunately, the trend appears to be completely on the side of Disney profits rather than guest satisfaction.

It's a different story for off-site hotels, which lack services like free shuttles and extra time in the theme parks. Very good third-party resorts, such as the Waldorf Astoria, adjacent to Disney property, offer rates 30–60% less than those of comparable Disney hotels. It helps considerably if you've got a car, even if you factor in the cost of gas.

How to Save $400 on Your Trip

THIS GUIDE DESCRIBES many techniques for saving money on a Walt Disney World vacation, including finding an inexpensive hotel, discounts on third-party admission tickets, and budget-friendly restaurants. But sometimes you can do all of that *and* still need to cut your budget. Not to worry—**touringplans.com** blogger **Kristi Fredericks** has you covered with five simple, painless ways to save more than $400 on your Disney vacation.

For each of these tips, assume a family of four traveling to Walt Disney World for a one week (six-day, seven-night) vacation. Our sample family includes two adults and two children ages 3 and 9.

TIP #1: BRING YOUR OWN RAIN PONCHOS

Disney World can be a rainy place no matter what time of year you visit. Bring your own rain ponchos instead of buying at the parks to save some dough.

DON'T Buy 2 adult ponchos x $8.50 and 2 kids' ponchos x $7.50 = **$33**

DO Buy 4 ponchos at local dollar store = **$4**   **SAVINGS** $33 – $4 = **$29**

TIP #2: BRING YOUR OWN STROLLER

Our sample family will need a stroller for their 3-year-old in the parks, and it's handy to have a stroller for the airport and resort areas as well. Remember that most airlines will gate-check your stroller for free.

DON'T Rent a stroller for $13 per day (length-of-stay rate) x 6 days = **$78**

DO Buy 1 umbrella stroller at Babies"R"Us = **$25**   **SAVINGS** $78 – $25 = **$53**

TIP #3: DRINK FREE WATER

All Disney restaurants will give you a free cup of ice water. Instead of wasting money and calories on sugary drinks, this is an easy way to save some cash. For our sample family, let's assume that everyone wants something other than water to drink at breakfast and that the kids' meals will include a drink at lunch and dinner. Only the adults will drink free water, and only at lunch and dinner.

DON'T Buy 1 beverage at $3 each x 2 adults x 2 meals x 6 days = **$72**

DO Drink free water x 2 adults x 2 meals x 6 days = **$0**

SAVINGS $72 – $0 = **$72**

TIP #4: BRING YOUR OWN SNACKS

It's amazing how much you can save by bringing your own nonperishable snacks into the park. A zip-top bag filled with cereal bars, granola, raisins, and crackers goes a long way toward staving off hunger.

DON'T Buy 1 snack at $4 each x 4 people x 2 times x 6 days = **$192**

DO Bring your own snacks = **$35**   **SAVINGS** $192 – $35 = **$157**

TIP 5: EAT BREAKFAST IN YOUR ROOM

This saves you time and a small fortune in food costs. Let's assume our family will grab two coffees and two milks from their hotel's food court each morning, so we won't include beverages in either cost.

DON'T Buy one $9 breakfast platter + one $6 yogurt parfait + two kid's Mickey waffle meals x $5 x 6 days = **$150**

DO Bring your own breakfast, including paper bowls, napkins, plastic spoons, cereal, breakfast pastries, mini-doughnuts, and cereal bars = **$30**

SAVINGS $150 – $30 = **$120**

TOTAL SAVINGS $431 *(about $72 per day)*

FOUR MORE TIPS FROM BOB

1. Buy your admission online from one of the sellers on page 64. Get tickets only for the number of days you plan to visit, and skip all add-ons.

2. Book a hotel outside of Walt Disney World. Hotels on US 192 (Irlo Bronson Memorial Highway) are usually the least expensive. Or consider renting a vacation home (see discussion starting on page 246) if you have four or more people in your group.

3. Avoid parking fees by using your hotel's shuttle service or by taking Disney transportation from Disney Springs or the water parks, where (for the moment) parking is free. The second suggestion eats up a lot of time, so do this only if you're budgeting to the penny.

4. Buy discounted Disney-brand apparel and souvenirs from one of Orlando's two Disney Character Warehouse outlets (see page 738).

WALT DISNEY WORLD ADMISSION OPTIONS

DISNEY OFFERS A NUMBER OF different admission options in order to accommodate various vacation needs. These range from the humble **1-Day Base Ticket,** good for a single day's entry into one Disney theme park, to the blinged-out **Premium Annual Pass,** good for 365 days of admission into every Disney theme or water park, plus DisneyQuest, Disney's Oak Trail Golf Course, and more. See the chart on pages 60–61 for a summary.

The number of ticket options available makes it difficult to sort out which option represents the least expensive way to see and do everything you want. The average family staying for a week at an off-World hotel and planning a couple of activities outside the theme parks has about a dozen different ticket options to consider.

Adding to the complexity, Disney's reservation agents are trained to avoid answering subjective questions about which ticket option is "best." Many families, we suspect, become overwhelmed trying to sort out the different options and simply purchase an expensive ticket with more features than they'll use.

As an example, a family of two adults and two children who want to visit the theme parks for five days and a water park for one day could buy everyone a 5-Day Base Ticket plus the Water Park Fun and More option, for $1,572 total. Or they could buy separate admissions to the theme and water parks from a third-party vendor for $1,376, a savings of $196. The problem is that comparing options requires detailed knowledge of the myriad perks included with specific admissions.

THIS IS A JOB FOR . . . A COMPUTER!

IT'S COMPLICATED ENOUGH that we wrote a computer program to solve it. Visit **touringplans.com** and try our **Park Ticket Calculator,** on the home page. It aggregates ticket prices from Disney and a number of online ticket vendors. Answer a few questions relating to the size of your party and the parks you intend to visit, and the calculator will identify your four cheapest ticket options. It'll also show you how much you'll save.

The program will also make recommendations for considerations other than price. For example, Annual Passes might cost more, but Disney often offers substantial resort discounts and other deals to Annual Pass holders. These resort discounts, especially during the off-season, can more than offset the price of the pass.

The Park Ticket Calculator has saved readers millions of dollars over the past few years, as this husband discovered:

You just saved me from making a $408 mistake and needless expense!

MAGIC YOUR WAY

WALT DISNEY WORLD OFFERS AN ARRAY of theme park ticket options, grouped into a program called Magic Your Way. The simplest option, visiting one theme park for one day, is called a **1-Day Base Ticket.** Other features, such as the ability to visit more than one park per day ("park hopping"), or the inclusion of admission to Disney's minor venues (Typhoon Lagoon, Blizzard Beach, DisneyQuest, mini-golf, and the like), are available as individual add-ons to the Base Ticket.

In 2013 Disney introduced separate pricing for a single day's admission to the Magic Kingdom versus the World's other theme parks. An adult 1-Day Base Ticket for the Magic Kingdom costs $111.83, while one day's admission to any other theme park is $103.31 (including tax).

Multiday pricing is still uniform across the parks. The more days of admission you buy, the lower the cost per day. For example, if you buy an adult 5-Day Base Ticket for $335.48 (tax included), each day costs $67.10, compared with $103.31 a day for a one-day pass to Epcot, the Studios, or Animal Kingdom and $111.83 for the Magic Kingdom. Tickets can be purchased from 1 up to 10 days and admit you to exactly one theme park per day; you can reenter your chosen park as many times as you like on that day.

Disney says its tickets expire within 14 days of the first day of use. In practice, they really mean 13 days after the first day of use. If, say, you purchase a 4-Day Base Ticket on June 1 and use it that day for admission to the Magic Kingdom, you'll be able to visit a single Disney theme park on any of your three remaining days from June 2 through June 14. After that, the ticket expires and any unused days will be lost.

WDW Theme Park Ticket Options

	1-DAY	2-DAY	3-DAY	4-DAY	5-DAY
BASE TICKET AGES 3–9					
MK: $105.44 EP/AK/DHS: $96.92	$190.64	$272.64	$303.53	$314.18
—	($95.32/day)	($90.88/day)	($75.88/day)	($62.84/day)
BASE TICKET AGE 10 AND UP					
MK: $111.83 EP/AK/DHS: $103.31	$204.48	$292.88	$324.83	$335.48
—	($102.24/day)	($97.63/day)	($81.21/day)	($67.10/day)

Base Ticket admits guest to one theme park each day of use.

PARK HOPPER ADD-ON *(1-day prices include admission)*					
Ages 3–9: $158.69 Age 10+: $165.08	$68.16 (+ admission)	$68.16 (+ admission)	$68.16 (+ admission)	$68.16 (+ admission)
—	($34.08/day)	($22.72/day)	($17.04/day)	($13.63/day)

Park Hopper option entitles guest to visit more than one theme park on each day of use.

WPFAM ADD-ON *(1-day prices include admission)*					
Ages 3–9: $173.60 Age 10+: $179.99	$63.90 (+ admission)	$63.90 (+ admission)	$63.90 (+ admission)	$63.90 (+ admission)
2 visits	2 visits	3 visits	4 visits	5 visits

Water Park Fun and More option entitles guest to a specified number of visits (between 2 and 10) to a choice of entertainment and recreation venues.

PARK HOPPER + WPFAM *(1-day prices include admission)*					
Ages 3–9: $201.29 Age 10+: $207.68	$95.85 (+ admission)	$95.85 (+ admission)	$95.85 (+ admission)	$95.85 (+ admission)
—	($47.93/day)	($31.95/day)	($23.96/day)	($19.17/day)

TICKET ADD-ONS

NAVIGATING THE MAGIC YOUR WAY PROGRAM is like ordering dinner à la carte at an upscale restaurant: many choices, mostly expensive, virtually all of which require some thought.

Two add-on options are offered with the Magic Your Way Ticket, each at an additional cost:

PARK HOPPER This add-on you lets you visit more than one theme park per day. The cost is about $37–$46 (including tax) on top of the price of an adult 1-Day Base Ticket and a flat $68.16 tacked on to adult or child 2- and 3-Day Base Tickets—exorbitant for one or two days, but more affordable the longer your stay. As an add-on to a 7-Day Base Ticket, the flat fee works out to $9.74 per day for park-hopping privileges. If you want to visit the Magic Kingdom in the morning and eat at Epcot in the evening, this is the feature to request.

Note: All ticket and add-on prices include 6.5% sales tax.				
6-DAY	**7-DAY**	**8-DAY**	**9-DAY**	**10-DAY**
BASE TICKET AGES 3–9				
$324.83	$335.48	$346.13	$356.78	$367.43
($54.14/day)	($47.93/day)	($43.27/day)	($39.64/day)	($36.74/day)
BASE TICKET AGE 10 AND UP				
$346.13	$356.78	$367.43	$378.08	$388.73
($57.69/day)	($50.97/day)	($45.93/day)	($42.01/day)	($38.87/day)
Park choices are Magic Kingdom, Epcot, Disney's Hollywood Studios, or Disney's Animal Kingdom.				
PARK HOPPER ADD-ON *(1-day prices include admission)*				
$68.16 (+ admission)	$68.16 (+ admission)	$68.16 (+ admission)	$68.16 (+ admission)	$68.16 (+ admission)
($11.36/day)	($9.74/day)	($8.52/day)	($7.57/day)	($6.82/day)
Park choices are any combination of Magic Kingdom, Epcot, Disney's Hollywood Studios, or Disney's Animal Kingdom on each day of use.				
WPFAM ADD-ON *(1-day prices include admission)*				
$63.90 (+ admission)	$63.90 (+ admission)	$63.90 (+ admission)	$63.90 (+ admission)	$63.90 (+ admission)
6 visits	7 visits	8 visits	9 visits	10 visits
Choices are Disney's Blizzard Beach water park, Disney's Typhoon Lagoon water park, DisneyQuest, Oak Trail Golf Course, ESPN Wide World of Sports Complex, or Winter Summerland or Fantasia mini-golf.				
PARK HOPPER + WPFAM *(1-day prices include admission)*				
$95.85 (+ admission)	$95.85 (+ admission)	$95.85 (+ admission)	$95.85 (+ admission)	$95.85 (+ admission)
($15.98/day)	($13.69/day)	($11.98/day)	($10.65/day)	($9.59/day)
Note: Check **touringplans.com** for the latest ticket prices, which are subject to change. All tickets expire 14 days after first use.				

WATER PARK FUN AND MORE (WPFAM) This option gives you a single admission to one of Disney's water parks (Blizzard Beach and Typhoon Lagoon), DisneyQuest, Oak Trail Golf Course, Fantasia Gardens or Winter Summerland mini-golf, or the ESPN Wide World of Sports Complex. The cost is a flat $63.90, including tax. Except for the single-day WPFAM ticket, which gives you two admissions, the number of admissions equals the number of days on your ticket. If you buy an 8-Day Base Ticket, for example, and add the WPFAM option, you get eight WPFAM admissions. What you *can't* do is, say, buy a 10-Day Base Ticket with only three WPFAM admissions or a 3-Day Base Ticket with four WPFAM admissions. You can, however, skip WPFAM entirely and buy an individual admission to any of these minor parks—that's frequently the best deal if you want to visit only one of the venues above.

Disney also offers a **Park Hopper–WPFAM combo** for $95.85, including tax. If you plan to spend a lot of time at the water parks and other WPFAM venues, the combo will save you $36 over buying the two options separately.

The foregoing add-ons are available for purchase in any combination. If you buy a ticket and then decide later on that you want one or more of the options, you can upgrade your ticket to add the feature(s) you desire. Disney doesn't prorate the cost, so you'll pay the same price regardless of when you buy the option: If you add the Park Hopper option on the last day of your trip, you'll pay the same $63.90 as if you'd bought it before you left home.

Annual Passes

An **Annual Pass** provides unlimited use of the major theme parks for one year; a **Premium Annual Pass** also provides unlimited use of the minor parks. Annual Pass holders also get perks, including free parking and seasonal offers such as room-rate discounts at Disney resorts. The Annual Pass is not valid for special events, such as admission to Mickey's Very Merry Christmas Party. Tax included, Annual Passes run $696.51 for both adults and kids age 3 and up. A Premium Annual Pass, at $829.64 for adults and kids age 3 and up, provides unlimited admission to Blizzard Beach, Typhoon Lagoon, DisneyQuest, and Oak Trail Golf Course, in addition to the four major theme parks, plus mini-golf discounts.

Florida Resident Passes

Disney offers several special admission options to Florida residents. The **Florida Resident Annual Pass** ($563.39 for adults and kids age 3 and up) and the **Florida Resident Premium Annual Pass** ($691.19 for adults and kids age 3 and up) both offer unlimited admission and park-hopping privileges to the four major theme parks. The Florida Resident Premium Annual Pass also provides unlimited admission to Blizzard Beach, Typhoon Lagoon, DisneyQuest, and Oak Trail Golf Course, in addition to the four major theme parks, plus mini-golf discounts. And the **Florida Resident Seasonal Pass** ($350.39 for adults and kids age 3 and up) provides unlimited admission to the four major theme parks except on selected blackout dates. In addition to Annual Passes, Florida residents are eligible for discounts on 1-Day Park Hopper passes (about $4) as well as on various add-on options.

unofficial **TIP**
The break-even point for an Annual Pass is 12 days of theme park visits. With Annual Pass resort discounts, the break-even is about six days at a Deluxe resort.

ANOTHER ONE BITES THE DUST

DISNEY CLOSES MONEY-SAVING LOOPHOLES each time it updates its admission prices and options. The most recent casualty was the No Expiration option, which allowed you to roll over any unused admission days on your ticket to a subsequent trip. Assuming you could keep that ticket in a safe place, you'd pay for two trips' worth of admission now and avoid years of ticket-price increases on your next visit. Well, they couldn't let *that* continue, could they?

HOW TO GET THE MOST FROM MAGIC YOUR WAY

FIRST, BE REALISTIC about what you want out of your vacation. A seven-day theme park ticket with seven WPFAM admissions might seem like a wonderful idea when you're snowbound in February and planning your trip. But actually trying to visit all those parks in a week in July might end up feeling more like Navy SEAL training. If you're going to visit only one water park, DisneyQuest, or the ESPN Wide World of Sports Complex, you're almost always better off purchasing that admission separately rather than in the WPFAM option. If you plan to visit two or more WPFAM venues, you're better off buying the add-on.

ANTICIPATING PRICE INCREASES

DISNEY USUALLY RAISES PRICES ONCE A YEAR, with the last couple of increases having gone into effect just before the crowds arrived: The latest hike came in February 2015 and the one before that in February 2014; the three before these came in June, and the five before those in August. Price increases have generally run about 5% a year, but specific ticket categories are frequently bumped much more. In 2015, the average increase for Base Tickets was 3%, and 4% for add-on options. If you're putting a budget together, assume at least a 5% increase, but know that it could be higher.

unofficial **TIP**
We wouldn't be surprised to see a second round of price hikes in late 2015, so save money on tickets by planning ahead—buy them before the next price increase.

A Georgia dad puts Disney's price hikes in perspective:

> In the spring of 1983 as a working student, I purchased a [pre–Magic Your Way] 3-Day Park Hopper for $35 (including tax). Minimum wage was $3.35/hour, meaning it took less than 11 hours of work to pay for that ticket. With the latest increase, a 3-Day Base Ticket plus Park Hopper costs $361, or about **50 hours** of work at today's minimum wage of $7.25/hour.

TICKETS, BIOMETRICS, WRISTBANDS, AND RFID

TO THIS POINT IN THE BOOK, we've used the word *ticket* to describe that thing you carry around as proof of your admission to the park. In fact, Disney admission media come in two forms—neither of which is a ticket. While we use *ticket* as shorthand for "admission medium," you'll be better prepared by knowing what you'll actually be handed when you plunk down your money.

If you're staying at a Disney resort, your admission medium is a rubber wristband about the size and shape of a small wristwatch. Called a **MagicBand,** it contains a tiny radio frequency identifier (RFID) chip, on which is stored a link to the record of your admission purchase in Disney's computers. Your MagicBand also functions as your hotel-room key, and it can (optionally) work as a credit card for most food and merchandise purchases throughout the park.

If you don't want a MagicBand, you get a **Key to the World Card,** which looks like a credit card. If you're staying off-property or you bought your admission from a third-party vendor, your ticket is a flexible, credit card–size piece of plastic-coated paper. Both alternatives also contain an RFID chip; upgrading them to a MagicBand costs $13. The inner workings of RFID are discussed in detail starting on page 67.

In addition to using RFID chips, Disney's computer systems store the dimensions of one finger from your right hand, a reference to which is also stored on your MagicBand or laminated card. Recording this biometric information requires a quick and painless measurement, taken the first time you use the ticket. When you use it again, you'll be asked to scan the same finger to validate your identity. If the scans don't match—say, you use a different finger—you may be asked to present photo ID.

If you're buying admission for your entire family and you're worried that you won't be able to keep everyone's tickets straight, Disney's computer system should have every family member's data linked to every ticket, allowing anyone in your group to enter with anyone else's ticket. We've confirmed this by having a platoon of *Unofficial Guide* researchers (including men, women, and children) swap MagicBands with each other; all were admitted.

WHERE TO PURCHASE MAGIC YOUR WAY TICKETS

YOU CAN BUY YOUR ADMISSION PASSES on arrival at Walt Disney World or buy them in advance. Passes are available at Walt Disney World resorts and theme parks, at some non-Disney hotels and shopping centers, and through independent ticket brokers. Because Disney admissions are only marginally discounted in the Walt Disney World–Orlando area, the chief reason for you to buy from an independent broker is convenience. Offers of free or heavily discounted tickets abound, but they generally require you to attend a time-share sales presentation.

Magic Your Way tickets are available at Disney Stores and at **disney world.com** for the same prices listed in the chart on pages 60 and 61.

If you're trying to keep costs to an absolute minimum, consider using an online ticket wholesaler, such as the **Official Ticket Center, Undercover Tourist, Kissimmee Guest Services,** or **Maple Leaf Tickets,** especially for trips with five or more days in the parks. All tickets sold are brand-new, and the savings can range from $4 to more than $60, depending on the ticket and options chosen. If any options don't make sense for your specific plans, the representatives will tell you so.

unofficial **TIP**
If you order tickets in advance, allow enough time for them to be mailed to your home.

All four companies offer discount tickets for almost all Central Florida attractions, including Disney, Universal, SeaWorld, and Cirque du Soleil. Discounts for the major theme parks range from about 6% to 12%; tickets for other attractions are more deeply discounted. The **Official Ticket Center** (3148 Vineland Rd., Kissimmee; daily, 8 a.m.–8:30 p.m. Eastern time; ☎ 407-396-9020 or 877-406-4836; fax 407-396-9323; **officialticketcenter.com**) offers USPS Certified Mail for free or Priority Mail for $10. For the same price, they'll also deliver to area hotels; pickup at their office is free. **Undercover Tourist** (US: ☎ 800-846-1302; Monday–Friday, 9 a.m.–4 p.m. Eastern time; UK: ☎ 0800 081 1702; Monday–Friday, 2 p.m.–9 p.m. Greenwich mean time; ☎ +1 386-239-8624 worldwide; fax +1 386-252-3469; **undercovertourist.com**) offers free delivery and has a sweetheart relationship with **MouseSavers** (**mousesavers.com**). If you subscribe to the MouseSavers e-newsletter, you can access Undercover Tourist through a special "secret" link that provides additional savings on top of the normal discount. **Kissimmee Guest Services** (950 Celebration Blvd., Suite H, Celebration; ☎ 888-206-6040 or 321-939-2057; Monday–Saturday, 8 a.m.–5 p.m., Sunday, 8 a.m.–noon, all Eastern time; UK: ☎ 0208 432 4024; **kgstickets.com**) offers free ticket delivery to area hotels for tickets ordered by phone, but tickets ordered online are cheaper. **Maple Leaf Tickets** (4647 W. Irlo Bronson Memorial Hwy., Kissimmee; daily, 8 a.m.–6 p.m. Eastern time; ☎ 407-396-0300 or 800-841-2837; fax 407-396-4127; **mapleleaftickets .com**) offers the same deal on pickup at their store and for $6.95 delivery to area hotels; USPS Priority Mail is a flat $6.95 per order.

Where *Not* to Buy Passes

In addition to the many authorized sellers of Disney admissions, a number of unauthorized sellers exist. They buy unused days on legitimately purchased passes and then resell them as if they were brand-new.

These resellers are easy to identify: They insist that you specify the exact days when you plan to use the ticket. They know, of course, how many days are left on the pass and when it expires. If you tell them you plan to use it tomorrow and the next two days, they'll sell you a ticket that has three days left on it and expires in three days. Naturally, because they don't tell you this, you assume the usual 14-day expiration period from the date of first use. In the case of your tickets, however, the original purchaser triggered the 14-day expiration period. If you decide to skip a day instead of using the pass on the next three consecutive days, you'll discover to your chagrin that it has expired.

unofficial **TIP**
Also steer clear of passes offered on eBay and Craigslist.

FOR ADDITIONAL INFORMATION ON PASSES

IF YOU HAVE A QUESTION OR CONCERN regarding admissions that can be addressed only through a person-to-person conversation, call **Disney Ticket Inquiries** at ☎ 407-566-4985 or e-mail **ticket.inquiries @disneyworld.com.** If you call, be aware that you may spend considerable time on hold; if you e-mail, be aware that it can take up to three days to get a response. In contrast, the ticket section of the Disney World website—**disneyworld.disney.go.com/tickets**—is surprisingly straightforward in showing how ticket prices break down.

WHERE THE REAL DEALS ARE

BOTH GREAT THEME PARKS, **Universal Studios Florida** and **Universal's Islands of Adventure** routinely offer admission discounts and specials at **universalorlando.com.** For a family of four—say, Mom, Dad, and two kids under age 10—the total cost to visit both Universal parks for two days is around $809, including tax. For the same family to spend two days at Disney parks with park-hopping privileges during the same period, it cost a whopping $1,003, tax included. Even in the absence of any discounts, two days of park hopping at Universal for our family of four cost $194 less than the same admission at Walt Disney World.

THE BRITISH ARE COMING!

IN THE UNITED KINGDOM, Disney offers advance-purchase tickets not available in the US. The **Seven-Day Premium Ticket** (£278 for adults and £258 for children) provides unlimited admission as well as park-hopping privileges to the major theme parks, and seven admissions to the minor venues. It expires 14 days from the date of first use.

Ultimate Tickets are priced at £275 for adults and £255 for kids for 7- or 14-day passes (the 14-day passes are on sale right now), and £305 and £285 for 21-day passes. The Ultimate Tickets provide unlimited admission to both major and minor parks along with park-hopping privileges to the major parks. The 7- and 14-day Ultimate Tickets expire 14 days after first use, and the 21-day Ultimate Ticket expires 21 days after first use. For additional information call ☎ 0870-242-4900 UK or ☎ 407-566-4985 US (Monday–Friday, 9 a.m.–8 p.m.; Saturday, 9 a.m.–7 p.m.; and Sunday, 10 a.m.–4 p.m.), or see **wdtc.disneyinternational.com/tickets** or the **Disney Information Bulletin Board** at **thedibb.co.uk.**

MORE DISCOUNTS ON ADMISSIONS

Discounts Available to Certain Groups and Individuals

DISNEY VACATION CLUB Members get a discount on Annual Passes.

CONVENTION-GOERS Disney World, Universal, SeaWorld, and other parks sometimes set up a link cited in convention materials to purchase discounted afternoon and evening admissions. See **tinyurl.com/disney conventiontix** and **tinyurl.com/seaworldconventiontix2016.**

DISNEY CORPORATE SPONSORS If you work for a Walt Disney World corporate sponsor, you may be eligible for discounted admissions or preferential treatment at the parks. Check with your workplace's employee-benefits office.

FLORIDA RESIDENTS get substantial savings on virtually all tickets. You'll need proof of residency, such as a driver's license or state-issued photo ID, to purchase these tickets.

MILITARY, DEPARTMENT OF DEFENSE, CIVIL SERVICE Active-duty and retired military, Department of Defense (DOD) civilian employees, some civil-service employees, and dependents of these groups can buy Disney multiday admissions at a 9–10% discount. At most military and DOD installations, the passes are available from the Morale, Welfare, and Recreation office. Civil-service employees should contact their personnel office to see if they're eligible. Military personnel can buy discounted admission for nonmilitary guests as long as the military member accompanies the nonmilitary member. If a group seeks the discount, at least half must be eligible for the military discount.

DISNEY YOUTH EDUCATION SERIES Disney runs programs for K–12 students to learn how the parks incorporate everything from performing arts to physics. The program runs every day and offers substantial ticket discounts (with substantial restrictions). Disney usually requires a 10-person minimum to attend these events, but it waives that requirement on occasion. See **disneyyouth.com** for more information.

Special Passes

Walt Disney World offers a number of special and situational passes that are not known to the general public and are not sold at any Disney World ticket booth. The best information we've found on these passes is available on the Internet at **tinyurl.com/wdwdiscounttix**.

HOW MUCH DOES IT COST PER DAY?

A TYPICAL DAY WOULD COST $738.52, excluding lodging and transportation, for a family of four—Mom, Dad, 12-year-old Abner, and 8-year-old Agnes—driving their own car and staying outside of Disney World. They plan to stay a week, so they buy 5-Day Base Tickets with the Park Hopper option.

unofficial **TIP**
Almost half the cost of a day in the parks is in food.

The biggest outlay is usually food costs, which increase at least twice a year. We think it's easier for Disney to raise food prices because most families look closely only at the cost of transportation, lodging, and tickets when budgeting for a Disney vacation.

HOW MUCH DOES A DAY COST?	
Breakfast for four at Denny's with tax and tip	**$43.15**
Epcot parking fee (free for pass holders and resort guests)	**$17.00**
Four day admission on a 5-Day Ticket with Park Hopper	**$318.66**
Dad: *Adult 5-Day with tax is $403.64 divided by five days = $80.73*	
Mom: *Adult 5-Day with tax is $403.64 divided by five days = $80.73*	
Abner: *Adult 5-Day with tax is $403.64 divided by five days = $80.73*	
Agnes: *Child 5-Day with tax is $382.34 divided by five days = $76.47*	
Morning break (soda or coffee)	**$11.25**
Fast-food lunch (sandwich or burger, fries, soda), no tip	**$58.28**
Afternoon break (soda and popcorn)	**$26.63**
Dinner at Italy (3 appetizers, 4 entrees, 3 desserts), with tax and tip	**$210.41**
Souvenirs (Mickey T-shirts for Abner and Agnes) with tax*	**$53.14**
One-day total (without lodging or transportation)	$738.52
Increase over last year's total ($712.18)	3.70%

*Cheer up—you won't have to buy souvenirs every day.

BACK TO THE SALT MINES! Our math could be off, but it appears that the cost of a Disney vacation has increased roughly three times faster than US workers' median wages (6% vs. 1.8%) since 2005. To put that in perspective, it took the average worker about 3.8 hours to earn enough money for a 1-Day Base Ticket in 2005. Today it's 4.2 hours.

RFID: IT'S ALL IN THE WRIST

WITH ITS MYMAGIC+ CAMPAIGN (see page 35), Disney introduced **MagicBands**—reusable rubber wristbands—as a sort of wearable theme park ticket. Small and reusable across trips, a MagicBand is imprinted with your first name, an ID number, and some legalese, along with a Mickey logo. A tiny radio-frequency-identification (RFID) chip embedded in the wristband holds your ticket and travel information.

Each RFID chip—not much larger than the end of a pencil—sends a unique serial number over short distances via radio waves. When you purchase theme park admission, Disney's computers will store that serial number, along with your ticket information. To enter a theme park, you touch your MagicBand to an RFID reader instead of going through a turnstile. The RFID reader collects your MagicBand's serial number, compares your biometric information, and verifies with Disney's computer systems that you've got the correct admission to enter the park.

> *un*official **TIP**
> Old non-RFID tickets must be converted to the new media before you can enter the theme parks or use FastPass+. You can get this done only at Guest Relations, just outside each park.

RFID technology has been used for many years in the retail and transportation industries to track everything from the location of cargo containers to the receipt, stocking, and purchase of T-shirts. Many bus and subway systems have switched to RFID-enabled cards from paper tickets. The US government also puts RFID chips in all new passports to prevent forgery.

Disney hotel guests get a MagicBand by default but may request a plastic **Key to the World (KTTW) Card** instead. If you're staying off-site or you bought your admission through a third party, you can upgrade to a MagicBand for $13; otherwise, you get a credit card–sized laminated ticket. Like the MagicBand, the two card options use RFID.

Each member of your family gets his or her own MagicBand, each with a unique serial number. Along with the wristband, each family member will be asked to select a four-digit personal-identification number (PIN) for purchases—more on that below. The wristbands are resizable and waterproof, and they have ventilation holes for cooling. Eight colors are available: red, black, blue, green, pink, orange, yellow, and gray (the default). You can choose your colors and personalize your bands when you book your resort stay at the Disney World website.

> *un*official **TIP**
> Get stickers of almost any color or design for your MagicBand at **magicyourbands.com**.

Using your MagicBand is a skill you need to get the hang of. The RFID chip in the band is located under a Mickey-head symbol about the size of a dime—to open your hotel-room door, use FastPass+, or enter a theme park, you have to line up the Mickey head pretty exactly with the RFID reader in question. Practice makes perfect, but many guests end up frustrated, contorting their wrists or simply taking the MagicBand off in order to align the chip with a reader. Quite a few guests, particularly men, simply carry their MagicBand in their pocket instead of wearing it.

Disney says using RFID at park entrances speeds admittance, because the readers are more reliable than the old magnetic-stripe kind.

RFID for Payment, Hotel-Room Access, and Photos

Disney's hotel-room doors have RFID readers, allowing you to enter your room simply by tapping your wristband or KTTW Card against the reader. The same technology has been in use for years at upscale hotels around the world.

RFID readers are also installed at virtually every Disney cash register on-property, allowing you to pay for food, drinks, and souvenirs by tapping your MagicBand/KTTW Card against the reader. You'll be asked to verify your identity by entering your PIN on a small keypad to complete your purchase. This technology, known as "contactless payment," has been in use worldwide for many years, too.

If you're using Disney's **Memory Maker** service (see page 479), your MagicBand/KTTW Card serves as the link between your photos and your family. Each photographer carries a small RFID reader, against which you tap your MagicBand before having your photo taken. The computers running the Memory Maker system will link your photos to you, and you'll be able to view them on the Disney World website.

Disney's onboard ride-photo computers incorporate RFID technology, too. As you begin down the big drop near the finale of Splash Mountain, for example, RFID sensors read the serial number on your MagicBand and pass it to Splash Mountain's cameras. When those cameras snap your family plunging into the briar patch, they attach your MagicBands' serial number to the photo, allowing you to see your ride photos together after you've returned home. Because ride sensors may not pick up the signal from an RFID card sitting in a wallet or purse, we're fairly sure that onboard ride photos require MagicBands.

unofficial **TIP** In early 2015, the **Yacht and Beach Club Resorts** and **Beach Club Villas** became the first Disney resorts to use MagicBands to validate parking. Other resorts are expected to join the rollout throughout 2015. Disney introduced the measure for "green" purposes, specifically to cut paper waste generated by parking permits.

The Future of RFID

Other innovative uses of RFID technology are rumored to be in the works. In one scenario we've heard, you'll provide Disney with some information about your child before your visit, such as his or her favorite color and pet's name. Later, when your child visits Cinderella, an RFID reader next to Cinderella will recognize your child's wristband and display the previously gathered information on a hidden prompter for Cinderella to work into conversation. And because Disney's computer systems will know from your MagicBand which rides you've been on and where you've eaten, Cinderella may mention those details, too.

But as impressive as all this sounds, many people are understandably concerned about multinational corporations tracking their movements. As noted earlier, guests who prefer not to wear MagicBands can instead obtain KTTW Cards, which are somewhat more difficult to track (inexpensive RFID-blocking wallets are available online). Disney claims that guests who opt out of MagicBands don't get the full range of ride experiences, though, so there's a trade-off to be made.

RFID and MagicBands are hot topics with our readers. First, from a Buckley, Michigan, mom:

MagicBands and MyMagic+: AMAZING! We had everything we needed right in our wristbands! If we didn't want to take anything with us when we left the room, we didn't have to! The MagicBands themselves acted as our room key, charge card, park passes, FastPasses, and Dining Plan vouchers!

This from a newlywed couple:

> *We can't say enough about how awesome the MagicBands are! Not having to root around for a room key after a long day of touring was bliss. The fact that they could be worn in the water made going to the pool or a water park a snap. Also, they were linked to my wife's credit card, so we didn't have to bring cash everywhere. Plus, they survived Summit Plummet! I think I've said enough.*

Finally, a mom from Plano, Texas, chipped in regarding unexpected MagicBand perks:

> *Love the MagicBands—they make it so convenient to spend lots of money! I noticed that you can use them at the Disney Store at the airport, too. In Epcot, we ate lunch at Sunshine Seasons—printed out at the bottom of my receipt was a coupon for 20% off a purchase at select stores in my Disney resort.*

ALLOCATING TIME

DURING DISNEY WORLD'S FIRST DECADE, a family with a week's vacation could enjoy the Magic Kingdom and the now-closed River Country and still have several days left for the beach or other area attractions. Since Epcot opened in 1982, however, Disney World has steadily been enlarging to monopolize the family's entire vacation. Today, with the addition of Blizzard Beach, Typhoon Lagoon, Disney's Hollywood Studios, Disney's Animal Kingdom, and Disney Springs, you should allocate 6 days for a whirlwind tour (7–10 if you insist on a little relaxation during your vacation). If you don't have that much time, be prepared to make some hard choices.

The theme parks and water parks are huge and require lots of walking and, sometimes, lots of waiting in lines. Approach Walt Disney World the same way you would an eight-course Italian dinner: with plenty of time between courses. Don't cram too much into too little time.

WHICH PARK TO SEE FIRST?

THIS QUESTION IS LESS ACADEMIC than it appears, especially if your party includes children or teenagers. Children who see the Magic Kingdom first expect the same type of entertainment at the other parks. At Epcot, they're often disappointed by the educational orientation and serious tone (as are many adults). Disney's Hollywood Studios offers some wild action along with family-friendly stage shows and attractions. Children may not find Animal Kingdom as exciting as the Magic Kingdom or DHS, because animals can't be programmed to entertain on cue.

First-time visitors should see Epcot first; you'll be able to enjoy it without having been preconditioned to think of Disney entertainment as solely fantasy or adventure.

See Disney's Animal Kingdom second. Like Epcot, it's educational, but its live animals provide a change of pace.

Next, see Disney's Hollywood Studios (DHS), which helps all ages transition from the educational Epcot and Animal Kingdom to the fanciful Magic Kingdom. Also, because DHS is smaller, you won't walk as much or stay as long. Save the Magic Kingdom for last—having said that, we know that most readers make a beeline for the Magic Kingdom, mostly for the reason that this North Carolina reader asserts:

> *Although you recommend sort of a reverse order for park visitation, ending up at the Magic Kingdom last, I disagree. We went to the Magic Kingdom first, which is Disney World for many of us.*

OPERATING HOURS

THE DISNEY WORLD WEBSITE publishes preliminary park hours 180 days in advance, but schedule adjustments can happen at any time, including the day of your visit. Check **disneyworld.com** or call ☎ 407-824-4321 for the exact hours before you arrive. Off-season, parks may be open as few as 8 hours (9 a.m.–5 p.m.). At busy times (particularly holidays), they may operate 8 a.m.–2 a.m.

OFFICIAL OPENING VERSUS REAL OPENING

WHEN YOU CALL, you're given "official hours." On many days, the parks open earlier. If the official hours are 9 a.m.–9 p.m., for instance, Main Street in the Magic Kingdom might open at 8:30 a.m. and the remainder of the park at 9 a.m.

Disney surveys local hotel reservations, estimates how many visitors to expect on a given day, and opens the theme parks early to avoid bottlenecks at parking facilities and ticket windows and to absorb crowds as they arrive.

Rides and attractions shut down at approximately the official closing time. Main Street in the Magic Kingdom remains open 30 minutes to an hour after the rest of the park has closed.

THE VACATION THAT FIGHTS BACK

VISITING DISNEY WORLD REQUIRES levels of stamina more often associated with running a marathon. A British gentleman, thinking we exaggerated about the walking required, measured his outings using a pedometer. His discovery:

> *I decided to wear a pedometer for our recent visit to WDW. Our visits to the theme parks were spread over five days, during which my wife and I (ages 51 and 55) walked a total of 68 miles for an average of 13 miles per day!*

The point is, at Walt Disney World less is more. Take the World in small doses, with plenty of swimming, napping, reading, and relaxing in between. If you don't see everything, you can always come back.

An articulate Anchorage, Alaska, teen and her family found out the hard way the importance of building in time to decompress:

> *We discovered that trying really hard to have lots of fun can get in the way of actually having fun. We crammed our schedule a little too full (seven parks—Disney, Universal, and SeaWorld—in eight full days). My older sisters would speed-walk from attraction to attraction while my parents straggled behind trying to keep up, while I was caught in the middle, both wanting to get to the next ride as fast as I could and wanting just to spend some quality time with my parents. No family*

*un**official* TIP
If your schedule permits
only one day of touring,
concentrate on one
theme park and save the
others for another visit.

*should spend more than two consecutive days at
the parks without a low-key day in the middle. I
wish I'd known this going in.*

Hitting the Wall

As you plan your time at Disney World, consider
your physical limitations. It's exhausting to rise
at dawn and run around a theme park for 8–12 hours day after day.
Sooner or later (usually sooner), you hit the wall. To avoid that, use
these two tips alone or in combination:

1. Take at least a morning off (preferably the entire day) after two consecutive days
   in the parks.
2. Return to your hotel for a 3- to 5-hour break each day you're in the theme parks.

A Suwanee, Georgia, reader discovered the first tip on his own:

*My initial plan for the family entailed a day at the Magic Kingdom;
one day each at Epcot, Animal Kingdom, Disney's Hollywood Studios, Universal Studios, and Islands of Adventure; one down day; and
a leftover day for a second visit to something we hadn't finished. By
day two, I became acutely aware that there was no way we would be
able to keep up that pace.*

A La Grange, Illinois, mother discovered the second tip through
her child:

*As I was planning, I was very sure we wouldn't be taking a swim/nap
break in the middle of the day. No way! On the very first day of touring (at the Magic Kingdom), my 7-year-old said (at 9:30 a.m.—after
only 2 hours at the park), "I'm hot—when can we go back to the
hotel and swim?" Needless to say, we took that little break every day.*

Finally, a Boston mom underscores the importance of timing:

*Don't make the decision about whether to take a break when the kids
are doing fine at noon. Think about that tired, cranky, sweaty child in
about 3 hours. Then imagine the same child at 5 p.m.!*

THE PRACTICALITY OF RETURNING TO YOUR HOTEL FOR REST

MANY READERS WRITE ABOUT the practicality of departing the
theme park for a nap and swim at the hotel. A dad from Sequim, Washington, made the following request:

*I would like to see nearness to the parks emphasized in your accom-
modation guide. We tried going back to the hotel for midday breaks,
but it was too time-consuming. By the time you got to the car, negotiated traffic, rested, and reversed the process to get back to the park,
it took 2–3 hours for a short rest and was not worth it!*

First, in response to the reader's request, we publish a chart in Part
Three, Accommodations, that provides the commuting times to each of
the Disney theme parks from many popular hotels within 20 miles of
Walt Disney World. But to address the larger issue, we think the reader
was overly anxious about the time away from the parks. Two to three

hours isn't make-or-break. Had he resigned himself to a 4- to 5-hour break, his family would've stayed rested and relaxed.

Here's the scoop: At Disney's Animal Kingdom, Disney's Hollywood Studios, and Epcot, you can get to your car in the parking lot in about 15–20 minutes. From the Magic Kingdom, it will take you 30–35 minutes. Obviously, if you're at the farthest point from the park entrance when you decide to return to the hotel, or you barely miss a parking-lot tram, it will take longer. But from most places in the parks, the previous times are correct. Once in your car, you'll be able to commute to most US 192 hotels, all Disney World hotels, all Lake Buena Vista hotels, and most hotels along the Interstate 4 corridor and south International Drive ("I-Drive") in 20 minutes or less. It will take about the same time to reach hotels on I-Drive north of Sand Lake Road and in the Universal Orlando area.

So, for most people, the one-way commute will average 35–40 minutes. But here's what you get for your time: a less-expensive lunch at a restaurant of your choosing, a swim, and a nap of up to an hour. If you add up the times, you'll be away from the parks about 4–5 hours, counting the commute. If you want, eat dinner outside the World before returning. Clearly, this won't work during times of year when the parks close early, but these aren't times when most families go to Disney World. If you visit when the parks close early, you'll see more attractions in less time, owing to reduced attendance, and you'll be able to leave the parks earlier and take your break in the late afternoon or early evening. Not ideal, but neither are the crowds and heat of summer.

ARRIVAL- AND DEPARTURE-DAY BLUES: WHAT TO DO WHEN YOU HAVE ONLY HALF A DAY

ON ARRIVAL AND DEPARTURE DAYS, you probably will have only part of a day for touring or other recreational pursuits. It's a common problem: You roll into the World about 1 p.m., excited and ready to go—but where?

The first question: Do you feel comfortable using a full day's admission to the parks when you have less than a full day to tour? The incremental cost to add another day of admission is small when you're visiting for three or more days, but significant if you're there for only a long weekend. Your arrival time and the parks' closing times are also considerations, but so is the touring disadvantage you suffer by not being on hand when a park opens. **FastPass+,** a reservation system for popular attractions (discussed starting on page 87), provides some relief from long afternoon lines, but it isn't available for every attraction, nor is there an unlimited supply of reservations.

Opting for a Partial Day at the Theme Parks

If you decide to use one day's admission on a half-day or less, refer to our *Unofficial Guide* Crowd Calendar at **touringplans.com** for the least-crowded park to visit.

You can make FastPass+ reservations for each park's most popular rides up to 60 days before your visit at **disneyworld.com** (it's 30 days in advance for Annual Pass holders and off-site guests with a valid ticket). You could try to obtain FastPass+ reservations when you arrive, but be aware that the daily allocation of FastPasses at popular rides may be gone by then.

One option, if you can reach the park before 1 p.m. and stay until closing (5–8 p.m., depending on season), is Disney's Animal Kingdom, which requires the least time to tour. Because guests who arrive at opening frequently complete their tour by about 3 p.m., crowds thin in late afternoon. Try to make FastPass+ reservations for Kilimanjaro Safaris or Expedition Everest in advance.

Whenever you arrive at a theme park (including Universal parks) after 10 a.m., you should go to higher-capacity attractions where waiting time is relatively brief, even during the most crowded part of the day. Besides FastPass+, another time-saver at Test Track in Epcot, Expedition Everest in Disney's Animal Kingdom, Rock 'n' Roller Coaster in Disney's Hollywood Studios, and several Universal Orlando attractions is the **singles line,** a separate line for individuals who are alone or don't mind riding alone. The objective is to fill odd spaces left by groups that don't quite fill the entire ride vehicle. Because there aren't many singles and most groups are unwilling to split up, singles lines are usually much shorter than regular lines.

Disney parks are better for partial-day touring than Universal parks because Disney parks generally operate more high-capacity attractions than Universal does. We like the Universal parks and admire their cutting-edge technology, but the best way to see them is to be there at opening and follow our touring plans.

Our clip-out Touring Plan Companions in the back of the book list attractions in each Disney park that require the least waiting during the most crowded part of the day. Although the queues for these attractions may seem humongous, they move quickly. Also check out parades, stage shows, and other live entertainment. Popular attractions generally stay packed until an hour or so before closing; however, they often require little waiting during evening parades, shows, or fireworks.

Alternatives to the Theme Parks on Arrival Day

Before you head out for fun on arrival day, you must check in, unpack, and buy admissions, and you probably will detour to the grocery or convenience store to buy snacks, drinks, and breakfast food. At all Disney resorts and many non-Disney hotels, you cannot occupy your room until after 3 p.m. (4 p.m. for DVC resorts); however, many properties will check you in, sell you tickets, and store your luggage before that hour.

The least expensive way to spend your arrival day is to check in, unpack, do your chores, and relax at your hotel swimming pool.

Other daytime options include a trip to a local water park. Because the Disney water parks are so crowded (during summer you need to be on hand for opening, just as you do at the other Disney parks), we recommend **Wet 'n Wild** (**wetnwildorlando.com**) on International Drive, which is generally less crowded than Disney's water parks but more expensive. What's great about Wet 'n Wild is that it stays open late in summer. Any water park that stays open past 5 p.m. is worth a look, because crowds at all parks clear out substantially after 4 p.m. If the park is open late and you get hungry, you'll find ample fast food. No matter which water park you choose, slather on broad-spectrum sunscreen. (For details on water parks, see Part Seventeen.)

If you want something drier, we heartily recommend **Gatorland,** a quirky attraction on US 441 near Kissimmee (about 20 minutes from Walt Disney World). Gatorland, a slice of pre-Disney Florida, is exceptionally interesting and well managed. It's perfect for a half-day outing, provided you like alligators, snakes, and lizards. For information, call ☎ 800-393-JAWS or go to **gatorland.com.**

If none of the previous fires your boiler, consider miniature golf (expensive in Walt Disney World, more reasonable outside it) or **The NBA Experience,** an upcoming pro basketball–themed venue at Disney Springs (see page 728). It will replace **DisneyQuest,** a significantly outdated interactive-games venue that's expensive and doesn't handle crowds particularly well.

In the Evening

Dinner provides a great opportunity to plan the next day's activities. If you're hungry for entertainment too, take in a show at or after dinner. If you go the show route, we recommend **Cirque du Soleil *La Nouba*** at Disney Springs. Cirque is expensive, but we think it's the single best thing in all of Walt Disney World. Disney also offers some dinner shows, of which the *Hoop-Dee-Doo Musical Revue* is our pick of the litter. Both Cirque and *Hoop-Dee-Doo* are extremely popular; make reservations far in advance.

If you're not up for Cirque or a dinner show, consider **CityWalk,** Universal's nighttime-entertainment complex. Other options include **Jellyrolls,** a dueling-pianos club at the BoardWalk, and **Raglan Road,** an Irish pub at Disney Springs with live music and good food. All are best appreciated by adults—energetic adults, at that.

Departure Days

Departure days don't seem to cause as much consternation as arrival days. If you want to visit a theme park on your departure day, get up early and be there when it opens. If you have a lot of time, check out and store your luggage with the bell desk or in your car. Or, if you can arrange a late checkout, you might want to return to your hotel for a shower and change of clothes before departing. Some hotels are quite lenient regarding late checkouts; others assess a charge.

THE CARDINAL RULES FOR SUCCESSFUL TOURING

MANY VISITORS DON'T HAVE SIX DAYS to devote to Disney. Some are en route to other destinations or may wish to sample additional Central Florida attractions. For these visitors, efficient touring is a must.

Even the most time-effective touring plan won't allow you to comprehensively cover two or more major theme parks in one day. Plan to allocate an entire day to each park (an exception to this is when the parks close at different times, allowing you to tour one park until closing, then proceed to another).

One-Day Touring

A comprehensive one-day tour of the Magic Kingdom, Epcot, Disney's Animal Kingdom, or Disney's Hollywood Studios is possible but requires knowledge of the park, good planning, good navigation, and plenty of energy and endurance. One-day touring leaves little time for sit-down meals, prolonged browsing in shops, or lengthy breaks. Yes, it can be fun and rewarding, but allocating two days per park, especially for the Magic Kingdom and Epcot, is the ideal.

A Connecticut couple in their 20s underscores the walking involved in seeing Walt Disney World:

> You don't realize how much you're going to walk on this vacation— take whatever amount you're thinking and double it. We averaged 9 miles a day, and we weren't going to every ride and attraction.

Successfully touring the Magic Kingdom, Epcot, Animal Kingdom, or Disney's Hollywood Studios hinges on three rules:

1. Determine in Advance What You Really Want to See

Which attractions appeal to you most? Which ones would you like to experience if you have time left? What are you willing to forgo?

To help you set your touring priorities, we describe the theme parks and their attractions in detail. In each description, we include the authors' evaluation of the attraction and the opinions of Disney World guests expressed as star ratings. Five stars is the highest rating.

Finally, because Disney attractions range from midway-type rides and horse-drawn trolleys to high-tech extravaganzas, we have developed a hierarchy of categories to pinpoint an attraction's magnitude:

SUPER-HEADLINERS The best attractions the theme park has to offer. Mind-boggling in size, scope, and imagination, they represent the cutting edge of attraction technology and design.

HEADLINERS Multimillion-dollar, full-scale, themed adventures and theater presentations. Modern in technology and design and employing a full range of special effects.

MAJOR ATTRACTIONS More modestly themed adventures, but ones that incorporate state-of-the-art technologies. Or larger-scale attractions of older design.

MINOR ATTRACTIONS Midway-type rides, small "dark" rides (cars on a track, zigzagging through the dark), small theater presentations, transportation rides, and elaborate walk-through attractions.

DIVERSIONS Exhibits, both passive and interactive; include playgrounds, video arcades, and street theater.

Though not every attraction fits neatly into these descriptions, the categories provide a comparison of attraction size and scope. Remember that bigger and more elaborate doesn't always mean better. Peter Pan's Flight, a minor attraction in the Magic Kingdom, continues to be one of the park's most beloved rides. Likewise, for many young children, no attraction, regardless of size, surpasses Dumbo.

2. Arrive Early! Arrive Early! Arrive Early!

This is the single most important key to efficient touring and avoiding long lines. First thing in the morning, there are no lines and fewer people. The same four rides you experience in 1 hour in early morning can take as long as 3 hours after 10:30 a.m. Eat breakfast before you arrive; don't waste prime touring time sitting in a restaurant.

The earlier a park opens, the greater your advantage. This is because most vacationers won't rise early and get to a park before it opens. Fewer people are willing to make an 8 a.m. opening than a 9 a.m. opening. If you visit during midsummer, arrive at the turnstile 30–40 minutes before opening. During holiday periods, arrive 45–60 minutes early.

Many readers share their experiences about getting to the parks before opening. From a 13-year-old girl from Bloomington, Indiana:

> Please stress this to your readers: If you want to ride anything with a short wait, you have to get up in the morning! If this is a sacrifice you aren't willing to make, reconsider a Disney World vacation.

A Pennsylvania mom of two found that slacking didn't pay:

> This is emphasized in the guide multiple times, but I want to say it again: Be at rope drop. I went during one of the slowest times of the year, and the morning I didn't wake up for rope drop I was able to experience less than half of what I did the other days.

A Minneapolis mother of three managed a compromise:

> Getting there early meant we could do the popular things without a long wait. That way I got my type-A "get things done" stuff out of the way in the morning and my husband got to indulge his "let's wander without a plan" personality the rest of the day.

If getting the kids up earlier than usual makes for rough sailing, don't despair: You'll have a great time no matter when you get to the park. Many families with young children have found that it's better to accept the relative inefficiencies of arriving at the park a bit late than to jar the children out of their routine. In our guide especially for families, *The Unofficial Guide to Walt Disney World with Kids*, we provide a number of special touring plans (including touring plans for sleepyheads) that we don't have room for in this guide.

3. Avoid Bottlenecks

Helping you avoid bottlenecks is what the *Unofficial Guide* is about. This involves being able to predict where, when, and why they occur. Concentrations of hungry people create bottlenecks at restaurants during lunch and dinner; concentrations of people moving toward the exit near closing time cause gift shops en route to clog; concentrations of visitors at new and popular rides, and at rides slow to load and unload, create logjams and long lines.

Our solution for avoiding bottlenecks is touring plans for the Magic Kingdom, Epcot, Disney's Animal Kingdom, Disney's Hollywood Studios, and the two Disney water parks. We also provide detailed information on rides and performances, enabling you to estimate how long you may have to wait in line and allowing you to compare rides for their crowd capacity.

All touring plans are in the back of this book, following the indexes. Plans for Magic Kingdom begin on page 806 and for Epcot on page 812. One-day touring plans for Animal Kingdom and Disney's Hollywood

Studios follow, on pages 817 and 818, respectively. Next come one-day touring plans for Universal's Islands of Adventure and Universal Studios Florida, on pages 819 and 820, respectively; a plan for both parks is on pages 821–822. Touring plans for Blizzard Beach and Typhoon Lagoon water parks are found on pages 823 and 824, respectively.

WHAT'S A QUEUE?

ALTHOUGH IT'S NOT COMMONLY USED in the United States, *queue* (pronounced "cue") is the universal English word for a line, such as one in which you wait to cash a check at the bank or to board a ride at a theme park. Queuing theory, a mathematical area of specialization within the field of operations research, studies and models how lines work. Because the *Unofficial Guide* draws heavily on this discipline, we use some of its terminology. In addition to the noun, the verb *to queue* means to get in line, and a *queuing area* is a waiting area that accommodates a line. When guests decline to join a queue because they perceive the wait to be too long, they're said to *balk*.

OF UTMOST IMPORTANCE: READ THIS!

IN ANALYZING READER SURVEYS, we were astonished by the percentage of readers who *don't* use our touring plans. Scientifically tested and proven, these plans can save you **4 entire hours** or more of waiting in line in a single day—4 fewer hours of standing, 4 hours freed up to do something fun. Our groundbreaking research that created the touring plans has been the subject of front-page articles in the *Dallas Morning News* and *The New York Times* and has been cited in numerous scholarly journals. So why would you not use them?

We get a ton of reader mail—98% of it positive—commenting on our touring plans. First, from a mother who planned a last-minute trip:

> We rode all of the main attractions in Epcot, Magic Kingdom, and Hollywood Studios over a three-day period, and we didn't wait more than 10 minutes for any ride—and this was during spring break! We had a five-day pass, so we used the evenings and another day to stroll through the parks, enjoying the sights and minor attractions.

From a Ferndown, England, mother of two:

> We were stunned by how effective the touring plans were straight out of the book. We would get to the given park early, and by the time the plan suggested lunch it could be about 10:30 (and this was at Easter!). We got straight on a clamshell at The Seas with Nemo & Friends, and as we took our seats we saw a line form after us.

An Ohio family felt the wind in their sails:

> The whole time we were in the Magic Kingdom, following the touring plan, it seemed that we were traveling in front of a hurricane—we'd wait 10 minutes or so for an attraction (or less—sometimes we just walked right on), but when we got out and started moving on to the next one, we could see the line building for what we just did.

For a Glasgow, Scotland, reader, touring the *Unofficial* way contributed to family harmony:

Trying to decide where to go next wasn't something we had to worry about. There was none of that "Whatever you think" / "I don't mind"– type discussion that can haunt even the best of holidays.

A 30-something mom of two from Oconomowoc, Wisconsin, found that the touring plans fanned the flames of *amour:*

My husband was a bit doubtful about using a touring plan, but on our first day at Magic Kingdom, after we'd done all the Fantasyland attractions and ridden Splash Mountain twice before lunch, he looked at me with amazement and said, "I've never been so attracted to you."

Finally, from an Edmonds, Washington, family who used the touring plans for Universal's Islands of Adventure:

This trip was the first time we were actually going to leave the property (gasp!) and go to Universal, and I was very happy that you included a touring plan for Islands of Adventure. It worked like a charm! I've always wondered how it feels to follow your plans not ever having seen the park before, and now I know—it was easy!

TOURING PLANS: WHAT THEY ARE AND HOW THEY WORK

See More, Do More, Wait Less

From the first edition of the *Unofficial Guide,* minimizing our readers' waits in line has been a top priority. We know from our research and that of others that theme park patrons measure overall satisfaction based on the number of attractions they're able to experience during a visit: the more attractions, the better. Thus, we developed and offered our readers field-tested touring plans that allow them to experience as many attractions as possible with the least amount of waiting in line.

Our touring plans have always been based on theme-park-traffic flow, attraction capacity, the maximum time a guest is willing to wait (called a *balking constraint*), walking distance between attractions, and waiting-time data collected at every attraction in every park, every day of the year. The plans derived from a combinatorial model (for anyone who cares) that married the well-known assignment problem of linear programming with queuing (waiting-line) theory. The model approximated the most time-efficient sequence in which to visit the attractions of a specific park. After we created a preliminary touring plan from the model, we field-tested it in the park, using a test group (who followed our plan) and a control group (who didn't have our plan and who toured according to their own best judgment).

unofficial TIP
The facts and figures in our books come from years of data collection and analysis by expert statisticians, programmers, field researchers, and lifelong Disney enthusiasts.

The two groups were compared, and the results were amazing. On days of heavy attendance, the groups touring without our plans spent an average of 4 hours more in line and experienced 37% fewer attractions than did those who did use the plans.

Over the years, this research has been recognized by both the travel industry and academe, having been cited by such diverse sources as the *Atlanta Journal-Constitution, Bottom Line,* the *Dallas Morning News,* the Mathematical Association of America, *Money, The New York Times, Operations Research Forum, Travel Weekly, USA Today,* and *Wired,* along with the BBC, CBS News, Fox News, and the Travel Channel. The methodology behind our touring plans was also used as a case study in the 2010 book *Numbers Rule Your World,* by Kaiser Fung, professor of statistics at New York University.

So how good *are* the touring plans in the *Unofficial Guide?* Our computer program typically gets within about 2% of the optimal touring plan and finds an optimal plan for most straightforward situations around 70% of the time. To put this in perspective, if the hypothetical "perfect" Adult One-Day Touring Plan took about 10 hours to complete, the *Unofficial* touring plan would take around 10 hours and 12 minutes. Because it would take about 30 years for a really powerful computer to find that "perfect" plan, the extra 12 minutes is a reasonable trade-off.

In the 2003 edition of this guidebook, we noted the possibility of using our software to see every attraction in the Magic Kingdom in one day. We dubbed this the Ultimate Magic Kingdom Touring Plan and offered it free to anyone up for the challenge. Dozens of otherwise-sane families have completed this plan since that time, and hundreds have come close. The current record-holders are Jordyn and Kenny White of Gun Barrel City, Texas, who saw 98 attractions in 23 hours and 54 minutes on May 23, 2014 (the Magic Kingdom was open for 24 consecutive hours). That works out to roughly 1 attraction every 15 minutes. Other "ultimate" plans exist for Epcot, DHS, and Disney's Animal Kingdom. Drop us a line or visit **touringplans.com/ultimate** if you're up for the challenge. Note that these plans aren't intended for families, first-time visitors, or anyone simply wanting a nice day in the parks. To the contrary, they're like running a marathon.

Customize Your Touring Plans

The attractions included in our touring plans are the most popular as determined by almost 57,000 reader surveys. If you've never been to Walt Disney World, we suggest using the plans in this book. Besides being the best our program can produce, these plans have been field-tested by tens of thousands of families. They'll ensure that you see the best Disney attractions with as little waiting in line as possible.

If you're a return visitor, your favorite attractions may be different. One way to customize the plans is to go to **touringplans.com** to create personalized versions. Tell the software the date, time, and park you've chosen to visit, along with the attractions you want to see. Your custom plan will tell you, for your specific travel date and time, the exact order in which to visit attractions to minimize your waits in line. Our touring plans also support "switching off" on thrill rides (see page 412). Besides attractions, you can schedule meals, breaks, character greetings, and more. You can even tell your plans how fast you plan to walk, and they'll make the necessary adjustments. Plus, the plans can handle any FastPass+ reservations you've already got and tell you which attractions would benefit most from using them.

Alternatively, some changes are simple enough to make on your own. If a plan calls for an attraction you're not interested in, simply skip it and move on to the next one. You can also substitute similar attractions in the same area of the park. If a plan calls for, say, riding Dumbo and you'd rather not, but you would enjoy the Mad Tea Party (which is not on the plan), then go ahead and substitute that for Dumbo. As long as the substitution is a similar attraction—substituting a show for a ride won't work—and is pretty close by the attraction called for in the touring plan, you won't compromise the plan's overall effectiveness.

A family of four from South Slocan, British Columbia, found they could easily tailor the touring plans to meet their needs:

> We amended your touring plans by taking out the attractions we didn't want to do and just doing the remainder in order. It worked great, and by arriving before the parks opened, we got to see everything we wanted, with virtually no waits!

As did a Jacksonville, Florida, family:

> We used a combination of the Two-Day Touring Plan for Parents with Small Children and the Two-Day Touring Plan for Adults. We were able to get on almost everything with a 10-minute wait or less.

Finally, from a Magnolia, Mississippi, family of four:

> One of the things we love most about the book and the website is the ability to adjust any of the plans to our family's preferences simply by omitting a step or two. The plans work for any style of touring, from commando to laid-back.

OVERVIEW OF THE TOURING PLANS

OUR TOURING PLANS ARE STEP-BY-STEP guides for seeing as much as possible with a minimum of standing in line. They're designed to help you avoid crowds and bottlenecks on any day of the year. The plans will save time on days when attendance is lighter (see "Selecting the Time of Year for Your Visit," page 39), but they won't be as critical to successful touring.

What You Can Realistically Expect from the Touring Plans

Though we present one-day touring plans for each theme park, be aware that the Magic Kingdom and Epcot have more attractions than you can reasonably expect to see in one day. Because the two-day plans for the Magic Kingdom and Epcot are the most comprehensive, efficient, and relaxing, we strongly recommend them over the one-day plans. However, if you must cram your visit into a single day, the one-day plans will allow you to see as much as is humanly possible. Because construction at Disney's Hollywood Studios has closed many attractions, seeing the attractions that remain open in one day is doable; likewise, Disney's Animal Kingdom is a one-day outing.

Variables That Affect the Success of the Touring Plans

The plans' success will be affected by how quickly you move from ride to ride; when and how many refreshment and restroom breaks you take;

when, where, and how you eat meals; and your ability (or lack thereof) to find your way around. Smaller groups almost always move faster than larger groups, and parties of adults generally cover more ground than families with young children. Switching off (page 412), also known as "The Baby Swap," among other things, inhibits families with little ones from moving expeditiously among attractions. Plus, some folks simply cannot conform to the plans' "early to rise" conditions, as this reader from Cleveland Heights, Ohio, recounts:

> Our touring plans were thrown totally off by one member who could not be on time for opening. Even in October, this made a huge difference in our ability to see attractions without waiting.

And a family from Centerville, Ohio, says:

> The toughest thing about your touring plans was getting the rest of the family to stay with them. Getting them to pass by attractions in order to hit something across the park was no easy task.

The Disney Dining Plan's required restaurant reservations impose a rigid schedule that can derail a touring plan, as this Wichita, Kansas, mom attests:

> The [printed] touring plans were impractical if used with the dining plan. The hour-long meals wreaked havoc on the itinerary, and we never seemed to be able to get back on track, even with low crowd levels and rainy afternoons.

Along with dining breaks, the appearance of a Disney character usually stops a touring plan in its tracks. While some characters stroll the parks, it's equally common that they assemble in a specific venue where families queue up for photos and autographs. Meeting characters, posing for photos, and getting autographs can burn hours of touring time.

If your kids collect character autographs, you need to anticipate these interruptions by including character greetings when creating your online touring plans, or else negotiate some understanding with your children about when you'll collect autographs. Note that queues for autographs, especially in the Magic Kingdom and Disney's Animal Kingdom, are sometimes as long as or longer than the queues for major attractions. The only time-efficient ways to collect autographs are to use FastPass+ where available (such as for Mickey Mouse and the Disney princesses at the Magic Kingdom) or to line up at the character-greeting areas first thing in the morning. Early morning is also the best time to experience popular attractions, so you may have some tough choices to make.

Some things are beyond your control. Chief among these are the manner and timing of bringing a particular ride to capacity. For example, Big Thunder Mountain Railroad, a roller coaster in the Magic Kingdom, has five trains. On a given morning, it may begin operation with two of the five, then add the other three when needed. If the waiting line builds rapidly before operators go to full capacity, you could have a long wait, even in early morning.

A variable that can give your touring plans a boost is the singles line (see page 74), as this English reader explains:

We used the touring plans to the letter and found that not only did they work, but they worked even better in conjunction with single-rider queues. The only rides that we queued up for normally were ones with a 20-minute-or-less queue time and wet rides.

Another variable is your arrival time for a theater show. You'll wait from the time you arrive until the end of the presentation in progress. Thus, if a show is 15 minutes long and you arrive 1 minute after it has begun, your wait will be 14 minutes. Conversely, if you arrive as the show is wrapping up, your wait will be only a minute or two.

While we realize that following the plans isn't always easy, we nevertheless recommend continuous, expeditious touring until around noon. After that, breaks and diversions won't affect the plans significantly.

What to Do if You Lose the Thread

If unforeseen events interrupt a plan:

1. If you're following a touring plan in our **Lines** app (**touringplans.com/lines**), just press "Optimize" when you're ready to start touring again. Lines will figure out the best possible plan for the remainder of your day.

2. If you're following a printed touring plan, skip a step on the plan for every 20 minutes' delay. For example, if you lose your wallet and spend an hour hunting for it, skip three steps and pick up from there.

3. Forget the plan and organize the remainder of the day using the standby wait times listed in Lines or the Clip-Out Touring Plan Companions in the back of the book.

What to Expect When You Arrive at the Parks

Because most touring plans are based on being present when the theme park opens, you need to know about opening procedures. Disney transportation to the parks begins 1½–2 hours before official opening. The parking lots open at around the same time.

Each park has an entrance plaza outside the turnstiles. Usually, you're held there until 30 minutes before the official opening time, when you're admitted. What happens next depends on the season and the day's crowds:

1. **STANDARD OPENING PROCEDURES** At Epcot, Disney's Hollywood Studios, and Animal Kingdom, all guests are permitted through the turnstiles, and you'll find that one or several specific attractions are open early.

   At Epcot, Spaceship Earth and sometimes Test Track or Soarin' will be operating. At Animal Kingdom, you may find it's Kilimanjaro Safaris, Expedition Everest, and TriceraTop Spin. At Hollywood Studios, look for Tower of Terror, Toy Story Midway Mania!, and/or Rock 'n' Roller Coaster.

   At the Magic Kingdom, you may be admitted past the turnstiles 15 minutes before park opening, but you'll usually be confined to a small section of the park, such as Main Street, U.S.A., until official opening time. A human wall of Disney cast members keeps you there until opening, when the wall speed-walks you back to the headliner attractions (to prevent anyone from running or getting trampled).

2. **HIGH-ATTENDANCE DAYS** When large crowds are expected, you'll usually be admitted through the turnstiles up to 30 minutes before official opening, and most of the park will be operating.

In the first scenario on the previous page, you gain a big advantage if you're already past the turnstiles when the park opens. While everyone else is stuck in line waiting for the people ahead to find their tickets and figure out how the biometric scans work, the lucky few already in the park will be in line for their first attraction. You'll probably be done and on your way to your second before many of them are even in the park, and the time savings accrue throughout the rest of the day.

Clip-Out Touring Plans

For your convenience, we've prepared graphical clip-out copies of all touring plans. These pocket versions combine touring plan itineraries with maps and directions. Select the plan appropriate for your party, and get familiar with it. Then clip the pocket version from the back of this guide and carry it with you as a quick reference at the theme park.

Will the Plans Continue to Work Once the Secret Is Out?

Yes! First, all the plans require that a patron be there when a park opens. Many Disney World patrons simply won't get up early while on vacation. Second, less than 2% of any day's attendance has been exposed to the plans—too few to affect results. Last, most groups tailor the plans, skipping rides or shows according to taste.

How Frequently Are the Touring Plans Revised?

We revise them every year, and updates are always available at **touringplans.com.** Be prepared for surprises, though: Opening procedures and showtimes may change, for example, and you can't predict when an attraction might break down.

"Bouncing Around"

Some readers object to crisscrossing a theme park as our touring plans sometimes require. A woman from Decatur, Georgia, told us she "got dizzy from all the bouncing around." Believe us, we empathize.

We've worked hard over the years to eliminate the need to crisscross a theme park in our touring plans. (In fact, our customized software can minimize walking instead of waiting in line, if that's important to you.) Occasionally, however, it's possible to save a lot of time in line with a few extra minutes of walking.

The reasons for this are varied. Sometimes a park is designed intentionally to require walking. In the Magic Kingdom, for example, the most popular attractions are positioned as far apart as possible—in the north, east, and west corners of the park—so that guests are more evenly distributed throughout the day. Other times, you may be visiting just after a new attraction has opened that everyone wants to try. In that case, a special trip to visit the new attraction may be required earlier in the day than normal, in order to avoid longer waits later. And live shows, especially at the Studios, sometimes have performance schedules so at odds with each other (and the rest of the park's schedule) that orderly touring is impossible.

If you want to experience headliner attractions in one day without long waits, you can see those first (requires crisscrossing the park), use

FastPass+ (if available), or hope to squeeze in visits during parades and the last hour the park is open (may not work).

If you have two days to visit the Magic Kingdom or Epcot, use the Two-Day Touring Plans (see pages 809 and 810 for the Magic Kingdom, pages 815 and 816 for Epcot). These spread the popular attractions over two mornings and work great even when the parks close early.

Touring Plans and the Obsessive-Compulsive Reader

We suggest sticking to the plans religiously, especially in the mornings, if you're visiting during busy times. The consequence of touring spontaneity in peak season is hours of standing in line. When using the plans, however, relax and always be prepared for surprises and setbacks.

If you find your type-A brain doing cartwheels, reflect on the advice of a woman from Trappe, Pennsylvania:

> I had planned for this trip for two years and researched it by use of guidebooks, computer programs, videotapes, and information received from WDW. On night three of our trip, I ended up taking an unscheduled trip to the emergency room. When the doctor asked what seemed to be the problem, I responded, "I don't know, but I can't stop shaking, and I can't stay here very long because I have to get up in a couple hours to go to Disney's Hollywood Studios." Diagnosis: an anxiety attack caused by my excessive itinerary.

An Omaha, Nebraska, couple devised their own way to cope:

> We created our own 4.25 x 5.5 guidebook for our trip that included a number of pages from the **touringplans.com** website. This was the first page:

The Type-A Spouse's Bill of Rights

1. We will not see everything in one vacation, and any attempt to do so may be met with blunt trauma.

2. Len Testa will not be vacationing with us. His plans don't schedule time for benches. Ours may.

3. We may deviate from the touring plans at some point. Really.

4. Even if it isn't on the Disney Dining Plan, a funnel cake or other snack may be purchased without a grouchy face from the nonpurchasing spouse.

5. Sometimes, sitting by the pool may sound more fun than going to a park, show, or other scheduled event. On this vacation, that will be fine.

6. "But I thought we were going to . . ." is a phrase that must be stricken from the discussion of any plans that had not been previously discussed as a couple.

7. Other items may be added as circumstances dictate at the parks.

> It was a much happier vacation with these generally understood principles in writing.

Touring Plan Rejection

Some folks don't respond well to the regimentation of a touring plan. If you encounter this problem with someone in your party, roll with the punches as this Maryland couple did:

The rest of the group was not receptive to the use of the touring plans. I think they all thought I was being a little too regimented about planning this vacation. Rather than argue, I left the touring plans behind as we ventured off for the parks. You can guess the outcome. We took our camcorder with us and watched the movies when we returned home. About every 5 minutes or so there's a shot of us all gathered around a park map trying to decide what to do next.

A reader from Royal Oak, Michigan, ran into trouble by not getting her family on board ahead of time:

The one thing I will suggest is if one member of the family is doing most of the research and planning (like I did), that they communicate what the book/touring plans suggest. I failed to do this and it led to some, shall we say, tense moments between my husband and me on our first day. However, once he realized how much time we were saving, he understood why I was so bent on following the plans.

Touring Plans for Low-Attendance Days

We receive a number of letters each year similar to the following one from Lebanon, New Jersey:

The guide always assumed there would be large crowds. We had no lines. An alternate tour for low-traffic days would be helpful.

There are, thankfully, still days on which crowds are low enough that a full-day touring plan isn't needed. However, some attractions in each park bottleneck even if attendance is low:

MAGIC KINGDOM *Enchanted Tales with Belle,* The Many Adventures of Winnie the Pooh, Peter Pan's Flight, Seven Dwarfs Mine Train, Space Mountain, Splash Mountain

EPCOT Soarin', Test Track

DISNEY'S ANIMAL KINGDOM Dinosaur, Expedition Everest, Kilimanjaro Safaris

DHS Rock 'n' Roller Coaster, Toy Story Midway Mania!, The Twilight Zone Tower of Terror

Immense lines also build for meet and greets involving characters from Disney's latest films. In early 2015, for example, it was common at park opening for a 2-hour line to form to meet the princesses from Disney's *Frozen.* For this reason, we recommend following a touring plan through the first five or six steps. If you're pretty much walking onto every attraction, scrap the remainder of the plan. Alternatively, see the attractions listed above right after the park opens, or use FastPass+.

EXTRA MAGIC HOURS AND THE TOURING PLANS

IF YOU'RE A DISNEY RESORT GUEST and use your morning Extra Magic Hours privileges, complete your early-entry touring before the general public is admitted, then position yourself to follow the touring plan. When the public is admitted, the park will suddenly swarm. A Wilmington, Delaware, mother advises:

The early-entry times went like clockwork. We were finishing up the Great Movie Ride when Disney's Hollywood Studios opened to the

*public, and we had to wait in line quite a while for Voyage of the Lit-
tle Mermaid, which sort of screwed up everything thereafter. Early-
opening attractions should be finished up well before regular opening
time so you can be at the plan's first stop as early as possible.*

In the Magic Kingdom, early-entry attractions currently operate in
Fantasyland and Tomorrowland. At Epcot, they're in the Future World
section. At Disney's Animal Kingdom, they're in DinoLand U.S.A.,
Asia, Discovery Island, and Africa. At Disney's Hollywood Studios,
they're dispersed. Practically speaking, see any attractions on the plan
that are open for early entry, crossing them off as you do. If you finish
all early-entry attractions and have time left before the general public
is admitted, sample early-entry attractions not included in the plan.
Stop touring about 10 minutes before the public is admitted, and position yourself for the first attraction on the plan that wasn't open for
early entry. During early entry in the Magic Kingdom, for example,
you can almost always experience Seven Dwarfs Mine Train and
Under the Sea: Journey of the Little Mermaid in Fantasyland, plus
Space Mountain in Tomorrowland. As official opening nears, go to the
boundary between Fantasyland and Liberty Square and be ready to
blitz Splash and Big Thunder Mountains according to the touring plan
when the rest of the park opens.

Evening Extra Magic Hours, when a designated park remains open
for Disney resort guests 2 hours beyond normal closing time, have less
effect on the touring plans than early entry in the morning. Parks are
almost never scheduled for both early entry and evening Extra Magic
Hours on the same day. Thus a park offering evening Extra Magic Hours
will enjoy a fairly normal morning and early afternoon. It's not until
late afternoon, when park hoppers coming from the other theme parks
descend, that the late-closing park will become especially crowded. By
that time, you'll be well toward the end of your touring plan.

FASTPASS+

THE LATEST EVOLUTION of this 15-year-old
ride-reservation system, FastPass+ is a milestone
in Disney's never-ending quest to create something
more complicated than the US tax code or the
Affordable Care Act.

The original iteration of FastPass (also styled
as *Fastpass* and *FASTPASS* over the years) was
introduced in 1999 as a way to moderate high
wait times at some of Disney's headliner attrac-
tions. A new version of the system, called FastPass+, completely replaced
the old one in January 2014. Whereas the old system printed your reservation times on small slips of paper dispensed from ATM-like kiosks
next to each attraction, the current FastPass+ system is (with one exception described later) entirely electronic: You must use a computer, mobile
device, or in-park terminal to make and modify FastPass+ reservations,
and you must use your RFID-enabled MagicBand, Key to the World
Card, or day-guest card to redeem the reservation. As before, FastPass+
is free of charge to all Walt Disney World guests.

unofficial **TIP**
Disney offers FastPass+
only for select attractions
—around 70 in all—and
only during busy times of
year for some. Specific
FastPass+ information
for each Disney theme
park is provided in its
respective chapter.

Because FastPass+ has a learning curve, understanding how to use it is important for success when using our touring plans, especially if you want to experience lots of attractions or you're unable to arrive at park opening. Somewhat like making a dinner reservation at a restaurant, FastPass+ allows you to reserve a ride on an attraction at a Disney theme park. You can request a specific time, such as 7:30 p.m., or you can let the system give you its "first available" reservation.

Although we take issue with the current system's complicated rules and procedures—enough that we lampooned them in the last edition's "The Importance of Being Goofy," which told the story of a married couple navigating the system for the first time, one rather overenthusiastically—we do concede that FastPass+ can help you see more with less waiting, *provided you know how to use it.* Like the old FastPass, it reduces waits for designated attractions by distributing guests at those attractions throughout the day. Also like the old system, FastPass+ provides an incentive—a shorter wait—for guests willing to postpone experiencing a given attraction until later in the day. The system also, in effect, imposes a penalty—standby status—on guests who don't use it. However, spreading out guest arrivals sometimes decreases waits for standby guests as well.

unofficial **TIP**
Because an attraction's FastPass+ availability is limited by its hourly rider capacity, those who book last-minute trips or buy admission at the gate may find that reservations are no longer available at their favorite attractions.

FastPass+ does *not* eliminate the need to arrive early at a theme park. Because each park offers a limited number of FastPass+ attractions, you still have to make an early start if you want to avoid long lines at non-FastPass+ attractions.

Making a FastPass+ Reservation

Anyone with an upcoming stay at a Walt Disney World hotel can make FastPass+ reservations up to 60 days in advance at **disneyworld.com** and through the My Disney Experience app; Annual Pass holders staying off-property may reserve up to 30 days in advance, as may day guests with a valid ticket.

If you buy your admission the day you arrive at the park or you want to change your previous FastPass+ selections once you're inside, you can do so using the mobile app or new in-park computer terminals.

You should set aside *at least* 30 minutes to complete the advance-booking process. Before you begin, make sure that you have the following items on hand:

- A valid admission ticket or purchase-confirmation number for everyone in your group
- Your hotel-reservation number, if you're staying on-site
- A computer, smartphone, or tablet connected to the Internet
- An e-mail account that you can access easily while traveling
- An account at **mydisneyexperience.com**
- A schedule of the parks you'll be visiting each day, including arrival and departure times, plus the times of any midday breaks
- The dates, times, and confirmation numbers of any dining or recreation reservations you've already made

- A fistful of Xanax
- The patience of Job

If you're coordinating travel plans with friends or family who live elsewhere, the following information is also good to have:

- The names and (optionally) e-mail addresses of the people you're traveling with
- A schedule of the parks these folks are visiting on each day of their trip, including their arrival, departure, and break times
- The dates and times of any dining or recreation reservations these folks have made

Again, the only way to make FastPass+ reservations before your trip is to use the My Disney Experience (MDE) website or app—you can't make them by phone, the way you would for a restaurant reservation. We think it's easier to use the website, so we'll describe that here; the steps for the app are similar.

1. E-MAIL ACCESS Because the MDE site uses your e-mail address to identify you and send you new login credentials should you forget your old ones (see next step), you need to make sure you'll have easy access to your account while you're in the parks. If you don't have a mobile app for your e-mail account, download and configure it before you leave home. And if you don't have an account with a web-based service such as Gmail, go ahead and set one up—it's much easier to configure for mobile devices than e-mail you get through your ISP.

2. MY DISNEY EXPERIENCE ACCESS Now go to the MDE site and click "Sign In or Create Account" in the upper-right corner; then click "Create Account" on the screen that follows. You'll be asked for your e-mail address, along with your name, home address, and birthdate. (Disney uses your home address to send your MagicBands and, if applicable, hotel-reservation information.) You'll also be asked to choose two security questions and answers—write these down and store them in a safe place, or save them as a text file. If you forget your MDE login information, Disney will ask you these questions to verify your identity.

3. DISNEY HOTEL INFORMATION Next, MDE asks whether you'll be staying at a Disney hotel. If you are, enter your reservation number. This associates your MDE account with your hotel stay in Disney's computer systems. If you've booked a travel package that includes theme park admission, Disney computers will automatically link the admission to your MDE account, allowing you to skip Step 5 below.

4. REGISTER FRIENDS AND FAMILY You'll now be asked for the names, ages, and e-mail addresses of everyone traveling with you. This is so you can make dining and FastPass+ reservations for your entire group at the same time later in the process. You can add family and friends at any time, but you might as well do it now.

5. REGISTER TICKETS If you've bought your admission from a third-party ticket reseller or you have tickets or MagicBands left over from a previous trip, you'll be asked to register those next. On each ticket is printed a unique ID code, usually a string of 12–20 numbers, located at one corner on the back; on MagicBands, look for a 12-digit number printed inside the band. Enter the ID code for each ticket you have.

You can make FastPass+ reservations for as many days as there are on your ticket. If you decide later to extend your stay, you'll be able to make reservations for additional days. If you've got a voucher that needs to be converted to a ticket at the parks, you can still register it by calling Disney tech support at ☎ 407-939-7765.

6. SELECT A DATE Click on the My Disney Experience logo in the upper-right corner of your screen. A menu should appear, with "FastPass+" as one of the choices. Click on "FastPass+."

The next screen should display a rolling seven-day calendar, beginning around the start of your trip's dates. Select one of these dates and click "Next."

7. SELECT TRAVEL PARTY On the screen that follows, you'll choose which of your friends and family will use the FastPass+ reservations you're making. Note that everyone you select during this step will get the same set of FastPass+ attractions and times: If your FastPass+ choices include, say, Space Mountain and your father-in-law doesn't do roller coasters, you'll need to tweak his selections in Step 10. For now, choose all the members of your group and click "Next."

8. SELECT ATTRACTIONS On this screen you choose your FastPass+ experiences from a list of eligible attractions. Because Disney has rules governing the combinations of FastPasses you can get at Epcot and Disney's Hollywood Studios (see page 93), the attractions will be grouped into the correct tiers for those parks, and you'll see how many opportunities you have in each tier. If all FastPasses for an attraction have been distributed, the message "Standby Available" will appear next to its name.

If you don't choose an attraction for every opportunity MDE gives you—for instance, if you choose only two attractions when MDE says you can choose three—you'll automatically be assigned random attractions for all remaining opportunities.

9. CHOOSE INITIAL RETURN TIMES Next, MDE will give you four different sets of FastPass+ return times, grouped as Options A, B, and C, plus Best Match. Each option contains one return time for each attraction that you selected in Step 8. Again, we're not sure how Disney assigns the return times or what Disney thinks "Best Match" means. We do know that you have to choose all of the return times in Options A–C and Best Match. For now, choose the set of return times that's closest to what you want, and you'll be able to modify them in the next step.

10. MODIFY RETURN TIMES OR ATTRACTIONS If the initial set of FastPass+ return times conflicts with your plans, you can check whether alternate times are available that better fit your schedule. The good news is that you can change each attraction's return times separately. Plus, if none of the return times for a particular attraction work for you, you can pick another attraction at this stage without having to start over.

OK, you've booked one set of FastPasses for one park visit—now you'll need to repeat Steps 6–10 for every park you plan to visit, on every day of your trip. Simple, no?

A reader from White Plains, New York, found it all too much work:

> It's frustrating that you have to pick three attractions, when often I wanted to choose just one or two. It was also tough to set up for a big group—we ended up just getting the same FastPasses for everyone.

You've gotta hand it to Disney—making FastPass+ reservations online combines the efficiency of a third-world bureaucracy with the excitement of double-entry bookkeeping.

unofficial **TIP** To see how Adolf Hitler feels about FastPass+, go to **tinyurl.com/hitlerfastpass.**

Buying Tickets and Making FastPass+ Reservations On Arrival

If (1) you buy your admission the day you arrive at the parks or (2) you have to delay making your FastPass+ selections until you're inside, Disney has placed new computer terminals throughout the parks where you can make on-the-spot reservations; we've listed the specific locations in each theme park's chapter. Each set of terminals—look for the FP+ KIOSK signs—is staffed by a group of cast members who can walk you through the reservation process.

If you're tech-challenged, not to worry: You can use a paper FastPass+ form, sort of like a cafeteria menu, that lets you tick off checkboxes next to the rides you want to experience. A cast member will take your form and enter your selections into the kiosk for you. You'll still need to provide your MDE username and password, however.

Be aware that the number of kiosks is limited, and most locations can process reservations for no more than 150 people per hour, as a Cleveland family found out:

On our first day, I had to wait in line for around a half-hour at a Fast-Pass+ kiosk, and by the time it was my turn they had run out of passes for two of the three selections I had wanted: Peter Pan's Flight and Enchanted Tales with Belle. I was a pro by our third day there, but I miss the old system, which was much more user-friendly.

RETURNING TO RIDE Each FastPass+ reservation lasts for an hour, and Disney officially enforces the ride return time. Thus, if you make a Fast-Pass+ reservation to ride Space Mountain at 7:30 p.m., you have until 8:30 p.m. to either use it or change it to something else. Just like a restaurant reservation, your FastPass+ may be canceled if you don't show up on time. In practice, however, we've found that you can usually be up to 5 minutes early or 15 minutes late to use your reservation.

unofficial **TIP**
You'll be notified of any issues with FastPass+ reservations through the My Disney Experience mobile app.

When you return to Space Mountain at the designated time, you'll be directed to a FAST-PASS+ RETURN line. Before you get in line, you'll have to validate your reservation by touching your MagicBand or RFID ticket to a reader at the FastPass+ Return entrance. Then you'll proceed with minimal waiting to the attraction's preshow or boarding area.

If technical problems cause an attraction to be closed during your return time, Disney will automatically adjust your FastPass+ reservation in one of three ways:

1. If it's early in the day, Disney will offer you the chance to return to the attraction at any point in the day after it reopens.

2. Alternatively, Disney may let you choose another FastPass+ attraction in the same park, on the same day.

3. If it's late in the day, Disney will automatically give you another selection good for any FastPass+ attraction at any park the following day.

At a number of FastPass+ attractions, listed in the following chart, the time gap between getting your pass and returning to ride can range from 3 to 7 hours. To ensure that you have enough time to ride on the day of your visit, either book FastPass+ in advance for these attractions or reserve them in the parks as early in the day as possible.

GET FASTPASS+ *BEFORE 11 A.M.* FOR THE FOLLOWING:							
MAGIC KINGDOM							
Buzz Lightyear's Space Ranger Spin	Evening Parade	Frozen Meet and Greet	Peter Pan's Flight	Seven Dwarfs Mine Train	Space Mountain	Splash Mountain	
EPCOT	Frozen Ever After, *IllumiNations*, Mission: Space (Orange), Soarin', Test Track						
ANIMAL KINGDOM	Expedition Everest	Kilimanjaro Safaris	Meet Mickey and Minnie at Adventurers Outpost				
DHS	Rock 'n' Roller Coaster, Tower of Terror, Toy Story Midway Mania!						

FastPass+ Rules

Disney has rules in place to prevent guests from obtaining certain combinations of FastPass+ reservations before they get to the parks:

RULE #1: You can obtain only one advance FastPass+ reservation per attraction, per day, but you can get more once you're in the park and you've used your first set of three. You can't make multiple advance FastPass+ reservations for, say, Toy Story Midway Mania!—you have to select three different attractions. But once you've entered Hollywood Studios for the day and your first three reservations have been used or have expired, you can obtain more for Toy Story Midway Mania! if they're available.

It's generally a bad idea to make advance FastPass+ reservations for any of the evening parades or fireworks, because you won't be able to get any more reservations while you're in the park. We suggest checking around 4 p.m. to see if any reservations are available for the fireworks and parades. If they are and you're done with the headliner attractions, go ahead and grab a FastPass+.

RULE #2: FastPass+ reservation times can't overlap—Disney's computer system doesn't allow it. If you have a FastPass+ reservation for 2–3 p.m., for instance, you can't make another reservation later than 1 p.m. or earlier than 3 p.m. in the same park.

FASTPASS+ TIERS Disney also prohibits guests from using FastPass+ on all of a park's headliner attractions. The practice, known informally as "FastPass+ tiers," was in effect only at Epcot and Disney's Hollywood Studios at press time but will probably be extended to all four parks eventually.

At Epcot, by way of example, the FastPass+ attractions are divided into the following two tiers:

TIER A (Choose 1)	TIER B (Choose 2)
• IllumiNations	• Captain EO
• Living with the Land	• Epcot Character Spot
• Soarin'	• Journey into Imagination
• Test Track	• Mission: Space (Green or Orange)
	• Spaceship Earth
	• The Seas with Nemo & Friends
	• Turtle Talk with Crush

FastPass+ lets you choose only one attraction from Tier A and two attractions from Tier B. Note that Tier A comprises the attractions with the longest lines: This ensures that most guests get to choose either Soarin' or Test Track. Also, note that few of the attractions in Tier B actually require FastPass+ for most of the year.

Again, though, the tiers don't apply beyond your first three advance FastPass+ reservations—any reservations you make beyond the first three when you're in the parks are totally up to you.

Clearly, these rules are designed to do three things: encourage you to stay at a Disney resort, book your trip well in advance, and tell Disney exactly where you plan to be every day. These three things increase Disney's revenue. They also decrease Disney's operating expenses, because Disney can adjust its staffing levels at each park based on how many people have made FastPass+ reservations. More importantly, by promising lower wait times in advance, Disney encourages you to spend more time at its parks and discourage you from last-minute trips to Universal or other parks.

How FastPass+ Affects Your Waits in Line

At press time, there were only about 10 Walt Disney World attractions at which FastPass+ was having a noticeable effect on standby lines. That's according to our initial analysis of 2 million standby wait times collected at Walt Disney World since FastPass+ went live in January 2014. We compared those with 8 million standby wait times collected across Walt Disney World since 2009 and adjusted for higher attendance levels from 2013 to 2015.

Standby wait times are down significantly at these attractions:

- Rock 'n' Roller Coaster (−14 minutes)
- Toy Story Midway Mania! (−13 minutes)
- Expedition Everest (−11 minutes)
- Test Track (−11 minutes)

One possible reason for the decrease in wait times is that before FastPass+, guests would use legacy Fastpass much more often. Now that there are limits on the number of FastPass+ reservations that guests can obtain in advance, coupled with the byzantine process for obtaining FastPasses online, people are riding these attractions less frequently.

Wait times are *up* at these attractions:

- Pirates of the Caribbean (+10 minutes)
- Dinosaur (+7 minutes)
- The Haunted Mansion (+7 minutes)
- Spaceship Earth (+7 minutes)
- The Magic Carpets of Aladdin (+6 minutes)
- Journey into Imagination (+5 minutes)
- Primeval Whirl (+4 minutes)

We think waits are up at Dinosaur because (1) Disney requires guests to choose three FastPass+ attractions and (2) Dinosaur appears at the top of the alphabetical list of attractions to choose from. In the past, people would have had to hike to a remote corner of the park to find Dinosaur's Fastpass machines. Now that Dinosaur is a more visible choice in the app, it's getting more traffic.

Pirates of the Caribbean, The Haunted Mansion, and Spaceship Earth didn't have Fastpass in the couple of years leading up to the introduction of FastPass+. Here, we think the increase in wait times here owes primarily to the preferential treatment FastPass+ guests get in boarding these rides. It's possible for cast members to load 10, 20, or 30 FastPass+ guests for every 1 standby guest in line, and enough people are selecting these attractions as their third FastPass+ choice for that policy to have an impact.

We're not sure what accounts for the small increases at The Magic Carpets of Aladdin or Primeval Whirl. Maybe, like Dinosaur, Primeval Whirl is the third choice of a lot of Animal Kingdom guests, or maybe people who would have otherwise skipped the Magic Carpets are trying them now. If you've chosen either of these two attractions for Fast-Pass+, write, e-mail, or message us to explain why.

How FastPass+ Affects Your Touring Plans

We think most *Unofficial Guide* readers probably spend fewer minutes per day walking around the parks, because they no longer need to walk to an attraction's Fastpass machines. The time saved by walking is slightly more than the overall increases in standby waits at secondary attractions, so FastPass+—when it works—is roughly a break-even proposition for folks using our touring plans.

We say "when it works" because on a recent trip to the Magic King-dom, we (Bob and Len) spent the better part of a day observing just how wrong things can go at a FastPass+ return point. The most common snafu we saw was a family arriving too early or too late for their reser-vation. That's understandable, because MagicBands don't display reser-vation times, and they're cumbersome to find on My Disney Experience.

The next most frequent issue we saw was from families, particularly those who don't speak English as their first language, who simply didn't get how FastPass+ works. For example, many families seemed to think that simply wearing the MagicBand allowed them access to the Fast-Pass+ line, without their having to make a reservation.

When a MagicBand doesn't work at a FastPass+ return point, a cast member can usually resolve the problem fairly quickly. When the problem is more complex, the line stops while the issue is sorted.

Consider what happens when an issue occurs at Pirates of the Carib-bean, which can handle around 2,800 people in a good hour. Roughly half the ride's capacity is dedicated to FastPass+, so on busy days about two new guests arrive at the FastPass+ entrance every 5 seconds. If the cast member at the FastPass+ return point takes 30 seconds to resolve a problem, then a line of 12 guests will have formed by time the issue is fixed. When the guest experiencing the issue needs to get his or her MagicBand serviced somewhere else in the park or doesn't understand English very well, then the interaction can easily take more time, and the line grows longer.

On the upside, Disney has made great progress in streamlining these "recovery" processes, and we expect them to continue to pour resources into further speed-ups.

Your FastPass+ Priorities at Each Park

Including the touring plans in this book and on our website, we've up-dated almost 200 touring plans to use FastPass+ exclusively. Each plan now lists the suggested FastPass+ start times for the attractions that will save you the most time in line, like this:

SUGGESTED START TIMES FOR FASTPASS+ RESERVATIONS

- Peter Pan's Flight: 10 a.m.
- Buzz Lightyear's Space Ranger Spin: 5 p.m.
- *Enchanted Tales with Belle*: 7 p.m.

When we updated the plans, we kept count of how many times each attraction was identified as needing FastPass+. It turns out that this is a prioritized list of the attractions for which you should use FastPass+ to avoid long waits in line. We've added this information to the FastPass+ section in each theme park's chapter.

Customized Touring Plans and FastPass+

The touring plans in this guide, which have all been revised to incorporate FastPass+, are our most efficient, provided you're willing to arrive at the park 35–60 minutes before opening. Likewise, both our custom plans and our Lines app support FastPass+.

You can update your FastPass+ reservations while you're in the park, too. If you decide to change a reservation from Splash Mountain to Big Thunder Mountain Railroad, you can tell Lines to reoptimize your plan based on your new FastPass+ times. This allows you to handle any situation while still minimizing your waits for the rest of the day.

That said, most of the Studios' and Animal Kingdom's shows never require FastPass+. The touring plans already do a good job of getting you to the show at least 15 minutes in advance (or earlier for *Fantasmic!*), in which case you'll almost always be able to get in to see that performance. In the worst-case scenario, you'll have to wait only until the next show. Also, because you can get a FastPass+ reservation for either *Fantasmic!* or Toy Story Midway Mania! at the Studios, you'll almost always end up with a shorter wait in line if you use the Toy Story FastPass+.

The same logic applies at Disney World's parades and fireworks. We don't usually recommend using FastPass+ for the Main Street Electrical Parade or *Wishes* fireworks at the Magic Kingdom, *IllumiNations* at Epcot, or many theater shows (unless you've got extra FastPasses at the end of your second day). Using FastPass+ for these usually guarantees you only somewhere to sit or stand. Because you still have to arrive early to claim a prime viewing location, you end up not saving much time—as this Charleston, South Carolina, reader figured out:

> *FastPass+ for* IllumiNations *and shows like* Beauty and the Beast *is a waste. They give away many more reservations for* IllumiNations *than actually provide a good view, so unless you arrive early and stake out a place (which you can do without FastPass+), there really is no point.*

Readers React to FastPass+

FastPass+ generates more comments than anything we've seen in years. A mother from Kansas likes the ability to schedule rides in advance:

> *It was great to schedule our FastPasses ahead of time and know when and where we were going to be. If a ride was closed during our scheduled time, we got an e-mail, and we were able to go back at any time the rest of the day or switch the attraction or time.*

Other readers speak less fondly of FastPass+. This woman from Minneapolis, for instance, says that it's made her rethink her opinion of Disney:

FastPass+ has made my trips less enjoyable, to the point that I've decided not to renew my Annual Pass. You were absolutely correct in your 2014 edition when you predicted that the new system would rescind privileges. If you ask me, they should rename it "FastPass Minus."

unofficial TIP
The Magic Kingdom offers the greatest variety in capacity and popularity, with vastly differing rides and shows.

A dad from Port St. Lucie, Florida, is blunt:

The only people who like FastPass+ are the ones who didn't know how to use the old system.

From a Round Rock, Texas, reader:

I tried to log in to make FastPass+ reservations right at midnight Eastern time on day 60 before our trip, as suggested by friends. Apparently, there was a glitch in the system, because I couldn't get in. When I tried again at 7 a.m., FastPasses for meeting Anna and Elsa and for Seven Dwarfs Mine Train were already gone for the entire day. I was able to schedule both for later in our visit—but if I'm staying at a Disney resort and I can't get FP+ for attractions 7 hours after I'm eligible, there is no way day guests are going to get the passes they want.

I am a type-A pre-planner, and even I can't stand the rigidity and stress involved with this new system! Finally, the choices you have to make in the tiers are ridiculous. The only two rides in Epcot that need a FastPass are Soarin' and Test Track, and with FastPass+ you have to pick one and stand in line for the other. Even with the touring plans (which I love), we have to wait 30–40 minutes for one or the other! Two thumbs down and two more from my husband for FP+.

From a Ross-on-Rye, United Kingdom, grandfather:

This was our first trip with our grandchildren and FastPass+, and I found the amount of planning required to get appropriate FastPasses for our multigenerational group intimidating.

A Pennsylvania mom of two found out that FastPass+ is inflexible when it comes to park hopping:

When we were about leave the Magic Kingdom for Hollywood Studios, it was frustrating to know that I couldn't make a reservation at the kiosk for any park other than one I was currently at.

A Fort Collins, Colorado, woman discovered that the FastPass+ times recommended by the My Disney Experience mobile app usually aren't the most convenient:

FastPass+ is a pain that people need to pay attention to. Disney doesn't make it really clear that you don't have to take the times they give you and that you can try times other than their recommended ones.

A common complaint is that FastPass+ is targeted to tech-savvy younger guests, as this 60-something from Bemidji, Minnesota, notes:

I know a lot of people can't go anywhere without their gadgets, but there are a LOT of us, young and old, who don't have them or don't want to use them on vacation. I have a laptop and an old-fashioned flip phone, and my husband has a Kindle for reading—that's it. It seems that those without iPhones, etc., are at a disadvantage.

As discussed earlier, you can make changes to your FastPass+ reservations, or set up new reservations, at FastPass+ kiosks in the park. An "up East" family of four reported their experience:

The in-park kiosks were crazy busy. There were almost always lines, especially after 11 a.m. We didn't even try to use the kiosks—by the time I'd used our first three selections (this was usually early afternoon), I noticed that there were rarely any FastPass+ times left for the rides we wanted to go on. (Disney sometimes had a sandwich board up around some of the kiosks, noting which attractions still had FastPass+ times available and their level of availability [e.g., very limited or available]. Although Disney says you can get an additional FastPass+ after you've used your selections, I wouldn't count on it, because the most popular attractions are usually out of FastPass+ times early in the day anyway. Also, Disney forces you to use the kiosks rather than letting you use your phone/device with the My Disney Experience app, but it's just a waste of time to wait in line for a FastPass+ time or attraction that you probably wouldn't have wanted anyway.

A Canadian family of three adults ventilates:

FastPass+ seems to be a "plus" only for Disney. For us, it was more like "FastPass Sucks." I can tolerate booking rides 60 days ahead. I can tolerate having only three plus the other fourth one that rolls over. What I really disliked most about it was that under the old system, you'd have your ticket and be on your way in less than 5 seconds. Now getting another FastPass is an involved, complicated process that eats up at least 30 minutes of touring time. Also, it's very difficult to keep track of them when your phone's battery dies.

A Chalfont, Pennsylvania, woman agrees:

I hated having to rely on my iPhone to check FP+ times. And the one time I tried to change them, it was just a royal PITA. (I must be one of those rare birds who like to disconnect when they're on vacation.) I don't mind booking ADRs six months out for a restaurant I know I'll want to eat at, but I loathe having to book a FastPass+ for Soarin' or Seven Dwarfs Mine Train, knowing that more than likely I won't be able to change it at the last minute if I need to.

We've been getting lots of good reader tips and advice about using FastPass+. First, from an Edmonton, Alberta, mom:

FastPass+ gives you great insight into which parks are going to be very busy on which days. For instance, I couldn't get decent FastPasses at Animal Kingdom for any of the days we wanted to go to the park, so after trying various permutations and combinations, I just accepted what I could get for quite late in the day, and we decided to go early and see how it went. I got most FastPasses for Epcot and Disney's Hollywood Studios at the times I wanted, but the Magic Kingdom was going to be so busy, based on the potential FastPass+ times I could get, that we decided as a family not to go there this trip.

A mom from Portage La Prairie, Saskatchewan, offers this:

The only piece of advice I would change is not to discourage people from getting FastPass+ for parades. I have two small children (2 and 4), and it was hard to find a good spot for them to see the parade properly.

An Albany, New York, reader found that poor wireless reception in the parks can mess with FastPass+ as well with apps:

I had a fabulous vacation, but I had planned on having full access to My Disney Experience and Lines from my phone. I use Verizon and usually have no problems with service, but I found that both apps were totally unusable in the parks. In fact, I had to visit a FastPass+ kiosk in Animal Kingdom because I couldn't view my reservations. The cast member at the kiosk recommended that I take a screen shot of my reservations each day to avoid this problem. While this did work, I never was able to change my reservations using MDE or use the touring plans in Lines during my trip. On my next visit, I'll print out the touring plans and follow them the old-fashioned way.

> *un**official* **TIP**
> Before you get in a 40-minute-or-longer line for a ride, check for a FastPass+—a reservation could pop up at any time. We saved lots of time doing this.
> —A Baton Rouge, Louisiana, mother of two teens

UNDERSTANDING WALT DISNEY WORLD ATTRACTIONS

DISNEY WORLD'S PRIMARY APPEAL IS IN ITS rides and shows. Understanding how these are engineered to accommodate guests is interesting and invaluable to developing an efficient itinerary.

All attractions, regardless of location, are affected by two elements: capacity and popularity. Capacity is how many guests the attraction can serve at one time. Popularity shows how well visitors like an attraction. Capacity can be adjusted at some attractions. It's possible, for example, to add trucks to Kilimanjaro Safaris at Disney's Animal Kingdom or put extra boats on the Magic Kingdom's Jungle Cruise. Generally, however, capacity remains relatively fixed.

Designers try to match capacity and popularity as closely as possible. A high-capacity ride that isn't popular is a failure. Lots of money, space, and equipment have been poured into the attraction, yet there are empty seats. Journey into Imagination at Epcot fits this profile.

It's extremely unusual for a new attraction not to measure up, but it's fairly common for an older ride to lose appeal. Some attractions, such as Space Mountain at the Magic Kingdom, have sustained great appeal years beyond their debut, while others declined in popularity after a few years. Most

> *un**official* **TIP**
> Generally, attractions are immensely popular when they're new, and thus have longer lines.

attractions, however, work through the honeymoon, then settle down to handle the level of demand for which they were designed. When this happens, there are enough interested guests during peak hours to fill almost every seat, but not so many that long lines develop.

Sometimes Disney correctly estimates an attraction's popularity but fouls the equation by mixing in a third variable such as location. Spaceship Earth, the ride inside the geosphere at Epcot, is a good example. Placing the ride squarely in the path of every person entering the park ensures that it will be inundated during morning when the park is filling. On the flip side, *The American Adventure,* at the opposite end of Epcot, has huge capacity but plays to a partially filled theater until midafternoon, when guests finally reach that part of the park.

If demand is high and capacity is low, large lines materialize. The Studios' Toy Story Midway Mania!, for instance, is the only headliner attraction that is open during morning Extra Magic Hours and has no minimum height requirement. Thus, it's the only headliner many families can experience, so demand quickly outstrips the ride's capacity. The result of this mismatch is that children and parents often suffer hour-long waits for a 6½-minute ride.

Capacity design is predicated on averages: the average number of people in the park, the normal distribution of traffic to specific areas, and the average number of staff needed to operate the ride. On a holiday weekend, when the averages are exceeded, all but a few attractions operate at maximum capacity, and even then they're overwhelmed by huge crowds. On days of low attendance in the fall, capacity is often not even approximated, and guests can ride without a wait.

Only the Magic Kingdom and Disney's Animal Kingdom offer low-capacity midway rides and spook-house "dark" rides. They range from state-of-the-art to antiquated. This diversity makes efficient touring of the Magic Kingdom much more challenging. If guests don't understand the capacity–popularity relationship and don't plan accordingly, they might spend most of the day in line.

Although Epcot, Animal Kingdom, and Disney's Hollywood Studios have fewer rides and shows than the Magic Kingdom, almost all their attractions are major features on par with the Magic Kingdom's Pirates of the Caribbean and The Haunted Mansion in scope, detail, imagination, and spectacle. All but a few Epcot, Animal Kingdom, and DHS rides are fast-loading, and most have large capacities. Because Epcot, Animal Kingdom, and DHS attractions are generally well engineered and efficient, lines may appear longer than those in the Magic Kingdom but usually move more quickly. There are no midway rides at Epcot or DHS, and fewer attractions at those parks are intended for kids.

In the Magic Kingdom, crowds are more a function of the popularity and engineering of individual attractions; at Epcot, Animal Kingdom, and DHS, traffic flow and crowding are more affected by park layout. For touring efficiency, it's important to understand how Magic Kingdom rides and shows operate. At Epcot and Animal Kingdom, this knowledge is less important.

To develop an efficient touring plan, it's necessary to understand how rides and shows are designed and function. We'll examine both.

CUTTING YOUR TIME IN LINE BY UNDERSTANDING THE RIDES

WALT DISNEY WORLD HAS MANY TYPES OF RIDES. Some, such as The Great Movie Ride at Disney's Hollywood Studios, can carry more than 3,000 people an hour. At the other extreme, TriceraTop Spin at Animal Kingdom can handle only around 500 people an hour. Most rides fall somewhere in between. Many factors figure into how long you'll wait to experience a ride: its popularity; how it loads and unloads; how many persons can ride at once; how many units (cars, rockets, boats, flying elephants, and the like) are in service at a time; and how many cast members are available to operate the ride. Let's take the factors one by one.

1. How Popular Is the Ride?

Newer rides such as the Magic Kingdom's Seven Dwarfs Mine Train attract a lot of people, as do such longtime favorites as the same park's Big Thunder Mountain Railroad. If a ride is popular, you need to know how it operates in order to determine the best time to ride. But a ride need not be especially popular to generate long lines; in some cases, such lines are due not to a ride's popularity but to poor traffic engineering. This is the case at the Mad Tea Party and The Barnstormer (among others) in Fantasyland. Both rides serve only a small percentage of any day's attendance at the Magic Kingdom, yet because they take so long to load and unload, long lines form regardless.

2. How Does the Ride Load and Unload?

Some rides never stop. They're like conveyor belts that go around and around. These are "continuous loaders." The Haunted Mansion and Under the Sea: Journey of the Little Mermaid at the Magic Kingdom, along with Spaceship Earth at Epcot, are continuous loaders. The number of people that can be moved through in an hour depends on how many cars—"doom buggies" or whatever—are on the conveyor. The Haunted Mansion and Spaceship Earth have lots of cars on the conveyor, and each consequently can move more than 2,000 people an hour.

Other rides are "interval loaders." Cars are unloaded, loaded, and dispatched at set intervals (sometimes controlled manually, sometimes by computer). Space Mountain in Tomorrowland is an interval loader. It has two tracks (the ride has been duplicated in the same facility). Each track can run as many as 14 space capsules, released at 36-, 26-, or 21-second intervals. (The bigger the crowd, the shorter the interval.)

In one kind of interval loader, empty cars, as in Space Mountain's space capsules, return to where they reload. In a second kind, such as Splash Mountain, one group of riders enters the vehicle while the previous group departs. Rides of the latter type are referred to as "in and out" interval loaders. As a boat docks, those who have just completed their ride exit to the left; at almost the same time, those waiting to ride enter the boat from the right. The reloaded boat is released to the dispatch point a few yards down the line, where it's launched according to the interval being used.

Interval loaders of both types can be very efficient people-movers if (1) the dispatch (launch) interval is relatively short and (2) the ride can accommodate many vehicles at one time. Since many boats can float through Pirates of the Caribbean at one time, and since the dispatch interval is short, almost 3,000 people can see this attraction each hour.

The least efficient rides, in terms of traffic engineering, are "cycle rides," also called "stop and go" rides. Those waiting to ride exchange places with those who have just ridden. Unlike in-and-out interval rides, cycle rides shut down during loading and unloading. While one boat is loading and unloading in It's a Small World (an interval loader), many other boats are advancing through the ride. But when Dumbo touches down, the whole ride is at a standstill until the next flight launches (ditto Prince Charming Regal Carrousel and the Mad Tea Party).

In cycle rides, the time in motion is "ride time." The time the ride idles while loading and unloading is "load time." Load time plus ride time equals "cycle time," or the time from the start of one run of the ride until the start of the next. The only cycle rides in Disney World are in the Magic Kingdom and Disney's Animal Kingdom.

3. How Many Persons Can Ride at One Time?

This figure expresses "system capacity," or the number of people who can ride at one time. The greater the carrying capacity of a ride (all other things being equal), the more visitors it can accommodate per hour. Some rides can add extra units (cars, boats, and such) as crowds build, to increase capacity; others, such as the Astro Orbiter in Tomorrowland, have a fixed capacity (it's impossible to add more rockets).

4. How Many Units Are in Service at a Given Time?

Unit is our term for the vehicle in which you ride. At the Mad Tea Party the unit is a teacup, at Peter Pan's Flight a pirate ship. On some rides (mostly cycle rides), the number of units operating at one time is fixed. There are always 32 flying elephants at Dumbo and 90 horses on Prince Charming Regal Carrousel. There's no way to increase the capacity of such rides by adding units. On a busy day, the only way to carry more people each hour on a fixed-unit cycle ride is to shorten the loading time or decrease the ride time. The bottom line: On a busy day for a cycle ride, you'll wait longer and possibly be rewarded with a shorter ride. This is why we steer you away from cycle rides unless you're willing to ride them early in the morning or late at night. These are the cycle rides:

THE MAGIC KINGDOM Astro Orbiter, The Barnstormer, Dumbo the Flying Elephant, Mad Tea Party, The Magic Carpets of Aladdin, Prince Charming Regal Carrousel

DISNEY'S ANIMAL KINGDOM TriceraTop Spin

Many other rides throughout Disney World can increase their capacity by adding units as crowds build. For example, if attendance is light, Big Thunder Mountain Railroad in Frontierland can start the day by running only one of its five mine trains from one of two available loading platforms. If lines build, the other platform is opened and more mine trains are placed into operation. At capacity, the five trains can carry about 2,400 persons an hour. Likewise, Star Tours at Disney's Hollywood Studios can increase its capacity by using all its simulators, and the Gran Fiesta Tour boat ride at Mexico in Epcot can add more boats. Sometimes a long queue will disappear almost instantly when new units are brought online. When an interval loader places more units into operation, it usually shortens the dispatch intervals, allowing more units to be dispatched more often.

5. How Many Cast Members Are Available to Operate the Ride?

Adding cast members to a ride can allow more units to operate or additional loading or holding areas to open. In the Magic Kingdom, Pirates of the Caribbean and It's a Small World can run two waiting lines and loading zones. The Haunted Mansion has a 1½-minute preshow staged in a "stretch room." On busy days, a second stretch room can be activated, permitting a more continuous flow of visitors to the actual loading area.

Additional staff makes a world of difference to some cycle rides. Often, the Mad Tea Party has only one attendant. This person alone must clear visitors from the ride just completed, admit and seat visitors for the upcoming ride, check that each teacup is secured, return to the control panel, issue instructions to the riders, and finally activate the ride (whew!). A second attendant divides these responsibilities and cuts loading time by 25–50%.

CUTTING YOUR TIME IN LINE BY UNDERSTANDING THE SHOWS

MANY FEATURED ATTRACTIONS AT WALT DISNEY WORLD are theater presentations. While they aren't as complex as rides, understanding them from a traffic-engineering standpoint may save you touring time.

Most theater attractions operate in three phases:

1. Guests are in the theater viewing the presentation.

2. Guests who have passed through the turnstile wait in a holding area or lobby. They will be admitted to the theater as soon as the show in progress concludes. Several attractions offer a preshow in their lobby to entertain guests until they're admitted to the main show. Examples include *Enchanted Tiki Room* and *Stitch's Great Escape!* in the Magic Kingdom; *Captain EO* at Epcot; and *Muppet-Vision 3-D* at Disney's Hollywood Studios.

3. A line waits outside. Guests in line enter the lobby when there's room and will ultimately move into the theater.

Theater capacity, the presentation's popularity, and park attendance determine how long lines will be at a show. Except for holidays and other days of heavy attendance, the longest wait for a show usually doesn't exceed the length of one performance. As almost all theater attractions run continuously, stopping only long enough for the previous audience to leave and the waiting audience to enter, a performance will be in progress when you arrive. *O Canada!* at Epcot's Canada Pavilion lasts 15 minutes; your longest wait under normal circumstances is about 15 minutes if you arrive just after the show has begun.

A WORD ABOUT DISNEY THRILL RIDES

READERS OF ALL AGES should try to be open-minded about Disney "thrill rides." In comparison with those at other theme parks, the Disney attractions are quite tame, with more emphasis on sights, atmosphere, and special effects than on the motion, speed, or feel of the ride. While

we suggest you take Disney's pre-ride warnings seriously, we can tell you that guests of all ages report enjoying rides such as Tower of Terror, Big Thunder Mountain, and Splash Mountain.

The Rock 'n' Roller Coaster and Expedition Everest, however, are a different story. Both are serious coasters that share more in common with Revenge of the Mummy at Universal Studios than they do with Space Mountain or Big Thunder Mountain.

Mission: Space, a high-tech simulation ride at Epcot, is a toss-up (pun intended)—it absolutely has the potential to make you sick. After many guest incidents, Disney made half of the ride a tamer, no-spin experience—one that's less likely to launch your lunch.

CENTRAL FLORIDA ROLLER COASTERS

IF YOU EVER GO to a party where folks are discussing Immelmanns, heartline rolls, dive loops, and LIM launchers, don't mistake the guests for fighter pilots. Incredibly, you'll be among the intelligentsia of roller-coaster aficionados. This growing population, along with millions of other not-quite-so-fanatical coaster lovers, is united in the belief that roller coasters are—or ought to be—the heart of every theme park.

Though Disney pioneered the concept of super-coasters with the **Matterhorn Bobsleds** at Disneyland in 1959, it took them 16 years to add another roller coaster, **Space Mountain** at Walt Disney World, to their repertoire. In relatively quick succession followed Space Mountain at Disneyland and **Big Thunder Mountain Railroad** at both Disneyland's and Walt Disney World's Magic Kingdoms. Irrespective of the Mountains' popularity, Disney didn't build another coaster in the United States for almost 20 years. In the interim, coasters enjoyed a technical revolution that included aircraft carrier–type launching devices and previously unimaginable loops, corkscrews, vertical drops, and train speeds. Through all this, Disney sat on the sidelines. After all, Disney parks didn't offer "rides" but, rather, "adventure experiences" in which the sensation of the ride itself was always secondary to storylines and visuals. But when archrival Universal announced plans for its Islands of Adventure theme park, featuring an entire arsenal of thrill rides, Disney—spurred by competition—went to work.

The upshot was a banner year in 1999 for Central Florida coasters, with **The Incredible Hulk Coaster, Dueling Dragons: Fire** and **Ice** (now **Dragon Challenge: Chinese Fireball** and **Hungarian Horntail**) opening at Universal's Islands of Adventure; **Rock 'n' Roller Coaster** coming online at Disney's Hollywood Studios; and **Gwazi**, a wooden coaster, premiering at Busch Gardens Tampa. Close on their heels in early 2000 was **Kraken** at SeaWorld. These six coasters made Space and Big Thunder Mountains look like cupcakes and wienie buns. All except Gwazi featured inversions, corkscrews, and rollovers. Best of all for coaster lovers, none of the players were content to rest on their laurels: Universal Studios came back with **Revenge of the Mummy** in 2004, followed by **SheiKra** at Busch Gardens in 2005 and the awe-inspiring **Expedition Everest** at Disney's Animal Kingdom in 2006.

The spring and summer of 2009 marked the debut of **Manta** at Sea World Orlando and **Hollywood Rip Ride Rockit** at Universal Studios Florida. Manta is an inverted steel coaster on which riders are suspended under the tracks, prone and facedown; Rip Ride Rockit is also a steel coaster, only here you sit as opposed to being suspended. The first hill is a 16-second *vertical* climb, followed by a 65-mph plunge. Two years later, **Cheetah Hunt,** a launched coaster, opened at Busch Gardens.

The Top 16 Central Florida Roller Coasters

COASTER	HOST PARK	CENTRAL FLORIDA RANK	INTER-NATIONAL RANK
MANTA	SeaWorld	1	36
EXPEDITION EVEREST	Animal Kingdom	2	104
CHINESE FIREBALL	Islands of Adventure	3	57
CHEETAH HUNT	Busch Gardens	4	72
MONTU	Busch Gardens	5	16
INCREDIBLE HULK COASTER	Islands of Adventure	6	66
KUMBA	Busch Gardens	7	29
HUNGARIAN HORNTAIL	Islands of Adventure	8	71
KRAKEN	SeaWorld	9	59
SHEIKRA	Busch Gardens	10	37
HOLLYWOOD RIP RIDE ROCKIT	Universal Studios FL	11	125
ROCK 'N' ROLLER COASTER	DHS	12	155
GWAZI	Busch Gardens	13	121
REVENGE OF THE MUMMY	Universal Studios FL	14	107
SPACE MOUNTAIN	Magic Kingdom	15	150
BIG THUNDER MOUNTAIN	Magic Kingdom	16	189
ESCAPE FROM GRINGOTTS	Universal Studios FL	N/A*	N/A
SEVEN DWARFS MINE TRAIN	Magic Kingdom	N/A	N/A
WHITE LIGHTNING	Fun Spot America	N/A	N/A

Source: **bestrollercoasterpoll.com**   *N/A = data unavailable at press time

The spring and summer of 2014 witnessed the unveiling of two new coasters: **Seven Dwarfs Mine Train** at the Magic Kingdom and **Harry Potter and the Escape from Gringotts** at Universal Studios Florida. Seven Dwarfs Mine Train, a family coaster, offers modest speeds, small hills, and a slow-mo look at the Dwarfs' cottage and gem mine; its ride vehicles swing slightly, almost imperceptibly, from side to side. Gringotts is a 3-D steel coaster ride through the bank vaults made famous in the Harry Potter books and movies. Stunning visual effects are emphasized over raw speed or height—there are no loops or inversions. And, unlike Seven Dwarfs Mine Train, Escape from Gringotts is totally indoors.

White Lightning debuted in 2013 at Orlando's Fun Spot America theme park. It offers a surprising amount of airtime for a small wooden coaster. With a max vertical of 58 feet and reaching speeds of 44 mph, it delivers a surprisingly smooth and satisfying thrill experience for a family coaster. Its Fun Spot sibling is **Freedom Flyer,** a low-to-the-ground inverted steel coaster. Also a family coaster, it hits speeds of 34 mph (the same as Seven Dwarfs Mine Train) as your feet dangle over pedestrian traffic below. It's known for its tight whiplash turns.

Upcoming in 2016 at Busch Gardens is **Cobra's Curse,** a combination roller coaster, wild mouse, and spin coaster that hits top speeds of

(Plus Three More)

TYPE	LENGTH (FEET)	HEIGHT (FEET)	INVERSIONS	SPEED (MPH)	RIDE TIME	RIDE FEEL
Steel/inverted	3,359	140	4	56	2:35	Very smooth
Steel/sit-down	4,424	112	0	50	3:45	Very smooth
Steel/inverted	3,200	125	5	60	2:25	Very smooth
Steel/sit-down	4,429	102	1	60	3:30	Smooth
Steel/inverted	3,983	150	7	60	3:00	Smooth
Steel/sit-down	3,700	110	7	67	2:15	Smooth
Steel/sit-down	3,978	143	7	60	2:54	Slightly rough
Steel/inverted	3,200	125	5	55	2:25	Very smooth
Steel/sit-down	4,177	149	7	65	2:02	Smooth
Steel/sit-down	3,188	200	1	70	3:00	Very smooth
Steel/sit-down	3,800	167	2	65	2:30	Rough
Steel/sit-down	3,403	80	3	57	1:22	Very smooth
Wood/sit-down	3,508	91	0	51	2:30	Very rough
Steel/sit-down	2,200	45	0	40	3:00	Very smooth
Steel/sit-down	3,196	90	0	27	2:35	Rough
Steel/sit-down	2,780	45	0	36	3:30	Smooth
Steel/sit-down	2,000	27	0	26	4:00	Smooth
Steel/sit-down	2,000	41	0	34	2:15	Very smooth
Wood/sit-down	2,032	70	0	44	1:15	Smooth

40+ mph over its 2,100 foot layout. The ride should be zippy enough, but the real Cobra's Curse is that it can handle only 1,000 riders an hour, a paltry number in the world of modern coasters.

Today there are 15 big-time roller coasters in Central Florida, 24 if you want to include the tamer Space Mountain, Seven Dwarfs Mine Train, and Big Thunder Mountain Railroad at Walt Disney World; **Flying School, Lego Technic Test Track,** and **Coastersaurus** at Legoland Florida; Escape from Gringotts at Universal Studios; and White Lightning and Freedom Flyer at Fun Spot America. Cheetah Hunt, The Incredible Hulk Coaster, Revenge of the Mummy, and Rock 'n' Roller Coaster feature accelerated launch systems in which the train is hurled, slingshot-like, up the first hill; Rock 'n' Roller Coaster and Revenge of the Mummy are indoor coasters augmented by mind-blowing visuals, special effects, and soundtracks. Expedition Everest is the most fully realized attraction of the 15, with a storyline, astounding attention to detail, and a track that plunges in and out of the largest (albeit artificial) mountain in Florida. Kraken, Cheetah Hunt, and Expedition Everest are the longest roller coasters of the lot, their tracks exceeding 4,000 feet long. **Montu** at Busch Gardens, along with Dragon Challenge at Universal, is inverted, meaning the track is overhead and your feet dangle.

Having ridden all of these until we could no longer walk straight, we rank them as follows. (For a glossary of roller-coaster terminology, see **ultimaterollercoaster.com/coasters/glossary.**)

1. MANTA, SEAWORLD There are coasters you barely survive and coasters you savor. Manta is clearly among the latter: a supersmooth experience that leaves you grinning from ear to ear. An inverted flying steel coaster, Manta gently lowers you into a suspended Superman position and you, well, fly. Many coaster fans consider the most memorable moments a sweeping loop in the first half of the ride and near-misses of a pond or rock wall (depending where you're sitting) in the second half. Technically, Manta has it all. After a first drop of 113 feet, it zooms through a pretzel loop, a 360-degree incline roll, and two corkscrews while reaching a height of 140 feet and speeds of 55 mph.

2. EXPEDITION EVEREST, DISNEY'S ANIMAL KINGDOM This coaster offers such a complete package, with something to dazzle each of the senses, that it overcomes its lack of loops and inversions. The segment where the train corkscrews downward in the dark may be the most unusual in roller-coaster annals. Though you begin the segment in reverse, you soon succumb to an almost disembodied and dreamlike state of drifting in a void, with an exhilarating sense of speed but with no certain sense of direction. When you can see, there's plenty to look at: The mountain, with its caverns, cliffs, and crags, is a work of art; then there's that pesky yeti who menaces you throughout the ride. And for those of you who hate rough coasters, Expedition Everest is oh-so-smooth.

3. DRAGON CHALLENGE: CHINESE FIREBALL, UNIVERSAL'S ISLANDS OF ADVENTURE Previously called Dueling Dragons, Dragon Challenge was given a new theme and incorporated into The Wizarding World of Harry Potter–Hogsmeade, which opened at Universal's Islands of Adventure in June 2010. The number-three ranking was disputed within our research group, with several of us placing Montu at Busch Gardens third. Dragon Challenge has two trains, Chinese Fireball and Hungarian Horntail (formerly Fire and Ice), that are launched in short succession, creating a sense of chase between the two. Though both trains have identical lift hills, their respective layouts are different, and Chinese Fireball offers the superior ride, with a 115-foot drop, five inversions, and speeds of 60 mph. Because this is an inverted coaster, your feet dangle throughout.

4. CHEETAH HUNT, BUSCH GARDENS With a 4,429-foot track, Cheetah Hunt is the longest coaster in Florida. A complete experience both tactilely and visually, Cheetah Hunt hurls you through the scenic, wildlife-rich Serengeti Plain section of the park. The ride emulates the hunting style of the cheetah with sudden bursts of speed, accomplished with linear-synchronous-motor launches similar to the accelerated launch systems of The Incredible Hulk Coaster at Universal and Rock 'n' Roller Coaster at DHS. With Cheetah Hunt, however, you're launched three times—once at the start of the ride and twice more during the circuit. The layout includes a 130-foot drop into a shallow canyon, overbanked turns, parabolas, and a heartline-roll inversion. The linear out-and-back course allows more opportunity for viewing the animals than would the more common concentric, twisting layouts from which it's almost impossible to take in your surroundings.

5. MONTU, BUSCH GARDENS Montu is a little longer than Chinese Fireball and features seven inversions—including loops of 104 and 60 feet and a 0-g roll—on a layout distinguished by very tight turns. With an initial drop of 128 feet, Montu posts top speeds of 60 mph and pulls 3.8 g's. Also inverted, Montu is intense and exhilarating but less visually interesting than and not as smooth as Chinese Fireball.

6. THE INCREDIBLE HULK COASTER, UNIVERSAL'S ISLANDS OF ADVEN-TURE No weak points here. A tire-propelled launch system takes you from 0 to 40 mph in 2 seconds up the first hill, hurling you into a twisting dive of 105 feet. From there it's two loops, two flat-spin corkscrews, a cobra roll, and a plunge through a 150-foot-long tunnel to the end. You hit speeds of 67 mph and pull as many as 4 g's. Unequivocally, the Hulk has the best start of any roller coaster in Central Florida. The ride, however, is not quite as smooth as Chinese Fireball's, and it's not inverted like Chinese Fireball and Montu, which is why we've ranked it sixth.

7. KUMBA, BUSCH GARDENS With a track of almost 4,000 feet, seven inversions, a 135-foot first drop, g-forces of 3.8, a top speed of 60 mph, and a very tight layout, Kumba can hold its own with any coaster. Features include a 114-foot-tall vertical loop, two rolls, and interlocking corkscrews, among others. We find Kumba a little rough, but sitting toward the back of the train mitigates the problem somewhat.

8. DRAGON CHALLENGE: HUNGARIAN HORNTAIL, UNIVERSAL'S ISLANDS OF ADVENTURE Hungarian Horntail is Chinese Fireball's slightly less evil twin, with speeds of 55 mph and a first drop of 95 feet, compared with Chinese Fireball's 60 mph and 115 feet. Hungarian Horntail's design elements are different as well, though both coasters hit you with five inversions bundled in a mix of rolls, corkscrews, and a loop. Like Chinese Fireball, Hungarian Horntail is an inverted coaster.

9. KRAKEN, SEAWORLD The Kraken was a ferocious sea monster kept caged by Poseidon, Greek god of the sea. Much of this Kraken's track is over water, and it takes a number of sweeping dives into subterranean caverns. A very fast coaster, Kraken hits speeds of 65 mph with one drop of 144 feet, and it boasts loops, rolls, and corkscrews for a total of seven inversions. Though not inverted, the cars are open-sided and floorless.

10. HOLLYWOOD RIP RIDE ROCKIT, UNIVERSAL STUDIOS "The Triple R," as some locals call it, opened in August 2009 as Universal's second roller coaster. A steel sit-down coaster, RRR trades full inversions for steep dives and tight corkscrew turns. The ride is a lot more jarring than we expected, with a fair amount of lateral shaking. The gimmick here is that you can select your own music to accompany the ride. Views from the top of the 167-foot lift hill are killer. The Triple R reaches top speeds of 65 mph.

11. SHEIKRA, BUSCH GARDENS While the higher-rated coasters do a lot of things well, SheiKra is pretty much one-dimensional—it drops like a rock straight down (a *sheikra* is an African hawk known for diving vertically on its prey). That's right: a no-slope, 90-degree free fall. After scaling the 200-foot lift hill, the coaster descends over the lip of the first drop and brakes to a stop. There you're suspended, dangling for a few anxious moments until the train is released. On the way down, you hit speeds of 70 mph and enjoy the best airtime of any Florida coaster.

(Airtime is the sensation of floating when your body is forced up from the seat bottom, creating air between the seat and your body.) Following a loop, the drill is repeated on a second, more modest drop. The cars on SheiKra are the widest we've seen, seating eight people across in each of three rows. Accordingly, the track is very wide. This width, among other things, makes for a plodding, uninspiring ride except during the two big drops. More compelling is the view of downtown Tampa from the top of the lift hill.

12. ROCK 'N' ROLLER COASTER, DISNEY'S HOLLYWOOD STUDIOS This wasn't a unanimous ranking either. The Rock 'n' Roller Coaster reaches a height of only 80 feet, lasts just 1 minute and 22 seconds, and incorporates just a couple of design elements, but that 0- to 57-mph launch in 2 seconds is totally sweet. Rock 'n' Roller Coaster is a dark ride (that is, it's indoors), and the story is that you're on your way to an Aerosmith concert in Hollywood in a big stretch limousine. Speakers in each car blast a soundtrack of the group's hits synchronized with the myriad visuals that erupt out of the gloom. The ride is smooth. Not the biggest or baddest coaster in the realm, but like Expedition Everest, it'll put a big grin on your face every time.

13. GWAZI, BUSCH GARDENS As the only traditional wooden coaster of the 15 rides ranked, Gwazi at first looked like a snore: no inversions, corkscrews, loops, barrel rolls, or any of the other stuff that had been rearranging our innards. Wrong! This coaster serves up an unbelievably wild ride that seems literally out of control most of the time. Teeth-rattlingly rough, with much side-to-side lurching, Gwazi reaches a top speed of 51 mph but feels twice that fast. In the best wooden-coaster tradition, riders attempt to hold their arms in the air, but on Gwazi it's impossible. Gwazi's coaster trains were replaced in 2011, making the ride marginally smoother (*marginally* being the operative word). Gwazi is a racing coaster (a dual-track roller coaster whose trains leave the station at the same moment and race each other through the circuit) with two trains, Lion/Yellow and Tiger/Blue. Of the two, Tiger/Blue gives you the biggest bang for your buck.

14. REVENGE OF THE MUMMY, UNIVERSAL STUDIOS If we were ranking attractions as opposed to coasters, this one would rank much higher. Revenge of the Mummy is a super-headliner hybrid, of which its coaster dimension is only one aspect. A complete description of the attraction can be found starting on page 677; for the moment, however, we can tell you that it's a dark ride full of tricks and surprises, and in roller-coaster mode only for about a third of the ride. The ride is wild, and the visuals and special effects are among the best you'll find.

15. SPACE MOUNTAIN, THE MAGIC KINGDOM When you strip away the theme of this beloved Disney favorite, you're left with a souped-up version of the Wild Mouse, a midway staple with sharp turns and small, steep drops that runs with two- or four-passenger cars instead of trains. But when you put a Wild Mouse in the dark—where you can't anticipate the turns and drops—it's like feeding the mouse steroid-laced cheese. With Space Mountain, Disney turned a dinky coaster with no inversions and a top speed of 27 mph into a fairly robust attraction that set the standard for Disney thrill rides until the debut of The Twilight Zone Tower of

Terror. Space Mountain may be close to the bottom of our ranking, but in the hearts of many theme park guests, it remains number one.

16. BIG THUNDER MOUNTAIN RAILROAD, THE MAGIC KINGDOM With its runaway-mine-train storyline, Big Thunder is long on great visuals but ranks as a very innocuous roller coaster. Though many riders consider it jerky and rough, it's a Rolls-Royce compared with the likes of Gwazi and Kumba at Busch Gardens. Unlike on Gwazi, it's not only possible but easy to ride with your arms in the air. Though a steel coaster, Big Thunder offers no inversions and a top speed of only 36 mph. Then again, the higher-ranked coasters don't offer falling boulders, flash floods, possums, buzzards, and dinosaur bones.

17. HARRY POTTER AND THE ESCAPE FROM GRINGOTTS, UNIVERSAL STUDIOS This was the most anticipated new attraction in the world in 2014, but like Seven Dwarfs Mine Train (below), Escape from Gringotts is mostly eye candy. This indoor steel coaster incorporates 3-D projection, amazingly detailed sets, and a storyline of the Potter Fab Three rumbling through the underground vaults of Gringotts Wizarding Bank as they try to escape archenemy Voldemort. There's a load of action, some nifty track-switching, and a free-fall simulation, but the ride itself is much tamer than that of Harry Potter and the Forbidden Journey, assuming you can handle the visuals. As far as the track goes, there's one 27-foot drop and one big up-launch, with no change in track elevation in between.

18. SEVEN DWARFS MINE TRAIN, THE MAGIC KINGDOM The mildest roller coaster on this list, Seven Dwarfs is designed to be the first or second roller-coaster experience for grade-schoolers. Its unique feature is that the ride vehicles swing slightly from side to side, which amplifies the turning sensation you feel in the ride's tight curves. Like Big Thunder, Seven Dwarfs is a steel coaster with no inversions, and it has a top speed of around 34 mph. Because the track is much smoother than Big Thunder's or Space Mountain's, you may not feel as if you're moving very fast.

PART THREE

ACCOMMODATIONS

 ## *The* BASIC CONSIDERATIONS

LOCATING A SUITABLE HOTEL OR CONDO is critical to planning any Walt Disney World vacation. The basic question is whether to stay inside the World. Luxury lodging can be found both in and out of Disney World. Budget lodging is another story. In the World, room rates range from about $100 on a weeknight during what Disney calls Value season to more than $1,600 per night during the holidays. Outside, rooms are as low as $35 a night.

Beyond affordability is convenience. We've lodged both in and out of Disney World, and there's special magic and peace of mind associated with staying inside the World. "I feel more a part of everything and less like a visitor," one guest writes.

There's no real hardship in staying outside Disney World and driving or taking a hotel shuttle to the theme parks. Meals can be less expensive, and rooming outside the World makes you more receptive to other Orlando-area attractions and eating spots. **Universal Studios** and **Universal's Islands of Adventure, Kennedy Space Center Visitor Complex, SeaWorld,** and **Gatorland** are well worth your attention.

Because Walt Disney World is so large, some off-property hotels are closer in both time and distance to many of the theme parks than are some Disney resorts. Check our Hotel Information Chart on pages 277–291, which lists commuting times from both Disney and non-Disney hotels. Lodging prices can change, but it's possible to get a hotel room comparable to one at a Disney's Moderate resort for half the cost during holidays, or a room twice the size for the same money, all within a 15-minute drive of the Magic Kingdom.

If you have young children, read Part Five, Walt Disney World with Kids, before choosing lodging. Seniors, couples on a honeymoon or romantic holiday, and disabled guests should read the applicable sections of Part Six, Special Tips for Special People, before booking.

THE TAX MAN COMETH

SALES AND LODGING TAXES can add a chunk of change to the cost of your hotel room. Cumulative tax in Orange County is 12.5% and in adjacent Osceola County, 13%. Lake Buena Vista, the Universal Orlando area, International Drive, and all the Disney resorts except the All-Star Resorts are in Orange County.

ABOUT HOTEL RENOVATIONS

WE INSPECT SEVERAL HUNDRED HOTELS in the Disney World area to compile the *Unofficial Guide*'s list of lodging choices. Each year we call each hotel to verify contact information and in-

***unofficial* TIP**
Request a renovated room at your hotel—these can be much nicer than the older rooms.

quire about renovations or refurbishments. If a hotel has been renovated or has refurbished its guest rooms, we reinspect it, along with any new hotels, for the next edition of the *Guide*. Hotels reporting no improvements are rechecked every two years. We inspect most Disney-owned hotels every 6–12 months, and no less than once every two years.

Many hotels more than five years old, both in and out of the World, refurbish 10–20% of their guest rooms each year. This incremental approach minimizes disruption, but it makes your room assignment something of a crapshoot—you might luck into a newly renovated room, or you might be assigned a threadbare one.

Disney reservationists won't guarantee you a recently refurbished room, but they will make a note of your request and will try to accommodate you. On the other hand, non-Disney hotels *will* often guarantee you an updated room when you book.

***unofficial* TIP**
Power shoppers, rejoice! If you're staying at a Disney-owned hotel, you can charge theme park and Disney Springs purchases to your hotel room.

BENEFITS OF STAYING IN THE WORLD

GUESTS WHO STAY ON DISNEY PROPERTY enjoy privileges and amenities unavailable to those staying outside the World. Though some of these perks are advertising gimmicks, others are real and potentially valuable. Here are the benefits and what they mean:

1. CONVENIENCE If you don't have a car, commuting to the parks is easy via the Disney transportation system. This is especially advantageous if you stay in a hotel connected by monorail or boat service. If you have a car, however, dozens of hotels outside Disney World are within 5–10 minutes of theme-park parking lots.

2. EARLY ACCESS TO RIDE AND RESTAURANT RESERVATIONS Disney hotel and campground guests, along with guest staying at the Swan and Dolphin resorts, can make FastPass+ ride reservations 60 days before they arrive—30 days earlier than the general public. Disney resort guests can also make dining reservations up to 190 days before their visit, 10 more than the general public.

3. EXTRA MAGIC HOURS AT THE THEME PARKS Disney World lodging guests are invited to enter a designated park 1 hour earlier than the general public each day or to enjoy a designated theme park for up to 2 hours after it closes to the general public in the evening.

Extra Magic Hours can be valuable if you know how to use them. They can also land you in gridlock. (See our detailed discussion of EMHs starting on page 86.)

4. BABYSITTING AND CHILD-CARE OPTIONS Disney hotel and camp-ground guests have several options for babysitting, child care, and children's programs. The **Polynesian Village Resort** and **Animal Kingdom Lodge,** along with several other Disney hotels, offer "clubs"—themed child-care centers where potty-trained children ages 3–12 can stay while the adults go out.

Though somewhat expensive, the clubs are highly regarded by children and parents. On the negative side, they're open only in the evening, and not all Disney hotels have them. If you're staying at a Disney hotel without a club, you're better off using a private in-room babysitting service (see page 426). In-room babysitting is also available at hotels outside Disney World.

5. DISNEY'S MAGICAL EXPRESS If you arrive in Orlando by air, Disney will collect your checked baggage and send it by bus directly to your Walt Disney World resort, allowing you to bypass baggage claim. Magical Express is available daily, 5 a.m.–10 p.m.; free bus service to your hotel is available 24 hours a day. Transportation to your resort hotel will usually include stops at other resorts. The time from deplaning to arriving at your resort will be anywhere from 45 to 90 minutes depending on your resort (35 minutes of that will be driving to Walt Disney World property).

unofficial **TIP**
You'll be asked to show your MagicBands (see page 67) to board Disney's Magical Express, so pack them in your carry-on stuff rather than your checked bags.

When it's time to go home, you can check your baggage and pick up your boarding pass at the front desk of your Disney resort. This service is available to all guests at Disney hotels (excluding the Swan, the Dolphin, Shades of Green, and hotels of the Downtown Disney Resort Area), even those who don't use Magical Express (folks who have rental cars, for example). Resort check-in counters are open 5 a.m.–1 p.m., and you must check in no later than 3 hours before your flight (within the US and Puerto Rico) or 4 hours for international flights. Participating airlines are **AirTran, Alaska, American, Delta, JetBlue, Southwest, United,** and **US Airways.** All of the preceding airlines have restrictions on the number of bags, checking procedures, and related items; consult your carrier before leaving home for specifics. For an in-depth discussion of Disney's Magical Express, see Part Seven, Arriving and Getting Around.

6. PRIORITY THEME PARK ADMISSIONS On days of unusually heavy attendance, Disney may restrict admission into the theme parks for all customers. When deciding whom to admit into the parks, priority is given to guests staying at Disney resorts. In practice, no guest is turned away until a park's parking lot is full. When this happens, that park will be packed to gridlock.

7. CHILDREN SHARING A ROOM WITH THEIR PARENTS There's no extra charge per night for children younger than 18 sharing a room with their parents. Many hotels outside Disney World also offer this perk.

8. FREE PARKING Disney resort guests with cars pay nothing to park in theme park lots or hotels. This saves $17 per day at the parks and up to $20 per day at the hotel.

9. RECREATIONAL PRIVILEGES Disney guests get preferential treatment for tee times at the golf courses.

STAYING IN OR OUT OF THE WORLD: WEIGHING THE PROS AND CONS

1. COST If cost is a primary consideration, you'll lodge much less expensively outside Disney World. Our ratings of hotel quality, cost, and commuting times to the theme parks encompass hotels both in and out of the World (see How the Hotels Compare and the Hotel Information Chart, both later in this chapter).

2. EASE OF ACCESS Even if you stay in Disney World, you're dependent on some mode of transportation. It may be less stressful to use the Disney transportation system, but with the single exception of commuting to the Magic Kingdom, the fastest, most efficient, and most flexible way to get around is usually a car. If you're at Epcot, for example, and want to take the kids back to Disney's Contemporary Resort for a nap, forget the monorail. You'll get back much faster by car.

A reader from Raynham, Massachusetts, who stayed at the Caribbean Beach Resort writes:

> Even though the resort is on the Disney bus line, I recommend renting a car if it fits one's budget. The buses don't go directly to many destinations, and often you have to switch buses. Getting a bus back to the hotel after a hard day can mean a long wait in line.

Readers complain about problems with the Disney transportation system more than most topics. These comments from a Havertown, Pennsylvania, dad are typical:

> WDW bus transportation is quite inefficient. When traveling from the BoardWalk to anywhere else, we had to pick up other passengers at the Swan, Dolphin, and Yacht and Beach Clubs before heading off to the parks. Same story upon return.

Although it's only for the use and benefit of Disney guests, the Disney transportation system is nonetheless public, and users must expect inconveniences: conveyances that arrive and depart on their schedule, not yours; the occasional need to transfer; multiple stops; time lost loading and unloading passengers; and, generally, the challenge of understanding and using a large, complex transportation network.

Relatively few Americans use public transportation frequently, but guests who do—as did this Heswall, England, reader—tend to be more satisfied with Disney's bus system:

> I really feel that you are a bit hard on the Disney transport service. This may be an American thing, but we Brits are more used to buses. We were told buses were running every 20 minutes, but in practice we never waited more than 10.

If you plan to have a car, consider this: Disney World is so large that some destinations within the World can be reached more quickly from off-property hotels than from Disney hotels. For example, guests at lodgings on US 192 (near the so-called Walt Disney World Maingate) are closer to Disney's Hollywood Studios, Animal Kingdom, and Blizzard Beach water park than guests at many hotels inside Disney World.

A Kentucky dad overruled his family about staying at a Disney resort and is glad he did:

My wife read in another guidebook that it can take 2 hours to commute to the parks if you stay outside Walt Disney World. I guess it could take 2 hours if you stayed in Tampa, but from our hotel on US 192 we could commute to any of the parks except the Magic Kingdom and have at least one ride under our belt in about an hour. (We found out later that the writer of the other guidebook worked for Disney Magazine.)

For commuting times from specific non-Disney hotels, see our Hotel Information Chart on pages 277–291.

3. YOUNG CHILDREN Although the hassle of commuting to most non-World hotels is only slightly (if at all) greater than that of commuting to Disney hotels, a definite peace of mind results from staying in the World. Regardless of where you stay, make sure you get your young children back to the hotel for a nap each day.

4. SPLITTING UP If you're in a party that will probably split up to tour (as frequently happens in families with teens or children of widely varying ages), staying in the World offers more transportation options and, thus, more independence. Mom and Dad can take the car and return to the hotel for a relaxed dinner and early bedtime while the teens remain in the park for evening parades and fireworks.

5. FEEDING THE ARMY OF THE POTOMAC If you have a large crew that chows down like cattle on a finishing lot, you may do better staying outside the World, where food is far less expensive.

6. VISITING OTHER ORLANDO-AREA ATTRACTIONS If you'll be visiting SeaWorld, Kennedy Space Center Visitor Complex, Universal Orlando, or other area attractions, it may be more convenient to stay outside the World.

The DISNEY RESORTS

DISNEY RESORTS 101

BEFORE YOU MAKE ANY DECISIONS, understand these basics regarding Disney resorts.

1. RESORT CLASSIFICATIONS Disney loves to categorize, so it's not surprising that they've developed a hierarchy of resort classifications and sub-classifications:

Deluxe resorts are Disney's top-of-the-line hotels, with extensive theming, luxurious rooms, and superior on-site dining, recreation, and services. **Disney's Wilderness Lodge & Villas** and **Animal Kingdom Lodge & Villas** are popular for their theming and their price, which is at the low end of this category. (Their rooms are also the smallest among the Deluxes.)

 unofficial TIP
Understand that Disney Reservation Center and Walt Disney Travel Company representatives don't have detailed personal knowledge of resorts.

Disney Deluxe Villa (DDV) resorts, also known as **Disney Vacation Club (DVC) resorts,** offer suites, some with full kitchens. DDV resorts, several of which are attached to Deluxe resorts, equal or surpass Deluxe resorts in quality. They can also be a better value: Unlike other Disney resorts, DDV resorts don't levy a nightly surcharge for each additional adult (age 18+) in a room beyond the standard two.

Moderate resorts are a step down from Deluxes in guest-room quality, amenities, and cost. The price difference among Moderates is perhaps a few dollars per night at most, so choosing a resort in this category generally comes down to which theme you prefer.

Also classified by Disney as a Moderate resort, **Fort Wilderness Resort & Campground** offers both campsites and fully equipped cabins.

At the bottom of the list are **Value resorts,** with the smallest rooms, most limited amenities, and lowest rates of any Disney-owned hotels. Because this category is so popular with budget-conscious families, Disney has four separate Value price tiers:

- The **All-Star Sports, Music,** and **Movies Resorts** are Disney's oldest and least-expensive Value resorts.
- **Disney's Pop Century Resort** sits in the middle of the Value price range—about $10 per night more than the All-Stars.
- **Disney's Art of Animation Resort** is the newest Value property, with the largest rooms, best food court, and best pools in this category. Standard rooms here cost about $25 per night more than those at the All-Stars.
- Two-room **Family Suites** are available at the All-Star Music and Art of Animation Resorts, from around $240 to $510 per night.

2. MAKING RESERVATIONS Whether you book through Disney, a travel agent, online, with a tour operator, or through an organization like AAA, you'll frequently save by booking the room exclusive of any vacation package. This is called a *room-only reservation.* Though later in this chapter we'll scrutinize the advantages and disadvantages of buying a package, we'll tell you now that Walt Disney World packages at list price rarely save you any money (though they can certainly be convenient).

In dealing with Disney for rooms only, use **disneyworld.com** instead of calling the Disney Reservation Center (DRC) at ☎ 407-W-DISNEY (934-7639). Because of some administrative and operational consolidation, reservationists at the DRC are trained to sell only Walt Disney Travel Company packages. Even if you insist that all you want is a room, they'll try to persuade you to bundle it with some small extra, like a miniature-golf pass, so that your purchase can be counted as a package. Seems innocuous enough, but that little upgrade allows Disney to apply various restrictions and cancellation policies that you wouldn't be saddled with if you bought a room by itself—for example, Disney might add trip insurance to your package automatically.

Regarding cancellation, know that there are trade-offs. If you book a package and cancel 2–44 days before arrival, you lose your $200 deposit. If you cancel fewer than 2 days before arrival, you lose the entire package cost, including airfare and insurance. If you reserve only a room and cancel fewer than five days before arrival (six days if you booked through Disney's website), you lose your deposit of one night's room charge, which can easily be more than $200 if you booked at a Moderate, Deluxe, or DDV resort. Further, Disney imposes a $65 fee for changing your package's details, including travel dates, moving to a cheaper resort, or adding a discount code.

unofficial **TIP**
Booking online is *much* faster than calling DRC. If you must call, do so before 11 a.m. or after 3 p.m. Eastern.

If you call, tell the agent what you want in terms of lodging and get a room-only rate quote. Then tell the agent what you're looking for in terms of admissions. When you've pinned down your room selection and lodging costs, ask the agent if he or she can offer any packages that beat the à la carte prices. But don't be swayed by little sweeteners included in a package unless they have real value for you. If the first agent you speak to isn't accommodating, hang up and call back. There are a couple hundred agents, some more helpful than others.

When dealing with Disney reservations, a careful shopper from West Lafayette, Indiana, advises both wariness and toughness:

> *Making reservations through W-DISNEY is like buying a car: You need to know the sales tricks, have a firm idea of what you want, and be prepared to walk away if you don't get what you want at a price you want to pay.*

If you need specific information, call the resort directly, ask for the front desk, and pose your question before phoning the DRC. If your desired dates aren't available, keep calling back or check online. Something might open up.

3. A MOST CONFUSING VIEW Rates at Disney hotels vary from season to season (see the next section) and from room to room according to view. Further, each Disney resort has its own seasonal calendar. Seasons such as "Regular," "Value," "Peak," and "Holiday" vary depending on the resort instead of that tired old January–December calendar that the rest of us use. But confusing as Disney seasons are, they're logic personified compared to the panoply of guest-room views the resorts offer. Depending on the resort, you can choose standard views, water views, pool views, lagoon views, garden views, or savanna views, among others. Standard view, the most ambiguous category, crops up at about three-fourths of Disney resorts. It's usually interpreted as a view of infrastructure or unremarkable scenery. At Animal Kingdom Lodge, for example, you have savanna views, Arusha views, pool views, and standard views. Savanna views overlook the replicated African savanna, Arusha views offer prime opportunities to see animals (particularly zebras), pool views overlook the swimming pool, and standard views offer stunning vistas of . . . rooftops and parking lots.

With a standard view, however, you can at least pinpoint what you *won't* be seeing. Every resort defines views of water differently. At the Grand Floridian Resort & Spa, for example, rooms with views of Seven Seas Lagoon are sensibly called lagoon-view rooms, while those with views of the marina or pools are enigmatically called garden-view rooms.

unofficial **TIP**
If you book a king room at a Moderate resort, you can request a water-view room at no extra charge (this isn't guaranteed, though).

Zip over to the Yacht Club Resort, another Deluxe property. Like the Grand Floridian, the

Yacht Club is on a lake and has a pool and a marina. Views of all three are lumped into one big lagoon- or pool-view category—anything wet counts! If somehow you can glimpse the lake or a swimming pool, you have a water view.

It's worth noting that scoring a Grand Floridian room with a view of the Magic Kingdom requires exacting verbiage, as a mom from Pontefract, England, attests:

> We stayed at the Grand Floridian, which was lovely. However, I paid extra for a Magic Kingdom view. I was soooo disappointed when all I could see from the balcony was Space Mountain (unless I hung out so far I risked falling over). I was so looking forward to sitting on the balcony with a glass of wine and watching the fireworks. I know that next time I will have to ask for a view of Cinderella Castle, not just a Magic Kingdom view.

For many readers a good view is considered essential to the enjoyment of their hotel room. Getting the view you want, however, doesn't necessarily mean that you'll have the experience you want, as a Rochester, New York, couple points out:

> We stayed in the Conch Key building at the Grand Floridian. The view was lovely, but all we heard was the boat's horn blasting every 20 minutes, 7 a.m.–midnight. It was obnoxious and kept us up.

Our favorite water views are at the Contemporary Resort's Garden Building, which extends toward Bay Lake to the east of the giant A-frame. Rooms in this three-story structure, such as room 6109, afford some of the best lake vistas in Disney World (see **tinyurl.com /contemporary6109** for a view from one of these rooms). Many rooms are so near the water, in fact, you could spit a prune pit into the lake from your window. And their category? Garden views.

We could go on and on, but pinning Disney down on precisely what will be outside your window is the point. In our discussion of individual resorts later in this chapter, we'll tell you which rooms have the good views.

Our website's **Hotel Room View** project uses more than 30,000 photos to show the view you get from every hotel room in Walt Disney World, plus instructions on how to request each specific room. It uses interactive maps for every building in every resort, so that you can search for rooms by cost, view, walking distance, noise, handicap accessibility, and more. As you read this chapter, visit **touringplans.com/walt-disney-world/hotels** to see photos of the rooms we recommend.

*un*official **TIP**
Disney will guarantee connecting rooms if your party includes more children than adults. (In Disney terms, *adjoining rooms* are next to each other and *connecting rooms* have a door between them.)

4. HOW TO GET THE ROOM YOU WANT Disney won't guarantee a specific room when you book but will post your request on your reservation record. The easiest way to make a request is to use our **Hotel Room View** tool, described above. Select the room you want, and we'll automatically fax your request to Disney five days before you arrive.

Our experience indicates that making a request by room number confuses the Disney reservationists; as a result, they're unsure where to place you if the room you've asked for is unavailable. To increase your odds of getting the room you want, tell the reservationist exactly what characteristics and amenities you desire—for example: "I'd like a room with a balcony on the second or third floor of the Contemporary Resort's Garden Building with an unobstructed view of the lake." (It's unnecessary to ask for a nonsmoking room at a Disney resort—all rooms were designated smoke-free in 2007.)

unofficial **TIP**
Three to four days before you arrive, call the resort front desk. Call late in the evening when they're not so busy, and reconfirm the requests that by now should be appearing in their computers.

Be direct and politely assertive when speaking to the Disney agent. At Port Orleans Riverside, for example, rooms with king beds have options for standard-, garden-, pool-, preferred-, and river-view rooms. If you want to overlook the river, say so; likewise, if you want a pool view, speak up. Similarly, state clearly such preferences as a particular floor, a corner room, a room near restaurants, or a room away from elevators and ice machines. If you have a long list of preferences, type it in order of importance and e-mail, fax, or snail-mail it to the hotel. Include your contact information and reservation-confirmation number. Use abbreviations where possible—we're told Disney's reservation system may hold only around 80 characters of preference text.

It will be someone from the resort who actually assigns your room. Call back in a few days to make sure your preferences were posted to your record.

We'll provide info needed for each resort to frame your requests, including a resort layout map and our recommendations for specific rooms or buildings. We'll use a dash (–) to indicate a range of rooms. Thus, "rooms 2230–2260" refers to the 31 rooms within that range. Sometimes we'll specify even- or odd-numbered rooms within a range, for example, "odd-numbered rooms 631–639." In this case we're referring to rooms 631, 633, 635, 637, and 639.

Again, note that our Hotel Room View tool (see previous page) will give you the exact wording to use when requesting a specific room, and it can automatically send your request to Disney at the appropriate tine before you arrive.

HOW TO GET DISCOUNTS ON LODGING

THERE ARE SO MANY GUEST ROOMS in and around Disney World that competition is brisk, and everyone, including Disney, wheels and deals to fill them. Disney, however, has its own atypical way of managing its room inventory. To uphold the brand integrity of its hotels, Disney prefers to use inducements rather than discounts per se. For example, Disney might include free dining if you reserve a certain number of nights at rack rate, or offer special deals only by e-mail to returning guests. Consequently, many of the strategies for obtaining discounted rates in most cities and destinations don't work well for Disney hotels. We'll explore these strategies in-depth when we discuss booking non-Disney hotels near Walt Disney World; for the moment, though, here are some tips for getting price breaks at Disney properties:

1. SEASONAL SAVINGS Save 15–35% per night or more on a Disney hotel room by visiting during the slower times of year. However, Disney uses so many adjectives (Regular, Holiday, Peak, Value, and the like) to describe its seasonal calendar that it's hard to keep up. Plus, the dates for each "season" vary among resorts. Disney also changes the price of its hotel rooms with the day of the week, charging more for the same room on Friday and Saturday nights. The increased rates range from $20 to $90 or more per room, per night.

2. ASK ABOUT SPECIALS When you talk to Disney reservationists, ask specifically about specials. For example, "What special deals or discounts are available at Disney hotels during the time of our visit?" Being specific and assertive paid off for a Warren Township, New Jersey, dad:

> Your tip on asking Disney employees about discounts was invaluable. They will not volunteer this information, but by asking we saved almost $500 on our hotel room.

Another New Jersey reader takes a high-calorie approach:

> My husband and I begin planning each WDW vacation the same way: Call the famous 407-W-DISNEY number and speak to someone with a ridiculous name (this time it was Flower and Buffy). I present my vacation plan to the operator, which consists of my specific date, WDW resort, and ticket choice. She quotes me a price; I thank her for her help and hang up. I call again and present my exact same plan to a new operator, who quotes me a totally different price! I repeat the phone process again and obtain another price for the same plan. After three years, my husband and I feel like we're playing "Spin the Wheel to Get a Price for the WDW Vacation." Now, instead of getting disgusted, we make it a night of calling with coffee and dessert.

A family from West Springfield, Massachusetts, discovered that if you keep on shopping even after you've booked, your efforts can really pay off:

> I booked our trip online with Disney using a special-offer discount we had received in the mail. Two months before our trip, and after I had already paid in full, Disney ran a special that was actually better than the one I had booked. I gave them a call, and they politely, quickly, and efficiently credited me with the difference.

Be aware that specials can include discounts on vacation packages in addition to discounts on rooms. Discounts on park admission or dining packages (see "Spring for 'Free Dining' " in "Disney Lodging for Less," page 224) can be substantial, depending on the number of people in your traveling party or where you're staying.

3. TRADE-UP OR UPSELL RATES If you request a room at a Disney Value resort and none are available, you may be offered a discounted room in the next category up (Moderate resorts, in this example). Similarly, if you ask for a room in a Moderate resort and none is available, Disney will usually offer a deal for Disney Deluxe Villa rooms or a Deluxe resort. You can angle for a trade-up rate by asking for a resort category that's more likely to be sold out.

4. KNOW THE SECRET CODE The folks at **MouseSavers (mousesavers .com)** maintain an updated list of discounts and reservation codes for

Disney resorts. The codes are separated into categories such as "for anyone," "for residents of certain states," and "for Annual Pass holders." Anyone calling ☎ 407-W-DISNEY can use a current code and get the discounted rate.

Be aware that Disney targets people with PIN codes in e-mails and direct mailings. PIN-code discounts are offered to specific individuals and are correlated with a given person's name and address. When you try to make a reservation using the PIN, Disney will verify that the street or e-mail address to which the code was sent is yours.

MouseSavers has a great historical list of when discounts were released and what they encompassed at **mousesavers.com/historical wdwdiscounts.html.** You can also sign up for the MouseSavers newsletter, with discount announcements, Disney news, and exclusive offers not available to the general public.

To get your name in the Disney system for a PIN code, call ☎ 407-W-DISNEY and request written info or the free trip-planning DVD. If you've been to Walt Disney World before, your name and address will of course already be on record, but you won't be as likely to receive a PIN-code offer as you would by calling and requesting that information be mailed to you. On the web, go to **disneyworld.com** and sign up (via the trip-planning DVD) to automatically be sent offers and news at your e-mail address. You might also consider getting a **Disney Rewards Visa Card,** which entitles you to around two days' advance notice when a discount is released (visit **disney.go.com/visa** for details).

unofficial **TIP**
To enhance your chances of receiving a PIN-code offer, you need to get your name and street or e-mail address into the Disney system.

5. INTERNET SELLERS Online travel sellers **Expedia (expedia.com), One Travel (onetravel.com), Priceline (priceline.com),** and **Travelocity (travelocity.com)** offer discounted rooms at Disney hotels, but usually at a price approximating the going rate obtainable from the Walt Disney Travel Company or Walt Disney World Central Reservations. Most breaks are in the 7–25% range, but they can go as deep as 40%. Always check these websites' prices against Disney's—while updating this guide, we noticed that for the same dates during summer 2015, Priceline was charging $30 more per night than Disney for the same standard-view room at the Beach Club.

6. WALT DISNEY WORLD WEBSITE Disney still offers deals when it sees lower-than-usual future demand. Go to **disneyworld.com** and look for "Explore Our Special Offers" on the home page. In the same place, also look for seasonal discounts, usually listed as "Summertime Savings" or "Fall Savings" or something similar. You can also go to "Places to Stay" at the top of the home page, where you'll find a link to Special Offers. You must click on the particular special to get the discounts: If you fill out the information on "Price Your Vacation," you'll be charged the full rack rate. Reservations booked online are subject to a penalty if canceled fewer than 45 days before you arrive. Before booking rooms on Disney's or any website, click "Terms and Conditions" and read the fine print.

7. RENTING DISNEY VACATION CLUB POINTS The Disney Vacation Club (DVC) is Disney's time-share-condominium program. DVC resorts (a.k.a. Disney Deluxe Villa [DDV] resorts) at Walt Disney World are **Animal Kingdom Villas, Bay Lake Tower at the Contemporary Resort,** the **Beach**

Club Villas, BoardWalk Villas, Grand Floridian Villas, Old Key West Resort, Polynesian Villas & Bungalows, Saratoga Springs Resort & Spa, Treehouse Villas at Saratoga Springs, and Wilderness Lodge Villas. Each DVC resort offers studios and one- and two-bedroom villas; some resorts also offer three-bedroom villas. (The new Polynesian Village DVC resort is limited to studios and two-bedroom bungalows.) Studios are equipped with kitchenettes, wet bars, and fridges; villas come with full kitchens. Most accommodations have patios or balconies.

DVC members receive a number of points annually that they use to pay for their Disney accommodations. Sometimes members elect to "rent" (sell) their points instead of using them in a given year. Though Disney is not involved in the transaction, it allows DVC members to make these points available to the general public. The going rental rate is usually in the neighborhood of $14 per point. Renting a studio for a summer week at Animal Kingdom Lodge & Villas would run you $3,252 with tax during Regular season if you booked through the DRC. The same studio costs the DVC member 95 points for a week. If you rented those points at $14 per point, the same studio would cost you $1,330 with tax—more than $1,900 less.

You have two options when renting points: go through a company that specializes in DVC points rental, or locate and deal directly with the selling DVC member. For a fixed rate of around $14 per point, the folks at David's Disney Vacation Club Rentals (dvcrequest.com) will act on your behalf as a points broker, matching your request for a specific resort and dates to their available supply. They'll also take requests months in advance and notify you as soon as something becomes available. We've used these folks for huge New Year's Eve events and last-minute trips, and they're tops. Plus they accept major credit cards.

In addition to David's, some readers, like this one from St. Louis, have had good results with The DVC Rental Store (dvcrentalstore.com):

> We rented DVC points for this trip through the DVC Rental Store, and we had a wonderful experience. Unlike David's, they don't make you pay the entire cost upon booking. For our stay at Wilderness Lodge Villas, we paid just over half what we were planning to pay for the Wilderness Lodge.

When you deal directly with the selling DVC member, you pay him or her directly, such as by certified check (few members take credit cards). The DVC member makes a reservation in your name and pays Disney the requisite number of points. Arrangements vary, but the going rate seems to be around $14 per point. Trust is required from both parties. Usually your reservation is documented by a confirmation sent from Disney to the owner and then passed along to you. Though the deal you cut is strictly up to you and the owner, you should always insist on receiving the aforementioned confirmation before making more than a one-night deposit.

We suggest checking online at one of the various Disney discussion boards (such as mouseowners.com) if you're not picky about where you stay and when you go and you're willing to put in the effort to ask around. If you're trying to book a particular resort, especially during a busy time of year, there's something to be said for the low-hassle approach of a points broker.

8. TRAVEL AGENTS are active players and particularly good sources of information on limited-time programs and discounts. We believe a good travel agent is the best friend a traveler can have. And though we at the *Unofficial Guide* know a thing or two about the travel industry, we always give our agent a chance to beat any deal we find. If she can't beat it, we let her book it anyway if she can get commission from it, thus nurturing the relationship.

As you might expect, some travel agents and agencies specialize, sometimes exclusively, in selling Walt Disney World. These agents have spent an incredible amount of time at the resorts; they've also completed extensive Disney-education programs. They're usually the most Disney-knowledgeable agents in the travel industry. Most of these specialists and their agencies display the Earmarked logo stating that they're Authorized Disney Vacation Planners.

These Disney specialists are so good we use them ourselves. The needs of our research team are many, and our schedules are complicated. When we work with an Authorized Disney Vacation Planner, we know we're dealing with someone who knows Disney inside and out, including where to find the deals and how to use all the tricks of the trade that keep our research budget under control. Simply stated, they save us time and money—sometimes lots of both.

Each year we ask our readers to rate the travel agent who helped plan their Disney vacation. We received more than 4,400 responses this year. The best of the best include **Sue Pisaturo** of **Small World Vacations,** whom we've used many times and who contributes to this guide (**sue@ smallworldvacations.com**); **Coleen Bolton** (**coleen@mei-travel.com**), who also made our list in the 2013 and 2014 editions of this guide; **Minnie Babb** (**minnie@smallworldvacations.com**) and **Darren Wittko** (**darren@ magicalvacationstravel.com**), both of whom made the list a second year in a row; and newcomers **Caroline Baggerly** (**caroline@mei-travel.com**), **Holly Biss** (**holly@magicalvacationstravel.com**), and **Belle Meyers** (**belle@ smallworldvacations.com**).

Our reader-survey results indicate that for Walt Disney World, you'll be much more satisfied using a travel agent who specializes in Disney and much more likely to recommend those agents to a friend. While the agents listed above are among the ones most consistently recommended in our surveys, you'll find good Disney specialists throughout the country if you prefer to work with someone close to home.

9. ORGANIZATIONS AND AUTO CLUBS Disney has developed time-limited programs with some auto clubs and organizations. AAA, for example, can often offer discounts on hotels and packages comparable to those Disney offers its Annual Pass holders. Such deals come and go, but the market suggests there will be more. If you're a member of AARP, AAA, or any travel or auto club, ask whether the group has a program before shopping elsewhere.

10. ROOM UPGRADES Sometimes a room upgrade is as good as a discount. If you're visiting Disney World during a slower time, book the least expensive room your discounts will allow. Checking in, ask very politely about being upgraded to a water-view or pool-view room. A fair percentage of the time, you'll get one at no additional charge. Understand, however, that a room upgrade should be considered a favor. Hotels are under no obligation to upgrade you, so if your request is not met, accept the decision graciously. Also, note that suites at Deluxe resorts are exempt from discount offers.

11. MILITARY DISCOUNTS The **Shades of Green Armed Forces Recreation Center,** near the Grand Floridian Resort & Spa, offers luxury accommodations at rates based on a service member's rank, as well as attraction tickets to the theme parks. For rates and other information, call ☎ 888-593-2242 or see **shadesofgreen.org.**

12. YEAR-ROUND DISCOUNTS AT THE SWAN AND DOLPHIN RESORTS Government workers, teachers, nurses, military, and AAA and *Entertainment Coupon Book* members can save on their rooms at the Dolphin or Swan (when space is available, of course). Call ☎ 888-828-8850.

CHOOSING A WALT DISNEY WORLD HOTEL

IF YOU WANT TO STAY IN THE WORLD but you don't know which hotel to choose, consider these factors:

1. COST Consider your budget. Hotel rooms start at about $100 a night at the **All-Star** and **Pop Century Resorts** during Value season and top out near $1,600 at the **Grand Floridian Resort & Spa** during Holiday season. Suites, of course, are more expensive than standard rooms.

Disney's Animal Kingdom Villas, Bay Lake Tower, Beach Club Villas, BoardWalk Villas, Grand Floridian Villas, Old Key West Resort, Saratoga Springs Resort & Spa and **Wilderness Lodge Villas** offer condotype accommodations with one-, two-, and (at Saratoga Springs, BoardWalk Villas, Old Key West, Animal Kingdom Villas, Grand Floridian Villas, and Bay Lake Tower) three-bedroom units with kitchens, living rooms, DVD players, and washers and dryers. The new **Polynesian Villas & Bungalows** consist solely of studios and two-bedroom freestanding units.

Studios have a kitchenette (with microwave, mini-fridge, and sink) but no washer or dryer. Prices range from $358 per night for a studio suite at Animal Kingdom Villas to more than $3,400 per night for a two-bedroom bungalow at Polynesian Village Villas. Fully equipped cabins (minus a washer and dryer) at **Fort Wilderness Resort & Campground** cost $336–$562 per night. The Family Suites at All-Star Music and Art of Animation have kitchenettes, separate bedrooms, and two bathrooms. A few suites without kitchens are available at the more expensive Disney resorts.

For any extra adults in a room (more than two), the nightly surcharge for each extra adult is $10 at Value resorts, $15 at Moderates, and $25 at Deluxes, plus tax. *DDV resorts levy no surcharge.*

Also at Disney World are the seven hotels of the **Downtown Disney Resort Area (DDRA).** Accommodations range from fairly luxurious to motel-like. While the DDRA is technically part of Disney World, staying there is like visiting a colony rather than the motherland. Free parking at theme parks isn't offered—nor is early entry, with one current exception, the Hilton—and hotels operate their own buses rather than use Disney transportation. For more information on DDRA properties, see the chart and discussion starting on page 211.

COSTS PER NIGHT OF DISNEY HOTEL ROOMS, LATE 2015 *(rack rate)*	
Rates are for standard rooms except where noted.	
All-Star Resorts	$104–$199
All-Star Music Resort Family Suites	$244–$443
Animal Kingdom Lodge	$320–$556
Animal Kingdom Villas *(studio, Jambo/Kidani)*	$358–$674
Art of Animation Family Suites	$304–$514
Art of Animation Resort	$129–$224
Bay Lake Tower at Contemporary Resort *(studio)*	$500–$740
Beach Club Resort	$400–$672
Beach Club Villas *(studio)*	$415–$687
BoardWalk Inn	$429–$683
BoardWalk Villas *(studio)*	$415–$687
Caribbean Beach Resort	$191–$285
Contemporary Resort *(Garden Building)*	$400–$630
Coronado Springs Resort	$197–$290
Dolphin *(Sheraton)*	$189–$430
Fort Wilderness Resort & Campground *(cabins)*	$336–$562
Grand Floridian Resort & Spa	$582–$856
Grand Floridian Villas *(studio)*	$570–$890
Old Key West Resort *(studio)*	$368–$531
Polynesian Village Resort	$483–$760
Polynesian Villas & Bungalows *(studio)*	$494–$772
Pop Century Resort	$115–$209
Port Orleans Resort *(French Quarter & Riverside)*	$191–$285
Saratoga Springs Resort & Spa *(studio)*	$368–$531
Swan *(Westin)*	$189–$430
Treehouse Villas	$818–$1,377
Wilderness Lodge	$325–$561
Wilderness Lodge Villas *(studio)*	$421–$621
Yacht Club Resort	$400–$672

2. LOCATION Once you determine your budget, think about what you want to do at Disney World. Will you go to all four theme parks or concentrate on one or two?

If you're going to be driving, your Disney hotel's location isn't especially important unless you plan to spend most of your time at the Magic Kingdom. (Disney transportation is always more efficient than your car in this case, because it bypasses the Transportation and Ticket Center, the World's transportation hub, and deposits you at the theme park entrance.) If you haven't decided whether you want a car for your Disney vacation, see "How to Travel Around the World" (page 456).

Most convenient to the Magic Kingdom are the three resort complexes linked by monorail: the **Grand Floridian** and its **Villas,** the

WHAT IT COSTS TO STAY IN THE DOWNTOWN DISNEY RESORT AREA	
Best Western Lake Buena Vista Resort Hotel	$80–$170
B Resort	$119–$237
Buena Vista Palace Hotel & Spa	$139–$169
DoubleTree Guest Suites	$119–$229
Hilton Orlando Lake Buena Vista	$139–$289
Holiday Inn in the WDW Resort	$104–$190
Wyndham Lake Buena Vista Resort	$104–$300

Contemporary and **Bay Lake Tower,** and the **Polynesian Village, Villas, & Bungalows.** Commuting to the Magic Kingdom by monorail is quick and simple, allowing visitors to return to their hotel for a nap, swim, or meal.

Contemporary Resort and Bay Lake Tower, in addition to being on the monorail, are only a 10- to 15-minute walk to the Magic Kingdom. Guests reach Epcot by monorail but must transfer at the Transportation and Ticket Center. Buses connect the resorts to Disney's Hollywood Studios, Disney's Animal Kingdom, the water parks, and Disney Springs. No transfer is required, but the bus makes several stops before reaching either destination.

> *un*official **TIP**
> If you plan to use Disney transportation to visit all four major parks and one or both of the water parks, book a centrally located resort that has good transportation connections. The Epcot resorts and the **Polynesian Village, Caribbean Beach, Art of Animation, Pop Century, Coronado Springs,** and **Port Orleans Resorts** fill the bill.

The Polynesian Village, Villas, & Bungalows is served by the monorail and is an easy walk from the transportation center, where you can catch an express monorail to Epcot. This makes the Polynesian Village the only Disney resort with direct monorail access to both Epcot and the Magic Kingdom. To minimize your walk to the transportation center, request a standard room in Tokelau or, once construction is complete, a DVC studio in Pago Pago or Moorea (see page 157).

Wilderness Lodge & Villas, along with **Fort Wilderness Resort & Campground,** are linked to the Magic Kingdom by boat and to everywhere else in the World by somewhat-convoluted bus service. The **Four Seasons Resort Orlando at Walt Disney World,** behind the former Osprey Ridge Golf Course, has its own bus service to the Magic Kingdom.

The most centrally located resorts in Walt Disney World are the Epcot hotels: the **BoardWalk Inn, BoardWalk Villas, Yacht & Beach Club Resorts, Beach Club Villas, Swan,** and **Dolphin**—and **Coronado Springs,** near Disney's Animal Kingdom. The Epcot hotels are within easy walking distance of Disney's Hollywood Studios and Epcot's International Gateway. Except at Coronado Springs, boat service is also available at these resorts, with vessels connecting to DHS. Epcot hotels are best for guests planning to spend most of their time at Epcot or DHS.

Caribbean Beach Resort, Pop Century Resort, and **Art of Animation Resort** are just south and east of Epcot and DHS. Along Bonnet Creek, **Disney's Old Key West** and **Port Orleans Resorts** also offer quick access to those parks.

Also along Bonnet Creek, pretty much surrounded by Walt Disney World, is a parcel of land that Disney was unable to acquire and that went undeveloped for decades. Now that property is home to the 70-acre **Bonnet Creek Resort,** comprising four non-Disney hotels: the **Waldorf Astoria Orlando;** the **Hilton Orlando Bonnet Creek;** and two **Wyndham** properties: the **Wyndham Bonnet Creek Resort** and its more luxurious sibling, the **Wyndham Grand Orlando Resort Bonnet Creek.** Technically, the complex isn't in Walt Disney World, but you can access it only via Disney property and roads—a real sore spot with Disney. The hotels of the Bonnet Creek Resort are as close to the theme parks as Disney's own, offer transportation to the parks and Disney Springs, and are every bit as good as Disney's best, often at around half the price. We profile the Hilton, the Waldorf Astoria, and the Wyndham Bonnet Creek later in this chapter in "Hotels Outside Walt Disney World."

Though not centrally located, the **All-Star Resorts** and **Animal Kingdom Lodge & Villas** have very good bus service to all Disney World destinations and are closest to Animal Kingdom.

If you plan to play golf, book **Old Key West Resort** or **Saratoga Springs Resort & Spa,** both of which are built around golf courses, or the **Four Seasons,** which has its own course and is a short drive to Disney's Palm and Magnolia courses. The military-only **Shades of Green** resort is adjacent to the Palm and Magnolia as well. Nearby but not on a golf course are the **Contemporary** and **Bay Lake Tower,** along with the **Grand Floridian, Polynesian Village,** and **Port Orleans Resorts.**

For boating and water sports, try the **Polynesian Village, Contemporary,** or **Grand Floridian Resorts, Fort Wilderness Resort & Campground,** or **Wilderness Lodge & Villas.** The lodge and campground are also great for hikers, bikers, and joggers.

3. ROOM QUALITY Few Disney guests spend much time in their hotel rooms, though these rooms are among the best designed and most well appointed anywhere. Plus, they're meticulously maintained. At the top of the line are the luxurious rooms of the **Contemporary, Grand Floridian,** and **Polynesian Village Resorts;** bringing up the rear are the small rooms of the **All-Star Resorts.** But even these economy rooms are sparkling-clean and quite livable.

The chart at right shows how Walt Disney World hotels (along with the **Swan** and **Dolphin,** which are Westin and Sheraton hotels, respectively) stack up for quality.

4. THE SIZE OF YOUR GROUP Larger families and groups may be interested in how many persons a Disney resort room can accommodate, but only Lilliputians would be comfortable in a room filled to capacity. Groups requiring two or more guest rooms should consider condo or villa accommodations in or out of the World. The most cost-efficient Disney resorts for groups of five are the **Alligator Bayou** section of **Port Orleans Riverside** and **Caribbean Beach Resort.** The cheapest digs for six are the **All-Star Music Family Suites.** If your party includes more than six people, you'll need either two hotel rooms, a suite, a villa, or a condo. The Disney room-layout schematics on the following pages show the rooms' relative sizes and configurations, along with the maximum number of persons per room.

HOTEL	ROOM-QUALITY RATING
1. BAY LAKE TOWER	95
2. CONTEMPORARY RESORT	93
3. GRAND FLORIDIAN VILLAS	93
4. POLYNESIAN VILLAGE RESORT (non-DVC rooms*)	92
5. ANIMAL KINGDOM VILLAS (studio)	91
6. BEACH CLUB RESORT	90
7. BEACH CLUB VILLAS (studio)	90
8. BOARDWALK VILLAS (studio)	90
9. DOLPHIN	90
10. GRAND FLORIDIAN RESORT & SPA	90
11. OLD KEY WEST RESORT (studio)	90
12. SARATOGA SPRINGS RESORT & SPA (studio)	90
13. SWAN	90
14. TREEHOUSE VILLAS	90
15. WILDERNESS LODGE VILLAS (studio)	90
16. ANIMAL KINGDOM LODGE	89
17. BOARDWALK INN	89
18. YACHT CLUB RESORT	89
19. FORT WILDERNESS CABINS	86
20. WILDERNESS LODGE	86
21. CORONADO SPRINGS RESORT	85
22. SHADES OF GREEN	85
23. PORT ORLEANS FRENCH QUARTER	84
24. PORT ORLEANS RIVERSIDE	83
25. CARIBBEAN BEACH RESORT	80
26. ART OF ANIMATION RESORT (standard rooms)	78
27. ALL-STAR RESORTS	73
28. POP CENTURY RESORT	71

*Polynesian Villas & Bungalows too new to rate

5. THEME All Disney hotels are themed. Each is designed to make you feel you're in a special place or period of history.

Some resorts carry off their themes better than others, and some themes are more exciting. **Wilderness Lodge & Villas,** for example, is extraordinary, reminiscent of a grand national-park lodge from the early 20th century. The lobby opens eight stories to a timbered ceiling supported by giant columns of bundled logs. One look eases you into the Northwest-wilderness theme. The lodge is a great choice for couples and seniors and is heaven for children.

Animal Kingdom Lodge & Villas replicates grand safari lodges of Kenya and Tanzania and overlooks its own African game preserve. By far the most exotic Disney resort, it's made to order for couples on romantic getaways and for families with children. Likewise dramatic, the **Polynesian Village Resort, Villas & Bungalows** conveys the feeling of the Pacific Islands. It's great for romantics and families. Many

DISNEY HOTELS BY THEME

ALL-STAR RESORTS: Sports, music, and movies

ANIMAL KINGDOM LODGE & VILLAS: African game preserve

ART OF ANIMATION RESORT: Disney's animated films

BAY LAKE TOWER: Upscale, ultramodern urban hotel

BEACH CLUB RESORT & VILLAS: New England beach club of the 1870s

BOARDWALK INN: East Coast boardwalk hotel of the early 1900s

BOARDWALK VILLAS: East Coast beach cottage of the early 1900s

CARIBBEAN BEACH RESORT: Caribbean islands

CONTEMPORARY RESORT: Future as perceived by past, present generations

CORONADO SPRINGS RESORT: Northern Mexico and the American Southwest

DOLPHIN: Modern Florida resort

GRAND FLORIDIAN RESORT & SPA, VILLAS: Turn-of-the-20th-century luxury hotel

OLD KEY WEST RESORT: Key West

POLYNESIAN VILLAGE RESORT, VILLAS & BUNGALOWS: Hawaii–South Seas

POP CENTURY RESORT: Icons from various decades of the 20th century

PORT ORLEANS FRENCH QUARTER RESORT: Turn-of-the-19th-century New Orleans

PORT ORLEANS RIVERSIDE RESORT: Antebellum Louisiana plantation, bayou-side retreat

SARATOGA SPRINGS RESORT & SPA: 1880s Victorian lake

SWAN: Modern Florida resort

TREEHOUSE VILLAS: Rustic vacation homes with modern amenities

WILDERNESS LODGE & VILLAS: National-park grand lodge of the early 1900s

YACHT CLUB RESORT: New England seashore hotel of the 1880s

waterfront rooms on upper floors offer a perfect view of Cinderella Castle and the Magic Kingdom fireworks across Seven Seas Lagoon.

Grandeur, nostalgia, and privilege are central to the **Grand Floridian Resort & Spa, Grand Floridian Villas, Yacht & Beach Club Resorts, BoardWalk Inn,** and **BoardWalk Villas.** Though modeled after Eastern-seaboard seaside hotels of different eras, the resorts are similar. **Saratoga Springs Resort & Spa,** supposedly representative of an upstate New York country retreat, looks like what you'd get if you crossed the Beach Club with the Wilderness Lodge. For all the resorts inspired by northeastern resorts, thematic distinctions are subtle and lost on many guests.

Port Orleans French Quarter Resort lacks the mystery and sultriness of the real New Orleans French Quarter but captures enough of its architectural essence to carry off the theme. **Port Orleans Riverside Resort** likewise succeeds with its plantation and bayou setting. **Old Key West Resort** gets the architecture right, but cloning its inspiration on such a large scale totally glosses over the real Key West's idiosyncratic patchwork personality. The **Caribbean Beach Resort**'s theme is much more effective at night, thanks to creative lighting. By day, it looks like a Miami condo development.

DISNEY DELUXE RESORTS ROOM DIAGRAMS

Contemporary Resort

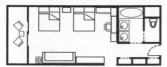

Typical room, 394 square feet
*Rooms accommodate 5 guests,
plus 1 child under age 3 in a crib.*

Polynesian Village Resort

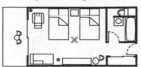

Typical room, 415 square feet
*Rooms accommodate 5 guests,
plus 1 child under age 3 in a crib.*

Grand Floridian Resort & Spa

Typical room, 440 square feet
*Rooms accommodate 5 guests,
plus 1 child under age 3 in a crib.*

BoardWalk Inn

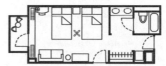

Typical room, 371 square feet
*Rooms accommodate 4 guests,
plus 1 child under age 3 in a crib.*

Beach Club Resort

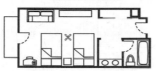

Typical room, 381 square feet
*Rooms accommodate 5 guests,
plus 1 child under age 3 in a crib.*

Yacht Club Resort

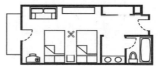

Typical room, 381 square feet
*Rooms accommodate 5 guests,
plus 1 child under age 3 in a crib.*

Wilderness Lodge

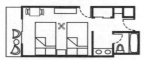

Typical room, 344 square feet
*Rooms accommodate 4 guests,
plus 1 child under age 3 in a crib.*

Animal Kingdom Lodge

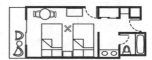

Typical room, 344 square feet
*Rooms accommodate 4 guests,
plus 1 child under age 3 in a crib.*

Coronado Springs Resort offers several styles of Mexican and southwestern American architecture. Though the lake setting is lovely and the resort is attractive and inviting, the theme (with the exception of the main swimming area) isn't especially stimulating—more like a Scottsdale, Arizona, country club than a Disney resort. Like Caribbean Beach, though, Coronado Springs is beautiful at night.

The **All-Star Resorts** comprise 30 three-story, T-shaped hotels with almost 6,000 guest rooms. There are 15 themed areas: 5 celebrate sports

Continued on page 134

DISNEY DELUXE VILLA RESORTS ROOM DIAGRAMS

Old Key West Resort

Studio (gray): 376 square feet
One-bedroom: 942 square feet
Two-bedroom: 1,333 square feet
Grand Villa: 2,202 square feet

Animal Kingdom Villas
(Jambo House & Kidani Village)

Studio (gray): 316–365 square feet (Jambo House),
366 square feet (Kidani Village)
One-bedroom: 629–710 square feet (Jambo House),
807 square feet (Kidani Village)
Two-bedroom: 945–1,075 square feet (Jambo House),
1,173 square feet (Kidani Village)
Grand Villa: 2,349 square feet (Jambo House),
2,201 square feet (Kidani Village)

Bay Lake Tower
at Contemporary Resort

Studio (gray): 339 square feet
One-bedroom: 803 square feet
Two-bedroom: 1,152 square feet
Grand Villa: 2,044 square feet

BoardWalk Villas

Studio (gray): 412 square feet
One-bedroom: 814 square feet
Two-bedroom: 1,236 square feet
Grand Villa: 2,491 square feet

Treehouse Villas at
Saratoga Springs Resort & Spa

Three-bedroom:
1,074 square feet

The Villas at
Grand Floridian Resort & Spa

Studio (gray): 374 square feet
One-bedroom (white): 844 square feet
Two-bedroom lock-off (gray and white):
1,232 square feet

DDV GUEST-OCCUPANCY LIMITS • **Studios:** 4 persons at all but Grand Floridian, Polynesian Villas, and Wilderness Lodge (5). • **One-bedroom villas:** 4 at Beach Club, BoardWalk, Saratoga Springs, and Wilderness Lodge; 4 or 5 at Animal Kingdom Lodge (Jambo House); 5 everywhere else. • **Two-bedroom villas:** 8 or 9 at Animal Kingdom Lodge (Jambo House); 9 at Animal Kingdom Lodge (Kidani Village), Bay Lake Tower, and Old Key West; 9 or 10 at Grand Floridian; 8 everywhere else. Three-bedroom and Grand Villas: 9 at Treehouse Villas; 12 everywhere else. *Note:* To all these limits you may add 1 child under age 3 in a crib.

DISNEY DELUXE VILLA RESORTS
ROOM DIAGRAMS (Continued)

Wilderness Lodge Villas

Studio (gray): 356 square feet
One-bedroom: 727 square feet
Two-bedroom: 1,080 square feet

Beach Club Villas

Studio (gray): 356 square feet
One-bedroom: 726 square feet
Two-bedroom: 1,083 square feet

Saratoga Springs Resort & Spa

Studio (gray): 355 square feet
One-bedroom: 714 square feet
Two-bedroom: 1,075 square feet

Polynesian Village Villas

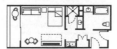

Studio: 460 square feet

Polynesian Village Bungalows

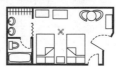

1,650 square feet

DISNEY MODERATE RESORTS ROOM DIAGRAMS

Coronado Springs Resort

Typical room, 314 square feet
Rooms accommodate 4 guests, plus 1 child under age 3 in a crib.

Port Orleans French Quarter Resort

Typical room, 314 square feet
Rooms accommodate 4 guests, plus 1 child under age 3 in a crib.

Caribbean Beach Resort

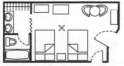

Typical room, 314 square feet
Rooms accommodate 4 guests, plus 1 child under age 3 in a crib.

Port Orleans Resort Riverside

Typical room, 314 square feet
Rooms accommodate 4 guests, plus 1 child under age 3 in a crib. Alligator Bayou has trundle bed for extra child (54" long) at no extra charge.

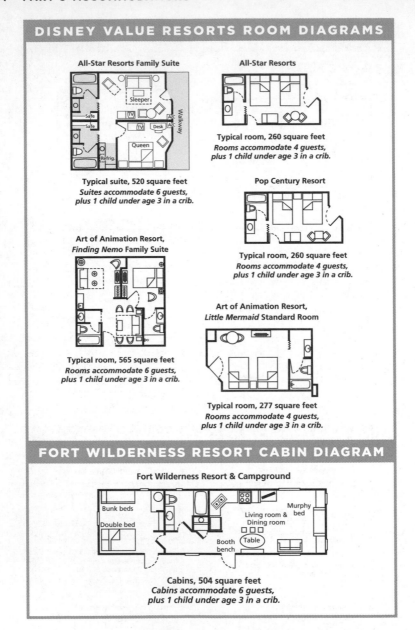

DISNEY VALUE RESORTS ROOM DIAGRAMS

All-Star Resorts Family Suite

Typical suite, 520 square feet
*Suites accommodate 6 guests,
plus 1 child under age 3 in a crib.*

All-Star Resorts

Typical room, 260 square feet
*Rooms accommodate 4 guests,
plus 1 child under age 3 in a crib.*

Pop Century Resort

Typical room, 260 square feet
*Rooms accommodate 4 guests,
plus 1 child under age 3 in a crib.*

**Art of Animation Resort,
Finding Nemo Family Suite**

Typical room, 565 square feet
*Rooms accommodate 6 guests,
plus 1 child under age 3 in a crib.*

**Art of Animation Resort,
Little Mermaid Standard Room**

Typical room, 277 square feet
*Rooms accommodate 4 guests,
plus 1 child under age 3 in a crib.*

FORT WILDERNESS RESORT CABIN DIAGRAM

Fort Wilderness Resort & Campground

Cabins, 504 square feet
*Cabins accommodate 6 guests,
plus 1 child under age 3 in a crib.*

Continued from page 131

(surfing, basketball, tennis, football, and baseball), 5 recall Hollywood movies, and 5 have musical motifs. The resort's design, with entrances shaped like giant Dalmatians, Coke cups, footballs, and the like, is pretty adolescent, sacrificing grace and beauty for energy and novelty. Guest rooms are small, with decor reminiscent of a teenage boy's bedroom. Despite the theme, there is neither sports nor music; however, movies are shown nightly at all three resorts. **Pop Century Resort** is pretty much a clone of All-Star Resorts, only here the giant icons symbolize decades of the 20th century (Big Wheels, 45-rpm records, silhouettes of people doing period dances, and such), and period memorabilia decorates the rooms. Across the lake from Pop Century Resort is the **Art of Animation Resort,** with icons and decor based on four animated features: *Cars, Finding Nemo, The Lion King,* and *The Little Mermaid.*

Pretense aside, the **Contemporary, Swan,** and **Dolphin** are essentially themeless though architecturally interesting. The original Contemporary Resort is a 15-story A-frame building with monorails running through the middle. Views from guest rooms here and in **Bay Lake Tower** are among the best at Disney World. The Swan and Dolphin are massive yet whimsical. Designed by Michael Graves, they're excellent examples of "entertainment architecture."

6. DINING The best resorts for dining quality and selection are the Epcot resorts: the **Beach Club Villas, BoardWalk Inn & Villas, Dolphin, Swan,** and **Yacht & Beach Club Resorts.** Each has good restaurants and is within easy walking distance of the others and of the 15 restaurants in Epcot's World Showcase section. If you stay at an Epcot resort, you have a total of 32 restaurants within a 5- to 12-minute walk.

The only other place in Disney World where restaurants and hotels are similarly concentrated is in the **Downtown Disney Resort Area.** In addition to restaurants in the hotels themselves, **B Resort, Best Western Lake Buena Vista Resort Hotel, Buena Vista Palace Hotel & Spa,** the **Hilton, Holiday Inn at Walt Disney World,** and **Wyndham Lake Buena Vista Resort,** along with **Saratoga Springs Resort & Spa,** are within walking distance of restaurants in Disney Springs.

Guests at the **Contemporary, Polynesian Village,** and **Grand Floridian** can eat in their hotels, or they can commute to restaurants in the Magic Kingdom (not recommended) or in other monorail-linked hotels. Riding the monorail to another hotel or to the Magic Kingdom takes about 10 minutes each way, plus waiting for the train.

The other Disney resorts are somewhat isolated. This means you're stuck dining at your hotel unless (1) you have a car or (2) you're content to eat at the theme parks or Disney Springs.

Here's the deal. Disney transportation works fine for commuting from hotels to theme parks and Disney Springs, but it's useless for getting from one hotel to another. If you're staying at Port Orleans and you want to dine at the Swan, forget it—it could take you up to an hour and a half each way by bus. You could take a bus to the Magic Kingdom and catch a train to one of the monorail-served hotels for dinner. That would take "only" 45 minutes each way. When all is said and done, your best strategy for commuting from hotel to hotel by road is to use your car or pony up for a cab.

Of the more-isolated resorts, **Wilderness Lodge & Villas** and **Animal Kingdom Lodge & Villas** serve the best food. **Coronado Springs, Port Orleans, Old Key West,** and **Caribbean Beach Resorts** each have a full-service restaurant, and all but Old Key West have a food court and pizza delivery. None of the isolated resorts, however, offer enough variety for the average person to be happy eating in his/her hotel every day. **Pop Century Resort, Art of Animation Resort,** and the **All-Star**

DISNEY RESORT AMENITIES

RESORT	SUITES	CONCIERGE FLOOR	NUMBER OF ROOMS	ROOM SERVICE (full)	FREE IN-ROOM WI-FI	FRIDGE/ MINI-FRIDGE
ALL-STAR RESORTS	•	—	5,406	—	•	•
ANIMAL KINGDOM LODGE	•	•	972	•	•	•
ANIMAL KINGDOM VILLAS	•	•*	458	•	•	•
ART OF ANIMATION RESORT	•	—	1,984	—	•	•
BAY LAKE TOWER	•	—	295	•	•	•
BEACH CLUB VILLAS	•	—	282	•	•	•
BOARDWALK INN	•	•	371	•	•	•
BOARDWALK VILLAS	•	—	532	•	•	•
CARIBBEAN BEACH RESORT	—	—	2,112	—	•	•
CONTEMPORARY RESORT	•	•	655	•	•	•
CORONADO SPRINGS RESORT	•	•	1,915	•	•	•
DOLPHIN	•	—	1,509	•	—	•
FORT WILDERNESS CABINS	—	—	409	—	•	•
GRAND FLORIDIAN RESORT & SPA, VILLAS	•	•	1,067	•	•	•
OLD KEY WEST RESORT	•	—	761	—	•	•
POLYNESIAN VILLAGE, VILLAS, & BUNGALOWS	•	•	866	•	•	•
POP CENTURY RESORT	—	—	2,880	—	•	•
PORT ORLEANS RESORT	—	—	3,056	—	•	•
SARATOGA SPRINGS RESORT & SPA	•	—	1,260	—	•	•
SHADES OF GREEN	•	—	586	•	•	•
SWAN	•	—	758	•	—	•
TREEHOUSE VILLAS	•	—	60	—	•	•
WILDERNESS LODGE & VILLAS	•	•	863	•	•	•
YACHT & BEACH CLUB RESORTS	•	•	1,197	•	•	•

*Jambo House only

Resorts (Disney's most isolated hotel complex) have nearly 10,500 guest rooms and suites, but no full-service restaurants. There are five food courts, but you have to get to them before 11 p.m. in most cases.

7. AMENITIES AND RECREATION Disney resorts offer a staggering variety of amenities and recreational opportunities (see charts above). All provide elaborate swimming pools, themed shops, restaurants or food courts, bars or lounges, and access to four Disney golf courses. The more you pay for your lodging, the more amenities and opportunities are at your disposal. **Animal Kingdom Lodge & Villas, BoardWalk Inn, Wilderness Lodge,** and the **Contemporary, Grand Floridian, Polynesian Village,** and **Yacht & Beach Club Resorts,** for example, all offer concierge floors.

For swimming and sunning, the **Contemporary** and **Bay Lake Tower, Polynesian Village & Villas, Wilderness Lodge & Villas,** and **Grand Floridian & Villas** offer both pools and white-sand nonswimming beaches on Bay Lake or Seven Seas Lagoon. **Caribbean Beach**

DISNEY RESORT RECREATION

RESORT	FITNESS CENTER	WATER SPORTS	MARINA	BEACH	TENNIS	BIKING
ALL-STAR RESORTS	–	–	–	–	–	–
ANIMAL KINGDOM LODGE & VILLAS	•	–	–	–	•*	–
ART OF ANIMATION RESORT	–	–	–	–	–	–
BAY LAKE TOWER	•	•	•	•	•	–
BEACH CLUB VILLAS	•	•	•	•	•	–
BOARDWALK INN	•	–	•	–	•	•
BOARDWALK VILLAS	•	–	•	–	•	•
CARIBBEAN BEACH RESORT	–	–	–	•	–	•
CONTEMPORARY RESORT	•	•	•	•	•	–
CORONADO SPRINGS RESORT	•	–	–	•	–	–
DOLPHIN	•	•	•	•	•	–
FORT WILDERNESS RESORT	–	•	•	•	•	•
GRAND FLORIDIAN RESORT & SPA, VILLAS	•	•	•	•	–	–
OLD KEY WEST RESORT	•	–	•	–	•	•
POLYNESIAN VILLAGE, VILLAS & BUNGALOWS	–	•	•	•	–	–
POP CENTURY RESORT	–	–	–	–	–	–
PORT ORLEANS RESORT	–	–	•	–	–	•
SARATOGA SPRINGS RESORT & SPA, TREEHOUSE VILLAS	•	–	–	–	•	•
SHADES OF GREEN	•	–	–	–	•	–
SWAN	•	–	•	•	•	–
WILDERNESS LODGE & VILLAS	•	•	•	•	–	•
YACHT & BEACH CLUB RESORTS	•	•	•	•	•	–

*Kidani Village only

Resort, the Dolphin, and the Yacht & Beach Club also provide both pools and nonswimming beaches. Though lacking a lakefront beach, Saratoga Springs Resort & Spa, Animal Kingdom Lodge & Villas, Port Orleans and Coronado Springs Resorts, and BoardWalk Inn & Villas have exceptionally creative pools. See the chart on page 139 for our rankings of the swimming facilities at each Disney resort.

Bay Lake and Seven Seas Lagoon are the best venues for boating. Resorts fronting these lakes are the Contemporary and Bay Lake Tower, Polynesian Village & Villas, Wilderness Lodge & Villas, Grand Floridian & Villas, and Fort Wilderness Resort & Campground.

Though on smaller bodies of water, the Dolphin and the Yacht & Beach Club also rent watercraft.

Most convenient for golf are Shades of Green, Saratoga Springs, Old Key West, Contemporary and Bay Lake Tower, Polynesian Village & Villas, Grand Floridian & Villas, and Port Orleans. Tennis is available at the resorts indicated with bullets (•) in the chart on the facing page. Disney resorts with fitness and weight-training facilities are

RESORT	FITNESS-CENTER RATING
1. Saratoga Springs Resort & Spa, Treehouse Villas	★★★★★
2. Grand Floridian Resort & Spa, Villas	★★★★½
3. Animal Kingdom Lodge & Villas	★★★★
4. BoardWalk Inn & Villas	★★★★
5. Yacht & Beach Club Resorts *(shared facility)*	★★★★
6. Contemporary Resort–Bay Lake Tower *(shared facility)*	★★★½
7. Coronado Springs Resort	★★★½
8. Wilderness Lodge & Villas	★★★½
9. Dolphin	★★★
10. Shades of Green	★★★
11. Swan	★★★
12. Old Key West Resort	★½

rated and ranked in the chart above (resorts not listed don't have such facilities).

While there are many places to bike or jog at Disney World (including golf-cart paths), the best biking and jogging are at **Fort Wilderness Resort & Campground** and the adjacent **Wilderness Lodge & Villas. Caribbean Beach Resort** offers a lovely hiking, biking, and jogging trail around the lake. Also good for biking and jogging is the area along Bonnet Creek extending through **Port Orleans** and **Old Key West** toward Disney Springs. Epcot resorts offer a lakefront promenade and bike path, as well as a roadside walkway suitable for jogging. Of the Value resorts, only **Art of Animation** and **Pop Century** have good jogging options.

On-site child-care programs are offered at **Animal Kingdom Lodge & Villas,** the **Dolphin,** the **Hilton Orlando Lake Buena Vista,** the **Polynesian Village & Villas,** the **Swan, Wilderness Lodge & Villas,** and the **Yacht & Beach Club Resorts.** All other resorts offer in-room babysitting (see page 425 for details).

Disney offers free public Wi-Fi at all resorts as well as at the theme parks, water parks, ESPN Wide World of Sports Complex, and several other public areas. The resort Wi-Fi, while free, is occasionally slow and unreliable. Two teens from Dallas groused:

> We wish the "free" Wi-Fi was better. We put free in quotes because the Wi-Fi sucks so much that it's not really free. It costs you the price of the two Advil you have to take trying to get it to work!

The Value resorts seem to have the most Wi-Fi problems, probably because of their high number of guest users compared with other resorts. If you find yourself unable to connect, try configuring your Wi-Fi adapter's wireless-mode setting to **802.11b.**

8. NIGHTLIFE The boardwalk at **BoardWalk Inn & Villas** has an upscale dance club (albeit one that has never lived up to its potential); a club

RESORT	POOL RATING
1. YACHT & BEACH CLUB RESORTS & BEACH CLUB VILLAS (shared complex)	★★★★★
2. GRAND FLORIDIAN RESORT & SPA, VILLAS	★★★★½
3. ANIMAL KINGDOM VILLAS (Kidani Village)	★★★★½
4. SARATOGA SPRINGS RESORT & SPA, TREEHOUSE VILLAS	★★★★½
5. WILDERNESS LODGE & VILLAS	★★★★½
6. ANIMAL KINGDOM LODGE & VILLAS (Jambo House)	★★★★
7. PORT ORLEANS RESORT	★★★★
8. CORONADO SPRINGS RESORT	★★★★
9. DOLPHIN	★★★★
10. POLYNESIAN VILLAGE, VILLAS, & BUNGALOWS	★★★★
11. SWAN	★★★★
12. BAY LAKE TOWER	★★★★
13. CARIBBEAN BEACH RESORT	★★★★
14. BOARDWALK INN & VILLAS	★★★½
15. CONTEMPORARY RESORT	★★★½
16. ALL-STAR RESORTS	★★★
17. ART OF ANIMATION RESORT	★★★
18. OLD KEY WEST RESORT	★★★
19. FORT WILDERNESS RESORT & CAMPGROUND	★★★
20. POP CENTURY RESORT	★★★
21. SHADES OF GREEN	★★★

featuring a live band, dueling pianos, and sing-alongs; a brewpub; and a sports bar. The BoardWalk clubs are within easy walking distance of all Epcot resorts. Most non-Disney hotels in **Disney Springs,** as well as **Saratoga Springs Resort & Spa,** are within walking distance of that area's nightspots. Nightlife at other Disney resorts is limited to lounges that stay open late.

At the Contemporary Resort's **California Grill** and its adjoining lounge, you can relax over dinner or cocktails and watch the *Wishes* fireworks at the nearby Magic Kingdom.

All the Goodies Without the Big Bucks

A Roanoke, Virginia, couple share how they enjoyed Disney's luxury resorts on the cheap:

> One thing I think you should emphasize in your guide is how lovely it is to enjoy the Deluxe resorts without having to pay to stay there. We had a rental car, so it was easy for us to drive to Animal Kingdom Lodge, the Grand Floridian, and Wilderness Lodge for dinner. We allowed enough time before our reservation to explore each resort, have a drink in the bar, and then be shown to our table. We felt very thrifty enjoying these expensive resorts and then going back to our moderately priced resort to sleep.

unofficial **TIP**
The best resort lounges are the DVC-only **Top of the World** at Bay Lake Tower (make friends with an owner for access) and **Victoria Falls** at Animal Kingdom Lodge. Honorable mention goes to the **Territory Lounge** at Wilderness Lodge, where you can sometimes order from the menu of the adjacent Artist Point restaurant.

DISNEY HOTELS: *Complaints and Comparisons*

	SOUND	LIGHTING	PILLOWS	OVERALL
ALL-STAR MOVIES	D	C	C	C–
ALL-STAR MUSIC	A	C	C	B
ALL-STAR SPORTS	A	C	C	B
ANIMAL KINGDOM LODGE & VILLAS (Jambo House)	F	A	B	C+
ANIMAL KINGDOM VILLAS (Kidani Village)	C	C	B	C
ART OF ANIMATION (standard rooms)	C	B	B	B–
ART OF ANIMATION (suites)	B	B+	B	B
BAY LAKE TOWER	A	C	B	B+
BEACH CLUB RESORT & VILLAS	B	C	B	C
BOARDWALK INN	B	C	B	B
BOARDWALK VILLAS	B	C	B	B
CARIBBEAN BEACH RESORT	B	B	B	B
CONTEMPORARY RESORT	D	A	A	B+
CORONADO SPRINGS RESORT	B	B+	B	B
DOLPHIN	A	D	A	B+
FORT WILDERNESS RESORT (cabins)	C	D	D	D
GRAND FLORIDIAN RESORT & SPA	F	A	A	B–
OLD KEY WEST RESORT	A	D	A	B+
POLYNESIAN VILLAGE & VILLAS	F	A	B	C+
POP CENTURY RESORT	B	D	C	C
PORT ORLEANS FRENCH QUARTER	B	C	C	C
PORT ORLEANS RIVERSIDE	A	C	C	B
SARATOGA SPRINGS RESORT & SPA	B	C	B	C
SWAN	A	D	A	B+
TREEHOUSE VILLAS AT SARATOGA SPRINGS RESORT & SPA	A	B	B	B+
WILDERNESS LODGE	F	A	A	B–
WILDERNESS LODGE VILLAS	B	C	B	C
YACHT CLUB RESORT	D	A	A	B+

RESEARCHING WALT DISNEY WORLD HOTELS

THE *UNOFFICIAL GUIDE* HOTEL TEAM inspects hundreds of hotel rooms each year throughout North America and stays abreast of current trends and issues in the lodging industry. One such issue is the list of frequent complaints hotel guests make regarding their rooms. Over the years, the most common complaints have included excessive noise, uncomfortable beds, poor lighting, outdated furnishings, and substandard towels. Because these complaints are ongoing concerns, the hotel team undertook a complete reevaluation of every Walt Disney World resort (including the **Swan** and **Dolphin**) in each of these areas.

In the Lab with Dr. Fluffy

Our tests included everything from the quality of the bed linens to the age of the mattresses to the fluffiness (loft) of the pillows. While evaluation criteria for linens and mattresses are fairly well known, we couldn't find any standard test to measure pillow fluffiness. A search of *Consumer Reports*' website failed to find anything, and fear of another restraining order kept us from making all the phone calls to the magazine that we wanted. So we had to invent our own.

The method we came up with is based on measuring how far a half-filled gallon jug of water sank into the middle of a pillow. (Two quarts of water weigh between one-third and one-half as much as a typical human head, according to most estimates. Also, a gallon jug is easy to find, and no one thinks twice if you bring one into a hotel lobby. Not so with a replica of a human head—trust us.)

Key to this experiment was determining the proper range of support a good pillow should provide. A test bottle that sank too deep into a pillow would indicate not enough support; on the other hand, a bottle that sank very little might indicate an experience akin to sleeping on a brick. We therefore evaluated a wide range of pillows before the test to establish the proper range of support.

The best pillows are found at the non-Disney-owned **Swan** and **Dolphin** resorts. It's probably no coincidence that they're made with goose feathers and down; Disney's Deluxes use down, too, while the rest use polyester fiberfill. Decent pillows are found at the **Grand Floridian, Contemporary, Wilderness Lodge & Villas,** and **Old Key West.** The pillows at the Value resorts are better than they were a few years ago, but certainly nothing you'd want to buy for home.

Mattresses at all the Walt Disney World resorts come from brand-name manufacturers such as Sealy and Simmons. Value resorts typically have either two full-size mattresses or one king; Moderate and Deluxe resorts have two queen beds (each about 20% larger than a full) or one king. Exceptions are found at two Moderates: **Fort Wilderness Cabins,** which use full mattresses, and **Caribbean Beach,** which has upgraded its rooms from full mattresses to queens, with some rooms featuring an additional Murphy bed. Another notable exception is the **Swan,** which uses Westin's aptly named Heavenly Bed mattresses. Throughout the resorts, almost all the mattresses we inspected were less than 2 years old, and about half were less than a year old. The oldest mattress we found on Disney property—in service for 8 years—was at Disney's **Fort Wilderness Cabins.** (Outside Disney, we've seen 17-year-old mattresses still in use.)

Disney's Value and Moderate resorts use the same brand of 180-thread-count sheets for their bed linens. Disney's Deluxe and DDV resorts and the independent **Swan** and **Dolphin** resorts all use 250-thread-count sheets or better.

unofficial **TIP** Many hotel air-conditioner systems have motion sensors that turn off the AC while you're sleeping. See **tinyurl.com /ac-override** for instructions on how to turn off the sensor.

Pipe Down Out There

Noisy rooms rank near the top of hotel guests' complaints every year. A well-designed room blocks both the noise coming from an adjacent room's television and from the swimming pool across the resort. Based on our initial tests of both interior and exterior soundproofing, and for the reasons outlined on the following page, we believe that a room's exterior door is the critical component in keeping sound out.

Chris Eliopoulos

Our test equipment consisted of a digital sound meter, a portable CD player, and a copy of The Who's greatest hits. We first calibrated the volume of the CD player until Roger Daltrey's ear-piercing wail in "Baba O'Riley" reached 70 decibels on the sound meter. Next, we took the CD player outside the room and placed the meter on top of the pillow of the bed closest to the exterior door. We replayed "Baba O'Riley" and recorded the decibel reading on the sound meter. For good measure, we also recorded the sound level in the room with and without the AC running, and around the resort in general.

Surprisingly, six of the seven worst results came from Disney Deluxe resorts, with **Animal Kingdom Lodge (Jambo House)**, the **Grand Floridian**, the **Polynesian Village**, and **Wilderness Lodge Villas** making up the bottom four. Eight hotels earned top marks: **All-Star Music**, **All-Star Sports**, **Bay Lake Tower**, the **Dolphin**, **Old Key West Resort**, **Port Orleans Riverside Resort**, the **Swan**, and **Treehouse Villas**. In addition to the Deluxe resorts mentioned previously, the **Contemporary** and **Wilderness Lodge** were near the bottom, along with the Value **All-Star Movies Resort**. (The new **Polynesian Villas & Bungalows** weren't yet open at the time of our research.)

Overall, Value and Moderate resorts did much better than Deluxe resorts when it came to blocking out exterior noise, with Disney's All-Star Music and All-Star Sports, both Value resorts, being the overall winners. That certainly runs counter to what consumers would expect, so we set about trying to find an explanation. Like any good detective, we looked for an economic motive first.

The explanation turns out to be fairly simple, and it does come down to money—Disney's money. At most Disney Value and Moderate resorts (and, notably, Disney Vacation Club resorts), each room's exterior door opens onto the great outdoors, just as the average home's exterior door opens to the outside world. These exterior doors must have extensive weather stripping to keep out wind and rain. Also, exterior-facing walls tend to be thicker and better insulated than interior walls, as these measures reduce Disney's costs to heat and cool the rooms. Such walls also work really well at blocking noise.

In contrast, Disney's Deluxe rooms typically have doors that open onto an interior hallway that Disney is already paying to heat and cool. Thus, there's little economic incentive for Disney to put the same materials into the outward-facing doors and walls of some Deluxe resorts, since the temperature range outside the room is relatively constant and there's no need to keep rain or wind out. (In fact, many Deluxe resorts have a small gap of ¼–¾ inch at the bottom of their doors to aid in getting fresh air *into* the rooms.) Unfortunately, this permits more sound to enter. Finally, the interior hallways themselves can function as giant echo chambers, allowing sounds to bounce off the walls back and forth, up and down the hallway. Not so at the other resorts, where many sounds bounce off an exterior wall and out into space.

Room soundproofing, however, is only half of the story. The other half, as any good real estate agent knows, is location; despite the resort's relatively good performance, a pool-view room at All-Star Sports is likely to pick up a lot more noise than an upper-floor corner room at the Grand Floridian, because the former faces a heavily used public space. So our next task was to determine the amount of external noise affecting every single room at Walt Disney World.

We assigned *Unofficial Guide* researcher Rich Vosburgh to the task. Using a combination of resort maps, aerial photography, and a whole lot of old-fashioned legwork, Rich created an External Noise Potential metric for each hotel room on Disney property, taking into account factors including the floor level, pedestrian traffic, proximity to public spaces, and number of nearby hotel rooms. Finally, the research team revisited every building in every resort to verify our rankings.

For the most part, we were spot on. But there were a couple of surprises that we're sure we would've overlooked had we not reviewed every single room. For example, the northwest-facing rooms in Buildings 4 and 5 of Disney's **All-Star Music** resort are situated well away from most public spaces in the resort and overlook the extreme end of a parking lot. There's not a lot of pedestrian traffic around, and the rooms themselves tested well for soundproofing—hey, these should be some quiet rooms, right? Well, when we visited the resort, we discovered that this particular section of parking lot, because it was away from most guest rooms, is where Disney decides to warm up its diesel buses in the morning before servicing the three All-Star Resorts. At 6 a.m., the area around these buildings sounded like Daytona International Speedway on race day.

Our research indicates that quiet rooms can be found in almost any resort. For readers who put peace and quiet at the top of their list, we've listed the 12 quietest spots among all WDW resorts in the chart below.

QUIETEST ROOMS IN WALT DISNEY WORLD
ALL-STAR MUSIC Buildings 5 and 6, rooms facing west
ALL-STAR SPORTS Building 3, rooms facing west; Building 2, rooms facing north
BAY LAKE TOWER Any room is good here—rooms are the quietest in WDW
BEACH CLUB Easternmost hallways, rooms facing east
BEACH CLUB VILLAS Rooms facing southeast
BOARDWALK INN All rooms facing courtyard, just east of main lobby
CARIBBEAN BEACH Trinidad South, Buildings 35 and 38, rooms facing lake; Barbados, Buildings 11 and 12, facing south
PORT ORLEANS RIVERSIDE Alligator Bayou, Buildings 26 and 28, rooms facing east; Acadian House, north wings, rooms facing west
PORT ORLEANS FRENCH QUARTER Building 1, rooms facing water; Building 7, north wing, rooms facing water; Building 6, north wing, rooms facing water
TREEHOUSE VILLAS Any room is good
WILDERNESS LODGE Middle of northernmost wing, rooms facing northwest (woods)
WILDERNESS LODGE VILLAS Southernmost part of the building, water-view rooms facing east

Let There Be Light

As with noise, poor lighting generally ranks near the top of hotel guests' complaints. Of particular concern is the lighting in the bathroom and grooming area, the head of the bed (for reading), and the desk or table area (for working). In fact, lighting here is so important that professional associations publish standards listing the minimum amount of lighting needed for each area. Our evaluations incorporate the standards and recommendations of the Illuminating Engineering Society of North America (IESNA), a leading institution for lighting research, technology, and its applications.

Our test equipment was an industrial-grade digital light meter, able to detect a wide range of light levels. In addition to testing the lighting at the grooming, desk, and bed areas, we also tested the bath/shower area, the armchair or sitting area (if the room had one), and the overall light level in the room. The results were weighted to emphasize the quality of light in the grooming, desk, and bed areas.

The rooms with the best lighting were found at **Animal Kingdom Lodge & Villas (Jambo House),** the **Contemporary,** the **Grand Floridian,** the **Polynesian Village,** and **Wilderness Lodge & Villas,** all Deluxe resorts. **Coronado Springs** was the highest-scoring Moderate resort. No Value resort posted acceptable scores in lighting.

Rooms at the Polynesian Village exceeded the IESNA's minimum recommendations in every area, and the Contemporary's rooms exceeded the recommendations in all except the armchair reading area. Disney seems to be giving special attention to room lighting when doing its resort rehabs, and it's paying off. (Rooms at the **Polynesian Villas & Bungalows** weren't yet open at the time of our research.)

Outside the Contemporary and Polynesian Village, the **Caribbean Beach** and **Grand Floridian** scored high with their grooming-and-bath-area lighting, while the **Wilderness Lodge Villas** and **Coronado Springs** had the best lighting in the desk/work area, with Coronado Springs using a specially designed ceiling lamp to ensure bright work surfaces; and **Wilderness Lodge** and **Port Orleans Riverside** had the best bed lighting. The worst scores were recorded at the **BoardWalk Inn,** the **Swan, Pop Century Resort,** and the **Yacht Club Resort.** How bad is the lighting? Rooms this dim are fertile ground for Barry White music as you gear up for sexy times with your sweetie.

Check-in and Checkout

Up to 60 days before you arrive, you can log on to **mydisneyreservation .com** to complete the check-in process, make room requests and Fast-Pass+ reservations, choose MagicBands, and note events such as birthdays and anniversaries you're celebrating during your trip. Depending on how much information you provide to the site before your trip, your resort check-in can be eliminated or streamlined considerably:

DIRECT-TO-ROOM CHECK-IN If you select your MagicBands and provide the website with a credit card number, a PIN for purchases, and your arrival and departure times, Disney will send you an e-mail or text confirmation that your check-in is complete. Next, Disney will e-mail or text you with your room number a few hours before you arrive at your resort, allowing you to go straight to your room without stopping at the front desk.

ONLINE CHECK-IN If you've checked in online but you haven't added a credit card or PIN to your account, or you don't have MagicBands, you'll still be able to bypass the regular check-in desk and head for the Online Check-In Desk to finish the check-in process. *Procrastinators, take note:* Online check-in should be completed at least 24 hours before you arrive; using your smartphone to check in online as you saunter up to the resort won't work.

If you're unable to check in online before your trip, don't worry. Disney has spent a lot of time and effort on reengineering the check-in process, cutting the average wait significantly. At the Value resorts, such as All-Star Sports, which get lots of tour and sports-team traffic, Disney has separate check-in areas for those groups, leaving the huge main check-in desk free for regular travelers. A cast member also roams the lobby and can issue an "all hands on deck" alert when lines develop.

The arrival of a busload of guests can sometimes overwhelm the front desk of Deluxe resorts, which have smaller front desks and fewer agents, but this is the exception rather than the rule.

If your room is unavailable when you arrive, Disney will either give you a phone number to call to check on the room or will offer to call or send a text message to your cell phone when it's ready.

A Cleveland mom shares her family's strategy for being content until their room is ready:

> My husband and I can't believe how people complain about the downtime people have while waiting for their room to be ready. We pack our swimsuits and sunscreen in our carry-ons. We arrive, check in, and leave our cell number for a text when the room is ready and head to the pool. By the time it's ready, we're rarin' to go!

Checking out is a snap. Your bill will be prepared and e-mailed, affixed to your doorknob, or slipped under your door the night before you leave. If everything is in order, you have only to pack up and depart. If there's a problem with your bill, however, you'll have to resolve it at the front desk, where the previous order of most efficient to least efficient is a good gauge of the probable hassle you're in for.

UNOFFICIAL GUIDE READERS SPEAK OUT

MANY READERS SHARE with us their experiences and criticisms regarding Disney hotels through our survey questionnaire (at **touringplans.com/walt-disney-world/survey**). Some copy us on letters of complaint sent to Disney. If you've written or copied us about a bad experience, you might be surprised that we haven't quoted your letter. Any business can have a bad day, even a Disney hotel, and a single incident might not be indicative of the hotel's general level of quality and service. In our experience, if a problem is endemic the same complaint will usually surface in a number of letters. But even with our voluminous reader mail, your comments often paint a mixed picture. For instance, for every letter we get that's critical of the Grand Floridian, it's not unusual for us to receive another letter telling us it's the best place the reader ever stayed.

READERS' 2015 DISNEY RESORT REPORT CARD

RESORT
ALL-STAR MOVIES
ALL-STAR MUSIC
ALL-STAR SPORTS
ANIMAL KINGDOM LODGE
ANIMAL KINGDOM VILLAS
ART OF ANIMATION RESORT
BAY LAKE TOWER
BEACH CLUB RESORT
BEACH CLUB VILLAS
BOARDWALK INN
BOARDWALK VILLAS
CARIBBEAN BEACH RESORT
CONTEMPORARY RESORT
CORONADO SPRINGS RESORT
DOLPHIN
FORT WILDERNESS CABINS
GRAND FLORIDIAN RESORT & SPA
OLD KEY WEST RESORT
POLYNESIAN VILLAGE RESORT*
POP CENTURY RESORT
PORT ORLEANS FRENCH QUARTER
PORT ORLEANS RIVERSIDE
SARATOGA SPRINGS RESORT & SPA
SHADES OF GREEN
SWAN
TREEHOUSE VILLAS
WILDERNESS LODGE
WILDERNESS LODGE VILLAS
YACHT CLUB RESORT
AVERAGE FOR DISNEY HOTELS
AVERAGE FOR OFF-SITE HOTELS

Polynesian Villas & Bungalows too new to rate

We tend to hear more often from readers when things go badly than when things go well. Whether your experience was positive or negative, we encourage you to share it with us. The more comments we receive, the more accurate and complete a picture we can provide.

READERS' 2015 DISNEY RESORT REPORT CARD

EACH YEAR, SEVERAL THOUSAND READERS send in their responses to our reader surveys. Found on the table above, the Resort Report Card documents their opinions of the Disney resorts as well as the Swan, the Dolphin, and Shades of Green. **Room quality** reflects readers' satisfaction with their rooms, while **Check-in efficiency**

ROOM QUALITY	CHECK-IN EFFICIENCY	QUIETNESS OF ROOM	SHUTTLE SERVICE	POOL	STAFF	DINING	OVERALL RATING
C	B	B–	B	B	A	C	B
B	B	B	B	B	B+	C	B
B	B	B–	B–	B	B+	C	B
B	B	B	C	A	A	C	B
B	A	B	B	B	A	C+	B+
B+	A	B	B+	B	A	C+	B+
A	B	B	B	B	A	C	B
B	B	C+	B	A	A	B+	B
B	A	A	B	A–	B	B	B
B	A	B–	B+	B	A	C	B
B	A	B	B–	C+	A	F	B
C	B	B	B–	B	B	D	B–
B+	B	B–	B	B–	B	B–	B
B	B–	B	B	B	B	D	B–
B+	A	A	C	A	B	D	B
B	B+	A	B–	A	A	C–	B
B	B	B	B	B	B	C	B
B	B	B	B	B	B	F	B
A	A	B	B+	B	A	D	B
C	B	C	B+	B	A–	C	B
B+	B+	B+	B+	B	A	C	B
B	B	B	B	B	B	C	B
A	B	A	C	B	A	C	B
A	C	A	F	C	B	D	B
A	B–	B	B–	C+	B+	C	B
A–	A–	B–	B	A	A–	D–	B
B	A	B–	B–	B+	A	B–	B
B	B	A	B–	A–	A	C+	B
B	B	B	B–	A	A	F	B
B	**B**	**B**	**B–**	**B**	**B+**	**C**	**B**
B	C+	B	F	C	B	F	B

rates the speed and ease of check-in. **Quietness of room** measures how well, in the guests' perception, their rooms are insulated from external noise. **Shuttle service** rates Disney bus, boat, and/or monorail service to and from the hotels. **Pool** reflects reader satisfaction with the resorts' swimming pools. **Staff** measures the friendliness and helpfulness of the resort's employees, and **Dining** rates resorts' overall food value.

Readers have ranked Disney resorts about the same over the past four years, with most properties receiving an overall B rating. Also for a fourth consecutive year, bus transportation and dining options are the areas where Disney scores lowest. Check-in efficiency is an area where they do better than most. Off-site hotels are, on average, rated slightly lower than Disney hotels, with problems noted in food courts and transportation. Disney has also reopened its ratings lead over off-site hotels, which had dropped during the recession.

Putting It All Together:
Reader Picks for Best and Worst Resorts

Deluxe and DDV resorts generally rank higher than other Disney hotels in our annual survey, and this edition is no exception. Apparently, a woodsy theme helps: Readers rated **Wilderness Lodge, Wilderness Lodge Villas,** and **Fort Wilderness Cabins** highly across our surveys. The **Beach Club Villas** also scored well. **Treehouse Villas at Saratoga Springs** was the lowest-scoring resort in this category—its lack of on-site dining dissatisfies many readers, and it does much worse than average on our "Would you stay here again?" and "Would you recommend this hotel to a friend?" questions.

WOULD YOU RECOMMEND THIS HOTEL TO A FRIEND?	
RESORT NAME	definitely recommend
Fort Wilderness Cabins	100%
Polynesian Village Resort	97%
Dolphin	96%
All-Star Movies	95%
Wilderness Lodge Villas	95%
Port Orleans French Quarter	94%
Animal Kingdom Lodge	93%
Contemporary Resort	93%
Animal Kingdom Villas	91%
Beach Club Villas	91%
Old Key West	91%
Wilderness Lodge	91%
Yacht Club Resort	91%
Art of Animation	90%
Beach Club Resort	90%
BoardWalk Inn	90%
BoardWalk Villas	89%
Port Orleans Riverside	88%
Shades of Green	88%
Grand Floridian Resort	87%
Bay Lake Tower	86%
All-Star Music	84%
Saratoga Springs Resort	82%
Coronado Springs Resort	76%
All-Star Sports	75%
Pop Century Resort	75%
Swan	75%
Caribbean Beach Resort	65%
Treehouse Villas	52%
Average for WDW hotels	**84%**
Average for off-site hotels	**91%**

WOULD YOU STAY AT THIS HOTEL AGAIN?	
RESORT NAME	would stay again
Beach Club Villas	100%
BoardWalk Inn	100%
Fort Wilderness Cabins	100%
Wilderness Lodge Villas	100%
Wilderness Lodge	98%
Dolphin	96%
Bay Lake Tower	95%
Grand Floridian Resort	95%
Contemporary Resort	94%
Polynesian Village Resort	94%
Shades of Green	94%
Art of Animation	92%
Beach Club Resort	92%
Port Orleans French Quarter	92%
Animal Kingdom Villas	91%
Port Orleans Riverside	91%
Yacht Club Resort	91%
All-Star Movies	89%
All-Star Music	89%
Animal Kingdom Lodge	89%
BoardWalk Villas	89%
Swan	86%
Old Key West	82%
Saratoga Springs Resort	82%
Pop Century Resort	79%
Coronado Springs Resort	76%
All-Star Sports	75%
Caribbean Beach Resort	73%
Treehouse Villas	52%
Average for WDW hotels	**84%**
Average for off-site hotels	**94%**

UNOFFICIAL PICKS FOR DISNEY ON-SITE RESORTS
ADULTS
Value: Pop Century For the nostalgic decor
Moderate: Coronado Springs For a bit of sophistication at reasonable rates
Deluxe: Swan and Dolphin For a great location, lots of adult-oriented restaurants nearby, and lower rates than the other Crescent Lake resorts
GROUPS OF FIVE OR MORE
Value: Art of Animation Newest suites with two baths
Moderate: Port Orleans Riverside One or two connecting rooms in Alligator Bayou
Deluxe: Old Key West Two-bedroom villa (booked with DVC rental points)
FAMILIES WITH YOUNG KIDS
Value: Art of Animation Kids will delight in the architecture and themed pools.
Moderate: Caribbean Beach Like a beach vacation while you're at Disney
Deluxe: Animal Kingdom Lodge Fantastic interactive and educational programs. *Alternate:* **Polynesian Village** after construction is finished in 2016.
FAMILIES WITH OLDER KIDS
Value: Pop Century A lively pool scene means meeting new friends. Very teen-friendly food court, with Art of Animation's within walking distance..
Moderate: Fort Wilderness There's plenty of opportunity for independent exploration of this massive resort, and having a kitchen means you don't have to take out a second mortgage to feed the bottomless pits of teen stomachs.
Deluxe: Yacht & Beach Club For Stormalong Bay and easy access to Epcot and Disney's Hollywood Studios

After Fort Wilderness Cabins, **Port Orleans French Quarter** was the next highest-rated Moderate resort, with **Caribbean Beach** the lowest. Among Disney's Value resorts, **Art of Animation** scored highest and **Pop Century** scored lowest.

As in years past, readers tended to be tougher than the *Unofficial Guide* hotel inspectors when it came to ratings. (For example, we really prefer Pop Century to the All-Stars.) But remember that readers are rating one guest room during a specific visit, while our inspectors provide a comparative rating of more than 250 Disney and non-Disney hotels in and around Walt Disney World. For our ratings, see How the Hotels Compare, on pages 272–276.

WALT DISNEY WORLD HOTEL PROFILES

FOR THOSE OF YOU WHO'VE PLOWED through the foregoing and remain undecided, here are our profiles of each Disney resort. For photos, video, and up-to-date information on the Walt Disney World resorts, check out our website, **touringplans.com.**

THE MAGIC KINGDOM RESORTS

Disney's Grand Floridian Resort & Spa

(See **tinyurl.com/ug-grandfloridian** *for extended coverage.)*

GRAND FLORIDIAN RESORT & SPA, GRAND FLORIDIAN VILLAS

STRENGTHS	WEAKNESSES
• Low guest-to-staff ratio	• Most expensive WDW resort
• Excellent dining options for adults	• Self-parking is across the street
• Large rooms with day beds	• Public areas often blocked by wedding parties
• Very good on-site spa	
• Fantastic kids' *Alice in Wonderland*–themed splash area	• Only one on-site restaurant suitable for younger children
• Boat and monorail transportation to the Magic Kingdom	• Close to ongoing construction at Polynesian Village through early 2016
• Diverse recreational options	• Bus transportation to DHS, Animal Kingdom, water parks, and Disney Springs is shared by the other monorail resorts
• Close to Palm, Magnolia, and Oak Trail Golf Courses	

WALT DISNEY WORLD'S FLAGSHIP HOTEL is inspired by Florida's grand Victorian seaside resorts. A complex of four- and five-story white frame buildings, the Grand Floridian integrates verandas, intricate latticework, dormers, and turrets beneath a red-shingle roof to capture the most memorable elements of 19th-century ocean-resort architecture. Covering 40 acres along Seven Seas Lagoon, the Grand Floridian offers lovely pools, white-sand beaches, and a multifaceted marina.

The 867 guest rooms, with wood trim and soft goods (curtains, linens, towels, and the like) in tones of deep red, gold, and tan, are luxurious, though we think the mocha-colored walls are a little dark at night. The woodwork, marble-topped sinks, and ceiling fans amplify the Victorian theme. Large by any standard, the typical room is 440 square feet (dormer rooms are smaller) and furnished with two queen beds, a daybed, a reading chair, and a small desk with chair. Many rooms have a balcony. All rooms have a coffeemaker and a large dresser–TV stand with mini-fridge.

Bathrooms are large, with plenty of counter space and fluffy towels. Two shelves under the sink provide a small amount of storage. A 1,500-watt, wall-mounted hair dryer is provided, but it's not very powerful; bring your own if you have lots of hair. Water pressure in the shower is average—probably less than what you get at home but still enough to rinse out shampoo.

A separate dressing area next to the bathroom includes two sinks and enough counter space to fit most of your toiletries. The dressing area includes a sliding door that separates it from the sleeping area. Combined with the bathroom, this means that three people can get dressed at the same time.

With a high ratio of staff to guests, service is outstanding. The resort has several full-service restaurants, and others are a short monorail ride away. The hotel is connected directly to the Magic Kingdom by monorail and to other Disney World destinations by bus. Walking time to the monorail and bus-loading areas from the most remote guest rooms is about 7–10 minutes.

The Grand Floridian's **Senses Spa,** modeled after Disney Cruise Line's, is one of the best in the Orlando area (see our review in Part Twenty). The resort's pools are among the nicest on Disney property.

Grand Floridian Resort & Spa & Grand Floridian Villas

The Courtyard Pool, large enough that local waterfowl mistake it for a lake, has a zero-entry ramp for small children to splash in. Cabanas are available to rent here, too. An *Alice in Wonderland*–themed splash area sits between the Grand Flo's main building and the Villas. If your kids like water and their college fund is paid up, this is the place to be.

The rest of the Grand Floridian's grounds are maintained to a very high standard. It's a lovely resort to walk around during the evening, with romantic light levels and charming background music. A stroll from the Grand Flo's marina, past the resort's main buildings, and over to the Polynesian for a nightcap is a nice way to end the evening.

Most reader comments concerning the Grand Floridian are positive. First, from a Durham, North Carolina, mother of two preschoolers:

> *The Grand Floridian pool with the waterslide was a big hit with our kids. They also loved taking the boat across the lagoon to return from the Magic Kingdom.*

GOOD (AND NOT-SO-GOOD) ROOMS AT THE GRAND FLORIDIAN *(See* **tinyurl.com/gfroomviews** *for photos.)* The resort is spread over a peninsula jutting into Seven Seas Lagoon. In addition to the main building, there are five dispersed rectangular buildings. Most rooms have a balcony, and most balconies are enclosed by a rail that affords good visibility. Dormer rooms, just beneath the roof in each building, have smaller enclosed balconies that limit visibility when you're seated. Most dormer rooms, however, have vaulted ceilings and a coziness that compensates for the less-desirable balconies.

If you want to be near the bus and monorail, most of the restaurants, and shopping, ask for a room in the main building (all concierge rooms). The best rooms are 4322–4329 and 4422–4429, which have full balconies and overlook the lagoon in the direction of the beach and the Polynesian Village. (*Note:* You'll be seeing a lot of the Polynesian Village's construction work through 2015.) Other excellent main-building rooms are 4401–4409, with full balconies overlooking the marina and an unobstructed view of Cinderella Castle across the lagoon.

Of the five lodges, three—Conch Key, Boca Chica, and Big Pine Key—have one long side facing the lagoon and the other facing inner courtyards and swimming pools. At Conch Key, full-balcony rooms 7229–7231, 7328, 7329, 7331, and 7425–7431 (except 7430) offer vistas across the lagoon to the Magic Kingdom and castle. Room 7427 is just about perfect. Less-expensive rooms in the same building that offer good marina views are 7212, 7312, 7412–7415, 7417, 7419, 7421, 7513–7515, and 7517. (Grand Floridian room numbers are coded. Take room 7213: 7 is the building number, 2 is the floor, and 13 is the room number.) In Boca Chica and Big Pine Key, ask for a lagoon-view room on the first, second, or third floor. Many garden-view rooms in Big Pine Key, and a few in Boca Chica, have views obstructed by a poolside building. These are the worst views from any Grand Floridian room.

The two remaining buildings, Sugar Loaf Key (concierge only) and Sago Key, face each other across the marina. The opposite side of Sugar Loaf Key faces a courtyard, while the other side of Sago Key faces a finger of the lagoon and a forested area. These views are pleasant but not in the same league as those from the rooms listed previously. Exceptions are end rooms in Sago Key that have a view of the lagoon and Cinderella Castle (rooms 5139, 5144, 5145, 5242–5245, and 5342–5345).

THE VILLAS AT DISNEY'S GRAND FLORIDIAN RESORT & SPA (See **tinyurl .com/ug-gfvillas** for extended coverage.) This Disney Deluxe Villa property opened in fall 2013. The 200-room T-shaped building sits with the main hotel along the shore of Seven Seas Lagoon. The Villas offer studio, one-, two-, and three-bedroom accommodations that sleep 5–12 adults; among DDV resorts, the studios were among the first to accommodate a maximum of 5.

Decorated in neutral tones with mostly green accents, rooms are the nicest of any DDV property. Most have vaulted living-room ceilings and faux-wood balconies or porches. Those balconies stretch the entire length of the room, giving everyone enough space for a good view.

The studios have a kitchenette with mini-refrigerator, sink, and coffeemaker, while the larger rooms have full kitchens. Those feature a stainless-steel oven range, with the dishwasher and refrigerator tucked behind white-wood panels that match the glass door cabinets. Other amenities in the full kitchens include a full-size coffeemaker, a toaster, frying pans, and the usual set of plates, glasses, cups, and cutlery. Also in the kitchen are a banquette seat and table with room for six.

The living room has a sofa that seats three comfortably, an upholstered chair and ottoman, a coffee table, and a large, flat-panel television. The sofa converts into a bed that sleeps two; a cabinet below the TV hides a small pulldown bed. We'd use these for kids, not adults.

Studio rooms have a queen bed in addition to the folding options listed above. One-bedroom villas have a king bed plus the folding options; two-bedroom villas have a king mattress in one bedroom and two queen mattresses in the other, plus the folding options; the Grand Villa's third bedroom has an additional two queen mattresses.

The one- and two-bedroom units and the Grand Villa bedrooms include a large writing desk, a flat-panel TV with DVD player, two nightstands with convenient electric plugs, and a side chair. They've also got large walk-in closets.

Bathrooms are large, with marble tile and, yes, flat-panel TVs built into the mirrors. Studio bathrooms have a separate toilet and shower area; in the one-bedroom configuration, a tub and dressing area sit adjacent to the bedroom. The bathroom and shower are connected by a pocket door, allowing two groups of people to get dressed at the same time. The tiled shower looks as if it could comfortably hold eight people should the need arise. (We're not kidding—it's large enough that if you stand right outside and yell "Echo!," it'll echo.)

The Villas have their own parking lot next to the building, but no on-site dining. Within walking distance, however, are the restaurants of both the main Grand Floridian and the Polynesian Village, giving you a bit more variety than other Magic Kingdom resorts. Room service is available from the Grand Floridian's in-room dining menu. Rates are high, as you might expect, but renting Disney Vacation Club points helps in that regard.

GOOD (AND NOT-SO-GOOD) ROOMS AT THE GRAND FLORIDIAN VILLAS *(See* **tinyurl.com/gfroomviews** *for photos.)* Rooms 1X14, 1X16, and 1X18 face the Magic Kingdom and have views of Space Mountain and the castle and fireworks; 1X14 has probably the best views of any room in all of the Villas. (X indicates a floor number.)

Even-numbered rooms 1X02–1X12 face west, toward the Polynesian Village and Seven Seas Lagoon, and have a good view of the nightly water pageant as it floats by. Until the Polynesian Village refurb is done in 2016, however, construction equipment and unfinished buildings will be a part of the views from these rooms.

Rooms 1X15, 1X17, 1X19–1X22, 1X24, 1X26, and 1X28 face Disney's Wedding Pavilion, the parking lot, the monorail, and landscaping. Odd-numbered rooms 1X03–1X13 and 1X25, 1X27, and 1X29 look out onto the pool facilities and landscaping.

Disney's Polynesian Village Resort, Villas, & Bungalows
(See **tinyurl.com/ug-poly** *for extended coverage.)*

SOUTH PACIFIC TROPICS ARE RE-CREATED at this Deluxe resort, which currently consists of two- and three-story Hawaiian "longhouses" situated around the four-story Great Ceremonial House. Buildings

POLYNESIAN VILLAGE RESORT, VILLAS, & BUNGALOWS

STRENGTHS	
• Most family-friendly dining on the monorail loop	• Close to Palm, Magnolia, and Oak Trail Golf Courses
• Fun South Seas theme	**WEAKNESSES**
• On-site child care	• Ongoing DVC/DDV construction through at least winter 2015
• Boat and monorail transportation to the Magic Kingdom	• No spa or exercise facilities (guests must use those at the Grand Floridian)
• Walking distance to Epcot monorail	• Bus transportation to DHS, Animal Kingdom, water parks, and Disney Springs is shared with the other monorail resorts
• Among the best club levels of the Deluxe resorts	

feature wood tones, with exposed-beam roofs and tribal-inspired geometric inlays in the cornices. The Great Ceremonial House contains restaurants, shops, and an atrium lobby with slate floors and many species of tropical plants. Spread across 39 acres along Seven Seas Lagoon, the resort has three white-sand beaches, some with volleyball courts. Its pool complex likewise captures the South Pacific theme. The Polynesian Village has no on-site fitness center, but its guests are welcome at the Grand Floridian's facilities, a short quarter-mile walk or 2-minute monorail ride away. Landscaping is superb—garden-view rooms are generally superior to garden- or standard-view rooms at other resorts.

The Polynesian Village's Moorea, Tokelau, and Pago Pago buildings are moving into Disney's time-share program. Rooms here will be remodeled to studio accommodations with kitchenettes.

The Polynesian Village construction should last through at least winter 2015. These various projects affect the entire resort, including parking, check-in, restaurants, pools, beaches, child-care facilities, and more. When the remodel is finished, the Polynesian Village will have fewer than 500 standard hotel rooms. If you haven't been to the Polynesian before, we recommend not booking a stay until the construction is done. A good resource for news and updates is **tikimanpages .com,** run by longtime *Unofficial Guide* friend Steve Seifert.

Along with the Polynesian DVC construction came a new bar called Trader Sam's. Modeled after the very successful lounge of the same name at the Disneyland Hotel in California, Sam's menu includes tasty mixed drinks and appetizers, plus interactive artwork, props, and "artifacts" stuffed into every available inch of space.

Although the Polynesian Village is one of Disney's oldest resorts, periodic refurbishments keep it well maintained. Refurbishments in 2013 included new paint, carpet, headboards, soft goods, and bathroom designs for all rooms.

Most rooms have two queen beds, a sofa, a reading chair, and a large dresser with a built-in flat-panel TV cabinet. A mini-fridge and coffeemaker sit between two large closets near the doorway and opposite the bathroom area. The dresser includes two horizontal shelves above and below the TV for extra storage capacity. The closets are spacious and light. Lighting throughout the room, including that for the desk and beds, is among the best on Disney property.

Polynesian Village Resort, Villas, & Bungalows

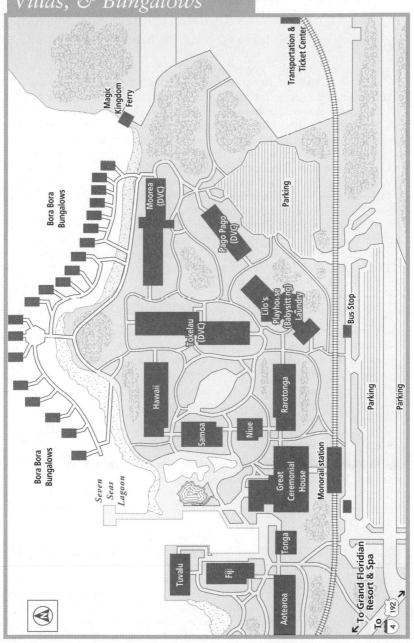

Transportation & Ticket Center

Magic Kingdom Ferry

Bora Bora Bungalows

Moorea (DVC)

Pago Pago (DVC)

Parking

Tokelau (DVC)

Lilo's Playhouse (Babysitting)

Laundry

Bus Stop

Hawaii

Rarotonga

Samoa

Niue

Bora Bora Bungalows

Seven Seas Lagoon

Great Ceremonial House

Monorail station

Parking

Parking

Tonga

Tuvalu

Fiji

Aotearoa

To Grand Floridian Resort & Spa

To 4 192

Seafoam–colored walls are offset by the dark wood of the desk and beds and by lighter woods used as accents on the remaining furniture. The color scheme is brightened by the use of white bed comforters. Woven straw headboards and carved wood tikis provide texture throughout the room.

King beds were added to some rooms in Fiji, Rarotonga, and Samoa. These can be booked directly through Disney's website or by phone. All are categorized as garden-view rooms.

The Poly's bathroom design is among our favorites in Walt Disney World, even if they're on the small side. Two large sinks offer plenty of counter space. A spacious bath and shower (with curved shower rod) provides plenty of room, with good water pressure. And the bathroom's cool tile floor feels great on your feet after a long day in the parks. The sink and shower share a door to separate them from the rest of the room. While that makes the bathroom area feel larger, it means that only two people can get ready at the same time.

Easily accessible by monorail are full-service restaurants at the Grand Floridian and Contemporary Resorts, as well as restaurants in the Magic Kingdom. The Polynesian Village has a monorail station on-site and is within easy walking distance of the Transportation and Ticket Center. Bus service is available to other Disney destinations. Walking time to the bus- and monorail-loading areas from the most remote rooms is 8–11 minutes.

Some readers, like this Summerville, South Carolina, family, wouldn't stay anywhere else on Disney property but the Polynesian Village:

> Polynesian Village was WONDERFUL. We could walk to the Transportation and Ticket Center to get on the buses to Disney's Hollywood Studios and Animal Kingdom without getting on the monorail. From now on, we will ONLY stay at the Polynesian Village.

A Maryland family of four found the guest-room soundproofing somewhat lacking, confirming our own research:

> We took towels from the pool and stuffed them under the door to deaden the noise coming from the connecting room.

GOOD (AND NOT-SO-GOOD) ROOMS AT THE POLYNESIAN VILLAGE RESORT *(See* **tinyurl.com/polyroomviews** *for photos.)* The Polynesian Village's 11 guest-room buildings, called *longhouses,* are spread over a long strip of land bordered by the monorail on one side and Seven Seas Lagoon on the other. All the buildings, except for the more recently added Moorea, Pago Pago, and Tokelau (now DVC buildings), opened with the Magic Kingdom in 1971. All buildings feature first-floor patios and third-floor balconies. The older buildings, comprising more than half the resort's rooms, have fake balconies on their second floors. (The newer buildings offer full balconies on both the second and third floors, and patios on the first.) A small number of patios in the first-floor rooms have views blocked by mature vegetation, but these patios provide more room than do the balconies on the third floor. If view is important and you're staying in one of the eight older longhouses, ask for a third-floor room.

Within the Great Ceremonial House are most restaurants and shops, as well as the resort lobby, guest services, and bus and monorail stations. Longhouses most convenient to the Great Ceremonial House (Fiji, Tonga suites, Rarotonga, Niue, and Samoa) offer views of the swimming complex, a small marina, or inner gardens (possibly with the monorail). There are no lagoon views except for oblique views from the upper floors of Fiji and Samoa, Aotearoa, and a tunnel view from Tonga (suites only). Samoa, however, by virtue of its proximity to the main swimming complex, is a good choice for families who plan to spend time at the pool. If your children are under age 8, request a first-floor room on the volcano pool side of Samoa.

You can specifically request a lagoon- or Magic Kingdom–view room at the Polynesian Village, if you're willing to pay extra. The best of these rooms are on the second and third floors in Moorea (which, again, will be a DVC building), the third floor in Tuvalu, and, if you're staying in a concierge room, the third floor in Hawaii.

There are some quirks in the way Disney categorizes room views at the Polynesian Village, and it's possible to get a view of the castle and fireworks while staying in a garden-view room. Second- and third-floor rooms in the DVC building Tokelau (rooms 2901–2913, 2939–2948, 3901–3913, and 3939–3948) offer the best shot at sideways views of the castle and fireworks, though readers say taller palm trees may block even these upper rooms. First-floor rooms (1901–1913 and 1939–1948) may also have landscaping blocking some of the Magic Kingdom views, but the patio provides more room to move to find a better spot, too.

In addition to second-floor rooms in the older buildings (the buildings with fake balconies), also avoid the monorail-side rooms in Rarotonga and the parking-lot side of Pago Pago (also a DVC building). Garden-view rooms in Aotearoa are especially nice, but the monorail, though quiet, runs within spitting distance.

Many of the first-floor rooms in Hawaii (1501–1518) have been downgraded from theme-park-view to garden- or lagoon-view rooms because their scenery is now blocked by the new bungalows. These rooms still offer a chance to see the evening fireworks, however, and are a little less expensive than similar rooms on higher floors.

If you plan to spend a lot of time at Epcot, Moorea and Pago Pago are within easy walking distance of the Transportation and Ticket Center (TTC) and the Epcot monorail. Even if you're going to the Magic Kingdom, it's a shorter walk from Moorea and Pago Pago to the TTC and Magic Kingdom monorail than to the monorail station at the Great Ceremonial House. Tuvalu, Fiji, and Aotearoa are the most distant accommodations from the Polynesian Village's bus stop. For large strollers or wheelchair access, take the ferry to the Magic Kingdom.

POLYNESIAN VILLAS & BUNGALOWS The Tokelau, Moorea, and Pago Pago longhouses hold DVC studio rooms that sleep five and are the largest studios in Walt Disney World's DVC inventory. They are also the first DVC studios to feature two bathrooms: The smaller bath has a small sink and step-in shower; the larger has a toilet, sink, and bath/shower combination. This allows three people to get ready simultaneously.

While these studios are otherwise similar to the Poly's standard rooms, there are enough small touches to make them different, including recessed ceilings, more stone and tile work in the baths, and a slightly darker color scheme.

The Polynesian's 20 new two-bedroom Pago Pago bungalows sit in front of the Hawaii, Tokelau, and Moorea buildings; they're connected to land by a wood walkway. The bungalows offer very good views of the Magic Kingdom and Seven Seas Lagoon, at some astounding prices (up to $3,400 per night). They're nice rooms, and we're sure that Disney will sell them, but we can't say that the view is worth that cost.

The Poly Villas should have a separate parking lot when construction is finished. Dining, child care, and transportation will be shared with the main resort.

Our planned review of the Polynesian Villas' studios was put on hold in late spring 2015 due to operational issues with the rooms; we'll have a review posted on **touringplans.com** and this e-book by the fall.

Disney's Wilderness Lodge & Villas

(See **tinyurl.com/ug-wlodge** *for extended coverage.)*

NOTE: Parts of Wilderness Lodge & Villas will be a construction zone from late 2015 through 2016, as Disney adds new time-share units to the shores of Bay Lake and the Wilderness Lodge building. Water-view (northeast-facing) rooms at the villas and northwest-facing woods-view rooms at the lodge may be subject to construction noise and views. We hear that some upper-floor hotel rooms in the lodge will also be converted to time-share lodging. If so, expect construction to affect more rooms on the northwest side of the lodge. Your best bet to avoid the mess is to request a courtyard view in the main building or a southwest-facing view in the villas, or choose another hotel.

This Deluxe resort is inspired by national-park lodges of the early 20th century. Situated on the shore of Bay Lake, the lodge consists of an eight-story central building augmented by two seven-story guest wings and a wing of studio and one- and two-bedroom condominiums. The hotel features exposed timber columns, log cabin–style facades, and dormer windows, and an 82-foot-tall stone fireplace in the lobby. Although the resort isn't on vast acreage, it does have a beach and a delightful pool modeled on a mountain stream.

The lodge's 727 guest rooms, refurbished in 2012, have darkly stained Mission-style furniture accented by soft goods done in blue-and-red

STRENGTHS	WEAKNESSES
• National-park-lodge theme is a favorite of kids and adults alike	• Transportation to Magic Kingdom is by bus or boat only
• Along with Animal Kingdom Lodge, it's the least expensive Disney Deluxe resort	• One of two Deluxe resorts without character dining
• Excellent lounge for adults	• Whispering Canyon Cafe noise can spill out into lobby and rooms near it
• Close to recreational options at Fort Wilderness	• Villas guests must access most services through main hotel
• Great views from guest rooms	• Bus transportation to Magic Kingdom sometimes shared with Fort Wilderness
• Rooms with bunk beds available	
• On-site child care	• Smallest rooms of Disney's Deluxe resorts
• Exceptionally peaceful location and public areas (Villas)	• Ongoing construction through 2016

Wilderness Lodge & Villas

Bay Lake

Future DVC Units

Future DVC Units

Wilderness Lodge Villas

Wilderness Lodge

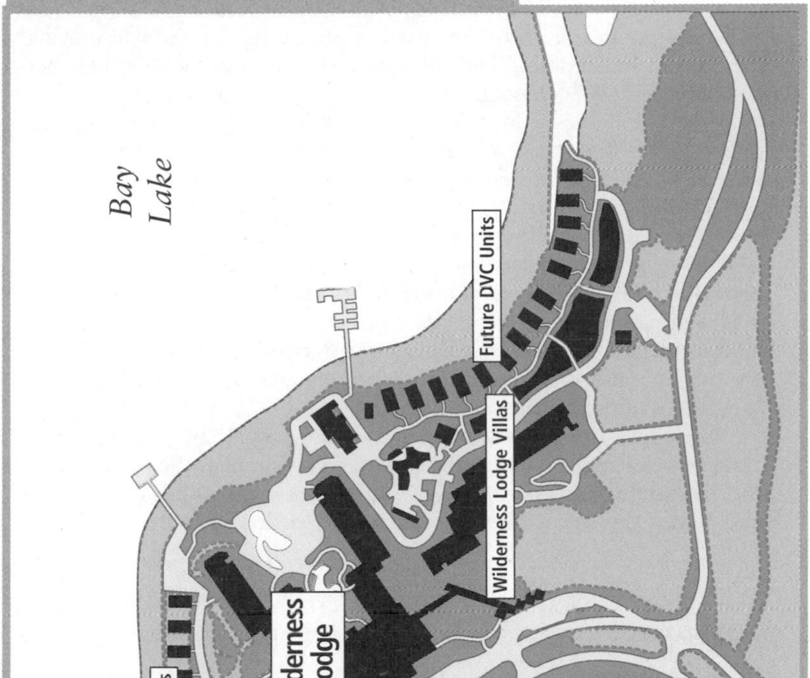

American Indian patterns. Carved-wood headboards, rough-hewn armoires, and rustic light fixtures create a log-cabin coziness. Typical rooms have two queen-size beds; some have one queen bed and bunk beds. All rooms have a table and chairs, a two-sink vanity outside the bathroom, a mini-fridge, and a coffeemaker. Rooms on the ground floor have patios; rooms above have balconies.

Part of the DVC time-share program, the 136 adjoining Villas at Disney's Wilderness Lodge are studio and one- and two-bedroom units in a freestanding building to the right of the lodge. Studios offer kitchen-ettes; one- and two-bedroom villas come with full kitchens. The villas' rustic decor was updated in 2014, with pine furniture, leaf-motif rugs and curtains, and woodland creatures from Disney's *Bambi* decorating the pillows and bedding. The villas share restaurants, pools, and other amenities with Wilderness Lodge.

Along with the 2014 update, the villas' studios got fold-down sleeper sofas like those at the Grand Floridian Villas. All villas got new armoires and flat-panel TVs; new stainless-steel kitchen appliances (one- and two-bedroom units); new bathroom tile and fixtures; and new flooring, wallpaper, and kitchen countertops.

There are two full-service restaurants on-site, with several more a boat ride away. The resort is connected to the Magic Kingdom by boat and to other Disney parks by bus. Boat service may be suspended during thunderstorms, so if it's raining or looks like it's about to, Disney will provide buses. Walking time to buses and boats from the most remote rooms is about 5–8 minutes.

The lodge's pool area was refurbished in late 2014, adding a new children's water-play area and expanded seating near the pool bar.

Two adult couples from Fort Smith, Arkansas, think the Wilderness Lodge is great, with one reservation (pardon the pun):

There has been a real downturn in our opinion in the efficacy of the bus transportation. The ambience of the lodge makes up for it, though.

A Boone County, Indiana, reader concurs about the transportation:

To paraphrase Mark Twain, rumors that Wilderness Lodge's transportation problems have been resolved are greatly exaggerated—it's an easy ride to the Magic Kingdom, but trips to the Studios and Animal Kingdom take nearly an hour, which is just inexcusable.

A mom from Oklahoma City piles on:

We have stayed at Disney's Wilderness Lodge on four occasions and have had good experiences on all except the most recent. The shuttle service from the hotel to the parks was the worst we have ever experienced in all our trips to WDW. We waited more than an hour at the hotel dock for a boat to Magic Kingdom. When it finally showed up and loaded, we made an unexplained trip to Fort Wilderness Campground and loaded 26 more people before heading to Magic Kingdom. It took 90 minutes to get from Wilderness Lodge to Magic Kingdom! The bus system was not much better. It's nearly impossible to get to the parks before opening using the Disney shuttle service!

Finally, a reader from Newport, Kentucky, doesn't think that Disney is doing itself any favors:

The bus transportation to the other parks left something to be desired. Often we would go to another resort, usually the Grand Floridian or the Fort Wilderness Campground, and pick up other guests. The bus ride from our hotel to Animal Kingdom went to the Grand Floridian then to Blizzard Beach and finally to Animal Kingdom. Disney should provide more adequate bus transportation to the parks given the amount they charge for rooms at the Deluxe hotels.

From a business standpoint, it doesn't make much sense to have long bus rides. The more time I spend on a bus, the less time I'm in the park spending money.

MORE TIME-SHARE UNITS AT WILDERNESS LODGE Disney filed plans in the spring of 2015 seeking approval to add 26 new lakeside villas to the Wilderness Lodge & Villas. While Disney hasn't said anything official about these, we think they'll be similar to the new bungalows over at the Polynesian Village Resort—two-bedroom units that sleep about eight. In addition, we've heard rumors that some upper-floor rooms at the lodge would be converted to time-share units as well. No prices, dates, or floor plans were available as we went to press.

GOOD (AND NOT-SO-GOOD) ROOMS AT WILDERNESS LODGE & VILLAS *(See* tinyurl.com/wlroomviews *for photos.)* The lodge is shaped like a very blocky V. The main entrance and lobby are at the closed end of the V. Next are middle wings that connect the lobby to the parallel end sections, which extend to the open part of the V. The V's open end flanks pools and gardens and overlooks Bay Lake directly or obliquely. Avoid rooms on the fourth, fifth, and sixth floors numbered 67–99; these overlook the main lobby and pick up every whoop, holler, and shout from the boisterous Whispering Canyon Cafe downstairs. The noise makes it difficult to get to sleep before Whispering Canyon closes, usually at 10 p.m.

The better rooms are on floors four, five, and six, toward the V's open end. On the very end of the V, rooms 4000–4003, 4166–4169, 5000–5003, 5166–5169, 6000–6003, and 6166–6169 offer a direct frontal view of Bay Lake. (The X000–X003 views include tall trees.) Toward the end of the V on the parallel wings, but facing inward, odd-numbered rooms 4005–4023, 4147–4165, 5005–5023, 5147–5165, 6005–6023, and 6147–6165 face the courtyard, but with excellent oblique lake views. Even-numbered rooms 5004–5034 and 6004–6034 front a woodland northwest of the lodge, and beyond the woodland, the Magic Kingdom. Odd-numbered rooms 5035–5041, 5123–5129, 6035–6041, and 6123–6129, on the lake end of the parallel middle wings, offer a direct but distant view of the lake, with pools and gardens in the foreground. Rooms looking southeast face the Wilderness Lodge Villas, a garden area, and woods. (The map suggests that these rooms offer a lake view, but trees block the line of sight.)

A handful of rooms overlook parking lots, service areas, and such—of these, avoid fourth- and fifth-floor rooms X042–X066. The rooms listed above afford the most desirable views, but if you can't score one, you're pretty much assured of a woodland view or a room fronting the faux rocks and creek in the V's inner courtyard. Concierge rooms on the seventh floor aren't recommended: Only those facing the Magic Kingdom have nice views, and even those have a service area in the foreground. Almost all rooms at the lodge have balconies. Avoid 1538, 1540, 1542, and 1544, which face a giant green electrical transformer.

Except for a few rooms overlooking the pool, rooms at Wilderness Lodge Villas offer woodland views. The best are odd-numbered rooms X531–X563 on floors three through five, which open to the lake (northeast) side of the resort (you usually can't see the lake, though). Rooms on the opposite side of the same wing offer similar views, but with some roads and parking lots visible, and with traffic noise.

Disney's Contemporary Resort and Bay Lake Tower

(See **tinyurl.com/ug-contemporary** *for extended coverage.)*

STRENGTHS	WEAKNESSES
• Iconic architecture; the only hotel that the monorail goes *through*	• "Magic Kingdom view" rooms mostly look out at parking lots and are overpriced
• Large, very attractive guest rooms with nice views of Bay Lake	• Very small studios in Bay Lake Tower sleep no more than two people comfortably
• Easy walk to the Magic Kingdom	
• Rooms in the Garden Building can be a relatively good value	• Hordes of bugs are attracted to the Garden Building's entry lighting
• Convenient parking	• Hallway decor at Bay Lake Tower can feel institutional
• Best lounge at Walt Disney World (Top of the World, Bay Lake Tower)	• Bus transportation to DHS, Animal Kingdom, water parks, and Disney Springs is shared with the other monorail resorts
• Recreation options on Bay Lake	
• Boat service to Fort Wilderness Resort & Campground	• No on-site child care

THIS 655-ROOM DELUXE RESORT ON BAY LAKE is unique in that its A-frame design permits the Magic Kingdom monorail to pass through the structure's cavernous atrium. The only real source of color in the atrium is a 90-foot mosaic depicting American Indian children and nature. The off-white central tower is augmented by a three-story Garden Building fronting Bay Lake to the south and by Bay Lake Tower, a 295-room, 15-story Disney Deluxe Villa development, to the north.

Standard rooms in the A-frame afford fantastic views of Bay Lake or the Magic Kingdom, and all have balconies. At 394 square feet each, they're only slightly smaller than equivalent rooms at the Grand Floridian.

The Contemporary's rooms are, in our opinion, among the nicest of any Disney resort. Rooms were refurbished in 2013, and the decor still lives up to the resort's name. Amenities include flat-panel LCD TVs, built-in closets, stylish soft goods, and comfortable beds. Wood accents in warm tones are a welcome relief from the bland beige that dominates so many hotel palettes. Orange and yellow accent pieces add just the right splash of color. The flat-panel TV is surrounded by a modern interpretation of the traditional family hearth: Two expansive curved shelves (perfect for storing small items) serve as the hearth's mantel, while a colorful tiled display underneath simulates the fireplace. Functional, attractive, and clever, it's the furniture equivalent of George Clooney.

A lot of thought went into the bathroom design, too. You enter the bath through a sliding pocket door instead of a traditional hinged model. The pocket door provides plenty of room and makes it easy to move around inside. (It's such a great idea that Len has adopted it in his own home.) A curved shower-curtain rod provides extra room. Combined with the pocket door, the curtain rod makes the bathroom feel much bigger than it is. Another thoughtful touch: A small motion sensor detects when you're up and moving at night, and turns on a dimmed bathroom light to help you find your way.

Contemporary Resort & Bay Lake Tower

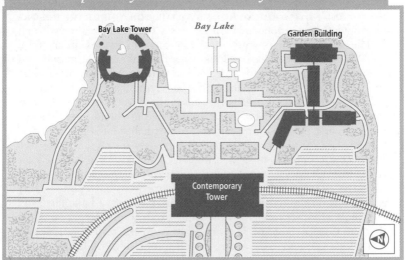

Bathroom sinks have an avant-garde flat-bottom design. If you can name a single Belgian architect or you own shoes made in Scandinavia, you'll probably love them; other folks think they look like lab equipment. When brushing your teeth, spit directly over the drain; otherwise, the toothpaste glob doesn't move. One minor gripe: You have to scoot around one of the sinks to get in the shower. (We're sure George Clooney has his quirks, too.)

The work area has ample surface space provided by an L-shaped, glass-topped desk; it looks high-tech, but rounded corners perfectly soften the piece. Lighting is superb, with top scores in the bathroom grooming, reading, and work areas. Small, stylish overhead lights are more than ample for reading in bed.

The Contemporary's beds are topped with 250-thread-count sheets and down-filled pillows. The air-conditioning system is a little louder than most. If you like to sleep with a bit of white noise in the background, however, you'll be in heaven.

Dining options abound. On the first floor is The Wave . . . of American Flavors, a 220-seat "health-conscious 21st-century" restaurant. What does *health-conscious* mean in Disney-speak? You can still get bacon for breakfast, but the coffee it comes with is certified organic and bird-friendly. The Contempo Cafe, a counter-service restaurant on the fourth floor's Grand Canyon Concourse, serves upscale sandwiches, salads, and flatbread pizzas. Chef Mickey's, also on the fourth floor, hosts a popular character buffet at breakfast, brunch, and dinner. On the 15th floor, the award-winning California Grill serves contemporary American cuisine.

The pool has slides for kids, and cabanas for rent. The resort has around a half-dozen shops, too. The Contemporary is within easy walking distance of the Magic Kingdom; monorail transportation is available to both the Magic Kingdom and Epcot. Other destinations can be accessed by bus or boat. Walking time to transportation loading areas from the most remote rooms is 6–9 minutes.

GOOD (AND NOT-SO-GOOD) ROOMS AT THE CONTEMPORARY RESORT
(See **tinyurl.com/crroomviews** *for photos.)* There are two guest-room buildings at the Contemporary: the A-frame tower and the Garden Building. Rooms in the A-frame overlook either Bay Lake and the marina and swimming complex on one side, or the parking lot with Seven Seas Lagoon and the Magic Kingdom in the background on the other. Except for most second- and third-floor rooms in the Garden Wing, each guest room has a balcony with two chairs and a table. If you stay on the Magic Kingdom side of the A-frame, ask for a room on the ninth floor or higher. The parking lot and connecting roads are less distracting there (see **tinyurl.com/cr-room4848** as an example). On the Bay Lake side, the view is fine from all floors, though higher floors are preferable.

In the Garden Building, all ground-floor rooms have patios. Only end rooms on the second and third floors facing Bay Lake have full balconies; all other rooms have balconies only a foot deep. Also, note that the Garden Building is a fair walk from the restaurants, shops, front desk, guest services, and monorail station in the A-frame.

On a recent visit, swarms of Florida love bugs circled the Garden Building's entrances at night, apparently attracted to the yellow lighting inside—you'll need to step over thousands of bug bodies if you leave through those doors in the morning. If you're grossed out at the prospect, try the westernmost entrance nearest the main building, and avoid the north-facing doors nearest the marina. Insects aside, the Garden rooms' isolation is a plus when it comes to scenery and tranquility.

There's a lot of boat traffic in the lake and canal alongside the Garden Building. Nearest the lake and quietest are rooms 6116–6123, 6216–6223, and 6316–6323. At the water's edge but noisier are rooms 6107–6115, 6207–6215, and 6307–6315. Flanking the canal connecting Bay Lake and Seven Seas Lagoon are rooms 5128–5151, 5228–5251, and 5328–5351. All these have nice canal and lake views, but they're subjected to a lot of noise from passing watercraft.

The Garden Building also has rooms facing the marina, pool, and playground; these work well for families with young children. The view isn't comparable to views from the rooms previously listed, but ground-floor rooms 5105–5125 provide easy access to the pool.

In addition to offering some of the most scenic and tranquil guest rooms in Disney World, the Garden Building likewise contains some of the most undesirable ones. Avoid rooms ending with numbers 52 through 70—almost all of these look directly onto a parking lot.

BAY LAKE TOWER AT DISNEY'S CONTEMPORARY RESORT (See **tinyurl .com/ug-blt** for extended coverage.) Opened in 2009, Bay Lake Tower is a 15-story, 295-unit DDV resort featuring studios and one-, two-, and three-bedroom villas, as well as two-story, three-bedroom Grand Villas with spectacular views of Bay Lake and the Magic Kingdom. Laid out in a semicircle, Bay Lake Tower is connected to the Contemporary by an elevated, covered walkway and shares the main resort's monorail service.

Rooms are well appointed, with flat-panel TVs, DVD players, mini-fridges, microwaves, and coffeemakers. Brightly colored accessories, paintings, and accent walls complement an otherwise-neutral color scheme. Wood tables and granite countertops add a natural touch. Each room has a private balcony or patio. The rooms we've stayed in tested as the quietest on Disney property but average for lighting and bedding.

Studios sleep up to four people and include one queen-size bed and one double sleeper sofa. The part of the studio with the bed, sofa, and TV measures about 170 square feet and feels small with just two people; four would be an adventure. A refurbishment of all studio rooms moved the bath's sink from the kitchen to the bathroom.

One-bedroom villas sleep five and provide a formal kitchen, a second bathroom, and a living room in addition to the studio bedroom. The living room's chair and sofa fold out to sleep three more people.

Two-bedroom villas sleep nine and include all of the kitchen amenities found in a one-bedroom, plus an extra bathroom. One of the baths is attached to a second bedroom with two queen beds or a queen bed plus a sleeper-sized sofa. As with the one-bedrooms, a sofa bed and sleeper chair in the living room provide extra places to snooze, though they're best suited to small children. Bathrooms in the two-bedroom villas are laid out a bit better than those in the one-bedrooms, with more room to move about. One odd feature in these (also found at other DVC resorts) is a folding door separating the tub from the master bedroom. Nevertheless, we think the two-bedroom villas are the best of Bay Lake Tower's standard offerings.

The two-story Grand Villas sleep 12 and include four bathrooms, the same master-bedroom layout, and two bedrooms with two queen beds apiece. An upstairs seating area overlooking the main floor provides a sleeper sofa and chair. These rooms have two-story windows that offer unparalleled views of either Bay Lake or the Magic Kingdom—with unparalleled prices to match.

Unofficial Guide reader opinions of Bay Lake Tower have been mostly positive. A Minnesota family of four loved it:

> We had a studio with a Magic Kingdom view. The balcony was a private oasis where my husband and I would relax and watch the fireworks together after the kids were asleep. On our second night he looked at me and said, "We're always going to stay here."

A Tennessee family wasn't in love with Bay Lake Tower's views:

> The Magic Kingdom view isn't as magical as Disney wants you to believe. You can see the fireworks from your room, but they're off-center over Space Mountain. During the day, your view is the Bay Lake Tower parking lot. The lake view, on the other hand, may be the most peaceful at Walt Disney World.

Bay Lake Tower has its own check-in desk as well as its own private pool and pool bar, plus a small fire pit on the beach. Its Top of the World Lounge is the best bar on Disney property but, alas, only for DVC owners. If need be, offer to buy a round of drinks in exchange for an invite.

A 1-mile jogging path loops around Bay Lake Tower and the Contemporary's garden wing. Dining, transportation, and other recreational activities are shared with the Contemporary Resort.

If you're paying for a Magic Kingdom view, request a room on an upper level—above the seventh floor, at least—if you don't want to look out on the parking lot. Even-numbered rooms XX06–XX16 have the best viewing angle of the park. Rooms XX24–XX30 may technically be described as having Magic Kingdom views, but they're oriented toward the Contemporary, and you have to turn the other way to see the park. (See **tinyurl.com/blt-roomviews** for photos.)

Shades of Green *(See **tinyurl.com/ug-shades** for extended coverage.)*

STRENGTHS	
• Large guest rooms	• Swimming complex, fitness center
• Discount tickets for military personnel with ID	• On-site car rental (Alamo)
• Quiet setting	**WEAKNESSES**
• Views of golf course from guest rooms	• No interesting theme
• Convenient self-parking	• Limited on-site dining
	• Limited bus service
	• Daily parking fee ($5)
	• No free parking at theme parks

THIS DELUXE RESORT is owned and operated by the US Armed Forces and is open to US military personnel (including members of the National Guard and reserves, retired military, and employees of the US Public Health Service and the Department of Defense) and their families, foreign military personnel attached to US units, and some civilian contractors. Shades of Green consists of one three-story and one five-story building nestled among three golf courses that are open to Disney guests.

At 455 square feet each, the 586 guest rooms at Shades of Green are larger than those at the Grand Floridian. Decor is pleasant though thoroughly unremarkable—pretty much the same as at any midpriced hotel. Most rooms have two queen-size beds, a daybed, and a table and four chairs, as well as a television in an armoire. All rooms have a patio or balcony.

A Minot AFB, North Dakota, father of three thinks Shades of Green is the way to go—mostly:

As an active-duty military member, I can tell you there's no better deal on a WDW vacation than at Shades of Green. A couple of drawbacks, though, were the midlevel quality of the food at the Italian restaurant and the lack of a place to get a drink.

A mom from Winchester, Virginia, weighs in:

Shades of Green has an AAFES [Army & Air Force Exchange Service] on-site. In addition to carrying everything one might find in a hotel gift/sundries shop, this small store carries Disney merchandise. It's also a Class Six [a military version of a package store]. We were able to purchase everything we needed there and never had to leave WDW in search of a grocery store. Plus there's no tax on purchases.

A military mom from Plainfield, Indiana, makes a case for exploring all your options:

While it's true that SoG is often a good deal for service members and veterans, military families should still do some comparison shopping.

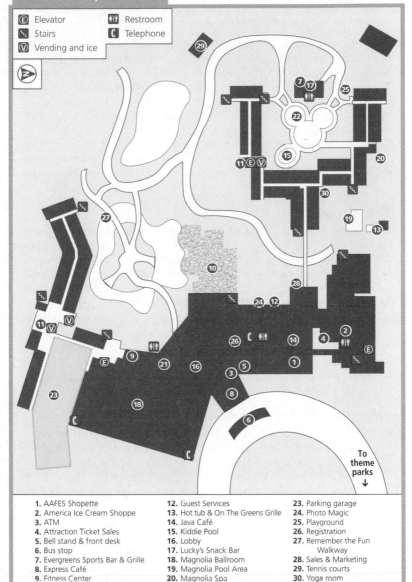

Shades of Green

Legend:
- Ⓔ Elevator
- Stairs
- Ⓥ Vending and ice
- Restroom
- Telephone

To theme parks ↓

1. AAFES Shopette
2. America Ice Cream Shoppe
3. ATM
4. Attraction Ticket Sales
5. Bell stand & front desk
6. Bus stop
7. Evergreens Sports Bar & Grille
8. Express Café
9. Fitness Center
10. The Garden Gallery Restaurant
11. Guest laundry
12. Guest Services
13. Hot tub & On The Greens Grille
14. Java Café
15. Kiddie Pool
16. Lobby
17. Lucky's Snack Bar
18. Magnolia Ballroom
19. Magnolia Pool Area
20. Magnolia Spa
21. Mangino's Bistro/Bistro To Go
22. Mill Pond Pool Area
23. Parking garage
24. Photo Magic
25. Playground
26. Registration
27. Remember the Fun Walkway
28. Sales & Marketing
29. Tennis courts
30. Yoga room

Room rates are tiered based on rank—the higher your rank, the higher your rate. Definitely check into military rates at Disney properties; when we traveled to WDW in 2009, it was cheaper for us to stay at a Disney Moderate resort than at SoG. Also, military-connected guests should check out the **Armed Forces Vacation Club** for condos near

*WDW [see **afvclub.com** for participating Orlando-area properties]. This time around, we rented a two-bedroom, two-bath condo with a full kitchen and awesome pool area for seven nights, and it cost us less than two nights at a Disney hotel.*

Even though the resort isn't operated by Disney, service is comparable to that at Disney Deluxe properties. Transportation to all theme parks is by bus, with a transfer required to almost all destinations. Walking time to the bus-loading area from the most remote rooms is about 5 minutes. If you're visiting during holidays or a long weekend, book as early as possible (up to seven months in advance).

You don't have to worry much about bad rooms at Shades of Green. Except for a small percentage that overlook the entrance road and parking lot, most offer views of the golf courses that surround the hotel, or the swimming area. When you reserve, make your preference known. Shades of Green has its own website, **shadesofgreen.org.**

THE EPCOT RESORTS

THE EPCOT RESORTS ARE ARRAYED around Crescent Lake between Epcot and Disney's Hollywood Studios (but closer to Epcot). Both theme parks are accessible by boat and on foot. No Epcot resort offers transportation to Epcot's main entrance, and it's between 0.7 and 1.1 miles to walk, depending on the hotel and route. As a Greenville, South Carolina, mom reports, this can be a problem:

The only transportation to Epcot is by boat or foot. There's no bus available to take you to the front gates. We had to walk through the International Gateway and all the way to the front of Epcot to ride Future World attractions. And if we finished Epcot at the end of the day near the front entrance, the only way back home was a long hike through Future World and the International Gateway.

A reader from Emporia, Kansas, overcame this obstacle:

We had no transportation to the front gate of Epcot for arrival before opening. So we decided to do early entry at Magic Kingdom (7 a.m.), take in one popular attraction, and then catch the monorail to Epcot. Worked like a charm. We were at Epcot by 8:20 a.m.

Disney's Yacht & Beach Club Resorts and Beach Club Villas
*(See **tinyurl.com/ug-yachtbeach** for extended coverage.)*

DISNEY'S BEACH CLUB RESORT will be undergoing an extensive refurbishment through late 2016, including new room decor and furniture and renovations to the lobby and other public spaces. From the length of the refurbishment, it appears as if Disney will be working on only a few rooms at a time, so impact to guests should be minimal. Before you make a reservation, check with Disney to see if any significant work is likely to affect your stay.

These adjoining Deluxe resorts are similarly themed. Both have clapboard facades with whitewashed-wood trim. The Yacht Club is painted a subdued gray, the Beach Club a brighter blue. The Yacht Club has a nautical theme with model ships and antique navigational

Yacht & Beach Club Resorts & Beach Club Villas

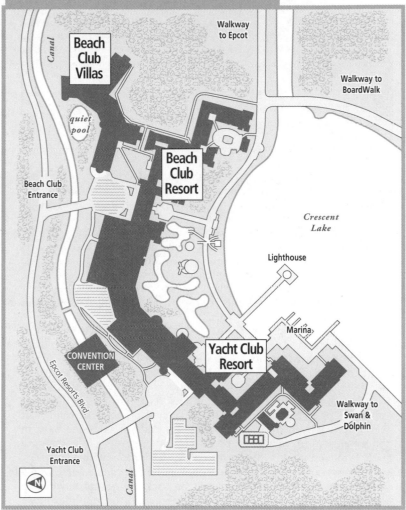

Walkway to Epcot

Canal

Beach Club Villas

Walkway to BoardWalk

quiet pool

Beach Club Resort

Beach Club Entrance

Crescent Lake

Lighthouse

Marina

Yacht Club Resort

CONVENTION CENTER

Epcot Resorts Blvd.

Yacht Club Entrance

Walkway to Swan & Dolphin

Canal

instruments in public areas. The Beach Club is embellished with beach scenes in foam-green and white. Both have themed lobbies, with a giant globe in the Yacht Club's and sea-horse fixtures in the Beach Club's. The resorts face the 25-acre Crescent Lake and share an elaborate swimming complex.

There are 621 rooms at the Yacht Club, 576 rooms at the Beach Club, and 282 studio and one- and two-bedroom villas at the Beach Club Villas, part of the DVC time-share program. Most of the rooms are 381 square feet and have two queen-size beds, a daybed, a reading chair, a mini-fridge, a coffeemaker, and a desk and a chair. Like

YACHT & BEACH CLUB RESORTS AND BEACH CLUB VILLAS

STRENGTHS	WEAKNESSES
• Best pool complex of any WDW resort	• Lack of good quick-service dining options
• Walking distance to Epcot's International Gateway	• Views and balcony size are hit-and-miss
• Relatively affordable full-service restaurant (Captain's Grille)	• Bus service to Magic Kingdom, Animal Kingdom, water parks, and Disney Springs is shared with other Epcot resorts
• Close to many BoardWalk and Epcot dining options	• No three-bedroom Grand Villas at the Beach Club Villas
• Well-themed public spaces	• Beach Club Villas have fewer baths per bedroom than newer DVC/DDV properties
• Bright and attractive guest rooms	
• Boat transportation to Disney's Hollywood Studios	

the Grand Floridian's, rooms have a lot of drawer space. Yacht Club rooms are decorated in blue and white with red accents; Beach Club offers light blue and tan tones. Some rooms have full balconies; many rooms have mini balconies.

The Beach Club Villas evoke seaside Victorian cottages. Studio accommodations offer kitchenettes; one- and two-bedroom villas have full kitchens. Subject to availability, villas are open to the public as well as to DVC (time-share) members. The villas share restaurants, pools, and other amenities with the Yacht & Beach Club Resorts. A small business center serves guests' work needs for both the Yacht and Beach Clubs and Beach Club Villas.

As Disney Deluxe resorts, the Yacht Club and Beach Club provide excellent service. They offer nine restaurants and lounges and are within walking distance of Epcot and the BoardWalk. Transportation to other destinations is by bus or boat. Walking time to the transportation loading areas from the most remote rooms is 7 minutes.

Although the Yacht & Beach Club Resorts are arrayed along Crescent Lake opposite Disney's BoardWalk, a relatively small percentage of guest rooms actually overlook the lake. Many additional rooms have an oblique view of the lake but face a courtyard or garden. To complicate matters, the resorts don't differentiate between a room with a lake view and one overlooking a swimming pool, pond, or canal. There's only one category for anything wet: lagoon or pool view. Go to **tinyurl.com /yacht-roomviews** or **tinyurl.com/beach-roomviews** to see specific views from these rooms.

The Beach Club consists of a long main building with several wings protruding toward Crescent Lake. Looking at the resort from Crescent Lake, the Beach Club adjoins the Yacht Club on the left and spreads toward Epcot on the right. The main building and the various wings range from three to five stories. Most rooms have full or mini balconies or, on the ground floor, patios. Full balconies are big enough for a couple of chairs, while mini balconies are about 6 inches deep (stand at the rail or sit in a chair inside the room). Top-floor rooms often have enclosed balconies set into the roof. Unless you're standing, visibility is somewhat limited from these dormer balconies. Our Hotel Room Views include descriptions of each room's balcony type.

We receive a lot of mail about the Yacht & Beach Club Resorts, most of it positive. First, these remarks from a Wayland, Massachusetts, mother of two:

> This was the first time we stayed at the Beach Club, and for us the amazing pool complex was worth the extra money. Several nights we climbed up to the top of the waterslide as the sun was setting, and it was an incredible sight—truly a memorable experience!

This mom from Brownsville, Texas, however, has some issues with the Beach Club:

> The room doors at the Beach Club don't fit very snugly, so any noise from the hall was practically broadcast into our room. Our room was close to the elevators, so it sounded like everyone in the hotel was stampeding past our door in the morning. If we go back, I'll ask for a more remote room way at the end of the hall.

GOOD (AND NOT-SO-GOOD) ROOMS AT THE BEACH CLUB RESORT *(See* **tinyurl.com/beach-roomviews** *for photos.)* The Beach Club's better views are from rooms that have full balconies, and from those that overlook the lake. Other good rooms include those facing woods, with Epcot in the background. The woods-facing rooms are the resort's quietest, most peaceful accommodations, in terms of both lack of noise and attractive scenery. These rooms are also nearest to Epcot's International Gateway entrance if you're walking, but farthest from the resort's main pool area, lobby, and restaurants.

Of the remaining rooms, most face courtyards, with some of these providing oblique views of the lake, and others overlooking parking lots and the resort's front entrance.

The following are our recommendations for good rooms at the Beach Club Resort. All room numbers are four digits, with the first digit specifying the floor and the remaining three digits specifying the room number. (The Beach Club will charge you for a water view if there's so much as a birdbath in sight. If you're going to spend the money, get a *real* water view.)

WATER-VIEW ROOMS WITH FULL BALCONIES FACING THE LAKE Odd-numbered rooms 2641–2645; suite 2647; 3501–3507; 3699–3725; club-level rooms 5699–5725

STANDARD-VIEW ROOMS WITH FULL BALCONIES FACING THE WOODS AND EPCOT Even-numbered rooms 2528–2596, 3512–3530, 4532–4596

GOOD (AND NOT-SO-GOOD) ROOMS AT THE YACHT CLUB RESORT *(See* **tinyurl.com/yacht-roomviews** *for photos.)* When you look at the Yacht Club from Crescent Lake, the resort is connected to the Beach Club on the right and angles toward the Dolphin hotel on the left. All Yacht Club rooms offer full balconies or, on the ground floor, patios. Rooms with the best views are as follows (the higher the last three digits in the room number, the closer to lobby, main pool area, and restaurants):

FIFTH-FLOOR ROOMS WITH FULL BALCONIES FACING THE LAKE, WITH THE BOARDWALK INN IN THE BACKGROUND Club-level rooms 5161, 5163, 5241

FIFTH-FLOOR ROOMS DIRECTLY FACING EPCOT Rooms 5195–5199, 5153

STANDARD-VIEW FOURTH-FLOOR ROOMS FACING EPCOT Rooms 4195–4199, 4153

Some other rooms face the BoardWalk or Epcot across Crescent Lake, but they're inferior to the rooms just listed.

Avoid standard-view rooms at either resort except for rooms 3512–3536 and 4578–4598 at the Beach Club; these overlook a dense pine thicket. In addition to offering a nice vista for a standard-view rate, these are the closest rooms to Epcot available at any resort on Crescent Lake.

BEACH CLUB VILLAS This Disney Deluxe Villa property is supposedly inspired by the grand Atlantic seaside homes of the early 20th century. We'll bet the villas don't resemble any seaside home you ever saw. Thematically, there's little to differentiate the Beach Club Villas from the Yacht & Beach Club Resorts, or from the parts of the BoardWalk Inn & Villas that don't front the BoardWalk.

Configured roughly in the shape of a fat Y or slingshot, the Beach Club Villas are set back away from the lake adjoining the front of the Beach Club Resort. Arrayed in connected four- and five-story taffy-blue sections topped with cupolas, the villas are festooned with white woodwork and slat-railed balconies. The effect is clean, breezy, and evocative . . . though of what we're not certain. Accommodations include studios, with a kitchenette, one queen bed, and a sofa sleeper; and one- and two-bedroom villas with full kitchens. The rooms are a bit small but attractively decorated in pastels with New England–style summer-home furniture. Patterned carpets and seashore-themed art complete the package.

We don't like the Beach Club Villas as well as the Wilderness Lodge Villas (they're more visually interesting) or the villas of Old Key West Resort (they're roomier, more luxurious, and more private). The Beach Club Villas have their own modest swimming pool but otherwise share the restaurants, facilities, and transportation options of the adjoining Yacht & Beach Club Resorts. The villas' strengths and weaknesses include all of those listed for the Yacht & Beach Club Resorts. Additional strengths include laundry and kitchen facilities in the one- and two-bedroom units, and self-parking directly adjacent to the building. The villas' one additional weakness is that they offer no lake view.

GOOD (AND NOT-SO-GOOD) ROOMS AT THE BEACH CLUB VILLAS *(See* **tinyurl.com/bcv-roomviews** *for photos.)* Though the studios and villas are attractive and livable, the location of the Beach Club Villas, between parking lots, roads, and canals, leaves much to be desired. Rooms facing the pool offer a limited view of a small canal but are subject to traffic noise. Ditto the rooms on the northeast side, but they don't face the pool. Only southeast-facing rooms provide both a scenic landscape (woods) and relative relief from traffic noise. The nearby road is two lanes only, and traffic noise probably won't bother you if you're indoors with the balcony door closed, but for the bucks you shell out to stay at the villas, you can find nicer, quieter accommodations elsewhere on Disney property. If you elect to stay at the Beach Club Villas, go for odd-numbered rooms 225–251, 325–351, 425–451, and 525–551.

Disney's BoardWalk Inn & Villas

(See **tinyurl.com/ug-bwinn** *for extended coverage.)*

ON CRESCENT LAKE ACROSS from the Yacht & Beach Club Resorts, the BoardWalk Inn is another of the Walt Disney World Deluxe resorts.

BoardWalk Inn & Villas

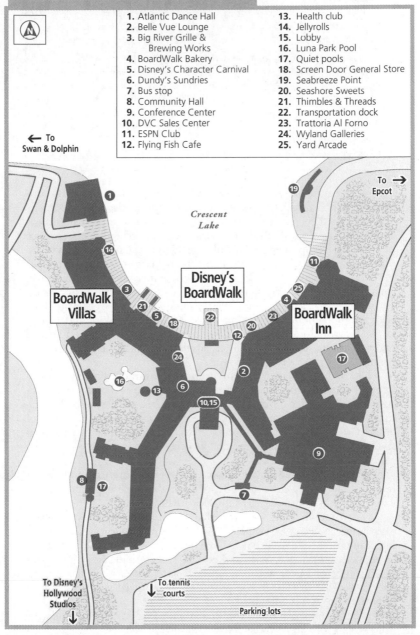

1. Atlantic Dance Hall
2. Belle Vue Lounge
3. Big River Grille & Brewing Works
4. BoardWalk Bakery
5. Disney's Character Carnival
6. Dundy's Sundries
7. Bus stop
8. Community Hall
9. Conference Center
10. DVC Sales Center
11. ESPN Club
12. Flying Fish Cafe
13. Health club
14. Jellyrolls
15. Lobby
16. Luna Park Pool
17. Quiet pools
18. Screen Door General Store
19. Seabreeze Point
20. Seashore Sweets
21. Thimbles & Threads
22. Transportation dock
23. Trattoria Al Forno
24. Wyland Galleries
25. Yard Arcade

← To Swan & Dolphin

To → Epcot

Crescent Lake

Disney's BoardWalk

BoardWalk Villas

BoardWalk Inn

To Disney's Hollywood Studios

To tennis courts

Parking lots

The complex is a detailed replica of an early-20th-century Atlantic coast boardwalk. Facades of hotels, diners, and shops create an inviting and exciting waterfront skyline. In reality, the BoardWalk Inn & Villas are

BOARDWALK INN & VILLAS

STRENGTHS	
• Walking distance to Epcot's International Gateway and Disney's Hollywood Studios	• Limited quick-service dining options suitable for children
• Unique garden suites	• Not as many rooms overlook the BoardWalk as you might think
• Vast selection of dining options for adults	• Clown pool may freak you out
• Fitness center is larger than Yacht & Beach Club's	• Bus service to Magic Kingdom, Animal Kingdom, water parks, and Disney Springs is shared with other Epcot resorts
• Clown pool is whimsical	
	• BoardWalk Villas have fewer baths per bedroom than newer DVC/DDV properties
WEAKNESSES	
• Long, confusing hallways	
• Some may find room theming overly fussy	

a single integrated structure behind the facades. Restaurants and shops occupy the boardwalk level, while accommodations rise up to six stories above. Painted bright red and yellow along with weathered pastel greens and blues, the BoardWalk resorts are the only Disney hotels that use neon signage as architectural detail. The complex shares a pool with an old-fashioned amusement park theme (there are also two quiet pools).

The BoardWalk Inn's 371 Deluxe rooms measure 371 square feet each. Most contain two queen-size beds with hardwood headboards, an upholstered sleeper sofa, a cherry desk and chair, an alarm clock with 30-pin iPhone dock, a mini-fridge, a coffeemaker, and ceiling fans. Decor includes yellow-and-white-striped wallpaper and striped green curtains. Closet space exceeds that in other Disney Deluxe rooms. Most rooms have balconies.

The 532 BoardWalk Villas are decorated in similar pastels—lots of light green, pink, and blue—with bright tiles in the kitchens and bathrooms. Villas range from 412 to 2,491 square feet (studio through three-bedroom) and sleep 4–12 people. Many villas have full kitchens, laundry rooms, and whirlpool tubs. The villas tend to be more expensive than similar accommodations at other Disney resorts—you pay for the address.

The BoardWalk Villas will finish a resort-wide interior and exterior refurbishment project by late 2015. Updates include new interior and exterior paint, plus updates to interior furnishings.

The inn and villas are well staffed and offer excellent service. They're also home to some of Disney World's better restaurants and shops, including the BoardWalk Bakery, serving lunch sandwiches and salads along with morning pastries and coffee. The complex is within walking distance of Epcot and is connected to other destinations by bus and boat. Walking time to transportation loading areas from the most remote rooms is 5–6 minutes.

Reader comments about the BoardWalk Inn & Villas include the following. From an Iowa City, Iowa, family:

We were surprised that so relatively few rooms at the BoardWalk Inn have interesting views. We were in a group staying there before a Disney cruise, and the one couple who actually had a view of the boardwalk said it was noisy.

A number of readers have complained about the bus service at the BoardWalk Inn. This comment is typical:

The transportation by bus (to Animal Kingdom and Magic Kingdom) was the worst. We waited at least 40 minutes every time and almost missed a dinner reservation (for which we had left 1½ hours early).

GOOD (AND NOT-SO-GOOD) ROOMS AT THE BOARDWALK INN & VILLAS *(See* **tinyurl.com/bwi-roomviews** *for photos.)* The complex comprises several wings that radiate from the lobby complex, in a rough H-shape. Crescent Lake and the Promenade (pedestrian boardwalk) are to the north, the entrance is to the south, and the canal that runs to Disney's Hollywood Studios is to the west. If you book a BoardWalk room through Disney's agents or website, *water view* means Crescent Lake and the BoardWalk area only; views of the canal or pool are considered standard view. But if you book a villa through a DVC member or the DVC site, the same pool and canal are called garden or pool view, and the view of the BoardWalk is called BoardWalk view. Two concierge floors cater to those wanting extra service.

Most rooms at the inn and villas have a balcony or patio, though balconies on the standard upper-floor rooms alternate between large and medium. The BoardWalk Inn & Villas each share about half the frontage on the Promenade, which overlooks Crescent Lake. The Promenade's clubs, stores, and attractions are spread about equally between the two sections, leading to similar levels of noise and commotion. However, the inn side is closer to Epcot and the nearby access road; this provides better views of Epcot fireworks and easier access to that park, but it also means more road noise.

Otherwise, the inn is actually less noisy than the more expensive villas; there's one tranquil, enclosed courtyard, and another half-enclosed area with a quiet pool (where BoardWalk's Garden Suites are). There are many rooms to avoid at the inn, starting with rooms overlooking access roads and parking lots, and rooms looking down on the roof of the adjacent conference center. And although the aforementioned quiet rooms face courtyards, the views are pretty ho-hum. When you get right down to it, the only rooms with decent views are those fronting the Promenade and lake, specifically odd-numbered rooms 3213–3259 and 4213–4259. We're told by Disney insiders that most of these rooms are reserved more than 10 months in advance, so snagging one requires advance planning and a lot of luck. As for the others, you're more likely to get a better view at the far less expensive Port Orleans, Caribbean Beach, or Coronado Springs Resort.

The villas are somewhat better. Most overlook a canal to the west with the Swan resort and its access road and parking lots on the far side. Worse are the rooms that front BoardWalk's entrance and car lots. As at the inn, the villas offer only a handful of rooms with good views. Odd-numbered rooms 3001–3047, 4001–4047, and 5001–5047 afford dynamic views of the Promenade and Crescent Lake, with Epcot in the background. Rooms X05, X07, X13, X15, X29, and X31 are studios. They're a little noisy if you open your balcony door but otherwise offer a glimpse of one of Disney World's more happening places. Unless you bag one of these rooms, however, you'll spend a bundle for a very average (or worse) view.

Promenade-facing villa rooms have noise issues identical to their inn counterparts. The midsection of the canal-facing villas look out on Luna Park Pool, a carnival-themed family-pool complex that gets extremely noisy during the day. Some of the quieter villas are away from the Promenade with views of the canal and a partially enclosed quiet pool. Noise is practically nonexistent; the only downside is that the rooms are relatively distant from the Promenade and Epcot. Rooms on the opposite side of this wing are almost as quiet, but they face BoardWalk's parking lot and thus are less desirable.

The Walt Disney World Swan and Walt Disney World Dolphin
(See **tinyurl.com/ug-swan** *and* **tinyurl.com/ug-dolphin** *for extended coverage.)*

ROOMS AT THE SWAN AND DOLPHIN are undergoing a complete renovation through late 2016. The refurbishment will be done in phases to minimize disruption to guests and will update all rooms in both resorts. Public spaces, including the lobby, restaurants, and pools, will not be affected.

Although these resorts are inside the World and Disney handles their reservations, they're owned by Sheraton (Dolphin) and Westin (Swan) and can be booked directly through their parent companies, too. Both are served by Disney transportation to the theme parks and participate in Extra Magic Hours and FastPass+, but neither offers Disney's Magical Express bus service to and from the airport or participates in the Disney Dining Plan.

Opened in 1990, the resorts face each other on either side of an inlet of Crescent Lake. The Dolphin is a 27-story triangular turquoise building. On its roof are two 56-foot-tall fish balanced with their tails in the air. The Swan has a 12-story main building flanked by two seven-story towers. Two 47-foot-tall swans adorn its roof, paralleling their marine counterparts across the way.

Both the Swan and the Dolphin have been described as bizarre and stylistically disjointed ("Art Deco gone haywire" comes to mind).

STRENGTHS	WEAKNESSES
• Best-priced location on Crescent Lake	• Conventioneers may be off-putting to vacationing families
• Both hotels participate in Starwood Preferred Guest program	• Daily resort and parking fees
• Good on-site and nearby dining	• No Disney's Magical Express or Disney Dining Plan
• Only hotels within walking distance to mini-golf (Fantasia Gardens)	• Bus service to Magic Kingdom, Animal Kingdom, water parks, and Disney Springs is shared with other Epcot resorts
• Large variety of upscale restaurants; 24-hour food available at Picabu	• Architecture that was on the cutting edge 25 years ago now seems dated
• On-site car rental through National and Alamo	• Self-parking is quite distant from the hotels' entrances
• Very nice pool complex	
• Impressive public spaces	
• Walking distance to both Epcot International Gateway and DHS	

Swan & Dolphin

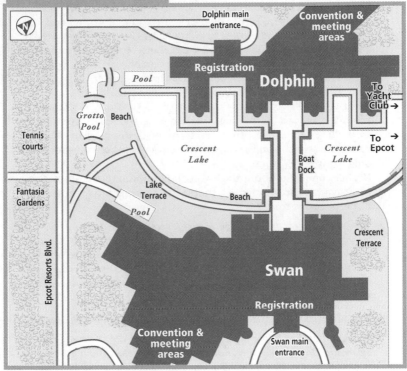

They're definitely architectural period pieces. The giant swans look swanlike, but the Dolphin's fish more closely resemble catfish from outer space. The effect could be described as adventurous or unsettling, depending on your point of view.

The Dolphin's lobby is the more ornate, featuring a rotunda with spokelike corridors branching off to shops, restaurants, and other public areas. At the other end of the spectrum, the Swan's lobby is so small that it seems an afterthought. Both resorts feature art of wildly different styles and eras (from Matisse to Roy Lichtenstein). The Dolphin's Grotto Pool is shaped like a seashell and has a waterfall, while the Swan's pool is a conventional rectangle.

The Dolphin's rooms' current design incorporates light-colored woods, floral earth-tone carpeting, and blue draperies. The plush Heavenly Beds are buttressed by oversize wood headboards adorned with vaguely modernist landscapes. A sleek, contemporary dresser–desk combo and a reading chair complete the furnishings. Some rooms have balconies.

The Swan's standard guest rooms are decorated similarly to the Dolphin's. Westin's Heavenly Beds make for ultracomfy sleeping. The reading light is great in or out of bed. A huge, round mirror hangs above the dresser. The bath, though small for a Disney World hotel, is well appointed.

Because the Swan and the Dolphin aren't run by Disney, service is less relentlessly cheerful than at other on-property resorts. They'll also nickel-and-dime you to death. For example, both tack on a $23-per-day resort fee and another $16 per day for self-parking. Even more shocking is the price the Dolphin's gift shop charges for sundries: We paid almost $10 for a pint of Ben & Jerry's ice cream—roughly $3 more than Disney charges in its gift shops (and twice as much as Publix). Whatever rate you're quoted at the Swan and the Dolphin, temper your expectations by adding another $50 per day in miscellaneous costs.

The two hotels collectively house more than a dozen restaurants and lounges and are within easy walking distance of Epcot and the BoardWalk. They're also connected to other destinations by bus and boat. Walking time from the most remote rooms to the transportation loading areas is 7–9 minutes.

Reader comments about the Swan and Dolphin touch on the same several themes. The following remarks are representative. First, from an El Paso, Texas, reader:

> We scored a great deal through MouseSavers and decided to give the Swan a try. The pool setup was super, and our room was beautiful and had a great view looking toward Epcot. Taking the two hotels together, the restaurant selection was the best I've seen in or out of the World. On the downside, both hotels are really spread out, and it was quite a hike from self-parking to the entrance of the Swan.

A couple from Nashua, New Hampshire, also touts the pools:

> We stayed at the Dolphin and found that neither the Disney nor the Swan and Dolphin websites, nor anything else, depicts how great the pool complex is. Not only are there multiple pools, a sandy beach, swan boats, whirlpools, a waterfall, a waterslide, and maybe the best poolside bar in all of Disney World, there's also a wonderfully green, restful grotto-in-tropical-forest theme.

Finally, thoughts from a woman writing from near Fort Worth, Texas:

> We stayed at the Dolphin, which I hadn't stayed at before because something within me screamed, "NOT DISNEY," and I couldn't shut it up. But then we decided to take a relatively last-minute trip to WDW (we booked 40 or so days out, I think). All the Disney resorts were booked, or we would've had to do a split stay. So I found the nurse discount at the Dolphin, and I was overjoyed! A great room, comfy beds, fantastic pool, and WDW transportation just like any Disney resort for $200 a night! Not bad.

GOOD (AND NOT-SO-GOOD) ROOMS AT THE SWAN AND THE DOLPHIN
These sprawling hotels are configured very differently, and their irregular shapes mean it's easier to discuss groups of rooms in relation to exterior landmarks and compass directions rather than by room numbers. When speaking with a Disney reservationist, use our tips to ask for a particular view or area.

THE SWAN East-facing rooms offer prime views, particularly in the upper half of the seven-story wing above Il Mulino New York Trattoria. From this vantage point, guests overlook a canal and the BoardWalk, with Epcot in the distance. *IllumiNations* fireworks enliven the view nightly. Balcony rooms are available on floors five, six, and seven for an additional $50 and up per night. However, rooms in the wing nearest the hotel's main section have the southern portion of their view obscured by the building's easternmost portion, which juts east beyond the seven-story wing. There are some east-facing rooms on that portion of the main section, sans balconies. Lofty palm trees obscure the view from east-facing rooms below the fourth floor. The best rooms with an Epcot view are 626 and 726.

North-facing rooms afford views of the Dolphin and (generally) of the courtyard. Exceptions are the north-facing rooms on the easternmost portion of the main section, which look across Crescent Terrace to the BoardWalk. These afford angled views of Epcot and are buffered by palms on the lowest three floors. The few north-facing rooms at the end of the Swan's two eight-story wings directly overlook Crescent Lake. However, the bulk of north-facing rooms are in the main section and overlook the courtyard, with greenery, fountains, and an indoor café in its center. Courtyard-facing rooms are subject to noise from below, though never much.

Above the eighth floor, north-facing rooms in the main section overlook roofs of the shorter wings. In these rooms, height enhances the vista from your window, but only near the center of the hotel is the view not seriously marred by rooftops below.

North-facing main-section rooms have a more direct view of the Dolphin across the lake than the courtyard-facing rooms in either eight-story wing. However, most wing rooms can view the lake at an angle. Those on the northern edge of the western wing also view the BoardWalk at an angle.

Most courtyard-facing rooms have balconies; 224 rooms are so equipped, and these balconies offer panoramic 180-degree views. Of course, from most rooms at the Swan, part of any 180-degree view will include another section of the hotel.

The Swan's worst views are from west-facing rooms above the fourth floor, which overlook the unsightly roof of the hotel's western wing. The northernmost rooms in the wing directly above Kimonos restaurant are an exception—their balconies overlook the pool and the beach on Crescent Lake's western shore. Rooms 680–691 offer nice pool views.

Above the Swan's main entrance, south-facing rooms overlook the parking lot, with forest and the Hollywood Studios in the distance. However, the canal is also visible to the east. These rooms lack balconies.

THE DOLPHIN Consisting of a central A-frame with large wings jutting off each side and four smaller arms extending from the rear of the building, the Dolphin is attached to a large conference center, which means that the majority of guests are ostensibly there on business. The same amenities found at Disney Deluxe resorts are found at the Dolphin. All parks are accessible from a shuttle stop or a boat dock between the Dolphin and the Swan.

If you want a room with easy access to shopping, dining, and transportation to and from the parks, almost any Dolphin room will do. The shuttle (outside the main entrance) and the boat dock are equidistant from the main front and rear exits. Restaurants and shopping are primarily on the first and third floors.

If, however, you also want a view of something other than parking-lot asphalt, your choices narrow considerably. Rooms in the Dolphin with pleasant views are in the four arms on the rear of the building. Rooms on all the arms sport balconies from the first through fourth floors, then offer balconies or windows alternately on floors five through nine.

One of the Dolphin's best views overlooks the Grotto Pool on the far west side of the building. An artificial beach with a small waterfall is visible from rooms at the very end of the large west wing. None of these rooms has a balcony, but that might be a blessing, since the pool comes with canned music and a bar. A better bet would be to ask for a room on the far west side of the first rear arm. These outer rooms have balconies and are more removed from the pool. Rooms on the inner, west part of that arm overlook a bladderwort-encrusted reflecting pool; these aren't recommended. Nor are the facing rooms on the next arm.

Between the second and third arms looms the monstrous Dolphin fountain; the better room choices here are on the top two floors. Here, from arm two you can see the BoardWalk (including any nighttime fireworks at Epcot), and from arm three you can see the Grotto Pool. Otherwise, you may find you have a view of massive green-concrete fish scales. The noise from the water is loud, and the fountain gushes continuously—it's either soothing or maddening depending on your temperament.

Arms three and four are situated around a reflecting pool. A concern for rooms in this area is that the ferry toots its horn every time it approaches and departs the dock. Its path runs right by these rooms, and the horn blows just as it passes. The first time that happens, it's quaint. By the 117th, your hair will be coming out in clumps.

The Crescent Lake side of arm four, and the small jut of the large Dolphin wing perpendicular to it, offer arguably the best views. You have an unobstructed view of the lake and Epcot fireworks, a fine BoardWalk view for people-watching, and, from higher floors, a view of the beach at Beach Club. There's ferry noise, but these rooms still have the most going for them. The best of the best in this arm are rooms 8015, 7015, 5015, 4015, and 3015. Rooms with balconies at the Dolphin generally run upwards of $40 a night more than rooms without.

Disney's Caribbean Beach Resort

*(See **tinyurl.com/ug-caribbean** for extended coverage.)*

STRENGTHS	WEAKNESSES
• Colorful Caribbean theme	• New Murphy beds in select rooms increase capacity to five people
• Rooms with *Pirates of the Caribbean* and *Finding Nemo* themes	**WEAKNESSES**
• Lakefront setting	• Check-in is far from rest of resort
• Large food court	• Sit-down dining is mediocre at best
• New queen bed mattresses replaced double beds	• Multiple bus stops
	• Some "villages" are a good distance from restaurants and shops

Caribbean Beach Resort

Beach   Playground
Bus stop   Pool

THE CARIBBEAN BEACH RESORT OCCUPIES 200 acres surrounding a 45-acre lake called Barefoot Bay. This midpriced resort, modeled after resorts in the Caribbean, consists of the registration area ("Custom House") and six two-story "villages" named after Caribbean islands. Each village has its own pool, laundry room, and beach. The Caribbean motif is maintained with blue metal roofs, widow's walks, and wooden railed porches. The atmosphere is cheerful, with buildings painted blue, lime green, and sherbet orange. In addition to the six village pools, the resort's main swimming pool is themed as an old Spanish fort, complete with slides and water cannons.

Most of the 2,112 guest rooms are 314 square feet. After a renovation in 2015, Caribbean Beach replaced its two double beds with two queen mattresses and added a fold-down Murphy bed to select rooms. Most rooms are decorated with neutral beach tones accented by bright tropical colors. All are outfitted with the same light-oak furniture. Rooms don't have balconies, but the access passageways are external and have railings. Rooms in Trinidad South are themed to a *Pirates of the Caribbean* motif. These rooms cost about $50–$75 more than comparable ones elsewhere in the resort. The soft goods and headboards in all non-*Pirates*-themed rooms have a subtle *Finding Nemo* theme.

South and east of Epcot and the Studios, Caribbean Beach offers transportation to all Disney World destinations by bus. Though it has one full-service restaurant and a food court, food service is woefully inadequate for a resort of this size. Walking time to the transportation loading area from the most remote rooms can be 7–9 minutes, so guests should seriously consider having a car.

Despite these limitations, many readers love the Caribbean Beach. An Edgewater, Colorado, couple comes to its defense:

Caribbean Beach was great. The hotel was full, but we saw very few people. It's laid out so you have some privacy, even though there was a bit of walking. However, the food court meals were always served at the same temperature and degree of staleness.

A Philadelphia dad with two tots in tow also had mostly positive things to say:

The Caribbean Beach Resort was beautiful. Our island (Barbados) was very quiet and relaxing on the courtyard/garden side, but the walk to the bus stop with a child was a bit of a haul.

A Kingwood, Texas, family of five also found the resort to be overly large but lucked out with the location of their room:

The Caribbean Beach Resort is a lovely property with a great pool and splash pad for our little guy. Fortunately, we had our own car with us because the thought of walking a half mile for food, drink, or the pool was daunting after a day in the parks. We felt like offering rides to others for a buck!

This 20-something couple from Kansas City, Missouri, wished they'd had a car:

The Caribbean Beach Resort is incredibly hard to navigate, and the bus service is horrendous. It often felt like there was only one bus running at a time, and we experienced several 30-plus-minute waits for the bus to and from parks. The resort is huge, and the bus circled the entire resort before it headed to the destination, so if you were unlucky enough to be on one of the last stops during a rush to the parks, the bus would pass right by if it was full. On multiple occasions we arrived at the bus stop 1-plus hour before our dining reservations but still found ourselves running from the park gates to make it to the restaurant on time!

From a Ridgeway, Virginia, mother of one:

The Caribbean Beach Resort was great—especially the housekeeping staff, who creatively rearranged my daughter's toys every day. Made coming back to the room much more fun. My only complaint with CBR was the inefficiency of checkout—although express checkout was available, someone had to be present to have luggage moved from the room to the main house for transport via Magical Express. We had scheduled a late-afternoon flight on our last day so we could all spend one last morning in the park—I missed most of it because I had to go and sit with the luggage. I was not happy AT ALL.

A mom from Fenton, Michigan, found bus service lacking:

We recommend renting a car and/or paying for a preferred room location—especially if you're going in the hotter months or are impatient. The buses just take way too long with all the stops, and we thought it was a long hike to the food court and pools in the heat.

GOOD (AND NOT-SO-GOOD) ROOMS AT THE CARIBBEAN BEACH RESORT *(See **tinyurl.com/cbrroomviews** for photos.)* The resort's grounds are quite pleasant. Landscaping—lots of ferns and palm trees—is verdant, especially in the courtyards. The six "islands," or groups of buildings clustered around Barefoot Bay, are identical. The two-story motel-style structures are arranged in various ways to face court-yards, pools, the bay, and so forth. The setup is similar to Disney's Coronado Springs Resort in nearly every way but theme.

In general, corner rooms are preferable since they have more windows. Standard-view rooms face either the parking lots or courtyards, and the usual broad interpretation of water views is in play here. Beyond that, your main choices will revolve around your preference for proximity to (or distance from) the Custom House, pools, parking lots, pirates, or beaches on Barefoot Bay. Each island has direct access to at least one beach, playground, bus stop, and parking lot.

The island of Barbados is nearest the Custom House, but its central location guarantees that it also experiences the most foot traffic and road noise. It also shares its only beach and playground with Martinique, which probably is the best area for families. Martinique has access to two beaches, is adjacent to the main pool and playground at Old Port Royale Centertown, and yet is removed enough from the Custom House to offer a little serenity for parents.

The islands of Aruba and Jamaica are similar in character to Martinique, but each has only one beach, and guests must cross a footbridge to reach Old Port Royale center. Trinidad North comprises three buildings, and its thin layout means that noise penetrates its courtyard from surrounding roads and from rambunctious kids at Old Port Royale next door. The quietest island is Trinidad South, which is most remote from resort facilities. It has its own playground and beach, and the beach has a bonus—the view across Barefoot Bay is of wild, undeveloped Florida forest, a rarity on Disney property.

After you've sorted out your convenience and location priorities, think about the view. Avoid the standard-view rooms; all look onto a parking lot, road, or tiny garden. Water views at the Caribbean overlook swimming pools or Barefoot Bay. Pool views are less than enchanting, and there's lots of noise and activity around the pools. Bay views are the pick of the litter at the Caribbean. Such rooms in Barbados, Martinique, Trinidad North, and Trinidad South catch the afternoon sun. Bay-view rooms in Aruba and Jamaica catch the morning sun. Because we like the sun at our back in the evening, we always go for rooms 4246–4252 in Jamaica, 1246–1248 in Barbados, or 5256–5260 and 5541–5548 (but not 5542 or 5545) in Aruba. If you don't mind the sun in your eyes during cocktail time, rooms 2254–2256, 2413–2416, and 2445–2448 in Martinique are good bets, as are lake-facing rooms 3533–3534, 3853–3858, and 3949 in Trinidad South. We're not crazy about any room in Trinidad North. Be aware that the aging air-conditioning units for individual buildings are pretty loud. One room with an especially nice bay view (2525 in Martinique) is nonetheless not recommended because of its proximity to a clunky AC unit. Try room 2558 instead.

THE BONNET CREEK RESORTS

Not to be confused with the Disney resorts that follow, the **Bonnet Creek Resort** *is a 70-acre hotel, golf, and convention complex along Bonnet Creek. Although adjacent to and accessible from the World, it is not owned by Disney. Two of its four hotels are reviewed in "Hotels Outside Walt Disney World."*

Disney's Saratoga Springs Resort & Spa
(See **tinyurl.com/ug-ssr** for extended coverage.)
Treehouse Villas at Disney's Saratoga Springs Resort & Spa
(see maps on following pages)

SARATOGA SPRINGS, A DISNEY DELUXE VILLA RESORT, has a theme wordily described by Disney as recalling an "1880s, Victorian, upstate New York lakeside retreat" amid "pastoral landscapes, formal gardens, bubbling springs, and natural surroundings." Saratoga Springs comprises 1,260 studio and one-, two-, and three-bedroom villas across the lake from Disney Springs. Housed in 12 buildings, most accommodations are of recent vintage, while the fitness center and check-in building are retooled vestiges of the erstwhile Disney Institute. An adjacent 60-unit DDV complex, **Treehouse Villas at Disney's Saratoga Springs Resort & Spa,** opened in 2009.

The fitness center is by far the best at Walt Disney World. The Senses spa, like the Grand Floridian's, was refurbished in 2013 along the lines of those on Disney's cruise ships. Service and decor are very good, and this Senses location is easier to get to than the one at the Grand Floridian if you're staying east of the World. See page 759 for a full review.

Surrounded on three sides by golf courses, Saratoga Springs is the only Disney-owned resort that affords direct access to the links (the military-only Shades of Green also provides golf on-property).

Furnishings and soft goods are less whimsical and more upscale and masculine than at other Disney resorts. Chairs, sofas, and tables are substantial—perhaps a little too substantial for the rooms they inhabit. The overall effect, however, is sophisticated and restful. A Gulf Shores, Alabama, family, however, takes a slight exception to the restful part:

> Saratoga Springs Resort was beautiful, comfortable, and exactly what we needed for our family of five. It was VERY quiet . . . except for the toilets. When you flushed, it sounded like the space shuttle launching.

A couple from Peru, Indiana, takes a more critical tack:

> Saratoga Springs is our least favorite resort. We didn't enjoy the theming, and unless you have a car, getting around by bus is a real hassle. The food court is very small and the food expensive. Also, checkout

SARATOGA SPRINGS RESORT & SPA

STRENGTHS
- Often available at discounted rates or as a DVC/DDV rental
- Attractive main pool; multiple well-themed quiet pools with snack bars
- Closest resort to Disney Springs and Typhoon Lagoon
- Convenient parking
- Only WDW-owned resort with dedicated golf (Lake Buena Vista Golf Course)
- Grocery options in gift shop
- Very nice spa and fitness center

WEAKNESSES
- On-site dining is limited for a resort of this size
- Theme is dull compared with those of other Disney resorts
- Villas are beginning to show some wear
- Fewer baths per bedroom than newer DVC/DDV properties
- Bus service can take some time to get out of the (huge) resort

*was very slow, and our room seemed smaller than comparable rooms
at BoardWalk Villas and Old Key West.*

A Cartersville, Georgia, reader echoes the previous complaint
about bus service:

*No matter when we tried to leave a park for Saratoga Springs, there
were no buses—45 minutes was the norm. Why pay the premium when
you end up driving or taking cabs so as not to waste 2–3 hours per day?*

**GOOD (AND NOT-SO-GOOD) ROOMS AT SARATOGA SPRINGS RESORT &
SPA** *(See* **tinyurl.com/ssrroomviews** *for photos.)* This resort's sprawling
size puts some of its best rooms very far away from the main lobby,
restaurants, and shops. If you don't have a car, the best rooms are those
in The Springs, numbered 3101–3436 and 3501–3836. Ask for a room
toward the northeast side of these buildings (away from the lobby), as
the southwest rooms border a well-traveled road. Avoid rooms 4101–
4436 in Building 14; a pedestrian walkway runs behind the patios of
this building and gets a lot of use in the early morning from guests
headed to breakfast.

If you have a car or you don't mind a couple of extra furlongs' walk
to the lobby, rooms 1101–1436 and 2501–2836 in Congress Park
offer quietness, a view of Disney Springs, and a relatively short walk
to the bus stop. Also good are rooms 4501–4826, 6101–6436, and
6501–6836 in The Paddock. Avoid rooms on the northeast side of the
5101–5435 building of The Paddock, as well as the northwest side of
the 5501–5836 building; these border a swimming pool and bus stop.

In addition to being quiet, rooms 1101–1436 of Congress Park and
rooms 6101–6436 and 6501–6836 of The Paddock afford the closest
walks to Disney Springs shops, restaurants, and entertainment.

TREEHOUSE VILLAS AT DISNEY'S SARATOGA SPRINGS RESORT & SPA
Opened in 2009, this complex of 60 three-bedroom villas lies between
Old Key West Resort and the Grandstand section of Saratoga Springs
proper, with a separate entrance off Disney Vacation Club Way. The
treehouses are bordered by Lake Buena Vista Golf Course to the northeast and a waterway to the southwest that feeds into Village Lake.

True to their name, the villas stand on stilts 10 feet off the ground
(ramps provide wheelchair access) and are surrounded by a densely

TREEHOUSE VILLAS

STRENGTHS	WEAKNESSES
• Spectacular stand-alone three-bedroom villas	• Long distance from Saratoga Springs services such as check-in and dining
• Quiet location	• Kids may find all that quiet boring
• Historical connection to the Treehouses from the 1970s	• Lackluster pool
• Innovative round design feels more spacious than other villas with the same square footage	• Limited number of units makes the Treehouses among the most difficult accommodations to book at WDW
	• Only two baths per villa
	• Bus travelers connect through Saratoga Springs

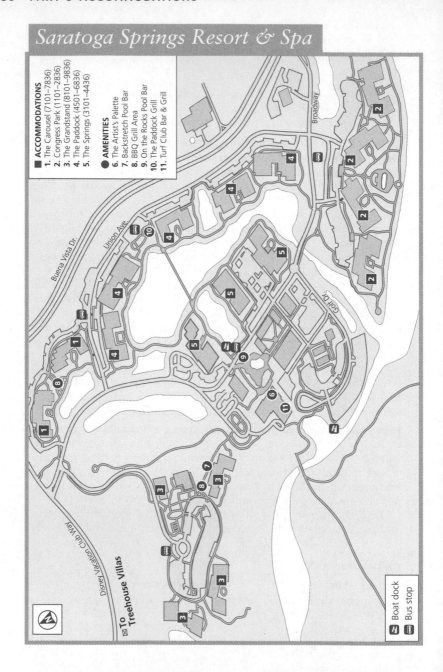

Saratoga Springs Resort & Spa

ACCOMMODATIONS
1. The Carousel (7101–7836)
2. Congress Park (1101–2836)
3. The Grandstand (8101–9836)
4. The Paddock (4501–6836)
5. The Springs (3101–4436)

AMENITIES
6. The Artist's Palette
7. Backstretch Pool Bar
8. BBQ Grill Area
9. On the Rocks Pool Bar
10. The Paddock Grill
11. Turf Club Bar & Grill

Boat dock
Bus stop

wooded landscape. Each villa is an eight-sided structure with three bedrooms and two full bathrooms in about 1,074 square feet.

Each villa holds nine people, about the same number as comparably sized rooms at the other DVC/DDV resorts. The master and second bedrooms have queen beds, and the third bedroom has bunk

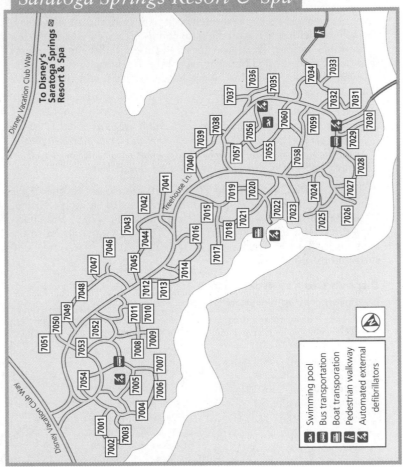

Treehouse Villas at Saratoga Springs Resort & Spa

beds. A sofa bed and sleeper chair in the living room round out the mattress lineup. As with sleeper sofas and chairs in general, we think these are more appropriate for kids than adults.

The three-bedroom Treehouses usually cost about $130–$230 more per night than a comparably sized two-bedroom villa elsewhere at Saratoga Springs. The trade-off, however, is that you get an extra bedroom and give up some living space elsewhere. You probably won't notice the missing space because the layout of the kitchen, dining, and living areas is so open. Beware the master-bathroom shower, which is next to the tub in an enclosed glass wall: Tilt down to shave your legs or grab a bottle of shampoo, and you could whack your head on the side of the tub.

The interior of each villa is decorated with natural materials, such as stone floors in the kitchen, granite countertops, and stained wood furniture. End tables, picture frames, and bunk beds are made from rustic logs. Bathrooms, outfitted in modern tile, have showers and tubs plus a decent amount of counter space.

Because of its location, Treehouse Villas has few amenities of its own: Each villa has a large wooden deck with grill, and all villas share a small pool with spa. A walking path connects the complex to the rest of Saratoga Springs; Treehouse guests can use all of the main resort's facilities. Two dedicated bus stops serve the Treehouses.

A family from Columbus, New Jersey, thinks a stay at the Treehouse Villas is money well spent:

> *I give them five stars for value. We were trying to be economical, as there were nine people in our party and it saved us about $700–$1,000 per night. Our villa had three rooms and a pullout couch that comfortably housed our group. It had a great eat-in kitchen as well, which further helped us save money on breakfast.*

Treehouses 7024–7034 and 7058–7060 are closest to one of the villas' two dedicated bus stops and the walkway to Saratoga Springs; 7026–7033 also have water views. Treehouses 7001–7011 and 7045–7054 are closest to the other bus stop; 7020–7023 are closest to the boat docks. Finally, Treehouses 7035–7037, 7055, 7056, and 7060 surround the pool.

Disney's Old Key West Resort

*(See **tinyurl.com/ug-okwest** for extended coverage.)*

STRENGTHS	
• Largest villas of the DVC/DDV resorts	• Grocery selection in gift shop
• Often available at discounted rates or as DVC rental	• Convenient parking
• Mature landscaping	**WEAKNESSES**
• Homey, well-themed lounge (The Gurgling Suitcase)	• Multiple bus stops
	• No elevators in many buildings
• Close to Lake Buena Vista Golf Course	• Fewer baths per bedroom than newer DVC/DDV properties
• Boat service to Disney Springs	• Mediocre on-site dining

THIS WAS THE FIRST DVC/DDV PROPERTY. Although the resort is a time-share property, units not being used by owners are rented on a nightly basis. Old Key West Resort is a large aggregation of two- to three-story buildings modeled after Caribbean-style residences and guesthouses of the Florida Keys. Set subdivision-style around a golf course and along Bonnet Creek, the buildings are arranged in small, neighborhood-like clusters. They feature pastel facades, white trim, and shuttered windows. The registration area is in Conch Flats Community Hall, along with a full-service restaurant, modest fitness center, marina, and sundries shop. Each cluster of accommodations has a quiet pool; a larger pool is at the community hall. (A waterslide in the shape of a giant sand castle highlights the main pool.)

This resort offers some of the roomiest accommodations at Walt Disney World, with all rooms having been refurbished in 2010. Studios are 376 square feet; one-bedroom villas, 942; and two-bedroom

Old Key West Resort

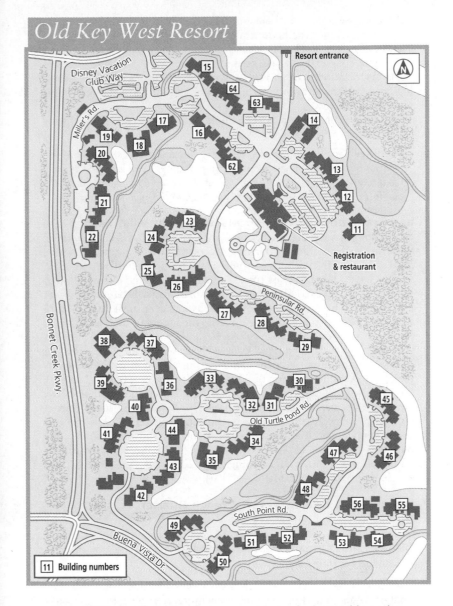

Resort entrance

Disney Vacation Club Way

Miller's Rd.

15
64
63
17
16
19
18
62
20
21
22
23
24
25
26
27
28
29

14
13
12
11

Registration & restaurant

Peninsular Rd.

Bonnet Creek Pkwy.

38
37
39
36
33
40
32 31
44
41
43
35
42

30
45
Old Turtle Pond Rd.
34
47
46
48

49
51 52
50

South Point Rd.

56 55
53 54

Buena Vista Dr.

11 Building numbers

villas, 1,333. Studios contain two queen-size beds, a table and two chairs, and an extra vanity outside the bathroom. One-bedroom villas have a king-size bed in the master bedroom, a queen-size sleeper sofa in the living room, a laundry room, and a full kitchen with coffeemaker. Two-bedroom villas feature a king-size bed in the master bedroom, a queen-size sleeper sofa and fold-out chair in the living room, and two queen beds in the second bedroom. All villas have enough closet space to contain your entire wardrobe. Studios and villas are tastefully decorated with leather and upholstered furniture in neutral tan or green color schemes. The wood kitchen table and chairs are painted white. One-bedroom and larger villas have wood flooring instead of carpet. Each villa has a private balcony that opens to views of the golf course, landscape, or a waterway.

Transportation to other Disney World destinations is by bus. Walking time to transportation loading areas from the most remote rooms is about 6 minutes.

An Erie, Pennsylvania, reader thinks Old Key West is Walt Disney World's most well-kept secret:

> Old Key West has the most spacious rooms and villas and the easiest access to your car—right outside your door! It's in a great location and built around a gorgeous golf course. There are a number of small, almost private pools, so you don't have to go to the main pool to swim.

GOOD (AND NOT-SO-GOOD) ROOMS AT OLD KEY WEST RESORT *(See* **tinyurl.com/okw-roomviews** *for photos.)* Old Key West is huge, with 49 three-story villa buildings offering a mix of studio and multiroom villas. Views are nice from almost all villas; all multiroom villas and some studios have a large balcony furnished with a table and chairs. Though nice vistas are easy to come by, quiet is more elusive. Because the resort is bordered by busy Bonnet Creek Parkway and even busier Buena Vista Drive, the best villas are those as far from the highway noise as possible. For quiet isolation and a lovely river view, ask for Building 46 or 45, in that order. For a lake and golf-course view away from road noise but closest to restaurants, recreation, the marina, the main swimming complex, and shopping, ask for Building 13. Nearby, Buildings 12 and 11 are likewise quiet and convenient but offer primarily golf-course views. Next-best choices are Buildings 32 and 34. Building 32 looks onto a lake with the golf course in the background, while 34 faces the golf course with tennis courts to the left and a lake to the right. None of the buildings recommended is more than a 2- to 5-minute walk to the nearest bus stop or pool. Avoid Buildings 19–22, 38 and 39, 41 and 42, and 49–54, which border Bonnet Creek Parkway and Buena Vista Drive.

Disney's Port Orleans Resort–French Quarter
(See **tinyurl.com/ug-pofq** *for extended coverage.)*

Disney's Port Orleans Resort–Riverside
(See **tinyurl.com/ug-por** *for extended coverage.)*

A MODERATE RESORT, Port Orleans is divided into two sections. The smaller, southern part is called the French Quarter; the larger section is labeled Riverside.

PORT ORLEANS RESORT–FRENCH QUARTER The 1,008-room French Quarter section is a sanitized Disney version of New Orleans's Vieux Carré. Consisting of seven three-story guest-room buildings next to the Sassagoula River, the resort suggests what New Orleans would look like if its buildings were painted every year and garbage collectors never went on strike. Prim pink-and-blue guest buildings are festooned with wrought-iron filigree, shuttered windows, and old-fashioned iron lampposts. In keeping with the Crescent City theme, French Quarter is

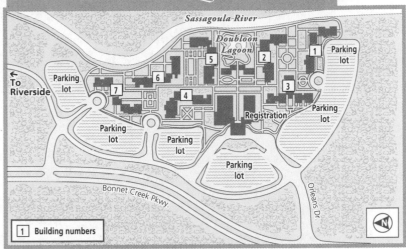

Port Orleans French Quarter Resort

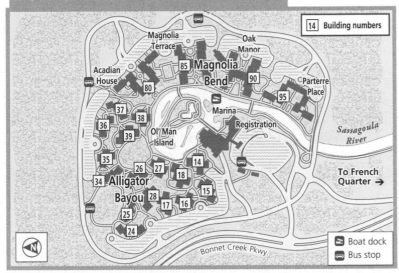

Port Orleans Riverside Resort

landscaped with magnolia trees and overgrown vines. The centrally located Mint contains the registration area and food court and is a reproduction of a turn-of-the-19th-century building where Mississippi Delta farmers sold their harvests.

The registration desk features a vibrant Mardi Gras mural and old-fashioned bank-teller windows. Doubloon Lagoon surrounds a colorful fiberglass creation depicting Neptune riding a sea serpent.

PORT ORLEANS-FRENCH QUARTER

STRENGTHS	
• Most compact of the WDW Moderate resorts	• Good place to walk or run for fitness
• One bus stop	**WEAKNESSES**
• Live entertainment in Scat Cat's Club	• Ho-hum pool
• Beignets in food court!	• Shares bus service with Port Orleans Riverside during slower times of year
• Attractively themed lobby	• No full-service dining
• Short walk to Port Orleans Riverside's restaurants and bars	

PORT ORLEANS RESORT-RIVERSIDE

STRENGTHS	
• Interesting narrative to theming	• Close driving distance to the Magic Kingdom
• Disney princess–themed rooms in Magnolia Bend	• Good place to walk or run for fitness
• Live entertainment in River Roost Lounge	• Recreation options (bikes, boats)
• A Moderate resort that can sleep five, in a Murphy bed at Alligator Bayou	**WEAKNESSES**
• Very nice feature pool	• Multiple bus stops; shares service with Port Orleans French Quarter during slower times of year
	• Mediocre full service restaurant

French Quarter rooms measure 314 square feet. Most contain two queen beds, a table and two chairs, a dresser–credenza, a mini-fridge, a coffeemaker, and a vanity outside the bathroom. With their cherry headboards, Mardi Gras–purple coverlets, cherry-wood credenzas, and olive carpet, the rooms are themed but tasteful. A privacy curtain separates the dressing area from the rest of the room, allowing three people to get ready at once. No rooms have balconies, but ornamental iron-railed accessways on each floor provide a good (though less private) substitute.

There's a food court but no full-service restaurant. The closest full-service eatery is in the adjacent Riverside section of the resort, about a 15-plus-minute walk. The commute to restaurants in other hotels may be 40–60 minutes each way. The Disney bus system links the French Quarter to all Disney World destinations. Walking time to bus-loading areas from the most remote French Quarter rooms is 5 minutes or less.

Most readers really like Port Orleans French Quarter. This comment from a Wynnewood, Pennsylvania, father of two is typical:

I highly recommend Port Orleans French Quarter. We stayed at All-Star Movies on our last trip and didn't think it made sense to stay anywhere else. Well, we were wrong. The price difference wasn't that big, and what we got for the difference was well worth it: uncrowded pool, bellhop service, front-door greeters with great tips for touring, and a bigger, more comfortable room. Totally worth the extra money.

One Philadelphia Gen Xer wasn't flush with joy about his stay:

The in-room toilets seem to be powered by jet thrusters. We were woken up far too many times in the night when someone in a neighboring room would flush.

An unidentified e-mailer backs him up:

The reader comment about the toilets is 100% correct. They're air-pressure-forced rather than water-flow-and-gravity-operated—like an airplane toilet, only MUCH louder. Every morning I was woken up at 7:30 a.m. with an hour's worth of whoooshing.

GOOD (AND NOT-SO-GOOD) ROOMS AT PORT ORLEANS FRENCH QUARTER *(See* **tinyurl.com/pofq-roomviews** *for photos.)* Seven guest-room buildings flank the pool and Guest Relations building and bus stop. The best views are from rooms facing the river and pine forest on the opposite bank. Wings of Buildings 1, 2, 5, 6, and 7 flank the river and provide the best river views in all of Port Orleans. River-view rooms in Buildings 1, 6, and 7 are a long walk from French Quarter public facilities, but they're the most tranquil. Families with children should request river-view rooms in Buildings 2 and 5, nearest the swimming complex. Make sure the reservationist understands that you're requesting a room with a river view, not just a water view. All river-view rooms are also water-view rooms, but not vice versa. Note that standard-view rooms look onto a courtyard or a parking lot.

Following are the best river-view rooms in each building:

BUILDING 1 Rooms 1127–1132, 1227–1232 (except 1229), 1327–1332
BUILDING 2 Rooms 2227–2232, 2327–2332
BUILDING 5 Rooms 5118–5123, 5218–5224, 5318–5325
BUILDING 6 Rooms 6123–6126, 6223–6226, 6323–6326, 6138–6139, 6236–6240, 6335–6340, 6145–6148, 6245–6248, 6345–6348
BUILDING 7 Rooms 7142–7147, 7242–7247, 7342–7347

Note that room 6X23 in Building 6 is a corner room with two windows, one of which faces the river. But Disney puts it in the less expensive garden-view category.

PORT ORLEANS RESORT–RIVERSIDE This resort draws on the lifestyle and architecture of Mississippi River communities in antebellum Louisiana. Spread along the Sassagoula River, which encircles Ol' Man Island (the section's main swimming area), Riverside is subdivided into two more themed areas: the mansion area, which features plantation-style architecture, and the bayou area, with tin-roofed rustic (imitation) wooden buildings. Mansions are three stories tall, while bayou guesthouses are a story shorter. Riverside's food court houses a working cotton press powered by a 32-foot waterwheel.

Each of Riverside's 2,048 rooms is 314 square feet. Most provide one king or two queen beds, a table and two chairs, a mini-fridge and coffeemaker, and two pedestal sinks outside the bathroom. Rooms in the Alligator Bayou section of Riverside feature brass bathroom fixtures, hickory-branch bedposts, Murphy beds, and quilted bedspreads. Rooms in the plantation-themed Magnolia Bend section of Riverside are more conventional, with light-green walls, chestnut-colored wood furnishings, olive carpets, and dark-blue bedding accents.

All four Riverside buildings contain exclusively Disney princess–themed rooms, similar in concept to the Disney-themed rooms at Caribbean Beach. Riverside's rooms are themed to *The Princess and the Frog*, with appearances by Tiana's other princess friends. These rooms cost around $70 more per night than other rooms.

Rooms in Alligator Bayou—along with those at Caribbean Beach—are unique among Disney's Moderate properties in that they sleep five people; the fifth is a fold-down, Murphy-style bed, more suitable for children than adults.

Many readers have written asking us to emphasize that, aside from the differences in guest rooms described previously, all the rooms are more or less the same regardless of the facade of your building, as a New York City reader observed:

Although the Riverside section is modeled after mansions of the Old South, the outside of each building is simply a shell—there's little or no decor inside your room that corresponds to the theme outside.

This reader didn't have room for all of his stuff:

Our room was adequate but lacked storage. We stayed in the Alligator Bayou section, so instead of a large dresser, we had a Murphy bed with three small drawers. The location was nice, but because we were two adults, being in a room with a Murphy bed didn't make sense.

A Lexington, Kentucky, mom touts Riverside's counter-service food:

The counter service at Riverside was the most convenient, efficient, and spacious of any we've experienced at Disney. The pasta bar was one of the most enjoyable meals we experienced—and we had counter service at the Grand Floridian, the Polynesian Village, and the Contemporary, plus we ate at Cinderella's Royal Table, Chef Mickey's, The Crystal Palace, the Biergarten, and Akershus.

GOOD (AND NOT-SO-GOOD) ROOMS AT PORT ORLEANS RIVERSIDE RESORT *(See* **tinyurl.com/por-roomviews** *for photos.)* Riverside is so large that we use bicycles whenever we work there. All told, there are 20 guest-room buildings (not counting flanking wings on two buildings). Divided into two sections, Alligator Bayou and Magnolia Bend, the resort is arrayed around two pine groves and a watercourse that Disney calls the Sassagoula River. Magnolia Bend consists of four three-story, grand plantation–style complexes named Acadian House, Magnolia Terrace, Oak Manor, and Parterre Place. Though Magnolia Bend is on the river, only about 15% of the guest rooms have an unobstructed view of the water. The vast majority of rooms overlook a courtyard or parking lot. Trees and other vegetation block the view of many rooms actually facing the river. The best views in Magnolia Bend are from the third-floor river side of Acadian House (Building 80), which overlooks the river and Ol' Man Island: rooms 8417–8419.

To the south are Magnolia Terrace (Building 85) and Oak Manor (Building 90), each in an H shape. They're nearer the front desk, restaurant, lounge, and shopping complex than Acadian House. Continuing south, Parterre Place (Building 95) has a number of rooms facing the river, but the views are blocked by trees or extend to the parking lot on the opposite shore. In general, with the few previous exceptions, if you want a nice river view, opt for Port Orleans French Quarter downriver.

Alligator Bayou, the other part of Port Orleans Riverside, forms an arch around the resort's northern half. Sixteen smaller, two-story guest-room buildings, set among pine groves and abundant gardens, offer a cozy alternative to the more-imposing structures of the Magnolia Bend section of Riverside and Port Orleans French Quarter. If you want a river view, ask for a second-story water-view room in Building 27 or 38. Building 14 also offers some river-view rooms and is convenient to shops, the front desk, and the restaurant, but it's in a noisy, high-traffic area. A good compromise for families is Building 18. It's insulated from traffic and noise by landscaping, yet is next to a satellite swimming pool and within an easy walk of the lobby and restaurant.

Disney's Port Orleans Riverside map shows two lakes north of the river bend, suggesting additional water views in Alligator Bayou. But these are dried-up lakes now forested with pine. This area, however, is richly landscaped to complement the "pine islands," and though out of sight of water, it offers the most peaceful and serene accommodations in the Port Orleans resort. In this area, we recommend Buildings 26, 25, and 39, in that order. Note that these buildings are somewhat distant from the resort's central facilities, and there's no adjacent parking. In Alligator Bayou, avoid Buildings 15, 16, 17, and 24, all of which are subject to traffic noise from nearby Bonnet Creek Parkway.

Remember: All Port Orleans guest buildings have exterior corridors. When you look out your window, a safety rail will be in the foreground, and other guests will periodically walk past.

THE ANIMAL KINGDOM RESORTS

Disney's Animal Kingdom Lodge & Villas: Jambo House
(See **tinyurl.com/ug-aklodge** *for extended coverage.*)

Disney's Animal Kingdom Villas: Kidani Village
(See **tinyurl.com/ug-kidani** *for extended coverage.*) **(see map next page)**

IN THE FAR SOUTHWEST CORNER OF THE WORLD and adjacent to Disney's Animal Kingdom theme park, Animal Kingdom Lodge opened in 2001. Designed by Peter Dominick of Wilderness Lodge fame, the resort fuses African tribal architecture with the rugged style of grand East African national-park lodges. Five-story thatched-roof guest-room wings fan out from a vast central rotunda housing the lobby. Public areas and about half of the rooms offer panoramic views of a private 43-acre wild-life preserve, punctuated with streams and elevated *kopje* (rock outcrops) and populated with some 200 free-roaming animals and 130 birds.

Most of the 972 guest rooms measure 344 square feet and boast hand-carved furnishings and richly colored soft goods. Standard amenities include a flat-panel TV, desk with two chairs, ceiling fan, mini-fridge, and coffeemaker. Behind each headboard sits faux mosquito netting. (Perhaps the tan curtains are supposed to be the folds of a safari tent.) Bathrooms have animal-themed wallpaper, two sinks, and a large mirror. Almost all rooms have full balconies.

The resort is divided into Jambo House, which has both regular hotel rooms and DDV units, and the all-DDV Kidani Village.

Animal Kingdom Lodge & Villas

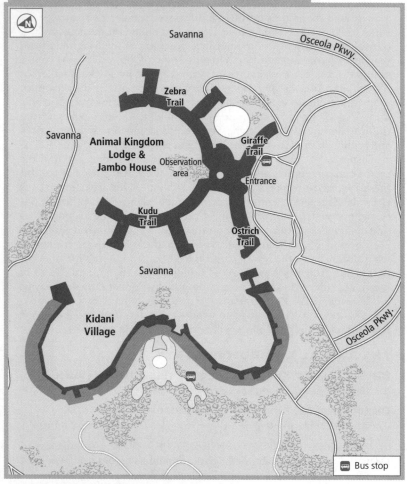

Jambo House offers fine dining in a casual setting at Jiko—The Cooking Place. Twin wood-burning ovens are the focal point of the restaurant, which serves meals inspired by the myriad cuisines of Africa. Boma—Flavors of Africa, the family restaurant, serves a buffet with food prepared in an exhibition kitchen featuring a wood-burning grill and rotisserie. Tables are under thatched roofs. The Mara, a quick-service restaurant with extended hours, and Victoria Falls, a delightful mezzanine lounge overlooking Boma, round out the hotel's food-and-beverage service. Other amenities include an elaborate swimming area, a village marketplace, and a 1-hour nighttime safari tour exclusively for Lodge guests ages 8 and up. The tour costs $70 per person and takes place nightly at 10 p.m.

Consisting of a separate building shaped like a backwards 3, Kidani Village comprises 324 units, a dedicated savanna, a well-themed pool

ANIMAL KINGDOM LODGE & VILLAS: JAMBO HOUSE

STRENGTHS	WEAKNESSES
• Magnificent lobby	• Jambo House villas are smaller than those at Kidani Village
• Excellent on-site dining options	
• Large, beautiful feature pool	• Rooms are among the smallest of the Deluxe resorts
• On-site cultural and nature programs	• No direct nonbus transportation to any theme park
• Best theming of any Disney hotel	

ANIMAL KINGDOM VILLAS: KIDANI VILLAGE

STRENGTHS	
• Nice pool with excellent splash area	• Close to Jambo House amenities and restaurants
• Underground parking close to elevators	• One of the nicest fitness rooms on-property
• Beautiful, understated lobby	**WEAKNESSES**
• Sanaa restaurant is an *Unofficial Guide* favorite	• Savanna views can be hit-and-miss
• Beautiful Grand Villas sleep 13	• No quick-service food other than pool bar

and splash zone, and Sanaa, a sit-down restaurant combining Indian and African cuisines. Other amenities include a fitness center, an arcade, a gift shop, and tennis, shuffleboard, and basketball courts. Kidani Village is connected to Jambo House by a half-mile walking trail; DDV guests at either resort can use the facilities at both buildings.

Both Jambo House and Kidani Village have studios and one-, two-, and three-bedroom villas. Most rooms at Kidani Village are larger, however, and the difference is anywhere from 50 square feet for a studio to more than 200 square feet for a two-bedroom unit. (The three-bedroom Grand Villas at Jambo House, 148 square feet larger than those in Kidani Village, are the exception.) Kidani's villas also have one more bathroom for one-, two-, and three-bedroom units. Because of the difference in area, one-bedroom units in Kidani Village can accommodate up to five people, and two-bedroom units can hold up to nine via a sleeper chair in the living room. At Jambo House, one-bedroom "value" rooms sleep four; standard, savanna, and Club Level rooms sleep five.

Having stayed at Kidani Village almost a dozen times, we think it's quiet and relaxed. The lobby and rooms have a smaller, more personal feel than Jambo House's. The exterior isn't anything special—essentially a set of green rectangles with oversize African-themed decorations attached. Kidani's distance from Jambo House makes it feel especially remote. The bus stops are a fair distance from the main building, too, and it's easy to head in the wrong direction when you're coming back from the parks at night.

Animal Kingdom Lodge & Villas is connected to the rest of Disney World by bus, but because of the resort's remote location, you should seriously consider having a car if you stay there.

A family of four from Lincoln, England, gives Animal Kingdom Lodge a mixed, though mostly positive, review:

We had a fab holiday, but we wouldn't recommend people paying the extra money to have a savanna room. The animals are scarce, and you don't really spend much time in your room. The pool and the kids' club were fantastic and the hotel stunning. The food court was fine, although we wished they'd change the menu, as after two weeks you're fed up of the same choices.

GOOD (AND NOT-SO-GOOD) ROOMS AT ANIMAL KINGDOM LODGE & VIL-LAS *(See* **tinyurl.com/akl-roomviews** *for photos.)* A glance at the resort map tells you where the best rooms and villas are. Kudu Trail and Zebra Trail, two wings branching from the rear of Jambo House, form a semi-circle around the central wildlife savanna. Along each wing are seven five-story buildings, with accommodations on floors two through five. Five buildings on each wing form the semicircle, while the remaining two buildings jut away from the center. The best rooms—on floors three and four, facing into the circle—are high enough to survey the entire savanna yet low enough to let you appreciate the ground-level detail of this amazing wildlife exhibit; plus, these rooms offer the easiest access to the lobby and restaurants. Second-floor rooms really can't take in the panorama, and fifth-floor rooms are a little too high for intimate views of the animals. Most of the fourth-floor rooms in Jambo House are reserved for concierge guests, and the fifth and sixth floors house the DDV units.

Most rooms in the outward-jutting buildings, as well as rooms facing away from the interior, also survey a savanna, but one not as compelling as that of the inner circle. On the Zebra Trail, the first two buildings plus the first jutting building provide savanna views on one side and look onto the swimming complex on the other.

Less attractive still are two smaller wings, Ostrich Trail and Giraffe Trail, branching from either side of the lodge near the main entrance. Some rooms on the left side of Ostrich Trail (see map on page 196) overlook a small savanna. Rooms on the opposite side of the same buildings overlook the front entrance. Least desirable is Giraffe Trail, extending from the right side of the lobby: Its rooms overlook either the pool (water view) or the resort entrance (standard view). A Portage, Indiana, family begs to differ with our assessment, however:

We stayed in a pool-view room in Giraffe Trail and loved it. The view was beautiful, even without the animals (which you can see elsewhere). The proximity to the pool, lobby, and restaurants was great, and we saved about $500 over what we would've spent on a savanna view.

The best views in Kidani Village are the north-facing rooms near the bottom and middle of the backwards 3. Try rooms 7X38–7X44, 7X46–7X52, 7X06–7X11, 7X68–7X82, and 7X61–7X67 (X = numbers 0–9). These overlook the savanna next to Jambo House's Kudu Trail rooms and beyond into undeveloped woods. West- and south-facing rooms in the bottom half of Kidani Village overlook the parking lot; west-facing rooms in the top half have either pool or savanna views. (See **tinyurl.com/kidani-roomviews** for photos.)

Disney's Coronado Springs Resort
(See **tinyurl.com/ug-coronado** *for extended coverage.)*

Coronado Springs Resort

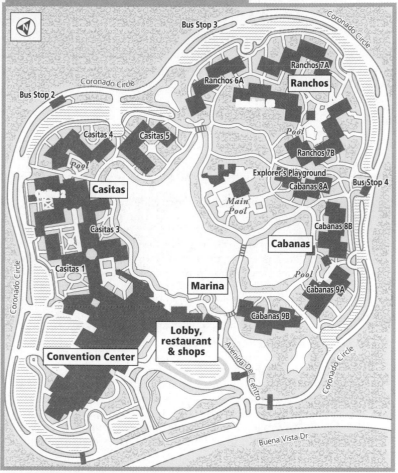

NEAR ANIMAL KINGDOM, Coronado Springs Resort is Disney's only midpriced convention property. Inspired by northern Mexico and the American Southwest, the resort is divided into three separately themed areas. The two- and three-story Ranchos call to mind Southwestern cattle ranches, while the two-story Cabanas are modeled after Mexican beach resorts. The multistoried Casitas embody elements of Spanish architecture found in Mexico's great cities. The lobby, part of the Casitas, features a mosaic ceiling and tiled floor.

The vast resort surrounds a 22-acre lake, and there are three small pools as well as one large swimming complex. The main pool features a reproduction of a Mayan step pyramid with a waterfall cascading down its side.

Most of the 1,915 guest rooms measure 314 square feet and contain two queen beds, a desk and chair, a mini-fridge, a coffeemaker,

CORONADO SPRINGS RESORT

STRENGTHS	WEAKNESSES
• Most sophisticated room decor of the Moderate resorts	• Conventioneers may be off-putting to vacationing families
• Setting is beautiful at night	• Some rooms are a long distance from check-in, lobby, and restaurants
• Themed swimming area with waterslides	• Multiple bus stops
• Large feature pool	
• On-site business center	
• Best public Wi-Fi at any Disney resort	

and a vanity outside the bathroom. Rooms are decorated with a subtle Southwestern theme, with turquoise accents. None of the rooms have their own balconies.

Coronado Springs completed a resort-wide room-refurbishment project in 2015. Updates included new interior paint, carpets, and bath vanities.

Perhaps because Coronado Springs is geared to conventions, getting work done here is easier than at any other Disney Moderate resort. A specially designed light fixture above the desk holds a down-pointing bulb and provides excellent illumination of the work area. Wi-Fi is available throughout the resort, and the business-center staff is friendly and knowledgeable.

Coronado Springs offers two full-service restaurants as well as Disney World's most interesting food court, plus Rix, a bar. Unfortunately, there's not nearly enough food service for a resort this large and remote. We suggest having a car to expand your dining options. The resort is connected to other Disney destinations by bus only. Walking time from the most remote rooms to the bus stop is 8–10 minutes.

Cabana 9B holds Coronado's Business Class rooms, with access to a private lounge for serving breakfast and snacks throughout the day. These rooms cost around $56 per night more than standard rooms, depending on the season.

Reader opinions concerning Coronado Springs are split. A family from Cumming, Georgia, was disappointed:

The convention center really interferes with a family vacation—everyone we met there was working and wanted to talk about work while we were trying to get away from work!

A Chester, Virginia, mother had a very different experience:

Coronado Springs was absolutely fabulous. The staff was friendly, the kids loved the pool, and we all loved Pepper Market. It was nice and quiet at night. There were many convention guests, but they did not interfere with our trip.

For a family from Kansas City, Kansas, Coronado Springs was their first accommodations in a Disney Moderate resort:

This was the first time we stayed at Coronado Springs. On our previous three trips, we stayed at Pop Century, and I was curious if the Moderate resorts were worth the extra money. At first, the size of the resort was daunting, and having the main building so far away from the rooms was a challenge at first. But we quickly settled into a routine and figured out the bus routes—for some of the buses, the main building was the last stop, and for other routes, the first. Maybe it was our bad luck, but finding the internal shuttle was like spotting a unicorn! The bus service was really the only major drawback. The room at Coronado was more spacious and came with a ceiling fan. The door separating the living area from the bath vanity was very useful because I was able to get ready in the morning without waking the kids. The kids really enjoyed the pool area, and I thought it was better themed than Pop Century. The size of the resort meant that we had more walking to and from the pool and main areas, but that also meant it felt less crowded. Overall, I thought the resort was worth the price difference.

A family from Indianapolis liked the swimming pools:

The pool at Coronado Springs was excellent—the kids loved the slide! Also utilized smaller pool close to our room—was good for kids to relax before bedtime.

Finally, a Canvey Island, England, reader was fair and balanced:

We stayed at Coronado Springs and were very satisfied overall. The Pepper Market food court was overly complicated (stamping tickets to pay at the end, multiple tickets per party), but the quality was good. The Maya Grill was a disappointment, overpriced for the quality of the food. The walk around the lake on a nice day is a delight.

As convention hotels go, Coronado Springs is an odd duck. Whereas at comparable hotels everything is centrally located and guest rooms are in close proximity, rooms here are spread around a huge lake. If you're assigned a room on the opposite side of the lake from the meeting area and restaurants, plan on an 11- to 15-minute hike every time you leave your room. If your organization books Coronado Springs for a meeting, consider having your meals catered—the restaurants simply don't have the capacity during a large convention to accommodate the breakfast rush or to serve a quick lunch between sessions.

GOOD (AND NOT-SO-GOOD) ROOMS AT CORONADO SPRINGS RESORT
*(See **tinyurl.com/csr-roomviews** for photos.)* Coronado Springs encircles a large artificial lake called Lago Dorado. In addition to the main building (El Centro), which contains shopping venues, restaurants, and a conference center, there are three communities of accommodations. Moving clockwise around the lake, the Casitas are near the lobby, restaurants, shops, and convention center. Standard-view rooms face parking lots or a courtyard. Water-view rooms cover pools, the lake, and so on. For a good view of Lago Dorado, book one of these rooms:

3220–3287 (except 3224, 3225–3240, 3260–3265, 3266, and 3274–3280)
3320–3383 (except 3324, 3330–3335, 3360–3365, 3374–3380, and 3384–3387)
3420–3487 (except 3424, 3430–3435, 3460–3465, 3474–3479, and 3483–3486)
4461–4464 *(Continued on next page)*

(Continued from previous page)

    5202–5212

    5303–5304, 5311–5312

    5400–5413, 5423–5463 (except 5403–5404, 5411–5412, and 5450)

Next come the Ranchos, set back from the lake. The desert theme translates to lots of cactus and gravel, not much water or shade, and almost no good views. The Ranchos are a hike from everything but the main swimming area. Rooms 6X00–6X04 afford the best views.

Now come the Cabanas, which offer some very nice lake views. Cabana 9B (all Business Class rooms) is our favorite, near restaurants and the convention center, and only a moderate walk to the main pool. Rooms with the best views are 9500–9507, 9528–9543, 9554–9557, 9600–9611, and 9650–9656, with lake views, and 9640–9647, with a view of a small lagoon. Rooms overlooking the lake are subject to some generally tolerable traffic noise.

Other lake-view rooms we recommend include the following:

    8129–8131 and 8142–8147

    8500–8510, 8550–8553, and 8573 (except 8505, 8507, and 8509)

    8600–8610, 8650–8653, and 8673 (except 8605, 8607, and 8609)

    9150–9152 and 9253

Disney's All-Star Resorts: Movies, Music, and Sports
*(See **tinyurl.com/ug-allstars** for extended coverage.)*

DISNEY'S ORIGINAL VERSION OF A BUDGET RESORT features three distinct themes executed in the same hyperbolic style. Spread over a vast expanse, the resorts comprise 30 three-story motel-style guest-room buildings. Although the three resorts are neighbors, each has its own lobby, food court, and registration area. All-Star Sports features huge sports equipment: bright football helmets, tennis rackets, and baseball bats—all taller than the buildings they adorn. Similarly, All-Star Music features 40-foot guitars, maracas, and saxophones, while All-Star Movies showcases giant popcorn boxes and icons from Disney films. The food courts were recently refurbished, and all three resorts offer in-room pizza delivery. Lobbies are loud (in both decibels and brightness) and cartoonish, with checkerboard walls and photographs of famous athletes, musicians, or film stars. There's even a photo of Mickey Mouse with Alice Cooper. Each resort has two main pools; Music's are shaped like musical instruments (the Piano Pool and the guitar-shaped Calypso Pool), and one of Movies' is star-shaped. All six pools feature plastic replicas of Disney characters, some shooting water pistols.

*un**official* **TIP**
Movies has the best food court. **Sports** has the best bus service.

At 260 square feet, standard rooms at the All-Star Resorts are very small—the same size as those at Pop Century Resort and slightly smaller than Art of Animation's standard rooms. All-Star rooms are so small, in fact, that a family of four attempting to stay in one room might redefine *family values* by week's end. Each room has two double beds or one king bed, mini-fridge (no coffeemaker), a separate vanity area, and a table and chairs. Bathrooms have curved shower rods, an improvement.

All-Star Resorts

Except for artwork and bathroom wallpaper, all three resorts' rooms are furnished identically. No rooms have balconies.

If you're planning to save for a Disney vacation, you may want to save enough for a bigger room at another resort if space is an important consideration. Also, the All-Stars are the noisiest Disney resorts,

ALL-STAR RESORTS

STRENGTHS	WEAKNESSES
• Least expensive of the Disney resorts	• Most likely Disney resorts to host large school groups
• Rooms recently refurbished	
• Family suites at All-Star Music are less expensive than those at Art of Animation	• Rooms are small
	• No full-service dining; food courts often overwhelmed at mealtimes
• Convenient parking	
• Lots of pools	• All three resorts share buses during slower times of year; bus stops often crowded
• Lovely landscaping, if you know where to look (Music)	
• In-room pizza delivery	• Perhaps *Fantasia 2000* and *The Mighty Ducks* weren't the best choices to theme two entire sections around?

though guest rooms are well soundproofed and quiet. We still use a white-noise app on our phones when we stay here, though.

Due to the low staff-to-guest ratio, service is mediocre. Also, there are no full-service restaurants, and the bus ride from the remote All-Stars to a sit-down restaurant at another resort is about 45 minutes one-way (there is, however, a McDonald's about a quarter-mile away). Bus service to the theme and water parks is pretty efficient. Walking time to the bus stop from the most remote guest rooms is about 8 minutes.

We receive a lot of letters commenting on the All-Star Resorts. From a family group of 13 from East Greenbush, New York:

The All-Star Resorts are perfectly family-oriented. Some nice touches that were not mentioned in your guide—a small amphitheater set up in the lobby to occupy the kids while you check in, and soft sidewalk material surrounding the kiddie pool. And the playground has two separate jungle gyms—one for older kids and one for younger kids.

A Baltimore family had a similarly positive experience:

We were pleasantly surprised by All-Star Movies. Yes, the rooms are small, but the overall magic there is amazing. The lobby played Disney movies, which is perfect if you get up early and the buses aren't running yet. Customer service was impeccable.

A Canadian family had a not-so-positive experience:

The guide didn't prepare us for the large groups of students who take over the resorts. They're very noisy and very pushy when it comes to getting on buses. Our scariest experience was when we tried getting on a bus and got mobbed by about 100 students.

From a Massachusetts family of four:

I would never recommend the All-Star for a family. It was like dormitory living. Our room was a long hike from the bus stop, and it was tiny—you needed to step into the bathroom, shut the door, then step around the toilet that blocked half the tub.

ALL-STAR MUSIC FAMILY SUITES In the Jazz and Calypso Buildings, the 192 suites measure roughly 520 square feet, slightly larger than the cabins at Fort Wilderness but slightly smaller than Art of Animation's Family Suites. Each suite, formed from the combination of two formerly separate rooms, includes a kitchenette with mini-refrigerator, microwave, and coffeemaker. Sleeping accommodations include a queen bed in the bedroom, plus a pullout sleeper sofa, a chair bed, and an ottoman bed. We're not sure we'd let adult friends (ones we want to keep, anyway) on the sofa bed or the chair or ottoman beds, but they're fine for children. A hefty door separates the two rooms.

The All-Star Music Family Suites also feature flat-panel TVs plus two bathrooms—one more than the Fort Wilderness cabins. The suites cost about 25% less than the cabins and about 20% less than the Art of Animation Family Suites, but they don't have the kitchen space or appliances to prepare anything more than rudimentary meals. If you're trying to save money by eating in your room, the cabins are your best bet. If you just want a little extra space and somewhere to nuke your Pop-Tarts in the morning, the All-Star suites are just fine.

Reader comments about the family suites are generally positive, though measured. First, from a North Carolina family of five:

> It was so nice to have a place to unwind without the kids at night, along with two bathrooms and extra space for breakfast/snacks/drinks in the kitchen area. My only issue was that we weren't comfortable leaving the kids on the foldouts because they're right next to the front door, plus my husband and I didn't want to be confined to the bedroom from the time we put the kids to bed, so we slept on a foldout. The first night was hell, but the second night we took the mattresses off the pullout chair and ottoman and put them on top of the mattress on the couch—MUCH better!

From a Skokie, Illinois, family of five:

> We found the All-Star Music Family Suite to be very roomy for the six of us. Our teenagers and preteen were quite comfortable on the pullout sofa, chair, and ottoman. Having the two bathrooms was a must, and the kitchen area was great; lots of shelf space for the food we had delivered from Garden Grocer (they're excellent, by the way) [see page 482]. Our only complaint is that from 7:30 a.m. until midnight there's always music playing—it can get annoying to always have that beat going in the background. The rooms are soundproofed but not enough; had to use earplugs.

GOOD (AND NOT-SO-GOOD) ROOMS AT THE ALL-STAR RESORTS *(See* **tinyurl.com/asmo-roomviews, tinyurl.com/asmu-roomviews,** *and* **tinyurl.com/assp-roomviews** *for photos.)* Although the layouts of All-Star Resorts' Movies, Music, and Sports sections are different, the buildings are identical three-story, three-winged structures. The T-shaped buildings are further grouped into pairs, generally facing each other, and share a common subtheme. For example, there's a *Toy Story* pair in the Movies section. In addition to being named by theme, such as *Fantasia*, buildings

*un*official **TIP**
Music 5654 may be the best room at the All-Star Resorts. This third-floor corner room overlooks a small pond in a wooded area behind the resort. See **tinyurl.com/music5654** for a photo of the view.

are numbered 1–10 in each section. Rooms are accessed via a motel-style outdoor walkway, but each building has an elevator.

Parking is plentiful, all of it in sprawling lots buffering the three sections. A room near a parking lot means easier loading and unloading but also unsightly views of the lot during your stay. The resort offers a luggage service, but it often takes up to an hour for your bags to arrive.

The sure way to avoid a parking-lot vista is to request a room facing a courtyard or pool. The trade-off is noise. The sound of cars starting in the parking lot is no match for shrieking children or hooting teenagers in the pool. But don't count on a good view of the pool, even if your room faces it directly. The buildings' themed facade decorations are placed on their widest face—the top of the T—which is also the side facing the pool or courtyard. In some cases, as with the surfboards in the Sports section, these significantly obstruct the view from nearby rooms. Floodlights are trained on these facades and if you step out of your room at night to view the action below, looking down may result in temporary blindness.

The sort of traveler you are should dictate the room you request. If you choose an All-Star Resort because you'd rather spend time and money at the parks, book a room near the bus stop, your link to the rest of the World. Note that buses leave from the central public buildings of each section, which are near the larger, noisier pools. If you're planning to return to your room for an afternoon nap, request a room farther from the pools. Also consider an upper-story room to minimize foot traffic past your door. On the other hand, if you choose All-Star for its kid-friendly aspects, consider roosting near the action. A bottom-floor room provides easy pool access, and a room looking out on a courtyard or pool allows you to keep an eye on children playing outside.

For travelers without young children (infants excluded), the best bets for privacy and quiet are buildings that overlook the forest behind the resort, Buildings 2 and 3 in All-Star Sports and 5 and 6 in All-Star Music. Interior-facing rooms in these buildings (and their partners) also fill the bill, since they overlook courtyards farthest from the large pools. The courtyards vary with theme but are generally only mildly amusing.

If you're traveling with children, opt for a section and building with a theme that appeals to your kids. Often, that will be a film—movies are the lifeblood of the Disney empire—but it might be a sport. If you're staying in Home Run Hotel, don't forget the ball and gloves to maximize the experience (just keep games of catch away from the pool). Older elementary- and middle-school children probably will want to spend hotel time in or near the bigger pools or arcades in nearby halls. Periodically, cadres of teenagers—too cool for their younger siblings—effectively commandeer the smaller secondary pools. Playgrounds are tucked behind Building 9 in All-Star Music and behind Building 6 in All-Star Sports. Rooms facing these are ideal for families with children too young or timid for the often-chaotic larger pools. In All-Star Movies, the playground is nearer to the food court than to any rooms.

The following tip from a former All-Star Resorts cast member from Fayetteville, Georgia, illustrates just how big these resorts are:

Rooms at the far end of the Mighty Ducks building of All-Star Movies are closer to the All-Star Music food court, pool, and buses than to

All-Star Movies' own facilities. Follow the walkway from the Ducks building north to All-Star Music's Melody Hall.

Disney's Pop Century Resort
*(See **tinyurl.com/ug-popcentury** for extended coverage.)*

STRENGTHS	WEAKNESSES
• Theming is fun for anyone over 35	• Theming may be lost on kids and teens
• Our favorite pool bar of the Value resorts	• Small rooms that are the same size as All-Stars' but slightly more expensive
• One bus stop	
• Walking trail around Hour Glass Lake and connecting bridge to Art of Animation	• Bus stops at theme parks are a long distance from park entrances
• In-room pizza delivery	
• Convenient parking	

ON VICTORY WAY near the ESPN Wide World of Sports Complex is Pop Century Resort. Originally designed to be completed in phases, the resort opened its first section in 2004. The second phase was canceled in favor of a new Value resort, Disney's Art of Animation (see page 209).

Pop Century is a near-clone of the All-Star Resorts—that is, four-story, motel-style buildings built around a central pool, food court, and registration area. Decorative touches make the difference. Where the All-Star

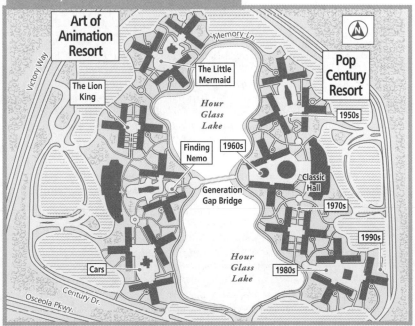

Pop Century Resort & Art of Animation Resort

Resorts display larger-than-life icons from sports, music, and movies, and Art of Animation is inspired by Disney cartoons, Pop Century draws its icons from decades of the 20th century and their attendant popular culture: building-sized Big Wheels, hula hoops, and the like, punctuated by silhouettes of people doing the jitterbug and the twist.

The public areas at Pop Century are marginally more sophisticated than the ones at the All-Star Resorts, with 20th-century period furniture and decor rolled up in a saccharine, those-were-the-days theme. A food court, a bar, a playground, pools, and so on emulate the All-Star Resorts model in size and location. A Pop Century departure from the All-Star precedent has merchandise retailers thrown in with the fast-food concessions in a combination dining-and-shopping area. This apparently is what happens when a giant corporation tries to combine selling pizza with hawking Goofy hats. (You just know the word *synergy* was used like cheap cologne in those design meetings.) As at the All-Star Resorts and Art of Animation, there's no full-service restaurant. The resort is connected to the rest of Walt Disney World by bus, but because of the limited dining options, we recommend having a car.

Running $107–$209 per night, guest rooms at Pop Century are small at 260 square feet. The decor is upbeat, with white bedspreads and blue walls. Wall art depicts pop memorabilia from decades past. Cherry-finish wood-inlaid furniture and blue-and-tan-patterned carpet provide an upscale touch, but these are not rooms you'd want to spend a lot of time in. Bathrooms are tiny and counter space a scarce commodity. Worst of all, we've received many complaints from readers that the soundproofing between rooms is inadequate. A lake separating Pop Century from the Art of Animation Resort offers water views not available at the All-Star Resorts.

A reader from Dublin, Georgia, thinks we underrate Pop:

> *I can't believe you don't like Pop Century. (1) It's far superior to the All-Star Resorts. (2) There's a lake at a Value resort and a view of fireworks. (3) The courtyards have Twister games and neat pools for little children. (4) The memorabilia is interesting to us of a certain age. (5) I love the gift shop, food court, and bar combo. The [dinner entrees are among] the best bargains and the best food anywhere. (6) Bus transportation is better than anywhere else, including Grand Floridian! (7) The layout is more convenient to the food court. (8) I never hear construction noise, and the noise from neighbors is not worse than anywhere else. (9) Where else do the cast members do the shag to oldies?*

Don't know what it is about Pop Century fans, but they seem to have a propensity for making lists—take this Waukee, Iowa, family:

> *We loved Pop Century Resort: (1) It was cheap enough that we had plenty of money left over for other fun things at Disney. (2) A shrimp [entrée] was one of the most awesome fast-food items we've had at Disney. (3) Although the rooms are a little small and the lighting isn't the best, the resort is affordable enough that without tax two rooms at the Pop Century are in the same price range as one room at other resorts. (4) It's not far from any park at Disney, nor from Disney Springs. (5) The combo food court–shopping area really works: My grandparents can eat breakfast in the food court while my brother,*

sister, parents, and I shop. (6) Food is actually pretty affordable for Disney. (7) Great pools that are not too far from our rooms. (8) You can request a room on the first floor, near the parking lot. They were really accommodating when we explained that I had to have a rather heavy oxygen tank brought to our room, so it would be easier on us to stay on the first floor. (9) Check-in takes probably the least amount of time that I have ever seen at a Disney resort.

But a Springfield, Illinois, dad gives Pop Century a mixed review:

We wanted something different from All-Star Movies (two stays in the previous three years), so we gave Pop Century a shot. Believe the noise complaints—they're true. It's like the walls were made of papier-mâché. Although the bus service was great and the pool (and splash pools) were nice for a Value resort, we'll be back at All-Star Movies the next time around.

A family from Spartanburg, South Carolina, was also disturbed by the noise:

The one thing I should have paid more attention to was the noise level rating at Pop Century. The resort itself was great, but it was hard to actually nap when we came back to the resort each afternoon due to music and games on the loudspeakers. Do not face the 1960s pool if you want some R&R.

GOOD (AND NOT-SO-GOOD) ROOMS AT POP CENTURY RESORT *(See* **tinyurl.com/pop-roomviews** *for photos.)* The best rooms for both view and convenience are the lake-view rooms in Buildings 4 and 5, representing the 1960s. Another option, though with a less compelling view, would be rooms in the same building facing east, toward the registration and food-court building. Next-best choices would be the east-facing rooms of Building 3 in the 1950s, and of Building 6 in the 1970s. Avoid south-facing rooms in 1980s Building 7 and 1990s Building 8. Both are echo chambers for noise from nearby Osceola Parkway. Finally, so-called preferred rooms at Pop Century, which are closer to the main pool and lobby, cost about $7–$17 more than others. They're definitely closer, but they probably save only 5 minutes of walking per day and subject you to more noise from guests walking past your room. We don't think these rooms are worth the extra cost. Finally, note that guest rooms don't have private patios or balconies.

Disney's Art of Animation Resort *(see map on page 207)*
(See **tinyurl.com/ug-artofanimation** *for extended coverage.)*

OPENED IN MAY 2012, Disney's Art of Animation is a Value resort across Hour Glass Lake from Pop Century. It was originally designed to be part of Pop Century and represent the years 1900–1949, but recessions and an abundance of hotel capacity prevented Disney from ever completing construction. When the time came for a new Value resort, Disney switched the theme to its animated movies, which still fit in well with the pop-culture motif across the lake.

As at Pop Century, Art of Animation's standard rooms are housed in four-story buildings and exterior-facing walkups, with a series of

ART OF ANIMATION RESORT

STRENGTHS	WEAKNESSES
• Exceptional theming, particularly *Cars* and *Lion King* areas	• Most expensive Value resort
• Best pool of the Value resorts	• Terrible in-room mobile reception
• Landscape of Flavors food court is an *Unofficial Guide* favorite	• The number of made-to-order meals at the food court can mean long waits in line
• Family Suites are innovatively designed and themed	• The resort's Family Suites are rarely discounted
• In-room pizza delivery	• Poor soundproofing
• Walking trail around Hour Glass Lake and connecting bridge to Pop Century	
• Just one bus stop	

themed swimming pools and a food court. However, the majority of the resort's accommodations are suites similar to those at Disney's All-Star Music Resort. All told, there are 864 standard rooms and 1,120 suites. The suites have interior hallways to the guest rooms instead of the exterior walkways found at Disney's other Value resorts.

Art of Animation's suites are around 565 square feet, about what you'd get by combining two standard rooms into one suite. Each suite has a master bedroom, a living room, two full bathrooms, and a kitchenette with mini-fridge, microwave, and coffeemaker. Sleeping accommodations include a queen bed in the bedroom, a sleeper sofa, and a living-room table that converts into a full-size bed. The bedroom and living room have flat-panel TVs.

Slightly larger than comparable rooms at other Value resorts, standard rooms are 277 square feet and include one king or two double beds, a flat-panel TV, a mini-fridge, and a table and chairs.

Theming incorporates characters from four Disney films: *Cars, Finding Nemo, The Lion King,* and *The Little Mermaid.* All but the *Mermaid*-themed rooms are suites. As at Pop Century, large, colorful icons stand in the middle of each group of buildings; here, though, they represent film characters rather than pop-culture touchstones. An interesting departure from the other Value resorts is the outside paint schemes: Rather than using pastels, Disney has decorated the exteriors with giant murals stretching the length of each structure. The *Cars* buildings, for example, each display a four-story panoramic vista of the American desert, with the movie's iconic characters in the middle, while the *Lion King* buildings capture a single verdant jungle scene. It's a great idea.

Three of the four sets of themed buildings have pools; the *Lion King* complex has a playground instead. Like the other Value resorts, Art of Animation has a central building—here called Animation Hall—for check-in and bus transportation; it also holds the resort's food court, Landscape of Flavors; a gift shop; and a video-game arcade.

Speaking of check-in, the wall behind the front desk is a dazzling rainbow of colors from floor to ceiling. In sharp contrast to the faded paints and photos at, say, the All-Stars, Art of Animation's backlight displays and wall art are bright and vibrant and should stand up well to Florida's weather.

Most comments concerning Art of Animation have been positive. A mom from Blountville, Tennessee, says:

> The Art of Animation Resort was the highlight of our trip! Out daughter loves The Little Mermaid, *and the rooms, while small and basic, were adorable. The courtyards, the pools, the main lobby areas, etc.— Disney is fantastic at attention to detail. Our daughter loved pointing out* Lion King, Nemo, *and* Little Mermaid *characters every day.*

Readers complain, however, about the long walk from the *Little Mermaid*–themed buildings to the food court and front desk. Mobile reception was also singled out as a problem. A woman from Houston related the following:

> There was no AT&T service inside the building where our rooms were. There was plenty of service outside the building, but the moment we stepped inside it was like a vacuum. It was very upsetting.

Noise and soundproofing are likewise issues. A mom from Boise, Idaho, comments:

> Art of Animation was great, but I'm not sure if we would stay there again because of the noise. The suites were great, but the pool area was very noisy. I think this is just how it is at the Value resorts.

A Guyton, Georgia, mom agrees:

> The room was very poorly soundproofed. I heard snoring and bathroom noises from other rooms that I should not have been able to hear. One afternoon my toddler and I returned to the room for a nap—I suppose housekeeping was cleaning the room above ours, but it sounded like someone was bowling up there.

GOOD (AND NOT-SO-GOOD) ROOMS AT ART OF ANIMATION The quietest suites are south- and east-facing rooms in Buildings 3 (*Cars*), 4 (*Finding Nemo*), and 6 (*The Lion King*). The quietest standard rooms are east-facing rooms in Building 8 and south-facing rooms in Building 7 (both *The Little Mermaid*). Avoid northwest-facing rooms in Building 1 and southwest-facing rooms in Building 10, which face the Disney bus route and Art of Animation's bus stops.

INDEPENDENT HOTELS OF THE DOWNTOWN DISNEY RESORT AREA

THE SEVEN HOTELS of the Downtown Disney Resort Area (DDRA) were created back when Disney had far fewer of its own resorts. The hotels—the **Best Western Lake Buena Vista Resort Hotel, B Resort,** the **Buena Vista Palace Hotel & Spa, DoubleTree Guest Suites,** the **Hilton Orlando Lake Buena Vista,** the **Holiday Inn in the Walt Disney World Resort,** and **Wyndham Lake Buena Vista Resort**—are chain-style affairs with minimal or nonexistent theming, though the Buena Vista Palace especially is pretty upscale. Several of the larger properties have shifted their focus to convention and business travelers.

The main advantage to staying in the DDRA is being in Disney World and next to Disney Springs. Guests at the Hilton, Wyndham Lake Buena Vista Resort, Buena Vista Palace, and Holiday Inn are an

AMENITIES AT DDRA HOTELS					
HOTEL	CHILDREN'S PROGRAMS	DINING	KID-FRIENDLY	POOL(S)	RECREATION
Best Western LBV Resort	None	★★½	★★★	★★½	★★
B Resort	None	★★★½	★★½	★★½	★★★
Buena Vista Palace	★★★★	★★	★★★½	★★★½	★★★★
DoubleTree Guest Suites	None	★★	★★★	★★½	★★½
Hilton Orlando LBV	None	★★½	★★½	★★★	★★½
Holiday Inn WDW Resort	None	★★	★★	★★★	★★
Wyndham LBV Resort	★★½	★★½	★★★	★★★	★★★

easy 5- to 15-minute walk from the Marketplace on the east side of Disney Springs. Guests at B Resort, the Best Western Lake Buena Vista, and DoubleTree Guest Suites are about 10 minutes farther by foot. Disney transportation can be accessed at Disney Springs, though the buses take a notoriously long time to leave due to the number of stops throughout the complex. Although all DDRA hotels offer shuttle buses to the theme parks, the service is provided by private contractors and is somewhat inferior to Disney transportation in frequency of service, number of buses, and hours of operation. Get firm details in advance about shuttle service from any DDRA hotel you're considering. All these hotels are easily accessible by car and are only marginally farther from the Disney parks than several of the Disney resorts; DDRA hotels are also quite close to Typhoon Lagoon water park.

DDRA hotels, even the business- and convention-focused ones, try to appeal to families. Some have pool complexes rivaling those at any Disney resort, whereas others offer a food court or all-suite rooms. A few sponsor character meals and organized kids' activities; all have counters for buying Disney tickets, and most have Disney gift shops.

A Difficult Value Proposition

With the exception of the Hilton and the B Resort, we find it difficult to recommend these hotels. The rooms at many are in need of refurbishment. Further, for much of the year there's little price difference between these rooms and those at Disney's Value resorts, especially when Disney offers discounts. If you're driving, note that the traffic near Disney Springs is an absolute gridlock throughout the evening too.

ADDITIONAL FEES AT THE DDRA RESORTS				
HOTEL	SELF-PARKING	RESORT FEE	INTERNET	TOTAL PER DAY
BEST WESTERN LBV RESORT	Free	$14	Free	$14
B RESORT	$16	$22.50	Free	$38.50
BUENA VISTA PALACE	Free	$22	Free	$22
DOUBLETREE GUEST SUITES	$17	None	$10	$27
HILTON ORLANDO LBV	$15	$24	$10	$49
HOLIDAY INN WDW RESORT	$12	None	Free	$12
WYNDHAM LBV RESORT	$8	$18	Free	$26

Speaking of prices, all of the DDRA resorts tack on daily charges for self-parking, Internet access, or some cockamamy "resort fee." These fees add $12–$49 per night to your stay, plus tax.

A special thumbed nose to the Hilton, which was tacking on $49 per day in fees (plus tax!) to a $159-per-night reservation in early 2015.

Heaven knows Disney's Deluxe resorts are overpriced, but it's hard to see how any DDRA property can compete with the value proposition of Disney's inexpensive hotels, which offer free airport transportation, better bus service, free parking, and extra time at the theme parks. We suspect most readers who choose the DDRA resorts do so either because they've earned enough rewards points to qualify for a free stay or the Disney resorts are sold out. We'd be hard-pressed to think of another reason to stay at these hotels, especially if we had a car.

Descriptions of each DDRA resort follow. Also take a peek at the combined website for the DDRA hotels at **downtowndisneyhotels .com**. Finally, check the comparative chart on the previous page.

B Resort ★★★½

1905 Hotel Plaza Blvd.
☎ 407-828-2828 or
800-66-BHOTELS
bresortlvb.com

B RESORTS, a Florida hotel chain, relaunched the former Royal Plaza in the summer of 2014 after an extensive multi-year renovation. Located within walking distance of shops and restaurants and situated 5 miles or less from the Disney parks, the 394-room hotel targets couples, families, groups, and business travelers.

Decorated in cool blues, whites, and grays, guest rooms and suites afford views of downtown Orlando, area lakes, and theme parks. Along with B Resorts–exclusive Blissful Beds, each room is outfitted with sleek modern furnishings and a large interactive flat-screen TV. Additional touches include a mini-fridge and gaming consoles (available on request). Some rooms are also equipped with bunk beds, kitchenettes, or wet bars.

Our most recent stay at the B Resort was in early 2015, and we enjoyed it quite a bit. Our standard room was spotlessly clean, and the room decor is fun without being faddy. The bathroom is spacious, with plenty of storage. The glass shower is well-designed and has good water pressure. There's absolutely nothing wrong with this hotel at this price point, except for the terrible traffic you have to endure every night because of Disney Springs. And that's a shame because it's not the hotel's doing. But if the B were on the other side of Disney Springs, we'd gladly stay here again.

A mom from Tennessee also likes the B Resort, especially when it's on sale:

The vibe of the B Resort was great—like a knockoff of the W, very bright and modern. The restaurant was great, and the zero-entry pool was good. The resort has a more adult feel, but I never felt out of place with my son. I found a deal on Orbitz for around $310 for three nights, with taxes and fees. If choosing between the B and Pop Century for a short stay, I'd take the B Resort hands down.

Amenities include free Wi-Fi, a spa, beauty salon, and fitness center. The main restaurant, American Q, serves a modern upscale take on classic barbecue in regional styles ranging from Carolina to Kansas City. Hungry guests can also choose from a poolside bar and grill; The Pickup, a grab-and-go shop just off the lobby that serves quick breakfasts, snacks, picnic lunches, and ice cream; and 24/7 in-room dining.

Other perks: a zero-entry pool with interactive water features; a kids' area; loaner iPads; Monscierge, a digital touchscreen concierge and destination guide in the lobby; and more than 25,000 square feet of meeting and multi-use space. Though not served by Disney transportation, B Resort provides bus service to the parks and other Disney World venues. A resort fee of $22.50 per day applies.

Best Western Lake Buena Vista Resort Hotel ★★★

2000 Hotel Plaza Blvd.
☎ 407-828-2424 or
800-348-3765
lakebuenavista
resorthotel.com

THE 18-STORY, 325-ROOM Best Western Lake Buena Vista has relatively few of the extras common to most other DDRA properties. The rooms are in need of refurbishment. Parking is a hike from many rooms, and to get to them you pass through hallways and areas that could use a good scrubbing. The most surprising thing was the attitude of general indifference from several of the staff when we needed help checking in.

A breakfast buffet and dinner service of American fare are available in the Trader's Island Grill, while the Parakeet Café offers sandwiches and snacks. The poolside Flamingo Cove Lounge provides its own menu of pub standards as well as alcoholic refreshment. The pool is small though pleasantly landscaped, and there's a kiddie pool as well. Other amenities include a fitness room and game room. Although there are no organized children's programs, the resort can arrange child care.

Buena Vista Palace Hotel & Spa ★★★½

1900 E. Buena Vista Dr.
Lake Buena Vista
☎ 407-827-2727 or
866-397-6516
buenavistapalace.com

THE BUENA VISTA PALACE IS upscale and convenient. Surrounded by an artificial lake and plenty of palms, the spacious pool area comprises three heated pools, the largest of which is partially covered; a whirlpool and sauna; a basketball court; and a sand volleyball court. A pool concierge will fetch your favorite magazine or fruity drink. On Sunday, the Watercress Café hosts a character brunch ($25 for adults and $12 for children). The 897 guest rooms are posh and spacious; each comes with desk, coffeemaker, hair dryer, satellite TV with pay-per-view movies, iron and board, and mini-fridge. There are also 117 suites. In-room babysitting is available. One lighted tennis court, a European-style spa offering 60 services, a fitness center, an arcade, a playground, and a beauty salon round out amenities. Two restaurants and a mini-market are on-site. And if you aren't wiped out after time in the parks, consider dropping by the Lobby Lounge or the full-menu sports bar for a nightcap. *Note:* All these amenities and services come at a price—a $22-per-night resort fee will be added to your bill.

DoubleTree Guest Suites ★★★½

2305 Hotel Plaza Blvd.
☎ 407-934-1000
doubletreeguestsuites.com

THIS GIANT WHITE BUNKER of a hotel is the only all-suite establishment on Disney property. What it lacks in atmosphere and creative attributes, it makes up for in convenience and comfort. Within walking distance of Disney Springs, the 229 suites are spacious for a family, although the decor is startling, with no apparent theme. No rooms have balconies, though ground floors offer patios.

Amenities include a safe, hair dryer, refrigerator, microwave, coffeepot, fold-out bed, and two TVs (bedroom and living room).

Children will enjoy their own check-in desk, the free chocolate-chip cookie, and the small playground. The heated pool, children's pool, and whirlpool spa are moderate in size; a minus is that traffic noise from Interstate 4 can be heard faintly from the pool deck. The tiny fitness center (more like a fitness closet), pool table, four tennis courts, and outdoor bar are adjacent to the pool. High-speed Internet and a business center in the lobby are convenient for those on working holidays. The Market

*un*official **TIP**

If you consider a non-Disney hotel, check its quality as reported in independent travel references such as the *Unofficial Guides*, AAA directories, *Forbes* guides, or *Frommer's* guides.

(open 7 a.m.–midnight) offers groceries, drinks, ice cream, and sundaes for those late-night munchies; the EverGreen Cafe serves breakfast, lunch, and dinner. Babysitting is available.

Hilton Orlando Lake Buena Vista ★★★★

THE HILTON IS THE ONLY DDRA HOTEL offering Disney's Extra Magic Hours program to its guests (although we hear

1751 Hotel Plaza Blvd.
☎ 407-827-4000
hilton-wdwv.com

the perk may be discontinued at the end of 2015). Although the resort fees are outrageous and the decor is dated, the rooms are comfortable and nicer than some others in the DDRA. On-site dining includes Covington Mill Restaurant, offering sandwiches and pasta; Andiamo, an Italian bistro; and Benihana, a Japanese steakhouse and sushi bar (the last two are reviewed in Part Four). Covington Mill hosts a Disney-character breakfast on Sundays. The two pools are matched with a children's spray pool and a 24-hour fitness center. An exercise room and a game room are on-site, as is a 24-hour market. Babysitting is available, but there are no organized children's programs.

A Denver family of five found the Hilton's shuttle service lacking:

The transportation, provided by a company called Mears, was unreliable. They did a better job of getting guests back to the hotel from the park than getting them to the park from the hotel. Shuttles from the hotel were randomly timed and went repeatedly to the same parks—skipping others and leaving guests to wait for up to an hour.

Holiday Inn in the Walt Disney World Resort ★★★½

COMPLETELY RENOVATED IN 2010, the Holiday Inn is modern and comfortable. The layout remains the same, with tower rooms grouped around an atrium and wing rooms overlooking the pool. The feel of the hotel is modern and contemporary yet relaxed and comfortable. Disney Springs is just a short walk away.

1805 Hotel Plaza Blvd.
☎ 407-828-8888
or 888-465-4329
hiorlando.com

The totally upgraded rooms feature pillow-top beds with triple sheeting and firm or soft pillows. Each room has a 32-inch flat-panel HDTV and free high-speed Internet. The bathrooms are clean and well designed—the nicest in any DDRA resort. Amenities include granite countertops and showerheads with a choice of comfort sprays.

The Palm Breezes Restaurant and Bar serves breakfast, lunch, and dinner at reasonable prices. A breakfast buffet is available, as well as à la carte items. The Grab n Go Outlet in the lobby offers quick snacks and sandwiches. Other amenities include a large and well-kept zero-entry pool, along with a Jacuzzi in the pool area. A separate entrance brings you into the convention center, ballroom, and meeting room areas, with a business center nearby.

Wyndham Lake Buena Vista Resort ★★★½

1850 Hotel Plaza Blvd.
☎ 407-828-4444
or 800-624-4109
wyndhamlakebuena
vista.com

ACROSS FROM DOWNTOWN DISNEY, the Wyndham Lake Buena Vista was formerly known as Regal Sun Resort. The lobby is bright and airy and check-in service friendly. Rooms are larger than most and have in-room refrigerators. Pool-facing rooms in the hotel's wings have exterior hallways that overlook the pool and center courtyard; these hallways can be noisy during summer months. Elevators are available, but they're unusually slow—it's probably faster to walk to the second and third floors, assuming you're up for the exercise. Disney-character breakfasts take place on Tuesdays, Thursdays, and Saturdays at LakeView Restaurant.

CAMPING AT WALT DISNEY WORLD

DISNEY'S FORT WILDERNESS RESORT & CAMPGROUND is a spacious area for tent and RV camping. Fully equipped, air-conditioned prefabricated log cabins are also available for rent.

Tent/Pop-Up campsites provide water, electricity, and cable TV and run $56–$120 a night depending on season. **Full Hook-Up** campsites have all the previous amenities, accommodate large RVs, and run $78–$145 per night. **Preferred Hook-Up** campsites for tents and RVs add sewer connections and run $89–$158 per night. **Premium** campsites add an extra-large concrete parking pad and run $96–$163 a night.

All sites are level and provide picnic tables, waste containers, grills, and free Wi-Fi. Fires are prohibited except in the grills. Pets are permitted in some Premium and Preferred loops.

Campsites are arranged on loops accessible from one of three main roads. There are 28 loops, with Loops 100–2000 for tent and RV campers, and Loops 2100–2800 offering cabins at $336–$562 per night. RV sites are roomy by eastern-US standards, with the Premium and Full Hook-Up campsites able to accommodate RVs more than 45 feet long, but tent campers will probably feel a bit cramped. (Note that tent stakes cannot be put into the concrete at the Premium sites.) On any given day, 90% or more of campers are RVers.

Fort Wilderness Resort & Campground arguably offers the most recreational facilities and activities of any Disney resort. Among them are two video arcades; nightly campfire programs; Disney movies; a dinner theater; two swimming pools; a beach; walking paths; bike, boat, canoe, golf-cart, and water-ski rentals; a petting zoo; horseback riding; hayrides; fishing; and tennis, basketball, and volleyball courts. There are two convenience stores, a restaurant, and a tavern. Comfort stations with toilets, showers, pay phones, ice machine, and laundry facilities are within walking distance of all campsites.

Access to the Magic Kingdom is by boat from Fort Wilderness Landing and to Epcot by bus, with a transfer at the Transportation and Ticket Center (TTC) to the Epcot monorail. Boat service may be suspended during thunderstorms, in which case Disney will provide buses. An alternate route to the Magic Kingdom is by internal bus to the

FORT WILDERNESS RESORT & CAMPGROUND

STRENGTHS	WEAKNESSES
• Informality	• Isolated location
• Children's play areas	• Complicated bus service
• Best recreational options at WDW	• Confusing campground layout
• Special day and evening programs	• Lack of privacy
• Campsite amenities	• Very limited on-site dining options
• Shower and toilet facilities	• Crowding at beaches and pools
• *Hoop-Dee-Doo Musical Revue* show	• Small baths in cabins
• Convenient self-parking	• Extreme distance to store and restaurant facilities from many campsites
• Off-site dining via boat at the Magic Kingdom	

TTC, then by monorail or ferry to the park. Transportation to all other Disney destinations is by bus. Motor traffic within the campground is permitted only when entering or exiting. Get around within the campground by bus, golf cart, or bike, the latter two available for rent.

For tent and RV campers, there's a fairly stark trade-off between sites convenient to pools, restaurant, trading posts, and other amenities, and those that are most scenic, shady, and quiet. RVers who prefer to be near guest services, the marina, the beach, and the restaurant and tavern should go for Loops 100, 200, 700, and 400 (in that order). Loops near the campground's secondary facility area with pool, trading post, bike and golf-cart rentals, and campfire program are 1400, 1300, 600, 1000, and 1500, in order of preference. If you're looking for a tranquil, scenic setting among mature trees, we recommend Loops 1800, 1900, 1700, and 1600, in that order, and the backside sites on the 700 loop. The best loop of all, and the only one to offer both a lovely setting and proximity to key amenities, is Loop 300. The best loops for tents and pop-up campers are 1500 and 2000, with 1500 being nearest a pool, a convenience store, and the campfire program.

With the exception of Loops 1800 and 1900, avoid sites within 40 yards of the loop entrance. These sites are almost always flanked by one of the main traffic arteries within Fort Wilderness. Further, sites on the outside of the loop are almost always preferable to those in the center of the loop. RVers should be forewarned that all sites are back-ins and that although most sites will accommodate large rigs, the loop access roads are pretty tight and narrow.

Rental cabins offer a double bed and two bunk beds in the only bedroom, augmented by a Murphy bed (pulls down from the wall) in the living room. There's one rather small bathroom with shower and tub.

The prefab log cabins (classified as Moderate resorts in the Disney hierarchy) are warm and homey, but the stem-to-stern interior wood paneling and smallish windows make for pretty dark accommodations at night. Neither the lighting fixtures provided nor the wattage of their bulbs are up to the job of lighting the cabins once the sun goes down.

All cabins offer air-conditioning, televisions with DVD players and/or VCRs, fully equipped kitchens, and dining tables. Housekeeping is

Continued on page 220

Fort Wilderness Resort & Campground

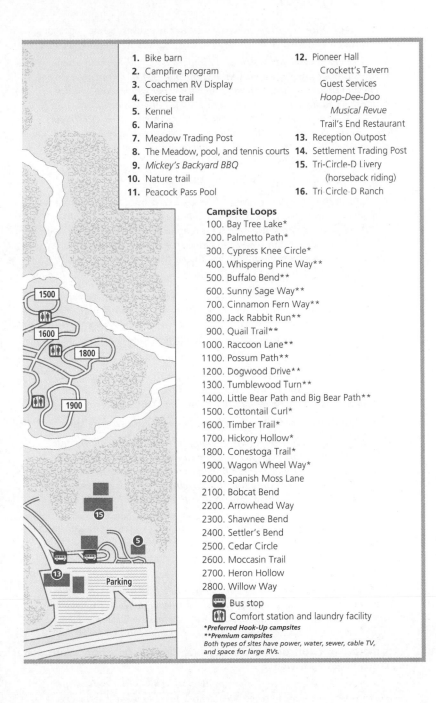

1. Bike barn
2. Campfire program
3. Coachmen RV Display
4. Exercise trail
5. Kennel
6. Marina
7. Meadow Trading Post
8. The Meadow, pool, and tennis courts
9. *Mickey's Backyard BBQ*
10. Nature trail
11. Peacock Pass Pool

12. Pioneer Hall
    Crockett's Tavern
    Guest Services
    Hoop-Dee-Doo
        Musical Revue
    Trail's End Restaurant
13. Reception Outpost
14. Settlement Trading Post
15. Tri-Circle-D Livery
    (horseback riding)
16. Tri-Circle-D Ranch

Campsite Loops
100. Bay Tree Lake*
200. Palmetto Path*
300. Cypress Knee Circle*
400. Whispering Pine Way**
500. Buffalo Bend**
600. Sunny Sage Way**
700. Cinnamon Fern Way**
800. Jack Rabbit Run**
900. Quail Trail**
1000. Raccoon Lane**
1100. Possum Path**
1200. Dogwood Drive**
1300. Tumblewood Turn**
1400. Little Bear Path and Big Bear Path**
1500. Cottontail Curl*
1600. Timber Trail*
1700. Hickory Hollow*
1800. Conestoga Trail*
1900. Wagon Wheel Way*
2000. Spanish Moss Lane
2100. Bobcat Bend
2200. Arrowhead Way
2300. Shawnee Bend
2400. Settler's Bend
2500. Cedar Circle
2600. Moccasin Trail
2700. Heron Hollow
2800. Willow Way

🚌 Bus stop
🚻 Comfort station and laundry facility
Preferred Hook-Up campsites
Premium campsites
*Both types of sites have power, water, sewer, cable TV,
and space for large RVs.*

Continued from page 217

provided daily. Most readers are crazy about the cabins. Some representative comments follow. A Wappingers Falls, New York, family writes:

> We stayed at Fort Wilderness in a cabin because (1) we wanted a separate bedroom area; (2) we wanted a kitchen; (3) our kids are very lively, and the cabins were apart from each other so we wouldn't disturb other guests; and (4) we thought the kids might meet other children to play with. The cabins worked out just right for us. Although the kids didn't meet any other children to play with, they had a ball chasing the little lizards and frogs, kicking around pinecones, sitting on the deck to eat ice pops, and sleeping in bunk beds.

From a Downers Grove, Illinois, family of five:

> We spent a LOT of time waiting for buses and ferries, more than we remember waiting a few years ago. While we liked having a stop at the Meadow area, there was always a long wait for a purple bus to take us back to the cabin when returning from the parks (from both depots). They need a separate bus route just for the cabins.

A Rochester, New York, dad agrees:

> If you're staying at Fort Wilderness, we highly recommend getting a golf cart. There's a lot going on at the campground, and the bus system can be cumbersome. Also, our 3-year-old wasn't always up for the walk—just getting from our cabin to the main loop was a lot for her.

This Mechanicsville, Virginia, mom concurs on the golf cart:

> Loved the cabins at Fort Wilderness. The location was perfect with the boat transportation to the Magic Kingdom. A golf cart is a must, though it drives the cost to stay there into the Deluxe price range.

A mother of two from Albuquerque, New Mexico, offers this:

> We stayed in a cabin and liked having all the space and the full kitchen. However, the pool nearest our cabin (a quarter-mile away!) never even had a lifeguard. I had hoped to be able to send the kids to swim when we needed some time to ourselves, but with the distance and lack of lifeguards, there was no way to do that.

Though the cabins are especially popular, RV and tent campers love Fort Wilderness, too. First from a Marietta, Georgia, multigenerational family:

> I do wish you'd stress more the advantages of Fort Wilderness. With sites for any size/type of camper/tent, it's FAR more affordable than any hotel inside the park. Additionally, you could theoretically (although not likely) prepare all of your own meals. We usually had breakfast, packed snacks, and returned for lunch and dinner every day.

A mother of two from Mechanicsville, Virginia, puts Fort Wilderness on a pedestal as well:

> The most important thing—the family time. This is the only resort where you're encouraged to go outside and play! You can bike, swim, visit two arcades, hike the nature trail, ride a horse, rent a boat, play

volleyball, go to the beach, attend a free character sing-along and marshmallow roast followed by a classic Disney movie that many younger families never knew existed (we were introduced to Snowball Express), enjoy multiple playgrounds, play tennis, rent a golf cart, walk around at night to see the festively decorated campsites (many Disney-themed), take a romantic carriage ride, take your first pony ride, and see a wild turkey. Don't forget the fishing or the great view of the fire-works from the beach or the up-close water light parade.

With all of this stuff, much of it free or very affordable, who needs the parks? We visited last June and never set foot in a park.

But an Apple Valley, California, woman doesn't think the RV campsites are very well designed:

Our RV site was a back-in site, as they all are, so be prepared for that, and we noticed that the hookup utilities were in awful positions for a trailer hookup. In particular, the sewer hookups were at the front of the site, which is completely opposite of where those hookups are in most RVs. It was a good thing we had an extra-long sewer hose and extension! Not good planning, Disney!

Bus service at Fort Wilderness leaves a lot to be desired, so much in fact that we wouldn't stay there unless we had our own car. To go anywhere, you first have to catch an internal bus that makes many, many stops. If your destination is outside Fort Wilderness, you then have to transfer to a second bus. To complicate things, buses serving destinations outside the campground depart from two locations, the Reception Outpost and Pioneer Hall. This means you have to keep track of which destinations each transfer center serves.

Finally, if you rent a cabin or camp in a tent or RV, particularly in fall or spring, keep abreast of local weather conditions.

A number of independent campgrounds are within 30 miles of Walt Disney World. Here are the closest:

Kissimmee-Orlando KOA ☎ 407-396-2400; **koa.com/campgrounds /kissimmee.** 96 licensed sites; about 6 miles to Walt Disney World US 192 (Maingate) entrance

Sherwood Forest RV Resort ☎ 800-548-9981; **rvonthego.com.** 531 licensed sites; about 4 miles to Walt Disney World US 192 (Maingate) entrance

Tropical Palms Resort ☎ 407-396-4595; **tropicalpalmsrv.com.** 365 licensed sites; about 2.5 miles to WDW US 192 (Maingate) entrance

HOW *to* EVALUATE *a* WALT DISNEY WORLD TRAVEL PACKAGE

HUNDREDS OF WALT DISNEY WORLD package vacations are offered each year. Some are created by the Walt Disney Travel Company, others by airlines, independent travel agents, and wholesalers. Almost all include lodging at or near Disney World plus theme park admissions. Packages offered by airlines include air transportation.

Prices vary seasonally; mid-March–Easter, summer, and holiday periods are the most expensive. Off-season, there are plenty of empty rooms, and you can negotiate great discounts, especially at non-Disney properties. Similarly, airfares and rental cars are cheaper off-peak.

Almost all package ads are headlined "5 Days at Walt Disney World from $645" (or such). The key word is *from:* The rock-bottom price includes the least desirable hotels; if you want better or more-convenient digs, you'll pay more—often much more.

Packages offer a wide selection of hotels. Some, like the Disney resorts, are very dependable. Others run the gamut of quality.

Checking two or three independent sources is best. Also, before you book, ask how old the hotel is and when the guest rooms were last refurbished. Locate the hotel on a map to verify its proximity to Disney World. If you won't have a car, make sure that the hotel has adequate shuttle service.

Packages with non-Disney lodging are much less expensive. But guests at Disney-owned properties get Extra Magic Hours privileges, the opportunity to make dining and FastPass+ reservations far in advance, free parking, and access to Disney transportation. These privileges (except Extra Magic Hours for Hilton guests) don't apply to guests at the Downtown Disney Resort Area hotels (see page 211).

Packages should be a win–win proposition for both buyer and seller. The buyer makes only one phone call and deals with one salesperson to set up the whole vacation (transportation, rental car, admissions, lodging, meals, and even golf and tennis). The seller, likewise, deals with the buyer only once. Some packagers also buy airfares in bulk on contract, not unlike a broker playing the commodities market. By buying a large number of airfares in advance, the packager saves significantly over posted fares. The practice is also applied to hotel rooms. Because selling packages is efficient and the packager often can buy package components in bulk at discount, the seller's savings in operating expenses are sometimes passed on to the buyer, making the package not only convenient but also an exceptional value.

In practice, however, the seller may realize all the economies and pass on no savings. Packages sometimes are loaded with extras that cost the packager almost nothing but run the package's price sky-high. Savings passed on to customers are still somewhere in Fantasyland.

Choose a package that includes features you're sure to use. You'll pay for all of them whether you use them or not. If price is more important than convenience, call around to see what the package would cost if you booked its components on your own. If the package price is less than the à la carte cost, the package is a good deal. If costs are about equal, the package probably is worth it for the convenience. Much of the time, however, you'll find you save significantly by buying the components individually.

CUT TO THE CHASE

IT'S MUCH FASTER TO BOOK a Disney resort room online than it is to call the Disney reservations number (☎ 407-W-DISNEY). If you call, you'll be subjected to about 5–10 minutes of recorded questions (many just fishing for nonrelevant personal information). If you actually want to make a reservation, slog on through. (When the question "Have you called us before?" pops up, answer "yes" unless you want to be corralled into an additional survey for "first-timers.") If you just want to ask a question or speak to a live person, touch 0 to bypass all the recorded stuff.

WALT DISNEY TRAVEL COMPANY MAGIC YOUR WAY PACKAGES

DISNEY'S MAGIC YOUR WAY travel-package program mirrors the admission-ticket program of the same name. Here's how it works: You begin with a base package room and tickets. Tickets can be customized to match the number of days you intend to tour the theme parks, and range in length from 1 to 10 days. As with theme park admissions, the package program offers strong financial incentives to book a longer stay. "The longer you play, the less you pay per day," is the way Disney puts it, borrowing a page from Sam Walton's concept of the universe. An adult 1-Day Base Ticket for the Magic Kingdom (with tax) costs $111.83, whereas if you buy a 7-Day Base Ticket, the average cost per day drops to $50.97. You can purchase options to add on to your Base Tickets, such as hopping between theme parks; playing mini-golf; or visiting water parks, DisneyQuest, or ESPN Wide World of Sports.

With Magic Your Way packages, you can avoid paying for features you don't intend to use. You need not purchase a package with theme park tickets for the entire length of your stay. With Magic Your Way you can choose to purchase as many days of admission as you intend to use. On a one-week vacation, for example, you might want to spend only five days in the Disney parks, saving a day each for Universal Studios and SeaWorld. With Magic Your Way you can buy only five days of admission on a seven-day package. Likewise, if you don't normally park-hop, you can purchase multiday admissions that don't include the Park Hopper feature. Best of all, you can buy the various add-ons at any time during your vacation.

Before we deluge you with a boxcar of options and add-ons, let's define the basic components of Disney's Magic Your Way package:

- One or more nights of accommodations at your choice of any Disney resort. Rates vary with lodging choice: The Grand Floridian is usually the most expensive, and the All-Star, Pop Century, and Art of Animation Resorts are the least expensive.
- Base Ticket for the number of days you tour the theme parks
- Unlimited use of the Disney transportation system
- Free theme park parking
- Official Walt Disney Travel Company luggage tag (one per person)

Magic Your Way Dining Plans

Disney offers dining plans to accompany its Magic Your Way ticket system. They're available to all Disney resort guests except those staying at the Swan, the Dolphin, the hotels of the Downtown Disney Resort Area, and Shades of Green. Guests must also purchase a Magic Your Way package from Disney (not through an online reseller), have Annual

DISNEY LODGING FOR LESS

Mary Waring, *former webmaster at* **MouseSavers** *(*mousesavers *.com; see page 38), knows more about Disney hotel packages than anyone on the planet. Here are her money-saving suggestions.*

BOOK "ROOM-ONLY." It's frequently a better deal to book a room-only reservation instead of buying a vacation package. Disney likes to sell vacation packages because they're easy and profitable. When you buy a package, you're typically paying a premium for convenience. You can often save money by putting together your own package. It's not hard: Just book room-only at a resort and buy passes, meals, and extras separately.

Disney now prices its standard packages at the same rates as if you had purchased individual components separately at full price. However, what Disney doesn't tell you is that components can usually be purchased separately at a discount—and those discounts are not reflected in the brochure prices of Disney's packages. (Sometimes you can get special-offer packages that do include discounts; see below.)

Keep in mind that Disney's packages often include extras you're unlikely to use. Also, packages require a $200 deposit and full payment 45 days in advance; plus, they have stringent change and cancellation policies. Generally, booking room-only requires a deposit of one night's room rate with the remainder due at check-in. Your reservation can be changed or canceled for any reason until five days before check-in.

Whether you decide to book a Disney vacation package or create your own, there are a number of ways to save:

- **USE DISCOUNT CODES TO REDUCE YOUR ROOM-ONLY OR PACKAGE RATE.** Disney uses these codes to push unsold rooms at certain times of year and occasionally offers packages that include resort discounts or value-added features. Check a website like **mousesavers.com** to learn about codes that may be available for your vacation dates. Some codes are available to anyone, while others are just for Florida residents, Annual Pass holders, and so on.

  Discount codes aren't always available for every hotel or every date, and they typically don't appear until two to six months in

Passes, or be members of the Disney Vacation Club (DVC) to participate in the plan. Except for DVC members, a three-night minimum stay is typically also required. Overall cost is determined by the number of nights you stay at a Disney resort.

You must purchase a Disney package vacation to be eligible for a dining plan, as a family of five from Waldron, Michigan, learned:

We read through the Unofficial Guide *and noticed that it said not to book a package during slow season. We were overwhelmed with the*

advance. The good news is that you can usually apply a code to an existing room-only reservation. Simply call the Disney Reservation Center at ☎ 407-W-DISNEY (934-7639) (or contact a Disney-savvy travel agent) and ask whether any rooms are available at your preferred hotel for your preferred dates using the code.

- **BE FLEXIBLE.** Buying a room or package with a discount code is a little like shopping for clothes at a discount store: If you wear size XX-small or XXXX-large, or you like green when everyone else is wearing pink, you're a lot more likely to score a bargain. Likewise, resort discounts are available only when Disney has excess rooms. You're more likely to get a discount during less-popular times (such as value season) and at larger or less-popular resorts. Animal Kingdom Lodge and Old Key West Resort seem to have discounted rooms available more often than the other resorts do.

- **BE PERSISTENT.** This is the most important tip. Disney allots a certain number of rooms to each discount. Once the discounted rooms are gone, you won't get that rate unless someone cancels. Fortunately, people change and cancel reservations all the time. If you can't get your preferred dates or hotel with one discount code, try another one (if available) or keep calling back first thing in the morning to check for cancellations—the system resets overnight, and any reservations with unpaid deposits are automatically released for resale.

- **SPRING FOR "FREE DINING."** One of Disney's biggest package bargains, this promotion has been offered since 2005 during less-busy times of year. When you purchase a full-price room and full-price tickets for each person in the room, you get a Disney Dining Plan for your entire stay. The trick is to choose one of Disney's cheapest rooms and enjoy all that free food: If you choose a Value resort, you get the Quick-Service Dining Plan; if you choose a Moderate resort, you get the standard Disney Dining Plan. You can also book a Value resort and pay the difference to upgrade from Quick-Service to the regular plan. Free Dining is always offered throughout September (a slow time due to heat, humidity, hurricane season, and kids going back to school); sometimes it's offered in late August or at other times during the year.

decisions that we had to make, so we booked the resort first, then the tickets, and then we wanted the dining plan. Well, they wouldn't add the dining plan on because we had already booked everything.

MAGIC YOUR WAY PLUS DINING PLAN This plan provides, for each member of your group, for each night of your stay, one counter-service meal, one full-service meal, and one snack at participating Disney dining locations and restaurants, including room service at some Disney resorts (type "Disney Dining Plan Locations" into your favorite search engine to find sites with the entire list). The plan also includes one refillable drink mug per person, per package, but it can be filled only at Disney resort counter-service restaurants. For guests age 10 and up, the price is $61.82, tax included; for guests ages 3–9, the price is $20.98 per night, tax included. Children younger than age 3 eat free from an adult's plate.

For instance, if you're staying for three nights, you'll be credited with three counter-service meals, three full-service meals, and three snacks for each member of your party. All those meals will be put into a group meal account. Meals in your account can be used by anyone in your group, on any combination of days, so you're not required to eat every meal every day. Thus, you can skip a full-service meal one day and have two on another day.

The counter-service meal includes:

- A main course (a sandwich, dinner salad, pizza, or the like) or a complete combo meal (such as a hamburger and fries); breakfast is typically a combination platter with eggs, bacon or sausage, potatoes, and a biscuit;
- A dessert (except breakfast, where Disney does not offer dessert);
- And a nonalcoholic drink.

The full-service sit-down meals include:

- A main course or entrée,
- A dessert (except breakfast, where Disney does not offer dessert);
- And a nonalcoholic drink.

If you're dining at a buffet, the full-service meal includes the buffet and a nonalcoholic drink. Tax is included in the dining plan, but gratuity is not.

The definition of *snacks* is detailed enough to read like a nuclear-disarmament specification:

- **All single-serving nonalcoholic beverages not in a souvenir cup or with a souvenir attachment.** The serving size must be less than 1 liter, and beverages served at recreation counters are excluded from the plan.
- **All soups served in counter-service locations,** including Disney resort food courts.
- **All items that are eligible as snacks and are on the menu as single items but have additional options at a separate price.** What the heck does that mean? If you want a pretzel with cheese sauce, then together they count as one snack.
- **All ice-cream novelties.** Also all hand-scooped ice cream not served in a souvenir container, including sundaes of up to two scoops.
- **All counter-service items identified as sides** or additions that are not considered entrées.
- **Fresh-popped popcorn.** Pre-bagged popcorn is not considered a snack. Oh.
- **Counter-service breakfast items that can be considered part of an entrée and that are also offered as separate sides,** such as cereal with milk; French toast sticks; create-your-own oatmeal or quinoa; grits; bacon; sausage; eggs; potatoes; or biscuits, with or without gravy. When in doubt, ask a cast member what else might count.

Disney's top-of-the-line restaurants (referred to as Disney Signature restaurants in the plan), along with Cinderella's Royal Table, all the dinner shows, regular room service, and in-room pizza delivery, count as two full-service meals on the standard (Plus) dining plan. If you dine at one of these locations, two full-service meals will be deducted from your account for each person dining.

In addition to the preceding, the following rules apply:

- Everyone staying in the same resort room must participate in the Disney Dining Plan.
- Children ages 3–9 must order from the kids' menu, if available. This rule is occasionally relaxed at Disney's counter-service restaurants, enabling older kids to order from the adult (ages 10+) menu.
- Alcoholic and some nonalcoholic beverages are not included in the plan.
- A full-service meal can be breakfast, lunch, or dinner. The greatest savings occur when you use your full-service-meal credits for dinner.
- The meal plan expires at midnight **on the day you check out** of your Disney resort. **Unused meals are nonrefundable.**
- Neither the Disney Dining Plan nor Disney's Free Dining can be added to a discounted room-only reservation.

QUICK-SERVICE DINING PLAN This plan includes meals, snacks, and nonalcoholic drinks at most counter-service eateries in Walt Disney World. The cost (including tax) is $42.77 per day for guests age 10 and up, $17.54 per day for kids ages 3–9. The plan includes two counter-service meals and one snack per day, in addition to one refillable drink mug per person, per package (eligible for refills only at counter-service locations in your Disney resort).

MAGIC YOUR WAY DELUXE DINING PLAN This plan offers a choice of full- or counter-service meals for three meals a day at any participating restaurant. In addition to the three meals a day, the plan also includes two snacks per day and a refillable drink mug. The Deluxe Plan costs $111.73 for adults and children age 10 and up and $32.56 for

unofficial **TIP**
In our survey of families who've purchased the Magic Your Way Plus Dining Plan, 57% said they'd buy it again.

children ages 3–9 for each night of your stay (prices include tax). Cranking it up another notch, there are even more extravagant dining plans associated with Magic Your Way Premium and Platinum Packages, both described a little later. These included tips at some sit-down and room-service meals, as well as slightly different rules for sit-down-meal credits.

Not only does the Deluxe Dining Plan cost a lot of money, it costs a lot of time, as a dad from Hudson Falls, New York, explains:

> The Deluxe Dining Plan gave us a chance to try restaurants we normally would never go to, but it felt like most of our trip revolved around food: get to the restaurant, wait to be seated, order drinks, wait, get drinks, wait, order meals, wait, get meals, wait, order dessert, wait, get dessert, wait, get the check, wait, give the wait staff your room card, wait, figure out the tip, and wait. With three meals a day, we lost 4.5–6 hours a day just on eating, plus the travel time.

In addition to food, all the plans include sweeteners, such as a free round of miniature golf, discounts on spa treatments and salon services, and deals on recreational activities like fishing and watersports.

Disney ceaselessly tinkers with the dining plans' rules, meal definitions, and participating restaurants. Here are some recent examples:

- You can exchange a sit-down meal credit for a counter-service meal, though doing this even once can negate any savings you get from using a plan in the first place.

- At sit-down restaurants, you can substitute dessert for a side salad, cup of soup, or fruit plate.

- For guests on the Deluxe, Premium, and Platinum Dining Plans, Disney makes no distinction between adult and child dining credits. If you have two child and two adult dining credits available and you'd like to pay for four adult meals using those credits, you can.

- You may exchange one sit-down or counter-service meal credit for three snacks, as long as you do so within the same transaction. It is not a good deal to exchange a sit-down credit for three snacks.

- Counter-service restaurants do not differentiate between adult and child meal credits. If you have two adult credits and two child credits on your account, you may purchase four adult counter-service meals with those credits.

- Finally, you can use your meal credits to pay for the meals of people who are not on any dining plan.

THINGS TO CONSIDER WHEN EVALUATING THE PLUS DINING PLAN The dining plan has been one of the most requested of Disney's package add-ons since its introduction; families report that their favorite aspect is the peace of mind that comes from knowing their meals are paid for ahead of time, rather than having to keep track of a budget while they're in the parks. Families also enjoy the communal aspect of sitting down together for a full meal, without having to worry about who's picking up the food or doing the dishes.

Costwise, however, it's difficult for many families to justify using the plan. If you prefer to always eat at counter-service restaurants, you'll be better off with the Quick-Service plan. You should also avoid the Plus plan if you have finicky eaters, you're visiting during holidays or summer, or you can't get reservations at your first- or second-choice sit-down restaurants. In addition, if you have children age 10 and up, be sure that they can eat an adult-sized dinner at a sit-down restaurant every night; if not, you'd probably come out ahead just paying for everyone's meals without the plan.

If you opt for the plan, skipping one full-service meal during a visit of five or fewer days can mean the difference between saving and losing money. In our experience, having a scheduled sit-down meal for every day of a weeklong vacation can be mentally exhausting, especially for kids. One option might be to schedule a meal at a Disney Signature restaurant, which requires two full-service credits, and have no scheduled sit-down meal on another night in the middle of your trip, allowing everyone to decide on the spot if they're up for something formal.

As already noted, many of the most popular restaurants are fully booked as soon as their reservation windows open. If you're still interested in the dining plan, book your restaurants as soon as possible, typically 180 days before you visit. Then decide whether the plan makes economic sense. For more on Advance Reservations—the term is Disney-speak (hence the capital letters) and not exactly what it implies—see Part Four.

If you're making reservations to eat at Disney hotels other than your own, a car allows you to easily access all the participating restaurants. When you use the Disney transportation system, dining at the various resorts can be a logistical nightmare. Those without a car may want to weigh the immediate services of a taxi—typically $10–$12 each way across Disney property, versus a 50- to 75-minute trip on Disney transportation each way.

When Disney offers Free Dining discounts (typically in September), they generally charge rack rate for the hotel. You should work out the math, but Free Dining is typically a good deal for families who have two children under age 10, are staying at a Value resort, and book lots of character meals. Light eaters and childless couples, especially those staying at Deluxe resorts, may find it cheaper to take a room discount and pay for food separately.

For an in-depth discussion of the various plans, including number crunching (with algebra, even!), visit **touringplans.com** (scroll down and click "Dining" on the home page, then "Disney Dining Plan").

Readers who tried the Disney dining plan had varying experiences, but frustration seems to be a common refrain. A St. Louis family of three comments:

> We purchased the dining plan and would never do it again. Far too expensive, far too much food, and then you have to tip on top of the expense. Much easier to purchase what you want, where and when you want.

A New Hampshire family concurs:

> Dining plans are NOT for us. Keeping track of the meals, figuring out what you can and can't buy, and rushing around on the last day trying to use up what's left is just too stressful. We'd rather just buy what we want, when and where we want it.

A reader from The Woodlands, Texas, laments that the plan has altered the focus of her vacation:

> For me, the Disney Dining Plan has taken a lot of the fun out of going to Disney World. Now, dining for each day must be planned months in advance unless one is to eat just hot dogs, pizza, and other walk-up items. I want to have fun. I don't want to be locked into a tight schedule, always worrying about where we need to be when it's time to eat, and I don't want to eat when I'm not hungry just because I have a reservation somewhere.

A Tennessee mother of a 3-year-old gives the plan two thumbs up:

> We LOVED the dining plan. It was wonderful to not have to stress every day about trying to keep up with a budget for food. The plan turned out to be a fantastic deal for us, especially since we did four character meals that would have cost at least $400 otherwise.

A mom from Baltimore agrees about character meals:

I'd recommend the Disney Dining Plan only to those who wish to use it for character dining—that's where the value is. Otherwise, save your money and pay out of pocket as you go.

And a Belmont, Massachusetts, dad is a fan of the Quick Service Dining Plan:

If you intend to eat Disney food, the counter-service meal plan is a good option. We didn't want the full plan because the restaurants seemed overpriced, and the necessity of reservations months in advance seemed crazy and a bar to flexibility. You get two counter-service meals (entree/combo, dessert, drink) and two snacks (food item or drink) per person per day as part of the plan, and even though kids' meals are cheaper, there's no distinction when you order—kids can order [more-expensive] adult meals.

A mom from Orland Park, Illinois, comments on the difficulty of getting Advance Reservations:

It's impossible to get table reservations anywhere good—the restaurants that are available are available for a reason. We found ourselves taking whatever was open and were unhappy with every sit-down meal we had, except for lunch at Liberty Tree Tavern. I don't enjoy planning my day exclusively around eating at a certain restaurant at a certain time, but that is what you must do six months in advance if you want to eat at a good sit-down restaurant in Disney.

As this reader from San Jose, California, explains, guests who are not on the dining plan need to know how the plan has affected obtaining Advance Reservations:

When planning 90 days out for the off-season, I was told by the Disney rep to make all my reservations then because the restaurants are booked by people on the dining plan. In fact, I was told that most of the sit-down restaurants don't even take walk-ins anymore. Sure enough, even though I was well over 90 days away from my vacation, a lot of my restaurant choices were unavailable. I had to rearrange my entire schedule to fit the open slots at the restaurants I didn't want to miss.

A family from Wilmington, Massachusetts, shared this:

We found the basic dining plan somewhat limiting, and it provided way too much food. Dessert came with both the counter-service and table-service meals. If you tell the server that you don't want dessert at either of these meals, he or she will try hard to convince you that you are making a life-altering mistake because you aren't getting your money's worth. I understand that the dining plan is a great value for many people, but we aren't a "strap on the feedbag" kind of group.

Many readers report that Disney cast members are more knowledgeable about the dining plan these days. A Washington, D.C.–area couple writes:

The kinks are worked out, and everyone at the parks we talked to *seemed to get it, but we still spent $40 or more at most sit-down dinners on drinks and tips.*

A Hickory, North Carolina, reader agrees:

Most cast members knew the plans well and were happy to explain to us what our options were.

A mum from Sutton Coldfield, England, warns that toddlers fall through the cracks:

We were traveling with two 6-year-olds and a 2-year-old. My youngest did not qualify for the dining plan, which worked well in the buffet-style restaurants where he could eat free. However, if you eat in a full-service restaurant and your 2-year-old is eating off the menu, there's no infant option—you have to pay for a child's meal.

A Land O' Lakes, Florida, dad bumped into this problem:

We had some trouble with our Deluxe Dining Plan being "invalidated" after checkout, though it was supposed to be valid until midnight of our checkout date. That was annoying, since calls to the resort were needed to verify the meals left on our passes for The Crystal Palace and for some snacks later.

From a Midwestern reader:

We could almost relate our dining experience to that of a person who receives food stamps—very restricted and always at the mercy of someone else for food selection.

The dining plan left a family of five from Nashville, Tennessee, similarly dazed and confused:

What was annoying was the inconsistency. You can get a 16-ounce chocolate milk on the kids' plan, but only 8 ounces of white milk at many places. At Earl of Sandwich, you can get 16 ounces of either kind. A pint of milk would count as a snack (price $1.52), but they wouldn't count a quart of milk (price $1.79) because it wasn't a single serving. However, in Animal Kingdom, my husband bought a water-bottle holder (price $3.75) and used a snack credit.

Reader Tips for Getting the Most Out of the Plan

A mom from Radford, Virginia, shares the following tip:

Warn people to eat lunch early if they have dinner reservations before 7 p.m. Disney doesn't skimp on food—if you eat a late lunch (where, by the way, they feed you the same ungodly amount of food), you WILL NOT be hungry for dinner.

A mom from Brick Township, New Jersey, found that the dining plan streamlined her touring:

We truly enjoyed our Disney trip, and this time we purchased the dining plan. This was great for the kids because we did a character-dining experience every day. This helped us in the parks because we didn't have to wait in line to see the characters. Instead, we got all of our autographs during our meals.

A Saskatoon, Saskatchewan, father of three says you have to watch vendors like a hawk:

We had a problem with a vendor who charged us meal service for each of the ice cream bars we purchased. This became evident at our final sit-down meal, when we didn't have any meal vouchers left. Check the receipts after every purchase!

A mom from Lawrence, Kansas, offers this tip:

The quick-service meals aren't really designated for kids or adults when they ring you up and subtract the food from your plan. I wish I'd have known early on that if they couldn't see I had a child under 9, I could have ordered a regular meal and gotten more food. We figured that out toward the end and started ordering bigger meals for our 7-year-old (we saved the desserts to share later).

Finally, a Brooklyn family of four warns that the plan doesn't always eliminate the need to use cash:

We ate dinner at Jiko—we each ordered a salad and a main course and skipped dessert—and while the food was good, we ended up leaving annoyed by Disney's cheapness. We were on the dining plan and were told that our meals would be two credits each. This translates to about $80 apiece. Fine. But when the check came, we were not only charged the two credits each, we were charged $12 each for the salads. Plus tips. I asked why we had been charged extra, and I was told that dessert was included in the meal plan but not first courses. It's pretty annoying to pay $80 per person for a one-course dinner and STILL have to put down more cash.

Magic Your Way Premium Package

With the Magic Your Way Premium Package you get lodging; Magic Your Way Base Tickets; breakfast, lunch, and dinner (including two snacks per day plus gratuities and one refillable resort drink mug per person), character meals, and dinner shows; unlimited golf, tennis, fishing excursions, and water sports; select theme park tours; Cirque du Soleil show tickets; unlimited use of child-care facilities—everything you can think of except for alcoholic beverages. The Premium Package costs $194 for adults and $144 for kids ages 3–9 (tax included) in addition to the cost of the standard Magic Your Way package. *Note:* A minimum three-night stay at Walt Disney World is required in order to book the Premium Package.

unofficial **TIP**
For all Magic Your Way plans, everyone in the room must be on the same package and ticket options. All tickets must be used within 14 days of first use.

Disney, needless to say, has built a nice profit into every component of the Magic Your Way Premium Package. If you don't use all the features, Disney makes out even better.

PLATINUM PACKAGE The favorite of high rollers who want to prepay for everything they might desire while at Walt Disney World, the Platinum Package gets you lodging; Base Tickets; breakfast, lunch, and dinner in full-service restaurants; unlimited golf, tennis, boating, and recreation; unlimited dinner shows and character breakfasts; primo Cirque du Soleil seats; private in-room child care; unlimited use of child-care facilities;

personalized itinerary planning; a ride on the Characters in Flight balloon at Disney Springs; a spa treatment; a fireworks cruise; admission to select tours; reserved seating for *Fantasmic!;* and (here's the kicker) nightly turndown service! Everything you can think of, in other words, except alcoholic beverages. Per diem prices (including tax) for the Platinum Package are $254 for adults and $184 for kids in addition to the cost of a standard Magic Your Way package—but anyone who buys this package doesn't give a Goofy fart what the prices are anyway. As with the Premium Package, a minimum three-night stay is required.

DOING THE MATH

COMPARING A MAGIC YOUR WAY PACKAGE with purchasing the package components separately is a breeze.

1. Pick a Disney resort and decide how many nights you want to stay.
2. Next, work out a rough plan of what you want to do and see so you can determine the admission passes you'll require.
3. When you're ready, call the Disney Reservation Center (DRC) at ☎ 407-W-DISNEY and price a Magic Your Way package with tax for your selected resort and dates. The package will include both admissions and lodging. It's also a good idea to get a quote from a Disney-savvy travel agent (see page 124).
4. Now, to calculate the costs of buying your accommodations and admission passes separately, call the DRC a second time. This time, price a room-only rate for the same resort and dates. Be sure to ask about the availability of any special deals. While you're still on the line, obtain the prices, with tax, for the admissions you require. If you're not sure which of the various admission options will best serve you, consult our free Ticket Calculator at **touringplans.com.**
5. Add the room-only rates and the admission prices. Compare this sum to the DRC quote for the Magic Your Way package.
6. Check for deals and discounts on packages and admission.

When you upgrade to a Premium Package, you load the plan with so many features that it's difficult to price them individually. For a rough comparison, price the plan of your choice using the previous steps. To complete the picture, work up a dining budget, excluding alcohol. Add your estimated dining costs to the room-only quote and admissions quote, and compare this to the price of the plan.

Regarding the economics of the dining plan, it's illustrative to know how the cost of one day on the plan is spent on each component. We'll spare you the math, but an approximate value for each item across every 2016 Disney Dining Plan is as follows:

- Each counter-service meal is worth **$16–$17.40.**
- Each table-service meal is worth **$34–$35.25.**
- Every snack is worth around **$4.35.**
- The refillable mug is worth **$4–$8.**

THROW ME A LINE!

IF YOU BUY A PACKAGE FROM DISNEY, don't expect reservationists to offer suggestions or help you sort out your options. Generally, they respond only to your specific questions, ducking queries that require an opinion. A reader from North Riverside, Illinois, complains:

> My wife made two telephone calls, and the representatives from WDW were very courteous. However, they only answered the questions posed and were not eager to give advice on what might be most cost-effective. I feel a person could spend 8 hours on the phone with WDW reps and not have any more input than you get from reading the literature.

If you can't get the information you need from Disney, contact a good travel agent. Chances are the agent can help you weigh your options.

PACKAGES FROM A DIFFERENT PERSPECTIVE

WE'VE ALWAYS EVALUATED PACKAGES from a dollars-and-cents point of view, paying scant attention to other considerations such as time, economy, and convenience. A reader from Westchester County, New York, finally got our attention, writing:

> I fully understand your position not to recommend the Premium plans in your guide, because they're expensive. However, when one books six rooms, as I have, with guests ages 4–59, including a wife, grandchildren, children, sons- and daughters-in-law, and a nanny, the thought of trying to find out what way each family segment would like to go and then arranging for it on a daily basis is a scary scenario. With the Premium Plan, they can go where they want, eat where they want, and Gramps and his roommate don't have the hassle.

A Mobile, Alabama, couple also liked the Premium Plan, although they had some reservations (pardon the pun) about dining:

> While we had plenty of time to see and do things, had we been there for a week or less we probably would've been frustrated with how much time it took to eat three table-service meals a day, once you calculate the secondary time expense of traveling to the restaurant (which may or may not be in the park you're in at the moment). One time we finished eating lunch and basically had to check in for dinner almost immediately!

Purchasing Room-Only Plus Passes Versus a Package

SUE PISATURO of **Small World Vacations** (**smallworldvacations.com**), a travel agency that specializes in Disney, also thinks there's more involved in a package-purchase decision than money.

> Should you purchase a Walt Disney World package or buy all the components of the package separately? There's no single answer to this confusing question.
>
> A Walt Disney World package is like a store-bought prepackaged kids' meal, the kind with the little compartments filled with meat, cheese, crackers, drink, and dessert: You just grab the package and go. It's easy, and if it's on sale, why bother doing it yourself? If it's not on sale, it still may be worth the extra money for convenience.
>
> Purchasing the components of your vacation separately is like buying each of the meal's ingredients, cutting them up into neat piles and packaging the lunch yourself. Is it worth the extra time and effort to do it this way? Will you save money if you do it this way?

You have two budgets to balance when you plan your Disney World vacation: time and money. Satisfying both is your ultimate goal. Research and planning are paramount to realizing your Disney vacation dreams. Create your touring plans before making a final decision with regard to the number of days and options on your theme park passes. Create your dining itinerary (along with Advance Reservations, if possible) to determine if Disney's dining plan can save you some money.

HOTELS *outside*
WALT DISNEY WORLD

SELECTING AND BOOKING A HOTEL OUTSIDE WALT DISNEY WORLD

LODGING COSTS OUTSIDE DISNEY WORLD vary incredibly. If you shop around, you can find a clean motel with a pool within 5–20 minutes of the World for as low as $40 a night. Because of hot competition, discounts abound, particularly for AAA and AARP members.

There are four primary out-of-the-World areas to consider:

1. INTERNATIONAL DRIVE AREA This area, about 15–25 minutes northeast of the World, parallels I-4 on its eastern side and offers a wide selection of hotels and restaurants. Prices range from $56 to $400 per night. The chief drawbacks are terribly congested roads, countless traffic signals, and inadequate access to westbound I-4. While I-Drive's biggest bottleneck is its intersection with Sand Lake Road, the mile between Kirkman and Sand Lake Roads is almost always gridlocked. We provide tips for avoiding this traffic in Part Seven (see "Sneak Routes," page 459).

Regarding traffic on International Drive (known locally as I-Drive), a convention-goer from Islip, New York, weighed in with this:

When I visited Disney World with my family last summer, we wasted huge chunks of time in traffic on International Drive. Our hotel was in the section between the big McDonald's [at Sand Lake Road] and Wet 'n Wild [at Universal Boulevard]. There are practically no left-turn lanes in this section, so anyone turning left can hold up traffic for a long time.

Traffic aside, a man from Ottawa, Ontario, sings the praises of his I-Drive experience:

International Drive is the place to stay when going to Disney. Your description of this location failed to point out that there are several discount stores, boutiques, restaurants, mini-putts, and other entertainment facilities, all within walking distance of remarkably inexpensive accommodations and a short drive away from WDW.

I-Drive hotels are listed in the **Orlando Official Visitors Guide,** published by Visit Orlando. To obtain a copy, call ☎ 800-972-3304 or 407-363-5872, or check **visitorlando.com.**

2. LAKE BUENA VISTA AND THE I-4 CORRIDOR A number of hotels are along FL 535 and west of I-4 between Disney World and I-4's intersection with Florida's Turnpike. They're easily reached from the interstate and are near many restaurants, including those on International Drive. The *Orlando Official Visitors Guide* (see page 28) lists most of them. For some traffic-avoidance tips, see "The I-4 Blues" (page 446) in Part Seven, Arriving and Getting Around. This area includes Disney's new Flamingo Crossings Value-priced resort area (see page 255).

3. US 192 (IRLO BRONSON MEMORIAL HIGHWAY) This is the highway to Kissimmee, to the southeast of Disney World. In addition to large full-service hotels, many small, privately owned motels often offer a good value. Several dozen properties on US 192 are nearer Disney parks than are more expensive hotels inside the World. The number and variety of restaurants on US 192 has increased markedly, compensating for the area's primary shortcoming. Locally, US 192 is called Irlo Bronson Memorial Highway. The section to the west of I-4 and the Disney Main-gate is designated Irlo Bronson Memorial Highway West, while the section from I-4 running southeast toward Kissimmee is Irlo Bronson Memorial Highway East.

The combined east and west sections have numbered mile markers that simplify navigation if you know which marker is closest to your destination. Though traffic is heavy on Irlo Bronson west of the Main-gate, it doesn't compare to the congestion east of the Maingate and I-4 between Mile Markers 8 and 13. This section can—and should—be avoided by using **Osceola Parkway,** a toll road that parallels Irlo Bronson to the north and terminates in Walt Disney World at the entrance to Animal Kingdom.

A senior citizen from Brookfield, Connecticut, was pleased with lodging in the US 192–Kissimmee area:

> We were amazed to find that from our cheaper and superior accommodations in Kissimmee it took only 5 minutes longer to reach the park turnstiles than it did from the Disney accommodations.

Hotels on US 192 and in Kissimmee are listed in the *Kissimmee Visitor's Guide.* Order a copy by calling ☎ 800-327-9159, or view it online at **experiencekissimmee.com.**

4. UNIVERSAL STUDIOS AREA In the triangular area bordered by I-4 on the southeast, Vineland Road on the north, and Turkey Lake Road on the west are Universal Orlando and the hotels most convenient to it. Running north–south through the middle of the triangle is Kirkman Road, which connects to I-4. On the east side of Kirkman are a number of independent hotels and restaurants. Universal hotels, theme parks, and CityWalk are west of Kirkman. Traffic in this area is not nearly as congested as on nearby International Drive, and there are good interstate connections in both directions.

DRIVING TIME TO THE PARKS FOR VISITORS LODGING OUTSIDE WALT DISNEY WORLD

OUR HOTEL INFORMATION CHART on pages 277–291 shows the commuting time to the Disney theme parks from each hotel listed. Those commuting times represent an average of several test runs. Your actual time may be shorter or longer depending on traffic, road construction (if any), and delays at traffic signals.

The commuting times in our Hotel Information Chart show conclusively that distance from the theme parks is not necessarily the dominant factor in determining commuting times. Among those we list, the hotels on Major Boulevard opposite the Kirkman Road entrance to Universal Orlando, for example, are the most distant (in miles) from the Disney parks. But because they're only one traffic signal from easy access to I-4, commuting time to the parks is significantly less than for many closer hotels.

Note that times in the chart differ from those in the Door-to-Door Commuting Times chart in Part Seven. The latter compares using the Disney transportation system with driving your own car *inside* Walt Disney World. These times include actual transportation time plus tram, monorail, or other connections required to get from the parking lots to the entrance turnstiles. The hotel chart's commuting times, by contrast, represent only the driving time to and from the entrance of the respective parking lot of each park, with no consideration for getting to and from the parking lot to the turnstiles.

Add to the commuting times in the Hotel Information Chart a few minutes for paying your parking fee and parking. Once you park at the Transportation and Ticket Center (Magic Kingdom parking lot), it takes 20–30 minutes more to reach the Magic Kingdom via monorail or ferry. To reach Epcot from its parking lot, add 7–10 minutes. At Disney's Hollywood Studios and Animal Kingdom, the lot-to-gate transit is 5–12 minutes. If you haven't purchased your theme park admission in advance, tack on another 10–20 minutes.

GOOD NEIGHBOR HOTELS

SOME HOTELS PAY DISNEY a marketing fee to display a Good Neighbor designation. Usually there is a ticket shop in the lobby that sells full-price Disney tickets. Other than that, the designation means nothing for the consumer. It doesn't guarantee quality—some Good Neighbor hotels are very nice, others not so much. Some are close to Walt Disney World, while others are quite far away. Disney requires Good Neighbor hotels to provide free shuttle service to Walt Disney World but prohibits them from offering shuttle service to Universal or SeaWorld.

HOTEL SHOPPING ON THE INTERNET: WELCOME TO THE WILD WEST

UNMATCHED AS AN EFFICIENT and timely distributor of information, the Internet has become the primary resource for travelers seeking to shop for and book their own air travel, hotels, rental cars, entertainment, and travel packages. It's by far the best direct-to-consumer distribution channel in history.

INTERNET ECONOMICS 101 The evolution of selling travel on the web has radically altered the way airlines, hotels, cruise lines, rental-car companies, and the like do business. Before the Internet, they depended on travel agents or direct contact with customers by phone. Transaction costs were high because companies were obligated to pay commissions and fund labor-intensive in-house reservations departments. With the advent of the

Continued on page 242

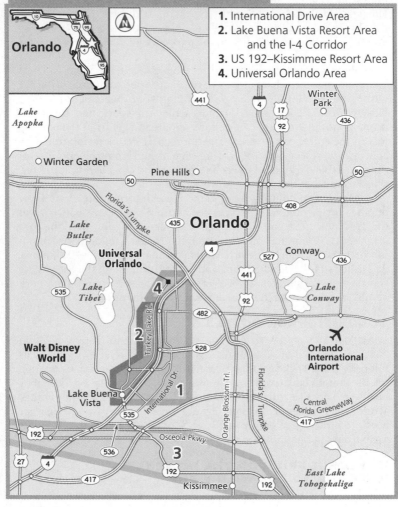

Hotel Concentrations Around Walt Disney World

1. International Drive Area
2. Lake Buena Vista Resort Area and the I-4 Corridor
3. US 192–Kissimmee Resort Area
4. Universal Orlando Area

International Drive & Universal Areas

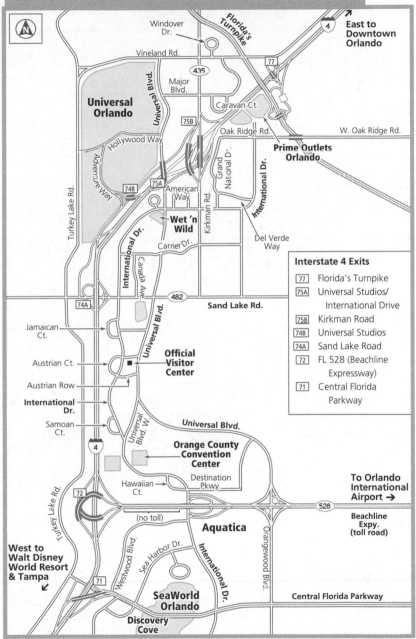

Lake Buena Vista Resort Area & the I-4 Corridor

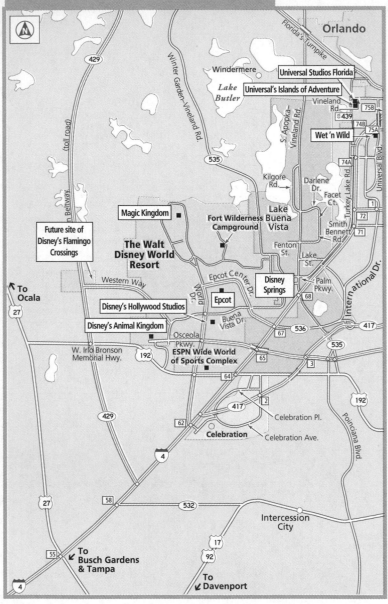

US 192–Kissimmee Resort Area

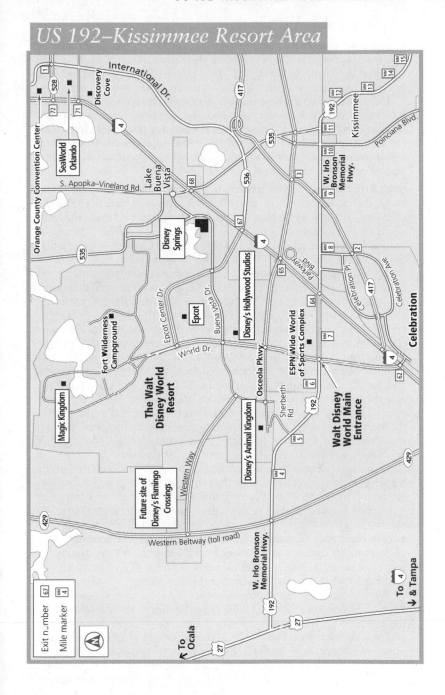

Orange County Convention Center

International Dr.

Discovery Cove

SeaWorld Orlando

S. Apopka–Vineland Rd.

Lake Buena Vista

Disney Springs

Epcot Center Dr.

Epcot

Fort Wilderness Campground

The Walt Disney World Resort

Magic Kingdom

World Dr.

Buena Vista Dr.

Disney's Hollywood Studios

Osceola Pkwy.

Disney's Animal Kingdom

Sherberth Rd.

ESPN Wide World of Sports Complex

Walt Disney World Main Entrance

Parkway Blvd.

Celebration Pl.

Celebration Ave.

Celebration

W. Irlo Bronson Memorial Hwy.

Kissimmee

Poinciana Blvd.

Future site of Disney's Flamingo Crossings

Western Way

Western Beltway (toll road)

W. Irlo Bronson Memorial Hwy.

To Ocala

To & Tampa

Exit number 67
Mile marker MM 4

Continued from page 237

Internet, inexpensive e-commerce transactions became possible: Airlines and rental-car companies began using their own websites to effectively cut travel agents out of the sales process. Hotels also developed websites but continued to depend on wholesalers and travel agents as well.

It didn't take long before independent websites sprang up that sold travel products from a wide assortment of suppliers, often at deep discounts. These sites, called **online travel agencies (OTAs),** include such familiar names as **Travelocity, Orbitz, Priceline, Expedia, Hotels.com,** and **Hotwire.** Those mentioned and others like them attract huge numbers of customers shopping for hotels.

OTAS AND THE MERCHANT MODEL In the beginning, hotels paid OTAs about the same commission that they paid travel agents, but then the OTAs began applying the thumbscrews, forcing hotels to make the transition from a simple commission model to what's called a merchant model. Under this model, hotels provide an OTA with a deeply discounted room rate that the OTA then marks up and sells. The difference between the marked-up price and the discounted rate paid to the hotel is the OTA's gross profit. If, for example, a hotel makes $120 rooms available to an OTA at a 33% discount, or $80, and the OTA sells the room at $110, the OTA's gross profit is $30 ($110 – $80).

The merchant model, originally devised for wholesalers and tour operators, has been around since long before the Internet. Wholesalers and tour operators, then and now, must commit to a certain volume of business, commit to guaranteed room allotments, pay deposits, and bundle the discounted rates with other travel services so that the actual hotel rate remains hidden within the bundle. This is known as *opaque pricing*. The merchant model costs the hotel two to three times the normal travel-agent commission—considered justifiable because the wholesalers and tour operators also promote the hotel through brochures, websites, trade shows, print ads, and events.

OTAs now demand the equivalent of a wholesale commission or higher but are subject to none of the requirements imposed on wholesalers and tour operators. For instance, they don't have to commit to a specified volume of sales or keep discounted room rates opaque. In return, hotels give up 20–50% of gross profit and are rewarded by having their rock-bottom rates plastered all over the Internet, with corresponding damage to their image and brand. (This last is why it's very rare to see a Disney hotel advertised on an OTA site at a price lower than what you can obtain from Disney itself.)

What's more, doing business with OTAs is very expensive for hotels. The cost for a hotel to sell a multiday booking on its own website is $10–$12, including site hosting and analytics, marketing costs, and management fees. This is 10–20 times cheaper than the cost of the same booking through an OTA. Let's say a hotel sells a $100 room for six nights on its own website. Again, the booking would cost the hotel around $12, or $2 per night. If an OTA books the same room having secured it from the hotel at a 30% discount, the hotel receives $70 per night from the OTA. Thus the hotel's cost for the OTA booking is $30 per night, or $180 for six nights—15 times as costly as selling the room online with no middleman.

In the hotel industry, occupancy rates are important, but simply getting bodies into beds doesn't guarantee a profit. A more critical metric is *revenue per available room* (RevPAR). For a hotel full of guests booked through an OTA, RevPAR will be 20–50% lower than for the same number of guests who booked the hotel directly, either through the hotel's website or by phone.

It's no wonder, then, that hotels and OTAs have a love–hate relationship. Likewise, it's perfectly understandable that hotels want to maximize direct bookings through their own websites and minimize OTA bookings. Problem is, the better-known OTAs draw a lot more web traffic than a given hotel's (or even hotel chain's) website. So the challenge for the hotel becomes how to shift room-shoppers away from the OTAs and channel them to its website. A number of hotel corporations, including Choice, Hilton, Hyatt, InterContinental, Marriott, and Wyndham, have risen to that challenge by forming their own OTA called **Room Key** (roomkey.com). The participating chains hope that working together will generate enough visitor traffic to make Room Key competitive with the Expedias and Travelocities of the world.

MORE POWER TO THE SHOPPER Understanding the market dynamics we've described gives you a powerful tool for obtaining the best rates for the hotel of your choice. It's why we tell you to shop the web for the lowest price available and then call your travel agent or the hotel itself to ask if they can beat it. Any savvy reservationist knows that selling you the room directly will both cut the hotel's cost and improve gross margin. If the reservationist can't help you, ask to speak to his or her supervisor. (We've actually had to explain hotel economics to more than a few clueless reservation agents.)

As for travel agents, they have clout based on the volume of business they send to a particular hotel or chain and can usually negotiate a rate even lower than what you've found on the Internet. Even if the agent can't beat the price, he or she can often obtain upgrades, preferred views, free breakfasts, and other deal sweeteners. When we bump into a great deal on the web, we call our agent. Often she can beat the deal or improve on it, perhaps with an upgrade. *Reminder:* Except for special arrangements agreed to by you, the fee or commission due to your travel agent will be paid by the hotel.

THE SECRET The key to shopping on the Internet is, well, shopping. When we're really hungry for a deal, there are a number of sites that we always check out:

OUR FAVORITE ONLINE HOTEL RESOURCES
mousesavers.com Best site for hotels in Disney World
hotelcoupons.com Self-explanatory
experiencekissimmee.com Primarily US 192–Kissimmee area hotels
orlandovacation.com Great rates for condos and home rentals
visitorlando.com Good info; not user-friendly for booking

We scour these sites for unusually juicy hotel deals that meet our criteria (location, quality, price, amenities). If we find a hotel that fills the bill, we check it out at other websites and comparative travel

244 PART 3 ACCOMMODATIONS

search engines such as **Kayak** (**kayak.com**) and **Mobissimo** (**mobissimo .com**) to see who has the best rate. (As an aside, Kayak used to be purely a search engine but now sells travel products, raising the issue of whether products not sold by Kayak are equally likely to come up in a search. Mobissimo, on the other hand, only links potential buyers to provider websites.) Your initial shopping effort should take about 15–20 minutes, faster if you can zero in quickly on a particular hotel.

Next, armed with your insider knowledge of hotel economics, call the hotel or have your travel agent call. Start by asking about specials. If there are none, or if the hotel can't beat the best price you've found on the Internet, share your findings and ask if the hotel can do better. Sometimes you'll be asked for proof of the rate you've discovered online—to be prepared for this, go to the site and enter the dates of your stay, plus the rate you've found to make sure it's available. If it is, print the page with this information and have it handy for your travel agent or for when you call the hotel. (*Note:* Always call the hotel's local number, not its national reservations number.)

INDEPENDENT AND BOUTIQUE HOTEL DEALS While chain hotels worry about sales costs and profit margins, independent and so-called boutique hotels are concerned about discoverability—making themselves known to the traveling public. The market is huge and it's increasingly hard for these hotels to get noticed, especially when they're competing with major chains. Independent and boutique hotels work on the premise that if they can get you through the front door, you'll become a loyal customer. For these hotels, substantially discounting rates is part of their marketing plan to build a client base. Because such hotels get lost on the big OTA sites and on search engines like Kayak and Google, they've jumped on the flash-sale bandwagon. Offering almost irresistible rates on daily-coupon sites like **Groupon** and **LivingSocial,** the independents can get their product in front of thousands of potential guests.

These offers are very generous but also time-limited. If you're in the market, though, you'll be hard-pressed to find better deals. While an OTA such as Expedia generally obtains rooms at a 20–35% discount off the hotel's published rate, flash sites cut deals at an extra-deep discount. This allows their subscribers to bid on or secure coupons for rooms that are often as much as 50% lower than the hotel's standard rate, and that frequently include perks such as meals, free parking, waived resort fees, shopping vouchers, spa services, and entertainment. On Groupon's home page, click "Getaways" or just wait for Getaway coupons by e-mail as part of your free subscription. On LivingSocial you have to specifically subscribe to "Adventures" and "Escapes"; otherwise, you'll receive only non-travel-related offers.

ANOTHER WRINKLE Finally, a quick word about a recent trend: bidding sites. On these sites you enter the type of accommodation you desire and your travel dates, and hotels will bid for your reservation. Some sites require that you already have a confirmed booking from a hotel before you can bid. A variation is that you reserve a room at a particular hotel (including Disney hotels) for a set rate. If the rate drops subsequently, you get money back; if the rate goes up, your original rate is locked in.

Late 2011 and early 2012 saw the launch of TripAdvisor's **Tingo** (**tIngo.com**) and Montreal-based **BackBid** (**backbid.com**), each claiming to be able to beat rates offered by hotel websites and OTAs.

Slamming the lodging industry in full-frontal assault is **Airbnb** (**airbnb.com**), a site that hooks up travelers with owner-hosted alternative options all over the world: bedrooms in people's homes, private apartments, vacation homes, and even live-on boats. The hotel industry is up in arms because Airbnb is not subject to most of the regulation and taxes that dedicated hotels must observe. Though an Airbnb reservation is a little dicier than one with a chain hotel, it's also considerably cheaper. Most reports on Airbnb have been positive, and we've had good experiences with them ourselves.

IS IT WORTH IT? You might be asking yourself if it's worth all this effort to save a few bucks. Saving $10 on a room doesn't sound like a big deal, but if you're staying six nights that adds up to $60. Earlier we referred to unusually juicy deals, deep discounts predicated by who-knows-what circumstances that add up to big money. They're available every day, and with a little perseverance you'll find them—not often for Disney hotels, but for hotels that are just as good. Good hunting!

New Is Better—and Sometimes Cheaper

New hotels rarely burst on the scene at 100% occupancy. During a hotel's first year, when it strives to generate buzz and attract clientele, it often offers deeply discounted rooms. This is true even of prestigious brands. One thing's for sure: A new hotel will charge less the first few months it's open than subsequently, and a hotel that opens during low season will discount more than hotels that come on line during high season.

Two Other Discount Sources Worth Mentioning

1. ORLANDO MAGICARD This discount program is sponsored by Visit Orlando. Cardholders are eligible for discounts of 12–50% at about 50 hotels. The Magicard is also good for discounts at some area attractions, three dinner theaters, museums, performing-arts venues, restaurants, shops, and more. Valid for up to six persons, the card isn't available for larger groups or conventions.

To obtain a free Magicard and a list of participating hotels and attractions, call ☎ 800-643-9492 or 407-363-5872. On the web, go to **visitorlando.com/magicard;** the Magicard and accompanying brochure can be printed from a personal computer. If you miss getting one before you leave home, obtain one at the Visit Orlando Official Visitors Center at 8723 International Dr. When you call for your Magicard, also request the *Orlando Official Visitors Guide.*

2. HOTELCOUPONS.COM *FLORIDA GUIDE* This book of coupons for lodging statewide is free in many restaurants and motels on main highways leading to Florida. Because most travelers make reservations before leaving home, picking up the book en route doesn't help much. To view it online or sign up for a free monthly guide sent by e-mail, visit **hotel coupons.com**. For a hard copy ($3 for handling, $5 if shipped to Canada), call ☎ 800-222-3948 Monday–Friday, 8 a.m.–5 p.m. Eastern time.

Scratch That Itch . . . for Information

Granted, it won't help you find good deals on hotels, but **The Bedbug Registry** (**bedbugregistry.com**), is nonetheless a useful resource, allowing you to peruse reports of bedbug and other insect infestations at any hotel in the US. Simply enter the name, city, and state of the property in question; you can also submit a report of your own. Understand that bedbug outbreaks are usually confined to particular rooms and that the creepy-crawlies were probably brought in by previous guests.

CONDOMINIUMS AND VACATION HOMES

VACATION HOMES ARE FREESTANDING, while condominiums are essentially one- to three-bedroom accommodations in a larger building housing a number of similar units. Because condos tend to be part of large developments (frequently time-shares), amenities such as swimming pools, playgrounds, game arcades, and fitness centers often rival those found in the best hotels. Generally speaking, condo developments don't have restaurants, lounges, or spas.

With a condo, if something goes wrong, there will be someone on hand to fix the problem. Vacation homes rented from a property-management company likewise will have someone to come to the rescue, though responsiveness varies from company to company. If you rent directly from an owner, correcting problems is often more difficult, particularly when the owner doesn't live in the same area as the rental home.

In a vacation home, all the amenities are contained in the home. Depending on the specific home, you might find a small swimming pool, hot tub, two-car garage, family room, game room, and even a home theater. Features found in both condos and vacation homes include full kitchens, laundry rooms, TVs, DVD players, and frequently stereos. Interestingly, though almost all freestanding vacation homes have private pools, very few have backyards. This means that, except for swimming, the kids are pretty much relegated to playing in the house.

Time-share condos are clones when it comes to furniture and decor, but single-owner condos and vacation homes are furnished and decorated in a style that reflects the taste of the owner. Vacation homes, usually one- to two-story houses in a subdivision, very rarely afford interesting views (though some overlook lakes or natural areas), while condos, especially the high-rise variety, sometimes offer exceptional ones.

The Price Is Nice

The best deals in lodging in the Walt Disney World area are vacation homes and single-owner condos. Prices range from about $65 a night for two-bedroom condos and town homes to $200–$500 a night for three- to seven-bedroom vacation homes. Forgetting about taxes to keep the comparison simple, let's compare renting a vacation home to staying at one of Disney's Value resorts. A family of two parents, two teens, and two grandparents would need three hotel rooms at Disney's All-Star Resorts. At the lowest rate obtainable, that would run you $110 per night, per room, or $330 total. Rooms are 260 square feet each, so you'd have a total of 780 square feet. Each room has a private bath and a television.

Renting at the same time of year from **All Star Vacation Homes** (no relation to Disney's All-Star Resorts), you can stay at a 2,053-square-foot, four-bedroom, three-bath vacation home with a private pool 3 miles from Walt Disney World for $289—not quite as economical as Disney's Value resorts, but plenty of value all the same: With four bedrooms, each of the teens can have his or her own room. Further, for the dates we checked, All Star Vacation Homes was running a special in which they threw in a free rental car with a one-week home rental.

But that's not all—the home comes with the following features and amenities: a flat-screen LED TV with a DVD player (assorted games and DVDs available for complimentary checkout at the rental office); a heatable private pool; five additional flat-screen TVs and DVD players (one in each bedroom and one in the game room); a fully equipped kitchen; a game room with an air-hockey table and video-game console; a hot tub; a full-size washer and dryer; a fully furnished private patio; and a child-safety fence.

The home is in a community with a 24-hour gated entrance. At the community center are a large swimming pool; a whirlpool; tennis, volleyball, and half-court basketball courts; a children's playground; a gym and exercise room; a convenience store; and a 58-seat cinema.

One thing we like about All Star Vacation Homes is that its website, **allstarvacationhomes.com,** offers detailed information, including a dozen or more photos of each specific home. When you book, the home you've been looking at is the actual one you're reserving. If you want to see how the home previously described is furnished, for instance, go to the home page, scroll down to "Select Code" and look for a small search window in the upper-right side of the photograph that reads "Search a Property Code." Enter **2-8137 SP-WP** in the search window. You'll be taken to another page with a description of the home, a slide show, a floor plan, and additional information.

On the other hand, some vacation-home companies, like rental-car agencies, don't assign you a specific home until the day you arrive. These companies provide photos of a typical home instead of making information available on each of the individual homes in their inventory. In this case, you have to take the company's word that the typical home pictured is representative and that the home you'll be assigned will be just as nice.

How the Vacation-Home Market Works

In the Orlando–Walt Disney World area, there are more than 26,000 rental homes, including stand-alone homes, single-owner condos (that is, not time-shares), and town homes. The same area has about 116,000 hotel rooms. Almost all the rental homes are occupied by their owners for at least a week or two each year; the rest of the year, the owners make the homes available for rent. Some owners deal directly with renters, while others enlist the assistance of a property-management company.

Incredibly, about 700 property-management companies operate in the Orlando–Kissimmee–Walt Disney World market. Most of these are mom-and-pop outfits that manage an inventory of 10 homes or

Continued on page 250

Rental-Home Developments Near WDW

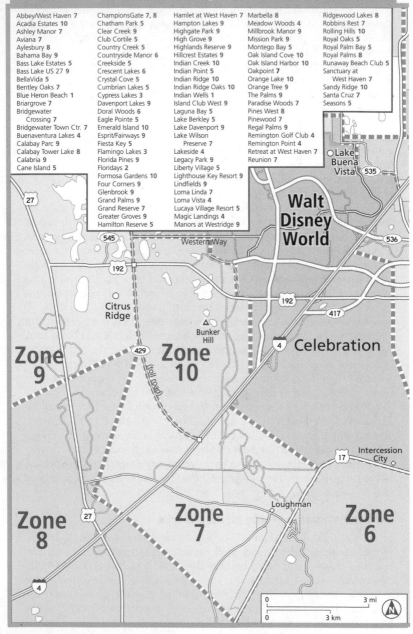

Abbey/West Haven 7
Acadia Estates 10
Ashley Manor 7
Aviana 7
Aylesbury 8
Bahama Bay 9
Bass Lake Estates 5
Bass Lake US 27 9
BellaVida 5
Bentley Oaks 7
Blue Heron Beach 1
Briargrove 7
Bridgewater
    Crossing 7
Bridgewater Town Ctr. 7
Buenaventura Lakes 4
Calabay Parc 9
Calabay Tower Lake 8
Calabria 7
Cane Island 5

ChampionsGate 7, 8
Chatham Park 5
Clear Creek 9
Club Cortile 5
Country Creek 5
Countryside Manor 6
Creekside 5
Crescent Lakes 6
Crystal Cove 5
Cumbrian Lakes 5
Cypress Lakes 3
Davenport Lakes 9
Doral Woods 6
Eagle Pointe 5
Emerald Island 10
Esprit/Fairways 9
Fiesta Key 5
Flamingo Lakes 3
Florida Pines 9
Floridays 2
Formosa Gardens 10
Four Corners 9
Glenbrook 9
Grand Palms 9
Grand Reserve 7
Greater Groves 9
Hamilton Reserve 5

Hamlet at West Haven 7
Hampton Lakes 9
Highgate Park 9
High Grove 9
Highlands Reserve 9
Hillcrest Estates 9
Indian Creek 10
Indian Point 5
Indian Ridge 10
Indian Ridge Oaks 10
Indian Wells 1
Island Club West 9
Laguna Bay 5
Lake Berkley 5
Lake Davenport 9
Lake Wilson
    Preserve 7
Lakeside 4
Legacy Park 9
Liberty Village 5
Lighthouse Key Resort 9
Lindfields 9
Loma Linda 7
Loma Vista 7
Lucaya Village Resort 5
Magic Landings 4
Manors at Westridge 9

Marbella 8
Meadow Woods 4
Millbrook Manor 9
Mission Park 9
Montego Bay 5
Oak Island Cove 10
Oak Island Harbor 10
Oakpoint 7
Orange Lake 10
Orange Tree 9
The Palms 9
Paradise Woods 7
Pines West 8
Pinewood 7
Regal Palms 9
Remington Golf Club 4
Remington Point 4
Retreat at West Haven 7
Reunion 7

Ridgewood Lakes 8
Robbins Rest 7
Rolling Hills 10
Royal Oaks 5
Royal Palm Bay 5
Royal Palms 8
Runaway Beach Club 5
Sanctuary at
    West Haven 7
Sandy Ridge 10
Santa Cruz 7
Seasons 5

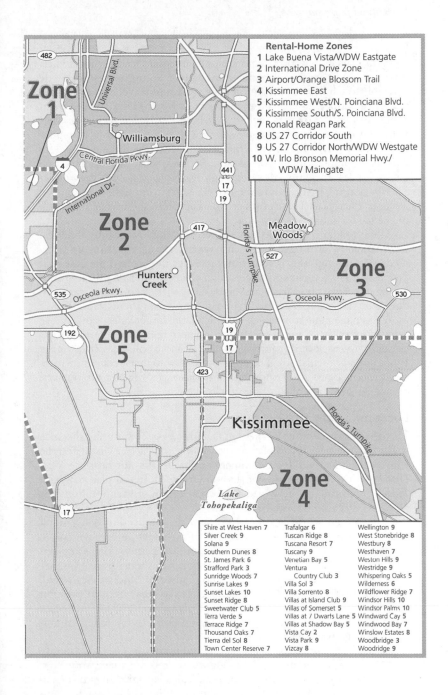

Rental-Home Zones
1 Lake Buena Vista/WDW Eastgate
2 International Drive Zone
3 Airport/Orange Blossom Trail
4 Kissimmee East
5 Kissimmee West/N. Poinciana Blvd.
6 Kissimmee South/S. Poinciana Blvd.
7 Ronald Reagan Park
8 US 27 Corridor South
9 US 27 Corridor North/WDW Westgate
10 W. Irlo Bronson Memorial Hwy./
   WDW Maingate

Zone 1
Zone 2
Zone 3
Zone 5
Zone 4

Williamsburg
Meadow Woods
Hunters Creek
Kissimmee
Lake Tohopekaliga

482
Universal Blvd.
4
Central Florida Pkwy.
International Dr.
441
17
19
417
Florida's Turnpike
527
535
Osceola Pkwy.
E. Osceola Pkwy.
530
192
19
17
423
Florida's Turnpike
17

Shire at West Haven 7	Trafalgar 6	Wellington 9
Silver Creek 9	Tuscan Ridge 8	West Stonebridge 8
Solana 9	Tuscana Resort 7	Westbury 8
Southern Dunes 8	Tuscany 9	Westhaven 7
St. James Park 6	Venetian Bay 5	Weston Hills 9
Strafford Park 3	Ventura	Westridge 9
Sunridge Woods 7	Country Club 3	Whispering Oaks 5
Sunrise Lakes 9	Villa Sol 3	Wilderness 6
Sunset Lakes 10	Villa Sorrento 8	Wildflower Ridge 7
Sunset Ridge 8	Villas at Island Club 9	Windsor Hills 10
Sweetwater Club 5	Villas of Somerset 5	Windsor Palms 10
Terra Verde 5	Villas at 7 Dwarfs Lane 5	Windward Cay 5
Terrace Ridge 7	Villas at Shadow Bay 5	Windwood Bay 7
Thousand Oaks 7	Vista Cay 2	Winslow Estates 8
Tierra del Sol 8	Vista Park 9	Woodbridge 3
Town Center Reserve 7	Vizcay 8	Woodridge 9

Continued from page 247

less (probably fewer than 70 companies oversee more than 100 rental homes).

Homeowners pay these companies to maintain and promote their properties and handle all rental transactions. Some homes are made available to wholesalers, vacation packagers, and travel agents in deals negotiated either directly by the owners or by property-management companies on the owners' behalf. A wholesaler or vacation packager will occasionally drop its rates to sell slow-moving inventory, but more commonly the cost to renters is higher than when dealing directly with owners or management companies: Because most wholesalers and packagers sell their inventory through travel agents, both the wholesaler/packager's markup and the travel agent's commission are passed along to the renter. These costs are in addition to the owner's cut and/ or the fee for the property manager.

Along similar lines, logic may suggest that the lowest rate of all can be obtained by dealing directly with owners, thus eliminating an intermediary. Although this is sometimes true, it's more often the case that property-management companies offer the best rates. With their marketing expertise and larger customer base, these companies can produce a higher occupancy rate than can the owners themselves. What's more, management companies, or at least the larger ones, can achieve economies of scale not available to owners regarding maintenance, cleaning, linens, even acquiring furniture and appliances (if a house is not already furnished). The combination of higher occupancy rates and economies of scale adds up to a win–win situation for owners, management companies, and renters alike.

Location, Location, Location

The best vacation home is one that is within easy commuting distance of the theme parks. If you plan to spend some time at SeaWorld and the Universal parks, you'll want something just to the northeast of Walt Disney World (between the World and Orlando). If you plan to spend most of your time in the World, the best selection of vacation homes is along US 192 to the south of the park.

Walt Disney World lies mostly in Orange County but has a small southern tip that dips into Osceola County, which, along with Polk County to the west of the World, is where most vacation homes and single-owner condos and town houses are. Zoning laws in Orange County (which also includes most of Orlando, Universal Studios, SeaWorld, Lake Buena Vista, and the International Drive area) used to prohibit short-term rentals of homes and single-owner condos, but in recent years the county has loosened its zoning restrictions in a few predominantly tourist-oriented areas.

By our reckoning, about half the rental homes in Osceola County and all the rental homes in Polk County are too far away from Walt Disney World for commuting to be practical. That said, an entrance to Walt Disney World off the FL 429 four-lane toll road halves the commute from many of the vacation-home developments arrayed around the intersection of US 192 and US 27. FL 429 runs north–south from

I-4 south of Walt Disney World to Florida's Turnpike. You might be able to save a few bucks by staying farther out, but the most desirable homes to be found are in Vista Cay and in developments no more than 4 miles from Disney World's main entrance on US 192 (Irlo Bronson Memorial Highway), in Osceola County.

To get the most from a vacation home, you need to be close enough to commute in 20 minutes or less to your Walt Disney World destination. This will allow for naps, quiet time, swimming, and dollar-saving meals you prepare yourself. Though traffic and road conditions are as important as the distance from a vacation home to your Disney destination, we recommend a home no farther than 5 miles away in areas northeast of Walt Disney World and no farther than 4.5 miles away in areas south of the park. Bear in mind that rental companies calculate distance from the vacation home to the absolute nearest square inch of Disney property, so in most instances you can expect to commute another 3 or more miles within Walt Disney World to reach your ultimate destination.

Shopping for a Vacation Home

The only practical way to shop for a rental home is on the web. This makes it relatively easy to compare different properties and rental companies; on the downside, there are so many owners, rental companies, and individual homes to choose from that you could research yourself into a stupor. Three main types of websites serve the home-rental game: those for property-management companies, which showcase a given company's homes and are set up for direct bookings; individual owner sites; and third-party listings sites, which advertise properties available through different owners and sometimes management companies as well. Sites in the last category will usually refer prospective renters to an owner's or management company's site for reservations.

We've found that most property-management sites are not very well designed and will test your patience to the max. You can practically click yourself into old age trying to see all the homes available or figure out where on earth they are. Nearly all claim to be "just minutes from Disney." (By that reasoning, we should list our homes; they're also just minutes from Disney . . . 570 minutes, to be exact!)

Many websites list homes according to towns (such as Auburndale, Clermont, Davenport, Haines City, and Winter Garden) or real estate developments (including Eagle Pointe, Formosa Gardens, Indian Ridge, and Windsor Palms) in the general Disney area, none of which you're likely to be familiar with. The information that counts is the distance of a vacation home or condo from Walt Disney World; for that you often must look for something like "4 miles from Disney" embedded in the home's description. If you visit a site that lists homes by towns or real estate developments, begin by looking at our map on pages 248–249, which shows where all these places are in relation to Walt Disney World. If the map is unhelpful in determining distance, we suggest that you find another location for your stay.

The best websites provide the following:

- Numerous photos and in-depth descriptions of individual homes to make comparisons quick and easy

- Overview maps or text descriptions that reflect how far specific homes or developments are from Walt Disney World
- The ability to book the rental home of your choice on the site
- An easy-to-find phone number for bookings and questions

The best sites are also easy to navigate, let you see what you're interested in without your having to log in or divulge any personal information, and list memberships in such organizations as the Better Business Bureau and the Central Florida Vacation Rental Managers Association (visit **cfvrma.com** for the association's code of ethics).

Recommended Websites

After checking out dozens upon dozens of sites, here are the ones we recommend. All of them meet the criteria listed above. If you're stunned that there are so few of them, well, so were we. (For the record, we elected not to list some sites that met our criteria but whose homes are too far away from Walt Disney World.)

All Star Vacation Homes (allstarvacationhomes.com) is easily the best of the management-company sites, with easily accessible photos and plenty of details about featured homes. All the company's rental properties are within either 4 miles of Walt Disney World or 3 miles of Universal Studios.

#1 Dream Homes (floridadreamhomes.com) has a good reputation for customer service and now has photos of and information about the homes in its online inventory.

Orlando's Finest Vacation Homes (orlandosfinest.com) represents both homeowners and property-management companies. Offering a broad inventory, the Orlando's Finest website features photos and information on individual homes. Although the info is not as detailed as that offered by the All Star Vacation Homes site, friendly sales agents can fill in the blanks.

Vacation Rentals by Owner (vrbo.com) is a nationwide vacation-homes listings service that puts prospective renters in direct contact with owners. The site is straightforward and always lists a large number of rental properties in Celebration, Disney's planned community situated about 8–10 minutes from the theme parks. Two similar listings services with good websites are **Vacation Rentals 411 (vacationrentals411.com)** and **Last Minute Villas (lastminutevillas.net)**.

The website for **Visit Orlando (visitorlando.com)** is the place to go if you're interested in renting a condominium at one of the many time-share developments (click on "Places to Stay" at the site's home page). You can call the developments directly, but going through this website allows you to bypass sales departments and escape their high-pressure invitations to sit through sales presentations. The site also lists hotels and vacation homes.

Making Contact

Once you've found a vacation home you like, check around the website for a Frequently Asked Questions (FAQ) page. If there's not a FAQ page, here are some of the things you'll want to check out on the phone with the owner or rental company.

1. How close is the property to Walt Disney World?
2. Is the home or condominium that I see on the Internet the one I'll get?
3. Is the property part of a time-share development?
4. Are there any specials or discounts available?
5. Is everything included in the rental price, or are there additional charges? What about taxes?
6. How old is the home or condo I'm interested in? Has it been refurbished recently?
7. What is the view from the property?
8. Is the property near any noisy roads?
9. What is your smoking policy?
10. Are pets allowed? (This consideration is as important to those who want to avoid pets as to those who want to bring them.)
11. Is the pool heated?
12. Is there a fenced backyard where children can play?
13. How many people can be seated at the main dining table?
14. Is there a separate dedicated telephone at the property?
15. Is high-speed Internet access available?
16. Are linens and towels provided?
17. How far are the nearest supermarket and drugstore?
18. Are child-care services available?
19. Are there restaurants nearby?
20. Is transportation to the parks provided?
21. Will we need a car?
22. What is required to make a reservation?
23. What is your change/cancellation policy?
24. When is checkout time?
25. What will we be responsible for when we check out?
26. How will we receive our confirmation and arrival instructions?
27. What are your office hours?
28. What are the directions to your office?
29. What if we arrive after your office has closed?
30. Whom do we contact if something goes wrong during our stay?
31. How long have you been in business?
32. Are you licensed by the state of Florida?
33. Do you belong to the Better Business Bureau and/or the Central Florida Vacation Rental Managers Association?

We frequently receive letters from readers extolling the virtues of renting a condo or vacation home. This endorsement by a family from Ellington, Connecticut, is typical:

> *Our choice to stay outside Disney was based on cost and sanity. We've found over the last couple of years that our children can't share the same bed. We have also gotten tired of having to turn off*

the lights at 8 p.m. and lie quietly in the dark waiting for our chil-
dren to fall asleep. With this in mind, we needed a condo/suite layout.
Anything in Disney offering this option [BoardWalk Villas, Beach
Club Villas, Old Key West, and the like] was going to cost $400–
$500 a night. This was not built into our Disney budget. We decided
on the Sheraton Vistana Resort. We had a two-bedroom villa with
full kitchen, living room, three TVs, and washer/dryer. I packed for
half the trip and did laundry almost every night. The facilities offered
a daily children's program and several pools, kiddie pools, and play-
scapes. Located on FL 535, we had a 5- to 10-minute drive to most
attractions, including SeaWorld, Disney, and Universal.

A St. Joe, Indiana, family had a good experience renting a vacation
home, writing:

We rented a home in Kissimmee this time, and we'll never stay in
a hotel at WDW again. It was by far the nicest, most relaxing time
we've ever had down there. Our rental home was within 10–15 min-
utes of all the Disney parks, and 25 minutes from SeaWorld. We
had three bedrooms, two baths, and an in-ground pool in a screened
enclosure out back. We paid $90 per night for the whole shootin'
match. We did spring for the pool heating, $25 per night extra in Feb-
ruary. We used AAA Dream Homes Rental Company and they did a
great job by us. They provided us with detailed info before we went
down so we'd know what we needed to bring.

A New Jersey family of five echoes the above:

I cannot stress enough how important it is if you have a large fam-
ily (more than two kids) to rent a house for your stay! We had vis-
ited WDW several times in the past by ourselves when we were newly-
weds. Fast-forward 10 years later, when we took our three kids, ages
6 years, 4 years, and 20 months. We stayed at Windsor Hills Resort,
*which I booked through **globalresorthomes.com**. I was able to see all*
the homes and check availability when I was reserving the house. This
development is 1.5 miles from the Disney Maingate. It took us about
10 minutes to drive there in the a.m., and we had no traffic issues at all.

THE BEST HOTELS FOR FAMILIES
OUTSIDE WALT DISNEY WORLD

WHAT MAKES A SUPER FAMILY HOTEL? Roomy accommoda-
tions, in-room fridge, great pool, complimentary breakfast, child-care
options, and programs for kids are a few of the things the *Unofficial
Guide* hotel team researched in selecting the top hotels for families
from among hundreds of properties in the Disney World area. Some
of our picks are expensive, others are more reasonable, and some are
a bargain. Regardless of price, be assured that these hotels understand
a family's needs.

Though all of the following hotels offer some type of shuttle to the
theme parks, some offer very limited service. Call the hotel before you
book and ask what the shuttle schedule will be when you visit. Since
families, like individuals, have different wants and needs, we haven't
ranked these properties; they're listed by zone and alphabetically.

Disney's Flamingo Crossings

In 2007, right before the global financial meltdown, Disney announced ambitious plans for a new 450-acre, Value-oriented hotel and restaurant complex, just beyond the western edge of the main Disney World property, at the intersection of Western Way and FL 429. Plans were quietly dropped when the Great Recession came. For years, nothing other than an abandoned website and some press releases remained.

Fast-forward to 2015, and construction has begun on the first two hotels, scheduled to open in early 2016. Both are Marriott brands: **TownePlace Suites,** an extended-stay hotel, and **SpringHill Suites** will have about 250 rooms each; we expect them to be near the $150- to $250-per-night price point. As budget suites, these rooms are targeting the sports groups that participate in events at Disney's Wide World of Sports complex. These two hotels will be adjacent and share parking, a pool, and a gym. Other planned amenities include batting cages, a basketball court, and a practice field capable of being configured for different sports. Assuming there's a market for these, the developer plans to build up to five more hotels in the same area.

INTERNATIONAL DRIVE & UNIVERSAL AREAS

CoCo Key Hotel and Water Resort–Orlando ★★★½

Rate per night $75–$108. **Pools ★★★★**. **Fridge in room** Yes. **Shuttle to parks** Yes (Aquatica, SeaWorld, Universal, Wet 'n Wild). **Maximum number of occupants per room** 4. **Special comments** Daily $24 resort fee for use of the water park; day guests may use the water park for $24.95/person Monday–Friday ($26.95 on weekends and $21.95 for Florida residents).

7400 International Dr. Orlando
☎ 407-351-2626 or 877-875-4681
cocokeyorlando.com

NOT FAR FROM THE UNIVERSAL ORLANDO theme parks, CoCo Key combines a tropical-themed hotel with a canopied water park featuring 3 pools and 14 waterslides, as well as poolside food and arcade entertainment. A full-service restaurant serves breakfast and dinner; a food court offers family favorites such as burgers, chicken fingers, and pizza.

A unique feature of the resort is its cashless payment system, much like that on a cruise ship. At check-in, families receive bar-coded wristbands that allow purchased items to be easily charged to their room.

The unusually spacious guest rooms include 37-inch flat-panel TVs, free Wi-Fi, granite showers and countertops, and plenty of accessible outlets for electronics.

DoubleTree by Hilton Orlando at SeaWorld ★★★★½

Rate per night $129–$179. **Pools ★★★½**. **Fridge in room** Standard in some rooms; available in others for $10/day. **Shuttle to parks** Yes. **Maximum number of occupants per room** 4. **Special comments** Good option if you're visiting SeaWorld or Aquatica. Pets welcome (1 per room, 25-pound limit, $75).

10100 International Dr. Orlando
☎ 407-352-1100 or 800-327-0363
doubletreeorlando idrive.com

ON 28 LUSH, TROPICAL ACRES with a Balinese feel, the DoubleTree is adjacent to SeaWorld and Aquatica water park. The 1,094 rooms and suites—classified as resort or tower—are suitable for business travelers or families. We recommend the tower rooms for good views and the resort rooms for maximum convenience. Laguna serves steak and seafood, along with breakfast; you can also get a quick bite at The Market or the pool bar. Relax and cool off at one of the three pools (there are two more just for kids), or indulge in a special spa treatment. A fitness center, mini-golf course and putting green, children's day camp, and game area afford even more diversions. The resort is about a 15-minute drive to Walt Disney World, a 12-minute drive to Universal, or a short walk to SeaWorld.

Nickelodeon Suites Resort ★★★½

Rate per night $149–$209. **Pools** ★★★★. **Fridge in room** Yes. **Shuttle to parks** Yes. **Maximum number of occupants per room** 8. **Special comments** Daily character breakfast; resort fee of $35/night.

14500 Continental Gateway
Orlando
☎ 407-387-5437
or 877-NICK-111
nickhotel.com

SPONGEBOB SQUAREPANTS, eat your heart out. This resort is as kid-friendly as they come. Decked out in all themes Nickelodeon, the hotel is sure to please any fan of TV shows the likes of *SpongeBob, Dora the Explorer,* and *Avatar: The Last Airbender,* to name a few. Nickelodeon characters from the channel's many shows hang out in the resort's lobby and mall area, greeting kids while parents check in.

Guests can choose from among 777 suites—one-bedroom Family Suites and two- and three-bedroom KidSuites—executed in a number of different themes—all very brightly and creatively decorated. All suites include kitchenettes or full kitchens; also standard are microwave, fridge, coffeemaker, TV, iron and board, hair dryer, and safe. KidSuites feature a semiprivate kids' bedroom with bunk or twin beds, pull-out sleeper bed, 32-inch TV, CD player, and activity table. The master bedroom offers ample storage space that the kids' bedroom lacks.

Additional amenities include a video arcade, Studio Nick (a game-show studio that hosts several game shows a night for the entertainment of a live studio audience), a buffet (kids age 3 and younger eat free with a paying adult), a food court offering Subway and other choices, the full-service Nicktoons Cafe (offers character breakfasts), a convenience store, a lounge, a gift shop, a fitness center, a washer and dryer in each courtyard, and a guest-activities desk (buy Disney tickets and get recommendations on babysitting). Not to be missed are the resort's two pools, Oasis and Lagoon. Oasis features a water park complete with water cannons, rope ladders, geysers, and dump buckets, as well as a hot tub for adults (with a view of the rest of the pool so you can keep an eye on little ones) and a smaller play area for younger kids. Kids will love the huge, zero-entry Lagoon Pool with 400-gallon dump bucket, plus a nearby basketball court and nine-hole mini-golf course. Pool activities for kids are scheduled several times a day, seasonally; some games feature the infamous green slime. Whatever you do, avoid letting your kids catch you saying the phrase "I don't know" while you're here—trust us.

Universal's Cabana Bay Beach Resort ★★★★

Rate per night $119–$210 standard rooms, $174–$294 suites. **Pools** ★★★★. **Fridge in room** Suites only. **Shuttle to parks** Yes (Universal,

SeaWorld, Discovery Cove, Aquatica, and Wet 'n Wild). **Maximum number of occupants per room** 4 for standard rooms, 6 for suites.

6550 Adventure Way
Orlando
☎ 407-503-4000 or
888-464-3617
tinyurl.com/cabanabay

OPENED IN SPRING 2014, Cabana Bay is Universal's first on-site hotel aimed at the value and moderate markets. The theme is midcentury modern, with lots of windows, bright colors, and period-appropriate lighting and furniture. We think the resort would be right at home in the deserts of Palm Springs or Las Vegas, while our British friends say the decor reminds them of Butlin's Bognor Regis resort circa 1985.

Whatever Cabana Bay reminds you of, we think you'll like it. Kids will love the two large and well-themed pools (one with a lazy river), the amount of space they have to run around in, the video arcade, and the vintage cars parked outside the hotel lobby. Adults will appreciate the sophisticated kitsch of the decor, the multiple lounges, the business center, and the on-site Starbucks. We think Cabana Bay is an excellent choice for price- and/or space-conscious families visiting Universal.

The hotel's closest competitor in the Orlando area is Disney's Art of Animation Resort, and the two share many similarities. Both have standard rooms and family suites. At 430 square feet per suite, Cabana Bay suites are about 135 square feet smaller than comparable suites at A of A and have only one bathroom. We found them well appointed for two to four people per room (though not for the six Loews claims as its capacity). Rack rates for the suites are about $140–$300 per night less than Art of Animation's.

Each family suite has a small bedroom with two queen beds, divided from the living area and kitchenette by a sliding screen; a foldout sofa in the living area offers additional sleeping space. (Standard rooms also have two queen beds.) The bath is divided into three sections: toilet, sink area, and shower room with additional sink. The kitchenette has a microwave, coffeemaker, and mini-fridge. A bar area allows extra seating for quick meals, and a large closet has enough space to store everyone's luggage. Built-in USB charging outlets for your devices are a thoughtful touch.

Recreational options include the 10-lane Galaxy Bowl (about $15 per person with shoe rental), poolside table tennis and billiards, and a large Jack LaLanne fitness center. (Fitness centers aren't found at any Disney Value or Moderate resort except Coronado Springs.) Outdoor movies are shown nightly near the pool. We're also told that Cabana Bay guests can use the pools at the other three Universal hotels.

In addition to the Starbucks, a food court with seating area shows 1950s TV clips. Swizzle Lounge in the lobby, two pool bars, in-room pizza delivery, and the Galaxy Bowl round out the on-site dining options. You'll find more restaurants and clubs nearby at the Royal Pacific Resort and Universal CityWalk.

Unlike the other Universal resorts, Cabana Bay offers no watercraft service to the parks—it's either take the bus or walk. In November 2014, a new pedestrian bridge opened connecting Cabana Bay to CityWalk and the rest of Universal Orlando, but we still recommend the bus service for most people. Cabana Bay guests are eligible for early entry at Universal but do not get a complimentary Universal Express pass.

At the time of this review, signage guiding guests to the resort from the Universal area was nearly nonexistent. In the meantime, use your GPS or follow the signs for the Pacifica Ballroom at the Royal Pacific until you see the one sign leading you to the drive into the resort.

Universal's Hard Rock Hotel ★★★★½

Rate per night $259–$464. **Pool ★★★★. Fridge in room** Yes. **Shuttle to parks** Yes (Universal, SeaWorld, Discovery Cove, Aquatica, and Wet 'n Wild). **Maximum number of occupants per room** 5 (double-queen) or 3 (king). **Special comments** Microwaves available for $15/day. Character dinner on Saturday. Pets welcome ($50/night).

5800 Universal Blvd. Orlando
☎ 407-503-2000 or 888-464-3617
hardrockhotel orlando.com

OPENED IN 2001, the Hard Rock Hotel is both Universal Orlando's least-expensive on-site resort and the closest resort to Universal's theme parks. The exterior has a California Mission theme, with white stucco walls, arched entryways, and rust-colored roof tiles. Inside, the lobby is a tribute to rock-and-roll style, all marble, chrome, and stage lighting.

The eight floors hold 650 rooms and 29 suites, with the rooms categorized into standard, deluxe, and club-level tiers. Standard rooms are 375 square feet, slightly larger than rooms at Disney's Moderate resorts and a bit smaller than most Disney Deluxe rooms. The Hard Rock Hotel completed a top-to-bottom "remastering" of its rooms in early 2015, giving the formerly masculine decor a major makeover, with light-gray walls and linens, pastel furniture, and colorful retro-inspired accents.

Standard rooms are furnished with two queen beds, with smooth, plush, comfortable linens and more pillows than you'll know what to do with. Rooms also include a flat-panel LCD television, refrigerator, coffeemaker, and an alarm clock with a 30-pin iPhone docking port.

A six-drawer dresser and separate closet with sliding doors ensure plenty of storage space. In addition, most rooms have a reading chair and a small desk with two chairs. An optional rollaway bed, available at an extra charge, allows standard rooms to sleep up to five people.

Each room's dressing area features a sink and hair dryer. The bathroom is probably large enough for most adults to get ready in the morning while another person gets ready in the dressing area.

Guests staying in standard rooms can choose from one of three views: standard, which can include anything from walkways and parking lots to lawns and trees; garden view, which includes the lawn, trees, and (in some rooms) the waterway around the resort; and pool view, which includes the Hard Rock's expansive pool.

Deluxe rooms with king beds are around 500 square feet and can accommodate up to three people with an optional rollaway bed rental. These rooms feature a U-shaped sitting area in place of the second bed, and the rest of the amenities are the same as in standard rooms. Deluxe queen rooms are also 500 square feet and can hold up to five people using a pullout sofa.

The pool is an attraction unto itself, and the place to see and be seen. Situated in the middle of the resort's C-shaped main building, the 12,000-square-foot pool includes a 250-foot waterslide, a sand beach, and underwater speakers so you can hear the music while you swim. Adjacent to the pool are a fountain play area for small children, a sand-volleyball court, hot tubs, and a poolside bar. The Hard Rock also has a small, functional fitness center. Like all Universal Orlando Resort hotels, the Hard Rock has a business center and video arcade.

On-site dining includes The Kitchen, a casual full-service restaurant open for breakfast, lunch, and dinner, featuring American food such as burgers, steaks, and salads. The Palm Restaurant is an upscale steakhouse available for dinner only. And, of course, the Hard Rock Café is just a short distance away at Universal CityWalk.

After its much-needed refurbishment, we rate the rooms at Hard Rock slightly ahead of the more-expensive Portofino Bay. While not exactly cheap (it charges $20 per day for self-parking and $15 for in-room Internet), Hard Rock is a good value compared to, say, Disney's Yacht & Beach Clubs. What you're paying for at the Hard Rock is a short walk to the theme parks and Universal Express Unlimited first, and the room second.

Universal's Portofino Bay Hotel ★★★★½

Rate per night $294–$479. **Pools** ★★★★. **Fridge in room** Minibar; fridge available for $15/day. **Shuttle to parks** Yes (Universal, SeaWorld, Discovery Cove, Aquatica, and Wet 'n Wild). **Maximum number of occupants per room** 5 (double-queen) or 3 (king). **Special comments** Character dinner on Friday. Pets welcome ($50/night).

5601 Universal Blvd.
Orlando
☎ 407-503-1000 or
888-464-3617
tinyurl.com
/portofinobay

UNIVERSAL'S TOP-OF-THE-LINE HOTEL evokes the Italian seaside city of Portofino, complete with a man-made Portofino Bay past the lobby. To Universal's credit, the layout, color, and theming of the guest-room buildings are a good approximation of the architecture around the harbor in the real Portofino (Universal's version has fewer yachts, however).

Inside, the lobby is decorated with pink marble floors, white-wood columns, and arches. The space is both airy and comfortable, with side rooms featuring seats and couches done in bold reds and deep blues.

Portofino Bay was refurbished in 2013. Most guest rooms are 450 square feet, larger than most at Disney's Deluxe resorts, and have either one king bed or two queen beds. King rooms sleep up to three people with an optional rollaway bed; the same option allows queen rooms to sleep up to five. Two room-view options are available: Garden rooms look out over the landscaping and trees (many of these are the east-facing rooms in the resort's east wing; others face one of the three pools); bay-view rooms face either west or south and overlook Portofino Bay, with a view of the piazza behind the lobby too.

Rooms come furnished with a 32-inch LCD flat-panel TV, a refrigerator, a coffeemaker, and an alarm clock with a 30-pin iPhone docking port. Other amenities include a small desk with two chairs, a comfortable reading chair with lamp, a chest of drawers, and a standing closet. Wi-Fi is $15 per day in guest rooms, free in the lobby. Beds are large, plush, and comfortable.

Guest bathrooms at Portofino Bay are the best on Universal property. We've seen smaller New York apartments! The best thing is the shower, which has enough water pressure to strip paint from old furniture, not to mention an adjustable spray nozzle that varies the water pulses to simulate everything from monsoon season in the tropics to the rhythmic thumps of wildebeest hooves during migrating season. We love it.

Portofino Bay has three pools, the largest of which is the Beach Pool, on the west side of the resort. Two smaller quiet pools sit at the far end of the east wing and to the west of the main lobby. The Beach Pool has a zero-entry design and a waterslide themed after a Roman aqueduct, plus a children's play area, hot tubs, and a poolside bar and grill. The Villa Pool has private cabana rentals for that Italian Riviera feeling. Rounding out the luxuries are the full-service Mandara Spa; a complete fitness center with weight machines, treadmills, and more; a business center; and a video arcade.

On-site dining includes three sit-down restaurants serving Italian cuisine; a deli; a pizzeria; and a café serving coffee and gelato. Some of the food prices go well beyond what we'd consider reasonable, even for a theme park hotel.

While we think Portofino Bay has some of Universal's best rooms, the prices put it on par with the Ritz-Carlton—something its good points can't quite justify. On the other hand, the Ritz isn't a short walk from The Wizarding World of Harry Potter.

Universal's Royal Pacific Resort ★★★★½

Rate per night $234–$404. **Pools** ★★★★. **Fridge in room** Yes. **Shuttle to parks** Yes (Universal, SeaWorld, Discovery Cove, Aquatica, and Wet 'n Wild). **Maximum number of occupants per room** 5 (double-queen) or 3 (king). **Special comments** Microwaves available for $15/day. Character breakfast on Sunday; character dinners on Monday, Wednesday, and Thursday. Pets welcome ($50/night).

6300 Hollywood Way
Orlando
☎ 407-503-1000 or
888-464-3617
tinyurl.com
/royalpacific

YOU MAY BE TEMPTED, as we were initially, to write off the Royal Pacific, which opened in 2002, as a knockoff of Disney's Polynesian Village Resort. There are indeed similarities, but the Royal Pacific is attractive enough, and has enough strengths of its own, for us to recommend that you try a stay there to compare for yourself.

The South Seas–inspired theming is both relaxing and structured. Guests enter the lobby from a walkway two stories above an artificial stream that surrounds the resort. Once you're inside, the lobby's dark teak-wood accents contrast nicely with the enormous amount of light coming in from the windows and three-story A-frame roof. Palms line the walkway through the lobby, and through these you see that the whole lobby surrounds an enormous outdoor fountain.

The 1,000 guest rooms are spread among three Y-shaped wings attached to the main building. Standard rooms are 335 square feet—about the size of a room at Disney's Moderate resorts—and feature one king or two queen beds. King rooms sleep up to three people with an optional rollaway bed; queen rooms sleep five with that rollaway bed. The beds, fitted with 300-thread-count sheets, are very comfortable.

The rooms and hallways of Royal Pacific's first tower were refurbished in 2015, and the remainder will be done by early 2016, with modern monochrome wall treatments and carpets, accented with boldly colored floral graphics. Rooms include a 32-inch flat-panel LCD TV, a refrigerator, a coffeemaker, and an alarm clock with a 30-pin iPhone docking port. Other amenities include a small desk with two chairs, a comfortable reading chair, a chest of drawers, and a large closet. Wi-Fi is $15 per day in guest rooms, free in the lobby.

A dressing area with sink is separated from the rest of the room by a wall. Next to the dressing area is the bathroom, with a tub, shower, and toilet. While they're acceptable, the bathroom and dressing areas at the Royal Pacific are our least favorite in the Universal resorts.

Guests in north- and west-facing rooms in Tower 1 are closest to the attractions at Islands of Adventure and can hear the roar from IOA's Incredible Hulk Coaster throughout the day and night. East-facing rooms in Towers 1 and 2 are exposed to traffic noise from Universal Boulevard and, more distantly, I-4. Quietest are south-facing pool-view rooms in Tower 1 and south-facing rooms in Tower 3.

As at the Hard Rock, the Royal Pacific's zero-entry pool includes a sand beach, volleyball court, play area for kids, hot tub, and cabanas for rent, plus a poolside bar and grill.

Amenities include a 5,000-square-foot fitness facility ($10 per day, free with club-level rooms), a business center, a video arcade, two full-service restaurants, three bars, and a luau. Of the table-service restaurants, only Islands Dining Room is open for breakfast. Emeril Lagasse's Tchoup Chop, the other table-service option, is open for lunch and dinner (reservations recommended).

Universal's Sapphire Falls Resort *(opening 2016)*

UNIVERSAL'S FIFTH ON-SITE LOEWS HOTEL, Sapphire Falls Resort, seeks to bring a sunny Caribbean island vibe to the moderate-price market when its 1,000 rooms open in summer 2016. Sandwiched between Royal Pacific and Cabana Bay—both physically and pricewise— Sapphire Falls will sport all of the amenities of Universal's three Deluxe hotels, including water taxi transportation to the parks, with the crucial exception of complimentary Express Passes.

6601 Adventure Way
Orlando
☎ 407-503-5000 or
888-464-3617
loewshotels.com
/sapphire-falls-hotel

Water figures heavily at Sapphire Falls, whose namesake waterfalls form the scenic centerpiece of the resort. The zero-entry main pool features a white-sand beach, waterslide, children's play areas, fire pit, and cabanas for rent. A fitness room holds a sauna and hot tub. For dinner, Amatista Cookhouse offers table-service Caribbean dining, with an open kitchen and waterfront views. Club Katine serves tapas-style small plates near the pool bar's fire pit. New Dutch Trading Co. is an island-inspired grab-and-go marketplace, and Strong Water Tavern in the lobby has rum tastings and tableside ceviche.

Sapphire Falls also contains 131,000 square feet of meeting space and a business center. Covered walkways connect to a parking structure, which in turn connects to the meeting facilities at Royal Pacific, making the new sister properties ideal for conventions.

The rooms range from 364 square feet in a standard queen or king to 529 square feet in the 36 Kids' Suites, up to 1,358 square feet in the 15 Hospitality Suites. All rooms have a 49-inch flat-panel HDTV, mini-fridge, and coffeemaker. Universal will begin accepting reservations in the spring of 2016. At press time, no official pricing information was available, but we expect rack rates to be between those of Royal Pacific and Cabana Bay.

LAKE BUENA VISTA & I-4 CORRIDOR

B Resort ★★★½

Rate per night $135–$172. **Pools** ★★★½. **Fridge in room** Yes. **Shuttle to parks** Yes (Disney only). **Maximum number of occupants per room** 4 plus child in crib. **Special comments** $20/night resort fee. *See full profile on page 213.*

Buena Vista Palace Hotel & Spa ★★★½

Rate per night $121–$226. **Pools** ★★★½. **Fridge in room** Yes. **Shuttle to parks** Yes (Disney only). **Maximum number of occupants per room** 4. **Special comments** Sunday character brunch available; $22/night resort fee. *See full profile on page 214.*

Four Seasons Resort Orlando at
Walt Disney World Resort ★★★★★

Rate per night $545–$845. **Pools** ★★★★★. **Fridge in room** Yes. **Shuttle to parks** Yes (Disney only). **Maximum number of occupants per room** 4 (3 adults or 2 adults and 2 children). **Special comments** The best pool complex in Walt Disney World.

10100 Dream Tree Blvd.
Golden Oak
☎ 407-313-7777
or 800-267-3046
fourseasons.com
/orlando

AT 444 GUEST ROOMS, the Four Seasons Resort Orlando is simultaneously the largest hotel in the Four Seasons chain and the smallest on Disney property. It's also the best deluxe resort in the area, with comfort, amenities, and personal service that far surpass anything Disney's Deluxes offer. If you're trying to fit a couple of days of relaxing, non-park time into your vacation, this is the hotel to choose.

Standard guest rooms average around 500 square feet and feature either one king bed with a sleeper sofa or two double beds (a crib is available in double rooms). Amenities include two flat-panel televisions, a coffeemaker, a small refrigerator, a work desk with two chairs, a personal digital video recorder (DVR) to record TV shows, and Bluetooth speakers for your personal audio. In keeping with the room's gadget-friendly spirit, each nightstand has four electrical outlets and two USB ports.

Bathrooms have glass-walled showers, a separate tub, marble vanities with two sinks, mosaic-tile floors, hair dryers, lighted mirrors, and a TV in the mirror above the sink.

Most rooms have an 80-square-foot balcony with table and chairs—perfect for your morning coffee or evening nightcap. Standard-view rooms look out onto the resort's lawns, gardens, and nearby homes in Golden Oak. Lake-view rooms—which overlook the lake, the Tom Fazio–designed Tranquilo Golf Club (formerly Osprey Ridge), or the pool—cost about $100 more per night than standard-view rooms. Park-view rooms, on floors 6–16, cost about $200 more per night than standard-view rooms and offer views of the Magic Kingdom's nightly fireworks. (Suites are available with views of Epcot, too.)

The resort's 5-acre pool area is the best on Walt Disney World property, and the least crowded. It features an adult pool, a family pool, an 11,000-square-foot lazy river, and a splash zone with two 242-foot waterslides. To put this in perspective, the Four Seasons' pool area is about twice as large as Stormalong Bay at the Beach and Yacht Club Resorts but with only a third as many guests. Private pool cabanas are available for rent (around $200/day).

Capa, a Spanish-themed rooftop restaurant, serves seafood and steaks (open nightly, 6–10 p.m.; dress is resort casual, and reservations are recommended). Ravello, on the first floor, serves American breakfasts (6:30–11 a.m.) and Italian dinners (5:30–10 p.m.; reservations are recommended, and dress is smart casual). PB&G (Pool Bar and Grill) serves barbecued meats and salads by the main pool (11 a.m.–6 p.m.).

Service is excellent at the Four Seasons. About 25% of the staff transferred from other Four Seasons properties, bringing years of experience and knowledge to this resort. On one visit, the front desk receptionist walked us to our room after check-in, and we were often greeted by name as we walked through the resort.

At the hotel's Disney Planning Center, Disney cast members can help with reservations or any other Disney needs. Disney will also deliver your in-park purchases to the Four Seasons, but staying at the Four Seasons does not qualify guests for Extra Magic Hours, 60-day FastPass+ reservations, or use of Magical Express from the airport.

The hotel has a full-service spa and fitness center, as well as a beautiful late-checkout lounge that allows use of the showers and bathrooms in the spa.

Hilton Orlando Lake Buena Vista ★★★★

Rate per night $161–$241. **Pools** ★★★½. **Fridge in room** Minibar; mini-fridge available free on request. **Shuttle to parks** Yes (Disney theme and water parks only). **Maximum number of occupants per room** 4. **Special comments** Sunday character breakfast and Disney Extra Magic Hours program; $22/night resort fee. *See full profile on page 215.*

Hilton Orlando Bonnet Creek ★★★★

Rate per night $119–$249. **Pool** ★★★★½. **Fridge in room** Yes. **Shuttle to parks** Yes. **Maximum number of occupants per room** 4. **Special comments** $22/night resort fee.

THE HILTON BONNET CREEK is one of our favorite non-Disney hotels in Lake Buena Vista, and the value for the money beats anything in Disney's Deluxe category. Behind Disney's Caribbean Beach and Pop Century Resorts, this Hilton is much nicer than the one in the Downtown Disney Resort Area.

14100 Bonnet Creek
Resort Lane
Orlando
☎ 407-597-3600
hiltonbonnetcreek.com

Standard rooms measure around 414 square feet—comparable to Disney's Deluxe resorts—and have either one king bed or two queen beds. The beds' mattresses and linens are very comfortable. Other features include a 37-inch flat-panel TV, a spacious work desk, an armoire, a small reading chair with floor lamp, a nightstand, and a digital clock. A coffeemaker, small refrigerator, ironing board, and iron are all standard, along with free wired and wireless Internet.

Bathrooms include tile floors with glass showers and a hairdryer. Unfortunately, the layout isn't as up-to-date as other hotels'—where many upscale hotel bathrooms have two sinks (so two people can primp at once), the Hilton's has only one. And where modern bathroom configurations often include a dressing area separate from the bath and a separate water closet for the commode, everything is in the bathroom here. That makes it harder for four-person families to get ready in the morning.

The Hilton's public areas are stylish and spacious. Families will enjoy the huge zero-entry pool, complete with waterslide, as well as the 3-acre lazy river. Even better, the Hilton staff run arts-and-crafts activities poolside during the day, allowing parents to grab a quick swim and a cocktail. Pool-facing cabanas are also available for rent at around $300 per day or $150 per half-day. If you're trying to stay in swimsuit shape, a nice fitness center sits on the ground floor.

The Hilton participates in the Waldorf Astoria's Kids Club next door, for children ages 5–12. A daytime program is available 10:30 a.m.–2:30 p.m., and an evening program is available 6–10 p.m. on Friday and Saturday. Price is $75 for the first child, $25 for each additional child.

There are more than a dozen restaurants and lounges between the Hilton and the Waldorf Astoria, with cuisine including an upscale steakhouse,

Italian, sushi, tapas, a coffee bar, an American bistro, and breakfast buffet choices. Breakfast hours usually run 7–11:30 a.m., lunch 11:30 a.m.–5 p.m., and dinner 5–10 p.m. Reservations are recommended for the fancy places.

Marriott Village at Lake Buena Vista   ★★★

Rate per night $74–$189. **Pools** ★★★. **Fridge in room** Yes. **Shuttle to parks** Disney only, $7. **Maximum number of occupants per room** 4 (Courtyard and Fairfield) or 5 (SpringHill). **Special comments** Free Continental breakfast at Fairfield and SpringHill.

8623 Vineland Ave.
Orlando
☎ 407-938-9001
or 800-761-7829
marriottvillage.com

THIS GATED HOTEL COMMUNITY INCLUDES a 388-room Fairfield Inn (★★★½), a 400-suite SpringHill Suites (★★★), and a 312-room Courtyard (★★★½). Whatever your budget, you'll find a room here to fit it. If you need a bit more space, book SpringHill Suites; if you're looking for value, try the Fairfield Inn; if you need limited business amenities, reserve at the Courtyard. Amenities at all three properties include fridge, cable TV, iron and board, hair dryer, and microwave. Cribs and roll-away beds are available at no extra charge at all locations. Swimming pools at all three hotels are attractive and medium-sized, featuring children's interactive splash zones and whirlpools; in addition, each property has its own fitness center. The incredibly convenient Village Marketplace food court includes Pizza Hut, Village Grill, Village Coffee House, and a 24-hour convenience store. Bahama Breeze and Golden Corral full-service restaurants are within walking distance. Other services and amenities include a Disney planning station and ticket sales, an arcade, and a Hertz car-rental desk. Shoppers will find the Orlando Premium Outlets adjacent. You'll get plenty of bang for your buck at Marriott Village.

Sheraton Vistana Resort Villas   ★★★★

Rate per night $127–$254. **Pools** ★★★½. **Fridge in room** Yes. **Shuttle to parks** Yes (Disney free; other parks for a fee). **Maximum number of occupants per room** 4–8. **Special comments** Though time-shares, the villas are rented nightly as well.

8800 Vistana Centre Dr.
Orlando
☎ 407-239-3100 or
866-208-0003
tinyurl.com/vistanaresort

THE SHERATON VISTANA is deceptively large, stretching across both sides of Vistana Centre Drive. Because Sheraton's emphasis is on selling the time-shares, the rental angle is little known. But families should consider it; the Vistana is one of Orlando's best off-Disney properties. If you want a serene retreat from your days in the theme parks, this is an excellent base. The spacious villas come in one-bedroom, two-bedroom, and two-bedroom-with-lock-off models (which can be reconfigured as one studio room and a one-bedroom suite). All are decorated in beachy pastels, but the emphasis is on the profusion of amenities. Each villa has a full kitchen (including fridge/freezer, microwave, oven/range, dishwasher, toaster, and coffeemaker, with an option to prestock with groceries and laundry products), clothes washer and dryer, TVs in the living room and each bedroom (one with DVD player), stereo with CD player in some villas, separate dining area, and private patio or balcony in most. Grounds offer seven swimming pools (three with bars), four playgrounds, two restaurants, game rooms, fitness centers, a mini-golf course, sports equipment rental (including bikes), and courts for basketball, volleyball, tennis, and shuffleboard. A mind-boggling array of activities for kids (and adults) ranges from crafts to games and sports tournaments. Of special note: Vistana is highly secure, with locked gates bordering all guest areas, so children can have the run of the place without parents worrying about them wandering off. The one downside: noise, both above (from being on the flight path of a helicopter tour company) and below (from International Drive). Bring a white noise machine or app for better sleep.

Waldorf Astoria Orlando ★★★★½

Rate per night $234–$424. **Pool** ★★★★. **Fridge in room** Yes. **Shuttle to parks** Yes (Disney only) **Maximum number of occupants per room** 4, plus child in crib. **Special comments** Good alternative to Disney Deluxe resorts; $30/night resort fee.

14200 Bonnet Creek Resort Lane
Orlando
☎ 407-597-5500
waldorfastoria
orlando.com

THE WALDORF ASTORIA is between I-4 and Disney's Pop Century Resort, near the Hilton Orlando at the back of the Bonnet Creek Resort property. Getting here requires a GPS or good directions, so be prepared with those before you travel. Once you arrive, however, you'll know the trip was worth it. Beautifully decorated and well manicured, the Waldorf is more elegant than any Disney resort. Service is excellent, and the staff-to-guest ratio is far lower than at Disney properties.

At just under 450 square feet, standard rooms feature either two queen beds or one king. A full-size desk allows you to get work done if it's absolutely necessary, and rooms also have flat-panel televisions, high-speed Internet, and Wi-Fi. The bathrooms are spacious and gorgeous, with cool marble floors, glass-walled showers, separate tubs, and enough counter space for a Broadway makeup artist. This space is so nice that we've debated whether we'd rather stay at Pop Century with three others or sleep in a Waldorf bathroom by ourselves.

Amenities include a fitness center, a spa, a golf course, six restaurants, and two pools (including one zero-entry pool for kids). Poolside cabanas are available for rent. The resort offers shuttle service to the Disney parks about every half-hour, but check with the front desk for the exact schedule when you arrive. Runners will enjoy the relative solitude—it's about a 1-mile round-trip to the nearest busy road.

Wyndham Bonnet Creek Resort ★★★★½

Rate per night $229–$359. **Pool** ★★★★. **Fridge in room** Yes. **Shuttle to parks** Yes (Disney only). **Maximum number of occupants per room** 4–12 depending on room/suite. **Special comments** A non-Disney suite hotel within Walt Disney World.

9560 Via Encinas
Lake Buena Vista
☎ 407-238-3500
or 888-743-2687
wyndhambonnet
creek.com

THIS CONDO HOTEL lies on the south side of Buena Vista Drive, about a quarter-mile east of Disney's Caribbean Beach Resort. The property has an interesting history: When Walt Disney began secretly buying up real estate in the 1960s under the names of numerous front companies, the land on which this resort stands was the last holdout and was never sold to Disney, though the company tried repeatedly to acquire it through the years. (The owners reportedly took issue with the way Disney went about acquiring land and preferred to see the site languish undeveloped.)

The 482-acre site was ultimately bought by Marriott, which put up a Fairfield Inn time-share development in 2004. The Wyndham is part of a luxury-hotel complex on the same site that includes a 500-room Waldorf Astoria (see previous profile), a 400-room Wyndham Grand, and a 1,000-room Hilton (see page 263). The development is surrounded on three sides by Disney property and on one side by I-4.

One- and two-bedroom condos have fully equipped kitchens, washers and dryers, jetted tubs, and balconies. Activities and amenities include two outdoor swimming pools, a lazy river float stream, a children's activities program, a game room, a playground, and miniature golf. Free scheduled transportation serves all the Disney parks. One-bedroom units are furnished with a king bed in the bedroom and a sleeper sofa in the living area; two-bedroom condos have two double beds in the second bedroom, a sleeper sofa in the living area, and an additional bath.

US 192 AREA

Clarion Suites Maingate ★★★½

7888 W. Irlo Bronson
Memorial Hwy.
Kissimmee
☎ 407-390-9888 or
888-390-9888
clarionsuites
kissimmee.com

Rate per night $99–$169. **Pool** ★★★. **Fridge in room** Yes. **Shuttle to parks** Yes (Disney, Universal, and SeaWorld). **Maximum number of occupants per room** 6 for most suites. **Special comments** Free Continental breakfast served daily for up to two guests; additional breakfast $5.99 advance, $6.99 day of.

THIS PROPERTY HAS 150 SPACIOUS one-room suites, each with double sofa bed, microwave, fridge, coffeemaker, TV, hair dryer, and safe. The suites aren't lavish, but they're clean and contemporary, with muted deep-purple and beige tones. Extra bathroom counter space is especially convenient for larger families. The heated pool is large and has plenty of lounge chairs and moderate landscaping. A kiddie pool, whirlpool, and poolside bar complete the courtyard. Other amenities include an arcade and a gift shop. But Maingate's big plus is its location next door to a shopping center with about everything a family could need. There, you'll find 10 dining options, including Outback Steakhouse, Red Lobster, Subway, T.G.I. Friday's, and Chinese, Italian, and Japanese eateries; a Winn-Dixie Marketplace; a liquor store; a bank; a dry cleaner; and a tourist-information center with park passes for sale, among other services. All this is a short walk from your room.

Gaylord Palms Resort & Convention Center ★★★★½

6000 W. Osceola Pkwy.
Kissimmee
☎ 407-586-2000
gaylordpalms.com

Rate per night $257–$283. **Pool** ★★★★. **Fridge in room** Yes. **Shuttle to parks** Yes (Disney only). **Maximum number of occupants per room** 4. **Special comments** Probably the closest you'll get to Disney-level extravagance out of the World. Resort fee of $20/day.

THIS DECIDEDLY UPSCALE RESORT has a colossal convention facility and caters strongly to business clientele, but it's still a nice (if pricey) family resort. Hotel wings are defined by the three themed, glass-roofed atriums they overlook. Key West's design is reminiscent of island life in the Florida Keys; Everglades is an overgrown spectacle of shabby swamp chic, complete with piped-in cricket noise and a robotic alligator; and the immense, central St. Augustine harks back to Spanish Colonial Florida. Lagoons, streams, and waterfalls cut through and connect all three, and walkways and bridges abound. A fourth wing, Emerald Bay Tower, overlooks the Emerald

Plaza shopping and dining area of the St. Augustine atrium. These rooms are the nicest and the most expensive, and they're mostly used by convention-goers. Though rooms have fridges and alarm clocks with CD players (as well as other perks such as high-speed Internet access), the rooms themselves really work better as retreats for adults than for kids. However, children will enjoy wandering the themed areas and playing in the family pool (with water-squirting octopus). In-room child care is provided by Kid's Nite Out (see page 426).

Orange Lake Resort ★★★★½

8505 W. Irlo Bronson Memorial Hwy. Kissimmee
☎ 407-239-0000 or 800-877-6522
orangelake.com

Rate per night $107–$159. **Pools** ★★★★. **Fridge in room** Yes. **Shuttle to parks** Yes (fee varies depending on destination). **Maximum number of occupants per room** Varies. **Special comments** This is a time-share property, but if you rent directly through the resort as opposed to the sales office, you can avoid time-share sales pitches; $8/night resort fee.

YOU COULD SPEND YOUR ENTIRE VACATION never leaving this property, about 6–10 minutes from the Disney theme parks. From its 10 pools and two mini-water parks to its golfing opportunities (36 holes of championship greens plus two 9-hole executive courses), Orange Lake offers an extensive menu of amenities and recreational opportunities. If you tire of lazing by the pool, try waterskiing, wakeboarding, tubing, fishing, or other activities on the 80-acre lake. There's also a live alligator show, exercise programs, organized competitive sports and games, arts-and-crafts sessions, and miniature golf. Activities don't end when the sun goes down. Karaoke, live music, a Hawaiian luau, and movies at the resort cinema are some of the evening options.

The 2,412 units are tastefully decorated and comfortably furnished, ranging from suites and studios to three-bedroom villas, all with fully equipped kitchens. If you'd rather not cook on vacation, try one of the seven restaurants scattered across the resort: two cafés, three grills, one pizzeria, and a fast-food eatery. If you need help with (or a break from) the kids, babysitters are available to come to your villa, accompany your family on excursions, or take your children to attractions for you.

HOTELS *and* MOTELS:
Rated and Ranked

IN THIS SECTION, WE COMPARE HOTELS in four main areas outside Walt Disney World (see page 235) with those inside the World.

In addition to Disney properties, we rate hotels in the four lodging areas defined earlier in this chapter. Additional hotels can be found at the intersection of US 27 and I-4, on US 441 (Orange Blossom Trail), and in downtown Orlando. Most of these require more than 30 minutes of commuting to Disney World and thus are not rated. We also haven't rated lodging east of Siesta Lago Drive on US 192.

WHAT'S IN A ROOM?

EXCEPT FOR CLEANLINESS, state of repair, and decor, travelers pay little attention to hotel rooms. There is, of course, a clear standard of quality that differentiates Motel 6 from Holiday Inn, Holiday Inn from Marriott, and so on. Many guests, however, fail to appreciate that some rooms are better engineered than others. Making the room usable to its occupants is an art that combines both form and function.

Decor and taste are important. No one wants to stay in a room that's dated, garish, or ugly. But beyond decor, how "livable" is the room? In Orlando, for example, we've seen some beautifully appointed rooms that aren't well designed for human habitation. Even more than decor, your room's details and design elements are the things that will make you feel comfortable and at home.

ROOM RATINGS

TO EVALUATE PROPERTIES FOR THEIR QUALITY, tastefulness, state of repair, cleanliness, and size of their standard rooms, we have grouped the hotels and motels into classifications denoted by stars—the overall star rating. Star ratings in this guide apply only to Orlando-area properties and don't necessarily correspond to ratings awarded by *Frommer's*, Mobil, AAA, or other travel critics. Because stars have little relevance when awarded in the absence of recognized standards of comparison, we have tied our ratings to expected levels of quality established by specific American hotel corporations.

Overall star ratings apply only to room quality and describe the property's standard accommodations. For most hotels, a standard accommodation is a room with one king bed or two queen beds. In an all-suite property, the standard accommodation is either a studio or a one-bedroom suite. In addition to standard accommodations, many hotels offer luxury rooms and special suites, which aren't rated in this guide. Star ratings for rooms are assigned without regard to whether a property has restaurant(s), recreational facilities, entertainment, or other extras.

In addition to stars (which delineate broad categories), we use a numerical rating system—the room-quality rating. Our scale is 0–100, with 100 being the best possible rating and zero (0) the worst. Numerical ratings show the difference we perceive between one property and another. For instance, rooms at both the Stay Sky Suites I-Drive Orlando and the Clarion Suites Maingate are rated three and a half stars (★★★½). In the supplemental numerical ratings, the former is an 82 and the latter a 76. This means that within the ★★★½ category, Stay Sky Suites has slightly nicer rooms than Clarion Suites.

The location column identifies the area around Walt Disney World where you'll find a particular property. The designation **WDW** means the property is inside Walt Disney World. A **1** means it's on or near International Drive. Properties on or near US 192 (a.k.a. Irlo Bronson Memorial Highway, Vine Street, and Space Coast Parkway) are indicated by a **3**, and those in the vicinity of Universal Orlando as **4**. All others are marked with **2** and for the most part are along FL 535 and the I-4 corridor, though some are in nearby locations that don't meet any other criteria.

Names of properties along US 192 also designate location (for example, Holiday Inn Maingate West). The consensus in Orlando seems to be that the main entrance to Disney World is the broad interstate-type road that runs off US 192. This is called the **Maingate**. Properties along US 192 call themselves Maingate East or West to differentiate their positions along the highway. So, driving southeast from Clermont or Florida's Turnpike, the properties before you reach the Maingate turnoff are called Maingate West, while the properties after you pass the Maingate turnoff are called Maingate East.

LODGING AREAS *(see map on page 238)*	
WDW Walt Disney World	
1 International Drive	**2** Lake Buena Vista and I-4 Corridor
3 US 192 (Irlo Bronson Memorial Highway)	**4** Universal Orlando Area

Cost estimates are based on the hotel's published rack rates for standard rooms. Each **$** represents $50. Thus a cost symbol of **$$$** means that a room (or suite) at that hotel will be about $150 a night; amounts over $200 are indicated by **$ x 5** and so on.

OVERALL STAR RATINGS		
★★★★★	Superior rooms	Tasteful and luxurious by any standard
★★★★	Extremely nice rooms	What you'd expect at a Hyatt Regency or Marriott
★★★	Nice rooms	Holiday Inn or comparable quality
★★	Adequate rooms	Clean, comfortable, and functional without frills—like a Motel 6
★	Super-budget	These exist but are not included in our coverage

We've focused on room quality and excluded consideration of location, services, recreation, or amenities. In some instances, a one- or two-room suite is available for the same price or less than that of a single standard hotel room.

If you've used an earlier edition of this guide, you'll notice that new properties have been added and many ratings and rankings have changed, some because of room renovation or improved maintenance or housekeeping. Lax housekeeping or failure to maintain rooms can bring down ratings.

unofficial **TIP**
The key to avoiding disappointment is to snoop in advance. Ask how old the hotel is and when its guest rooms were last renovated.

Before you shop for a hotel, consider this letter from a man in Hot Springs, Arkansas:

We canceled our room reservations to follow the advice in your book and reserved a hotel highly ranked by the Unofficial Guide. *We wanted inexpensive, but clean and cheerful. We got inexpensive, but also dirty, grim, and depressing. The room spoiled the holiday for me aside from our touring.*

This letter was as unsettling to us as the bad room was to the reader—our integrity as travel journalists is based on the quality of the information we provide. When rechecking the hotel, we found our rating was representative, but the reader had been assigned one of a small number of threadbare rooms scheduled for renovation.

Be aware that some chains use the same guest-room photo in promotional literature for all their hotels and that the rooms at a specific property may bear no resemblance to the photo in question. When you or your travel agent calls, ask how old the property is and when the guest room you're being assigned was last renovated. If you're assigned a room that is inferior to your expectations, demand to be moved.

A WORD ABOUT TOLL-FREE TELEPHONE NUMBERS

AS WE'VE REPEATED SEVERAL TIMES in this chapter, it's essential to communicate with the hotel directly when shopping for deals and stating your room preferences. Most toll-free numbers are routed directly to a hotel chain's central reservations office, and the customer-service agents there typically have little or no knowledge of the individual hotels in the chain or of any specials those hotels may be offering. In our Hotel Information Chart (pages 277–291), therefore, we list the toll-free number only if it connects directly to the hotel in question; otherwise, we provide the hotel's local phone number. We also provide local numbers for the Disney resorts in the Hotel Information Chart and in the Walt Disney World Phone Numbers chart on pages 30 and 31, but note that these hotels must be booked through the Disney Reservation Center (☎ 407-W-DISNEY). After you've reserved your room, you can check online to make sure the reservation is in order.

THE 30 BEST HOTEL VALUES

IN THE CHART ON THE FACING PAGE, we look at the best combinations of quality and value in a room. Rankings are calculated without consideration for location or the availability of restaurant(s), recreational facilities, entertainment, and/or amenities.

A reader wrote to complain that he had booked one of our top-ranked rooms in terms of value and had been very disappointed in the room. We noticed that the room the reader occupied had a quality rating of ★★½. Remember that the list of top deals is intended to give you some sense of value received for dollars spent. A ★★½ room at $40 may have the same *value* as a ★★★★ room at $115, but that doesn't mean the rooms will be of comparable *quality*. Regardless of whether it's a good deal, a ★★½ room is still a ★★½ room.

THE TOP 30 BEST DEALS

HOTEL	LODGING AREA	OVERALL QUALITY	ROOM QUALITY	($ = $50)
1. Rodeway Inn Maingate	3	★★½	59	$–
2. Monumental Hotel	1	★★★★½	94	$$–
3. Shades of Green	WDW	★★★★½	91	$$–
4. Extended Stay America Orlando Lake Buena Vista	2	★★★★	83	$$–
5. Extended Stay America Convention Center/Westwood	1	★★★★	84	$$–
6. Holiday Inn Main Gate East	3	★★★★½	90	$$+
7. Monumental MovieLand Hotel	1	★★★	68	$+
8. Vacation Village at Parkway	3	★★★★½	91	$$+
9. Motel 6 Orlando–I-Drive	1	★★★	66	$+
10. Westgate Vacation Villas	2	★★★★½	90	$$+
11. Super 8 Kissimmee/Maingate	3	★★★	70	$+
12. Radisson Resort Orlando-Celebration	3	★★★★	86	$$
13. The Inn at Calypso	3	★★★½	82	$$–
14. Westgate Town Center	2	★★★★½	93	$$+
15. Hampton Inn & Suites Orlando–South Lake Buena Vista	3	★★★½	80	$$–
16. Super 8 Kissimmee	3	★★½	60	$–
17. Hilton Grand Vacations Club at SeaWorld	1	★★★★½	95	$$$–
18. Extended Stay America Deluxe Orlando Theme Parks	4	★★★½	75	$$–
19. Extended Stay America Orlando Theme Parks	4	★★★½	75	$$–
20. Hilton Orlando Bonnet Creek	1	★★★★	88	$$+
21. Four Points by Sheraton Orlando Studio City	1	★★★½	90	$$$–
22. Legacy Vacation Club Orlando	3	★★★½	80	$$$–
23. Knights Inn Maingate Kissimmee/Orlando	3	★★★	58	$–
24. Extended Stay America Orlando Convention Center	1	★★★	72	$+
25. Orange Lake Resort	3	★★★★½	94	$$$–
26. La Quinta Inn Orlando I-Drive	1	★★★	73	$$–
27. Barefoot'n Resort	3	★★★★	85	$$+
28. Ramada Convention Center I-Drive	1	★★★	65	$+
29. Celebration Suites	3	★★½	61	$+
30. Galleria Palms Kissimmee Hotel	3	★★★	74	$$–

How the Hotels Compare

HOTEL	LODGING AREA	OVERALL QUALITY	ROOM QUALITY	($ ≈ $50)
Four Seasons Resort Orlando at Walt Disney World Resort	WDW	★★★★★	98	$ x 9
Omni Orlando Resort at ChampionsGate	2	★★★★★	96	$+ x 5
Hilton Grand Vacations Club at SeaWorld	1	★★★★½	95	$$$-
Rosen Centre Hotel	1	★★★★½	95	$$$+
Disney's Animal Kingdom Villas (Kidani Village)	WDW	★★★★½	95	$- x 10
Bay Lake Tower at Disney's Contemporary Resort	WDW	★★★★½	95	$- x 12
Monumental Hotel	1	★★★★½	94	$$-
Orange Lake Resort	3	★★★★½	94	$$$-
Gaylord Palms Hotel & Convention Center	3	★★★★½	94	$$$+
The Ritz-Carlton Orlando, Grande Lakes	1	★★★★½	94	$+ x 5
Westgate Town Center	2	★★★★½	93	$$+
Waldorf Astoria Orlando	2	★★★★½	93	$$$$+
JW Marriott Orlando Grande Lakes	1	★★★★½	93	$+ x 5
Universal's Hard Rock Hotel	4	★★★★½	93	$ x 8
Disney's Contemporary Resort	WDW	★★★★½	93	$+ x 9
The Villas at Disney's Grand Floridian Resort & Spa	WDW	★★★★½	93	$- x 13
Disney's Grand Floridian Resort & Spa	WDW	★★★★½	93	$- x 14
DoubleTree by Hilton Orlando at SeaWorld	1	★★★★½	92	$$$+
Marriott's Grande Vista	1	★★★★½	92	$$$+
Westgate Lakes Resort & Spa	2	★★★★½	92	$$$+
Villas of Grand Cypress	2	★★★★½	92	$- x 5
Hyatt Regency Grand Cypress	2	★★★★½	92	$- x 5
Marriott's Sabal Palms	2	★★★★½	92	$+ x 6
Universal's Portofino Bay Hotel	4	★★★★½	92	$+ x 8
Disney's Polynesian Village, Villas & Bungalows (studios)	WDW	★★★★½	92	$+ x 11
Disney's Polynesian Village Resort	WDW	★★★★½	92	$- x 12
Shades of Green	WDW	★★★★½	91	$$-
Vacation Village at Parkway	3	★★★★½	91	$$+
Disney's Animal Kingdom Villas (Jambo House)	WDW	★★★★½	91	$ x 8
Holiday Inn Main Gate East	3	★★★★½	90	$$+
Westgate Vacation Villas	2	★★★★½	90	$$+
Four Points by Sheraton Orlando Studio City	1	★★★★½	90	$$$-
Polynesian Isles Resort (Diamond Resorts)	3	★★★★½	90	$$$
Bohemian Celebration Hotel	2	★★★★½	90	$$$+
Renaissance Orlando at SeaWorld	1	★★★★½	90	$$$+
Marriott's Harbour Lake	2	★★★★½	90	$$$$-
Hyatt Regency Orlando	1	★★★★½	90	$$$$-
Lighthouse Key Resort & Spa	3	★★★★½	90	$$$$-
Liki Tiki Village	3	★★★★½	90	$$$$-
Grand Beach	1	★★★★½	90	$$$$-

How the Hotels Compare (Continued)

HOTEL	LODGING AREA	OVERALL QUALITY	ROOM QUALITY	($ = $50)
Walt Disney World Dolphin	WDW	★★★★½	90	$$$$+
Walt Disney World Swan	WDW	★★★★½	90	$$$$+
Orlando World Center Marriott Resort	2	★★★★½	90	$$$$+
Wyndham Bonnet Creek Resort	2	★★★★½	90	$$$$+
Universal's Royal Pacific Resort	4	★★★★½	90	$+ x 6
Disney's Old Key West Resort	WDW	★★★★½	90	$+ x 8
Disney's Saratoga Springs Resort & Spa	WDW	★★★★½	90	$+ x 8
Disney's Beach Club Resort	WDW	★★★★½	90	$+ x 9
The Villas at Disney's Wilderness Lodge	WDW	★★★★½	90	$- x 10
Disney's Beach Club Villas	WDW	★★★★½	90	$- x 10
Disney's BoardWalk Villas	WDW	★★★★½	90	$- x 10
Treehouse Villas at Disney's Saratoga Springs Resort & Spa	WDW	★★★★½	90	$- x 20
DoubleTree Universal	4	★★★★	89	$$$-
Courtyard Orlando Lake Buena Vista at Vista Centre	2	★★★★	89	$$$-
Sheraton Vistana Resort Villas	2	★★★★	89	$$$$-
Disney's Animal Kingdom Lodge	WDW	★★★★	89	$ x 8
Disney's Yacht Club Resort	WDW	★★★★	89	$- x 10
Disney's BoardWalk Inn	WDW	★★★	89	$+ x 10
Hilton Orlando Bonnet Creek	1	★★★★	88	$$+
WorldQuest Orlando Resort	1	★★★★	88	$$$-
Caribe Royale All-Suite Hotel & Convention Center	1	★★★★	88	$$$+
Hilton Garden Inn Lake Buena Vista/Orlando	2	★★★★	88	$$$+
Hilton Grand Vacations Club on I-Drive	1	★★★★	88	$$$+
Sheraton Lake Buena Vista Resort	2	★★★★	88	$$$+
Universal's Cabana Bay Beach Resort	4	★★★★	88	$$$$-
Hilton Orlando Lake Buena Vista	WDW	★★★★	87	$$$-
Mystic Dunes Resort & Golf Club	3	★★★★	87	$$$-
Wyndham Cypress Palms	3	★★★★	87	$$$
Westin Orlando Universal Boulevard	1	★★★★	87	$$$$+
Radisson Resort Orlando-Celebration	3	★★★★	86	$$
Embassy Suites Orlando–LBV Resort	2	★★★★	86	$$$+
Floridays Resort Orlando	1	★★★★	86	$$$$
Marriott's Cypress Harbour	1	★★★★	86	$ x 6
Disney's Fort Wilderness Resort (cabins)	WDW	★★★★	86	$- x 8
Disney's Wilderness Lodge	WDW	★★★★	86	$- x 9
Marriott's Imperial Palms	1	★★★★	86	$- x 9
Barefoot'n Resort	3	★★★★	85	$$+
Hawthorn Suites Lake Buena Vista	2	★★★★	85	$$+
Wyndham Orlando Resort I-Drive	1	★★★★	85	$$+
Residence Inn Orlando at SeaWorld	2	★★★★	85	$$$-

How the Hotels Compare *(Continued)*

HOTEL	LODGING AREA	OVERALL QUALITY	ROOM QUALITY	($ = $50)
Legacy Vacation Club Lake Buena Vista	2	★★★★	85	$$$-
Homewood Suites by Hilton LBV-Orlando	2	★★★★	85	$$$$-
Marriott's Royal Palms	1	★★★★	85	$- x 6
Extended Stay America Convention Center/ Westwood	1	★★★★	84	$$-
Star Island Resort & Club	3	★★★★	84	$$$+
Hyatt Place Orlando/Universal	4	★★★★	84	$$$+
Disney's Port Orleans Resort–French Quarter	WDW	★★★★	84	$- x 5
Extended Stay America Orlando LBV	2	★★★★	83	$$-
Buena Vista Suites	1	★★★★	83	$$$+
Disney's Coronado Springs Resort	WDW	★★★★	83	$- x 5
Disney's Port Orleans Resort–Riverside	WDW	★★★★	83	$- x 5
The Inn at Calypso	3	★★★½	82	$$-
Courtyard Orlando LBV in Marriott Village	2	★★★½	82	$$+
Stay Sky Suites I-Drive Orlando	1	★★★½	82	$$+
CoCo Key Water Resort–Orlando	1	★★★½	82	$$+
The Point Universal Orlando Resort	1	★★★½	82	$$+
Holiday Inn Resort Lake Buena Vista	2	★★★½	82	$$+
Castle Hotel	1	★★★½	82	$$$
Radisson Hotel Orlando Lake Buena Vista	2	★★★½	82	$$$-
B Resort	WDW	★★★½	82	$$$+
Nickelodeon Suites Resort	1	★★★½	82	$$$$
Parkway International Resort	3	★★★½	82	$- x 5
Westgate Towers	2	★★★½	81	$$+
Hampton Inn & Suites Orlando–South LBV	3	★★★½	80	$$-
Legacy Vacation Club Orlando	3	★★★½	80	$$$-
Comfort Inn Orlando–Lake Buena Vista	2	★★★½	80	$$
Hilton Garden Inn Orlando I-Drive North	1	★★★½	80	$$+
Hawthorn Suites Orlando Convention Center	1	★★★½	80	$$+
Fairfield Inn & Suites Near Universal Orlando Resort	4	★★★½	80	$$$-
Hilton Garden Inn Orlando at SeaWorld	1	★★★½	80	$$$-
Embassy Suites Orlando I-Drive/ Jamaican Court	1	★★★½	80	$$$-
Residence Inn Orlando Convention Center	1	★★★½	80	$$$-
Buena Vista Palace Hotel & Spa	WDW	★★★½	80	$$$-
Disney's Art of Animation Resort	WDW	★★★½	80	$$$$-
SpringHill Suites Orlando Convention Center	1	★★★½	80	$$$$-
Orbit One Vacation Villas	3	★★★½	80	$$$$-
Disney's Caribbean Beach Resort	WDW	★★★½	80	$$$$+
Fairfield Inn & Suites Orlando Lake Buena Vista	2	★★★½	79	$$+
Holiday Inn in the Walt Disney World Resort	WDW	★★★½	79	$$$+

How the Hotels Compare (Continued)

HOTEL	LODGING AREA	OVERALL QUALITY	ROOM QUALITY	($ = $50)
Courtyard Orlando I-Drive	1	★★★½	78	$$+
Park Inn by Radisson Resort and Conference Center	3	★★★½	78	$$$-
Clarion Suites Maingate	3	★★★½	76	$$
The Palms Hotel & Villas	3	★★★½	76	$$+
Grand Lake Resort	1	★★★½	76	$$+
Hampton Inn Orlando/Lake Buena Vista	2	★★★½	76	$$$-
Quality Suites Lake Buena Vista	2	★★★½	76	$$$-
Quality Suites Royale Parc Suites	3	★★★½	76	$$$+
Extended Stay America Deluxe Orlando Theme Parks	4	★★★½	75	$$-
Extended Stay America Orlando Theme Parks	4	★★★½	75	$$-
Best Western Plus Universal Inn	4	★★★½	75	$$-
Hawthorn Suites Orlando I-Drive	1	★★★½	75	$$+
Fairfield Inn & Suites Orlando LBV in Marriott Village	2	★★★½	75	$$+
Holiday Inn & Suites Orlando Universal	4	★★★½	75	$$$-
Wyndham Lake Buena Vista Resort	WDW	★★★½	75	$$+
DoubleTree Guest Suites	WDW	★★★½	75	$$$
Residence Inn Orlando Lake Buena Vista	2	★★★½	75	$$$+
Best Western Premier Saratoga Resort Villas	3	★★★½	75	$$$$-
Galleria Palms Kissimmee Hotel	3	★★★	74	$$-
Crown Club Inn	3	★★★	74	$$-
Best Western Lake Buena Vista Resort Hotel	WDW	★★★	74	$$$+
La Quinta Inn Orlando I-Drive	1	★★★	73	$$-
Disney's All-Star Movies Resort	WDW	★★★	73	$$$-
Disney's All-Star Music Resort	WDW	★★★	73	$$$-
Disney's All-Star Sports Resort	WDW	★★★	73	$$$-
Extended Stay America Orlando Convention Center	1	★★★	72	$+
Baymont Inn & Suites Celebration	3	★★★	72	$$
Staybridge Suites Lake Buena Vista	2	★★★	72	$$$+
SpringHill Suites Orlando LBV in Marriott Village	2	★★★	71	$$$+
Disney's Pop Century Resort	WDW	★★★	71	$$$+
Super 8 Kissimmee/Maingate	3	★★★	70	$+
Hampton Inn I-Drive/Convention Center	1	★★★	70	$$+
Comfort Suites Universal	4	★★★	70	$$+
Monumental MovieLand Hotel	1	★★★	68	$+
Westgate Palace	1	★★★	68	$$$$-
Maingate Lakeside Resort	3	★★★	67	$$-
The Enclave Hotel & Suites	1	★★★	67	$$$-
Hampton Inn Universal	4	★★★	67	$$$-

How the Hotels Compare *(Continued)*

HOTEL	LODGING AREA	OVERALL QUALITY	ROOM QUALITY	($ = $50)
Motel 6 Orlando–I-Drive	1	★★★	66	$+
Comfort Inn I-Drive	1	★★★	66	$$−
Ramada Convention Center I-Drive	1	★★★	65	$+
Rosen Inn International Hotel	1	★★★	65	$$+
Best Western I-Drive	1	★★★	65	$$+
Magnuson Grand Hotel Maingate West	3	★★★	65	$$+
Clarion Inn & Suites at I-Drive	1	★★½	64	$+
Clarion Inn Lake Buena Vista	2	★★½	64	$$−
Hampton Inn South of Universal	1	★★½	64	$$$−
Silver Lake Resort	3	★★½	64	$$$
The Floridian Hotel & Suites	1	★★½	63	$$−
La Quinta Inn Orlando–Universal Studios	4	★★½	63	$$−
Country Inn & Suites Orlando Universal	1	★★½	63	$$
Comfort Inn Maingate	3	★★½	62	$$+
Celebration Suites	3	★★½	61	$+
Super 8 Kissimmee	3	★★½	60	$−
Destiny Palms Maingate West	3	★★½	60	$+
Royal Celebration Inn	3	★★½	60	$+
Rodeway Inn Maingate	3	★★½	59	$−
Knights Inn Maingate Kissimmee/Orlando	3	★★	58	$−
Red Roof Inn Orlando Convention Center	1	★★	58	$+

Hotel Information Chart

B Resort ★★★½
1905 Hotel Plaza Blvd.
Lake Buena Vista, FL 32830
☎ 407-828-2828
bresortlbv.com

LOCATION	WDW
ROOM RATING	82
COST ($=$50)	$$$+

Commuting times to parks *(in minutes)*

MAGIC KINGDOM	15:45
EPCOT	11:00
ANIMAL KINGDOM	15:00
DHS	12:45

Barefoot'n Resort ★★★★
2754 Florida Plaza Blvd.
Kissimmee, FL 34746
☎ 407-589-2127
barefootn.com

LOCATION	3
ROOM RATING	85
COST ($=$50)	$$+

Commuting times to parks *(in minutes)*

MAGIC KINGDOM	17:00
EPCOT	14:00
ANIMAL KINGDOM	14:00
DHS	12:00

Bay Lake Tower at Disney's Contemporary Resort ★★★★½
4600 N. World Dr.
Lake Buena Vista, FL 32830
☎ 407-824-1000
tinyurl.com/baylaketower

LOCATION	WDW
ROOM RATING	95
COST ($=$50)	$- X 12

Commuting times to parks *(in minutes)*

MAGIC KINGDOM	on monorail
EPCOT	11:00
ANIMAL KINGDOM	17:15
DHS	14:15

Baymont Inn & Suites Celebration ★★★
7601 Black Lake Rd.
Celebration, FL 34747
☎ 407-396-1100
tinyurl.com/baymontcelebration

LOCATION	3
ROOM RATING	72
COST ($=$50)	$$

Commuting times to parks *(in minutes)*

MAGIC KINGDOM	8:30
EPCOT	8:15
ANIMAL KINGDOM	5:30
DHS	7:45

Best Western I-Drive ★★★
8222 Jamaican Ct.
Orlando, FL 32819
☎ 407-345-1172
tinyurl.com/bwidrive

LOCATION	1
ROOM RATING	65
COST ($=$50)	$$+

Commuting times to parks *(in minutes)*

MAGIC KINGDOM	8:30
EPCOT	8:15
ANIMAL KINGDOM	11:15
DHS	10:45

Best Western Lake Buena Vista Resort Hotel ★★★
2000 Hotel Plaza Blvd.
Lake Buena Vista, FL 32830
☎ 407-828-2424
lakebuenavistaresorthotel.com

LOCATION	WDW
ROOM RATING	74
COST ($=$50)	$$$+

Commuting times to parks *(in minutes)*

MAGIC KINGDOM	16:00
EPCOT	11:15
ANIMAL KINGDOM	15:15
DHS	13:00

Best Western Plus Universal Inn ★★★½
5618 Vineland Rd.
Orlando, FL 32819
☎ 407-226-9119
tinyurl.com/bwuniversal

LOCATION	4
ROOM RATING	75
COST ($=$50)	$$-

Commuting times to parks *(in minutes)*

MAGIC KINGDOM	17:30
EPCOT	13:00
ANIMAL KINGDOM	16:00
DHS	15:30

Best Western Premier Saratoga Resort Villas ★★★½
4787 W. 192*
Kissimmee, FL 34746
☎ 407-997-3300
bestwesternpremierkissimmee.com

LOCATION	3
ROOM RATING	75
COST ($=$50)	$$$$-

Commuting times to parks *(in minutes)*

MAGIC KINGDOM	20:00
EPCOT	14:00
ANIMAL KINGDOM	16:00
DHS	23:45

Bohemian Celebration Hotel ★★★★½
700 Bloom St.
Celebration, FL 34747
☎ 407-566-6000
celebrationhotel.com

LOCATION	2
ROOM RATING	90
COST ($=$50)	$$$+

Commuting times to parks *(in minutes)*

MAGIC KINGDOM	13:30
EPCOT	13:00
ANIMAL KINGDOM	13:00
DHS	12:30

Buena Vista Palace Hotel & Spa ★★★½
1900 E. Buena Vista Dr.
Lake Buena Vista, FL 32830
☎ 407-827-2727
buenavistapalace.com

LOCATION	WDW
ROOM RATING	80
COST ($=$50)	$$$-

Commuting times to parks *(in minutes)*

MAGIC KINGDOM	16:00
EPCOT	11:15
ANIMAL KINGDOM	15:15
DHS	13:00

Buena Vista Suites ★★★★
8203 World Center Dr.
Orlando, FL 32821
☎ 407-239-8588
bvsuites.com

LOCATION	1
ROOM RATING	83
COST ($=$50)	$$$+

Commuting times to parks *(in minutes)*

MAGIC KINGDOM	9:15
EPCOT	4:30
ANIMAL KINGDOM	7:30
DHS	8:15

Caribe Royale All-Suite Hotel & Convention Center ★★★★
8101 World Center Dr.
Orlando, FL 32821
☎ 407-238-8000
cariberoyale.com

LOCATION	1
ROOM RATING	88
COST ($=$50)	$$$+

Commuting times to parks *(in minutes)*

MAGIC KINGDOM	9:15
EPCOT	4:45
ANIMAL KINGDOM	7:45
DHS	8:15

Hotel Information Chart *(Continued)*

Castle Hotel ★★★½		
8629 International Dr.		
Orlando, FL 32819		
☎ 407-345-1511		
castlehotelorlando.com		
LOCATION	1	
ROOM RATING	82	
COST ($ = $50)	$$$	
Commuting times to parks *(in minutes)*:		
MAGIC KINGDOM	22:30	
EPCOT	17:45	
ANIMAL KINGDOM	20:45	
DHS	20:15	

Celebration Suites ★★½		
5820 W. US 192*		
Kissimmee, FL 34746		
☎ 407-396-7900		
suitesatoldtown.com		
LOCATION	3	
ROOM RATING	61	
COST ($=$50)	$+	
Commuting times to parks *(in minutes)*		
MAGIC KINGDOM	11:15	
EPCOT	11:00	
ANIMAL KINGDOM	9:15	
DHS	10:30	

Clarion Inn & Suites at I-Drive ★★½		
9956 Hawaiian Ct.		
Orlando, FL 32819		
☎ 407-351-5100		
tinyurl.com/clarionidrive		
LOCATION	1	
ROOM RATING	64	
COST ($=$50)	$+	
Commuting times to parks *(in minutes)*		
MAGIC KINGDOM	19:30	
EPCOT	14:15	
ANIMAL KINGDOM	17:15	
DHS	16:45	

Comfort Inn I-Drive ★★★		
8134 International Dr.		
Orlando, FL 32819		
☎ 407-313-4000		
tinyurl.com/comfortidrive		
LOCATION	1	
ROOM RATING	66	
COST ($=$50)	$$–	
Commuting times to parks *(in minutes)*		
MAGIC KINGDOM	20:00	
EPCOT	15:30	
ANIMAL KINGDOM	18:30	
DHS	18:00	

Comfort Inn Maingate ★★½		
7675 W. US 192*		
Kissimmee, FL 34747		
☎ 407-396-4000		
comfortinnkissimmee.com		
LOCATION	3	
ROOM RATING	62	
COST ($=$50)	$$+	
Commuting times to parks *(in minutes)*		
MAGIC KINGDOM	8:30	
EPCOT	8:00	
ANIMAL KINGDOM	5:30	
DHS	7:30	

Comfort Inn Orlando– Lake Buena Vista ★★★½		
8686 Palm Pkwy.		
Orlando, FL 32836		
☎ 407-239-8400		
tinyurl.com/comfortinnlbv		
LOCATION	2	
ROOM RATING	80	
COST ($=$50)	$$	
Commuting times to parks *(in minutes)*		
MAGIC KINGDOM	14:15	
EPCOT	9:45	
ANIMAL KINGDOM	12:45	
DHS	12:15	

Courtyard Orlando Lake Buena Vista at Vista Centre ★★★★		
8501 Palm Pkwy.		
Lake Buena Vista, FL 32836		
☎ 407-239-6900		
tinyurl.com/courtyardlbv		
LOCATION	2	
ROOM RATING	89	
COST ($=$50)	$$$–	
Commuting times to parks *(in minutes)*		
MAGIC KINGDOM	13:15	
EPCOT	8:30	
ANIMAL KINGDOM	11:30	
DHS	11:00	

Courtyard Orlando LBV in Marriott Village ★★★½		
8623 Vineland Ave.		
Orlando, FL 32821		
☎ 407-938-9001		
tinyurl.com/courtyardlbv marriottvillage		
LOCATION	2	
ROOM RATING	82	
COST ($=$50)	$$+	
Commuting times to parks *(in minutes)*		
MAGIC KINGDOM	12:00	
EPCOT	7:15	
ANIMAL KINGDOM	10:15	
DHS	9:45	

Crown Club Inn ★★★		
105 Summer Bay Blvd.		
Clermont, FL 34711		
☎ 407-239-8315		
crownclubinn.com		
LOCATION	3	
ROOM RATING	74	
COST ($=$50)	$$–	
Commuting times to parks *(in minutes)*		
MAGIC KINGDOM	14:00	
EPCOT	9:15	
ANIMAL KINGDOM	11:30	
DHS	13:15	

Disney's All-Star Sports Resort ★★★		
1701 W. Buena Vista Dr.		
Lake Buena Vista, FL 32830		
☎ 407-939-5000		
tinyurl.com/allstarsports		
LOCATION	WDW	
ROOM RATING	73	
COST ($=$50)	$$$–	
Commuting times to parks *(in minutes)*		
MAGIC KINGDOM	6:15	
EPCOT	5:45	
ANIMAL KINGDOM	4:15	
DHS	5:15	

Disney's Animal Kingdom Lodge ★★★★		
2901 Osceola Pkwy.		
Lake Buena Vista, FL 32830		
☎ 407-938-3000		
tinyurl.com/aklodge		
LOCATION	WDW	
ROOM RATING	89	
COST ($=$50)	$ X 8	
Commuting times to parks *(in minutes)*		
MAGIC KINGDOM	8:15	
EPCOT	6:15	
ANIMAL KINGDOM	2:15	
DHS	6:00	

Disney's Animal Kingdom Villas *(Jambo House)* ★★★★½		
2901 Osceola Pkwy.		
Lake Buena Vista, FL 32830		
☎ 407-938-3000		
tinyurl.com/akjambo		
LOCATION	WDW	
ROOM RATING	91	
COST ($=$50)	$ X 8	
Commuting times to parks *(in minutes)*		
MAGIC KINGDOM	8:15	
EPCOT	6:15	
ANIMAL KINGDOM	2:15	
DHS	6:00	

*US 192 is known locally as Irlo Bronson Memorial Highway.

Clarion Inn Lake Buena Vista
★★½
8442 Palm Pkwy.
Lake Buena Vista, FL 32836
☎ 407-996-7300
clarionlbv.com

LOCATION	2
ROOM RATING	64
COST ($=$50)	$$-

Commuting times to parks (in minutes)
MAGIC KINGDOM	13:15
EPCOT	8:30
ANIMAL KINGDOM	11:30
DHS	11:00

Clarion Suites Maingate ★★★½
7888 W. US 192*
Kissimmee, FL 34747
☎ 407-390-9888
clarionsuiteskissimmee.com

LOCATION	3
ROOM RATING	76
COST ($=$50)	$$

Commuting times to parks (in minutes)
MAGIC KINGDOM	10:00
EPCOT	9:15
ANIMAL KINGDOM	7:00
DHS	9:00

CoCo Key Water Resort–Orlando
★★★½
7400 International Dr.
Orlando, FL 32819
☎ 407-351-2626
cocokeyorlando.com

LOCATION	1
ROOM RATING	82
COST ($=$50)	$$+

Commuting times to parks (in minutes)
MAGIC KINGDOM	21:00
EPCOT	16:30
ANIMAL KINGDOM	19:00
DHS	19:30

Comfort Suites Universal ★★★
5617 Major Blvd.
Orlando, FL 32819
☎ 407-363-1967
tinyurl.com/csuniversal

LOCATION	4
ROOM RATING	70
COST ($=$50)	$$+

Commuting times to parks (in minutes)
MAGIC KINGDOM	17:45
EPCOT	13:15
ANIMAL KINGDOM	16:15
DHS	15:15

Country Inn & Suites Orlando Universal ★★½
7701 Universal Blvd.
Orlando, FL 32819
☎ 407-313-4200
countryinns.com/orlandofl_universal

LOCATION	1
ROOM RATING	63
COST ($=$50)	$$

Commuting times to parks (in minutes)
MAGIC KINGDOM	21:00
EPCOT	16:15
ANIMAL KINGDOM	19:15
DHS	18:45

Courtyard Orlando I-Drive
★★★½
8600 Austrian Ct.
Orlando, FL 32819
☎ 407-351-2244
tinyurl.com/courtyardidrive

LOCATION	1
ROOM RATING	78
COST ($=$50)	$$+

Commuting times to parks (in minutes)
MAGIC KINGDOM	21:45
EPCOT	17:00
ANIMAL KINGDOM	20:00
DHS	19:30

Destiny Palms Maingate West
★★½
8536 W. US 192*
Kissimmee, FL 34747
☎ 407-396-1600
destinypalmshotel.com

LOCATION	3
ROOM RATING	60
COST ($=$50)	$+

Commuting times to parks (in minutes)
MAGIC KINGDOM	13:45
EPCOT	13:15
ANIMAL KINGDOM	11:00
DHS	13:00

Disney's All-Star Movies Resort
★★★
1901 W. Buena Vista Dr.
Lake Buena Vista, FL 32830
☎ 407-939-7000
tinyurl.com/allstarmovies

LOCATION	WDW
ROOM RATING	73
COST ($=$50)	$$$-

Commuting times to parks (in minutes)
MAGIC KINGDOM	6:15
EPCOT	5:45
ANIMAL KINGDOM	4:15
DHS	5:15

Disney's All-Star Music Resort
★★★
1801 W. Buena Vista Dr.
Lake Buena Vista, FL 32830
☎ 407-939-6000
tinyurl.com/allstarmusicresort

LOCATION	WDW
ROOM RATING	73
COST ($=$50)	$$$-

Commuting times to parks (in minutes)
MAGIC KINGDOM	6:15
EPCOT	5:45
ANIMAL KINGDOM	4:15
DHS	5:15

Disney's Animal Kingdom Villas
(Kidani Village) ★★★★½
3701 Osceola Pkwy.
Lake Buena Vista, FL 32830
☎ 407-938-7400
tinyurl.com/akkidani

LOCATION	WDW
ROOM RATING	95
COST ($=$50)	$- X 10

Commuting times to parks (in minutes)
MAGIC KINGDOM	8:15
EPCOT	6:15
ANIMAL KINGDOM	2:15
DHS	6:00

Disney's Art of Animation Resort
★★★½
1850 Animation Way
Lake Buena Vista, FL 32830
☎ 407-938-7000
tinyurl.com/artofanimationresort

LOCATION	WDW
ROOM RATING	80
COST ($=$50)	$$$$-

Commuting times to parks (in minutes)
MAGIC KINGDOM	12:00
EPCOT	10:00
ANIMAL KINGDOM	12:00
DHS	3:00

Disney's Beach Club Resort
★★★★½
1800 Epcot Resorts Blvd.
Lake Buena Vista, FL 32830
☎ 407-934-8000
tinyurl.com/beachclubresort

LOCATION	WDW
ROOM RATING	90
COST ($=$50)	$+ X 9

Commuting times to parks (in minutes)
MAGIC KINGDOM	7:15
EPCOT	5:15
ANIMAL KINGDOM	6:45
DHS	4:00

Hotel Information Chart *(Continued)*

Disney's Beach Club Villas
★★★★½
1800 Epcot Resorts Blvd.
Lake Buena Vista, FL 32830
☎ 407-934-8000
tinyurl.com/beachclubvillas

LOCATION	WDW
ROOM RATING	90
COST ($=$50)	$- X 10

Commuting times to parks *(in minutes)*
MAGIC KINGDOM 7:15
EPCOT 5:15
ANIMAL KINGDOM 6:45
DHS 4:00

Disney's BoardWalk Inn ★★★★
2101 N. Epcot Resorts Blvd.
Lake Buena Vista, FL 32830
☎ 407-939-6200
tinyurl.com/boardwalkinn

LOCATION	WDW
ROOM RATING	89
COST ($=$50)	$+ X 10

Commuting times to parks *(in minutes)*
MAGIC KINGDOM 7:15
EPCOT 5:30
ANIMAL KINGDOM 7:00
DHS 3:00

Disney's BoardWalk Villas
★★★★½
2101 N. Epcot Resorts Blvd.
Lake Buena Vista, FL 32830
☎ 407-939-6200
tinyurl.com/boardwalkvillas

LOCATION	WDW
ROOM RATING	90
COST ($=$50)	$- X 10

Commuting times to parks *(in minutes)*
MAGIC KINGDOM 7:15
EPCOT 5:30
ANIMAL KINGDOM 7:00
DHS 3:00

Disney's Fort Wilderness Resort
(cabins) ★★★★
4510 N. Fort Wilderness Trail
Lake Buena Vista, FL 32830
☎ 407-824-2837
tinyurl.com/ftwilderness

LOCATION	WDW
ROOM RATING	86
COST ($=$50)	$- X 8

Commuting times to parks *(in minutes)*
MAGIC KINGDOM 13:15
EPCOT 8:30
ANIMAL KINGDOM 20:00
DHS 14:00

Disney's Grand Floridian Resort & Spa ★★★★½
4401 Floridian Way
Lake Buena Vista, FL 32830
☎ 407-824-3000
tinyurl.com/grandflresort

LOCATION	WDW
ROOM RATING	93
COST ($=$50)	$- X 14

Commuting times to parks *(in minutes)*
MAGIC KINGDOM on monorail
EPCOT 4:45
ANIMAL KINGDOM 11:45
DHS 6:45

Disney's Old Key West Resort
★★★★½
1510 North Cove Rd.
Lake Buena Vista, FL 32830
☎ 407-827-7700
tinyurl.com/oldkeywest

LOCATION	WDW
ROOM RATING	90
COST ($=$50)	$+ X 8

Commuting times to parks *(in minutes)*
MAGIC KINGDOM 10:45
EPCOT 6:00
ANIMAL KINGDOM 14:30
DHS 10:30

Disney's Port Orleans Resort–French Quarter ★★★★
2201 Orleans Dr.
Lake Buena Vista, FL 32830
☎ 407-934-5000
tinyurl.com/portorleansfq

LOCATION	WDW
ROOM RATING	84
COST ($=$50)	$- X 5

Commuting times to parks *(in minutes)*
MAGIC KINGDOM 12:00
EPCOT 8:00
ANIMAL KINGDOM 16:15
DHS 12:30

Disney's Port Orleans Resort–Riverside ★★★★
1251 Riverside Dr.
Lake Buena Vista, FL 32830
☎ 407-934-6000
tinyurl.com/portorleansriverside

LOCATION	WDW
ROOM RATING	83
COST ($=$50)	$- X 5

Commuting times to parks *(in minutes)*
MAGIC KINGDOM 12:00
EPCOT 8:00
ANIMAL KINGDOM 16:15
DHS 12:30

Disney's Saratoga Springs Resort & Spa ★★★★½
1960 Broadway
Lake Buena Vista, FL 32830
☎ 407-827-1100
tinyurl.com/saratogawdw

LOCATION	WDW
ROOM RATING	90
COST ($=$50)	$+ X 8

Commuting times to parks *(in minutes)*
MAGIC KINGDOM 14:45
EPCOT 8:45
ANIMAL KINGDOM 18:15
DHS 14:30

DoubleTree Guest Suites ★★★½
2305 Hotel Plaza Blvd.
Lake Buena Vista, FL 32830
☎ 407-934-1000
doubletreeguestsuites.com

LOCATION	WDW
ROOM RATING	75
COST ($=$50)	$$$

Commuting times to parks *(in minutes)*
MAGIC KINGDOM 13:00
EPCOT 8:30
ANIMAL KINGDOM 12:30
DHS 10:00

DoubleTree Universal ★★★★
5780 Major Blvd.
Orlando, FL 32819
☎ 407-351-1000
doubletreeorlando.com

LOCATION	4
ROOM RATING	89
COST ($=$50)	$$$-

Commuting times to parks *(in minutes)*
MAGIC KINGDOM 19:00
EPCOT 14:15
ANIMAL KINGDOM 17:15
DHS 16:45

Embassy Suites Orlando I-Drive/Jamaican Court ★★★½
8250 Jamaican Ct.
Orlando, FL 32819
☎ 407-345-8250
orlandoembassysuites.com

LOCATION	1
ROOM RATING	80
COST ($=$50)	$$$-

Commuting times to parks *(in minutes)*
MAGIC KINGDOM 20:15
EPCOT 15:30
ANIMAL KINGDOM 18:30
DHS 18:00

*US 192 is known locally as Irlo Bronson Memorial Highway.

Disney's Caribbean Beach Resort
★★★½
900 Cayman Way
Lake Buena Vista, FL 32830
☎ 407-934-3400
tinyurl.com/caribbeanbeachresort

LOCATION	WDW
ROOM RATING	80
COST ($=$50)	$$$$+

Commuting times to parks (in minutes)
MAGIC KINGDOM	8:00
EPCOT	6:00
ANIMAL KINGDOM	7:15
DHS	4:15

Disney's Contemporary Resort
★★★★½
4600 N. World Dr.
Lake Buena Vista, FL 32830
☎ 407-824-1000
tinyurl.com/contemporarywdw

LOCATION	WDW
ROOM RATING	93
COST ($=$50)	$+ X 9

Commuting times to parks (in minutes)
MAGIC KINGDOM	on monorail
EPCOT	11:00
ANIMAL KINGDOM	17:15
DHS	14:15

Disney's Coronado Springs Resort
★★★★
1000 W. Buena Vista Dr.
Lake Buena Vista, FL 32830
☎ 407-939-1000
tinyurl.com/coronadosprings

LOCATION	WDW
ROOM RATING	83
COST ($=$50)	$- X 5

Commuting times to parks (in minutes)
MAGIC KINGDOM	5:30
EPCOT	4:00
ANIMAL KINGDOM	4:45
DHS	4:45

Disney's Polynesian Village Resort
★★★★½
1600 Seven Seas Dr.
Lake Buena Vista, FL 32830
☎ 407-824-2000
tinyurl.com/polynesianresort

LOCATION	WDW
ROOM RATING	92
COST ($=$50)	$- X 12

Commuting times to parks (in minutes)
MAGIC KINGDOM	12:00
EPCOT	8:00
ANIMAL KINGDOM	16:15
DHS	12:30

Disney's Polynesian Village, Villas & Bungalows (studios) ★★★★½
1600 Seven Seas Dr.
Lake Buena Vista, FL 32830
☎ 407-824-2000
tinyurl.com/polynesianresort

LOCATION	WDW
ROOM RATING	92
COST ($=$50)	$+ X 11

Commuting times to parks (in minutes)
MAGIC KINGDOM	12:00
EPCOT	8:00
ANIMAL KINGDOM	16:15
DHS	12:30

Disney's Pop Century Resort
★★★
1050 Century Dr.
Lake Buena Vista, FL 32830
☎ 407-938-4000
tinyurl.com/popcenturywdw

LOCATION	WDW
ROOM RATING	71
COST ($=$50)	$$$+

Commuting times to parks (in minutes)
MAGIC KINGDOM	8:30
EPCOT	6:30
ANIMAL KINGDOM	6:15
DHS	5:00

Disney's Wilderness Lodge
★★★★
901 Timberline Dr.
Lake Buena Vista, FL 32830
☎ 407-824-3200
tinyurl.com/wildernesslodge

LOCATION	WDW
ROOM RATING	86
COST ($=$50)	$- X 9

Commuting times to parks (in minutes)
MAGIC KINGDOM	N/A*
EPCOT	10:00
ANIMAL KINGDOM	15:15
DHS	13:30

Disney's Yacht Club Resort
★★★★
1700 Epcot Resorts Blvd.
Lake Buena Vista, FL 32830
☎ 407-934-7000
tinyurl.com/yachtclubwdw

LOCATION	WDW
ROOM RATING	89
COST ($=$50)	$- X 10

Commuting times to parks (in minutes)
MAGIC KINGDOM	7:15
EPCOT	5:15
ANIMAL KINGDOM	6:45
DHS	4:00

DoubleTree by Hilton Orlando at SeaWorld ★★★★½
10100 International Dr.
Orlando, FL 32821
☎ 407-352-1100
doubletreeorlandoidrive.com

LOCATION	1
ROOM RATING	92
COST ($=$50)	$$$+

Commuting times to parks (in minutes)
MAGIC KINGDOM	17:45
EPCOT	13:00
ANIMAL KINGDOM	16:00
DHS	15:30

Embassy Suites Orlando–Lake Buena Vista Resort ★★★★
8100 Lake Ave.
Orlando, FL 32836
☎ 407-239-1144
embassysuiteslbv.com

LOCATION	2
ROOM RATING	86
COST ($=$50)	$$$+

Commuting times to parks (in minutes)
MAGIC KINGDOM	12:45
EPCOT	8:00
ANIMAL KINGDOM	11:00
DHS	10:30

The Enclave Hotel & Suites ★★★
6165 Carrier Dr.
Orlando, FL 32819
☎ 407-351-1155
enclavesuites.com

LOCATION	1
ROOM RATING	67
COST ($=$50)	$$$-

Commuting times to parks (in minutes)
MAGIC KINGDOM	20:45
EPCOT	16:15
ANIMAL KINGDOM	19:15
DHS	18:45

Extended Stay America Convention Center/Westwood ★★★★
6443 Westwood Blvd.
Orlando, FL 32821
☎ 407-351-1982
tinyurl.com/extendedstaywestwood

LOCATION	1
ROOM RATING	84
COST ($=$50)	$$-

Commuting times to parks (in minutes)
MAGIC KINGDOM	17:30
EPCOT	12:45
ANIMAL KINGDOM	15:45
DHS	15:30

**Primary transportation to Wilderness Lodge and Wilderness Lodge Villas is by ferry rather than by car.

Hotel Information Chart *(Continued)*

Extended Stay America Deluxe Orlando Theme Parks ★★★½	
5610 Vineland Rd.	
Orlando, FL 32819	
☎ 407-370-4428	
tinyurl.com/esvineland	
LOCATION	4
ROOM RATING	75
COST ($=$50)	$$-
Commuting times to parks (in minutes)	
MAGIC KINGDOM	18:00
EPCOT	14:15
ANIMAL KINGDOM	18:00
DHS	16:00

Extended Stay America Orlando Convention Center ★★★	
6451 Westwood Blvd.	
Orlando, FL 32821	
☎ 407-352-3454	
tinyurl.com/extendedstayocc	
LOCATION	1
ROOM RATING	72
COST ($=$50)	$+
Commuting times to parks (in minutes)	
MAGIC KINGDOM	17:30
EPCOT	12:45
ANIMAL KINGDOM	15:45
DHS	15:30

Extended Stay America Orlando Lake Buena Vista ★★★★	
8100 Palm Pkwy.	
Orlando, FL 32836	
☎ 407-239-4300	
tinyurl.com/extendedlbv	
LOCATION	2
ROOM RATING	83
COST ($=$50)	$$-
Commuting times to parks (in minutes)	
MAGIC KINGDOM	13:45
EPCOT	9:00
ANIMAL KINGDOM	12:00
DHS	11:30

Fairfield Inn & Suites Orlando LBV in Marriott Village ★★★½	
8615 Vineland Ave.	
Orlando, FL 32821	
☎ 407-938-9001	
tinyurl.com/fairfieldlbvmarriott village	
LOCATION	2
ROOM RATING	75
COST ($=$50)	$$+
Commuting times to parks (in minutes)	
MAGIC KINGDOM	12:00
EPCOT	7:15
ANIMAL KINGDOM	10:15
DHS	9:45

Floridays Resort Orlando ★★★★	
12562 International Dr.	
Orlando, FL 32821	
☎ 407-238-7700	
floridaysresortorlando.com	
LOCATION	1
ROOM RATING	86
COST ($=$50)	$$$$
Commuting times to parks (in minutes)	
MAGIC KINGDOM	14:30
EPCOT	9:45
ANIMAL KINGDOM	12:45
DHS	12:15

The Floridian Hotel & Suites ★★½	
7531 Canada Ave.	
Orlando, FL 32819	
☎ 407-212-3021	
thefloridianhotel.com	
LOCATION	1
ROOM RATING	63
COST ($=$50)	$$-
Commuting times to parks (in minutes)	
MAGIC KINGDOM	20:15
EPCOT	15:45
ANIMAL KINGDOM	18:45
DHS	18:15

Gaylord Palms Hotel & Convention Center ★★★★½	
6000 W. Osceola Pkwy.	
Kissimmee, FL 34746	
☎ 407-586-0000	
gaylordpalms.com	
LOCATION	3
ROOM RATING	94
COST ($=$50)	$$$+
Commuting times to parks (in minutes)	
MAGIC KINGDOM	9:00
EPCOT	8:45
ANIMAL KINGDOM	7:00
DHS	8:15

Grand Beach ★★★★½	
8317 Lake Bryan Beach Blvd.	
Orlando, FL 32821	
☎ 407-238-2500	
diamondresorts.com/grand-beach	
LOCATION	1
ROOM RATING	90
COST ($=$50)	$$$$-
Commuting times to parks (in minutes)	
MAGIC KINGDOM	17:00
EPCOT	11:00
ANIMAL KINGDOM	18:00
DHS	12:00

Grand Lake Resort ★★★½	
7770 W. US 192*	
Kissimmee, FL 34747	
☎ 407-396-3000	
dailymanagementresorts.com	
LOCATION	1
ROOM RATING	76
COST ($=$50)	$$+
Commuting times to parks (in minutes)	
MAGIC KINGDOM	9:15
EPCOT	8:30
ANIMAL KINGDOM	6:15
DHS	8:30

Hampton Inn South of Universal ★★½	
7110 S. Kirkman Rd.	
Orlando, FL 32819	
☎ 407-345-1112	
tinyurl.com/hamptonkirkman	
LOCATION	1
ROOM RATING	64
COST ($=$50)	$$$-
Commuting times to parks (in minutes)	
MAGIC KINGDOM	21:15
EPCOT	16:45
ANIMAL KINGDOM	19:45
DHS	19:15

Hampton Inn Universal ★★★	
5621 Windhover Dr.	
Orlando, FL 32819	
☎ 407-351-6716	
tinyurl.com/hamptonuniversal	
LOCATION	4
ROOM RATING	67
COST ($=$50)	$$$-
Commuting times to parks (in minutes)	
MAGIC KINGDOM	19:00
EPCOT	14:15
ANIMAL KINGDOM	17:15
DHS	16:45

Hawthorn Suites Lake Buena Vista ★★★★	
8303 Palm Pkwy.	
Orlando, FL 32836	
☎ 407-597-5000	
hawthornlakebuenavista.com	
LOCATION	2
ROOM RATING	85
COST ($=$50)	$$+
Commuting times to parks (in minutes)	
MAGIC KINGDOM	20:15
EPCOT	15:30
ANIMAL KINGDOM	18:30
DHS	18:00

*US 192 is known locally as Irlo Bronson Memorial Highway.

Extended Stay America Orlando Theme Parks ★★★½
5620 Major Blvd.
Orlando, FL 32819
☎ 407-351-1788
tinyurl.com/extendeduniversal

LOCATION	4
ROOM RATING	75
COST ($=$50)	$$-

Commuting times to parks (in minutes)
MAGIC KINGDOM	18:00
EPCOT	14:15
ANIMAL KINGDOM	18:00
DHS	16:00

Fairfield Inn & Suites Near Universal Orlando Resort ★★★½
5614 Vineland Rd.
Orlando, FL 32819
☎ 407-581-5600
tinyurl.com/fairfielduniversal

LOCATION	4
ROOM RATING	80
COST ($=$50)	$$$-

Commuting times to parks (in minutes)
MAGIC KINGDOM	17:30
EPCOT	12:45
ANIMAL KINGDOM	15:45
DHS	15:15

Fairfield Inn & Suites Orlando Lake Buena Vista ★★★½
12191 S. Apopka-Vineland Rd.
Lake Buena Vista, FL 32836
☎ 407-239-1115
tinyurl.com/fairfieldlbv

LOCATION	2
ROOM RATING	79
COST ($=$50)	$$+

Commuting times to parks (in minutes)
MAGIC KINGDOM	14:00
EPCOT	9:15
ANIMAL KINGDOM	12:15
DHS	11:45

Four Points by Sheraton Orlando Studio City ★★★★½
5905 International Dr.
Orlando, FL 32819
☎ 407-351-2100
fourpointsorlandostudiocity.com

LOCATION	1
ROOM RATING	90
COST ($=$50)	$$$-

Commuting times to parks (in minutes)
MAGIC KINGDOM	20:30
EPCOT	15:45
ANIMAL KINGDOM	18:45
DHS	18:15

Four Seasons Resort Orlando at Walt Disney World Resort ★★★★★
10100 Dream Tree Blvd.
Golden Oak, FL 32836
☎ 407-313-7777
fourseasons.com/orlando

LOCATION	WDW
ROOM RATING	98
COST ($=$50)	$ X 9

Commuting times to parks (in minutes)
MAGIC KINGDOM	9:00
EPCOT	8:00
ANIMAL KINGDOM	15:00
DHS	8:00

Galleria Palms Kissimmee Hotel ★★★
3000 Maingate Ln.
Kissimmee, FL 34747
☎ 407-396-6300
galleriakissimmeehotel.com

LOCATION	3
ROOM RATING	74
COST ($=$50)	$$-

Commuting times to parks (in minutes)
MAGIC KINGDOM	8:15
EPCOT	7:30
ANIMAL KINGDOM	5:15
DHS	7:15

Hampton Inn & Suites Orlando-South Lake Buena Vista ★★★½
4971 Calypso Cay Way
Kissimmee, FL 34746
☎ 407-396-6100
tinyurl.com/hamptonsouthlbv

LOCATION	3
ROOM RATING	80
COST ($=$50)	$$-

Commuting times to parks (in minutes)
MAGIC KINGDOM	21:00
EPCOT	15:00
ANIMAL KINGDOM	17:00
DHS	15:00

Hampton Inn I-Drive/Convention Center ★★★
8900 Universal Blvd.
Orlando, FL 32819
☎ 407-354-4447
tinyurl.com/hamptonocc

LOCATION	1
ROOM RATING	70
COST ($=$50)	$$+

Commuting times to parks (in minutes)
MAGIC KINGDOM	21:30
EPCOT	17:00
ANIMAL KINGDOM	20:00
DHS	19:30

Hampton Inn Orlando/Lake Buena Vista ★★★½
8150 Palm Pkwy.
Orlando, FL 32836
☎ 407-465-8150
tinyurl.com/hamptonlbv

LOCATION	2
ROOM RATING	76
COST ($=$50)	$$$-

Commuting times to parks (in minutes)
MAGIC KINGDOM	12:45
EPCOT	8:00
ANIMAL KINGDOM	11:00
DHS	10:30

Hawthorn Suites Orlando Convention Center ★★★½
6435 Westwood Blvd.
Orlando, FL 32821
☎ 407-351-6600
hawthornsuitesorlando.com

LOCATION	1
ROOM RATING	80
COST ($=$50)	$$+

Commuting times to parks (in minutes)
MAGIC KINGDOM	17:30
EPCOT	12:45
ANIMAL KINGDOM	15:45
DHS	15:30

Hawthorn Suites Orlando I-Drive ★★★½
7975 Canada Ave.
Orlando, FL 32819
☎ 407-345-0117
tinyurl.com/hawthornidrive

LOCATION	1
ROOM RATING	75
COST ($=$50)	$$+

Commuting times to parks (in minutes)
MAGIC KINGDOM	20:00
EPCOT	15:15
ANIMAL KINGDOM	18:15
DHS	17:45

Hilton Garden Inn Lake Buena Vista/Orlando ★★★★
11400 Marbella Palm Ct.
Orlando, FL 32836
☎ 407-239-9550
tinyurl.com/hgilakebuenavista

LOCATION	2
ROOM RATING	88
COST ($=$50)	$$$+

Commuting times to parks (in minutes)
MAGIC KINGDOM	18:00
EPCOT	12:00
ANIMAL KINGDOM	18:00
DHS	14:00

Hotel Information Chart (Continued)

Hilton Garden Inn Orlando at SeaWorld ★★★½
6850 Westwood Blvd.
Orlando, FL 32821
☎ 407-354-1500
tinyurl.com/hgiseaworld

LOCATION	1
ROOM RATING	80
COST ($=$50)	$$$-

Commuting times to parks (in minutes)
MAGIC KINGDOM	15:30
EPCOT	11:00
ANIMAL KINGDOM	14:00
DHS	13:30

Hilton Garden Inn Orlando I-Drive North ★★★½
5877 American Way
Orlando, FL 32819
☎ 407-363-9332
tinyurl.com/hiltonidrive

LOCATION	1
ROOM RATING	80
COST ($=$50)	$$+

Commuting times to parks (in minutes)
MAGIC KINGDOM	21:15
EPCOT	16:30
ANIMAL KINGDOM	19:30
DHS	19:00

Hilton Grand Vacations Club at SeaWorld ★★★★½
6924 Grand Vacations Way
Orlando, FL 32821
☎ 407-239-0100
tinyurl.com/hgvseaworld

LOCATION	1
ROOM RATING	95
COST ($=$50)	$$$-

Commuting times to parks (in minutes)
MAGIC KINGDOM	17:00
EPCOT	12:30
ANIMAL KINGDOM	16:30
DHS	15:30

Holiday Inn & Suites Orlando Universal ★★★½
5905 Kirkman Rd.
Orlando, FL 32819
☎ 407-351-3333
hiuniversal.com

LOCATION	4
ROOM RATING	75
COST ($=$50)	$$$-

Commuting times to parks (in minutes)
MAGIC KINGDOM	19:00
EPCOT	14:15
ANIMAL KINGDOM	17:15
DHS	16:45

Holiday Inn in the Walt Disney World Resort ★★★½
1805 Hotel Plaza Blvd.
Lake Buena Vista, FL 32830
☎ 407-828-8888
hiorlando.com

LOCATION	WDW
ROOM RATING	79
COST ($=$50)	$$$+

Commuting times to parks (in minutes)
MAGIC KINGDOM	15:30
EPCOT	10:45
ANIMAL KINGDOM	12:30
DHS	14:45

Holiday Inn Main Gate East ★★★★½
5711 W. US 192*
Kissimmee, FL 34746
☎ 407-396-4222
holidayinnmge.com

LOCATION	3
ROOM RATING	90
COST ($=$50)	$$+

Commuting times to parks (in minutes)
MAGIC KINGDOM	12:15
EPCOT	12:00
ANIMAL KINGDOM	10:15
DHS	11:30

Hyatt Regency Grand Cypress ★★★★½
1 Grand Cypress Blvd.
Orlando, FL 32836
☎ 407-239-1234
grandcypress.hyatt.com

LOCATION	2
ROOM RATING	92
COST ($=$50)	$- X 5

Commuting times to parks (in minutes)
MAGIC KINGDOM	13:30
EPCOT	8:45
ANIMAL KINGDOM	11:45
DHS	11:15

Hyatt Regency Orlando ★★★★½
9801 International Dr.
Orlando, FL 32819
☎ 407-284-1234
orlando.regency.hyatt.com

LOCATION	1
ROOM RATING	90
COST ($=$50)	$$$$-

Commuting times to parks (in minutes)
MAGIC KINGDOM	19:30
EPCOT	15:15
ANIMAL KINGDOM	18:15
DHS	17:45

The Inn at Calypso ★★★½
5001 Calypso Cay Way
Kissimmee, FL 34746
☎ 407-997-1400
calypsocay.com/the-inn.php

LOCATION	3
ROOM RATING	82
COST ($=$50)	$$-

Commuting times to parks (in minutes)
MAGIC KINGDOM	13:30
EPCOT	13:00
ANIMAL KINGDOM	11:30
DHS	12:30

La Quinta Inn Orlando–Universal Studios ★★½
5621 Major Blvd.
Orlando, FL 32819
☎ 407-313-3100
tinyurl.com/lquniversal

LOCATION	4
ROOM RATING	63
COST ($=$50)	$$-

Commuting times to parks (in minutes)
MAGIC KINGDOM	18:00
EPCOT	13:15
ANIMAL KINGDOM	16:15
DHS	16:00

Legacy Vacation Club Lake Buena Vista ★★★★
8451 Palm Pkwy.
Lake Buena Vista, FL 32836
☎ 407-238-1700
legacyvacationresorts.com

LOCATION	2
ROOM RATING	85
COST ($=$50)	$$$-

Commuting times to parks (in minutes)
MAGIC KINGDOM	13:15
EPCOT	8:30
ANIMAL KINGDOM	11:30
DHS	11:00

Legacy Vacation Club Orlando ★★★½
2800 N. Poinciana Blvd.
Kissimmee, FL 34746
☎ 407-997-5000
legacyvacationresorts.com

LOCATION	3
ROOM RATING	80
COST ($=$50)	$$$-

Commuting times to parks (in minutes)
MAGIC KINGDOM	16:30
EPCOT	16:15
ANIMAL KINGDOM	14:30
DHS	15:30

*US 192 is known locally as Irlo Bronson Memorial Highway.

Hilton Grand Vacations Club on I-Drive ★★★★
8122 Arrezzo Way
Orlando, FL 32821
☎ 407-465-2600
tinyurl.com/hgvidrive

LOCATION	1
ROOM RATING	88
COST ($=$50)	$$$+

Commuting times to parks (in minutes)

MAGIC KINGDOM	16:15
EPCOT	14:00
ANIMAL KINGDOM	17:00
DHS	16:30

Hilton Orlando Bonnet Creek ★★★★
14100 Bonnet Creek Resort Ln.
Orlando, FL 32821
☎ 407-597-3600
hiltonbonnetcreek.com

LOCATION	1
ROOM RATING	88
COST ($=$50)	$$+

Commuting times to parks (in minutes)

MAGIC KINGDOM	8:00
EPCOT	6:00
ANIMAL KINGDOM	7:15
DHS	4:15

Hilton Orlando Lake Buena Vista ★★★★
1751 Hotel Plaza Blvd.
Lake Buena Vista, FL 32830
☎ 407-827-4000
hilton-wdwv.com

LOCATION	WDW
ROOM RATING	87
COST ($=$50)	$$$-

Commuting times to parks (in minutes)

MAGIC KINGDOM	15:15
EPCOT	10:30
ANIMAL KINGDOM	14:30
DHS	12:15

Holiday Inn Resort Lake Buena Vista ★★★½
13351 FL 535
Orlando, FL 32821
☎ 407-239-4500
hiresortlbv.com

LOCATION	2
ROOM RATING	82
COST ($=$50)	$$+

Commuting times to parks (in minutes)

MAGIC KINGDOM	10:45
EPCOT	6:00
ANIMAL KINGDOM	9:00
DHS	8:30

Homewood Suites by Hilton LBV-Orlando ★★★★
11428 Marbella Palm Ct.
Orlando, FL 32836
☎ 407-239-4540
tinyurl.com/homewoodsuiteslbv

LOCATION	2
ROOM RATING	85
COST ($=$50)	$$$$-

Commuting times to parks (in minutes)

MAGIC KINGDOM	18:00
EPCOT	12:00
ANIMAL KINGDOM	18:00
DHS	14:00

Hyatt Place Orlando/Universal ★★★★
5895 Caravan Ct.
Orlando, FL 32819
☎ 407-351-0627
orlandouniversal.place.hyatt.com

LOCATION	4
ROOM RATING	84
COST ($=$50)	$$$+

Commuting times to parks (in minutes)

MAGIC KINGDOM	19:00
EPCOT	14:15
ANIMAL KINGDOM	17:45
DHS	16:45

JW Marriott Orlando Grande Lakes ★★★★½
4040 Central Florida Pkwy.
Orlando, FL 32837
☎ 407-206-2300
jw-marriott.grandelakes.com

LOCATION	1
ROOM RATING	93
COST ($=$50)	$+ X 5

Commuting times to parks (in minutes)

MAGIC KINGDOM	23:00
EPCOT	18:15
ANIMAL KINGDOM	21:30
DHS	20:45

Knights Inn Maingate Kissimmee/ Orlando ★★
7475 W. US 192*
Kissimmee, FL 34747
☎ 407-396-4200
tinyurl.com/knightsinnmgk

LOCATION	3
ROOM RATING	58
COST ($=$50)	$-

Commuting times to parks (in minutes)

MAGIC KINGDOM	8:15
EPCOT	7:45
ANIMAL KINGDOM	5:45
DHS	7:30

La Quinta Inn Orlando I-Drive ★★★
8300 Jamaican Ct.
Orlando, FL 32819
☎ 407-351-1660
tinyurl.com/lqidrive

LOCATION	1
ROOM RATING	73
COST ($=$50)	$$-

Commuting times to parks (in minutes)

MAGIC KINGDOM	21:45
EPCOT	17:15
ANIMAL KINGDOM	20:15
DHS	19:45

Lighthouse Key Resort & Spa ★★★★½
8545 W. US 192*
Kissimmee, FL 34747
☎ 321-329-7000
lighthousekeyresort.com

LOCATION	3
ROOM RATING	90
COST ($=$50)	$$$$-

Commuting times to parks (in minutes)

MAGIC KINGDOM	20:00
EPCOT	21:00
ANIMAL KINGDOM	16:00
DHS	16:00

Liki Tiki Village ★★★★½
17777 Bali Blvd.
Winter Garden, FL 34787
☎ 407-239-5000
likitiki.com

LOCATION	3
ROOM RATING	90
COST ($=$50)	$$$$-

Commuting times to parks (in minutes)

MAGIC KINGDOM	9:00
EPCOT	8:45
ANIMAL KINGDOM	5:15
DHS	8:15

Magnuson Grand Hotel Maingate West ★★★
7491 W. US 192*
Kissimmee, FL 34747
☎ 407-396-6000
tinyurl.com/magnusongrand

LOCATION	3
ROOM RATING	65
COST ($=$50)	$$+

Commuting times to parks (in minutes)

MAGIC KINGDOM	8:15
EPCOT	7:30
ANIMAL KINGDOM	5:00
DHS	7:15

Hotel Information Chart (Continued)

Maingate Lakeside Resort ★★★
7769 W. US 192*
Kissimmee, FL 34747
☎ 407-396-2222
maingatelakesideresort.com

LOCATION	3
ROOM RATING	67
COST ($=$50)	$$−

Commuting times to parks (in minutes)
MAGIC KINGDOM	9:15
EPCOT	8:30
ANIMAL KINGDOM	6:30
DHS	8:30

Marriott's Cypress Harbour ★★★★
11251 Harbour Villa Rd.
Orlando, FL 32821
☎ 407-238-1300
tinyurl.com/cypressharbourvillas

LOCATION	1
ROOM RATING	86
COST ($=$50)	$ X 6

Commuting times to parks (in minutes)
MAGIC KINGDOM	17:45
EPCOT	13:15
ANIMAL KINGDOM	17:45
DHS	16:15

Marriott's Grande Vista ★★★★½
5925 Avenida Vista
Orlando, FL 32821
☎ 407-238-7676
tinyurl.com/marriottsgrandevista

LOCATION	1
ROOM RATING	92
COST ($=$50)	$$$+

Commuting times to parks (in minutes)
MAGIC KINGDOM	15:00
EPCOT	12:45
ANIMAL KINGDOM	15:45
DHS	15:15

Marriott's Sabal Palms ★★★★½
8805 World Center Dr.
Orlando, FL 32821
☎ 407-238-6200
tinyurl.com/marriottssabalpalms

LOCATION	2
ROOM RATING	92
COST ($=$50)	$+ X 6

Commuting times to parks (in minutes)
MAGIC KINGDOM	15:00
EPCOT	9:00
ANIMAL KINGDOM	16:00
DHS	10:00

Monumental Hotel ★★★★½
12120 International Dr.
Orlando, FL 32821
☎ 407-239-1222
monumentalhotelorlandofl.com

LOCATION	1
ROOM RATING	94
COST ($=$50)	$$−

Commuting times to parks (in minutes)
MAGIC KINGDOM	14:45
EPCOT	10:00
ANIMAL KINGDOM	13:00
DHS	12:30

Monumental MovieLand Hotel
★★★
6233 International Dr.
Orlando, FL 32819
☎ 407-351-3900
monumentalmovielandhotel.com

LOCATION	1
ROOM RATING	68
COST ($=$50)	$+

Commuting times to parks (in minutes)
MAGIC KINGDOM	20:30
EPCOT	15:45
ANIMAL KINGDOM	18:45
DHS	18:15

Omni Orlando Resort at ChampionsGate ★★★★★
1500 Masters Blvd.
ChampionsGate, FL 33896
☎ 407-390-6664
tinyurl.com/omnichampionsgate

LOCATION	2
ROOM RATING	96
COST ($=$50)	$+ X 5

Commuting times to parks (in minutes)
MAGIC KINGDOM	15:30
EPCOT	15:00
ANIMAL KINGDOM	15:00
DHS	14:30

Orange Lake Resort ★★★★½
8505 W. US 192*
Kissimmee, FL 34747
☎ 407-239-0000
tinyurl.com/orangelakeresort orlando

LOCATION	3
ROOM RATING	94
COST ($=$50)	$$$−

Commuting times to parks (in minutes)
MAGIC KINGDOM	8:45
EPCOT	8:30
ANIMAL KINGDOM	5:30
DHS	8:00

Orbit One Vacation Villas ★★★½
2950 Entry Point Blvd.
Kissimmee, FL 34741
☎ 407-396-1300
tinyurl.com/orbit1villas

LOCATION	3
ROOM RATING	80
COST ($=$50)	$$$$−

Commuting times to parks (in minutes)
MAGIC KINGDOM	15:00
EPCOT	14:00
ANIMAL KINGDOM	7:00
DHS	9:00

Parkway International Resort
★★★½
6200 Safari Trail
Kissimmee, FL 34746
☎ 407-396-6600
parkwayresort.com

LOCATION	3
ROOM RATING	82
COST ($=$50)	$− X 5

Commuting times to parks (in minutes)
MAGIC KINGDOM	8:30
EPCOT	8:15
ANIMAL KINGDOM	6:15
DHS	7:45

The Point Universal Orlando Resort
★★★½
7389 Universal Blvd.
Orlando, FL 32819
☎ 407-956-2000
thepointorlando.com

LOCATION	1
ROOM RATING	82
COST ($=$50)	$$+

Commuting times to parks (in minutes)
MAGIC KINGDOM	23:00
EPCOT	17:00
ANIMAL KINGDOM	23:00
DHS	19:00

Polynesian Isles Resort
(Diamond Resorts) ★★★★½
3045 Polynesian Isles Blvd.
Kissimmee, FL 34746
☎ 407-396-1622
polynesianisle.com

LOCATION	3
ROOM RATING	90
COST ($=$50)	$$$

Commuting times to parks (in minutes)
MAGIC KINGDOM	14:30
EPCOT	14:15
ANIMAL KINGDOM	12:30
DHS	14:00

*US 192 is known locally as Irlo Bronson Memorial Highway.

Marriott's Harbour Lake
★★★★½
7102 Grand Horizons Blvd.
Orlando, FL 32821
☎ 407-465-6100
tinyurl.com/harbourlake

LOCATION	2
ROOM RATING	90
COST ($=$50)	$$$$-

Commuting times to parks (in minutes)
MAGIC KINGDOM	18:00
EPCOT	13:30
ANIMAL KINGDOM	18:00
DHS	16:30

Marriott's Imperial Palms ★★★★
8404 Vacation Way
Orlando, FL 32821
☎ 407-238-6200
tinyurl.com/imperialpalmvillas

LOCATION	1
ROOM RATING	86
COST ($=$50)	$- X 9

Commuting times to parks (in minutes)
MAGIC KINGDOM	9:45
EPCOT	5:00
ANIMAL KINGDOM	8:00
DHS	7:30

Marriott's Royal Palms ★★★★
8404 Vacation Way
Orlando, FL 32821
☎ 407-238-6200
tinyurl.com/marriottsroyalpalms

LOCATION	1
ROOM RATING	85
COST ($=$50)	$- X 6

Commuting times to parks (in minutes)
MAGIC KINGDOM	9:45
EPCOT	5:00
ANIMAL KINGDOM	8:00
DHS	7:30

Motel 6 Orlando-I-Drive ★★★
5909 American Way
Orlando, FL 32819
☎ 407-351-6500
tinyurl.com/motel6idrive

LOCATION	1
ROOM RATING	66
COST ($=$50)	$+

Commuting times to parks (in minutes)
MAGIC KINGDOM	20:15
EPCOT	16:00
ANIMAL KINGDOM	19:00
DHS	18:30

Mystic Dunes Resort & Golf Club ★★★★
7600 Mystic Dunes Ln.
Kissimmee, FL 34747
☎ 407-396-1311
mystic-dunes-resort.com

LOCATION	3
ROOM RATING	87
COST ($=$50)	$$$-

Commuting times to parks (in minutes)
MAGIC KINGDOM	10:45
EPCOT	10:30
ANIMAL KINGDOM	7:45
DHS	10:00

Nickelodeon Suites Resort
★★★½
14500 Continental Gateway
Orlando, FL 32821
☎ 407-387-5437
nickhotel.com

LOCATION	1
ROOM RATING	82
COST ($=$50)	$$$$

Commuting times to parks (in minutes)
MAGIC KINGDOM	9:45
EPCOT	5:00
ANIMAL KINGDOM	8:00
DHS	7:30

Orlando World Center Marriott Resort ★★★★½
8701 World Center Dr.
Orlando, FL 32821
☎ 407-239-4200
marriottworldcenter.com

LOCATION	2
ROOM RATING	90
COST ($=$50)	$$$$+

Commuting times to parks (in minutes)
MAGIC KINGDOM	9:45
EPCOT	5:00
ANIMAL KINGDOM	8:00
DHS	7:30

The Palms Hotel & Villas ★★★½
3100 Parkway Blvd.
Kissimmee, FL 34747
☎ 407-396-2229
thepalmshotelandvillas.com

LOCATION	3
ROOM RATING	76
COST ($=$50)	$$+

Commuting times to parks (in minutes)
MAGIC KINGDOM	8:30
EPCOT	8:15
ANIMAL KINGDOM	6:30
DHS	7:45

Park Inn by Radisson Resort and Conference Center ★★★½
3011 Maingate Ln.
Kissimmee, FL 34747
☎ 407-396-1400
parkinn.com/hotel-orlando

LOCATION	3
ROOM RATING	78
COST ($=$50)	$$$-

Commuting times to parks (in minutes)
MAGIC KINGDOM	8:15
EPCOT	7:45
ANIMAL KINGDOM	5:45
DHS	7:45

Quality Suites Lake Buena Vista
★★★½
8200 Palm Pkwy.
Orlando, FL 32836
☎ 407-465-8200
qualitysuiteslbv.com

LOCATION	2
ROOM RATING	76
COST ($=$50)	$$$-

Commuting times to parks (in minutes)
MAGIC KINGDOM	13:45
EPCOT	9:15
ANIMAL KINGDOM	12:15
DHS	11:45

Quality Suites Royale Parc Suites
★★★½
5876 W. US 192*
Kissimmee, FL 34746
☎ 407-396-8040
royaleparcsuitesorlando.com

LOCATION	3
ROOM RATING	76
COST ($=$50)	$$$+

Commuting times to parks (in minutes)
MAGIC KINGDOM	11:15
EPCOT	11:00
ANIMAL KINGDOM	9:15
DHS	10:30

Radisson Hotel Orlando Lake Buena Vista ★★★½
12799 Apopka-Vineland Rd.
Orlando, FL 32836
☎ 407-597-3400
tinyurl.com/radissonlbv

LOCATION	2
ROOM RATING	82
COST ($=$50)	$$$-

Commuting times to parks (in minutes)
MAGIC KINGDOM	13:45
EPCOT	9:00
ANIMAL KINGDOM	12:00
DHS	11:30

Hotel Information Chart *(Continued)*

Radisson Resort Orlando-Celebration ★★★★	
2900 Parkway Blvd.	
Kissimmee, FL 34747	
☎ 407-396-7000	
tinyurl.com/radissonoc	
LOCATION	3
ROOM RATING	86
COST ($=$50)	$$
Commuting times to parks *(in minutes)*	
MAGIC KINGDOM	8:30
EPCOT	8:00
ANIMAL KINGDOM	6:30
DHS	7:45

Ramada Convention Center I-Drive ★★★	
8342 Jamaican Ct.	
Orlando, FL 32819	
☎ 407-363-1944	
tinyurl.com/ramadaidrive	
LOCATION	1
ROOM RATING	65
COST ($=$50)	$+
Commuting times to parks *(in minutes)*	
MAGIC KINGDOM	20:15
EPCOT	15:30
ANIMAL KINGDOM	18:30
DHS	18:00

Red Roof Inn Orlando Convention Center ★★	
9922 Hawaiian Ct.	
Orlando, FL 32819	
☎ 407-352-1507	
tinyurl.com/redroofkiss	
LOCATION	1
ROOM RATING	58
COST ($=$50)	$+
Commuting times to parks *(in minutes)*	
MAGIC KINGDOM	19:00
EPCOT	14:15
ANIMAL KINGDOM	17:15
DHS	16:45

Residence Inn Orlando Lake Buena Vista ★★★½	
11450 Marbella Palm Ct.	
Orlando, FL 32836	
☎ 407-465-0075	
tinyurl.com/residenceinnlbv	
LOCATION	2
ROOM RATING	75
COST ($=$50)	$$$+
Commuting times to parks *(in minutes)*	
MAGIC KINGDOM	15:40
EPCOT	11:00
ANIMAL KINGDOM	14:00
DHS	13:30

The Ritz-Carlton Orlando, Grande Lakes ★★★★½	
4012 Central Florida Pkwy.	
Orlando, FL 32837	
☎ 407-206-2400	
grandelakes.com	
LOCATION	1
ROOM RATING	94
COST ($=$50)	$+ X 5
Commuting times to parks *(in minutes)*	
MAGIC KINGDOM	23:00
EPCOT	18:15
ANIMAL KINGDOM	21:30
DHS	20:45

Rodeway Inn Maingate ★★½	
5995 W. US 192*	
Kissimmee, FL 34747	
☎ 407-396-4300	
tinyurl.com/rodewaymaingate	
LOCATION	3
ROOM RATING	59
COST ($=$50)	$-
Commuting times to parks *(in minutes)*	
MAGIC KINGDOM	11:15
EPCOT	11:00
ANIMAL KINGDOM	9:15
DHS	10:30

Shades of Green ★★★★½	
1950 W. Magnolia Palm Dr.	
Lake Buena Vista, FL 32830	
☎ 407-824-3400	
shadesofgreen.org	
LOCATION	WDW
ROOM RATING	91
COST ($=$50)	$$-
Commuting times to parks *(in minutes)*	
MAGIC KINGDOM	3:30
EPCOT	4:45
ANIMAL KINGDOM	9:30
DHS	6:15

Sheraton Lake Buena Vista Resort ★★★★	
12205 S. Apopka–Vineland Rd.	
Orlando, FL 32836	
☎ 407-239-0444	
sheratonlakebuenavistaresort.com	
LOCATION	2
ROOM RATING	88
COST ($=$50)	$$$+
Commuting times to parks *(in minutes)*	
MAGIC KINGDOM	13:45
EPCOT	9:00
ANIMAL KINGDOM	12:00
DHS	11:30

Sheraton Vistana Resort Villas ★★★★	
8800 Vistana Centre Dr.	
Orlando, FL 32821	
☎ 407-239-3100	
tinyurl.com/vistanavillas	
LOCATION	2
ROOM RATING	89
COST ($=$50)	$$$$-
Commuting times to parks *(in minutes)*	
MAGIC KINGDOM	11:15
EPCOT	6:30
ANIMAL KINGDOM	9:30
DHS	9:00

Star Island Resort & Club ★★★★	
5000 Avenue of the Stars	
Kissimmee, FL 34746	
☎ 407-997-8000	
star-island.com	
LOCATION	3
ROOM RATING	84
COST ($=$50)	$$$+
Commuting times to parks *(in minutes)*	
MAGIC KINGDOM	15:45
EPCOT	15:15
ANIMAL KINGDOM	14:15
DHS	13:30

Stay Sky Suites I-Drive Orlando ★★★½	
7601 Canada Ave.	
Orlando, FL 32819	
☎ 407-581-2151	
stayskysuitesidriveorlando.com	
LOCATION	1
ROOM RATING	82
COST ($=$50)	$$+
Commuting times to parks *(in minutes)*	
MAGIC KINGDOM	20:15
EPCOT	15:45
ANIMAL KINGDOM	18:45
DHS	19:15

Staybridge Suites Lake Buena Vista ★★★	
8751 Suiteside Dr.	
Orlando, FL 32836	
☎ 407-238-0777	
tinyurl.com/staybridgelbv	
LOCATION	2
ROOM RATING	72
COST ($=$50)	$$$+
Commuting times to parks *(in minutes)*	
MAGIC KINGDOM	14:15
EPCOT	9:30
ANIMAL KINGDOM	12:30
DHS	12:00

*US 192 is known locally as Irlo Bronson Memorial Highway.

Renaissance Orlando at SeaWorld
★★★★½
6677 Sea Harbor Dr.
Orlando, FL 32821
☎ 407-351-5555
tinyurl.com/renorlandoseaworld

LOCATION	1
ROOM RATING	90
COST ($=$50)	$$$+

Commuting times to parks *(in minutes)*

MAGIC KINGDOM	16:45
EPCOT	12:15
ANIMAL KINGDOM	15:15
DHS	14:45

**Residence Inn Orlando at
SeaWorld** ★★★★
11000 Westwood Blvd.
Orlando, FL 32821
☎ 407-313-3600
tinyurl.com/residenceinnseaworld

LOCATION	2
ROOM RATING	85
COST ($=$50)	$$$-

Commuting times to parks *(in minutes)*

MAGIC KINGDOM	15:45
EPCOT	11:15
ANIMAL KINGDOM	14:15
DHS	13:45

**Residence Inn Orlando
Convention Center** ★★★½
8800 Universal Blvd.
Orlando, FL 32819
☎ 407-226-0288
tinyurl.com/resinnconventioncenter

LOCATION	1
ROOM RATING	80
COST ($=$50)	$$$-

Commuting times to parks *(in minutes)*

MAGIC KINGDOM	22:00
EPCOT	17:30
ANIMAL KINGDOM	20:30
DHS	20:00

Rosen Centre Hotel ★★★★½
9840 International Dr.
Orlando, FL 32819
☎ 407-996-9840
rosencentre.com

LOCATION	1
ROOM RATING	95
COST ($=$50)	$$$+

Commuting times to parks *(in minutes)*

MAGIC KINGDOM	19:45
EPCOT	15:15
ANIMAL KINGDOM	18:15
DHS	17:45

Rosen Inn International Hotel
★★★
7600 International Dr.
Orlando, FL 32819
☎ 407-996-1600
roseninn7600.com

LOCATION	1
ROOM RATING	65
COST ($=$50)	$$+

Commuting times to parks *(in minutes)*

MAGIC KINGDOM	19:45
EPCOT	15:00
ANIMAL KINGDOM	18:00
DHS	17:30

Royal Celebration Inn ★★½
4944 W. US 192*
Kissimmee, FL 34746
☎ 407-396-4455
royalcelebrationorlando.com

LOCATION	3
ROOM RATING	60
COST ($=$50)	$+

Commuting times to parks *(in minutes)*

MAGIC KINGDOM	15:45
EPCOT	15:30
ANIMAL KINGDOM	13:45
DHS	15:00

Silver Lake Resort ★★½
7751 Black Lake Rd.
Kissimmee, FL 34747
☎ 407-397-2828
silverlakeresort.com

LOCATION	3
ROOM RATING	64
COST ($=$50)	$$$

Commuting times to parks *(in minutes)*

MAGIC KINGDOM	8:15
EPCOT	8:00
ANIMAL KINGDOM	4:30
DHS	7:30

**SpringHill Suites Orlando
Convention Center** ★★★½
8840 Universal Blvd.
Orlando, FL 32819
☎ 407-345-9073
tinyurl.com/shsconventioncenter

LOCATION	1
ROOM RATING	80
COST ($=$50)	$$$$-

Commuting times to parks *(in minutes)*

MAGIC KINGDOM	22:30
EPCOT	17:50
ANIMAL KINGDOM	20:45
DHS	20:20

**SpringHill Suites Orlando LBV in
Marriott Village** ★★★
8601 Vineland Ave.
Orlando, FL 32821
☎ 407-938-9001
**tinyurl.com/springhill
marriottvillage**

LOCATION	2
ROOM RATING	71
COST ($=$50)	$$$+

Commuting times to parks *(in minutes)*

MAGIC KINGDOM	12:00
EPCOT	7:15
ANIMAL KINGDOM	10:15
DHS	9:45

Super 8 Kissimmee ★★½
1815 W. Vine St.
Kissimmee, FL 34741
☎ 407-847-6121
tinyurl.com/super8kiss

LOCATION	3
ROOM RATING	60
COST ($=$50)	$-

Commuting times to parks *(in minutes)*

MAGIC KINGDOM	11:45
EPCOT	11:15
ANIMAL KINGDOM	11:00
DHS	9:45

Super 8 Kissimmee/Maingate
★★★
5875 W. US 192*
Kissimmee, FL 34746
☎ 407-396-8883
tinyurl.com/super8maingate

LOCATION	3
ROOM RATING	70
COST ($=$50)	$+

Commuting times to parks *(in minutes)*

MAGIC KINGDOM	8:30
EPCOT	8:00
ANIMAL KINGDOM	7:45
DHS	5:45

**Treehouse Villas at Disney's
Saratoga Springs Resort & Spa**
★★★★½
1960 Broadway
Lake Buena Vista, FL 32830
☎ 407-827-1100
tinyurl.com/saratogawdw

LOCATION	WDW
ROOM RATING	90
COST ($=$50)	$- X 20

Commuting times to parks *(in minutes)*

MAGIC KINGDOM	12:45
EPCOT	7:15
ANIMAL KINGDOM	16:45
DHS	12:30

Hotel Information Chart *(Continued)*

Universal's Cabana Bay Beach Resort ★★★★
6550 Adventure Way
Orlando, FL 32819
☎ 407-503-2000
tinyurl.com/cabanabay

LOCATION	4
ROOM RATING	88
COST ($=$50)	$$$$–

Commuting times to parks *(in minutes)*
MAGIC KINGDOM	20:00
EPCOT	15:00
ANIMAL KINGDOM	17:00
DHS	14:00

Universal's Hard Rock Hotel ★★★★½
5800 Universal Blvd.
Orlando, FL 32819
☎ 407-503-2000
hardrockhotelorlando.com

LOCATION	4
ROOM RATING	93
COST ($=$50)	$ X 8

Commuting times to parks *(in minutes)*
MAGIC KINGDOM	21:45
EPCOT	17:00
ANIMAL KINGDOM	20:00
DHS	19:30

Universal's Portofino Bay Hotel ★★★★½
5601 Universal Blvd.
Orlando, FL 32819
☎ 407-503-1000
tinyurl.com/portofinobay

LOCATION	4
ROOM RATING	92
COST ($=$50)	$+ X 8

Commuting times to parks *(in minutes)*
MAGIC KINGDOM	21:45
EPCOT	17:15
ANIMAL KINGDOM	20:15
DHS	19:45

The Villas at Disney's Wilderness Lodge ★★★★½
901 Timberline Dr.
Lake Buena Vista, FL 32830
☎ 407-824-3200
tinyurl.com/wlvillas

LOCATION	WDW
ROOM RATING	90
COST ($=$50)	$– X 10

Commuting times to parks *(in minutes)*
MAGIC KINGDOM	N/A*
EPCOT	10:00
ANIMAL KINGDOM	15:15
DHS	13:30

Villas of Grand Cypress ★★★★½
1 N. Jacaranda
Orlando, FL 32836
☎ 407-239-4700
grandcypress.com

LOCATION	2
ROOM RATING	92
COST ($=$50)	$– X 5

Commuting times to parks *(in minutes)*
MAGIC KINGDOM	14:00
EPCOT	12:00
ANIMAL KINGDOM	19:00
DHS	15:00

Waldorf Astoria Orlando ★★★★½
14200 Bonnet Creek Resort Ln.
Lake Buena Vista, FL 32830
☎ 407-597-5500
waldorfastoriaorlando.com

LOCATION	2
ROOM RATING	93
COST ($=$50)	$$$$+

Commuting times to parks *(in minutes)*
MAGIC KINGDOM	8:00
EPCOT	6:00
ANIMAL KINGDOM	7:15
DHS	4:15

Westgate Palace ★★★
6145 Carrier Dr.
Orlando, FL 32819
☎ 407-996-6000
westgateresorts.com/palace

LOCATION	1
ROOM RATING	68
COST ($=$50)	$$$$–

Commuting times to parks *(in minutes)*
MAGIC KINGDOM	20:45
EPCOT	16:15
ANIMAL KINGDOM	19:15
DHS	18:45

Westgate Towers ★★★½
7600 West US 192*
Kissimmee, FL 34747
☎ 407-396-2500
westgateresorts.com/towers

LOCATION	2
ROOM RATING	81
COST ($=$50)	$$+

Commuting times to parks *(in minutes)*
MAGIC KINGDOM	8:45
EPCOT	8:30
ANIMAL KINGDOM	5:45
DHS	8:00

Westgate Town Center ★★★★½
7700 Westgate Blvd.
Kissimmee, FL 34747
☎ 407-396-2500
westgateresorts.com/town-center

LOCATION	2
ROOM RATING	93
COST ($=$50)	$$+

Commuting times to parks *(in minutes)*
MAGIC KINGDOM	8:45
EPCOT	8:30
ANIMAL KINGDOM	5:45
DHS	8:00

Wyndham Bonnet Creek Resort ★★★★½
9560 Via Encinas
Lake Buena Vista, FL 32830
☎ 407-238-3500
wyndhambonnetcreek.com

LOCATION	2
ROOM RATING	90
COST ($=$50)	$$$$+

Commuting times to parks *(in minutes)*
MAGIC KINGDOM	8:00
EPCOT	6:00
ANIMAL KINGDOM	7:15
DHS	4:15

Wyndham Cypress Palms ★★★★
5324 Fairfield Lake Dr.
Kissimmee, FL 34746
☎ 407-397-1600
cypresspalms.com

LOCATION	3
ROOM RATING	87
COST ($=$50)	$$$

Commuting times to parks *(in minutes)*
MAGIC KINGDOM	15:15
EPCOT	15:00
ANIMAL KINGDOM	14:45
DHS	14:45

Wyndham Lake Buena Vista Resort ★★★½
1850 Hotel Plaza Blvd.
Lake Buena Vista, FL 32830
☎ 407-828-4444
wyndhamlakebuenavista.com

LOCATION	WDW
ROOM RATING	75
COST ($=$50)	$$+

Commuting times to parks *(in minutes)*
MAGIC KINGDOM	15:15
EPCOT	10:45
ANIMAL KINGDOM	14:45
DHS	12:15

*US 192 is known locally as Irlo Bronson Memorial Highway.

Universal's Royal Pacific Resort
★★★★½
6300 Hollywood Way
Orlando, FL 32819
☎ 407-503-3000
tinyurl.com/royalpacific

LOCATION	4
ROOM RATING	90
COST ($=$50)	$+ X 6

Commuting times to parks (in minutes)

MAGIC KINGDOM	20:00
EPCOT	15:15
ANIMAL KINGDOM	18:15
DHS	17:45

Vacation Village at Parkway
★★★★½
2949 Arabian Nights Blvd.
Kissimmee, FL 34747
☎ 407-396-9086
dailymanagementresorts.com

LOCATION	3
ROOM RATING	91
COST ($=$50)	$$+

Commuting times to parks (in minutes)

MAGIC KINGDOM	8:30
EPCOT	8:15
ANIMAL KINGDOM	6:45
DHS	7:45

The Villas at Disney's Grand Floridian Resort & Spa
★★★★½
4401 Floridian Way
Lake Buena Vista, FL 32830
☎ 407-824-3000
tinyurl.com/grandfloridianvillas

LOCATION	WDW
ROOM RATING	93
COST ($=$50)	$- X 13

Commuting times to parks (in minutes)

MAGIC KINGDOM	on monorail
EPCOT	4:45
ANIMAL KINGDOM	11:45
DHS	6:45

Walt Disney World Dolphin ★★★★½
1500 Epcot Resorts Blvd.
Lake Buena Vista, FL 32830
☎ 407-934-4000
swandolphin.com

LOCATION	WDW
ROOM RATING	90
COST ($=$50)	$$$$+

Commuting times to parks (in minutes)

MAGIC KINGDOM	6:45
EPCOT	5:00
ANIMAL KINGDOM	6:15
DHS	4:00

Walt Disney World Swan ★★★★½
1200 Epcot Resorts Blvd.
Lake Buena Vista, FL 32830
☎ 407-934-3000
swandolphin.com

LOCATION	WDW
ROOM RATING	90
COST ($=$50)	$$$$+

Commuting times to parks (in minutes)

MAGIC KINGDOM	6:30
EPCOT	4:45
ANIMAL KINGDOM	6:15
DHS	4:00

Westgate Lakes Resort & Spa ★★★★½
10000 Turkey Lake Rd.
Orlando, FL 32819
☎ 407-345-0000
westgateresorts.com/lakes

LOCATION	2
ROOM RATING	92
COST ($=$50)	$$$+

Commuting times to parks (in minutes)

MAGIC KINGDOM	17:30
EPCOT	14:30
ANIMAL KINGDOM	19:15
DHS	18:00

Westgate Vacation Villas
★★★★½
7700 Westgate Blvd.
Kissimmee, FL 34747
☎ 407-239-0510
westgateresorts.com/vacation-villas

LOCATION	2
ROOM RATING	90
COST ($=$50)	$$+

Commuting times to parks (in minutes)

MAGIC KINGDOM	8:45
EPCOT	8:30
ANIMAL KINGDOM	5:45
DHS	8:00

Westin Orlando Universal Boulevard ★★★★
9501 Universal Blvd.
Orlando, FL 32819
☎ 407-233-2200
westinorlandouniversal.com

LOCATION	1
ROOM RATING	87
COST ($=$50)	$$$$+

Commuting times to parks (in minutes)

MAGIC KINGDOM	19:45
EPCOT	15:00
ANIMAL KINGDOM	18:15
DHS	17:30

WorldQuest Orlando Resort
★★★★
8849 Worldquest Blvd.
Orlando, FL 32821
☎ 407-387-3800
worldquestorlando.com

LOCATION	1
ROOM RATING	88
COST ($=$50)	$$$-

Commuting times to parks (in minutes)

MAGIC KINGDOM	17:00
EPCOT	11:00
ANIMAL KINGDOM	17:00
DHS	13:00

Wyndham Orlando Resort I-Drive
★★★★
8001 International Dr.
Orlando, FL 32819
☎ 407-351-2420
wyndham.com/hotels/MCOWD

LOCATION	1
ROOM RATING	85
COST ($=$50)	$$+

Commuting times to parks (in minutes)

MAGIC KINGDOM	19:45
EPCOT	15:00
ANIMAL KINGDOM	18:15
DHS	17:30

PART FOUR

DINING *in* AND *around* WALT DISNEY WORLD

DINING *outside* WALT DISNEY WORLD

UNOFFICIAL GUIDE RESEARCHERS love good food and invest a fair amount of time scouting new places to eat. And because food at Walt Disney World is so expensive, we (like you) have an economic incentive for finding palatable meals outside the World. Alas, the surrounding area isn't exactly a culinary nirvana. If you thrive on fast food and the fare at chain restaurants (Denny's, T.G.I. Friday's, Olive Garden, and the like), you'll be as happy as an alligator at a chicken farm. But if you're in the market for a superlative dining experience, you'll find the pickings outside the World of about the same quality as those inside, only less expensive. Plus, some ethnic cuisines aren't represented in WDW restaurants.

Among specialty restaurants both in and out of the World, location and price will determine your choice. For instance, both Walt Disney World and adjoining tourist areas have some decent Italian restaurants—which one you select depends on how much money you want to spend and how convenient the place is to reach. Our recommendations for specialty and ethnic fare served outside of Disney World are summarized in the table that starts on page 296.

Better restaurants outside Walt Disney World cater primarily to adults. That's a plus, however, if you're looking to escape children or you want to eat in peace and quiet.

DINING AT UNIVERSAL CITYWALK

DINING AND SHOPPING are the focus at CityWalk, whose restaurants tends to cater more to adult tastes than do the theme park restaurants. Probably the best of the bunch is **Emeril's Orlando,** but each restaurant has a couple of decent options if you know what to look for. One thing all of them have in common is noise: Your fussy toddler will have to fight to be heard in some of these places. Some of the restaurants use **OpenTable** (**opentable.com**) for online reservations, and you can make reservations to the other venues from **universalorlando.com** via **NexTable,** making it easy to get seats before you go park-hopping.

ANTOJITOS ☎ 407-224-3663; **tinyurl.com/antojitoscitywalk.** The name means "little cravings," the Mexican equivalent of Spain's small-plate *tapas,* so it's only natural that the best dishes are the appetizers. Try the empanada trio (beef, chicken, and mushroom) and the *esquites asados,* roasted corn-off-the-cob with queso fresco and mayo. Free custompainted luchador masks are handed out Wednesday–Sunday. Antojitos carries more than 200 tequila brands, too, and makes a tasty margarita.

BOB MARLEY—A TRIBUTE TO FREEDOM ☎ 407-224-3663; **tinyurl .com/bobmarleytribute.** Set in a replica of the reggae singer's Jamaica home, the building is filled with memorabilia and photos showcasing his career and life. The Caribbean-inspired dishes—beef patties, yucca fries, oxtail stew, and such—aren't particularly memorable, but the laid-back atmosphere makes it worth a visit.

BUBBA GUMP SHRIMP CO. ☎ 407-903-0044; **bubbagump.com/locations /orlando.** This seafood eatery is part of an international chain inspired by *Forrest Gump.* Take a wild guess what the specialty here is.

THE COWFISH Combination burger joint and sushi bar (burgers are a touch better than the sushi). Unusual but delicious. Try the Crab Rangoon appetizer and order the bacon coleslaw as a side. Good service.

EMERIL'S ORLANDO ☎ 407-224-2424; **emerilsrestaurants.com/emerils -orlando.** Not to be confused with Emeril Lagasse's fancier and more expensive Asian-inspired Tchoup Chop at the nearby Royal Pacific Resort, this is the Florida outpost of Emeril's original restaurant in New Orleans. The cuisine—CityWalk's best—is Louisiana-style with creative flair. The smoked-mushroom appetizer is outstanding, and the banana cream pie will renew your faith in humanity.

HARD ROCK CAFE ☎ 407-351-7625; **hardrock.com/orlando.** The best meals we've had here have consisted of drinks and appetizers or desserts. The entrees—burgers, sandwiches, steaks, and such—aren't especially memorable. More remarkable is the collection of music memorabilia, including a pink 1959 Cadillac revolving over the bar. It's the biggest such collection on display anywhere in the Hard Rock chain.

HOT DOG HALL OF FAME The menu is inspired by the food served at baseball stadiums around the US, complete with bleacher seating and broadcasts of live and classic baseball games.

JIMMY BUFFETT'S MARGARITAVILLE ☎ 407-224-2155; **margaritaville orlando.com.** A boisterous tribute to the head Parrothead. The focal point is a volcano that spews margarita mix instead of lava. The food is Floridian–Caribbean, so expect lots of seafood and jerk seasoning and Key lime pie. If you're not a Buffett fan, it isn't worth a special trip.

NBC SPORTS GRILL & BREW (NOT OPEN AT PRESS TIME) Opening in fall 2015 on the site of the former NASCAR Sports Grille, NBC Sports Grill will feature 90 big-screen HDTVs and more than 100 beers—including a special draft available only here. The open design will evoke a luxury skybox in a sports stadium, and the central show kitchen will sport a signature open-flame kettle grill. The exterior will be distinguished by supersize video screens that will broadcast games to all of CityWalk, as well as an outdoor beer garden to relax in. The menu will offer burgers, steaks, and other sports-bar fare (crab Scotch eggs, anyone?).

In or Out of the World for These Cuisines?

AMERICAN Good selections both in and out of the World.

BARBECUE Better out of the World.

BUFFETS A toss-up—Disney buffets are expensive but offer excellent quality and variety. Out-of-World buffets aren't as upscale but are inexpensive.

CHINESE Better out of the World.

FRENCH Toss-up; good but expensive both in and out of the World.

GERMAN Passable but not great, in or out of the World.

ITALIAN Tie on quality; better value out of the World.

JAPANESE/SUSHI **Teppan Edo** in the Japan Pavilion at Epcot is tops for teppanyaki (table grilling). For sushi and sashimi, try **Tokyo Dining,** also in Japan, or visit **Kimonos** at the Swan resort.

MEXICAN **La Hacienda de San Angel** at Epcot is good but expensive, with more-affordable food right next door at the quick-service **La Cantina de San Angel.** For decent Tex-Mex, try **El Patron** outside the World.

MIDDLE EASTERN More choice and better value out of the World.

SEAFOOD Toss-up.

STEAK/PRIME RIB Try **Shula's Steak House** at the Dolphin or **The Capital Grille** on International Drive out of the World. For more-affordable but nevertheless-delicious wads o' meat, try one of the **Black Angus** steakhouses on International Drive, Lake Buena Vista, or US 192.

PAT O'BRIEN'S ☎ 407-224-2106; **patobriens.com/orlando.** This and **CityWalk's Rising Star** are mostly music venues that serve some food. Pat O'Brien's, behind a facade that looks remarkably similar to the New Orleans original, has the best bites (try the jambalaya).

RED OVEN PIZZA BAKERY ☎ 407-224-3663; **tinyurl.com/redoven pizza.** Artisan pizza baked in a 900°F oven. Choose from five white and five red Neapolitan-style pies, made with San Marzano tomatoes, organic extra-virgin olive oil, buffalo mozzarella, fine-ground "00" flour, and filtered water. Pizzas run $9–$14 and serve two people.

VIVO ITALIAN KITCHEN ☎ 407-224-2253; **tinyurl.com/vivocitywalk.** Upscale Italian restaurant with pasta made on-site nightly. Good, inexpensive appetizers. Try the Nonna Cake for dessert.

A food court on CityWalk's upper level offers serviceable quick bites: **Bread Box Handcrafted Sandwiches, BK Whopper Bar, Moe's Southwest Grill, Panda Express,** and **Fusion Bistro Sushi & Sake Bar.**

BUFFETS AND MEAL DEALS OUTSIDE WALT DISNEY WORLD

BUFFETS, RESTAURANT SPECIALS, and discount dining abound in the area surrounding Walt Disney World, especially on US 192 (a.k.a. Irlo Bronson Memorial Highway) and along International Drive. The local visitor magazines, distributed free at non-Disney hotels, among other places, are packed with advertisements and discount coupons for seafood feasts, Chinese buffets, Indian buffets, breakfast buffets, and a host of other specials.

For a family trying to economize, some of the come-ons are mighty sweet. But are these places any good? Is the food fresh, tasty, and appealing? Are the restaurants clean and inviting? Armed with little more than a roll of Tums, the *Unofficial* research team tried all the eateries that advertise heavily in the tourist magazines. Here's what we discovered.

CHINESE SUPER BUFFETS *Whoa!* Talk about an oxymoron. If you've ever tried preparing Chinese food, especially a stir-fry, you know that split-second timing is required to avoid overcooking. So it should come as no big surprise that Chinese dishes languishing on a buffet lose their freshness, texture, and flavor in a hurry.

For the past few editions of this guide, we were able to find several Chinese buffets that we felt comfortable recommending; unfortunately, we would return the next year only to discover that their quality had slipped precipitously. We then searched for new buffets to replace the ones we deleted from the book, and we can tell you that wasn't fun work. At the end of the day, **Dragon Court Chinese Buffet & Sushi Bar** (12384 S. Apopka–Vineland Road, just after FL 535 turns 90 degrees to the west; ☎ 407-238-9996; **dragoncourtchinese.com**) and **Ace Plus Chinese Buffet** (8701 W. Irlo Bronson Memorial Hwy.; ☎ 407-390-7588; **acepluschinesebuffet.com**) are the only Asian buffets that we've elected to list. Dragon Court is friendly and low-key, with a good selection of mainly Chinese dishes; Ace Plus is a good choice if you're staying near where US 192 intersects the FL 429 toll road. We rate both buffets at two and a half stars: Dragon Court has fewer selections than Ace Plus, but the overall quality is less hit-and-miss; Ace Plus, while not as good as Dragon Court, has so much to choose from that if you pick your way through the minefield, you'll find enough for an enjoyable meal. Finally, sushi at Chinese buffets is, almost without exception, pretty dismal—if it's sushi that lures you, go to a Japanese restaurant.

INDIAN BUFFETS Indian food works better on a buffet than Chinese food; in fact, it actually improves as the flavors marry. In the Disney World area, most Indian restaurants offer a buffet at lunch only—not too convenient if you're spending your day at the theme parks. If you're out shopping or taking a day off, these Indian buffets are worth trying:

AASHIRWAD INDIAN CUISINE 5748 International Dr., at the corner of International Drive and Kirkman Road; ☎ 407-370-9830

PUNJAB INDIAN RESTAURANT 7451 International Dr.; ☎ 407-352-7887

CHURRASCARIAS A number of these South American–style meat emporiums have sprung up along International Drive. Our picks are **Café Mineiro** (6432 International Dr.; ☎ 407-248-2932; **cafemineirosteak house.com**), a Brazilian steakhouse north of Sand Lake Road, and **Boi Brazil Churrascaria** (5668 International Dr.; ☎ 407 354-0260; **boibrazil .com**). Both offer good value. More expensive are the Argentinean churrasco specialties at **The Knife** (12501 FL 535; ☎ 786-866-3999; **theknife restaurant.com**); be sure to try the sweetbreads, an Argentine specialty rarely found in the US. If you prefer chain restaurants, the pricey **Texas de Brazil** and **Fogo de Chão** also have locations in Orlando.

Continued on page 298

Where to Eat Outside Walt Disney World

AMERICAN

JOHNNIE'S HIDEAWAY 12551 FL 535, Orlando; ☎ 407-827-1111; **johnnies hideaway.com;** moderate–expensive. Seafood and steaks, with an emphasis on Florida cuisine.

THE RAVENOUS PIG* 1234 N. Orange Ave., Winter Park; ☎ 407-628-2333; **theravenouspig.com;** moderate–expensive. New American cuisine with an award-winning menu that changes frequently depending on seasonal ingredients.

SEASONS 52 7700 W. Sand Lake Rd., Orlando; ☎ 407-354-5212; **seasons 52.com;** moderate–expensive. Delicious, creative New American food that's low in fat and calories. Extensive wine list.

BARBECUE

BUBBALOU'S BODACIOUS BAR-B-QUE 5818 Conroy Rd., Orlando (near Universal Orlando); ☎ 407-295-1212; **bubbalous.com;** inexpensive. Tender, smoky barbecue; tomato-based Killer Sauce.

4 RIVERS SMOKEHOUSE 11764 University Blvd., Orlando; ☎ 844-474-8377; **4rsmokehouse.com;** inexpensive. Award-winning beef brisket; fried pickles, cheese grits, fried okra, and collard greens.

CARIBBEAN

BAHAMA BREEZE 8849 International Dr., Orlando; ☎ 407-248-2499; **bahamabreeze.com;** moderate. A creative and tasty version of Caribbean cuisine from the owners of the Olive Garden and Red Lobster chains.

CHINESE

MING COURT 9188 International Dr., Orlando; ☎ 407-898-9672; **ming -court.com;** inexpensive. Dim sum, crispy roast pork, and roast duck.

CUBAN/SPANISH

COLUMBIA 649 Front St., Celebration; ☎ 407-566-1505; **columbiarestau rant.com;** moderate. Authentic Cuban and Spanish creations, including paella and the famous 1905 Salad.

ETHIOPIAN

NILE ETHIOPIAN RESTAURANT 7040 International Dr., Orlando; ☎ 407-354-0026; **nile07.com;** inexpensive–moderate. Authentic stews and delicious vegetarian dishes. Bob's favorite Orlando/WDW-area restaurant.

FRENCH

LE COQ AU VIN* 4800 S. Orange Ave., Orlando; ☎ 407-851-6980; **lecoq auvinrestaurant.com;** moderate–expensive. Country French cuisine in a relaxed atmosphere. Reservations suggested.

INDIAN

MEMORIES OF INDIA 8204 Crystal Clear Ln., Suite 1600, Orlando; ☎ 407-370-3277; **memoriesofindiacuisine.com;** inexpensive–moderate. Tandoori dishes, samosas, tikka masala, Sunday Champagne brunch with buffet.

ITALIAN

ANTHONY'S COAL-FIRED PIZZA 8031 Turkey Lake Rd., Orlando; ☎ 407-363-9466; **anthonyscoalfiredpizza.com;** inexpensive. Pizzas, eggplant, pastas, beer and wine.

*20 minutes or more from Walt Disney World

BICE ORLANDO RISTORANTE Loews Portofino Bay Hotel, Universal Orlando Resort, 5601 Universal Blvd., Orlando; ☎ 407-503-1415; **orlando .bicegroup.com;** expensive. Authentic Italian; great wines.

JAPANESE/SUSHI

AMURA 7786 W. Sand Lake Rd., Orlando; ☎ 407-370-0007; **amura.com;** moderate. A favorite sushi bar for locals. The tempura is popular, too.

HANAMIZUKI 8255 International Dr., Orlando; ☎ 407-363-7200; **hana mizuki.us;** moderate–expensive. Pricey but very authentic.

NAGOYA SUSHI 7600 Dr. Phillips Blvd., Suite 66, in the very rear of The Marketplace at Dr. Phillips; ☎ 407-248-8558; **nagoyasushi.com;** moderate. A small, intimate restaurant with great sushi and an extensive menu.

MEXICAN

CHEVYS FRESH MEX 12547 FL 535, Lake Buena Vista; ☎ 407-827-1052 or 407-827-1119; **chevys.com;** inexpensive–moderate. Conveniently located across from the FL 535 entrance to WDW.

EL PATRON 12167 S. Apopka–Vineland Rd., Orlando; ☎ 407-238-5300; **elpatronorlando.com;** inexpensive. Family-owned restaurant serving freshly prepared Mexican dishes. Full bar.

MOE'S SOUTHWEST GRILL 7541-D W. Sand Lake Rd., Orlando; ☎ 407-264-9903; **moes.com;** inexpensive. Cheap, dependable Southwestern fare.

TAQUITOS JALISCO* 1041 S. Dillard St., Winter Garden; ☎ 407-654-0363; inexpensive. Low-key atmosphere; flautas, chicken mole, fajitas, hearty burritos, good vegetarian.

NEW WORLD

NORMAN'S 4012 Central Florida Pkwy., in the Ritz-Carlton Orlando; ☎ 407-393-4333; **normans.com;** expensive. Norman Van Aken, dean of New World cuisine, offers a menu that changes often—but you'll always find his sinfully delicious conch chowder. World-class wine menu.

SEAFOOD

BONEFISH GRILL 7830 W. Sand Lake Rd., Orlando; ☎ 407-355-7707; **bonefishgrill.com;** moderate. Casual setting along busy Restaurant Row on Sand Lake Road. Choose your fish, and then choose a favorite sauce to accompany. Also steaks and chicken.

CELEBRATION TOWN TAVERN 721 Front St., Celebration; ☎ 407-566-2526; **thecelebrationtowntavern.com;** moderate. Popular hangout for locals, with New England–style seafood. Clam chowder is a big hit.

OCEAN PRIME 7339 W. Sand Lake Rd., Orlando; ☎ 407-781-4880; **ocean -prime.com;** expensive. Elegant supper-club ambience; classic fare focusing on fresh seafood, perfectly cooked meats. Outdoor dining and piano bar.

STEAK/PRIME RIB

BULL & BEAR Waldorf Astoria Orlando, 14200 Bonnet Creek Resort Ln., Orlando; ☎ 407-597-5500; **waldorfastoriaorlando.com/dining/bull-and -bear;** expensive. Classic steakhouse with a clubby ambience. Steaks, seafood, lamb chops, and more.

THE CAPITAL GRILLE Pointe Orlando, 9101 International Dr., Orlando; ☎ 407-370-4392; **thecapitalgrille.com;** expensive. Dry-aged steaks, good wine list, and classic decor.

TEXAS DE BRAZIL 5259 International Dr., Orlando; ☎ 407-355-0355; **texas debrazil.com;** expensive. All-you-care-to-eat in an upscale Brazilian-style *churrascaria*. Filet mignon, sausage, pork ribs, chicken, lamb, and more. Kids age 6 and under free, ages 7–12 half-price. Salad bar with 40+ options.

Where to Eat Outside WDW *(continued)*

STEAK/PRIME RIB *(continued)*

VITO'S CHOP HOUSE 8633 International Dr., Orlando; ☎ 407-354-2467; **vitoschophouse.com;** moderate. Surprisingly upscale meat house with a taste of Tuscany.

THAI

THAI SILK 6803 S. Kirkman Rd. at International Drive, Orlando; ☎ 407-226-8997; **thaisilkorlando.com;** moderate. Housed in an unassuming strip-mall location and acclaimed by Orlando dining critics for its authentic Thai dishes. Delicious vegetarian options; impressive wine list. Try the distinctly non-Thai fried cheesecake for dessert.

THAI THANI 11025 International Dr., Orlando; ☎ 407-239-9733; 600 Market St., Celebration, ☎ 407-566-9444; **thaithani.net;** moderate. Specializes in Thai duck preparations. Some Chinese stir-fry.

Continued from page 295

SEAFOOD AND LOBSTER BUFFETS These affairs don't exactly fall under the category of inexpensive dining. The main draw (no pun intended) is all the lobster you can eat. The problem is that lobsters, like Chinese food, don't wear well on a steam table. After a few minutes on the buffet line, they make better tennis balls than dinner, so try to grab your lobster immediately after a fresh batch has been brought out.

Two lobster buffets are on International Drive, and another is on US 192. Although all three do a reasonable job, we prefer **Boston Lobster Feast** (6071 W. Irlo Bronson Memorial Hwy.; ☎ 407-396-2606; and 8731 International Dr., five blocks north of the Convention Center; ☎ 407-248-8606; **bostonlobsterfeast.com**). Both locations are distinguished by a vast variety of seafood in addition to the lobster. The International Drive location is cavernous and noisy, which is why we prefer the Irlo Bronson location, where you can actually have a conversation over dinner. The International Drive location has ample parking, while the Irlo Bronson restaurant does not. At about $40 for early birds (4–6 p.m.) and $44 after 6 p.m., dining is expensive at both locations.

SALAD BUFFETS The most popular of these in the Walt Disney World area is **Sweet Tomatoes** (6877 S. Kirkman Rd., ☎ 407-363-1616; 12561 S. Apopka–Vineland Rd., ☎ 407-938-9461; 3236 Rolling Oaks Blvd., off US 192 near the FL 429 western entrance to Disney World, ☎ 407-966-4664; **souplantation.com**). During lunch and dinner, you can expect a line out the door, but fortunately one that moves fast. The buffet features prepared salads and an extensive array of ingredients for building your own. In addition to salads, Sweet Tomatoes offers a variety of soups, a modest pasta bar, a baked-potato bar, an assortment of fresh fruit, and ice-cream sundaes. Dinner runs $11.79 for adults, $6 for children ages 6–12, and $4 for children ages 3–5. Lunch is $9.79 for adults and the same prices as dinner for children.

BREAKFAST AND ENTREE BUFFETS Most chain steakhouses in the area, including **Ponderosa, Sizzler,** and **Golden Corral,** offer entree buffets. Among them, they have 15 locations in the Walt Disney World area. All serve breakfast, lunch, and dinner. At lunch and dinner, you get the buffet when you buy an entree, usually a steak; breakfast is a straightforward buffet (that is, you don't have to buy an entree). As for the food, it's chain-restaurant quality but decent all the same. Prices are a bargain, and you can get in and out at lightning speed—important at breakfast when you're trying to get to the parks early. Some locations offer lunch and dinner buffets at a set price without your having to buy an entree.

Though you can argue about which chain serves the best steak, **Golden Corral** wins the buffet contest hands-down, with at least twice as many offerings as its three competitors. While buffets at Golden Corral and Ponderosa are pretty consistent from location to location, the buffets at the different Sizzlers vary a good deal. Our pick of the Sizzlers is the one at 7602 W. Irlo Bronson Memorial Hwy. (☎ 407-397-0997). In addition to the steakhouses, WDW-area **Shoney's** also offer breakfast, lunch, and dinner buffets. Local freebie visitor magazines are full of discount coupons for all of the previous restaurants.

A New Hampshire reader notes that some off-site breakfast buffets don't open early enough:

> *You mention quite a few buffets for off-site dining, but it would have been nice to know their normal morning business hours. Some buffets (like Ponderosa) didn't open until 8 a.m. for breakfast. This is way too late if you're trying to get to the park at opening time.*

unofficial **TIP** Most chain-restaurant breakfast buffets have a number of locations in the Disney World area, but their operating hours aren't always the same. If you want to eat early or late, your best bet is to contact the restaurant to confirm that it will be open at your preferred time.

DISNEY BUFFETS VS OFF-SITE BUFFETS Most off-site buffets are long on selection but don't compare favorably to Disney buffets in terms of quality; likewise, the setting and ambiance of Disney buffets is generally superior. If you're trying to save money, however, non-Disney buffets offer excellent value. At a Disney buffet, you can expect well-prepared dishes across all food categories. At an off-site buffet, though some dishes may be below par, you should find enough that's palatable to put together a more-than-acceptable meal. At *any* buffet, we recommend starting with small samples to sort out the winners and losers, then going back for larger portions of your favorites.

MEAL DEALS Discount coupons are available for a wide range of restaurants, including some wonderful upscale-ethnic places such as **Ming Court** (Chinese; 9188 International Dr., Orlando; ☎ 407-351-9988; **ming-court.com**).

A meat eater's delight is the Feast for Four at **Sonny's Real Pit Bar-B-Q**. For $44 per family of four, you get sliced pork and beef plus chicken, ribs, your choice of three sides (choose from beans, slaw, fries, among others), garlic bread or corn bread, and soft drinks or tea, all served family-style. The closest Sonny's location to Walt Disney World and Universal is at 7423 S. Orange Blossom Trail in Orlando (☎ 407-859-7197; **sonnysbbq.com**.) No coupons are available (or needed) for Sonny's, but they're available for the other "meateries."

A meatery to approach with caution is **Western Sizzlin's Wood Grill Buffet** (11701 International Dr.; ☎ 407-778-4844), whose ubiquitous ads tantalizingly depict steak, ribs, and the like. In point of fact, none of these items are available for lunch, and we advise calling ahead to see what's available for dinner.

COUPONS Find discounts and two-for-one coupons for many of the restaurants mentioned in freebie visitor guides available at most hotels outside Walt Disney World. The **Visit Orlando Official Visitors Center** (8723 International Dr.; ☎ 407-363-5872; **visitorlando.com;** open daily, 8:30 a.m.–6:30 p.m., except Christmas) offers a treasure trove of coupons and free visitor magazines. In Kissimmee, visit the **Osceola County Welcome Center and History Museum** (4155 W. Vine St.; ☎ 407 396-8644; **osceolahistory.org**). In addition to visitor information and restaurant coupons, the center also houses an excellent free museum tracing the colorful history of Central Florida. On the Internet, check out **coupons alacarte.com** and **orlandocoupons.com** for printable coupons.

THE GREAT ORLANDO PIZZA SCAM Plenty of reputable local pizza joints deliver to hotels in and around the theme parks; many Disney and Universal resorts offer pizza delivery as well. But for a few years now, con artists have been distributing flyers advertising delivery to hotel guests—they ask for your credit card number over the phone, but the pizza never arrives. Disregard any such flyers you find.

DINING *in* WALT DISNEY WORLD

THIS SECTION AIMS TO HELP YOU find good food without going broke or tripping over a culinary land mine. More than 140 restaurants operate within the World, including about 90 full-service establishments, more than 30 of which are inside the theme parks. Disney restaurants offer exceptional variety, serving everything from Moroccan lamb to Texas barbecue. Most restaurants are expensive, and many serve less-than-distinguished fare, but there are good choices in every area of Walt Disney World.

GETTING IT RIGHT

ALTHOUGH WE WORK HARD to be fair, objective, and accurate, many readers, like this woman from Charleston, West Virginia, think we're too critical of Walt Disney World restaurants:

> Get a life! It's crazy and unrealistic to be so snobbish about restaurants at a theme park. Considering the number of people Disney feeds each day, I think they do a darn good job. Also, you act so surprised that the food is expensive. Have you ever eaten at an airport? HELLO IN THERE? . . . Surprise, you're a captive! It's a theme park!

And a mom from Erie, Pennsylvania, struck a practical note:

> Most of the food at Walt Disney World is OK. If you pay attention to what other visitors say and what's in the guidebooks, you can avoid the yucky places. It's true that you pay more than you should, but it's more convenient to eat in Walt Disney World than to run around trying to find cheaper restaurants somewhere else.

As you may infer from these reader comments, researching and reviewing restaurants is no straightforward endeavor—to the contrary, it's fraught with peril. We have read dining reviews by writers who turn up their noses at anything except four-star French restaurants. We've read reviews absolutely devoid of criticism, written by "experts" unwilling to risk offending the source of their free meals. Finally, we've seen reviews in dining guides that are wholly based on surveys submitted by diners whose credentials for evaluating fine dining are mysterious at best and questionable at least.

unofficial **TIP**
Our research team has eaten at every restaurant, kiosk, bar, cart, and food stand in Walt Disney World many times.

How, then, do we go about presenting the best possible dining coverage? At the *Unofficial Guide,* we begin with highly qualified culinary experts and then balance their opinions with those of our readers— which, by the way, don't always coincide. (Likewise, the coauthors' assessments don't always agree with those of our dining experts.)

In the spirit of democracy, we encourage you to fill out our online reader survey at **touringplans.com/walt-disney-world/survey.** If you'd like to share your dining experience in greater depth, we also invite you to write us at the address on page 12 or send us an e-mail: **unofficial guides@menasharidge.com.**

DISNEY DINING 101

DISNEY DINING PLANS

DISNEY OFFERS SEVERAL DINING PLANS. If you choose to sign up for a plan, you must do so when you book your Disney resort room or package vacation; for this reason, we explore the topic in-depth in Part Three, Accommodations (see page 223).

WAITER, THESE PRICES ARE GIVING ME HEARTBURN!

INCREASES IN DISNEY'S TICKET COSTS are always sure to grab headlines, but most people don't notice that Disney's restaurant prices rise about as fast. For example, while the cost of a one-day theme park ticket has increased about 33% since 2010, the average entree price at Le Cellier has gone from around $30 to just under $42—an increase of 39%. Plus, Disney sometimes levies a "dining surcharge" during the summer and other busy times of year. Factoring in the surcharge, an adult breakfast at The Crystal Palace has increased almost 45% during the same time.

You might need a stiff drink after seeing those menu prices, but booze is no bargain either. While the average bottle of wine in WDW costs three times as much as retail, some wines have much higher markups. For example, a $6 bottle of Placido Pinot Grigio costs $39 in Epcot and various Disney resort lounges—six-and-a-half times as much as the retail price. If you rent a car and eat dinner each day at non-Disney restaurants, you'll save enough to more than pay for the rental cost.

This comment from a New Orleans mom spells it out:

> *Disney keeps pushing prices up and up. For us, the sky is NOT the limit. We won't be back.*

BEHIND THE SCENES AT ADVANCE RESERVATIONS

THOUGH THEY'RE CALLED Advance Reservations, most reservations at Disney World don't guarantee you a table at a specific time as they would at your typical hometown restaurant. Disney restaurants operate on what they call a "template system." Instead of scheduling Advance Reservations for actual tables, reservations fill time slots. The number of slots available is based on the average length of time that guests occupy a table at a particular restaurant, adjusted for seasonality.

Here's a rough example of how it works: Let's say Coral Reef Restaurant at Epcot has 40 tables for four and 8 tables for six, and that the average length of time for a family to be seated, order, eat, pay, and depart is 40 minutes. Add 5 minutes to bus the table and set it up for the next guests, and the table is turning every 45 minutes. The restaurant provides Disney's central dining-reservations system **(CDRS)** with a computer template of its capacity, along with the average time the table is occupied. When you use Disney World's dining website (**disney world.disney.go.com/dining**) or call its dining hotline (☎ 407-WDW-DINE, 939-3463), both access CDRS for your requests.

Thus, when you use the website to make Advance Reservations for four people at 6:15 p.m., CDRS removes one table for four from overall capacity for 45 minutes. The template on the system indicates that the table will be unavailable for reassignment until 7 p.m. (45 minutes later). So it goes for all tables in the restaurant, each being subtracted from overall capacity for 45 minutes, then listed as available again, then assigned to other guests and subtracted again, and so on, throughout the meal period. CDRS tries to fill every time slot for every seat in the restaurant, or come as close to filling every slot as possible. No seats—repeat, none—are reserved for walk-ins.

unofficial **TIP**
Disney charges a $10- to-$25-per-person penalty for missing an Advance Reservation, or if you cancel on the day of the meal.

Templates are filled differently depending on the season and restaurant. All Disney restaurants now charge a no-show fee; this has reduced the no-show rate to virtually zero, and these restaurants are booked every day according to their actual capacity.

A couple of tips: Only one person needs to dine at the restaurant for Disney to consider your reservation fulfilled, even if you've got a reservation for more people. Also, while Disney says it requires 24 hours' notice, you can cancel up until midnight of the day before your meal. The upside to the no-show fee is that it's easier to book most restaurants closer to the date of your visit, as the fee discourages tentative plans.

With Advance Reservations, your wait will usually be less than 20 minutes during peak hours, and often less than 10 minutes. If you're a walk-in, especially during busier seasons, expect to either wait 40–75 minutes or be told that no tables are available.

GETTING ADVANCE RESERVATIONS AT POPULAR RESTAURANTS

BREAKFAST AND DINNER AT THE MAGIC KINGDOM'S **Be Our Guest** restaurant, in Fantasyland, and the 8 a.m. breakfast slots at **Cinderella's Royal Table,** in Cinderella Castle, are the two hardest-to-get reservations in Walt Disney World. Why? Be Our Guest has arguably the best food in the park, awesome special effects, and good word of mouth; Cinderella's Royal Table is Disney's tiniest character-meal restaurant, accommodating only about 130 diners at a time. You'll have to put in some effort to secure an Advance Reservation at these places.

The easiest and fastest way to get a reservation is go to **disneyworld .disney.go.com/dining** starting at 6 a.m. Eastern time, a full hour before phone reservations open. To familiarize yourself with how the site works, try it out a couple of days before you actually make reservations. You'll also save time by setting up an account online before your 180-day booking window, making sure to enter any credit card information needed to guarantee your reservations.

If you live in California and have to get up at 3 a.m. Pacific time to make a reservation, Disney couldn't care less: There's no limit to the number of hoops they can make patrons jump through if demand exceeds supply.

Disney's website is usually within a few seconds of the official time as determined by the US Naval Observatory or the National Institute of Standards and Technology, accessible online at **time.gov.** Using this site, synchronize your computer to the second the night before your 180-day window opens.

Early on the morning you want to make reservations, take a few moments to type the date of your visit into a word processor in MM/DD/YYYY format (for example, 11/16/2015 for November 16, 2015). Select the date and copy it to your computer's clipboard by pressing the **Ctrl** and **C** keys simultaneously (**Command-C** on Mac) or right-clicking your mouse and selecting "Copy"). This will save you from having to type in the date when the site comes online.

Next, start trying Disney's website about 3 minutes before 6 a.m. You'll see a text box where you can specify the date of your visit. Click the text box and press **Ctrl-A,** then **Ctrl-V** (substitute **Command** for **Ctrl** on Mac) to paste the date; then press the tab key on your keyboard. (You can also click on the blue calendar icon to flip through a month-by-month calendar, or you can select the entire date in the text box, right-click your mouse, and select "Paste," but these are slower.) You'll also see a place to specify the time of your meal and your party size; you can fill these in ahead of time, too.

Above the "Party Size" widget is a text box with the words "Search Within Dining." Start typing your restaurant name in that text box. As soon as you start typing, the website will start guessing which restaurant you want and offer a list of suggestions. It's faster if you just type a few letters—*bog* or *cin* is enough for the site to know you mean Be Our Guest or Cinderella's Royal Table, respectively. Click on the desired restaurant in the list of suggestions. Finally, click "Find a Table" or hit the Enter key on your keyboard—both submit your request to CDRS.

If your date isn't yet available, a message will appear saying "There is a problem searching for reservations at this time" or something similar. If this happens, refresh the browser page and start over. If you don't see an error message, however, the results returned will tell you whether your restaurant has a table available.

Advance Reservations: The Official Line

YOU CAN RESERVE THE FOLLOWING up to 180 days in advance:

AFTERNOON TEA AND CHILDREN'S PROGRAMS at the Grand Floridian Resort & Spa

ALL DISNEY TABLE-SERVICE RESTAURANTS and character-dining venues

FANTASMIC! **DINING PACKAGE** at Disney's Hollywood Studios

HOOP-DEE-DOO MUSICAL REVUE at Fort Wilderness Resort & Campground

MICKEY'S BACKYARD BBQ at Fort Wilderness Resort & Campground

SPIRIT OF ALOHA DINNER SHOW at the Polynesian Village Resort

Guests staying at Walt Disney World resorts—these do not include the Swan, the Dolphin, Shades of Green, or the hotels of the Downtown Disney Resort Area—can book their dining 180 days before their arrival date and can book dining reservations for their entire length of stay (up to 10 days).

Note that while you're typing, other guests are trying to make Advance Reservations, too, so you want the transaction to go down as quickly as possible. Flexibility on your part counts—it's much harder to get a seating for a large group, so give some thought to breaking your group into numbers that can be accommodated at tables for four. Also make sure that you have your credit card out where you can read it.

All Advance Reservations for Cinderella's Royal Table character meals, the *Fantasmic!* Dining Package, the *Hoop-Dee-Doo Musical Revue,* the *Spirit of Aloha Dinner Show,* and Mickey's Backyard BBQ require complete prepayment with a credit card at the time of the booking. The name on the booking can't be changed after the Advance Reservation is made. Reservations may be canceled, with the deposit refunded in full, by calling ☎ 407-WDW-DINE at least 24 hours (Cindy's) or 48 hours (*Fantasmic!* and the dinner shows) before seating time.

While many readers have been successful using our strategies, some have not:

> I got up extra-early 180 days before our trip to get Thanksgiving reservations at Le Cellier for my husband's birthday. Even though I logged on to Disney's website right at 6 a.m., by the time I got done typing and clicking the only table that was available was for 8:40 p.m.—too late for our children, and we would have missed IllumiNations.

On most days, a couple hundred users slam Disney's computer system within milliseconds of one another. With this volume, a 20th of a second or less can make the difference between getting a table and not getting one. As it happens, there are variables beyond your control. One is the number of computers through which your request passes before it reaches Disney's reservation system. The explanation is somewhat technical, but the same principle applies whether you're trying to get dining reservations online with Disney or concert seats through Ticketmaster.

When you enter a URL into your browser, the request for that page gets passed through a series of intermediate computers spread throughout the Internet. The specific route is chosen based on network speed and traffic volume, and preference is given to faster routes. For example,

Advance Reservations: The *Unofficial* Scoop

BECAUSE DISNEY CHARGES a $10-to-$25-per-person no-show penalty at its restaurants, no-show rates are close to zero. The penalty ensures that serious diners have some chance to get into Disney's better restaurants.

These days you'll need to reserve only a few breakfast venues in advance most times of the year. The most popular of these are **Be Our Guest** and **Cinderella's Royal Table** at the Magic Kingdom. If you don't care what time you eat, you'll need to call about 10 weeks out to get in for breakfast. If you're visiting during a holiday or peak season, or you want a specific time such as 8 a.m., you'll need to call a full 180 days in advance. If BOG or Cindy's is unavailable, we recommend **'Ohana** at the Polynesian Village Resort, which can be booked as little as a week before your trip.

Likewise, only a handful of restaurants require lunch reservations. The most popular are are Be Our Guest, which fills six months in advance; Epcot's **Le Cellier Steakhouse,** in the Canada Pavilion, which fills up about three months in advance; Cinderella's Royal Table, which fills up during about the same time frame; and **Akershus Royal Banquet Hall** in the Norway Pavilion, which fills up about 7–10 weeks out.

Except for Be Our Guest, for which reservations are snapped up as soon as they're available, dinner reservations are generally easy to get within 60 days at most locations, as long as you're not particular about the time you eat. (If that's critical to your family's happiness, click or call 180 days in advance.)

from Len Testa's house in Greensboro, North Carolina, the request for Disney's dining page usually goes from his computer to a small Time Warner Cable facility in Greensboro. From there it's routed through Raleigh, North Carolina, to Washington, D.C. From Washington it goes through Chicago, then Denver, and then Las Vegas before finally making it to Disney's computers. (This also tells us that Disney's computers may be hosted somewhere out west—nowhere near Orlando.)

Distance counts too, though we're talking milliseconds. Thus, it takes just a bit longer for a request to reach Disney's computers from Chicago than from Atlanta, longer yet if you're trying from New York.

If you don't have access to a computer at 6 a.m. on the morning you need to make reservations, be ready to call ☎ 407-WDW-DINE at 7 a.m. Eastern time and follow the prompts to speak to a live person. You may still get placed on hold if call volume is higher than usual, and you'll be an hour behind the early birds with computers. Still, you'll be well ahead of those who couldn't make it up before sunrise.

Also, if you're on the Disney Dining Plan and you want to book the *Fantasmic!* package, Cinderella's Royal Table, or one of the dinner shows, you may be better off reserving by phone. The online system may not recognize your table-service credits, but you can book and pay with a credit card and then call ☎ 407-WDW-DINE after 7 a.m. and have them credit the charge for the meal back to your card (a potential hassle if you get an uncooperative cast member). When you get to Walt Disney World, you'll use credits from your dining plan to "pay" for the meal. (Sometimes the online system has glitches and shows no availability; in this case, call after 7 a.m. to confirm if the online system is correct.)

NEVER, NEVER, NEVER, NEVER GIVE UP Not getting what you want the first time you try doesn't mean the end of the story. A mom from Cincinnati advises persistence in securing Advance Reservations:

I was crushed when I called and tried to reserve Chef Mickey's and couldn't. I decided not to give up and would go online once or twice a day to check reservations for Chef Mickey's and the other restaurants I wanted. It took me about a week, but sooner or later I ended up booking every single reservation I wanted except 'Ohana.

LAST-MINUTE ADVANCE RESERVATIONS Because Advance Reservations require a credit card, and because a fee is charged for failing to cancel in time, you can often score a last-minute reservation. This is attributable to reservation-holders who are tired or have last-minute conflicts calling in at the last moment to avoid paying the $10-per-head penalty. As long as the reservation-holder calls to cancel before midnight the day before, he or she won't be charged. So your best shot at picking up a canceled reservation is to repeatedly call or ping **disneyworld.disney.go .com/dining** as often as possible between 10 and 11 p.m.

***STILL* CAN'T GET AN ADVANCE RESERVATION?** Go to the restaurant on the day you wish to dine and try for a table as a walk-in (most full-service restaurants take walk-ins between 2:30 and 4:30 p.m.). This is a long shot, though you may be able to swing it during the least busy times of year or on cold or rainy days during busier seasons. If you try to walk in then, your chances are best during the last hour of serving.

unofficial **TIP**
Smoking is banned at all restaurants and lounges at Walt Disney World.

Landing an Advance Reservation for Cinderella's Royal Table at dinner is somewhat easier than for breakfast or lunch, but the price is a whopping $73 for adults and $43 for children ages 3–9. If you're unable to lock up a table for breakfast or lunch, a dinner reservation will at least get your kids inside the castle.

NO-SHOW FEES As noted earlier, Disney charges a per-person penalty if you fail to show up for an Advance Reservation the day of the meal. A $10 no-show fee is enforced at all Disney sit-down restaurants; at **Victoria & Albert's,** it's $25 for the main dining room, $50 for Queen Victoria's Room and Chef's Table (the latter two also require 48 hours' notice to cancel an Advance Reservation).

DRESS

DRESS IS INFORMAL at most theme park restaurants, but Disney has a "business casual" dress code for some of its resort restaurants: khakis, dress slacks, jeans, or dress shorts with a collared shirt for men and capris, skirts, dresses, jeans, and dress shorts for women. Restaurants with this dress code are **Jiko—The Cooking Place** at Animal Kingdom Lodge & Villas, the **Flying Fish Cafe** at the BoardWalk, the **California Grill** at the Contemporary Resort, **Monsieur Paul** at Epcot's France Pavilion, **Cítricos** and **Narcoossee's** at the Grand Floridian Resort & Spa, **Artist Point** at Wilderness Lodge & Villas, **Yachtsman Steakhouse** at the Yacht Club Resort, **Todd English's bluezoo** and **Shula's Steak House** at the Dolphin, and **Il Mulino New York Trattoria** at the Swan. **Victoria & Albert's** at the Grand Floridian is the only Disney restaurant that requires men to wear a jacket to dinner.

FOOD ALLERGIES AND SPECIAL REQUESTS

IF YOU HAVE SPECIAL DIETARY NEEDS, make them known when you make your Advance Reservations. For more information, see Part Six, Special Tips for Special People.

A Phillipsburg, New Jersey, mom reports her family's experience:

My 6-year-old has many food allergies. When making my Advance Reservations, I indicated these to the clerk. When we arrived at the restaurants, the staff was already aware of my child's allergies and assigned our table a chef who double-checked the list of allergies with us. The chefs were very nice and made my son feel very special.

A FEW CAVEATS

BEFORE YOU BEGIN EATING your way through the World, you need to know a few things:

1. Theme park restaurants rush their customers in order to make room for the next group of diners. Dining at high speed may appeal to a family with young, restless children, but for people wanting to relax, it's more like eating in a pressure chamber than fine dining.

2. Disney restaurants have comparatively few tables for parties of two, and servers are generally disinclined to seat two guests at larger tables. If you're a duo, you might have to wait longer—sometimes much longer—to be seated.

3. At full-service Disney restaurants, an automatic gratuity of 18% is added to your tab for parties of six or more—even at buffets where you serve yourself.

4. If you're dining in a theme park and cost is an issue, make lunch your main meal. Lunch entrees are similar to dinner entrees, but they're significantly cheaper.

WALT DISNEY WORLD RESTAURANT CATEGORIES

IN GENERAL, food and beverage offerings at Walt Disney World are defined by service, price, and convenience:

FULL-SERVICE RESTAURANTS Full-service restaurants are in all Disney resorts (except the All-Star Resorts, Art of Animation, Port Orleans French Quarter, and Pop Century) and all major theme parks, and Disney Springs (Marketplace, The Landing, and West Side). Disney operates most of the restaurants in the theme parks and its hotels, while contractors or franchisees operate the restaurants in hotels of the Downtown Disney Resort Area (DDRA); the Swan and Dolphin resorts; and some in Disney's Animal Kingdom, Epcot, the BoardWalk, and Disney Springs. Advance Reservations (see pages 302–306) are recommended for most full-service restaurants except those in the DDRA. The restaurants accept American Express, Carte Blanche, Diners Club, Japan Credit Bureau, MasterCard, and Visa.

BUFFETS AND FAMILY-STYLE RESTAURANTS Many of these have Disney characters in attendance, and most have a separate children's menu featuring dishes such as hot dogs, burgers, chicken nuggets, pizza, macaroni and cheese, and spaghetti and meatballs. In addition to the buffets, several restaurants serve a family-style, all-you-can-eat, fixed-price meal.

Advance Reservations are required for character buffets and recommended for all other buffets and family-style restaurants. Most credit cards are accepted. As noted earlier, an automatic 18% gratuity is added to the bill for parties of six or more, but when the tipping is at your discretion, a North Carolina reader urges generosity with waitstaff:

> I've seen diners leave a dollar or two per person at buffets. I've also heard of people protesting Disney's prices by leaving a small tip or none at all. This is unacceptable—these servers keep your drinks full, keep your plates clean, and check on you constantly. They deserve at least 15–18%. If you can't afford to tip, you shouldn't eat there.

If you want to eat a lot but don't feel like standing in yet another line, then consider one of the all-you-can-eat family-style restaurants. These feature platters of food brought to your table in courses by a server. You can eat as much as you like—even go back to a favorite appetizer after you finish the main course. The food tends to be a little better than what you'll find on a buffet line.

The table at right lists buffets and family-style restaurants (where you can belly up for bulk loading) at Walt Disney World.

FOOD COURTS Featuring a collection of counter-service eateries under one roof, food courts can be found at the Moderate resorts (Coronado Springs, Caribbean Beach, Port Orleans) and Value resorts (All-Star, Art of Animation, and Pop Century). (The closest thing to a food court at the theme parks is **Sunshine Seasons** at Epcot; see below and full profile on page 331.) Advance Reservations are neither required nor available at these restaurants.

COUNTER SERVICE Counter-service fast food is available in all theme parks and at the BoardWalk and Disney Springs. The food compares in quality with Captain D's, McDonald's, or Taco Bell but is more expensive, though often served in larger portions.

FAST CASUAL Somewhere between burgers and formal dining are the establishments in Disney's "fast casual" category, including three in the theme parks: **Be Our Guest** in the Magic Kingdom (lunch service), **Sunshine Seasons** in Epcot, and **Studio Catering Co.** in Disney's Hollywood Studios. Fast-casual restaurants feature menu choices a cut above what you'd normally see at a typical counter-service location. At Sunshine Seasons, for example, chefs will prepare grilled salmon on an open cooking surface while you watch, or you can choose from rotisserie chicken or pork, tasty noodle bowls, or large sandwiches made with artisanal breads. Entrees cost about $2 more on average than traditional counter service, but the variety and food quality more than make up for the difference.

VENDOR FOOD Vendors abound at the theme parks, Disney Springs, and the BoardWalk. Offerings include popcorn, ice-cream bars, churros (Mexican pastries), soft drinks, bottled water, and (in theme parks) fresh fruit. Prices include tax; many vendors are set up to accept credit cards, charges to your room at a Disney resort, and the Disney Dining Plan. Others take only cash (look for a sign near the cash register).

Walt Disney World Buffets and Family-Style Restaurants

RESTAURANT	LOCATION	CUISINE	MEALS SERVED	CHAR- ACTERS
Akershus Royal Banquet Hall	Epcot	American (B), Norwegian (L, D)	B, L, D	Yes
Biergarten	Epcot	German	L, D	No
Boma—Flavors of Africa	Animal Kingdom Lodge	African (D), American (B)	B, D	No
Cape May Cafe	Beach Club Resort	American	B, D	Yes (B)
Captain's Grille	Yacht Club Resort	American	B*, L, D	No
Chef Mickey's	Contemporary Resort	American	B, Br, D	Yes
Cinderella's Royal Table	The Magic Kingdom	American	B*, L, D	Yes
The Crystal Palace	The Magic Kingdom	American	B, L, D	Yes
The Garden Grill	Epcot	American	D	Yes
Garden Grove	Swan	American	B***, L, D***	Yes (B**)
Hollywood & Vine	Disney's Hollywood Studios	American	B, L, D	Yes (B, L)
Hoop-Dee-Doo Musical Revue	Fort Wilderness	American	D	No
Liberty Tree Tavern	The Magic Kingdom	American	L, D*	No
Mickey's Backyard BBQ	Fort Wilderness	American	D	Yes
1900 Park Fare	Grand Floridian	American	B, D	Yes
'Ohana	Polynesian Village	Polynesian	B, D	Yes (B)
Spirit of Aloha Dinner Show	Polynesian Village	American	D	No
Trail's End Restaurant	Fort Wilderness	American	B***, L, D***	No
Tusker House Restaurant	Disney's Animal Kingdom	African (L, D), American (B)	B, L, D	Yes (B, L, D)
Whispering Canyon Cafe	Wilderness Lodge	American	B, L, D	No

* Serves family-style meals only at the meal(s) indicated.
** Character-breakfast buffet served only on weekends.
*** Serves buffet-style meals only at the meal(s) indicated.

HARD CHOICES

DINING DECISIONS WILL DEFINITELY affect your Walt Disney World experience. If you're short on time and you want to see the theme parks, avoid full service. Ditto if you're short on funds. If you do want full service, arrange Advance Reservations—again, they won't actually reserve you a table, but they can minimize your wait.

Integrating Meals into the *Unofficial Guide* Touring Plans

Arrive before the park of your choice opens. Tour expeditiously, using your chosen plan (taking as few breaks as possible), until about 11 or 11:30 a.m. Once the park becomes crowded around midday, meals and other breaks won't affect the plan's efficiency. If you intend to stay in the park for evening parades, fireworks, or other events, eat dinner early enough to be finished in time for the festivities.

Character Dining

A number of restaurants, primarily those that serve all-you-can-eat buffets and family-style meals, offer character dining. At character meals, you pay a fixed price and dine in the presence of one to five Disney characters who circulate throughout the restaurant, hugging children (and sometimes adults), posing for photos, and signing autographs. Character breakfasts, lunches, and dinners are served at restaurants in and out of the theme parks. For an extensive discussion of character dining, see the section starting on page 418 in Part Five, Walt Disney World with Kids.

FULL-SERVICE DINING FOR FAMILIES WITH YOUNG CHILDREN

DISNEY RESTAURANTS OFFER an excellent (though expensive) opportunity to introduce young children to the variety and excitement of ethnic food. No matter how formal a restaurant appears, the staff is accustomed to fidgety, impatient, and often boisterous children. **Les Chefs de France** at Epcot, for instance, may be the only French restaurant in the United States where most patrons wear shorts and T-shirts and at least two dozen young diners are attired in basic black . . . mouse ears.

unofficial TIP
Disney Kids' Meals are for kids ages 3–9.

Almost all Disney restaurants offer kids' menus, and all have booster seats and high chairs. Servers understand how tough it may be for children to sit still for an extended period of time, and they'll supply little ones with crackers and rolls and serve your dinner much faster than in comparable restaurants elsewhere. Reader letters suggest that being served too quickly is much more common than having a long wait.

Good Walt Disney World Theme Park Restaurants for Children

In Epcot, preschoolers most enjoy the **Biergarten** in Germany, **San Angel Inn** in Mexico, and **Coral Reef Restaurant** at the Seas with Nemo & Friends Pavilion in Future World. The Biergarten combines a rollicking and noisy atmosphere with good basic food, including roast chicken; a German oompah band entertains, and kids can often participate in Bavarian dancing. San Angel Inn is in the Mexico village marketplace. From the table, children can watch boats on the Gran Fiesta Tour drift beneath a smoking volcano. With a choice of chips, tacos, and other familiar items, picky kids usually have no difficulty finding something to eat. (Be aware, though, that the service here is sometimes glacially slow.) Coral Reef, with tables beside windows looking into The Seas' aquarium, offers a satisfying mealtime diversion for all ages. If your children don't eat fish, Coral Reef also serves beef and chicken.

Biergarten offers reasonable value, plus good food. Coral Reef and San Angel Inn are overpriced, though the food is pretty good.

Be Our Guest Restaurant and **Cinderella's Royal Table,** both in Fantasyland, are the hot tickets in the Magic Kingdom, but reservations are often unobtainable. (At present, there are no characters at Be Our Guest.) We think the best kids' fare is served at the **Liberty Tree Tavern.**

At Disney's Hollywood Studios, all ages enjoy the atmosphere and entertainment at **Hollywood & Vine,** the **Sci-Fi Dine-In Theater Restaurant,** and the **50's Prime Time Cafe.** Unfortunately, the Sci-Fi's food is close to dismal except for dessert, and the Prime Time's is uneven.

The three full-service restaurants at Disney's Animal Kingdom are **Tusker House Restaurant** (actually a buffet); **Rainforest Cafe,** a great favorite of children; and **Yak & Yeti Restaurant.**

QUIET, ROMANTIC PLACES TO EAT

RESTAURANTS WITH GOOD FOOD and a couple-friendly ambience are rare in the theme parks. Only a handful of dining locales satisfy both requirements: **Coral Reef Restaurant,** an alfresco table at **Tutto Italia Ristorante,** the terrace at the **Rose & Crown Dining Room,** and the upstairs tables at the France Pavilion's **Monsieur Paul,** all in Epcot; and the corner booths at **The Hollywood Brown Derby** in Disney's Hollywood Studios. Waterfront dining (though not necessarily quiet or romantic) is available at **Fulton's Crab House, Paradiso 37,** and **Portobello** at Disney Springs and **Narcoossee's** at the Grand Floridian.

unofficial **TIP**
The **California Grill** atop the Contemporary Resort has the best view at Walt Disney World.

Victoria & Albert's at the Grand Floridian is the World's showcase gourmet restaurant; expect to pay big bucks. Other good choices for couples include **Artist Point** at Wilderness Lodge, **Yachtsman Steakhouse** at the Yacht Club, **Shula's Steak House** at the Dolphin, **Jiko** at Animal Kingdom Lodge, and **Flying Fish Cafe** at the BoardWalk.

Eating later in the evening and choosing a restaurant we've mentioned will improve your chances for intimate dining; nevertheless, children—well behaved or otherwise—are everywhere at Walt Disney World, and there's no way to escape them. These honeymooners from Slidell, Louisiana, write:

> *We made dinner reservations at some of the nicer Disney restaurants. We made sure to reserve past dinner hours, and we tried to stress that we were on our honeymoon. In every restaurant we went to, we were seated next to large families. The kids were usually tired and cranky. It's very difficult to enjoy a romantic dinner when there are small children crawling around under your table. Our suggestion: Seat couples without children together and families with kids elsewhere.*

FAST FOOD IN THE THEME PARKS

BECAUSE MOST MEALS DURING a Disney World vacation are consumed on the run while touring, we'll tackle counter-service and vendor foods first. Plentiful in all theme parks are hot dogs, hamburgers, chicken

THE COST OF COUNTER-SERVICE FOOD

BAGEL OR MUFFIN	$2.79-$2.99
BROWNIE	$2.99-$3.99
BURRITO	$7.09-$7.59
CAKE OR PIE	$3.59-$5.19
CEREAL WITH MILK	$3.19-$3.69
CHEESEBURGER WITH FRIES	$8.79-$11.49
CHICKEN BREAST SANDWICH	$9.19-$9.99
CHICKEN NUGGETS WITH FRIES	$7.59-$9.29
CHILDREN'S MEAL *(various)*	$5.49-$5.99
CHIPS	$2.79-$3.25
COOKIE	$2.50-$3.99
FRIED-FISH BASKET WITH FRIES	$7.99-$9.49
FRENCH FRIES	$2.99
FRUIT *(whole)*	$1.69-$3.59
FRUIT CUP / FRUIT SALAD	$3.79-$3.99
HOT DOG	$5.75-$10.29
ICE CREAM / FROZEN NOVELTIES	$3.99-¢4.99
NACHOS WITH CHEESE	$3.99-$7.69
PB&J SANDWICH	$5.49 *(kids' meal)*
PIZZA *(personal)*	$9.19-$10.69
POPCORN	$3.50-$5.50
PRETZEL	$2.95-$4.79
SALAD *(entree)*	$7.99-$11.69
SALAD *(side)*	$3.29
SMOKED TURKEY LEG	$10.50-$13.29
SOUP / CHILI	$3.29-$7.99
SUB / DELI SANDWICH	$7.50-$10.49
TACO SALAD	$8.19
VEGGIE BURGER	$8.59-¢9.99

THE COST OF COUNTER-SERVICE DRINKS

DRINKS	SMALL	LARGE
BEER	$5.75-$7.00	$7.50-$12.50
BOTTLED WATER *(one size)*	$2.50-$4.00	$2.50-$4.00
LATTE *(one size)*	$3.99	$3.99-$5.19
COFFEE *(one size)*	$2.29	$2.29
FLOAT, MILKSHAKE, OR SUNDAE *(one size)*	$4.49-$5.39	$4.49-$5.39
FRUIT JUICE	$2.59-$2.99	$3.29-$3.79
HOT TEA AND COCOA *(one size)*	$2.09-$2.29	$2.09-$2.29
MILK	$1.79	$2.39-$2.59
SOFT DRINKS, ICED TEA, AND LEMONADE	$2.59-$2.99	$3.29

Refillable souvenir mugs cost $16.49 with tax (free refills) at Disney resorts and around $11 at the water parks. Each person on a Disney Dining Plan gets a free mug, refillable at their Disney resort.

sandwiches, salads, and pizza. They're augmented by special items that relate to the park's theme or the part of the park you're touring. In Epcot's Germany, for example, counter-service bratwurst and beer are sold. In Frontierland in the Magic Kingdom, vendors sell smoked turkey legs. Counter-service prices are fairly consistent from park to park. Expect to pay the same for your coffee or hot dog at Disney's Animal Kingdom as at Disney's Hollywood Studios.

Getting your act together in regard to counter-service restaurants in the parks is more a matter of courtesy than necessity. Rude guests rank fifth among reader complaints. A mother from Fort Wayne, Indiana, points out that indecision can be as maddening as outright discourtesy, especially when you're hungry:

> *Every fast-food restaurant has menu signs the size of billboards, but do you think anybody reads them? People waiting in line spend enough time in front of these signs to memorize them and still don't have a clue what they want when they finally get to the counter. If by some miracle they've managed to choose between the hot dog and the hamburger, they then fiddle around another 10 minutes deciding what size Coke to order. Folks, PULEEEZ get your orders together ahead of time!*

A North Carolina reader offers a tip for helping things along:

> *Many counter-service registers serve two queues each, one to the left and one to the right of each register. People are not used to this and will instinctively line up in one queue per register, typically on the right side, leaving the left vacant. We had register operators wave us up to the front several times to start a left queue instead of waiting behind others on the right.*

Healthful Food at Walt Disney World

One of the most commendable developments in food service at Walt Disney World has been the introduction of healthier foods and snacks. People who have diabetes, vegetarians, dieters, those requiring kosher meals, and the like should have no trouble finding something to eat. The same goes for anyone seeking wholesome, nutritious food. Health-conscious choices such as fresh fruit are available at most fast-food counters and even from vendors.

unofficial **TIP**
Look for the **Mickey Check** icon on healthy menu items such as fresh fruit and low-fat milk.

News for Java Junkies

Starbucks are on the Magic Kingdom's Main Street, in Epcot's Future World, on Hollywood Boulevard in the Studios, and in Disney Springs (with Animal Kingdom coming soon).

Beyond Counter Service: Tips for Saving Time and Money

Even if you confine your meals to quick-service fare, you lose a lot of time getting food in the theme parks. Here are some ways to minimize the time you spend hunting and gathering:

1. Eat breakfast before you arrive. Restaurants outside the World offer some outstanding breakfast specials. Plus, some hotels furnish small refrigerators in their guest rooms, or you can rent a fridge or bring a cooler. If you can get by on cold cereal, rolls, fruit, and juice, this will save a ton of time.

2. After a good breakfast, buy snacks from vendors in the parks as you tour, or stuff some snacks in a fanny pack.

3. All theme park restaurants are busiest between 11:30 a.m. and 2:15 p.m. for lunch and 6 and 9 p.m. for dinner. For shorter lines and faster service, don't eat during these hours, especially 12:30–1:30 p.m.

4. Many counter-service restaurants sell cold sandwiches. Buy a cold lunch minus drinks before 11:30 a.m., and carry it in small plastic bags until you're ready to eat (within an hour or so of purchase). Ditto for dinner. Buy drinks at the appropriate time from any convenient vendor.

5. Most fast-food eateries have more than one service window. Regardless of the time of day, check the lines at all windows before queuing. Sometimes a window that's staffed but out of the way will have a much shorter line or none at all. Note, however, that some windows may offer only certain items.

6. If you're short on time and the park closes early, stay until closing and eat dinner outside Disney World before returning to your hotel. If the park stays open late, eat dinner about 4 or 4:30 p.m. at the restaurant of your choice. You should sneak in just ahead of the dinner crowd.

Our readers use variations on these tips with great success. A Missouri mom writes:

We arrived at WDW with our steel Coleman cooler well stocked with milk and sandwich fixings. I froze a block of ice in a milk bottle, and we replenished it daily with ice from the resort ice machine. I also froze small packages of deli-type meats for later in the week. We ate cereal, milk, and fruit each morning, with boxed juices.

Each child had a belt bag of his own, which he filled from a special box of "goodies" each day with things like packages of crackers and cheese, packets of peanuts and raisins. Each child also had a small, rectangular plastic water bottle that could hang on the belt. We filled these at water fountains before getting into lines.

We left the park before noon, ate sandwiches, chips, and soda in the room, and napped. We purchased our evening meal in the park, at a counter-service eatery. We budgeted for both morning and evening snacks from a vendor but often didn't need them.

A Whiteland, Indiana, mom suggests:

If you're traveling with younger kids, take a supply of small paper or plastic cups to split drinks, which are both huge and expensive.

DISNEY DINING SUGGESTIONS

FOLLOWING ARE SUGGESTIONS for dining at each of the major theme parks. If you want to try a full-service restaurant at one of the parks, be aware that the restaurants continue to serve after the park's official closing time. We once showed up at The Hollywood Brown Derby just as Disney's Hollywood Studios closed at 8 p.m. We were seated almost immediately and enjoyed a leisurely dinner while the crowds cleared out.

THE MAGIC KINGDOM

OF THE PARK'S SIX full-service restaurants, **Be Our Guest** (breakfast, dinner) in Fantasyland is the best, followed by **Liberty Tree Tavern** in Liberty Square and **The Plaza Restaurant** on Main Street. **Cinderella's Royal Table** in the castle and **The Crystal Palace** on Main Street serve a decent-but-expensive character buffet. Avoid **Tony's Town Square Restaurant** on Main Street.

AUTHORS' FAVORITE COUNTER-SERVICE RESTAURANTS

Be Our Guest (breakfast, lunch) *Fantasyland*
Columbia Harbour House *Liberty Square*

These two restaurants' menus have the most variety within the Magic Kingdom. Be Our Guest serves a tasty tuna niçoise salad (with seared tuna), a grilled-ham-and-cheese sandwich that's better than you'd expect, and a savory braised-pork entree. Columbia Harbour House's offerings include lobster rolls, grilled salmon, and a delicious hummus sandwich on multigrain bread. Beyond these, the Magic Kingdom's fast-food eateries are undistinguished, not to mention about twice as expensive as McDonald's, for about the same quality. On the positive side, portions are large, sometimes large enough for children to share. Check our mini-profiles of the park's counter-service restaurants before you queue up.

unofficial **TIP**
Don't worry about dining late if you're depending on Disney transportation: Buses, boats, and monorails run 1–2 hours after the parks close.

Our dining recommendations for a day at the Magic Kingdom:

1. Obtain an Advance Reservation for lunch at Be Our Guest. See point 3 below for details.

2. Take the monorail to one of the hotels for lunch. The trip takes very little time, and because most guests have left the hotels for the parks, the resorts' restaurants are often uncrowded. The food is better than the Magic Kingdom's, the service is faster, the atmosphere is more relaxed, and mixed drinks are available.

3. Full-service restaurants that accept Advance Reservations fill quickly in the summer and during holidays. To obtain Advance Reservations, visit **disneyworld.disney.go.com/reservations/dining,** call ☎ 407-939-3463, or hotfoot it to your chosen restaurant as soon as you enter the park. Advance Reservations are explained starting on page 302, and Magic Kingdom full-service and counter-service restaurants are profiled later in this chapter.

4. A good rule at any full-service restaurant is to keep it simple. Order sandwiches or basic dishes (such as roast turkey and mashed potatoes).

Here are some comments from readers about Magic Kingdom full-service and counter-service restaurants. First, regarding Cinderella's Royal Table, two perspectives from two different readers:

Reader 1: Our whole family did Cinderella's Royal Table for lunch. Our two little boys (ages 3 and 4) loved it even more than their

6-year-old sister. They loved all the princesses paying special attention to them since they were the only guys in the whole place. My 3-year-old left with his face covered in lipstick and even managed to propose to Cinderella—who, sadly, mentioned she was already married.

Reader 2: The food was OK, but the characters spent a lot of time at each table—so much time that we only got to meet Snow White and Belle. Wasn't worth the trouble of getting the seating.

A mom from Glen Burnie, Maryland, says she was given plenty of time to eat her (mediocre) food:

The many comments I read about Cinderella's Royal Table rushing guests out the door aren't consistent with our experience. It's a character meal—it's not like guests are eating a leisurely 3-hour multicourse feast at a French restaurant. The food wasn't particularly good, but we never felt rushed. Our server was attentive, and the princesses all spent quite a bit of time making our princess feel like an honored guest.

There are two things everyone agrees on concerning Be Our Guest: The food is good and it's hard to get into. First, from a Burlington, Ontario, dad:

The best thing about the vacation: eating lunch at Be Our Guest. The atmosphere and quality of food were unlike any quick-service I'd ever had at Disney.

From a Kansas City, Missouri, mom:

Be Our Guest must be the new Cinderella's Royal Table. I tried to get a dinner reservation when we first planned our vacation four months ahead, and I couldn't get one. Fortunately, you can line up for lunch to see the inside of the castle.

And finally, from a Belgium, Wisconsin, reader:

Disney artificially inflates the exclusivity of this restaurant by not utilizing one of the dining rooms at less-than-peak periods and by having, at best, minimal staff, causing my table to have to wait 40 minutes for dessert.

The Crystal Palace gets mixed reviews. A sampling:

The food quality and selection were the worst I've seen in 10 years of going there, and the characters were stretched way too thin—only two came to our table in an hour and a half.

Of all the restaurants we visited, I can't rave enough about The Crystal Palace or Liberty Tree Tavern. The food was great, the service was wonderful, and the characters were awesome.

Like the previous reader, the following reader really liked the Liberty Tree Tavern:

Didn't expect much here but made a reservation based on your book. What a surprise! The food was great as well as the atmosphere.

So did this Broussard, Louisiana, couple—though their enthusiasm isn't exactly unqualified:

We booked a reservation for dinner at Liberty Tree Tavern. What we didn't realize is that it was a set menu. The food was excellent—like Thanksgiving dinner—but the price was crazy! Dinner for two with drinks and tip ran us $90. Not what we were expecting.

A mom of four from Charleston, South Carolina, enjoyed Columbia Harbour House:

The lobster roll was yummy. My teen daughter said the shrimp was the best she had ever had, and my teen son loved his salmon. We all left full and happy.

EPCOT

SINCE THE BEGINNING, dining has been an integral component of Epcot's entertainment product. The importance of dining is reflected in the number of restaurants and their ability to serve consistently interesting and well-prepared meals. World Showcase has many more restaurants than attractions, and Epcot has added bars, tapas-style eateries, and full-service restaurants faster than any park in memory.

unofficial **TIP**
Epcot has 17 full-service restaurants: 2 in Future World and 15 in World Showcase. With a couple of exceptions, these are among the best restaurants at Walt Disney World, in or out of the theme parks.

FULL-SERVICE RESTAURANTS IN EPCOT	
FUTURE WORLD	
Coral Reef Restaurant **The Seas**	Garden Grill Restaurant **The Land**
WORLD SHOWCASE	
Akershus Royal Banquet Hall **Norway**	Rose & Crown Dining Room **United Kingdom**
Biergarten **Germany**	San Angel Inn Restaurante **Mexico**
Le Cellier Steakhouse **Canada**	Spice Road Table **Morocco**
Les Chefs de France **France**	Teppan Edo **Japan**
La Hacienda de San Angel **Mexico**	Tokyo Dining **Japan**
Monsieur Paul **France**	Tutto Italia Ristorante **Italy**
Nine Dragons Restaurant **China**	Via Napoli **Italy**
Restaurant Marrakesh **Morocco**	

For the most part, Epcot's restaurants have always served decent food, though the World Showcase restaurants have occasionally been timid about delivering honest representations of their host nations' cuisine. That seems to be changing faster in some areas (Mexico) than others (Morocco), but we're hopeful that we see a trend. It's still true that the less adventuresome diner can find steak and potatoes on virtually every menu, but the same kitchens will serve up the real thing for anyone willing to ask.

Many Epcot restaurants are overpriced, most conspicuously **Monsieur Paul** (France) and **Coral Reef Restaurant** (The Seas). Combining attractive ambience and well-prepared food with good value are **Via Napoli** (Italy), **Biergarten** (Germany), and **La Hacienda de San Angel** (Mexico). Biergarten (along with **Restaurant Marrakesh** in Morocco) also features live entertainment.

While eating at Epcot can be a consummate hassle, an afternoon without Advance Reservations for dinner in World Showcase is like not having a date on the day of the prom. Each pavilion (except United States) has a beautifully seductive ethnic restaurant or two, offering the gastronomic delights of the world. To tour these exotic settings and not partake is almost beyond the limits of willpower. And while the fare in some World Showcase restaurants isn't always compelling, the overall experience is exhilarating. If you fail to dine in World Showcase, you'll miss one of Epcot's most delightful features.

AUTHORS' FAVORITE COUNTER-SERVICE RESTAURANTS

Les Halles Boulangerie–Pâtisserie *France*   **Sunshine Seasons** *The Land*
Sommerfest *Germany*   **Tangierine Cafe** *Morocco*

Les Halles Boulangerie–Pâtisserie sells pastries, sandwiches, and quiches. The pastries are made on-site, and the sandwiches are as close to actual French street food—in taste, size, and price—as you'll get anywhere in Epcot. (We had one of those *Ratatouille* flashback scenes while eating one, only ours was in the Marais.) Another favorite is the chicken-and-lamb *shawarma* platter at Morocco's **Tangierine Cafe.** Besides juicy lamb, it comes with some of the best tabbouleh we've tasted in Florida.

In addition to these, we recommend the following ethnic counter-service specialties:

GERMANY	**Sommerfest** for bratwurst and Beck's beer
JAPAN	**Katsura Grill** for noodle dishes, teriyaki, and tempura
NORWAY	**Kringla Bakeri og Kafe** for pastries, open-face sandwiches, and Carlsberg beer (our favorite)
UNITED KINGDOM	**Rose & Crown Pub** for Guinness, Harp, and Bass beers

Unofficial Guide readers have diverse opinions of Epcot's full-service restaurants. Concerning Coral Reef Restaurant in The Seas with Nemo & Friends:

Tried Coral Reef for the first time, despite reviews. Waited 40 minutes beyond our reserved time, and the food was mediocre and pricey. Next time I'll cook a burger next to my daughter's goldfish bowl.

We were surprised by how much everyone loved Coral Reef. We had great service, and the food was awesome. We had a booth directly in front of the tank and didn't even request it!

Restaurant Marrakesh likewise garnered mixed reviews:

Restaurant Marrakesh is overrated. It may be a walk on the wild side for someone from, say, Wichita, but I can find better and more exotic food at a dozen places in my neighborhood.

(For all you folks in Wichita who are wondering where this reader is from: Arlington, Virginia.) More comments from a Royal Oak, Michigan, woman:

We'd been to Morocco and wanted to see how the Disney version compared. Of course, they're not the same, but the food was excellent and the setting was nearly as exotic as the real thing. The big shock came when the bill arrived and there was a per-person charge for the musical entertainment and belly dancing. They played for maybe 30 minutes, and after the expensive meal, the music charge was off-putting. I had to laugh, though, because that unexpected charge made me feel like I really was back in Morocco.

Le Cellier is one of the most coveted reservations in Epcot:

Le Cellier is one of the hardest restaurants for which to get Advance Reservations [see page 302]. It wasn't available any of the 10 days of my trip, and I called more than 90 days in advance.

The filet mignon I got at Le Cellier may indeed have been the best steak I've ever had—and it had better have been for that price.

A couple of pointed comments about Nine Dragons in China:

The food was horrible, and the noise level was extremely high. I've had better Chinese at our local strip mall.

I think they should rename it Nine Tums.

Akershus Royal Banquet Hall in the Norway Pavilion has become quite the favorite of character-dining enthusiasts:

I took my 4-year-old daughter and 4-year-old niece, who were of course obsessed with seeing the princesses. The girls got to see Belle, Ariel, Cinderella, Aurora, and Jasmine. Each princess came to the table one at a time, the food was great, the dessert was to die for, and the waitstaff was extremely friendly and outgoing. The princesses were really engaged with the girls, and the best thing was that Ariel saw my daughter outside while she was leaving the restaurant. Ariel swooped down and planted a kiss on her cheek—my daughter wouldn't wash her cheek for the rest of the day!

And, finally, about the San Angel Inn:

Expensive, but where else can you drink Corona beer and dine under a moonlit sky at the base of a vaulted pyramid while boats drift by?

But a Bristol, Tennessee, reader complained of cramped conditions:

At San Angel Inn, the tables are so close together you could easily swipe food off a plate at the next table and they might never notice.

Drinking Around the World (Showcase)

A popular adult pastime at Epcot is to make a complete circuit of the World Showcase, sampling the exceptional alcoholic drinks native to each nation represented. Perhaps knowing this, Disney has added stand-alone bars to five pavilions.

LA CAVA DEL TEQUILA, MEXICO Inside the pyramid, La Cava stocks more than 100 kinds of tequila and mezcal (similar to tequila, with a smoky flavor), almost a dozen kinds of margaritas, and various light appetizers. La Cava seats just over 50 people but is far more popular than that. On weekends and on special events such as the Food & Wine Festival or Cinco de Mayo, expect a wait to get a table.

La Cava is Len's favorite bar in Walt Disney World. Two things set it apart: First, a dedicated tequila expert is on hand most days to explain the different types of tequila and provide tasting notes. (Her name is Hilda, and she's from the town of Tequila in Jalisco, Mexico—tell her Len sent you.) Second, the team that runs La Cava is very engaged with the Disney community on social media, which makes it easy to ask questions about the drinks and menus. As of this writing, folks who follow **@cavadeltequila** on Twitter get free chips and salsa.

SAKE BAR, JAPAN It isn't much more than a small circular table at the far end of the retail space on the first floor of the Japan Pavilion. It's common to see customers lined up two deep to sip and discuss their favorite rice wines. A decent and affordable selection of sakes can be purchased from a shelf right next to the bar-table. Frankly, we're amazed that this hasn't been expanded into a proper dedicated room.

SPICE ROAD TABLE, MOROCCO Offering waterside food and drinks, Spice Road Table is a surprisingly uncrowded spot for *IllumiNations* dining. Unique cast-member costuming, a highly detailed interior, and an open-air patio are the highlights of the setting and atmosphere. Choose from beer, wine, cocktails, and tapas-style small plates, including mussels, calamari, and stuffed grape leaves For dessert, the almond ice cream is made on-site. The food is decent, but at $8–$30, the prices are on the high side for what you get.

TUTTO GUSTO WINE CELLAR, ITALY Tutto Gusto serves wine, spirits, and light appetizers in a setting reminiscent of an underground wine cellar. Perhaps learning from La Cava, which opened first, Tutto Gusto has seating for 113. Our favorite spot is a small room just inside the entrance, to the right, with a fireplace, a couple of comfy chairs, and tables big enough to hold your food and drinks.

The menu is divided into three sections. The "small plates" section offers four choices that each serve two people: combinations of cured meats and salamis, cheeses, olives, veggies, and seafood. Prices start at $24 each. Besides these, there's a selection of sandwichlike panini available, but the bread isn't as good as you'd expect. The best, and most reasonably priced, thing on the menu is the pasta. Try the hand-rolled *pici* (like spaghetti, only fatter) with lamb. When it comes to dessert, the cannoli are some of the best we've ever had. The wine list is extensive. Service is good.

That said, Tutto Gusto is a poster child for how Disney's restaurant management can ruin a good thing. We loved it when it first opened— the menu had lots of à la carte options and was (for Epcot) reasonably priced. Within a year, however, Disney made it just another restaurant by jacking up the prices and condensing the menu (for example, getting rid of the charcuterie selections we loved).

WEINKELLER, GERMANY Decorated in stone, dark woods, heavy chandeliers, and thick wood tables, Weinkeller serves wines by the glass (around $5) and in flights of three 2-ounce pours (about $10). If you like sweet white wines, this is the place to be. Selections usually include a couple of Rieslings, a Liebfraumilch, dessert wines, and ice wines. The bar has no seating and serves no food, but the wine pours are generous— and that counts for something.

In addition to the preceding, the UK Pavilion has had the **Rose & Crown Pub** for years. But with the growing popularity of watering holes in World Showcase, we wouldn't be surprised if Disney added a few more.

EPCOT AFTER HOURS WIND DOWN Last held in the summer and fall of 2014, these wine-and-spirits tastings begin at Epcot's closing time and run through 11 p.m. or later. Wind Down menus vary by location and typically include a flight of three or four small drinks, plus appetizers that complement the beverages. An experienced member of the bar staff usually leads a discussion on how the alcohol is made and how to taste each drink. La Cava del Tequila is almost always the most crowded venue (and frequently sells out), followed by Tutto Gusto, the Rose & Crown, and Spice Road Table. Full bar and food menus are available during the event, too. It's a lot of fun. Check the Disney website or **touringplans.com** for news on future Wind Downs.

DISNEY'S ANIMAL KINGDOM

BECAUSE TOURING ANIMAL KINGDOM takes less than a day, crowds are heaviest from 9:30 a.m. until about 3:30 p.m. Expect a mob at lunch and thinner crowds at dinner. We recommend you tour early after a good breakfast, then eat a very late lunch or graze on vendor food. If you tour later in the day, eat lunch before you arrive, then enjoy dinner in or out of the theme park. Animal Kingdom full-service and counter-service restaurants are profiled later in this chapter.

Animal Kingdom isn't particularly exotic. You'll find a lot of counter-service fast food, along with **Tusker House,** a buffet-style restaurant, and **Yak & Yeti,** a table-service restaurant, in Asia. You'll also find plenty of traditional theme park food—hot dogs, burgers, and the like—but even the fast food is superior to typical Disney fare. Our two counter-service favorites: **Flame Tree Barbecue** in Discovery Island, with its waterfront dining pavilions, and **Yak & Yeti Local Food Cafes** (just outside the full-service Yak & Yeti) for casual Asian dishes from egg rolls to crispy honey chicken.

The new **Harambe Market,** to the right as you approach Kilimanjaro Safaris, has four windows, each serving a different specialty food. Choices include spice-rubbed ribs, batter-fried sausages, and grilled chicken or beef kebabs. Beer and South African wines are also available.

A Whitestone, New York, dad thinks we sell Tusker House short:

You really underestimate Tusker House. It was easily the best buffet, and the characters at lunch ended up making it a great meal.

A Cambridge, England, reader loved the full-service Yak & Yeti:

Our meal was the best we had in the World—in fact, some of the best Asian cuisine we had tried since our travels in Southeast Asia—yet we were dismayed to see tables of Americans next to us ordering burgers with so many Asian specialties to choose from.

AUTHORS' FAVORITE COUNTER-SERVICE RESTAURANT
Flame Tree Barbecue *Discovery Island*

The third full-service restaurant in Animal Kingdom, **Rainforest Cafe,** has entrances both inside and outside the park, meaning you don't have to buy park admission to eat there. Both Rainforest Cafes (the other is at Disney Springs) accept Advance Reservations.

DISNEY'S HOLLYWOOD STUDIOS

DINING AT DHS is more interesting than at the Magic Kingdom but less ethnic than at Epcot. The park has five restaurants where Advance Reservations are recommended or required: **The Hollywood Brown Derby, 50's Prime Time Cafe, Sci-Fi Dine-In Theater Restaurant, Mama Melrose's Ristorante Italiano,** and the **Hollywood & Vine** buffet. The upscale Brown Derby is by far the best restaurant at the Studios. For simple Italian food, including pizza, Mama Melrose's is fine; just don't expect anything fancy. At the Sci-Fi Dine-In, you eat in little cars at a simulated drive-in movie from the 1950s. Though you won't find a more entertaining restaurant in Walt Disney World, the food is quite disappointing. Somewhat better is the 50's Prime Time Cafe, where you sit in Mom's time-warp kitchen and scarf down meat loaf while watching clips of classic sitcoms. It's fun and the food is a step up. The best way to experience either restaurant is to stop in for dessert or a drink between 2:30 and 4:30 p.m. Hollywood & Vine features singing and dancing characters from the Disney Channel during breakfast and lunch. DHS full-service and counter-service restaurants are profiled later in this chapter.

AUTHORS' FAVORITE COUNTER-SERVICE RESTAURANTS

ABC Commissary *Echo Lake*	**Min and Bill's Dockside Diner** *Echo Lake*
Backlot Express *Echo Lake*	**Toluca Legs Turkey Company** *Sunset Boulevard*

We receive considerable mail from readers recounting their DHS dining experiences. A reader from Sumter, South Carolina, writes:

We had lunch at the Sci-Fi Dine-In. You gave it a terrible review, but I've always felt you guys are too hard on the Disney restaurants, so we went ahead and ate there. Well, you were right on target! The atmosphere was fun, but the food was lousy . . . and expensive!

From an East Lansing, Michigan, woman who'd had it to here with togetherness:

I disagree with your review of the Sci-Fi Dine-In. After a busy and hot day of touring, it's heaven to be in a dark, air-conditioned room.

The 50's Prime Time Cafe is always a hot topic. First, from a Maryland reader:

50's Prime Time Cafe was fun, but the food was mediocre at best. If my mom cooked that way, I would've run away from home.

But a West Newton, Massachusetts, family loved the Prime Time:

We know you guys didn't rate it very well, but we decided to go against your recommendation and give it a shot. We're so glad we did! For the five of us (ages 16–20), it was a blast. "Leroy," our waiter and "big brother" for the meal, came and sat at our table and helped us set our places so we wouldn't get in trouble with "Mom." When one member of our party cursed, "Mom" arrived to punish him, making him clear the table onto her tray, which he did shamefully. Overall, it was a total kick that we talked about for the rest of the trip.

The Hollywood Brown Derby was a favorite of a San Diego reader:

Delicious food, great selections, and an excellent end to an evening at the Studios.

If you arrive at DHS without having arranged Advance Reservations for meals, you can make them at the Advance Reservations kiosk at the corner of Hollywood and Sunset Boulevards or at the restaurants. **The Hollywood Brown Derby,** expensive but tasty, is usually among the last to fill. If you have no Advance Reservations and you get hungry, try **Studio Catering Co.** or **Min & Bill's Dockside Diner,** both of which sometimes fly under the radar of the teeming hordes.

MORE READER COMMENTS ABOUT WALT DISNEY WORLD DINING

EATING IS A POPULAR TOPIC among *Unofficial Guide* readers. In addition to participating in our annual restaurant survey, many readers share their thoughts. The following comments are representative.

Here's a 13-year-old girl from Omaha, Nebraska, who doesn't get bent out of shape over one bad meal:

Honestly, when was the last time you came home from Disney World and said, "Gosh, my vacation really sucked because I ate at a bad restaurant"? Disney World is Disney World, no matter what.

A reader from Carbondale, Illinois, exhorts other readers to be adventuresome in their choice of restaurants:

We had a blast dining at Akershus and Marrakesh! The service was great; food was different but not weird. My husband is a picky eater, but even he was able to say that he tried Norwegian and Moroccan food at the end of our vacation!

A big thumbs-up from a Troup, Texas, reader for the California Grill:

You recommended the California Grill for the view of the Magic Kingdom fireworks show, but you didn't mention being able to see IllumiNations. We scheduled a 9:15 dinner and arrived early. The staff allowed us to have a drink in the lounge area and watch the fireworks at the Magic Kingdom. When we were seated at 8:20, the hostess told us that we had a great view of Epcot and we should watch for the fireworks at 9 o'clock. The food was exceptional, the service was outstanding, and the view was amazing.

Note: Much of *IllumiNations* takes place below tree line, so only the higher aerial fireworks can be seen from the California Grill. Still, it's a treat. A Canadian mom raises a caution, however:

We ate dinner on our last night at the California Grill. It was wonderful, but it took 3 hours. This is not a great place to take your kids. We were there from 7 to 10 p.m., and it was just too much for them.

From a reader in the United Kingdom:

We had the most fantastic meal at California Grill and I'd definitely recommend it. Being central London–living foodie-types, we're very hard to please, but the meal there really was second to none.

A family of five loved Whispering Canyon Cafe at Wilderness Lodge:

Our best experience for dining was at the Whispering Canyon. My girls (ages 6, 10, and 11) thought the servers were great. They joked with each other, shouted, and laughed with the kids. Our waiter even sat down with our kids and helped my oldest "finish" her salad and showed my youngest how to eat whipped cream off her nose.

An Albuquerque, New Mexico, couple is very enthusiastic about Artist Point, also at Wilderness Lodge:

Our meal at Artist Point was one of the best we've ever experienced. Our steaks were so good we're still talking about them months later.

Sanaa, in the Kidani Village section of Animal Kingdom Lodge, really impressed an Ellicott City, Maryland, family:

Sanaa is a beautiful restaurant with delicious and inexpensive (for Disney) food that you can't find anywhere else in Walt Disney World. We had a fabulous adults-only evening here, but I would bring children too for an early dinner overlooking the savanna.

A woman from Verona, Wisconsin, praises character dining:

We think the character meals are underrated. These meals are in pleasant settings and provide an easy, efficient way for little kids to interact with characters while providing adults with an opportunity to relax. Yes, they're a little pricey, but you get more than food.

This reader tried several character meals, commenting:

The Crystal Palace (Magic Kingdom): A HUGE hit with my kids! We met Eeyore, Pooh, Tigger, and Piglet. The food was great, too—lots of choices, and all done very well.

Chef Mickey's (Contemporary Resort): By far the best dining experience we had. And with it being Chef Mickey's, you of course get to meet Mickey, Minnie, Pluto, Goofy, and Donald. A must-do!

Akershus (Epcot): We did this one for breakfast. It was a little different than the others, as it was half-buffet, half–family style (big community plate to be shared with the table) We met Belle, Ariel, Cinderella, and Aurora. Plus, we got to try some Norwegian dishes!

Hollywood and Vine (Hollywood Studios): We didn't care for this one at all—if it hadn't been for meeting the Disney Junior characters (Sofia the First, Jake, Handy Manny, and Doc McStuffins), we probably wouldn't have picked this one. The food was subpar, but the worst was the seating and organization of the characters: Most of the table were booths, which made it very hard for children to get in and out to meet the characters and/or go to the buffet to get food. There was no rhyme or reason to which way the characters were going, and the handlers were nowhere to be found.

Evidently, Hollywood and Vine is also slow, as a Salinas, California, mom reports:

We were able to finish most of the meals before the parks opened, but the Hollywood Studios breakfast took too long due to the characters not visiting people when they needed to do a little show. We ended up leaving without seeing all of the characters after 2 hours.

A couple from Oxford, England, had a discount coupon and still didn't like Planet Hollywood:

We got $15 off at Planet Hollywood, but it was so noisy with loud music that children were covering their ears—it ruined the meal.

A Pennsylvania Gen Y guy likes PH—and clearly knows how to deal with the LM (loud music, that is):

Planet Hollywood had the best (strongest) mixed drinks, and great ribs and ravioli.

A mother of three from Jamaica, New York, waited 2 hours and 40 minutes for a table at the Rainforest Cafe and still had a good time:

The Rainforest Cafe was an absolute delight. Our 6-year-old sat right next to a gorilla that ranted every few minutes, our 10-month-old loved the huge fish tanks, and they both loved the food. Our wait for a table was over 2 hours, but it was worth it.

But a Richardson, Texas, family had this to say:

It was wild, wet, and loud, and the service was the worst in WDW.

(Most negative reader comments concerning Rainforest Cafe pertain to the Disney Springs location, not the one at Animal Kingdom.)

We get lots of comments about the dinosaur-themed T-REX restaurant at Disney Springs. A Dartmouth, Nova Scotia, mom writes:

Terrible experience! Overpriced, bad food, VERY LOUD—we couldn't even hear each other. They put us in the ice-cave room, which has no dinosaur; it felt like I was taking my toddlers to a mini-rave with all the flashing lights.

But what was a negative for the previous parent was a blessing for a Beaverton, Oregon, mother of two:

The best place for your kids to have a tantrum is T-REX. No one can hear them screaming!

And finally, Raglan Road at Disney Springs was a big hit with another mom of two, this one from Los Angeles:

Cannot say enough about this amazing Irish pub. The ambience, the food, the entertainment were all absolutely top-notch. I feel like its presence could be overshadowed by other more flashy restaurants at Disney Springs, but it was a HUGE highlight of our trip.

COUNTER-SERVICE *Mini-Profiles*

TO HELP YOU FIND palatable fast food that suits your tastes, we provide thumbnail profiles of the theme park counter-service restaurants, listed alphabetically by park. They're rated for quality, portion size, and value. (The average thumbs-up rating for all Disney counter-service restaurants is 83%, with a standard deviation of 3.6%.) Value ratings range from A to F, as follows:

A	Exceptional value; a real bargain	**D**	Somewhat overpriced
B	Good value	**F**	Extremely overpriced
C	Fair value; you get exactly what you pay for		

THE MAGIC KINGDOM
Aloha Isle

QUALITY Excellent	VALUE B+	PORTION Medium	LOCATION Adventureland
READER-SURVEY RESPONSES 97%	3%	DISNEY DINING PLAN? No	

Selections Soft-serve ice cream; ice-cream floats; fresh pineapple spears; chips; juice, bottled water, coffee, tea.

Comments The pineapple Dole Whip soft-serve is a must-try. Formerly located across from the Swiss Family Treehouse, Aloha Isle is now next door to *Walt Disney's Enchanted Tiki Room.*

Be Our Guest Restaurant

QUALITY Excellent	VALUE B+	PORTION Medium	LOCATION Fantasyland
READER-SURVEY RESPONSES 91%	9%	DISNEY DINING PLAN? Yes	

Selections Breakfast: cured meats and cheeses, open-faced bacon and poached egg sandwich with Brie, eggs Florentine in puff pastry, steel-cut oatmeal, scrambled egg whites with roasted tomatoes, signature fried doughnuts. Lunch: tuna niçoise salad, *croque monsieur,* carved turkey and roast-beef sandwiches, braised pork with bacon mashed potatoes, veggie quiche, quinoa salad. Kids' meals include seared mahimahi, carved turkey sandwich, slow-cooked pork, a tasty meat loaf, grilled cheese and tomato soup, or whole-grain macaroni with marinara sauce.

Comments The best counter-service restaurant in the Magic Kingdom, and one of the best in all of Disney World. Our favorite breakfast selections are the open-faced bacon-and-egg sandwich with Brie and the fried doughnuts topped with banana-caramel sauce and chocolate ganache. For lunch we like the slow-cooked pork coq au vin–style, with mushrooms, carrots, onions, and bacon; it's served with mashed potatoes for soaking up the rich sauce, plus a side of green beans. The *croque monsieur* sandwich is a grown-up version of grilled ham and cheese, with carved ham, Gruyère cheese, and béchamel sauce and *pommes frites* on the side. If we're behaving, the generous seared-tuna niçoise salad hits the spot.

    Note: Breakfast is served for just 2 hours (8–10 a.m.), and lines for lunch start forming as early as 9:30 a.m. Expect at least a 30-minute wait if you go between 11 a.m. and 1 p.m. Advance Reservations for lunch are available online at **disneyworld.disney.go.com/dining.** Disney has also rolled out advance ordering for lunch via its My Disney Experience mobile app. See page 342 for a review of Be Our Guest's sit-down dinner service.

Casey's Corner

QUALITY Good	VALUE B	PORTION Medium	LOCATION Main Street, U.S.A.
READER-SURVEY RESPONSES 84%	16%	DISNEY DINING PLAN? Yes	

Selections Hot dogs, corn-dog nuggets, fries, and brownies.

Comments Best to stop at Casey's when it's extra-busy—that's the best guarantee of a fresh bun and hot fries. Len recommends the barbecue slaw dog; our dining insider favors the Polish sausage with grilled onions and stone-ground mustard, or the addictive corn-dog nuggets.

Columbia Harbour House

QUALITY Good	VALUE B	PORTION Medium	LOCATION Liberty Square
READER-SURVEY RESPONSES 94% 👍 6% 👎		DISNEY DINING PLAN? Yes	

Selections You can behave with the grilled salmon with couscous and broccoli, tuna on multigrain bread, broccoli peppercorn salad, or Lighthouse Sandwich with hummus and broccoli slaw. Or you can indulge with fried shrimp or battered fish. The lobster roll falls somewhere in between. Other choices: fried chicken or fish nuggets; New England clam chowder; vegetarian chili; coleslaw; garden salad; chocolate cake, seasonal cobbler, or strawberry yogurt for dessert. For kids: macaroni and cheese, PB&J sandwich, chicken nuggets, or tuna sandwich with grapes.

Comments No trans fats in the fried items, and the soups and sandwiches are a cut above most fast-food fare.

Cosmic Ray's Starlight Cafe

QUALITY Good	VALUE B	PORTION Large	LOCATION Tomorrowland
READER-SURVEY RESPONSES 80% 👍 20% 👎		DISNEY DINING PLAN? Yes	

Selections Rotisserie chicken and ribs; burgers (and vegetarian burgers); hot dogs; Greek salad; chicken, turkey, and vegetable sandwiches; chicken nuggets; chili-cheese dog; barbecue-pork sandwich; chicken-noodle soup; chili-cheese fries; gelato and cake for dessert. Kosher choices available by request.

Comments Plenty of options, but the setup can be a little confusing. Each of the three "bays" has different offerings, so make sure you look at each menu before deciding—and note that some items show up on more than one menu. Generous toppings bar.

Friar's Nook

QUALITY Good	VALUE B	PORTION Medium-large	LOCATION Fantasyland
READER-SURVEY RESPONSES 92% 👍 8% 👎		DISNEY DINING PLAN? Yes	

Selections Hot dogs, specialty macaroni and cheese (bacon cheeseburger, beef pot roast), veggies and chips with hummus, freshly made potato chips, lemonade slush.

Comments We prefer the plain version of the mac and cheese, with crunchy panko topping. A little pricey, but filling.

Gaston's Tavern

QUALITY Good	VALUE C	PORTION Medium	LOCATION Fantasyland
READER-SURVEY RESPONSES 91% 👍 9% 👎		DISNEY DINING PLAN? Yes	

Selections Roast pork shank (the porcine equivalent of the giant turkey leg), hummus with chips, cinnamon rolls, chocolate croissants, LeFou's Brew (frozen apple juice flavored with toasted marshmallow).

Comments Clever setting, limited menu. Most everyone is here for the ginormous pork shank or a cinnamon roll. The supersweet Le Fou's Brew is basically expensive apple juice.

Golden Oak Outpost

QUALITY Good	VALUE B+	PORTION Medium-large	LOCATION Frontierland
READER-SURVEY RESPONSES 76% 👍 24% 👎		DISNEY DINING PLAN? Yes	

Selections Waffle fries topped with barbecue pork and slaw or brown gravy and white Cheddar; BLT waffle fries with bacon, lettuce, tomato, and ranch dressing; Tex-Mex waffle fries with black-bean relish, jalapeños, Cheddar, and sour cream.

Comments Served with apple slices or carrots. Sweet potato nuggets with powdered sugar for dessert.

The Lunching Pad

QUALITY Good	VALUE B-	PORTION Medium	LOCATION Tomorrowland
READER-SURVEY RESPONSES	71% 👍	29% 👎	DISNEY DINING PLAN? Yes

Selections Sweet cream-cheese pretzel; frozen sodas; classic Coney Island dog with chili, onion, and mustard.

Comments The frozen carbonated drinks—cola, cherry, blue raspberry—are a treat in summer's heat.

Pecos Bill Tall Tale Inn & Cafe

QUALITY Good	VALUE B	PORTION Medium–large	LOCATION Frontierland
READER-SURVEY RESPONSES	84% 👍	16% 👎	DISNEY DINING PLAN? Yes

Selections One-third-pound Angus cheeseburger; grilled-chicken sandwich with bacon and pepper jack cheese; barbecue-pork sandwich; veggie burgers; Southwest chicken salad; chili; child's plate with burger, grilled cheese, turkey sandwich, or barbecue-pork sandwich and child's beverage; fries and chili-cheese fries; chocolate cake, yogurt, and carrot cake.

Comments Garnish your burger at the fixin's station. The popular taco salad has moved over to Tortuga Tavern.

The Pinocchio Village Haus

QUALITY Fair	VALUE C	PORTION Medium	LOCATION Fantasyland
READER-SURVEY RESPONSES	78% 👍	22% 👎	DISNEY DINING PLAN? Yes

Selections Flatbread pizzas; Italian flatbread sub; chicken nuggets; fries; Caesar salad with chicken; meatball sub sandwiches; Mediterranean salad; kids' meal of pizza, chicken nuggets, mac and cheese, or PB&J.

Comments An easy stop for families in Fantasyland, but it's usually crowded. Consider Columbia Harbour House (see previous page) instead—it's just a few minutes' walk away, and tastier, too.

Tomorrowland Terrace Restaurant *(open seasonally)*

QUALITY Fair	VALUE C	PORTION Medium–large	LOCATION Tomorrowland
READER-SURVEY RESPONSES	83% 👍	17% 👎	DISNEY DINING PLAN? Yes

Selections One-third-pound Angus bacon cheeseburger; chicken nuggets; pasta primavera with chicken; lobster roll; beef-and-blue-cheese salad; citrus shrimp salad; chocolate cake, carrot cake, or yogurt for dessert.

Comments The lobster roll, served with homemade potato chips, is our favorite item on the menu.

Tortuga Tavern *(open seasonally)*

QUALITY Fair	VALUE B	PORTION Medium–large	LOCATION Adventureland
READER-SURVEY RESPONSES	86% 👍	14% 👎	DISNEY DINING PLAN? Yes

Selections Beef taco salad; beef nachos with black beans; chicken, beef, or vegetarian burritos; chicken Caesar salad; quesadillas and PB&J sandwiches for kids.

Comments Large, shaded eating area. Generous toppings bar with tomatoes, lettuce, cheese, and salsa.

EPCOT
L'Artisan des Glaces

QUALITY Excellent	VALUE C	PORTION Large	LOCATION France
READER-SURVEY RESPONSES 97% 👍	3% 👎	DISNEY DINING PLAN? Yes	

Selections Flavors change but can include vanilla, chocolate, mint chocolate, pistachio, hazelnut, profiterole, caramel with salt, cherry, white chocolate with coconut, and coffee ice creams. Sorbet flavors can include strawberry, mango, melon, lemon, pomegranate, and mixed berry. Over-21s can enjoy two scoops in a martini glass, topped with a shot of Grand Marnier, rum, or whipped cream–flavored vodka.

Comments Hands-down, this is the best ice cream at Disney World, freshly made on the spot. Our profiterole sample had chunks of chocolate-covered cookie pieces, and our white chocolate–coconut had fresh shaved coconut in it. The chocolate macaron ice-cream sandwich is worth every calorie.

La Cantina de San Angel

QUALITY Good	VALUE B	PORTION Medium–large	LOCATION Mexico
READER-SURVEY RESPONSES 84% 👍	16% 👎	DISNEY DINING PLAN? Yes	

Selections Tacos with seasoned beef; nachos with ground beef; fried cheese empanada; Mexican salad with cabbage, lettuce, black beans, and corn; guacamole and chips; churros and frozen fruit pops; margaritas. For kids, empanadas or chicken tenders.

Comments The Cantina is a popular spot for a quick meal, with 150 covered outdoor seats. When it's extra-busy, they open up the back of La Hacienda's dining room for air-conditioned seating.

Crêpes des Chefs de France

QUALITY Excellent	VALUE B+	PORTION Medium	LOCATION France
READER-SURVEY RESPONSES 84% 👍	16% 👎	DISNEY DINING PLAN? No	

Selections Crepes filled with chocolate, strawberry preserves, ice cream, or sugar; ice cream; specialty beer (Kronenbourg 1664); espresso.

Comments These crepes rate high—even with French guests. Look for the kiosk at the front of the France Pavilion.

Electric Umbrella

QUALITY Fair	VALUE B–	PORTION Medium	LOCATION Innoventions East
READER-SURVEY RESPONSES 67% 👍	33% 👎	DISNEY DINING PLAN? Yes	

Selections Angus bacon cheeseburger; French Dip burger; sausage-and-pepper sub; veggie flatbread; veggie naan-wich with tofu; Caesar salad with chicken; chicken nuggets; child's plate with cheeseburger, mac and cheese, vegetarian flatbread, or chicken wrap; cheesecake, no-sugar-added brownie, chocolate cupcake.

Comments In a word, uninspired. Much better choices elsewhere.

Fife & Drum Tavern

QUALITY Fair	VALUE C	PORTION Large	LOCATION United States
READER-SURVEY RESPONSES 86% 👍	14% 👎	DISNEY DINING PLAN? Yes	

Selections Turkey legs, popcorn, pretzels, ice cream, frozen slushes, beer.

Comments Great place to grab a bite for a show at the America Gardens Theatre. Seating also available in and around the Liberty Inn, behind the Fife & Drum.

Fountain View

QUALITY Fair	VALUE C	PORTION Small	LOCATION Future World Plaza
READER-SURVEY RESPONSES 94% 👍 6% 👎		DISNEY DINING PLAN? Yes	

Selections Coffee drinks and teas; breakfast sandwiches and pastries.
Comments Disney-themed Starbucks, with the same food and drinks you'd find in any other.

Katsura Grill

QUALITY Good	VALUE B	PORTION Small-medium	LOCATION Japan
READER-SURVEY RESPONSES 89% 👍 11% 👎		DISNEY DINING PLAN? Yes	

Selections Sushi; noodle bowls (beef, curry, and tempura shrimp); chicken, beef, or salmon teriyaki; chicken-cutlet curry; Japanese curry rice with beef; edamame; miso soup; green-tea cheesecake; green-tea and azuki-bean ice cream; teriyaki chicken kids' plate; Kirin beer, sake, and plum wine.
Comments Great spot to grab some sushi and sit outside.

Kringla Bakeri og Kafe

QUALITY Good-excellent	VALUE B	PORTION Small-medium	LOCATION Norway
READER-SURVEY RESPONSES 95% 👍 5% 👎		DISNEY DINING PLAN? Yes	

Selections Pastries and cakes; rice cream; sandwiches such as the smoked-salmon-and-egg or the Norwegian Club with lingonberry mayo; vegetable torte; espresso, cappuccino, and imported beers.
Comments Try the ham-and-apple sandwich with Jarlsberg and Muenster. Ditto the rice cream (not a typo, by the way). Shaded outdoor seating.

Les Halles Boulangerie–Pâtisserie

QUALITY Good	VALUE A	PORTION Small-medium	LOCATION France
READER-SURVEY RESPONSES 96% 👍 4% 👎		DISNEY DINING PLAN? Yes	

Selections The beautiful deli–bakery case is stocked with goodies such as tuna niçoise salad; sandwiches (ham and cheese; grilled eggplant; Brie, cranberry, and apple); imported-cheese plates; quiches; soups; and delicate pastries.
Comments Les Halles opens at 9 a.m.—2 hours before World Showcase—so it's a wonderful spot for a quiet breakfast. For an authentic Parisian experience, grab a baguette or baguette sandwich and eat it while walking around France. Usually crowded starting at lunch and throughout the day.

Liberty Inn

QUALITY Fair	VALUE C	PORTION Medium	LOCATION United States
READER-SURVEY RESPONSES 80% 👍 20% 👎		DISNEY DINING PLAN? Yes	

Selections Angus bacon cheeseburger; surf-and-turf burger with beef and crab; Louisiana-style shrimp with rice; grilled-chicken BLT; Maryland crab cakes; New York strip with red-wine butter, fries, and steamed broccoli; chili; Southwest salad with chicken and black-bean salsa; red, white, and blue salad with dried cranberries, pecans, apples, and blue cheese; hot dogs; veggie "chicken" sandwich; chicken nuggets; child's plate of grilled chicken or pasta with marinara.
Comments They've freshened up the menu here, but quality could be better. Still, the New York strip is a relative bargain at $11.49. Kosher items also available.

Lotus Blossom Cafe

QUALITY Fair	VALUE C	PORTION Medium	LOCATION China
READER-SURVEY RESPONSES 70% 👍 30% 👎		DISNEY DINING PLAN? Yes	

Selections Pork and vegetable egg rolls, pot stickers, Hong Kong–style vegetable curry (chicken optional), sesame chicken salad, shrimp fried rice, orange chicken, beef-noodle soup bowl, caramel-ginger or lychee ice cream, plum wine, Tsingtao beer.

Comments The menu never changes, and the food remains mediocre.

Promenade Refreshments

QUALITY Fair	VALUE C	PORTION Large	LOCATION World Showcase Promenade
READER-SURVEY RESPONSES 79% 👍 21% 👎		DISNEY DINING PLAN? Yes	

Selections Chili dogs, hot dogs, frozen yogurt, beer.

Comments Seating is limited to nonexistent—be prepared to walk and chew.

Refreshment Cool Post

QUALITY Good	VALUE B–	PORTION Small	LOCATION Between Germany and China
READER-SURVEY RESPONSES 85% 👍 15% 👎		DISNEY DINING PLAN? Yes	

Selections Hot dogs, soft-serve in a waffle cone, slushes, coffee or tea, draft Safari Amber beer ($7).

Comments Home of the Doofenslurper—frozen lemonade topped with passion-fruit sorbet foam.

Refreshment Port

QUALITY Good	VALUE B–	PORTION Medium	LOCATION Near Canada
READER-SURVEY RESPONSES 93% 👍 7% 👎		DISNEY DINING PLAN? Yes	

Selections Fried favorites—croissant doughnut, chicken nuggets and fries—plus flavored coffees, hot chocolate, and soft-serve ice cream.

Comments Almost everyone in line is here for the trendy and calorie-laden croissant doughnut.

Rose & Crown Pub

QUALITY Good	VALUE C+	PORTION Medium	LOCATION United Kingdom
READER-SURVEY RESPONSES 91% 👍 9% 👎		DISNEY DINING PLAN? No	

Selections Fish and chips; Scotch egg (hard-boiled, wrapped in sausage, and deep-fried); corned beef; shepherd's pie; bangers and mash; British cheese plate; Guinness, Harp, and Bass beers, as well as other spirits.

Comments Most of the crowd is here to drink in an authentic British pub with ales, lagers, and stouts. Outside the pub is Yorkshire County Fish Shop (see next page), which serves food to go.

Sommerfest

QUALITY Good	VALUE B–	PORTION Medium	LOCATION Germany
READER-SURVEY RESPONSES 86% 👍 14% 👎		DISNEY DINING PLAN? Yes	

Selections Bratwurst, curry wurst, *nudelgratin* (baked macaroni with Cheddar and Swiss), cold potato salad, house-made paprika chips, apple strudel, Black Forest cake, cheesecake, German wine and beer.

Comments Grab a spot in the courtyard to indulge in one of the hearty sausages and a cold pilsner. Skip the *nudelgratin.*

Sunshine Seasons

QUALITY Excellent	VALUE A	PORTION Medium	LOCATION The Land
READER-SURVEY RESPONSES 95% 👍 5% 👎		DISNEY DINING PLAN? Yes	

Selections Comprise the following four areas: (1) wood-fired grills and rotisseries, with rotisserie half-chicken or slow-roasted pork chop and wood-grilled fish with seasonal vegetables; (2) sandwich shop with made-to-order sandwiches such as oak-grilled veggie flatbread, spicy fish tacos, and turkey-and-cheese on ciabatta; (3) Asian shop, with noodle bowls and various stir-fry combos; (4) soup-and-salad shop, with soups made daily and unusual creations such as the Power Salad (quinoa, almonds, and chicken) and roasted-beet-and-goat-cheese salad. Breakfast includes the usual suspects: pastries, bacon, eggs, and the like.

Comments One of the best quick-service spots in Epcot. The breakfast panini (eggs, bacon, roast pork, and cheese) is an *Unofficial* favorite.

Tangierine Cafe

QUALITY Good	VALUE B	PORTION Medium	LOCATION Morocco
READER-SURVEY RESPONSES 93% 👍 7% 👎		DISNEY DINING PLAN? Yes	

Selections Chicken and lamb *shawarma;* hummus; tabbouleh; lentil salad; couscous salad; chicken, lamb, and falafel wraps; marinated olives; child's burger or chicken tenders; Moroccan wine and beer; baklava.

Comments It's rarely busy, and the food is decent if not totally authentic. Grab a seat outdoors and people-watch along World Showcase Promenade.

Yorkshire County Fish Shop

QUALITY Good	VALUE B+	PORTION Medium	LOCATION United Kingdom
READER-SURVEY RESPONSES 94% 👍 6% 👎		DISNEY DINING PLAN? Yes	

Selections Fish and chips, shortbread, Bass Ale draft and Harp Lager.

Comments There's usually a line for the crisp, hot fish and chips at this convenient fast-food window attached to the Rose & Crown Pub (see full-service profile on page 369). Outdoor seating overlooks the lagoon.

DISNEY'S ANIMAL KINGDOM

Creature Comforts

QUALITY Fair	VALUE C	PORTION Small	LOCATION Discovery Island near Africa
READER-SURVEY RESPONSES Too new to rate		DISNEY DINING PLAN? Yes	

Selections Coffee drinks and teas; breakfast sandwiches and pastries.

Comments Disney-themed Starbucks. The fare is largely the same you'd find at any other, plus the occasional Animal Kingdom–themed treat.

Flame Tree Barbecue

QUALITY Excellent	VALUE B–	PORTION Large	LOCATION Discovery Island
READER-SURVEY RESPONSES 92% 👍 8% 👎		DISNEY DINING PLAN? Yes	

Selections Half-slab St. Louis–style ribs; smoked half-chicken; smoked-pork sandwich; smoked-chicken salad; jumbo turkey leg; fruit plate with honey yogurt; child's plate of baked chicken drumstick, chicken sandwich, hot dog, or PB&J sandwich; French fries, coleslaw, and onion rings; Key lime or chocolate mousse; Safari Amber beer, Bud Light, and wine.

Comments Expanded outdoor seating provides more shaded space overlooking the water. One of our favorites for lunch.

Harambe Market

QUALITY Good	VALUE B	PORTION Large	LOCATION Africa
READER-SURVEY RESPONSES Too new to rate		DISNEY DINING PLAN? Yes	

Selections Spice-rubbed ribs with green papaya–carrot slaw and chickpea, cucumber, and tomato salad; curry corn dog, grilled-chicken kebabs, ground beef–kebab flatbread sandwich, each served with a roasted broccoli–tomato salad. Beer and South African wines are also available. Kids' menu includes child-size versions of the adult selections or a snack pack with yogurt, apple slices, carrots, and crackers.

Comments Plenty of shaded seating. Disney Imagineers modeled the marketplace setting after a typical real-life market in an African nation during the 1960s colonial era. The curry corn dog and the chicken skewers are our favorites.

Kusafiri Coffee Shop and Bakery

QUALITY Good	VALUE B	PORTION Medium	LOCATION Africa
READER-SURVEY RESPONSES 92% 👍 8% 👎		DISNEY DINING PLAN? Yes	

Selections Cupcakes, turnovers, Danish, muffins, croissants, cookies, brownies, cake, fruit cups, yogurt, coffee, cocoa, and juice. Breakfast wrap (egg, sausage, spinach, and goat cheese) served until 10:30 a.m.

Comments The only savory offering is the breakfast wrap. The colossal cinnamon roll is a favorite anytime.

Pizzafari

QUALITY Fair	VALUE B	PORTION Medium	LOCATION Discovery Island
READER-SURVEY RESPONSES 80% 👍 20% 👎		DISNEY DINING PLAN? Yes	

Selections Cheese, pepperoni, or veggie personal pizza; meatball sub; wedge salad with chicken; pasta Bolognese. For kids, mac and cheese, pasta with turkey marinara, cheese pizza, or PB&J. Chocolate mousse or tiramisu for dessert. Beer and wine available.

Comments The pizza is unimpressive. Kosher menu available.

Restaurantosaurus

QUALITY Good	VALUE B+	PORTION Medium-large	LOCATION DinoLand U.S.A.
READER-SURVEY RESPONSES 77% 👍 23% 👎		DISNEY DINING PLAN? Yes	

Selections Angus bacon cheeseburger; chicken nuggets; black-bean burger; mac-and-cheese hot dog; chicken BLT salad; grilled-chicken sandwich; kids' turkey wrap, corn-dog nuggets, cheeseburger, or PB&J.

Comments Good burger-toppings bar. Plenty of seating.

Royal Anandapur Tea Company

QUALITY Good	VALUE B	PORTION Medium	LOCATION Asia
READER-SURVEY RESPONSES 91% 👍 9% 👎		DISNEY DINING PLAN? No	

Selections Wide variety of hot and iced teas and coffees (fantastic frozen chai); lattes; coffee, espresso, and cappuccino; pastries.

Comments Halfway between Expedition Everest and Kali River Rapids, this is the kind of small, eclectic, Animal Kingdom–specific food stand that you wish other parks had. Nine loose teas from Asia and Africa can be ordered hot or iced.

Yak & Yeti Local Food Cafes

QUALITY Fair	VALUE B	PORTION Large	LOCATION Asia
READER-SURVEY RESPONSES 90% 👍 10% 👎		DISNEY DINING PLAN? Yes	

Selections Crispy honey chicken with steamed rice, Korean stir-fry barbecue chicken, ginger chicken salad, Asian chicken sandwich, roasted-vegetable couscous wrap, egg rolls, chicken fried rice. Kids' menu: chicken tenders, PB&J, or cheeseburger with applesauce and carrots.

Comments For filling up when you're in a hurry. Everything is a little too sweet except the couscous wrap.

DISNEY'S HOLLYWOOD STUDIOS

ABC Commissary

QUALITY Fair	VALUE B–	PORTION Medium-large	LOCATION Echo Lake
READER-SURVEY RESPONSES 69% 👍 31% 👎		DISNEY DINING PLAN? Yes	

Selections New York strip steak; roasted salmon; Asian salad (chicken or salmon); chicken club sandwich; Angus cheeseburger with Sriracha aioli and fried shrimp; shrimp platter; seafood platter; couscous, quinoa, and arugula salad; child's chicken nuggets, cheeseburger, or turkey sandwich; chocolate mousse; cupcakes; no-sugar-added strawberry parfait; wine and beer.

Comments You're bound to find something to like on this diverse menu. Indoors and centrally located, but hard to find. Offers kosher meals.

Backlot Express

QUALITY Fair	VALUE C	PORTION Medium-large	LOCATION Echo Lake
READER-SURVEY RESPONSES 83% 👍	17% 👎	DISNEY DINING PLAN? Yes	

Selections Angus cheeseburger; spicy Buffalo chicken nuggets; chili dog; Southwest salad with chicken, black-bean relish, and avocado; pressed turkey club; grilled-vegetable sandwich; cantaloupe-and-cucumber salad. For kids, chicken nuggets, PB&J, or grilled-veggie sandwich. Soft drinks and beer.

Comments Fun props—some actually used in movies—decorate this spacious dining space.

Catalina Eddie's

QUALITY Fair	VALUE B	PORTION Medium-large	LOCATION Sunset Boulevard
READER-SURVEY RESPONSES 60% 👍	40% 👎	DISNEY DINING PLAN? Yes	

Selections Cheese and pepperoni pizzas, hot Italian deli sandwich, Caesar salad, banana parfait, cupcakes, and vanilla cake with chocolate custard.

Comments The lowest-rated counter-service restaurant in the park. Seldom crowded. Go figure.

Fairfax Fare

QUALITY Fair	VALUE B	PORTION Medium-large	LOCATION Sunset Boulevard
READER-SURVEY RESPONSES 81% 👍	19% 👎	DISNEY DINING PLAN? Yes	

Selections Barbecue chicken and ribs; pulled-pork sandwiches; "designer" hot dogs (barbecue pork and coleslaw, macaroni and cheese with truffle oil); chili dogs; turkey legs; Fairfax Salad with barbecue pork, bacon, and corn-tomato salsa; banana parfait; vanilla cake.

Comments Like Charo on *The Love Boat,* the mac-and-cheese–truffle-oil hot dog is a standout in a sea of forgettable supporting players. Ask to have your bun warmed before your dog is served.

Min and Bill's Dockside Diner

QUALITY Fair	VALUE C	PORTION Small-medium	LOCATION Echo Lake
READER-SURVEY RESPONSES 81% 👍	19% 👎	DISNEY DINING PLAN? Yes	

Selections Italian sausage, jumbo turkey legs, frankfurter on a pretzel roll, specialty mac and cheese (Buffalo chicken, barbecue pork), shakes and soft drinks, chips and cookies, beer.

Comments Stir the toppings into the warm mac and cheese for a hearty meal in a bowl. Limited seating at nearby picnic tables.

Pizza Planet

QUALITY Good	VALUE B+	PORTION Medium	LOCATION Streets of America
READER-SURVEY RESPONSES 76% 👍	24% 👎	DISNEY DINING PLAN? Yes	

Selections Cheese, pepperoni, and vegetarian pizzas; meatball sub; salads; child's chicken sub or cheese pizza; cookies and cupcakes.

Comments It's all about the arcades. Repair to the outdoor seating with umbrella-shaded tables if you want to avoid the din inside.

Rosie's All-American Cafe

QUALITY Fair	VALUE C	PORTION Medium	LOCATION Sunset Boulevard
READER-SURVEY RESPONSES	97% 👍	3% 👎	DISNEY DINING PLAN? Yes

Selections Cheeseburgers; black-bean burgers; chicken nuggets; soups; child's turkey sandwich or chicken nuggets with carrot sticks or applesauce; banana parfait, cupcakes, or vanilla cake with chocolate custard.
Comments A quick stop on the way to Tower of Terror or Rock 'n' Roller Coaster. Plenty of shaded seating and a good fixin's bar.

Starring Rolls Cafe

QUALITY Good	VALUE B	PORTION Small–medium	LOCATION Sunset Boulevard
READER-SURVEY RESPONSES	93% 👍	7% 👎	DISNEY DINING PLAN? Yes

Selections Deli sandwiches, sushi, pastries and desserts, coffee.
Comments Slowest counter service in the Studios.

Studio Catering Co.

QUALITY Good	VALUE B	PORTION Small–medium	LOCATION Streets of America
READER-SURVEY RESPONSES	85% 👍	15% 👎	DISNEY DINING PLAN? Yes

Selections Grilled-veggie sandwiches, pressed turkey clubs, buffalo chicken sandwiches, toasted Tuscan deli sandwiches, sloppy joes, Greek salad. PB&J, veggie sandwich, or chicken nuggets for kids. The adjacent High Octane Refreshments serves margaritas and other cocktails.
Comments You might miss this spot unless your kids are burning off energy at Honey, I Shrunk the Kids Movie Set Adventure. Grab a frozen piña colada to sip while the youngsters play. Plenty of shaded seating.

Toluca Legs Turkey Company

QUALITY Good	VALUE B	PORTION Medium–large	LOCATION Sunset Boulevard
READER-SURVEY RESPONSES	83% 👍	17% 👎	DISNEY DINING PLAN? Yes

Selections Smoked turkey legs and pork shanks; bottled soda and beer.
Comments For fans of giant meat.

Trolley Car Cafe

QUALITY Fair	VALUE C	PORTION Small	LOCATION Sunset Boulevard
READER-SURVEY RESPONSES	90% 👍	10% 👎	DISNEY DINING PLAN? Yes

Selections Coffee drinks and teas; breakfast sandwiches and pastries.
Comments Former retail shop turned Disney-themed Starbucks. The building is the real attraction: The pink-stucco Spanish Colonial exterior calls to mind old Hollywood, while the industrial-style interior is themed to evoke a trolley-car switching station. The fare is largely the same you'd find at any other Starbucks, plus such signature Studios treats as the mountainous chocolate-Butterfinger cupcake.

FULL-SERVICE RESTAURANTS:
Rated and Ranked

THE PROFILES IN THIS SECTION allow you to quickly check the cuisine, location, star rating, cost range, quality rating, and value rating of every full-service restaurant at Walt Disney World. Profiles are listed alphabetically by restaurant.

OVERALL RATING This encompasses the entire dining experience: style, service, ambience, and food quality. Five stars is the highest rating attainable. Four-star restaurants are above average; three-star restaurants serve good, though not necessarily memorable, meals. Two-star restaurants are mediocre, and one-star restaurants are below average. Our star ratings don't correspond to those awarded by AAA, Mobil, Zagat, or other restaurant reviewers.

COST RANGE This tells you how much you'll spend on a full-service entree. Appetizers, sides, soups/salads, desserts, drinks, and tips aren't included. Costs are categorized as **inexpensive** (less than $13), **moderate** ($13–$23), or **expensive** ($24 and up).

To give you a clearer idea of your options, we've also compiled the number of sit-down entrees available in each price range, as follows:

INEXPENSIVE: 600   **MODERATE:** 1,300   **EXPENSIVE:** 600

QUALITY RATING Food quality is rated from one to five stars, five being the best. The criteria are taste, freshness of ingredients, preparation, presentation, and creativity of food served. Price is not a consideration.

VALUE RATING If, on the other hand, you're looking for both quality *and* value, then you should check this rating, also expressed as stars.

PAYMENT All Disney restaurants take American Express, Carte Blanche, Diners Club, Discover, Japan Credit Bureau, MasterCard, and Visa.

Readers' Restaurant-Survey Responses

For each Disney World restaurant profiled, we include the results of the previous year's Reader-Survey Responses. Results are expressed as a percentage of readers who liked the restaurant well enough to eat there again (thumbs-up 👍) versus the percentage who didn't (thumbs-down 👎). (Readers tend to be less critical than we are, for what it's worth.) The average thumbs-up rating for all Disney full-service restaurants is 86%, with a standard deviation of 7%. If you'd like to participate in the ratings, go to **touringplans.com/walt-disney-world/survey.**

This edition, with more than 30 restaurants achieving scores of at least 90%, we decided that only those with ratings of 95% or above could be deemed substantially better than average. At the top, with 100%, is **Splitsville,** the bowling alley–cum–restaurant at Disney Springs. (We're pretty sure the draw is the concept rather than the food, which is just *meh.*) Tied for second, at 97%, are the Beach Club Resort's **Beaches & Cream Soda Shop,** serving made-to-order burgers and milkshakes in a 1950s-style diner, and **Cítrico's,** one of the Grand Floridian's fine-dining establishments. Coming in third is the Grand Floridian's **Victoria & Albert's**—the most exclusive restaurant in Walt Disney World—back up from 92% last year to 96% this year. Rounding out this elite group are the **Grand Floridian Cafe** and **Trail's End** at Fort Wilderness Resort & Campground, both at 95%.

The biggest movers this edition were **Monsieur Paul,** up from 64% to 93%, and **Turf Club Bar & Grill,** down from 92% to 63%—a respective gain and loss of 29 percentage points.

New this edition, **Trattoria Al Forno,** the new Italian restaurant at the BoardWalk, comes in at 82%. This is the third dining concept in this space in recent years, having replaced Kouzzina by Cat Cora and, before that, Spoodles. Also new is **The Boathouse,** a high-end waterfront seafood eatery at Disney Springs, but we didn't have survey results for it at press time.

The Boathouse will soon be joined in Disney Springs by **Blaze Fast-Fire'd Pizza,** serving artisanal pies; an East Coast outpost of **The Edison,** an industrial-themed restaurant and live-music venue (the original is in downtown L.A.); **Morimoto Asia,** a pan-Asian restaurant from chef Masaharu Morimoto, of *Iron Chef* fame; **Jock Lindsey's Hangar Bar,** an aviation-themed restaurant and watering hole named for Indiana Jones's pilot; and **STK Orlando,** part of a chain of high-concept steakhouses.

Remember that our survey results report overall reader satisfaction, not just food quality. Also, the star ratings represent the opinions of our research team and our dining insider—your experience may vary.

FULL-SERVICE RESTAURANT PROFILES

Akershus Royal Banquet Hall ★★

NORWEGIAN/BUFFET	EXPENSIVE	QUALITY ★★	VALUE ★★★★
READER-SURVEY RESPONSES	89% 👍 11% 👎	DISNEY DINING PLAN?	Yes

Norway, World Showcase, Epcot; ☎ 407-939-3463

Reservations Required for breakfast and recommended for lunch and dinner. A credit card is required to reserve breakfast and lunch. **Dining Plan credits** 1 per person, per meal. **When to go** Anytime. **Cost range** Breakfast $40 (child $24), lunch $42 (child $25), dinner $47 (child $25). **Service** ★★★★. **Friendliness** ★★★★. **Parking** Epcot lot. **Bar** Full service. **Wine selection** Good. **Dress** Casual. **Disabled access** Yes. **Customers** Theme park guests. **Character breakfast** Daily, 8–11:10 a.m. **Character lunch** Daily, 11:55 a.m.–3:30 p.m. **Character dinner** Daily, 4:55–8:35 p.m.

SETTING AND ATMOSPHERE The inside of Akershus looks like every child's vision of a fairy-tale castle: high ceilings, stone archways, sumptuous purple carpets, regal banners flying. What's mildly surprising, given the attention to authenticity elsewhere in Epcot, is that it doesn't look more like the real Akershus Castle in Oslo, which has plain wooden floors; flat, simple ceilings; and painted brick arches. Disney's version is almost as ungodly expensive as the real thing, though, and you're apt to hear *norsk* spoken by your servers. Close enough for us.

HOUSE SPECIALTIES Breakfast: smoked salmon, herring, mackerel, and *gjetost* (goat cheese). Lunch and dinner: *koldtbord* ("cold board" of meats, cheeses, seafood, and salads), oven-roasted chicken breast with potato dumplings, pan-seared salmon, house-made butternut-squash ravioli, and *kjøttkake* (ground-beef-and-pork dumplings served with mashed potatoes, seasonal vegetables, and lingonberry sauce). For kids: thinly sliced strip sirloin, pasta with grilled chicken, cheese pizza, salmon with steamed rice, and meatballs with mashed potatoes.

OTHER RECOMMENDATIONS Cold Carlsberg beer on tap.

SUMMARY AND COMMENTS Akershus has never been on our "you've just gotta try this" list, but if you have kids who love princesses, they won't be disappointed. There was a time when the buffet was noteworthy, but these days all the attention in the kitchen goes to feeding families fast. And as for the prices, you're paying for the privilege of princess face-time.

Continued on page 341

WALT DISNEY WORLD Restaurants by Cuisine

CUISINE	LOCATION	OVERALL RATING	COST	QUALITY RATING	VALUE RATING
AFRICAN					
JIKO—THE COOKING PLACE	Animal Kingdom Lodge	★★★★½	Exp	★★★★½	★★★½
BOMA—FLAVORS OF AFRICA	Animal Kingdom Lodge	★★★★	Exp	★★★★	★★★★½
TUSKER HOUSE RESTAURANT	Animal Kingdom	★★★	Mod	★★★	★★★
AMERICAN					
CALIFORNIA GRILL	Contemporary	★★★★★	Exp	★★★★★	★★★
THE HOLLYWOOD BROWN DERBY	DHS	★★★★	Exp	★★★★	★★★
ARTIST POINT	Wilderness Lodge	★★★½	Exp	★★★★	★★★
CAPE MAY CAFE	Beach Club	★★★½	Mod	★★★½	★★★★
WHISPERING CANYON CAFE	Wilderness Lodge	★★★	Mod	★★★½	★★★★
CAPTAIN'S GRILLE	Yacht Club	★★★	Mod	★★★½	★★★
THE CRYSTAL PALACE	Magic Kingdom	★★★	Mod	★★★½	★★★
HOUSE OF BLUES	Disney Springs	★★★	Mod	★★★½	★★★
50'S PRIME TIME CAFE	DHS	★★★	Mod	★★★	★★★
LIBERTY TREE TAVERN*	Magic Kingdom	★★★	Mod	★★★	★★★
TUSKER HOUSE RESTAURANT	Animal Kingdom	★★★	Mod	★★★	★★★
CINDERELLA'S ROYAL TABLE	Magic Kingdom	★★★	Exp	★★★	★★
OLIVIA'S CAFE	Old Key West	★★★	Mod	★★★	★★
T-REX	Disney Springs	★★★	Mod	★★	★★
THE WAVE . . . OF AMERICAN FLAVORS	Contemporary	★★★	Mod	★★	★★
CHEF MICKEY'S	Contemporary	★★½	Exp	★★★	★★★
ESPN CLUB	BoardWalk	★★½	Mod	★★★	★★★
ESPN WIDE WORLD OF SPORTS GRILL	ESPN Wide World of Sports Complex	★★½	Mod	★★★	★★★
HOLLYWOOD & VINE	DHS	★★½	Mod	★★★	★★★
1900 PARK FARE	Grand Floridian	★★½	Mod	★★★	★★★
BOATWRIGHT'S DINING HALL	Port Orleans	★★½	Mod	★★★	★★
GRAND FLORIDIAN CAFE	Grand Floridian	★★½	Mod	★★★	★★
BEACHES & CREAM SODA SHOP	Beach Club	★★½	Inexp	★★½	★★½
SPLITSVILLE	Disney Springs	★★½	Mod	★★½	★★
PLANET HOLLYWOOD	Disney Springs	★★½	Mod	★★	★★
RAINFOREST CAFE	Animal Kingdom and Disney Springs	★★½	Mod	★★	★★
GARDEN GROVE	Swan	★★	Mod	★★★	★★
WOLFGANG PUCK GRAND CAFE	Disney Springs	★★	Exp	★½	★½
LAS VENTANAS	Coronado Springs	★★	Mod	★★½	★★

Closed for renovations through November 2015

AMERICAN *(continued)*

SCI-FI DINE-IN THEATER RESTAURANT	DHS	★★	Mod	★★½	★★
GARDEN GRILL RESTAURANT	Epcot	★★	Exp	★★	★★★
BIG RIVER GRILLE & BREWING WORKS	BoardWalk	★★	Mod	★★	★★
THE FOUNTAIN	Dolphin	★★	Mod	★★	★★
THE PLAZA RESTAURANT	Magic Kingdom	★★	Mod	★★	★★
TURF CLUB BAR & GRILL	Saratoga Springs	★★	Mod	★★★	★★
TRAIL'S END RESTAURANT	Fort Wilderness Resort	★★	Mod	★★	★★
MAYA GRILL	Coronado Springs	★	Mod	★	★

BUFFET

BOMA— FLAVORS OF AFRICA	Animal Kingdom Lodge	★★★★	Exp	★★★★	★★★★½
CAPE MAY CAFE	Beach Club	★★★½	Mod	★★★½	★★★★
BIERGARTEN	Epcot	★★★½	Exp	★★★	★★★★
THE CRYSTAL PALACE	Magic Kingdom	★★★	Mod	★★★½	★★★
TUSKER HOUSE RESTAURANT	Animal Kingdom	★★★	Mod	★★★	★★★
CHEF MICKEY'S	Contemporary	★★½	Exp	★★★	★★★
HOLLYWOOD & VINE	DHS	★★½	Mod	★★★	★★★
1900 PARK FARE	Grand Floridian	★★½	Mod	★★★	★★★
GARDEN GROVE	Swan	★★	Mod	★★★	★★
AKERSHUS ROYAL BANQUET HALL	Epcot	★★	Exp	★★	★★★★
TRAIL'S END RESTAURANT	Fort Wilderness Resort	★★	Mod	★★	★★

CHINESE

NINE DRAGONS RESTAURANT	Epcot	★★★	Mod	★★★	★★

CUBAN

BONGOS CUBAN CAFE	Disney Springs	★★	Mod	★★	★★

ENGLISH

ROSE & CROWN DINING ROOM	Epcot	★★★	Mod	★★★½	★★

FRENCH

MONSIEUR PAUL	Epcot	★★★★	Exp	★★★★½	★★★
BE OUR GUEST RESTAURANT	Magic Kingdom	★★★★	Exp	★★★★	★★★★
LES CHEFS DE FRANCE	Epcot	★★★	Exp	★★★	★★★

GERMAN

BIERGARTEN	Epcot	★★	Exp	★★	★★★★

GLOBAL

PARADISO 37	Disney Springs	★★½	Inexp	★★★	★★★

GOURMET

VICTORIA & ALBERT'S	Grand Floridian	★★★★★	Exp	★★★★★	★★★★

WDW Restaurants by Cuisine *(cuisine)*

CUISINE	LOCATION	OVERALL RATING	COST	QUALITY RATING	VALUE RATING
INDIAN/AFRICAN					
SANAA	Animal Kingdom Villas–Kidani Village	★★★★	Exp	★★★★	★★★★
IRISH					
RAGLAN ROAD IRISH PUB & RESTAURANT	Disney Springs	★★★★	Mod	★★★½	★★★
ITALIAN					
TUTTO ITALIA RISTORANTE	Epcot	★★★★	Exp	★★★★	★★★
VIA NAPOLI	Epcot	★★★★	Mod	★★★½	★★★
TRATTORIA AL FORNO	BoardWalk	★★★½	Mod	★★★½	★★
RAVELLO	Four Seasons	★★★	Mod	★★★	★★★
IL MULINO NEW YORK TRATTORIA	Swan	★★★	Exp	★★★	★★
MAMA MELROSE'S RISTORANTE ITALIANO	DHS	★★½	Mod	★★★	★★
PORTOBELLO	Disney Springs	★★½	Exp	★★★	★★
TONY'S TOWN SQUARE RESTAURANT	Magic Kingdom	★★½	Mod	★★★	★★
JAPANESE/SUSHI					
KIMONOS	Swan	★★★★	Mod	★★★★½	★★★
TEPPAN EDO	Epcot	★★★½	Exp	★★★★	★★★
TOKYO DINING	Epcot	★★★	Mod	★★★★	★★★
BENIHANA	Hilton	★★★	Exp	★★★½	★★★
MEDITERRANEAN					
CÍTRICOS	Grand Floridian	★★★½	Exp	★★★★½	★★★
FRESH MEDITERRANEAN MARKET	Dolphin	★★½	Mod	★★½	★★
MEXICAN					
LA HACIENDA DE SAN ANGEL	Epcot	★★★	Exp	★★★½	★★½
SAN ANGEL INN RESTAURANTE	Epcot	★★★	Exp	★★★	★★
MAYA GRILL	Coronado Springs	★	Exp	★	★
MOROCCAN					
SPICE ROAD TABLE	Epcot	★★★½	Mod	★★★★	★★★
RESTAURANT MARRAKESH	Epcot	★★	Mod	★★½	★★
NORWEGIAN					
AKERSHUS ROYAL BANQUET HALL	Epcot	★★	Exp	★★	★★★★
POLYNESIAN/PAN-ASIAN					
'OHANA	Polynesian Village	★★★	Mod	★★★½	★★★
KONA CAFE	Polynesian Village	★★★	Mod	★★★	★★★★

TRADER SAM'S GROG GROTTO	Polynesian Village	★★★	Mod	★★★	★★★
YAK & YETI RESTAURANT	Animal Kingdom	★★	Exp	★★½	★★
SEAFOOD					
NARCOOSSEE'S	Grand Floridian	★★★★½	Exp	★★★½	★★
FLYING FISH CAFE	BoardWalk	★★★★	Exp	★★★★	★★★
ARTIST POINT	Wilderness Lodge	★★★½	Exp	★★★★	★★★
TODD ENGLISH'S BLUEZOO	Dolphin	★★★	Exp	★★★★	★★
THE BOATHOUSE	Disney Springs	★★★	Exp	★★★	★★½
FULTON'S CRAB HOUSE	Disney Springs	★★½	Exp	★★½	★★
CORAL REEF RESTAURANT	Epcot	★★½	Exp	★★	★★
SHUTTERS AT OLD PORT ROYALE	Caribbean Beach	★★	Mod	★★½	★★
STEAK					
CAPA	Four Seasons	★★★★	Exp	★★★★	★★★
SHULA'S STEAK HOUSE	Dolphin	★★★★	Exp	★★★★	★★
LE CELLIER STEAKHOUSE	Epcot	★★★½	Exp	★★★½	★★★
YACHTSMAN STEAKHOUSE	Yacht Club	★★★	Exp	★★★½	★★
SHUTTERS AT OLD PORT ROYALE	Caribbean Beach	★★	Mod	★★½	★★

Continued from page 337

Artist Point ★★★½

AMERICAN	EXPENSIVE	QUALITY ★★★★	VALUE ★★★
READER-SURVEY RESPONSES 93% 👍	7% 👎	DISNEY DINING PLAN? Yes	

Wilderness Lodge & Villas; ☎ 407-824-3200

Reservations Required. **Dining Plan credits** 2 per person, per meal. **When to go** Anytime. **Cost range** $29–$49 (child $8–$13). **Service** ★★★★★. **Friendliness** ★★★★★. **Parking** Hotel lot. **Bar** Full service. **Wine selection** All wines from the Pacific Northwest. **Dress** Dressy casual. **Disabled access** Yes. **Customers** Hotel guests, locals. **Dinner** Daily, 5:30–9:30 p.m.

SETTING AND ATMOSPHERE Understated Arts and Crafts decor, reminiscent of the grand national-park lodges of the West: massive landscape paintings, heavy wooden tables, cast-iron chandeliers. Get a table by the window and you might see the erupting geyser near the waterfront.

HOUSE SPECIALTIES The smoky portobello soup, a worthy starter, never leaves the menu. Ditto the cedar-plank salmon and kettle-steamed mussels.

OTHER RECOMMENDATIONS Grilled buffalo strip steak, roasted Berkshire pork loin, pan-seared fish, seasonal berry cobbler. For kids, baked salmon, grilled chicken, and pasta.

SUMMARY AND COMMENTS Don't be put off by the cavernous dining room— the food and friendly service warm up the place.

Beaches & Cream Soda Shop ★★½

AMERICAN	INEXPENSIVE	QUALITY ★★½	VALUE ★★½
READER-SURVEY RESPONSES 97% 👍	3% 👎	DISNEY DINING PLAN? Yes	

Beach Club Resort; ☎ 407-934-8000

Reservations Recommended. **Dining Plan credits** 1 per person, per meal. **When to go** Anytime. **Cost range** $8–$16.50. **Service** ★★★. **Friendliness** ★★★★. **Parking** Hotel lot. **Bar** Beer only. **Wine selection** None. **Dress** Casual. **Disabled access** Yes. **Customers** Resort guests. **Lunch and dinner** Daily, 11 a.m.–11 p.m.

SETTING AND ATMOSPHERE Casual eats and retro soda-fountain decor. Guests in bathing suits and flip-flops queue up for hearty burgers, sandwiches (such as pork-belly Cuban, seared salmon, or grilled chicken), and piles of hot fries.

HOUSE SPECIALTIES Burgers (singles and doubles) and fries; giant hot dogs; hand-scooped ice cream including the gargantuan $29 Kitchen Sink dessert, with five flavors of ice cream smothered in toppings.

OTHER RECOMMENDATIONS Chef salad, roasted turkey on brioche, vegetarian falafel, root beer float.

SUMMARY AND COMMENTS Beaches & Cream exists mainly to give guests an excuse to eat all the things they're not supposed to. But hey, it's vacation—indulge! Seating is scarce during peak hours.

Benihana ★★★

JAPANESE	EXPENSIVE	QUALITY ★★★½	VALUE ★★★
READER-SURVEY RESPONSES	Not enough to rate	DISNEY DINING PLAN?	No

Hilton in the Walt Disney World Resort, Downtown Disney Resort Area; ☎ 407-827-4865

Reservations Recommended. **When to go** Anytime. **Cost range** $19–$45 (child $8.50–$10.50). **Service** ★★★★★. **Friendliness** ★★★★★. **Parking** Hotel lot. **Bar** Full service. **Wine selection** Good. **Dress** Casual. **Disabled access** Yes. **Customers** Hotel guests, some locals. **Dinner** Monday–Thursday, 4–10 p.m.; Friday–Sunday, 2–10 p.m.

SETTING AND ATMOSPHERE Find your spot around the large teppanyaki tables with built-in grills, and get ready for the Japanese chefs' antics. Lighting is low and focused on the stage: the chef's grill.

HOUSE SPECIALTIES Steak, chicken, seafood, and hibachi vegetables cooked as you watch. Upgrade to filet mignon and lobster tails.

OTHER RECOMMENDATIONS Spicy tofu steak.

ENTERTAINMENT AND AMENITIES Dinner is the show at this restaurant, where the chefs do a lot of noisy chopping and grilling. Or opt for the sushi lounge, with happy hour prices Monday–Thursday, 4:30–7 p.m.

SUMMARY AND COMMENTS Benihana never changes, and that's what we like about it. Put on the red chef's toque and get in the spirit. If you're looking for a nice, quiet dinner, this isn't it: The place is noisy, and you'll be sharing a table for eight.

Be Our Guest Restaurant ★★★★

FRENCH/AMERICAN	EXPENSIVE	QUALITY ★★★★	VALUE ★★★★
READER-SURVEY RESPONSES	91% 👍 9% 👎	DISNEY DINING PLAN?	Yes

Fantasyland, Magic Kingdom; ☎ 407-939-3463

Reservations Accepted. **Dining Plan credits** 1 per person, per meal (Quick-Service credits for breakfast and lunch, Table-Service credit for dinner). **When to go** Breakfast, lunch, or dinner. **Cost range** Breakfast, $20, Lunch $9.50–$14 (child $6.99–$8.50), dinner $18.50–$33.50 (child $9–$11). **Service** ★★★★. **Friendliness** ★★★★. **Parking** Magic Kingdom lot. **Bar** Wine and beer only. **Wine selection** Solid wine list that's mostly French to match the restaurant's theming—from sparkling starters to a sweet Sauternes. A handful of popular

California vintages are on the list. **Dress** Casual. **Disabled access** Yes. **Customers** Magic Kingdom guests. **Breakfast** Daily, 8–10 a.m. **Lunch** Daily, 10:30 a.m.–2:30 p.m. **Dinner** Daily, 4–9:30 p.m.

SETTING AND ATMOSPHERE Beast's Castle is so popular that they've added quick-service breakfast from 8 to 10 a.m., in one of three themed rooms inspired by *Beauty and the Beast:* the Grand Ballroom, the mysterious West Wing, and the pretty Rose Gallery. (Dinner reservations are still the most difficult to snag.) The rooms fill up fast, with a noise level to match the hordes (550 seats). The lights are dimmed at dinner, which offers table service and a tad more serenity. And grown-ups love a beverage menu that includes wine and beer. (See page 326 for counter-service profile.)

HOUSE SPECIALTIES Pan-seared salmon on leek fondue, New York strip.

OTHER RECOMMENDATIONS Grilled strip steak with *pommes frites.* For dessert, cupcakes and a no-sugar-added lemon-raspberry fruit puff.

SUMMARY AND COMMENTS Be Our Guest does a fine job of feeding the masses. If you already have a breakfast or lunch reservation, you can preorder online up to 30 days in advance. For a slightly less hectic experience, choose a table in the West Wing, which is smaller, darker, and a little quieter.

Biergarten ★★

GERMAN	EXPENSIVE		QUALITY ★★		VALUE ★★★★
READER-SURVEY RESPONSES	87% 👍	13% 👎	DISNEY DINING PLAN? Yes		

Germany, World Showcase, Epcot; ☎ 407-939-3463

Reservations Accepted. **Dining Plan credits** 1 per person, per meal. **When to go** Lunch or dinner. **Cost range** Lunch $23 (child $13), dinner $38 (child $18). **Service** ★★★★. **Friendliness** ★★★★. **Parking** Epcot lot. **Bar** Full service. **Wine selection** German. **Dress** Casual. **Disabled access** Yes. **Customers** Theme park guests. **Lunch** Daily, noon–3:45 p.m. **Dinner** Daily, 4 p.m.–park closing.

SETTING AND ATMOSPHERE Biergarten is a hefty German buffet set inside a nighttime Teutonic town square. You're seated at long tables lined up in rows, emanating like the moon's rays, from a central dance floor and stage. A lederhosen-clad oompah band plays and encourages diners to sing and dance. (If you do, mercifully low light levels mean your friends' cell phone videos can't positively ID you.) Just as in the real Germany, table space is assigned community-style, so you may be seated with other families.

HOUSE SPECIALTIES Beet salad, various sausages, homemade spaetzle with gravy, *nudelgratin* (baked macaroni with cheese custard), and sauerbraten. There's also carved-to-order pork roast with German mustard and breaded pork schnitzel.

OTHER RECOMMENDATIONS *Rouladen* (thinly sliced beef rolled and stuffed with onions) braised red cabbage, potato dumplings (dinner only), and German beer.

ENTERTAINMENT AND AMENITIES Oompah band and German dancers perform after 1:15 p.m.

SUMMARY AND COMMENTS The quality of the food continues to dip, but the lively 25-minute dinner show (one every hour) and noisy dining room are part of the fun, especially for families.

Big River Grille & Brewing Works ★★

AMERICAN	MODERATE		QUALITY ★★		VALUE ★★
READER-SURVEY RESPONSES	65% 👍	35% 👎	DISNEY DINING PLAN? Yes		

BoardWalk; ☎ 407-560-0253

Reservations Not accepted. **Dining Plan credits** 1 per person, per meal. **When to go** Anytime. **Cost range** $10.50–$26.50. **Service** ★★★. **Friendliness** ★★★★. **Parking** BoardWalk lot. **Bar** Full service. **Wine selection** Minimal. **Dress** Casual. **Disabled access** Yes. **Customers** Tourists. **Lunch and dinner** Sunday–Thursday, 11 a.m.–11 p.m., Friday and Saturday until midnight.

SETTING AND ATMOSPHERE Situated for prime people-watching on Disney's BoardWalk, the outdoor tables fill up fast on a pretty day. A minimalist interior focuses on the craft beer that is made on the premises, with glass walls to see the process as ales and lagers are microbrewed. The place is small—it seems like the huge copper brewing tanks take up more room than that allotted to the diners.

HOUSE SPECIALTIES Beer-cheese soup, flame-grilled meat loaf.

SUMMARY AND COMMENTS The food is just OK, but with the popularity of craft beer, Big River is a hot spot on the BoardWalk. Their house brews include a light lager, a robust ale, and seasonal choices. A good late-night-dining choice, with everything from salads and sandwiches to rib-eye steak.

The Boathouse ★★★

SEAFOOD	EXPENSIVE	QUALITY ★★★	VALUE ★★½
READER-SURVEY RESPONSES	Too new to rate	DISNEY DINING PLAN?	Yes

The Landing, Disney Springs; ☎ 407-939-3463

Reservations Accepted. **Dining Plan credits** 2 per person, per meal. **When to go** Lunch or dinner. **Cost range** $17–$135 (child $10). **Service** ★★★. **Friendliness** ★★★★. **Parking** Lot and garage at Disney Springs. **Bar** Full service. **Wine selection** Good. **Dress** Casual. **Disabled access** Yes. **Customers** Locals and Disney guests. **Lunch and dinner** Daily, 11 a.m.–11 p.m.

SETTING AND ATMOSPHERE The first things you notice about The Boathouse, on the waterfront at Disney Springs, are the vintage Amphicars (amphibious autos produced in the 1960s and completely restored) and the Italian water taxis floating next to the front door—a multimillion-dollar fleet of 19 rare boats from private collectors, museums, and boat shows around the world. The big, airy restaurant seats up to 600 (200 outdoors) in nautically themed dining rooms (two private). The three bars include one built over the water and attached to more than 300 feet of boardwalk and docks.

HOUSE SPECIALTIES Seafood of every sort: a raw bar with three to five varieties of fresh oysters and wild-caught Baja shrimp; fish and shellfish, including Florida seasonal varieties; jumbo lump crab cake; lobster; Florida-farmed caviar; dry-aged long-bone rib chop ($115 for two); filet mignon topped with jumbo lump crab; baked Alaska.

SUMMARY AND COMMENTS Expensive, but the servings are big enough to share, and the food is fresh—even the fries are hand-cut. While seafood is the star, the steaks are top-notch as well. Hop a ride in an Amphicar ($125) or a water taxi ($75 adults, $50 kids) before or after your meal.

Boatwright's Dining Hall ★★½

AMERICAN/CAJUN	MODERATE	QUALITY ★★★	VALUE ★★
READER-SURVEY RESPONSES	84% 👍 16% 👎	DISNEY DINING PLAN?	Yes

Port Orleans Resort Riverside; ☎ 407-939-3463

Reservations Accepted. **Dining Plan credits** 1 per person, per meal. **When to go** Early evening. **Cost range** Dinner $17–$34 (child $8.59). **Service** ★★★. **Friendliness** ★★★★★. **Parking** Hotel lot. **Bar** Full service. **Wine selection** Fair. **Dress** Casual. **Disabled access** Yes. **Customers** Hotel guests. **Dinner** Daily, 5–10 p.m.

SETTING AND ATMOSPHERE This cavernous, casual dining room is meant to serve the masses. Wooden tables are set with a boatwright's tool kit that contains condiments, and a giant skeleton of a riverboat completes the theme.

HOUSE SPECIALTIES Sweet tea–brined pork chop, jambalaya with chicken and andouille sausage.

OTHER RECOMMENDATIONS Buttermilk-marinated crispy chicken breast, prime rib, blackened sustainable fish, bananas Foster angel-food cake.

SUMMARY AND COMMENTS With seating for 200, Boatwright's covers all the bases: steaks, chops, ribs, pasta, and vegetarian, with a little Cajun flair (crawfish bites, fried oysters, barbecued shrimp) thrown in. Because it's the only table-service restaurant in Port Orleans, there can be waits, so settle in with an Abita beer, brewed in small batches near New Orleans.

Boma—Flavors of Africa ★★★★

AFRICAN	EXPENSIVE	QUALITY ★★★★	VALUE ★★★★½
READER-SURVEY RESPONSES	92% 👍 8% 👎	DISNEY DINING PLAN?	Yes

Animal Kingdom Lodge & Villas–Jambo House; ☎ 407-938-3000

Reservations Recommended for dinner. **Dining Plan credits** 1 per person, per meal. **When to go** Anytime. **Cost range** Breakfast $20 (child $12), dinner $38 (child $18). **Service** ★★★★. **Friendliness** ★★★★. **Parking** Valet ($20) or hotel lot. **Bar** Full service. **Wine selection** All South African. **Dress** Casual. **Disabled access** Yes. **Customers** Hotel guests. **Breakfast** Daily, 7:30–11 a.m. **Dinner** Daily, 4:30–10 p.m.

SETTING AND ATMOSPHERE Boma's big, open floor allows a lot of tables to be packed in, making it somewhat cramped and noisy. That's good for families with small children, though: A crying baby (or adult) won't get even a glance from anyone nearby. Theming includes concrete floors colored to look like mud, faux-bamboo railings, and patterned sheets decorating the ceiling. The quality of Boma's long buffet encourages diners to roam and graze, just like the animals you'll see wandering outside.

HOUSE SPECIALTIES Pecan-caramel bread pudding at breakfast; papaya, avocado, and grapefruit salad; lamb curry; beef bobotie; house-made soups.

OTHER RECOMMENDATIONS Hummus and breads; roasted salmon, pork, chicken, and beef; Zebra Dome dessert.

SUMMARY AND COMMENTS Boma is a favorite of both locals and visitors because it's all-you-care-to-eat and the food is well prepared. If you like a major bang for your buck, try Boma. And make a reservation.

Bongos Cuban Cafe ★★

CUBAN	MODERATE	QUALITY ★★	VALUE ★★
READER-SURVEY RESPONSES	65% 👍 35% 👎	DISNEY DINING PLAN?	Yes

Disney Springs West Side; ☎ 407-828-0999

Reservations Recommended. **Dining Plan credits** 1 per person, per meal. **When to go** Anytime. **Cost range** $10–$45 (child $6–$8). **Service** ★★★★. **Friendliness** ★★★★. **Parking** Disney Springs lot. **Bar** Full service. **Wine selection** Moderate. **Dress** Casual. **Disabled access** Elevator to second level. **Customers** Fans of Cuban culture and cuisine; Disney guests. **Lunch and dinner** Sunday–Thursday, 11 a.m.–11 p.m., Friday and Saturday until midnight.

SETTING AND ATMOSPHERE Bongos is one of the Downtown Disney originals that remains untouched during the big makeover to Disney Springs. The three-story pineapple icon and beautiful tropical decor—banana-leaf roof, banana-leaf ceiling fans, and palm tree–shaped columns—take diners on a trip to Havana. Hand-painted murals and mosaics lend an artistic air, and an open wraparound porch provides pleasant outdoor dining.

HOUSE SPECIALTIES Cuban sandwich, Cuban-style skirt steak, and *ropa vieja* (shredded beef in tomato sauce).

ENTERTAINMENT AND AMENITIES Latin music.

SUMMARY AND COMMENTS Gloria Estefan and her husband-producer, Emilio, created this large restaurant that marries salsa music with Cuban cuisine. Start with a mojito, then try a classic Cuban dish—it may not be as authentic as Miami's Cuban restaurants, but if you're craving hearty dishes with beans, rice, fried sweet plantains, roast chicken or pork, or slow-cooked beef, Bongos fills the bill.

California Grill ★★★★★

AMERICAN	EXPENSIVE	QUALITY ★★★★★	VALUE ★★★
READER-SURVEY RESPONSES	92% 👍 8% 👎	DISNEY DINING PLAN? Yes	

Contemporary Resort; ☎ 407-939-3463

Reservations Required. **Dining Plan credits** 2 per person, per meal. **When to go** During evening fireworks. **Cost range** $32–$49 (child $9–$18). **Service** ★★★★★. **Friendliness** ★★★★★. **Parking** Valet ($20) or hotel lot. **Bar** Full service. **Wine selection** Fantastic. **Dress** Dressy casual. **Disabled access** Yes. **Customers** Hotel guests and locals. **Dinner** Daily, 5–10 p.m.

SETTING AND ATMOSPHERE The beautiful California Grill remains one of the top choices for Disney dining, both for its remarkable view from the 15th floor of the Contemporary Resort and its bustling open kitchen, which turns out spectacular fare. It can be crowded and noisy, filled with families who want a view of the Magic Kingdom fireworks, so book a table early or late for a somewhat quieter experience. A show-stopping wine display comprises 1,600 bottles in a climate-controlled case just off the elevator. If you don't have a reservation, ask for a seat at the sushi bar or in the lounge, where you can order appetizers (but not entrees).

HOUSE SPECIALTIES Sushi, three-meat signature meatballs, Sonoma goat cheese ravioli; crispy rock-shrimp salad, pork two ways (grilled tenderloin and lacquered pork belly), oak-fired filet of beef, chocolate pudding cake. Outstanding wine list and craft cocktails.

ENTERTAINMENT AND AMENITIES Magic Kingdom fireworks are the star of the show—but only guests with reservations may watch from the 15th floor.

SUMMARY AND COMMENTS In spite of the noise, California Grill is one of Walt Disney World's top dining experiences.

Capa ★★★★

STEAK	EXPENSIVE	QUALITY ★★★★	VALUE ★★★
READER-SURVEY RESPONSES	Too new to rate	DISNEY DINING PLAN? No	

Four Seasons Resort Orlando at Walt Disney World; ☎ 407-313-7777

Reservations Required. **When to go** Dinner. **Cost range** $32–$110. **Service** ★★★★. **Friendliness** ★★★. **Parking** Lot at Four Seasons Resort; valet. **Bar** Full service. **Wine selection** Excellent. **Dress** Upscale resort. **Disabled access** Yes. **Customers** Locals and Disney guests. **Dinner** Daily, 5–11 p.m.

SETTING AND ATMOSPHERE Even getting to the Four Seasons Resort is an interesting challenge—you must go through the gates at Golden Oak (Disney's tony private residential community) to reach the resort, and it's worth the trip. Head to the 17th-floor rooftop bar and dining room, which has a casual style and fabulous views of the fireworks at the Magic Kingdom, Epcot, and Disney's Hollywood Studios from the expansive open-air patio. Don't look for white linens, but rather clean lines and stark elegance: gorgeous red art on the walls, oversize chairs, and cozy banquettes.

HOUSE SPECIALTIES Spanish-style tapas, including Ibérico and Serrano hams; small bites such as deviled eggs, shrimp, pork belly, and salt cod; larger plates, including grilled octopus, Wagyu beef, veal cheeks, and foie gras; entrees including Arctic char, duck, and lobster; and, from the grill, fish, lamb, and big, juicy steaks including a porterhouse for two, plus sauces to accompany. The wine list offers more than 50 selections from Spain, along with house-made sangria. End with fancy churros and chocolate.

SUMMARY AND COMMENTS Capa vies with California Grill for the most fabulous views at Disney World. If you're not hungry for steak, tapas and cocktails are the most fun and affordable way to enjoy this stunning dining room. We've heard it eventually may be closed to non–resort guests, so grab a seat on the 1,200-square-foot patio and enjoy the views while you can.

Cape May Cafe ★★★½

AMERICAN/BUFFET	MODERATE	QUALITY ★★★½	VALUE ★★★★
READER-SURVEY RESPONSES	94% 👍	6% 👎	DISNEY DINING PLAN? Yes

Beach Club Resort; ☎ 407-934-3358

Reservations Recommended. **Dining Plan credits** 1 per person, per meal. **When to go** Anytime. **Cost range** Breakfast $29 (child $16), dinner $38 (child $18). **Service** ★★★★★. **Friendliness** ★★★★★. **Parking** Hotel lot. **Bar** Full service. **Wine selection** Limited. **Dress** Casual. **Disabled access** Yes. **Customers** Epcot and hotel guests. **Breakfast** Daily, 7:30–11 a.m. **Dinner** Daily, 5–10 p.m.

SETTING AND ATMOSPHERE Just off the lobby at the Beach Club, Cape May Cafe features nautical New England decor in two dining rooms and lots of comfortable seating.

HOUSE SPECIALTIES The buffet includes shrimp, both peel-and-eat and fried; steamed mussels; calamari and clams (each offered on different days); salmon; chicken; corn on the cob; lots of salads; and a good dessert bar. The kids' bar includes chicken nuggets and mac and cheese.

OTHER RECOMMENDATIONS The tart Key lime pie from the dessert bar.

ENTERTAINMENT AND AMENITIES Character breakfast with Goofy, Minnie, and Chip 'n' Dale.

SUMMARY AND COMMENTS Cape May's all-you-can-eat menu isn't terribly exciting, but you can get your money's worth in decent seafood. Advance Reservations are recommended. Because Cape May is within easy walking distance of the World Showcase entrance to Epcot, it's a convenient and affordable place to dine before *IllumiNations*.

Captain's Grille ★★★

AMERICAN	MODERATE	QUALITY ★★★½	VALUE ★★★
READER-SURVEY RESPONSES	84% 👍	16% 👎	DISNEY DINING PLAN? Yes

Yacht Club Resort; ☎ 407-939-3463

Reservations Accepted. **Dining Plan credits** 1 per person, per meal. **When to go** Breakfast or lunch. **Cost range** Breakfast buffet $18.99, lunch $14–$30 (child $8.59), dinner $16–$33 (child $8.59). **Service** ★★★★★. **Friendliness** ★★★★★. **Parking** Hotel lot. **Bar** Full service. **Wine selection** Good. **Dress** Casual. **Disabled access** Yes. **Customers** Hotel guests. **Breakfast** Daily, 7:30–11:25 a.m. **Lunch** Daily, 11:30 a.m.–2 p.m. **Dinner** Daily, 5–9 p.m.

SETTING AND ATMOSPHERE Just off the lobby and open for breakfast, lunch, and dinner, Captain's Grille's large, open dining room has a casual feel with nautical touches to match the hotel's decor. A favorite of Disney cast members for lunch (because there's always a table available and you don't need reservations), the kitchen turns out better-than-average fare.

HOUSE SPECIALTIES Breakfast features a buffet or an à la carte menu, with such selections as a butter-poached lobster omelet and lemon-ricotta hot cakes. Lunch includes New England lobster sliders, burgers, fish and chips, and crab cakes (get a side order of hand-cut salt-and-vinegar fries). Dinner features grilled New York strip, Cabernet-braised short ribs, rosemary-brined pork tenderloin, seasonal fish, and snow crab legs.

SUMMARY AND COMMENTS If you want a quiet break from Epcot, Captain's Grille is an ideal spot that's a short walk from the World Showcase entrance. Service can be a little slow, but the food is well prepared.

Le Cellier Steakhouse ★★★½

STEAK	EXPENSIVE	QUALITY ★★★½	VALUE ★★★
READER-SURVEY RESPONSES	90% 👍 10% 👎	DISNEY DINING PLAN? Yes	

Canada, World Showcase, Epcot; ☎ 407-939-3463

Reservations Required. **Dining Plan credits** 2 per person, per meal. **When to go** Before 6 p.m. **Cost range** Lunch and dinner $29–$50 (child $8–$12). **Service** ★★★★. **Friendliness** ★★★★★. **Parking** Epcot lot. **Bar** Full bar. **Wine selection** Canadian wines are featured. **Dress** Casual. **Disabled access** Yes. **Customers** Theme park guests. **Lunch** Daily, 11:30 a.m.–3 p.m. **Dinner** Daily, 4–8:50 p.m.

SETTING AND ATMOSPHERE Walk past the Canada Pavilion's pretty gardens into this small, darkened dining room, intended to evoke the look and feel of a wine cellar. Given the escalated prices, it doesn't feel upscale, with heavy wooden tables and no linens, but the crowd doesn't seem to mind—the steaks make up for the ambience. Service is "cheerful Canadian," meaning servers will apologize to *you* if you spill something on *them.*

HOUSE SPECIALTIES Mushroom filet mignon, Canadian Cheddar cheese soup.

OTHER RECOMMENDATIONS Dry-aged boneless rib eye, braised lamb shank, pan-seared flounder, sumac-crusted salmon. Excellent wine selection.

SUMMARY AND COMMENTS They've scaled back the prices a bit—the rib eye Is down to $50!—and the menu is the same for lunch and dinner, so go anytime you can snag a reservation (more about that on page 302). If you're looking for a good steak in a theme park setting, Le Cellier is the place.

Chef Mickey's ★★½

AMERICAN/BUFFET	EXPENSIVE	QUALITY ★★★	VALUE ★★★
READER-SURVEY RESPONSES	87% 👍 13% 👎	DISNEY DINING PLAN? Yes	

Contemporary Resort; ☎ 407-939-3463

Reservations Required. **Dining Plan credits** 1 per person, per meal. **When to go** Early evening. **Cost range** Breakfast and brunch $38 (child $20), dinner $47 (child $24). **Service** ★★★★. **Friendliness** ★★★★★. **Parking** Valet ($20) or hotel lot. **Bar** Full service. **Wine selection** Fair. **Dress** Casual. **Disabled access** Yes. **Customers** Theme park guests. **Character breakfast** Daily, 7–11:30 a.m. **Character brunch** Daily, 11:30 a.m.–2:30 p.m. **Character dinner** Daily, 5–9:30 p.m.

SETTING AND ATMOSPHERE Can we say *madhouse*? This big, open dining room with the monorail whizzing by overhead is a cacophony of children's and parents' voices. The food is secondary—everyone's here to meet Mickey and his pals (usually Goofy, Minnie, Donald and Pluto), who promise a stop at every single table. The buffet circles the center of the room.

HOUSE SPECIALTIES Breakfast: pancakes, carved ham, pastries. Brunch: breakfast faves (Mickey waffles, etc.), plus lunch choices such as barbecued ribs and baked salmon. Dinner: carved beef and turkey, sundae bar.

OTHER RECOMMENDATIONS Salads and sushi. And Mom and Dad can have a cocktail for dinner—even tequila on the rocks!

ENTERTAINMENT AND AMENITIES Character visits.

SUMMARY AND COMMENTS The food takes a backseat to the characters, but you won't leave hungry, and the kids' buffet (mac and cheese, mini-corn dogs) will satisfy picky eaters. Best of all, nobody cares if the kids are loud.

Les Chefs de France ★★★

FRENCH	EXPENSIVE	QUALITY ★★★	VALUE ★★★
READER-SURVEY RESPONSES 82% 👍	18% 👎	DISNEY DINING PLAN? Yes	

France, World Showcase, Epcot; ☎ 407-939-3463

Reservations Recommended. **Dining Plan credits** 1 per person, per meal. **When to go** Anytime. **Cost range** Lunch $15–$29 (child $7–$8), dinner $19–$36 (child $7–$8). **Service** ★★★★★. **Friendliness** ★★★★★. **Parking** Epcot lot. **Bar** Beer. **Wine selection** Very good. **Dress** Casual. **Disabled access** Yes. **Customers** Theme park guests. **Lunch** Daily, noon–3 p.m. **Dinner** Daily, 5–9 p.m.

SETTING AND ATMOSPHERE It's like stepping into a busy Parisian bistro, and with young French students in the States for the Disney College Program making up much of the waitstaff, the sound of French feels very Continental. The smells are delicious, with the on-site bakery's baguettes on every table. White tablecloths and padded banquettes accentuate the classic bistro decor of the main dining room, where window tables make for fun people-watching on the World Showcase Promenade.

HOUSE SPECIALTIES Dishes inspired by the three great French chefs for whom the restaurant is named: Paul Bocuse, the late Gaston Lenôtre, and Roger Vergé. At lunch, try the prix fixe bowl of onion soup topped with Gruyère and a *croque monsieur* for the classic French experience; at dinner, bouillabaisse, duck breast with cherries, or grilled tenderloin of beef.

OTHER RECOMMENDATIONS Baked goat cheese salad; short ribs braised in Cabernet; crème brûlée.

SUMMARY AND COMMENTS Here's your chance to eat at a restaurant created by three of France's best chefs. Jerome Bocuse, the son of Paul Bocuse, runs the restaurant with executive chef Bruno Vrignon, who trained in Lyon with Bocuse. If you're on a budget, go at lunch: Many dinner entrees are available midday at reduced prices.

Cinderella's Royal Table ★★★

AMERICAN	EXPENSIVE	QUALITY ★★★	VALUE ★★
READER-SURVEY RESPONSES 92% 👍	8% 👎	DISNEY DINING PLAN? Yes	

Cinderella Castle, Fantasyland, Magic Kingdom; ☎ 407-939-3463

Reservations Required; credit card required to reserve; must prepay in full. **Dining Plan credits** 2 per person, per meal. **When to go** Early. **Cost range** Character breakfast, $58 adults, $35 children; character lunch, $61 adults, $38 children; character dinner, $73 adults, $43 children. **Service** ★★★★. **Friendliness** ★★★★. **Parking** Magic Kingdom lot. **Bar** No alcohol served. **Dress** Casual. **Disabled access** Limited. **Customers** Theme park guests. **Character breakfast** Daily, 8:05–10:40 a.m. **Character lunch** Daily, 11:45 a.m.–2:40 p.m. **Character dinner** Daily, 3:50–10 p.m.

SETTING AND ATMOSPHERE A recent spiffing-up of the medieval banquet hall included new carpet and new costumes for the servers, but most guests won't recognize the difference. It's still the top spot for dining in the Disney theme parks, and while the food is better than average, it's more about experiencing a character meal on the second floor of Cinderella Castle.

HOUSE SPECIALTIES All meals are fixed-price character affairs, and the kitchen is upping its game—at breakfast there's banana-bread French toast; crepes with spinach, sauteed lobster, and blue crab, topped with a poached egg and Hollandaise; or a healthy plate with scrambled egg whites, hot 10-grain cereal, Greek yogurt, house-made granola, walnut-sunflower bread, and fresh fruit. At lunch you'll find pan-seared cod, gnocchi or farro with seasonal vegetables, and pork on ciabatta bread. Dinner fare may include slow-roasted pork loin, grilled swordish, tomato risotto, flourless chocolate cake, or espresso cheesecake.

ENTERTAINMENT AND AMENITIES Assorted princesses attend all three meals.

SUMMARY AND COMMENTS It isn't cheap to eat here, but no matter—families can't seem to get enough of this "Disney magic." For more on reserving a spot at the Royal Table (and the travails thereof), see page 302.

Cítricos ★★★½

MEDITERRANEAN	EXPENSIVE	QUALITY ★★★★½	VALUE ★★★
READER-SURVEY RESPONSES	97% 👍	3% 👎	DISNEY DINING PLAN? Yes

Grand Floridian Resort & Spa; ☎ 407-939-7429

Reservations Required; credit card required to reserve the Chef's Domain. **Dining Plan credits** 2 per person, per meal. **When to go** Anytime. **Cost range** $33–$49 (child $9–$17). Chef's Domain: $800 (!) minimum, minus tax and tips. **Service** ★★★★★. **Friendliness** ★★★★★. **Parking** Valet ($20); self-parking is deceptively far away. **Bar** Full service. **Wine selection** Very good. **Dress** Dressy casual. **Disabled access** Yes. **Customers** Hotel guests and locals. **Dinner** Daily, 5:30–10 p.m.

SETTING AND ATMOSPHERE The golds and yellows of the Mediterranean color this stylish dining room on the second floor of the Grand Floridian. Diners often find chef Phil Ponticelli working his culinary magic in the full-view show kitchen.

HOUSE SPECIALTIES Sautéed Florida rock shrimp with lemon, feta, tomatoes, and white wine; crispy pan-fried veal chop; oak-grilled seasonal fish.

OTHER RECOMMENDATIONS Charcuterie platter, oak-grilled filet mignon, warm chocolate-banana torte.

SUMMARY AND COMMENTS Ponticelli appreciates local and seasonal produce and seafood, so the menu always has a few delicious surprises based on what's freshest. If you're flush with cash, reserve the Chef's Domain, a private room for up to 12 guests where Ponticelli creates a special menu.

Coral Reef Restaurant ★★½

SEAFOOD	EXPENSIVE	QUALITY ★★	VALUE ★★
READER-SURVEY RESPONSES	73% 👍	27% 👎	DISNEY DINING PLAN? Yes

The Seas with Nemo & Friends, Future World, Epcot; ☎ 407-939-3463

Reservations Required. **Dining Plan credits** 1 per person, per meal. **When to go** Lunch. **Cost range** Lunch $16–$33 (child $9), dinner $20–$33 (child $9). **Service** ★★★★. **Friendliness** ★★★★. **Parking** Epcot lot. **Bar** Full service. **Wine selection** Good. **Dress** Casual. **Disabled access** Yes. **Customers** Theme park guests. **Lunch** Daily, 11:30 a.m.–3:20 p.m. **Dinner** Daily, 4 p.m.–park closing.

SETTING AND ATMOSPHERE Though the decor could use a face-lift, you can't beat the view in this darkened dining room, which faces the world's largest saltwater aquarium; tiered seating gives everyone a pretty good view of the multitude of fishes (and sometimes Mickey in a SCUBA suit). The ethereal entryway gives the impression that you're going under the sea; special light fixtures throw ripple patterns on the ceiling.

HOUSE SPECIALTIES Creamy lobster soup with tarragon and brandy, on the menu since the restaurant opened; seared rainbow trout; grilled New York strip steak; Chocolate Wave dessert. For kids: grilled fish or chicken, pork tenderloin.

SUMMARY AND COMMENTS Certainly the best restaurant in Future World, Coral Reef is a great escape from the Florida sun. Grab a souvenir fish guide and check out the 4,000 sea creatures that call this place home.

The Crystal Palace ★★★

AMERICAN/BUFFET	MODERATE	QUALITY ★★★½	VALUE ★★★
READER-SURVEY RESPONSES	91% 👍 9% 👎	DISNEY DINING PLAN? Yes	

Main Street, U.S.A., Magic Kingdom; ☎ 407-939-3463

Reservations Required. **Dining Plan credits** 1 per person, per meal. **When to go** Anytime. **Cost range** Breakfast $27 (child $15), lunch $30 (child $16), dinner $42 (child $20). **Service** ★★★. **Friendliness** ★★★★. **Parking** Magic Kingdom lot. **Bar** No alcohol served. **Dress** Casual. **Disabled access** Yes. **Customers** Park guests. **Character breakfast** Daily, 8–10:30 a.m. **Character lunch** Daily, 11:30 a.m.–2:45 p.m. **Character dinner** Daily, 3:15 p.m.–park closing.

SETTING AND ATMOSPHERE A breakfast or lunch visit to The Crystal Palace surrounds you with cool sunlight and decorative plants, along with a large, easy-to-navigate buffet area. The restaurant's white steel supports, arched ceilings, and glass roof (especially the atrium) are tributes to its namesake, built to house London's 1851 Great Exhibition—the first world's fair—and among the first structures to use plate glass in large quantities. Because of all the windows, the setting is less distinctive for dinner after dark.

HOUSE SPECIALTIES The buffet items change often but may include waffles and pancakes layered with fresh fruit for breakfast and, for lunch and dinner, flank steak, roasted chicken, and barbecued pork tenderloin; Thai curry mussels; grilled vegetables with balsamic glaze; pasta with wild mushrooms and chicken; shrimp; and a sundae bar. The salads are exceptionally fresh. Kids get their own buffet with macaroni and cheese and chicken fingers.

ENTERTAINMENT AND AMENITIES Winnie the Pooh and friends schmooze and pose with the kids.

SUMMARY AND COMMENTS The best dining value in the Magic Kingdom—go hungry and fill up. The food is consistently good, but eating seems somehow secondary to the desire to get lots of photos with Pooh and his pals.

ESPN Club ★★½

AMERICAN/SANDWICHES	MODERATE	QUALITY ★★★	VALUE ★★★
READER-SURVEY RESPONSES	74% 👍 26% 👎	DISNEY DINING PLAN? Yes	

BoardWalk; ☎ 407-939-1177

Reservations Not accepted. **Dining Plan credits** 1 per person, per meal. **When to go** Anytime. **Cost range** $13–$23.50 (child $8.59). **Service** ★★★. **Friendliness** ★★★★. **Parking** Valet ($20) or BoardWalk lot. **Bar** Full service. **Wine selection** Minimal. **Dress** Casual. **Disabled access** Yes. **Customers** Tourists. **Hours** Daily, 11:30 a.m.–1 a.m.

SETTING AND ATMOSPHERE A sports bar to the *n*th degree, with basketball-court flooring, sports memorabilia, and more television monitors than a network affiliate. The bar area features satellite sports-trivia video games. A large octagonal space with a wall of TVs serves as the main dining room.

HOUSE SPECIALTIES PB&J burger, ESPN wings, char-crusted tuna burger, "Boo-Yah!" chili.

SUMMARY AND COMMENTS If you plan to watch a big sports event, go early, as the line often spills out the door. It's noisy and fun, with large portions and decent quality. And don't worry about missing a play—there are even TVs in the restrooms.

ESPN Wide World of Sports Grill ★★½

AMERICAN	MODERATE	QUALITY ★★★	VALUE ★★★
READER-SURVEY RESPONSES	Not enough to rate	DISNEY DINING PLAN?	Yes

ESPN Wide World of Sports Complex; ☎ 407-939-2196

Reservations Not necessary. **Dining Plan credits** 1 per person, per meal. **When to go** When an event is going on. *Note:* You must pay admission to the sports complex to eat here. **Cost range** $8–$14 (child $8.59). **Service ★★★. Friendliness ★★½. Parking** ESPN Wide World of Sports lot. **Bar** Full service. **Wine selection** Minimal. **Dress** Jerseys if you've got 'em. **Disabled access** Yes. **Customers** Sports fans. **Hours** Open only on event days.

SETTING AND ATMOSPHERE Think the Hard Rock Cafe with sports memorabilia instead of musical instruments. More than 20 big-screen TVs play whatever games are on.

HOUSE SPECIALTIES Salads, BLTs, pastrami on rye, burgers.

ENTERTAINMENT AND AMENITIES Televised sporting events.

SUMMARY AND COMMENTS The grill feeds the hungry fans at the sports complex, so the fare is basic and filling.

50's Prime Time Cafe ★★★

AMERICAN	MODERATE	QUALITY ★★★	VALUE ★★★
READER-SURVEY RESPONSES	85% 👍 15% 👎	DISNEY DINING PLAN?	Yes

Echo Lake, Disney's Hollywood Studios; ☎ 407-939-3463

Reservations Recommended. **Dining Plan credits** 1 per person, per meal. **When to go** Lunch or dinner. **Cost range** Lunch and dinner, $13.50–$22 (child $8.59). **Service ★★★★★. Friendliness ★★★★★. Parking** DHS lot. **Bar** Full service. **Wine selection** Limited. **Dress** Casual. **Disabled access** Yes. **Customers** Theme park guests. **Lunch** Daily, 11 a.m.–3:55 p.m.; opens at 10:30 a.m. on Sunday and Wednesday. **Dinner** Daily, 4 p.m.–park closing.

SETTING AND ATMOSPHERE Dine in a 1950s kitchen stocked with antique refrigerators, boomerang-patterned laminate tabletops, sunburst clocks, and decoupage art made from preserved fruit. Black-and-white TVs play vintage sitcom clips while you wait for your entrees; then you order dessert from a menu shown on GAF View-Master reels.

HOUSE SPECIALTIES Pot roast, chicken potpie, PB&J milkshake, and other retro fare. There's a nod to contemporary cuisine with a multigrain pasta, but it's hard to pass up fried chicken and meat loaf.

SUMMARY AND COMMENTS Though the restaurant is usually packed and noisy, the waitstaff makes it worthwhile, nagging you just like Mom did to "Take your elbows off the table!" and "Finish every last bite!" If the place is packed, grab a spot at the bar in the equally kitschy Tune-In Lounge next door—they don't serve food, but they will make you a PB&J shake or a Dad's Electric Lemonade (with rum).

Flying Fish Cafe ★★★★

SEAFOOD	EXPENSIVE	QUALITY ★★★★	VALUE ★★★
READER-SURVEY RESPONSES	83% 👍 17% 👎	DISNEY DINING PLAN?	Yes

BoardWalk; ☎ 407-939-3463

Reservations Required. **Dining Plan credits** 2 per person, per meal. **When to go** Anytime. **Cost range** $37–$47 (child $8–$15). **Service ★★★★★. Friendliness**

★★★★★. **Parking** Valet ($20) or BoardWalk lot. **Bar** Full service. **Wine selection** Excellent but pricey. **Dress** Dressy casual. **Disabled access** Good. **Customers** Tourists and locals. **Dinner** Sunday–Thursday, 5:30–10 p.m.; Friday and Saturday, 5:30–10:30 p.m.

SETTING AND ATMOSPHERE Right along the BoardWalk, the Flying Fish has upscale decor inspired by a 1930s Coney Island coaster—the booths are designed with swooping backs to resemble the climbs. Whimsical fish fly overhead; columns are clad in oversize gold fish scales for a dreamy effect. Seating in front of the on-stage kitchen is home to the Chef's Counter, where chef Tim Keating crafts a tasting menu based on what's seasonal (reservations required). It's pricey, but Keating sources best-of-the-best Florida seafood and produce.

HOUSE SPECIALTIES Keating, a repeat James Beard Foundation finalist, is a big proponent of Florida products; he also sources vegetables from The Land at Epcot. Repeat guests always expect to find the restaurant's signature dish: potato-wrapped red snapper with creamy leek fondue and a red wine–butter sauce; char-crusted New York strip; and lump crab cakes. Desserts are seasonal, but the house-made sorbets and caramelized-banana Napoleon are divine.

OTHER RECOMMENDATIONS Florida seafood, artisanal cheeses, grilled Berkshire pork tenderloin, oak-grilled Maine sea scallops.

SUMMARY AND COMMENTS Locals love the Flying Fish, and for good reason: Keating runs a tight kitchen and pays attention to each plate. Though this is food for grown-ups, you'll often see children in the noisy dining room because of the BoardWalk location.

The Fountain ★★

AMERICAN	MODERATE	QUALITY ★★	VALUE ★★
READER-SURVEY RESPONSES 88% 👍	12% 👎	DISNEY DINING PLAN? No	

Dolphin Resort; ☎ 407-934-1609

Reservations Not taken. **When to go** Anytime. **Cost range** $7.50–$16 (child $9). **Service** ★★★★. **Friendliness** ★★★★. **Bar** Beer and wine only. **Wine selection** Limited. **Parking** Hotel lot ($17). **Dress** Casual. **Disabled access** Yes. **Customers** Hotel guests. **Lunch and dinner** Daily, 11 a.m.–11 p.m.

SETTING AND ATMOSPHERE Informal soda-shop ambience.

HOUSE SPECIALTIES Build-your-own burgers and hot dogs, BLTs, milkshakes (we love the PB&J), and ice-cream cones.

OTHER RECOMMENDATIONS Philly cheesesteak, lamb gyro, big salads including seared salmon and chicken Caesar.

SUMMARY AND COMMENTS Probably not the best choice if you're counting calories.

Fresh Mediterranean Market ★★½

MEDITERRANEAN/AMERICAN	MODERATE	QUALITY ★★½	VALUE ★★
READER-SURVEY RESPONSES 57% 👍	43% 👎	DISNEY DINING PLAN? No	

Dolphin Resort; ☎ 407-934-1609

Reservations Available but not necessary. **When to go** Breakfast or lunch. **Cost range** Breakfast (buffet or à la carte) $5–$23 (child $14), lunch $14–$18 (child $12). **Service** ★★★★. **Friendliness** ★★★★. **Parking** Hotel lot ($17). **Bar** Beer, wine, and limited cocktails. **Wine selection** Limited. **Dress** Casual. **Disabled access** Yes. **Customers** Hotel guests. **Breakfast** Daily, 6:30–11 a.m. **Lunch** Monday–Friday, 11:30 a.m.–1 p.m.; Saturday and Sunday, noon–2 p.m. Days of operation may vary according to hotel occupancy.

SETTING AND ATMOSPHERE Spare decor with brightly colored tiles, light woods, and big windows. Ask for a veranda table if you want to have a quiet conversation away from the action in the open kitchen.

HOUSE SPECIALTIES Breakfast: fresh fruit and vegetable juices, made-to-order omelets, "Paleo" cereal. Lunch: burgers and salads.

OTHER RECOMMENDATIONS Sangria with organic fruit juices.

SUMMARY AND COMMENTS The menu is as spartan as the setting, but If you're looking for healthful and organic choices, this is the spot.

Fulton's Crab House ★★½

SEAFOOD	EXPENSIVE	QUALITY ★★½	VALUE ★★
READER-SURVEY RESPONSES 87% 👍	13% 👎	DISNEY DINING PLAN? Yes	

Disney Springs; ☎ 407-939-3463

Reservations Accepted. **Dining Plan credits** 2 per person, per meal. **When to go** Early evening. **Cost range** Lunch $13–$29 (child $8–$12), dinner $21–$199 (child $8–$12). **Service** ★★★★. **Friendliness** ★★★★. **Parking** Lot near the old Pleasure Island complex. **Bar** Full service. **Wine selection** Good; mostly American. **Dress** Casual. **Disabled access** Yes. **Customers** Locals and Disney guests. **Lunch** Daily, 11:30 a.m.–3:30 p.m. **Dinner** Daily, 4–11 p.m.

SETTING AND ATMOSPHERE On a permanently anchored boat at Disney Springs, Fulton's consists of separate dining areas that feel completely different: the Market Room, a tribute to New York City's Fulton Fish Market (the restaurant's namesake); the Constellation Room, a semicircular room with a starlit night sky; and the Industry Room, a tribute to the fishing industry. We prefer the back deck on pretty days. Usually packed.

HOUSE SPECIALTIES Seafood tower for two or four; Florida stone crab in season; fresh oysters; Ultimate Crab Experience for four with Alaskan king, Canadian snow, and Pacific Northwest Dungeness crab.

OTHER RECOMMENDATIONS Florida grouper, Maine lobster, fried jumbo shrimp, baby back ribs, filet mignon.

SUMMARY AND COMMENTS Even with all the new restaurants coming to Disney Springs, Fulton's is still a good spot for savoring seafood classics: raw oysters, giant crab, Maine lobster, seasonal Florida fish. During busy times of year, waits can be long—more than an hour even on weeknights. But if you don't get fresh seafood back home, go early, request a table outside, order a seafood tower, and enjoy.

Garden Grill Restaurant ★★

AMERICAN	EXPENSIVE	QUALITY ★★	VALUE ★★★
READER-SURVEY RESPONSES 92% 👍	8% 👎	DISNEY DINING PLAN? Yes	

The Land, Future World, Epcot; ☎ 407-939-3463

Reservations Required. **Dining Plan credits** 1 per person, per meal. **When to go** Dinner. **Cost range** $38 (child $19). **Service** ★★★★. **Friendliness** ★★★★★. **Parking** Epcot lot. **Bar** Wine, beer, and some mixed drinks. **Wine selection** Fair. **Dress** Casual. **Disabled access** Yes. **Customers** Theme park guests. **Character dinner** Daily, 4:30–8 p.m.

SETTING AND ATMOSPHERE With the popular Soarin' attraction nearby, the all-you-can-eat Garden Grill stays busy, even though the concept and the dining room have grown rather dated. Even so, it's a classic: The floor revolves slowly as you peer down into scenes from Living with the Land, the Land Pavilion's ride-through attraction (see page 553). At about the time you finish a meal, you've revolved once, past scenes of a desert, a rainforest, and a farm, along with a few mural-painted walls in between. Much more exciting for kids are the Disney characters—Mickey, Chip 'n' Dale, and others make stops at tables for photo ops and greetings.

HOUSE SPECIALTIES Beef filet, turkey breast with stuffing and gravy, and sustainable fish of the day; buttermilk mashed potatoes, veggies, and salads made with ingredients from The Land's greenhouses. Dessert is a seasonal cobbler with vanilla-bean whipped cream. The kids' menu includes turkey breast with whole-grain rice pilaf, mac and cheese, chicken drumsticks, sweet potato sticks, and broccoli.

ENTERTAINMENT AND AMENITIES The view. Character dining. Free nonalcoholic beverages included with meals.

SUMMARY AND COMMENTS The food is filling, and the retro-Disney setting is worth experiencing at least once.

Garden Grove ★★

AMERICAN	MODERATE	QUALITY ★★★	VALUE ★★
READER-SURVEY RESPONSES 71% 👍	29% 👎	DISNEY DINING PLAN? No	

Swan Resort; ☎ 407-934-1609

Reservations Recommended. **When to go** Anytime. **Cost range** Breakfast $12–$15 (child $7 or $8), lunch $14–$19 (child $9–$12), dinner $30–$37 (child $18); weekend Disney-character breakfast buffet $25 (child $16), Disney-character seafood buffet (Friday and Saturday nights) $36 (child $17). **Service** ★★★. **Friendliness** ★★★. **Parking** Valet ($20) or hotel lot ($17). **Bar** Full service. **Wine selection** Good. **Dress** Casual. **Disabled access** Yes. **Customers** Hotel guests, some locals, tourists. **Breakfast, lunch, and dinner** Daily, 6:30 a.m.–9:30 p.m.; character breakfast, Saturday and Sunday, 8–11 a.m.

SETTING AND ATMOSPHERE Disney characters are the stars every night for dinner—and for breakfast on weekends—in this spacious dining room with a 25-foot faux oak tree in the center. At night, the lights are dimmed and the oak tree is illuminated with lanterns and twinkling lights.

HOUSE SPECIALTIES For lunch, burgers, short-rib salad, fish tacos. For dinner, a new concept with unlimited salad and soup for starters, then a protein (beef, salmon, chicken) or vegetarian entree, and finally a dessert buffet. The weekend seafood buffet features a raw bar, jumbo scallops, fried-seafood basket, paella, and salmon.

SUMMARY AND COMMENTS Garden Grove probably isn't worth a special trip if you aren't already staying at the Swan. But the food is plentiful, and the character meals are a bargain compared with, say, Chef Mickey's.

Grand Floridian Cafe ★★½

AMERICAN	MODERATE	QUALITY ★★★	VALUE ★★
READER-SURVEY RESPONSES 95% 👍	5% 👎	DISNEY DINING PLAN? Yes	

Grand Floridian Resort & Spa; ☎ 407-824-2496

Reservations Accepted. **Dining Plan credits** 1 per person, per meal. **When to go** Anytime. **Cost range** Breakfast $11–$19 (child $6), lunch $9–$29 (child $8.59), dinner $17.50–$33 (child $8.50). **Service** ★★★. **Friendliness** ★★★★. **Parking** Valet ($20); self-parking is far away. **Bar** Full service. **Wine selection** Good. **Dress** Casual. **Disabled access** Yes. **Customers** Hotel guests. **Breakfast** Daily, 7–11:30 a.m. **Lunch** Daily, 11:30 a.m.–2 p.m. **Dinner** Daily, 5–9 p.m.

SETTING AND ATMOSPHERE Light and airy decor with lots of sunlight, servers dressed in Victorian costumes, and pretty views of the pool and courtyard. Open three meals a day for casual dining.

HOUSE SPECIALTIES The expansive breakfast menu includes omelets, lobster eggs Benedict, seasonal pancakes, and steel-cut oatmeal. At lunch,

Florida fish tacos, Reuben sandwich, falafel burger with chipotle hummus. For dinner, surf and turf burger with Angus beef and poached lobster, shrimp and grits, sustainable fish, New York strip steak.

OTHER RECOMMENDATIONS Chocolate fondue, Boston cream pie.

SUMMARY AND COMMENTS A quick place to grab a tasty bite. Scrumptious desserts by the same team of pastry chefs who service all of the Grand Floridian's dining rooms.

La Hacienda de San Angel   ★★★

MEXICAN	EXPENSIVE	QUALITY ★★★½	VALUE ★★½
READER-SURVEY RESPONSES	81% 👍	19% 👎	DISNEY DINING PLAN? Yes

Mexico, World Showcase, Epcot; ☎ 407-939-3463

Reservations Required. **Dining Plan credits** 1 per person, per meal. **When to go** Dinner. **Cost range** $24–$59 (child $8.50–$9.50). **Service** ★★★★. **Friendliness** ★★★★★. **Parking** Epcot lot. **Bar** Full. **Wine selection** All Mexican. **Dress** Casual. **Disabled access** Yes. **Customers** Theme park guests. **Dinner** 4–8:35 p.m.

SETTING AND ATMOSPHERE Right along the waterfront at the Mexico Pavilion, La Hacienda is a primo spot for watching fireworks through the tall windows. The interior has authentic touches of Mexico in its lighting and decor.

HOUSE SPECIALTIES The simplest dishes on the menu are the best: *queso fundido;* corn cakes stuffed with chorizo; the taco trio with pork, beef, and chicken; fried-shrimp tacos with chipotle-lime aioli. The margaritas are the real deal—or just go for a flight of fine sipping tequila.

SUMMARY AND COMMENTS We're not too Impressed with the pricey mixed grill, and we advise making a meal of appetizers and a signature cocktail, like the avocado margarita with a hibiscus–Himalayan salt rim. There's also a vegetarian menu if you ask.

Hollywood & Vine   ★★½

AMERICAN	MODERATE	QUALITY ★★★	VALUE ★★★
READER-SURVEY RESPONSES	83% 👍	17% 👎	DISNEY DINING PLAN? Yes

Echo Lake, Disney's Hollywood Studios; ☎ 407-939-3463

Reservations Recommended; credit card required to reserve *Fantasmic!* Dining Package (see page 304). **Dining Plan credits** 1 per person, per meal. **When to go** Anytime. **Cost range** Breakfast buffet $27 (child $15); lunch buffet $34 (child $18); dinner buffet $34–$56 (child $17–$33), depending on *Fantasmic!* seating. **Service** ★★★★. **Friendliness** ★★★★★. **Parking** DHS lot. **Bar** Full service. **Wine selection** Limited. **Dress** Casual. **Disabled access** Yes. **Customers** DHS guests. **Character breakfast** Daily, 8–11:20 a.m.; **Character lunch** Daily, 11:40 a.m.–2:25 p.m. **Dinner** Daily, 5–9 p.m.

SETTING AND ATMOSPHERE Just off Hollywood Boulevard near the park entrance, this 1930s-era diner has a sleek Art Deco design (think chrome and tile) that gets lost amid all the Disney-character frenzy, with little ones happy to see their favorite Disney Channel pals at breakfast and lunch. About every 30 minutes, Sofia the First, Doc McStuffins, Handy Manny, and Jake from *Jake and the Never Land Pirates* perform for cheering fans under the age of 6. .Dinner is subdued.

HOUSE SPECIALTIES Salads, soups, create-your-own pasta, fish of the day, carved and grilled meats, fresh fruits and breads, sundae bar and chocolate fountain. (Menu changes often.)

SUMMARY AND COMMENTS Family-friendly, so expect lots of noisy kids.

The Hollywood Brown Derby ★★★★

AMERICAN	EXPENSIVE	QUALITY ★★★★	VALUE ★★★
READER-SURVEY RESPONSES 90% 👍 10% 👎		DISNEY DINING PLAN? Yes	

Hollywood Boulevard, Disney's Hollywood Studios; ☎ 407-939-3463

Reservations Accepted; credit card required to reserve the *Fantasmic!* Dining Package (see page 304). **Dining Plan credits** 2 per person, per meal. **When to go** Early evening. **Cost range** Lunch and dinner $16–$43 (child $6–$14). **Service** ★★★★★. **Friendliness** ★★★★★. **Parking** DHS lot. **Bar** Full service. **Wine selection** Very good. **Dress** Casual. **Disabled access** Yes. **Customers** Theme park guests. **Lunch** Daily, 11:30 a.m.–3 p.m. **Dinner** Daily, 3:30 p.m.–park closing.

SETTING AND ATMOSPHERE An oasis of civility in the middle of a theme park, this is a replica of the original Brown Derby (not the one shaped like a hat) in California. The sunken dining room has a certain elegance, with tuxedoed waiters, curved booths, and white linen. Tall palm trees in huge pots stand in the center of the room and reach for the high ceiling.

HOUSE SPECIALTIES Cobb salad (named for Bob Cobb, the original restaurant's owner), grapefruit cake made from the original Brown Derby recipe, grilled Wagyu-beef burger, and original fettuccine Alfredo at lunch; pan-seared black grouper and char-glazed filet of beef at dinner. The kids' menu includes grilled black grouper, whole-grain penne pasta, and grilled chicken breast.

OTHER RECOMMENDATIONS Crispy spiced duck breast, Thai noodle bowl with wok-fried coconut tofu, crispy jumbo lump crab cake appetizer.

SUMMARY AND COMMENTS The Brown Derby is one of the top theme park restaurants at Disney World. It's expensive, yes, but also a wonderful way to relax and regenerate. The decor is so perfect you'll feel as if you're in a Fred Astaire–Ginger Rogers movie. Service is outstanding, as is the food.

   If you don't have reservations, the patio lounge opens at noon and is first-come, first-served, with a menu of small plates and cocktails. Shaded by big umbrellas, the outdoor tables are great spots for people-watching. The menu ($9–$29) is all small plates: Cobb salad, artisanal cheeses, charcuterie, Wagyu-beef sliders with Cognac-mustard aioli and Gouda cheese, steamed mussels, and desserts. (You can also order from the regular menu.) Drink choices include various flights—martinis, margaritas, Champagnes, white and red wines, Scotches, and Grand Marnier vintages—along with wines by the glass or half-bottle and classic cocktails.

House of Blues ★★★

REGIONAL AMERICAN	MODERATE	QUALITY ★★★½	VALUE ★★★
READER-SURVEY RESPONSES Not enough to rate		DISNEY DINING PLAN? Yes	

Disney Springs West Side; ☎ 407-934-2623

Reservations Recommended. **Dining Plan credits** 1 per person, per meal. **When to go** Lunch or early dinner; Sunday gospel brunch. **Cost range** $12–$29 (child $7–$10), brunch $40 (child $22). **Service** ★★★★. **Friendliness** ★★★. **Parking** Disney Springs lot. **Bar** Full service. **Wine selection** Modest. **Dress** Casual. **Disabled access** Good. **Customers** Blues lovers. **Brunch** 2 seatings on Sunday, 10:30 a.m. and 1 p.m. **Lunch and dinner** Sunday–Tuesday, 11:30 a.m.–11 p.m.; Wednesday and Thursday, 11:30 a.m.–midnight; Friday and Saturday, 11:30 a.m.–1 a.m.

SETTING AND ATMOSPHERE Adjacent to Cirque du Soleil, House of Blues has a ramshackle look that's almost out of place in Disney Springs, but it's a solid stop for lunch or dinner before or after a show. And with its own separate concert hall, there's often great live music—including the lively Sunday gospel brunch. A quick-service window, along with outdoor bar and seating (sometimes with live music), draws passersby. But if you've got time for a sit-down meal, the fabulous folk art in the restaurant is worth a look.

HOUSE SPECIALTIES Barbecue sandwiches (pulled pork, brisket, and chicken), ribs, and smoked turkey legs at The Smokehouse walk-up window; inside, choose from flatbreads, burgers, shrimp and grits, ribs, New York strip steak, and Voodoo Shrimp simmered in amber beer.

OTHER RECOMMENDATIONS Jambalaya, tacos, lobster mac and cheese, Bourbon bread pudding.

SUMMARY AND COMMENTS The best food on the West Side, in a fun, casual setting. If you're planning on taking in one of the musical acts next door, see the show first so you can get a good seat, and then come back afterward to eat.

Il Mulino New York Trattoria ★★★

ITALIAN	EXPENSIVE		QUALITY ★★★		VALUE ★★
READER-SURVEY RESPONSES	64% 👍	36% 👎	DISNEY DINING PLAN? No		

Swan Resort; ☎ 407-934-1609

Reservations Accepted. **When to go** Dinner. **Cost range** $16–$45 (child $12–$16). **Service** ★★. **Friendliness** ★★. **Parking** Valet (free with validation) or hotel lot ($17). **Bar** Full service. **Wine selection** Good. **Dress** Dressy casual. **Disabled access** Yes. **Customers** Mostly hotel guests and conventioneers. **Dinner** 5–11 p.m. nightly.

SETTING AND ATMOSPHERE A spin-off of the New York City restaurant, Il Mulino takes an upscale-casual approach to Italian cuisine, with family-style platters for sharing. Tables are dark wood; an open kitchen creates a bustle. You can request private dining in one of the smaller rooms.

HOUSE SPECIALTIES The cuisine focuses on Italy's Abruzzi region, with hearty pastas and big cuts of meat. Try the spaghetti carbonara or the veal saltimbocca.

OTHER RECOMMENDATIONS Charcuterie, mussels in white wine, pizzas, rib eye with sautéed spinach.

SUMMARY AND COMMENTS Predictable menu with a little bit of everything you'd expect in a bustling Italian restaurant: pizza, pasta, meat, seafood. Il Mulino is perfect for conventioneers—and there appear to be many of them sharing the big tables—but adventurous eaters may want to go elsewhere.

Jiko—The Cooking Place ★★★★½

AFRICAN/FUSION	EXPENSIVE		QUALITY ★★★★½		VALUE ★★★½
READER-SURVEY RESPONSES	91% 👍	9% 👎	DISNEY DINING PLAN? Yes		

Animal Kingdom Lodge & Villas–Jambo House; ☎ 407-938-3000

Reservations Required. **Dining Plan credits** 2 per person, per meal. **When to go** Dinner. **Cost range** $30–$49 (child $7–$12). **Service** ★★★★★. **Friendliness** ★★★★★. **Parking** Valet ($20) or hotel lot. **Bar** Full bar. **Wine selection** All South African. **Dress** Dressy casual. **Disabled access** Good. **Customers** Hotel guests and locals. **Dinner** Daily, 5:30–10 p.m.

SETTING AND ATMOSPHERE Downstairs from the lobby, young African exchange students greet guests as they enter a dining room with decor inspired by the opening scenes of *The Lion King,* with a flock of white birds appearing to fly overhead. A pair of large wood-burning ovens dominates the center of the room.

HOUSE SPECIALTIES African-inspired dips and breads, oak-grilled filet mignon with South African red wine sauce, maize-crusted tilefish.

OTHER RECOMMENDATIONS Grilled wild-boar tenderloin, seafood curry, and Nigerian-spiced double-cut pork chop with braised greens. The kids' menu includes grilled turkey or chicken breast, vegetables and whole-grain rice pilaf, fish, steak, and mac and cheese.

SUMMARY AND COMMENTS Jiko has won numerous accolades (including AAA's Four Diamond Award) for its interesting fare and stellar wine list—one of the largest collections of South African wines in any North American restaurant, with more than 1,800 bottles. Dishes are beautifully spiced and full of flavor. Start with the Taste of Africa dips and warm bread, and wrap up with Ghanaian chocolate and Kenyan coffee pot de crème, or a cup of Kenyan press-pot coffee or a specialty tea. Special menus for the glucose- and lactose-intolerant, vegans, and vegetarians.

Kimonos ★★★★

JAPANESE	MODERATE	QUALITY ★★★★½	VALUE ★★★
READER-SURVEY RESPONSES	80% 👍 20% 👎	DISNEY DINING PLAN? No	

Swan Resort; ☎ 407-934-1609

Reservations Accepted for parties of 6 or more. **When to go** Dinner. **Cost range** Sushi and rolls à la carte, $5.25–$18. **Service** ★★★★★. **Friendliness** ★★★★★. **Parking** Valet ($20) or hotel lot ($17). **Bar** Full service. **Wine selection** Very good. **Dress** Casual. **Disabled access** Yes. **Customers** Hotel guests and locals. **Dinner** Daily, 5:30 p.m.–midnight; bar opens at 5 p.m.

SETTING AND ATMOSPHERE Sushi and nightly karaoke—what a combo! Go early if you want a zen experience with sushi and sake in the serene setting: black-lacquered tabletops and counters, tall pillars rising to bamboo rafters with rice-paper lanterns, and elegant kimonos that hang outstretched on the walls and between the dining sections. The chefs will greet you with a friendly welcome, and you'll be offered a hot towel to clean your hands.

HOUSE SPECIALTIES Both cooked and raw sushi and hot dishes. Classic rolls include California, tuna, and soft-shell crab; the Kimonos roll features tuna, salmon, yellowtail, and wasabi mayo. Small plates include beef satay, pork belly, and *tori no karaage* (Japanese fried chicken).

SUMMARY AND COMMENTS The skill of the sushi artists is as much a joy to watch as is eating the wonderfully fresh creations. Karaoke starts at 9 p.m., with mostly the convention crowd at the microphone.

Kona Cafe ★★★

POLYNESIAN/PAN-ASIAN	MODERATE	QUALITY ★★★	VALUE ★★★★
READER-SURVEY RESPONSES	88% 👍 13% 👎	DISNEY DINING PLAN? Yes	

Polynesian Village Resort; ☎ 407-939-3463

Reservations Accepted. **Dining Plan credits** 1 per person, per meal. **When to go** Anytime. **Cost range** Breakfast $9–$14.50 (child $6.50), lunch $12–$18 (child $8.59), dinner $11–$33 (child $8.59). **Service** ★★★★. **Friendliness** ★★★★★. **Parking** Valet ($20) or hotel lot. **Bar** Full service. **Wine selection** OK. **Dress** Casual. **Disabled access** Yes. **Customers** Mostly hotel guests; some locals. **Breakfast** Daily, 7:30–11:45 a.m. **Lunch** Daily, noon–2:45 p.m. **Dinner** Daily, 5–9:45 p.m.

SETTING AND ATMOSPHERE With the remake of the Polynesian Village Resort, Kona Cafe remains the hotel's coffee shop, open three meals a day. Right next to the monorail station, the casual, open dining room is an easy ride from the Magic Kingdom by boat or monorail should you want to escape the theme park for lunch or dinner.

HOUSE SPECIALTIES Breakfast: The indulgent Tonga Toast (French toast layered with bananas) Is still the most-requested dish. Lunch: sushi, pan-Asian noodles with shrimp, beef, or vegetables; sticky wings; banana-chocolate crème brûlée. Dinner: sushi, *togarashi*-spiced ahi tuna, grilled curry-crusted lamb chop, New York strip steak, and sustainable fish.

OTHER RECOMMENDATIONS Charcuterie and cheese, Kilauea torte (chocolate cake with a warm chocolate center), and Kona coffee served in a press pot.

SUMMARY AND COMMENTS The menu is themed to the island decor, and though the dining room Isn't fancy, the food is on a higher plane than your average java joint's. An adjacent sushi bar serves the full restaurant menu for dinner and offers coffee and pastries during breakfast and lunch hours.

Liberty Tree Tavern ★★★
(closed for renovations through November 2015)

AMERICAN	MODERATE	QUALITY ★★★	VALUE ★★★
READER-SURVEY RESPONSES	91% 👍 9% 👎	DISNEY DINING PLAN? Yes	

Liberty Square, Magic Kingdom; ☎ 407-939-3463

Reservations Accepted. **Dining Plan credits** 1 per person, per meal. **When to go** Lunch or dinner. **Cost range** Lunch $15–$20 (child $8.59), dinner $34 (child $17). **Service** ★★★★★. **Friendliness** ★★★★★. **Parking** Magic Kingdom lot. **Bar** No alcohol served. **Dress** Casual. **Disabled access** Yes. **Customers** Theme park guests. **Lunch** Daily, 11:30 a.m.–3 p.m. **Character dinner** Daily, 4–9 p.m.

SETTING AND ATMOSPHERE The Liberty Tree's six dining rooms take their cues from Revolutionary War–era American decor, with furnishings from different colonies. For example, the Philadelphia Room has burgundy carpet, Federal-style furniture, and a portrait of Ben Franklin; other themes include a Virginia pub and New England seaside inn, with corresponding tables, chairs, and art. The Colonial theme and low ceilings—along with the 1970s-era floor plan—make the tavern feel smaller than it is, especially after dark.

HOUSE SPECIALTIES For lunch: New England–style pot roast, roast turkey, and the Liberty Boys BLT with pork belly. Family-style character dining at dinner, with all-you-can-eat turkey breast, carved beef, and sliced pork, all served with mashed potatoes, stuffing, and mac and cheese.

OTHER RECOMMENDATIONS Crab-and-lobster dip for two, Colony Salad with seared salmon.

SUMMARY AND COMMENTS Though nothing much changes at Liberty Tree (the servers still wear those Colonial-style getups), it's still among the best of the Magic Kingdom's full-service restaurants. Make Advance Reservations here for about an hour or so before parade time—after you eat, you can walk right out and watch the parade. And you can enjoy Thanksgiving turkey and stuffing any day of the year.

Mama Melrose's Ristorante Italiano ★★½

ITALIAN	MODERATE	QUALITY ★★★	VALUE ★★
READER-SURVEY RESPONSES	87% 👍 13% 👎	DISNEY DINING PLAN? Yes	

Streets of America, Disney's Hollywood Studios; ☎ 407-939-3463

Reservations Required; credit card required to reserve the *Fantasmic!* Dining Package (see page 304). **Dining Plan credits** 1 per person, per meal. **When to go** Lunch or dinner. **Cost range** $13–$33 (child $8.59). **Service** ★★★. **Friendliness** ★★★★★. **Parking** DHS lot. **Bar** Full service. **Wine selection** Limited.

Dress Casual. **Disabled access** Yes. **Customers** Theme park guests. **Lunch** Daily, noon–3:30 p.m. **Dinner** Daily, 3:30 p.m.–park closing.

SETTING AND ATMOSPHERE Tucked at the back of Disney's Hollywood Studios, Mama Melrose's is easy to miss. This casual restaurant is inspired by "red-sauce Italian" joints that you still can find all over America: red-and-white checkered tablecloths, red vinyl booths, and grapevines hanging from the rafters. Ambience is generally quiet unless it's peak season.

HOUSE SPECIALTIES Fresh mozzarella, penne alla vodka with chicken or shrimp, flatbreads, seasonal pastas. Whole-wheat pasta available.

OTHER RECOMMENDATIONS Charred strip steak, oak-fired mussels, tiramisu and cannoli for dessert.

SUMMARY AND COMMENTS Because of Mama Melrose's out-of-the-way location, you can sometimes just walk in, especially in the evening. The food won't win any awards—the red sauce is a little heavy, for instance—but for family-style Italian, it's fine.

Maya Grill ★

MEXICAN/AMERICAN	EXPENSIVE		QUALITY ★	VALUE ★
READER-SURVEY RESPONSES	77%	23%	DISNEY DINING PLAN?	Yes

Coronado Springs Resort; ☎ 407-939-3463

Reservations Accepted. **Dining Plan credits** 1 per person, per meal. **When to go** Dinner. **Cost range** $20–$58 (child $7–$9.50). **Service** ★★★. **Friendliness** ★★★. **Parking** Hotel lot. **Bar** Full service. **Wine selection** Fair. **Dress** Casual. **Disabled access** Yes. **Customers** Hotel guests. **Breakfast** Daily, 7–11 a.m. **Dinner** Daily, 5–10 p.m.

SETTING AND ATMOSPHERE The dining room was designed to evoke the ancient world of the Maya, achieving "a harmony of fire, sun, and water." But the idea falls short. The kitchen is open to view—but so is the barren and starkly lit walkway outside. We keep waiting for the rumored renovation to materialize.

HOUSE SPECIALTIES Overpriced Tex-Mex and Nuevo Latino dinner fare, such as a $58 rib eye, fajita skillet, and slow-cooked pork with corn tortillas.

SUMMARY AND COMMENTS Maya Grill is owned by the same folks who run the restaurants at the Mexico Pavilion In Epcot, but execution falls short here considering the high prices ($23 for shrimp tacos). Still, conventioneers keep it busy.

Monsieur Paul ★★★★

FRENCH	EXPENSIVE	QUALITY ★★★★½	VALUE ★★★
READER-SURVEY RESPONSES	93%	7%	DISNEY DINING PLAN? YES

France, World Showcase, Epcot; ☎ 407-939-3463

Reservations Required. **Dining Plan credits** 2 per person, per meal on Plus and Deluxe Plans; 1 per person, per meal on Premium and Platinum Plans. **When to go** Late dinner. **Cost range** $39–$44 (child $13–$16). **Service** ★★★★. **Friendliness** ★★★★★. **Parking** Epcot or BoardWalk lot; enter through back gate. **Bar** Full service. **Wine selection** Good but pricey. **Dress** Casual. **Disabled access** Elevator to second level. **Customers** Theme park guests. **Dinner** Daily, 5:30–8:35 p.m.

SETTING AND ATMOSPHERE Light and modern, Monsieur Paul is tucked away upstairs at the France Pavilion. Access lies up a stairway (there's also an elevator) lined with photos of legendary French chef Paul Bocuse. His son, Jerôme, runs the restaurants started In 1982 In Epcot by his father and two other famous French chefs, Gaston Lenôtre and Roger Vergé.

Despite Monsieur Paul's relaxed ambience, this is definitely upscale cuisine, with sublime sauces and classic French preparations. Open only for dinner; request a table at the windows to watch the world go by on World Showcase Lagoon. Seats just 120.

HOUSE SPECIALTIES Chef Bocuse's black-truffle soup, available only on the fixed-price menu; red snapper in potato "scales"; *pot-au-feu* of scallops.

SUMMARY AND COMMENTS Monsieur Paul may be a bit formal and high-priced for many park guests, but if you can get past the sticker shock, this is *the* spot for a quiet dinner and conversation. Young chef Francesco Santin, who worked at Bocuse's restaurant in Lyon, France, wows diners with classic French tastes, including escargot, roasted duck breast with apple fondant, grilled beef tenderloin with mushroom crust and bordelaise sauce, and flourless chocolate cake with praline crunch. There's also a three-course fixed-price menu ($89 per person) that doesn't include anything on the regular menu, along with a solid wine list. A rather grown-up kids' menu includes roasted chicken breast and filet mignon.

Narcoossee's ★★★★½

SEAFOOD	EXPENSIVE	QUALITY ★★★½	VALUE ★★
READER-SURVEY RESPONSES 94% 👍	6% 👎	DISNEY DINING PLAN? Yes	

Grand Floridian Resort & Spa; ☎ 407-939-3463

Reservations Required. **Dining Plan credits** 2 per person, per meal. **When to go** Early evening. **Cost range** $33–$75 (child $7–$15). **Service** ★★★★★. **Friendliness** ★★★★★. **Parking** Valet ($20); self-parking is deceptively far away. **Bar** Full service. **Wine selection** Good. **Dress** Dressy casual. **Disabled access** Yes. **Customers** Hotel guests and locals. **Dinner** Daily, 5:30–10 p.m.

SETTING AND ATMOSPHERE At the edge of Seven Seas Lagoon, Narcoossee's (which gets its name from a Creek Indian word that means "little bear" and is also the name of a nearby town in Osceola County) has a prime spot on the grounds of the Grand Floridian, but the decor desperately needs updating—it hasn't changed since the resort opened in 1988. Hardwood floors and wooden chairs and tables make it a noisy choice for dinner, but the great food and service more than make up for the ambience. Plus you can step out on the back porch for a perfect view of the nightly Electrical Water Pageant or Magic Kingdom fireworks.

HOUSE SPECIALTIES Two-pound steamed Maine lobster, crispy whole yellowtail snapper, day boat scallops, and grilled filet mignon or Black Ángus New York strip steak. Kids' menu includes oven-roasted shrimp, grilled chicken, veggie burger, and pasta.

OTHER RECOMMENDATIONS Barbecued grilled shrimp and grits, sustainable Carolina blue-crab cake, Narcoossee's Candy Bar.

SUMMARY AND COMMENTS Narcoossee's has excellent service, a very good wine list—and steep prices (the lobster-tail-and-steak entree costs $75). Still, it's one of the few places at Disney with an upscale, seafood-centric menu, and one of the few where you can find fresh steamed lobster. Grab a seat at the bar if you don't have a reservation.

Nine Dragons Restaurant ★★★

CHINESE	MODERATE	QUALITY ★★★	VALUE ★★
READER-SURVEY RESPONSES 69% 👍	31% 👎	DISNEY DINING PLAN? Yes	

China, World Showcase, Epcot; ☎ 407-939-3463

Reservations Recommended. **Dining Plan credits** 1 per person, per meal. **When to go** Lunch or dinner. **Cost range** Lunch $13–$19 (child $8–$10), dinner

$13–$27 (child $8–$10). **Service** ★★★. **Friendliness** ★★★★. **Parking** Epcot lot. **Bar** Full service. **Wine selection** Minimal. **Dress** Casual. **Disabled access** Yes. **Customers** Theme park guests. **Lunch** Daily, 11:30 a.m.–4 p.m. **Dinner** Daily, 4:30 p.m.–park closing.

SETTING AND ATMOSPHERE Nine Dragons' attractive interior—subdued wood tones, colorful lanterns, beautiful backlit glass sculptures from China—and efficient service create a respite from the bustle of World Showcase. Ask for a window seat for a view of passersby on the promenade.

HOUSE SPECIALTIES Pot stickers, shrimp-and-taro lollipops, honey-sesame chicken, five-spice fish.

OTHER RECOMMENDATIONS Vegetarian stir-fry, noodle sampler with fresh vegetables and pork and chicken dipping sauces.

SUMMARY AND COMMENTS You can usually get a table without a wait in the spacious dining room, and while Nine Dragons gets a bad rap for being pricey, we think the food and the service are above average.

1900 Park Fare ★★½

AMERICAN/BUFFET	MODERATE	QUALITY ★★★	VALUE ★★★
READER-SURVEY RESPONSES	92% 👍	8% 👎	DISNEY DINING PLAN? Yes

Grand Floridian Resort & Spa; ☎ 407-824-3000

Reservations Recommended. **Dining Plan credits** 1 per person, per meal. **When to go** Breakfast or dinner. **Cost range** Breakfast $27 (child $15), dinner $45 (child $21). **Service** ★★★★. **Friendliness** ★★★★. **Parking** Valet ($20); self-parking is deceptively far away. **Bar** Full service. **Wine selection** Limited. **Dress** Casual. **Disabled access** Yes. **Customers** Hotel and resort guests. **Character breakfast** Daily, 8–11 a.m. **Character dinner** Daily, 4:30–8:30 p.m.

SETTING AND ATMOSPHERE Everyone is here to see the Disney characters—the food and decor are afterthoughts, though the tables are set with linen and service is first-rate in the bright, cavernous, high-ceilinged room. An antique band organ, "Big Bertha," periodically pumps out music to dine by. It's all very Grand Floridian.

HOUSE SPECIALTIES The buffet includes beef tenderloin, pork loin with chutney, prime rib, spice-crusted salmon, sushi,

OTHER RECOMMENDATIONS Separate buffet for kids includes pasta marinara, mini–corn dogs, chicken nuggets, and mac and cheese.

ENTERTAINMENT AND AMENITIES Character dining with Mary Poppins, Winnie the Pooh, Tigger, and Alice at breakfast, Cinderella, Prince Charming, and others at dinner.

SUMMARY AND COMMENTS A good, relatively inexpensive choice for character dining, but too bright and loud for adults without children.

'Ohana ★★★

POLYNESIAN	MODERATE	QUALITY ★★★½	VALUE ★★★
READER-SURVEY RESPONSES	94% 👍	6% 👎	DISNEY DINING PLAN? Yes

Polynesian Village Resort; ☎ 407-939-3463

Reservations Recommended. **Dining Plan credits** 1 per person, per meal. **When to go** Breakfast or dinner. **Cost range** Character breakfast $29 (child $16), dinner $33 (child $16). **Service** ★★★★. **Friendliness** ★★★★★. **Parking** Hotel lot. **Bar** Full service. **Wine selection** Limited. **Dress** Casual. **Disabled access** Yes. **Customers** Resort guests. **Character breakfast** Daily, 7:30–11 a.m. **Dinner** Daily, 5–10 p.m.

SETTING AND ATMOSPHERE Columns of carved tiki gods support the raised thatched roof in the center of 'Ohana's main dining room, while the dining tables, arranged in rows, resemble long, segmented surfboards. The centerpiece of the main room is a large, open-pit grill, on which your food is prepared with flair *and* flare: From time to time, the chef will pour some liquid on the fire, causing huge flames to shoot up. This is usually in response to something one of the strolling entertainers has said, evoking a sign from the fire gods.

'Ohana is perfect for families with young children. At any given moment, there may be a hula-hoop contest or a coconut race, where kids are invited to push coconuts around the dining room with broomsticks.

HOUSE SPECIALTIES Skewer service is the specialty here—there's no menu. As soon as you're seated, the feeding frenzy begins. Starters include honey-glazed chicken wings, fried pork dumplings, pineapple-coconut bread, and lettuce wraps. The main course is steak, pork loin, chicken, and grilled peel-and-eat shrimp, accompanied by stir-fried vegetables and egg noodles with pineapple in peanut sauce, all placed on a lazy Susan in the center of the table.

ENTERTAINMENT AND AMENITIES Strolling singers, games, and Mickey, Pluto, Lilo, and Stitch at breakfast.

SUMMARY AND COMMENTS Our readers adore 'Ohana, which means "family." The food is hearty and honest, and if you love meat and you come hungry, it's a great place to fill up. The method of service and the fact that it just keeps coming make it all taste a little better. Request a seat in the main dining room, where the fire pit is.

Olivia's Cafe ★★★

AMERICAN	MODERATE	QUALITY ★★★	VALUE ★★
READER-SURVEY RESPONSES	86% 👍 14% 👎	DISNEY DINING PLAN?	Yes

Old Key West Resort; ☎ 407-939-3463

Reservations Accepted. **Dining Plan credits** 1 per person, per meal. **When to go** Lunch. **Cost range** Breakfast $10–$14 (child $6.50), lunch and dinner $18.50–$33 (child $8.59). **Service** ★★★★. **Friendliness** ★★★★. **Parking** Hotel lot. **Bar** Full service. **Wine selection** Limited. **Dress** Casual. **Disabled access** Yes. **Customers** Resort guests. **Breakfast** Daily, 7:30–10:30 a.m. **Lunch** Daily, 11:30 a.m.–5 p.m. **Dinner** Daily, 5–10 p.m.

SETTING AND ATMOSPHERE Old Key West was the first Disney Vacation Club. Many DVC members consider Olivia's their home kitchen, and their photos decorate the walls. The decor is Disneyfied Key West, with pastels, mosaic-tile floors, potted palms, and tropical trees in the center of the room. There is some outside seating, which looks out over the waterway. Tile, wood siding, and no tablecloths add up to one noisy dining room.

HOUSE SPECIALTIES Breakfast: crab-cake eggs Benedict, banana-bread French toast, and poached eggs with sweet potato hash. Lunch and dinner: conch fritters and conch chowder; Olivia's Classic Burger, with applewood-smoked bacon; Plantation Key Pork Chop with smoked-Gouda fondue; slow-cooked prime rib; shrimp and grits; barbecue pork ribs.

OTHER RECOMMENDATIONS Catch of the day, banana bread pudding sundae, Key lime tart.

SUMMARY AND COMMENTS Service is super-friendly, and the kitchen turns out tasty casual fare. Take a stroll on the boardwalk with a Rum Runner or frozen margarita after your meal.

Paradiso 37 ★★½

GLOBAL	INEXPENSIVE	QUALITY ★★★	VALUE ★★★
READER-SURVEY RESPONSES	71% 👍 29% 👎	DISNEY DINING PLAN?	Yes

FULL-SERVICE RESTAURANTS: RATED AND RANKED

Disney Springs; ☎ 407-934-3700

Reservations Accepted. **When to go** Lunch or dinner. **Dining Plan credits** 1 per person, per meal. **Cost range** $10–$27 (child $8). **Service** ★★★. **Friendliness** ★★★★. **Parking** Disney Springs lot. **Bar** Full service. **Wine selection** Limited. **Dress** Casual. **Disabled access** Yes. **Customers** Theme park guests, locals. **Lunch and dinner** Sunday–Wednesday, 11:30 a.m.–midnight; Thursday–Saturday, 11:30 a.m.–1 a.m.

SETTING AND ATMOSPHERE In keeping with all the development going on at Disney Springs, Paradiso recently expanded, nearly doubling its seating, adding more terrace dining, and installing a new outdoor performance stage along the waterfront. Ambience is festive and casual, with an open kitchen. Food is inspired by street foods of Central, South, and North America, from mac-and-cheese bites to enchiladas and barbecue pork.

HOUSE SPECIALTIES Ceviche, jalapeño burger, Argentinean skirt steak, whole crispy chicken and Chilean-style salmon, and the "mangled margarita," a combo of a margarita and sangria. (The *37* in the name refers to the number of varieties of tequila.)

OTHER RECOMMENDATIONS Quesadillas, burritos, deep-fried mac and cheese.

SUMMARY AND COMMENTS The construction at Disney Springs makes it a bit of a challenge to get here, and the drinks outshine the food, but Paradiso 37 is one of the few Disney spots that cooks burgers medium-rare. And the joint boasts "the coldest beer in the world," served at a crisp 29°F–32°F.

Planet Hollywood ★★½

AMERICAN	MODERATE	QUALITY ★★	VALUE ★★
READER-SURVEY RESPONSES 66% 👍	34% 👎	DISNEY DINING PLAN? Yes	

Disney Springs; ☎ 407-827-7827

Reservations Recommended. **Dining Plan credits** 1 per person, per meal. **When to go** Late lunch. **Cost range** $11–$31 (child $8). **Service** ★★. **Friendliness** ★★. **Parking** Lot near the old Pleasure Island complex. **Bar** Full service. **Wine selection** Limited. **Dress** Casual. **Disabled access** Yes. **Customers** Tourists, locals. **Lunch and dinner** Daily, 11 a.m.–1 a.m.

SETTING AND ATMOSPHERE By early 2016, Planet Hollywood's makeover—part of the overall transformation of Downtown Disney into Disney Springs—will be complete. The trademark globe structure is being reimagined as a four-story observatory, in keeping with Disney Springs' turn-of-the-century design aesthetic. The interior will feature spherical, planet-shaped lighting fixtures and new finishes, but the movie memorabilia will stay. A new outdoor terrace and bar space, called Stargazers, will present live entertainment, while a DJ will spin in the main dining room.

HOUSE SPECIALTIES World Famous Chicken Crunch, Kobe sliders, watermelon-and-feta salad, barbecue ribs, shrimp fajitas, L.A. Lasagna, bananas Foster cheesecake.

OTHER RECOMMENDATIONS Lobster roll; Thanksgiving Every Day (turkey legs, spicy sausage stuffing, gravy, and mashed potatoes); hand-dipped shakes.

SUMMARY AND COMMENTS It was time for a makeover at Planet Hollywood, recognized by guests from around the world as an American icon.

The Plaza Restaurant ★★

AMERICAN	MODERATE	QUALITY ★★	VALUE ★★
READER-SURVEY RESPONSES 90% 👍	10% 👎	DISNEY DINING PLAN? Yes	

Main Street, U.S.A., Magic Kingdom; ☎ 407-939-3463

Reservations Required. **Dining Plan credits** 1 per person, per meal. **When to go** Lunch or dinner. **Cost range** $12–$18 (child $8.59). **Service** ★★★★. **Friendliness** ★★★★. **Parking** Magic Kingdom lot. **Bar** No alcohol served. **Dress** Casual. **Disabled access** Yes. **Customers** Theme park guests. **Lunch and dinner** 11 a.m.–15 minutes before park closing.

SETTING AND ATMOSPHERE The Plaza, a quaint and cozy spot tucked away on a side street at the end of Main Street as you head to Tomorrowland, adds Art Nouveau touches to Main Street's Victorian theming. Decor aside, it's air-conditioned heaven on a sweltering Florida day.

HOUSE SPECIALTIES Chicken-strawberry salad, tuna salad on croissant, beef brisket–onion burger, Reuben sandwich, ice-cream desserts such as the Plaza banana split or sundae.

OTHER RECOMMENDATIONS Plaza Club; veggie sandwich with fresh mozzarella, hummus, and basil pesto. For kids, turkey sandwich, grilled chicken strips, grilled cheese, cheeseburger, PB&J.

SUMMARY AND COMMENTS While it's not on anyone's Disney-dining bucket list, The Plaza is a true blast from the past—it was one of the first restaurants at the Magic Kingdom when the park opened in 1971. So go and enjoy an old-fashioned indulgence like a hot-fudge sundae or banana split.

Portobello ★★½

ITALIAN	EXPENSIVE	QUALITY ★★★	VALUE ★★
READER-SURVEY RESPONSES 86% 👍	14% 👎	DISNEY DINING PLAN? Yes	

Disney Springs; ☎ 407-934-8888

Reservations Recommended. **Dining Plan credits** 1 per person, per meal. **When to go** Anytime. **Cost range** Lunch $9–$15 (child $7–$11), dinner $10–$29 (child $7–$13). **Service** ★★★. **Friendliness** ★★★★. **Parking** Lot near the old Pleasure Island complex. **Bar** Full service. **Wine selection** Very good; heavily Italian. **Dress** Casual. **Disabled access** Yes. **Customers** Tourists, locals. **Lunch** Daily, 11:30 a.m.–4 p.m. **Dinner** Daily, 4–11 p.m.

SETTING AND ATMOSPHERE On the waterfront at Disney Springs, Portobello has a faux-Tuscan interior designed to look like a "country Italian trattoria." A very *large* trattoria.

HOUSE SPECIALTIES Antipasti platter, wood-burning-oven pizzas, house-made lasagna, meatball sub.

OTHER RECOMMENDATIONS Grilled flat-iron steak, milk-braised pork shoulder, Italian gelato and sorbet.

SUMMARY AND COMMENTS The best seats are on the shaded porch. Service is spotty, food is ordinary.

Raglan Road Irish Pub & Restaurant ★★★★

IRISH	MODERATE	QUALITY ★★★½	VALUE ★★★
READER-SURVEY RESPONSES 92% 👍	8% 👎	DISNEY DINING PLAN? Yes	

Disney Springs; ☎ 407-938-0300

Reservations Recommended. **Dining Plan credits** 1 per person, per meal. **When to go** Monday–Saturday after 8 p.m. **Cost range** Weekend brunch $8–$19, lunch $15–$27 (child $7–$14), dinner $15–$29 (child $7–$14); family-style roasts (6+ people) $35–$55. **Service** ★★★½. **Friendliness** ★★★★★. **Parking** Marketplace lot or lot near the old Pleasure Island complex. **Bar** Irish whiskeys and beers. **Wine selection** Better than a pub's but not extensive. **Dress** Casual. **Disabled access** Yes. **Customers** Tourists and locals. **Weekend brunch, lunch, and dinner** 11 a.m.–11 p.m., with pub grub available until closing (1 a.m.-ish).

SETTING AND ATMOSPHERE Many elements of this pub, including the bar, were hand-crafted from hardwoods in Ireland and sent to the United States for reassembly ("lock, stock, and beer barrel," as the website advises). The venue is huge by Irish-pub standards, but the dark polished-wood paneling, as well as the snugs (small, private cubbyholes), preserves the feel of the traditional pub. The pentagonal main room sits beneath an impressive but very unpublike dome. In the middle of the room is a tall, tablelike platform accessible to Celtic dancers via a permanently attached short staircase. A modest bandstand is situated along the wall in front of a large pseudo-hearth. Branching from the cavernous domed center room are cozy dining areas and snugs.

HOUSE SPECIALTIES Celebrity chef Kevin Dundon, star of the Irish reality shows *Guerrilla Gourmet* and *Heat* as well as *Kevin Dundon's Modern Irish Food* on PBS, oversees the kitchen, which turns out classic Irish fare with a twist. The must-try appetizer is the Dalkey Duo: batter-fried cocktail sausages with a mustard dipping sauce. And while you could order a burger, we recommend branching out and trying something different— say, Kevin's Heavenly Ham (glazed loin of bacon with cabbage and potatoes), Cluck Curry (chicken curry with almond rice), or Sod the Stew (beef stew infused with a hint of Guinness). And of course, beer-battered fish and chips.

Fun "Host the Roast" family-style brunches—offered weekends and including sides and dessert—serve six or more and must be ordered 48 hours in advance. Choose from lemon-thyme chicken, stuffed leg of lamb, pork loin, or beef rib roast. Brunch also includes boxty (a "sandwich" of Irish ham and Cheddar between two hash-brown cakes, topped with a fried egg), omelets, pancakes, sausages, and the requisite Bloody Marys and mimosas.

ENTERTAINMENT AND AMENITIES Though you could consider a great selection of Irish lagers and stouts an amenity, the real draw here is the Celtic music. A talented band plays daily. Starting in the early evening with a couple of superb acoustic sets, the band sets up as the diners filter out and the pub crawlers settle in. A Celtic dancer wanders in and dances on the aforementioned table to some of the numbers. (Think *Riverdance,* not stripper pole.)

SUMMARY AND COMMENTS A night in a good Irish pub, Raglan Road included, is a joyous and uplifting experience. As the Irish say, it'll set you right up.

Rainforest Cafe ★★½

AMERICAN	MODERATE	QUALITY ★★	VALUE ★★
READER-SURVEY RESPONSES† 83% 👍		17% 👎	DISNEY DINING PLAN? Yes

†*Average of Animal Kingdom (84% 👍) and Disney Springs (81% 👍)*

Disney's Animal Kingdom; ☎ 407-938-9100
Disney Springs Marketplace; ☎ 407-827-8500

Reservations Recommended. **Dining Plan credits** 1 per person, per meal. **When to go** After the lunch crunch, in late afternoon, and before dinner hour. **Cost range** $13–$26 (child $6–$7). **Service** ★★★. **Friendliness** ★★★★. **Parking** Marketplace lot. **Bar** Full bar. **Wine selection** Limited. **Dress.** Casual. **Disabled access** Yes. **Customers** Tourists, locals. **Hours** *Disney's Animal Kingdom:* Daily, 8:30 a.m.–park closing; *Disney Springs Marketplace:* Sunday–Thursday, 11 a.m.–11 p.m.; Friday and Saturday, 11 a.m.–midnight. (Animal Kingdom location serves breakfast; Disney Springs location does not.)

SETTING AND ATMOSPHERE It's always packed, and there's usually a wait, but families flock to this now-familiar restaurant for big plates of food in a noisy dining room with lots to keep the kids entertained. Look for the giant volcano that can be seen, and heard, erupting all over the Marketplace; the smoke coming from the volcano is nonpolluting, in accordance with the restaurant's conservation theme. The dining room looks like a jungle—imagine all the silk plants in the world tacked to the ceiling—complete with animatronic elephants, bats, and monkeys (not the most realistic we've seen). There's occasional thunder and even some rainfall.

HOUSE SPECIALTIES House-made crab dip, Caribbean coconut shrimp, burgers, ribs, brownie cake with ice cream.

ENTERTAINMENT AND AMENITIES After the wait you endure, a chair and some sustenance are all the entertainment you'll need. If you're willing to pay to avoid the long wait, stop by the day before and buy a Landry's Select Club membership for $25. By presenting your card on the day you want to dine, you'll be seated much faster (and get 10% off retail and other benefits).

SUMMARY AND COMMENTS While we've never been impressed by the Rainforest Cafes, a lot of our readers rave about them. The shopping and the kid appeal must be the attractions, because it certainly isn't the food: Preparations are spotty, and waits can be horrendous.

Ravello ★★★

ITALIAN	MODERATE	QUALITY ★★★	VALUE ★★★
READER-SURVEY RESPONSES	Too new to rate	DISNEY DINING PLAN?	No

Four Seasons Resort Orlando at Walt Disney World; ☎ 407-313-7777

Reservations Required. **When to go** Breakfast and dinner. **Cost range** Breakfast $11–$32, dinner $16–$49. **Service** ★★★. **Friendliness** ★★★. **Parking** Lot at Four Seasons Resort; valet. **Bar** Full service. **Wine selection** Good. **Dress** Casual. **Disabled access** Yes. **Customers** Locals and Disney guests. **Breakfast** 6:30–11 a.m. **Dinner** 5:30–10 p.m.

SETTING AND ATMOSPHERE Ravello is designed with floor-to-ceiling windows, light woods, and sleek furniture, with an open kitchen as the centerpiece. There's also outdoor seating. And it's the spot at the Four Seasons to meet the Disney characters—Goofy and his pals—for breakfast on Thursdays and Saturdays.

HOUSE SPECIALTIES For breakfast, Key lime curd–stuffed brioche French toast, smoked beef brisket Benedict, huevos rancheros; buffet with omelet station. For dinner, steamed mussels with San Marzano tomatoes and lemon bread; ravioli stuffed with veal, spinach, and ricotta; spinach gnocchi; wood-grilled pizzas; grilled rib eye; pan-seared duck breast.

SUMMARY AND COMMENTS Most non–Four Seasons guests head to the resort to dine at Capa (see page 346), but Ravello is less expensive, and the food is authentic "modern Italian." If you want a quiet spot, ask for an outside table (especially during character breakfasts).

Restaurant Marrakesh ★★

MOROCCAN	MODERATE	QUALITY ★★½	VALUE ★★
READER-SURVEY RESPONSES	86% 👍 14% 👎	DISNEY DINING PLAN?	Yes

Morocco, World Showcase, Epcot; ☎ 407-939-3463

Reservations Accepted. **Dining Plan credits** 1 per person, per meal. **When to go** Lunch or dinner. **Cost range** Lunch $15–$22 (child $8), dinner $21–$45 (child $8). **Service** ★★★★. **Friendliness** ★★★★. **Parking** Epcot lot. **Bar** Full service. **Wine selection** Limited. **Dress** Casual. **Disabled access** Yes. **Customers** Theme park guests. **Lunch** Daily, noon–3:15 p.m. **Dinner** Daily, 3:30 p.m.–park closing.

SETTING AND ATMOSPHERE At the very back of the Morocco Pavilion, Marrakesh re-creates a Moroccan palace with tile mosaics, inlaid-wood ceilings, brass chandeliers, subdued lighting, and red Bukhara carpets. Moroccan artisans crafted the decor when the pavilion opened in 1982, and nothing has changed, including the menu.

HOUSE SPECIALTIES The appetizer combo is a good way to sample the beef *brewat* (pastry filled with beef, deep-fried, and sprinkled with cinnamon sugar), *bastilla* (a minced-chicken pie sprinkled with cinnamon sugar), and *jasmina* salad. Follow with shish kebab, roast lamb, or lemon chicken. Picky kids can choose from chicken tenders, pasta, and burgers.

OTHER RECOMMENDATIONS If you're hungry, curious, or both, try the Berber Feast, with tastes of several courses.

ENTERTAINMENT AND AMENITIES Moroccan band and belly dancing.

SUMMARY AND COMMENTS Marrakesh is one of the least-busy World Showcase restaurants, mainly because the cuisine has been homogenized for American palates—nothing is overly spicy or too unfamiliar. But it's fun to watch the belly dancers and hear some beautiful Middle Eastern music.

Rose & Crown Dining Room ★★★

ENGLISH	MODERATE	QUALITY ★★★½	VALUE ★★
READER-SURVEY RESPONSES	90% 👍	10% 👎	DISNEY DINING PLAN? Yes

United Kingdom, World Showcase, Epcot; ☎ 407-939-3463

Reservations Accepted. **Dining Plan credits** 1 per person, per meal. **When to go** Lunch or dinner. **Cost range** Lunch $15–$29 (child $8.59), dinner $16–$32 (child $8.50). **Service** ★★★★★. **Friendliness** ★★★★★. **Parking** Epcot lot. **Bar** Full bar with Bass, Guinness, and Harp beers on tap. **Wine selection** Limited. **Dress** Casual. **Disabled access** Yes. **Customers** Epcot guests. **Lunch** Daily, noon–3:20 p.m. **Dinner** Daily, 4:30 p.m.–park closing.

SETTING AND ATMOSPHERE Pub in the front, dining room in the back. The pub hops with activity from open to close and has the look and feel of a traditional English watering hole: a large, cozy bar with rich wood appointments, beamed ceilings, and a hardwood floor. The adjoining dining room is rustic and simple.

HOUSE SPECIALTIES Fish and chips, bangers and mash (sausage and mashed potatoes), pan-roasted salmon, and shepherd's pie (the vegetarian version is delicious, too), washed down with Bass ale.

OTHER RECOMMENDATIONS Trio of UK cheeses, Scotch egg (a hard-boiled egg with a deep-fried sausage coating), cider-braised corned beef, the requisite New York strip steak, and sticky toffee pudding for dessert.

SUMMARY AND COMMENTS At dinnertime, the Rose & Crown is packed with folks bogarting tables for *IllumiNations*. The food is good, so branch out and try something new—you can always get fish and chips at the adjacent walk-up window.

Sanaa ★★★★

INDIAN/AFRICAN	EXPENSIVE	QUALITY ★★★★	VALUE ★★★★
READER-SURVEY RESPONSES	91% 👍	9% 👎	DISNEY DINING PLAN? Yes

Animal Kingdom Villas–Kidani Village; ☎ 407-939-3463

Reservations Accepted. **Dining Plan credits** 1 per person, per meal. **When to go** Lunch or dinner. **Cost range** Lunch $15–$24 (child $8.59), dinner $18–$34 (child $8.59). **Service** ★★★★. **Friendliness** ★★★★. **Parking** Valet ($20) or garage. **Bar** Full service. **Wine selection** Good. **Dress** Casual. **Disabled access** Yes. **Customers** Theme park guests, locals, Disney Vacation Club guests. **Lunch** Daily, 11:30 a.m.–4 p.m. **Dinner** Daily, 4:30 p.m.–park closing.

SETTING AND ATMOSPHERE A floor down from the Kidani Village lobby, Sanaa's casual dining room is inspired by African outdoor markets, with baskets, beads, and art on the walls. It's a cozy space, with 9-foot-tall windows that look out on the resort's savanna—giraffes, water buffalo, and other animals wander within yards of you as you dine.

HOUSE SPECIALTIES Starters include Indian-style breads (naan, onion *kulcha,* and *paneer paratha*) served with red-chile sambal, spicy jalapeno-lime pickle, coriander chutney, and cucumber raita; tandoori chicken; sustainable fish with shrimp and scallops. For lunch, lamb kefta sliders and tandoori shrimp sandwich; for dinner, butter chicken, chicken vindaloo, seafood curry, and sustainable fish. Diverse Old and New World wines pair beautifully with the food.

OTHER RECOMMENDATIONS Tandoori-marinated pork tenderloin, Tanzanian chocolate mousse.

SUMMARY AND COMMENTS Sanaa (sah-**NAH**) has become a favorite of Disney cast members and locals—the flavors are addicting. It's not as upscale as Jiko, the resort's fine-dining restaurant (page 358), offering instead a casual take on African-Indian fusion cuisine.

San Angel Inn Restaurante ★★★

MEXICAN	EXPENSIVE	QUALITY ★★★	VALUE ★★
READER-SURVEY RESPONSES	79% 👍	21% 👎 DISNEY DINING PLAN?	Yes

Mexico, World Showcase, Epcot; ☎ 407-939-3463

Reservations Accepted. **Dining Plan credits** 1 per person, per meal. **When to go** Lunch or dinner. **Cost range** Lunch $18–$24.50 (child $8.50–$9.50), dinner $23.50–$28.50 (child $8.50–$9.50). **Service** ★★★. **Friendliness** ★★★. **Parking** Epcot lot. **Bar** Full service. **Wine selection** Limited. **Dress** Casual. **Disabled access** Yes. **Customers** Theme park guests. **Lunch** Daily, 11:30 a.m.–4 p.m. **Dinner** Daily, 4:30 p.m.–park closing.

SETTING AND ATMOSPHERE Step inside the Aztec pyramid in Mexico, navigate the busy marketplace, and end up at San Angel Inn, which overlooks a starry sky and the Gran Fiesta Tour boat ride. Its decor is inspired by the original San Angel Inn in Mexico City.

HOUSE SPECIALTIES Appetizers include *tlacoyos de chilorio,* corn cakes topped with refried beans, pork, *queso fresco,* sour cream, and green-tomatillo sauce; and quesadillas *repozadas,* battered corn quesadillas stuffed with corn, *huitlacoche* (Mexican truffle), mushrooms, and queso fresco. Still on the menu is the classic mole poblano—chicken in a sauce made from several kinds of chiles and unsweetened Mexican chocolate.

OTHER RECOMMENDATIONS Chile relleno, carne asada, cheesecake with *cajeta* (caramel sauce).

ENTERTAINMENT AND AMENITIES Mariachi or marimba bands in the courtyard.

SUMMARY AND COMMENTS The prices are steep, but the menu goes beyond the typical tacos and such, offering special and regional dishes that are difficult to find in the United States. And the dining room is a cool, quiet respite from the theme park.

Sci-Fi Dine-In Theater Restaurant ★★

AMERICAN	MODERATE	QUALITY ★★½	VALUE ★★
READER-SURVEY RESPONSES	86% 👍	14% 👎 DISNEY DINING PLAN?	Yes

Commissary Lane, Disney's Hollywood Studios; ☎ 407-939-3463

Reservations Recommended. **Dining Plan credits** 1 per person, per meal. **When to go** Anytime. **Cost range** $14–$32 (child $9). **Service** ★★★★★. **Friendliness** ★★★★★. **Parking** DHS lot. **Bar** Full service. **Wine selection** Limited. **Dress**

Casual. **Disabled access** Yes. **Customers** Theme park guests. **Lunch** Sunday and Wednesday, 10:30 a.m.–4 p.m.; Monday and Tuesday and Thursday–Saturday, 11 a.m.–4 p.m. **Dinner** Daily, 4 p.m.–park closing.

SETTING AND ATMOSPHERE Walk through the doors and into the back of a simulated soundstage; then round the corner into a stage set that re-creates a drive-in from the 1950s, with faux classic cars instead of tables. Hop in, order, and watch campy black-and-white clips. Servers, some on roller skates, take your order from the driver's seat.

HOUSE SPECIALTIES Same menu at lunch and dinner, with everything from burgers to pasta and New York strip.

ENTERTAINMENT AND AMENITIES Cartoons and clips of vintage horror and sci-fi movies, such as *Attack of the 50 Foot Woman, Robot Monster,* and *The Blob.*

SUMMARY AND COMMENTS We consider the Sci-Fi an attraction, not a dining destination: The concept is fun, but the prices are too high for what you get. Stick with simple fare (the Reuben is delicious), fill up on appetizers, or just order a shake or hot-fudge sundae. If you must try Sci-Fi, we recommend making late-afternoon or late-evening Advance Reservations. Otherwise, try walking in around 11 a.m. or 3 p.m.

Shula's Steak House ★★★★

STEAK	EXPENSIVE	QUALITY ★★★★	VALUE ★★
READER-SURVEY RESPONSES 90% 👍	10% 👎	DISNEY DINING PLAN? No	

Dolphin Resort; ☎ 407-934-1362

Reservations Required. **When to go** Dinner. **Cost range** $28–$130 (for the Australian lobster tail). *Note:* Everything is à la carte. **Service** ★★★★. **Friendliness** ★★★★. **Parking** Valet (free with validation) or hotel lot ($17). **Bar** Full service. **Wine selection** Good; expensive. **Dress** Dressy. **Disabled access** Yes. **Customers** Hotel guests and locals. **Dinner** Daily, 5–11 p.m.

SETTING AND ATMOSPHERE Shula's feels more like a men's club than a resort restaurant, but the appeal to conventioneers is obvious: dark woods, even darker lighting, large gilt-framed black-and-white photographs of football players in action, and high prices that get passed on to expense accounts.

HOUSE SPECIALTIES In a word, meat—really expensive but very high-quality meat. Only certified Angus beef is served: filet mignon, porterhouse (including a 48-ounce cut), and prime rib.

OTHER RECOMMENDATIONS Barbecued shrimp stuffed with basil, seasonal oysters, 4-pound Maine lobster, catch of the day.

SUMMARY AND COMMENTS Shula's is classier than it is kitschy, though printing the menu on the side of a football and placing it on a kickoff tee in the center of the table is a bit much. We could also do without the rehearsed spiel from the waiters and the pretentious parading of raw beef and live lobster at each table. But if you've got deep pockets and you're in the mood for red meat, Shula's has you covered.

Shutters at Old Port Royale ★★

STEAK AND SEAFOOD	MODERATE	QUALITY ★★½	VALUE ★★
READER-SURVEY RESPONSES 88% 👍	13% 👎	DISNEY DINING PLAN? Yes	

Caribbean Beach Resort; ☎ 407-939-3463

Reservations Accepted. **Dining Plan credits** 1 per person, per meal. **When to go** Dinner. **Cost range** $18–$34 (child $8.59). **Service** ★★★. **Friendliness** ★★★★★. **Parking** Hotel lot. **Bar** Full service. **Wine selection** Moderate. **Dress** Casual. **Disabled access** Yes. **Customers** Hotel guests. **Dinner** Daily, 5–10 p.m.

SETTING AND ATMOSPHERE In the Old Port Royale section of Caribbean Beach, Shutters is the resort's table-service restaurant. The sparsely decorated dining room has kind of a neglected feel, but the chef is having fun in the kitchen whipping up Caribbean-inspired dishes.

HOUSE SPECIALTIES Barbecue pork brisket, Island Pasta with chorizo and shrimp, grilled rib eye, jerk-rubbed mahimahi.

OTHER RECOMMENDATIONS Chicken wings in habanero–brown sugar glaze, barbecue shrimp and grits, braised beef–pepper jack cheese empanada.

SUMMARY AND COMMENTS You likely wouldn't go to Shutters if you weren't already staying at the hotel, but the food is fine, the service is friendly, and you don't need a reservation.

Spice Road Table ★★★½

MOROCCAN	MODERATE	QUALITY ★★★★	VALUE ★★★
READER-SURVEY RESPONSES	88% 👍 13% 👎	DISNEY DINING PLAN? No	

Morocco, World Showcase, Epcot; ☎ 407-939-3463

Reservations Not accepted. **When to go** Anytime, but primo spot for nightly fireworks. **Cost range** $8–$10 small plates, $22–$30 entrees (child $6–$8). **Service** ★★★★★. **Friendliness** ★★★★★. **Parking** Epcot lot. **Bar** Full service. **Wine selection** Limited. **Dress** Casual. **Disabled access** Yes. **Customers** Epcot guests. **Hours** Daily, 11 a.m.–park closing.

SETTING AND ATMOSPHERE Along the waterfront at Epcot, Spice Road Table is a fantastic spot for watching nightly fireworks from either the covered terrace or the small dining room, tastefully appointed with Moroccan art. Friendly servers usher theme park guests into the cool interior; a well-stocked bar is the centerpiece as you walk through the front door The best seats, 120 in all, are on the terrace, unless it's a hot Florida day.

HOUSE SPECIALTIES Tapas, Mediterranean-style: hummus and olives, mussels tagine, fried calamari, lamb sliders, rice-stuffed grape leaves. Entrees include rack of lamb and beef and chicken kebabs.

OTHER RECOMMENDATIONS Coriander-crusted rack of lamb; yellowfin tuna with eggplant, zucchini, capers, and basil oil.

SUMMARY AND COMMENTS The small plates are made for sharing; pair them with organic sangria, a Mediterranean beer, or a signature cocktail. If you just want something cold on a hot afternoon, the adjacent Spice Road Juice Bar is the spot for a Moroccarita, Habibi Daiquiri, Sultan's Colada, or nonalcoholic Royal Blue Oasis Slushie; beer, sangria, and wine; or house-made ice cream in unusual flavors such as toasted almond and rosewater.

Splitsville ★★½

AMERICAN	MODERATE	QUALITY ★★½	VALUE ★★
READER-SURVEY RESPONSES	100% 👍 0% 👎	DISNEY DINING PLAN? Yes	

Disney Springs West Side; ☎ 407-938-PINS (7467)

Reservations Accepted. **Dining Plan credits** 1 per person, per meal. **Cost range** $7–$16 (child $7). **Service** ★★½. **Friendliness** ★★★. **Parking** Disney Springs lot. **Bar** Full service. **Wine selection** Don't expect Lafite Rothschild. **Dress** Casual. **Disabled access** Yes. **Customers** Tourists. **Hours** Monday–Friday, 10:30 a.m.–late, opens Saturday and Sunday at 10 a.m.

SETTING AND ATMOSPHERE Splitsville is part of a multistate chain of "luxury lanes"—hybrid bowling alleys–restaurants. The decor is vaguely mid-century modern, with Sputnik lamps and other Space Age touches. It's loud, obviously, but there's plenty to see and also room for rambunctious kids to roam while you wait for your food.

HOUSE SPECIALTIES The sushi—salmon, shrimp, tuna, crab, and various combinations thereof—is the best thing on the menu.

OTHER RECOMMENDATIONS Meat eaters will like the steak chimichurri or pulled-pork sandwich. The Birthday Cake Martini, garnished with sprinkles, is like having Betty Crocker as your bartender.

SUMMARY AND COMMENTS The menu is more spread-out than a 7/10 split: Burgers, sushi, pizza, seafood, barbecue, Mexican, and Italian are represented, plus nachos and other bar food. It would be a stretch for any kitchen to make half of these things well, let alone a kitchen in a bowling alley. We've tried almost everything on the menu, and while all of it was OK, the only thing we'd order again is the sushi.

Teppan Edo ★★★½

JAPANESE	EXPENSIVE		QUALITY ★★★★	VALUE ★★★
READER-SURVEY RESPONSES	93% 👍	7% 👎	DISNEY DINING PLAN?	Yes

Japan, World Showcase, Epcot; ☎ 407-939-3463

Reservations Recommended. **Dining Plan credits** 1 per person, per meal. **When to go** Lunch or dinner. **Cost range** $18–$32 (child $9.50–$13.50). **Service** ★★★★★. **Friendliness** ★★★★★. **Parking** Epcot lot. **Bar** Full service. **Wine selection** Limited. **Dress** Casual. **Disabled access** Via elevator. **Customers** Epcot guests. **Lunch** Daily, noon–3:45 p.m. **Dinner** Daily, 4 p.m.–park closing.

SETTING AND ATMOSPHERE Six Japanese dining rooms with grills on tables and entertaining chefs chopping, slicing, and dicing.

HOUSE SPECIALTIES Chicken, shrimp, beef, scallops, and Asian vegetables stir-fried on a teppanyaki grill by a knife-juggling chef.

ENTERTAINMENT AND AMENITIES Watching the teppanyaki chefs.

SUMMARY AND COMMENTS A popular dining option for families—the communal tables are a fun way to meet other guests. You'll get plenty to eat, but the starters include sushi, tempura, ribs, edamame, and miso soup.

Todd English's bluezoo ★★★

SEAFOOD	EXPENSIVE		QUALITY ★★★★	VALUE ★★
READER-SURVEY RESPONSES	71% 👍	29% 👎	DISNEY DINING PLAN?	No

Dolphin Resort; ☎ 407-934-1111

Reservations Recommended. **When to go** Dinner. **Cost range** $28–$60 (child $10–$16). *Note:* Everything is à la carte. **Service** ★★★★. **Friendliness** ★★★. **Parking** Valet (free with validation) or hotel lot ($17). **Bar** Full service. **Wine selection** Excellent. **Dress** Dressy casual. **Disabled access** Yes. **Customers** Hotel guests, locals. **Dinner** Daily, 5–11 p.m.

SETTING AND ATMOSPHERE One of our favorite dining rooms at Disney, swathed in blues with iridescent bubbles suspended from the lights. The name is courtesy of celebrity chef Todd English's son, who as a young boy saw an under-the-sea movie and said it looked like a "blue zoo." Open kitchen, raw bar, and a unique circular rotisserie that makes the fish being grilled on it seem to dance on the coals.

HOUSE SPECIALTIES "Dancing fish" (from the rotisserie), 2-pound Maine lobster in sticky soy glaze, 72-hour short ribs, mesquite beef tenderloin.

OTHER RECOMMENDATIONS New England–style clam chowder with salt-cured bacon, teppan-seared jumbo sea scallops, raw-bar platter, grass-fed lamb.

SUMMARY AND COMMENTS English's stylish Florida outpost is frequented mainly by conventioneers who don't mind the high prices—$3 for a single oyster, $60 for the 2-pound lobster—or the expensive wine list. Although bluezoo is primarily a seafood place, the beef tenderloin is excellent as well.

Tokyo Dining ★★★

JAPANESE	MODERATE	QUALITY ★★★★	VALUE ★★★
READER-SURVEY RESPONSES 90% 👍	10% 👎	DISNEY DINING PLAN? Yes	

Japan, World Showcase, Epcot; ☎ 407-939-3463

Reservations Accepted. **Dining Plan credits** 1 per person, per meal. **When to go** Lunch. **Cost range** $9–$30 (child $10.50–$11.50). **Service** ★★★★. **Friendliness** ★★★. **Parking** Epcot lot. **Bar** Full service. **Wine selection** Limited. **Dress** Casual. **Disabled access** Yes. **Customers** Theme park guests. **Lunch** Daily, noon–3:45 p.m. **Dinner** Daily, 4 p.m.–park close.

SETTING AND ATMOSPHERE Gracious service, modern Asian decor, and a beautifully lit sushi bar distinguish this restaurant. There are no seats at the sushi bar, but the sushi chefs are great entertainment for the entire dining room. Tables near the windows have a wonderful second-floor view of World Showcase.

HOUSE SPECIALTIES Tempura shrimp, chicken, and vegetables; panko oysters; sushi; bento box with sliced steak, sashimi, California roll, tempura shrimp, and vegetables served with sukiyaki beef rice.

SUMMARY AND COMMENTS The dining room is sleek, the sushi is super-fresh, and the overall experience is relaxing and congenial.

Tony's Town Square Restaurant ★★½

ITALIAN	MODERATE	QUALITY ★★★	VALUE ★★
READER-SURVEY RESPONSES 79% 👍	21% 👎	DISNEY DINING PLAN? Yes	

Main Street, U.S.A., Magic Kingdom; ☎ 407-939-3463

Reservations Recommended. **Dining Plan credits** 1 per person, per meal. **When to go** Late lunch or early dinner. **Cost range** Lunch $13.50–$20 (child $8.59), dinner $17–$30 (child $8.59). **Service** ★★★★. **Friendliness** ★★★★★. **Parking** Magic Kingdom lot. **Bar** No alcohol served. **Dress** Casual. **Disabled access** Yes. **Customers** Magic Kingdom guests. **Lunch** Daily, 11:30 a.m.–2:45 p.m. **Dinner** Daily, 5 p.m.–park closing.

SETTING AND ATMOSPHERE Just inside the Magic Kingdom on Main Street, with a glass-windowed porch that's wonderful for watching the action outside, Tony's Town Square is a bit worn around the edges, but it's another rite of passage for Disney fans—you *must* have a plate of spaghetti in the restaurant that commemorates *Lady and the Tramp*.

HOUSE SPECIALTIES Lunch: sausage-and-pepperoni flatbread, spaghetti with meatballs. Dinner: shrimp scampi, chicken Parmigiana, New York strip.

SUMMARY AND COMMENTS It's not haute cuisine, but Tony's does a decent job with pasta (multigrain and gluten-free options available). Go at lunch, when it's cheaper, and ask for a seat on the porch when you book.

Trader Sam's Grog Grotto ★★★

PAN-ASIAN	MODERATE	QUALITY ★★★	VALUE ★★★
READER-SURVEY RESPONSES Too new to rate	DISNEY DINING PLAN? No		

Disney's Polynesian Village Resort; ☎ 407-824-2000

Reservations Not accepted. **When to go** After 4 p.m. **Cost range** $8.49–$15 (small plates only). **Service** ★★★. **Friendliness** ★★★★. **Parking** Polynesian Village lot or valet ($20). **Bar** Full service. **Wine selection** Good. **Dress** Casual. **Disabled access** Yes. **Customers** Locals and Disney guests. **Hours** Daily, 4 p.m.–midnight.

SETTING AND ATMOSPHERE Fans of Trader Sam's Enchanted Tiki Bar at the Disneyland Hotel couldn't wait for Disney World to get a version of its own. But while the two share nostalgic interactive props and animatronics (the ones here are a nod to the old 20,000 Leagues Under the Sea attraction) and even a few menu items, the Grog Grotto has its own vibe. Off the Polynesian Village's main lobby and featuring views of the marina and Seven Seas Lagoon, this tiki bar has its own lore built in: It was started by Trader Sam, Adventureland's famous "head" salesman, who welcomes you to his enchanted South Seas hideaway to explore a menu of "magical tropical drinks and food."

HOUSE SPECIALTIES Cocktails are the big draw, with names like Castaway Crush, Tahitian Torch, and the over-the-top Uh-Oa!—Myers's and Bacardi rums mixed with various fruit juices and served in a communal tiki bowl with straws all around; there are also "No Booze Brews" for teetotalers.

OTHER RECOMMENDATIONS Small plates include chicken lettuce cups with hoisin-ginger sauce, ahi poke with wasabi yuzu, kalua pork tacos with shredded cabbage and pickled vegetables, pan-fried dumplings with soy-sesame dipping sauce, roasted chicken and pork-pâté *bánh mì* sliders with pickled vegetables, salmon *oshizushi* (pressed sushi), corn-battered Portuguese sausages with curry ketchup, and the Headhunter Sushi Roll.

SUMMARY AND COMMENTS Trader Sam's is already a hit with Disneyphiles, so get there early—there are just 50 seats inside and 80 on the patio.

Trail's End Restaurant ★★

AMERICAN/BUFFET	MODERATE	QUALITY ★★	VALUE ★★
READER-SURVEY RESPONSES 95% 👍	15% 👎	DISNEY DINING PLAN? Yes	

Fort Wilderness Resort & Campground; ☎ 407-939-3463

Reservations Recommended. **Dining Plan credits** 1 per person, per meal. **When to go** Breakfast or dinner. **Cost range** Breakfast $18 (child $11), lunch $12–$17 (child $8.59), dinner $25 (child $14). **Service** ★★★. Friendliness ★★★. **Parking** Fort Wilderness lot. **Bar** Full-service bar next door. **Wine selection** Limited. **Dress** Casual. **Disabled access** Yes. **Customers** Fort Wilderness campers, theme park guests. **Breakfast** 7:30–11:30 a.m. **Lunch** 11:30 a.m.–2 p.m. **Dinner** 4:30–9:30 p.m. Sunday–Thursday, 4:30–10 p.m. Friday and Saturday.

SETTING AND ATMOSPHERE At Fort Wilderness, next to the *Hoop-Dee-Doo Musical Revue,* Trail's End is what a restaurant would've looked like had America's settlers built one out of a log cabin. The interior features exposed log beams, oak tabletops, and walls hung with enough old-timey kitchen equipment to start a flea market. The theming is fun, although the decor could use some freshening up.

HOUSE SPECIALTIES Breakfast and dinner are served buffet-style; lunch transitions to an à la carte menu. Breakfast features eggs, sausage, bacon, waffles, and biscuits and gravy, along with fruit and pastries. Lunch is an odd hodgepodge of everything from Florida rock-shrimp dumplings to flatbreads and chicken and waffles, with s'mores and warm sticky-bun sundaes for dessert. The dinner menu (buffet or carryout) includes fried chicken, ribs, pasta, catch of the day, pizza, and chili.

OTHER RECOMMENDATIONS Fried green tomatoes and beans-and-greens soup at lunch.

SUMMARY AND COMMENTS With its "everything but the kitchen sink" philosophy, Trail's End offers something for everyone.

Trattoria Al Forno ★★★½

ITALIAN	MODERATE	QUALITY ★★★½	VALUE ★★
READER-SURVEY RESPONSES 82% 👍	18% 👎	DISNEY DINING PLAN? Yes	

Disney Springs Marketplace; ☎ 407-939-3463

Reservations Accepted. **Dining Plan credits** 2 per person, per meal. **When to go** Breakfast or dinner. **Cost range** Breakfast $7–$13.50 (child $6.50), dinner $17–$37 (child $8.59). **Service** ★★★. **Friendliness** ★★★★. **Parking** Lot for Disney's BoardWalk and valet. **Bar** Full service. **Wine selection** Good; all Italian. **Dress** Casual. **Disabled access** Yes. **Customers** Locals and Disney guests. **Breakfast** Daily, 7:30–11 a.m. **Dinner** Daily, 5–10 p.m.

SETTING AND ATMOSPHERE The big dining room feels a little more personal with three different "dining areas" and a private room at the back, with an open kitchen for watching the action, including a wood-burning oven. Our favorite spot is the "formal dining room" right in front of the kitchen, where it's a little less noisy (and carpeted), or one of the booths at the back. Servers tend to be a little overattentive, as most of them have been here for years—before its current incarnation, it was Spoodles and then Kouzzina by Cat Cora.

HOUSE SPECIALTIES For breakfast: poached egg over polenta with fennel sausage, red sauce, and Parmesan; waffle with espresso-mascarpone cream; cured Italian meats with hard-boiled egg, tomatoes, and cheeses. For dinner: Thin-sliced cured Italian meats; pizzas; linguini with clams; tagliatelle alla carbonara; T-bone steak; sauteed shrimp with lemon-caper butter and polenta; tiramisu and bomboloni (fried doughnuts).

SUMMARY AND COMMENTS The kitchen is doing things right—making mozzarella and ciabatta daily, rolling out fresh pasta (cavatelli), slicing cured meats with a beautiful Italian flywheel. The wine list is carefully curated, with labels from all of Italy's major regions and more than 30 available by the glass or *quartino*. Breakfast is one of the best on Disney property.

T-REX ★★★

AMERICAN	MODERATE	QUALITY ★★	VALUE ★★
READER-SURVEY RESPONSES	79% 🙂	21% 😣	DISNEY DINING PLAN? Yes

Disney Springs Marketplace; ☎ 407-828-8739

Reservations Recommended. **Dining Plan credits** 1 per person, per meal. **When to go** Lunch or dinner. **Cost range** $13–$32 (child $7–$8). **Service** ★★★. **Friendliness** ★★★. **Parking** Disney Springs lot. **Bar** Full service. **Wine selection** Minimal. **Dress** Casual. **Disabled access** Yes. **Customers** Families. **Lunch and dinner** Daily, 11 a.m.–11 p.m.; open until midnight Friday and Saturday.

SETTING AND ATMOSPHERE Sensory overload in a cavernous dining room with life-size robotic dinosaurs, giant fish tanks, bubbling geysers, waterfalls, fossils in the bathrooms, and crystals in the walls. Volume: loud and louder, with meteor showers and growling dinos.

HOUSE SPECIALTIES Gigantosaurus Burger, Pork-asaurus Sandwich, Prehistoric Pasta, Saber-Tooth Sundae.

OTHER RECOMMENDATIONS Cretaceous Chicken-Fried Steak, Triassic Tortellini, Chocolate Tarpit. (Have you figured out there's a theme here?)

SUMMARY AND COMMENTS Expect a wait unless there's an empty seat at the bar. But nobody's here just for the ordinary, overpriced food—it's nonstop "eatertainment," with kid-friendly food served in huge portions. The coolest spot for dining is the Ice Cave at the back of the restaurant, with glowing blue walls.

Turf Club Bar & Grill ★★

AMERICAN	MODERATE	QUALITY ★★★	VALUE ★★
READER-SURVEY RESPONSES	63% 🙂	37% 😣	DISNEY DINING PLAN? Yes

Saratoga Springs Resort & Spa; ☎ 407-939-3463

Reservations Accepted. **Dining Plan credits** 1 per person, per meal. **When to go** Dinner. **Cost range** Dinner $17–$31.50 (child $8.59). **Service** ★★★. **Friendliness** ★★★★. **Parking** Lot. **Bar** Full service. **Wine selection** Good. **Dress** Casual. **Disabled access** Good. **Customers** Hotel guests. **Dinner** Daily, 5–9 p.m.

SETTING AND ATMOSPHERE If you're looking for an out-of-the-way spot that's quiet with decent food, Turf Club is a good bet. When the weather is nice, ask for an outdoor table; you can spot golfers on the adjacent Lake Buena Vista Golf Course and look across the way to Disney Springs. Just off the lobby of Saratoga Springs Resort, the dining room is equestrian-themed.

HOUSE SPECIALTIES Signature grilled-romaine salad, prime rib, Turf Club pasta.

OTHER RECOMMENDATIONS Grilled lamb chops, sustainable fish, crispy free-range chicken breast with three-cheese mac and cheese.

SUMMARY AND COMMENTS Because this tucked-away spot caters mainly to the Disney Vacation Club crowd, it's rarely crowded. The cuisine won't wow you, but the grilled-romaine salad (with Caesar dressing, balsamic reduction, and roasted cherry tomatoes) is one of Disney's best.

Tusker House Restaurant ★★★

AMERICAN/AFRICAN/BUFFET	MODERATE	QUALITY ★★★	VALUE ★★★
READER-SURVEY RESPONSES 92% 👍	8% 👎	DISNEY DINING PLAN? Yes	

Africa, Disney's Animal Kingdom; ☎ 407-939-3463

Reservations Required for character meals. **Dining Plan credits** 1 per person, per meal. **When to go** Anytime. **Cost range** Breakfast $29 (child $16), lunch $38 (child $19), dinner $44 (child $21). **Service** ★★★. **Friendliness** ★★★. **Parking** Animal Kingdom lot. **Bar** Full-service bar next door. **Dress** Casual. **Disabled access** Yes. **Customers** Theme park guests. **Character breakfast** Daily, 8–10:30 a.m. **Character lunch** Daily, 11:30 a.m.–3:30 p.m. **Character dinner** Daily, 4 p.m.–park closing.

SETTING AND ATMOSPHERE Tusker House's character meals feature Mickey, Donald, Daisy, and Goofy. The setting—inside the Harambe Village square—is plainer than Disney's promotional photos would indicate, especially after dark. The food is good, though not as varied or as interesting as the surroundings would lead you to expect; still, it's fine for filling up families and visiting with the Disney characters.

HOUSE SPECIALTIES Carved sirloin, rotisserie pork and chicken, chicken curry, seafood stew, spiced tofu.

OTHER RECOMMENDATIONS African- and Indian-influenced dishes such as chutney, couscous, and curry.

SUMMARY AND COMMENTS Tusker House appeals to kids who want to meet the Disney characters and grown-ups who appreciate the convenience and value of a buffet. You can try something different, such as beef bobotie at breakfast and curries and chutneys at lunch and dinner, but there are plenty of familiar tastes, too.

Tutto Italia Ristorante ★★★★

ITALIAN	EXPENSIVE	QUALITY ★★★★	VALUE ★★★
READER-SURVEY RESPONSES 83% 👍	17% 👎	DISNEY DINING PLAN? Yes	

Italy, World Showcase, Epcot; ☎ 407-939-3463

Reservations Recommended. **Dining Plan credits** 1 per person, per meal. **When to go** Midafternoon. **Cost range** Lunch $17–$30 (child $10), dinner $23–$30 (child $10). **Service** ★★★★. **Friendliness** ★★★★. **Parking** Epcot lot. **Bar** Beer and wine only. **Wine selection** All Italian. **Dress** Casual. **Disabled access**

Yes. **Customers** Theme park guests. **Lunch** Daily, 11:30 a.m.–3:30 p.m. **Dinner** Daily, 4:30–park closing.

SETTING AND ATMOSPHERE Tutto Italia feels like a big restaurant in Rome or Milan, with huge murals of a piazza along the wall behind the upholstered banquettes, but it can get noisy in the dining room, which is nearly always full. If the weather is pleasant, request a table on the piazza.

HOUSE SPECIALTIES *Fior di latte* mozzarella with roasted peppers and basil; Fettuccine Campagnole (with arugula, spinach, basil, and burrata cheese); chicken scallopine with white asparagus; grilled butcher's steak; panna cotta and gelati for dessert.

OTHER RECOMMENDATIONS Any of the pastas (fettuccine, gnochetti, ravioli, spaghetti); fried calamari.

SUMMARY AND COMMENTS Pricey for relatively simple Italian, but the service is polished, the cuisine is authentic, and the servings are ample.

Las Ventanas   ★★

AMERICAN	MODERATE	QUALITY ★★½	VALUE ★★
READER-SURVEY RESPONSES Too new to rate		DISNEY DINING PLAN? Yes	

Coronado Springs Resort; ☎ 407-939-3463

Reservations Recommended. **Dining Plan credits** 1 per person, per meal. **When to go** Breakfast, lunch, or dinner. **Cost range** Entrees $18–$24, pizzas $19 (individual)–$41 (serves 3–5). Service ★★★★. Friendliness ★★★★. **Parking** Epcot lot. **Bar** Beer and wine only. **Dress** Casual. **Disabled access** Yes. **Customers** Coronado Springs guests. **Breakfast** Daily, 7 a.m.–10:30 a.m. **Lunch** Daily, 11 a.m.–2 p.m. **Dinner** Daily, 4–10 p.m.

SETTING AND ATMOSPHERE Tucked discreetly inside one of the main hallways connecting Coronado's food court with its convention space, Las Ventanas theming is more refined and subdued than the nearby Pepper Market, with high ceilings, dark slate floors, and rust-colored walls.

HOUSE SPECIALTIES Huevos rancheros at breakfast. Prime rib at dinner.

SUMMARY AND COMMENTS Las Ventanas isn't anything special; it's more like additional capacity for when the resort is crowded. Because it's tucked away, it can be a welcome, quiet place for a simple breakfast. Stick to the basics (waffles, eggs, sandwiches, and burgers) and you'll be fine.

Via Napoli   ★★★★

ITALIAN	MODERATE	QUALITY ★★★½	VALUE ★★★
READER-SURVEY RESPONSES 89% 👍 11% 👎		DISNEY DINING PLAN? Yes	

Italy, World Showcase, Epcot; ☎ 407-939-3463

Reservations Recommended. **Dining Plan credits** 1 per person, per meal. **When to go** Lunch or dinner. **Cost range** Entrees $18–$24, pizzas $19 (individual)–$41 (serves 3–5). **Service** ★★★★. **Friendliness** ★★★★. **Parking** Epcot lot. **Bar** Beer and wine only. **Dress** Casual. **Disabled access** Yes. **Customers** Theme park guests. **Lunch** Daily, 11:30 a.m.–3:15 p.m. **Dinner** Daily, 4:30–9 p.m.

SETTING AND ATMOSPHERE The three big pizza ovens are the stars of the show in this loud, cavernous dining room with tile floors and stucco walls, but there are enough staff and guests moving around that it feels like a bustling Italian market. Shaded outdoor seating is also available for those who want a quieter dining spot.

HOUSE SPECIALTIES The best pizza in Walt Disney World. The rest of the menu is average, with the possible exception of the salads.

SUMMARY AND COMMENTS Because the pizzas are cooked at inferno-like temperatures, they don't stay in the oven for long and vegetable toppings stay crunchy. The Capriciossa (eggplant, artichokes, prosciutto, and mushrooms) and four-cheese pies are our favorites.

Victoria & Albert's ★★★★★

GOURMET	EXPENSIVE	QUALITY ★★★★★	VALUE ★★★★
READER-SURVEY RESPONSES	96% 👍 4% 👎	DISNEY DINING PLAN? No	

Grand Floridian Resort & Spa; ☎ 407-939-3862

Reservations Mandatory; must confirm by noon the day of your seating; credit card required to reserve; call at least 180 days in advance to reserve. **When to go** Anytime. **Cost range** Fixed price, $150 per person or $215 with wine pairings; Chef's Table and Queen Victoria's Room, $210 or $315 with wine pairings. **Service** ★★★★★. **Friendliness** ★★★★. **Parking** Valet (free); self-parking is deceptively far away. **Wine selection** 700 on the menu, 4,200 more in the cellar. **Dress** Jacket required for men, evening wear for women. **Disabled access** Yes. **Customers** Hotel guests, locals. **Dinner** 2 seatings nightly at 5:45–6:30 p.m. and 9–9:45 p.m., plus 1 seating at 6 p.m. for the Chef's Table. *Note:* No children under age 10 admitted except at Chef's Table.

SETTING AND ATMOSPHERE Frette linens, Riedel crystal, Christofle silver—with only 18 tables in the main dining room and Queen Victoria's Room with seating for 8, this is the top dining experience at Disney World. A winner of AAA's Five Diamond Award—the only restaurant in Central Florida so honored—Victoria & Albert's is civilized, lavish, and expensive.

HOUSE SPECIALTIES The menu changes daily, but you might find Minnesota elk tenderloin, Alaskan salmon, local free-range Poulet Rouge chicken, and Australian Kobe-style beef on chef Scott Hunnel's menu. Pastry chef Erich Herbitschek's desserts are divine.

ENTERTAINMENT AND AMENITIES A harpist or violinist entertains from the foyer. But the best show is in the kitchen when you book the Chef's Table, where Hunnel crafts a personalized menu.

SUMMARY AND COMMENTS Hunnel (a James Beard Foundation nominee) and his team prepare modern American cuisine with the best of the best from around the world. While the main dining room and Queen Victoria's Room are whisper-quiet, the convivial Chef's Table is a different experience altogether. For epicures, it's a bargain.

The Wave . . . of American Flavors ★★★

NEW AMERICAN	MODERATE	QUALITY ★★	VALUE ★★
READER-SURVEY RESPONSES	94% 👍 6% 👎	DISNEY DINING PLAN? Yes	

Contemporary Resort; ☎ 407-939-3463

Reservations Accepted. **Dining Plan credits** 1 per person, per meal. **When to go** Anytime. **Cost range** Breakfast $9–$12.50 à la carte, $18.50 buffet (child $6.50); lunch $12–$19.50 (child $9); dinner $16.50–$33 (child $9). **Service** ★★★. **Friendliness** ★★★. **Parking** Valet ($20) or hotel lot. **Bar** Full service. **Wine selection** All New World screw-caps. **Dress** Casual. **Disabled access** Yes. **Customers** Hotel guests, locals. **Breakfast** Daily, 7:30–11 a.m. **Lunch** Daily, noon–2 p.m. **Dinner** Daily, 5:30–10 p.m.

SETTING AND ATMOSPHERE On the first floor of the Contemporary just past the front desk, you walk into The Wave's lounge, with the dining room to the left—the lounge is usually packed after 5 p.m., and it's hard to snag a seat. The adjoining dining room has the feel of an upscale coffee shop, with wooden tables and white-linen napkins.

HOUSE SPECIALTIES For breakfast, a generous buffet, organic Colombian press-pot coffee, mega-berry smoothie, multigrain French toast, and make-your-own muesli. For lunch, lump crab–Florida rock shrimp cakes, build-your-own Florida-raised beef burger. For dinner: grilled Colorado lamb chops, sustainable fish, potato gnocchi with braised short rib, vegetarian curry stew.

OTHER RECOMMENDATIONS Pork belly with local eggs, charcuterie board, no-sugar-added crème brûlée.

SUMMARY AND COMMENTS While it's not a dining destination, the kitchen has stayed the course with healthful, locally sourced dining options. Organic beers and coffees, hip cocktails, and all-screw-cap wines—focusing on New World bottlings from Argentina, Australia, Chile, New Zealand, and South Africa—are part of the forward-thinking beverage lineup.

Whispering Canyon Cafe ★★★

AMERICAN	MODERATE	QUALITY ★★★½	VALUE ★★★★
READER-SURVEY RESPONSES	83% 👍 17% 👎	DISNEY DINING PLAN?	Yes

Wilderness Lodge & Villas; ☎ 407-939-3463

Reservations Accepted. **Dining Plan credits** 1 per person, per meal. **When to go** Anytime. **Cost range** Breakfast $10.50–$16.50 (child $7–$8.50), lunch $14–$22 (child $9), dinner $17.50–$34 (child $9). **Service** ★★★★. **Friendliness** ★★★★. **Parking** Hotel lot. **Bar** Full service. **Wine selection** Limited. **Dress** Casual. **Disabled access** Yes. **Customers** Hotel guests. **Breakfast** Daily, 7:30–11:30 a.m. **Lunch** Daily, 11:30 a.m.–2:30 p.m. **Dinner** Daily, 5–10 p.m.

SETTING AND ATMOSPHERE Big, open dining room just off the lobby with whimsical Wild West decor. Despite its name, Whispering Canyon is anything but quiet, with servers encouraging diners to let loose and have fun (pony races, anyone?). Tables have a barrel-top lazy Susan where food is placed for an all-you-can-eat experience.

HOUSE SPECIALTIES For breakfast, the all-you-can-eat platter offers bacon, sausage, scrambled eggs, home fries, buttermilk biscuits and gravy. For lunch and dinner, big skillets loaded with corn bread, pulled pork, smoked pork ribs, roasted chicken, sausage, mashed potatoes, baked beans, and corn on the cob are crowd-pleasers.

OTHER RECOMMENDATIONS New York strip steak, citrus-glazed rainbow trout, s'mores with marshmallow gelato.

SUMMARY AND COMMENTS Whispering Canyon is rowdy fun for families, and the all-you-can-eat skillets give hungry folks their money's worth.

Wolfgang Puck Grand Cafe ★★

CREATIVE CALIFORNIAN	EXPENSIVE	QUALITY ★½	VALUE ★½
READER-SURVEY RESPONSES	94% 👍 6% 👎	DISNEY DINING PLAN?	Yes

Disney Springs West Side; ☎ 407-938-9653

Reservations Recommended. **Dining Plan credits** 1 per person, per meal (downstairs only). **When to go** Early evening. **Cost range** Cafe $12–$29 (child $6–$9), upstairs $25–$45 (child $10–$18). **Service** ★★★. **Friendliness** ★★★. **Parking** Disney Springs lot. **Bar** Full service. **Wine selection** Very good. **Dress** Casual in the cafe; upstairs, collared and sleeved shirts for men and no jeans. **Disabled access** Yes. **Customers** Tourists, locals. **Hours** *Cafe:* Lunch and dinner daily, 11:30 a.m.–11 p.m. *Upstairs:* Dinner Sunday–Wednesday, 6–9 p.m.; Thursday–Saturday, 6–10 p.m.

SETTING AND ATMOSPHERE This is actually two restaurants in one—four if you count the attached Wolfgang Puck Express and the sushi bar that flows into the restaurant's lounge area. Downstairs is the actual cafe, with several open kitchen areas, colorful tile, and plenty of pictures of Puck hanging around. The upstairs is a more formal dining room, but in name only. Both spaces are inordinately loud, making conversation difficult.

HOUSE SPECIALTIES Puck's famous wood-fired pizzas—including barbecue chicken and spicy shrimp—are the best things on the menu. Sushi is also a good bet. Upstairs, the menu features fresh fish, chicken, and beef.

SUMMARY AND COMMENTS With the new Disney Springs overlay, we're hoping this once-delicious dining option makes a comeback. Quality has taken a nosedive in recent years, but visitors still know Puck's name and keep the place busy—in spite of the less-than-stellar food, there's usually a crowd. Try the sushi bar, or skip the entree and go straight for dessert.

Yachtsman Steakhouse ★★★

STEAK	EXPENSIVE	QUALITY ★★★½	VALUE ★★
READER-SURVEY RESPONSES 89% 👍 11% 👎		DISNEY DINING PLAN? Yes	

Yacht Club Resort; ☎ 407-939-3463

Reservations Required. **Dining Plan credits** 2 per person, per meal. **When to go** Dinner. **Cost range** Dinner $31–$110 (child $8–$12). **Service** ★★★★. **Friendliness** ★★★★. **Parking** Hotel lot. **Bar** Full service. **Wine selection** Very good. **Dress** Dressy casual. **Disabled access** Yes. **Customers** Hotel guests and locals. **Dinner** Daily, 5:30–10:30 p.m.

SETTING AND ATMOSPHERE Wooden beams, white linens, and a view of the Yacht Club's sandy lagoon make Yachtsman feel light and airy rather than dark and masculine like the typical steakhouse. Beef is the star, of course, but there are other options on the menu, even vegetarian. The adjacent Crew's Cup Lounge is a fun place to start the evening.

HOUSE SPECIALTIES The 32-ounce porterhouse for two ($110) is a worthy splurge. Outstanding cheese and charcuterie selections, too.

OTHER RECOMMENDATIONS Grilled lamb chop, duck à l'orange; seared ahi tuna, Yachtsman Sundae with gelato and Amarena cherries.

SUMMARY AND COMMENTS Yachtsman Steakhouse has a cult following of local meat-lovers who don't mind the sky-high prices ($45 for prime rib, $59 for a strip steak). The quality is outstanding: The dry-aged steaks are cut and trimmed on the premises, and vintages from every major wine-producing region of the world complement the menu.

Yak & Yeti Restaurant ★★

PAN-ASIAN	EXPENSIVE	QUALITY ★★½	VALUE ★★
READER-SURVEY RESPONSES 85% 👍 15% 👎		DISNEY DINING PLAN? Yes	

Asia, Disney's Animal Kingdom; ☎ 407-939-3463

Reservations Recommended. **Dining Plan credits** 1 per person, per meal. **When to go** Dinner. **Cost range** $17–$26 (child $8.50). **Service** ★★★★. **Friendliness** ★★★★. **Parking** Animal Kingdom lot. **Bar** Full service. **Wine selection** Limited. **Dress** Casual. **Disabled access** Yes. **Customers** Theme park guests. **Lunch** Daily, 11 a.m.–3:30 p.m. **Dinner** Daily, 4 p.m.–park closing.

SETTING AND ATMOSPHERE A rustic two-story Nepalese inn . . . with seating for hundreds. Windows on the second floor overlook the Asia section of the theme park. The Asian artifacts are more interesting than the food.

HOUSE SPECIALTIES Seared miso salmon, Thai-chili chicken wings, wok-fried green beans, teriyaki mahimahi, chicken tikka masala.

SUMMARY AND COMMENTS Yak & Yeti isn't as good as it used to be—with Chinese, Indian, Japanese, and Thai cuisines represented, there's just too much going on. The kitchen should pare down the menu and then fine-tune what's left.

PART FIVE

WALT DISNEY WORLD *with* KIDS

▌▇ The **ECSTASY** *and the* **AGONY**

SO OVERWHELMING IS THE DISNEY MEDIA and advertising presence that any child who watches TV or shops with Mom is likely to get revved up about going to Walt Disney World. Parents, if anything, are even more susceptible. Almost all parents brighten at the prospect of guiding their children through this special place. But the reality of taking a young child (particularly during the summer) can be closer to the agony than to the ecstasy.

A Dayton, Ohio, mother who took her 5-year-old to Disney World one summer recalls:

> *I felt so happy and excited before we went. I guess it was all worth it, but when I look back I think I should have had my head examined. The first day we went to the Magic Kingdom, it was packed. By 11 in the morning, we had walked so far and stood in so many lines that we were all exhausted. Kristy cried about going on anything that looked or even sounded scary and was frightened by all of the Disney characters (they're so big!) except Minnie and Snow White.*
>
> *We got hungry about the same time as everyone else, but the lines for food were too long and my husband said we'd have to wait. By 1 in the afternoon we were just plugging along, not seeing anything we were really interested in, but picking rides because the lines were short, or because whatever it was, was air-conditioned. At around 2:30, we finally got something to eat, but by then we were so hot and tired that it felt like we had worked in the yard all day. At the end, we were so P.O.'d and uncomfortable that we weren't having any fun.*

Before you stiffen in denial, let us assure you that this family's experience is not unusual. Most young children are as picky about rides as they are about what they eat, and many preschoolers are intimidated by the Disney characters. Few humans (of any age) are mentally or physically equipped to march all day in a throng of 50,000 people in the hot Florida sun. And would you be surprised to learn that almost 60% of preschoolers said the thing they liked best about their Disney vacation was the hotel swimming pool?

But even somewhat older kids will surprise you, as this Windsor, Ontario, mom relates:

> On day three, we were in World Showcase and our two girls suddenly stopped in their tracks between Italy and Germany. They looked around for a minute and we asked what was wrong. Turns out they'd finally seen something other than characters that appealed to them. "Could we just run around on that grass over there for a few minutes?" they asked. "We won't take too long." So away they went to chase each other on the grass for 10 minutes. Years later, that is what they remember about the trip. Ever since, we've tried to include time in each trip plan to "run around on that grass over there," wherever "there" might be.

With good planning and a sense of humor, you'll be e-mailing us messages like this one from a Harrisburg, Pennsylvania, mom:

> I knew it would be fun for my daughter, but what I didn't expect was just how much fun it would be for me.

REALITY TESTING: WHOSE DREAM IS IT?

REMEMBER WHEN YOU WERE LITTLE and you got that nifty remote control car for Christmas, the one Dad wouldn't let you play with? Did you wonder who the car was really for? Ask yourself a similar question about your vacation to Walt Disney World. Whose dream are you trying to make come true: yours or your child's?

Young children read their parents' emotions. When you ask, "Honey, how would you like to go to Disney World?" your child will respond more to your smile and enthusiasm than to any notion of what Disney World is all about. The younger the child, the more this holds true. From many preschoolers, you could elicit the same excitement by asking, "Sweetie, how would you like to go to Cambodia on a dogsled?"

unofficial **TIP** When considering a trip to Walt Disney World, think about whether your kids are old enough to enjoy what can be a very fun but taxing trip.

So is your happy fantasy of introducing your child to Disney magic a pipe dream? Not necessarily, but you have to be open to reality testing. For example, would you increase the probability of a successful visit by waiting a year or two? Will your child have sufficient endurance and patience to cope with long lines and large crowds?

RECOMMENDATIONS FOR MAKING THE DREAM COME TRUE

WHEN YOU'RE PLANNING A DISNEY WORLD VACATION with young children, consider the following:

AGE Although Walt Disney World's color and festivity excite all children and specific attractions delight toddlers and preschoolers, Disney entertainment is generally oriented to older children and adults. Children should be a fairly mature 7 years old to *appreciate* the Magic Kingdom and Disney's Animal Kingdom, a year or two older to get much out of Epcot or Disney's Hollywood Studios.

Readers continually debate how old a child should be or the ideal age to go to Disney World. A Rockaway, New Jersey, mom writes:

I found myself rereading your section "The Ecstasy and the Agony." Unfortunately, our experience was pure agony, with the exception of our hotel pool. It was the one and only thing our kids enjoyed. I had planned and saved for this trip for over a year, and I cried all week at the disappointment that our kids just wanted to swim.

A dad from Columbus, Ohio, felt like he was in a maternity ward:

We were shocked to see so many newborns as well. I could have sworn that one woman gave birth at the bus stop, her baby was so small.

An overly ambitious mother of a toddler received a reality check:

It took me a day to realize that I had to let some things go. We were traveling with a 3-year-old, and it wasn't fun for anyone when I was seeing Disney as one big to-do list. I still made sure that we hit the highlights for her—Pooh, Little Mermaid, characters, princesses, and so on—but we didn't make it to many things on my list. I had to accept that and be OK with it.

A Lawrenceville, Georgia, mother of two toddlers advises maintaining the children's normal schedule:

The first day, we tried your suggestion about an early start, so we woke the children (ages 4 and 2) and hurried them to get going. BAD IDEA with toddlers. This put them off-schedule for naps and meals the rest of the day.

WHEN TO VISIT Avoid the hot, crowded summer months, especially if you have preschoolers. Go in October, November (except Thanksgiving), early December, January, February, or May. If you have children of varied ages and they're good students, take the older ones out of school and visit during the cooler and less congested off-season.

Most readers who've tried Disney World at various times agree. A New Hampshire parent writes:

I took my grade-school children out of school for a few days to go during a slow time and would highly recommend it. We communicated with the teachers about a month before traveling to seek their preference for whether classwork and homework should be completed before, during, or after our trip. It's so much more enjoyable to be at Disney when your children can experience rides and attractions and all that is Disney rather than standing in line. And traveling at a time of year when it's not unbearably hot makes such a difference as well.

There's another side to this story, and we've received some well-considered letters from parents and teachers who don't think taking kids out of school is such a hot idea. From a father in Fairfax, Virginia:

My wife and I are disappointed that you seem to be encouraging families to take their children out of school to avoid the crowds at WDW during the summer months. My wife is an eighth-grade teacher of chemistry and physics. She has parents pull their children, some honor-roll students, out of school for vacations, only to discover when they return that the students are unable to comprehend the material.

A Martinez, California, teacher offers this compelling analogy:

There are a precious 180 days for us as teachers to instruct our students, and there are 185 days during the year for Disney World. I have seen countless students during my 14 years of teaching struggle to catch up the rest of the year due to a week of vacation during critical instructional periods. The analogy I use with my students' parents is that it's like walking out of a movie after watching the first 5 minutes, then returning for the last 5 minutes and trying to figure out what happened.

But a teacher from Penn Yan, New York, sees things differently:

As a teacher and a parent, I disagree with the comments from teachers saying that it's horrible for a parent to take a child out for a vacation. If a parent takes the time to let us know that a child is going to be out, we help them get ready for upcoming homework the best we can. If the child is a good student, why shouldn't they go have a wonderful experience with their family?

If possible, have your child's teacher create special assignments relating to the educational aspects of Disney World. If your children can't afford to miss school, take your vacation as soon as the school year ends. Alternatively, try late August, before school starts. Understand that you don't have to visit during one of the more ideal times of year to have a great vacation.

BUILD NAPS AND REST INTO YOUR ITINERARY The parks are huge: Don't try to see everything in one day. Tour in the early morning and return to your hotel around 11:30 a.m. for lunch, a swim, and a nap. Even during off-season, when crowds are smaller and the temperature is more pleasant, the major parks' size will exhaust most children younger than age 8 by lunchtime. Return to the park in late afternoon or early evening and continue touring. A family from Texas underlines the importance of naps and rest:

unofficial **TIP** If you must rent a car to make returning to your hotel practicable, do it.

Probably the most important tip your guide gave us was going to the hotel to swim and regroup during the day. The parks became unbearable by noon—and so did my husband and boys. The hotel was an oasis that calmed our nerves! After about 3 hours of playtime, we headed out to a different park for dinner and a cool evening of fun.

Regarding naps, this mom doesn't mince words:

For parents of small kids: Take the book's advice, get out of the park, and take the nap, take the nap, TAKE THE NAP!

A Matthews, North Carolina, family pooped out in two days:

This was our first trip to Disney, and we learned the hard way why it's important to rest and get out of the parks awhile. Our first two days were packed with touring, followed by a princess makeover and dining with the princesses in Cinderella Castle. Needless to say, by day three we were exhausted, grumpy, and beginning to see no magic in Disney. We ended our third day by noon at Epcot and headed back to the resort to rest and relax for the rest of the night. After that, I rearranged all of our touring plans for rest and relaxing time, which allowed us to finish our vacations with happy (most of the time) children and parents.

If you plan to return to your hotel at midday and want your room made up, let housekeeping know. before you leave in the morning.

WHERE TO STAY The time and hassle involved in commuting to and from the theme parks will be less if your hotel is close by. This doesn't necessarily mean you have to lodge inside Disney World. Because the World is so geographically dispersed, many off-property hotels are closer to the parks than some Disney resorts (see our Hotel Information Chart in Part Three, showing commuting times from Disney and non-Disney hotels). Regardless of where you stay, it's imperative that you take young children out of the parks each day for a few hours of rest. Neglecting to relax can ruin the day—or the vacation—for everyone.

If you have young children, book a hotel that's within a 20-minute drive from the theme parks. It's true that you can revive somewhat by retreating to a Disney hotel for lunch or by finding a quiet restaurant in the parks, but there's no substitute for returning to the comfort of your hotel.

If you're traveling with children 12 years old and younger and you want to stay in Walt Disney World, we recommend the **Polynesian Village & Villas, Grand Floridian & Villas,** or **Wilderness Lodge & Villas** (in that order), if they fit your budget. For less-expensive rooms, try **Port Orleans French Quarter.** The least expensive on-site rooms are available at the **All-Star Resorts.** In addition to standard hotel rooms, the **All-Star Music** and **Art of Animation Resorts** offer two-room Family Suites that can sleep as many as six and provide kitchenettes. Log cabins at **Fort Wilderness Resort & Campground** and the DVC resorts are another option for families who need a little more space. Outside the World, check our top hotels for families (see page 254), but know that many more good options exist.

unofficial **TIP**
The way to protect your considerable investment in your Disney vacation is to stay happy and have a good time. You don't have to meet a quota for experiencing attractions. *Do what you want.*

BE IN TOUCH WITH YOUR FEELINGS When you or your kids get tired and irritable, call time-out. Trust your instincts. What would feel best? Another ride, an ice-cream break, or going back to the room for a nap?

LEAST COMMON DENOMINATORS Somebody is going to run out of steam first, and when he or she does, the whole family will be affected. Sometimes a snack break will revive the flagging member. Sometimes, however, it's better to return to your hotel. Pushing the tired or discontented beyond their capacity will spoil the day for them—and you. Energy levels vary. Be prepared to respond to members of your group who poop out. *Hint:* "We've driven a thousand miles to take you to Disney World and now you're ruining everything!" is not an appropriate response.

BUILDING ENDURANCE Though most children are active, their normal play usually doesn't condition them for the exertion required to tour a Disney park. Start family walks four to six weeks before your trip to get in shape. A mother from Wescosville, Pennsylvania, reports:

We had our 6-year-old begin walking with us a bit every day one month before leaving—when we arrived at Disney World, her little legs could carry her, and she had a lot of stamina.

From a Middletown, Delaware, mom::

You recommended walking for six weeks prior to the trip, but we began months in advance, just because. My husband lost 10 pounds, my daughter never once complained, and we met a lot of neighbors!

SETTING LIMITS AND MAKING PLANS In order to avoid arguments and disappointment, establish guidelines for each day and get everybody committed. Include the following:

1. Wake-up time and breakfast plans
2. When to depart for the park
3. What to take with you
4. A policy for splitting the group or for staying together
5. What to do if the group gets separated or someone is lost
6. What you want to see, including plans in the event an attraction is closed or too crowded
7. A policy on what you can afford for snacks
8. How long you plan to tour in the morning and what time you'll return to your hotel to rest
9. When you'll return to the park and how late you'll stay
10. Dinner plans
11. A policy for buying souvenirs, including who pays (kids or parents)
12. Bedtimes

BE FLEXIBLE Any day at Disney World includes surprises; be prepared to adjust your plan. Listen to your intuition.

WHAT KIDS WANT According to the travel-research firm Yesawich, Pepperdine, Brown, and Russell, 71% of children between the ages of 6 and 17 say they need a vacation because school and homework get them down. The chart below shows what kids want and don't want when taking a vacation. Kids surveyed have a lot in common about what they do want, not as much concerning what they don't.

WHAT DO KIDS WANT?	WHAT DO KIDS NOT WANT?
To go swimming/have pool time **85%**	To get up early **52%**
To eat in restaurants **78%**	To ride in a car **36%**
To stay at a hotel or resort **76%**	To play golf **34%**
To visit a theme park **76%**	To go to a museum **31%**
To stay up late **73%**	

Other high-ranking wants include throwing water balloons and eating ice cream.

MAINTAINING SOME SEMBLANCE OF ORDER AND DISCIPLINE OK, OK, wipe that smirk off your face. Order and discipline on the road may seem like an oxymoron to you, but you won't be hooting when your 5-year-old launches a tantrum in the middle of Fantasyland. Your willingness to give this subject serious consideration before you leave home may well be the most important element of your pre-trip preparation.

Discipline and maintaining order are more difficult when traveling than at home because everyone is, as a Boston mom put it, "in and out"—in strange surroundings and out of the normal routine. For children, it's hard to contain excitement and anticipation that pop to the surface in the form of fidgety hyperactivity, nervous energy, and sometimes, acting out. Confinement in a car, plane, or hotel room only exacerbates the situation, and kids often tend to be louder than normal, more aggressive with siblings, and much more inclined to push the envelope of parental patience. Once you're in the theme parks, it doesn't get much better. There's more elbow room, but there are also overstimulation, crowds, heat, and miles of walking. All this, coupled with marginal or inadequate rest, can lead to a meltdown in the most harmonious of families.

Sound parenting and standards of discipline practiced at home, applied consistently, will suffice to handle most situations on vacation.

unofficial **TIP**
Just because the kids are on vacation doesn't mean you should let them monopolize your trip— maintain some of your everyday rules, and you'll all have a better time together.

Still, it's instructive to study the hand you're dealt when traveling. For starters, aside from being jazzed and ablaze with adrenaline, your kids may believe that rules followed at home are somehow suspended when traveling. Parents reinforce this misguided intuition by being inordinately lenient in the interest of maintaining peace in the family. While some of your home protocols (like cleaning your plate and going to bed at a set time) might be relaxed to good effect on vacation, differing from your normal approach to discipline can precipitate major misunderstanding and possibly disaster.

Children, not unexpectedly, are likely to believe that a vacation (especially a vacation to Walt Disney World) is intended just for them. This reinforces their focus on their own needs and largely erases any consideration of yours. Such a mind-set dramatically increases their sense of hurt and disappointment when you correct them or deny them something they want. An incident that would hardly elicit a pouty lip at home could well escalate to tears or defiance when traveling. It's important before you depart on your trip, therefore, to discuss your vacation needs with your children, and to explore their wants and expectations as well.

The stakes are high for everyone on a vacation—for you because of the cost in time and dollars, but also because your vacation represents a rare opportunity for rejuvenation and renewal. The stakes are high for your children, too. Children tend to romanticize travel, building anticipation to an almost unbearable level. Discussing the trip in advance can ground expectations to a certain extent, but a child's imagination will, in the end, trump reality every time. The good news is that you can take advantage of your children's emotional state to establish preset rules and conditions for their conduct while on vacation. Because your children want what's being offered *sooooo* badly, they will be unusually accepting and conscientious regarding whatever rules are agreed upon.

According to *Unofficial Guide* child psychologist Karen Turnbow, PhD, successful response to (or avoidance of) behavioral problems on the road begins with a clear-cut disciplinary policy at home. Both at home and on vacation the approach should be the same, and should be based on the following key concepts:

1. LET EXPECTATIONS BE KNOWN Discuss what you expect from your children, but don't try to cover every imaginable situation (that's what lawyers are for—just kidding). Cover expectations regarding compliance with parental directives, treatment of siblings, resolution of disputes, schedules (including morning wake-up and bedtimes), courtesy and manners, staying together, and who pays for what.

2. EXPLAIN THE CONSEQUENCES OF NONCOMPLIANCE Detail very clearly and firmly the consequence of not meeting expectations. This should be very straightforward and unambiguous: "If you do X (or don't do X), this is what will happen."

3. WARNING You're dealing with excited, expectant children, not machines, so it's important to issue a warning before meting out discipline. It's critical to understand that we're talking about one unequivocal warning rather than multiple warnings or nagging. These last undermine your credibility and make your expectations appear relative or less than serious. Multiple warnings or nagging also effectively pass control of the situation from you to your child (who sometimes may continue acting out as an attention-getting strategy).

4. FOLLOW THROUGH If you say you're going to do something, do it. Period. Children must understand that you mean business.

5. CONSISTENCY Inconsistency makes discipline a random event in the eyes of your children. Random discipline encourages random behavior, which translates to a nearly total loss of parental control. Long term, both at home and on the road, your response to a given situation or transgression must be perfectly predictable. Structure and repetition, essential for a child to learn, cannot be achieved in the absence of consistency.

Although the previous methods are the five biggies, several corollary concepts and techniques are worthy of consideration as well.

Understand that whining, tantrums, defiance, sibling friction, and even holding up the group are ways in which children communicate with parents. Frequently the object or precipitant of a situation has little or no relation to the unacceptable behavior. A fit may on the surface appear to be about the ice cream you refused to buy little Robby, but there's almost always something deeper, a subtext that is closer to the truth (this is why ill behavior often persists after you give in to a child's demands). As often as not, the real cause is a need for attention. This need is so powerful in some children that they will subject themselves to certain punishment and parental displeasure to garner the attention they crave, even if it's negative.

*un**official* **TIP** Teaching your kids to tell you clearly what they want or need will help make the trip more enjoyable for everyone.

To get at the root cause of the behavior in question requires both active listening and empowering your child with a "feeling vocabulary." Active listening is a concept that's been around a long time. It involves being alert not only to what a child says, but also to the context in which it's said, to the words used and possible subtext, to the child's emotional state and body language, and even to what's not said. Sounds complicated, but it's basically being attentive to the larger picture and, more to the point, being aware that there *is* a larger picture.

Helping your child develop a feeling vocabulary involves teaching your child to use words to describe what's going on. The idea is to teach the child to articulate what's really troubling him, to be able to identify and express emotions and mood states in language. Of course, learning to express feelings is a lifelong learning experience, but it's much less dependent on innate sensitivity than on being provided with the tools for expression and being encouraged to use them.

Children are almost never too young to begin learning a feeling vocabulary. And helping your child to get in touch with—and to communicate—his or her emotions will stimulate you to focus on *your* feelings and mood states in a similar way. With persistence and effort, the whole family can achieve a vastly improved ability to communicate.

A Shelby, North Carolina, reader touts a resource for parents whose kids need a little help with their feeling vocabularies:

> *I use a therapy technique at work called the **Alert Program** that helps kids develop self-regulation skills, including a feeling vocabulary. The website (**alertprogram.com**) provides an explanation and additional resources [some free, some for sale]. You can use many analogies to make it work, but an especially fun one is to use Disney characters: A child might feel like Winnie the Pooh if he's "just right," Tigger if he's hyper or needs a movement break, or Eeyore if he's feeling tired or sad. Practicing these indicators before your trip can help your child communicate his/her needs effectively and can help you have a more pleasant trip by warding off meltdowns!*

Until you get the hang of active listening and a feeling vocabulary, be careful not to become part of the problem. There's a laundry list of not-so-adult responses to bad behavior that only make things worse: hitting, yelling, belittling, pleading, nagging, and inducing guilt.

Responding to a child appropriately in a disciplinary situation requires thought and preparation. Following are things to keep in mind and techniques to try when your world blows up while waiting in line for Dumbo.

1. BE THE ADULT It's well understood that children can push their parents' buttons faster and more skillfully than just about anyone or anything else. They've got your number, know precisely how to elicit a response, and are not reluctant to go for the jugular. Fortunately (or unfortunately), you're the adult, and to deal with a situation effectively, you've got to act like one. If your kids get you ranting and caterwauling, you effectively abdicate your adult status. Worse, you suggest by way of example that being out of control is an acceptable expression of hurt or anger. No matter what happens, repeat the mantra, "I am the adult in this relationship."

2. FREEZE THE ACTION Being the adult and maintaining control almost always translates to freezing the action, to borrow a sports term. Instead of responding in knee-jerk fashion (that is, at a maturity level closer to your child's than yours), freeze the action by disengaging. Wherever you are or whatever the family is doing, stop in place and concentrate on one thing, and one thing only: getting all involved calmed down. Practically speaking this usually means initiating a time-out. It's essential that you take this action immediately. Grabbing your child by the arm or collar and dragging him toward the car or hotel room only escalates the turmoil by prolonging the confrontation and by adding a coercive physical dimension to an already volatile emotional event. For the sake of everyone involved, including the people around you (as when a toddler throws a tantrum in church), it's essential to retreat to a more private place. Choose the first place available. Firmly sit the child down and refrain from talking to him until you've both cooled off. This might take a little time, but the investment is worthwhile. Truncating the process is like trying to get on your feet too soon after surgery.

3. ISOLATE THE CHILD You'll be able to deal with the situation more effectively and expeditiously if the child is isolated with one parent. Dispatch the uninvolved members of your party for a snack break or have them go on with the activity or itinerary without you (if possible) and arrange to rendezvous later at an agreed time and place. In addition to letting the others get on with their day, isolating the offending child with one parent relieves him of the pressure of being the group's focus of attention and object of anger. Equally important, isolation frees you from the scrutiny and expectations of the others in regard to how to handle the situation.

4. REVIEW THE SITUATION WITH THE CHILD If, as discussed a few pages back, you've made your expectations clear, stated the consequences of failing to meet those expectations, and administered a warning, review the situation with the child and follow through with the discipline warranted. If, as often occurs, things are not so black-and-white, encourage the child to communicate his feelings. Try to uncover what occasioned the acting out. Lectures and accusatory language don't work well here, nor do threats. Dr. Turnbow suggests that a better approach (after the child is calm) is to ask, "What can we do to make this a better day for you?"

5. FREQUENT TANTRUMS OR ACTING OUT The preceding four points relate to dealing with an incident as opposed to a chronic condition. If a child frequently acts out or throws tantrums, you'll need to employ a somewhat different strategy.

Tantrums are cyclical events evolved from learned behavior. A child learns that he can get your undivided attention by acting out. When you respond, whether by scolding, admonishing, threatening, or negotiating, your response further draws you into the cycle and prolongs the behavior. When you accede to the child's demands, you reinforce the effectiveness of the tantrum and raise the cost of capitulation next time around. When a child thus succeeds in monopolizing your attention, he effectively becomes the person in charge.

To break this cycle, you must disengage from the child. The object is to demonstrate that the cause-and-effect relationship (that is, tantrum elicits parental attention) is no longer operative. This can be accomplished by refusing to interact with the child as long as the untoward behavior continues. Tell the child that you're unwilling to discuss his problem until he calms down. You can ignore the behavior, remove yourself from the child's presence (or vice versa), or isolate the child with a time-out. It's important to disengage quickly and decisively with no discussion or negotiation.

Most children don't pick the family vacation as the time to start throwing tantrums. The behavior will be evident before you leave home, and home is the best place to deal with it. Be forewarned, however, that bad habits die hard, and that a child accustomed to getting attention by throwing tantrums will not simply give up after a single instance of disengagement. More likely, the child will at first escalate the intensity and length of his tantrums. By your consistent refusal over several weeks (or even months) to respond to his behavior, however, he will finally adjust to the new paradigm.

Children are cunning as well as observant. Many understand that a tantrum in public is embarrassing to you and that you're more likely to cave in than you would at home. Once again, consistency is the key, along with a bit of anticipation. When traveling, it's not necessary to retreat to the privacy of a hotel room to isolate your child. You can carve out space for a time-out almost anywhere: on a theme park bench, in a park, in your car, in a restroom, even on a sidewalk.

You can often spot the warning signs of an impending tantrum and head it off by talking to the child before he reaches an explosive emotional pitch. And don't forget that tantrums are about getting attention. Giving your child attention when things are on an even keel often preempts acting out.

6. SALVAGE OPERATIONS Kids are full of surprises, and sometimes those surprises are, well, not good. What if your sweet precious pulls a stunt so beyond the pale that it threatens to derail your entire trip? In the case of one Ohio boy visiting Disney World with his family, his offense resulted in his being grounded more or less for life. For starters, his parents split up the group: One parent escorted the miscreant back to the hotel room, where he was effectively confined for the duration. That evening, Mom and Dad arranged for in-room sitters for the rest of the stay. Expensive? Yep, but better than ruining the vacation for everybody else.

In another case, a child acted out at the Magic Kingdom, though the offense was of a milder order of magnitude. Because it was the family's last day at Disney World, the parents elected to place the misbehaver in time-out for the rest of their day in the park—one parent would monitor the culprit while the other parent and the siblings enjoyed the attractions. At agreed-upon times, the parents would switch places.

Parenting Advice: Readers Weigh In

Though the foregoing section was developed by top child psychologists, it rubs some readers, like this teacher from Corryton, Tennessee, the wrong way:

> *The one thing I don't like is the section on how to make your kids behave. As a preschool teacher, I can honestly say that people who need this advice won't take it anyway—so why bother?*

But a North Carolina psychiatrist disagrees:

The section of the Unofficial Guide *dealing with child behavioral issues while traveling is one of the most concise and well-articulated presentations on this subject that I have encountered anywhere. I recommend it to many of my patients who are contemplating traveling with their children.*

A New Hampshire father of two had this to say:

Your advice on touring with children was fabulous. Your book gave us confidence to do the parks without being deer caught in the headlights.

ABOUT THE *UNOFFICIAL GUIDE* TOURING PLANS

PARENTS WHO USE OUR TOURING PLANS are often frustrated by interruptions and delays caused by their young children. Here's what to expect:

1. CHARACTER ENCOUNTERS CAN WREAK HAVOC WITH THE TOURING PLANS. Many children will stop in their tracks whenever they see a Disney character. Attempting to haul your child away before he has satisfied his curiosity is likely to cause anything from whining to full-scale revolt. Either go with the flow or specify a morning or afternoon for photos and autographs. Be aware that queues for autographs can be as long as the queues for major attractions; our touring plans use FastPass+ (see page 87) to minimize waits in line.

2. OUR TOURING PLANS CALL FOR VISITING ATTRACTIONS IN A SEQUENCE, OFTEN SKIPPING ATTRACTIONS ALONG THE WAY. Children don't like to skip *anything*! If something catches their eye, they want to see it right there and then. Some can be persuaded to skip attractions if parents explain their plans in advance, but other kids flip out at skipping something, particularly in Fantasyland. A mom from Charleston, South Carolina, writes:

We didn't have much trouble following the touring plans at Hollywood Studios and Epcot. The Magic Kingdom plan, on the other hand, turned out to be a train wreck. While we were on Dumbo, my 5-year-old saw eight dozen other things in Fantasyland she wanted to do. Long story short: After Dumbo, there was no getting her out of there.

A mother of two from Burlington, Vermont, adds:

My kids were very curious about the castle because we had read Cinderella at home. Whenever I wanted to leave Fantasyland, I would just say, "Let's go to the castle and see if Cinderella is there." Once we got as far as the front door to the castle, it was no problem going out to the Central Plaza and then to another land.

3. IF YOU'RE USING A STROLLER, YOU WON'T BE ABLE TO TAKE IT INTO ATTRACTIONS OR ONTO RIDES. This includes rides such as the Walt Disney World Railroad that are included in the touring plans as in-park transportation. (An exception: Folding strollers are permitted on the railroad.) Well-marked stroller parking is available throughout the theme parks.

4. USE TECHNOLOGY TO GET BACK ON TRACK. Kids and touring plans are sort of like tossing back tequila shots: Sometimes unexpected things happen. Fortunately, we've built our Lines app (see page 83) to recover from such unforeseen events. If you find yourself out of sync with your plan and you're using Lines, just press the "Optimize" button when you're ready to get started again. Lines will redo your touring plan from that moment forward, using the current crowd conditions in the park.

While our touring plans help you make the most of your time at the parks, it's impossible to define what "most" will be. If you have two young children, you probably won't see as much as two adults will; if you have four children, you probably won't see as much as a couple with only two.

STUFF TO THINK ABOUT

OVERHEATING, SUNBURN, AND DEHYDRATION These are the most common problems of younger children at Disney World. Carry and use sunscreen. Apply it on children in strollers, even if the stroller has a canopy. To avoid overheating, stop for rest regularly—say, in the shade, or in a restaurant or at a show with air-conditioning.

BLISTERS AND SORE FEET In addition to wearing comfortable shoes, bring along some blister bandages if you or your children are susceptible to blisters. These bandages (which are also available at First Aid, if you didn't heed our warnings) offer excellent protection, stick well, and won't sweat off. Remember, a preschooler may not say anything about a blister until it's already formed, so keep an eye on things during the day. For an expanded discussion, see pages 476 and 477.

unofficial **TIP**
Keep little ones well covered in sunscreen and hydrated with fluids. Carry plastic bottles of water (bottles with screw caps are sold in all major parks for about $3). And remember: Excited kids may not tell you if they're thirsty or hot.

FIRST AID Each major theme park has a **First Aid Center**. In the Magic Kingdom, it's at the end of Main Street to your left, between Casey's Corner and The Crystal Palace. At Epcot, it's on the World Showcase side of Odyssey Center. At Disney's Hollywood Studios, it's in the Guest Relations Building inside the main entrance. At Disney's Animal Kingdom, it's in Discovery Island, on your left just before you cross the bridge to Africa, across from the ice-cream stand. And in all four parks, First Aid and the Baby Care Center are right next to each other. If you or your children have a medical problem, go to a First Aid Center. They're friendlier than most doctor's offices and are accustomed to treating everything from paper cuts to allergic reactions.

KIDS WITH ADHD Some parents of children prescribed Ritalin or similar medication let their child take a "drug holiday" when school lets out. If you've cut your child's dosage or discontinued her medication altogether, be aware that she might experience sensory overload at Disney World. Consult your child's physician before altering his or her drug regimen.

GLASSES AND SUNGLASSES If your kids (or you) wear them, attach a strap or string to the frames so the glasses will stay on during rides and can hang from the child's neck while indoors.

THINGS YOU FORGOT OR RAN OUT OF Rain gear, diapers, baby formula, sunburn treatments, memory cards, and other sundries are sold at all major theme parks and at Typhoon Lagoon, Blizzard Beach, and Disney Springs. If you don't see something you need, ask if it's in stock. Basic over-the-counter meds are often available free in small quantities at the First Aid Centers in the parks.

INFANTS AND TODDLERS AT THE THEME PARKS The major parks have **Baby Care Centers.** Everything necessary for changing diapers, preparing formulas, and warming bottles and food is available. Supplies are sold, and rockers and special chairs for nursing mothers are provided. At the Magic Kingdom, the Baby Care Center is next to The Crystal Palace at the end of Main Street. At Epcot, it's in the Odyssey Center, between Test Track in Future World and Mexico in World Showcase. At Disney's Hollywood Studios, it's in the Guest Relations Building, left of the main entrance. At Disney's Animal Kingdom, the Baby Care Center is behind First Aid, near the Discovery Island entrance to Africa. Dads are welcome at the centers and can use most services. In addition, many men's restrooms in the major parks have changing stations.

If your baby is on formula, this New Berlin, Wisconsin, mom has a handy tip:

> We got hot water from the food vendors and mixed the formula as needed. It eliminated keeping bottles cold and then warming them up.

Infants and toddlers are allowed in any attraction that doesn't have minimum height or age restrictions. But as a Minneapolis mother reports, some attractions are better for babies than others:

> Theater and boat rides are easier for babies (ours was almost a year old, not yet walking). Rides where there's a bar that comes down are doable, but harder—Peter Pan was our first encounter with this type of ride, and we had barely gotten situated when I realized my son might fall out of my grasp.

The same mom also advises:

> We used a baby sling on our trip and thought it was great when standing in lines—much better than a stroller, which you have to park before getting in line (and navigate through crowds).

If you're a mother who wants to nurse during a theater attraction, note that most shows run about 17–20 minutes. Exceptions are *The Hall of Presidents* at the Magic Kingdom and *The American Adventure* at Epcot, which run 23 and 29 minutes, respectively.

We should pause to state unambiguously that mothers are free to nurse whenever and wherever they choose. A Georgia mom, not sure that all nursing mothers understand this, writes:

> Many women have no problem nursing uncovered, and they have the right to do so in public without being criticized. Even women who do want to cover up may have a baby who won't cooperate and flings off the cover; plus, it's not necessary to sit through all of The Hall of Presidents to feed your child. I understand that peace and quiet help, but nursing mothers will tell you that their babies will eat almost

anywhere, and they shouldn't feel pressured to sneak off when a baby is hungry. A lot of people read your books, and it would be nice to see you refer to breastfeeding as normal and not something that needs to be hidden or covered.

A Lake Charles, Louisiana, mom is more blunt:

Don't tell me that men who'll do almost anything to see a boob will faint dead away at the sight of a nursing mother's breast. Ladies, feed your babies and tell the offended men and other prudes to get over themselves!

RUNNING OUT OF GAS When Bob was preparing to hike from the Colorado River to the rim of the Grand Canyon—a 5,000-foot ascent—a park ranger advised him to mix an electrolyte-replacement powder in his water and eat an energy-boosting snack at least twice every hour. While there's not much ascending to do at Walt Disney World, battling the heat, humidity, and crowds contributes to poop-out, especially where kids are concerned. Limiting calorie consumption to mealtimes just won't get it, as an experienced and wise grandma points out:

Children who get cranky during a visit often do so from all that time and energy expended without food. Feed them! A snack at any price goes a long way toward keeping little ones happy and parents sane!

STROLLERS

STROLLERS ARE AVAILABLE for rent at all four theme parks and Disney Springs area (single stroller, $15 per day with no deposit, $13 per day for the entire stay; double stroller, $31 per day with no deposit, $27 per day for the entire stay; stroller rentals at Disney Springs require a $100 credit card deposit; double strollers not available at Disney Springs). Strollers are welcome at Blizzard Beach and Typhoon Lagoon, but no rentals are available. With multiday rentals, you can skip the rental line entirely after your first visit—just head over to the stroller-handout area, show your receipt, and you'll be wheeling out of there in no time. If you rent a stroller at the Magic Kingdom and you decide to go to Epcot, Disney's Animal Kingdom, or Disney's Hollywood Studios, turn in your Magic Kingdom stroller and present your receipt at the next park. You'll be issued another stroller at no additional charge.

You can rent a stroller in advance—this lets you bypass the "paying" line and head straight to the "pickup" line. Disney resort guests can pay ahead at their resort's gift shop—save the receipts!

Obtain strollers at the Magic Kingdom entrance, to the left of Epcot's Entrance Plaza and at Epcot's International Gateway, and at **Oscar's Super Service** just inside the entrance of Disney's Hollywood Studios. At Disney's Animal Kingdom, they're at **Garden Gate Gifts,** to the right just inside the entrance. Returning the stroller is a breeze— you can ditch it anywhere in the park when you get ready to leave. To see what these rental strollers look like, Google "rental strollers at Walt Disney World" or the like.

Strollers are a must for infants and toddlers, but we've seen many sharp parents rent strollers for somewhat older children—the stroller

spares parents from having to carry kids when they sag, and it provides a convenient place to tote water and snacks.

A family from Tulsa, Oklahoma, recommends springing for a double stroller:

We rent a double for baggage room or in case the older child gets tired of walking.

But a New Lenox, Illinois, family advocates not leaving anyone out:

If your kids are 8 or under, RENT STROLLERS for all of them! An 8-year-old will fit in a stroller, and you can fit up to four kids in two doubles. My husband suggested getting a stroller for our 6-year-old and the two "babies" (ages 4 and 3). We plowed through crowds, and the kids didn't get nearly as tired since they could be seated whenever they wanted.

We've always advocated using strollers for any child who will fit; however, a McKean, Pennsylvania, reader thinks the situation has gotten out of hand:

Please tell parents their children don't have to be in strollers if (a) they're old enough to vote, (b) they've served in the armed services, (c) they smoke, and/or (d) they have kids of their own. It's gotten really ridiculous—this last visit we saw more 10+-year-olds in strollers than sub-10-year-olds. Strollers add congestion, especially with dingbat parents using them to blast through crowds like child-first battering rams. I never knew walking was bad for you.

A Charleston, West Virginia, mom recommends a backup plan:

Strollers are not allowed in lines for rides, so if you have a small child (ours was 4) who needs to be held, you might end up holding him a long time. If I had it to do over, I'd bring along some kind of child carrier for when he was out of the stroller.

If you go to your hotel for a break and intend to return to the park, leave your rental stroller in stroller parking near the park entrance, marking it with something personal like a bandanna. When you return, your stroller will be waiting.

Rental strollers are too large for all infants and many toddlers. If you plan to rent a stroller for your infant or toddler, bring pillows, cushions, or rolled towels to buttress him in.

Bringing your own stroller is permitted. However, only collapsible strollers are allowed on monorails, parking-lot trams, and buses. Your stroller is unlikely to be stolen, but mark it with your name.

Having her own stroller was indispensable to a Mechanicsville, Virginia, mother of two toddlers:

How I was going to manage to get the kids from the parking lot to the park was a big worry for me before I made the trip. I didn't read anywhere that it was possible to walk to the entrance of the parks instead of taking the tram, so I wasn't sure I could do it.

Since I have two kids ages 1 and 2, it was easier to walk to the entrance of the park from the parking lot with the kids in my own stroller than to take the kids out of the stroller, fold the stroller (while trying to control the two kids and associated gear), load the stroller and the kids onto the tram, etc. No matter where I was parked, I could always just walk to the entrance. It sometimes took a while, but it was easier for me.

A Secaucus, New Jersey, mom weighed all the considerations in exemplary type-A fashion:

If your child is under age 2, bring your own stroller. Three reasons to bring your own: First, you have all the way from your car to the Transportation and Ticket Center to the monorail (or ferry) to the stroller rental without a stroller, but with your child, diaper bag, and own self and stuff in tow. Not half as bad as doing it in reverse when leaving, when you're exhausted and have added to your luggage with purchases and the toddler who might have walked in wants to be carried out. Second, the WDW stroller is simply too large for most children under age 2 to be comfortable without significant padding. The seat is so low that the child is forced to keep their legs straight out in front of them. Third, despite being soooo big, there's NO PLACE to store anything.

Now, if your child is past needing a diaper bag, the WDW strollers seem like a pretty good deal. You won't need the storage space, and they do maneuver very well. They seem especially good for children who no longer need a stroller at home (ages 4–6) but who won't make it walking all day.

If your child is 2 or 3, it's a toss-up. If you're a type-A mom, like me, who carries extra clothes, snacks, toys, enough diapers for three days, along with a pocketbook and extra-jackets-for-everyone-just-in-case, you've probably found a stroller that suits your needs and will be miserable with the WDW kind. If you're a type-B "we can get everything else we need at the park; I'll just throw a diaper in my back pocket" mom, you'll probably be tickled with the WDW strollers.

An Oklahoma mom, however, reports a bad experience with bringing her own stroller:

It's much easier to rent a stroller in the park. The one we brought was nearly impossible to get on the buses and was a hassle at the airport. I remember feeling dread when a bus pulled up—people look at you like you have a cage full of chickens.

PARKING YOUR STROLLER Well-marked stroller parking is available in all the "lands" of every park. If you leave your stroller in front of an attraction instead of a designated parking area, it will be moved.

STROLLER-RENTAL OPTIONS With Disney pricing its own stroller rentals so high, a number of Orlando rental companies have sprung up, able to undercut Disney's prices, provide more comfortable strollers, and deliver them to your hotel. Most of the larger companies offer the same stroller models (the Baby Jogger City Mini Single, for example), so the primary differences between the companies are price and service.

Regarding the latter, Disney currently allows just a handful of stroller companies to drop off and pick up at a Disney hotel without your having to be physically present to meet the delivery person, thus freeing you to run around the parks instead of waiting around at your hotel. The two companies reviewed below are part of the **Disney Featured Stroller Provider** program, a fact they mention prominently on their websites. Before renting from another company, check to see if they're on the featured list, too.

We had mom and **touringplans.com** blogger **Angela Dahlgren** rent strollers from different companies, use them in the parks, then return them. Her evaluations cover the overall experience, from the ease with which the stroller was rented to the delivery of the stroller, its condition upon arrival, usability in the parks, and the return process.

Kingdom Strollers (☎ 407-271-5301; **kingdomstrollers.com**) topped Angela's list, getting top marks for website ease of use, stroller selection, condition, and overall service. The stroller was also much easier to use than Disney's standard model, had more storage, and had an easier-to-use braking system. A rental of one to three nights costs $40; four to seven nights is $60. That makes the break-even point for choosing Kingdom Strollers over Disney somewhere around five days.

Angela also recommends **Orlando Stroller Rentals**, LLC (☎ 800-281-0884; **orlandostrollerrentals.com**), which has the same prices, plus an excellent website that allows you to easily compare the features of different strollers.

STROLLER WARS Sometimes strollers disappear while you're enjoying a ride or show. Disney staff will often rearrange strollers parked outside an attraction. This may be done to tidy up or to clear a walkway. Don't assume that your stroller is stolen because it isn't where you left it. It may be neatly arranged a few feet away—or perhaps more than a few feet away, as this Skokie, Illinois, dad reports:

> The stroller reorganizations while you're on rides are a bit unnerving. More than once, our stroller was moved out of visible distance from the original spot. On one occasion, it was moved to a completely different stroller-parking area near another ride, and no sign or cast member was around to advise where. We had to track a cast member down, and she had to call in to find out where it had been moved. Be prepared for this.

Sometimes, however, strollers are taken by mistake or ripped off by people not wanting to spend time replacing one that's missing. Don't be alarmed if yours disappears. You won't have to buy it, and you'll be issued a new one.

While replacing a stroller is no big deal, it's inconvenient. A Minnesota family complained that their stroller was taken six times in one day at Epcot and five times in a day at Disney's Hollywood Studios. Even with free replacements, larceny on this scale represents a lot of wasted time. Through our own experiments and readers' suggestions, we've developed a technique for hanging on to a rented stroller: Affix something personal (but expendable) to the handle. Evidently, most strollers are pirated by mistake (they all look alike) or because it's easier to swipe someone else's than to replace one that has disappeared. Because most stroller "theft" results from confusion or laziness, the average pram-pincher will hesitate to haul off a stroller containing another person's property. We tried several items and concluded that a bright, inexpensive scarf or bandanna tied to the handle works well as identification. A sock partially stuffed with rags or paper works even better (the weirder and more personal the object, the greater the deterrent).

A multigenerational family from Utah went a step further and made their stroller difficult to move:

> We decorated our stroller with electrical tape to make it stand out, and my son added a small cowbell to make it clang if moved.

STROLLERS AS LETHAL WEAPONS A middle-aged couple from Brunswick, Maine, lobbies for a temporary stroller ban:

> As an over-45 couple, we couldn't believe the number and sizes of strollers and those ubiquitous scooters. You had to be constantly vigilant or you would have your foot run over or path slowed down by them. We've decided that one day a week, in one theme park, there should be a "no wheels" day. (Ah, but we live in Fantasyland!)

You'd be surprised at how many people are injured by strollers pushed by parents who are driving aggressively or in a hurry. Given the number of strollers, pedestrians, and tight spaces, mishaps are inevitable on both sides. A simple apology and a smile are usually the best remediation.

LOST CHILDREN

ALTHOUGH IT'S AMAZINGLY EASY TO LOSE a child (or two) in the theme parks, it usually isn't a serious problem: Disney employees are schooled in handling the situation. If you lose a child in the Magic Kingdom, report it to a Disney employee, and then check at the Baby Care Center and at City Hall, where lost-children logs are kept. At Epcot, report the loss, then check at the Baby Care Center in the Odyssey Center. At Disney's Hollywood Studios, report the loss at the Guest Services Building, at the entrance end of Hollywood Boulevard. At Disney's Animal Kingdom, go to the Baby Care Center in Discovery Island. Paging isn't used, but in an emergency, an "all-points bulletin" can be issued throughout the park(s) via internal communications. If a Disney employee encounters a lost child, he or she will take the child immediately to the park's Baby Care Center.

Sew a label into each child's shirt that states his or her name, your name, the name of your hotel, and your cell phone number. You can also write the information on a strip of masking tape or attach a

MagicBand to the child's clothing (but resist the urge to put it on like a dog collar).

An easier and trendier option is a temporary tattoo with your child's name and your phone number. Unlike labels, ID bracelets, or wristbands, the tattoos cannot fall off or be lost. Temporary tattoos last about two weeks, won't wash or sweat off, and are not irritating to the skin. They can be purchased online from SafetyTat at **safetytat .com,** or from Tattoos With A Purpose at **tattooswithapurpose.com.** Special tattoos are available for children with food allergies or cognitive impairment such as autism.

A Kingston, Washington, reader recommends recording vital info for each child on a plastic key tag or luggage tag and affixing it to the child's shoe. This reader also snaps a photo of the kids each morning to document what they're wearing. A Rockville, Maryland, mom shared a strategy one step short of a cattle brand:

unofficial **TIP**
We suggest that kids younger than 8 be color-coded by dressing them in purple T-shirts or equally distinctive clothes.

> *Traveling with a 3-year-old, I was very anxious about losing him, so I wrote my cell phone number on his leg with a permanent marker. I felt much more confident that he'd get back to me quickly if he became lost.*

One way to better keep track of your family is to buy each person a "Disney uniform"—in this case, the same brightly and distinctively colored T-shirt. A Yuma, Arizona, family tried this with great success:

> *We all got the same shirts (bright red) so that we could easily spot each other in case of separation (VERY easy to do). It was a lifesaver when our 18-month-old decided to get out of the stroller and wander off. As I've heard before, Dumbo seems to draw them in, and lo and behold, guess where we found him (still dragging his leash but with a nice cast member following him). No matter what precautions you may try, it seems there are always those opportunities to lose a child, but the recognizable shirts helped tremendously.*

HOW KIDS GET LOST

CHILDREN GET SEPARATED FROM THEIR PARENTS every day at Disney theme parks under remarkably similar (and predictable) circumstances:

1. PREOCCUPIED SOLO PARENT The party's only adult is preoccupied with something like buying refreshments, reading a map, or using the restroom. Junior is there one second and gone the next.

2. THE HIDDEN EXIT Sometimes parents wait on the sidelines while two or more young children experience a ride together. Parents expect the kids to exit in one place and the youngsters pop out elsewhere. Exits from some attractions are distant from entrances. Know exactly where your children will emerge before you allow them to ride by themselves.

unofficial **TIP**
Children under age 14 must be accompanied by someone age 14 or older when entering Disney World's theme parks and water parks, as well as DisneyQuest.

3. AFTER THE SHOW At the end of many shows and rides, a Disney staffer announces, "Check for personal belongings and take small children by the hand." When dozens, if not hundreds, of people leave an attraction simultaneously, it's easy for parents to lose their children unless they have direct contact.

4. POTTY PROBLEMS Mom tells 6-year-old Tommy, "I'll be sitting on this bench when you come out of the restroom." Three possibilities: One, Tommy exits through a different door and becomes disoriented (Mom may not know there's another door). Two, Mom decides she also will use the restroom, and Tommy emerges to find her gone. Three, Mom pokes around in a shop while keeping an eye on the bench but misses Tommy when he comes out.

If you can't find a companion- or family-accessible restroom, make sure there's only one exit. The restroom on a passageway between Frontierland and Adventureland in the Magic Kingdom is the all-time worst for disorienting visitors. Children and adults alike have walked in from the Adventureland side and walked out on the Frontierland side (and vice versa). Adults realize quickly that something is wrong. Children, however, sometimes fail to recognize the problem.

Designate a distinctive meeting spot and give clear instructions: "I'll meet you by this flagpole. If you get out first, stay right here." Have your child repeat the directions back to you. When children are too young to leave alone, sometimes you have to think outside the box, as our Rockville, Maryland, mom (quoted on the previous page) did:

> It was very scary for me at times, being alone with children who had just turned 1 and 2. I'm reminded of the time on the trip when I couldn't fit the double stroller into the bathroom. I was at Epcot inside one of the buildings and I had to leave my kids with a WDW employee outside of the restroom because the stroller just wouldn't fit inside with me. Thinking about the incident now makes me laugh. The good news is that I found that most WDW bathrooms can accommodate a front-and-back double stroller inside the handicapped stall with you.

5. PARADES There are many parades and shows at which the audience stands. Children tend to jockey for a better view. By moving a little this way and that, the child quickly puts distance between you and him before either of you notices.

6. MASS MOVEMENTS Be on guard when huge crowds disperse after fireworks or a parade, or at park closing. With 20,000–40,000 people at once in an area, it's very easy to get separated from a child or others in your party. Use extra caution after the evening parade and fireworks in the Magic Kingdom, *Fantasmic!* at Disney's Hollywood Studios, and *Illumi-Nations* at Epcot. Plan where to meet in the event you get separated.

7. CHARACTER GREETINGS When the Disney characters appear, children can slip out of sight. (See "Then Some Confusion Happened," page 417.)

8. GETTING LOST AT DISNEY'S ANIMAL KINGDOM It's especially easy to lose a child in Animal Kingdom, particularly at the Oasis entryway, on the Maharajah Jungle Trek, and on the Pangani Forest Exploration Trail. Mom and Dad will stop to observe an animal. Junior stays close for a minute or so, and then, losing patience, wanders to the exhibit's other side or to a different exhibit.

Especially in the multipath Oasis, locating a lost child can be maddening, as a Safety Harbor, Florida, mother describes:

Manny wandered off in the paths that lead to the jungle village while we were looking at a bird. It reminded me of losing somebody in the supermarket, when you run back and forth looking down each aisle but can't find the person you're looking for because they're running around too. I was nutso before we even got to the first ride.

A mother from Flint, Michigan, came up with yet another way to lose a kid: abandonment.

From the minute we hit the park it was gripe, whine, pout, cry, beg, scream, pick, pester, and aggravate. When he went to the restroom for the ninth time before 11 a.m., I thought, "I'm outta here! Let the little snothead walk back to Flint." Unfortunately, I was brought up Catholic with lots of guilt, so I didn't follow through.

DISNEY, KIDS, *and* SCARY STUFF

 unofficial **TIP**
Monsters and special effects at Disney's Hollywood Studios are more real and sinister than those in the other parks.

DISNEY RIDES AND SHOWS are adventures, and they focus on themes of all adventures: good and evil, death, beauty and ugliness, fellowship and enmity. As you sample the attractions at Walt Disney World, you'll transcend the spinning and bouncing of midway rides to thought-provoking and emotionally powerful entertainment. All the endings are happy, but the adventures' impact, given Disney's gift for special effects, often intimidates and occasionally frightens young children.

There are attractions with menacing witches, burning towns, skeletons, and ghouls popping out of their graves, all done with humor, provided you're old enough to understand the joke.

If your child has difficulty coping with the ghouls of The Haunted Mansion, then you should think twice about exposing him at the Studios to battle scenes in Star Tours or machine-gun battles and the creature from *Alien* in The Great Movie Ride.

You can reliably predict that Walt Disney World will, at one time or another, send a young child into system overload. Be sensitive, alert, and prepared for almost anything, even behavior that is out of character for your child. Most children take Disney's macabre trappings in stride, and others are easily comforted by an arm around the shoulder or a squeeze of the hand. Parents who know that their children tend to become upset should take it slow and easy, sampling benign adventures like the Jungle Cruise, gauging reactions, and discussing with the children how they felt about what they saw.

Sometimes young children will rise above their anxiety in an effort to please their parents or siblings. This doesn't necessarily indicate a mastery of fear, much less enjoyment. If children leave a ride in apparently good shape, ask if they would like to go on it again (not necessarily now, but sometime). The response usually will indicate how much they actually enjoyed the experience.

Continued on page 407

SMALL-CHILD FRIGHT-POTENTIAL CHART

This is a quick reference to identify attractions to be wary of, and why. The chart represents a generalization, and all kids are different. It relates specifically to kids ages 3–7. On average, children at the younger end of the range are more likely to be frightened than children in their sixth or seventh year.

The Magic Kingdom

SORCERERS OF THE MAGIC KINGDOM Loud but not frightening.

MAIN STREET, U.S.A.

MAIN STREET VEHICLES Not frightening in any respect.

WALT DISNEY WORLD RAILROAD Not frightening in any respect.

ADVENTURELAND

JUNGLE CRUISE Moderately intense, some macabre sights. A good test attraction for little ones.

PIRATES OF THE CARIBBEAN Slightly intimidating queuing area; intense boat ride with gruesome (though humorously presented) sights and a short, unexpected slide down a flume.

THE MAGIC CARPETS OF ALADDIN Much like Dumbo. A favorite ride of young children.

SWISS FAMILY TREEHOUSE Kids who are afraid of heights may want to skip it.

WALT DISNEY'S ENCHANTED TIKI ROOM A thunderstorm, loud volume level, and simulated explosions frighten some preschoolers.

FRONTIERLAND

BIG THUNDER MOUNTAIN RAILROAD Visually intimidating from outside, with moderately intense visual effects. The roller coaster is wild enough to frighten many adults, particularly seniors. Switching-off option provided (see page 412).

COUNTRY BEAR JAMBOREE Not frightening in any respect.

FRONTIERLAND SHOOTIN' ARCADE Frightening to kids who are scared of guns.

SPLASH MOUNTAIN Visually intimidating from the outside, with moderately intense visual effects. The ride culminates in a 52-foot plunge down a steep chute. Switching-off option provided (see page 412).

TOM SAWYER ISLAND AND FORT LANGHORN Some very young children are intimidated by dark walk-through tunnels that can be easily avoided.

LIBERTY SQUARE

THE HALL OF PRESIDENTS Not frightening, but boring for young ones.

THE HAUNTED MANSION Name raises anxiety, as do sounds and sights of waiting area. Intense attraction with humorously presented macabre sights. The ride itself is gentle.

LIBERTY BELLE RIVERBOAT Not frightening in any respect.

FANTASYLAND

ARIEL'S GROTTO Not frightening in any respect.

DUMBO THE FLYING ELEPHANT A tame midway ride that's a great favorite of most young children.

THE BARNSTORMER May frighten some preschoolers.

ENCHANTED TALES WITH BELLE Not frightening in any respect.

IT'S A SMALL WORLD Not frightening in any respect.

MAD TEA PARTY Midway-type ride can induce motion sickness in all ages.

THE MANY ADVENTURES OF WINNIE THE POOH Frightens a few preschoolers.

PETER PAN'S FLIGHT Not frightening in any respect.

PETE'S SILLY SIDESHOW Not frightening in any respect.

PRINCE CHARMING REGAL CARROUSEL Not frightening in any respect.

PRINCESS FAIRYTALE HALL Long lines may have parents running for the hills.

FANTASYLAND (continued)

SEVEN DWARFS MINE TRAIN May frighten some preschoolers.

UNDER THE SEA: JOURNEY OF THE LITTLE MERMAID Animatronic octopus character frightens some preschoolers.

TOMORROWLAND

ASTRO ORBITER Visually intimidating from the waiting area, but the ride is actually relatively tame.

BUZZ LIGHTYEAR'S SPACE RANGER SPIN May frighten some preschoolers.

MONSTERS, INC. LAUGH FLOOR May frighten some preschoolers.

SPACE MOUNTAIN Very intense roller coaster in the dark; the Magic Kingdom's wildest ride and a scary roller coaster by any standard. Switching-off option provided (see page 412).

STITCH'S GREAT ESCAPE! Very intense (and smelly). May frighten children age 9 and younger. Switching-off option provided (see page 412).

TOMORROWLAND SPEEDWAY The noise of the waiting area slightly intimidates preschoolers; otherwise, not frightening.

TOMORROWLAND TRANSIT AUTHORITY PEOPLEMOVER Not frightening in any respect.

WALT DISNEY'S CAROUSEL OF PROGRESS Not frightening in any respect.

Epcot

FUTURE WORLD

SUM OF ALL THRILLS Intense roller-coaster simulator may frighten some kids.

IMAGINATION!: *CAPTAIN EO* Extremely intense visual effects and loudness can frighten many young children.

JOURNEY INTO IMAGINATION WITH FIGMENT Loud noises and unexpected flashing lights startle younger children.

THE LAND: *THE CIRCLE OF LIFE* Not frightening in any respect.

THE LAND: LIVING WITH THE LAND Not frightening in any respect.

THE LAND: SOARIN' May frighten kids age 7 and younger, or anyone with a fear of heights. Otherwise a very mellow ride.

MISSION: SPACE Extremely intense space-simulation ride that has been known to frighten guests of all ages. Switching-off option provided (see page 412).

THE SEAS: THE SEAS WITH NEMO & FRIENDS Very sweet but may frighten some toddlers.

THE SEAS: MAIN TANK AND EXHIBITS Not frightening in any respect.

THE SEAS: *TURTLE TALK WITH CRUSH* Not frightening in any respect.

SPACESHIP EARTH Dark, imposing presentation intimidates a few preschoolers.

TEST TRACK Intense thrill ride may frighten guests of any age. Switching-off option provided (see page 412).

UNIVERSE OF ENERGY: *ELLEN'S ENERGY ADVENTURE* Dinosaur segment frightens some preschoolers; visually intense, with some intimidating effects.

WORLD SHOWCASE

CANADA: *O CANADA!* Not frightening, but audience must stand.

CHINA: *REFLECTIONS OF CHINA* Not frightening in any respect.

FRANCE: *IMPRESSIONS DE FRANCE* Not frightening in any respect.

GERMANY Not frightening in any respect.

ITALY Not frightening in any respect.

JAPAN Not frightening in any respect.

MEXICO: GRAN FIESTA TOUR Not frightening in any respect.

MOROCCO Not frightening in any respect.

UNITED KINGDOM Not frightening in any respect.

UNITED STATES: *THE AMERICAN ADVENTURE* Not frightening in any respect.

SMALL-CHILD FRIGHT-POTENTIAL CHART
(Continued)

Disney's Animal Kingdom

THE OASIS Not frightening in any respect.

RAFIKI'S PLANET WATCH Not frightening in any respect.

DISCOVERY ISLAND

THE TREE OF LIFE/*IT'S TOUGH TO BE A BUG!* Very intense and loud, with special effects that startle viewers of all ages and potentially terrify little kids.

WILDERNESS EXPLORERS Not frightening in any respect.

AFRICA

FESTIVAL OF THE LION KING A bit loud, but otherwise not frightening.

KILIMANJARO SAFARIS A "collapsing" bridge and the proximity of real animals make a few young children anxious.

PANGANI FOREST EXPLORATION TRAIL Not frightening in any respect.

WILDLIFE EXPRESS TRAIN Not frightening in any respect.

ASIA

EXPEDITION EVEREST Can frighten guests of all ages. Switching-off option provided (see page 412).

FLIGHTS OF WONDER Swooping birds alarm a few small children.

KALI RIVER RAPIDS Potentially frightening and certainly wet for guests of all ages. Switching-off option provided (see page 412).

MAHARAJAH JUNGLE TREK Some children may balk at the bat exhibit.

DINOLAND U.S.A.

THE BONEYARD Not frightening in any respect.

DINOSAUR High-tech thrill ride rattles riders of all ages. Switching-off option provided (see page 412).

PRIMEVAL WHIRL A beginner roller coaster. Most children age 7 and older will take it in stride. Switching-off option provided (see page 412).

THEATER IN THE WILD/*FINDING NEMO—THE MUSICAL* Not frightening in any respect, but loud.

TRICERATOP SPIN A midway-type ride that will frighten only a small percentage of younger children.

Disney's Hollywood Studios

HOLLYWOOD BOULEVARD

THE GREAT MOVIE RIDE Intense in parts, with very realistic special effects and some visually intimidating sights. Frightens many preschoolers.

SUNSET BOULEVARD

FANTASMIC! Terrifies some preschoolers.

ROCK 'N' ROLLER COASTER The wildest coaster at Walt Disney World. May frighten guests of any age. Switching-off option provided (see page 412).

THEATER OF THE STARS/*BEAUTY AND THE BEAST—LIVE ON STAGE* Not frightening in any respect.

THE TWILIGHT ZONE TOWER OF TERROR Visually intimidating to young children; contains intense and realistic special effects. The plummeting elevator at the ride's end frightens many adults as well as kids. Switching-off option provided (see page 412).

ECHO LAKE

INDIANA JONES EPIC STUNT SPECTACULAR! An intense show with powerful special effects, including explosions, but young kids generally handle it well.

ECHO LAKE *(continued)*
STAR TOURS—THE ADVENTURES CONTINUE Extremely intense visually for all ages; too intense for kids under age 8. Switching-off option provided (see page 412).
STREETS OF AMERICA
HONEY, I SHRUNK THE KIDS MOVIE SET ADVENTURE Not scary (though oversized).
JIM HENSON'S MUPPET-VISION 3-D Intense and loud, but not frightening.
LIGHTS, MOTORS, ACTION! EXTREME STUNT SHOW Super stunt spectacular; intense with loud noises and explosions, but not threatening in any way.
PIXAR PLACE
TOY STORY MIDWAY MANIA! Dark ride may frighten some preschoolers.
MICKEY AVENUE
WALT DISNEY: ONE MAN'S DREAM Not frightening in any respect.
ANIMATION COURTYARD
DISNEY JUNIOR—LIVE ON STAGE! Not frightening in any respect.
VOYAGE OF THE LITTLE MERMAID Some children are creeped out by Ursula.

Continued from page 403

Evaluating a child's capacity to handle the visual and tactile effects of Disney World requires patience, understanding, and experimentation. Each of us has our own demons. If a child balks at or is frightened by a ride, respond constructively. Let your children know that lots of people, adults and children, are scared by what they see and feel. Help them understand that it's OK if they get frightened and that their fear doesn't lessen your love or respect. Take pains not to compound the discomfort by making a child feel inadequate; try not to undermine self-esteem, impugn courage, or ridicule. Most of all, don't induce guilt by suggesting the child's trepidation might be ruining the family's fun. It's also sometimes necessary to restrain older siblings' taunting.

A reader from New York City expresses strong feelings about pressuring children:

> As a psychologist who works with children, I felt ethically torn (and nearly filed a report!) watching parents force their children to go on rides they didn't want to ride (especially the Tower of Terror and Dinosaur). The Disney staff were more than willing to organize a parental swap to save these children from such abuse!

A visit to Disney World is more than an outing or an adventure for a young child. It's a testing experience, a sort of controlled rite of passage. If you help your little one work through the challenges, the time can be immeasurably rewarding and a bonding experience for you both.

THE FRIGHT FACTOR

WHILE EACH YOUNGSTER IS DIFFERENT, following are seven attraction elements that alone or combined could push a child's buttons and indicate that a certain attraction isn't age appropriate for that child:

1. NAME OF THE ATTRACTION Young children will naturally be apprehensive about something called, say, The Haunted Mansion or Tower of Terror.

2. VISUAL IMPACT OF THE ATTRACTION FROM OUTSIDE Splash Mountain, the Tower of Terror, and Big Thunder Mountain Railroad look scary enough to give adults second thoughts, and they terrify many little kids. A Utah family of six reports the following:

> At 5 years old, my granddaughter was big enough and willing to go on almost everything. The problem was with the preliminary introductions to Haunted Mansion and Tower of Terror. Walking through and learning the stories before the actual rides were what frightened her and made her opt out without going in. The rides themselves would not have been bad; she loved Splash Mountain and Big Thunder Mountain, but she could SEE those rides before entering.

3. VISUAL IMPACT OF THE INDOOR-QUEUING AREA The caves at Pirates of the Caribbean and the dungeons and "stretch rooms" of The Haunted Mansion can frighten children.

4. INTENSITY OF THE ATTRACTION Some attractions inundate the senses with sights, sounds, movement, and even smell. Animal Kingdom's *It's Tough to be a Bug!*, for example, combines loud sounds, lights, smoke, and animatronic insects with 3-D cinematography to create a total sensory experience.

A Johnston, Iowa, mom describes the situation well:

> The 3-D and 4-D experiences are way too scary for even a very brave 5-year-old girl. The shows that blew things on her, shot smells in the air, had bugs flying, etc. scared the bejesus out of her. We escorted her crying from It's Tough to Be a Bug!, Mickey's PhilharMagic, and Stitch's Great Escape!

5. VISUAL IMPACT OF THE ATTRACTION Sights in various attractions range from falling boulders to lurking buzzards, from grazing dinosaurs to waltzing ghosts. What one child calmly absorbs may scare the pants off of another the same age.

6. DARK Many Disney World attractions operate indoors in the dark. For some children, this triggers fear. A child who gets frightened on one dark ride (The Haunted Mansion, for example) may be unwilling to try other indoor rides.

7. THE TACTILE EXPERIENCE Some rides are wild enough to cause motion sickness, wrench backs, and discombobulate guests of any age.

As a footnote to the preceding, be aware that gaining the courage and confidence in regard to the attractions is not necessarily an upwardly linear process. A dad from Maryland explains:

> As a 4-year-old, my daughter absolutely adored The Haunted Mansion. At 5 she was scared to death on it! At 6 she was fine again. Just because a child loves a ride at one age doesn't mean that he or she will love it on the next trip.

A BIT OF PREPARATION

WE RECEIVE MANY TIPS FROM PARENTS telling how they prepared their young children for the Disney experience. A common strategy is to acquaint children with the characters and stories behind the attractions by reading Disney books and watching Disney videos at home. A more direct approach is to watch videos that show the attractions. Of the latter, a Lexington, Kentucky, mom reports:

> *My timid 7-year-old daughter and I watched ride and show videos on YouTube, and we cut out all the ones that looked too scary. At the parks, she still didn't like, and cried at, It's Tough to Be a Bug! Ellen's Energy Adventure made her tense up, but she loved, loved, loved Kali River Rapids.*

A Gloucester, Massachusetts, mom solved the problem on the spot:

> *My 3½-year-old was afraid of The Haunted Mansion. We just pulled his hat over his face and quietly talked to him while we rode.*

You can order a free **Walt Disney World Vacation Planning DVD** by clicking on "Free Planning DVD" at the **disneyworld.com** home page or by calling ☎ 407-W-DISNEY (934-7639). As a YouTube supplement, it gives your kids an adequate sense of what they'll see. Allow at least one month for delivery. For more-immediate gratification, you can also watch the **Travel Channel**'s Walt Disney World specials on Hulu or Netflix streaming.

ATTRACTIONS THAT EAT ADULTS

YOU MAY SPEND SO MUCH ENERGY worrying about Junior that you forget to take care of yourself. The attractions listed below can cause motion sickness or other problems for older kids and adults:

POTENTIALLY PROBLEMATIC ATTRACTIONS FOR GROWN-UPS
THE MAGIC KINGDOM
FANTASYLAND Mad Tea Party
FRONTIERLAND Big Thunder Mountain Railroad, Splash Mountain
TOMORROWLAND Space Mountain
EPCOT
FUTURE WORLD Mission: Space, Sum of All Thrills, Test Track
DISNEY'S ANIMAL KINGDOM
ASIA Expedition Everest, Kali River Rapids
DINOLAND U.S.A. Dinosaur
DISNEY'S HOLLYWOOD STUDIOS
ECHO LAKE Star Tours—The Adventures Continue
SUNSET BOULEVARD Rock 'n' Roller Coaster, The Twilight Zone Tower of Terror

A WORD ABOUT HEIGHT REQUIREMENTS

A NUMBER OF ATTRACTIONS REQUIRE children to meet minimum height and age requirements. If you have children too short or too young to ride, you have several options, including switching off (see page 412). Although the alternatives may resolve some practical and logistical issues, your smaller children may nonetheless be resentful of their older (or taller) siblings who qualify to ride. A mom from Virginia writes of such a situation:

ATTRACTION AND RIDE RESTRICTIONS

THE MAGIC KINGDOM

The Barnstormer	35" minimum height
Big Thunder Mountain Railroad	40" minimum height
Seven Dwarfs Mine Train	38" minimum height
Space Mountain	44" minimum height
Splash Mountain	40" minimum height
Stitch's Great Escape!	40" minimum height
Tomorrowland Speedway	32" to ride, 54" to drive unassisted

EPCOT

Mission: Space	44" minimum height
Soarin'	40" minimum height
Sum of All Thrills	48" minimum height, 54" for inversions
Test Track	40" minimum height

DISNEY'S ANIMAL KINGDOM

Dinosaur	40" minimum height
Expedition Everest	44" minimum height
Kali River Rapids	38" minimum height
Primeval Whirl	48" minimum height

DISNEY'S HOLLYWOOD STUDIOS

Honey, I Shrunk the Kids Movie Set Adventure	10 yrs. maximum recommended age
Rock 'n' Roller Coaster	48" minimum height
Star Tours—The Adventures Continue	40" minimum height
The Twilight Zone Tower of Terror	40" minimum height

BLIZZARD BEACH WATER PARK

Chair Lift	32" minimum height
Downhill Double Dipper slide	48" minimum height
Slush Gusher slide	48" minimum height
Summit Plummet slide	48" minimum height
T-Bar (in Ski Patrol Training Camp)	60" maximum height
Tike's Peak children's area	48" maximum height

TYPHOON LAGOON WATER PARK

Bay Slides	60" minimum height
Crush 'n' Gusher	48" minimum height
Humunga Kowabunga slide	48" minimum height
Ketchakiddee Creek children's area	48" maximum height
Shark Reef saltwater reef swim	10 yrs. minimum age unless accompanied by adult
Wave Pool	*Adult supervision required*

DISNEYQUEST

Buzz Lightyear's AstroBlasters	51" minimum height
CyberSpace Mountain	51" minimum height
Mighty Ducks Pinball Slam	48" minimum height
Pirates of the Caribbean—Battle for Buccaneer Gold	35" minimum height

You mention height requirements for rides but not the intense sibling jealousy this can generate. Frontierland was a real problem in that respect. Our very petite 5-year-old, to her outrage, was stuck hanging around while our 8-year-old went on Splash Mountain and Big Thunder Mountain with her grandma and granddad, and the nearby alternatives weren't helpful (too long a line for rafts to Tom Sawyer Island, etc.). The best areas had a playground or other quick attractions for short people near the rides with height requirements, like The Boneyard near the Dinosaur ride at Animal Kingdom.

The reader makes a point, though splitting the group and meeting later can be more complicated than she imagines. If you split up, ask the Disney attendant (called a greeter) at the entrance to the attraction(s) with height requirements how long the wait is. If you tack 5 minutes for riding on to the anticipated wait and add 5 or so minutes to exit and reach the meeting point, you'll have a sense of how long the younger kids (and their supervising adult) will have to do other stuff. Our guess is that even with a long line for the rafts, the reader would've had sufficient time to take her daughter to Tom Sawyer Island while the sibs rode Splash Mountain and Big Thunder Mountain with the grandparents. For sure, she had time to tour the Swiss Family Treehouse in adjacent Adventureland.

For more information, see the chart on the facing page.

WAITING-LINE STRATEGIES *for* ADULTS *with* YOUNG CHILDREN

CHILDREN HOLD UP BETTER through the day if you limit the time they spend in lines. Arriving early and using our touring plans greatly reduce waiting. Here are other ways to reduce stress for children:

1. LINE GAMES Anticipate that children will get restless in line, and plan activities to reduce the stress and boredom. In the morning, have waiting children discuss what they want to see and do during the day. Later, watch for and count Disney characters or play simple games such as 20 Questions. Lines move continuously; games requiring pen and paper are impractical. Waiting in the holding area of a theater attraction is a different story. Here, tic-tac-toe, hangman, drawing, and coloring make the time fly.

A Springfield, Ohio, mom reports on an unexpected but welcome assist from her brother:

I have a bachelor brother who joined my 5-, 7-, and 9-year-olds and me for vacation. Pat surprised all of us with a bunch of plastic animal noses he had in his hip pack. When the kids got restless or cranky in line, he'd turn away and pull out a pig nose or a parrot nose or something. When he turned back around with the nose on, the kids would majorly crack up.

A Waco, Texas, dad broke out the bubbly:

I took bubbles along with us. My boys loved them and so did the other children waiting in line. (I bought wedding-size bottles that would fit into everyone's fanny pack.)

2. SWITCHING OFF Several attractions have minimum height and/or age requirements. Some couples with children too small or too young forgo these attractions, while others take turns riding. Missing some of Disney's best rides is an unnecessary sacrifice, and waiting in line twice for the same ride is a tremendous waste of time.

ATTRACTIONS WHERE SWITCHING OFF IS COMMON	
THE MAGIC KINGDOM	**DISNEY'S ANIMAL KINGDOM**
• The Barnstormer • Big Thunder Mountain Railroad • Seven Dwarfs Mine Train • Space Mountain • Splash Mountain • *Stitch's Great Escape!* • Tomorrowland Speedway	• Dinosaur • Expedition Everest • Kali River Rapids • Primeval Whirl
EPCOT	**DISNEY'S HOLLYWOOD STUDIOS**
• Mission: Space • Soarin' • Test Track	• Rock 'n' Roller Coaster • Star Tours— The Adventures Continue • The Twilight Zone Tower of Terror

Instead, take advantage of "switching off," also known variously as "The Baby Swap," "The Rider Swap," or "The Baby/Rider Switch." For switching off to work, there must be at least two adults. Adults and kids wait in line together. When you reach a cast member, say you want to switch off. The cast member will allow everyone, including young children, to enter the attraction. When you reach the loading area, one adult rides while the other exits with the kids. Then the riding adult disembarks and takes charge of the children while the other adult rides. A third member of the party, either an adult or an older child, can ride twice, once with each switching-off adult, so the grown-ups don't have to ride alone.

3. COMBINING THE FASTPASS+ SYSTEM WITH SWITCHING OFF On most FastPass+ attractions, Disney handles switching off somewhat differently. When you tell the cast member that you want to switch off, you'll get a special "rider exchange" FastPass good for three people. One parent and the nonriding child (or children) will at that point be asked to leave the line. When those riding reunite with those waiting, the waiting adult and two others from the party can ride using the special FastPass. This eliminates confusion at the boarding area while sparing the nonriding adult and child the tedium of waiting in line.

4. LAST-MINUTE COLD FEET If your young child gets cold feet just before boarding a ride where there's no age or height requirement, you usually can arrange a switch-off with the loading attendant. (This happens frequently in Pirates of the Caribbean's dungeon waiting area.)

No law says you have to ride. If you reach the boarding area and someone is unhappy, tell an attendant you've changed your mind and you'll be shown the way out.

5. THROW YOURSELF ON THE GRENADE, MILDRED! For long-suffering parents who are determined to sacrifice themselves on behalf of their children, we provide a Magic Kingdom One-Day Touring Plan called the Dumbo-or-Die-in-a-Day Touring Plan for Parents with Small Children. This plan (see page 811) will ensure that you run yourself ragged. Designed to help you forfeit everything of personal interest for your children's pleasure, the plan guarantees you'll go home battered and exhausted, with extraordinary stories of devotion and perseverance. By the way, it really works. Anyone under age 8 will love it.

The DISNEY CHARACTERS

THE LARGE AND FRIENDLY costumed versions of Mickey, Minnie, Donald, Goofy, and others—known as the Disney characters—provide a link between Disney animated films and the theme parks. To those emotionally invested, the characters in Disney films are as real as next-door neighbors, never mind that they're drawings on plastic. In recent years, theme park personifications of the characters also have become real to us. It's not a person in a mouse costume; it's Mickey himself. Similarly, meeting Belle or Elsa isn't an encounter with a pretty cast member but a real celebrity—a memory to be treasured.

unofficial **TIP**
Don't underestimate your child's excitement at meeting the Disney characters—but also be aware that very small children may find the large costumed characters a little frightening.

While Disney animated-film characters number in the hundreds, only about 250 have been brought to life in costume. Of these, fewer than a fifth mix with guests; the others perform in shows or parades. Originally confined to the Magic Kingdom, the Disney characters are now found in all major theme parks and at Disney Deluxe resorts that host character meals.

We receive hundreds of reader comments telling us how much the Disney characters enhanced their theme park experience. This e-mail from a Wisconsin mom is representative:

> *I can't say enough about the characters and how they react to the children and just people in general. They are obviously highly trained in people skills and just add an extra dimension to the park.*

CHARACTER WATCHING Watching characters has become a pastime. Families once were content to meet a character occasionally. They now pursue them relentlessly, armed with autograph books and cameras. Because some characters are only rarely seen, character watching has become character collecting. (To cash in on character collecting, Disney sells autograph books throughout the World.) Mickey, Minnie, and Goofy are a snap to bag; they seem to be everywhere. But some characters, like the Queen of Hearts and Friar Tuck, seldom come out, and quite a few appear only in parades or stage shows. Other characters appear only in a location consistent with their starring role. The Fairy Godmother is often near Cinderella Castle in Fantasyland, while Buzz Lightyear appears close to his eponymous attraction in Tomorrowland.

unofficial **TIP**
Many kids take special delight in meeting the "face characters," such as Anna, Elsa, Tiana, and Cinderella, who can speak to them and engage them in a way that the mute animal characters can't.

A Brooklyn dad complains that character collecting has gotten out of hand:

> *This year, when we took our youngest child (who is now 8 years old), he had already seen his siblings' collection and was determined to outdo them. However, rather than random meetings, the characters are now available practically all day long at different locations, according to a printed schedule, which our son was old enough to*

read. We spent more time standing in line for autographs than we did for the most popular rides!

A family from Birmingham, Alabama, found some benefit in their children's pursuit of characters:

We had no idea we'd be caught up in this madness, but after my daughters grabbed your guidebook to get Pocahontas to sign it (we had no blank paper), we quickly bought a Disney autograph book and gave in. It was actually the highlight of their trip, and my son even got into the act by helping get places in line for his sisters. It was an amazing, totally unexpected part of our visit.

PREPARING YOUR CHILDREN TO MEET THE CHARACTERS Almost all characters are quite large; several, like Baloo, are huge. Small children don't expect this, and preschoolers especially can be intimidated.

Discuss the characters with your children before you go. On first encounter, don't thrust your child at the character. Allow the little one to deal with this big thing from whatever distance feels safe. If two adults are present, one should stay near the youngster while the other approaches the character and demonstrates that it's safe and friendly. Some kids warm to the characters immediately; some never do. Most take a little time and several encounters.

There are two kinds of characters: "furs," or those whose costumes include face-covering headpieces (including animal characters and such humanlike characters as Captain Hook), and "face characters," those for whom no mask or headpiece is necessary. These include Anna and Elsa, Aladdin and Jasmine, Ariel, Belle, Cinderella, Mary Poppins, Merida, Prince Charming, Snow White, and Tiana, among others.

Only face characters speak. Because cast members couldn't possibly imitate the furs' distinctive cinema voices, Disney has determined that it's more effective to keep such characters silent. Lack of speech notwithstanding, headpiece characters are warm and responsive, and they communicate effectively with gestures. Tell children in advance that these characters don't talk. As an aside, Disney has been implementing technology for making some of the furs talk, most notably Mickey and Minnie.

> *un*official **TIP**
> If you're using our Lines app in the parks, don't worry about losing time for meet and greets. Just tap "Optimize" after getting your autograph, and we'll tell you where to go next.

Some character costumes are cumbersome and give the cast members inside very poor visibility. (Eyeholes frequently are in the mouth of the costume or even on the neck or chest.) Children who approach the character from the back or side may not be noticed, even if the child touches the character. It's possible in this situation for the character to accidentally step on the child or knock him down. A child should approach a character from the front, but occasionally not even this works—Donald and Daisy, for example, have to peer around their bills. If a character appears to be ignoring your child, the character's handler will get its attention. Finally, some characters, such as Buzz Lightyear, can't sign autographs because of their costumes but will gladly pose for photos.

WDW CHARACTER-GREETING VENUES

THE MAGIC KINGDOM

MICKEY AND HIS POSSE

Chip 'n' Dale Liberty Square
Daisy, Donald, Goofy, Minnie Pete's Silly Sideshow (FastPass+)
Mickey Town Square Theater (FastPass+)
Pluto Town Square

DISNEY ROYALTY (*Princesses, Princes, Suitors, and Such*)

Aladdin, Jasmine Adventureland
Anna and Elsa Princess Fairytale Hall (FastPass+)
Ariel Ariel's Grotto (FastPass+)
Cinderella, Rapunzel Princess Fairytale Hall (FastPass+)
Aurora, Belle *Enchanted Tales with Belle* (FastPass+)
The Fairy Godmother, the Tremaines Near Bibbidi Bobbidi Boutique in Cinderella Castle
Gaston Fountain outside Gaston's Tavern
Merida Fairytale Garden
Naveen, Tiana Liberty Square
Snow White Outside the Town Square Theater exit

FAIRIES

Tinker Bell and Friends Town Square Theater (FastPass+)

MISCELLANEOUS

ALICE IN WONDERLAND
  Alice, the White Rabbit, Tweedledum and Tweedledee Mad Tea Party
  The Queen of Hearts Mad Tea Party, Town Square
THE ARISTOCATS **Marie** Town Square
LILO AND STITCH **Stitch** Tomorrowland
THE INCREDIBLES **Frozone, Mr. and Mrs. Incredible** Tomorrowland
PETER PAN **Peter, Wendy, Hook, Smee** Adventureland
TOY STORY **Bullseye, Jessie, Woody** Frontierland near Splash Mountain
  Buzz Lightyear Tomorrowland

EPCOT

MICKEY AND HIS POSSE

Chip 'n' Dale Outside on the Land side of the Epcot Character Connection
Daisy, Pluto On the right as you enter Epcot through the main turnstiles
Donald Mexico, at the Mexico Promenade
Goofy, Minnie, Mickey Epcot Character Spot (FastPass+)

DISNEY ROYALTY

Aladdin, Jasmine Morocco   **Anna and Elsa** Norway   **Aurora, The Beast, Belle** France
Mulan China   **Snow White** Germany

MISCELLANEOUS

Alice, Mary Poppins and Bert, Winnie the Pooh United Kingdom
Duffy the Disney Bear World Showcase Plaza
Geppetto, Pinocchio Italy

It's OK for your child to touch, pat, or hug the character. Under-standing the unpredictability of children, the character will keep his feet still, particularly refraining from moving backward or sideways. Most characters will pose for pictures or sign autographs. Costumes make it difficult for characters to wield a normal pen. If your child collects autographs, carry a pen the width of a Magic Marker.

DISNEY'S ANIMAL KINGDOM

MICKEY AND HIS POSSE

Chip 'n' Dale Rafiki's Planet Watch, at Conservation Station; The Oasis, just past the entrance turnstiles and to the right
Daisy Character Landing, Discovery Island
Donald DinoLand U.S.A., to the left of the Dinosaur exit on Cretaceous Trail
Goofy, Pluto DinoLand U.S.A., near Primeval Whirl
Mickey, Minnie Adventurers Outpost, Discovery Island (FastPass+)

DISNEY ROYALTY

Pocahontas Discovery Island trails that run behind the Tree of Life

MISCELLANEOUS

THE JUNGLE BOOK **King Loule and Baloo** On the walkway between Asia and Africa
THE LION KING **Rafiki** Rafiki's Planet Watch, at Conservation Station!
UP **Russell, Dug** By *It's Tough to Be a Bug!*

DISNEY'S HOLLYWOOD STUDIOS

MICKEY AND HIS POSSE

Chip 'n' Dale, Goofy, Minnie, Pluto, Sorcerer Mickey Check *Times Guide* for latest info

CURRENT-MOVIE PALS

Various characters Check *Times Guide* for latest info

DISNEY CHANNEL STARS

Phineas and Ferb Streets of America
Sofia the First, Jake (*Jake and the Never Land Pirates*) Animation Courtyard near *Disney Junior—Live on Stage!*

MISCELLANEOUS

THE INCREDIBLES
Frozone, Mr. and Mrs. Incredible Check *Times Guide* for latest info
MONSTERS, INC. **Mike, Sulley** Streets of America
STAR WARS **Darth Maul, Darth Vader, Stormtroopers** Near Star Tours
TOY STORY **Buzz, Jessie, Woody** Pixar Place

"THEN SOME CONFUSION HAPPENED" Kids sometimes become lost at character encounters. Usually, there's a lot of activity around a character, with both adults and children touching it or posing for pictures. Most commonly, Mom and Dad stay in the crowd while Junior approaches the character. In the excitement and with the character moving around, Junior heads in the wrong direction to look for Mom and Dad. In the words of a Salt Lake City mom: "Milo was shaking hands with Dopey one minute, then some confusion happened and Milo was gone."

We recommend that parents with preschoolers stay with them when they meet characters, stepping back only to take a quick picture.

CHARACTER HOGS While we're on the subject of cameras, give other families a chance. Especially if you're shooting video, consider the perspective of this Houston mom:

One of the worst things to deal with is people who shoot about 3 minutes of their child with Mickey, asking everyone else to move. A photo takes about 2 seconds.

MEETING CHARACTERS FOR FREE

DISNEY HAS CREATED many permanent greeting locations intended to satisfy its guests' inexhaustible desire to meet characters. The chart on pages 416 and 417 lists them by park and character.

Meeting characters at the greeting locations may be free, but it can eat up of hours of time. A reader from Panama City, Florida, offers this advice:

> Use FastPass+ for character greetings whenever you can. We did this for Ariel in Fantasyland and with Rapunzel at Princess Fairytale Hall, and we got in superfast!

CHARACTER DINING

BECAUSE OF THE INCREDIBLE POPULARITY of character dining, reservations can be hard to come by if you wait until a couple of months before your vacation to book your choices. What's more, if you want to book a character meal, you must provide Disney with a credit card number. Your card will be charged $10 *per person* if you no-show or cancel your reservation less than 24 hours in advance; you may, however, reschedule with no penalty. See "Getting Advance Reservations at Popular Restaurants" (page 302) for the full story.

At very popular character meals like the breakfast at Cinderella's Royal Table, you're required to make a for-real reservation and guarantee it with a for-real deposit.

WHAT TO EXPECT

CHARACTER MEALS ARE BUSTLING AFFAIRS held in the largest full-service restaurants at the theme parks and on-property resorts, plus the Walt Disney World Swan and select hotels in the Downtown Disney Resort Area and the Bonnet Creek Resort (including the Four Seasons).

Character breakfasts offer a fixed menu served individually, family-style, or on a buffet. The typical breakfast includes scrambled eggs; bacon, sausage, and ham; hash browns; waffles or French toast; biscuits, rolls, or pastries; and fruit. With family-style service, the meal is served in large skillets or platters at your table. The character breakfast at Akershus Royal Banquet Hall, for example, is served family-style and consists of typical breakfast fare such as eggs, bacon and sausage, and Danish pastries. Seconds (or thirds) are free. Buffets offer much the same fare, but you fetch it yourself.

Character dinners range from a set menu to buffets to ordering off the menu. Character-dinner buffets, such as those at 1900 Park Fare at the Grand Floridian and Chef Mickey's at the Contemporary Resort, separate the kids' fare from the grown-ups', though everyone is free to eat from both lines. Typically, the children's buffet includes hamburgers, hot dogs, pizza, fish sticks, chicken nuggets, macaroni and cheese, and peanut-butter-and-jelly sandwiches. Selections at the adult buffet usually include prime rib or other carved meat, baked or broiled Florida seafood, pasta, chicken, an ethnic dish or two, vegetables, potatoes, and salad.

At all meals, characters circulate around the room while you eat. During your meal, each of the three to five characters present will visit your table, arriving one at a time to cuddle the kids (and sometimes the adults), pose for photos, and sign autographs. Keep autograph books (with pens) handy and cameras or mobile phones at the ready. For the best photos, adults should sit across the table from their children. Seat the children where characters can easily reach them. If a table is against a wall, for example, adults should sit with their backs to the wall and children on the aisle.

Theresa Brown posted this great tip for getting the best photos at the independent Disney website **allears.net:**

> We did several character meals. At first, we would only use our cameras to take pictures of our children with the characters after they had signed the autograph books and were posing with them. But after the second meal, we started snapping away as soon as the characters approached our table. We're so glad we did this, because we captured a very funny sequence of events while at 1900 Park Fare at the Grand Floridian. These candid shots tell a funny story showing the playful interaction between my sons and the characters. After that, we started snapping away at all of the character meals, and now that we're back, we see that the candid shots usually gave us better pictures than the posed ones! Of course, you want the posed pictures, but the candid ones just might end up being your favorite memories of the meals!

At some larger restaurants, including 'Ohana at the Polynesian Village Resort and Chef Mickey's at the Contemporary, character meals involve impromptu parades of characters and children around the room, group singing, napkin waving, and other organized madness.

Even without parades and such, character meals are pretty frenetic, as this mother of a 3-year-old attests:

> The character meals are NOT relaxing. I wish I had known how frantic and rushed I would be. I was literally sprinting to the buffet to

throw food on my plate, so I wouldn't miss a character at our table. I still HIGHLY recommend them, as the food was actually pretty good, and the meals were the BEST part of our daughter's trip. But just be prepared for it to be a semi-hectic affair.

WHEN TO GO

ATTENDING A CHARACTER BREAKFAST usually prevents you from arriving at the theme parks in time for opening. Because early morning is best for touring and you don't want to burn daylight lingering over breakfast, we suggest:

1. Schedule your in-park character breakfast for the first seating if the park opens at 9 a.m. or later. You'll be admitted to the park before other guests (admission is still required) through a special line at the turnstiles. Arrive early to be among the first parties seated.

2. Go to a character dinner or lunch instead of breakfast. It'll be a nice break.

3. Schedule the last seating for breakfast. Have a light snack such as cereal or bagels before you head to the parks for opening, hit the most popular attractions until 10:15 or so, and then head for brunch. The buffet should keep you fueled until dinner, especially if you eat another light snack in the afternoon.

4. Go on arrival or departure day. The day you arrive and check in is usually good for a character dinner. Settle at your hotel, swim, then dine with the characters. This strategy has the added benefit of exposing your children to the characters before chance encounters at the parks. Some children, moreover, won't settle down to enjoy the parks until they have seen Mickey. Departure day also is good for a character meal. Schedule a character breakfast on your check-out day before you head for the airport or begin your drive home.

5. Go on a rest day. If you plan to stay five or more days, you'll probably take a day or half-day from touring to rest or do something else. These are perfect days for a character meal.

HOW TO CHOOSE A CHARACTER MEAL

MANY READERS ASK FOR ADVICE about character meals. This question from a Waterloo, Iowa, mom is typical:

Are all character breakfasts pretty much the same or are some better than others? How should I go about choosing one?

In fact, some *are* better, sometimes much better. When we evaluate character meals, we look for the following:

1. THE CHARACTERS The meals offer a diverse assortment of characters. Pick a meal that features your kids' favorites. Check out our Character-Meal Hit Parade chart (see pages 422 and 423) to see which characters are assigned to each meal. Most restaurants stick with the same characters. Even so, check the lineup when you call to make your Advance Reservations.

2. ATTENTION FROM THE CHARACTERS At all character meals, characters circulate among guests, hugging children, posing for pictures, and signing autographs. How much time a character spends with you and your children depends primarily on the ratio of characters to guests. The more characters and fewer guests, the better. Because many character-meal venues never fill to capacity, the character-to-guest ratios in our Character-Meal Hit Parade chart have been adjusted to reflect an average attendance. Even so, there's quite a range. The best ratio is at Cinderella's Royal Table, where there's about 1 character to every 26 guests.

The worst ratio is theoretically at the Swan resort's Garden Grove, where there could be as few as 1 character for every 198 guests. We say "theoretically," however, because in practice there are far fewer guests at the Garden Grove than at character meals in Disney-owned resorts, and often more characters. (During one meal, friends of ours were literally the only guests in the restaurant for breakfast and had to ask the characters to leave them alone to eat.)

A Jerseyville, Illinois, mom gives the face characters high marks:

Our 7-year-old daughter wanted to have dinner with Sleeping Beauty, so we scheduled a character dinner with the princesses in the Norway Pavilion. The princesses were so accessible and took their time with our child, answering questions and smiling for pictures. In fact, our daughter told us she "had the best day of her life," and parents want to hear that from their child.

An Indiana mother of two relates the importance of keeping tabs on the characters:

For character meals, take note of which characters are there when you arrive, and mentally check them off as they visit your table. If the last one or two seem slow to arrive, seek out the "character manager" and let him or her know ASAP.

3. THE SETTING Some character meals are in exotic settings. For others, moving the event to an elementary-school cafeteria would be an improvement. Our chart rates each meal's setting with the familiar scale of zero (worst) to five (best) stars. Two restaurants, Cinderella's Royal Table in the Magic Kingdom and Garden Grill Restaurant in the Land Pavilion at Epcot, deserve special mention. Cinderella's Royal Table is on the first and second floors of Cinderella Castle in Fantasyland, offering guests a look inside the castle. Garden Grill is a revolving restaurant overlooking several scenes from the Living with the Land boat ride. Also at Epcot, the popular Princess Storybook Meals are held in the castlelike Akershus Royal Banquet Hall. Though Chef Mickey's at the Contemporary Resort is rather sterile in appearance, it affords a great view of the monorail running through the hotel. Themes and settings of the remaining character-meal venues, while apparent to adults, will be lost on most children.

4. THE FOOD Although some food served at character meals is quite good, most is average (palatable but nothing to get excited about). In variety, consistency, and quality, restaurants generally do a better job with breakfast than with lunch or dinner (if served).

Some restaurants offer a buffet, while others opt for "one-skillet" family-style service, in which all hot items are served from the same pot or skillet. Regarding the latter, a Texas mom notes:

The family-style meals are much better for character dining. At the buffet, you're scared to leave your table in case you miss a character or other action.

CHARACTER-MEAL HIT PARADE

1. CINDERELLA'S ROYAL TABLE   MAGIC KINGDOM

MEALS SERVED Breakfast, lunch, and dinner   **SETTING** ★★★★

CHARACTERS Cinderella, Ariel, Aurora, Jasmine, Snow White

TYPE OF SERVICE Fixed menu   **FOOD VARIETY & QUALITY** ★★★

NOISE LEVEL Quiet   **CHARACTER–GUEST RATIO** 1:26

2. AKERSHUS ROYAL BANQUET HALL   EPCOT

MEALS SERVED Breakfast, lunch, and dinner   **SETTING** ★★★★

CHARACTERS 4–6 characters chosen from Ariel, Belle, Jasmine, Mary Poppins, Mulan, Sleeping Beauty, Snow White

TYPE OF SERVICE Family-style and menu (all you care to eat)

FOOD VARIETY & QUALITY ★★★½   **NOISE LEVEL** Quiet

CHARACTER–GUEST RATIO 1:54

3. CHEF MICKEY'S   CONTEMPORARY

MEALS SERVED Breakfast, brunch, dinner   **SETTING** ★★★

CHARACTERS *All three meals:* Mickey, Minnie, Donald, Goofy, Pluto (sometimes Chip 'n' Dale)

TYPE OF SERVICE Buffet

FOOD VARIETY & QUALITY Breakfast ★★★   Brunch ★★★   Dinner ★★★½

NOISE LEVEL Loud   **CHARACTER–GUEST RATIO** 1:56

4. THE CRYSTAL PALACE   MAGIC KINGDOM

MEALS SERVED Breakfast, lunch, and dinner   **SETTING** ★★★

CHARACTERS Pooh, Eeyore, Piglet, Tigger   **TYPE OF SERVICE** Buffet

FOOD VARIETY & QUALITY Breakfast ★★½   Lunch and dinner ★★★

NOISE LEVEL Very loud   **CHARACTER–GUEST RATIO** Breakfast 1:67 Lunch and dinner 1:89

5. 1900 PARK FARE   GRAND FLORIDIAN

MEALS SERVED Breakfast, dinner   **SETTING** ★★★

CHARACTERS *Breakfast:* Mary Poppins, Alice, Mad Hatter, Pooh, Tigger
Dinner: Cinderella, Prince Charming, Lady Tremaine, the two stepsisters

TYPE OF SERVICE Buffet   **FOOD VARIETY & QUALITY** Breakfast ★★★   Dinner ★★★½

NOISE LEVEL Moderate   **CHARACTER–GUEST RATIO** Breakfast 1:54 Dinner 1:44

6. GARDEN GRILL RESTAURANT   EPCOT

MEAL SERVED Dinner   **SETTING** ★★★★½

CHARACTERS Mickey, Pluto, Chip 'n' Dale   **TYPE OF SERVICE** Family-style

FOOD VARIETY & QUALITY ★★★½   **NOISE LEVEL** Very quiet

CHARACTER–GUEST RATIO 1:46

To help you sort everything out, we rate the food at each character meal in our chart using the five-star scale.

5. THE PROGRAM Some larger restaurants stage modest performances where the characters dance, head a parade around the room, or lead songs and cheers. For some guests, these activities give the meal a celebratory air; for others, they turn what was already mayhem into absolute chaos. Either way, the antics consume time the characters could spend with families at their table.

7. TUSKER HOUSE RESTAURANT   DISNEY'S ANIMAL KINGDOM

MEALS SERVED Breakfast, lunch, dinner	**SETTING** ★★★
CHARACTERS Donald, Daisy, Mickey, Goofy	**TYPE OF SERVICE** Buffet
FOOD VARIETY & QUALITY ★★★ **NOISE LEVEL** Very loud	
CHARACTER–GUEST RATIO 1:112	

8. CAPE MAY CAFE   BEACH CLUB

MEAL SERVED Breakfast **SETTING** ★★★ **CHARACTERS** Goofy, Donald, Minnie	
TYPE OF SERVICE Buffet **FOOD VARIETY & QUALITY** ★★½	
NOISE LEVEL Moderate **CHARACTER–GUEST RATIO** 1:67	

9. 'OHANA   POLYNESIAN VILLAGE

MEAL SERVED Breakfast **SETTING** ★★	
CHARACTERS Lilo and Stitch, Mickey, Pluto **TYPE OF SERVICE** Family-style	
FOOD VARIETY & QUALITY ★★½ **NOISE LEVEL** Moderate	
CHARACTER–GUEST RATIO 1:57	

10. HOLLYWOOD & VINE   DISNEY'S HOLLYWOOD STUDIOS

MEALS SERVED Breakfast, lunch **SETTING** ★★½	
CHARACTERS Handy Manny, Sofia the First, Doc McStuffins, Jake (*Jake and the Never Land Pirates*)	
TYPE OF SERVICE Buffet **FOOD VARIETY & QUALITY** ★★★	
NOISE LEVEL Moderate **CHARACTER–GUEST RATIO** 1:71	

11. GARDEN GROVE   SWAN

MEALS SERVED Breakfast (Sat and Sun), dinner (Fri and Sat) **SETTING** ★★★	
CHARACTERS Chip 'n' Dale, Goofy, Pluto **TYPE OF SERVICE** Buffet	
FOOD VARIETY & QUALITY ★★★½ **NOISE LEVEL** Moderate	
CHARACTER–GUEST RATIO 1:198, but frequently much better	

12. RAVELLO   FOUR SEASONS RESORT ORLANDO

MEALS SERVED Breakfast (Thursday and Saturday) **SETTING** ★★★	
CHARACTERS Goofy and pals **TYPE OF SERVICE** Buffet	
FOOD VARIETY & QUALITY ★★★½ **NOISE LEVEL** Moderate	
CHARACTER–GUEST RATIO 1:39	

6. NOISE If you want to eat in peace, character meals are a bad choice. That said, some are much noisier than others. Our chart gives you an idea of what to expect.

7. WHICH MEAL? Although breakfasts seem to be most popular, character lunches and dinners are usually more practical because they don't interfere with early-morning touring. During hot weather, a character lunch can be heavenly.

8. COST Dinners cost more than lunches and lunches more than breakfasts. Prices for meals (except at Cinderella Castle) vary considerably from the least expensive to the most expensive restaurant. Breakfasts run $27–$58 for adults and $15–$38 for kids ages 3–9. For character lunches, expect to pay $31–$61 for adults and $16–$38 for kids. Dinners are $31–$73 for adults and $16–$43 for children. Little ones age 2 years and younger eat free. The meals at the high end of the price range are at **Cinderella's Royal Table** in the Magic Kingdom and **Akershus Royal Banquet** Hall at Epcot. The reasons for the sky-high prices: (1) Cinderella's Royal Table is small but in great demand and (2) both Akershus and Cindy's are Disney-princess central.

9. ADVANCE RESERVATIONS Disney makes Advance Reservations for character meals 180 days before you wish to dine (Disney resort guests can reserve 190 days out, or 10 additional days in advance); moreover, Disney resort guests can make Advance Reservations for all meals during their stay. Advance Reservations for most character meals are easy to obtain even if you call only a couple of weeks before you leave home. Meals at Cinderella's Royal Table and Be Our Guest are another story. For these two, you'll need our strategy (see Part Four), as well as help from Congress and the Pope.

If you don't get what you want at first, try again later, advises a London, England, mother of two:

> When a booking window opens, many people overbook and then either get buyer's remorse or find alternative bookings and cancel. When my booking window first opened, I was able to book barely 20% of what I wanted, but within two to three weeks, I had 100%.

10. CHECKING IT TWICE Disney occasionally shuffles the characters and theme of a character meal. If your little one's heart is set on Pooh and Piglet, getting Hook and Mr. Smee is just a waste of time and money. Reconfirm all character-meal Advance Reservations three weeks or so before you leave home by calling ☎ 407-WDW-DINE.

11. "FRIENDS" For some venues, Disney has stopped specifying characters scheduled for a particular meal. Instead, they say it's a given character "and friends"—for example, "Pooh and friends," meaning Eeyore, Piglet, and Tigger, or some combination thereof, or "Mickey and friends" with some assortment chosen among Minnie, Goofy, Pluto, Donald, Daisy, Chip, and Dale.

12. THE BUM'S RUSH Most character meals are leisurely affairs, and you can usually stay as long as you want. An exception is Cinderella's Royal Table at the Magic Kingdom. Because Cindy's is in such high demand, the restaurant does everything short of pre-chewing your food to move you through, as this European mother of a 5-year-old can attest:

> We dined a lot, did three character meals and a few signature restaurants, and every meal was awesome except for lunch with Cinderella in the castle. While I'd often read it wouldn't be a rushed affair, it was exactly that. We had barely sat down when the appetizers were thrown on our table, the princesses each spent just a few seconds with our daughter—almost no interaction—and the side dishes were cold. We were out of there within 40 minutes and felt very stressed. Considering the price for the meal, I cannot recommend it.

GETTING AN ADVANCE RESERVATION AT CINDERELLA'S ROYAL TABLE

ONCE UPON A TIME, breakfast was the only character meal served at Cinderella Castle in the Magic Kingdom. Reservations for every table were gone within minutes of becoming available each morning. Disney

responded to this popularity by adding character lunches and dinners—
and jacking up the price to almost $60–$70 per adult. As a result, it's now
much easier to get into Cinderella's Royal Table for some meals during
your stay. Also, the opening of the wildly popular **Be Our Guest** restaurant
in Fantasyland has taken a lot of pressure off Cindy's. If you're visiting
during peak periods or you've got to have a reservation at a specific,
popular time, see our Advance Reservation tips starting on page 302.

DISNEY'S ROYAL ALTERNATIVES If you're unwilling to fund Cinderella's
shoe habit or you simply weren't able to get an Advance Reservation
before young Ariel graduates from college, rest assured there are other
venues that will feed you in the company of princesses.

Akershus Royal Banquet Hall, in the Norway Pavilion of Epcot's
World Showcase, serves family-style breakfast, lunch, and dinner. Disney tends to define *princess* quite loosely, so you may see any character who's ever donned a dress (with the exception of Cinderella)
at this meal. Entrees are a combination of traditional buffet fare and
Scandinavian-style dishes.

Dinner at the Grand Floridian's **1900 Park Fare** features the whole
crew from *Cinderella,* including Lady Tremaine and the stepsisters
(breakfast is a character buffet with Winnie the Pooh and friends). At
$44 per adult and $22 for children age 9 and under, this is a far more
economical option for diners wishing to get their princess on, and the
wicked stepsisters are an absolute hoot. This meal is also a little more
boy-friendly if you're entertaining a mixed crowd. Finally, remember
that your own little princess may be feeding off your own excitement
over eating in the Castle—she might be just as happy with a plastic
crown purchased in the gift shop and a burger from Cosmic Ray's.

OTHER CHARACTER EVENTS

A CAMPFIRE AND SING-ALONG are held nightly (times vary with
the season) near the Meadow Trading Post and Bike Barn at **Fort Wilderness Resort & Campground.** Chip 'n' Dale lead the songs, and a Disney
film is shown. The program is free and open to resort guests (☎ 407-
824-2900). Another character encounter at Fort Wilderness is *Mickey's
Backyard BBQ,* held seasonally on Thursdays and Saturdays. See page
746 for details.

▮▮ BABYSITTING

CHILD-CARE CENTERS Child care isn't available
inside the theme parks, but two Magic Kingdom
resorts connected by monorail or boat (Polynesian
Village and Wilderness Lodge & Villas), four Epcot

*un*official **TIP**
Child-care clubs close
at or before midnight. If
you intend to stay out
late, in-room babysitting
is your best bet.

resorts (the Yacht & Beach Club Resorts, the Swan, and the Dolphin),
and Animal Kingdom Lodge, along with the Hilton at Walt Disney
World, have child-care centers for potty-trained children age 3 and older
(see chart on page 427). Services vary, but children generally can be left
between 5 p.m. and midnight. Milk and cookies and blankets and pillows are provided at all centers, and dinner is provided at most. Play is
supervised but not organized, and toys, videos, and games are plentiful.
Guests at any Disney resort or campground may use the services.

BABYSITTING SERVICES

KID'S NITE OUT	FAIRY GODMOTHERS
☎ 407-828-0920 or 800-696-8105 **kidsniteout.com**	☎ 407-277-3724 (24 hours)
HOTELS SERVED All Walt Disney World and Orlando-area hotels	**HOTELS SERVED** All WDW hotels and those in the general WDW area
SITTERS Men and women	**SITTERS** Mothers and grandmothers, female college students
MINIMUM CHARGES 4 hours	**MINIMUM CHARGES** 4 hours
BASE HOURLY RATES 1 child, $18 2 children, $21 3 children, $24 4 children, $26	**BASE HOURLY RATES** 1 child, $16 2 children, $16 3 children, $16 4 children or more, $18
EXTRA CHARGES Transportation fee, $10; starting before 8 a.m. or after 9 p.m., +$2 per hour; additional fee for holidays	**EXTRA CHARGES** Transportation fee, $16; starting after 10 p.m., +$2 per hour
CANCELLATION DEADLINE 24 hours before service	**CANCELLATION DEADLINE** 3 hours before service
FORM OF PAYMENT AE, D, MC, V; tips in cash	**FORM OF PAYMENT** Cash or traveler's checks for actual payment; tips in cash
THINGS SITTERS WON'T DO Transport children in private vehicle, take children swimming, give baths	**THINGS SITTERS WON'T DO** Transport children, give baths. Swimming is at sitter's discretion.

The most elaborate of the child-care centers (variously called "clubs" or "camps") is **Lilo's Playhouse** at the Polynesian Village Resort. The rate for ages 3–12 is $15 per hour, per child (2-hour minimum).

All the clubs accept reservations (some six months in advance!) with a credit card guarantee. Call the club directly, or reserve through Disney at ☎ 407-WDW-DINE. Most clubs require a 24-hour cancellation notice and levy a hefty penalty of 2 hours' time or $30 per child for no-shows. A limited number of walk-ins are usually accepted on a first-come, first-served basis.

If you're staying in a Disney resort that doesn't offer a child-care club and you *don't* have a car, then you're better off using in-room babysitting. Trying to take your child to a club in another hotel by Disney bus requires a 50- to 90-minute trip each way. By the time you've deposited your little one, it will almost be time to pick him or her up again.

IN-ROOM BABYSITTING Two companies provide in-room sitting in Walt Disney World and surrounding areas: **Kid's Nite Out** and **Fairy Godmothers** (no kidding). Kid's Nite Out also serves hotels in the greater Orlando area, including downtown. All three provide sitters older than age 18 who are insured, bonded, screened, reference-checked, police-checked, and trained in CPR. In addition to caring for your kids in your room, the sitters will, if you direct (and pay), take your children to the theme parks or other venues. Both services offer bilingual sitters. (See the chart above for details.)

SPECIAL PROGRAMS
for CHILDREN

SEVERAL CHILDREN'S PROGRAMS ARE AVAILABLE at Walt Disney World parks and resorts. While all are undoubtedly fun, we find them somewhat lacking in educational focus.

CHILD-CARE CLUBS*

HOTEL	NAME OF PROGRAM	AGES	PHONE
ANIMAL KINGDOM LODGE •	Simba's Cubhouse •	3–12 •	☎ 407-938-4785
DOLPHIN AND SWAN •	Camp Dolphin •	4–12 •	☎ 407-934-4241
POLYNESIAN VILLAGE RESORT •	Lilo's Playhouse •	3–12 •	☎ 407-824-2000
YACHT & BEACH CLUB RESORTS •	Sandcastle Club •	3–12 •	☎ 407-934-3750
WILDERNESS LODGE & VILLAS •	Cub's Den •	3–12 •	☎ 407-824-1083

*Child-care clubs operate afternoons and evenings. Before 4 p.m., call the hotels rather than the numbers listed above. All programs require reservations; call ☎ 407-WDW-DINE (939-3463).

DISNEY'S FAMILY MAGIC TOUR This is a 1½- to 2-hour guided tour of the Magic Kingdom for the entire family. Even children in strollers (no younger than age 3) are welcome. The tour combines information about the Magic Kingdom with the gathering of clues that ultimately solve "diabolical" problems. There's usually a marginal plot such as saving Wendy from Captain Hook, in which case the character at the end of the tour is Wendy. The tour departs daily at 10 a.m. The cost is about $34 per person with tax, plus a valid Magic Kingdom admission. The maximum group size is 20 persons. Reservations can be made up to one year in advance by calling ☎ 407-WDW-TOUR (939-8687).

DISNEY'S PIRATE ADVENTURE Children ages 4–12 get to don bandannas, hoist the Jolly Roger, and set out on a boat trip to search for buried treasure by following a map. At the final port of call, the kids find the treasure (doubloons, beads, and rubber bugs!) and wolf down snacks. The treasure is split among the kids. The adventure costs about $40 per child with tax and is offered at Port Orleans Riverside (Bayou Pirate Adventure), the Grand Floridian (Pirate Adventure), the Yacht Club (Albatross Treasure Cruise), and the Caribbean Beach Resort (Islands of the Caribbean). All programs are offered daily, 9:30–11:30 a.m., weather permitting; call ☎ 407-WDW-PLAY (939-7529) for days offered and other information. Boys and girls alike really love this outing—many report it as the highlight of their vacation. *Note:* No parents allowed!

DISNEY'S THE MAGIC BEHIND OUR STEAM TRAINS Kids must be age 10 or older for this 3-hour tour, presented Monday–Saturday. At the 7:30 a.m. start time, join the crew of the Walt Disney World Railroad as they prepare their steam locomotives for the day. Cost is about $54 per person with tax, plus a valid Magic Kingdom admission. Call ☎ 407-WDW-TOUR for information and reservations.

MY DISNEY GIRL'S PERFECTLY PRINCESS TEA PARTY It certainly takes a princely sum to cover the tab on this Grand Floridian gathering, hosted by Rose Petal, an enchanted storytelling rose. Your little princess gets dressed up in her favorite regal attire and sips tea with Princess Aurora. Girls receive an 18-inch My Disney Girl doll dressed in a matching Princess Aurora gown plus accessories. Other loot includes a ribbon tiara, silver link bracelet, fresh rose, scrapbook set, and "Best Friend" certificate. A luncheon is served as well. The cost is about $250 with tax and tip for one adult and one child ages 3–11; add an additional adult for $85 or an additional child for $165. *Note:* **This event is not covered by the Disney Dining Plan.** The tea party is held every Sunday, Monday, and Wednesday–Friday, 10:30 a.m.–noon. Call ☎ 407-939-6983 for reservations and information.

WONDERLAND TEA PARTY Held at 1900 Park Fare restaurant in the Grand Floridian Monday–Friday afternoons at 2 p.m. for $43 per child (ages 4–12, with tax), the program consists of decorating (and eating) cupcakes and having lunch and tea with characters from Alice in Wonderland. Reservations can be made by calling ☎ 407-WDW-DINE 90 days in advance.

An Illinois mom ponied up for two of the programs:

> We splurged on the Perfectly Princess Tea Party. It was nice but a bit too long with all the singing and stories. Not easy for a 4-year-old to sit that long. I'm not sure it was worth it, and I would not do it again. We also booked the Wonderland Tea Party. That was a much better cost, and I thought my daughter would love decorating a cupcake. She was so freaked out by the Mad Hatter that the nice workers there called me and asked me to come get her. They said many kids are scared of him, so I'm not sure why they don't have Alice and another character.

BIRTHDAYS *and* SPECIAL OCCASIONS

IF SOMEONE IN YOUR FAMILY CELEBRATES A BIRTHDAY while you're at Disney World, don't keep it a secret. A Lombard, Illinois, mom put the word out and was glad she did:

> My daughter was turning 5 while we were there; our hotel asked me who her favorite character was and did the rest. We came back to our room on her birthday and there were helium balloons, a card, and a Cinderella photo autographed in ink! When we entered the Magic Kingdom, we received an "It's My Birthday Today" pin (FREE!), and at the restaurant she got a huge cupcake with whipped cream, sprinkles, and a candle. IT PAYS TO ASK!

PART SIX

SPECIAL TIPS *for* SPECIAL PEOPLE

WALT DISNEY WORLD *for* PEOPLE *with* BAD ATTITUDES

YOU'D BE AMAZED at how many people are dragged unwillingly to Walt Disney World by their friends and families. But for skeptics and cynics who've never visited, there's hope, as described by a 25-year-old woman from Williamstown, Massachusetts:

> My boyfriend is sort of anti-Disney, so to save our relationship and vacation, I steered us clear of some traditional must-sees. (It's a Small World, for example, might have sent him over the edge.) I made sure that Soarin' was one of the first rides we went on. He absolutely loved it, and it opened his mind to the rest of the Disney experience.

A Louisiana mom—the lone Disney fan in her family—chimed in with this:

> This year I DRAGGED two teenage boys and an outdoorsman, all Disney haters, to Orlando. None of them wanted to go, but I promised them that I wouldn't force them to go again. After the trip, my 16-year-old son said, "Mom, I'll go with you again," and my husband said, "I'm shocked that I had a great time." (I didn't remind him of what happened on Harry Potter and the Forbidden Journey— the man in the seat next to him puked, and yes, some of it landed on my husband!)

WALT DISNEY WORLD *for* SINGLES

DISNEY WORLD IS GREAT FOR SINGLES. It's safe, clean, and low-pressure. Safety and comfort are unsurpassed, especially for women traveling alone. Parking lots are well lit and constantly patrolled.

If you're looking for a place to relax without being hit on, Disney World is perfect. The bars, lounges, and nightclubs are among the most

TIPS FOR GOING SOLO

SINGLE CAN MEAN TRAVELING ALONE as well as unmarried, and being by yourself doesn't mean that you can't have a great time at Walt Disney World. **Deb Wills,** creator of the all-things-Disney website **allears.net**, offers this advice:

- One of the best parts about traveling solo is that you can be your own boss. Sleep in, have leisurely morning coffee on the balcony, relax by the pool . . . or not. If you'd rather get up and go early, who's to stop you?

- Put some spontaneity into your day. If you're taking Disney transportation, get on the first park bus that arrives.

- Get on the resort monorail (not the Express!) at the Magic Kingdom, and visit each of the resorts it stops at. Each resort has its own theme and character, with lots to see and explore.

- Did you know that you can walk through the queues and view the preshows of the thrill rides even if you don't want to ride? Wander through at your own pace, then tell the cast member before boarding that you don't wish to ride, and you'll be shown to a nearby exit.

- If you *do* want to experience the thrill rides, take advantage of the single-rider lines for the Rock 'n' Roller Coaster, Expedition Everest, and Test Track. They can cut your wait time significantly.

- If you encounter folks taking photos of each other, ask if they'd like to be in one photo, then offer to snap the picture. This is a great way to make friends.

- Get your favorite Disney snack, find a bench, and people-watch. You'll be amazed at what you see: the honeymooning couple wearing bride-and-groom

laid-back and friendly you're likely to find. Between the BoardWalk and Disney Springs, nightlife abounds; virtually every type of entertainment is available at a reasonable price. If you overimbibe and you're a Disney resort guest, Disney buses will return you safely to your hotel.

See "Tips for Going Solo," above, for more ways to enjoy Walt Disney World on your own.

WALT DISNEY WORLD *for* COUPLES

MANY COUPLES THINK Walt Disney World is strictly for kids. Not so, an Evans City, Pennsylvania, woman attests:

> *I have many friends who think I was crazy to travel to Walt Disney World without my children (ages 9 and 12). I absolutely loved it! Instead of rushing from thrill ride to thrill ride with all the other hordes of people, we were able to slow down and enjoy all of the amazing details that make WDW the incredibly special place that it is. It is an entirely different, but equally magical, experience.*

So many couples tie the knot or honeymoon in the World that Disney has a dedicated department to help arrange the day of your mouse ears, toddlers giving Mickey and the characters their first hugs, grand-parents smiling indulgently as their grandchildren smear ice cream all over their faces. If you're missing the smiles of your own children, buy a couple of balloons and give them away. You'll help make the kids near you very, very happy.

- Learn how some of the magic is created. Take a behind-the-scenes tour (see Part Eighteen) or one of the Deluxe hotel tours.

- Visit Animal Kingdom Lodge and relax at an animal-viewing area. Find an animal keeper; they'll gladly discuss care of the wild animals at the resort.

- Don't hesitate to strike up conversations with cast members or guests in line with you. Foreign cast members in Epcot's World Showcase are happy to share stories about their homelands.

- Enjoy a leisurely shopping adventure around the World. Some stores (**Arribas Brothers** in Disney Springs and **Mitsukoshi Department Store** in the Japan Pavilion at World Showcase) have really neat displays and exhibits.

- Go to that restaurant you've always wanted to try but your picky eater has always declined. You don't have to order a full meal; try several appetizers or, better yet, just dessert.

- Use common sense about your personal security. I feel very comfortable and safe traveling alone at Disney World and have done so many times, but I still don't do things that I wouldn't do at home (like announce to anyone listening that I'm traveling solo). If you aren't comfortable walking to your room alone, ask at the front desk for a security escort. Use extra caution in the parking lots at night, just as you would at home.

dreams. **Disney's Fairy Tale Weddings & Honeymoons** (☎ 321-939-4610; **disneyweddings.com**) offers a range of ceremony venues and services, plus honeymoon planning and registries.

WEDDINGS, COMMITMENT CEREMONIES, AND VOWS RENEWALS

FOR COUPLES WISHING TO GET HITCHED, all packages include a bouquet, a two-tier cake and Champagne toast (not part of the Memories Collection), live music (an organist or violinist, depending on the venue), photo package, limousine service or in-room wedding decoration, wedding-planning website, a wedding coordinator, and Annual Passes to Disney World for the happy couple (not part of the Memories Collection). The officiant and marriage certificate are not included with any package. Disney has a list of local officiants from which to choose, or the couple may bring their own.

Many couples make a special trip to Walt Disney World to plan their weddings in person, though it's entirely possible to make all arrangements by phone and online. While it may seem that a Disney wedding is the ultimate cookie-cutter event, many options exist for making your day personal and special. The best resource for planning a Disney wedding is *Passporter's Disney Weddings & Honeymoons,* by Carrie Hayward (available in print at Amazon or as an e-book at **passporter.com/weddings.asp**).

LEGALITIES

TO MARRY IN THE WORLD, you need a marriage license, issued at any Florida courthouse. There is no waiting period. Florida residents must complete a 4-hour premarital counseling session to marry sooner than 3 days after obtaining their license; all weddings must occur within 60 days of getting the license. Blood tests aren't required, but both parties must present identification and their Social Security numbers. If you were widowed or divorced within 30 days of the wedding, you must present a certified copy of the deceased spouse's death certificate or your divorce decree.

unofficial **TIP**
Contact Disney as soon as you have a date in mind for your event— popular dates may not be available on short notice. If you wish to hold your ceremony inside a theme park, you're restricted to very early in the morning or late at night, when the park is closed to guests.

HONEYMOONS AND HONEYMOON REGISTRIES

HONEYMOON PACKAGES are adaptations of regular Disney World travel packages, though you may purchase add-ons such as flowers and in-room gifts to make your trip more special. Some couples who honeymoon at Walt Disney World create a registry that allows friends and family to bestow gifts of tours, spa packages, special dinners, and the like. (Couples receive gift funds by bank transfer or check.) For more information on honeymoon registries, visit **disney.honeymoonwishes.com.**

ROMANTIC GETAWAYS

DISNEY WORLD IS A FAVORITE GETAWAY FOR COUPLES, but not all Disney hotels are equally romantic. Some are too family-oriented; others swarm with convention-goers. For romantic (though expensive) lodging, we recommend **Animal Kingdom Lodge & Villas; Bay Lake Tower** at the Contemporary; the **Polynesian Village & Villas; Wilderness Lodge & Villas;** the **Grand Floridian Resort, Spa, & Villas; BoardWalk Inn & Villas;** and the **Yacht & Beach Club Resorts.** The Alligator Bayou section at **Port Orleans Riverside,** a Disney Moderate resort, also has secluded rooms.

CELEBRATING . . . EVERYTHING!

WALT DISNEY WORLD IS ALL ABOUT CELEBRATING—marriages, birthdays, anniversaries, the works—and can add a special touch to your big day, but only if you let somebody know. A St. Louis newlywed offers this advice:

> If you're celebrating, ask for Celebration Buttons when you check into your hotel or at any park's Guest Relations, then WEAR THEM! Cast members regularly congratulated us, and I'm relatively certain we were seated at better tables for dinner based solely on our buttons.

WALT DISNEY WORLD
"At Large"

YOU'VE JUST SPENT A SMALL FORTUNE for your vacation. If you're a person of size, you don't want to worry about whether you'll have trouble fitting in the ride vehicles. Fortunately, Walt Disney World realizes that its guests come in all shapes and sizes and is quite accommodating. Deb Wills and Debra Martin Koma, experts on Walt Disney World travel for those with special challenges, offer these suggestions.

- Remember that you'll be on your feet for hours at a time, so wear comfortable, broken-in shoes. Pay attention to your feet: If you feel a blister starting, take care of it quickly. (Each theme park has a First Aid Center stocked with bandages and other necessities. For more on blister prevention, see page 476.)

- If you're prone to chafing, consider bringing a commercial antifriction product (such as Bodyglide) designed to control or eliminate rubbing. You can find this and similar products at most pharmacies and sporting-goods stores.

- Not all attractions have the same kinds of vehicles or seating. Some have bench seats, while others have individual seats; some have overhead harnesses, while others have seat belts or lap bars. Learn what type of seating or vehicle each attraction has before you go so you know what to expect (check out **tinyurl.com/allears-ride-gallery** for details). If the attraction has a seat belt, pull it all the way out before you sit down to make it easier to strap yourself in. Note that some attractions even have seat-belt extenders—ask a cast member about these.

- Several attractions (Expedition Everest, for example) offer a sample ride vehicle for you to try out before you get in line. Ask a cast member for the location.

- Front seats (such as those in the Rock 'n' Roller Coaster and Test Track) often have more legroom.

- In restaurants, look for chairs without arms. If you don't see any, the host or hostess should be able to provide one for you.

- Request a resort hotel room with a king-size bed. It may cost a bit more, but the good sleep you'll get will be more than worth it!

WALT DISNEY WORLD
for EXPECTANT MOTHERS

WHEN IT COMES TO PREGNANT WOMEN visiting Walt Disney World, the authors, alas, have no wisdom of their own to impart. (Try as they might, Bob and Len have never been in the family way.)

Enter **Debbie Grubbs,** a Colorado reader. During her fifth month of pregnancy, she waddled intrepidly all over the World, compiling observations and tips for expectant moms that she shares below.

Magic Kingdom:

Splash Mountain is a no-go, obviously, due to the drop—or so I thought. It turns out that the seat configuration in the "logs" has more to do with it than the drop. The seats are made so that your knees are higher than your rear, causing compression on the abdomen (when it's this large). This is potentially harmful to the baby. As always, better safe than sorry.

Big Thunder Mountain Railroad is also restricted for obvious reasons. It's just not a good idea to ride roller coasters when pregnant.

Mad Tea Party may be OK if you don't spin the cups. We didn't ride this one because my doctor advised me to skip rides with centrifugal [or centripetal] force. Dumbo in Fantasyland and the Astro Orbiter in Tomorrowland are OK, though.

Space Mountain is one of my favorite rides . . . but a roller coaster nonetheless.

Tomorrowland Speedway isn't recommended due to the amount of rear-ending by overzealous younger drivers.

(We also think Debbie would have passed on Seven Dwarfs Mine Train and its swinging cars.)

Disney's Animal Kingdom: *Both Dinosaur and Primeval Whirl are very jerky and should be avoided.*

(We think Debbie would've avoided Expedition Everest, too.)

Epcot: *Mission: Space and Test Track are restricted, as are all simulator rides—they're way too rough and jerky. [Nonmoving seats are available in some simulation attractions—ask a cast member.] Soarin' is fine.*

Disney's Hollywood Studios: *Tower of Terror is out of the question for the drop alone, and Star Tours is restricted because it's a simulator. The Rock 'n' Roller Coaster is clearly off-limits.*

Water Parks: *Slides are off-limits. Pregnant women can, however, do Shark Reef at Typhoon Lagoon with an extra-large wet-suit vest. The wave pools and floating creeks are great for getting the weight off your feet.*

A mother of three from Bethesda, Maryland, adds:

Go to a golf shop and buy one of those walking sticks with a seat attached to it—I would've been a goner without one. They're light-weight and easy to carry. Also, a support garment (such as a BellyBra) is a must for relieving the weight on your lower back.

MORE TIPS FOR MOMS-TO-BE

IN ADDITION TO DEBBIE'S TIPS, here are a few of ours:

1. Discuss your Disney World plans with your obstetrician before your trip.
2. Start walking at home to build up your stamina for walking in the parks. Once in the World, however, try to use in-park transportation whenever you can so that you're not having to walk *all* the time.
3. Get as much rest as you need—even if you have to sacrifice some time at the parks to get it. (Staying at a Disney resort will make it easier for you to return to your room for naps.)
4. Eat properly and hydrate throughout the day, especially when it's hot.

WALT DISNEY WORLD
for SENIORS

SENIOR CITIZENS have much the same problems and concerns as all Disney visitors. Older guests do, however, get into predicaments caused by touring with younger people. Pressured by their grandchildren to endure a frantic pace, many seniors concentrate on surviving Disney World rather than enjoying it. Seniors must either set the pace or dispatch the young folks to tour on their own.

An older reader in Alabaster, Alabama, writes:

Being a senior is not for wussies. At Walt Disney World in particular, it requires courage and pluck. Things that used to be easy take a lot of effort, and sometimes your brain has to wait for your body to catch up. Half the time, your grandchildren treat you like a crumbling ruin; then they turn around and trick you into getting on a roller coaster in the dark. What you need to tell seniors is that they have to be alert and not trust anyone—not their children, not the Disney people, and especially not their grandchildren. When your grandkids want you to go on a ride, don't follow along blindly like a lamb to the slaughter. Make sure you know what the ride is all about. **He who hesitates is launched!**

Most seniors we interview enjoy Disney World much more when they tour with folks their own age. If, however, you're considering visiting with your grandchildren, we recommend making an orientation visit without them first. This way, it'll be easier to establish limits, maintain control, and set a comfortable pace later on.

If you're *determined* to take the grandkids, read carefully the sections of this book that discuss family touring. (*Hint:* The Dumbo-or-Die-in-a-Day Touring Plan has been known to bring grown-ups of all ages to their knees.)

And when it comes to attractions, we feel that personal taste trumps age. We hate to see seniors pass up a full-blown adventure like Splash Mountain because it's a so-called thrill ride—it gets its appeal more from music and visual effects than from the thrill of the ride. Use our attraction profiles to help you make informed decisions.

GETTING AROUND

MANY SENIORS LIKE TO WALK, but a 7-hour visit to a theme park includes 4–10 miles on foot. Not up to that? Consider renting a wheelchair or mobility vehicle.

Wheelchairs rent (minus tax) for $12 with no deposit required, $10 per day for multiday rentals, and free at your Disney resort ($315 deposit). Rentals are available at all Disney World theme parks (see Parts Nine through Twelve for specific locations) and at Disney Springs. ECVs and ESVs cost $50 per day, plus a $20 refundable deposit

($100 at Disney Springs); call ☎ 407-824-5217 to reserve a vehicle. Wheelchairs are welcome at Disney's Blizzard Beach and Typhoon Lagoon water parks but are unavailable for rent.

Buena Vista Scooters (☎ 866-484-4797 or 407-938-0349; **buena vistascooters.com**) rents ECVs for $30 per day, with free delivery to and pickup from your Disney resort.

Your wheelchair-rental deposit slip is good for a replacement wheelchair in any park during the same day. You can rent a chair at the Magic

Kingdom in the morning, return it, go to Epcot, present your deposit slip, and get another chair at no additional charge.

TIMING YOUR VISIT

RETIREES SHOULD MAKE THE MOST of their flexible schedules and go to Disney World in fall or spring (excluding holiday weeks), when the weather is nicest and crowds are thinnest. Crowds are also sparse from late January through early February, but the weather can be unpredictable. If you visit in winter, take coats and sweaters, plus warm-weather clothing. Be prepared for anything from near-freezing rain to afternoons in the 80s. See Part One, page 39, for more information on the best times of year to visit.

LODGING

IF YOU CAN AFFORD IT, STAY IN WALT DISNEY WORLD. Rooms are among the Orlando–Kissimmee area's nicest, and transportation is always available to any Disney destination at no additional cost.

Disney hotels reserve rooms close to restaurants and transportation for guests of any age who can't tolerate much walking. They also provide golf carts to pick up and deliver guests at their rooms. Service can vary dramatically depending on the time of day and the number of guests requesting carts. At check-in time (around 3 p.m.), for example, the wait for a ride can be as long as 40 minutes.

Here are four reasons to consider staying in Disney World:

1. The quality of the properties is consistently above average.
2. Buses run only hourly or so for "outside" hotels. Disney buses run about every 20 minutes. Staying in the World guarantees transportation when you need it. On the flip side, the buses that serve out-of-the-World areas usually operate on a fixed schedule so you know exactly what time to be at the loading point.
3. You get free parking in major theme parks' lots.
4. You get preferential tee times on resort golf courses.

Walt Disney World hotels are spread out. It's easy to avoid most stairs, but it's often a long hike to your room from parking lots or bus stops. Seniors intending to spend more time at Epcot and Hollywood Studios than at the Magic Kingdom or Animal Kingdom should consider the **BoardWalk Inn & Villas**, the **Dolphin, Swan,** or the **Yacht & Beach Club Resorts.**

The **Contemporary Resort** and **Bay Lake Tower** are good choices for seniors who want to be on the monorail system. So are the **Grand Floridian** and the **Polynesian Village,** though they cover many acres, necessitating a lot of walking. For a restful, rustic feeling, choose **Wilderness Lodge & Villas.** If you want a kitchen and the comforts of home, book **Animal Kingdom Villas, Beach Club Villas, BoardWalk Villas, Grand Floridian Villas, Old Key West Resort,** or **Polynesian Villas & Bungalows.** If you enjoy watching birds and animals, try **Animal Kingdom Lodge & Villas.** Try **Saratoga Springs** for golf.

RVers will find pleasant surroundings at **Disney's Fort Wilderness Resort & Campground.** Several independent campgrounds are within

30 minutes of Disney World (see page 221). None offer the wilderness setting or amenities that Disney does, but they cost less.

TRANSPORTATION

ROADS IN DISNEY WORLD CAN BE DAUNTING. Armed with a decent sense of direction and a great sense of humor, however, even the most timid driver can get around.

If you drive, parking isn't a problem. Lots are served by trams linking the parking area and the theme park's entrance. Parking for the disabled is available adjacent to each park's entrance. Pay-booth attendants will provide a dashboard ticket and direct you to the reserved spaces. Disney requires that you be recognized officially as disabled to use this parking, but temporarily disabled or injured persons also are permitted access.

SENIOR DINING

EAT BREAKFAST AT YOUR HOTEL RESTAURANT or save money by having juice and rolls in your room. Carry snacks in a fanny pack supplemented by fruit, fruit juice, and soft drinks purchased from vendors. Make Advance Reservations for lunch before noon to avoid the crowds. Follow with an early dinner and be out of the restaurants, ready for evening touring and fireworks, long before the main crowd even thinks about dinner.

We recommend that seniors fit dining and rest into each day. Plan lunch as a break. Sit back, relax, and enjoy. Then return to your hotel for a nap or swim during the hot, crowded hours of the day.

WALT DISNEY WORLD *for* GUESTS *with* SPECIAL NEEDS

DISNEY WORLD IS SO ATTUNED TO GUESTS with physical challenges that unscrupulous people have been known to fake a disability in order to take unfair advantage. If you have a disability, Disney World is prepared to meet your needs.

Each theme park offers a free booklet describing disabled services and facilities at **disneyworld.disney.go.com/guest-services/guests-with -disabilities.** Or get it when you enter the parks, at resort front desks, and at wheelchair-rental locations inside the parks. More-limited information is available online at **disneyworld.disney.go.com/plain-text.**

For specific requests, such as those for special accommodations at hotels or on the Disney transportation system, call ☎ 407-939-7807 (voice) or 407-939-7670 (TTY). When the recorded menu comes up, press *1*. Limit your questions and requests to those regarding disabled services and accommodations (address other questions to ☎ 407-824-4321 or 407-827-5141 [TTY]). If you'll be staying at a Disney resort, let the reservation agent know of any special needs you have when you book your room.

The following equipment, services, and facilities are available at Disney hotels, though not all hotels offer all items:

• Accessible vanities	• Portable commodes
• Bed and bathroom rails	• Refrigerators
• Braille on signs and elevators	• Rubber bed padding
• Closed-captioned televisions	• Shower benches
• Double peepholes in doors	• Strobe-light smoke detectors
• Handheld showerheads	• Roll-in showers
• Knock and phone alerts	• TTYs
• Lowered beds	• Wheelchairs
• Phone amplifiers	• Widened bathroom doors

Service animals are welcome at all Disney resorts.

Much of the Disney transportation system is disability-accessible. Monorails can be accessed by ramp or elevator, and all bus routes are served by vehicles with wheelchair lifts, though unusually wide or long wheelchairs (or motorized chairs) may not fit the lift. Watercraft accommodations for wheelchairs are iffier. If you plan to stay at Wilderness Lodge & Villas, Fort Wilderness Campground, or an Epcot resort, call ☎ 407-939-7807 (voice) or 407-939-7670 (TTY) for the latest information on watercraft accessibility.

Food and merchandise locations at theme parks, Disney Springs, and hotels are generally accessible, but some fast-food queues and shop aisles are too narrow for wheelchairs. At these locations, ask a cast member or member of your party for assistance.

Disabled guests and their families give Disney high marks for accessibility and sensitivity. An Arlington, Virginia, woman writes:

> Disney is dynamite in its treatment of handicapped vacationers. My mom has mobility problems that got a lot worse between the time my dad made reservations and the time we arrived, and she was worried about getting around. Disney supplied a free wheelchair, every bus had kneeling steps for wheelchair users, and the cast members sprang into action when they saw us coming.

VISITORS WITH DISABILITIES

WHOLLY OR PARTIALLY NONAMBULATORY guests may rent wheelchairs. Most rides, shows, attractions, restrooms, and restaurants accommodate the nonambulatory disabled. If you're in a park and need assistance, go to Guest Relations.

A limited number of electric carts, ECVs (electric convenience vehicles), and ESVs (electric standing vehicles) are available for rent. They give nonambulatory guests tremendous freedom and mobility.

All Disney lots have close-in parking for disabled visitors. Request directions when you pay your parking fee. All monorails and most rides, shows, restrooms, and restaurants accommodate wheelchairs.

Even if an attraction doesn't accommodate wheelchairs, ECVs, or ESVs, nonambulatory guests may ride if they can transfer from their wheelchair to the ride's vehicle. Disney staff, however, aren't trained or permitted to assist with transfers—guests must be able to board the ride unassisted or have a member of their party assist them. Either way, members of the nonambulatory guest's party will be permitted to ride with him or her.

Because the waiting areas of most attractions won't accommodate wheelchairs, nonambulatory guests and their parties should ask a cast member for boarding instructions as soon as they arrive at an attraction. Almost always, the entire group will be allowed to board without a lengthy wait.

A reader from New Orleans who traveled to Disney World with a friend who uses a wheelchair writes:

> I went with a very dear friend of mine who is paraplegic. It was his first trip to WDW, and we were a little apprehensive about how much we'd be able to do. The official brochure is helpful but implies limits to accessibility. The reality is that nonambulatory visitors are able to do much more; one has only to ask the cast members what is really allowed. Brian is a very active person who is able to transfer from his wheelchair without too much difficulty, so we were able to ride almost everything we wanted.

DIETARY RESTRICTIONS AND ALLERGIES Walt Disney World restaurants work very hard to accommodate guests' special dietary needs. When you make a dining reservation online or by phone, you'll be asked about food allergies and the like. The host or hostess and your server will also ask about this and may send the chef out to discuss the menu; if you're not asked, just talk to your server when you're seated. For counter-service restaurants or kiosks, ask at Guest Relations or at the venue itself. For more information, e-mail **special.diets@disneyworld.com** or visit **tinyurl .com/wdwspecialdiets.**

An Idaho mom and her teenage daughter found Disney restaurants very responsive to their dietary needs:

> My daughter and I both have a gluten allergy. I have never felt so well cared for and safe eating anywhere else in the world. From our resort (both the food court and Boatwright's) to every single quick-service or sit-down restaurant, we had several choices, and we never waited longer than 8 minutes for our "special" orders.

To request kosher meals at table-service restaurants, call ☎ 407-WDW-DINE 48 hours in advance. All Disney menus have vegetarian options; vegans may have to talk to the chef. Vegetarians, vegans, and pescetarians should speak up when making dining reservations.

Folks with special diets *and* a sweet tooth should try the vegan, gluten-free, and kosher treats from **Erin McKenna's Bakery NYC,** with locations at Disney Springs, many Disney hotel food courts, and Animal Kingdom's Garden Kiosk. Besides sweets, the bakery does a tasty line of savory focaccia every once in a while. You can also order special-occasion cakes and baked goods by phone or online (☎ 407-938-9044; **erinmc kennasbakery.com/orlando**).

For guests who are subject to allergic reactions that can be severe or life-threatening, Disney provides epinephrine injectors (**EpiPens**) at First Aid Centers and other locations throughout the parks. These locations are shown on guide maps. Nurses and emergency responders are trained in EpiPen use, but guests with known conditions should always travel with their own supplies.

SIGHT- AND/OR HEARING-IMPAIRED GUESTS Guest Relations at the parks provides free assistive-technology devices to visually and hearing-impaired guests ($25 refundable deposit, depending on the device). Sight-impaired guests can customize the given information (such as architectural details, restroom locations, and descriptions of attractions and restaurants) through an interactive audio menu that is guided by a GPS in the device. Hearing-impaired guests can benefit from amplified audio and closed-captioning for attractions loaded into the same device.

Braille guidebooks are available from Guest Relations at all parks ($25 refundable deposit), and Braille menus are available at some theme park restaurants. Some rides provide closed-captioning; many theater attractions provide reflective captioning.

Disney provides sign-language interpretations of live shows at the theme parks on certain designated days of the week:

THE MAGIC KINGDOM: Mondays and Thursdays
EPCOT: Tuesdays and Fridays
DISNEY'S ANIMAL KINGDOM: Saturdays
DISNEY'S HOLLYWOOD STUDIOS: Sundays and Wednesdays

Get confirmation of the interpreted-performance schedule a minimum of one week in advance by calling Disney World information at ☎ 407-824-4321 (voice) or 407-827-5141 (TTY). You'll be contacted before your visit with a show schedule that lists the names, dates, and times of the interpreted performances.

NONAPPARENT DISABILITIES We receive many letters from readers whose traveling companion or child requires special assistance but who, unlike a person in a wheelchair, is not visibly disabled. Autism, for example, can make it very difficult or impossible for someone with the disorder to wait in line for more than a few minutes or in queues surrounded by a crowd.

A trip to Disney World can be nonetheless positive and rewarding for guests who are on the autism spectrum. And while any Disney vacation requires planning, a little extra effort to accommodate the affected person will pay large dividends.

Disney's PDF **Guide for Guests with Cognitive Disabilities** is available for download at **tinyurl.com/cognitivedisabilitiesguide**. *Note:* The guide is generally updated only when a reprint is required, so its Fast-Pass+ information may be out of date.

Disney's Disability Access Service (DAS)

Disney revised its procedures for assisting disabled guests in late 2013, in response to media reports that its then-current Guest Assistance Card (GAC) program was being abused rampantly.

The updated program, called Disability Access Service (DAS), is still designed to accommodate guests who can't wait in regular standby lines, and as with the old GAC program, you must still obtain a DAS card at the Guest Relations window of the first theme park you visit. The same card works in every subsequent park you visit.

When you get to Guest Relations, you'll need to present identification and describe your or your family member's limitations. You don't need to disclose a disease or medical condition—what Disney's looking for is a description of how the condition affects you in the parks. Disney's goal here is to get you the right level of assistance, not to obligate you to prove that you or your family member qualifies.

Be as detailed as possible in describing limitations. For instance, if your child is on the autism spectrum and has trouble waiting in long lines or sensory issues that make it difficult for him or her to stand or be subjected to loud noises, you need to let the cast member know each of these things. "He doesn't wait in lines" isn't enough to go on.

unofficial **TIP**
You can have only one active return time on your DAS card. If you choose to return to ride after your specified time, you may not ride any other attraction until the active attraction on your card has been ridden or a cast member has crossed it off because you've decided not to ride.

The DAS card requires a photograph. Pictures are taken with an iPad; the cast member will come to you if you can't make it up to the counter. If the card is for a child, you may either use the child's photo or substitute your own if you'd rather not use the child's. Finally, you must sign the card and agree to be bound by its rules.

DAS cards may be used at any attraction or meet and greet that has a FastPass+ line. Present the card to a cast member; if the standby wait time is less than 10 minutes, you'll usually be escorted through the standby entrance or FastPass+ entrance. If the standby time is higher, the cast member will enter on the back of the card the attraction, time of day, wait time, and a time for you to return to ride. The return time will be the current wait time minus 10 minutes—if, say, you get to Splash Mountain at 12:20 p.m. and the standby time is 40 minutes, your return time will be 12:50 p.m.

You may return at the specified time or at any time thereafter. When you return, you'll be given access to the FastPass+ line. The cardholder need not be present to obtain a return time but must be present with his or her party for anyone to gain admission.

DAS cards are good for parties of up to six people. For parties of more than six, all members of the party must be present when the card is used. DAS cards are good (1) for the duration of your vacation, (2) for 14 days, or (3) until the back of the card is full, whichever of these times is shortest. If you fill your card, you must return to Guest Relations and get another.

Finally, note that you can use FastPass+ while you're using the DAS. In fact, cast members will suggest that you do so. It may take some extra planning on the front end, but using FastPass+ helps your DAS access.

FRIENDS OF BILL W.

ALCOHOLICS ANONYMOUS MEETINGS convenient to Walt Disney World take place at 3 p.m. Monday–Saturday; visit **tinyurl.com/friends ofbillworlando** for additional information. For information on other meetings in the surrounding area (including Celebration, Four Corners, Kissimmee, and St. Cloud), visit **osceolaintergroup.org**. For information on **Al-Anon/Alateen** meetings in the area, visit **alanon-orlando.com**.

INTERNATIONAL VISITORS

DISNEY HAS DEVELOPED A WIRELESS DEVICE called **Ears to the World** that provides synchronized narration in French, German, Japanese,

Portuguese, or Spanish for more than 30 attractions in the theme parks. The wireless, lightweight headsets provide real-time translation and are available for a $25 refundable deposit at Guest Relations in all parks.

A mom from Minorca, Spain, offers advice to readers who are making the long haul to Walt Disney World:

> *You cannot predict how the time difference is going to affect you or the little people. Coming from Spain, we were looking at a 9-hour flight (from the UK) and a 6-hour time difference, and we spent our first few days in a haze of tiredness after trying to do too much too soon. We tried to fight it—don't!*

Londoner and *Unofficial* friend Andrew Dakoutros sent us this grab bag of tips and warnings for other Disney-bound Brits:

> *(1) Magical Express doesn't automatically take your bags from the carousel; (2) Jellyrolls [the piano bar at Disney's BoardWalk] doesn't accept UK driving licences as ID for entry; (3) MagicBands are not mailed to addresses in the UK; (4) many MouseSavers codes [see page 38] can't be used from the UK; (5) the Twinings tea at The Tea Caddy [at Epcot] doesn't taste as good as in London.*
>
> *Additionally, you need to emphasise how hot Florida is and the importance of sunscreen. Most Britons holiday in Spain or Greece, where the sun is nowhere near as strong.*
>
> *Brits also like to go shopping, and at two stores in particular: Abercrombie and Hollister. We consider these luxury brands—prices in Florida are about 30% less than in the UK—so every holiday to the US tends to involve a visit to one of those two stores.*

PART SEVEN

ARRIVING *and* GETTING AROUND

GETTING THERE

DIRECTIONS

YOU CAN DRIVE to any Walt Disney World destination via **World Drive** off US 192; via **Epcot Center Drive** off Interstate 4; via **FL 536** and **Osceola Parkway West** from FL 417/Central Florida GreeneWay; or from the **Western Way** interchange off FL 429, also known as the Western Beltway (see all maps in this chapter).

FROM INTERSTATE 10 Take I-10 east across Florida to I-75 southbound at Exit 296A/Tampa, and then take Florida's Turnpike (a toll road) southbound at Exit 328 (on the left) toward Orlando. Take FL 429 (another toll road) to Exit 267A/Tampa southbound off the turnpike. Leave FL 429 at Exit 8, the Western Way interchange, in the direction of Walt Disney World, and follow the signs to your Disney destination. Also use these directions to reach hotels along US 192 (Irlo Bronson Memorial Highway).

FROM INTERSTATE 75 SOUTHBOUND Take I-75 south onto Florida's Turnpike via Exit 328 (on the left) toward Orlando. Take FL 429 (toll) southbound off the turnpike. Leave FL 429 at Exit 8, the Western Way interchange, in the direction of Walt Disney World, and follow the signs to your Disney destination. Also use these directions to reach hotels along US 192 (Irlo Bronson Memorial Highway).

FROM INTERSTATE 95 SOUTHBOUND Exit I-95 onto I-4 west toward Orlando and Tampa. Outside of rush hour, continue on I-4 through downtown Orlando to Walt Disney World Exit 64, 65, 67, or 68, depending on your Disney World destination. During rush hour, take I-4 Exit 101B just south of Seminole Town Center onto FL 417/Central Florida GreeneWay. Skirt Orlando to the southwest and continue on FL 417 to Exit 6/FL 536, marked for Epcot/Downtown Disney.

FROM DAYTONA, SANFORD INTERNATIONAL AIRPORT, OR ORLANDO Head west on I-4 through Orlando, then take Exit 67/FL 536, marked

unofficial **TIP**
Interstate 4 is technically an east–west highway, but it actually runs diagonally (northeast–southwest) across Florida. In metro Orlando, it runs mostly north–south—and that can complicate getting your bearings if you're not familiar with the area. Most highways branching off I-4 run east and west here, not north and south as logic might suggest.

I-4 & Walt Disney World Area

Orlando

Florida's Turnpike

429

Winter Garden-Vineland Rd.

Windermere

Lake Butler

Universal Studios Florida

Universal's Islands of Adventure

Vineland Rd.

439

75B

74B

75A

Wet 'n Wild

74A

Universal Blvd.

S. Apopka-Vineland Rd.

535

Kilgore Rd. →

Darlene Dr.

Facet Ct.

Turkey Lake Rd.

1

72

Magic Kingdom

Fort Wilderness Campground

Lake Buena Vista

Smith Bennett Rd.

71

Future site of Disney's Flamingo Crossings

The Walt Disney World Resort

Fenton St.

Lake St.

Palm Pkwy.

To Ocala

Western Beltway

Western Way

Epcot Center Dr.

World Dr.

Epcot

Disney Springs

68

27

Disney's Hollywood Studios

Buena Vista Dr.

67

536

417

Disney's Animal Kingdom

Osceola Pkwy.

535

W. Irlo Bronson Memorial Hwy.

192

ESPN Wide World of Sports Complex

65

3

64

International Dr.

2

417

Celebration Pl.

62

192

4

Celebration

Celebration Ave.

Poinciana Blvd.

58

532

Intercession City

27

55

To Busch Gardens & Tampa

17

92

4

To Davenport

Epcot/Downtown Disney (or take another appropriate exit—see the next two pages for the full list of I-4 exits), and follow the signs.

FROM ORLANDO INTERNATIONAL AIRPORT Two routes lead from the airport to Walt Disney World (see the South Orlando and Walt Disney

World Area map on pages 22 and 23). Both routes take almost exactly the same time to drive except during rush-hour traffic, when Route One via FL 417 is far less congested than Route Two via the Beachline Expressway. Also, Route One eliminates the need to drive on I-4, which is always very congested.

Route One: Drive southwest on FL 417/Central Florida GreeneWay, a toll road. Take Exit 6/International Drive toward FL 535. FL 536 will cross I-4 and become Epcot Center Drive. From here, follow the signs to your Walt Disney World destination. If you're going to a hotel on US 192 (Irlo Bronson Memorial Highway), follow the same route until you reach I-4. Take I-4 west toward Tampa. Take the first US 192 exit if your hotel is on West Irlo Bronson, the second exit if your hotel is on East Irlo Bronson. If your hotel is in Lake Buena Vista, take Exit 6 onto FL 536 as described previously, then turn right on FL 535 to the Lake Buena Vista area. If you're headed to Animal Kingdom, Animal Kingdom Lodge, Pop Century, Art of Animation, the All-Star Resorts, or ESPN Wide World of Sports, the quickest route is to take Exit 3/Osceola Parkway and follow the signs to your destination.

unofficial TIP
If you take either of these two routes from the airport, you'll need money for tolls. Some exits are unmanned and require exact change, so be sure you have *at least $2 in quarters.* Also, note that while the manned toll booths take bills up to $20, they don't take credit cards. For details, see **sunpass.com**.

Route Two: Take FL 528/Beachline Expressway, a toll road, west for about 19 miles to the intersection with I-4. Go west on I-4 to Exit 67/FL 536, marked Epcot/Downtown Disney, and then follow the signs to your Walt Disney World destination. This is also the route to take if your hotel is on International Drive or Universal Boulevard, near Universal Studios, near SeaWorld, or near the Orange County Convention Center. For these destinations, take I-4 east toward Orlando.

FROM MIAMI, FORT LAUDERDALE, AND SOUTHEASTERN FLORIDA Head north on Florida's Turnpike to Exit 249/Osceola Parkway West, and follow the signs.

FROM TAMPA AND SOUTHWESTERN FLORIDA Take I-75 northbound to I-4; then drive east on I-4, take Exit 64 onto US 192 West, and follow the signs.

Walt Disney World Exits off I-4

East to west (in the direction of Orlando to Tampa), five I-4 exits serve Walt Disney World:

EXIT 68 (FL 535/LAKE BUENA VISTA) primarily serves the Downtown Disney Resort Area and Disney Springs, including the Marketplace and the West Side. It also serves non-Disney hotels with a Lake Buena Vista address. This exit puts you on a road with lots of traffic signals. Avoid it unless you're headed to one of the preceding destinations.

EXIT 67 (FL 536/EPCOT/DOWNTOWN DISNEY) delivers you to a four-lane expressway into the heart of Disney World. It's the fastest and most convenient way for westbound travelers to access almost all Disney destinations except Disney's Animal Kingdom and ESPN Wide World of Sports Complex.

EXIT 65 (OSCEOLA PARKWAY) is the best exit for westbound travelers to access Disney's Animal Kingdom, Animal Kingdom Lodge, Pop Century Resort, Art of Animation Resort, the All-Star Resorts, and ESPN Wide World of Sports Complex.

EXIT 64 (US 192/MAGIC KINGDOM) is the best route for eastbound travelers to all Disney destinations.

EXIT 62 (DISNEY WORLD/CELEBRATION) is the first Disney exit you'll encounter heading east. This four-lane, controlled-access highway connects to the Walt Disney World Maingate. Accessing Disney World via the next exit, Exit 64, also routes you through the main entrance.

THE I-4 BLUES

OVER MANY YEARS of covering Walt Disney World, we've watched I-4 turn from a highway into a parking lot. The greatest congestion used to be between the Universal Orlando–International Drive area and downtown Orlando, but the section to the southwest serving the Disney World exits has become the new choke point, seemingly irrespective of the time of day. If you're going from Walt Disney World toward Orlando (east), the jam usually breaks up after you've passed the FL 535 exit. As you head west toward Tampa, traffic eases up after the US 192 interchange.

Ameliorating (or complicating) the situation, the state of Florida is renovating a 21-mile stretch of I-4, from FL 434 in the northeast to Kirkman Road in the southwest, to improve traffic flow and capacity in these areas. The project will update 15 of the busiest interchanges, build 56 new bridges, and replace more than 70 overpasses, plus add four toll lanes to help defray the $2 billion estimated cost. The bad news is that construction is likely to last through 2021—two years later than it was supposed to be finished. Check **i4ultimate.com** for construction updates on the northern section, between Kirkman Road (near Universal) and downtown Orlando, or **i4express.com** for updates on the southern section, from Kirkman Road to US 27 in Polk County.

If you're considering a hotel on or near International Drive, try to find one toward the southern end of I-Drive. If the I-4 traffic becomes intolerable, it's pretty easy to commute from the Universal Orlando–International Drive area to Walt Disney World on (1) **Turkey Lake Road,** connecting to Palm Parkway and FL 535 on the northwest side of I-4; (2) the southernmost section of I-Drive, connecting to FL 536 on the southeast side of the interstate; or (3) **Daryl Carter Parkway,** which bridges I-4 just northeast of FL 535, connecting Palm Parkway and International Drive near the Orlando Vineland Premium Outlets.

TECH TIP On long road trips, use a GPS device that's smart enough to accept traffic updates and route you around delays. **TomTom** GPS units, for example, have a $5 accessory cable that picks up traffic signals from HD radio broadcasts. If you've got a newer smartphone, the app **Waze** (free; iOS, Android, and Windows Phone; **waze.com**), also does this trick.

ALTERNATIVE AIRPORTS

A SHORT DISTANCE northeast of Orlando is **Sanford International Airport (SFB; orlandosanfordairport.com).** Small, convenient, and easily accessible, it's low-hassle compared with the huge Orlando International Airport (MCO) and its block-long security-checkpoint lines.

The primary domestic carrier serving Sanford International is **Allegiant Air** (☎ 702-505-8888; **allegiantair.com**), with service from large and small airports throughout the East Coast and the Midwest. European carriers include **ArkeFly** (Netherlands; ☎ 855-808-4015; **arkefly.nl**), **Icelandair** (☎ 800-223-5500; **icelandair.com**), **Monarch** (UK: ☎ +44 (0) 1582 398 036; **flymonarch.com**), and **Thomson Airways** (UK: ☎ 0871 231 4691; **thomson.co.uk**). Finally, **SST Air** (☎ 407-288-8820; **sstair.com**) offers seasonal charter flights between Sanford and various cities in Brazil.

A reader from Roanoke, Virginia, uses Sanford frequently, writing:

> *The 45-minute drive to WDW is more than made up for by avoiding the chaos at Orlando International, and it's stress-free.*

From another reader:

> *I couldn't be happier with our car service out of Sanford. Bob Martinez of* **Better Deal Transport** *(***betterdealtransport.com***) was our driver. It was $180 round-trip, no hidden fees, gratuity included. He was great—flexible, patient, and in touch through the day as we dealt with delays. That part of the experience couldn't have been better.*

Other readers, like this couple from White Township, New Jersey, prefer flying into Tampa instead:

> *We've found that flying from Newark to Tampa instead of Orlando saves us money and our sanity. It means significantly lower fares, fewer children on the plane, and shorter security lines.*

Be aware, however, that it's an 80-mile drive from Tampa International Airport to the Magic Kingdom—about an hour and 15 minutes.

SECURITY AT ORLANDO INTERNATIONAL AIRPORT

THIS AIRPORT HANDLES about 35 million passengers a year. It's not unusual to see lines from the checkpoints snaking out of the terminal and into the main shopping corridor and food court. Airport officials sometimes actually shut down moving sidewalks to use them for more queuing space.

> *un**official* TIP**
> We recommend arriving at MCO 90 minutes–2 hours before your scheduled departure.

A number of passengers have reported missing their flights even when they arrived at the airport 90 minutes before departure. System improvements through 2014 have alleviated some, but by no means all, of the congestion. Most waits to clear security average less than 15 minutes, compared with 55 minutes or longer before the improvements. Even so, there are substantial fluctuations, with peak waits nearing an hour.

GETTING TO DISNEY WORLD FROM THE AIRPORT

YOU CURRENTLY HAVE FOUR OPTIONS for getting from Orlando International Airport (**MCO**) to Walt Disney World:

1. TAXI Taxis carry four to eight passengers (depending on vehicle type). Rates vary according to distance. If your hotel is in the World, your fare will be about $48–$65, plus tip. For the US 192 Maingate area, it will cost about $55. To International Drive or downtown Orlando, expect to pay in the neighborhood of $38–$50.

2. SHUTTLE SERVICE Mears Transportation Group (☎ 855-463-2776; **mearstransportation.com**) provides your transportation if your vacation package includes airport transfers. Nonpackage travelers can also use the service. The shuttles collect passengers until they fill a van (or bus). They're then dispatched. Mears charges *per-person* rates (children under age 3 ride free). One-way and round-trip services are available. See the chart below for a fare breakdown.

You might have to wait at the airport until a vehicle fills. Once under way, the shuttle will probably stop several times to discharge passengers before reaching your hotel. Obviously, it takes less time to fill a van than a bus, and less time to deliver and unload those passengers.

From your hotel to the airport, you're likely to ride in a van (unless you're part of a tour group, for which Mears might send a bus). Because shuttles make several pickups, you must leave much earlier than if you were taking a cab or returning a rental car.

FROM THE AIRPORT TO:	ONE-WAY ADULT/CHILD	ROUND-TRIP ADULT/CHILD
INTERNATIONAL DRIVE	$20/$15	$32/$24
DOWNTOWN ORLANDO (leaves hourly)	$19/$15	$31/$23
DDRA RESORTS–LAKE BUENA VISTA	$22/$17	$36/$27
US 192 MAINGATE AREA	$22/$17	$36/$27

3. TOWN-CAR SERVICE Like a taxi, town-car service will transport you directly from the airport to your hotel. The driver will usually be waiting for you in your airline's baggage-claim area. If saving time and hassle is worth the money, book a town car.

Each town-car service we surveyed offers large, well-appointed late-model sedans or limousines, which hold four passengers (to reserve a child's car seat, call ahead). Trunks easily hold golf bags.

Tiffany Towncar Service (☎ 888-838-2161 or 407-370-2196; **tiffany towncars.com**) provides a prompt, clean ride. The round-trip fee to a Disney or non-Disney resort in a town car is $130–$140 plus tip; one-way is about $75–$80. Tiffany offers a free 30-minute stop at a Publix supermarket en route to your hotel.

Quicksilver Tours & Transportation (☎ 888-GO-TO-WDW [468-6939] or 407-299-1434; **quicksilver-tours.com**) offers 8-person limos and 10-person vans as well as 4-person town cars. Round-trip town-car rates range from $125 to $130, depending on location; round-trip van rates range from $140 to $145; round-trip limo rate is $240.

Mears Transportation Group (☎ 855-463-2776; **mearstransportation .com**) also offers a town-car service for around $180 round-trip.

4. RENTAL CARS Short- and long-term rentals are available. Most companies allow drop-off at certain hotels or subsidiary locations in the Disney area if you don't want the vehicle for your entire stay. Likewise, at any time during your stay, you can pick up a car at those hotels and locations. Check **mousesavers.com** for rental-car discount codes.

The preferred routes to Walt Disney World, Universal Orlando, Sea-World, I-Drive, and US 192 all involve toll roads. Some roads require exact change to enter or exit via automated gates, and manned toll booths will not accept any currency denomination larger than a $20 bill. So before you leave the airport, make sure you're armed with at least a couple of dollars in quarters and some ones, fives, and tens.

SO WHAT'S THE BEST DEAL? If you're traveling solo or with one other person and you're pretty sure you won't need to rent a car, the shuttle is your least expensive bet. A cab will cost about $53–$70, including tip, or $27–$35 per person; the shuttle will cost you $22 each (one-way), saving $5–$13 per person. If all you care about is getting to your hotel as quickly as possible, choose the cab. A one-day car rental costs $40–$70, but you have to fill out the paperwork, pick up the vehicle, and gas it up before you return it. The more people in your group, the more economical the cab and the rental car become versus the shuttle; again, though, the cab will be quicker.

Ride-Sharing Services

Lyft (lyft.com), **Uber (uber.com)**, and similar services use ordinary people and their cars as an informal taxi service. Customers use a mobile app to find drivers in their area and estimate the length and cost of the ride.

Because they promote base fares some 30–40% cheaper than a traditional taxi service's—and because their business model is hostile to regulation—these companies frequently run into local opposition. After Lyft and Uber came to Orlando, the city banned them outright. In late 2014, the ban was lifted, but drivers became subject to more or less the same rules that govern their cab-driving counterparts. Orlando has also mandated that Uber and Lyft start charging the same minimum fares as local taxis, although for now they're still charging their lower rates while they negotiate with the city. And at press time, both services were still banned from picking up at MCO (drop-offs are allowed, however).

Local Lyft and Uber drivers have been slow to comply with the new laws, citing the various fees involved, which can be prohibitive for drivers who work just a few hours a week to make extra money. (Uber, in fact, gives its drivers a disincentive to go legal by paying their fines if they get ticketed.) Although Orlando police have pledged to be vigilant about going after noncompliant drivers, they may have their work cut out for them: Uber vehicles are unmarked, while Lyft vehicles have only a small pink plastic mustache—the company's symbol—affixed to their dashboards. As for the airport ban, a few drivers are willing to make clandestine pickups near (but not actually on) MCO property.

For the time being, both Uber and Lyft can save you money versus a regular cab. On a recent trip from Saratoga Springs Resort to the Magic Kingdom via Fort Wilderness, for example, Uber charged us $8.60, while the return taxi ride along the same route, in the same traffic, was $21.40. To avoid the potential hassle of a traffic stop, make sure your driver is city-compliant: Look for a blue sticker on the vehicle's windshield, and check that the driver is wearing an ID badge.

DISNEY'S MAGICAL EXPRESS

THIS FREE BUS SERVICE shuttles guests of Disney-owned and -operated resorts between MCO and Walt Disney World. (The Swan, the Dolphin, Shades of Green, and the hotels of Bonnet Creek Resort and the Downtown Disney Resort Area don't participate.) Magical Express also provides free luggage delivery to your resort, except between 10 p.m. and 5 a.m.—if your flight arrives between those hours, you'll need to pick up your stuff from baggage claim before boarding the bus.

First, register your flight information with your resort reservation, either at the time of booking or as soon as you've booked your flights, by calling ☎ 866-599-0951 or using **mydisneyexperience.com.**

US and Canadian travelers will receive their Magical Express paperwork in the mail 20–40 days before they arrive. The packet contains detailed instructions for getting around the airport, bus vouchers, and tags for checked luggage (two per traveler); **MagicBands** (see page 67) also work as bus vouchers. When it's time for your trip, you'll check your bags as you normally would and plan to see them again in your hotel room. If you've ever been on a cruise, the procedure is similar.

Non-Canadian international travelers won't get their vouchers or tags in the mail—instead, they'll need to go through Customs with bags in hand. Disney will collect the bags for transport at the Magical Express Welcome Center, where international guests will also receive their bus vouchers.

The Magical Express Welcome Center is on the B side of the airport's lower level. Cast members are stationed throughout the area to help you find your way. You can pick them out by their nautical costumes, the signs they're holding, and the big white Mickey gloves they wear.

If you already have your bus vouchers or MagicBands, just head straight to the bus check-in. A cast member will scan your vouchers/bands and direct you to a holding area for your resort's bus line. If you've lost or accidentally packed your vouchers/bands or you need other assistance, you'll be directed to the Welcome Center desk.

unofficial **TIP**
This is a good place to remind you of Disney's online check-in (see page 145), which will save you time registering at your hotel.

There's no seating inside the holding area, so if you know that a member of your party will have trouble standing for more than a very short time, let a cast member know. Lines generally move quickly, though, with waits to board rarely exceeding 20 minutes. Once on the bus, try to get a seat up front, since you'll be among the first to get off (and get in line at your hotel). Passengers must be at least 12 years old to ride unaccompanied by an adult.

Buses are shared among resorts—for example, a bus to Old Key West may also stop at Saratoga Springs or Port Orleans. Most of the time, Disney will try to fill a bus before sending it on its way. Each bus has 55 seats, and five buses may load at once. On more than one occasion, particularly for flights arriving very early in the morning or late at night, we've been the only passengers on our bus.

We've usually arrived at our resorts within 90 minutes of stepping off our plane. When you consider that you don't have to wait for your bags and that the trip takes 30 minutes regardless of who's driving, Magical Express is about as efficient an operation as you could hope for.

Your checked bags are picked up at the airport, sorted by destination, and sent directly on to your room—if it's ready. If not, bell services will hold your bags until you're able to get into your room. Because you may be separated from your checked bags for a few hours, remember the following:

- Don't check valuables such as cameras, laptops, or jewelry. This is good advice whether you use Magical Express or not.

- Likewise, don't check anything you'll need quick access to—MagicBands, phone chargers, travel documents, glasses, medication, and such.

- Pack swimsuits and sunscreen in your carry-on bag and enjoy the pool before your bags arrive.

- It's not necessary to check strollers and wheelchairs—these can be stored in your bus's luggage compartment.

If you booked your trip too late to get luggage tags, you can still use the delivery service: Just give the baggage-claim numbers that your airline gave you to the cast members at the Magical Express check-in desk, and they'll pick up and deliver your bags. We've done this before and it worked without a hitch.

THE TRIP HOME The day before you check out of your resort, you'll get a notification from Disney with your return information on it. This will include a time for you to board your bus back to MCO.

If you're checking bags, you'll need to pick up luggage tags separately at your resort lobby's Airline Check-in Desk. As of this edition, seven airlines participate in advance check-in: **Alaska, American, Delta, JetBlue, Southwest, United,** and **US Airways;** guests using these airlines for international flights may use the service as well. As this is also your airline check-in, you'll need to show ID just as you would at the airport. (When you drop off your bags, you'll also get your boarding passes if your flight leaves before noon, otherwise the passes will be delivered to your room on the morning of your departure.)

As this Bloomington, Illinois, couple discovered, the major downside to using Magical Express for your return trip is that you'll board your bus only about 3 hours before your flight is scheduled to depart (4 hours for international flights):

> On departure day, we stopped at three resorts after we were picked up, arriving at the last resort 50 minutes after we had departed ours. We were on the bus a total of 1 hour and 40 minutes, and our flight began boarding less than 15 minutes after we reached the gate. That's cutting it a little close in our opinion.

A group of adults from Manchester, Connecticut, reports a similarly nail-biting experience:

> Our flight out was at 8 a.m.—virtually impossible to get there from the hotel using Magical Express unless you leave at 5 a.m.! Next time we'll rent a car.

Magical Express Considered

What's our take on Magical Express? Well, when we see the word *free* attached to a travel package, our first question is, "So what's the catch?" Disney is nothing if not crafty, and the goal of getting folks to use their bus service is to keep people and their wallets inside Walt Disney World. If seeing other area sights (such as Universal Orlando) or eating at off-site restaurants is a priority for you, consider renting a car either at the airport or at one of the Disney on-site rental desks (see the next section, "Renting a Car").

A Provo, Utah, mom loved Magical Express:

Magical Express was heavenly. Not worrying about lugging six suit-cases around and arriving and departing quickly and comfortably was the cherry on top of the vacation.

A dad from Monroe, Washington, didn't:

Your guide needs to stress planning around Magical Express. It took us more than 2 hours to get from the airport to Animal Kingdom Lodge, which was the last stop on the schedule. Luckily, we were able to push our dinner reservations out, but next time we'll take a shuttle or a cab.

A dad from Ontario, Canada, warns:

On the return trip to the airport, [some international travelers'] bags don't automatically go on the Magical Express—you must get them using claim tickets and put them on the bus yourself. Had it not been for the bus driver, I would have left the resort without my baggage and arrived at the airport thinking all I had to do was show the driver my claim ticket.

Finally, *not* using Magical Express turned out to be liberating for this Mansfield, Texas, reader. His comments bolster our earlier assertion regarding why Disney offers Magical Express in the first place:

We rented a car from the airport, which helped us decide to go to Universal for Harry Potter, which made us want to try Discovery Cove. Because we didn't use Magical Express, we ended up spending hundreds of dollars that could have been Disney's.

RENTING A CAR

READERS PLANNING TO STAY in Walt Disney World ask frequently if they'll need a car. If your plans don't include restaurants, attractions, or destinations outside Disney World, then the answer is a very qualified no. But take into account the thoughts of this reader from Snohomish, Washington:

We rented a car and were glad we did. With a car we could drive to the grocery store to restock our snack supply. It also came in handy for our night out. I shudder at how long it might have taken us to get from the Caribbean Beach to the Polynesian Village to leave our kids at the child-care facility, then back to the Polynesian Village to get the kids, and then back to the Caribbean Beach.

A dad from Avon Lake, Ohio, adds:

Although we stayed at the Grand Floridian, we found the monorail convenient only for the Magic Kingdom. Of the six nights we stayed, we used our car five days.

From an Ann Arbor, Michigan, mother of three:

During our stay it was almost impossible to get into any of the Disney restaurants. Purely out of desperation, we rented a car so we could eat outside WDW. We had no problem finding good places to eat at a fraction of what you'd pay inside.

A dad from Vancouver, British Columbia, implores readers to get their act together before they reach the rental counter:

> When I arrived at the Dollar counter at Orlando Airport, there were 20 customers waiting in line and 5 agents. Everyone in front of me took at least 10 minutes with an agent; one guy spent most of his time talking to someone on his phone, trying to decide what to get! When it was my turn—45 minutes later—it took me 2 minutes because I knew what I wanted and I had already filled out my rental info online.

PLAN TO RENT A CAR

1. If your hotel is outside Walt Disney World.
2. If your hotel is in the World but you want to eat someplace other than the theme parks and your hotel.
3. If you plan to return to your hotel for naps or swimming during the day.
4. If you plan to visit other area theme parks or water parks (including Disney's).

unofficial **TIP** Orlando is one of the least expensive US cities in which to rent a car, with an average rate of $25 a day for the most affordable car. (New York is the most expensive city, at $76 a day.)

Renting a Car at Orlando International Airport

MCO has two terminals: **A** and **B**. Airlines serving Orlando are assigned to one or the other. Each terminal has three levels and a parking garage. Ticket counters are on Level Three. Baggage claim is on Level Two. Level One is where the car-rental counters are or where you can catch a courtesy vehicle to an off-site rental location.

Orlando is the world's largest rental-car market. At last count, 31 companies vied for your business. Eleven—**Alamo, Avis, Budget, Dollar, Enterprise, E-Z Rent-A-Car, Firefly Car Rental, Hertz, L&M, National,** and **Thrifty**—have counters at each terminal. **Payless** and 19 other companies have locations near the airport and provide courtesy shuttles outside Level One at both terminals. We prefer renting inside the airport, though, because (1) you can complete your paperwork while you wait for your checked luggage to arrive at baggage claim and (2) it's just a short walk to the garage to pick up your car.

If you rent on-site, you'll return your car to the garage adjacent to the terminal where your airline is located. If you return your car to the wrong garage, you'll have to schlep your luggage from one side of the airport to the other to reach your check-in.

Most rental companies charge about $5–$8 a gallon to fill the gas tank. If you plan to drive a lot, prepay for a fill-up so you can return the car empty, or fill up near your hotel on your way back to the airport. If you're taking FL 417, turn right at the Airport/Boggy Creek Road exit and drive about a mile to find the closest gas station to MCO.

How the Orlando Rental-Car Companies Stack Up

When it comes to renting a car, most *Unofficial Guide* readers are looking for the following, as reflected in the table on the next page:

1. Quick, courteous, and efficient processing on pickup.
2. A nice, well-maintained, late-model automobile.
3. A car that is clean and odor-free.

4. Quick, courteous, and efficient processing on return.

5. If applicable, an efficient shuttle between the rental agency and airport.

COMPANY	PICKUP EFFICIENCY	CONDITION OF CAR	CLEANNESS OF CAR	RETURN EFFICIENCY	SHUTTLE EFFICIENCY	OVERALL RATING
ADVANTAGE	C	A	C	B	—	B
ALAMO	B	A	A	A	—	A
AVIS	B	A	B	B	—	B
BUDGET	C	B+	B+	B	—	B
DOLLAR	B	B	B	B	—	B
ENTERPRISE	B	B	B	B	—	B
E-Z RENT-A-CAR	C	B	A	B	—	B
HERTZ	C+	B	A	A	—	B
NATIONAL	B	B	B	B	—	B
THRIFTY	C	C	B	B	—	C

On a scale from A (best) to F (worst), the table shows how readers rate the Orlando operations of each company based on the criteria shown. If you'd like to participate in our survey, go to **touringplans .com/walt-disney-world/survey.**

Unofficial Guide readers rated **Alamo** as the top rental company in Orlando last year, ending **National Car Rental**'s seven-year streak at the top. **Hertz** moved up to second place, National down to third. All of the major rental companies in our survey seem to be delivering consistently good service.

If you're looking to rent something distinctive yet remain within a budget, consider **Sixt** (**sixt.com**) or **Fox** (**foxrentacar.com**). Sixt has affordable vehicles from Mercedes and VW (including the Eos convertible), while Fox has the *adorabile* Fiat 500 at bargain prices.

If you rent a car, a 6–7% sales tax, $2.50-per-day airport-facility surcharge, and 45¢- to $2.02-per-day vehicle-license-recovery fee will be heaped onto your final bill. Some companies, including Hertz, are still adding a "fuel surcharge" fee, even with gas now under $2.25 a gallon. Luckily, you can rent a car at your hotel on the day you actually need it.

The Insurance Thing

Anyone who rents a car should know what his or her auto insurance does and doesn't cover. If you have the slightest question about your coverage, call your agent. A corollary discussion pertains to added coverage from your credit card company if the rental fee is charged on the card. Usually, credit card coverage picks up deductibles and some ancillary charges that your auto-insurance policy doesn't cover. The tune is the same, however: Make sure you understand what is and isn't covered.

The Public-Transportation Alternative

Some hotel shuttles outside of Walt Disney World don't operate early enough to get you to the parks before opening. An alternative is the **LYNX** public bus system. If you're staying in downtown Orlando, on International Drive south of the Beachline Expressway, or along Palm Parkway in Lake Buena Vista, you can take the LYNX **#50 bus** to the

DISCOUNT-CODE *Whac-A-Mole*

IN PAST EDITIONS OF THIS BOOK, we've published the best car-rental discount codes we could find. Then, within a few weeks of the book's release, the rental companies would discontinue the best of the ones we'd printed.

Enter the website **Zalyn** (**zalyn.com**). It starts off like any other car-rental site, asking for your travel destination, dates, and car preferences. Here's where the genius comes in: Zalyn knows of virtually every discount and coupon available for every car-rental agency, and it will apply all of them to see which gives you the lowest overall cost.

Once you find a rate you like, you usually have to book it through another service such as Priceline. But the savings are substantial, and it beats spending half an hour entering obscure discount codes on a bunch of different sites.

Walt Disney World Transportation and Ticket Center (TTC). The bus runs outbound daily from 5:15 a.m. to 11:48 p.m. and inbound from 5:23 a.m. to 1:05 a.m. Precise hours of service vary depending on where along the route you are. Use the online trip planner at **golynx.com** or call ☎ 407-841-LYNX for travel information. A Slaughter, Louisiana, woman gives the service high marks:

> We stayed at a hotel that was on the LYNX #50 bus line. It was perfect for getting to and from the park without having to wait for the hotel shuttles to start, which would have had us arriving after park opening. For 8 bucks, we couldn't beat it!

The downside is that the trip on the #50 bus takes almost 2 hours terminal-to-terminal; figure about 50 minutes or so if you board south of the Beachline Expressway. The **#56 bus** runs from Kissimmee to the TTC along US 192 (Irlo Bronson Memorial Highway), a trip of 1.25 hours one-way. The closer you are to Disney World and the farther you are from downtown Kissimmee, the shorter the trip.

GETTING ORIENTED

A GOOD MAP

READERS FREQUENTLY COMPLAIN about the quality of signs and maps provided by Disney. While it's easy to find the theme parks, locating other Disney destinations can be challenging: Disney-supplied maps are often hard to read or lacking in detail. Your best bet, in addition to the maps in this guide, is a Walt Disney World road map created by **Alamo Rent A Car.** Get it from the front desk or concierge at the resorts.

A very good map of the Orlando–Kissimmee–Disney World area is available free at the **Car Care Center** operated by Goodyear, near the Magic Kingdom parking lot.

GPS COORDINATES FOR THE THEME PARKS

CHECK WHETHER YOUR GPS already includes Disney's theme parks as points of interest. If not, use these GPS coordinates to guide you. Supplement them with Disney's road signs, which will direct you to parking lots as you get close.

DESTINATION PARKING LOT	GPS ADDRESS	LATITUDE AND LONGITUDE
THE MAGIC KINGDOM	3111 World Dr. Lake Buena Vista, FL 32830	N28° 25.124' W81° 34.871'
EPCOT	200 Epcot Center Dr. Lake Buena Vista, FL 32830	N28° 22.869' W81° 32.964'
ANIMAL KINGDOM	2801 Osceola Pkwy. Lake Buena Vista, FL 32380	N28° 21.480' W81° 35.426'
DHS	351 S. Studio Dr. Lake Buena Vista, FL 32830	N28° 21.425' W81° 33.618'
BLIZZARD BEACH	1534 Blizzard Beach Dr. Lake Buena Vista, FL 32830	N28° 21.338' W81° 34.384'
TYPHOON LAGOON	1145 E. Buena Vista Dr. Lake Buena Vista, FL 32830	N28° 22.162' W81° 31.576'
DISNEY SPRINGS	1490 E. Buena Vista Dr. Lake Buena Vista, FL 32830	N28° 22.064' W81° 31.167'

FINDING YOUR WAY AROUND

WALT DISNEY WORLD IS LIKE ANY BIG CITY: It's easy to get lost. Signs for the theme parks are excellent, but finding a restaurant or hotel is often confusing. The easiest way to orient yourself is to think in terms of five major areas, or clusters:

1. The first encompasses all hotels and theme parks around Seven Seas Lagoon. This includes the Magic Kingdom; hotels connected by the monorail; Shades of Green Resort; and the Palm, Magnolia, and Oak Trail Golf Courses.

2. The second includes developments on and around Bay Lake: Wilderness Lodge & Villas, Fort Wilderness Campground, and the Four Seasons Resort Orlando and Tranquilo Golf Club.

3. Cluster three contains Epcot, Disney's Hollywood Studios, the BoardWalk, ESPN Wide World of Sports, Epcot resort hotels, Pop Century Resort, Art of Animation Resort, and Caribbean Beach Resort.

4. The fourth cluster encompasses Disney Springs (including the Marketplace and West Side); Typhoon Lagoon water park; Lake Buena Vista Golf Course; the Downtown Disney Resort Area; and the Port Orleans, Saratoga Springs, and Old Key West resorts.

5. The fifth cluster contains Disney's Animal Kingdom; Blizzard Beach water park; and Animal Kingdom Lodge & Villas, the All-Star Resorts, and Coronado Springs Resort.

HOW *to* TRAVEL *around the* WORLD *(or, The Real Mr. Toad's Wild Ride)*

TRYING TO COMMUTE around Walt Disney World can be frustrating. A Magic Kingdom street vendor, telling us how to get to Epcot, proposed, "You can take the ferry or the monorail to the Transportation and Ticket Center. Then you can get another monorail, or you can catch the bus, or you can take a tram out to your car and drive over there yourself." What he didn't say was that it would be easier to ride a mule than to take any conceivable combination from this transportation smorgasbord.

TRANSPORTATION TRADE-OFFS FOR GUESTS LODGING OUTSIDE WALT DISNEY WORLD

DAY GUESTS (those staying outside the World) can use the monorail, bus, and boat systems. Our most important advice for these guests is to park in the lot of the theme park (or other Disney destination) where they plan to finish their day. This is critical if you stay at a park until closing.

Moving Your Car from Lot to Lot on the Same Day

Once you've paid to park in any major theme park lot ($17 per day), show your receipt and you'll be admitted into another park's lot on the same day without further charge. Annual Pass holders and Disney resort guests park free in any theme park lot.

ALL YOU NEED TO KNOW ABOUT DRIVING TO THE THEME PARKS

1. POSITIONING OF THE PARKING LOTS The Animal Kingdom, Epcot, and DHS lots are adjacent to each park's entrance. The Magic Kingdom lot is adjacent to the Transportation and Ticket Center (TTC). From the TTC, take a ferry or monorail to the park's entrance. Electronic displays at each will show you which option is faster.

2. PAYING TO PARK Disney resort guests and Annual Pass holders park free. All others pay. If you pay to park and you move your car during that day, show your receipt and you won't have to pay at the new lot.

3. FINDING YOUR CAR WHEN IT'S TIME TO DEPART Jot down, text, or take a phone picture of the section and row where you park. If you're driving a rental car, note the license-plate number.

4. GETTING FROM YOUR CAR TO THE PARK ENTRANCE Each lot provides trams to the park entrance or, at the Magic Kingdom, to the TTC. If you arrive early in the morning, it may be faster to walk to the entrance (or TTC) than to take the tram. At the TTC, Disney has added digital wait-time boards, showing you how long the wait is to board the express monorail to the Magic Kingdom or board the ferry. Choose the shorter of the two lines.

5. GETTING TO DISNEY'S ANIMAL KINGDOM FOR PARK OPENING If you're staying on-property and are planning to be at this theme park when it opens, take a Disney bus from your resort instead of driving. For some reason, Animal Kingdom's parking lot frequently opens 15 minutes before the park itself—which doesn't leave you enough time to park, hop on a tram, and pass through security before park opening.

6. HOW MUCH TIME TO ALLOT FOR PARKING AND GETTING TO THE PARK ENTRANCE At Epcot and Disney's Animal Kingdom, figure about 10–15 minutes to pay, park, and walk or ride to the entrance. At Disney's Hollywood Studios, allow 8–12 minutes; at the Magic Kingdom, 10–15 minutes to the TTC and another 20–30 to reach the park entrance via the monorail (most of which is waiting to board) or ferry (slower but usually less in demand). If you haven't purchased your theme park admission in advance, tack on another 10–20 minutes before you actually enter the park.

7. COMMUTING FROM PARK TO PARK You can commute among the theme parks via Disney bus, to and from the Magic Kingdom and Epcot by monorail, or to and from Epcot and Disney's Hollywood Studios by boat or on foot. You can, of course, commute in your own car as well. Using Disney transportation or your car, allow 45–60 minutes one-way, entrance to entrance. If you plan to park-hop, leave your car in the lot of the park where you'll finish the day.

8. LEAVING THE PARK AT THE END OF THE DAY If you stay at a park until closing, expect the parking-lot trams, monorails, and ferries to be mobbed. (The Magic Kingdom has wait-time displays showing the lines for the monorail and ferry.) If the wait for the tram is unacceptable, walk to your car, or walk to the first stop on the tram route and wait there for a tram. When someone gets off, you can get on.

9. DINNER AND A QUICK EXIT One way to beat closing crowds at the Magic Kingdom is to arrange reservations for dinner at a restaurant in the Contemporary Resort. When you leave the Magic Kingdom for dinner, move your car from the TTC lot to the Contemporary lot. After dinner, walk (8–10 minutes) or take the monorail back to the Magic Kingdom. When the park closes and everyone else is fighting to board the monorail or ferry, you can stroll back to the Contemporary, claim your car, and get on your way. Use the same strategy at Epcot by arranging a reservation at an Epcot resort. When the park closes after *IllumiNations*, exit via the International Gateway and walk to the resort where you parked.

10. CAR TROUBLE All parking lots have security patrols. If you have a dead battery or minor automotive problem, the patrols will help you.

For more serious trouble, the **Car Care Center** (☎ 407-824-0976), operated by Goodyear near the Magic Kingdom parking lot, can help. Prices for most services are comparable to those at home. The facility stays busy, so expect to leave your car unless the fix is simple. Hours are Monday–Friday, 7 a.m.–7 p.m.; Saturday, 7 a.m.–4 p.m.; and Sunday, 8 a.m.–3 p.m.

11. SCORING A GREAT PARKING PLACE If you arrive at a park after noon or move your car from park to park, there will be empty parking spaces near the entrance vacated by early guests who have left. Instead of following Disney signage or being directed by staff to a distant space, drive to the front and hunt a space, or use the approach of a Coopersburg, Pennsylvania, couple:

> *After leaving Epcot for lunch, we returned to find a fullish parking lot. We were unhappy because we had left a third-row parking spot. My husband told the attendant that we had left just an hour ago and that there were lots of spaces up front. Without a word of protest, he waved us to the front, and we got our same spot back!*

GOOD FUZZ, BAD FUZZ

FOR AS LONG AS ANYONE CAN REMEMBER, Disney World security imposed little to no restraint on speeding drivers. However, we've been alerted to the increasing presence of Orange County law enforcement busting speeders on Disney World property. So for the lead-footed among you, there will be no more Fairy Godmother treatment, and the character with the flashing blue lights isn't Goofy.

SNEAK ROUTES

SNEAK ROUTE IS A WHITEWATER-PADDLING TERM for an easy way through tough rapids. Unfortunately, not all difficult rapids have a sneak route. For those that don't, there's only one way through: the hard way. As we research this guide, we're constantly looking for ways to avoid traffic snarls. For some roads and areas, there are no alternative routes. For others, we've discovered sneak routes.

THE LIGHTS OF DISNEY SPRINGS Although dozens of searchlights blaze at Disney Springs after dark, what we're talking about here are the many multifunction traffic signals on **Buena Vista Drive** in front of Disney Springs, which mark a traffic bottleneck of the first order. Heaven help you if you're traveling from Coronado Springs Resort to Disney Springs—you'll encounter up to 15 traffic signals in the 5-mile drive, or roughly one every third of a mile. In the evening especially, this commute can take up to half an hour. It wouldn't be so bad if only traffic to Disney Springs were affected, but because Buena Vista Drive is one of Walt Disney World's most important traffic arteries, the traffic jam is on the order of a blocked coronary ventricle.

Most traffic entering and exiting Walt Disney World from the FL 535 entrance must run this traffic-signal gauntlet, and so too must guests staying at the seven hotels of the Downtown Disney Resort Area and Saratoga Springs Resort when traveling to Epcot, Disney's Hollywood Studios, the Magic Kingdom, Disney's Animal Kingdom, and Typhoon Lagoon. To avoid the bottlenecked area requires long but nearly traffic-free circumnavigation. Coming from the theme parks, you can bypass the mess by taking **I-4** or alternatively by looping around on **Bonnet Creek Parkway** and **Disney Vacation Club Way.** If you're going back to an Epcot or Magic Kingdom resort from Disney Springs, it may be faster to take I-4 West and follow the signs back to Disney property. Any way you look at it, though, it's a congested World after all.

INTERNATIONAL DRIVE (I-DRIVE) This is by far the most difficult area to navigate without long traffic delays. Most hotels on I-Drive are between **Kirkman Road** to the north and **FL 417 (Central Florida GreeneWay)** to the south. Between Kirkman Road and FL 417, three major roads cross I-Drive: From north to south on I-Drive (in the direction of Disney World), the first is **Universal Boulevard.** Next is **Sand Lake Road (FL 482),** pretty squarely in the middle of the hotel district. Finally, the **Beachline Expressway (FL 528)** connects I-4 and the airport.

unofficial **TIP**
To locate your I-Drive hotel, check **iridetrolley.com** or **Google Maps** (zoom way in for hotel names to appear).

The southern third of I-Drive can be accessed via **Central Florida Parkway,** connecting I-4 and Palm Parkway with the SeaWorld area of I-Drive, and by **Daryl Carter Parkway,** connecting Palm Parkway with the Orlando Vineland Premium Outlets.

I-Drive is a mess for a number of reasons: scarcity of left-turn lanes, long multidirectional traffic signals, and, most critically, limited access to westbound I-4 (toward Disney). From the Orange County Convention Center south to the Beachline Expressway and FL 417/Central Florida GreeneWay, getting on westbound I-4 is easy, but in the stretch where the hotels are concentrated (from Kirkman to about a mile south of Sand Lake), the only way most visitors know to access I-4 westbound

Disney Springs Sneak Routes

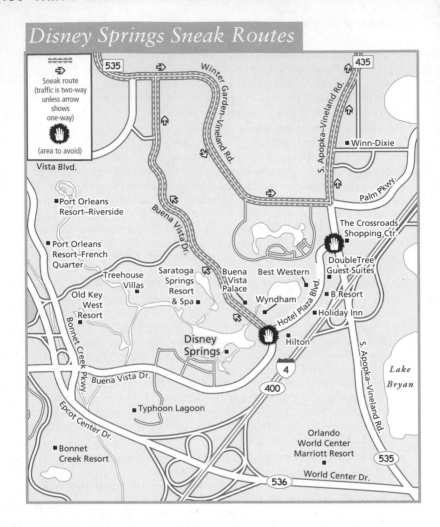

is to slog through the gridlock of the I-Drive–Sand Lake Road intersection en route to the I-4–Sand Lake Road interchange. A combination of a long, long traffic signal, a sea of motorists, and insufficient turn lanes makes this about as much fun as a root canal.

The object, then, is to access I-4 westbound *without* getting on Sand Lake Road. If your hotel is north of Sand Lake, access **Kirkman Road** by going north on I-Drive (in the opposite direction of the heaviest traffic) to the Kirkman Road intersection and turning left, or by cutting over to Kirkman via eastbound **Carrier Drive**. In either case, take Kirkman north over I-4 and, at the first traffic signal (at the entrance to Universal Orlando), make a U-turn. This will put you directly onto a westbound I-4 ramp. You can also go north on **Universal Boulevard,** which parallels I-Drive to the east; after you cross I-4 onto Universal property, stay left and follow the signs through two left turns to I-4—the signs are small, so stay alert.

International Drive Area Sneak Routes

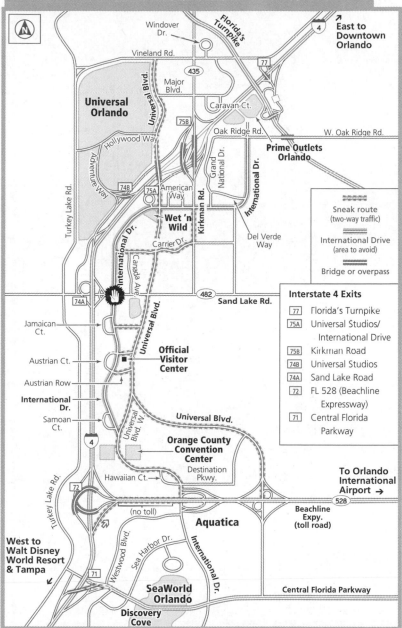

If your hotel is south of Sand Lake Road but north of Austrian Court, use **Austrian Row** to cut over to Universal Boulevard. Turn right (south) on Universal and continue until you intersect the **Beachline Expressway (FL 528)**; then take the Beachline west to I-4 (no toll).

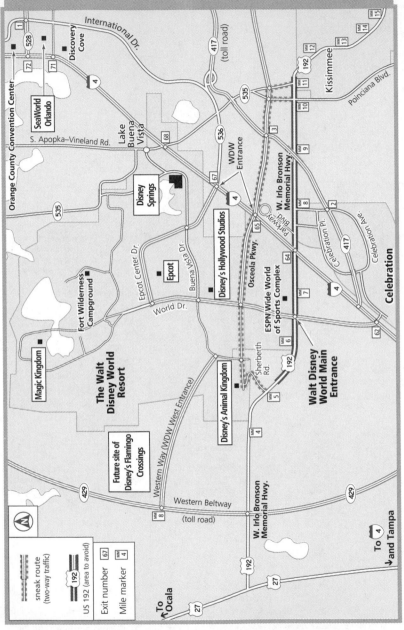

US 192–Kissimmee Resort Area Sneak Routes

US 192 (IRLO BRONSON MEMORIAL HIGHWAY) This road runs east–west along the southern border of Walt Disney World. From the Disney World entrance west on US 192/Irlo Bronson toward Clermont and east toward Kissimmee is a concentration of hotels. The highway, though heavily used,

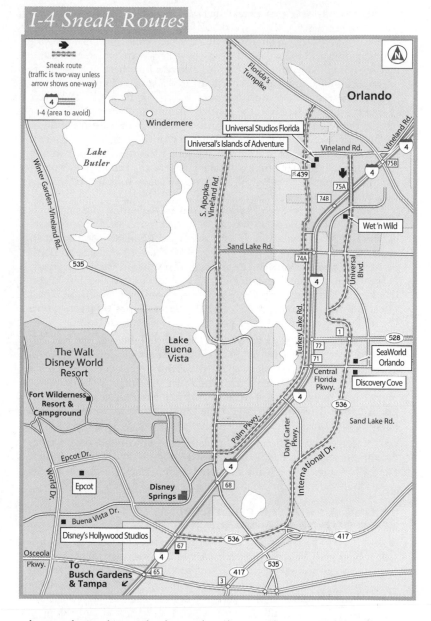

I-4 Sneak Routes

Sneak route
(traffic is two-way unless
arrow shows one-way)

I-4 (area to avoid)

Windermere

Lake
Butler

Winter Garden–Vineland Rd.

Orlando

Florida's Turnpike

Universal Studios Florida

Universal's Islands of Adventure

Vineland Rd.

Vineland Rd.

439

75B

4

74B

75A

74A

Wet 'n Wild

S. Apopka–Vineland Rd.

Sand Lake Rd.

535

Lake
Buena
Vista

The Walt
Disney World
Resort

Fort Wilderness
Resort &
Campground

Turkey Lake Rd.

Universal Blvd.

4

1

77

71

528

SeaWorld
Orlando

Discovery Cove

Central
Florida
Pkwy.

4

536

Sand Lake Rd.

Palm Pkwy.

Daryl Carter Pkwy.

International Dr.

4

Epcot Dr.

World Dr.

Epcot

Disney
Springs

68

Buena Vista Dr.

Disney's Hollywood Studios

Osceola
Pkwy.

67

4

65

To
Busch Gardens
& Tampa

536

417

535

3

417

has ample turn lanes. The downside is the many long, poorly timed multi-directional traffic signals. Even so, driving US 192 is easy compared with International Drive. Best of all, there are no godawful intersections like the one at I-Drive and Sand Lake Road.

Conspicuous mile markers are posted along US 192. If you know which marker is closest to your hotel, navigation is a snap. The main entrance (Maingate) to Disney World is between Mile Markers 6 and 7, and almost all US 192 hotels and restaurants are between Mile

Markers 4 and 15. If your hotel is between Markers 5 and 8, no sneak routes are necessary; if it's between Markers 1 and 5, save time by entering Disney property via **Sherberth Road,** which runs into Disney's Animal Kingdom and the west end of Osceola Parkway. This road existed before Animal Kingdom or Osceola Parkway, but there are few signs on US 192 indicating that Sherberth affords a shortcut into and out of Disney property. After you turn onto Sherberth from US 192, bear right almost immediately at the fork. Continue until you reach a major intersection with Disney signage. Turn right and then continue straight to Osceola Parkway and most of Disney World, or go left to Animal Kingdom Lodge. To get to Animal Kingdom, turn right and look immediately for the turn lane that will take you into the theme park's parking lot. Osceola Parkway, a toll road, doesn't levy tolls until it crosses I-4 and leaves Disney property.

If your hotel is between Markers 8 and 15, save time (but pay modest tolls) by taking **Osceola Parkway** west to Disney World. If your hotel is between Markers 8 and 11, go north on **Poinciana Boulevard** to access Osceola. If your hotel is between Markers 11 and 15, go north on **FL 535 (Apopka–Vineland Road)** and turn west on Osceola to reach Disney's Animal Kingdom and Disney's Hollywood Studios. For Epcot, the Magic Kingdom, and Disney Springs, continue on FL 535 past Osceola to the intersection with **FL 536/World Center Drive;** then turn left on FL 536 and follow the signs to your Disney destination.

FL 535 (APOPKA–VINELAND ROAD) There are a number of hotels northeast and southwest of I-4 on FL 535 and on streets connecting to it. Though many guests commute to the parks through Disney property via Hotel Plaza Drive to Disney Springs and then via Buena Vista Drive, it's much easier to take I-4 west from FL 535 and enter Disney property on **Epcot Center Drive** for Epcot and the Magic Kingdom, or on **Osceola Parkway** for Disney's Hollywood Studios and Disney's Animal Kingdom.

I-4 Expect heavy traffic and possible delays westbound on I-4 from 7 to about 9:30 a.m. Eastbound toward Orlando, expect heavy traffic from 4 to 7 p.m. If you want to avoid I-4 altogether, check out our I-4 sneak routes, detailed in the map on the previous page.

TAKING A SHUTTLE BUS FROM YOUR OUT-OF-THE-WORLD HOTEL

MANY INDEPENDENT HOTELS and motels near Disney World provide trams and buses. They're fairly carefree, depositing you near theme park entrances and saving you parking fees. The rub is that they might not get you there as early as you desire (a critical point if you take our touring advice) or be available when you wish to return to your lodging. Each service is different; check details before you make reservations.

*un*official **TIP**
Warning: Most shuttles don't add vehicles at park-opening or -closing times. In the mornings, you may not get a seat.

Some shuttles go directly to Disney World, while others stop at other hotels en route. This can be a problem if your hotel is the second or third stop on the route. During periods of high demand, buses frequently fill up at the first stop, leaving little or no room for passengers at subsequent stops. Before booking, inquire how many hotels are on the route and the sequence of the stops. The different hotels are often so close together that you can easily walk to the first hotel on the route and board there. Similarly, if there's a large hotel nearby, it might have its own dedicated bus service that is more efficient. Use it instead of the service provided by your hotel. The majority of out-of-the-World shuttles work on a fixed schedule instead of arriving and departing somewhat randomly like the Disney buses. Knowing exactly when a bus will depart makes it easier to plan your day.

A multigenerational family from Seattle shares their experience:

> *We stayed at a hotel off-site and it was fine, but I think next time we'll stay in the World. The shuttles weren't all that convenient or frequent, so we ended up taking taxis more than we thought we would.*

At closing or during a hard rain, more people will be waiting for the shuttle than it can hold, and some will be left behind. Most shuttles return for stranded guests, but guests may wait 20 minutes to more than an hour.

If you're depending on shuttles, leave the park at least 45 minutes before closing. If you stay until closing and don't want the hassle of the shuttle, take a cab. Cab stands are near the Bus Information buildings at Disney's Animal Kingdom, Epcot, Disney's Hollywood Studios, and the TTC. If no cabs are on hand, a cast member will call one for you. If you're leaving the Magic Kingdom at closing, it's easier to take the monorail to a hotel and hail a cab from there rather than at the TTC.

unofficial **TIP**
If you want to go from resort to resort or almost anywhere else, you'll have to transfer at a bus hub.

THE DISNEY TRANSPORTATION SYSTEM

THE DISNEY TRANSPORTATION SYSTEM (**DTS**) is large, diversified, and generally efficient, but sometimes it's also overwhelmed, particularly at park-opening and -closing times. If you could be assured of getting on a bus, boat, or monorail at these critical times, we would advise you to leave your car at home. However, when huge crowds want to go somewhere at the same time, delays are unavoidable. In addition, some destinations are served directly, while many others require one or more transfers. Finally, it's sometimes difficult to figure how the buses, boats, and monorails interconnect.

Basically, Disney has a "hub and spoke" system. Hubs include the TTC, Disney Springs, and all four major theme parks (from 2 hours before official opening time to 1 hour after closing). With some exceptions, direct service is available from Disney resorts to the major theme parks and Disney Springs, as well as between parks.

If a hotel offers boat or monorail service, its bus service will be limited; you'll have to transfer at a hub for many destinations. If you're staying at a Magic Kingdom resort that's served by the monorail (**Contemporary and Bay Lake Tower, Grand Floridian & Villas, Polynesian Village & Villas**), you'll be able to commute efficiently to the Magic Kingdom. If you want to visit Epcot, you must take the monorail to the TTC and transfer to the Epcot monorail. (Guests at the Polynesian Village &

Villas can eliminate the transfer by walking 5–10 minutes to the TTC and catching the direct monorail to Epcot.)

If you're staying at an Epcot resort (**BoardWalk Inn & Villas, Dolphin, Swan, Yacht & Beach Club Resorts**), you can walk or commute by boat to Epcot's International Gateway (rear) entrance. Although direct buses link Epcot resorts to the Magic Kingdom and Disney's Animal Kingdom, there's no direct bus to Epcot's main entrance or Disney's Hollywood Studios. To reach the Studios from the Epcot resorts, you must take a boat or walk.

The **Caribbean Beach, Pop Century, Art of Animation, Saratoga Springs, Port Orleans, Coronado Springs, Old Key West, Animal Kingdom Lodge & Villas,** and **All-Star Resorts** offer direct buses to all theme parks. The rub is that guests sometimes must walk a long way to bus stops or endure more than a half-dozen additional pickups before actually heading for the park(s). Commuting in the morning from these resorts is generally easy, though you may have to ride standing. Returning in the evening, however, can be a different story. Shades of Green runs continuous shuttles from the resort to the TTC, where guests can transfer to their final destinations.

Hotels of the **Downtown Disney Resort Area (DDRA)** provide shuttle service through an independent company. (The exception is the **Hilton,** which runs its own service.) The DDRA shuttles constitute a negative for guests at these hotels—the service is simply substandard. Before you book a DDRA hotel, check the nature and frequency of its shuttles.

Guests staying at **Fort Wilderness Resort & Campground** must use its buses to reach boat landings or the Settlement Depot and Reception Outpost bus stops. From these points, guests can travel directly by boat to the Magic Kingdom or by bus to other destinations. Except for going to the Magic Kingdom, the best way for Fort Wilderness guests to commute is in their own car.

The Disney Transportation System vs. Driving Your Own Car

To help you assess your transportation options, we've developed a chart (see pages 468 and 469) comparing the approximate commuting times from Disney resorts to various Walt Disney World destinations, using Disney transportation or your own car.

DISNEY TRANSPORTATION Times on the chart in the "Disney System" columns represent an average-case and worst-case scenario. For example, if you want to go from the Caribbean Beach Resort to Epcot, the chart indicates the times as 35 (49). The first number, 35, indicates how many minutes your commute will take on an average day. It assumes that buses run every 17 minutes, there are no major delays, and everything else is as usual. It represents the average time we observed during our research of the transportation system. For the pessimists, the number in parentheses (49) indicates the worst-case scenario. (*Example:* The bus is pulling away as you arrive at the stop, and you must wait 17 minutes for the next one. When you finally board, the bus makes a number of additional stops before heading for Epcot. Once en route, the bus hits every red light.) When planning your transportation time, you'll do best to assume that your trip will take about the same time as the average in the chart (the first number). If you're running on a rigid schedule and you need to be sure of your arrival time, you can use the maximum time (the second number) to plan conservatively.

By far the biggest influence on your travel time between two points on the DTS is the amount of time you have to wait for your bus to arrive. Once you hop on your bus, the travel time is pretty consistent barring any unusual traffic problems; but your time waiting for the bus can vary greatly. Most cast members will tell you that buses run every 20 minutes. Our data indicates they run slightly more often—about every 16 minutes, an improvement of 1 minute over last year's numbers. Service at Old Key West and Saratoga Springs has improved the most: On average a bus arrives every 17 minutes now, down from 25 minutes last year.

Bus schedules are also adjusted based on demand and fuel costs. We observed and timed almost 560 bus routes for this edition of the book: The intervals between any two buses arriving at a resort and headed for the same destination ranged from 1 minute to 56 minutes, although the average wait is, as noted, around 17 minutes. Still, if you've ever waited for an Epcot bus while three empty Disney Springs buses drive past, you know that Disney still has a lot of opportunity to optimize its bus-routing system.

The first number in the chart expresses the average transportation time, but our data shows that about 20% of the time your actual travel time will be less than half the average. So don't be surprised if your trip from Caribbean Beach Resort to Epcot takes only 15 minutes instead of the 35 (49) listed. Consider yourself lucky and enjoy the extra 20 minutes, doing something fun.

DRIVING YOUR OWN CAR The "Your Car" column indicates the average case and worst-case scenarios for driving. To make these times directly comparable to DTS times, we added the time needed to get from your parked car to the park's entrance. While buses and monorails deposit guests at the park's entrance, those who drive must take a tram from their car to the gate or walk. At the Magic Kingdom, you must take a tram from the parking lot to the TTC, then catch a monorail or ferry to the entrance.

The Disney Transportation System for Teenagers

If you're staying at Disney World and have teens in your party, familiarize yourself with the Disney bus system. Safe, clean, and operating until 1 hour after the parks close (until 2 a.m. from Disney Springs), buses are a great way for teens to get around. Note that children under age 14 must be accompanied by someone age 14 or older to be admitted to the theme parks, water parks, and DisneyQuest.

Walt Disney World Bus Service

Disney buses have an illuminated panel above the windshield that flashes the bus's destination. Theme parks also have designated waiting areas for each Disney destination. To catch the bus to the Caribbean Beach Resort from Disney's Hollywood Studios, for example, go to the bus stop and wait in the area marked TO THE CARIBBEAN BEACH RESORT. At the resorts, go to any bus stop and wait for the bus displaying your destination on the illuminated panel. Directions to Disney

Door-to-Door Commuting Times to and from the Disney Resorts and Parks

AVERAGE TIME (maximum time) IN MINUTES FROM	TO MAGIC KINGDOM		TO EPCOT		TO DHS	
	YOUR CAR	DISNEY SYSTEM	YOUR CAR	DISNEY SYSTEM	YOUR CAR	DISNEY SYSTEM
ALL-STAR RESORTS	37 (47)	20 (26)	18 (23)	25 (32)	16 (20)	17 (24)
ANIMAL KINGDOM	37 (48)	50 (68)	16 (17)	27 (38)	16 (17)	24 (34)
ANIMAL KINGDOM LODGE & VILLAS	39 (50)	19 (37)	19 (21)	27 (41)	18 (19)	22 (32)
ART OF ANIMATION RESORT	40 (51)	20 (30)	23 (28)	19 (30)	20 (24)	18 (28)
BEACH CLUB	36 (46)	23 (33)	16 (21)	18 (29*)	14 (18)	26 (37)
BLIZZARD BEACH	36 (46)	28 (39)	18 (23)	51 (70)	18 (22)	39 (54)
BOARDWALK INN & VILLAS	36 (46)	19 (31)	16 (21)	11 (22*)	14 (18)	26 (37)
CARIBBEAN BEACH	37 (47)	31 (43)	18 (23)	35 (49)	15 (19)	23 (33)
CONTEMPORARY-BAY LAKE	—	12 (17)	21 (26)	21 (29)	23 (27)	29 (39)
CORONADO SPRINGS	37 (47)	23 (32)	18 (23)	20 (28)	16 (20)	18 (26)
DHS	36 (46)	25 (35)	19 (24)	25 (35)	—	—
DISNEY SPRINGS	Bus service only back to your Disney resort					
DOLPHIN	35 (45)	20 (30)	15 (20)	24 (36*)	15 (19)	22 (32)
DOWNTOWN DISNEY RESORT AREA	41 (51)	69 (91)	21 (26)	47 (62)	20 (24)	45 (60)
EPCOT	36 (46)	26 (37)	—	—	19 (23)	21 (30)
FORT WILDERNESS	37 (47)	17 (27)	18 (23)	49 (67)	19 (23)	39 (54)
GRAND FLORIDIAN & VILLAS	—	7 (8)	18 (23)	33 (45)	20 (24)	23 (33)
MAGIC KINGDOM	—	—	26 (39)	33 (45)	22 (29)	24 (34)
OLD KEY WEST	36 (46)	24 (40)	18 (23)	24 (36)	18 (22)	25 (44)
POLYNESIAN VILLAGE	—	11 (14)	17 (22)	38 (53**)	19 (23)	19 (29)
POP CENTURY RESORT	40 (51)	26 (32)	23 (28)	23 (30)	20 (24)	18 (30)
PORT ORLEANS FRENCH QUARTER	37 (47)	25 (43)	19 (24)	24 (41)	19 (23)	25 (44)
PORT ORLEANS RIVERSIDE	38 (48)	24 (46)	20 (25)	20 (34)	20 (24)	25 (47)
SARATOGA SPRINGS	38 (48)	25 (41)	18 (23)	29 (43)	20 (24)	31 (45)
SHADES OF GREEN	28 (36)	35 (49)	18 (23)	33 (45)	20 (24)	20 (28)
SWAN	35 (45)	19 (43)	15 (20)	24 (36*)	15 (19)	22 (32)
TREEHOUSE VILLAS	37 (47)	27 (38)	18 (23)	27 (38)	19 (23)	25 (36)
TYPHOON LAGOON	37 (47)	41 (56)	18 (23)	51 (70)	15 (19)	62 (85)
WILDERNESS LODGE	—	20 (35)	20 (25)	22 (35)	22 (26)	27 (45)
YACHT CLUB	36 (46)	25 (40)	16 (21)	26 (57*)	14 (18)	34 (45)

\# Transportation between Disney Springs and the parks requires transfers at a nearby resort.

* This hotel is within walking distance of Epcot; time given is for boat transportation to the International Gateway (Epcot's rear entrance).

** By foot to Transportation and Ticket Center and then by Epcot monorail

† Driving time vs. time on DTS. Driving times include time in your car, stops to pay tolls, time to park, and transfers on Disney trams and monorails where applicable.

in Your Car Versus the Disney Transportation System †

	TO ANIMAL KINGDOM		TO TYPHOON LAGOON		TO DOWNTOWN DISNEY		TO BLIZZARD BEACH	
	YOUR CAR	DISNEY SYSTEM	YOUR CAR	DISNEY SYSTEM	YOUR CAR	DISNEY SYSTEM	YOUR CAR	DISNEY SYSTEM
	11 (12)	19 (35)	12 (13)	28 (50)	13 (14)	29 (51)	6 (7)	29 (39)
	—	—	17 (19)	45 (63)	19 (21)	—	10 (13)	21 (30)
	9 (10)	17 (31)	19 (21)	44 (62)	22 (24)	32 (54)	11 (14)	27 (39)
	14 (16)	18 (27)	12 (14)	26 (42)	15 (16)	29 (44)	10 (12)	22 (31)
	17 (18)	24 (36)	9 (10)	29 (41)	10 (11)	22 (33)	12 (13)	28 (40)
	10 (13)	26 (38)	13 (14)	60 (83)	14 (15)	—	—	—
	17 (18)	20 (32)	9 (10)	24 (51)	10 (11)	25 (52)	12 (13)	20 (32)
	17 (18)	31 (45)	6 (7)	26 (38)	7 (8)	30 (42)	12 (13)	40 (56)
	20 (21)	25 (37)	17 (18)	27 (39)	16 (17)	37 (52)	15 (16)	42 (58)
	11 (12)	18 (27)	12 (13)	17 (25)	13 (14)	27 (39)	6 (7)	24 (35)
	16 (17)	20 (30)	8 (9)	57 (79)	9 (10)	—	11 (12)	36 (51)
Bus service only back to your Disney resort								
	16 (17)	23 (35)	10 (11)	33 (47)	11 (12)	27 (39)	11 (12)	19 (28)
	21 (22)	48 (64)	9 (10)	6 (9)	6 (7)	—	16 (17)	46 (61)
	16 (17)	33 (48)	12 (13)	30 (42)	13 (14)	—	11 (12)	31 (45)
	24 (25)	41 (57)	10 (11)	37 (52)	11 (12)	45 (63)	19 (20)	42 (58)
	18 (19)	23 (35)	15 (16)	39 (55)	16 (17)	49 (68)	13 (14)	30 (44)
	17 (18)	45 (63)	23 (31)	39 (55)	27 (36)	—	12 (13)	41 (57)
	19 (20)	31 (57)	8 (9)	22 (33)	9 (10)	27 (40)	14 (15)	35 (50)
	17 (18)	19 (31)	14 (15)	44 (62)	15 (16)	54 (75)	12 (13)	32 (46)
	14 (16)	23 (29)	12 (14)	28 (48)	15 (16)	31 (50)	10 (12)	41 (51)
	19 (20)	29 (42)	9 (10)	26 (52)	10 (11)	27 (53)	14 (15)	24 (37)
	20 (21)	33 (54)	10 (11)	24 (41)	11 (12)	26 (53)	15 (16)	20 (28)
	21 (22)	36 (49)	9 (10)	24 (35)	6 (7)	29 (44)	16 (17)	34 (49)
	18 (19)	22 (33)	15 (16)	39 (55)	18 (20)	49 (68)	13 (14)	30 (44)
	16 (17)	19 (44)	10 (11)	33 (47)	11 (12)	35 (46)	11 (12)	19 (28)
	17 (19)	41 (59)	—	—	6 (7)	16 (24)	13 (14)	42 (60)
	20 (21)	28 (40)	9 (10)	23 (34)	8 (9)	—	15 (16)	35 (50)
	20 (21)	30 (47)	17 (18)	33 (51)	18 (19)	30 (48)	15 (16)	25 (42)
	17 (18)	22 (38)	8 (10)	37 (49)	10 (12)	29 (59)	12 (13)	36 (48)

destinations are available when you check in or at your hotel's Guest Relations desk. Guest Relations can also answer questions about the transportation system.

Service from resorts to major theme parks is fairly direct. You may have intermediate stops, but you won't have to transfer. Service to the water parks and other Disney resorts sometimes requires transfers.

The fastest way to commute among resorts by bus is to take a bus from your resort to one of the major theme parks and then transfer there to a bus for your resort destination. This works, of course, only when the parks are open—actually, from 1 hour before opening until 1 hour after closing. (Disney buses stop taking passengers *to* the theme parks when they close, but they'll take passengers *from* the parks for an hour afterward.) If you're trying to commute to another resort for a late dinner during the off-season, when parks close early, you'll have to transfer at Disney Springs—which Disney, in its transportation instructions, lists somewhat disingenuously as the transfer point for *all* resort-to-resort commuting, hoping you'll stop and drop some dough en route. If the theme park buses are running, however, proceed to the park closest to your resort and transfer to the bus going to the resort where you'll be dining.

Despite what Disney's official schedule says, bus service to the theme parks begins about 7:30 a.m. on days when official park opening is 9 a.m. Generally, the buses run every 20 minutes. Buses to all four parks deliver you to the park entrance.

To be on hand for opening time (when official opening is 9 a.m.), catch direct buses to Epcot, Disney's Animal Kingdom, and Disney's Hollywood Studios between 7:30 and 8 a.m. Catch direct buses to the Magic Kingdom between 8 and 8:15 a.m. If you must transfer to reach your park, leave 15–20 minutes earlier. On days when official opening is 7 or 8 a.m., move up your departure time accordingly.

For your return bus trip in the evening, leave the park 40 minutes to an hour before closing to avoid the rush. If you're caught in the exodus, you may be inconvenienced, but you won't be stranded. Buses, boats, and monorails continue to operate for 1 hour after the parks close.

A woman from Charlotte, North Carolina, thinks Disney bus service needs some work:

> The bus service to the parks from Animal Kingdom Lodge was poor in the evenings. Twice we had to wait an hour because there were so many people. I think Animal Kingdom Lodge should use the chain system [i.e., create an organized queuing area] like the Value resorts do to maintain the queue. Guests pushed their way to the front when others had clearly been waiting longer.

From a Decatur, Georgia, reader:

> I was really gung-ho about staying on-site and using the buses, but having done it, I probably wouldn't do it again. The buses were just too crowded and unpleasant. Even staying at one of the closest resorts (by bus), we found it took about an hour each way by the time we walked to the bus stations, waited, and walked back to our rooms.

A reader who stayed at Port Orleans reports:

> The Disney transportation system was wildly erratic, but we ended up with more luck than not. For every time we had to wait a half-hour at the bus stop, there were two or three times with no wait at all.

If you're planning on riding a bus from Port Orleans Riverside to a park around opening time, going to the West or North bus stop may be your best option. These are the first stops on the route, and the bus is sometimes full or standing-room-only before it gets to all the stops.

From a Huntsville, Alabama, mother of three:

> Best advice given was driving to the park instead of relying on buses.

Not All Hubs Are Created Equal

All major theme parks, Disney Springs, and the TTC are hubs on the bus system. If your route requires you to transfer at a hub, transfer at the closest park or the TTC, except at park closing time. Avoid Disney Springs as a transfer point—traffic around the complex slows everything to a crawl.

As elsewhere in Walt Disney World, bus service at Disney Springs is a crapshoot. A Lindenhurst, New York, mom who stayed at the All-Star Resorts recounts her experience:

> The one big problem we had was the bus coming back from Disney Springs. We waited for an hour, and during that time six buses came for Pop Century and five for Art of Animation. Only two buses came to service the All-Star hotels, but because they were already full from picking up people at the other stop, they couldn't take any more passengers! We called to try to get more buses sent, but they just kept telling us that another bus would come in 15–20 minutes.
>
> Finally, we gave up and took a taxi back to the hotel. As we were leaving, two workers reprimanded me for stepping out into the road to get around the line, which was now at least 75–100 people long. Really? You do nothing about the line, you don't try to get us another bus, but that you do? Once we got back to the hotel, though, the person I spoke to was very understanding and reimbursed me for the cab.

This reader likewise found himself in bus hell:

> I budgeted an HOUR for the return trip from Disney Springs to Animal Kingdom Lodge on the morning of our departure, and I STILL found myself on the phone with Magical Express 30 minutes before our bus was supposed to leave for the airport, asking when the next bus after that would leave AKL. We barely made the backup bus. This was NOT a "magical" ending to my vacation.

Except at Fort Wilderness, no buses run between the TTC and the Disney resorts. If you're commuting from resort to resort, you must transfer at Disney Springs or one of the major theme parks during park operating hours. If you're parked at the TTC and you want to travel to a Disney resort, go to the right of the Magic Kingdom entrance to catch a bus to your destination.

When All Else Fails, Take a Cab

Sometimes depending on Disney transportation, especially buses, is just too stressful if you absolutely have to be at a certain place at a certain time. Happily, taxi service is available at all resorts, the theme parks, Disney Springs, and many other Disney World locations. Fares for short hauls within the World generally run $8–$18. The time saved, plus the peace of mind, makes the expenditure worthwhile to many guests, including this Washington, DC, reader:

> I found Disney transportation unreliable when I really needed it at park opening and closing times. My first night at Epcot, after Illumi-Nations, the bus line was so long—and so stalled—that I decided it made more sense to shell out for a cab than to wait another hour to get back to my hotel. Likewise at other busy times throughout the World.

Even shelling out $80 or so for a few cab fares cost less than renting a car for a week.

Walt Disney World Monorail Service

Picture the monorail system as three loops. Loop A is an express route that runs counterclockwise connecting the Magic Kingdom with the TTC. Loop B runs clockwise alongside Loop A, making all stops, with service (in order) to the TTC, Polynesian Village & Villas, Grand Floridian & Villas, the Magic Kingdom, Contemporary Resort and Bay Lake Tower, and back to the TTC. The long Loop C dips southeast, connecting the TTC with Epcot. The hub for all loops is the TTC (where you usually park to visit the Magic Kingdom).

unofficial **TIP**
Monorails run for 1 hour after the Magic Kingdom and Epcot close. If a train is too crowded or you need transportation after the monorails have stopped (for example, during Evening Extra Magic Hours), catch a bus or boat. *Note:* As a safety measure, Disney prohibits guests from riding in the front of a train.

The monorail that serves the Magic Kingdom resorts usually starts running an hour and a half before official park opening. If you're staying at a Magic Kingdom resort and you wish to be among the first into the Magic Kingdom when official opening is 9 a.m., board the monorail at these times:

From the Contemporary Resort and Bay Lake Tower	7:45–8 a.m.
From the Polynesian Village Resort	7:50–8:05 a.m.
From the Grand Floridian Resort & Villas	8–8:10 a.m.

If you're a day guest, you'll be allowed on the monorail at the TTC between 8:15 and 8:30 a.m. when official opening is 9 a.m. If you want to board earlier, walk from the TTC to the Polynesian Village Resort and board there.

The monorail connecting Epcot and the TTC begins operating at 7:30 a.m. when Epcot's official opening is 9 a.m. To be at Epcot when it opens, catch the Epcot monorail at the TTC by 8:05 a.m.

While your Park Hopper pass suggests you can flit among parks, getting there is more complicated. For example, you can't go directly from the Magic Kingdom to Epcot. You must catch the express monorail (Loop A) to the TTC and transfer to the Loop C monorail to Epcot. If lines to board either monorail are short, you can usually reach Epcot in 30–40 minutes. But should you want to go to Epcot for dinner (as many do) and you're departing the Magic Kingdom in late afternoon, you may have to wait 30 minutes or longer to board the Loop A monorail. Adding this delay boosts your commute to 50–60 minutes.

PART EIGHT

BARE NECESSITIES

 ## MONEY, *Etc.*

CREDIT CARDS, MOBILE PAYMENTS, AND DISNEY GIFT CARDS

ACCEPTED THROUGHOUT WALT DISNEY WORLD are **American Express, Diners Club, Discover, Japan Credit Bureau, MasterCard,** and **Visa.** If you've got one of these credit cards linked to an iPhone 6 or newer, you can use **Apple Pay,** too.

Disney Gift Cards can be used at most Disney-owned and-operated stores and restaurants, and for recreational activities, tickets, and parking. See **disneygiftcard.com** for details.

BANKING SERVICES

AT THE THEME PARKS, banking is limited to ATMs, which are marked on park maps and are plentiful throughout Walt Disney World; most MasterCard and Visa cards are accepted. To get cash with an American Express card, you must sign an agreement with Amex before your trip.

If your card won't work in the ATMs, tellers at **SunTrust Bank** full-service locations will process your transaction. The SunTrust closest to the World is at 1675 E. Buena Vista Dr., across from Disney Springs Marketplace; for other Orlando-area branches, visit **suntrust.com.**

CURRENCY EXCHANGE

IN THE MAGIC KINGDOM, it's at **Guest Relations** in City Hall, on Main Street, U.S.A., at the park entrance. In Epcot, it's at Guest Relations on the west side of the Epcot Entrance Plaza. In the Studios or Animal Kingdom, exchange your euros, krones, or zloty at Guest Relations to the left of the entrance turnstiles. Disney Springs' two Guest Relations locations are at the Marketplace and the West Side.

A LICENSE TO PRINT MONEY

ONE OF DISNEY'S MORE SUBLIME PLOYS for separating you from your money is the printing and issuing of **Disney Dollars.** Available throughout Disney World or in advance by phone (☎ 407-566-4985) in denominations of $1, $5, and $10, each emblazoned with a Disney character or ride, the colorful cash can be used for purchases in Disney World, Disneyland, and Disney Stores nationwide; it can also be exchanged one-for-one with US currency, but only while you're in Disney World (you'll need your sales receipt for the exchange).

Some guests keep the money as souvenirs; others forget to spend or exchange it before they leave the World, then forget to redeem it at a Disney Store after their trip. A Michigan family, however, found a way to make their Disney Dollars useful:

> Since we had planned on going to Disney a year ahead of time, we asked people who were our children money for birthdays, Christmas, Tooth Fairy, etc., to give Disney Dollars instead. This forced both of our children (ages 5 and 7) to save the money for the trip.

VISITING MORE THAN ONE PARK IN A SINGLE DAY

IF YOUR ADMISSION ALLOWS YOU to visit all four theme parks in the same day, it will be validated with the date when you enter your first park. To enter another park, present your pass or MagicBand and have the fingertip of your index finger scanned by a biometric reader. Your admission must include the Park Hopper option—you can't use two "days" of admission to visit two parks on the same date.

PROBLEMS *and* UNUSUAL SITUATIONS

ATTRACTIONS CLOSED FOR REPAIRS

FIND OUT IN ADVANCE what rides and attractions may be closed during your visit. For complete refurbishment schedules, check online at **touringplans.com** or use our mobile app, **Lines.**

CAR TROUBLE

SECURITY PATROLS WILL HELP if you lock the keys in your parked car or find the battery dead. For more serious problems, the closest repair facility is the **Car Care Center,** near the Magic Kingdom parking lot (☎ 407-824-0976; open Monday–Friday, 7 a.m.–7 p.m.; Saturday, 7 a.m.–4 p.m., and Sunday, 8 a.m.–3 p.m.).

The nearest off-World repair center is **Maingate Citgo,** on US 192 west of I-4; (7424 W. Irlo Bronson Memorial Hwy., ☎ 407-396-2721). Farther away but highly recommended by local *Unofficial Guide* researchers is **Riker's Automotive & Tire** (5700 Central Florida Pkwy., near SeaWorld; ☎ 407-238-9800; **rikersauto.com**).

CELL PHONE SNAFUS

THIS WOMAN from Leawood, Kansas, spells out the problem:

> In our group, we were using three different carriers, and we all had problems sending and receiving texts and making calls.

The problem of signal strength is compounded by crowd noise and the ambient music played throughout the parks. Even if you have a decent signal, it's an exasperating challenge to find someplace quiet enough to have a conversation. When possible, text instead of call.

GASOLINE

THERE ARE THREE **Hess** gas stations on Disney property. One station is adjacent to the Car Care Center on the exit road from the Transportation and Ticket Center (Magic Kingdom) parking lot. It's also convenient to the Shades of Green, Grand Floridian, and Polynesian Village resorts. Most centrally located is the station at the corner of Buena Vista Drive and Epcot Resorts Boulevard, near the BoardWalk Inn. A third station, also on Buena Vista Drive, is across from Disney Springs.

LOST AND FOUND

IF YOU LOSE (OR FIND) SOMETHING in the Magic Kingdom, go to **City Hall.** At Epcot, Lost and Found is behind Spaceship Earth. At Disney's Hollywood Studios, it's at **Hollywood Boulevard Guest Relations,** and at Disney's Animal Kingdom, it's at **Guest Relations** at the main entrance. If you discover you've lost something after you've left the parks, call ☎ 407-824-4245 (for all parks); see page 30 for the numbers to call while in the parks.

It's unusual for readers to send us tips about Lost and Found, but a mom from Indianapolis sent two!

If you lose something on a ride and it has medication in it, Disney cast members will shut down a ride for 45 seconds to try to retrieve it. If they can't find it or it didn't contain meds, you have to come back to Lost and Found for it at the end of the day.

Also, don't forget to write down the serial numbers on your passes (if you have them). With the serial number, a cast member can look up when it was last used, giving you an idea of where it was lost.

LOST MAGICBANDS Duplicates can be made at Guest Relations at any theme park or resort.

LOST CARS Don't forget where you parked—write down your section and row, send yourself a text, or snap a picture with your phone or digital camera.

MEDICAL MATTERS

HEADACHE RELIEF Aspirin and other sundries are sold at the **Emporium** on Main Street, U.S.A. in the Magic Kingdom (behind the counter; you have to ask); at most retail shops in Epcot's Future World and World Showcase, Disney's Hollywood Studios, and Disney's Animal Kingdom; and at each Disney resort's gift shop.

ILLNESSES REQUIRING MEDICAL ATTENTION For the locations of the **First Aid Centers** in the theme parks, see the respective park chapters. Guests who use the service are generally very positive about it. This Hickory, North Carolina, reader's experience is representative:

We visited First Aid a time or two in the parks (my wife needed her blood pressure checked because she was worried about the heat and her pregnancy). We found trained medical staff, no wait, and all the friendliness and knowledge you would expect from Disney.

Off-property, a **Centra Care** walk-in clinic is located at 12500 S. Apopka–Vineland Rd. (☎ 407-934-CARE [2273]; open 8 a.m.–midnight weekdays and 8 a.m.–8 p.m. weekends). Centra Care also offers a 24-hour house-call service and runs a free shuttle (☎ 407-938-0650).

A North Carolina family of four had a good experience at **Buena Vista Urgent Care** (8216 World Center Dr., Suite D; ☎ 407-465-1110):

> We started day one needing medical care for our son, who has asthma and had developed croup. We found great care at Buena Vista Urgent Care. We waited 20 minutes, and then we were off to the parks.

The Medical Concierge (☎ 855-932-5252; themedicalconcierge .com) has board-certified physicians available 24-7 for house calls to your hotel room. They offer in-room X-rays and IV therapy service as well as same-day dental and specialist appointments. They also rent medical equipment. Insurance receipts, insurance billing, and foreign-language interpretation are provided. Walk-in clinics are also available.

DOCS (Doctors on Call Service; ☎ 407-399-DOCS; **doctorsoncall service.com**) also offers 24-hour house-call service. All physicians are certified by the American Board of Medical Specialties. A father of two from O'Fallon, Illinois, gives them a thumbs-up:

> My wife's cold developed into an ear infection that required medical attention, and DOCS was able to respond in 40 minutes. The doctor had medicine with him and was very professional and friendly.

Physician Room Service (☎ 407-238-2000; **physicianroomservice** .com) provides board-certified-doctor house calls to Disney World–area guest rooms for adults and children.

DENTAL NEEDS Call **Celebration Dental Group** (☎ 407-361-9704).

PRESCRIPTION MEDICINE Two drugstores nearby are **Walgreens** (12100 S. Apopka–Vineland Rd.; ☎ 407-238-0600) and **Turner Drugs** (12500 S. Apopka–Vineland Rd.; ☎ 407-828-8125; **turnerdrug.com**). Turner Drugs charges $7.50 to deliver a filled prescription to your Disney hotel's front desk, $10–$15 for non-Disney hotels. The fee is charged to your hotel account.

SGT. BLISTERBLASTER'S GUIDE TO HAPPY FEET

1. ON YOUR FEET! Get up, La-Z-Boy rider: When you go to Walt Disney World, you'll have to walk a lot farther than to the refrigerator. You can log 5–12 miles a day at the parks, so now's the time to shape up them dogs. Start with short walks around the neighborhood. Increase your distance gradually until you can do 6 miles without CPR.

2. A-TEN-SHUN! During your training program, pay attention when those puppies growl. They'll give you a lot of information about your feet and the appropriateness of your shoes. Listen up! No walking in flip-flops, loafers, or sandals. Wear well-constructed, broken-in running or hiking shoes. If you feel a "hot spot," that means a blister is developing. The most common sites for blisters are heels, toes, and balls of the feet. If you develop a hot spot in the same place every time you walk (a clue!), cover it with a Johnson & Johnson blister bandage or cushion (in drugstores without a prescription) before you set out.

3. SOCK IT UP, TRAINEE! Good socks are as important as good shoes. When you walk, your feet sweat like a mule in a peat bog, and the moisture only increases friction. To minimize friction, wear a pair of sock made from material such as SmartWool or CoolMax, which wicks perspiration away from your feet (SmartWool socks come in varying thicknesses). To further combat moisture, dust your dogs with antifungal talcum powder.

4. WHO DO YOU THINK YOU ARE, JOHN WAYNE? Don't be a hero. Take care of a foot problem the minute you notice it. Carry a small foot-emergency kit for your platoon. Include gauze, antibiotic ointment, disinfectant, moleskin or Johnson & Johnson blister bandages, scissors, a sewing needle or something else sharp (to drain blisters), and matches to sterilize the needle. Extra socks and talcum powder are optional.

5. BITE THE BULLET! If you develop a hot spot, cover it ASAP with a blister bandage. Cut the material large enough to cover the skin surrounding the spot. If you develop a blister, air out and dry your foot. Next, drain the fluid, but don't remove the top skin. Clean the area with disinfectant and place a blister bandage over the blister. The bandages come in several sizes, including specially shaped ones for fingers and toes; they're also good for covering hot spots. If you don't have blister bandages, don't cover the hot spot or blister with Band-Aids (they'll slip and wad up)—head to a park First Aid Center instead.

6. TAKE CARE OF YOUR PLATOON. If you have young, green troops in your outfit, they might not sound off when a hot spot develops. Stop several times a day and check their feet. If you forgot your emergency kit and a problem arises, stop by a First Aid Center. They have all the stuff you need to keep your command in action.

RAIN

WEATHER BAD? Go to the parks anyway. The crowds are lighter, and most attractions and waiting areas are under cover. Showers, especially during warmer months, are short.

Ponchos are about $8, umbrellas about $12. All ponchos sold at Disney World are made of clear plastic, so picking out somebody in your party on a rainy day can be tricky. Amazon sells an inexpensive orange poncho that will make your family pumpkin-colored beacons in a plastic-covered sea of humanity.

unofficial **TIP**
Raingear isn't always displayed in shops, so you have to ask for it.

A Wilmington, North Carolina, mom thinks high-quality raingear is worth the investment:

> *We're outdoor-sports people, so we have very good raincoats. It rained every day on this trip, driving many people out of the parks and leaving others looking miserable in their ponchos. Meanwhile, we hardly noticed the rain from inside our high-end jackets as we walked right onto many of the attractions.*

Some unusually heavy rain precipitated (no pun intended) dozens of reader suggestions for dealing with soggy days. The best came from this Memphis, Tennessee, mom:

1. Rain gear should include ponchos *and* umbrellas. When rain isn't beating down on your ponchoed head, it's easier to ignore.

2. If you're using a stroller, bring a plastic sheet or an extra poncho to protect it from rain. (Ponchos cover only Disney's single strollers.) Carry a towel in a plastic bag to wipe off your stroller after experiencing an attraction during a rainfall.

Unofficial Guide researcher Connie Wolosyk adds, "Wear a baseball cap under the poncho hood—without it, the hood never covers your head properly and your face always gets wet."

HOW TO LODGE A COMPLAINT WITH DISNEY

COMPLAINING ABOUT A LEAKY FAUCET or not having enough towels is pretty straightforward, and you usually will find Disney folks highly responsive. But a more global gripe, or one beyond an on-site manager's ability to resolve, is likely to disappear in the labyrinth of Disney bureaucracy.

One of our readers' foremost gripes relates to Disney's unresponsiveness in fielding complaints. A Providence, Rhode Island, dad's remarks are typical:

It's all warm fuzzies and big smiles until you have a problem—then everybody plays hide-and-seek. The only thing you know for sure is it's never the responsibility of the Disney person you're talking to.

A Mobile, Alabama, mother echoes his comment:

I made call after call, with one Disney person passing me on to the next, until finally I ran out of steam. Basically, I had to choose between getting my problem addressed, which was pretty much a full-time job, or going ahead with my vacation.

A Portland, Maine, reader summed it up in quintessential New England style:

Lodging a complaint with Disney is like shouting at a brick.

Like most companies, Disney would rather hear from you when the news is good. Regarding complaints, Disney prefers to receive them in writing, but by the time you get home and draft a letter, it's often too late to correct the problem. And though Disney would have you believe that it's a touchy-feely outfit, it generally isn't a company that will make things right for you after the fact. You may receive a letter thanking you for writing and expressing regret without actually acknowledging responsibility (for example, "We're sorry you felt inconvenienced"—as if the perception somehow arose from your imagination). It's unlikely, though, that they'll offer to fix anything.

If you still want to lodge a complaint, write to **Walt Disney World Guest Communications, PO Box 10040, Lake Buena Vista, FL 32830-0040.** If you're *really* steamed, you can fire off a letter to the following higher-ups:

Robert Iger, CEO	Bob Chapek, Chairman	George Kalogridis, President
The Walt Disney Company	Walt Disney Parks & Resorts	Walt Disney World
500 S. Buena Vista St.	500 S. Buena Vista St.	PO Box 10040
Burbank, CA 91521	Burbank, CA 91521	Lake Buena Vista, FL 32830

If Disney still doesn't respond, you can always go public:

Letters to the Editor, *Orlando Sentinel*
633 N. Orange Ave., MP-218
Orlando, FL 32801-1349
☎ 407-420-5000; fax 407-420-5286; **insight@orlandosentinel.com**

SERVICES

MESSAGES

MESSAGES LEFT at **City Hall** in the Magic Kingdom, **Guest Relations** at Epcot, **Hollywood Boulevard Guest Relations** at Disney's Hollywood Studios, or **Guest Relations** at Disney's Animal Kingdom can be retrieved at any of the four.

PET CARE

ACROSS FROM THE PORT ORLEANS RESORTS, the plush **Best Friends Pet Resort** accommodates up to 270 dogs in a variety of standard and luxury suites, some with private outdoor patios and play yards; the Kitty City pavilion houses up to 30 felines in two- and four-story cat condos. There's also a separate area just for birds and "pocket pets" such as hamsters. Encompassing more than 17,000 square feet of air-conditioned indoor space plus 10,000 square feet of covered outdoor runs and play areas, the resort is open to both Walt Disney World resort guests and visitors staying off-property. For more information, call ☎ 877-4-WDW-PETS (877-493-9738) or visit **bestfriendspetcare .com**. (*Note:* Pet parents must provide written proof of current vaccination from a vet, either at check-in or by fax at 203-840-5266.)

PHOTOS

FOR YEARS NOW, Walt Disney World has employed roving bands of photographers to take digital photos of families who don't use their own cameras. And, of course, Disney sells those pictures back to you through a website, where you can choose the images you want to keep, customize them with text and colorful borders, order photo CDs, and so on.

The latest iteration of the photo program, called **Memory Maker** (**disneyworld.disney.go.com/memory-maker**), costs $169 if you buy it in advance, $199 if you buy it in the parks. Memory Maker replaces Disney's PhotoPass system and adds to your package photos taken of your family on rides, such as Splash Mountain and Tower of Terror. Because Memory Maker is linked to your My Disney Experience (MDE) account (see page 36), you're also able to see photos of friends and family you've linked to there. Here's how it works:

unofficial **TIP**
You must have a My Disney Experience account to buy a Memory Maker package.

1. Find a Memory Maker photographer to take your first picture. Photographers roam throughout the theme parks and water parks, including near park entrances, in restaurants (and during character meals), and around iconic attractions such as Splash Mountain.

2. The photographer will scan your RFID ticket or MagicBand. This links your pictures to your MDE account. Onboard ride-photo systems should automatically detect your MagicBand and link the photos to your account.

3. Visit the MDE website within 45 days of your trip to view your photos. You can add decorative borders and short captions to your pictures, too, as well as share photos online.

If you're already logged in to MDE, your purchase will be automatically linked to your account. If not, you'll be asked to do so (or sign up for MDE) to complete the purchase.

You can download Memory Maker photos as many times as you want, subject to a few restrictions: First, if you prepurchase, you must do so at least three days before your trip in order to have all of your photos included. If you prepurchase fewer than three days before you arrive, you'll have to buy separately any photos taken during that three-day window. Next, Disney will store your photos for 45 days, so you'll need to download them promptly once you return home (you can also pay for extra time). Finally, once you've downloaded the first photo, you've got 30 days to download the rest. Disney grants you a limited license to reproduce the photos for personal use.

Because any two families can share a Memory Maker package via MDE, folks in the *Unofficial Guide* online community often split the cost with others traveling around the same time. It's a great way to get your photos at half-price. Visit **tinyurl.com/share-memory-maker** to find a partner on our discussion boards.

As of 2015, Walt Disney World no longer includes photo packages in the prices of its character meals.

EXCUSE ME, BUT WHERE CAN I FIND . . .

RELIGIOUS SERVICES IN THE WALT DISNEY WORLD AREA? See **allears .net/btp/church.htm** for a complete list.

SOMEPLACE TO CHARGE MY CELL PHONE? Charging stations are available near the *Tangled*-themed restrooms in Fantasyland in the Magic Kingdom; they're built into the faux-wood posts near the seating area. If you prefer to charge on the go, we use **Mophie** and **New Trent** external batteries for our devices. Both are available on **Amazon.com**.

SOMEPLACE TO PUT ALL THESE PACKAGES? Lockers are located on the ground floor of the Main Street railroad station in the Magic Kingdom, to the right of Spaceship Earth in Epcot, and on the Transportation and Ticket Center's east and west ends. At DHS, lockers are to the right of the entrance at Oscar's Super Service. Animal Kingdom lockers are to the left inside the entrance. Cost is $8 a day for small lockers and $10 a day for large lockers; prices include a $5 refundable deposit. Lockers at Blizzard Beach and Typhoon Lagoon water parks cost the same.

unofficial **TIP**
Be aware that Package Pick-Up closes 2 hours before the park. Disney resort guests can have their purchases delivered to their hotel's gift shop.

Package Pick-Up is available at the theme parks. Ask the salesperson to send your purchases to Package Pick-Up; when you leave the park, they'll be waiting for you. Epcot has two exits, thus two Package Pick-Ups; specify the main entrance or the International Gateway. If you're staying at a Disney resort, you can also have packages delivered to your resort's gift shop for pickup the following day. If you're leaving within 24 hours, though, take them with you or use the in-park pickup location.

AN OLD-FASHIONED CAMERA? Camera Centers at the parks sell disposable point-and-shooters with flash for around $18 plus tax ($21 for a waterproof version). Memory cards run $40–$60, so bring yours from home. Film developing is unavailable at Walt Disney World.

A GROCERY STORE? Avoid the **Gooding's Supermarket** in Crossroads Shopping Center. Its convenient location, across FL 535 from the Disney World entrance, is canceled out by poor selection and high prices. Instead, try the **Publix** just north of the intersection of Silverlake Park Drive and FL 535 or the **Winn-Dixie** on Apopka–Vineland Road, about a mile north of Crossroads Shopping Center.

The **Winn-Dixie** at US 192 on the west side of I-4 (7840 W. Irlo Bronson Memorial Hwy.; ☎ 407-397-2210) is the closest and largest grocery for visitors staying near the Sherberth Road or World Drive entrances to Disney World. The **Super Target** at 3200 Rolling Oaks Blvd. (☎ 407-321-3971) is the closest to the Western Way entrance.

We compiled a list of common vacation grocery items and went shopping (no item was on sale). The chart below shows how prices at **Garden Grocer** (see next page), the **Publix** at the Water Tower Shoppes in Celebration, the **Super Target** above, and the first **Winn-Dixie** above compare.

ITEM	GARDEN GROCER	PUBLIX	SUPER TARGET	WINN-DIXIE
12 DOUGHNUTS (store brand)	$8.38	$6.58	3.49	$4.49
MAXWELL HOUSE COFFEE (11.5 oz.)	$6.29	$4.31	$3.59	$4.79
COFFEE FILTERS (store brand, 200 count)	$2.49	$1.39	$2.04	$2.19
1 GALLON MILK (store brand)	$5.39	$3.79	$3.79	$4.09
TROPICANA ORANGE JUICE (59 oz.)	$5.99	$3.99	$3.79	$4.49
CHEERIOS (8.9 oz.)	$4.49	$3.83	$2.99	$3.79
COCA-COLA (12-pack, 12-oz. cans)	$6.99	$4.99	$5.99	$4.99
LAY'S POTATO CHIPS (10.5 oz.)	$5.39	$4.29	$4.29	$4.29
SUGAR (2 lbs., store brand)*	$4.19	$1.69	$2.64	$1.79
JIF PEANUT BUTTER (12 oz.)	$4.69	$2.99	$2.79	$3.19
CHIPS AHOY! COOKIES (13.72 oz.)	$4.49	$3.59	$2.54	$3.99
BANANAS (4 lbs.)**	$1.96	$2.76	$2.48	$2.76
WONDER BREAD (1 loaf)	$2.79	$2.69	$1.69	$1.99
BUDWEISER (12-pack, 12-oz. cans)	$13.99	$10.89	$11.49	$11.79
WELCH'S GRAPE JELLY (18 oz.)***	$3.49	$2.35	$1.99	$2.79
COLGATE TOOTHBRUSH	$2.49	0.99	$0.94	$1.99
BANANA BOAT SPORT SPF 30 SUNSCREEN (8 oz.)	$6.99	$7.99	$6.49	$8.99
TOTALS	**$90.49**	**$69.11**	**$63.02**	**$72.40**

   * *Super Target and Garden Grocer sell only 4-pound bags of sugar.*

  ** *Garden Grocer prices by the banana rather than by the pound.*

*** *Garden Grocer carries only Welch's jelly in the 30-ounce jar.*

GROCERY MARKETS THAT DELIVER? If you don't have a car or you don't want to take the time to go to the supermarket, **Garden Grocer (garden grocer.com)** will shop for you and deliver your groceries. The best way to compile your order is on Garden Grocer's website before you leave home. It's simple, the selection is huge, and it's easier to use (and cheaper) than its local competitor, **wegoshop.com.** If there's something you want that's not on their list of available items, they'll try to find it for you (including alcohol). Delivery arrangements are per your instructions. If you're staying at a hotel, you can arrange for your groceries to be left with bell services. For the sake of order-fulfillment accuracy and customer service, Garden Grocer is primarily set up for online ordering. If you can't get online, though, you can order by phone (☎ 866-855-4350). For orders of $200 or more, there's a $2 delivery fee; for orders less than $200, the delivery charge is $14; a minimum order of $40 is required. As of this writing, Garden Grocer doesn't deliver to the Swan or Dolphin. Also note that Garden Grocer's delivery schedule may fill completely around holidays, at which point they'll stop accepting orders for delivery on those dates.

We get lots of positive reader feedback about Garden Grocer. The following review from an Eagan, Minnesota, family is representative:

Garden Grocer was fabulous. I ordered our groceries online about one week before our arrival. I had a few questions, so I called and actually spoke with a human who was very helpful! Our flight got in about 7 p.m., and I called to let them know we were on our way. They arrived about 20 minutes after we did with everything we ordered.

WINE, BEER, AND LIQUOR? Wine and beer are sold in grocery stores. The best range of adult beverages is sold at the **ABC Fine Wine & Spirits** store less than a mile north of the Crossroads shopping center (11951 S. Apopka–Vineland Rd.; ☎ 407-239-0775).

PART NINE

The MAGIC KINGDOM

OPENED IN 1971, THE MAGIC KINGDOM was the first built of Walt Disney World's four theme parks. Many of the attractions found here are originals from that park opening, and a few—including **Cinderella Castle, Pirates of the Caribbean,** and **Splash Mountain**—have helped define the basic elements of theme park attractions the world over. Undoubtedly, the Magic Kingdom is what most people think of when they think of Walt Disney World.

Much of the Magic Kingdom was built by the same Disney staff who had built Disneyland almost two decades earlier. The remarkable achievement that Disney wrought in Orlando isn't that they could build a second, equally compelling theme park; rather, it's that they could do so on a much larger scale while keeping many of the fine details that make visiting a Disney park such a completely immersive experience.

NOT TO BE MISSED AT THE MAGIC KINGDOM	
ADVENTURELAND	• A Pirate's Adventure • Pirates of the Caribbean
FANTASYLAND	• Peter Pan's Flight • *Mickey's PhilharMagic* • Seven Dwarfs Mine Train
FRONTIERLAND	• Big Thunder Mountain Railroad • Splash Mountain
LIBERTY SQUARE	• The Haunted Mansion
SPECIAL EVENTS	• *Celebrate the Magic* • Evening Parade • *Wishes*
TOMORROWLAND	• *Space Mountain*

ARRIVING

IF YOU DRIVE, the Magic Kingdom **Transportation and Ticket Center (TTC)** parking lot opens about 2 hours before the park's official opening. For driving directions, see page 443. After paying a fee, you're directed to a parking space, then transported by tram to the TTC, where you catch either a monorail or a ferry to the park's entrance.

If you bring a stroller, a Ridgewood, New Jersey, family recommends the ferry (which starts operating 30–60 minutes before park opening):

The ferry from the TTC to the Magic Kingdom dock is a must if you're using a stroller. You can drive the stroller right onto the ferry and then just head to the back of the ferry to be the first ones off when it docks.

Continued on page 486

The Magic Kingdom

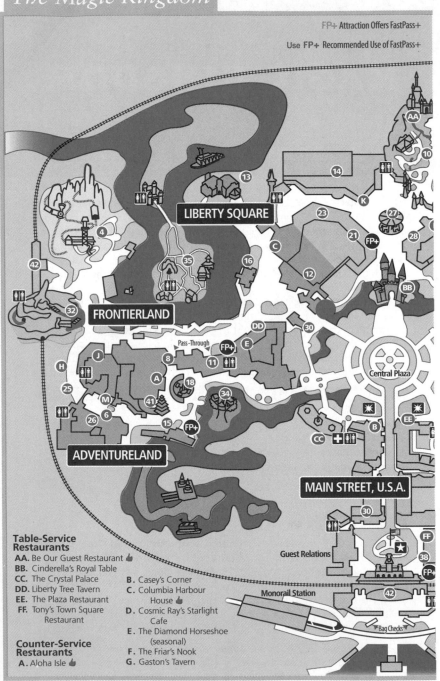

FP+ Attraction Offers FastPass+

Use FP+ Recommended Use of FastPass+

LIBERTY SQUARE

FRONTIERLAND

Pass-Through

Central Plaza

ADVENTURELAND

MAIN STREET, U.S.A.

Guest Relations

Monorail Station

Bag Checks

Table-Service Restaurants

AA. Be Our Guest Restaurant
BB. Cinderella's Royal Table
CC. The Crystal Palace
DD. Liberty Tree Tavern
EE. The Plaza Restaurant
FF. Tony's Town Square Restaurant

B. Casey's Corner
C. Columbia Harbour House
D. Cosmic Ray's Starlight Cafe
E. The Diamond Horseshoe (seasonal)
F. The Friar's Nook
G. Gaston's Tavern

Counter-Service Restaurants

A. Aloha Isle

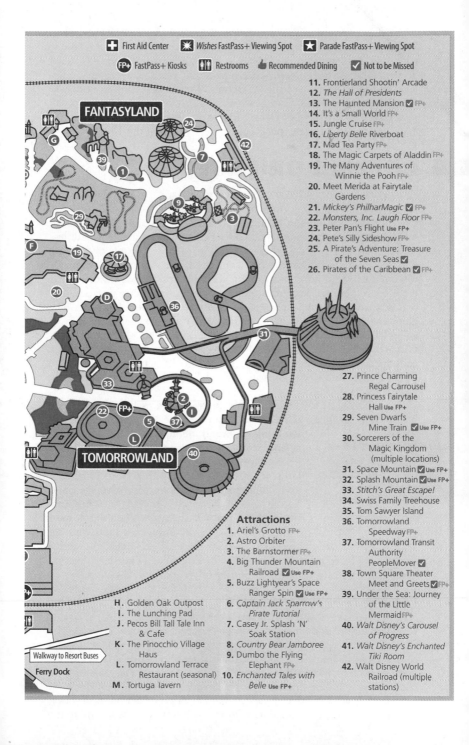

First Aid Center 　 Wishes FastPass+ Viewing Spot 　 Parade FastPass+ Viewing Spot

FP+ FastPass+ Kiosks 　 Restrooms 　 Recommended Dining 　 Not to be Missed

FANTASYLAND

TOMORROWLAND

Walkway to Resort Buses

Ferry Dock

11. Frontierland Shootin' Arcade
12. *The Hall of Presidents*
13. The Haunted Mansion ☑ FP+
14. It's a Small World FP+
15. Jungle Cruise FP+
16. *Liberty Belle* Riverboat
17. Mad Tea Party FP+
18. The Magic Carpets of Aladdin FP+
19. The Many Adventures of
    Winnie the Pooh FP+
20. Meet Merida at Fairytale
    Gardens
21. *Mickey's PhilharMagic* ☑ FP+
22. *Monsters, Inc. Laugh Floor* FP+
23. Peter Pan's Flight Use FP+
24. Pete's Silly Sideshow FP+
25. A Pirate's Adventure: Treasure
    of the Seven Seas ☑
26. Pirates of the Caribbean ☑ FP+

27. Prince Charming
    Regal Carrousel
28. Princess Fairytale
    Hall Use FP+
29. Seven Dwarfs
    Mine Train ☑ Use FP+
30. Sorcerers of the
    Magic Kingdom
    (multiple locations)
31. Space Mountain ☑ Use FP+
32. Splash Mountain ☑ Use FP+
33. *Stitch's Great Escape!*
34. Swiss Family Treehouse
35. Tom Sawyer Island
36. Tomorrowland
    Speedway FP+
37. Tomorrowland Transit
    Authority
    PeopleMover ☑
38. Town Square Theater
    Meet and Greets ☑ FP+
39. Under the Sea: Journey
    of the Little
    Mermaid FP+
40. *Walt Disney's Carousel
    of Progress*
41. *Walt Disney's Enchanted
    Tiki Room*
42. Walt Disney World
    Railroad (multiple
    stations)

Attractions

1. Ariel's Grotto FP+
2. Astro Orbiter
3. The Barnstormer FP+
4. Big Thunder Mountain
   Railroad ☑ Use FP+
5. Buzz Lightyear's Space
   Ranger Spin ☑ Use FP+
6. *Captain Jack Sparrow's
   Pirate Tutorial*
7. Casey Jr. Splash 'N'
   Soak Station
8. Country Bear Jamboree
9. Dumbo the Flying
   Elephant FP+
10. *Enchanted Tales with
    Belle* Use FP+

H. Golden Oak Outpost
I. The Lunching Pad
J. Pecos Bill Tall Tale Inn
   & Cafe
K. The Pinocchio Village
   Haus
L. Tomorrowland Terrace
   Restaurant (seasonal)
M. Tortuga Tavern

Continued from page 483

If you're staying at the Contemporary, Bay Lake Tower, Polynesian Village, or Grand Floridian resorts, you can commute to the Magic Kingdom by monorail (guests at the Contemporary and Bay Lake Tower can walk to the park more quickly). If you're staying at Wilderness Lodge & Villas or Fort Wilderness Resort & Campground, you can take a boat or bus. Guests at other Walt Disney World resorts can reach the park by bus. All Disney lodging guests, regardless of conveyance, are deposited at the park's entrance, bypassing the TTC.

GETTING ORIENTED

AT THE MAGIC KINGDOM, stroller, wheelchair, and ECV/ESV rentals are in the train station; lockers are on the right, just inside the entrance. On your left as you enter **Main Street, U.S.A.** is **City Hall,** the center for information, lost and found, guided tours, and entertainment schedules.

The guide map found there lists all attractions, shops, and eating places; provides information about first aid, baby care, and assistance for the disabled; and gives tips for good photos. It lists times for the day's special events, live entertainment, Disney-character parades, and concerts, and it also tells when and where to find Disney characters. The guide map is supplemented by a daily entertainment schedule known as the *Times Guide.* In addition to listing performance times, the *Times Guide* provides info on Disney-character appearances and what Disney calls Special Hours. This term usually refers to attractions that open late or close early and to the operating hours of park restaurants. The My Disney Experience app (see page 36) has this same information.

Main Street, U.S.A. ends at the **Central Plaza,** a hub from which branch the entrances to five other sections of the Magic Kingdom: **Adventureland, Frontierland, Liberty Square, Fantasyland,** and **Tomorrowland.**

unofficial **TIP**
Because Cinderella Castle is so large, designate a very specific meeting spot, such as the entrance to Cinderella's Royal Table restaurant at the rear of the castle.

Cinderella Castle, at the entrance to Fantasyland, is the Magic Kingdom's architectural icon and visual center. If you start in Adventureland and go clockwise around the Magic Kingdom, the castle spires will always be roughly on your right; if you start in Tomorrowland and go counterclockwise through the park, the spires will always be roughly on your left. The castle is an excellent meeting place if your group decides to split up or is separated accidentally.

FANTASYLAND EXPANSION

WITH THE OPENING OF **Seven Dwarfs Mine Train** in 2014, the Magic Kingdom completed the expansion of Fantasyland begun in 2010. The first phase of "New Fantasyland" opened in 2012, with attractions and restaurants that quickly joined the Magic Kingdom's must-do list. Parents with small children now race each morning to **Princess Fairytale Hall**—a character-greeting experience—for the chance to meet *Frozen*'s Anna and Elsa the way teens head for Space Mountain. Families get online to book Advance Reservations at **Be Our Guest,** which serves the best food in the

Magic Kingdom (all three meals require Advance Reservations 180 days before your visit). And Seven Dwarfs Mine Train draws Disney roller-coaster fans to Fantasyland for the first time.

Our Magic Kingdom touring plans reflect the latest developments. Check **touringplans.com** for updates.

FASTPASS+ ATTRACTIONS IN THE MAGIC KINGDOM

ADVENTURELAND
- Jungle Cruise
- The Magic Carpets of Aladdin
- Pirates of the Caribbean

FANTASYLAND
- Ariel's Grotto
- The Barnstormer
- Dumbo the Flying Elephant
- *Enchanted Tales with Belle*
- It's a Small World
- Mad Tea Party
- The Many Adventures of Winnie the Pooh
- *Mickey's PhilharMagic*
- Peter Pan's Flight
- Princess Fairytale Hall
- Seven Dwarfs Mine Train
- Under the Sea: Journey of the Little Mermaid

FRONTIERLAND
- Big Thunder Mountain Railroad
- Splash Mountain

LIBERTY SQUARE
- The Haunted Mansion

MAIN STREET, U.S.A.
- Town Square Theater Meet and Greets (Mickey, Tinker Bell)

TOMORROWLAND
- Buzz Lightyear's Space Ranger Spin
- *Monsters, Inc. Laugh Floor*
- Space Mountain
- Tomorrowland Speedway

ENTERTAINMENT & PARADES
- *Celebrate the Magic*
- Festival of Fantasy Parade
- Main Street Electrical Parade
- *Wishes* Fireworks

WHILE THE MAGIC KINGDOM offers FastPass+ for more than two dozen attractions, as listed above, our touring plan software identifies only five as frequently needing FastPass+: **(1) Peter Pan's Flight, (2)** *Enchanted Tales with Belle,* **(3) Big Thunder Mountain Railroad, (4) Splash Mountain,** and **(5) Space Mountain.**

Why is Peter Pan's Flight listed first? First of all, it's really nobody's choice as the first attraction to visit. If you've got small children, you're probably headed to *Enchanted Tales with Belle* or Seven Dwarfs Mine Train; if you've got older kids, you're probably headed to Space Mountain or Seven Dwarfs. And no matter where you go first, you'll probably visit at least one other attraction nearby next. That means you're not getting to Peter Pan within the first 30 minutes the park is open.

Second, Peter Pan appears on virtually every Magic Kingdom touring plan. It's a classic, if simple, Disney ride with universal appeal.

Third, although it's not a headliner attraction, Peter Pan develops long lines throughout the day. Wait times during Christmas, for example, can exceed 150–180 minutes fairly often. The ride's hourly capacity is around 1,100 guests—a little more than half of Buzz Lightyear's and far less than half of Pirates of the Caribbean's.

We think *Enchanted Tales with Belle* came in second because seeing it first thing in the morning usually doesn't make sense. Counting walking time and the elaborate preshow, you'd probably be committing about 30 minutes to that one attraction—you could probably

488 PART 9 THE MAGIC KINGDOM

visit two or three other attractions in Fantasyland in the same amount of time.

Big Thunder Mountain Railroad and Splash Mountain don't normally get a huge influx of guests immediately at park opening, but lines of 20–40 minutes can develop around midmorning at both as crowds make their way from Tomorrowland and Fantasyland.

Space Mountain probably made the list because of Seven Dwarfs Mine Train. The latter is not only the newest attraction in the Magic Kingdom, it has a less stringent height requirement than Space Mountain. Plus, it's listed as the first attraction to visit in a lot of our touring plans, and it's usually followed by other Fantasyland attractions to minimize walking. All this is to say, if you're going to Seven Dwarfs first, you'll need FastPass+ for Space Mountain when you visit it later.

Note that we haven't included the popular **Anna and Elsa Meet and Greet** at Princess Fairytale Hall among our FastPass+ musts. Lines do get incredibly long—approaching 4 hours in some cases!—but hourly capacity is only around 45–50 families, or roughly 500–600 people per day. You definitely need FastPass+, but your chances of scoring reservations are very low. If by some miracle you do snag them, our touring plan software can incorporate the *Frozen* princesses into your day.

On the other hand, six Magic Kingdom attractions *never* seem to need FastPass+, either because our touring plans get you to them before long lines develop or because the attractions rarely see long waits: **The Barnstormer, It's a Small World, Mad Tea Party, The Magic Carpets of Aladdin, *Mickey's PhilharMagic,*** and ***Monsters, Inc. Laugh Floor.*** You can almost always get in to the next seating for the two shows—and if the park is so crowded that you can't, the headliner attractions will be mobbed and remain your best use of FastPass+. As for the other four, their lines never get as long as those for more-popular rides.

FastPass+ kiosk locations in the Magic Kingdom are as follows:

- In the walkway between Adventureland and Liberty Square, near the Diamond Horseshoe Saloon and Swiss Family Treehouse
- At the entrance to Jungle Cruise in Adventureland
- Outside *Mickey's PhilharMagic* in Fantasyland
- Near *Stitch's Great Escape!* in Tomorrowland

Same-Day FastPass+ Availability

The preceding tells you which attractions to focus on when making your *advance* FastPass+ reservations before you get to the park. Once you're in the park, you can make more FastPass+ reservations once the originals have been used or have expired. How do you know which attractions are likely to have these day-of reservations? And when will they run out? Hush, *bubeleh,* the chart opposite has your answers.

You'll notice that many attractions have more day-of FastPass+ availability on days with moderate crowds than with low crowds. That seems backwards, but it's not: Disney can change how much of each ride's hourly capacity is dedicated to FastPass+ and increases this number on days of higher attendance. For example, on days of low crowds, Peter Pan's Flight might dedicate 50% of its hourly capacity to Fast-Pass+ riders, 75% on days of moderate crowds.

MAGIC KINGDOM
When Same-Day FP+ Runs Out, by Crowd Level

ATTRACTION	LOW CROWDS*	MODERATE CROWDS*	HIGH CROWDS*
Ariel's Grotto	5 p.m.	6-9 p.m.	9-10 p.m.
The Barnstormer	6-7 p.m.	8-9 p.m.	10-11 p.m.
Big Thunder Mountain	4-6 p.m.	5 p.m.	2-3 p.m.
Buzz Lightyear's Space Ranger Spin	5-6 p.m.	7-8 p.m.	6-8 p.m.
Dumbo the Flying Elephant	6-7 p.m.	8-9 p.m.	10-11 p.m.
Enchanted Tales with Belle	5-6 p.m.	6-7 p.m.	7-9 p.m.
Festival of Fantasy Parade	3 p.m.	Unlikely day-of availability	Unlikely day-of availability
The Haunted Mansion	6 p.m.	7-8 p.m.	5-8 p.m.
It's a Small World	6-7 p.m.	8-9 p.m.	9-10 p.m.
Jungle Cruise	5-6 p.m.	7-9 p.m.	8-10 p.m.
Monsters, Inc. Laugh Floor	5-6 p.m.	8-9 p.m.	9-10 p.m.
Mad Tea Party	6-7 p.m.	8-9 p.m.	10-11 p.m.
The Magic Carpets of Aladdin	6-7 p.m.	8-9 p.m.	11 p.m.
Main Street Electrical Parade	Noon-3 p.m.	Until first performance	Unlikely day-of availability
The Many Adventures of Winnie the Pooh	6-7 p.m.	8-9 p.m.	10-11 p.m.
Peter Pan's Flight	2-3 p.m.	3-4 p.m.	1-3 p.m.
Mickey's PhilharMagic	6-7 p.m.	7 p.m.	8-9 p.m.
Pirates of the Caribbean	5-6 p.m.	7-8 p.m.	3-5 p.m.
Princess Fairytale Hall: Cinderella and Rapunzel	5 p.m.	Unlikely day-of availability	Unlikely day-of availability
Princess Fairytale Hall: Anna and Elsa	5 p.m.	Unlikely day-of availability	Unlikely day-of availability
Seven Dwarfs Mine Train	1 p.m.	Unlikely day-of availability	Unlikely day-of availability
Splash Mountain	2-4 p.m.	3-6 p.m.	2-4 p.m.
Tomorrowland Speedway	5-6 p.m.	6-9 p.m.	7-9 p.m.
Town Square Mickey Mouse Meet and Greet	5-6 p.m.	5-9 p.m.	9-11 p.m.
Town Square Tinker Bell Meet and Greet	6 p.m.	8-10 p.m.	9-11 p.m.
Under the Sea: Journey of the Little Mermaid	5-6 p.m.	7-9 p.m.	8-9 p.m.
Wishes	3 p.m.	Until first performance	Unlikely day-of availability

* LOW CROWDS (Levels 1-3 on TouringPlans.com Crowd Calendar)

* MODERATE CROWDS (Levels 4-7 on TouringPlans.com Crowd Calendar)

* HIGH CROWDS (Levels 8-10 on TouringPlans.com Crowd Calendar)

DINING IN THE MAGIC KINGDOM

HERE'S A QUICK RECAP of the Magic Kingdom's major restaurants, rated by readers from highest to lowest. See Part Four for details.

MAGIC KINGDOM RESTAURANT REFRESHER	
COUNTER-SERVICE	**FULL-SERVICE**
Columbia Harbour House (94% 👍), Liberty Square	**Cinderella's Royal Table** (B, L, D) (92% 👍), Fantasyland
Sleepy Hollow Refreshments (94% 👍), Liberty Square	**Be Our Guest** (D) (91% 👍), Fantasyland
Main Street Bakery (Starbucks) (93% 👍), Main Street, U.S.A.	**Liberty Tree Tavern*** (L, D) (91% 👍), Liberty Square
Be Our Guest (B, L) (91% 👍), Fantasyland	**The Crystal Palace** (B, L, D) (91% 👍), Main Street, U.S.A.
Gaston's Tavern (91% 👍), Fantasyland	**The Plaza Restaurant** (L, D) (90% 👍), Main Street, U.S.A.
Casey's Corner (84% 👍), Main Street, U.S.A.	**Tony's Town Square** (L, D) (79% 👍), Main Street, U.S.A.
Pecos Bill Tall Tale Inn and Cafe (84% 👍), Frontierland	**Closed for renovations through November 2015*
Cosmic Ray's Starlight Cafe (80% 👍), Tomorrowland	
Pinocchio Village Haus (78% 👍), Fantasyland	

MAIN STREET, U.S.A.

BEGIN AND END YOUR VISIT ON MAIN STREET, which may open 30 minutes before and closes 30 minutes–1 hour after the rest of the park. The Walt Disney World Railroad stops at Main Street Station; get on to tour the park or ride to Frontierland or Fantasyland.

Main Street is a Disneyfied turn-of-the-20th-century small-town American thoroughfare. Its buildings are real, not elaborate props. Attention to detail is exceptional: Furnishings and fixtures are true

MAGIC KINGDOM Services

MOST PARK SERVICES are centered on Main Street, U.S.A., including:

Baby Care Center Next to The Crystal Palace, left around the Central Plaza (toward Adventureland)

Banking Services ATMs underneath the Main Street railroad station

Cell Phone Charging In Fantasyland, near the *Tangled*-themed restrooms between It's a Small World and The Haunted Mansion, and behind Big Top Treats in Storybook Circus

First Aid Center Next to The Crystal Palace, left around the Central Plaza (toward Adventureland)

Live Entertainment and Parade Information City Hall, at the railroad-station end of Main Street

Lost and Found City Hall

Lost Persons City Hall

Storage Lockers Underneath the Main Street railroad station

Walt Disney World and Local Attraction Information City Hall

Wheelchair, ECV/ESV, and Stroller Rentals Ground floor of the railroad station at the end of Main Street

DISNEY DISH WITH JIM HILL

WALKING THE BACK STREETS IN STYLE To keep guests who use the new overflow walkways behind Main Street, U.S.A., from having to see unthemed infrastructure, even for a minute, Disney recently added turn-of-the-20th-century theming to the back sides of all the buildings along the paths.

to the period. Along the street are shops, character-greeting venues, eating places, City Hall, and a fire station. Occasionally, horse-drawn trolleys, fire engines, and horseless carriages transport visitors along Main Street to the Central Plaza.

Two recently completed construction projects should help Main Street better handle large crowds. First, the huge circular area around the Central Plaza has been paved over and rebuilt into a FastPass+ viewing area for the Magic Kingdom's parades and fireworks. See "Parade Route and Vantage Points" on page 525 and "Vantage Points for Fireworks" on page 527 for more information.

Second, the areas behind the shops on either side of Main Street have been repurposed as pedestrian walkways for use during parades and fireworks during peak times, allowing guests to exit and enter the park from either side of Main Street when it would be otherwise impassable. One arcade, the one most frequently used, runs from just past Tony's Town Square Restaurant to the Tomorrowland side of The Plaza Restaurant; the other runs from near the First Aid Center next to The Crystal Palace to the Fire Station near City Hall on Main Street.

Main Street Characters

DESCRIPTION AND COMMENTS Colorful characters, including the mayor of Main Street, roam the area for photos, autographs, and lively conversation. Not as engaging as the characters who populate Hollywood Boulevard in Disney's Hollywood Studios, but still fun.

TOURING TIPS Characters are usually available from park opening until around 2 p.m. They're fun to talk to if you're in the area, but don't make a special trip.

Sorcerers of the Magic Kingdom ★★★

APPEAL BY AGE	PRESCHOOL ★★★★	GRADE SCHOOL ★★★★½	TEENS ★★★★½
YOUNG ADULTS ★★★★		OVER 30 ★★★★	SENIORS ★★★½

What it is Interactive video game. **Scope and scale** Minor attraction. **When to go** Before 11 a.m. or after 8 p.m. **Special comments** Long lines to play. **Authors' rating** Great idea; ★★★. **Duration of presentation** About 2 minutes per step, 4 or 5 steps per game. **Probable waiting time per step** 10–15 minutes.

DESCRIPTION AND COMMENTS Sorcerers of the Magic Kingdom combines aspects of role-playing games such as Dungeons and Dragons with Disney characters and theme park attractions. Your objective: to help the wizard Merlin keep evildoers from taking over the Magic Kingdom. Merlin sends you on adventures in different parts of the park to fight these villains. Each land hosts a different adventure within the game.

This free game is played with a set of trading cards—similar to baseball cards or Magic: The Gathering cards—with a different Disney character on each card. Each character possesses special properties that help it fight certain villains. Pick up the cards, plus a map showing where in the park you can play the game, at either the Fire Station on Main Street, U.S.A., or across from Sleepy Hollow Refreshments in Liberty Square.

You'll need your park ticket or MagicBand to pick up your first set of cards and start the game. One card, known as your "key," is special because it links you to your game. You'll need to present your key card when you pick up a set of cards to start your next adventure.

When you pick up your first set of cards, you'll view an instructional video explaining how to use them and the object of the game. Then you'll be sent to another location to start your first adventure. Each location in the park is associated with a unique symbol: an eye, a feather, a dragonfly, or something along those lines. Look for these symbols on the map to find the best route to your starting point.

Each adventure consists of four or five stops in a particular land. At each stop, another story will play on a video screen, outlining what your villain is trying to do. Merlin will ask you to cast a spell to stop the villain—to do so, hold one or more of your cards up to the video display. Cameras in the display read your card, deploy the spell, and show you the results.

The game has three levels: easy, medium, and hard. The easy version is the default and is appropriate for small children; holding up any one of your character cards is enough to defeat any villain. In more-advanced levels of the game, you need to display two or more character cards in specific combinations to defeat a particular villain. Different card combinations produce different spells, and only some spells work on certain characters in those advanced levels.

The audio at each step holds clues to which cards you should use against advanced villains. For example, if a villain says something like "Don't toy with me!" then you should look for cards with characters that are toys, such as the *Toy Story* characters; references to "being spotted" suggest using cards with characters from *101 Dalmatians;* and so on.

The game launched with an initial series of around 70 unique cards; you can obtain 5 new ones per day. Don't worry if you play more than once and end up with duplicate cards—a small trading market exists within the park. Disney issues new card series over time.

An Anchorage, Alaska, couple offers these tips for playing the game:

(1) Unless you plan to stick with every member of your group every single minute, make sure they all get their own portal keys. (2) Every card has a "rarity," located above the card number. If you want to trade cards, only trade for similar rarities. The symbol designates its rarity: planet (looks like a circle) is common, moon is uncommon, star is rare, lightning bolt is super-rare. You

can only obtain lightning-bolt cards by buying card packs at the Emporium when they're in stock. They usually sell out by lunchtime, and the days they have them are random (to help increase scarcity). (4) When you're playing, be prepared for a LOT of people to come up to you and ask what you're doing. (5) Also, be prepared for people to walk in front of you when you're playing. This can cause the card reader to time out. (6) You can buy T-shirts with special designs on them that increase your power when you play at medium and hard levels.

This Stamford, Connecticut, reader stresses that it takes a while to play:

Be warned—if you want to beat the game, it takes a lot longer than you think.

TOURING TIPS You'll probably encounter a line of 5–10 people ahead of you at each portal, especially if you play during the afternoon. One complete adventure should take about 30–60 minutes to play, depending on how crowded the park is. If the line to pick up cards is too long at the Main Street Fire Station, try the Liberty Square distribution point. If the game sounds too confusing, A Pirate's Adventure in Adventureland (see page 495) is easier.

Town Square Theater Meet and Greets: Mickey Mouse, Tinker Bell and Friends *(FastPass+)* ★★★★

APPEAL BY AGE PRESCHOOL ★★★★★ GRADE SCHOOL ★★★★★ TEENS ★★★★½
YOUNG ADULTS ★★★★ OVER 30 ★★★★½ SENIORS ★★★★½

What it is Character-greeting venue. **Scope and scale** Minor attraction. **When to go** Before 10 a.m. or after 4 p.m., or use FastPass+. **Special comments** Mickey and the fairies have 2 separate queues, requiring 2 separate waits in line. **Authors' rating** It all started with this mouse; ★★★★. **Duration of experience** 2 minutes per character. **Probable waiting time** 15–25 minutes. **Queue speed** Slow.

DESCRIPTION AND COMMENTS Meet Mickey, along with Tinker Bell and her Pixie Hollow friends, throughout the day at the Town Square Theater on Main Street, to your right as you enter the park.

TOURING TIPS Lines usually drop off after the afternoon parade. Oddly enough, meeting Mickey rarely requires FastPass+.

Transportation Rides

DESCRIPTION AND COMMENTS Trolleys, buses, and the like.
TOURING TIPS Will save you a walk to the Central Plaza. Not worth a wait.

Walt Disney World Railroad ★★★

APPEAL BY AGE PRESCHOOL ★★★★ GRADE SCHOOL ★★★★ TEENS ★★★★
YOUNG ADULTS ★★★½ OVER 30 ★★★★ SENIORS ★★★★

What it is Scenic railroad ride around the perimeter of the Magic Kingdom; provides transportation to Frontierland and Fantasyland. **Scope and scale** Minor attraction. **When to go** Anytime. **Special comments** Main Street is usually the least congested station. **Authors' rating** Plenty to see; ★★★. **Duration of ride** About 20 minutes for a complete circuit. **Average wait in line per 100 people ahead of you** 8 minutes; assumes 2 or more trains operating. **Loading speed** Moderate.

DESCRIPTION AND COMMENTS A transportation ride blending an unusual variety of sights with an energy-saving way to get around the park. The train provides a glimpse of all "lands" except Adventureland, with most of the interesting stuff (American Indian village, animatronic animals, frontier structures) on the leg between Frontierland and Fantasyland.

TOURING TIPS Save the train until after you've seen the featured attractions, or use it when you need transportation. On busy days, lines form at the Frontierland Station but rarely at the Main Street Station. Wheelchair access is available at the Frontierland and Fantasyland Stations.

Only folded strollers are permitted on the train, so you can't board with your rented Disney stroller. You can, however, obtain a replacement at your destination (keep your stroller name card and rental receipt with you).

Finally, note that the railroad shuts down immediately before and during parades; check your park guide map or *Times Guide* for parade times. Needless to say, this is not the time to queue up for the train.

ADVENTURELAND

ADVENTURELAND IS THE FIRST LAND to the left of Main Street, U.S.A. It combines an African-safari theme with a tropical-island atmosphere.

A new restaurant is scheduled open in Adventureland in late 2015 or early 2016, in the area across from Swiss Family Treehouse. The working name is **Skipper's Cantina,** the theme is reportedly tied to the Jungle Cruise, and it will reportedly operate along the lines of Fantasyland's Be Our Guest (see pages 326 and 342), with counter-service lunches and sit-down dinners. As fans of the old Adventureland Veranda, which used to occupy this spot, we're excited.

DISNEY DISH WITH JIM HILL

WE JUST USED WHAT WAS LION AROUND When Skipper's Cantina opens, you may notice a lot of familiar decor. According to the backstory the Imagineers cooked up for this new Magic Kingdom restaurant, the skippers "borrowed" a number of items from the Jungle Cruise to set up their restaurant. As you wander through the dining room, keep an eye out for items that used to be found in the attraction's queue or dangling from Trader Sam's belt.

Captain Jack Sparrow's Pirate Tutorial ★★★½

APPEAL BY AGE PRESCHOOL ★★★★½ GRADE SCHOOL ★★★★½ TEENS ★★★½
YOUNG ADULTS ★★★½   OVER 30 ★★★½   SENIORS ★★★½

What it is Outdoor stage show with guest participation. **Scope and scale** Diversion. **When to go** See *Times Guide* for show schedule. **Authors' rating** Sign us up; ★★★½. **Duration of presentation** About 20 minutes.

DESCRIPTION AND COMMENTS Outside Pirates of the Caribbean, Cap'n Jack and a crew member teach would-be knaves the skills needed for a career in piracy. Some kids go on stage to train in the finer points of dueling, similar to *Jedi Training Academy* at Hollywood Studios (see page 615). The show finishes with everyone taking the probably-not-legally-binding pirate's oath and singing a rousing round of "A Pirate's Life for Me." If you or your kids are fans of the Pirates ride or the movie series, this show is worth a look as well.

TOURING TIPS The shows attract decent crowds, but the first and last show seem to be the least popular. Standing-room-only outdoors.

Jungle Cruise *(FastPass+)* ★★★½

APPEAL BY AGE	PRESCHOOL ★★★★	GRADE SCHOOL ★★★★	TEENS ★★★½
YOUNG ADULTS ★★★★		OVER 30 ★★★★	SENIORS ★★★★

What it is Outdoor safari-themed boat ride. **Scope and scale** Major attraction. **When to go** Before 10:30 a.m., during the last 2 hours before closing, or use FastPass+. **Special comments** Fun to ride at night! **Authors' rating** A classic, but kinda long in the tooth; ★★★½. **Duration of ride** 8–9 minutes. **Average wait in line per 100 people ahead of you** 3½ minutes; assumes 10 boats operating. **Loading speed** Moderate.

DESCRIPTION AND COMMENTS An outdoor excursion through jungle waterways. Passengers encounter animatronic elephants, lions, hostile natives, and a menacing hippo. The boatman's spiel adds to the fun. Once one of the most elaborate attractions at the Magic Kingdom, the Jungle Cruise now seems dated. Since the advent of Disney's Animal Kingdom, the attraction's appeal has diminished, but in its defense, you can always depend on the robotic critters being present as you motor past. A Pelham, Alabama, woman agrees that it's past its prime:

> Jungle Cruise severely needs an update. Our tour guide indulged in annoying comedy to make up for the lack of excitement. I would rather have been eaten by the animatronic hippos.

TOURING TIPS Jungle Cruise is a FastPass+ attraction. Before you make a same-day reservation, however, ask a cast member what the estimated wait in the standby line is.

The Magic Carpets of Aladdin *(FastPass+)* ★★½

APPEAL BY AGE	PRESCHOOL ★★★★½	GRADE SCHOOL ★★★★	TEENS ★★★½
YOUNG ADULTS ★★★½		OVER 30 ★★★	SENIORS ★★★½

What it is Elaborate midway ride. **Scope and scale** Minor attraction. **When to go** Before 11 a.m. or after 7 p.m. **Authors' rating** A visually appealing children's ride; ★★½. **Duration of ride** 1½ minutes. **Average wait in line per 100 people ahead of you** 16 minutes. **Loading speed** Slow.

DESCRIPTION AND COMMENTS The Magic Carpets of Aladdin is a midway ride like Dumbo, except with magic carpets instead of elephants. A spitting camel sprays jets of water on carpet riders. Riders can maneuver their carpets up and down and side to side to avoid the water. The front seat controls vehicle height, while the backseat controls tilt—if you let the kids sit up front, prepare to get wet!

TOURING TIPS Like Dumbo, this ride has great eye appeal but extremely limited capacity (that is, it loads slowly). Try to get younger kids on during the first 30 minutes the park is open, or try just before park closing. FastPass+ is almost never needed.

A Pirate's Adventure: Treasure of the Seven Seas ★★★½

APPEAL BY AGE	PRESCHOOL ★★★½	GRADE SCHOOL ★★★★½	TEENS ★★★★
YOUNG ADULTS ★★★½		OVER 30 ★★★½	SENIORS ★★★★

What it is Interactive game. **Scope and scale** Diversion. **When to go** Anytime. **Authors' rating** Simple, fast, and fun—especially at night; not to be missed; ★★★½. **Duration of experience** About 20 minutes to play the entire game.

DESCRIPTION AND COMMENTS Similar to Agent P's World Showcase Adventure at Epcot, A Pirate's Adventure features interactive areas with physical props and narrations that lead guests through a quest to find lost treasure, all within Adventureland.

Guests begin their journey at an old Cartography Shop near Golden Oak Outpost—this is the central hub for adventurers helping to locate missing treasure. Groups of up to six people are given a talisman (a RFID card) that will help them on their journey. The talisman activates a video screen that assigns your group to one of five different missions. Your group is then given a map and sent off to find your first location.

Once at the location, one member of the party touches the talisman to the symbol at the station, and the animation begins. Each adventure has four or five stops throughout Adventureland, and each stop contains 30–45 seconds of activity. No strategy or action is required: Watch what unfolds on the screen, get your next destination, and head off.

We like how well each station integrates into its surroundings, and how the stations' artifacts and props tie together the attraction and movie storylines. A Pirate's Adventure also serves as a good introduction to other interactive games, such as Sorcerers of the Magic Kingdom (see page 491).

A Maryland mom writes:

The very best thing we did with our 4-year-old was A Pirates' Adventure. It was incredible. Located in its own building next to the arch in Adventureland, it was five scavenger hunts—we did all of them and it took 2 hours—our most fun 2 hours at the park! It's high-tech, magical, imaginative, active, and individualized. And you can keep the beautiful maps!

TOURING TIPS The effects are better at night. While we think everyone should try A Pirate's Adventure, it isn't a must if time is tight.

Pirates of the Caribbean (*FastPass+*) ★★★★
(*closed through September 2015 for refurbishment*)

**APPEAL BY AGE PRESCHOOL ★★★½ GRADE SCHOOL ★★★★ TEENS ★★★★½
YOUNG ADULTS ★★★★   OVER 30 ★★★★½   SENIORS ★★★★½**

What it is Indoor pirate-themed boat ride. **Scope and scale** Headliner. **When to go** Before 11 a.m., after 7 p.m., or use FastPass+. **Special comments** Frightens some kids. **Authors' rating** Disney Audio-Animatronics at their best; not to be missed; ★★★★. **Duration of ride** About 7½ minutes. **Average wait in line per 100 people ahead of you** 3 minutes; assumes one FastPass+ line, one standby line. **Loading speed** Fast.

DESCRIPTION AND COMMENTS An indoor cruise through a series of sets that depict a pirate raid on an island settlement, from bombardment of the fortress to debauchery after the victory. Arguably one of the most influential theme park attractions ever created, the Magic Kingdom's version retains the elaborate queuing area, grand scale, and detailed scenes that have awed audiences since its debut in Disneyland in 1967. The successful *Pirates of the Caribbean* movies have boosted the ride's popularity, and guests' demands led to the addition of animatronic figures of the film's Captain Jack Sparrow and Captain Barbossa in scenes.

Speaking of debauchery, Pirates of the Caribbean displays a strong dose of political correctness. Even so, a Rockville, Maryland, mother was not prepared for what she saw:

I had no idea that it would be as visually violent and historically accurate as it was. I really didn't look forward to explaining to my son why those women had ropes around their necks and such.

TOURING TIPS Undoubtedly one of the park's most timeless attractions. Engineered to move large crowds in a hurry, Pirates is a good attraction to see in the late afternoon.

DISNEY DISH WITH JIM HILL

TRIDENT, TRICYCLE, TRI-WHATEVER It's become a tradition for the Imagineers to pay tribute to a new *Pirates* movie by adding a character or a prop from that film to the Pirates attraction. This time around, Disney is looking for the right spot for the mythical Trident of Poseidon. As you'll see when *Pirates of the Caribbean: Dead Men Tell No Tales* hits theaters on July 7, 2017, Jack Sparrow needs this trident to defeat Captain Salazar and his ghastly crew of ghostly pirates.

Swiss Family Treehouse ★★★

APPEAL BY AGE PRESCHOOL ★★★½ GRADE SCHOOL ★★★½ TEENS ★★★
YOUNG ADULTS ★★★ OVER 30 ★★★½ SENIORS ★★★

What it is Outdoor walk-through treehouse. **Scope and scale** Minor attraction. **When to go** Anytime. **Special comments** Requires climbing a lot of stairs. **Authors' rating** Incredible detail and execution; ★★★. **Duration of tour** 10–15 minutes. **Average wait in line per 100 people ahead of you** 7 minutes.

DESCRIPTION AND COMMENTS An immense replica of the shipwrecked Swiss Family Robinson's arboreal abode. With its multiple stories and mechanical wizardry, it's the queen of all treehouses.

TOURING TIPS A self-guided walk-through tour involves a lot of stairs up and down, but no ropes, ladders, or anything fancy. Looky-loos or people stopping to rest sometimes create bottlenecks that slow the crowd flow. Visit in late afternoon or early evening if you're on a one-day tour, or in the morning of your second day.

Walt Disney's Enchanted Tiki Room ★★★½

APPEAL BY AGE PRESCHOOL ★★★½ GRADE SCHOOL ★★★½ TEENS ★★★
YOUNG ADULTS ★★★ OVER 30 ★★★½ SENIORS ★★★★

What it is Audio-Animatronic Pacific-island musical-theater show. **Scope and scale** Minor attraction. **When to go** Before 11 a.m. or after 3:30 p.m. **Special comments** Frightens some preschoolers. **Authors' rating** Very, very . . . unusual; ★★★½. **Duration of presentation** 15½ minutes. **Preshow entertainment** Talking birds. **Probable waiting time** 15 minutes.

DESCRIPTION AND COMMENTS The current show here is a shortened version of the original attraction, which premiered at Disneyland in 1963. Starring four singing, wisecracking parrots—José, Fritz, Michael, and Pierre—*Enchanted Tiki Room* remains a favorite of many, including us. The show is a series of musical numbers sung by dozens of birds, plants, and tikis that come to life all around the large seating area.

Although most readers like the show, they caution that it may be frightening to younger children. Concerning the scary parts, a mother of three from Coleman, Michigan, is outspoken:

The Tiki Room *show was very scary, with a thunder-and-lightning storm and a loud volcano. Can't Disney do anything without scaring young children?*

TOURING TIPS Usually not too crowded. We go in the late afternoon, when we appreciate sitting in air-conditioned comfort with our brains in park.

◼▯ FRONTIERLAND

THIS "LAND" ADJOINS ADVENTURELAND as you move clockwise around the Magic Kingdom. Frontierland's focus is on the Old West, with stockade-type structures and pioneer trappings.

Big Thunder Mountain Railroad *(FastPass+)* ★★★★

APPEAL BY AGE	PRESCHOOL ★★½	GRADE SCHOOL ★★★★½	TEENS ★★★★½
YOUNG ADULTS ★★★★½		OVER 30 ★★★★½	SENIORS ★★★★

What it is Tame Western mining–themed roller coaster. **Scope and scale** Headliner. **When to go** Before 10 a.m., in the hour before closing, or use FastPass+. **Special comments** 40″ minimum height requirement; children younger than age 7 must ride with an adult. Switching-off option provided (see page 412). **Authors' rating** Great effects; relatively tame ride; not to be missed; ★★★★. **Duration of ride** About 3½ minutes. **Average wait in line per 100 people ahead of you** 2½ minutes; assumes 5 trains operating. **Loading speed** Moderate–fast.

DESCRIPTION AND COMMENTS Roller coaster through and around a Disney "mountain." The idea is that you're on a runaway mine train during the Gold Rush. We put this coaster at about a 5 on a "scary scale" of 10. Big Thunder contains first-rate examples of Disney creativity: a realistic mining town, falling rocks, and an earthquake, all humorously animated with swinging possums, petulant buzzards, and the like. Ride it after dark if you can. Seats in the back offer the best experience.

We love the interactive props in the queue. Spin a metal wheel and push on a dynamite plunger to trigger an "explosion" (of water, steam, or noise) near a passing train; watch "home movies" of the workers in the mines; see (and smell!) what some proverbial canaries experience underground; and more. Best of all, these toys are spaced just far apart for little kids to have something to do the entire time in line. Great thinking.

TOURING TIPS A superb Disney experience, but not too wild a roller coaster. Emphasis is more on the sights than on the thrill of the ride.

Nearby Splash Mountain affects traffic flow to Big Thunder Mountain Railroad—adventuresome guests ride Splash Mountain first, then go next door to ride Big Thunder. All this means large crowds in Frontierland all day and long waits for Big Thunder. The best way to experience the Magic Kingdom's "mountains" is to ride Seven Dwarfs Mine Train and Space Mountain one morning as soon as the park opens, then Splash Mountain and Big Thunder Mountain the next morning. If you have only one day, the order should be (1) Seven Dwarfs, (2) Splash Mountain, (3) Big Thunder, and (4) Space Mountain.

A Midwestern mom offers this tip to families with kids too short to ride:

If you're switching off on Thunder Mountain or Splash Mountain and have young kids to entertain, there's a fantastic little playground nearby where you can pass the time. It's completely covered and near the restrooms too! It's next to Splash Mountain, under the train tracks.

Guests experience Disney attractions differently. Consider this letter from a lady in Brookline, Massachusetts:

Being senior citizens and having limited time, my friend and I confined our activities to attractions rated as four or five stars for seniors. Because of your recommendation, we waited an hour to board Big Thunder Mountain Railroad, which you rated a 5 on a scary scale of 10. After living through 3½ minutes of pure terror, I will rate it a 15. We were so busy holding on and screaming and even praying for our safety that we didn't see any falling rocks, a mining town, or an earthquake. The Big Thunder Mountain Railroad should not be recommended for seniors or preschool children.

A woman from Vermont discovered that there's more to consider about Big Thunder than being scared:

Big Thunder Mountain Railroad was rated a 5 on the scary scale, but it was much higher on the lose-your-lunch meter. One more sharp turn and the kids in front of me would've needed a dip in Splash Mountain!

However, a reader from West Newton, Massachusetts, dubbed the ride "a roller coaster for people who don't like roller coasters."

Country Bear Jamboree ★★★½

APPEAL BY AGE PRESCHOOL ★★★½ GRADE SCHOOL ★★★½ TEENS ★★★
YOUNG ADULTS ★★★ OVER 30 ★★★½ SENIORS ★★★★

What it is Audio-Animatronic country hoedown. **Scope and scale** Major attraction. **When to go** Anytime. **Authors' rating** Old and worn but pure Disney; ★★★½. **Duration of presentation** 11 minutes. **Preshow entertainment** None. **Probable waiting time** It's not terribly popular but has a comparatively small capacity. Waiting time between noon and 5:30 p.m. on a busy day will average 11–22 minutes.

DESCRIPTION AND COMMENTS A charming cast of animatronic bears sings and stomps in a Western-style revue. It's an air-conditioned refuge on hot days, but the *Jamboree* has run for so long that the geriatric bears are a step away from assisted living. Reader comments tend to echo the need for something new. From a Sandy Hook, Connecticut, mom:

I know they consider it a classic, and kids always seem to love it, but could they PLEASE update it after half a century?

A woman from Carmel, Indiana, put her experience in perspective:

Here is a half-hour of my life that I can never get back.

But a Mississippi dad defends the show:

I find it interesting how my reactions and those of my family change to certain attractions. Take Country Bear Jamboree, *for instance: In my 30s I enjoyed it considered it hokey and lame, yet I thoroughly enjoyed my daughter's intense love of it at ages 3 and 8 on two previous trips. This time, at age 54, I sat up fairly close with my wife and loved it—we even sang along! Of course, this was partly to embarrass my now-16-year-old daughter, who sat hunched down in the very last row. She says we have creeping senility, but I told her, "Just wait till you bring YOUR kids!"*

TOURING TIPS On hot and rainy days and during peak seasons, the *Jamboree* draws large crowds from midmorning on.

Frontierland Shootin' Arcade ★½

APPEAL BY AGE PRESCHOOL ★★★½ GRADE SCHOOL ★★★½ TEENS ★★★★½
YOUNG ADULTS ★★★★ OVER 30 ★★★½ SENIORS ★★★★

What it is Electronic shooting gallery. **Scope and scale** Diversion. **When to go** Anytime. **Special comments** Costs $1 per play. **Authors' rating** Absolutely not a must; ★½.

DESCRIPTION AND COMMENTS One of a few attractions not included in Magic Kingdom admission. Would-be gunslingers get around 30 shots per $1 play. Each shot is followed by a short delay before the next shot can be taken—this prevents small children from accidentally using all 30 shots in 5 seconds. It's barely noticeable for adults. Despite our low rating, many *Unofficial Guide* staff gladly spend a few bucks here when they visit the World. It's a small bit of you're-in-control interactivity in a park with a lot of sitting and watching.

TOURING TIPS Not a place to blow your time if you're on a tight schedule. The fun is entirely in the target practice—no prizes can be won.

Splash Mountain *(FastPass+)* ★★★★★

| APPEAL BY AGE | PRESCHOOL ★★★★† | GRADE SCHOOL ★★★★½ | TEENS ★★★★½ |
| YOUNG ADULTS ★★★★½ | OVER 30 ★★★★½ | SENIORS ★★★★½ |

†Many preschoolers are too short to ride, and others freak out when they see it from the waiting line. Among preschoolers who actually ride, most love it.

What it is Indoor/outdoor water-flume adventure ride. **Scope and scale** Super-headliner. **When to go** As soon as the park opens, during afternoon or evening parades, just before closing, or use FastPass+. **Special comments** 40" minimum height requirement; children younger than age 7 must ride with an adult. Switching-off option provided (see page 412). **Authors' rating** A soggy delight, and not to be missed; ★★★★★. **Duration of ride** About 10 minutes. **Average wait in line per 100 people ahead of you** 3½ minutes; assumes ride is operating at full capacity. **Loading speed** Moderate.

DESCRIPTION AND COMMENTS Splash Mountain tells the story of Br'er Rabbit, who goes off in search of adventure and finds it . . . along with a hungry fox and bear. Steep chutes and animatronics alternate with at least one special effect for each of the senses. The ride covers more than half a mile, splashing through swamps, caves, and backwoods bayous before climaxing in a five-story plunge and Br'er Rabbit's triumphant return home. More than 100 Audio-Animatronic characters, including Br'er Rabbit, Br'er Bear, and Br'er Fox, regale riders with songs, including "Zip-a-Dee-Doo-Dah."

TOURING TIPS This happy, adventuresome ride vies with Space Mountain in Tomorrowland and Seven Dwarfs Mine Train in Fantasyland as one of the park's most popular attractions. Crowds build fast in the morning, and waits of more than 2 hours can be expected once the park fills on busy days. Get in line first thing, certainly no later than 45 minutes after the park opens during warmer months. Long lines will persist all day.

If you have only a day to see the Magic Kingdom, make FastPass+ reservations in advance for around 9:30 a.m. at Big Thunder Mountain Railroad and around 3:30 p.m. at Space Mountain. On the day of your visit, ride Seven Dwarfs Mine Train as soon as the park opens, then hotfoot it to Splash Mountain to ride immediately. Your FastPass+ reservation for Big Thunder will be valid by the time you're done, and you'll have experienced three of the park's four headliners in about an hour.

DISNEY DISH WITH JIM HILL

THIS IDEA *DIDN'T* MAKE A SPLASH When Tony Baxter came up with the Splash Mountain idea back in 1983, he wanted to name the ride "Zip-A-Dee-Doo-Dah River Run," tying it to the hit song from *Song of the South.* But then–Disney CEO Michael Eisner hated the name, preferring to keep the "mountain" theme going for Disney's thrill rides.

If you have two mornings, do the Fantasyland and Frontierland attractions—Seven Dwarfs Mine Train, Splash Mountain, and Big Thunder Mountain Railroad—on one day and Space Mountain the next. Spreading your visits over two mornings eliminates a lot of walking.

Other FastPass+ strategies combining the park's "mountains" with other headliners have been incorporated into our Magic Kingdom touring plans (see pages 806–811).

As with Space Mountain, hundreds are poised to dash to Splash Mountain when the park opens. The best strategy is to go to the end of Main Street and turn left at The Crystal Palace restaurant. In front of the restaurant is a bridge that provides a shortcut to Adventureland. Stake out a position at the barrier rope. When the park opens, move as fast as you comfortably can and cross the bridge to Adventureland.

Another shortcut: Just past the first group of buildings on your right, roughly across from the Swiss Family Treehouse, is a small passageway containing restrooms and phones. Easy to overlook, it connects Adventureland to Frontierland. Go through here into Frontierland and take a hard left. As you emerge along the waterfront, Splash Mountain is straight ahead. If you miss the passageway, don't fool around looking for it. Continue straight through Adventureland to Splash Mountain.

Less exhausting in the morning is commuting to Splash Mountain via the Walt Disney World Railroad. Board at Main Street Station and wait for the park to open. The train will pull out of the station a few minutes after the rope drops at the Central Plaza end of Main Street. Ride to Frontierland Station and disembark. As you come down the stairs at the station, the entrance to Splash Mountain will be on your left. Because of the time required to unload at the station, train passengers will arrive at Splash Mountain a little after the lead element from the Central Plaza.

If you ride in the front seat, you almost certainly will get wet. Riders elsewhere get splashed but usually not doused. Since you don't know which seat you'll be assigned, go prepared. On a cool day, carry a plastic garbage bag and tear holes in the bottom and sides to make a water-resistant (not waterproof) sack dress (be sure to tuck the bag under your bottom). Or store a change of clothes, including footwear, in one of the park's rental lockers. Leave your camera or smartphone with a nonriding member of your group or wrap it in plastic. For any attraction where there's a distinct possibility of getting soaked, wear Tevas or some other type of waterproof sandal, and change back to regular shoes after the ride.

The scariest part of this adventure ride is the steep chute you see when standing in line, but the drop looks worse than it is. Despite reassurances, however, many children wig out when they see it. A mom from Grand Rapids, Michigan, recalls her kids' rather unique reaction:

We discovered after the fact that our children thought they would go under water after the drop and tried to hold their breath throughout the ride in preparation. They were really too preoccupied to enjoy the clever story.

Tom Sawyer Island and Fort Langhorn ★★★

APPEAL BY AGE PRESCHOOL ★★★★ GRADE SCHOOL ★★★★½ TEENS ★★★★
YOUNG ADULTS ★★★½ OVER 30 ★★★½ SENIORS ★★★

What it is Outdoor walk-through exhibit and rustic playground. **Scope and scale** Minor attraction. **When to go** Midmorning–late afternoon. **Special comments** Closes at dusk. **Authors' rating** The place for rambunctious kids; ★★★.

DESCRIPTION AND COMMENTS Tom Sawyer Island is a getaway within the park. It has hills to climb; a cave, windmill, and pioneer stockade (Fort Langhorn) to explore; a tipsy barrel bridge to cross; and paths to follow. You can watch riverboats chug past. It's a delight for adults and a godsend for children who have been in tow and closely supervised all day.

TOURING TIPS Tom Sawyer Island isn't one of the Magic Kingdom's more celebrated attractions, but it's one of the park's better-conceived ones. Attention to detail is excellent, and kids revel in its frontier atmosphere. It's a must for families with children ages 5–15. If your group is made up of adults, visit on your second day or on your first day after you've seen the attractions you most wanted to see.

Although children could spend a whole day on the island, plan on at least 20 minutes. Access is by raft from Frontierland; two operate simultaneously, and the trip is pretty efficient, although you may have to stand in line to board both ways. For a mother from Duncan, South Carolina, Tom Sawyer Island is as much a refuge as an attraction:

In the afternoon, when the crowds were at their peak and the weather at its hottest, our organization began to suffer. We retreated over to Tom Sawyer Island, which proved to be a true haven. My husband and I found a secluded bench and regrouped while the kids ran in the shade.

Walt Disney World Railroad

DESCRIPTION AND COMMENTS Stops in Frontierland on its circle tour of the park. See the description under Main Street, U.S.A. (page 493), for additional details.

TOURING TIPS Pleasant, feet-saving link to Main Street and Fantasyland, but the Frontierland station is more congested than those stations.

▎ LIBERTY SQUARE

LIBERTY SQUARE re-creates America at the time of the American Revolution. The architecture is Federal or Colonial. The **Liberty Tree,** a live oak more than 130 years old, lends dignity and grace to the setting.

The Hall of Presidents ★★★½

APPEAL BY AGE	PRESCHOOL ★★½	GRADE SCHOOL ★★★	TEENS ★★★½
YOUNG ADULTS ★★★½	OVER 30 ★★★★		SENIORS ★★★★½

What it is Audio-Animatronic historical theater presentation. **Scope and scale** Major attraction. **When to go** Anytime. **Authors' rating** Impressive and moving; ★★★½. **Duration of presentation** Almost 23 minutes. **Preshow entertainment** None. **Probable waiting time** The lines for this attraction look intimidating once you're inside the lobby, but they're swallowed up as the theater exchanges audiences. It would be exceptionally unusual not to be admitted to the next show.

DESCRIPTION AND COMMENTS The last update was in 2009, when Barack Obama was added and the entire presentation revamped, including a new narration by Morgan Freeman and a new speech by George Washington. The Father of Our Country joins Presidents Lincoln and Obama as the only Chief Executives with speaking parts. Although the show is updated roughly every decade, the presentation remains strongly inspirational and patriotic, highlighting milestones in American history. It's also one of Disney's best and most ambitious Audio-Animatronic efforts.

Throughout its periodic refurbishments, we've had a high opinion of *The Hall of Presidents*. That said, we receive a lot of mail from readers who get more than entertainment from it. A woman in St. Louis writes:

We always go when my husband gets cranky, so he can take a nice nap.

A young mother in Marion, Ohio, adds:

The Hall of Presidents *is a great place to breast-feed.*

Finally, from a New Jersey teen:

Mom and Dad both fell asleep during The Hall of Presidents. *Only I, a 15-year-old high school freshman, actually paid attention. It's not the most exciting thing in Disney World, but I find it very difficult to fall asleep when Morgan Freeman is speaking. His voice is way too awesome.*

TOURING TIPS Detail and costumes are masterful. This attraction is one of the park's most popular among older visitors. Don't be put off by long lines. The theater holds more than 700 people, thus swallowing large lines at a single gulp when visitors are admitted.

The Haunted Mansion *(FastPass+)* ★★★★½

APPEAL BY AGE   PRESCHOOL ★★★½ GRADE SCHOOL ★★★★   TEENS ★★★★½
YOUNG ADULTS ★★★★½   OVER 30 ★★★★½   SENIORS ★★★★½

What it is Haunted-house dark ride. **Scope and scale** Major attraction. **When to go** Before 11 a.m. or during the last 2 hours before closing. **Special comments** Frightens some very young children. **Authors' rating** A masterpiece of detail and not to be missed; ★★★★½. **Duration of ride** 7-minute ride plus a 1½-minute preshow. **Average wait in line per 100 people ahead of you** 2½ minutes; assumes both "stretch rooms" operating. **Loading speed** Fast.

DESCRIPTION AND COMMENTS Only slightly scarier than a whoopee cushion, The Haunted Mansion serves up some of the Magic Kingdom's best visual effects. "Doom Buggies" on a conveyor belt transport you through the house from parlor to attic, then through a graveyard. The effects change tone with the setting: Those found in the house are generally spooky, while the graveyard effects, such as a ghostly opera singer wearing a Viking helmet, are there for laughs. Some kids become anxious about what they think they'll see; almost nobody actually gets scared.

Unofficial Guide writer Eve Zibart, a Haunted Mansion fan, says:

This is one of the best attractions in the Magic Kingdom, jam-packed with visual puns, special effects, hidden Mickeys, and lovely Victorian-spooky sets. It's not scary except in the sweetest of ways, and it will remind you of the days before ghost stories gave way to slasher flicks.

A Temple, Texas, mom isn't convinced when we say it isn't scary:

You say the actual sights aren't really frightening. What isn't *frightening about a hanging corpse, a coffin escapee, and an axe-wielding skeleton bride?*

DISNEY DISH WITH JIM HILL

OLD-HAT IN A GOOD WAY As part of Disneyland's 60th-anniversary celebration, the long-gone-but-not-forgotten Hatbox Ghost returned to that theme park's Haunted Mansion. Walt Disney World's 50th anniversary is coming up in 2021, and according to what Imagineering insiders have recently told me, Disney World may get a hatbox-shaped birthday present at that time. But probably not sooner.

A mom from Victoria, British Columbia, wishes teens would shut their pieholes:

My 4-year-old daughter loved Space Mountain, but The Haunted Mansion really scared her. Our experience was that teenagers deliberately scream and pretend to be scared on this ride. This scares the crap out of the little ones.

Interactive elements in the left side of the outdoor queue ensure that guests have something to occupy them when lines are long. Features include a music-playing monument and a ship captain's tomb that squirts water.

TOURING TIPS Lines here ebb and flow more than those at most other Magic Kingdom hot spots because the Mansion is near *The Hall of Presidents* and the *Liberty Belle* Riverboat. These two attractions disgorge 700 and 450 people, respectively, when each show or ride ends, and many of these folks head straight for the Mansion. If you can't go before 11:30 a.m. or after 8 p.m., try to slip in between crowds.

If you're touring the Magic Kingdom in a single day, you'll find that Fast-Pass+ saves more time at other attractions than it does here. On the other hand, you may find it useful if you're touring over two or more days, or if the Mansion is your fourth FastPass.

Liberty Belle Riverboat ★★½

APPEAL BY AGE	PRESCHOOL ★★★½	GRADE SCHOOL ★★★½	TEENS ★★★
YOUNG ADULTS ★★★½		OVER 30 ★★★½	SENIORS ★★★★

What it is Outdoor scenic boat ride. **Scope and scale** Major attraction. **When to go** Anytime. **Authors' rating** Slow, relaxing, and scenic; ★★½. **Duration of ride** About 16 minutes. **Average wait to board** 10–14 minutes.

DESCRIPTION AND COMMENTS Large-capacity paddle-wheel riverboat navigates the waters around Tom Sawyer Island and Fort Langhorn, passing settler cabins, old mining paraphernalia, an Indian village, and a small menagerie of animatronic wildlife. A beautiful craft, the *Liberty Belle* provides a lofty perspective of Frontierland and Liberty Square.

TOURING TIPS The riverboat, which departs roughly every half-hour, is a good attraction for the busy middle of the day. If you encounter huge crowds, chances are that the attraction has been inundated by a wave of guests coming from a just-concluded performance of *The Hall of Presidents*.

FANTASYLAND

FANTASYLAND IS THE HEART OF THE MAGIC KINGDOM— a truly enchanting place spread gracefully like a miniature Alpine village beneath the steepled towers of Cinderella Castle.

Fantasyland is divided into three distinct sections. Directly behind Cinderella Castle and set upon a snowcapped mountain is **Beast's Castle,** part of a *Beauty and the Beast*–themed area. Most of this section holds dining and shopping, such as **Be Our Guest** restaurant (see reviews in Part Four); **Gaston's Tavern,** a small quick-service restaurant; and a gift shop. The far-right corner of Fantasyland—including **Dumbo, The Barnstormer** kiddie coaster, and the Fantasyland train station—is called **Storybook Circus** as an homage to Disney's *Dumbo* film. These are low-capacity amusement park rides appropriate for younger children. A covered seating area with plush chairs, electrical outlets, and USB chargers is available behind **Big Top Souvenirs.**

DISNEY DISH WITH JIM HILL

BEAUTIFUL FIXTURE, BEASTLY PROBLEM
The enormous chandelier that dangles over the Grand Ballroom in Be Our Guest Restaurant—12 feet tall and 11 feet wide, with 84 candles and 100 jewels—had to be partly disassembled at the last minute to fit through the restaurant's doors for installation.

The middle of Fantasyland holds the headliners, including **Under the Sea** and **Seven Dwarfs Mine Train.** The placement of these two attractions allows good traffic flow either to the left (toward Beast's Castle) for dining, to the right for attractions geared to smaller children, or back to the original part of Fantasyland for classic attractions such as **Peter Pan's Flight** and **The Many Adventures of Winnie the Pooh.**

The original part of Fantasyland also hosts the incredibly popular **Princess Fairytale Hall** meet and greet, with waits of 5 hours or more to meet *Frozen*'s Anna and Elsa. Even so, Len's daughter, Hannah, thinks it's the best character-greeting venue in Walt Disney World. (Lines for the B-list princesses are shorter.)

Finally, when nature (or technology) calls, don't miss the ***Tangled*-themed restrooms and outdoor seating** (with phone-charging stations), near Peter Pan's Flight and It's a Small World.

Ariel's Grotto *(FastPass+)* ★★★

APPEAL BY AGE	PRESCHOOL ★★★★½	GRADE SCHOOL ★★★★½	TEENS ★★★★
YOUNG ADULTS ★★★★		OVER 30 ★★★½	SENIORS ★★★★

What it is Character-greeting venue. **Scope and scale** Minor attraction. **When to go** Before 10:30 a.m., during the last 2 hours before closing, or use FastPass+. **Authors' rating** Not as themed as other character greetings; ★★★. **Duration of experience** About 30–90 seconds. **Probable waiting time** 45 minutes. **Queue speed** Slow.

DESCRIPTION AND COMMENTS This is Ariel's home turf, next to the Under the Sea ride. In the base of the seaside cliffs under Prince Eric's Castle, Ariel (in mermaid form) greets guests from a seashell throne.

An older couple from San Antonio visited the Grotto but didn't find what they were expecting:

The description of Ariel's Grotto on the park map read, "Visit Ariel and all her treasures," which led us to believe it was some sort of walk-through gallery. Curious, we were ushered into Ariel's Treasure Room. Imagine our surprise when we saw a young woman dressed only in a clamshell bra and a fish tail. When we told her that we didn't want to have our picture taken with her—I could just imagine having a picture of a scantily clad woman on my desk—she looked hurt and said, "You don't want a picture of me?"

TOURING TIPS The Grotto may close an hour before the rest of the park. The greeting area is set up almost as if to encourage guests to linger with Ariel, which keeps the line long. The queue isn't air-conditioned, which is surprising for a venue that's supposed to store fish.

The Barnstormer *(FastPass+)* ★★

APPEAL BY AGE	PRESCHOOL ★★★★	GRADE SCHOOL ★★★★	TEENS ★★★½
YOUNG ADULTS ★★★		OVER 30 ★★★	SENIORS ★★★½

What it is Small roller coaster. **Scope and scale** Minor attraction. **When to go** Before 11 a.m., during parades, during the last 2 hours before closing, or use FastPass+. **Special comments** 35″ minimum height requirement. **Authors' rating** Great for little ones, but not worth the wait for adults; ★★. **Duration of ride** About 53 seconds. **Average wait in line per 100 people ahead of you** 7 minutes. **Loading speed** Slow.

DESCRIPTION AND COMMENTS The Barnstormer is a very small roller coaster. The ride is zippy but supershort. In fact, of the 53 seconds the ride is in motion, 32 seconds are consumed in leaving the loading area, being ratcheted up the first hill, and braking into the off-loading area. The actual time you spend careering around the track is 21 seconds.

A 42-year-old woman from Westport, Connecticut, warns adults that the ride may not be as tame as it looks:

A nightmare that should have gone in your "Eats Adults" section. It looked so innocent—nothing hidden in the dark, over quickly—but my 8-year-old son and I were terrified, and it took me hours to stop feeling nauseated.

Though the reader's point is well taken, The Barnstormer is a fairly benign introduction to the roller-coaster genre and a predictably positive way to help your children step up to more-adventuresome rides. Simply put, a few circuits will increase your little one's confidence and improve his or her chances for enjoying Disney's more adult attractions. (Seven Dwarfs Mine Train would be the next to try.)

TOURING TIPS The cars of this dinky coaster are too small for most adults and tend to whiplash taller people. Parties without children should skip this one. If you're touring with children, you have a problem: The ride is visually and aurally appealing, and most kids want to ride, subjecting the whole family to slow-moving lines. If The Barnstormer is high on your children's hit parade, try to ride within the first 2 hours that Fantasyland is open. This attraction is rarely a good use of FastPass+.

A Cary, North Carolina, mother of preschoolers offers a heads-up for solo parents:

There are some fussy rules for riding The Barnstormer. Each of the ride cars holds only two people, and every child under 7 must be accompanied by an adult. That means a single parent can't take two small children on the ride alone; you either need to rustle up another adult to help or skip it entirely.

Casey Jr. Splash 'N' Soak Station ★★★

APPEAL BY AGE	PRESCHOOL ★★★★½	GRADE SCHOOL ★★★★½	TEENS ★★★
YOUNG ADULTS ★★½		OVER 30 ★★½	SENIORS ★★★

What it is Opportunity to get wet. **Scope and scale** Diversion. **When to go** When it's hot. **Authors' rating** Great way to cool off; ★★★.

DESCRIPTION AND COMMENTS Casey Jr., the circus train from *Dumbo,* plays host to an absolutely drenching experience outside the Fantasyland Train Station in the Storybook Circus area. Expect a cadre of captive circus beasts to spray water on you in this elaborate water-play area.

TOURING TIPS Puts all other theme park splash areas to soaking shame. Bring a change of clothes and a big towel.

Dumbo the Flying Elephant (*FastPass+*) ★★★½

APPEAL BY AGE	PRESCHOOL ★★★★½	GRADE SCHOOL ★★★★	TEENS ★★★
YOUNG ADULTS ★★★½		OVER 30 ★★★½	SENIORS ★★★½

What it is Disneyfied midway ride. **Scope and scale** Minor attraction. **When to go** Before 10:30 a.m., after 3 p.m., or use FastPass+. **Authors' rating** Disney's signature ride for children; ★★★½. **Duration of ride** 1½ minutes. **Average wait in line per 100 people ahead of you** 10 minutes. **Loading speed** Slow.

DESCRIPTION AND COMMENTS A tame, happy children's ride based on the lovable flying pachyderm. Parents and children sit inside small fiberglass "elephants" mounted on long metal arms, which spin around a central axis. Controls inside each vehicle allow you to raise the arm, making you spin higher off the ground. Despite being little different from rides at state fairs and amusement parks, Dumbo is the favorite Magic Kingdom attraction of many younger children.

As part of the Fantasyland expansion, Dumbo moved to the upper-right corner of the land. The attraction's capacity has doubled with the ad-dition of a second ride—a clone of the first. These two changes, along with the addition of the newer Fantasyland attractions, have drastically reduced waits to ride. If you do find yourself with a wait, Dumbo also includes a cov-ered queue featuring interactive elements (read: things your kids can play with to pass the time in line).

From a Glenelg, Maryland, mother of two preschoolers:

The Dumbo waiting area is fantastic for young kids. That's right—what my kids look forward to most is not the actual Dumbo ride but the playground that Disney created as the waiting area.

TOURING TIPS If Dumbo is essential to your child's happiness, ride within the first 2 hours the park is open or after dinner—not only are crowds smaller at night, but the lighting and effects make the ride much prettier then. Or try Dumbo following the afternoon parade.

If you want to ride Dumbo twice with a minimal wait, have both adults get in line on the same side of Dumbo, and allow between 32 and 64 peo-ple to get between the first adult and child and the second adult. Pass the child to the second adult when the first ride is over.

Finally, with increased capacity and a remote location moderating its lines, Dumbo is almost never a good choice for FastPass+.

Enchanted Tales with Belle (FastPass+)   ★★★★

APPEAL BY AGE	PRESCHOOL ★★★★½	GRADE SCHOOL ★★★★½	TEENS ★★★½
YOUNG ADULTS ★★★½	OVER 30 ★★★★		SENIORS ★★★★

What it is Interactive character show. **Scope and scale** Minor attraction. **When to go** As soon as the park opens, during the last 2 hours before closing, or use FastPass+. **Authors' rating** The prettiest meet-and-greet location in the park; ★★★★. **Duration of presentation** About 20 minutes. **Preshow entertainment** As described below. **Probable waiting time** 25 minutes. **Queue speed** Slow.

DESCRIPTION AND COMMENTS This multiscene *Beauty and the Beast* experi-ence takes guests into Maurice's workshop, through a magic mirror, and into Beast's library, where the audience shares a story with Belle.

You enter the attraction by walking through Maurice's cottage, where you see mementos tracing Belle's childhood, including her favorite books, and lines drawn on one wall showing how fast Belle grew every year.

From there you'll enter Maurice's workshop at the back of the cottage. An assortment of Maurice's odd wood gadgets covers every inch of the floor, walls, and ceiling. Take a moment to peruse the gadgets, then focus your at-tention on the mirror on the wall to the left of the entry door.

Soon enough, the room gets dark and the mirror begins to sparkle. With magic and some really good carpentry skills, the mirror turns into a full-size doorway, through which guests enter into a wardrobe room. Once in the wardrobe room, the attraction's premise is explained: You're supposed to re-enact the story of *Beauty and the Beast* for Belle on her birthday, and guests are chosen to act out key parts in the play.

Once the parts are cast, everyone walks into the castle's library and takes a seat. Cast members explain how the play will take place and introduce Belle, who gives a short speech about how thrilled she is for everyone to be there. The play is acted out within a few minutes, and all of the actors get a chance to take photos with Belle and receive a small bookmark as a memento.

During our visits, only those who were chosen to act in the play got to take photos with Belle. Also, those who took photos with Belle received a separate Memory Maker card for those photos.

Enchanted Tales with Belle is surely the prettiest and most elaborate meet-and-greet station in Walt Disney World. For the relative few who get to act in the play, it's also a chance to interact with Belle in a way that isn't possible in other character encounters. We also like how Disney "stages" guests in the cottage, workshop, and wardrobe rooms—it's an efficient way to handle the wait in line, and it keeps guests from getting bored. Sure, it can still be a 30-minute wait for a 3-minute play, but it's the best of its kind in Orlando, and your kids will love it.

An enthusiastic review from an Austin, Texas, mom:

> Enchanted Tales with Belle *surprised us with how well it was done. In the skit, my husband was a knight, my daughter was Mrs. Potts, and my son was silver-ware. It was so much fun, and the kids were so proud.*

TOURING TIPS *Enchanted Tales* has long lines from the time the park opens. In fact, its popularity has made it one of the hardest tickets at the Magic Kingdom, as a Lansing, Michigan, mom explains:

> *We found the wait for* Enchanted Tales with Belle *was never below 40 minutes. But our girls completely loved it, and so did I.*

Since it's slow-loading, make *Enchanted Tales* the first thing on your touring plan if you want to see it. Alternatively, try to visit during the last 2 hours the park is open, or use FastPass+.

It's a Small World (FastPass+) ★★★½

APPEAL BY AGE PRESCHOOL ★★★★½ GRADE SCHOOL ★★★★ TEENS ★★★ YOUNG ADULTS ★★★½ OVER 30 ★★★½ SENIORS ★★★★

What it is World brotherhood–themed indoor boat ride. **Scope and scale** Major attraction. **When to go** Before 11 a.m., during parades, after 7 p.m., or use FastPass+ **Authors' rating** Exponentially "cute"; ★★★½. **Duration of ride** About 11 minutes. **Average wait in line per 100 people ahead of you** 3½ minutes; assumes busy conditions with 30 or more boats operating. **Loading speed** Fast.

DESCRIPTION AND COMMENTS It's a Small World is a happy, upbeat indoor attraction with a mind-numbing tune that only a backhoe can remove from your brain. Small boats carry visitors on a tour around the world, with singing and dancing dolls showcasing the dress and culture of each nation. One of Disney's oldest entertainment offerings, Small World first unleashed its brainwashing song and lethally cute ethnic dolls on the real world at the 1964 New York World's Fair—the original exhibit was moved to Disneyland after the fair, and a duplicate was created for Walt Disney World when it opened in 1971.

Though it bludgeons you with its sappy redundancy, almost everyone enjoys It's a Small World (the first time, anyway). It stands, however, with *Enchanted Tiki Room* in the "What were they smokin'?" category.

A reader from Campbellton, New Brunswick, has developed a unique mechanism for coping with the annoying repetition of the theme song:

If, like me, you can't stand It's a Small World but get dragged on anyway, (1) ask to sit at the back of the boat, then (2) once you're in the building, pull out your iPhone and headphones and blast some heavy metal. You'd be amazed at how different and deceptively funny the ride becomes!

A teen from Calgary, Alberta, took the previous reader's advice:

I compromised with my dad that I'd ride provided I could listen to metal on my iPod. It worked, and I was satisfied.

TOURING TIPS Cool off here when it's hot. Lines are usually 30 minutes or less, so you don't need FastPass+. If you wear a hearing aid, *turn it off.*

Mad Tea Party *(FastPass+)* ★★

Motion Sickness

What it is Midway-type spinning ride. **Scope and scale** Minor attraction. **When to go** Before 11 a.m., after 5 p.m., or use FastPass+. **Special comments** You can make the teacups spin faster by turning the wheel in the center of the cup. **Authors' rating** Not worth the wait; ★★. **Duration of ride** 1½ minutes. **Average wait in line per 100 people ahead of you** 7½ minutes. **Loading speed** Slow.

DESCRIPTION AND COMMENTS Riders whirl feverishly in big teacups. *Alice in Wonderland*'s Mad Hatter provides the theme. Teenagers like to lure adults onto the teacups, then turn the wheel in the middle (making the cup spin faster) until the adults are plastered against the sides and on the verge of throwing up. Don't even *consider* getting on this one with anybody younger than 21.

A reader we've dubbed Melba the Human Centrifuge advises:

If you want to spin your teacup, don't put more than three people in one cup.

TOURING TIPS Mad Tea Party is notoriously slow-loading. Ride the morning of your second day if your schedule is more relaxed. Not a good choice for FastPass+.

The Many Adventures of Winnie the Pooh *(FastPass+)* ★★★½

What it is Indoor track ride. **Scope and scale** Minor attraction. **When to go** Before 10 a.m., in last hour park is open, or use FastPass+. **Authors' rating** As cute as the Pooh Bear himself; ★★★½. **Duration of ride** About 4 minutes. **Average wait in line per 100 people ahead of you** 4 minutes. **Loading speed** Moderate.

DESCRIPTION AND COMMENTS Pooh is sunny, upbeat, and fun. You ride a Hunny Pot through the pages of a huge picture book into the Hundred Acre Wood, where you encounter Pooh, Piglet, Eeyore, Owl, Rabbit, Tigger, Kanga, and Roo as they contend with a blustery day. There's even a dream sequence with Heffalumps and Woozles.

A 30-something couple from Lexington, Massachusetts, thinks Pooh has plenty to offer adults:

The attention to detail and special effects make it worth seeing even if you don't have children in your party. The Pooh dream sequence was great!

A Richmond, Indiana, mom loved Pooh's interactive queue:

The queue for The Many Adventures of Winnie the Pooh was amazing! There were so many things for little kids to do, and consequently fewer meltdowns! I wish there were more queues like that.

TOURING TIPS Pooh is a good choice for FastPass+ if you have small children and you're touring over two or more days.

Meet Merida at Fairytale Gardens   ★★★½

APPEAL BY AGE   PRESCHOOL ★★★★★   GRADE SCHOOL ★★★★½   TEENS ★★★½
YOUNG ADULTS ★★★½   OVER 30 ★★★½   SENIORS ★★★

What it is Storytelling session and character meet and greet. **Scope and scale** Diversion. **When to go** See *Times Guide* for schedule. **Authors' rating** Lovely lass, lovely locale; ★★★½. **Duration of presentation** About 10 minutes. **Probable waiting time** 1 hour or more. **Queue speed** Slow.

DESCRIPTION AND COMMENTS Merida, the flame-haired Scottish princess from *Brave,* greets guests in Fairytale Gardens, in front of Cinderella Castle on the Tomorrowland side, between the castle and Cosmic Ray's Starlight Cafe.

A mom from Shelby, North Carolina, saw red and liked it:

I was unaware that many of the princesses give red-lipstick kisses, and this delighted both of my children!

TOURING TIPS Princess meet and greets tend to be exceedingly popular, especially those involving princesses from recent movies, so expect long lines. If meeting Merida is a must-do for your family, get in line early in the morning.

Mickey's PhilharMagic (FastPass+)   ★★★★

APPEAL BY AGE   PRESCHOOL ★★★★   GRADE SCHOOL ★★★★½   TEENS ★★★★
YOUNG ADULTS ★★★★½   OVER 30 ★★★★½   SENIORS ★★★★½

What it is 3-D movie. **Scope and scale** Major attraction. **When to go** Before 11 a.m., during parades, or use FastPass+. **Authors' rating** A zany masterpiece, not to be missed; ★★★★. **Duration of presentation** About 12 minutes. **Probable waiting time** 12–30 minutes.

DESCRIPTION AND COMMENTS The Magic Kingdom's 3-D movie, *Mickey's PhilharMagic* features an odd collection of Disney characters, mixing Mickey and Donald with Simba and Ariel as well as Jasmine and Aladdin. Presented in a theater large enough to accommodate a 150-foot-wide screen—huge by 3-D standards—the movie is augmented by an arsenal of special effects built into the theater. The plot involves Mickey, as the conductor of the PhilharMagic, leaving the theater to solve a mystery. In his absence, Donald attempts to take charge, with disastrous results.

Brilliantly conceived, furiously paced, and laugh-out-loud funny, *Mickey's PhilharMagic* will leave you grinning. And where other Disney 3-D movies are loud, in-your-face affairs, this one is softer and cuddlier. Things pop out of the screen, but they're really not scary. It's the rare child who is frightened—but there are always exceptions, as was the case with the 3-year-old child of this North Carolina mom:

Our family found PhilharMagic way too violent (what seemed like minutes on end of Donald getting the crap kicked out of him by various musical instruments). I had to haul my screaming child out of the theater and submit to a therapeutic carousel ride afterwards.

Happily, an Oregon mom has an easy way to nip the willies in the bud:

My advice to parents is simply to have their kids not wear the 3-D glasses. We took my daughter's off right away, and then she began giggling and having a good time watching the movie.

TOURING TIPS The theater is large, so don't be alarmed to see a gaggle of people in the lobby. *PhilharMagic* never needs FastPass+.

Peter Pan's Flight *(FastPass+)* ★★★★

APPEAL BY AGE PRESCHOOL ★★★★½   GRADE SCHOOL ★★★★   TEENS ★★★½
YOUNG ADULTS ★★★★   OVER 30 ★★★★   SENIORS ★★★★

What it is Indoor track ride. **Scope and scale** Minor attraction. **When to go** First or last 30 minutes the park is open, or use FastPass+. **Authors' rating** Nostalgic, mellow, and well done; not to be missed; ★★★★. **Duration of ride** A little over 3 minutes. **Average wait in line per 100 people ahead of you** 5½ minutes. **Loading speed** Moderate–slow.

DESCRIPTION AND COMMENTS Peter Pan's Flight is superbly designed and absolutely delightful, with a happy theme uniting some favorite Disney characters, beautiful effects, and charming music. This indoor ride begins in the Darling family's house before taking you on a relaxing trip in a "flying pirate ship" over old London and thence to Never-Never Land, where Peter saves Wendy from walking the plank and Captain Hook rehearses for *Dancing with the Stars* on the snout of the ubiquitous crocodile. There's nothing here that will jump out at you or frighten young children.

A new themed queue for Peter Pan opened in early 2015. Besides air-conditioning, the updated preshow area features a walk through the Darling's street and home, where you'll see family portraits and various rooms of the house, play a few games to pass the time, and get sprinkled with a bit of pixie dust.

TOURING TIPS Because Peter Pan's Flight is very popular, count on long lines all day. Fortunately, the new queue runs under the roof of the building, out of direct sun and rain, and has tons of new art and interactive games to help pass the time. Ride in the first 30 minutes the park is open, during a parade, just before the park closes, or use FastPass+.

Our touring plan software suggests using FastPass+ for Peter Pan's Flight more than any other Walt Disney World attraction (see page 87).

Pete's Silly Sideshow *(FastPass+)* ★★★½

APPEAL BY AGE PRESCHOOL ★★★★½ GRADE SCHOOL ★★★★½ TEENS ★★★★
YOUNG ADULTS ★★★★   OVER 30 ★★★★   SENIORS ★★★★½

What it is Character-greeting venue. **Scope and scale** Minor attraction. **When to go** Before 11 a.m., during the last 2 hours before closing, or use FastPass+. **Authors' rating** Well themed with unique character costumes; ★★★½. **Duration of experience** 7 minutes per character. **Probable waiting time** 25 minutes. **Queue speed** Slow.

DESCRIPTION AND COMMENTS Pete's Silly Sideshow is a circus-themed character-greeting area in the Storybook Circus part of Fantasyland. The characters' costumes are distinct from the ones normally worn around the parks. Characters include Goofy as The Great Goofini, Donald Duck as The Astounding Donaldo, Daisy Duck as Madame Daisy Fortuna, and Minnie Mouse as Minnie Magnifique.

TOURING TIPS On non–Extra Magic Hour days, Pete's opens 45 minutes later than the rest of the park and usually closes at the same time as the first

Wishes fireworks show. The queue is indoors and air-conditioned. There's one queue for Goofy and Donald and a second queue for Minnie and Daisy; you can meet two characters at once, but you have to line up twice to meet all four. Rarely a good use of FastPass+.

Prince Charming Regal Carrousel ★★★

APPEAL BY AGE	PRESCHOOL ★★★★½	GRADE SCHOOL ★★★★	TEENS ★★★½
YOUNG ADULTS ★★★½		OVER 30 ★★★½	SENIORS ★★★½

What it is Merry-go-round. **Scope and scale** Minor attraction. **When to go** Anytime. **Authors' rating** A beautiful ride for children; ★★★. **Duration of ride** About 2 minutes. **Average wait in line per 100 people ahead of you** 5 minutes. **Loading speed** Slow.

DESCRIPTION AND COMMENTS One of the most elaborate and beautiful merry-go-rounds you'll ever have the pleasure of seeing, especially when its lights are on.

A shy and retiring 9-year-old girl from Rockaway, New Jersey, thinks our rating of the carousel for grade-schoolers should be higher:

I want to complain. I went on the Prince Charming Regal Carrousel four times and I loved it! Raise those stars right now!

TOURING TIPS Unless young children in your party insist on riding, appreciate this attraction from the sidelines. While lovely to look at, the carousel loads and unloads very slowly.

Princess Fairytale Hall *(FastPass+)* ★★★

APPEAL BY AGE	PRESCHOOL ★★★★★	GRADE SCHOOL ★★★★½	TEENS ★★★★
YOUNG ADULTS ★★★★		OVER 30 ★★★½	SENIORS ★★★½

What it is Character-greeting venue. **Scope and scale** Minor attraction. **When to go** Before 10:30 a.m., after 4 p.m., or use FastPass+. **Authors' rating** You want princesses? Disney's got 'em! ★★★. **Duration of ride** 7-10 minutes (estimated). **Average wait in line per 100 people ahead of you** 35 minutes (estimated). **Loading speed** Slow.

DESCRIPTION AND COMMENTS Princess Fairytale Hall is Disney-princess central in the Magic Kingdom. Inside are two greeting venues, with each holding a small reception area for two princesses. Thus, there are four princesses meeting and greeting at any time, and you can see two of them at once. Signs outside the entrance tell you which line leads to which princess pair and how long the wait will be. Rapunzel usually leads one side, typically paired with Snow White, Cinderella, or another princess, while Anna and Elsa from *Frozen* hold forth on the other side.

Around 5-10 guests at a time are admitted to each greeting area, where there's plenty of time for small talk, a photo, and a hug from each princess.

DISNEY DISH WITH JIM HILL

WILL FANTASYLAND GET *FROZEN* OUT? Epcot managers are counting on the new *Frozen* meet and greet in Norway to help boost attendance. That's why they've proposed having Anna and Elsa leave the Magic Kingdom's Princess Fairytale Hall for at least six months, so that Epcot has the sisters exclusively. Magic Kingdom managers aren't thrilled with this idea, pointing out that Disney's Hollywood Studios isn't being asked to put *For the First Time in Forever: A Frozen Sing-Along Celebration* on ice.

Enough time is given to each family, in fact, that we ran out of things to say to Rapunzel and shuffled quietly over to Snow White.

Fairytale Hall first opened with Cinderella headlining one of the attraction's two rooms, but Cindy was drawing roughly half the crowds Rapunzel did. When Anna and Elsa debuted to 5-hour lines at Epcot's Norway Pavilion, Cinderella was demoted to backup and the Scandinavians moved to the Magic Kingdom.

TOURING TIPS Anna and Elsa are the hottest character-greeting ticket in all of Walt Disney World. If your child absolutely must meet them, use Fast-Pass+ (good luck with that!) or head to Fairytale Hall first thing in the morning. Understand, though, that even if you're on hand at park opening, waits can easily top 2 hours—and often much, much more than that, as this frustrated Richmond, Virginia, mom found out:

My 8-year-old daughter wanted meet Anna and Elsa, so we rushed there at rope drop. We had a 2-hour wait, but others waited as long as 5.5 hours. Please tell your readers that the only way to see the Frozen princesses is to get a FastPass+ at least 60 days in advance or spend several hours in line, forgoing food, water, and bathroom breaks, and losing all sanity!

A Texas mom's teenage daughter didn't find it hard to see Anna and Elsa at all—to the contrary, they were all over the place:

My 13-year-old daughter amused herself by keeping count of how many Elsas and Annas she saw in the park and texting her counts to her friends. Just for the record, her final count was Elsa 90, Anna 67.

Seven Dwarfs Mine Train *(FastPass+)* ★★★★

APPEAL BY AGE PRESCHOOL ★★★★   GRADE SCHOOL ★★★★½ TEENS ★★★★
YOUNG ADULTS ★★★★   OVER 30 ★★★★   SENIORS ★★★★½

What it is Indoor/outdoor roller coaster. **Scope and scale** Major attraction. **When to go** As soon as the park opens, or use FastPass+. **Special comments** 38″ minimum height requirement. **Authors' rating** Great family coaster; not to be missed; ★★★★. **Duration of ride** About 2 minutes. **Average wait in line per 100 people ahead of you** About 4½ minutes. **Loading speed** Fast.

DISNEY DISH WITH JIM HILL

MINING INSPIRATION FROM THE PAST In Seven Dwarfs Mine Train's main mine scene, the Imagineers built the animation of the marching Seven Short Dudes using rotoscoped images directly from the "Heigh-Ho" number in the movie.

DESCRIPTION AND COMMENTS In the pantheon of Disney coasters, Seven Dwarfs Mine Train fits somewhere between The Barnstormer and Big Thunder Mountain Railroad—that is, it's geared to older grade-school kids who've been on amusement park rides before. There are no loops, inversions, or rolls in the track, and no massive hills or steep drops; rather, the Mine Train's trick is that your ride vehicle's seats swing side-to-side as you go through turns. And—what a coincidence!—Disney has designed a curvy track with steep turns. There's also an elaborate indoor section showing the Seven Dwarfs' underground operation.

The exterior design includes waterfalls, forests, and landscaping and is meant to join together all of the surrounding Fantasyland's various locations, including France and Germany. The swinging effect is more noticeable the farther back you're seated in the train.

New Disney attractions always generate a lot of reader comments, and Seven Dwarfs Mine Train is no exception. First, from a Rhode Island couple:

As far as new rides go, we give high marks to Seven Dwarfs Mine Train. It's faster than it looks in videos, and the animatronics are top-notch. It broke down during our FastPass+ window, so we were given an additional pass. On our next day in the Magic Kingdom, we rode it at night. Much like Big Thunder and Splash Mountain, this ride is even better at night!

From an Aurora, Illinois, woman:

It's a pretty easy coaster, somewhere between Big Thunder and The Barnstormer in intensity, and I'd ride it just to see the mine scene over and over again!

A Chester, Virginia, mom offers a little cost–benefit analysis:

Seven Dwarfs Mine Train was a great ride, but not worth a 90-minute wait.

A mom from Horsham, Pennsylvania, felt let down:

Our family's rating of the 7 D Mine Train is two stars at most. The detail and activities in line were great, and I thought that the animation of the characters' faces was amazing. But we were all sadly disappointed in the ride—it's over so quickly, it really isn't worth your time. Realistically, if we only had to wait 15–20 minutes, we still would only give it two and a half stars at best.

Finally, from a Hesston, Kansas, dad:

The Mine Train was fairly forgettable to my wife and I, but my 5-year old loved it. The middle dark-ride section was amazing, but the rest was over very fast. It's a perfect step between The Barnstormer and the bigger Mountains, but without FastPass+ or being there first, it can be skipped.

TOURING TIPS If you have only a day to see the Magic Kingdom, make Fast-Pass+ reservations in advance for around 9:30 a.m. at Big Thunder Mountain Railroad and around 3:30 p.m. at Space Mountain. On the day of your visit, ride Seven Dwarfs Mine Train as soon as the park opens, then hotfoot it to Splash Mountain to ride immediately. Your FastPass+ reservation for Big Thunder Mountain will be valid by the time you're done, and you'll have experienced three of the park's four headliners in about an hour.

If you have two mornings, do the Fantasyland and Frontierland attractions—Seven Dwarfs Mine Train, Splash Mountain, and Big Thunder Mountain Railroad—on one day and Space Mountain the next. Spreading your visits over two mornings eliminates a lot of walking.

Other FastPass+ strategies combining the park's "mountains" with other headliners have been incorporated into our Magic Kingdom touring plans (see pages 806–811).

Under the Sea: Journey of the Little Mermaid
(FastPass+) ★★★½

APPEAL BY AGE   PRESCHOOL ★★★★½   GRADE SCHOOL ★★★★   TEENS ★★★½
YOUNG ADULTS ★★★★   OVER 30 ★★★★   SENIORS ★★★★

What it is Dark ride retelling the film's story. **Scope and scale** Major attraction. **When to go** Before 10:30 a.m., during the last 2 hours before closing, or use Fast-Pass+. **Authors' rating** Colorful, but most effects are too simple for an attraction this big; ★★★½. **Duration of ride** About 5½ minutes. **Average wait in line per 100 people ahead of you** 3 minutes. **Loading speed** Fast.

DESCRIPTION AND COMMENTS Under the Sea takes riders through almost a dozen scenes retelling the story of *The Little Mermaid,* with animatronics, video effects, and a vibrant 3-D set the size of a small theater.

Guests board a clamshell-shaped ride vehicle running along a continuously moving track (similar to The Haunted Mansion's). Then the ride "descends" under water, past Ariel's grotto and on to King Triton's undersea kingdom. The most detailed animatronic is of Ursula, the octopus, and she's a beauty. Other scenes hit the film's highlights, including Ariel meeting Prince Eric, her deal with Ursula to become human, and, of course, the couple's happy ending.

The attraction's exterior is attractive, with detailed rock work, water, and story elements. (Our favorite effect is a "hidden Mickey"—the shape of Mickey's head and ears—that is created through a special alignment of the sun's shadow and the rock work, and only at noon on November 18, Mickey's birthday.) Our problems with the attraction are: (1) Most of the effects throughout the ride are simple and unimaginative, such as starfish that do nothing but spin on a central axis or lobsters that simply turn left and right; and (2) virtually the entire second half of the story is condensed into a handful of small scenes crammed together at the end of the ride.

An early 2015 update to the ride brought improved lighting, a few more animatronic sea creatures in the main show scene, and more-realistic hair for some of the animatronics.

TOURING TIPS Expect moderate waits most of the day. If you can, ride early in the morning or late at night. Rarely a good choice for FastPass+.

Walt Disney World Railroad

DESCRIPTION AND COMMENTS The railroad stops in Fantasyland on its circle tour of the park. See the description under Main Street, U.S.A. (page 493), for additional details.

TOURING TIPS Pleasant, feet-saving link to Main Street and Frontierland . . . but so crowded in the afternoon during times of peak attendance that you'll almost certainly find it faster to walk anywhere in the park.

▌▊ TOMORROWLAND

AT VARIOUS POINTS IN ITS HISTORY, Tomorrowland's attractions presented life's possibilities in adventures ranging from the modern-day (If You Had Wings' round-the-world travel in the 1970s) to the distant future (Mission to Mars). The problem that stymied Disney repeatedly was that the future came faster and looked different than what they'd envisioned.

Today, Tomorrowland's theme makes the least sense of any area in any Disney park. Its current attractions are based on gas-powered race cars, rocket travel (two rides), a look back at 20th-century technology, two rides with aliens, and a comedy show with monsters. It's not so much a vision of the future as it is a collection of attractions that don't fit anywhere else in the park.

Astro Orbiter ★★

APPEAL BY AGE	PRESCHOOL ★★★★	GRADE SCHOOL ★★★★	TEENS ★★★½
YOUNG ADULTS ★★★		OVER 30 ★★★	SENIORS ★★½

What it is Buck Rogers–style rockets revolving around a central axis. **Scope and scale** Minor attraction. **When to go** Before 11 a.m. or during the last hour before closing. **Special comments** Not as innocuous as it appears. **Authors' rating** Not worth the wait; ★★. **Duration of ride** 1½ minutes. **Average wait in line per 100 people ahead of you** 13½ minutes. **Loading speed** Slow.

DESCRIPTION AND COMMENTS Though visually appealing, the Astro Orbiter is still a slow-loading carnival ride. The fat little rocket ships simply fly in circles. The best thing about the Astro Orbiter is the nice view when you're aloft.

TOURING TIPS Expendable on any schedule. If you ride with preschoolers, seat them first, then board. The Astro Orbiter flies higher and faster than Dumbo and frightens some young children. It also apparently messes with some adults. A mother from Lev HaSharon, Israel, writes:

It was a nightmare—people should be forewarned. I was able to sit through all the "Mountains," the "Tours," and the like without my stomach reacting even a little, but after Astro Orbiter I thought I would be finished for the rest of the day. Very quickly I realized that my only chance for survival was to pick a point on the toe of my shoe and stare at it (and certainly not lift my eyes out of the "jet") until the ride was over. My 4-year-old was my copilot; she loved it (go figure), and she had us up high the whole time.

Buzz Lightyear's Space Ranger Spin (FastPass+) ★★★★

APPEAL BY AGE PRESCHOOL ★★★★½ GRADE SCHOOL ★★★★½ TEENS ★★★★
YOUNG ADULTS ★★★★   OVER 30 ★★★★   SENIORS ★★★★

What it is Whimsical space travel–themed indoor ride. **Scope and scale** Minor attraction. **When to go** First or last hour the park is open, or use FastPass+. **Authors' rating** Surreal shooting gallery; ★★★★. **Duration of ride** About 4½ minutes. **Average wait in line per 100 people ahead of you** 3 minutes. **Loading speed** Fast.

DESCRIPTION AND COMMENTS This attraction is based on the space-commando character Buzz Lightyear from the film *Toy Story*. The marginal storyline has you and Buzz trying to save the universe from the evil Emperor Zurg. The indoor ride is interactive to the extent that you can spin your car and shoot simulated laser cannons at Zurg and his minions. The first room's mechanical claw and red robot contain high-value targets, so aim for these.

TOURING TIPS Each car is equipped with two laser cannons and two score-keeping displays, enabling you to compete with your riding partner. A joystick allows you to spin the car to line up the various targets. Each time you pull the trigger, you release a red laser beam that you can see hitting or missing the target.

Most folks spend their first ride learning how to use the equipment (fire off individual shots as opposed to keeping the trigger depressed) and figuring out how the targets work. On the next ride, you'll be surprised by how much better you do. If you're hopeless at games of skill, check out our tips at **tinyurl.com/buzzfortheunskilled.**

Unofficial readers are unanimous in their praise of Buzz Lightyear. Some, in fact, spend several hours on it, riding again and again. The following comment from a Snow Hill, Maryland, dad is representative:

Buzz Lightyear was so much fun it can't be legal! We hit it first on early-entry day and rode it 10 times without stopping. The kids had fun, but it was Dad who spun himself silly trying to shoot the Z's.

Experience Buzz Lightyear after riding Space Mountain first thing in the morning, or use FastPass+.

Monsters, Inc. Laugh Floor *(FastPass+)* ★★★½

APPEAL BY AGE	PRESCHOOL ★★★★	GRADE SCHOOL ★★★★½	TEENS ★★★★
YOUNG ADULTS ★★★★		OVER 30 ★★★★	SENIORS ★★★★½

What it is Interactive animated comedy show. **Scope and scale** Major attraction. **When to go** Before 11 a.m., after 4 p.m., or use FastPass+. **Special comments** Audience members may be asked to participate in skits. **Authors' rating** Good concept, but the jokes are hit-and-miss; ★★★½. **Duration of presentation** About 15 minutes.

DESCRIPTION AND COMMENTS We learned in Disney-Pixar's *Monsters, Inc.* that children's screams could be converted to electricity, which was used to power a town inhabited by monsters. During the film, the monsters discovered that kids' laughter worked even better as an energy source, so in this attraction the monsters have set up a comedy club to capture as many laughs as possible. Mike Wazowski, the one-eyed green monster, emcees the club's three comedy acts. Each act consists of an animated monster (most not seen in the film) trying out various bad puns, knock-knock jokes, and Abbott and Costello–like routines. Using the same cutting-edge technology as Epcot's popular *Turtle Talk with Crush,* behind-the-scenes Disney employees voice the characters and often interact with audience members during the skits. As with any comedy set, some performers are funny and some are not, but Disney has shown a willingness to experiment with new routines and jokes.

A Sioux Falls, South Dakota, mom is a big fan:

> Laugh Floor *was great. It's amazing how the characters interact with the audience—I got picked on twice without trying. Plus, kids can text jokes to Roz.*

TOURING TIPS The theater holds several hundred people, so there's no need to rush here first thing in the morning. Try to arrive late in the morning after you've visited other Tomorrowland attractions, or after the afternoon parade when guests start leaving the park. *Laugh Floor* is never a good choice for FastPass+.

Space Mountain *(FastPass+)* ★★★★

APPEAL BY AGE	PRESCHOOL ★★★†	GRADE SCHOOL ★★★★½	TEENS ★★★★★
YOUNG ADULTS ★★★★½		OVER 30 ★★★★½	SENIORS ★★★½

†*Some preschoolers love Space Mountain; others are frightened by it.*

What it is Roller coaster in the dark. **Scope and scale** Super-headliner. **When to go** When the park opens or use FastPass+. **Special comments** Great fun and action; much wilder than Big Thunder Mountain Railroad. 44″ minimum height requirement; children younger than age 7 must be accompanied by an adult. Switching-off option provided (see page 412). **Authors' rating** An unusual roller coaster with excellent special effects; not to be missed; ★★★★. **Duration of ride** Almost 3 minutes. **Average wait in line per 100 people ahead of you** 3 minutes; assumes 2 tracks, with 1 dedicated to FastPass+ riders, dispatching at 21-second intervals. **Loading speed** Moderate–fast.

Motion Sickness

DESCRIPTION AND COMMENTS Totally enclosed in a mammoth futuristic structure, Space Mountain has always been the Magic Kingdom's most popular attraction. The theme is a space flight through dark recesses of the galaxy. Effects are superb, and the ride is the fastest and wildest in the Magic Kingdom. As a roller coaster, Space Mountain is much zippier than Big Thunder Mountain Railroad, but much tamer than the Rock 'n' Roller Coaster at Hollywood Studios or Expedition Everest at Animal Kingdom.

As a headliner, Space Mountain goes through periodic refurbishments to add effects and maintain ride quality. Past improvements include new lighting and effects, an improved sound system and soundtrack, and interactive games in the queue to help pass the time in line. Roller-coaster aficionados will tell you (correctly) that Space Mountain is a designer version of the Wild Mouse, a midway ride that's been around for almost 60 years. There are no long drops or swooping hills as there are on a traditional roller coaster—only quick, unexpected turns and small drops. Disney's contribution essentially was to add a space theme to the Wild Mouse and put it in the dark. And this does indeed make the Mouse seem wilder.

An Elburn, Illinois, reader recommends bracing yourself—literally:

> They should require you to wear a neck brace on Space Mountain. That ride is painful.

TOURING TIPS People who can handle a fairly wild roller-coaster ride will take Space Mountain in stride. What sets Space Mountain apart is that cars plummet through darkness, with only occasional lighting. Half the fun of Space Mountain is not knowing where the car will go next.

Space Mountain is a favorite of many Magic Kingdom visitors ages 7–60. Each morning before opening, particularly during summer and holiday periods, several hundred Space Mountain junkies await the signal to head to the ride's entrance. To get ahead of the competition, be one of the first in the park. Proceed to the end of Main Street and wait at the entrance to Tomorrowland.

Couples touring with children too small to ride Space Mountain can both ride without waiting twice in line by taking advantage of "switching off." Here's how it works: When you enter the Space Mountain line, tell the first Disney attendant (Greeter One) that you want to switch off. The attendant will allow you, your spouse, and your small child (or children) to continue together, phoning ahead to tell Greeter Two to expect you. When you reach Greeter Two (at the turnstile near the boarding area), you'll be given specific directions. One of you will proceed to ride, while the other stays with the kids. Whoever rides will be admitted by the unloading attendant to stairs leading back up to the boarding area. Here you switch off. The second parent rides, and the first parent takes the kids down the stairs to the unloading area where everybody is reunited and exits together. Switching off is also available at Big Thunder Mountain Railroad and Splash Mountain (and other attractions), and for FastPass+ users.

Seats are one behind another, as opposed to side by side—meaning parents can't sit next to their kids if they meet the height requirement.

If you don't catch Space Mountain first thing in the morning, use FastPass+ or try again during the 30 minutes before closing. To avoid overwhelming Space Mountain's air-conditioning system on hot days, would-be riders are sometimes held in line outside the entrance until the lines have subsided. The appearance from the outside is that the line is enormous when, in fact, most of the people waiting are those visible. This crowd-control technique, known as "stacking," discourages visitors from getting in line. (Stacking is also used at several Disney attractions during the hour before closing to ensure that the ride will be able to close on schedule.) Despite the apparently long line, the wait is usually no longer than if you had been allowed to queue inside.

Stitch's Great Escape!   ★★

APPEAL BY AGE	PRESCHOOL ★★½	GRADE SCHOOL ★★½	TEENS ★★½
YOUNG ADULTS ★★½		OVER 30 ★★	SENIORS ★★½

What it is Theater-in-the-round sci-fi adventure show. **Scope and scale** Minor attraction. **When to go** Before 11 a.m. or after 6 p.m.; try during parades. **Special comments** Frightens children of all ages; 40″ minimum height requirement. Switching-off option provided (see page 412). **Authors' rating** P.U.; ★★. **Duration of presentation** About 12 minutes. **Preshow entertainment** About 6 minutes. **Probable waiting time** 5–15 minutes.

DESCRIPTION AND COMMENTS *Stitch's Great Escape!* stars the havoc-wreaking little alien from the Disney animated feature *Lilo & Stitch*. In this show, Stitch is a prisoner of the galactic authorities and is being transferred to a processing facility en route to his final place of incarceration. He manages to escape by employing an efficient though gross trick, knocking out power to the facility in the process. (One wonders why aliens smart enough to master teleportation haven't yet invented a backup power source.) The rest of the show consists of Stitch lumbering around in the dark while cheap sound and odor effects are unleashed on the audience.

Guest response to *Stitch's Great Escape!* is so negative that Disney has stopped trying to improve it. Our readers likewise think it stinks, although this Norton Shores, Michigan, mom at least gave it a chance going in:

I love Lilo and Stitch *and am a huge fan of Stitch in particular. I got on the ride just knowing it would be great—then the lights went out. From that point on, it was just a big miserable fail. My 13-year-old actually heaved from the smell of Stitch's breath, and the bouncing [overhead restraints] jabbed us all painfully and repeatedly in the shoulders. The movie is still awesome, but the ride is a giant zit on the face of Disney that needs to be popped out of existence.*

A Las Vegas reader thinks he knows why an attraction that doesn't move has safety restraints:

Stitch's Great Escape! *has to be seen to understand just how awful an attraction can be. I had a glimmer of hope when they put the restraint on me. Looking back, I'm convinced the restraint was for the sole purpose of preventing the audience from leaving until they had been sufficiently tortured.*

Stitch's height requirement is 40 inches—the same as Big Thunder Mountain Railroad—in an attempt to keep out easily frightened younger children. The fact that Big Thunder is a roller coaster and that this ride doesn't move should be a warning to parents about its fright potential.

TOURING TIPS *Stitch* is more than enough to scare the pants off many kids ages 6 and younger. *Parents, note:* You're held in your seat by overhead restraints that will prevent you from getting up to comfort your child if the need arises.

Tomorrowland Speedway *(FastPass+)* ★★

APPEAL BY AGE	PRESCHOOL ★★★★½	GRADE SCHOOL ★★★★½	TEENS ★★★½
YOUNG ADULTS ★★★		OVER 30 ★★★	SENIORS ★★★

What it is Drive-'em-yourself miniature cars. **Scope and scale** Major attraction. **When to go** Before 10 a.m., during the last 2 hours before closing, or use FastPass+. **Special comments** Kids must be 54″ tall to drive unassisted. **Authors' rating** Boring for adults (★★); great for preschoolers. **Duration of ride** About 4¼ minutes. **Average wait in line per 100 people ahead of you** 4½ minutes; assumes 285-car turn-over every 20 minutes. **Loading speed** Slow.

DESCRIPTION AND COMMENTS An elaborate miniature raceway with gasoline-powered cars that travel up to 7 mph. The raceway, with its sleek cars and racing noises, is quite alluring. The cars poke along on a guide rail, leaving the driver little to do, but teens and many adults still enjoy it.

TOURING TIPS This ride is visually appealing, and the 9-and-under crowd loves it (adults, not so much). If your child is too short to drive, ride along and allow him or her to steer the car while you work the foot pedal.

A mom from North Billerica, Massachusetts, writes:

I was truly amazed by the number of adults in line—the only reason I could think of for that would be an insane desire to go on absolutely every ride at Disney World. The cars aren't a whole lot of fun, and they tend to pile up at the end, so it takes almost as long to get off as it did to get on.

The line for the speedway snakes across a pedestrian bridge to the ride's loading areas. For a shorter wait, turn right off the bridge and head to the first loading area rather than continuing to the second one.

Tomorrowland Transit Authority PeopleMover ★★★½

APPEAL BY AGE   PRESCHOOL ★★★★   GRADE SCHOOL ★★★★   TEENS ★★★★
YOUNG ADULTS ★★★★   OVER 30 ★★★★   SENIORS ★★★★½

What it is Scenic tour of Tomorrowland. **Scope and scale** Minor attraction. **When to go** Anytime, but especially during hot, crowded times of day (11:30 a.m.–4:30 p.m.). **Special comments** A good way to check out the line at Space Mountain and the Speedway. **Authors' rating** Scenic and relaxing; ★★★½. **Duration of ride** 10 minutes. **Average wait in line per 100 people ahead of you** 1½ minutes; assumes 39 trains operating. **Loading speed** Fast.

DESCRIPTION AND COMMENTS A once-unique prototype of a linear induction–powered mass-transit system, the PeopleMover has tramlike cars that carry riders on a leisurely tour of Tomorrowland, including a peek inside Space Mountain. In ancient times, the attraction was called the WEDway PeopleMover ("WED" = Walter Elias Disney).

A Delafield, Wisconsin, family offers only the faintest of praise:

Tomorrowland is best at night. With the lights, it turns boring rides like the PeopleMover into something less boring.

TOURING TIPS A relaxing ride where lines move quickly. It's a good choice during busier times of day.

Walt Disney's Carousel of Progress ★★★

APPEAL BY AGE   PRESCHOOL ★★★   GRADE SCHOOL ★★★   TEENS ★★★½
YOUNG ADULTS ★★★★   OVER 30 ★★★★   SENIORS ★★★★½

What it is Audio-Animatronic theater production. **Scope and scale** Major attraction. **When to go** Anytime. **Authors' rating** Nostalgic, warm, and happy; ★★★. **Duration of presentation** 21 minutes. **Preshow entertainment** Documentary on the attraction's long history. **Probable waiting time** Less than 10 minutes.

DESCRIPTION AND COMMENTS *Walt Disney's Carousel of Progress* offers a nostalgic look at how technology and electricity have changed the lives of an animatronic family over several generations, from about 1900 to 1990. Adults will be amused by the references to laser discs and car phones; kids will be confused.

TOURING TIPS *Carousel* handles big crowds effectively and is a good choice during busier times of day. Because of its age, it seems to have more minor operational glitches than most attractions, so you may be subjected to the same dialogue and songs several times. Look at it as extra air-conditioning.

LIVE ENTERTAINMENT *in* the **MAGIC KINGDOM**

unofficial **TIP**

Note: If you're short on time, it's impossible to see Magic Kingdom feature attractions and the live performances.

BANDS, DISNEY-CHARACTER APPEARANCES, parades, ceremonies, and singing and dancing further enliven the Magic Kingdom. For specific events the day you visit, check the live-entertainment schedule in your guide map (free as you enter the park or at City Hall) or in the *Times Guide* available along with the guide map. WDW live-entertainment guru Steve Soares usually posts the Magic Kingdom's performance schedule about a week in advance at **wdwent.com.**

Our one-day touring plans exclude live performances in favor of seeing as much of the park as time permits; parades and shows siphon crowds away from popular rides, thus shortening lines. Nonetheless, the color and pageantry of live events are integral to the Magic Kingdom— and a persuasive argument for a second day of touring. Here's a list of some regular performances and events that don't require reservations:

BAY LAKE AND SEVEN SEAS LAGOON FLOATING ELECTRICAL PAGEANT ★★★★ Usually performed at nightfall (9 p.m. at the Polynesian Village Resort, 9:15 at the Grand Floridian Resort & Spa, and 10:15 at the Contemporary Resort) on Seven Seas Lagoon and Bay Lake, this is one of our favorites among the Disney extras, but it's necessary to leave the Magic Kingdom to view it. The pageant is a stunning electric-light show aboard small barges and set to nifty electronic music. Leave the Magic Kingdom and take the monorail to the Polynesian Village, Grand Floridian, or Contemporary.

CASTLE FORECOURT STAGE ★★★½ The 20-minute *Dream-Along with Mickey* live show features Mickey, Minnie, Donald, Goofy, and a peck of princesses and other secondary characters, plus human backup dancers, in a show built around the premise that—*quelle horreur!*—Donald doesn't believe in the power of dreams. Crisis is averted through a frenetic whirlwind of song and dance.

The show is performed several times a day according to the season, with showtimes listed in the daily *Times Guide*. The Castle Forecourt Stage is elevated well above ground level, so good viewing spots are available all around Main Street's Central Plaza.

CELEBRATE THE MAGIC ★★★★½ In one of the most imaginative shows yet, videos and special effects are set to music and projected nightly onto Cinderella Castle. The effects are tremendous: In one vignette, the entire castle becomes a kaleidoscope of brightly colored Mickeys and Donalds; in another, flames appear throughout the castle's windows to emulate a scene from the Pirates of the Caribbean ride. Best of all, Disney regularly updates the show's content to keep it fresh (read: the *Frozen* princesses appear). While the show's soundtrack is invariably excessively sentimental, the visuals more than make up for it. We rate this as not to be missed.

For the winter holidays, *Celebrate the Magic* gets a *Frozen*-inspired retheming. Titled **A Frozen Holiday Wish,** the castle's projections include Anna, Elsa, Olaf, and other stars from that blockbuster, plus the usual cavalcade of classic Disney characters.

DISNEY-CHARACTER SHOWS AND APPEARANCES A number of characters are usually on hand to greet guests when the park opens. Because they snarl pedestrian traffic and stop most children dead in their tracks, this is sort of a mixed blessing. Most days, a character is on duty for photos and autographs 9 a.m.–10 p.m. next to City Hall. Mickey, Tinker Bell, and miscellaneous fairies can be found in Main Street's Town Square Theater, to the right as you enter the park; Disney princesses are found in Fairytale Hall in Fantasyland. Check the daily *Times Guide* for character-greeting locations and times.

FLAG RETREAT At 5 p.m. daily at Town Square (Walt Disney World Railroad end of Main Street). Sometimes performed with large college marching bands, sometimes with a smaller Disney band.

MAGIC KINGDOM BANDS Banjo, Dixieland, steel drum, marching, and fife-and-drum bands play daily throughout the park.

MOVE IT! SHAKE IT! DANCE AND PLAY IT! STREET PARTY ★★★½ Starting at the Walt Disney World Railroad end of Main Street, U.S.A., and working toward the Central Plaza, this short walk incorporates about a dozen guests with a handful of floats, Disney characters (including Mickey, Minnie, and Goofy), and entertainers. The parade's soundtrack, updated in late 2014, includes recent pop hits by Disney and non-Disney artists; there's a good amount of interaction between the entertainers and the crowd. Unless you're already on Main Street, however, or too pooped for anything else, we don't recommend making a special trip to view this parade.

TINKER BELL'S FLIGHT This nice special effect in the sky above Cinderella Castle heralds the beginning of the *Wishes* fireworks show (when the park is open late).

TOMORROWLAND FORECOURT STAGE This two-story space behind the Astro Orbiter occasionally hosts DJ-led dance parties. We wouldn't make a special trip to see these, but they're a nice 2-minute stop if you're passing by.

WISHES FIREWORKS SHOW *FASTPASS+/*★★★★★ Memorable vignettes and music from beloved Disney films combine with a stellar fireworks display while Jiminy Cricket narrates a lump-in-your-throat story about making wishes come true. (See page 527 for good viewing spots.)

A spot we'd previously recommended, in the Tomorrowland Terrace area, was apparently so good that Disney decided to start charging for it. To view *Wishes* from this location now costs $49 per adult and $29 per child. The viewing area is available starting 1 hour before *Wishes*, and the event includes a dessert buffet and nonalcoholic beverages. Reservations can be made 60 days in advance by calling ☎ 407-WDW-DINE (939-3463). If you make a reservation more than two weeks in advance, you'll be given a default reservation time of 6 p.m. for the dessert party and told to call back within two weeks of your trip for the actual time.

A St. Louis reader tried the dessert buffet:

We did the Wishes *Fireworks Dessert Party against my better judgment. While the vantage point was pretty good and the desserts were tasty, it was definitely not worth the price. We also were able to witness firsthand how we have become a nation of morbidly obese people.*

FastPass+ is also available for *Wishes,* giving you access to a special viewing area near the Central Plaza in front of Cinderella Castle. We don't recommend FastPass+ as one of your first three or four choices, however, since (1) you still need to show up well in advance to claim a good spot and (2) you're going to wait in a very long line for one of the park's headliner attractions. You're better off staking out a decent viewing spot about 20 minutes before the show, or trying for a same-day FastPass after you've used your first three or four.

WISHES **FIREWORKS CRUISE** For a different view, you can watch the fireworks from Seven Seas Lagoon aboard a chartered pontoon boat. The charter costs $293 for up to 8 people and just under $350 for 10 (tax included). Chips, soda, and water are provided; sandwiches and more-substantial food items may be arranged through reservations. Your Disney captain will take you for a little cruise and then position the boat in a perfect place to watch the fireworks. (A major indirect benefit of the charter is that you can enjoy the fireworks without fighting the mob afterward.) Because this is a private charter rather than a tour, only your group will be aboard. Life jackets are provided, but wearing them is at your discretion. To reserve a charter, call ☎ 407-WDW-PLAY (939-7529) at exactly 7 a.m. Eastern time about 180 days before the day you want to cruise. Because the Disney reservations system counts days in a somewhat atypical manner, we recommend phoning about 185 days out to have a Disney agent specify the exact morning to call for reservations.

MICKEY'S HALLOWEEN *and* CHRISTMAS PARTIES *and* 24-HOUR EVENTS

THE MAGIC KINGDOM HOSTS special after-hours, holiday-themed events in September, October, November, and December, celebrating Halloween and Christmas. These events require separate admission (see "The Walt Disney World Calendar" on page 48 in Part One for details) and can sell out. Space doesn't permit us to cover these events in the book, but we provide full details, including photos, best days to go, touring advice, and more, at **blog.touringplans.com.** Search for "Halloween Party" or "Christmas Party" to see the coverage.

It's become a tradition for the Magic Kingdom to stay open for 24 consecutive hours on one day of the year. The first such event was held on Leap Day, February 29 in 2012. Disney scheduled it for the Friday before Memorial Day in later years, including 2015. The 2016 date hasn't been announced yet, but 2016 is a leap year, so either date is possible. See **tinyurl.com/wdw-24hours** for a sample of the entertainment offered during this all-nighter.

PARADES

PARADES AT THE MAGIC KINGDOM ARE FULL-FLEDGED spectaculars with dozens of Disney characters and amazing special effects.

We rate the afternoon parade as outstanding and the evening parade as not to be missed.

In addition to providing great entertainment, parades lure guests away from the attractions. If getting on rides appeals to you more than watching a parade, you'll find substantially shorter lines just before and during parades. Because the parade route doesn't pass through Adventureland, Tomorrowland, or Fantasyland, attractions in these lands are particularly good bets.

Be forewarned: The parade path disrupts pedestrian traffic throughout most of the Magic Kingdom. If you're on the left side of Main Street (facing the castle), anywhere in Adventureland, or anywhere from Pecos Bill's in Frontierland through the Liberty Tree Tavern in Liberty Square (that is, the side opposite the Rivers of America), you're cut off from the rest of the park.

If you're on the right hand side of Main Street, however, you can walk counterclockwise around the Magic Kingdom from the Main Street train station, through all of Tomorrowland, all of Fantasyland, and the parts of Liberty Square and Frontierland that border the Rivers of America, ending at Splash Mountain in Frontierland.

If you plan to skip the parades in favor of attractions, plan on being on the "correct" side of the parade route 15 minutes before the parade starts. If you absolutely must cross the parade route, look for special crosswalks, typically near Casey's Corner on Main Street, U.S.A., and near the Liberty Tree Tavern in Liberty Square.

A Massachusetts mom recalls being trapped by the parade:

> The only major glitch in my plan was that I thought the WDW Railroad (which I had been planning to use as our escape from the crowds) would reopen after the first parade. Maybe either Disney or the Unofficial Guide should mention this, in case anyone else might be planning a similar escape route.

AFTERNOON PARADE

USUALLY STAGED AT 3 P.M., the afternoon parade features bands, floats, and marching Disney characters. A new production, **Festival of Fantasy** (★★★★), debuted in 2014, with an original score and new floats paying tribute to *The Little Mermaid, Brave,* and *Frozen,* among other

unofficial TIP

FastPass+ is available for premium areas to view the afternoon and evening parades. You still need to show up early for a good spot, though.

Disney films. Many of the floats' pieces spin and swing to extremes not normally found in Disney parades: The *Tangled* platform has characters riding swinging wood hammers from one side of the street to the other. The most talked-about float is Maleficent (the villain from *Sleeping Beauty,* and the star of her own feature film) in dragon form—she spits actual fire at a couple of points along the route.

EVENING PARADE

THIS HIGH-TECH AFFAIR employs electroluminescent and fiber-optic technologies, light-spreading thermoplastics (don't try this at home!), and clouds of underlit liquid-nitrogen smoke. For those who flunked chemistry and physics, the parade also offers music, Mickey Mouse, and twinkling lights.

Evening-parade performances vary by season, happening as often as twice a night during the busy times of year, to two or three times a week during less busy seasons. We rate it as not to be missed.

The **Main Street Electrical Parade** (MSEP; ★★★★) is the current nightly cavalcade at the Magic Kingdom. Its soundtrack—*Baroque Hoedown*—is a synthesizer-heavy testament to what prog rock might have been with access to modern technology and antidepressants. In our opinion, the Magic Kingdom's nighttime parade is always the best in Walt Disney World, and the Electrical Parade is the standard against which everything else is judged. Disney is known to swap out parades (MSEP replaced SpectroMagic in 2010), and may do so at any time. If you're at Disney World while MSEP is running, make a special trip to see it.

unofficial **TIP**
Call ☎ 407-824-4321 before you go to be sure the evening parade is on, or check the Lines or My Disney Experience apps..

PARADE ROUTE AND VANTAGE POINTS

MAGIC KINGDOM PARADES circle Town Square, head down Main Street, go around the Central Plaza, and cross the bridge to Liberty Square. In Liberty Square, they follow the waterfront and end in Frontierland. Sometimes they begin in Frontierland and run the route in the opposite direction. Most guests watch from the Central Plaza or from Main Street. One of the best and most popular vantage points is the upper platform of the Walt Disney World Railroad station at the Town Square end of Main Street. This is also a good place for watching the *Wishes* fireworks show, as well as for ducking out of the park ahead of the crowd when the fireworks end. The problem is, you have to stake out your position 30–60 minutes before the events begin.

If you have a FastPass+ reservation for a parade, the reserved viewing area is at the end of Main Street closest to the train station and park entrance, in the area around the flagpole in the middle of the square.

Because most spectators not using FastPass+ pack Main Street and the Central Plaza, we recommend watching the parade from Liberty Square or Frontierland. Great vantage points frequently overlooked are as follows:

1. Sleepy Hollow snack-and-beverage shop, immediately to your right as you cross the bridge into Liberty Square. If you arrive early, buy refreshments and claim a table closest to the rail. You'll have a perfect view of the parade as it crosses Liberty Square Bridge, but only when the parade begins on Main Street.

2. The pathway on the Liberty Square side of the moat from Sleepy Hollow snack-and-beverage shop to Cinderella Castle. Any point along this path offers an unobstructed view as the parade crosses Liberty Square Bridge. Once again, this spot works only for parades coming from Main Street.

3. The covered walkway between Liberty Tree Tavern and The Diamond Horseshoe Saloon. This elevated vantage point is perfect (particularly on rainy days) and usually goes unnoticed until just before the parade starts.

4. Elevated platforms in front of the Frontierland Shootin' Arcade, Frontier Trading Post, and the building with the sign reading FRONTIER MERCANTILE. These spots usually get picked off 10–12 minutes before parade time.

5. Benches on the perimeter of the Central Plaza, between the entrances to Liberty Square and Adventureland. Usually unoccupied until after the parade begins, they offer a comfortable resting place and an unobstructed (though somewhat distant) view of the parade as it crosses Liberty Square Bridge.

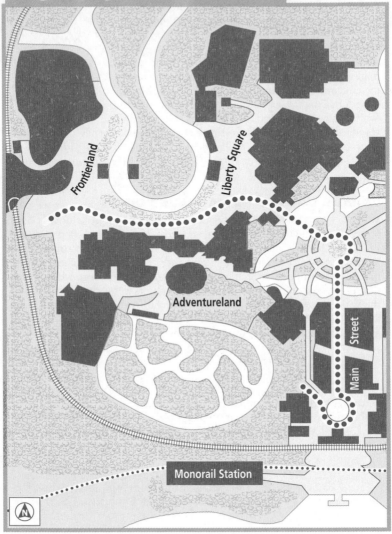

Magic Kingdom Parade Route

6. Liberty Square and Frontierland dockside areas; spots here usually go early.

7. The porch of Tony's Town Square Restaurant on Main Street provides an elevated viewing platform and an easy exit path when the fireworks are over.

Assuming it starts on Main Street (evening parades normally do), the parade takes 16–20 minutes to reach Liberty Square or Frontierland.

On evenings when the parade runs twice, the first parade draws a huge crowd, siphoning guests from attractions. Many folks leave the park after the early parade, with many more departing following the fireworks (which are scheduled on the hour between the two parades).

Continue to tour after the fireworks. This is a particularly good time to ride Splash Mountain and enjoy attractions in Adventureland. If you're touring Adventureland and the parade begins on Main Street, you won't have to assume your viewing position in Frontierland until 15 minutes after the parade kicks off (the time it takes the parade to reach Frontierland). If you watch from the Splash Mountain side of the street and head for the attraction as the last float passes, you'll be able to ride with only a couple minutes' wait. You might even have time to work in a last-minute ride on Big Thunder Mountain Railroad.

VANTAGE POINTS FOR FIREWORKS

IF YOU'VE GOT FASTPASS+ RESERVATIONS for the fireworks, your viewing location will be somewhere in the Central Hub area, between the end of Main Street, U.S.A., and Cinderella Castle. These areas, known as **Plaza Gardens East and West,** were specifically constructed for fireworks viewing. Of the two, we prefer Plaza Gardens East (the same side of the park as Tomorrowland) because the configuration of light and audio poles is slightly less obtrusive when viewing the castle.

If you don't have FastPass+ reservations, then anywhere along Main Street is fine for the fireworks, especially if you plan to leave the park immediately afterward. Watching from the train-station end of Main Street is the easiest way to facilitate a quick departure.

Our two favorite spots if we intend to remain in the park are:

1. **In Fantasyland between Seven Dwarfs Mine Train and *Enchanted Tales with Belle.*** Some of the minor fireworks that float above the castle will be behind you, but all of the major effects will be right in front of you. The explosions are loud, and the echo off the back of Cinderella Castle is memorable.

2. **On the bridge between the Central Hub and Tomorrowland.** It's a slightly sideways view of the fireworks, and there are a few trees that block some of the castle, but if Tinker Bell does her pre-fireworks flight from the castle, she'll fly directly over this area.

LEAVING THE PARK AFTER EVENING PARADES AND FIREWORKS

ARMIES OF GUESTS leave the Magic Kingdom after evening parades and fireworks. The Disney transportation system (buses, ferries, and monorail) is overwhelmed, causing long waits in boarding areas.

A mom from Kresgeville, Pennsylvania, recounts:

unofficial **TIP**
Digital displays at the Magic Kingdom exit show the wait to board the monorails and ferry—take the one with the shorter line.

Our family of five made the mistake of going to the Magic Kingdom the Saturday night before Columbus Day to watch the parade and fireworks. Afterwards, we lingered at The Crystal Palace to wait for the crowds to lessen, but it was no use. We started walking toward the gates and soon became trapped by the throng, not able to go forward or back. There was no way to get to the ferry to our hotel. Our group became separated, and it became a nightmare. We left the park at 10:30 p.m. and didn't get back to the Polynesian (less than a mile away) until after midnight. Even if they were to raise Walt Disney himself from cryogenic sleep and parade him down Main Street, I would never go to the Magic Kingdom on a Saturday night again!

An Oklahoma City dad offers this advice:

Never, never leave the Magic Kingdom just after the 10 p.m. fireworks. Go for another ride—no lines because everyone else is trying to get out!

Congestion persists from the end of the early evening parade until closing time. Most folks watch the early parade and then the fireworks a few minutes later. If you're parked at the Transportation and Ticket Center (TTC) and are intent on beating the crowd, view the early parade from the Town Square end of Main Street, leaving the park as soon as the parade ends.

unofficial **TIP**
For optimum touring and less congestion, enjoy attractions during the early parade, then break to watch the fireworks.

Here's what happened to a family from Cape Coral, Florida:

We tried to leave the park before the parade began, but Main Street was already packed and we didn't see any way to get out of the park—we were stuck. In addition, it was impossible to move across the street, and even the shops were so crowded it was virtually impossible to maneuver a stroller through them to get close to the entrance.

If you don't have a stroller (or are willing to forgo the $1 return refund for rental strollers), catch the Walt Disney World Railroad in Frontierland and ride to the park exit at Main Street. Again, don't cut it too close—the train stops running after the parade.

NEW MAIN STREET PASSAGEWAYS The good news is that Disney has built two pedestrian walkways behind the shops on either side of Main Street, U.S.A., specifically for guests who want to get in or out of the park without walking down the middle of Main Street. If you're on the Tomorrowland side of the park, a passageway runs from between The Plaza Restaurant and Tomorrowland Terrace, back behind the east side of Main Street, to Tony's Town Square Restaurant near the park exit. If you're on the Adventureland side of the park, the passageway runs from the First Aid area to the Main Street Fire Station near the park exit. However, these passageways aren't used every night, so there's no guarantee they'll be available.

unofficial **TIP**
Be aware that the railroad shuts down during parades because the floats must cross the tracks when entering or exiting the parade route in Frontierland.

If the passageways aren't open and you're on the Tomorrowland side of the park, it's still possible for you to exit during a parade. Leaving Tomorrowland, cut through Tomorrowland Terrace. Before you reach Main Street, bear left into the side door of the corner shop. Once inside, you'll see that Main Street shops have interior doors allowing you to pass from one shop to the next without having to get on Main Street. Work your way from shop to shop until you reach Town Square (easy, because people will be outside watching the parade). At Town Square, bear left and move to the train station and the park exit.

This strategy won't work if you're on the Adventureland side of the park. You can make your way through Casey's Corner restaurant to Main Street and then work your way through the interior of the Main Street shops, but when you pop out of the Emporium at Town Square, you'll be trapped by the parade. As soon as the last float passes, however, you can bolt for the exit.

Another strategy for beating the masses out of the park (if your car is at the TTC lot) is to watch the early parade and then leave before the fireworks begin. Line up for the ferry; one will depart about every 8–10 minutes. Try to catch the ferry that will be crossing Seven Seas Lagoon while the fireworks are in progress. The best vantage point is on the top deck to the right of the pilothouse as you face the Magic Kingdom; the sight of fireworks silhouetting the castle and reflecting off Seven Seas Lagoon is unforgettable. While there's no guarantee that a ferry will load and depart within 3 or 4 minutes of the fireworks, your chances are about 50–50 of catching it just right. If you're in the front of the line for the ferry and don't want to board the boat that's loading, stop at the gate and let people pass you. You'll be the first to board the next boat.

Strollers, wheelchairs, and ECVs make navigating the crowds even more difficult. If you've got one of these, or you're staying at a Disney hotel not served by the monorail and you have to depend on Disney transportation, watch the early parade and fireworks, then enjoy the attractions until about 20–25 minutes before the late parade is scheduled to begin. Then leave the park using one of the strategies listed above, and catch the Disney bus or boat back to your hotel.

TRAFFIC PATTERNS *in* *the* MAGIC KINGDOM

WHEN WE RESEARCH THE MAGIC KINGDOM, we study its traffic patterns, asking:

1. WHICH SECTIONS OF THE PARK AND WHICH ATTRACTIONS DO GUESTS VISIT FIRST? When the park opens, guest traffic to Fantasyland and Tomorrowland is heaviest, followed by Frontierland. Seven Dwarfs Mine Train pulls more people than ever into the back reaches of the park, and because the *Frozen* meet and greet at Princess Fairytale Hall is such a low-capacity attraction, it's a race to get there early. The girls (and parents) dressed up like Anna and Elsa, rushing through the park, look like an episode of *Toddlers and Tiaras* meets *The Amazing Race*.

Our researchers tested the frequent claim that most people turn right into Tomorrowland and tour the Magic Kingdom in a counterclockwise sequence. We found the claim to be baseless.

ATTRACTIONS THAT GET CROWDED EARLY
FANTASYLAND   • *Enchanted Tales with Belle*   • Peter Pan's Flight   • Princess Fairytale Hall (Anna and Elsa)   • Seven Dwarfs Mine Train
FRONTIERLAND   • Big Thunder Mountain Railroad   • Splash Mountain
TOMORROWLAND   • Buzz Lightyear's Space Ranger Spin   • Space Mountain   • Tomorrowland Speedway

2. HOW LONG DOES IT TAKE FOR THE PARK TO FILL UP? HOW ARE THE VISITORS DISPERSED IN THE PARK? A surge of early birds arrives before or around opening time but is quickly dispersed throughout the empty park. After the initial wave is absorbed, there's a lull lasting about an hour after opening. Then the park is inundated for about 2 hours, peaking between 10 a.m. and noon. Arrivals continue in a steady but diminishing stream until around 2 p.m. The lines we sampled were longest between 1 and 2 p.m., indicating more arrivals than departures into the early afternoon. For touring purposes, most attractions develop long lines between 10 and 11:30 a.m.

> *unofficial* **TIP**
> As the park fills up, visitors head for the top attractions before lines get long. This, more than anything else, determines morning traffic patterns.

From late morning until early afternoon, guests are equally distributed through all the lands. However, guests concentrate in Fantasyland, Liberty Square, and Frontierland in late afternoon, with a decrease of visitors in Adventureland and Tomorrowland. Adventureland's Jungle Cruise and Tomorrowland's Buzz Lightyear and Space Mountain continue to be crowded, but most other attractions in those lands are readily accessible.

3. HOW DO MOST VISITORS TOUR THE PARK? Do first-time visitors tour differently from repeat guests? Many first-time visitors are guided by friends or relatives familiar with the Magic Kingdom. These tours may or may not follow an orderly sequence. First-time visitors without personal guides tend to be more orderly in their touring. Many first-time visitors, however, are drawn to Cinderella Castle upon entering the park and thus begin their rotation from Fantasyland. Repeat visitors usually go directly to their favorite attractions.

4. HOW DOES FASTPASS+ AFFECT CROWD DISTRIBUTIONS? In Part Two, we discussed which attractions' average wait times were increasing or decreasing under FastPass+. When it comes to the Magic Kingdom, FastPass+ is moving guests from the right side of the park—Tomorrowland and Storybook Circus in Fantasyland—to Adventureland and the Liberty Square area, all on the left side of the park.

We've done our fair share of criticizing FastPass+, and there are still parts of it that are just plain goofy (see what we did there?). But as far as reaching its goal of more evenly distributing crowds throughout the park, FastPass+ has to be one of the big industrial-engineering-and-technology success stories of the past few years.

5. HOW DO SPECIAL EVENTS, SUCH AS PARADES AND LIVE SHOWS, AFFECT TRAFFIC PATTERNS? Parades pull huge numbers of guests away from attractions and provide a window of opportunity for experiencing the more popular attractions with less of a wait. Castle Forecourt Stage shows also attract crowds but only slightly affect lines.

6. WHAT ARE THE TRAFFIC PATTERNS NEAR AND AT CLOSING TIME? On our sample days, in busy times and off-season at the park, departures outnumbered arrivals beginning in midafternoon. Many visitors left in late afternoon as the dinner hour approached. When the park closed early, guests departed steadily during the 2 hours before closing, with a huge exodus at closing time. When the park closed late, a huge exodus began immediately after the early-evening parade and fireworks, with a second mass departure after the late parade, continuing until closing. Because Main Street and the transportation services remain open after the other five lands close, crowds leaving at closing mainly affect conditions on Main Street and at the monorail-, ferry-, and bus-boarding areas. In the hour before closing, the other five lands are normally uncrowded.

To get a complete view of the actual traffic patterns while you're in the park, use our mobile app, **Lines** (**touringplans.com/lines**). The app gives you current wait times and future estimates in half-hour increments for today and tomorrow. A quick glance shows how traffic patterns affect wait times throughout the day.

MAGIC KINGDOM TOURING PLANS

STARTING ON PAGE 806, our step-by-step touring plans are field-tested for seeing *as much as possible* in one day with a minimum of time wasted in lines. They're designed to help you avoid crowds and bottlenecks on days of moderate-to-heavy attendance. Understand, however, that there's more to see in the Magic Kingdom than can be experienced in one day. Since we first began covering the Magic Kingdom, four headliner attractions have been added and an entire land created and destroyed.

On days of lighter attendance (see "Selecting the Time of Year for Your Visit," page 39), our plans will save you time but won't be as critical to successful touring as on busier days.

To help with FastPass+, we've listed the approximate return times for which you should try to make reservations. (The plans should work with anything close to the times shown.) Because Disney limits how many FastPass+ reservations you can get, we've listed which attractions are most likely to need FastPass+, too. Check **touring plans.com** for the latest information.

*un*official **TIP**
Don't worry that other people will be following the plans and render them useless. Fewer than 4 in every 100 people in the park will have been exposed to this info.

CHOOSING THE APPROPRIATE TOURING PLAN

WE PRESENT FIVE MAGIC KINGDOM TOURING PLANS:

- Magic Kingdom One-Day Touring Plan for Adults
- Magic Kingdom Authors' Selective One-Day Touring Plan for Adults
- Magic Kingdom One-Day Touring Plan for Parents withSmall Children
- Magic Kingdom Two-Day Touring Plan
- Magic Kingdom Dumbo-or-Die-in-a-Day Touring Plan for Parents with Small Children

If you have two days (or two mornings) at the Magic Kingdom, the Two-Day Touring Plan is *by far* the most relaxed and efficient. The two-day plan takes advantage of early morning, when lines are short and the park hasn't filled with guests. This plan works well year-round and eliminates much of the extra walking required by the one-day plans. No matter when the park closes, our two-day plan guarantees the most efficient touring and the least time in lines. The plan is perfect for guests who wish to sample both the attractions and the atmosphere of the Magic Kingdom.

If you have only one day to visit but you wish to see as much as possible, then use the One-Day Touring Plan for Adults. It's exhausting, but it packs in the maximum. If you prefer a more relaxed visit, use the Authors' Selective One-Day Touring Plan. It includes the best the park has to offer (in the authors' opinion), eliminating the less-impressive attractions.

If you have children younger than age 8, adopt the One-Day Touring Plan for Parents with Small Children. It's a compromise, blending the preferences of younger children with those of older siblings and adults. The plan includes many children's rides in Fantasyland but omits roller-coaster rides and other attractions that frighten young children or are off-limits because of height requirements. Or use the One-Day Touring Plan for Adults or the Authors' Selective One-Day Touring Plan for Adults, and take advantage of switching off, a technique whereby children accompany adults to the loading area of a ride with age and height requirements but don't board (see page 412).

unofficial **TIP**
Switching off allows adults to enjoy the more adventuresome attractions while keeping the group together.

The Dumbo-or-Die-in-a-Day Touring Plan for Parents with Small Children is designed for parents who will withhold no sacrifice for their kids. On the Dumbo-or-Die Plan, adults generally stand around, sweat, wipe noses, pay for stuff, and watch the children enjoy themselves. It's great!

"Not a Touring Plan" Touring Plans

For the type-B reader, these touring plans (see page 804) avoid detailed step-by-step strategies for saving every last minute in line. To paraphrase one of our favorite movies, they're more guidelines than actual rules. Use these to avoid the longest waits in line while having maximum flexibility to see whatever interests you in a particular part of the park.

For the Magic Kingdom, these "not" touring plans include advice for adults and parents with one day in the park, for anyone with two days, and for anyone with an afternoon and a full day to tour.

Two-Day Touring Plan for Families with Small Children

If you have young children and are looking for a two-day itinerary, combine the Magic Kingdom One-Day Touring Plan for Parents with Small Children with the second day of the Magic Kingdom Two-Day Touring Plan.

Two-Day Touring Plan for Early-Morning Touring on Day One and Afternoon–Evening Touring on Day Two

Many of you enjoy an early start at the Magic Kingdom on one day, followed by a second day with a lazy, sleep-in morning, resuming your touring in the afternoon and/or evening. If this appeals to you, use the Magic

Kingdom One-Day Touring Plan for Adults or the Magic Kingdom One-Day Touring Plan for Parents with Small Children on your early day. Adhere to the touring plan for as long as it feels comfortable (many folks leave after the afternoon parade). On the second day, pick up where you left off. If you intend to use FastPass+ on your second day, make reservations well in advance, before they're all gone. Customize the remaining part of the touring plan to incorporate parades, fireworks, and other live performances according to your preferences.

MAGIC KINGDOM TOURING PLAN COMPANION

WE'VE CONSOLIDATED A GREAT DEAL OF INFORMATION about the Magic Kingdom in its Touring Plan Companion, at the back of the guide just after the touring plans. Like the plans, the companions are designed to clip out and take with you to the park. The Magic Kingdom Touring Plan Companion includes the best days to go, the best times to visit each attraction, the authors' rating, height requirements, small-child fright potential, and info on dining and cool places to take a break.

THE SINGLE-DAY TOURING CONUNDRUM

TOURING THE MAGIC KINGDOM IN A DAY is complicated by the fact that the premier attractions are at almost opposite ends of the park: Splash Mountain and Big Thunder Mountain Railroad in Frontierland, Space Mountain and Buzz Lightyear in Tomorrowland, and Under the Sea: Journey of the Little Mermaid and Seven Dwarfs Mine Train in the top center. It's virtually impossible to ride all six without encountering lines at one or another. If you ride Space Mountain and see Buzz Lightyear immediately after the park opens, for example, you won't have much of a wait, if any. By the time you leave Tomorrowland and hurry to Fantasyland, however, the line for Seven Dwarfs will be substantial. The same situation prevails if you ride the Fantasyland duo first: Seven Dwarfs Mine Train and Under the Sea, no problem; Space Mountain and Buzz Lightyear, however, have fair-sized lines. From 10 minutes after opening until just before closing, lines are long at these headliners.

The best way to ride all six without long waits is to use FastPass+ and tour over two mornings. Make midmorning FastPass+ reservations at Big Thunder for your first day. When you arrive, ride Seven Dwarfs Mine Train as soon as the park opens, then head directly for Splash Mountain. By the time you're done riding, your FastPass+ reservation should be ready for Big Thunder. On your second day, ride Space Mountain immediately after the park opens, then ride Buzz Lightyear.

If you have only a day to see the Magic Kingdom, make FastPass+ reservations in advance for around 9:30 a.m. at Big Thunder Mountain, and around 3:30 p.m. at Space Mountain. Then, on the day of your visit, ride Seven Dwarfs Mine Train as soon as the park opens, then ride Under the Sea, then hotfoot it to Splash Mountain. Your FastPass+ reservation for Big Thunder will be valid by the time you're done, and you'll have completed three of the park's four headliners in about an hour. Save Buzz Lightyear for around 3 p.m., when everyone is watching the parade, and hop on Space Mountain afterwards.

PRELIMINARY INSTRUCTIONS FOR ALL MAGIC KINGDOM TOURING PLANS

BECOME FAMILIAR WITH THE Magic Kingdom's opening procedures, as described on page 83 of Part Two. On days of moderate-to-heavy attendance, follow your chosen touring plan exactly, deviating only:

1. When you're not interested in an attraction it lists. Simply skip that attraction and proceed to the next.

2. When you encounter a very long line at an attraction the touring plan calls for. If this is the case, skip the attraction in question and go to the next step, returning later to retry.

BEFORE YOU GO

1. Call ☎ 407-824-4321 or check **disneyworld.com** the day before you go to verify official opening time.

2. Purchase admission and make FastPass+ reservations before you arrive.

3. Get familiar with park-opening procedures (see previous section) and reread the plan you've chosen so you know what you're likely to encounter.

MAGIC KINGDOM ONE-DAY TOURING PLAN FOR ADULTS *(page 806)*

FOR Adults without young children.

ASSUMES Willingness to experience all major rides (including roller coasters) and shows.

This plan requires a lot of walking and some backtracking to avoid lines. Extra walking and morning hustling will spare you 4 or more hours of standing in line. How far you get depends on how quickly you move from ride to ride, how many times you rest or eat, how quickly the park fills, and what time the park closes.

MAGIC KINGDOM AUTHORS' SELECTIVE ONE-DAY TOURING PLAN FOR ADULTS *(page 807)*

FOR Adults touring without young children.

ASSUMES Willingness to experience all major rides (including roller coasters) and shows.

This plan includes only the attractions we think are best. It requires a lot of walking and some backtracking to avoid lines. How far you get depends on how quickly you move from ride to ride, how many times you rest or eat, how quickly the park fills, and what time the park closes.

MAGIC KINGDOM ONE-DAY TOURING PLAN FOR PARENTS WITH SMALL CHILDREN *(page 808)*

FOR Parents with children younger than age 8.

ASSUMES Periodic stops for rest, restrooms, and refreshments.

This plan represents a compromise between the observed tastes of adults and those of younger children. Included are many amusement park rides that children may have the opportunity to experience at fairs and amusement parks back home. Although these rides are included in the plan, omit them if possible. These cycle-loading rides often have long lines, consuming valuable touring time:

- **THE BARNSTORMER**
- **DUMBO THE FLYING ELEPHANT**
- **MAD TEA PARTY**
- **THE MAGIC CARPETS OF ALADDIN**

This time could be better spent experiencing the many attractions that better demonstrate the Disney creative genius and are found only in the Magic Kingdom. Try instead either of the one-day plans for adults and take advantage of switching off (see page 412). This allows parents and young children to enter the ride together; at the boarding area, one parent watches the children while the other rides. Families using this plan should review Magic Kingdom attractions in our Small-Child Fright-Potential Chart in Part Five (see pages 404–407).

We recommend taking a break and returning to your hotel for a swim and a nap (even if you're not staying in the World). You won't see as much, but everyone will be more relaxed and happy.

This touring plan requires a lot of walking and some backtracking to avoid long lines. A little extra walking and some morning hustle will spare you 2–3 hours of standing in line. You may not complete the tour. How far you get depends on how quickly you move from ride to ride, how many times you rest or eat, how quickly the park fills, and what time the park closes.

To Convert This One-Day Touring Plan into a Two-Day Touring Plan

For Day 1, make FastPass+ reservations well in advance for Peter Pan's Flight around 11 a.m., The Many Adventures of Winnie the Pooh around 6:15 p.m., and *Enchanted Tales with Belle* around 7:15 pm. When the park opens, ride Seven Dwarfs Mine Train immediately, followed by Under the Sea. See the Storybook Circus attractions next, then Splash Mountain and The Haunted Mansion, before riding Peter Pan and leaving the park for lunch. Return to the park and work in the Frontierland and Liberty Square attractions around your FastPass+ reservations.

For Day 2, ride Buzz Lightyear, Astro Orbiter, and the Tomorrowland Speedway as soon as the park opens, then visit the Adventureland attractions, starting with the Magic Carpets of Aladdin. End your day with the PeopleMover and *Monsters, Inc.,* show in Tomorrowland, followed by the evening parade and fireworks.

MAGIC KINGDOM TWO-DAY TOURING PLAN
(pages 809 and 810)

FOR Those wishing to spread their Magic Kingdom visit over two days.

ASSUMES Willingness to experience all major rides and shows.

This two-day touring plan takes advantage of early-morning touring. Each day, you should complete the structured part of the plan by about 4 p.m. This leaves plenty of time for live entertainment. If the park is open late (after 8 p.m.), consider returning to your hotel at midday for a swim and a nap. Eat an early dinner outside Walt Disney World, and return refreshed to enjoy the park's nighttime festivities.

MAGIC KINGDOM DUMBO-OR-DIE-IN-A-DAY TOURING PLAN FOR PARENTS WITH SMALL CHILDREN
(page 811)

FOR Adults compelled to devote every waking moment to the pleasure and entertainment of their young children, or rich people who are paying someone else to take their children to the theme park.

PREREQUISITE This plan is designed for days when the Magic Kingdom doesn't close until 9 p.m. or later.

ASSUMES Frequent stops for rest, restrooms, and refreshments.

Name aside, this plan is no joke. Whether you're loving, guilty, masochistic, selfless, or insane, this itinerary will provide a youngster with about as perfect a day as is possible at the Magic Kingdom. Families using this plan should review Magic Kingdom attractions in our Small-Child Fright-Potential Chart in Part Five (see pages 404–407).

This plan is a concession to adults determined to give their young children the ultimate Magic Kingdom experience. If you left the kids with a sitter yesterday or wouldn't let little Marvin eat frosting for breakfast, the plan will expiate your guilt.

To Convert This One-Day Touring Plan into a Day-and-a-Half Touring Plan

The idea is to split the park in half so that Tomorrowland, Storybook Circus, and a few of the other Fantasyland attractions are on the second day. Here's how:

For the day of your afternoon visit, make FastPass+ reservations well in advance for Splash Mountain around 4 p.m., Pirates of the Caribbean around 5 p.m., and Jungle Cruise around 6:30 p.m. Work in the other rides, shows, and dinner around these, and end the day with the evening parade.

For your full-day visit, make FastPass+ reservations well in advance for Peter Pan's Flight around 10:30 a.m., *Enchanted Tales with Belle* around 6:30 p.m., and Buzz Lightyear around 8 p.m. Ride Seven Dwarfs Mine Train as soon as the park opens, then Winnie the Pooh on the way to Astro Orbiter and Tomorrowland Speedway. Visit Storybook Circus as you loop back to Under the Sea, then continue clockwise through Fantasyland before leaving the park for a midday break. Return to the park for dinner before your *Enchanted Tales* reservation, then see *Mickey's PhilharMagic*, the *Monsters, Inc.*, show in Tomorrowland, and Buzz Lightyear. See the parade and fireworks if you've not already done so, and try to get same-day FastPass+ reservations after you've used your first three or four.

PART TEN

EPCOT

EDUCATION, INSPIRATION, AND CORPORATE IMAGERY are the focus at Epcot, the most adult of the Disney theme parks. What it gains in taking a futuristic, visionary, and technological look at the world, it loses just a bit in warmth, happiness, and charm. Some people find the attempts at education superficial, while others want more entertainment and less education. Most visitors, however, find plenty of both.

Epcot is more than twice as big as the Magic Kingdom and Disney's Hollywood Studios and, though smaller than Disney's Animal Kingdom, has more territory to be covered on foot. Epcot rarely sees the congestion so common in the Magic Kingdom, but its popular rides have lines every bit as long as those at headliners such as Seven Dwarfs Mine Train and Space Mountain.

Epcot's size means that you can't see it all in one day without skipping an attraction or two and giving others a cursory glance. A major difference between Epcot and the other parks, however, is that some of its attractions can be savored slowly or skimmed, depending on personal interests. For example, the first section of Chevrolet's **Test Track** is a thrill ride, the second a collection of walk-through exhibits. Nearly all visitors take the ride, but many people, lacking time or interest, bypass the exhibits.

We rate several Epcot attractions as not to be missed. But part of the enjoyment of the park is that there's something for everyone.

NOT TO BE MISSED AT EPCOT
FUTURE WORLD • Living with the Land • Mission: Space • Soarin' • Spaceship Earth • Sum of All Thrills • Test Track • *Turtle Talk with Crush*
WORLD SHOWCASE • *The American Adventure* • *IllumiNations* (or its replacement)

THE EPCOT ACRONYM

IN THE BEGINNING, Epcot was EPCOT. When envisioned by Walt Disney as a utopian working city of the future, EPCOT was the acronym for **E**xperimental **P**rototype **C**ommunity **o**f **T**omorrow. Corporate Disney ultimately scrubbed Walt's vision, and the city became a theme park, but

Continued on page 540

Epcot

Attractions

1. Agent P's World Showcase Adventure *(multiple locations)*
2. *The American Adventure* ✓
3. *Captain EO* FP+
4. *The Circle of Life*
5. Club Cool
6. Epcot Character Spot FP+
7. *Frozen Ever After (opens 2016–17)* FP+
8. Frozen Royal Sommerhus meet and greet *(opens 2016–17)* FP+
9. Gran Fiesta Tour Starring the Three Caballeros
10. *IllumiNations: Reflections of Earth* ✓ FP+
11. *Impressions de France*
12. Innoventions East
13. Innoventions West
14. Journey into Imagination with Figment FP+
15. Living with the Land ✓ FP+
16. Mission: Space ✓ Use FP+
17. *O Canada!*
18. *Reflections of China*
19. The Seas Main Tank and Exhibits
20. The Seas with Nemo & Friends Use FP+
21. Soarin' ✓ Use FP+
22. Spaceship Earth ✓ FP+
23. Sum of All Thrills ✓
24. Test Track ✓ Use FP+
25. *Turtle Talk with Crush* ✓ FP+
26. Universe of Energy: *Ellen's Energy Adventure*

FUTURE WORLD

Outpost

China

Norway

Mexico

Test Track

Odyssey Center

IllumiNations FP+ Viewing

Festival Center *(seasonal)*

Lighter Traffic Bag Check

Bag Check

The Seas

FP+ Attraction Offers FastPass+

Use FP+ Recommended Use of FastPass+

First Aid Center

FP+ FastPass+ Kiosks

IllumiNations Top Viewing Spot

"Mom, I Can't Believe It's Disney" Fountains

✓ Not to be Missed

Recommended Dining

Restrooms

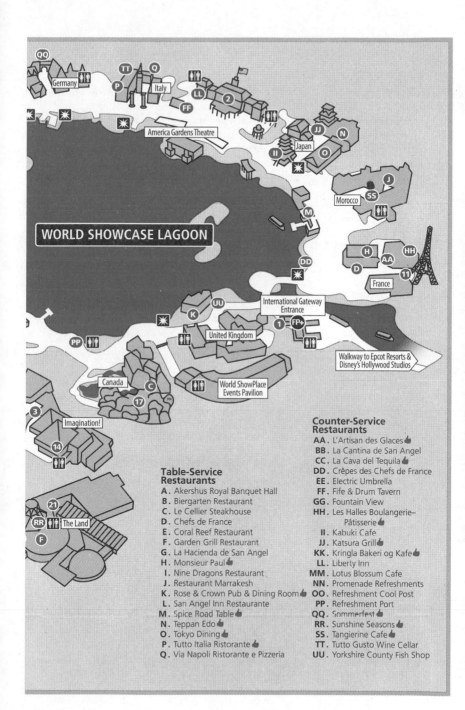

Table-Service Restaurants

A. Akershus Royal Banquet Hall
B. Biergarten Restaurant
C. Le Cellier Steakhouse
D. Chefs de France
E. Coral Reef Restaurant
F. Garden Grill Restaurant
G. La Hacienda de San Angel
H. Monsieur Paul
I. Nine Dragons Restaurant
J. Restaurant Marrakesh
K. Rose & Crown Pub & Dining Room
L. San Angel Inn Restaurante
M. Spice Road Table
N. Teppan Edo
O. Tokyo Dining
P. Tutto Italia Ristorante
Q. Via Napoli Ristorante e Pizzeria

Counter-Service Restaurants

AA. L'Artisan des Glaces
BB. La Cantina de San Angel
CC. La Cava del Tequila
DD. Crêpes des Chefs de France
EE. Electric Umbrella
FF. Fife & Drum Tavern
GG. Fountain View
HH. Les Halles Boulangerie–Pâtisserie
II. Kabuki Cafe
JJ. Katsura Grill
KK. Kringla Bakeri og Kafe
LL. Liberty Inn
MM. Lotus Blossum Cafe
NN. Promenade Refreshments
OO. Refreshment Cool Post
PP. Refreshment Port
QQ. Sommerfest
RR. Sunshine Seasons
SS. Tangierine Cafe
TT. Tutto Gusto Wine Cellar
UU. Yorkshire County Fish Shop

Continued from page 537

the name remained. And because EPCOT was clearly nothing of the sort, the acronym EPCOT became the name *Epcot*.

OPERATING HOURS

EPCOT HAS TWO THEMED AREAS, **Future World** and **World Show-case,** each with its own operating hours. Though schedules change throughout the year, Future World always opens before World Showcase. While most of Future World's attractions stay open until the entire park closes, a few close around 7 p.m. most of the year. World Showcase generally opens 2 hours later than Future World; moreover, some attractions open late or close early.

For park hours, call ☎ 407-824-4321 or visit **disneyworld.com.** For the operating schedules of specific attractions, check the park map or the supplemental *Times Guide.*

DINING IN EPCOT

HERE'S A QUICK RECAP of Epcot's major restaurants, rated by readers from highest to lowest. See Part Four for details.

EPCOT RESTAURANT REFRESHER	
COUNTER-SERVICE	**FULL-SERVICE**
L'Artisan des Glaces (97% 👍), France, World Showcase	**Tutto Gusto Wine Cellar** (100% 👍), Italy, World Showcase
Les Halles Boulangerie–Pâtisserie (96% 👍), France, World Showcase	**Monsieur Paul** (93% 👍), France, World Showcase
Kringla Bakeri og Kafe (95% 👍), Norway, World Showcase	**Teppan Edo** (93% 👍) Japan, World Showcase
Sunshine Seasons (95% 👍), The Land, Future World West	**Le Cellier Steakhouse** (90% 👍), Canada, World Showcase
Fountain View (Starbucks) (94% 👍), To the right of the big fountain in the back of Future World	**Rose & Crown Dining Room** (90% 👍), UK, World Showcase
Tangierine Cafe (93% 👍), Morocco, World Showcase	**Tokyo Dining** (90% 👍), Japan, World Showcase

◖ ARRIVING

IF YOU'RE A GUEST AT ONE OF THE EPCOT RESORTS, it will take you about 20–30 minutes to walk the mile or so from your hotel to the International Gateway (back entrance of Epcot) and from there to Future World. Instead of walking, you can catch a boat from your Epcot resort hotel to the International Gateway and then walk about 8 minutes to Future World. To reach the front (Future World) entrance of Epcot from the Epcot resorts, either take a boat from your hotel to Disney's Hollywood Studios and transfer to an Epcot bus, take a bus to Disney Springs and transfer to an Epcot bus, or take a cab.

unofficial **TIP**
Plan to arrive at the turnstiles 30–40 minutes before official opening time. Give yourself an extra 10 minutes or so to park and make your way to the entrance.

Arriving at the park by car is easy and direct (for driving directions, see page 443). Epcot has its own parking lot, and, unlike at the Magic Kingdom, you don't have to take a monorail or ferry to reach the entrance. Trams service the parking lot, or you can walk to the front gate. Monorail service connects Epcot with the Transportation and Ticket Center, the Magic Kingdom (transfer required), and Magic Kingdom resorts (transfer required).

For unknown reasons, getting through entrance security at Epcot is more cumbersome and time-consuming than at the other parks. In fact, it's a royal pain, as this unidentified reader relates:

My biggest complaint was the amount of time it took to actually get into Epcot: 35 minutes at 10:30 a.m. to get bags checked (park had opened at 9) and another 10 minutes to get in. It took nowhere near as long at the other parks, even with the same crowd size.

Take these delays into consideration if you're using one of the Epcot touring plans. A second, often overlooked, security checkpoint is on the other (east) side of the main checkpoint. If the main lines look too long, have one member of your group peek around to see if the east lines are shorter.

This reader from Sacramento, California, suggests using the International Gateway (World Showcase) entrance instead:

Thanks to MagicBands and FastPass+, the International Gateway entrance is convenient for getting into Epcot first thing in the morning. We entered there by boat from the Dolphin hotel and were met inside the gate by cast members who set up our FastPass+ reservations for the day.

GETTING ORIENTED

EPCOT'S TWO THEMED AREAS are markedly different: **Future World** examines where mankind has come from and where it's going; **World Showcase** features the landmarks, cuisine, and culture of almost a dozen nations and is meant to be a sort of permanent World's Fair.

Navigating Epcot is unlike getting around at the Magic Kingdom. The Magic Kingdom is designed so that nearly every location is part of a discrete environment—Liberty Square and Main Street, U.S.A., for example. All environments are visually separated to preserve the integrity of the theme.

Epcot, by contrast, is visually open. And while it seems strange to see a Japanese pagoda and the Eiffel Tower on the same horizon, getting around is fairly simple. An exception is Future World, where the enormous **Innoventions East and West** buildings hide everything on their opposite sides.

At Epcot, the architectural symbol is **Spaceship Earth.** This shiny, 180-foot geosphere is visible from almost everywhere in the park. Like Cinderella Castle at the Magic Kingdom, Spaceship Earth can help you keep track of where you are in Epcot. But it's in a high-traffic area and isn't centrally located, so it isn't a good meeting place.

Any of the World Showcase pavilions make good meeting places, but be specific. "Hey, let's meet in Japan!" sounds fun, but each pavilion is a mini-town with buildings, monuments, gardens, and plazas. Pick a specific place in Japan—the sidewalk side of the pagoda, for example.

FASTPASS+ ATTRACTIONS IN EPCOT

EPCOT OFFERS FASTPASS+ for 11 attractions in two tiers:

TIER A (Choose one per day)	TIER B (Choose two per day)
• *IllumiNations*	• *Captain EO*
• Living with the Land	• Epcot Character Spot
• Soarin'	• Journey into Imagination
• Test Track	• Mission: Space (Green or Orange)
	• Spaceship Earth
	• The Seas with Nemo & Friends
	• *Turtle Talk with Crush*

Because the tiers limit the number and combinations of FastPass+ attractions you can experience, much of our Epcot touring strategy is dictated by the attractions in Tier A, which include **Soarin'** and **Test Track.** Because you can't use FastPass+ for both, your best bet is to visit one as the first step in a touring plan, then use FastPass+ for the other. *Exception:* **Living with the Land** just doesn't get crowds comparable to the others, so it's rarely a good use of FastPass+.

Our most frequent FastPass+ recommendation is for **Spaceship Earth,** usually around lunch. Longer lines develop at Soarin' and Test Track than at Spaceship Earth, so it's important to get one of those done first thing in the morning. But because Spaceship Earth's wait times can reach 30–40 minutes, it's one of the best choices in Tier B.

Another attraction that affects Epcot touring is **Sum of All Thrills,** in which you design and then ride in your own virtual roller coaster. Though it's not to be missed, it's also not a FastPass+ attraction—that's probably because it can handle just a few hundred guests per hour and thus doesn't have enough rider capacity to allocate to reservations.

As an example, our Epcot One-Day Touring Plan for Adults minimizes the capacity constraints at Sum of All Thrills by sandwiching it between FastPass+ reservations for Test Track and Mission: Space, its neighbors in Future World:

1. **Soarin'**
2. **Living with the Land**
3. **Test Track:** FastPass+ for 9:15 a.m.
4. **Sum of All Thrills**
5. **Mission: Space (Orange):** FastPass+ for 10:15 a.m.

Get to Test Track in the second half of your 1-hour FastPass+ time window. By the time you've experienced Test Track and Sum of All Thrills, your FastPass+ window for Mission: Space will have started, plus it's a short walk there from Innoventions East. This strategy saves you both time in line and time walking from attraction to attraction.

In general, our touring plan software recommends FastPass+ for Soarin' more than twice as often as Test Track. Both have 40-inch height

EPCOT
When Same-Day FP+ Runs Out, by Crowd Level

ATTRACTION	LOW CROWDS*	MODERATE CROWDS*	HIGH CROWDS*
Captain EO (if open)	6 p.m.		Until 6-7 p.m.
Epcot Character Spot	4-5 p.m. (all crowd levels)		
IllumiNations (or replacement)	1-2 p.m.	Noon-1 p.m.	11 a.m.-noon
Journey into Imagination	6 p.m.	5-6 p.m.	4-5 p.m.
Living with the Land	6 p.m. (all crowd levels)		
Mission: Space (Orange)	1-3 p.m.	11 a.m.-noon	10 a.m.-noon
The Seas with Nemo and Friends	6-7 p.m.		3-5 p.m.
Soarin'	1-3 p.m.	Noon-1 p.m.	11 a.m.
Spaceship Earth	6-7 p.m.	4-5 p.m.	Noon-1 p.m.
Test Track	1-3 p.m.	Noon-1 p.m.	10 a.m.-noon
Turtle Talk with Crush	6-7 p.m. (all crowd levels)		

* LOW CROWDS (Levels 1-3 on TouringPlans.com Crowd Calendar)

* MODERATE CROWDS (Levels 4-7 on TouringPlans.com Crowd Calendar)

* HIGH CROWDS (Levels 8-10 on TouringPlans.com Crowd Calendar)

requirements, but Test Track is a harsher ride, with sudden stops, turns, and acceleration. For that reason, Test Track doesn't appear on many of our touring plans for parents with small children or those for seniors (the plan on the facing page is our standard one for adults).

A second reason to use FastPass+ at Soarin' is **Test Track's single-rider line,** a feature Soarin' doesn't have. Test Track's single-rider wait times are typically less than half those of its standby (non-FastPass+) wait times. If you're willing to split up your group, the single-rider line is a good way to mitigate Test Track's standby waits.

We've also identified four attractions for which FastPass+ is *never* necessary. First, waits for *Captain EO* and **Journey into Imagination with Figment** are almost always less than 10 minutes; similarly, waits for the nonspinning **Mission: Space (Green)** are almost always lower than those for the spinning (Orange) version.

Epcot Character Spot doesn't require FastPass+ in our Epcot touring plans for parents with small children. Because you can get a FastPass+ for Soarin' (if your kids are old enough to ride), and because Test Track and Mission: Space aren't in our plans due to their intensity and height requirements, our software usually puts the Character Spot as one of the first steps in your plan.

IllumiNations (or its successor—see page 566) is a must-see, and Fast-Pass+ gets you into a special viewing area for the show, but you still have to arrive a good 30–40 minutes in advance to get a good spot. Plus, there are so many other good viewing spots around World Showcase Lagoon that it's difficult to recommend FastPass+ for *IllumiNations;* the consequence is an hour-long wait at either Soarin' or Test Track. The exceptions are if you're visiting World Showcase for an evening—there are no other Tier A attractions here—or if you've used your first three FastPass+ reservations and *IllumiNations* FastPasses are still available.

When they open in 2016, **Frozen Ever After** and the **Royal Sommer-hus Meet and Greet** with Anna and Elsa (see page 560) will in all likelihood be FastPass+ attractions, too. Check the e-book version of this guide and **touringplans.com** for updates.

Look for Epcot FastPass+ kiosks in the following locations:

- At the Soarin' entrance, downstairs in The Land
- At the MyMagic+ Service Center, between Spaceship Earth and Innoventions East
- At the International Gateway entrance to the park
- In the Future World East walkway, on the way to Mission: Space
- In the Future World West walkway, on the way to The Land

Same-Day FastPass+ Availability

The preceding advice tells you which attractions to focus on when making your *advance* FastPass+ reservations before you get to the park. Once you're in the park, you can make more FastPass+ reservations once your advance reservations have been used or have expired. The chart on the previous page shows which attractions are likely to have day-of FastPasses available, and the approximate times at which they'll run out.

FUTURE WORLD

IMMENSE, GLEAMING FUTURISTIC STRUCTURES define the first themed area beyond Epcot's main entrance. Broad thoroughfares are punctuated with billowing fountains, all reflected in shiny space-age facades. Front and center is **Spaceship Earth,** flanked by **Innoventions East and West.** Pavilions dedicated to mankind's past, present, and future technological achievements ring the perimeter of Future World.

EPCOT Services

EPCOT'S SERVICE FACILITIES, most located in Future World, include:

Baby Care Center On the World Showcase side of the Odyssey Center

Banking Services ATMs outside the main entrance, on the Future World bridge, and in World Showcase at the US Pavilion and International Gateway entrance

Cell Phone Charging Outlets available in The Seas, upstairs near the women's restroom; in The Land, upstairs near The Garden Grill; and in Mexico, near the bench against the ramp that leads to the market

Dining Reservations At Guest Relations, to the left of Spaceship Earth

First Aid Center Next to the Baby Care Center

Live-Entertainment Information At Guest Relations

Lost and Found At the main entrance at the gift shop

Lost Persons At Guest Relations and the Baby Care Center

Walt Disney World and Local Attraction Information At Guest Relations

Wheelchair, ECV, ESV, and Stroller Rentals Inside the main entrance and to the left, toward the rear of the Entrance Plaza

Spaceship Earth (*FastPass+*) ★★★★

**APPEAL BY AGE   PRESCHOOL ★★★★   GRADE SCHOOL ★★★★   TEENS ★★★★
YOUNG ADULTS ★★★★   OVER 30 ★★★★   SENIORS ★★★★½**

What it is Educational dark ride through past, present, and future. **Scope and scale**
Headliner. **When to go** Before 10 a.m., after 4 p.m., or use FastPass+. **Special comments** If lines are long when you arrive, try again after 4 p.m. **Authors' rating** One
of Epcot's best; not to be missed; ★★★★. **Duration of ride** About 16 minutes.
Average wait in line per 100 people ahead of you 3 minutes. **Loading speed** Fast.

DESCRIPTION AND COMMENTS This ride spirals through the 18-story interior of
   Epcot's premier landmark, taking visitors past animatronic scenes depicting mankind's developments in communications, from cave painting
   to printing to television to space communications and computer networks. The ride shows an amazing use of the geosphere's interior.
      Spaceship Earth's scenes are periodically refreshed. The most recent include a 1970s-era computer room and a home garage showing what looks
   suspiciously like the invention of the Apple personal computer (perhaps an
   homage to Steve Jobs, who before his death was Disney's largest individual shareholder). Interactive video screens on the ride vehicles allow you
   to customize the ride's ending animated video. A postshow area with
   games and interactive exhibits rounds out the attraction.
TOURING TIPS Because it's near Epcot's main entrance, Spaceship Earth
   attracts arriving guests throughout the morning. If you want to ride Soarin' and Test Track, try to get a FastPass+ reservation for around 1 p.m.
   You should be almost done with Future World's attractions by then and
   ready to head to World Showcase. Or, if you plan on spending the afternoon in Future World and don't want to use FastPass+, try Spaceship
   Earth after 3 p.m.

Innoventions East and West ★★½

**APPEAL BY AGE   PRESCHOOL ★★★½   GRADE SCHOOL ★★★★   TEENS ★★★½
YOUNG ADULTS ★★★   OVER 30 ★★★½   SENIORS ★★★½**

What it is Static and hands-on exhibits relating to products and technologies of the
near future. **Scope and scale** Minor diversion. **When to go** On your second day at
Epcot or after you've seen all the major attractions. **Special comments** Most exhibits demand time and participation to be rewarding. **Authors' rating** We're hoping
for a spectacular refurbishment; ★★½.

*Note: Currently all of Innoventions West and a good chunk of Innoventions East
are closed for refurbishment, with no reopening date announced.*

DISNEY DISH WITH JIM HILL

WILL THE FORCE AWAKEN IN INNOVENTIONS WEST?
The Imagineers have a temporary solution to the problem of
technology progressing faster than Disney can build shows: to
turn this part of Future World into an exhibition of props and
costumes from the upcoming *Star Wars Episode VII: The Force
Awakens.* Why Epcot instead of Hollywood Studios? Because
the current plan for 2016 is to start building the new *Star Wars*
land at the Studios, making it a major construction zone.

DESCRIPTION AND COMMENTS Innoventions is a huge, busy collection of hands-
   on and walk-through exhibits sponsored by corporations and used to
   showcase their products and technology. It's so big that it takes two

buildings—Innoventions East and West, on either side of Future World Plaza—to contain everything. Electronics and entertainment-technology exhibits play prominent roles, as do ecology and "how things work" displays.

The problem that Disney faces with Innoventions is the same one it faces with Tomorrowland in the Magic Kingdom: The future arrives faster and different than expected. In the case of Innoventions, this means that exhibits based on cutting-edge technology will have approximately the same shelf life as a sesame bagel. As a result, large chunks of Innoventions are either closed or somewhat outdated.

Some exhibits are definitely worth stopping for, however. Our favorite is Raytheon's **Sum of All Thrills**, a roller-coaster simulator in which you design the coaster track on a tabletop computer, then climb aboard a giant robotic arm to experience your creation. We also like **Habit Heroes,** which requires you to do calisthenics to save the planet from sloth and gluttony (not kidding).

TOURING TIPS Spend time at Innoventions on your second day at Epcot. If you have only one day, visit late if you have the time and endurance. (The exception is Sum of All Thrills, which you should visit in the morning after Soarin', Test Track, and Mission: Space.) Skip exhibits with waits of more than 10 minutes, or experience them first thing in the morning on your second day, when there are no lines.

CLUB COOL

DESCRIPTION AND COMMENTS Attached to the fountain side of Innoventions West, this Coca-Cola–sponsored retail space–soda fountain provides free unlimited samples of soft drinks from around the world. Some will taste strange to Americans, but others will please. Perhaps because it's free and indoors, kids and teens rate Club Cool higher than all Epcot offerings except Soarin' and Test Track.

SUM OF ALL THRILLS ★★★★

APPEAL BY AGE	PRESCHOOL ★★★½	GRADE SCHOOL ★★★★½	TEENS ★★★★½
YOUNG ADULTS ★★★★½		OVER 30 ★★★★½	SENIORS ★★★★

What it is Hands-on exhibit and ride simulator. **Scope and scale** Minor attraction. **When to go** Before 10:30 a.m. or after 5 p.m. **Special comments** 48″ minimum height requirement, 54″ for track designs with inversions. **Authors' rating** Not to be missed; ★★★★. **Duration of attraction** 15 minutes. **Average wait in line per 100 people ahead of you** 40 minutes; assumes all simulators operating. **Loading speed** Slow.

DESCRIPTION AND COMMENTS Sum of All Thrills is a design-your-own-roller-coaster simulator in which you use a computer program to specify the drops, curves, and loops of a coaster track before boarding an industrial robotic arm to experience your creation. Three vehicle options are available: bobsled, roller coaster, and jet aircraft. It's possible to program actual loops into both the coaster and jet courses, and the robot arm will swing you upside down.

In addition to the vehicle, you select the kinds of turns, loops, and hills in your track design. Choices range from mild, broad curves to extreme multiple-loop inversions. Using computer-design tools, you can further customize these components by changing the height and width of each piece as you go. This customization makes it easy to ride Sum of All Thrills many times without experiencing the same track twice.

A New Jersey couple thinks Sum of All Thrills is simply awesome:

Sum of All Thrills has to be the most unheralded attraction anywhere in the World. With the chance to design your own attraction and waits usually under 20 minutes, it's one of the best things to do in Future World.

Touring Tips Not a high-capacity attraction, but also not on most guests' radar. Ride as early in the morning as possible.

Epcot Character Spot *(FastPass+)*   ★★★

APPEAL BY AGE   PRESCHOOL ★★★★½ **GRADE SCHOOL** ★★★★½ **TEENS** ★★★★
YOUNG ADULTS ★★★★   **OVER 30** ★★★★   **SENIORS** ★★★

What it is Character-greeting venue. **Scope and scale** Diversion. **When to go** Before 11 a.m., or use FastPass+. **Authors' rating** Indoors and air-conditioned; ★★★. **Duration of experience** 8 minutes. **Probable waiting time** 20–40 minutes. **Queue speed** Slow.

DESCRIPTION AND COMMENTS In Future World West, to the right of The Fountain restaurant, Epcot Character Spot offers the chance to meet Disney characters indoors, in air-conditioned comfort. Characters on hand typically include Mickey Mouse, Minnie Mouse, and Pluto. You may also find Chip 'n' Dale nearby outside.

TOURING TIPS The Character Spot should be your first stop if you have small children. Make FastPass+ reservations for Soarin' for around 9:30 a.m. so you can proceed there directly after getting autographs. The venue typically stays open until 9 p.m., even when other Future World attractions close at 7 p.m., and usually until around 10:45 p.m. during evening Extra Magic Hours, when Epcot is open until 11 p.m. or later.

Universe of Energy: *Ellen's Energy Adventure*   ★★★½

APPEAL BY AGE   PRESCHOOL ★★★   **GRADE SCHOOL** ★★★½ **TEENS** ★★★
YOUNG ADULTS ★★★½   **OVER 30** ★★★   **SENIORS** ★★★★

What it is Combination dark ride–theater presentation. **Scope and scale** Major attraction. **When to go** Anytime. **Special comments** Don't be dismayed by long lines—580 people enter the pavilion each time the theater changes audiences. **Authors' rating** Fun and informative, but showing its age; ★★★½. **Duration of presentation** About 26½ minutes. **Preshow entertainment** 8 minutes. **Probable waiting time** 14 minutes.

DESCRIPTION AND COMMENTS This attraction begins with a preshow film starring Ellen DeGeneres. While watching TV, Ellen dozes off and dreams that she's competing on *Jeopardy!* against her know-it-all former college roommate Judy (Jamie Lee Curtis). All of the categories deal with energy, and unfortunately for Ellen, Judy has a PhD in the subject.

Luckily, Ellen's next-door neighbor happens to be Bill Nye the Science Guy, who convinces Ellen—along with everyone else in the audience—to take a time-traveling crash course in the history of energy.

You move from the preshow hall to what appears to be an ordinary theater to watch another film, this one about energy sources. Then the seats divide into six 97-passenger traveling cars that carry you from the Big Bang (the beginning of Ellen's energy lessons) to the swamps and animatronic dinosaurs of a prehistoric forest. Special effects include the feel of warm, moist swamp air and the smell of sulfur from an erupting volcano.

The dialogue between DeGeneres and Nye is humorous and upbeat, but the script was written almost 20 years ago, when ExxonMobil was sponsoring the attraction. Don't expect to hear calls to action on climate change or carbon footprints, or much more than a passing reference to alternative energy sources.

For children, it's a toss-up. The dinosaurs frighten some preschoolers, and kids of all ages lose the thread during the educational segments.

A Zionsville, Indiana, reader agrees with us that *Ellen's Energy Adventure* is more than a little dated:

Ellen is genuinely funny, but this attraction is so old that the video quality is only slightly better than the Zapruder film's.

TOURING TIPS Because the theater has a ride component, the line doesn't move while the show is in progress. When the theater empties, however, a large chunk of the line disappears as people are admitted for the next show. Because of this, waits are generally tolerable.

Mission: Space *(FastPass+)* ★★★★

APPEAL BY AGE	PRESCHOOL ★★★½	GRADE SCHOOL ★★★★	TEENS ★★★★
YOUNG ADULTS ★★★★		OVER 30 ★★★★	SENIORS ★★★½

Motion Sickness

What it is Space-flight-simulator ride. **Scope and scale** Super-headliner. **When to go** First or last hour the park is open, or use FastPass+. **Special comments** Not recommended for pregnant women or people prone to motion sickness or claustrophobia; 44" minimum height requirement; a gentler nonspinning version is also available. **Authors' rating** Impressive; not to be missed; ★★★★. **Duration of ride** About 5 minutes plus preshow. **Average wait in line per 100 people ahead of you** 4 minutes. **Loading speed** Moderate–fast.

DESCRIPTION AND COMMENTS Mission: Space was one of the most popular rides at Disney World until two guests died after riding it in 2005 and 2006. While neither death was linked directly to the attraction, the negative publicity caused many guests to skip it entirely. In response, Disney added a tamer nonspinning version of Mission: Space in 2006.

Disney's lawyers probably clocked as much time as the ride engineers in designing the "lite" version. Even before you walk into the building, you're asked whether you want your ride with or without spin. Choose the spinning version and you're on the Orange team; the Green team trains on the no-spin side. Either way, you're immediately handed the appropriate "launch ticket" containing the first of myriad warnings about the attraction, as this *Unofficial Guide* reader discovered:

I chose the more intense version and was handed the Orange launch ticket to read. Basically, it explained that if I had ever had a tonsillectomy or even a mild case of pattern baldness, I should take the less intense ride.

This San Antonio reader says you don't give up much by choosing the Green option:

I am 65 and have ridden the Orange version a number of times. On our latest trip, we went on the Orange version again and felt a little uncomfortable. My wife suggested that we try the Green version, which I mistakenly believed was some sort of boring mission-control exercise where we would sit behind a computer. We were pleased to discover that the Green version was the full-blown ride but less intense—it gave us a great experience, including the feeling of lift-off and zero gravity, without the nausea.

Guests for both versions of the attraction enter the International Space Training Center, where they're introduced to the deep-space exploration program and then divided into groups for flight training. After orientation, they're strapped into space capsules for a simulated flight, where, of course, the unexpected happens. Each capsule accommodates a crew consisting of a group commander, pilot, navigator, and engineer, with a guest functioning in each role. The crew's skill and finesse (or, more often, lack thereof) in handling their respective responsibilities have no effect on the outcome of the flight.

The capsules are small, and both ride versions are amazingly realistic. The nonspinning version doesn't subject your body to g-forces, but it does bounce and toss you around in a manner roughly comparable to other Disney motion simulators. A Bradenton, Florida, mom found motion sickness to be the least of her problems:

I'd like to see warnings here about claustrophobia—I had no clue until the capsule closed that it would be so tight in there. I went into full panic mode.

TOURING TIPS Disney can reconfigure the ride's four centrifuges to either version based on guest demand. In general, the kinder, gentler version has a wait time of about half that of its more harrowing counterpart.

Having experienced the industrial-strength version of Mission: Space under a variety of circumstances, we've always felt icky when riding it on an empty stomach, especially first thing in the morning, so we looked around for an expert to tell us why. Because NASA is a codeveloper of Mission: Space and an authority on the effect of g-forces on the human body, we called them. Amazingly, a spokesman told us that NASA no longer does much high-g training these days. And the agency was reluctant to pass along anything resembling medical advice to the general public.

Fortunately, a longtime friend put us in touch with a real NASA astronaut who was willing to share (anonymously) some ideas on what causes the nausea, as well as some tips for preventing it. Our expert guesses, as we do, that low blood sugar is the culprit and suggests eating a normal meal 1–2 hours before experiencing the ride. Avoid milk and tomatoes; they're difficult to keep down and, as our contact noted with the voice of experience, particularly unpleasant if they come back up. A banana, we hear, is a good choice for your preflight meal. Another trick of the astronaut trade is to keep a piece of hard candy or a mint in your mouth; it's not clear, though, whether the candy helps keep blood-sugar levels high or is just a placebo. If all else fails, there are airsickness bags in each simulator.

Hit the john before you get in line—you'll think your bladder really has been to Mars and back before you get out of this one. We recommend securing a midmorning FastPass+ reservation for Mission: Space (Orange).

Few things delight our readers more than kibitzing about rides that can make you puke, and Mission: Space is at the top of this particular heap. From a Yakima, Washington, reader:

Mission: Space is awesome. A number of people we spoke to didn't ride because they were intimidated by the warnings about motion sickness.

A woman from Lisbon, Connecticut, used Mission: Space as her own personal relationship lab:

We now understand why husbands and wives will probably never go to space together after I (the "navigator") pushed his (the "pilot's") button during the flight. I couldn't help being a backseat driver—we could have crashed!

TEST TRACK PAVILION

DESCRIPTION AND COMMENTS Sponsored by Chevrolet, this pavilion consists of the **Test Track** attraction and **Inside Track,** a collection of transportation-themed exhibits and multimedia presentations. The pavilion is the last on the left before the World Showcase. Many readers tell us that Test Track "is one big commercial" for Chevrolet. We agree that promotional hype is more heavy-handed here than in most other business-sponsored attractions. But Test Track is nonetheless one of the most creatively conceived attractions in Disney World.

Test Track (FastPass+) ★★★★

What it is Auto-test-track simulator ride. **Scope and scale** Super-headliner. **When to go** The first 30 minutes the park is open or just before closing, or use FastPass+. **Special comments** 40″ minimum height requirement. **Authors' rating** Not to be missed; ★★★★. **Duration of ride** About 4 minutes. **Average wait in line per 100 people ahead of you** 4½ minutes. **Loading speed** Moderate–fast.

DESCRIPTION AND COMMENTS Test Track takes guests through the process of designing a new vehicle and then "testing" their car in a high-speed drive through and around the pavilion.

Guests entering the pavilion walk past displays of sleek, futuristic concept cars and glossy video screens where engineers discuss the work of car design and consumers explain the characteristics of their perfect car.

After hearing about auto design, guests are admitted into the Chevrolet Design Studio to create their own concept car. Using a large touchscreen interface (like a giant iPad), groups of up to three guests drag their fingers to design their car's body, engine, wheels, trim, and color. The computer screen reflects each design decision's impact on the car's capability, efficiency, responsiveness, and power. (For example, designing a large truck with a huge V-8 engine increases the car's capability and power but drastically reduces its efficiency.) The entire creative experience takes 5–8 minutes.

Next, guests board a six-seat ride vehicle, attached to a track on the ground, for an actual drive through Chevrolet's test track. The idea here is that guests are taking part in a computer simulation designed to test their vehicle's performance characteristics. The vehicle's tests include braking maneuvers, cornering, and acceleration, culminating in a spin around the outside of the pavilion at speeds of up to 65 miles per hour.

The ride visuals are sleek and eye-catching, but trying to understand them as a coherent narrative is pointless—like fuzzy dice and reality-TV contestants, they're there to look good, not to be useful. At various points during the ride, video screens show the virtual cars designed by the guests in your vehicle and a status update on how the vehicle's tests are progressing. Most guests figure out quickly that absolutely nothing in their car's design has any effect whatsoever on their ride experience.

Test Track's postshow area continues the design process by allowing guests to create commercials for their concept cars. Farther into the pavilion are displays of actual Chevys, many of which you can sit in. We've never heard of anyone attempting to buy a car from Test Track, but let us know if you have.

TOURING TIPS It's always been a challenge to keep Test Track running, especially in humid or wet conditions. When it's working properly, it's one of the park's better attractions—but for this London, Ontario, mom, such instances never materialized:

Test Track breaks down more than any ride I've ever seen. We went back there over and over again, got in line, and then had to get out. FastPass+ lines would have a 40-minute wait because no one got to ride at the proper time.

A repeat visitor from East Aurora, New York, suggests that all is not lost when the ride malfunctions:

If the ride breaks down, tell a cast member. They'll most likely give you a slip that allows you to skip the line and ride again. This happened to us twice during the busiest time of the year, and we rode again with no problem.

Be aware that FastPass+ reservations often run out by afternoon. In that case, try the single-rider line. Because most groups are unwilling to split up, this line is usually much shorter than the regular (standby) line.

IMAGINATION! PAVILION

DESCRIPTION AND COMMENTS Multiattraction pavilion on the west side of Innoventions West. Outside are an "upside-down" waterfall and one of our favorite Future World landmarks, the "jumping" water, a fountain that hops over the heads of unsuspecting passersby.

TOURING TIPS We recommend late-morning touring. See individual attractions for specifics.

Captain EO (FastPass+) ★★★

APPEAL BY AGE	PRESCHOOL ★★★	GRADE SCHOOL ★★★	TEENS ★★★
YOUNG ADULTS ★★½		OVER 30 ★★½	SENIORS ★★★

What it is 3-D film and 1980s pop-culture artifact with special effects. **Scope and scale** Headliner. **When to go** When it's playing, anytime—FastPass+ is unnecessary. **Special comments** The high decibels frighten some young children. **Authors' rating** ★★★. **Duration of presentation** About 17 minutes. **Preshow entertainment** 8 minutes. **Probable waiting time** 15 minutes.

DISNEY DISH WITH JIM HILL

EO OUT, INSIDE OUT IN Anticipating that Pixar's *Inside Out* (2015) is going to be a huge success, Disney is considering putting Joy, Sadness, Anger, Fear, and Disgust in the 3-D theater that housed *Honey, I Shrunk the Audience* and currently shows *Captain EO*. Pixar is reportedly already hard at work on a brand-new, only-at-the-Disney-parks adventure that would take place at Headquarters (that is, inside Riley's brain).

DESCRIPTION AND COMMENTS In response to Michael Jackson's death in 2009, Disney brought back his space-themed 3-D musical film *Captain EO,* which originally ran in Epcot from 1986 to 1994, for a "limited" engagement in its theme parks.

A few years into its second run, however, *Unofficial Guide* readers were rating *Captain EO* as the worst attraction in Epcot, and most other park visitors probably felt the same. In early 2015, Disney preempted *EO* to show previews of upcoming theatrical releases. *EO* returned for the summer, but its long-term status is tenuous. It's possible that *EO* could stick around, the previous film (*Honey, I Shrunk the Audience*) could make a comeback, or something else entirely could appear (see Disney Dish above). Stay tuned.

We think *Captain EO* is still worth seeing if it's playing. It hasn't aged as well as Jackson's other long-form video work, notably *Thriller,* but it's still one of the ultimate 1980s-era music videos. Directed by Francis Ford Coppola, it's a 3-D space fantasy with lasers, fiber optics, cannons, and other special effects in the theater, plus some audience participation. It remains, as one *Unofficial Guide* child of the '80s says, evocative of a certain time and place.

TOURING TIPS Shows typically begin on the hour and half-hour. The sound level is earsplitting, frightening some young children. The theater rarely fills when *EO* is running, making FastPass+ unnecessary.

Journey into Imagination with Figment *(FastPass+)* ★★½

APPEAL BY AGE **PRESCHOOL** ★★★★ **GRADE SCHOOL** ★★★½ **TEENS** ★★★
YOUNG ADULTS ★★★ **OVER 30** ★★★ **SENIORS** ★★★½

What it is Dark fantasy-adventure ride. **Scope and scale** Major attraction wannabe.
When to go Anytime. **Authors' rating** ★★½. **Duration of ride** About 6 minutes.
Average wait in line per 100 people ahead of you 2 minutes. **Loading speed** Fast.

DESCRIPTION AND COMMENTS Journey into Imagination takes you on a tour
of the zany Imagination Institute. Sometimes you're a passive observer
and sometimes you're a test subject as the ride provides a glimpse of the
fictitious lab's inner workings. Stimulating all your senses and then some,
it hits you with optical illusions, an experiment in which noise generates
colors, a room that defies gravity, and other brain teasers. All along the
way, Figment (a purple dragon) makes surprise appearances. After the
ride, you can adjourn to an interactive exhibit area offering the latest in
unique, hands-on imagery technology.

   Reader responses to Figment and company are pretty consistent. From
a Franklin, Tennessee, family of three:

*Journey into Imagination should be experienced only if you're a HUGE Fig-
ment fan—we, on the other hand, hated it. My husband was convinced after
our touring plan sent us to Figment that all touring plans were a waste of time.*

   The ride falls short of the promise suggested by its name. Will you go
to sleep? No. Will you find it amusing? Probably. Will you remember it tomorrow? Only Figment knows.

TOURING TIPS The standby wait for this attraction rarely exceeds 20 minutes, so no need for FastPass+ here. You can enjoy the interactive postshow exhibit without taking the ride, so save it for later in the day.

THE LAND PAVILION

DESCRIPTION AND COMMENTS The Land is a huge themed area containing
three attractions and two restaurants. When the pavilion was built, its
emphasis was on farming, but it now focuses on the environment.

TOURING TIPS This is a good place to grab a fast-food lunch. If you're coming here to see the attractions, however, stay away during mealtimes. Be
forewarned that strollers aren't allowed inside the pavilion—those with
babes in arms might want to bring an infant carrier.

The Circle of Life ★★★½

APPEAL BY AGE **PRESCHOOL** ★★★½ **GRADE SCHOOL** ★★★½ **TEENS** ★★★½
YOUNG ADULTS ★★★½ **OVER 30** ★★★ **SENIORS** ★★★½

What it is Film exploring humans' relationship with the environment. **Scope and scale**
Minor attraction. **When to go** Anytime. **Authors' rating** Inspiring and enlightening;
★★★½. **Duration of presentation** About 20 minutes. **Preshow entertainment** Ecological slide show and trivia. **Probable waiting time** 10–15 minutes.

DESCRIPTION AND COMMENTS This playful yet educational film, starring Pumbaa, Simba, and Timon from Disney's animated feature *The Lion King,* spot-
lights the environmental interdependency of all creatures, demonstrating
how easily the ecological balance can be upset. The message is sobering,
but one that enlightens.

   A reader e-mailed us this comment:

The Circle of Life *seems hypocritical. Simba berates Timon and Pumbaa because they don't understand the ecological impact of putting up a resort.
Hello—am I missing something, or didn't Disney do just that?*

TOURING TIPS Every visitor should see this film.

Living with the Land *(FastPass+)* ★★★★

What it is Indoor boat ride chronicling the past, present, and future of farming and agriculture in the United States. **Scope and scale** Major attraction. **When to go** Before 11 a.m., after 1 p.m., or use FastPass+. **Special comments** Go early in the morning and save other Land attractions (except for Soarin') for later in the day. The ride is on the pavilion's lower level. **Authors' rating** Informative without being dull; not to be missed; ★★★★. **Duration of ride** About 14 minutes. **Average wait in line per 100 people ahead of you** 3 minutes; assumes 15 boats operating. **Loading speed** Moderate.

DESCRIPTION AND COMMENTS The boat ride takes visitors through swamps, past inhospitable farm environments, and through a futuristic greenhouse where real crops are grown using the latest agricultural technologies. The greenhouse exhibits change constantly: Along with familiar fruits and grains such as tomatoes, corn, and rice, recent plantings include fluted pumpkins, hot peppers, and more exotic foods such as Malabar nuts, pandan, caimito, and amaranth.

Many Epcot guests assume that Living with the Land will be too dry and educational for their tastes. A woman from Houston writes:

I had a bad attitude about Living with the Land—I just didn't think I was up for a movie about wheat farming. Wow, was I surprised!

TOURING TIPS See this attraction before the lunch crowd hits The Land's restaurants. Living with the Land is rarely a good use of FastPass+. If you have a special interest in the agricultural techniques being demonstrated, take the **Behind the Seeds at Epcot** tour (see page).

Soarin' *(FastPass+)* ★★★★½

What it is Flight simulator ride. **Scope and scale** Super-headliner. **When to go** First 30 minutes the park is open, or use FastPass+. **Special comments** Entrance on the lower level of the Land Pavilion. May induce motion sickness; 40" minimum height requirement. Switching-off option provided (see page 412). **Authors' rating** Thrilling and mellow at the same time; not to be missed; ★★★★½. **Duration of ride** 5½ minutes. **Average wait in line per 100 people ahead of you** 4 minutes; assumes 2 concourses operating. **Loading speed** Moderate.

DISNEY DISH WITH JIM HILL

THERE'S BEEN A CHANGE TO YOUR FLIGHT You're going to have to be a pretty attentive air-traffic controller to keep tabs on what's going with Soarin' in 2016. With the third theater open, complete with a state-of-the-art digital-projection system, look for the other two theater domes to close separately for upgrades. Then expect more closures in 2017 as the original ride film is swapped out for a brand-new, international, up-in-the-air experience.

DESCRIPTION AND COMMENTS Soarin' is a thrill ride for all ages, as exhilarating as a hawk on the wing and as mellow as swinging in a hammock. If you've ever experienced flying dreams, you'll have a sense of how Soarin' feels.

Motion Sickness

Once you enter the main theater, you're secured in a seat not unlike those on inverted roller coasters. When everyone is in place, the rows of seats swing into position, making you feel as if the floor has dropped away, and you're suspended with your legs dangling. Thus hung out to dry, you embark on a simulated hang-glider tour, with IMAX-quality images projected all around you and with the flight simulator moving in sync with the movie. The images are well chosen and drop-dead beautiful. Special effects include wind, sound, and even smell. The ride itself is thrilling but perfectly smooth.

We think Soarin' is a must-experience for guests of any age who meet the height requirement—and yes, we've interviewed senior citizens who absolutely loved it—but this North Carolina mom has reservations:

Soarin' was VERY cool, but also on the scary side for people who are afraid of heights or who don't like that unsteady feeling. While we were "soaring" up, I was fine, but when we were going down, I had to keep telling myself, "This is only an illusion. I cannot fall out. This is only an illusion. . . . "

A new ride film is expected to debut at Soarin' in 2016, along with a third ride theater to increase ride capacity by 50%. We hear the new ride film will incorporate flyover sequences from around the world, possibly with different, random sequences each time you ride.

TOURING TIPS Having Soarin' opposite Test Track and Mission: Space in Future World takes some crowd pressure off both sides of the park. Keep in mind, however, that Test Track and Mission: Space serve up a little too much thrill for some guests. Soarin', conversely, is an almost platonic ride for any age. For that reason, it's at the top of the hit parade. See it before 9:30 a.m. or book FastPass+ reservations up to 60 days in advance; expect same-day reservations to be gone by 1 p.m. on days of moderate attendance or as early as 11 a.m. on busier days.

THE SEAS WITH NEMO & FRIENDS PAVILION

FEATURING CHARACTERS FROM DISNEY-PIXAR'S *FINDING NEMO*, this area encompasses one of America's top marine aquariums, a ride that tunnels through the aquarium, an interactive animated film, and a number of first-class educational walk-through exhibits. Altogether it's a stunning package, and not to be missed.

The Seas Main Tank and Exhibits ★★★½

APPEAL BY AGE PRESCHOOL ★★★★½ GRADE SCHOOL ★★★★½ TEENS ★★★★
YOUNG ADULTS ★★★★ OVER 30 ★★★★ SENIORS ★★★★

What it is A huge saltwater aquarium, plus exhibits on oceanography, ocean ecology, and sea life. **Scope and scale** Major attraction. **When to go** Before 11:30 a.m. or after 5 p.m., especially on Extra Magic Hours evenings. **Authors' rating** Excellent; ★★★½. **Average wait in line per 100 people ahead of you** 3½ minutes. **Loading speed** Fast.

DESCRIPTION AND COMMENTS The Seas is among Future World's most ambitious offerings, housed in a 200-foot-diameter, 27-foot-deep main tank containing fish, mammals, and crustaceans in a simulation of an ocean ecosystem. Visitors can watch the activity through 8-inch-thick windows below the surface (including some in the Coral Reef restaurant). On entering The Seas, you're directed to the loading area for The Seas with Nemo & Friends (see next profile), an attraction that conveys you via a Plexiglas tunnel through The Seas' main tank. You disembark at Sea Base Alpha, where you can enjoy the other attractions. (If the wait for Nemo & Friends is too long, head straight for the exhibits by going through the pavilion's exit, around back, and to the left of the main entrance.)

The Seas' fish population is substantial, but the strength of this attraction lies in the dozen or so exhibits offered after the ride. Visitors can view fish-breeding experiments, watch short films about sea life, and more. A delightful exhibit showcases clown fish (Nemo), regal blue tang (Dory), and other species featured in *Finding Nemo*. Other highlights include a hypnotic jellyfish tank; a sea horse aquarium; a stingray exhibit; and a manatee tank.

About two-thirds of the main aquarium is home to reef species, including sharks, rays, and a number of fish that you've seen in quiet repose on your dinner plate. The other third, separated by an inconspicuous divider, houses bottle-nosed dolphins and sea turtles. As you face the main aquarium, the most glare-free viewing windows for the dolphins are on the ground floor to the left by the escalators. For the reef species, it's the same floor on the right by the escalators. Stay as long as you like.

TOURING TIPS With The Seas with Nemo & Friends and *Turtle Talk with Crush*, The Seas is one of Epcot's more popular venues. Experience the ride and *Turtle Talk* in the morning before the park gets crowded, saving the excellent exhibits for later.

The Seas is uncrowded during evening Extra Magic Hours, making it a perfect time to have large swaths of the aquarium to yourself. We try to stop by every late night we can.

The Seas with Nemo & Friends *(FastPass+)*   ★★★

APPEAL BY AGE PRESCHOOL ★★★★½ GRADE SCHOOL ★★★★ TEENS ★★★½
YOUNG ADULTS ★★★½   OVER 30 ★★★½   SENIORS ★★★★

What it is Ride through a tunnel in The Seas' main tank. **Scope and scale** Major attraction. **When to go** Before 10:30 a.m., after 3 p.m., or use FastPass+. **Authors' rating** ★★★. **Duration of ride** 4 minutes. **Average wait in line per 100 people ahead of you** 3½ minutes. **Loading speed** Fast.

DESCRIPTION AND COMMENTS The Seas with Nemo & Friends is a high-tech ride featuring characters from the animated hit *Finding Nemo*. The ride likewise deposits you at the heart of The Seas, where the exhibits, *Turtle Talk with Crush,* and viewing platforms for the main aquarium are.

Upon entering The Seas, you're given the option of experiencing the ride or proceeding directly to the exhibit area. If you choose the ride, you'll be ushered to its loading area, where you'll be made comfortable in a "clamobile" for your journey through the aquarium. The attraction features technology that makes it seem as if the animated characters are swimming with live fish. Very cool. Almost immediately you meet Mr. Ray and his class and learn that Nemo is missing. The remainder of the odyssey consists of finding Nemo with the help of Dory, Bruce, Marlin, Squirt, and Crush. Unlike the film, however, the ride ends with a musical finale.

A mom from Asheville, North Carolina, thinks we underestimate the fright factor:

The Seas with Nemo & Friends is scary—sharks, jellyfish, and anglerfish, along with growling, and so on. My 8-year-old hated it!

TOURING TIPS The earlier you ride, the better (ditto for *Turtle Talk with Crush*). If waits are too much, come back after 3 p.m. or so, or use FastPass+.

Turtle Talk with Crush *(FastPass+)*   ★★★★

APPEAL BY AGE PRESCHOOL ★★★★½ GRADE SCHOOL ★★★★½ TEENS ★★★★
YOUNG ADULTS ★★★★   OVER 30 ★★★★   SENIORS ★★★★

What it is Interactive animated film. **Scope and scale** Minor attraction. **When to go** Before 11 a.m., after 3 p.m., or use FastPass+. **Authors' rating** A real spirit-lifter; not to be missed; ★★★★. **Duration of presentation** 17 minutes. **Preshow entertainment** None. **Probable waiting time** 10–20 minutes.

DESCRIPTION AND COMMENTS *Turtle Talk with Crush* is an interactive theater show starring the 153-year-old surfer-dude turtle from *Finding Nemo*. Although it starts like a typical Disney-theme-park movie, *Turtle Talk* quickly turns into a surprise interactive encounter as the on-screen Crush begins to have actual conversations with guests in the audience. Real-time computer graphics are used to accurately move Crush's mouth when forming words, and he's voiced by a guy who went to the Jeff Spicoli School of Diction.

A mom from Henderson, Colorado, has a crush on Crush:

> Turtle Talk with Crush *is a must-see. Our 4-year-old was picked out of the crowd by Crush, and we were just amazed by the technology. It was adorable and enjoyed by everyone from Grammy and Papa to the 4-year-old!*

TOURING TIPS It's unusual to wait more than one or two shows to get in. If you find long lines in the morning, try back after 3 p.m. when more of the crowd has moved on to World Showcase, or use FastPass+.

The "Mom, I Can't Believe It's Disney!" Fountains ★★★★

APPEAL BY AGE PRESCHOOL ★★★★★ GRADE SCHOOL ★★★★★ TEENS ★★★★
YOUNG ADULTS ★★★★ OVER 30 ★★★★ SENIORS ★★★★★

What it is Combination fountains and showers. **Scope and scale** Diversion. **When to go** When it's hot. **Special comments** Secretly installed by Martians during *Illumi-Nations*. **Authors' rating** Yes! ★★★★. **Duration of experience** As long as you like. **Probable waiting time** None.

DESCRIPTION AND COMMENTS These simple fountains—one on the walkway linking Future World to World Showcase, the other in Future World East, on the way to Test Track—aren't much to look at, but they offers a truly spontaneous experience: a rarity in Walt Disney World, where everything is controlled, from the snow peas in your stir-fry to how frequently the crocodile yawns in the Jungle Cruise.

Spouts of water erupt randomly from the sidewalk. You can frolic in the water or let it cascade down on you, or blow up your britches. On a broiling Florida day, when you think you might spontaneously combust, fling yourself into the fountain and cut loose. Dance, skip, sing, jump, splash, cavort, roll around, stick your toes down the spouts, or catch the water in your mouth as it descends. You can do all of this with your clothes on or, depending on your age, with your clothes off.

TOURING TIPS We don't know if the fountains' creator has been drummed out of the corps by the Disney Tribunal of People Who Sit on Sticks (probably), but we're grateful for his courage in introducing one thing that's not super-controlled. We do know that your kids will be right in the middle of the fun before your brain sounds the alert. Our advice: Pack a few pairs of dry shorts and turn the kids loose. You might even want to bring a spare pair for yourself. Or maybe not.

WORLD SHOWCASE

EPCOT'S OTHER THEMED AREA, World Showcase is an ongoing World's Fair encircling a picturesque 40-acre lagoon. The cuisine, culture, history, and architecture of almost a dozen countries (and one make-believe kingdom) are permanently displayed in individual national pavilions spaced along a 1.2-mile promenade. Pavilions replicate familiar landmarks and present representative street scenes from the host countries.

World Showcase features some of the loveliest gardens in the United States. In Germany, France, United Kingdom, Canada, and, to a lesser extent, China, they're sometimes tucked away and out of sight of pedestrian traffic on the World Showcase promenade. They're best appreciated during the day, as a Clio, Michigan, woman explains:

> Visit World Showcase in the daylight in order to view the beautiful gardens. We were sorry we didn't do this because we were following the guide and riding rides that we could have done later in the dark.

Most adults enjoy World Showcase, but many children find it boring. To make it more interesting to children, most Epcot retail shops sell **Passport Kits** for about $11. Each kit contains a blank "passport" and stamps for every World Showcase country. As kids accompany their folks to each country, they tear out the appropriate stamp and stick it in the passport. Disney has built a lot of profit into this little product, but guests—namely, parents—don't seem to mind the cost. As this dad from Birmingham, Alabama, relates, the Passport Kit helps get the kids through World Showcase with a minimum of impatience, whining, and tantrums:

unofficial **TIP**
If you don't want to spring for the Passport Kit, the Disney folks will be happy to stamp an autograph book or just about anything else—even your forehead.

> Adding stamps from the Epcot countries was the only way I was able to see all the displays with cheerful children.

Children also enjoy **Kidcot Fun Stops**, designed to make World Showcase more interesting for the 5- to 12-year-old set. The stops are usually nothing more than a large table set up somewhere in each pavilion. Tables are staffed by Disney cast members who stamp passports and lead modest craft projects relating to the host countries.

A mom from Billerica, Massachusetts, is a fan of the Fun Stops:

> The Kidcot project at Epcot was amazing! Our 2- and 5-year-olds loved making masks and collecting stamps.

An adult version of passport-stamp collecting is known as **Drinking Around the World** (see page 319), an activity enthusiastically endorsed by a woman from party-hearty New Orleans:

> We drank a beer in each country at Epcot—Dad was the designated driver—and posed for photos in each, and it quickly became hilarious, as were the progression-of-drunkenness photos that followed.

World Showcase offers some of the most diverse and interesting shopping in Walt Disney World. See Part Nineteen for details.

Agent P's World Showcase Adventure ★★★★

APPEAL BY AGE	PRESCHOOL ★★★½	GRADE SCHOOL ★★★★	TEENS ★★★★½
YOUNG ADULTS ★★★½		OVER 30 ★★★½	SENIORS ★★★½

What it is Interactive scavenger hunt in select World Showcase pavilions. **Scope and scale** Minor attraction. **When to go** Anytime. **Authors' rating** One of our favorite additions to the parks; ★★★★. **Duration of presentation** Allow 30 minutes per adventure. **Preshow entertainment** None. **Probable waiting time** None.

DESCRIPTION AND COMMENTS In their eponymous Disney Channel show, Phineas and Ferb have a pet platypus named Perry. In the presence of humans, Perry doesn't do a whole lot. (To be fair, we're not experts on typical platypus behavior, but read on.) When the kids aren't looking, though, Perry takes on the role of Agent P—a fedora-wearing, James Bond-esque secret agent who battles the nefarious Dr. Doofenshmirtz to prevent world domination.

In Agent P's World Showcase Adventure, you're a secret agent helping Perry, and you receive a cell phone–like device before you're dispatched on a mission to your choice of seven World Showcase pavilions. Once you arrive at the pavilion, the device's video screen and audio provide various clues to help you solve a set of simple puzzles necessary for defeating Doofenshmirtz's plan. As you discover each clue, you'll find special effects such as talking statues and flaming lanterns, plus live "secret agents" stationed in the pavilions just for this attraction. For example, in a prior version of the game you were instructed to utter the phrase "Danger is my cup of tea" to someone working behind the counter at the United Kingdom's tea shop; he or she would respond by handing you a Twinings tea packet on which was printed a clue to solve a puzzle.

Agent P makes static World Showcase pavilions more interactive and kid-friendly. The adventures have simple clues, fast pacing, and neat rewards for solving the puzzles. Len's teenage daughter, Hannah, will happily spend an entire afternoon in World Showcase playing this game and drinking Japanese sodas. Don't be surprised if, having completed one pavilion's adventure, your child wants to do the same.

TOURING TIPS Playing the game is free, and no deposit is required for the device. You'll need proof of park admission to sign up before you play, and you can choose both the time and location of your adventure. Register and pick up your devices at the Italy or Norway Pavilion, the International Gateway (near the UK Pavilion), or the east side of the main walkway from Future World to World Showcase.

Each group can have up to three devices for the same adventure. Because you're working with a device about the size of a cell phone, it's best to have one device for every two people in your group.

A Tucker, Georgia, mother of a 7-year-old is a fan:

My daughter and I thoroughly enjoyed Agent P's World Showcase Adventure. The interactivity was clever and exciting, plus NO LINES!

A Granger, Indiana, mom discovered a practical dimension to Agent P:

A great activity if it's raining: Do the adventure in Mexico. It's all inside, and by the time you're done, the rain usually is, too.

A Massillon, Ohio, mom was surprised at how long it took to play:

At Epcot, our 9- and 6-year-olds really enjoyed the Agent P mission, but it took way longer than the 25 minutes we were told (at least for the UK, the country we chose). It ended up being fine, but people should be aware.

NOW, MOVING CLOCKWISE around the World Showcase promenade, here are the nations represented and their attractions:

MEXICO PAVILION

DESCRIPTION AND COMMENTS Pre-Columbian pyramids dominate the pavilion's architecture. One pyramid forms Mexico's facade; the other overlooks the restaurant and plaza alongside the **Gran Fiesta Tour** indoor boat ride.

The village scene inside the pavilion is beautiful and exquisitely detailed. A retail shop occupies most of the left half of the inner pavilion, while Mexico's Kidcot Fun Stop is in the first entryway inside the pyramid. On the opposite side of the main floor is **La Cava del Tequila,** a bar serving more than 100 varieties of tequila as well as margaritas and mezcal.

TOURING TIPS The pyramids contain many authentic and valuable artifacts—take the time to stop and see these treasures.

Gran Fiesta Tour Starring the Three Caballeros ★★½

APPEAL BY AGE **PRESCHOOL** ★★★★ **GRADE SCHOOL** ★★★½ **TEENS** ★★★½
YOUNG ADULTS ★★★ **OVER 30** ★★★½ **SENIORS** ★★★½

What it is Scenic indoor boat ride. **Scope and scale** Minor attraction. **When to go** Before noon or after 5 p.m. **Authors' rating** Visually appealing, light, and relaxing; ★★½. **Duration of ride** About 7 minutes (plus 1½-minute wait to disembark). **Average wait in line per 100 people ahead of you** 4½ minutes; assumes 16 boats in operation. **Loading speed** Moderate.

DESCRIPTION AND COMMENTS The Gran Fiesta Tour incorporates animated versions of Donald Duck, José Carioca, and Panchito—an avian singing group called The Three Caballeros, from Disney's 1944 film of the same name—to spice up what's basically a slower-paced, Mexican-style It's a Small World.

The storyline has the Caballeros scheduled to perform at a fiesta when Donald suddenly goes missing; large video screens show him enjoying Mexico's sights and sounds while José and Panchito try to track him down. Everyone is reunited in time for a rousing concert near the end of the ride.

At the risk of sounding like the Disney geeks we are, we must point out that Panchito is technically the only Mexican Caballero—José Carioca is from Brazil and Donald is from Burbank. In any case, more of the ride's visuals seem to be on the left side of the boat, so have small children sit nearer the left to keep their attention, and listen for Donald's humorous monologue as you wait to disembark at the end of the ride.

A Fanwood, New Jersey, reader feels the ride is culturally insensitive:

The Gran Fiesta Tour was dreadful. If the idea was to rid the ride of derogatory Mexican stereotypes, the designers woefully missed the mark.

A Wilmington, Delaware, woman blames Gran Fiesta Tour's lack of pizzazz on . . . who else?

Donald Duck has ruined even the minimal value of the Mexico ride.

TOURING TIPS If the line looks longer than 5 minutes, grab a margarita (or several) at La Cava del Tequila and come back in 15.

"NORWAY" PAVILION

DESCRIPTION AND COMMENTS This pavilion encapsulates both everything we love about Epcot and everything we hate about corporate Disney. Parts of the pavilion—those based on the actual country of Norway—are complex, beautiful, and diverse. Highlights include replicas of the 14th-century Akershus Castle in Oslo; a miniature version of a stave church built in 1212 in Gol, Norway (go inside—the doors open!); and various other buildings that accurately represent traditional Scandanavian architecture. We were even inspired to visit Norway specifically because of how great this pavilion *was.*

For years after it was built, Epcot's Norway sat in a state of mostly benign neglect. The boat ride, Maelstrom, was a relatively short and lightly themed float-through of the country's history. The postride film was imbued with the same "our spirit is our people" platitudes that are repeated, in one way or another, in every World Showcase presentation ever made. But at least it was based on an actual country, at an actual point in time.

Fast-forward to today and the monster hit that is 2013's *Frozen,* set in the mythical Scandinavian-ish kingdom of Arendelle. Disney's bean counters, who couldn't design a pavilion if given Walt's own cryogenically preserved brain, must have looked at all the money *Frozen* made, seen Epcot's need to attract more customers, and decided that whatever World Showcase *really* is, it should include a made-up country whose main attractions are a hastily repurposed boat ride and a chance to meet unionized laborers dressed as cartoon toffs. Frankly, we're surprised that Disney hasn't replaced the actual Norwegian staff with Orlando teens taught to *bork-bork-bork* like The Muppets' Swedish Chef . . . yet.

Don't get us wrong—a hit like *Frozen* comes along once every 20 years, and Disney has to make hay while the sun shines. It's putting a pretend kingdom smack in the middle of World Showcase that sticks in our craw. And it's not as if there weren't already an entire Disney theme park within walking distance with so many closed or outdated attractions that charging $100 for admission is essentially petty larceny with a better marketing department. This *Frozen* stuff—which, not to put too fine a point on it, is an offshoot of a film, made by The Walt Disney Studios, in Hollywood—should have gone in Disney's Hollywood Studios instead.

Frozen Ever After *(opens 2016)*

What it is Indoor boat ride and Disney film–shilling vehicle. **Scope and scale** Major attraction. **When to go** Before noon., after 7 p.m., or use FastPass+. **Special comments** Expect long waits from the moment it opens. **Authors' rating** N/A. **Duration of ride** About 4½ minutes. **Average wait in line per 100 people ahead of you** 4 minutes; assumes 12 or 13 boats operating. **Loading speed** Fast.

DISNEY DISH WITH JIM HILL

WILL *FROZEN* HEAT UP EPCOT? Get ready to see even more of Anna, Elsa, Kristoff, and Olaf next spring. Ahead of the April 2016 opening of Frozen Ever After, Disney World will be mounting one of the largest promotional campaigns in its history, with full-page print ads and as many spots on prime-time TV as The Mouse can buy. Disney thinks tying the film to the redo of the defunct Maelstrom ride could result in a 20% bump in Epcot's attendance levels.

DESCRIPTION AND COMMENTS Frozen Ever After replaces Maelstrom, Norway's original boat ride from 1988. Expect to see all of the major *Frozen* characters, including Marshmallow, Olaf, Sven, and Wandering Oaken. Scenes in the ride will include Troll Valley and, of course, Elsa belting out "Let It Go."

TOURING TIPS Epcot hasn't opened many major new rides in recent years, and because this one is based on a wildly successful film, you should expect Frozen Ever After to be mobbed from the day it opens. Your likely best bet will be to arrive as soon as World Showcase opens, then backtrack to Mexico; otherwise, use FastPass+. Speaking of which, Disney hadn't announced at press time whether this will be a Tier 1 or Tier 2 attraction. (Maelstrom appeared in both tiers at different times.)

Royal Sommerhus Meet and Greet *(opens 2016)*

What it is Meet and greet with the *Frozen* princesses. **Scope and scale** Minor attraction. **When to go** Before noon, after 7 p.m., or use FastPass+. **Special comments** Expect long waits at the outset that should moderate over time. **Authors' rating** N/A. **Duration of greeting** N/A. **Average wait in line per 100 people ahead of you** N/A. **Loading speed** N/A.

DESCRIPTION AND COMMENTS Scheduled to open in 2016 along with Frozen Ever After is a character greeting for Anna and Elsa. While *Frozen* wasn't explicitly set in Norway, Disney alleges the meet and greet will feature traditional Norwegian architecture and crafts.

TOURING TIPS We've heard that this meet and greet will have multiple rooms with Anna and Elsa operating simultaneously. This, coupled with Epcot's lower average attendance, means that once the initial crowds die down after opening, waits should be somewhat shorter than those to see the same princesses at the Magic Kingdom's Princess Fairytale Hall. As with Frozen Ever After, Disney hadn't said at press time whether Royal Sommerhus will be a Tier 1 or Tier 2 FastPass+ attraction.

CHINA PAVILION

DESCRIPTION AND COMMENTS A half-sized replica of the Temple of Heaven in Beijing identifies this pavilion. Gardens and reflecting ponds simulate those found in Suzhou, and an art gallery features a lotus-blossom gate and formal saddle roofline. The China Pavilion offers two restaurants: the **Lotus Blossom Cafe,** a fast-food eatery, and **Nine Dragons Restaurant,** a full-service establishment (Advance Reservations recommended) that serves lamentably lackluster Chinese food in a lovely setting. **The Joy of Tea,** a tea stand and specialty-drink vendor, will feed your caffeine addiction until you can make it to Morocco's espresso bar.

    The pavilion also hosts exhibits on Chinese history and culture. Past exhibits have covered everything from China's indigenous peoples to the layout of Hong Kong Disneyland. The current exhibit displays scaled-down replicas of the terra-cotta "tomb warriors" buried with the Qin Dynasty emperor in the second century B.C. to guard him in the afterlife.

Reflections of China ★★★½

APPEAL BY AGE   PRESCHOOL ★★★   GRADE SCHOOL ★★★½   TEENS ★★★★
YOUNG ADULTS ★★★★   OVER 30 ★★★★   SENIORS ★★★★½

What it is Film about the Chinese people and culture. **Scope and scale** Major attraction. **When to go** Anytime. **Special comments** Audience stands throughout performance. **Authors' rating** ★★★½. **Duration of presentation** About 14 minutes. **Preshow entertainment** None. **Probable waiting time** 10 minutes.

DESCRIPTION AND COMMENTS Pass through the Hall of Prayer for Good Harvest to view this Circle-Vision 360 film. Warm and appealing (albeit politically sanitized), it's a brilliant introduction to the people and natural beauty of China.

TOURING TIPS The pavilion is truly beautiful—serene yet exciting. *Reflections of China* plays in a theater where guests must stand, but the film can usually be enjoyed anytime without much waiting.

GERMANY PAVILION

DESCRIPTION AND COMMENTS Dominated by a clock tower with boy and girl figures and a fountain depicting St. George's victory over the dragon, the

562   PART 10 EPCOT

pavilion's *platz* (plaza) is encircled by buildings in traditional architectural styles. The main attraction is **Biergarten,** a buffet that serves rib-sticking German food and beer (see Part Four, page 343). Yodeling, folk dancing, and oompah-band music are part of the mealtime festivities.

The biggest draw in Germany may be **Karamell-Küche** ("Caramel Kitchen"), offering small caramel-covered sweets including apples, fudge, and cupcakes. We love coming here for a midday snack to tide us over before dinner. Check out the large and elaborate model railroad just beyond the restrooms as you walk from Germany toward Italy.

TOURING TIPS The pavilion is pleasant and festive. Tour anytime.

ITALY PAVILION

DESCRIPTION AND COMMENTS The entrance to Italy is marked by an 83-foot-tall campanile (bell tower) modeled after the tower in St. Mark's Square in Venice. Left of the campanile is a replica of the 14th-century Doge's Palace, also in the famous square. The pavilion has a waterfront on the lagoon where gondolas are tied to striped moorings.

TOURING TIPS Streets and courtyards in Italy are among the most realistic in World Showcase. For a quick lunch, **Via Napoli** occasionally offers pizza—the best in Walt Disney World—by the slice; **Tutto Gusto Wine Cellar** serves small plates along with libations. Because there's no film or ride, you can tour the pavilion at any hour.

UNITED STATES PAVILION
The American Adventure ★★★★

APPEAL BY AGE	PRESCHOOL ★★½	GRADE SCHOOL ★★★½	TEENS ★★★½
YOUNG ADULTS ★★★★	OVER 30 ★★★★		SENIORS ★★★★½

What it is Mixed-media and Audio-Animatronic theater presentation on US history. **Scope and scale** Headliner. **When to go** Anytime. **Authors' rating** Disney's best historical and patriotic attraction; not to be missed; ★★★★. **Duration of presentation** About 29 minutes. **Preshow entertainment** Voices of Liberty choral singing. **Probable waiting time** 25 minutes.

DESCRIPTION AND COMMENTS The United States Pavilion consists of a fast-food restaurant (the **Liberty Inn**) and a patriotic show.

The American Adventure is a composite of everything Disney does best. Housed in an imposing brick structure reminiscent of Colonial Philadelphia, the 29-minute show is a stirring, albeit sanitized, rendition of American history narrated by an animatronic Mark Twain (who carries a burning cigar) and Ben Franklin. Behind a stage almost half the size of a football field is a 28-by-155-foot rear-projection screen—the largest ever used—on which motion picture images are interwoven with action on stage.

Though the production rouses patriotic emotion in some viewers, others find it deadly dull. A man from Fort Lauderdale, Florida, writes:

I saw The American Adventure *about 10 years ago and snoozed through it. We tried it again since you said it was updated, and it was still ponderous. I kept checking my watch, waiting for it to be over. I'll try it again in 10 years.*

An Erie, Pennsylvania, couple resented what they saw as Disney's squeaky-clean take on American history:

The American Adventure *glosses over the dark points of American history. For example, it neatly cuts out the audio about who bombed Pearl Harbor (at Epcot, after all, Japan is right next door). Why not focus on the natural beauty of America, its ethnic diversity, its contributions to world society?*

(To be fair, the presentation isn't as squeaky-clean as it once was—both Tiger Woods and Lance Armstrong are held up as heroes in the film.)

TOURING TIPS *The American Adventure* is the best patriotic attraction in the Disney repertoire. It usually plays to capacity audiences from around 1:30 to 3:30 p.m., but it isn't hard to get into: Because of the theater's large capacity, it's highly unusual not to be admitted to the next performance.

JAPAN PAVILION

DESCRIPTION AND COMMENTS A five-story, blue-roofed pagoda, inspired by a 17th-century shrine in Nara, sets this pavilion apart. A hill garden behind it features waterfalls, rocks, flowers, lanterns, paths, and rustic bridges. On the right, as one faces the entrance, a building inspired by the ceremonial and coronation hall at Kyoto's Imperial Palace contains restaurants and a branch of Japan's **Mitsukoshi** department store. Through the center entrance and to the left is **Bijutsu-kan Gallery,** exhibiting colorful displays on Japanese pop culture. Recent subjects have included everything from postwar tin toys to comics devoted to heroes with "animal spirits."

A new meet-and-greet area opened in early 2015, behind the pagoda, on the small hill in front of Katsura Grill. Here, female cast members wearing offbeat street fashion answer questions about Japan's youth culture, especially that of Tokyo's Harajuku district. Check the *Times Guide* for a schedule.

TOURING TIPS Japan blends simplicity, architectural grandeur, and natural beauty. Tour anytime.

MOROCCO PAVILION

DESCRIPTION AND COMMENTS A bustling market, winding streets, lofty minarets, and stuccoed archways re-create the romance and intrigue of Marrakesh and Casablanca. The pavilion also has a museum of Moorish art and **Restaurant Marrakesh,** featuring North African specialties. **Spice Road Table** serves up tapas-style Mediterranean dishes and excellent views of *IllumiNations,* along with high prices.

A Northfield, Minnesota, mother of two exploring Morocco found, of all things, peace and quiet:

We found an awesome resting place in Morocco—an empty air-conditioned gallery with padded benches. No one came in during the 15 minutes that we rested there, which was quite a difference from the rest of the park! Look for the red doors on your left when you enter.

TOURING TIPS Morocco has neither a ride nor a theater. Tour anytime.

FRANCE PAVILION

DESCRIPTION AND COMMENTS A replica of the Eiffel Tower is, *naturellement,* this pavilion's centerpiece. The streets recall La Belle Époque, France's "beautiful time" between 1870 and 1910. The restaurants, along with the bakery and ice-cream shop, are very popular—perhaps explaining why readers rank France as the best World Showcase pavilion.

Impressions de France ★★★½

**APPEAL BY AGE   PRESCHOOL ★★★½   GRADE SCHOOL ★★★½   TEENS ★★★½
YOUNG ADULTS ★★★★   OVER 30 ★★★★   SENIORS ★★★★½**

What it is Film essay on France and its people. **Scope and scale** Major attraction. **When to go** Anytime. **Authors' rating** Exceedingly beautiful film; ★★★½. **Duration**

of presentation About 18 minutes. **Preshow entertainment** None. **Probable waiting time** 15 minutes (at suggested times).

DESCRIPTION AND COMMENTS *Impressions de France* is an 18-minute movie projected over 200 degrees onto five screens. Unlike at China and Canada, the audience sits to view this well-made film showcasing France's people, cities, and natural wonders.

TOURING TIPS Usually begins on the hour and half-hour. France's streets are small and become congested when visitors queue for the film.

UNITED KINGDOM PAVILION

DESCRIPTION AND COMMENTS A hodgepodge of period architecture attempts to capture Britain's urban and rural sides. One street alone has a thatched-roof cottage, a four-story Tudor half-timber building, a pre-Georgian plaster building, a formal Palladian facade of dressed stone, and a city square with a Hyde Park bandstand (whew!).

   The pavilion is composed mostly of shops. **The Rose & Crown Pub** and **Rose & Crown Dining Room** offer dining on the water side of the promenade. For fish and chips to go, try **Yorkshire County Fish Shop.**

TOURING TIPS There are no attractions here, so tour anytime. Alice in Wonderland, Mary Poppins, and/or Pooh meet fans in the character-greeting area; check the *Times Guide* for a schedule. Advance Reservations aren't required for the Rose & Crown Pub, making it a nice place to stop for a beer.

CANADA PAVILION

DESCRIPTION AND COMMENTS Canada's cultural, natural, and architectural diversity are reflected in this large, impressive pavilion. Thirty-foot-tall totem poles embellish an Indian village at the foot of a replica of a magnificent château-style hotel. **Le Cellier,** a steakhouse on Canada's lower level, is one of Disney World's highest-rated restaurants. Dinner almost always requires Advance Reservations; lunch is a bit easier to arrange.

DISNEY DISH WITH JIM HILL

BREWING NEW IDEAS Back in the late 2000s, Disney seriously considered an "Anne of Green Gables" store in the Hôtel du Canada, the iconic building of the Canada Pavilion, but the financial crisis put and end to those plans. Now that the economy is on the rebound, the latest idea is to use the space for a Canadian craft-brew pub that would offer Epcot visitors a terrific view of *IllumiNations.*

O Canada!   ★★★½

APPEAL BY AGE	PRESCHOOL ★★★	GRADE SCHOOL ★★★	TEENS ★★★★
YOUNG ADULTS ★★★★		OVER 30 ★★★★	SENIORS ★★★★

What it is Film essay on Canada and its people. **Scope and scale** Major attraction. **When to go** Anytime. **Special comments** Audience stands to watch. **Authors' rating** Makes you want to catch the first plane up there; ★★★½. **Duration of presentation** About 15 minutes. **Preshow entertainment** None. **Probable waiting time** 9 minutes.

DESCRIPTION AND COMMENTS *O Canada!* showcases the country's natural beauty and the diversity of its people. Narrated by Martin Short, the film features scenes of Canada's stunning landscapes. Visitors leave the theater through **Victoria Gardens,** inspired by the famed Butchart Gardens of British Columbia.

Cast members often conduct a preshow Canadian-trivia quiz outside the theater. Helpful tips for Americans: Canada's capital is Ottawa; its $1 coin is nicknamed the Loonie, after the bird engraved on it; and the $2 coin is the Toonie—not, unfortunately, the Doubloonie.

TOURING TIPS This large-capacity attraction (guests must stand) gets fairly heavy late-morning attendance, as Canada is the first pavilion encountered as one travels counterclockwise around World Showcase Lagoon.

LIVE ENTERTAINMENT
in EPCOT

LIVE ENTERTAINMENT IN EPCOT is more diverse than in the Magic Kingdom. In World Showcase, it reflects the nations represented. Future World provides a perfect setting for new and experimental offerings. Information about live entertainment on the day you visit is contained in the Epcot guide map, often supplemented by a *Times Guide*. WDW live-entertainment guru Steve Soares usually posts the Epcot performance schedule about a week in advance at **wdwent.com.**

Here are some of the venues, performers, and performances you'll encounter:

AMERICA GARDENS THEATRE This large amphitheater, near the US Pavilion, faces World Showcase Lagoon. It hosts pop and oldies musical acts throughout much of the year, as well as Epcot's popular **Candlelight Processional** for the Christmas holidays, and sometimes the **Voices of Liberty** (see below).

AROUND WORLD SHOWCASE Impromptu performances take place in and around the pavilions. Among the acts are a strolling mariachi group in Mexico; a flag corps and juggler in Italy; two singing groups (**Voices of Liberty** and **American Music Machine**) at the US Pavilion; traditional songs, drums, and dances in Japan; more traditional music in Morocco; acrobats in France; a Scottish folk group in the United Kingdom; and a lumberjack show in Canada. Performances occur about every half-hour.

In 2014, Disney retired four longtime World Showcase acts, eliciting disappointment from guests such as this Minnesota woman:

> *There is a void in the park with the termination of Off Kilter [the Canada Pavilion's popular Celtic-rock band]. The replacements are not as entertaining. I mean no disrespect to the Canadian lumberjacks, but I don't go to Epcot or anywhere else to hear chainsaws.*

Live entertainment in World Showcase exceeded the expectations of this Ayden, North Carolina, reader:

> *I don't think you emphasize the street shows at Epcot enough. My husband and I loved the Japanese drumming, the Chinese acrobats, and the street players in United Kingdom. These performances were much more indicative of foreign cultures than the rides.*

A Vero Beach, Florida, couple love Voices of Liberty:

> *Voices of Liberty is one of our favorite acts. Their period costuming, rousing folk and patriotic songs, incredible a cappella sound,*

and heartwarming spirit bring forth a huge, sincere response from the audience.

(Note that Disney changes up VOL's song set on some days. When they're not in the US Pavilion, their repertoire consists of tunes from Disney movies—including, yes, "Let It Go.")

DINNER AND LUNCH SHOWS Restaurants in World Showcase serve up healthy portions of live entertainment with the victuals. Find folk dancing and an oompah band in Germany, singing waiters in Italy, and belly dancers in Morocco. Shows take place only at dinner in Italy and Morocco but at both lunch and dinner in Germany. Advance Reservations are required.

DISNEY CHARACTERS Characters appear at the Epcot Character Spot (see page 547), elsewhere throughout the park (see page 416), and in live shows at America Gardens Theatre and the Showcase Plaza between Mexico and Canada. Times are listed in the *Times Guide*. Finally, **Garden Grill Restaurant** in The Land and **Akershus Royal Banquet Hall** in Norway offer character meals.

IN FUTURE WORLD A musical crew of drumming janitors works near the front entrance and at Innoventions Plaza (between the two Innoventions buildings and by the fountain) according to the daily entertainment schedule. They're occasionally complemented by an electric-keyboard band that plays what the kids today would call oldies.

INNOVENTIONS FOUNTAIN SHOW Several times each day, the fountain between the two Innoventions buildings comes alive with pulsating, arching plumes of water synchronized to a musical score. Because no performance schedule is posted, the show comes as a pleasant surprise to many readers, such as this man from Berwickshire, England:

> *The musical fountain is an unexpected treat. I sat down and listened to it from start to finish on two different occasions. The music is catchy, and the soaring effects of both music and water are really beautiful.*

ILLUMINATIONS: REFLECTIONS OF EARTH
(FastPass+)

EPCOT'S GREAT OUTDOOR SPECTACLE (★★★★½) integrates fireworks, laser lights, neon, and music in a stirring tribute to the nations of the world. It's the climax of every Epcot day, and not to be missed.

IllumiNations has a plot and a theme, both fairly freighted with symbolism. The show kicks off with colliding stars that suggest the Big Bang, following which "chaos reigns in the universe." This display is soon replaced by twittering songbirds and various other manifestations signaling the nativity of the Earth. Next comes a brief history of time, from the dinosaurs to ancient Rome, all projected in images on a huge, floating globe. Man's art and inspiration then flash across the globe "in a collage of creativity." All this stimulates the globe to unfold "like a massive flower," bringing on the fireworks crescendo heralding the dawn of a new age.

Word around the lagoon is that a new nighttime extravaganza will replace *IllumiNations* sometime in late 2015 or early 2016. While we don't know the plot, we're reasonably sure the show will contain lasers, fireworks, and music. There are hints that it'll have some sort of interactive element, too, but no information of any substance.

Getting Out of Epcot After *IllumiNations* (Read This Before Selecting a Viewing Spot!)

IllumiNations ends the day at Epcot. When it's over, only a couple of gift shops remain open. Because there's nothing to do, everyone leaves at once. This creates a great snarl at Package Pick-Up, the Epcot monorail station, and the Disney bus stop. It also pushes to the limit the tram system hauling guests to their cars in the parking lot. It's important, then, to decide how quickly you want to leave the park after the show, and then pick your vantage point.

If you're staying at an Epcot resort (Swan, Dolphin, Yacht & Beach Club Resorts, and BoardWalk Inn & Villas), watch the show from somewhere on the southern (US Pavilion) half of World Showcase Lagoon, then leave through the International Gateway between France and the United Kingdom. You can walk or take a boat back to your hotel from the International Gateway. If you have a car and you're visiting Epcot in the evening for dinner and *IllumiNations,* park at the Yacht Club or Beach Club. After the show, duck out the International Gateway and be on the road to your hotel in 15 minutes.

If you're staying at any other Disney hotel and you don't have a car, the fastest way home is to join the mass exodus through the main gate after *IllumiNations* and catch a bus or the monorail.

Those who have a car in the Epcot lot have a more problematic situation. To beat the crowd, find a viewing spot at the end of World Showcase Lagoon nearest Future World (and the exits). Leave as soon as the show concludes, trying to exit ahead of the crowd (note that thousands of people will be doing exactly the same thing). To get a good vantage point between Mexico and Canada on the northern end of the lagoon, stake out your spot 60–100 minutes before the show (45–90 minutes during less-busy periods), or use FastPass+. Otherwise, you may squander more time holding your spot before *IllumiNations* than you would if you watched from the less-congested southern end of the lagoon and took your chances with the crowd upon departure.

More groups get separated and more kids get lost following *IllumiNations* than at any other time. In summer, you'll be walking in a throng of up to 30,000 people. If you're heading for the parking lot, anticipate this congestion and preselect a point in the Epcot entrance area where you can meet if someone gets separated from the group. We recommend the fountain just inside the main entrance.

For those with a car, the main problem is reaching the parking lot. Once you're there, traffic leaves the parking lot pretty well. If you paid close attention to where you parked, consider skipping the tram and walking. If you walk, watch your children closely and hang on to them for all they're worth—the parking lot is pretty wild at this time of night, with hundreds of moving cars.

Good Locations for Viewing *IllumiNations* and Other World Showcase Lagoon Performances

The best place to be for any presentation on World Showcase Lagoon is in a seat on the lakeside veranda of **La Cantina de San Angel** in Mexico. Come early—at least 90 minutes before *IllumiNations*—and relax with a cold drink or snack while you wait for the show.

Where to View IllumiNations

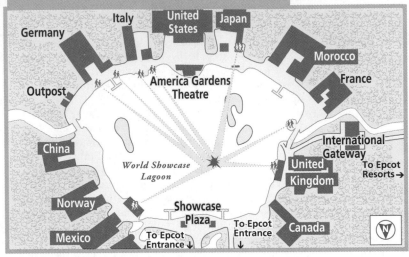

A woman from Pasadena, California, nailed down the seat but missed the relaxation. She writes:

> Stake out a prime site for IllumiNations *at least an hour and a half ahead—and be prepared to defend it. We got a lakeside table at Cantina de San Angel at 6:30 p.m.; unfortunately, we had to put up with troops of people asking us to share our table and trying to wedge themselves between our table and the fence.*

La Hacienda de San Angel in Mexico, the **Rose & Crown Pub** in the United Kingdom, and **Spice Road Table** in Morocco also have lagoon-side seating. Because of a small wall at the Rose & Crown, however, the view isn't quite as good as from the Cantina.

If you want to combine dinner at these sit-down locations with *IllumiNations,* make an Advance Reservation for about 1 hour and 15 minutes before showtime. Report a few minutes early for your seating and tell the host that you want a table outside where you can watch the show. Our experience is that the staff will bend over backward to accommodate you. If you can't snag an outside table, eat inside and hang out until showtime. When the lights dim, indicating the start of *IllumiNations,* you'll be allowed to join the diners to watch the show.

Because most guests run for the exits after a presentation and islands in the southern (US Pavilion) half of the lagoon block the view from some places, the most popular spectator positions are along the northern waterfront from Norway and Mexico to Canada and the United Kingdom. Although the northern half of the lagoon unquestionably offers excellent viewing, it's usually necessary to claim a spot 60–100 minutes before *IllumiNations* begins.

For those who are late finishing dinner, can't use FastPass+, or don't want to spend an hour or more standing by a rail, here are some good viewing spots along the southern perimeter (moving counterclockwise from the United Kingdom to Germany) that often go unnoticed until 10–30 minutes before showtime:

1. **International Gateway Island** The pedestrian bridge across the canal near International Gateway spans an island that offers great viewing. This island normally fills 30 minutes or more before showtime.

2. **Second-Floor (Restaurant-Level) Deck of the Mitsukoshi Building in Japan** An Asian arch slightly blocks your sight line, but this covered deck offers a great vantage point, especially if the weather is iffy. Only La Hacienda de San Angel in Mexico is more protected. If you take up a position on the Mitsukoshi deck and find the wind blowing directly at you, you can be reasonably sure that the smoke from the fireworks won't be far behind.

3. **Gondola Landing at Italy** An elaborate waterfront promenade offers excellent viewing. Claim a spot at least 30 minutes before showtime.

4. **The Boat Dock Opposite Germany** Another good vantage point, the dock generally fills 30 minutes before *IllumiNations*. Note that this area may be exposed to more smoke from the fireworks because of Epcot's prevailing winds.

5. **Waterfront Promenade by Germany** Views are good from the 90-foot-long lagoonside walkway between Germany and China.

None of the viewing locations are reservable, and good spots go early on busier nights. But speaking personally, we refuse to hold down a slab of concrete for 2 hours before *IllumiNations* as some people do. Most nights, you can find an acceptable vantage point 15–30 minutes before the show. Don't position yourself under a tree, an awning, or anything that blocks your overhead view.

A New Yorker who staked out his turf well in advance made this suggestion for staying comfortable until showtime:

> *Your excellent guide also served as a seat cushion while I waited seated on the ground. Make future editions thicker for greater comfort.*

IllumiNations and FastPass+

We don't recommend *IllumiNations* as a good use of one of your first three advance FastPass+ reservations, but if you have only one day to tour Epcot and you're using our standard touring plan, you should be able to pick up a same-day FastPass+ reservation for *IllumiNations* just after 1 p.m., after you've experienced all of Epcot's headliners.

The new *Frozen*-themed boat ride and princess meet and greet in Norway (see page 560), scheduled to open in 2016, will likely both be FastPass+ attractions. That could make for some tough choices under the current FastPass+ system: Reservations for *IllumiNations* generally run out by 1–2 p.m., but it's unlikely that most guests would be finished with their Norway FastPass+ experiences by then. However, plenty of excellent *IllumiNations*-viewing locations that don't require FastPass+ can be found around World Showcase Lagoon, so it's not critical to have a reservation.

Readers confirm that even when you do have a FastPass+ reservation for *IllumiNations*, it doesn't work very well. These comments are representative:

> *It wasn't worth it to me. There were a LOT of people and a small amount of railing space, which everyone was jostling for. I'm vertically challenged (5'4"), and I couldn't see the globe very well.*

*The lineup to get into the spot was INSANE. We went early and had
to wait in line for about 20 minutes just to get into the viewing area.*

ILLUMINATIONS CRUISE

FOR A REALLY GOOD VIEW, you can charter a pontoon boat for
$346 with tax. Captained by a Disney cast member, the boat holds up to
10 guests. Your captain will take you for a little cruise and then position
the boat in a perfect place to watch *IllumiNations*. Chips, soda, and water
are provided; sandwiches and more-substantial food items may be arranged through Disney reservations or Yacht Club Private Dining at
☎ 407-934-3160. Cruises depart from Bayside Marina. A major indirect
benefit of the charter is that you can enjoy *IllumiNations* without fighting
the mob afterward. Because this is a private charter rather than a tour,
only your group will be aboard. Life jackets are provided, but you can
wear them at your discretion. Because there are few boats, charters sell
out fast. To reserve, call ☎ 407-WDW-PLAY (939-7529) at exactly 7 a.m.
Eastern time 180 days before the day you want to charter. Because the
Disney reservations system counts days in a somewhat atypical manner,
we recommend phoning about 185 days out to have a Disney agent specify the exact morning to call for reservations. Similar charters are available on the Seven Seas Lagoon to watch the Magic Kingdom fireworks.

TRAFFIC PATTERNS
in EPCOT

IN THE MAGIC KINGDOM, Main Street, U.S.A., with its shops and
eateries, serves as a huge gathering place when the park opens and funnels visitors to the Central Plaza, where entrances branch off to the
lands. Thus, crowds are first welcomed and entertained (on Main
Street), then distributed almost equally to the lands.

At Epcot, by contrast, Spaceship Earth, the park's premier landmark and one of its headliner attractions, is just inside the main
entrance. When visitors enter the park, they almost irresistibly head
for it. Hence, a bottleneck forms less than 75 yards from the turnstiles
as soon as the park opens.

Early-morning crowds form in Future World because most of the
park's rides and shows are there. Except at Mission: Space, Soarin',
and Test Track, visitors are fairly equally distributed among Future World attractions. Mission: Space, Soarin', Spaceship Earth, and Test
Track are the major early-morning magnets.
These four biggies draw so many guests that the
other attractions in Future World don't develop
long waits until 11 a.m. or later.

Between 9 and 11 a.m., crowds build in Future World. Even when World Showcase opens
(usually 11 a.m.), more people are entering Fu-
ture World than are leaving for the Showcase. Attendance continues
building in Future World between noon and 2 p.m. World Showcase

***unofficial* TIP**
Visitors aware of the
congestion at Spaceship
Earth can take advantage
of the excellent oppor-
tunities it provides for
escaping waits at other
Future World attractions.

attendance builds rapidly as lunchtime approaches. Exhibits at the far end of World Showcase Lagoon report large audiences from about noon through 6:30 or 7:30 p.m.

The Magic Kingdom's premier attractions are situated on the far perimeters of its lands to distribute crowds evenly. Epcot's cluster of attractions in Future World holds the greater part of the throng in the smaller part of the park. World Showcase has just one major draw— *The American Adventure*—but it's not in the same league as the three super-headliners in Future World, and consequently you have no compelling reason to rush to see them. The bottom line: Crowds build all morning and into early afternoon in Future World. Not until the evening meal approaches do crowds equalize in Future World and World Showcase. Evening crowds in World Showcase, however, don't compare in size with morning and midday crowds in Future World. Attendance throughout Epcot is normally lighter in the evening.

Some guests leave Epcot in the early evening, but most of them exit en masse after *IllumiNations*. Upward of 30,000 people head for the parking lot and monorail station at once. Still, this congestion doesn't compare with the post-fireworks gridlock at the Magic Kingdom. One primary reason for the easier departure from Epcot is that its parking lot is adjacent to the park, not separated from it by a lake as at the Magic Kingdom. At the Magic Kingdom, departing visitors form bottlenecks at the monorail to the Transportation and Ticket Center and main parking lot. At Epcot, they proceed directly to their cars.

To get a complete view of the actual traffic patterns while you're in the park, use our mobile app, **Lines** (**touringplans.com/lines**). The app gives you current wait times and future estimates in half-hour increments for today and tomorrow. A quick glance shows how traffic patterns affect wait times throughout the day.

EPCOT TOURING PLANS

TOURING EPCOT IS MUCH MORE STRENUOUS and demanding than touring the other theme parks. Epcot requires about twice as much walking. And, unlike the Magic Kingdom, Epcot has no effective in-park transportation; wherever you want to go, it's always quicker to walk. Our plans will help you avoid crowds and bottlenecks on days of moderate-to-heavy attendance, but they can't shorten the distance you have to walk. (Wear comfortable shoes.) On days of lighter attendance, when crowd conditions aren't a critical factor, the plans will help you organize your tour. We offer four touring plans:

- Epcot One-Day Touring Plan
- Epcot Authors' Selective One-Day Touring Plan
- Epcot One-Day Touring Plan for Parents with Small Children
- Epcot Two-Day Early-Riser Touring Plan

The One-Day Touring Plan packs as much as possible into one long day and requires a lot of hustle and stamina. The Authors' Selective One-Day Touring Plan eliminates some lesser (in the authors' opinion) attractions and offers a somewhat more relaxed tour if you have only one day. The One-Day Touring Plan for Parents with Small Children gives little ones the best of Epcot while also building in needed rest time. Finally, the Two-Day Early-Riser Touring Plan is the most efficient, eliminating 90% of the backtracking and extra walking required by the other plans while still providing a comprehensive tour.

To help with FastPass+, we've listed the approximate return times for which you should attempt to make reservations. (The touring plan should work with anything close to the times shown.) Check **touring plans.com** for the latest developments and information.

"Not a Touring Plan" Touring Plans

For the type-B reader, these touring plans (see page 804) avoid detailed step-by-step strategies for saving every last minute in line. For Epcot, these "not" touring plans include advice for adults and parents with one day in the park, for anyone with two days, and for anyone with an afternoon and a full day to tour.

BEFORE YOU GO

1. Call ☎ 407-824-4321 or check the day before you go to verify official opening time.
2. Make reservations at the Epcot full-service restaurant(s) of your choice 180 days before your visit.
3. Make FastPass+ reservations 60 or 30 days in advance.

EPCOT ONE-DAY TOURING PLAN FOR ADULTS
(page 812)

FOR Adults and children age 8 or older.

ASSUMES Willingness to experience all major rides and shows.

This plan requires a lot of walking and a small amount of backtracking in order to avoid long waits in line. A little extra walking and some early-morning hustle will spare you 2–3 hours of standing in line. You might not complete the tour. How far you get depends on how quickly you move from attraction to attraction, how many times you rest and eat, how quickly the park fills, and what time it closes.

This plan is not recommended for families with very young children. If you're touring with young children and have only one day, use the Epcot Authors' Selective One-Day Touring Plan or the Epcot One-Day Touring Plan for Parents with Small Children. Break after lunch and relax at your hotel, returning to the park in late afternoon. If you can allocate two days to Epcot, use the Epcot Two-Day Early-Riser Touring Plan.

EPCOT AUTHORS' SELECTIVE ONE-DAY TOURING PLAN FOR ADULTS *(page 813)*

FOR All parties.

ASSUMES Willingness to experience major rides and shows.

This touring plan includes only what the authors believe is the best that Epcot has to offer. Families with children younger than age 8 should review Epcot attractions in our Small-Child Fright-Potential Chart in

Part Five (see pages 404–407). Rent a stroller for any child small enough to fit in one, and take your young children back to the hotel for a nap after lunch. If you can allocate two days to Epcot, use the Epcot Two-Day Early-Riser Touring Plan (see below).

EPCOT ONE-DAY TOURING PLAN FOR PARENTS WITH SMALL CHILDREN *(page 814)*

FOR Parents with children younger than age 8.

This touring plan is for parents and kids who want to experience Epcot's best attractions in a single day. It's the most popular Epcot touring plan at **touringplans.com.**

The plan includes a midday break of 3–4 hours. Make time for this break by skipping intense attractions such as Test Track and Mission: Space and by forgoing many World Showcase exhibits. Regarding World Showcase, we encourage families to sign up for a free interactive game called Agent P's World Showcase Adventure (see page 557), which most kids find endlessly entertaining.

Families with children younger than age 8 should review Epcot attractions in our Small-Child Fright-Potential Chart in Part Five (see pages 404–407). Rent a stroller for any child small enough to fit in one.

EPCOT TWO-DAY EARLY-RISER TOURING PLAN
(pages 815 and 816)

FOR All parties.

This is the most efficient of the Epcot touring plans. It takes advantage of easy touring made possible by morning's light crowds. Most folks will complete each day of the plan by midafternoon. While the plan doesn't include *IllumiNations* or other evening festivities, these activities, along with dinner at an Epcot restaurant, can be added at your discretion.

Families with children younger than age 8 should review Epcot attractions in our Small-Child Fright-Potential Chart in Part Five (see pages 404–407). Rent a stroller for any child small enough to fit in one.

PART ELEVEN

DISNEY'S ANIMAL KINGDOM

WITH ITS LUSH FLORA, WINDING STREAMS, meandering paths, and exotic setting, Disney's Animal Kingdom is a stunningly beautiful theme park. The landscaping alone conjures images of rainforest, veldt, and formal gardens. Soothing, mysterious, and exciting, every vista is a feast for the eye. Add to this loveliness a population of more than 1,000 animals, replicas of Africa's and Asia's most intriguing architecture, and a diverse array of singularly original attractions, and you have the most distinctive of all the Disney theme parks.

At 500 acres, Animal Kingdom is five times the size of the Magic Kingdom and almost twice the size of Epcot. But most of Animal Kingdom's vast geography is accessible only on guided tours or as part of attractions. Animal Kingdom consists of five sections, or "lands": **The Oasis, Discovery Island, DinoLand U.S.A., Africa,** and **Asia.**

Its size notwithstanding, Animal Kingdom offers a limited number of attractions. To be exact, there are seven rides, several walk-through exhibits, an indoor theater, three amphitheaters, a conservation exhibit, and a children's playground.

Animal Kingdom's opening was seen as Disney taking dead aim at Busch Gardens in Tampa, a theme park known for its exceptional zoological exhibits. Up to that time, Disney had preferred the neatly controlled movements of Audio-Animatronic animals to the unpredictable behaviors of real critters. Unfortunately for Disney, however, the combination of creative natural-habitat zoological exhibits and coasters developed by Busch Gardens became immensely popular, and as any student of The Walt Disney Company can attest, there's nothing like a successful competitor to make the Disney folks change their tune. So, all the press releases aside, Disney's Animal Kingdom was designed as a combination of natural-habitat zoological exhibits and thrill rides. Big surprise!

unofficial **TIP**
Three attractions—
Dinosaur, Expedition Everest, and **Kilimanjaro Safaris**—are among the best in the Disney repertoire.

Even if the recipe was copied, the Disney version serves up more than its share of innovations. For starters, there's lots of space, thus allowing for the sweeping vistas that Discovery Channel viewers would expect in, say, an African veldt setting. Then there are the enclosures, natural

NOT TO BE MISSED AT DISNEY'S ANIMAL KINGDOM	
DISCOVERY ISLAND • *It's Tough to Be a Bug!* • Wilderness Explorers	
AFRICA • *Festival of the Lion King* • Kilimanjaro Safaris	
ASIA • Expedition Everest	
DINOLAND U.S.A. • Dinosaur • *Finding Nemo—The Musical*	

in appearance, with few or no apparent barriers between you and the animals. The operative word, of course, is *apparent*. That flimsy stand of bamboo separating you from a gorilla is actually a neatly disguised set of steel rods embedded in concrete. The Imagineers even take a crack at certain animals' stubborn unwillingness to be on display: A lion that would rather sleep out of sight under a bush, for example, is lured to center stage with nice, cool, climate-controlled artificial rocks.

Animal Kingdom has received mixed reviews since it opened in 1998. Guests complain loudly about the park layout, the necessity of backtracking through Discovery Island in order to access the various themed areas, congested walkways, and lack of shade. However, most of the attractions have been well received, as have the animal exhibits and the park's architecture and landscaping. We marvel at the fact that readers of similar backgrounds come away with such vastly differing opinions.

In truth, Animal Kingdom is a park to linger over and savor—two things that Disney, with its crowds, lines, and regimentation, has conditioned us not to do. But many people intuit that Animal Kingdom must be approached in a different way, including this mother of three (ages 5, 7, and 9) from Hampton Bay, New York:

> To enjoy Animal Kingdom, you must have the right attitude. It's an educational experience, not a thrill park. We spoke to a cast member who played games with the kids—my daughter found a drawer full of butterflies, and the boys located a hidden ostrich egg and lion skull.

And though we offer a one-day touring plan for Animal Kingdom, a Cleveland reader argues for more time:

> I can't see how Animal Kingdom takes less than a day. There is so much to look at, animal-wise, architecturally, street performances— we kept going back at different times, and each time we saw the place literally in a new light or with different animals active.

These readers are right: Animal Kingdom's best features are its animals, nature trails, and cast members. We think the **Wilderness Explorers** scavenger hunt (see page 585) ties together all of the park's best elements, so we've added it to our Animal Kingdom touring plan. It's a lot of fun to play, and you just might learn something along the way.

Finally, a major construction project currently under way will bring the flora and fauna of James Cameron's *Avatar* to the park sometime in 2017. What used to be known as Camp Minnie-Mickey has been demolished and its attractions relocated to other areas of the park to make way for the new themed area, tentatively named **Pandora: The Land of Avatar.** Most of the construction will be confined to backstage areas, so impact to guests should be limited.

Continued on page 578

Disney's Animal Kingdom

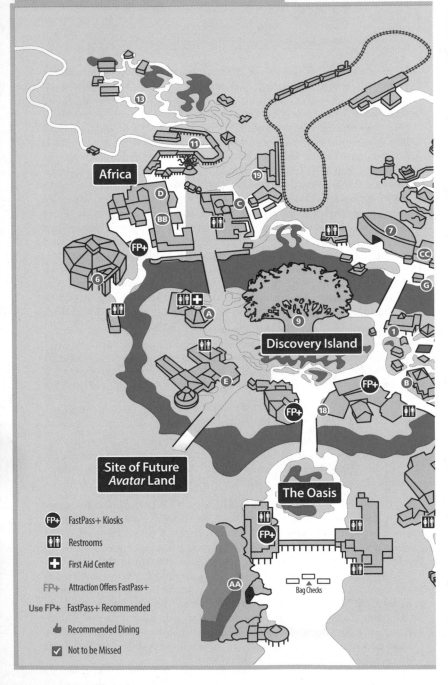

Africa

Discovery Island

Site of Future *Avatar* Land

The Oasis

Bag Checks

FP+ FastPass+ Kiosks

👫 Restrooms

➕ First Aid Center

FP+ Attraction Offers FastPass+

Use FP+ FastPass+ Recommended

👍 Recommended Dining

✓ Not to be Missed

Attractions

1. Adventurers Outpost Use FP+
2. The Boneyard
3. Conservation Station and Affection Section
4. DINOSAUR ☑ Use FP+
5. Expedition Everest ☑ Use FP+
6. *Festival of the Lion King* ☑ FP+
7. *Flights of Wonder*
8. Habitat Habit!
9. *It's Tough to be a Bug!*/The Tree of Life ☑
10. Kali River Rapids Use Use FP+
11. Kilimanjaro Safaris ☑ Use FP+
12. Maharajah Jungle Trek
13. Pangani Forest Exploration Trail
14. Primeval Whirl FP+
15. *Rivers of Light* (opens 2016) FP+
16. Theater in the Wild/*Finding Nemo–The Musical* FP+
17. TriceraTop Spin
18. Wilderness Explorers Sign-Up Station ☑
19. Wildlife Express Train

Rafiki's Planet Watch

Asia

DinoLand U.S.A.

Table-Service Restaurants

AA. Rainforest Cafe
BB. Tusker House Restaurant
CC. Yak & Yeti Restaurant

Counter-Service Restaurants

A. Creature Comforts
B. Flame Tree Barbecue
C. Harambe Market
D. Kusafiri Coffee Shop & Bakery
E. Pizzafari
F. Restaurantosaurus
G. Royal Anandapur Tea Company
H. Yak & Yeti Local Food Cafes

Continued from page 575

DISNEY DISH WITH JIM HILL

LIKE NIGHT AND DAY When Pandora: The Land of Avatar opens in 2017, be sure to allow enough time to visit Animal Kingdom twice. As impressive as this area will be during the day, the way it'll look at night will blow your mind—picture an enormous bioluminescent landscape that responds to your every footprint and slightest touch.

ARRIVING

DISNEY'S ANIMAL KINGDOM is off Osceola Parkway in the southwest corner of Walt Disney World and is not too far from Blizzard Beach, Coronado Springs Resort, and the All-Star Resorts. For driving directions, see page 443. Animal Kingdom Lodge is about a mile away from the park on its west side. From Interstate 4, take Exit 64B, US 192, to the so-called Walt Disney World main entrance (World Drive) and follow the signs to Animal Kingdom. Animal Kingdom has its own vast pay parking lot with close-in parking for the disabled. Once parked, you can walk to the entrance or catch a ride on one of Disney's trams.

The park is connected to other Walt Disney World destinations by the Disney bus system. If you're staying at a Disney resort and plan to arrive at Animal Kingdom before park opening, use Disney transportation rather than taking your own car.

OPERATING HOURS

ANIMAL KINGDOM'S OPENING TIME corresponds to that of the other parks. Thus, you can expect a 9 a.m. opening during less busy times of the year and an 8 a.m. opening during holidays and high season. This park usually closes well before the others in Disney World, however—as early as 5 p.m., in fact, during off-season. More common is a 6 or 7 p.m. closing.

Animal Kingdom's standard park-opening procedure lets all guests through the turnstiles about 15–30 minutes before official park opening. When this happens, you'll usually find Kilimanjaro Safaris, Expedition Everest, and TriceraTop Spin already open.

During slower or colder times of year, Disney may delay the daily opening of Kali River Rapids in Asia, as well as the Boneyard playground, the Wildlife Express Train, and Conservation Station. These procedures may change, so check the *Times Guide* or our mobile app, **Lines,** for the exact schedule when you arrive. The rest of the attractions come online at official park opening time.

On holidays and other days of projected heavy attendance, Disney will open the park 30–60 minutes early.

Animal Kingdom currently holds two morning Extra Magic Hours sessions per week, although we don't think they save you all that much time in line. Our advice is to get an extra hour of sleep and visit when early entry is not in effect.

For now, Kilimanjaro Safaris and the Pangani Forest Exploration Trail close around 30–60 minutes before sunset. Thus, as days get shorter with the change of seasons, the attractions close earlier in the day. A nighttime version of Kilimanjaro Safaris is expected to open in late 2015 or early 2016; the Pangani Trail may also stay open past dark, though nothing official has been announced.

In the fall, Disney closes all animal exhibits as early as 4:45 p.m.

unofficial **TIP**
Arrive, at the entrance turnstiles, admission in hand, 40 minutes before official opening during the summer and holiday periods, and 30 minutes before official opening the rest of the year.

GETTING ORIENTED

AT THE ENTRANCE PLAZA ARE TICKET KIOSKS fronting the main entrance. To your right, before the turnstiles, is an ATM. After you pass through the turnstiles, wheelchair and stroller rentals are to your right. **Guest Relations**—park headquarters for information, guide maps, entertainment schedules (*Times Guides*), missing persons, and lost and found—is to the left. Nearby are restrooms, public phones, and rental lockers. Beyond the entrance plaza, you enter **The Oasis,** a lushly vegetated network of converging pathways winding through a landscape punctuated with streams, waterfalls, and misty glades and inhabited by what Disney calls "colorful and unusual animals."

The park is arranged somewhat like the Magic Kingdom, in a hub-and-spoke configuration. The lush, tropical Oasis serves as Main Street, funneling visitors to **Discovery Island** at the center of the park. Dominated by the park's central icon, the 14-story hand-carved **Tree of Life,** Discovery Island is the park's retail and dining center. From Discovery

ANIMAL KINGDOM Services

MOST OF THE PARK'S SERVICE FACILITIES are inside the main entrance and on Discovery Island, as follows:

Baby Care Center On Discovery Island, behind the MyMagic+ Service Center

Banking Services ATMs at the main entrance, by the turnstiles, and near Dinosaur in DinoLand U.S.A.

Camera Memory Cards and Supplies Just inside the main entrance at Garden Gate Gifts, in Africa at Mombasa Marketplace, and at other retail shops throughout the park

Cell Phone Charging Outlets available at Pizzafari, Restaurantosaurus, Tusker House, and Conservation Station

Entertainment Information In the *Times Guide,* available at Guest Relations

First Aid Center On Discovery Island, next to the MyMagic+ Service Center

Guest Relations/Information Inside the main entrance to the left

Lost and Found Inside the main entrance to the left

Lost Persons Can be reported at Guest Relations and the Baby Care Center

Storage Lockers Inside the main entrance to the left

Wheelchair, ECV/ESV, and Stroller Rentals Inside the main entrance, to the right

Island, guests can access the respective themed areas of **Africa, Asia,** and **DinoLand U.S.A.** Discovery Island additionally hosts a theater attraction in The Tree of Life, and a number of short nature trails.

Even if you dawdle in the shops and linger over the wildlife exhibits, you should easily be able to take in Animal Kingdom in one day.

FASTPASS+ ATTRACTIONS IN DISNEY'S ANIMAL KINGDOM

FASTPASS+ IS OFFERED at 9 (soon to be 10) attractions:

AFRICA	**DINOLAND U.S.A.**
• *Festival of the Lion King*	• Dinosaur
• Kilimanjaro Safaris	• *Finding Nemo—The Musical*
	• Primeval Whirl
ASIA	
• Expedition Everest	**DISCOVERY ISLAND**
• Kali River Rapids	• *It's Tough to Be a Bug!*
• *Rivers of Light* (opens 2016)	• Meet Favorite Disney Pals at Adventurers Outpost

Our print and online touring plans most frequently suggest FastPass+ reservations for **Kali River Rapids.** Why? Similarly to Peter Pan's Flight at the Magic Kingdom, people go elsewhere first thing in the morning and come back to Kali after they've seen a few other attractions. In Animal Kingdom, adults and teens head to Expedition Everest in Asia first, while parents with children too small for Everest head for Kilimanjaro Safaris in Africa. Using FastPass+ at Kali River Rapids allows you to experience other important attractions early in the morning, when lines are short, while still giving you a relatively short line at Kali to contend with when you arrive. Another advantage to using FastPass+ for this attraction is that you can schedule your ride for either right before you leave the park (to avoid sloshing around all day) or during the warmer part of an otherwise cool day.

Our second most frequent recommendation for FastPass+ is Africa's **Kilimanjaro Safaris.** Most of our touring plans for tweens, teens, and adults start off at Expedition Everest and try to get through Dinosaur and Primeval Whirl in DinoLand U.S.A. before the crowds arrive. This also keeps backtracking to a minimum. Those plans generally visit the Safaris around either lunchtime or late afternoon, and using FastPass+ then will save you a lot of time in line.

Dinosaur and the **Adventurers Outpost** character meet and greet show up on our Animal Kingdom touring plans for parents with small children. Like Kali River Rapids, these aren't going to be the first stop of your day, and using FastPass+ at these attractions will generally save more time in line than using FastPass+ at any other child-friendly attraction in our plans.

Expedition Everest is our least frequently suggested FastPass+ attraction. This is because our software generally puts it as the first step in any Animal Kingdom touring plan. While posted wait times at Expedition Everest can average 60–80 minutes during summer and more during holidays, getting to Everest first thing in the morning lets you avoid those lines and save FastPass+ for something else. What's more,

ANIMAL KINGDOM
WHEN SAME-DAY FP+ RUNS OUT, BY CROWD LEVEL

ATTRACTION	LOW CROWDS*	MODERATE CROWDS*	HIGH CROWDS*
Dinosaur	3-4 p.m.	4 p.m.	11 a.m.-2 p.m.
Expedition Everest	3-4 p.m.	4 p.m.	11 a.m.-2 p.m.
Festival of the Lion King	2-3 p.m.	2-3 p.m.	1-2 p.m. (Levels 8-9), 5 p.m. (Level 10)
Finding Nemo—The Musical	3-4 p.m.	4 p.m.	1-3 p.m.
It's Tough to Be a Bug!	3-4 p.m.	4-5 p.m.	5-6 p.m.
Kali River Rapids	2-3 p.m.	3-4 p.m.	1-4 p.m.
Kilimanjaro Safaris (daytime version)	1-2 p.m.	1-2 p.m.	Noon-1 p.m.
Meet Mickey and Minnie at Adventurers Outpost	Noon-1 p.m.	Noon-3 p.m.	1-2 p.m.
Primeval Whirl	3-4 p.m.	4-5 p.m.	5-6 p.m.
* **LOW CROWDS** (Levels 1-3 on TouringPlans.com Crowd Calendar)			
* **MODERATE CROWDS** (Levels 4-7 on TouringPlans.com Crowd Calendar)			
* **HIGH CROWDS** (Levels 8-10 on TouringPlans.com Crowd Calendar)			

Expedition Everest has a single-rider line—if you can't get a FastPass+ reservation and you don't mind splitting up your group for one ride, the single-rider line is a great option.

Opening in 2016, **Rivers of Light** (page 593), a nighttime spectacular combining live music, floating lanterns, water screens, and animal imagery, will likely be a good choice for a day-of FastPass after the initial crowds have dissipated somewhat, after you've covered the other attractions. If you're visiting right after the show debuts, though, you might be better off reserving FastPass+ before your trip.

FastPass+ kiosk locations in Animal Kingdom are as follows:

- To the left of Expedition Everest's entrance in Asia
- Near Dawa Bar in Asia
- In front of the Disney Outfitters store on Discovery Island and across the walkway near Island Mercantile
- In front of the MyMagic+ Service Center, to the left of the entrance at The Oasis

Same-Day FastPass+ Availability

The preceding advice tells you which attractions to focus on when making your *advance* FastPass+ reservations before you get to the park. Once you're in the park, you can make more FastPass+ reservations once your advance reservations have been used or have expired. The chart above shows which attractions are likely to have day-of FastPasses available, and the approximate times at which they'll run out.

SPECIAL EVENTS IN DISNEY'S ANIMAL KINGDOM

THE MAGIC KINGDOM regularly hosts after-hours events such as Mickey's Not So Scary Halloween Party and Very Merry Christmas Party (see Part One). These are big moneymakers for Disney, because the theme park closes early to regular guests (who've paid full price for admission) and a separate entrance fee is charged for attending the party. In 2014, Disney was trying out an after-hours event at Animal Kingdom; though at press time it wasn't on the schedule for 2015, we think it may eventually come back.

Called **Harambe Nights,** the event was held on Saturday nights in summer 2014. It featured a retelling of the *Lion King* story, including a live orchestra and digital special effects, at the *Festival of the Lion King* theater in Africa; appetizers, desserts, wine, and beer; and a postshow "street party" with live music, Disney characters, and an Indian-African fusion buffet, designed by chefs from Boma, Jiko, and Sanaa, the three acclaimed restaurants at Animal Kingdom Lodge).

DINING IN DISNEY'S ANIMAL KINGDOM

HERE'S A QUICK RECAP of Animal Kingdom's top few restaurants, rated by readers from highest to lowest. See Part Four, Dining In and Around Walt Disney World, for details.

ANIMAL KINGDOM RESTAURANT REFRESHER	
COUNTER-SERVICE	FULL-SERVICE
Flame Tree Barbecue (92% 👍), Discovery Island	**Tusker House Restaurant** (92% 👍), Africa
Kusafiri Coffee Shop and Bakery (92% 👍), Africa	**Yak & Yeti Restaurant** (85% 👍), Asia
Royal Anandapur Tea Company (91% 👍), Asia *(coffee, tea, and pastries)*	**Rainforest Cafe** (84% 👍), to the left of the main entrance to the park
Yak & Yeti Local Food Cafes (90% 👍), Asia	

The OASIS

DESCRIPTION AND COMMENTS Though the functional purpose of The Oasis is the same as that of Main Street in the Magic Kingdom—that is, to funnel guests to the center of the park—it also serves as what Disney calls a "transitional experience." In plain English, this means that it sets the stage and gets you into the right mood to enjoy Animal Kingdom.

The minute you pass through the turnstiles, you'll know that this isn't just another central hub. Where Main Street, Hollywood Boulevard at the Studios, and the Epcot entrance plaza direct you like an arrow straight into the heart of the respective parks, The Oasis immediately envelops you in an environment replete with choices. There's no one broad thoroughfare, but rather multiple paths. Each delivers you to Discovery Island at the center of the park, but the route you choose and what you see along the way are up to you. Nothing obvious clues you in about where you're going—there's no fairy-tale castle or giant golf ball to beckon you. Instead you'll find a lush, green, canopied landscape with streams, grottoes, and waterfalls.

The natural-habitat zoological exhibits in The Oasis are representative of those throughout the park. Although extraordinarily lush and beautiful, the exhibits are primarily designed for the comfort and well-being of the animals. A sign identifies the animal(s) in each exhibit, but there's no guarantee that the animals will be immediately visible. Because most habitats are large and provide ample terrain for the occupants to hide, you must linger and concentrate, looking for small movements in the vegetation. When you do spot the animal, you may make out only a shadowy figure, or perhaps only a leg or a tail.

TOURING TIPS The Oasis is a place to savor and appreciate, but it will be largely lost on Disney-conditioned guests who blitz through at warp speed to queue up for the big attractions. If you're a blitzer in the morning, plan to spend some time in The Oasis on your way out of the park. The Oasis usually closes 30–60 minutes after the rest of the park.

DISCOVERY ISLAND

DISCOVERY ISLAND COMBINES a profusion of tropical greenery with whimsical equatorial African architecture. Connected to the other lands by bridges, the island is the hub from which guests can access the park's various themed areas. A village is arrayed in a crescent around the base of Animal Kingdom's iconic landmark, **The Tree of Life.** Towering 14 stories above the village, it's this park's version of Cinderella Castle or Spaceship Earth. Flanked by pools, meadows, and exotic gardens populated by a diversity of birds and animals, The Tree of Life houses a theater attraction inspired by the Disney-Pixar film *A Bug's Life.*

As you enter Discovery Island over the bridge from The Oasis and the park entrance, you'll see The Tree of Life directly ahead, at 12 o'clock. The bridge to Asia is to the right of the tree at 2 o'clock, with the bridge to DinoLand U.S.A. at roughly 4 o'clock. The bridge connecting The Oasis to Discovery Island is at 6 o'clock, the bridge to the future *Avatar* land is at 8 o'clock, and the bridge to Africa is at 11 o'clock.

Discovery Island is also the park's central headquarters for shopping, dining, and services. Here you'll find the **First Aid** and **Baby Care Centers,** plus FastPass+ kiosks. For Disney merchandise, try **Island Mercantile.** Counter-service food and snacks are available, but there are no sit-down eateries—the three full-service restaurants in the park are the **Rainforest Cafe,** to the left of the main entrance; **Tusker House Restaurant,** in Africa; and **Yak & Yeti Restaurant,** in Asia.

DISCOVERY ISLAND TRAILS Winding behind The Tree of Life is a series of walking trails that include around a dozen animal-viewing opportunities, from otters and kangaroos to lemurs, storks, and porcupines. One end of the path begins just before the bridge from Discovery Island to Africa, on the right side of the walkway; the other is to the right of the entrance to The Tree of Life. Besides the animals, you'll find verdant landscaping, waterfalls, and quiet spots to sit and reflect on your relationship with nature. Or nap. As we think Thoreau said, "Not until we have dozed do we begin to understand ourselves."

Meet Favorite Disney Pals at Adventurers Outpost
(FastPass+) ★★★½

APPEAL BY AGE	PRESCHOOL ★★★★	GRADE SCHOOL ★★★★½	TEENS ★★★★
YOUNG ADULTS ★★★★		OVER 30 ★★★★	SENIORS ★★★★

What it is Character-greeting venue. **Scope and scale** Minor attraction. **When to go** First thing in the morning, after 5 p.m., or use FastPass+. **Authors' rating** Nicely themed (and air-conditioned); ★★★½. **Duration of experience** About 2 minutes. **Probable waiting time** About 20 minutes. **Queue speed** Fast.

DESCRIPTION AND COMMENTS An indoor, air-conditioned character-greeting location for Mickey and Minnie Mouse, Adventurers Outpost is decorated with photos, memorabilia, and souvenirs from the Mouses' world travels.

TOURING TIPS The Outpost features two greeting rooms with two identical sets of characters, so lines move fairly quickly. Good use of FastPass+ if you have kids too small to ride Expedition Everest or Dinosaur.

The Tree of Life / *It's Tough to Be a Bug!* (FastPass+)
★★★★

APPEAL BY AGE PRESCHOOL ★★★½   GRADE SCHOOL ★★★★   TEENS ★★★★
YOUNG ADULTS ★★★★   OVER 30 ★★★★   SENIORS ★★★★½

What it is 3-D theater show. **Scope and scale** Major attraction. **When to go** Anytime. **Special comments** The theater is inside the tree. **Authors' rating** Zany and frenetic and not to be missed; ★★★★. **Duration of presentation** About 8 minutes. **Probable waiting time** 12–20 minutes.

DESCRIPTION AND COMMENTS The Tree of Life, apart from its size, is quite a work of art—we think it's the most visually compelling structure in any Disney park. Although from afar it's certainly magnificent and imposing, it's not until you examine the tree at close range that you truly appreciate its rich detail. What appears to be ancient gnarled bark is, in fact, hundreds of carvings depicting all manner of wildlife, each integrated seamlessly into the trunk, roots, and limbs of the tree. New "roots" were added to the tree in 2015, including crocodile and ram's head carvings. Look for these along the Discovery Island walkway to Africa, on the front left side of the tree.

In sharp contrast to the grandeur of the tree is the subject of the attraction housed within its trunk. Called *It's Tough to Be a Bug!*, this humorous 3-D presentation is about the difficulties of being a very small creature. Lighthearted and whimsical, the show is similar to *Mickey's PhilharMagic* at the Magic Kingdom in that it combines a 3-D film with an arsenal of tactile and visual special effects. We rate *Bug* as not to be missed.

TOURING TIPS *It's Tough to Be a Bug!* is rarely crowded even on the busiest days. Go in the morning after Kilimanjaro Safaris, Kali River Rapids, Expedition Everest, and Dinosaur. If you miss the bugs in the morning, try again in the late afternoon.

Note that *It's Tough to Be a Bug!* is very intense and the special effects will do a number on guests of all ages who are squeamish about insects. A mother of two from Williamsville, New York, shared this experience:

It's Tough to Be a Bug! was my girls' first Disney experience, and almost their last. The storyline was nebulous and difficult to follow—all they were aware of was the torture of sitting in a darkened theater being overrun with bugs. A constant stream of parents headed to the exits with terrorized children. Those who were left behind were screaming and crying as well. The 11-year-old refused to talk for 20 minutes after the fiasco, and the 3½-year-old wanted to go home—not back to the hotel, but home.

Most readers, however, loved the bugs, including this mom from Brentwood, Tennessee:

Comments from your readers make It's Tough to Be a Bug! *sound worse than* Stitch's Great Escape! *Well, it's not. It's intense, but mostly funny. The bugs are cute and charming instead of realistic and icky, so I can't understand what all the fuss is about. Kids go nuts to meet a cartoon rodent the size of a Porta John, but they freak out over some cartoon bugs? Get a grip!*

Wilderness Explorers ★★★★

APPEAL BY AGE	PRESCHOOL ★★★★	GRADE SCHOOL ★★★★½	TEENS ★★★½
YOUNG ADULTS ★★★★		OVER 30 ★★★★	SENIORS ★★★★★

What it is Park-wide scavenger hunt and puzzle-solving adventure game. **Scope and scale** Diversion. **When to go** Sign up first thing in the morning and complete activities throughout the day. **Special comments** Collecting all 32 badges takes 3–5 hours, which can be done over several days. **Authors' rating** One of the best attractions in any Disney park; not to be missed; ★★★★.

DESCRIPTION AND COMMENTS Walt Disney World offers several interactive games in its theme parks, and Wilderness Explorers is the best of the bunch—a scavenger hunt based on Russell's Boy Scout–esque troop from the movie *Up*. Players earn "badges" (stickers given out by cast members) for completing predefined activities throughout the park. For example, to earn the Gorilla Badge, you walk the Pangani Forest Exploration Trail to observe how the primates behave, then mimic that behavior back to a cast member to show what you've seen.

Register for the game near the bridge from The Oasis to Discovery Island. You'll be given an instruction book and a map showing the park location for each badge to be earned.

Cast members have been specially trained for this game and can tailor the activities based on the age of the child playing: Small children might get an explanation about what deforestation means, for example, while older kids may have to figure out why tigers have stripes. It's tons of fun for kids and adults, and we play it every time we're in the park.

TOURING TIPS Activities are spread throughout the park, including areas to which many guests never venture. You have to ride specific attractions to earn certain badges, so using FastPass+ for those will save time.

▋▋ AFRICA

THE LARGEST OF ANIMAL KINGDOM'S LANDS, Africa is entered through **Harambe,** a Disneyfied version of a modern rural African town. A market is equipped with modern cash registers; dining options consist of a sit-down buffet, limited counter service, and snack stands. What distinguishes Harambe is its understatement: Far from the stereotypical great-white-hunter image of an African town, Harambe is definitely (and realistically) *not* exotic. The buildings, while interesting, are architecturally simple. Though better maintained and more idealized than the real McCoy, Disney's Harambe would be a lot more at home in Kenya than the Magic Kingdom's Main Street would be in Missouri.

Harambe serves as the gateway to the African veldt habitat, Animal Kingdom's largest and most ambitious zoological exhibit. Access to the veldt is via the **Kilimanjaro Safaris** attraction, at the end of Harambe's main drag near the fat-trunked baobab tree. Harambe is also the departure point for the train to **Rafiki's Planet Watch** and **Conservation Station** (the park's veterinary headquarters), as well as the home of a long-running live theatrical show.

Festival of the Lion King (FastPass+) ★★★★

APPEAL BY AGE	PRESCHOOL ★★★★½	GRADE SCHOOL ★★★★½	TEENS ★★★★½
YOUNG ADULTS ★★★★½		OVER 30 ★★★★½	SENIORS ★★★★★

What it is Theater-in-the-round stage show. **Scope and scale** Major attraction. **When to go** Before 11 a.m., after 4 p.m., or use FastPass+. Check your park map or *Times Guide* for showtimes. **Authors' rating** Upbeat, energetic, and spectacular; not to be missed; ★★★★. **Duration of presentation** 30 minutes. **Preshow entertainment** None. **When to arrive** 20–30 minutes before showtime.

DESCRIPTION AND COMMENTS Inspired by the Disney animated feature, *Festival of the Lion King* is part stage show, part parade, part circus; in 2014, it relocated from Camp Minnie-Mickey to Africa, behind and to the left of Tusker House. Guests sit in four sets of bleachers surrounding the stage and organized into cheering sections, which are called on to make elephant, warthog, giraffe, and lion noises. (You won't be alone if you don't know what a giraffe or warthog sounds like.) There's a great deal of strutting around, some acrobatics, and a lot of singing and dancing. By our count, every tune from *The Lion King* is belted out and reprised several times—if you didn't know the words to the songs before the show, you definitely will after.

Unofficial Guide readers are almost unanimous in their praise of *Festival of the Lion King.* This letter from a Naples, Florida, mom is typical:

Festival of the Lion King *was the best thing we experienced at Animal Kingdom. The singers, dancers, fire twirlers, acrobats, and sets were spectacular.*

TOURING TIPS *Festival of the Lion King* is a big draw, so try to see the first show in the morning or one of the last two shows at night. For midday performances, you'll need to queue up at least 35–45 minutes before showtime; to minimize waiting in the hot sun, don't hop in line until cast members give the word to do so. The bleachers can make viewing difficult for the height-deficient—If you have small children or short adults in your party, try to snag a seat higher up. Rarely a good use of FastPass+.

Kilimanjaro Safaris *(FastPass+)* ★★★★★

APPEAL BY AGE	PRESCHOOL ★★★★½	GRADE SCHOOL ★★★★½	TEENS ★★★★½
YOUNG ADULTS ★★★★½	OVER 30 ★★★★½	SENIORS ★★★★★	

What it is Simulated ride through an African wildlife reservation. **Scope and scale** Super-headliner. **When to go** As soon as the park opens or in the 2 hours before closing, or use FastPass+. **Authors' rating** Not to be missed; ★★★★★. **Duration of ride** About 20 minutes. **Average wait in line per 100 people ahead of you** 4 minutes; assumes full-capacity operation with 18-second dispatch interval. **Loading speed** Fast.

DESCRIPTION AND COMMENTS Animal Kingdom's premier zoological attraction, Kilimanjaro Safaris offers an exceptionally realistic, albeit brief, imitation of an actual African photo safari. Thirty-two guests at a time board tall, open safari vehicles and are dispatched into a simulated African veldt habitat. Animals such as zebras, wildebeests, impalas, Thomson's gazelles, giraffes, and even rhinos roam apparently free, while predators such as lions, as well as potentially dangerous large animals like hippos, are separated from both prey and guests by all-but-invisible, natural-appearing barriers. Although the animals have more than 100 acres of savanna, woodland, streams, and rocky hills to call home, careful placement of water holes, forage, and salt licks ensures that the critters are hanging out by the road when safari vehicles roll by.

Having traveled in Kenya and Tanzania, I (Bob) can tell you that Disney has done an amazing job of replicating the sub-Saharan east-African landscape. The main difference that a Kenyan or Tanzanian would notice is that Disney's version is greener and, generally speaking, less barren. As on a real African safari, what animals you see, and how many, is pretty much a matter of luck. We've experienced Kilimanjaro Safaris more than 100 times and had a different experience on each trip.

Winding through the Safaris is Disney's **Wild Africa Trek,** a behind-the-scenes tour of Animal Kingdom that takes you into several of Kilimanjaro Safaris' animal enclosures. As you drive past the hippo pool or over the crocodile pool, look up for a series of rope bridges towering far above the ground—you may see Trekkers on tour. See page 721 of Part Eighteen for a complete description.

We hear the Safaris will begin offering nighttime tours in late 2015 or early 2016, probably around the time that *Rivers of Light* (see page 593) debuts. This will give Animal Kingdom guests additional after-dark entertainment options and be a unique viewing experience. No word on whether the animal lineup will change to include more-nocturnal creatures.

TOURING TIPS Kilimanjaro Safaris is Animal Kingdom's number-two draw behind Expedition Everest. From a touring standpoint, this is good news: By distributing guests evenly throughout the park, Expedition Everest makes it unnecessary to run to Kilimanjaro Safaris first thing in the morning. Our Animal Kingdom touring plan has you obtain FastPass+ reservations for the Safaris in the afternoon—while you wait for your FastPass+ return window, you'll have plenty of time to eat and tour the rest of Africa.

Waits for Kilimanjaro Safaris diminish in late afternoon, sometimes as early as 3:30 p.m. but more commonly somewhat later.

If you want to take photos, keep in mind that the vehicle isn't guaranteed to stop at any location, although the drivers try their best to do so when big animals are sighted. Be prepared to snap at any time. As for the ride, it's not that rough. Finally, the only thing that a young child might find scary is crossing an "old bridge" that seems to collapse under your truck.

Pangani Forest Exploration Trail ★★★★

APPEAL BY AGE   PRESCHOOL ★★★★   GRADE SCHOOL ★★★★   TEENS ★★★★
YOUNG ADULTS ★★★★½   OVER 30 ★★★★   SENIORS ★★★★½

What it is Walk-through zoological exhibit. **Scope and scale** Major attraction. **When to go** Anytime. **Authors' rating** ★★★★. **Duration of tour** About 20–25 minutes.

DESCRIPTION AND COMMENTS As the trail winds between the domain of two troops of lowland gorillas, it's hard to see what, if anything, separates you from the primates. Also on the trail is a hippo pool with an underwater viewing area, plus a naked-mole-rat exhibit. A highlight of the trail is an exotic-bird aviary so craftily designed that you can barely tell you're in an enclosure.

TOURING TIPS The Pangani Forest Exploration Trail is lush, beautiful, and jammed to the gills with people much of the time. Guests exiting Kilimanjaro Safaris can choose between returning to Harambe or walking the Pangani Forest Exploration Trail. Many opt for the trail. Thus, when the Safaris are operating at full tilt, it spews hundreds of guests every couple of minutes onto the Exploration Trail. The one-way trail in turn becomes so clogged that nobody can move or see much of anything. After a minute or two, however, you catch the feel of the mob moving forward in small lurches. From then on you shift, elbow, grunt, and wriggle your way along, every so often coming to an animal exhibit. Here you endeavor to work your way close to the rail but are opposed by people trapped against the rail who are trying to rejoin the surging crowd. The animals, as well as their natural-habitat enclosures, are pretty nifty if you can fight your way close enough to see them.

Clearly this attraction is either badly designed, misplaced, or both. Your only real chance for enjoying it is to walk through before 10 a.m.—that is, before the Safaris hit full stride—or after 2:30 p.m.

Another strategy, especially if you're more into the wildlife than the thrill rides, is to schedule a FastPass+ reservation for the Safaris 60–90 minutes after the park opens. That's long enough for an uncrowded, leisurely tour of the Pangani Forest Exploration Trail and a quick snack before you go on safari.

RAFIKI'S PLANET WATCH

THIS AREA ISN'T REALLY a "land" and not really an attraction either. Our best guess is that Disney uses the name as an umbrella for Conservation Station, the petting zoo, and the environmental exhibits accessible from Harambe via the Wildlife Express Train. Presumably, Disney hopes that invoking Rafiki (a beloved character from *The Lion King*) will stimulate guests to make the effort to check out things in this far-flung outpost of the park.

DISNEY DISH WITH JIM HILL

PLANET WATCH DUE FOR A TOON-UP If Disney's *Zootopia* (2016)—an animated comedy-mystery about a metropolis populated exclusively by animals—proves to be a hit, the Imagineers plan to give Rafiki's Planet Watch an extreme makeover. Rafiki would get the boot in favor of ritzy *Zootopia*-themed digs for the animals here, with names such as Savannah Square and Tundratown.

Conservation Station and Affection Section ★★★½

APPEAL BY AGE	PRESCHOOL ★★★½	GRADE SCHOOL ★★★★	TEENS ★★★
YOUNG ADULTS ★★★½	OVER 30 ★★★½		SENIORS ★★★★

What it is Behind-the-scenes educational exhibit and petting zoo. **Scope and scale** Minor attraction. **When to go** Anytime. **Special comments** Opens 30 minutes after the rest of the park. **Authors' rating** Not bad; ★★★½. **Probable waiting time** None.

DESCRIPTION AND COMMENTS Conservation Station is Animal Kingdom's veterinary and conservation headquarters. On the perimeter of the African section of the park, Conservation Station is, strictly speaking, a backstage working facility. Here guests can meet wildlife experts, observe some of the Station's ongoing projects, and learn about the behind-the-scenes operations of the park. The Station includes a rehabilitation area for injured animals and a nursery for recently born (or hatched) critters. Vets and other experts are on hand to answer questions.

While there are several permanent exhibits, including Affection Section (an animal-petting area), what you see at Conservation Station will largely depend on what's going on when you arrive. On most days when we've visited, there isn't enough happening to justify waiting in line twice (coming and going) for the train.

Most of our readers tell us that Conservation Station isn't worth the hassle. A Tinley Park, Illinois, mom writes:

Skip Conservation Station. Between the train ride to get to it and being there, we wasted a precious 1½ hours!

A Denver family had a better experience:

We really enjoyed Conservation Station. We saw a 13-foot python eating a rat!

And a reader from Kent in the United Kingdom was amused by both the goings-on and the other guests:

The most memorable part of Animal Kingdom for me was watching a veterinary surgeon and his team at Conservation Station perform an operation on a rat snake that had inadvertently swallowed a golf ball, presumably believing it to be an egg! This operation caused at least one onlooker to pass out.

You can access Conservation Station by taking the Wildlife Express Train directly from Harambe. To return to the center of the park, continue the loop from Conservation Station back to Harambe.

TOURING TIPS To enjoy Conservation Station, you have to invest a little effort and be inquisitive. Because it's so removed from the rest of the park, you'll never bump into it unless you take the train.

Habitat Habit!

DESCRIPTION AND COMMENTS On the pedestrian path between the train station and Conservation Station, Habitat Habit! consists of a tiny collection of signs about wildlife and a few animals. Park maps call it an attraction, which we find absurd.

Wildlife Express Train ★★

APPEAL BY AGE	PRESCHOOL ★★★★	GRADE SCHOOL ★★★½	TEENS ★★★½
YOUNG ADULTS ★★★	OVER 30 ★★★½		SENIORS ★★★½

What it is Scenic railroad ride to Rafiki's Planet Watch and Conservation Station. **Scope and scale** Minor attraction. **When to go** Anytime. **Special comments** Opens 30 minutes after the rest of the park. **Authors' rating** Ho-hum; ★★. **Duration of ride** About 5–7 minutes one-way. **Average wait in line per 100 people ahead of you** 9 minutes. **Loading speed** Moderate.

DESCRIPTION AND COMMENTS This ride snakes behind the African wildlife reserve as it makes its loop connecting Harambe to Rafiki's Planet Watch and Conservation Station. En route, you see the nighttime enclosures for the animals that populate Kilimanjaro Safaris. Similarly, returning to Harambe, you see the backstage areas of Asia. Regardless of which direction you're heading, the sights aren't especially stimulating.

TOURING TIPS Most guests embark for Conservation Station after experiencing Kilimanjaro Safaris and the Pangani Forest Exploration Trail. Thus, the train begins to get crowded between 10 and 11 a.m.

❙❙ ASIA

CROSSING THE ASIA BRIDGE from Discovery Island, you enter Asia through the village of **Anandapur,** a veritable collage of Asian themes inspired by the architecture and ruins of India, Thailand, Indonesia, and Nepal. Situated near the bank of the Discovery River and surrounded by lush vegetation, Anandapur provides access to a gibbon exhibit and Asia's two feature attractions: the **Kali River Rapids** whitewater raft ride and **Expedition Everest.** Also in Asia is *Flights of Wonder,* a bird show.

Expedition Everest—yep, another mountain, and at 200 feet, the tallest in Florida—is a super-headliner roller coaster. You board an old mountain railway destined for the foot of Mount Everest and end up racing both forward and backward through caverns and frigid canyons en route to paying a social call on the Abominable Snowman. Expedition Everest is billed as a "family thrill ride," which means simply that it's more like Big Thunder Mountain Railroad than Rock 'n' Roller Coaster.

Debuting in 2016, the nighttime *Rivers of Light* show (see page 593) will combine music, water screens, video projections, and more on the Discovery River, with sections around Asia and DinoLand U.S.A.

Expedition Everest *(FastPass+)* ★★★★½

APPEAL BY AGE PRESCHOOL ★★★½ GRADE SCHOOL ★★★★½ TEENS ★★★★★
YOUNG ADULTS ★★★★★ OVER 30 ★★★★★ SENIORS ★★★★

What it is High-speed outdoor roller coaster through Nepalese mountain village. **Scope and scale** Super-headliner. **When to go** Before 9:30 a.m. or after 3 p.m., or use FastPass+. **Special comments** 44″ minimum height requirement. Switching-off option provided (see page 412). **Authors' rating** Contains some of the park's most stunning visual elements; not to be missed; ★★★★½. **Duration of ride** 3½ minutes. **Average wait in line per 100 people ahead of you** Just under 4 minutes; assumes 2 tracks operating. **Loading speed** Moderate–fast.

DESCRIPTION AND COMMENTS The first true roller coaster in Animal Kingdom, Expedition Everest earned the park's longest waits in line from the moment it opened—and for good reason. Your journey begins in an elaborate waiting area modeled after a Nepalese village; then you board an old train headed for the top of Mount Everest. Throughout the waiting area are posted notes from previous expeditions, some with cryptic observations regarding a mysterious creature said to guard the mountain. These ominous signs are ignored (as if you have a choice!), resulting in a high-speed encounter with the Abominable Snowman himself.

The ride consists of tight turns (some while traveling backward), hills, and dips, but no loops or inversions. From your departure at the loading station through your first high-speed descent, you'll see some of the most spectacular panoramas available in Walt Disney World. On a clear day, you can see the buildings of Coronado Springs Resort, Epcot's Spaceship Earth, and possibly downtown Orlando. But look quickly, because you'll immediately be propelled, projectile-like, through the inner and outer reaches of the mountain. The final drop and last few turns are among the best coaster effects Disney has ever designed.

A few minor criticisms: At a couple of points, your vehicle stops while the ride's track is reconfigured, affecting the attraction's continuity. And while the Audio-Animatronic Yeti is undoubtedly impressive, he breaks down more than a 30-year-old Fiat. Most days Disney just simulates the Yeti moving by flashing a strobe light on his motionless body. But don't let these small shortcomings stop you from riding.

The coaster reaches a top speed of around 50 mph, just about twice that of Space Mountain, so expect to see the usual warnings for health and safety. The first few seats of these vehicles offer the best front-seat experience of any Disney coaster, indoor or out. If at all possible, ask to sit up front. Also, look for the animal poop on display in the FastPass+ return line—a deliberate attempt at verisimilitude, or did Disney run out of money for ride props and use whatever they could find? You decide.

As you might expect of a super-headliner attraction, Expedition Everest is the subject of much reader mail. A Seattle family rated Expedition Everest four thumbs up:

Expedition Everest is tremendous. It has enough surprises and runaway speed to make it one of the more enjoyable thrill rides in the whole Orlando area.

A Macon, Georgia, teen recruited the aged:

Expedition Everest was so smooooth! I went right out and brought my granny back to ride it. She didn't throw up or anything!

Beating the morning crowds to Expedition Everest is also a hot topic. From a Yonkers, New York, man:

At opening, we went toward DinoLand U.S.A. and followed the path around the lake to Everest. We arrived about 90 seconds ahead of the crowd being walked in and were the first to ride. Upon exiting, we noticed the line was already enormous; to our delight, the wait at the other major rides was negligible.

A Brookfield, Connecticut, reader had great luck with the singles line:

The single-rider line at Expedition Everest is amazing! I rode seven times in a row. I think my longest wait was 3–5 minutes, but often I just walked on!

TOURING TIPS Ride Everest as soon as the park instead of using FastPass+ This way you can save your reservations for other attractions or another Everest ride later. In the latter case, try riding during the last hour the park is open, or use the single-rider line.

Flights of Wonder ★★★★

APPEAL BY AGE	PRESCHOOL ★★★★	GRADE SCHOOL ★★★★½	TEENS ★★★★
YOUNG ADULTS ★★★★½		OVER 30 ★★★★½	SENIORS ★★★★½

What it is Stadium show about birds. **Scope and scale** Major attraction. **When to go** Anytime. **Special comments** Performance times listed in handout park map or *Times Guide*. **Authors' rating** Unique; ★★★★. **Duration of presentation** 30 minutes. **Preshow entertainment** None. **When to arrive** 20–30 minutes before showtime.

DESCRIPTION AND COMMENTS *Flights of Wonder* is well paced and showcases a surprising number of bird species. The focus is on the natural talents and characteristics of the various species, so don't expect to see parrots riding bicycles—the birds' natural behaviors far surpass any tricks learned from humans. A Brattleboro, Vermont, reader found *Flights of Wonder* especially compelling, writing:

The ornithologist guide is not only a wealth of information but a talented, comedic entertainer. The birds are thrilling, and we especially appreciated the fact that their antics were not the results of training against the grain but actual survival techniques the birds use in the wild.

Flights of Wonder exceeded the expectations of a Colorado Springs family with two elementary-school-age kids:

A coworker with kids the same age as ours said her kids loved Flights of Wonder. *Midway through the show I stopped taking pictures of the birds and began taking pictures of the expressions of amazement and joy on the faces of my kids and husband.*

TOURING TIPS *Flights of Wonder* plays at the stadium near the Asia Bridge on the walkway into Asia. Though the stadium is covered, it's not air-conditioned; thus, early-morning and late-afternoon performances are more comfortable. To play it safe, get to the stadium about 10–15 minutes before showtime.

Kali River Rapids *(FastPass+)* ★★★½

APPEAL BY AGE	PRESCHOOL ★★★★	GRADE SCHOOL ★★★★½	TEENS ★★★★
YOUNG ADULTS ★★★★½		OVER 30 ★★★★½	SENIORS ★★★★½

What it is Whitewater raft ride. **Scope and scale** Headliner. **When to go** First or last hour the park is open, or use FastPass+. **Special comments** You're guaranteed to get wet. Opens 30 minutes after the rest of the park. 38″ minimum height requirement. Switching-off option provided (see page 412). **Authors' rating** Short but scenic; ★★★½. **Duration of ride** About 5 minutes. **Average wait in line per 100 people ahead of you** 5 minutes. **Loading speed** Moderate.

DESCRIPTION AND COMMENTS   Whitewater raft rides have been a hot-weather favorite of theme park patrons for more than 20 years. The ride itself consists of an unguided trip down an artificial river in a circular rubber raft with a top-mounted platform seating 12 people. The raft essentially floats free in the current and is washed downstream through rapids and waves. Because the river is fairly wide, with numerous currents, eddies, and obstacles, there's no telling exactly where the raft will drift. Thus, each trip is different and exciting.

What distinguishes Kali River Rapids from other theme park raft rides is Disney's trademark attention to visual detail. Where many raft rides essentially plunge down a concrete ditch, Kali River Rapids flows through a dense rainforest and past waterfalls, temple ruins, and bamboo thickets, emerging into a cleared area where greedy loggers have ravaged the forest, and finally drifting back under the tropical canopy as the river cycles back to Anandapur. Along the way, your raft runs a gauntlet of raging cataracts, logjams, and other dangers.

The queuing area, which winds through an ancient Southeast Asian temple, is one of the most striking and visually interesting settings of any Disney attraction. And though the sights on the raft trip itself are also first-class, the attraction is marginal in two important respects. First, it's only about 3½ minutes on the water, and second, well . . . it's a weenie ride. Sure, you get wet, but otherwise the drops and rapids aren't all that exciting, as this Kansas family points out:

It was boiling hot, so we were happy about the prospect of being drenched. At the end, we all looked at each other and said, "Is that IT?" We couldn't believe we'd stood in line, sweating half to death, for 75 minutes just for that.

How wet do you get? A Plymouth, Michigan, reader has the answer:

Rather than just getting a little wet like on Splash Mountain, you get soaked— not the fun kind of wet. Poncho sales were brisk the day we were there.

TOURING TIPS   Kali River Rapids is hugely popular on hot summer days. Ride during the first or last hour the park is open or use FastPass+. Again, you'll probably get drenched—we recommend wearing shorts to the park and bringing along a jumbo trash bag or can liner, as well as a smaller plastic bag. Before boarding the raft, take off your socks and punch a hole in your jumbo bag for your head. Though you can also cut holes for your arms, you'll probably stay drier with your arms inside the bag. Use the smaller plastic bag to wrap around your shoes. If you're worried about mussing your 'do, bring a third bag for your head.

A Shaker Heights, Ohio, family who donned our *couture de garbage* discovered that staying dry on Kali River Rapids is not without its social costs:

Cast members and the other people in our raft looked at us like we'd just beamed down from Mars. (One cast member asked whether we needed wet suits and snorkels.) Plus, we didn't cut arm holes in our trash bags because we thought we'd stay drier that way—problem was, once we sat down we couldn't fasten our seat belts. After a lot of wiggling and adjusting and helping each other, we finally got belted in, and off we went, looking like sacks of fertilizer with little heads poking out. Very embarrassing, but we stayed nice and dry.

A family from Humble, Texas, who rode early in the morning on a cool day, shares this:

Our plan hit a definite wall upon experiencing Kali River Rapids as number two on the schedule. We didn't read about the precautions for this ride in your book until after we rode. The 6-year-old and Mom were COMPLETELY drenched—so much so that we had to leave the park and go back to our room at Port Orleans to change clothes. Since the temperature was around 60 degrees that morning, we were pretty miserable by the time we got back to our room. Needless to say, our schedule was shot by then.

Using FastPass+ to ride later in the day would have been a better option in this case.

Kali River Rapids offers free 2-hour locker rental (to the left of the attraction entrance, near the restrooms). Store a change of clothes in these to keep dry. Alternatively, wear as little as the law and Disney allow. If you're wearing closed shoes, try to prop your feet up above the bottom of the raft—slogging around in wet shoes and socks is a surefire recipe for blisters.

Maharajah Jungle Trek ★★★★

APPEAL BY AGE	PRESCHOOL ★★★★	GRADE SCHOOL ★★★★	TEENS ★★★★
YOUNG ADULTS ★★★★½	OVER 30 ★★★★		SENIORS ★★★★½

What it is Walk-through zoological exhibit. **Scope and scale** Headliner. **When to go** Anytime. **Special comments** Opens 30 minutes after the rest of the park. **Authors' rating** A standard-setter for natural habitat design; ★★★★. **Duration of tour** About 20–30 minutes.

DESCRIPTION AND COMMENTS The Maharajah Jungle Trek is a zoological nature walk similar to the Pangani Forest Exploration Trail, but with an Asian setting and Asian animals. You start with Komodo dragons and then work up to Malayan flying foxes. Next is a cave with fruit bats. Ruins of the maharaja's palace provide the setting for Bengal tigers. From the top of a parapet in the palace you can view a herd of blackbuck antelope and Asian deer. The trek concludes with an aviary.

Labyrinthine, overgrown, and elaborately detailed, the temple ruin would be a compelling attraction even without the animals. Throw in a few bats, bucks, and Bengals and you're in for a treat. Most readers, such as this Washington, D.C., couple, agree:

The Maharajah Jungle Trek was absolutely amazing. We were able to see all the animals, which were awake by that time (9:30 a.m.), including the elusive tigers. The part of the trek with the birds was fabulous. If you looked, you could spot hundreds of birds, some of which were eating on the ground a mere 3 feet away from us. Take your time walking through, since most of the animals are not obvious to the breezing eye and you must look for them.

TOURING TIPS The Jungle Trek doesn't get as jammed up as the Pangani Forest Exploration Trail and is a good choice for midday touring when most other attractions are crowded. The downside, of course, is that the exhibit showcases tigers, bats, and other creatures that might not be as active in the heat of the day as mad dogs and Englishmen.

Rivers of Light (opens 2016)

What it is Nighttime spectacular. **Scope and scale** Major attraction. **When to go** Check your *Times Guide* for showtimes.

DESCRIPTION AND COMMENTS Animal Kingdom has never had a nighttime event along the lines of the Magic Kingdom's *Wishes* or DHS's *Fantasmic!* One reason is that fireworks would startle the animals; another was that up to now there simply weren't enough attractions to keep the park open for 12–14 hours per day. In preparation for the 2017 opening of Pandora: The

DISNEY DISH WITH JIM HILL

ROCKIN' OUT THE RHINOS When *Rivers of Light* opens, it will dazzle Animal Kingdom visitors with its mix of music, live performers, and elaborate pageantry. What it *won't* do, or so Disney hopes, is frighten the animals in the park: For months before the show begins, the show's soundtrack will be played in the backstage barns and corrals where the animals bed down for the night. The idea is to familiarize the animals with the show's sounds, effects, and even audience noise.

Land of Avatar, though, Animal Kingdom is adding both the *Rivers of Light* nighttime spectacular and, rumor has it, a nighttime safari (see page 582).

The show will be staged in the middle of the Discovery River. Disney hasn't released many details about the show's plot, but we do know it'll feature sprayed water screens onto which animal- and nature-related films will be projected. Disney also promises "floating lanterns" and live music. We think there'll also be dramatic lighting effects, but no fireworks.

TOURING TIPS Judging from the construction going on around the Discovery River, we expect there to be two seating areas, at least one of them dedicated to FastPass+. One seating area will be in Asia, on the riverfront next to Expedition Everest; the second will be in DinoLand U.S.A.

DINOLAND U.S.A.

THIS MOST TYPICALLY DISNEY of Animal Kingdom's lands is a cross between an anthropological dig and a quirky roadside attraction. Accessible via the bridge from Discovery Island, DinoLand U.S.A. is home to a children's play area, a nature trail, a 1,500-seat amphitheater, and **Dinosaur**, one of Animal Kingdom's three thrill rides.

Also in DinoLand are a couple of natural-history exhibits, including **Dino-Sue**, an exact replica of the largest, most complete *Tyrannosaurus rex* discovered to date. Named after fossil hunter Sue Hendrickson, the replica (like the original) is 40 feet long and 13 feet tall. It doesn't dance, sing, or whistle, but it will get your attention nonetheless.

The Boneyard ★★★

APPEAL BY AGE	PRESCHOOL ★★★★½	GRADE SCHOOL ★★★★½	TEENS ★★★★
YOUNG ADULTS ★★★½		OVER 30 ★★★	SENIORS ★★★

What it is Elaborate playground. **Scope and scale** Diversion. **When to go** Anytime. **Special comments** Opens 30 minutes after the rest of the park. **Authors' rating** Stimulating fun for children; ★★★. **Duration of visit** Varies. **Probable waiting time** None.

DESCRIPTION AND COMMENTS Arranged in the form of a rambling open-air dig site, this elaborate playground is particularly appealing to kids age 12 and younger, but visually appealing to all ages. Playground equipment consists of the skeletons of *Triceratops, Tyrannosaurus rex, Brachiosaurus,* and the like, on which children can swing, slide, and climb. There are also sandpits where little ones can scrounge for bones and fossils.

TOURING TIPS Not the most pristine of Disney attractions, but certainly one where younger children will want to spend some time. And aside from being dirty, or at least sandy, The Boneyard gets mighty hot in the Florida sun. Keep your kids well hydrated, and drag them into the shade from time to time. Try to save the playground until after you've experienced the main attractions. Because The Boneyard is so close to the center of the park, it's easy to drop in whenever your kids get antsy. While the little ones clamber around on giant femurs and ribs, you can sip a tall cool one in the shade (still keeping an eye on them, of course).

As a Michigan family attests, kids love The Boneyard:

The highlight for our kids was The Boneyard, especially the dig site. They just kept digging and digging to uncover the bones of the woolly mammoth.

Be aware, however, that The Boneyard rambles over about a half-acre and is multistoried, making it' easy to lose sight of a small child in the playground. Fortunately, there's only one entrance and exit. A mother of two from Stillwater, Minnesota, found the playground too large for her liking:

If you're a parent who likes to have your eyes on your kids at all times, you won't like The Boneyard. Kids climb to the top of the slides, then you can't see them and you don't know what chute they'll be exiting from.

Dinosaur *(FastPass+)*   ★★★★

APPEAL BY AGE	PRESCHOOL ★★★	GRADE SCHOOL ★★★★	TEENS ★★★★½
YOUNG ADULTS ★★★★		OVER 30 ★★★★	SENIORS ★★★★

What it is Motion-simulator dark ride. **Scope and scale** Super-headliner. **When to go** Before 10:30 a.m., after 4:30 p.m., or use FastPass+. **Special comments** 40" minimum height requirement. Switching-off option provided (see page 412). **Authors' rating** Not to be missed; ★★★★. **Duration of ride** 3½ minutes. **Average wait in line per 100 people ahead of you** 3 minutes; assumes full-capacity operation with 18-second dispatch interval. **Loading speed** Fast.

DESCRIPTION AND COMMENTS Dinosaur is a combination track ride and motion simulator. In addition to moving along a cleverly hidden track, the ride vehicle also bucks and pitches (the simulator part) in sync with the visuals and special effects.

The plot has you traveling back in time on a mission of rescue and conservation. Your objective: to haul back a living dinosaur before the species becomes extinct. Whoever is operating the clock, however, cuts it a little close, and you arrive on the prehistoric scene just as a giant asteroid is hurtling toward Earth. General mayhem ensues as you evade carnivorous predators, catch Barney, and get the heck out of Dodge before the asteroid hits.

Dinosaur serves up nonstop action from beginning to end, with brilliant visual effects. Elaborate even by Disney standards, its tense, frenetic ride is embellished by the entire Imagineering arsenal of high-tech gimmickry.

To its credit, Disney is unafraid to keep Dinosaur a dark, fast ride. A mother from Kansasville, Wisconsin, liked it a lot:

Dinosaur is the best ride at WDW. Our group of 10, ranging in age from 65 (grandma) to 8 (grandson), immediately—and unanimously!—got back in line immediately after finishing.

That said, the menacing dinosaurs, along with the overall intensity of the experience, make Dinosaur a no-go for younger kids, as this Michigan family discovered:

Our 7-year-old son withstood every ride Disney threw at him, from Space Mountain to Tower of Terror. Dinosaur, however, did him in. By the end, he was riding with his head down, scared to look around.

TOURING TIPS Disney situated Dinosaur in such a remote corner of the park that guests have to poke around to find it. This, in conjunction with the overwhelming popularity of Kilimanjaro Safaris and Expedition Everest, makes Dinosaur the easiest super-headliner attraction at Disney World to get on. Even so, try to ride early in the day, after Expedition Everest.

Primeval Whirl *(FastPass+)* ★★★

APPEAL BY AGE   PRESCHOOL ★★★½   GRADE SCHOOL ★★★★   TEENS ★★★★ YOUNG   ADULTS   ★★★½   OVER 30   ★★★½   SENIORS   ★★★

What it is Small coaster. **Scope and scale** Minor attraction. **When to go** First or last hour the park is open or use FastPass+. **Special comments** 48″ minimum height requirement. Switching-off option provided (see page 412). **Authors' rating** "Wild mouse" on steroids; ★★★. **Duration of ride** Almost 2½ minutes. **Average wait in line per 100 people ahead of you** 4½ minutes. **Loading speed** Slow.

DESCRIPTION AND COMMENTS A small coaster with short drops and curves, Primeval Whirl runs through the jaws of a dinosaur, among other things. What makes this coaster different is that the cars also spin. You can't control the spinning—it starts and stops according to how the ride is programmed. Sometimes the spin is braked to a jarring halt after half a revolution, and sometimes it's allowed to make one or two complete turns. The complete spins are fun, but the screeching-stop half-spins are almost painful. If you subtract the time it takes to ratchet up the first hill, the actual ride time is about 90 seconds.

A Queens, New York, reader thinks Primeval Whirl is more evil than prime:

Primeval Whirl is a terrible ride on so many levels. My daughter nicknamed it "Primeval Hurl."

TOURING TIPS As with Space Mountain, Primeval Whirl is duplicated side-by-side, but with only one queue. When it runs smoothly, about 700 people per side can whirl in an hour—a goodly number for this type of attraction, but not enough to preclude long waits on busy-to-moderate days. If you want to ride, try to get on before 10 a.m.

Theater in the Wild / *Finding Nemo—The Musical* *(FastPass+)* ★★★★

APPEAL BY AGE   PRESCHOOL ★★★★½   GRADE SCHOOL ★★★★½   TEENS ★★★★ YOUNG   ADULTS   ★★★★½   OVER 30   ★★★★½   SENIORS   ★★★★½

What it is Enclosed venue for live stage shows. **Scope and scale** Major attraction. **When to go** Anytime. **Special comments** Performance times are listed in the handout park map or *Times Guide*. **Authors' rating** Not to be missed; ★★★★. **Duration of presentation** About 35 minutes. **When to arrive** 30 minutes before showtime.

DESCRIPTION AND COMMENTS *Finding Nemo—The Musical* is arguably the most elaborate live show in any Disney World theme park. Incorporating dancing, special effects, and sophisticated digital backdrops of the undersea world, it features on-stage human performers retelling Nemo's story with colorful, larger-than-life puppets. To be fair, "puppets" doesn't adequately convey the size or detail of these props, many of which are as big as a car and require two people to manipulate.

A few scenes, such as one in which Nemo's mom is eaten, may be too intense for some very small children. Some of the midshow musical numbers slow the pace, so the main concern for parents is whether the kids can sit still for an entire show. With that in mind, we advise parents to catch an afternoon performance—around 3 p.m. would be great—after seeing most of the rest of Animal Kingdom. If the kids get restless, you can either leave the show and catch the afternoon parade, or end your day at the park.

New Jersey drama critics have their own way with words, as this family of five demonstrates.

The Finding Nemo *musical is da bomb! The musical was amazing! It's a flaw-less package of puppetry, effects, music, and lots of Disney magic!*

TOURING TIPS To get a seat, show up 20–25 minutes in advance for morning and late-afternoon shows, and 30–35 minutes in advance for shows scheduled between noon and 4:30 p.m. Access to the theater is via a relatively narrow pedestrian path—if you arrive as the previous show is letting out, you'll feel like a salmon swimming upstream. *Finding Nemo* is rarely a good use of FastPass+.

Rivers of Light (opens 2016)   See description on page 593.

TriceraTop Spin   ★★

APPEAL BY AGE   PRESCHOOL ★★★★½   GRADE SCHOOL ★★★★   TEENS ★★★
YOUNG ADULTS ★★★   OVER 30 ★★★   SENIORS ★★★½

What it is Hub-and-spoke midway ride. **Scope and scale** Minor attraction. **When to go** Before noon or after 3 p.m. **Authors' rating** Dumbo's prehistoric forebear; ★★. **Duration of ride** 1½ minutes. **Average wait in line per 100 people ahead of you** 10 minutes. **Loading speed** Slow.

DESCRIPTION AND COMMENTS Another Dumbo-like ride for young children. Here you spin around a central hub until a dinosaur pops out of the top of the hub. You would think Disney could come up with something a little more creative.

TOURING TIPS Come back later if the wait exceeds 20 minutes.

LIVE ENTERTAINMENT
in DISNEY'S ANIMAL KINGDOM

WDW LIVE-ENTERTAINMENT GURU Steve Soares usually posts the Animal Kingdom performance schedule about a week in advance at **wdwent.com.**

ANIMAL ENCOUNTERS Throughout the day, Disney staff conduct impromptu short lectures on specific animals at the park. Look for a cast member in safari garb holding a bird, reptile, or small mammal.

A small interactive event titled *Winged Encounters—The Kingdom Takes Flight,* featuring macaws and their handlers, takes place on Discovery Island in front of The Tree of Life. Guests can talk to the animal's trainers and see the birds fly around the middle of the park. The concept is similar to *Flights of Wonder* (see page 591) on a much smaller scale. Check the *Times Guide* for showtimes and the exact location.

STREET PERFORMERS Can be found most of the time at Harambe in Africa and at Anandapur in Asia. Far and away the most intriguing of these performers is a stilt walker named **DiVine** (★★★★). Bedecked in foliage and luxuriant vines, she blends so completely with Animal Kingdom's dense flora that you don't notice her until she moves. We've seen guests standing less than a foot away gasp in amazement as DiVine brushes them with a leafy tendril. Usually found on the path between

Asia and Africa, DiVine is a must-see. Video of her is available at **YouTube** (search for "DiVine Disney's Animal Kingdom").

TRAFFIC PATTERNS *in* DISNEY'S ANIMAL KINGDOM

THE FOUR CROWD MAGNETS ARE **Kilimanjaro Safaris** in Africa, **Dinosaur** in DinoLand U.S.A., and **Kali River Rapids** and **Expedition Everest** in Asia. Because the park hosts large crowds for relatively few attractions, expect those attractions to be extremely busy, and for Expedition Everest and Kilimanjaro Safaris to be mobbed.

Most guests arrive in the morning, with a sizable number on hand before opening and a larger wave arriving before 10 a.m. Guests continue to stream in through the late morning and into the early afternoon, with crowds peaking at around 2 p.m. From about 2:30 p.m. on, departing guests outnumber arriving guests, as those who arrived early complete their tour and leave. Crowds thin appreciably by late afternoon and continue to decline into the early evening, although when *Rivers of Light* and the nighttime version of Kilimanjaro Safaris open in 2016, we expect crowds to pick up at those times. There should still be a midafternoon lull, however.

Because the number of attractions and shows is limited, most guests can complete a fairly comprehensive tour in two-thirds of a day if they arrive either at park opening or at about 3 p.m. (if the park stays open until 7 or 8 p.m.), when the early birds are heading for the exits.

unofficial **TIP**
If you visit during late afternoon, you'll almost certainly have to return another afternoon to finish seeing everything.

How guests tour Animal Kingdom depends on their prior knowledge of the park and its attractions. Newbies make their way to Discovery Island and depend on their park map to decide what to do next. Animal Kingdom vets heads straight for Kilimanjaro Safaris and Expedition Everest, with Kali River Rapids another early-morning favorite.

With so many guests heading first thing for either the Safaris or Everest, DinoLand and Discovery Island are lightly trafficked backwaters until late morning. As the day wears on, the masses who have experienced these two attractions turn their attention to other rides and shows, and the crowds become more equally distributed. Less-popular attractions don't experience high traffic until 11:30 a.m.

Our mobile app, **Lines** (**touringplans.com/lines**), gives you current wait times and future estimates in half-hour increments for today and tomorrow. A quick glance shows how traffic patterns affect wait times throughout the day.

DISNEY'S ANIMAL KINGDOM TOURING PLAN

TOURING ANIMAL KINGDOM isn't as complicated as touring the other parks because it has fewer attractions. Also, most rides, shows, and exhibits are oriented to the entire family, eliminating differences of opinion regarding how to spend the day.

Because Animal Kingdom has fewer attractions than the other parks, you can expect crowds to be more concentrated. If a line seems unusually long, ask a cast member what the estimated wait is. Or try the same attraction again after 3 p.m., while a show is in progress at the Theater in the Wild in DinoLand U.S.A., or while some special event is going on.

We've listed the estimated FastPass+ return times for which you should try to make reservations. (The touring plan should work with anything close to the times shown.) Because Disney limits how many FastPass+ reservations you can get, we've listed in the plans the attractions most likely to need FastPass+, too. Check **touringplans.com** for the latest information.

> *unofficial* **TIP**
> Until Pandora: The Land of Avatar opens in 2017, the limited number of attractions in Animal Kingdom can work to your advantage.

"Not a Touring Plan" Touring Plans

For the type-B reader, these touring plans (see page 804) dispense with detailed step-by-step strategies for saving every last minute in line. For Animal Kingdom, these "not" touring plans include advice for adults and parents with one day in the park, for anyone with two days, and for anyone with an afternoon and a full day to tour.

BEFORE YOU GO

1. Call ☎ 407-824-4321 or check the day before you go to verify official opening time.
2. Make reservations at the Epcot full-service restaurant(s) of your choice 180 days before your visit.
3. Make FastPass+ reservations 60 or 30 days in advance.

DISNEY'S ANIMAL KINGDOM ONE-DAY TOURING PLAN *(page 817)*

THIS TOURING PLAN ASSUMES a willingness to experience all major rides and shows. If you have children under age 8, see the Small-Child Fright-Potential Chart on pages 404–407. When you're following the touring plan, simply skip any attraction you don't wish to experience.

Many readers have asked us whether fewer animals are visible from Kilimanjaro Safaris around lunchtime than at park opening, out of concern that the animals might be less active in the midday heat. Our research indicates that you'll probably see the same number of animals regardless of when you visit.

PART TWELVE

DISNEY'S HOLLYWOOD STUDIOS

DHS: *A* BRIEF HISTORY

THE THEME PARK ORIGINALLY KNOWN as Disney-MGM Studios was hatched from a corporate rivalry and a wild, twisted plot. At a time when Disney was weak and fighting off "greenmail"—hostile-takeover bids—Universal's parent company at the time, MCA, announced that it was going to build an Orlando clone of its wildly successful Universal Studios Hollywood theme park. Behind the scenes, MCA was courting the billionaire Bass brothers of Texas, hoping to secure their investment in the project. The Basses, however, defected to the Disney camp and were front and center when Michael Eisner suddenly announced that Disney, too, would build a movie theme park in Florida.

A construction race ensued, but Universal, in the middle of developing new attraction technologies, was no match for Disney, which could import proven concepts and attractions from its other parks. In the end, Disney-MGM Studios opened May 1, 1989, more than a year before Universal Studios Florida.

THE EARLY YEARS

ONCE UPON A TIME, the Studios' soundstages and facilities produced many television shows and films, both live-action and animated. The 2003 Disney film *Brother Bear* was largely drawn—by hand, yet!— at what used to be Disney Feature Animation Florida; cinema nerds will recognize the park's landscape in the background of Jim Varney's magnum opus, *Ernest Saves Christmas.* Television series filmed here spanned everything from a revival of the classic game show *Let's Make a Deal* to the syndicated Hulk Hogan fiasco *Thunder in Paradise.* There were also attractions adapted from popular TV shows, including *Who Wants to Be a Millionaire—Play It!* and *The American Idol Experience.*

The Studios also hosted attractions that educated guests about TV and film production, the best known being a tram ride through and walking tour of the park's back lot. Others included the *Monster Sound Show,* which used audience volunteers to show how sound effects were added to films, and *SuperStar Television,* which reenacted famous TV scenes using "green screen" technology and park guests as actors.

THE END OF THE MGM CONNECTION

SO WHAT HAPPENED to "Disney-MGM Studios"? Disney purchased Pixar Animation Studios after partnering with the company on a series of highly successful films, including *Toy Story; A Bug's Life; Monsters, Inc.; Finding Nemo;* and *The Incredibles.* The cost of continuing an association with MGM, coupled with Pixar's arguably greater popularity, probably influenced Disney's decision to rename the park in 2008. But rather than replace *MGM* with *Pixar,* Disney went with the generic *Hollywood.*

DHS TODAY

THE *STUDIOS* IN "Disney's Hollywood Studios" is of little significance. Movie and television production ceased here long ago, and only a handful of aging attractions remain that offer a peek behind the scenes. DHS is now simply an amusement park whose theme is movies and TV.

In a public acknowledgment of the above, Disney CEO Bob Iger announced in 2015 that the park will be renamed again in the near future. The new moniker hasn't been chosen yet, but expect something along the lines of "Disney's Hollywood Adventure."

HELP US, OBI-WAN KENOBI Disney management knows that the Studios' appeal has been damaged badly by years of creative neglect, not to mention the 800-pound gorilla that is Universal Orlando's Wizarding World of Harry Potter. While no specifics have been announced, Disney has made no secret of its intent to redevelop large swaths of the Studios to include "lands" dedicated to *Star Wars, Toy Story,* and *Cars;* however, these projects aren't scheduled to be completed until around 2019 or 2020.

The STUDIOS *in* PERSPECTIVE

IF YOU'VE GOT JUST two or three days to visit Disney World, skip the Studios. It's hard for us to recommend spending $80–$100 on a park that has so little to offer. To wit: Several major attractions, among them *The American Idol Experience,* The Magic of Disney Animation, and the Studio Backlot Tour, have closed without being replaced. (The closing of The Magic of Disney Animation was, in fact, announced the day this edition of the *Guide* went to the printer.) Others, such as the **Indiana Jones Epic Stunt Spectacular!** and **Rock 'n' Roller Coaster,** haven't been updated in years. Except for the fireworks that happen at park closing, the few attractions that we rate as not to be missed (see page 608) can be seen easily in as little as 4 hours—not enough to justify the cost of admission. Finally, DHS's new themed areas are still in the concept stages.

For now, **Universal Studios Florida** is the superior choice if you want to visit a theme park devoted to movies, TV, and music.

DHS *at a* GLANCE

HOW MUCH TIME TO ALLOCATE

WHEREAS IT'S IMPOSSIBLE to see all of Epcot or the Magic Kingdom in one day, DHS is doable: There's far less ground to cover by foot

Continued on page 604

Disney's Hollywood Studios

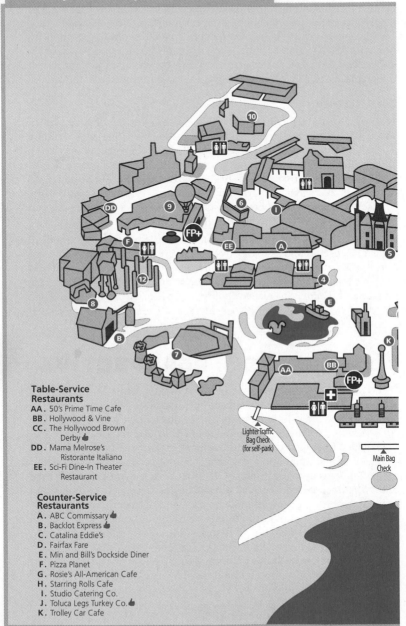

Table-Service Restaurants

AA. 50's Prime Time Cafe
BB. Hollywood & Vine
CC. The Hollywood Brown Derby 👍
DD. Mama Melrose's Ristorante Italiano
EE. Sci-Fi Dine-In Theater Restaurant

Counter-Service Restaurants

A. ABC Commissary 👍
B. Backlot Express 👍
C. Catalina Eddie's
D. Fairfax Fare
E. Min and Bill's Dockside Diner
F. Pizza Planet
G. Rosie's All-American Cafe
H. Starring Rolls Cafe
I. Studio Catering Co.
J. Toluca Legs Turkey Co. 👍
K. Trolley Car Cafe

Lighter Traffic
Bag Check
(for self-park)

Main Bag
Check

Attractions

1. *Beauty and the Beast—Live on Stage*/Theater of the Stars FP+
2. *Disney Junior—Live on Stage!* FP+
3. *Fantasmic!* ✓ Use FP+
4. *For the First Time in Forever: A Frozen Sing-Along Celebration* FP+
5. The Great Movie Ride ✓ Use FP+
6. Honey, I Shrunk the Kids Movie Set Adventure
7. *Indiana Jones Epic Stunt Spectacular!* FP+
8. *Jedi Training Academy*
9. *Jim Henson's Muppet-Vision 3-D* ✓ FP+
10. *Lights, Motors, Action! Extreme Stunt Show* FP+
11. Rock 'n' Roller Coaster ✓ Use FP+
12. Star Tours—The Adventures Continue ✓ Use FP+
13. Toy Story Midway Mania! ✓ Use FP+
14. The Twilight Zone Tower of Terror ✓ Use FP+
15. *Voyage of the Little Mermaid* FP+
16. *Walt Disney: One Man's Dream*

FP+ FastPass+ Kiosks

👫 Restrooms

✚ First Aid Center

👍 Recommended Dining

FP+ Attraction Offers FastPass+

Use FP+ FastPass+ Recommended

✓ Not to be Missed

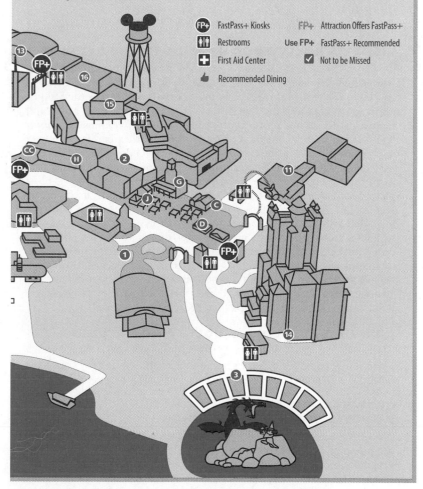

Continued from page 601

because its attractions are concentrated in an area about the size of Main Street, Tomorrowland, and Frontierland combined.

One fly in the ointment, however, is the park's perverse way of scheduling live shows. A West Chester, Pennsylvania, mom explains:

> *If I had it to do over, I'd skip the Studios. The shows were good, but we kept missing showtimes because either all the shows started at the same time or the walk between them was too long with little ones.*

Because DHS is small and many of its attractions have closed, it's more affected by large crowds. Our touring plan will help you stay a step ahead of the mob and minimize waiting in line. It'll also help with the show-schedule problem, but even when the park is crowded, you can see everything in well under a day.

DISNEY'S HOLLYWOOD STUDIOS IN THE EVENING

BECAUSE ALL OF DHS can be seen in as little as 8 hours, many guests who arrive early in the morning run out of things to do by 5 p.m. or so and leave. Their departure greatly thins crowds and makes the Studios ideal for evening touring. Lines for most attractions are bearable, and the park is cooler and more comfortable. The *Indiana Jones Epic Stunt Spectacular!* and productions at other outdoor theaters are infinitely more enjoyable during the evening than in the sweltering heat of the day.

DHS is the home of **Fantasmic!** (see page 609), the most dazzling nighttime-entertainment event in the Disney repertoire. Staged most nights (sometimes twice a night), weather permitting, in its own theater behind The Twilight Zone Tower of Terror, *Fantasmic!* is not to be missed. It's also a crowd magnet, owing to DHS guests sticking around or guests from other parks arriving after dinner to see the show. Although the crowds thin in the late afternoon, they build again as showtime approaches, making *Fantasmic!* a challenge to get into. Also adversely affected are **Rock 'n' Roller Coaster** and, to a lesser extent, **The Twilight Zone Tower of Terror,** both nearby. Crowd levels elsewhere remain generally light, except at **Toy Story Midway Mania!**

ARRIVING AT DISNEY'S HOLLYWOOD STUDIOS

DHS HAS ITS OWN PARKING LOT and is served by Disney transportation. If you drive, Disney's ubiquitous trams will convey you to the ticketing area and entrance gate. For driving directions, see page 443.

GETTING ORIENTED AT DISNEY'S HOLLYWOOD STUDIOS

ON YOUR LEFT AS YOU ENTER, **Guest Relations** serves as the park headquarters and information center, similar to City Hall in the Magic Kingdom and Guest Relations at Epcot and Disney's Animal Kingdom. Go there for a park map, a schedule of live performances (*Times Guide*), lost persons, Package Pick-Up, lost and found (on the right side of the entrance), baby-care facilities, and general information. To the right of the entrance are locker, stroller, and wheelchair rentals.

As at the Magic Kingdom, you enter the park and pass down a main street. In this case, it's the **Hollywood Boulevard** of the 1930s and '40s.

HOLLYWOOD STUDIOS Services

MOST PARK SERVICES are on Hollywood Boulevard, including:

Baby Care Center At Guest Relations; baby food and other necessities available at Oscar's Super Service

Banking Services ATM outside the park to the right of the turnstiles and on Streets of America near Pizza Planet restaurant

Camera Supplies At The Darkroom on the right side of Hollywood Boulevard as you enter the park, just past Oscar's Super Service

Cell Phone Charging Outlets in the Hollywood Brown Derby lobby, inside Backlot Express, and near the restrooms next to Toy Story Midway Mania!

First Aid Center At Guest Relations

Live Entertainment and Character Information Available free at Guest Relations and elsewhere in the park

Lost and Found At Package Pick-Up, to the right of the park entrance

Lost Persons Report at Guest Relations

Lockers To the right of the entrance, to the left of Oscar's Super Service

Wheelchair, ECV/ESV, and Stroller Rentals To the right of the entrance, at Oscar's Super Service

At the end of Hollywood Boulevard is a replica of the iconic **Grauman's Chinese Theatre.**

Though modest in size, the open-access areas of the Studios are confusingly arranged. As you face Grauman's Chinese, two themed areas— **Sunset Boulevard** and **Animation Courtyard**—branch off of Hollywood Boulevard to the right. Branching left off Hollywood Boulevard is **Echo Lake. Streets of America** wraps around the back of Echo Lake, while **Pixar Place**'s attractions are behind the Chinese Theatre and to the left of Animation Courtyard. Between Pixar Place and Animation Courtyard is **Mickey Avenue,** with its one minor attraction.

Still farther to the rear is an area comprising soundstages, technical facilities, wardrobe shops, offices, and sets. This area was closed to the public after the Studio Backlot Tour was discontinued in 2014.

FASTPASS+ ATTRACTIONS IN DISNEY'S HOLLYWOOD STUDIOS

LIKE EPCOT, DHS USES tiering (see page 93) to restrict the number of FastPass+ reservations you can have at its headliner attractions:

TIER A *(Choose one per day)*
- *Beauty and the Beast—Live on Stage*
- *Fantasmic!*
- Rock 'n' Roller Coaster
- The Great Movie Ride
- Toy Story Midway Mania!

TIER B *(Choose two per day)*
- *Disney Junior—Live on Stage!*
- *For the First Time in Forever: A Frozen Sing-Along Celebration*

- *Indiana Jones Epic Stunt Spectacular!*
- *Jim Henson's Muppet-Vision 3-D*
- *Lights, Motors, Action! Extreme Stunt Show*
- Star Tours—The Adventures Continue
- The Twilight Zone Tower of Terror
- *Voyage of the Little Mermaid*

ENTERTAINMENT & PARADES
- *The Comedy Warehouse Holiday Special* (seasonal)

DISNEY'S HOLLYWOOD STUDIOS
When Same-Day FP+ Runs Out, by Crowd Level

ATTRACTION	LOW CROWDS*	MODERATE CROWDS*	HIGH CROWDS*
Beauty and the Beast—Live on Stage	4-5 p.m.	4-5 p.m.	2-3 p.m.
Disney Junior—Live on Stage!	4-5 p.m.	3 p.m.	1-3 p.m.
Fantasmic!	3 p.m.	4-6 p.m.	6-8 p.m.
For the First Time in Forever: A Frozen Sing-Along Celebration	2-4 p.m.	1-3 p.m.	Noon
The Great Movie Ride	6-7 p.m.	6-7 p.m.	5-7 p.m.
Indiana Jones Epic Stunt Spectacular!	5 p.m.	5 p.m.	2-4 p.m.
Lights, Motors, Action! Extreme Stunt Show	4 p.m.	3-4 p.m.	1-2 p.m.
Voyage of the Little Mermaid	5-6 p.m.	2-4 p.m.	2-4 p.m.
Muppet-Vision 3-D	6-7 p.m.	7-8 p.m.	8-9 p.m.
Rock 'n' Roller Coaster	2-4 p.m.	Noon-1 p.m.	10 a.m.-noon
Star Tours	6 p.m.	2-5 p.m.	Noon-2 p.m.
Tower of Terror	2-4 p.m.	10 a.m.-noon	Noon
Toy Story Midway Mania!	Noon-1 p.m.	10 a.m.-noon	No day-of availability

* **LOW CROWDS** (Levels 1-3 on TouringPlans.com Crowd Calendar)

* **MODERATE CROWDS** (Levels 4-7 on TouringPlans.com Crowd Calendar)

* **HIGH CROWDS** (Levels 8-10 on TouringPlans.com Crowd Calendar)

These restrictions mean that having a good touring plan is essential to avoid long lines. The good news is that while FastPass+ is offered at more than a dozen attractions at Disney's Hollywood Studios, there are really only four that you need to be concerned with most of the year. Here's why:

Our print and online touring plans emphasize FastPass+ for **Toy Story Midway Mania!** Families with children too small to ride Rock 'n' Roller Coaster or Tower of Terror make a beeline to Toy Story Midway Mania! first thing in the morning, and lines grow quickly. Waits at Toy Story can reach 90 minutes or more on a busy day—in fact, the lines grow so fast that in about one-third of our touring plans, we recommend getting a FastPass+ reservation for 9–10 a.m., even when Toy Story is the first step in the plan. The two benefits to doing this are that (1) you'll shave off at least 10 minutes of waiting, and (2) you don't have to line up as early at park opening to join the mad rush to Toy Story.

Next, like Peter Pan's Flight in the Magic Kingdom, **Star Tours** isn't going to be anyone's first choice to visit. For teens and adults especially, the initial morning priorities will be Toy Story, Rock 'n' Roller Coaster, and Tower of Terror, possibly with The Great Movie Ride while they're in the area. This makes Star Tours a great choice for a mid- or late-morning FastPass+ reservation.

We really like how our touring plan software places **The Twilight Zone Tower of Terror** after lunch in many of our touring plans. This lets to check for day-of FastPass+ availability at *Fantasmic!* right after you ride the Tower of Terror.

Finally, our software thinks **The Great Movie Ride** is a good Fast-Pass+ choice for afternoon touring plans, especially if you can't get reservations for Toy Story or Rock 'n' Roller Coaster.

So why isn't **Rock 'n' Roller Coaster** among our four musts? Because it's in the same FastPass+ tier as Toy Story Midway Mania!, and you may choose only one of them. Because Toy Story almost always has the longer waits, it should be your FastPass+ choice. If you can get FastPass+ reservations for Toy Story, Star Tours—The Adventures Continue, and Tower of Terror, our touring plan software will usually make Rock 'n' Roller Coaster your first stop, where you'll find the shortest waits of the day.

We don't think *Fantasmic!* is a good choice for FastPass+ in most cases. For one thing, your reservation doesn't guarantee you a seat: You must still arrive 30–60 minutes beforehand to be guaranteed a good spot. Arrive 5 minutes before the show starts, and you're likely to be turned away even with FastPass+. Finally, using FastPass+ at *Fantasmic!* prevents you from using FastPass+ at Toy Story Midway Mania! and Rock 'n' Roller Coaster. The one situation in which FastPass+ *does* make sense is if you've used all of your three reservations and same-day *Fantasmic!* FastPasses are still available.

FastPass+ kiosk locations at the Studios are as follows:

- At the MyMagic+ Service Center, immediately to the left just past the entrance turnstiles
- At the wait-times board on the corner of Hollywood and Sunset Boulevards
- Near Toy Story Midway Mania!, on Pixar Place
- Near *Muppet-Vision 3-D,* just off Streets of America

Same-Day FastPass+ Availability

The preceding advice tells you which attractions to focus on when making your *advance* FastPass+ reservations before you get to the park. Once you're in the park, you can make more FastPass+ reservations once your advance reservations have been used or have expired. The chart on the previous page shows which attractions are likely to have day-of FastPasses available, and the approximate times at which they'll run out.

Some attractions have more day-of FastPass+ availability on days with moderate crowds than with low crowds. That seems backwards, but it's not: Disney can change how much of each ride's hourly capacity is dedicated to FastPass+ and increases this number on days of higher attendance. For example, on days of low crowds, Muppet-Vision 3-D might dedicate 50% of its hourly capacity to FastPass+ riders, perhaps 75% on days of moderate crowds.

DINING IN DISNEY'S HOLLYWOOD STUDIOS

HERE'S A QUICK RECAP of the Studios' top restaurants, rated by readers from highest to lowest. See Part Four for details.

DHS RESTAURANT REFRESHER *(continues on next page)*	
COUNTER-SERVICE	**FULL-SERVICE**
Starring Rolls Cafe (93% 👍), Sunset Boulevard	**The Hollywood Brown Derby** (90% 👍), Hollywood Boulevard

DHS RESTAURANT REFRESHER	
COUNTER-SERVICE	**FULL-SERVICE**
Trolley Car Cafe (Starbucks) (90% 👍), Sunset Boulevard	**Mama Melrose's Ristorante Italiano** (87% 👍), Streets of America
Writer's Stop (89% 👍), Streets of America	**50's Prime Time Cafe** (85% 👍), Echo Lake
Backlot Express (83% 👍), Echo Lake	**Hollywood & Vine** (83% 👍), Echo Lake
Fairfax Fare (81% 👍), Sunset Boulevard	

> **NOT TO BE MISSED AT DISNEY'S HOLLYWOOD STUDIOS**
>
> • *Fantasmic!* • *Jim Henson's Muppet-Vision 3-D* • Rock 'n' Roller Coaster
>
> • Star Tours—The Adventures Continue • Toy Story Midway Mania!
>
> • The Twilight Zone Tower of Terror

DISNEY'S HOLLYWOOD STUDIOS ATTRACTIONS

HOLLYWOOD BOULEVARD

THIS PALM-LINED THOROUGHFARE re-creates Tinseltown's main drag during the Golden Age of Hollywood. Most service facilities are here, interspersed with eateries and shops. Merchandise includes Disney trademark items and movie-related souvenirs.

Hollywood characters and roving performers entertain on the boulevard, and other happenings pass this way.

The Great Movie Ride *(FastPass+)* ★★★½

APPEAL BY AGE	PRESCHOOL ★★★	GRADE SCHOOL ★★★½	TEENS ★★★½
YOUNG ADULTS ★★★½	OVER 30 ★★★½		SENIORS ★★★★

What it is Indoor movie-history ride. **Scope and scale** Headliner. **When to go** Before 11 a.m., during dinner, after 8 p.m., or use FastPass+. **Special comments** Elaborate, with several surprises. **Authors' rating** The recent update is welcome but doesn't go far enough; ★★★½. **Duration of ride** About 19 minutes. **Average wait in line per 100 people ahead of you** 2 minutes; assumes all cars operating. **Loading speed** Fast.

DESCRIPTION AND COMMENTS Entering through a re-creation of Grauman's Chinese Theatre, guests board vehicles for a fast-paced tour of soundstage sets from classic films, including *Casablanca, Tarzan, The Wizard of Oz, Alien,* and *Raiders of the Lost Ark.* Each set is populated with Disney Audio-Animatronic characters, as well as the occasional human, all augmented by sound and lighting effects. One of Disney's larger and more ambitious dark rides, The Great Movie Ride encompasses 95,000 square feet and showcases some of the most famous scenes in filmmaking. Life-size animatronic sculptures of stars, including Gene Kelly, John Wayne, James Cagney, and Julie Andrews, inhabit some of the largest sets ever constructed for a Disney ride.

In early 2015, as part of an agreement with Turner Classic Movies, the Great Movie Ride's preshow film trailer and ride-film finale were updated with commentary from TCM host and film historian Robert Osborne. In addition, the finale was entirely reedited with a mix of classic clips, new scenes from previously featured films, and a handful of more-recent movies.

(Refreshingly, this is the first Disney movie montage we've seen in a while that gives *Tangled* more screen time than *Frozen.*)

The updated preshow and finale are first-rate—it's the attraction's meat that merits a "meh." Don't strain yourself searching for signs of improved animatronics or new effects in old sets, much less any all-new scenes.

TOURING TIPS It's rare to see waits of more than 30 minutes at The Great Movie Ride except during peak season. For one thing, it's an interval-loading, high-capacity attraction; for another, many of the clips don't ring a bell with anyone under age 40. Actual wait times usually run about one-third shorter than the times posted.

SUNSET BOULEVARD

EVOKING THE 1940s, Sunset Boulevard—the first right off Hollywood Boulevard—provides another venue for dining, shopping, and street entertainment.

Fantasmic! *(FastPass+)* ★★★★½

APPEAL BY AGE	PRESCHOOL ★★★★	GRADE SCHOOL ★★★★½	TEENS ★★★★½
YOUNG ADULTS ★★★★½	OVER 30 ★★★★½		SENIORS ★★★★½

What it is Mixed-media nighttime spectacular. **Scope and scale** Super-headliner. **When to go** Check *Times Guide* for schedule; if 2 shows are offered, the second is less crowded. **Special comments** Disney's very best nighttime event. **Authors' rating** Not to be missed; ★★★★½. **Duration of presentation** 25 minutes. **Probable waiting time** 50–90 minutes for a seat, 35–40 minutes for standing room.

DESCRIPTION AND COMMENTS Off Sunset Boulevard behind the Tower of Terror, this mixed-media show is staged on an island opposite the 7,900-seat Hollywood Hills Amphitheater. By far the largest theater facility ever created by Disney, the amphitheater can accommodate an additional 2,000 standing guests for an audience of nearly 10,000.

Fantasmic! is the most innovative outdoor spectacle ever attempted at any theme park. Starring Mickey Mouse in his role as the Sorcerer's Apprentice from *Fantasia,* the production uses lasers, images projected on a shroud of mist, fireworks, lighting effects, and music in combinations so stunning you can scarcely believe what you're seeing. The plot is simple: good versus evil. The story gets lost in all the special effects at times, but no matter: It's the spectacle, not the storyline, that's powerful.

A Pearland, Texas, mom found *Fantasmic!* too intense for her young child:

Fantasmic! should come with a warning label. The characters' larger-than-life laser visages, loud and ominous music, and thundering explosions sent hordes of parents with screaming children fleeing for the exits.

We don't receive many reports of young children being terrified by *Fantasmic!*, but the reader's point is well taken. Spend some time preparing your kids for what they will see. You can mitigate the fright factor somewhat by sitting back a bit. Also, hang on to your kids after *Fantasmic!* and give them instructions for regrouping should you get separated.

TOURING TIPS *Fantasmic!* is presented one or more times most evenings, but Disney has been known to change the schedule, so verify before you go. *Fantasmic!* is to the Studios what *IllumiNations* is to Epcot. While it's hard to imagine a 10,000-person stadium running out of space, that's just what happens almost every time the show is staged. On evenings when there are two shows, the second will always be less crowded. If you attend the first (or only) scheduled performance, then arrive at least an hour in advance; if you opt for the second, arrive 50 minutes early.

Fantasmic! is a FastPass+ attraction, but we don't think it should be one of your first three choices. See page 607 for an in-depth explanation.

A Cross Junction, Virginia, woman offers this advance-planning tip:

Buy deli sandwiches outside the park, pack them with snacks and water in your backpack, and get a seat early.

A multigenerational family from Barrie, Ontario, makes this suggestion for guests who are short on nature's upholstery:

Bring pillows or towels to sit on. We were sitting on those benches from 6 p.m. for the 7:30 show, and boy, did our rears hurt by the end!

Rainy and windy conditions sometimes cause *Fantasmic!* to be cancelled. Unfortunately, Disney officials usually don't make a final decision about whether to proceed or cancel until just before showtime. We've seen guests wait stoically for over an hour with no assurance that their patience and sacrifice will be rewarded. We don't recommend arriving more than 20 minutes before showtime on rainy or especially windy nights. On nights like these, pursue your own agenda until 10 minutes or so before showtime, then head to the stadium to see what happens.

Exiting *Fantasmic!* via the show's single exit can be hair-raising, as this retired elementary-school teacher attests:

It was like a cattle stampede, but at a snail's pace! Twice I almost ran over toddlers whose mothers were too tired to carry them.

From a veteran of both Disneyland and Walt Disney World:

I visit Disneyland a lot, and their [crowd-control] cast members push the throngs of guests through the park like clockwork, even when it's bursting at the seams. At Disney World, it's basically every man for himself at the end of the spectacles as the cast members retreat, leaving very tired, very cranky guests to duke it out. Such is the case at Fantasmic!—while I was very happy to see a backstage corridor wide open for a quick reroute, the presence of cast members was extremely rare. I was stunned!

Finally, a couple from Alberta, Canada, sums it up for all of us:

For a show so deservedly hyped, I would hope WDW finds ways to make seeing it less stressful.

FANTASMIC! DINING PACKAGE If you eat lunch or dinner at **Hollywood & Vine, The Hollywood Brown Derby,** or **Mama Melrose's Ristorante Italiano,** you can obtain a voucher for the members of your dining party to enter *Fantasmic!* via a special entrance and sit in a reserved section of seats. In return for your patronage of the restaurant, you can avoid 30–90 minutes waiting in the regular line to be admitted. If you know you're going to eat dinner at one of these locations, the dining package is a better way to see *Fantasmic!* than using FastPass+.

You must call ☎ 407-WDW-DINE (939-3463) 180 days in advance and request the package for the night you want to see the show. *Note:* This is a real reservation, not an Advance Reservation, and it must be guaranteed with a credit card at the time of booking. There's no additional charge for the package itself, but there is a $10 charge for cancelling a reservation with less than 48 hours' notice.

Included in the package are fixed-price menus for all three restaurants as follows; respective prices are for adults and kids ages 3–9: *Hollywood & Vine:* buffet dinner, $40/$21; *The Hollywood Brown Derby:* lunch and dinner, $57/$17; *Mama Melrose's:* lunch and dinner,

$38/$13. Nonalcoholic drinks and tax are included; park admission and gratuity are not. Prices fluctuate according to season, so call WDW-DINE to find out the exact price for a particular date.

You'll receive your vouchers at the restaurant. After dinner, report to the Highlands Gate on Sunset Boulevard—between Theater of the Stars and the Once Upon a Time store—30–45 minutes before showtime. A cast member will collect your vouchers and escort you to the reserved-seating section of the amphitheater. Though you're required to arrive early, you can be seated immediately. The reserved seats are in the center of the stadium; you won't have assigned seats—it's first-come, first-served—so arrive early for the best choice. Finally, understand that if *Fantasmic!* is canceled due to weather or other circumstances, you won't receive a refund or even a voucher for another performance.

Weather notwithstanding, a Waldorf, Maryland, couple thinks the dining package is the only way to go:

> We booked dinner at Hollywood & Vine, got our passes for the package, and waltzed on in to the show. We felt like VIPs, and it was so relaxing to see the show without the rush of the crowds.

Rock 'n' Roller Coaster *(FastPass+)* ★★★★

APPEAL BY AGE PRESCHOOL ★★½   GRADE SCHOOL ★★★★½   TEENS ★★★★★
YOUNG ADULTS ★★★★★   OVER 30 ★★★★½   SENIORS ★★★★

What it is Rock music–themed roller coaster. **Scope and scale** Headliner. **When to go** First 30 minutes the park is open, or use FastPass+. **Special comments** 48" minimum height requirement; children younger than age 7 must ride with an adult. Switching-off option provided (see page 412). Note that this attraction has a single-rider line. **Authors' rating** Disney's wildest American coaster; not to be missed; ★★★★. **Duration of ride** Almost 1½ minutes. **Average wait in line per 100 people ahead of you** 2½ minutes; assumes all trains operating. **Loading speed** Moderate–fast.

DISNEY DISH WITH JIM HILL

VARIETY IS THE SPICE OF LIFE Disney is building a "flex theater" right next door to Rock 'n' Roller Coaster. This multipurpose venue, slated to open in 2016, should be able to host everything from cheerleading competitions to high school band and choral groups. Those performances currently take place at the *Indiana Jones* show and at the Premiere Theater (behind *Muppet-Vision 3-D*). But Disney may be eyeing those spots for its *Star Wars* land, so building a flex theater makes sense.

Motion Sickness

DESCRIPTION AND COMMENTS Exponentially wilder than Space Mountain or Big Thunder Mountain Railroad in the Magic Kingdom, Rock 'n' Roller Coaster is an attraction for fans of high-speed thrill rides. Although the presence of Aerosmith and the synchronized music add measurably to the experience, the ride itself is the focus. Rock 'n' Roller Coaster's loops, corkscrews, and drops make Space Mountain seem like It's a Small World. What really makes this metal coaster unusual, however, is that first, it's in the dark (like Space Mountain, only with Southern California nighttime scenes instead of space), and second, you're launched up the first hill like a jet off a carrier deck. By the time you crest the hill, you'll have gone from 0 to 57 mph in less than 3 seconds. When you enter the first loop, you'll be pulling 5 g's—2 more than astronauts used to experience at liftoff on a space shuttle.

Reader opinions of Rock 'n' Roller Coaster are predictably mixed, colored invariably by how the reader feels about roller coasters. First, from a mother of two from High Mills, New York:

You can't warn people enough about Rock 'n' Roller Coaster. My daughter and I refused to go on it at all. My 9-year-old son, who had no problems with any ride, including Tower of Terror, went on with my husband and came off so shaken he was "done for" the rest of the day. My husband just closed his eyes and hoped for the best.

And from a Longmont, Colorado, dad:

The first 15 seconds of this ride are spectacular. I've never experienced anything like the initial take-off.

From an Australian couple who traveled a long way to ride a coaster:

My wife and I are definitely not roller-coaster people. However, we found Rock 'n' Roller Coaster quite exhilarating—and because it's dark, we didn't always realize that we were being thrown upside down. We rode it twice!

TOURING TIPS Rock 'n' Roller Coaster is not for everyone—if Space Mountain or Big Thunder pushes your limits, stay away.

Expect long lines except in the first 30 minutes after opening and during the late-evening performance of *Fantasmic!* Ride as soon as possible in the morning, or use the single-rider line or FastPass+.

A good strategy for riding Rock 'n' Roller Coaster, Toy Story Midway Mania!, and Tower of Terror with minimum wait is to make a midmorning FastPass+ reservation for Toy Story Midway Mania! and an evening FastPass+ reservation Tower of Terror up to 60 days in advance. Then, when you visit, rush first thing after opening to ride Rock 'n' Roller Coaster. If you can't make FastPass+ reservations before you arrive, ride Rock 'n' Roller Coaster or Toy Story Midway Mania! first, then find the nearest FastPass+ kiosk to make the other reservations.

Theater of the Stars / *Beauty and the Beast— Live on Stage* (FastPass+) ★★★★

APPEAL BY AGE	PRESCHOOL ★★★★½	GRADE SCHOOL ★★★★	TEENS ★★★★
YOUNG ADULTS ★★★★	OVER 30 ★★★★		SENIORS ★★★★½

What it is Live Hollywood-style musical, usually featuring Disney characters; performed in an open-air theater. **Scope and scale** Major attraction. **When to go** Anytime; evenings are cooler. **Special comments** Check your *Times Guide* for showtimes. **Authors' rating** Excellent; ★★★★. **Duration of presentation** 25 minutes. **Preshow entertainment** None. **When to arrive** 20–30 minutes before showtime.

DESCRIPTION AND COMMENTS Theater of the Stars combines Disney characters with singers and dancers in upbeat and humorous Hollywood musicals. The *Beauty and the Beast* show, in particular, is outstanding. The theater offers a clear field of vision from almost every seat. Best of all, a canopy protects the audience from the Florida sun (or rain), but the theater still gets mighty hot in the summer.

TOURING TIPS Unless you visit during the cooler months, see this show in the late afternoon or the evening. The production is so popular that you should show up 25–35 minutes early to get a good seat.

The Twilight Zone Tower of Terror (FastPass+) ★★★★★

APPEAL BY AGE	PRESCHOOL ★★★	GRADE SCHOOL ★★★★	TEENS ★★★★½
YOUNG ADULTS ★★★★★	OVER 30 ★★★★½		SENIORS ★★★★

What it is Sci-fi–themed indoor thrill ride. **Scope and scale** Super-headliner. **When to go** First or last 30 minutes the park is open, or use FastPass+. **Special comments** 40" minimum height requirement. Switching-off option provided (see page 412). **Authors' rating** Walt Disney World's best attraction; not to be missed; ★★★★★. **Duration of ride** About 4 minutes plus preshow. **Average wait in line per 100 people ahead of you** 4 minutes; assumes all elevators operating. **Loading speed** Moderate.

DESCRIPTION AND COMMENTS The Tower of Terror is a different species of Disney thrill ride, though it borrows elements of The Haunted Mansion at the Magic Kingdom. The story is that you're touring a once-famous Hollywood hotel gone to ruin. As at Star Tours, the queuing area immerses guests in the adventure as they pass through the hotel's once-opulent public rooms. From the lobby, guests are escorted into the hotel's library, where Rod Serling, speaking from an old black-and-white television, greets the guests and introduces the plot.

The Tower of Terror is a whopper, at 13-plus-stories tall. Breaking tradition in terms of visually isolating themed areas, it lets you see the entire Studios from atop the tower . . . but you have to look quick.

The ride vehicle, one of the hotel's service elevators, takes guests to see the haunted hostelry. The tour begins innocuously, but at about the fifth floor things get pretty weird. Guests are subjected to a full range of eerie effects as they cross into the Twilight Zone. The climax occurs when the elevator reaches the top floor—the 13th, of course—and the cable snaps.

The Tower of Terror is an experience to savor. Though the final plunges—yep, plural—are calculated to thrill, the meat of the attraction is its extraordinary visual and audio effects. There's richness and subtlety here, enough to keep the ride fresh and stimulating after many repetitions. Disney has also programmed random lift-and-drop sequences into the mix, making the attraction faster and keeping you guessing about when, how far, and how many times the elevator will fall.

A senior from the United Kingdom tried the Tower of Terror and liked it very much, writing:

I was thankful I had read your review of the Tower of Terror, or I would certainly have avoided it. As you say, it's so full of magnificent detail that it's worth riding even if you don't fancy the drops involved.

The Tower has great potential for terrifying young children and rattling more-mature visitors. If you have teenagers in your party, use them as experimental probes. If they report back that they really, really liked the Tower of Terror, run like hell in the opposite direction.

TOURING TIPS If you're on hand when the park opens and you want to ride Tower of Terror first, be aware that about 65% of the folks walking down Sunset Boulevard head for Rock 'n' Roller Coaster. If you're not positioned on the far right of the street, it will be hard to move through the crowd to make a right turn into Tower of Terror.

To save time once you're inside the queuing area, when you enter the library waiting room, stand in the far back corner across from the door where you entered and at the opposite end of the room from the TV. When the doors to the loading area open, you'll be the first admitted.

If you have young children (or anyone) who are apprehensive about this attraction, ask the attendant about switching off (see page 412).

Our touring plan on page 818 incorporates an optimal strategy for riding Tower of Terror, Rock 'n' Roller Coaster, and Toy Story Midway Mania! with minimum waits.

ECHO LAKE

AN ACTUAL MINIATURE LAKE near the middle of the Studios, to the left of Hollywood Boulevard, Echo Lake pays homage to its real-life California counterpart, which served as the backdrop to many early motion pictures. It also provides a visual transition from Hollywood Boulevard's retro theming to Streets of America's film-set ambience.

For the First Time in Forever: A Frozen Sing-Along Celebration (FastPass+) ★★★

APPEAL BY AGE	PRESCHOOL ★★★★½	GRADE SCHOOL ★★★★★	TEENS ★★★★½
YOUNG ADULTS ★★★★		OVER 30 ★★★	SENIORS ★★★

What it is Sing-along stage show retelling the story of *Frozen,* with appearances by Anna and Elsa. **Scope and scale** Minor attraction. **When to go** Check your *Times Guide* for showtimes. **Authors' rating** You'll learn all the words whether you want to or not; ★★★. Duration of presentation 25 minutes.

DESCRIPTION AND COMMENTS This attraction started out as a hastily assembled stage show during the summer of 2014, when DHS was closing other attractions and needed something for guests to do. The show retells the plot of *Frozen* in 25 minutes. That's enough time to sing every song in the movie and have a quick visit from Anna and Elsa—but nothing new.

A mom from Richmond, Virginia, says that even with *Frozen* overload, the sing-along is a definite upper:

The sing-along was fantastic—along with Fantasmic, *it was the highlight of the day. Even if you're a bit sick of* Frozen, *the atmosphere and the humor involved make it a lot of fun.*

TOURING TIPS FastPass+ gets you access to a preferred-seating section near the front of the stage.

Indiana Jones Epic Stunt Spectacular! (FastPass+) ★★★½

APPEAL BY AGE	PRESCHOOL ★★★½	GRADE SCHOOL ★★★★½	TEENS ★★★★
YOUNG ADULTS ★★★★		OVER 30 ★★★★	SENIORS ★★★★

What it is Movie-stunt demonstration and action show. **Scope and scale** Headliner. **When to go** First two shows or last show. **Special comments** Performance times posted on a sign at the entrance to the theatre. **Authors' rating** Done on a grand scale; ★★★½. **Duration of presentation** 30 minutes. **Preshow entertainment** Selection of "extras" from audience. **When to arrive** 20–30 minutes before showtime.

DESCRIPTION AND COMMENTS Educational though somewhat unevenly paced, the popular production showcases professional stunt men and women who offer behind-the-scenes demonstrations of their craft. Sets, props, and special effects are very elaborate.

TOURING TIPS The Stunt Theater holds 2,000 people; capacity audiences are common. The first performance is always the easiest to see. If the first show is at 10 a.m. or earlier, you can usually walk in, even if you arrive 5 minutes late. For the second performance, show up about 15–20 minutes ahead of time; for the third and subsequent shows, arrive 20–30 minutes early. If you plan to tour during late afternoon and evening, attend the last performance of the day. To beat the crowd out of the stadium, sit on the far right (as you face the staging area) and near the top.

To be chosen from the audience to be an "extra" in the stunt show, arrive early, sit down front, and display unbridled enthusiasm. A woman from Richmond, Virginia, explains:

After the first performance, I realized the best way to get picked was to stand up, wave my arms, and shout when the "casting director" called for volunteers. (Sitting toward the front helps, too.)

Jedi Training Academy ★★★½

APPEAL BY AGE   PRESCHOOL ★★★★½   GRADE SCHOOL ★★★★★   TEENS ★★★★
YOUNG ADULTS ★★★★   OVER 30 ★★★★½   SENIORS ★★★★

What it is Outdoor stage show. **Scope and scale** Minor attraction. **When to go** First 2 shows of the day. **Special comments** To sign up your children to go on stage, visit the ABC Sound Studio building early in the morning, or look for cast members near the entrance just before and after park opening. Spots are first-come, first-served. **Authors' rating** A treat for young *Star Wars* lovers; ★★★½. **Duration of show** About 15 minutes. **When to arrive** 15 minutes before showtime.

DESCRIPTION AND COMMENTS *Jedi Training Academy* is staged several times daily to the left of the Star Tours building entrance, opposite Backlot Express. If you want your young Skywalkers-in-training to appear on stage, visit the sign-up area at the ABC Sound Studio building (across from Star Tours) as early in the morning as possible; also, cast members are sometimes stationed outside the entrance just before and after the park opens. Spots go quickly and are first-come, first-served.

A Windham, New Hampshire, mom describes a common conundrum:

I'm guessing many families will have to choose between racing to Toy Story Midway Mania! to ride or racing to sign up for Jedi Training Academy (children MUST be present at sign-up). We hopped on TSMM, then crossed the park to sign up for JTA. By the time we got there, we were pushed to the 2:20 p.m. show, which eliminated the possibility of leaving for a nap after lunch.

Once on stage, these miniature Jedi are trained in the ways of The Force and do battle against Darth Vader. If all this sounds too intense, it's not—Storm Troopers provide comic relief, and just as in the movies, the good guys always win.

TOURING TIPS Surprisingly popular, given that Disney hasn't promoted it at the same level of hype as other shows. In the summer, grab drinks at Backlot Express, right next door, about 20 minutes before the show starts.

Star Tours—The Adventures Continue
(FastPass+) ★★★½

APPEAL BY AGE   PRESCHOOL ★★★★   GRADE SCHOOL ★★★★½   TEENS ★★★★½
YOUNG ADULTS ★★★★½   OVER 30 ★★★★½   SENIORS ★★★★

What it is Indoor space-flight-simulation ride. **Scope and scale** Headliner. **When to go** Before 10 a.m., after 6 p.m., or use FastPass. **Special comments** Expectant mothers and anyone prone to motion sickness are advised against riding. Too intense for many children younger than age 8; 40" minimum height requirement. **Authors' rating** A classic adventure; not to be missed; ★★★½. **Duration of ride** About 7 minutes. **Average wait in line per 100 people ahead of you** 5 minutes; assumes all simulators operating. **Loading speed** Moderate-fast.

Motion Sickness

DESCRIPTION AND COMMENTS Based on the *Star Wars* movie series, this was Disney's first modern simulator ride. Guests ride in a flight simulator modeled after those used for training pilots and astronauts. You experience dips, turns, twists, and climbs as your vehicle

DISNEY DISH WITH JIM HILL

A GALAXY FAR, FAR AWAY GETS A LITTLE CLOSER It's taken far longer than expected for Disney's board of directors to approve plans for the Studios's new *Star Wars*–themed land, planned for the vicinity of Streets of America and Mickey Avenue. But since Disney is reportedly spending upwards of $500 million, they want enough "wow" to ensure they can compete with the Wizarding World attractions at Universal. Look for construction to get started in 2016.

goes through an intergalactic version of the chariot race in *Ben-Hur.* The ride film is projected in high-definition 3-D and has more than 50 combinations of opening and ending scenes. You could ride Star Tours all day without seeing the same film segment twice.

An interactive show, *Jedi Training Academy* (see previous page), is staged several times daily to the left of the Star Tours building entrance.

TOURING TIPS Try to ride before 10 a.m., or use FastPass+. If you have young children (or anyone) who are apprehensive about this attraction, ask the attendant about switching off (see page 412). Watch for throngs arriving from performances of the *Indiana Jones Epic Stunt Spectacular!*—if you encounter a long line, try again later.

STREETS OF AMERICA

FORMERLY A WALK-THROUGH back-lot movie set, Streets of America is now a themed area that's home to four attractions. The street sets remain intact and serve as the primary pedestrian thoroughfare.

Honey, I Shrunk the Kids Movie Set Adventure ★★½

APPEAL BY AGE PRESCHOOL ★★★★½ GRADE SCHOOL ★★★★½ TEENS ★★★½
YOUNG ADULTS ★★★ OVER 30 ★★★ SENIORS ★★★

What it is Small but elaborate playground. **Scope and scale** Diversion. **When to go** Before 11 a.m. or after dark. **Special comments** Opens an hour later than the rest of the park; kids must be age 10 or younger to play. **Authors' rating** Great for young children, more of a curiosity for adults; ★★½. **Duration of presentation** Varies. **Average wait in line per 100 people ahead of you** 20 minutes.

DESCRIPTION AND COMMENTS This elaborate playground appeals to kids age 10 and younger. The story is that you've been "miniaturized" and must make your way through a yard full of 20-foot-tall blades of grass, giant ants, lawn sprinklers, and other oversize props. There are also tunnels, slides, and rope ladders to play on. All areas are padded, and cast members are on hand to maintain some semblance of control.

TOURING TIPS While this attraction undoubtedly looked good on paper, it has problems that are hard to "miniaturize" in practice. First of all, it's nowhere near large enough to accommodate all the kids who would like to play. Only 240 people are allowed "on the set" at a time, and many of these are supervising parents or curious adults who hopped in line without knowing what they were waiting for. Frequently by 10:30 or 11 a.m., the playground is full, with dozens waiting outside (some impatiently).

Also, kids get to play as long as parents allow. This creates uneven traffic flow and unpredictable waits. If it weren't for the third flaw—that the attraction is poorly ventilated (read: as hot and sticky as an Everglades swamp)—there's no telling when anyone would leave.

A Tolland, Connecticut, mom found the playground exasperating:

*We let the kids hang out here because we thought it would be relaxing. NOT!
You have three choices: (1) Let your kids go anywhere and hope if they try
to get out without your permission, someone will stop them. (2) Go everywhere with your kids—this takes stamina, athleticism, and a high tolerance
for humiliation (you look pretty stupid coming down those slides). (3) Try to
visually keep track of your kids. This is impossible, so you'll be either on the
edge of or in the middle of an anxiety attack the whole time you're there.*

If you visit during warmer months, get your kids in and out before
11 a.m.—by late morning, this attraction is way too hot and crowded for anyone to enjoy. Access is via Streets of America or Pixar Place.

Jim Henson's Muppet-Vision 3-D *(FastPass+)*   ★★★★

APPEAL BY AGE	PRESCHOOL ★★★★	GRADE SCHOOL ★★★★	TEENS ★★★★
YOUNG ADULTS ★★★★	OVER 30 ★★★★		SENIORS ★★★★½

What it is 3-D movie starring the Muppets. **Scope and scale** Major attraction. **When
to go** Anytime. **Authors' rating** Uproarious; not to be missed; ★★★★. **Duration of
presentation** 17 minutes. **Preshow entertainment** Muppets on television. **Probable
waiting time** 12 minutes.

DESCRIPTION AND COMMENTS *Muppet-Vision 3-D* provides a total sensory
experience, with wild 3-D action augmented by auditory, visual, and tactile special effects. If you're tired and hot, this zany presentation will make
you feel brand-new. Arrive early and enjoy the hilarious video preshow.

A New Brunswick, Canada, reader thinks the Muppets are heaven-sent:

*I think Muppet-Vision 3-D is a godsend for five reasons: (1) It NEVER has a
line (even on our visit on New Year's Day). (2) Everyone ages 1–100 gives the
show high marks. (3) Between the preshow and the movie, it's half an hour
seated comfortably in an air-conditioned theater. (4) Between the live actors
and animatronics, it's so much more than just another silly 3-D movie. (5) IT'S
THE MUPPETS! Who doesn't love these hysterical creatures and their 3-D
shenanigans?*

TOURING TIPS This production is popular, but the theater's capacity is almost
always sufficient. Waits peak around lunchtime, and it's unusual to see a
wait of more than 20 minutes except during holidays. Watch for throngs
arriving from performances of the *Indiana Jones Epic Stunt Spectacular!*—if
you do encounter a long line, try again later.

Lights, Motors, Action! Extreme Stunt Show *(FastPass+)*   ★★★½

APPEAL BY AGE	PRESCHOOL ★★★★	GRADE SCHOOL ★★★½	TEENS ★★★½
YOUNG ADULTS ★★★★½	OVER 30 ★★★★		SENIORS ★★★★

What it is Auto stunt show. **Scope and scale** Headliner. **When to go** Anytime.
Authors' rating Good stunt work, slow pace; ★★★½. **Duration of presentation** 25–
30 minutes. **Preshow entertainment** Selection of audience volunteers. **When to
arrive** 25–30 minutes before showtime.

DESCRIPTION AND COMMENTS This show, which originated at Disneyland Paris,
features cars and motorcycles in a blur of chases, crashes, jumps, and
explosions. The secrets behind the special effects are explained after each
stunt sequence, with replays and different camera views shown on an
enormous movie screen; the replays also serve to pass the time needed to
place the next stunt's props into position. While the stunt driving is excellent, the show plods between tricks, and you'll probably have had your fill

by the time the last stunt ends. Expect about 6–8 minutes of real action in a show that runs 25–30 minutes.

TOURING TIPS At the end of the Streets of America, *Lights, Motors, Action!* presents two to five shows daily. It's popular, but its remoteness—it's the most distant attraction from the park entrance—helps distribute and moderate crowds. The 3,000-person stadium ensures that you can find a seat except on the busiest days, but a family of four from Mount Pleasant, South Carolina, notes that it's easier to get into the stadium than out:

When we exited the arena (which was full the day we visited), it was horrible! The cast members directed us all to the same exit, and it was a HUGE bottleneck that took us 20 minutes to break free from.

PIXAR PLACE

THE WALKWAY BETWEEN *Voyage of the Little Mermaid* and the Backlot Express restaurant holds the popular **Toy Story Midway Mania!** attraction. To emphasize the importance of the *Toy Story* franchise, this section of the park is called Pixar Place.

DISNEY DISH WITH JIM HILL

PUMPING UP PIXAR PLACE Disney wants to turn Hollywood Studios into a full-day theme park. To do that, a number of Pixar-themed rides are now in the works. Some will be simple spinners and flat rides similar to the ones that were recently installed at Hong Kong Disneyland and Walt Disney Studios in Paris. Others will be wildly ambitious, such as an indoor version of Radiator Springs Racers at Disneyland. It's going to take almost five years to complete this Pixar Place expansion, but it should be a real winner once it's running.

Toy Story Midway Mania! *(FastPass+)* ★★★★½

APPEAL BY AGE	PRESCHOOL ★★★★½	GRADE SCHOOL ★★★★★	TEENS ★★★★½
YOUNG ADULTS ★★★★½		OVER 30 ★★★★½	SENIORS ★★★★½

What it is 3-D ride through indoor shooting gallery. **Scope and scale** Headliner. **When to go** As soon as the park opens, or use FastPass+. **Authors' rating** Not to be missed; ★★★★½. **Duration of ride** About 6½ minutes. **Average wait in line per 100 people ahead of you** 4½ minutes. **Loading speed** Fast.

DESCRIPTION AND COMMENTS Toy Story Midway Mania! ushered in a whole new generation of Disney attraction: the "virtual dark ride." Since Disneyland opened in 1955, ride vehicles have moved past two- and three-dimensional sets often populated by Audio-Animatronic (AA) figures. These amazingly detailed sets and robotic figures defined the Disney Imagineering genius in attractions such as Pirates of the Caribbean, The Haunted Mansion, and Peter Pan's Flight. Now for Toy Story Midway Mania!, the elaborate sets and endearing AA characters are gone. Imagine long corridors, totally empty, covered with reflective material. There's almost nothing there . . . until you put on your 3-D glasses. Instantly, the corridor is full and brimming with color and activity, thanks to projected computer-graphic (CG) images.

Conceptually, this is an interactive shooting gallery much like Buzz Lightyear's Space Ranger Spin (see page 516), but in Toy Story Midway Mania!, your ride vehicle passes through a totally virtual midway, with booths offering such games as ring tossing and ball throwing. You use a cannon on your ride vehicle to play as you move along from booth to booth. Unlike the laser guns in Buzz Lightyear, however, the pull-string cannons in Toy Story Midway Mania! take advantage of CG Image technology to toss rings, shoot balls, even throw eggs and pies. Each game booth is manned by a *Toy Story* character who is right beside you in 3-D glory, cheering you on. In addition to 3-D imagery, you experience vehicle motion, wind, and water spray.

The ride begins with a training round to familiarize you with the games, then continues through a number of "real" games in which you compete against your riding mate. The technology has the ability to self-adjust the level of difficulty, and there are plenty of easy targets for small children to reach. *Tip:* Let the pull-string retract all the way back into the cannon before pulling it again.

Finally, a 6-foot-tall Mr. Potato Head interacts with and talks to guests in real time in the queuing area (similar to *Turtle Talk with Crush* at Epcot).

TOURING TIPS Because it's a ton of fun and it has a relatively low rider-per-hour capacity, Toy Story Midway Mania! is the biggest bottleneck in Walt Disney World, surpassing even Test Track at Epcot. The only way to get aboard without a horrendous wait is to be one of the first through the turnstiles when the park opens and zoom to the attraction. Another alternative is to obtain FastPass+ reservations for Toy Story Midway Mania! But you'll need to act fast: Even on days of moderate attendance, all reservations for the day are usually gone by 11 a.m.

Families with children too small to ride Rock 'n' Roller Coaster or Tower of Terror make a beeline to Toy Story Midway Mania! first thing in the morning, and lines grow quickly. Waits at Toy Story can reach 90 minutes or more on a busy day. In fact, the lines grow so fast that in about a third of our touring plan variations, we recommend getting a FastPass+ reservation for 9 a.m.–10 a.m., even when Toy Story is the first step in the plan. The two benefits to doing this are that you'll shave off at least 10 minutes of waiting, and you don't have to line up as early at the park entrance to join the mad run to Toy Story.

Readers generally love the ride but hate the wait. A Nashville, Tennessee, mom was mostly positive:

Toy Story Midway Mania! was already swamped fairly early in the day. We had to resort to getting some of the last FastPass+ reservations, and it extended our day to wait until our return time came up. But oh my gosh, it was worth the wait!

But a woman from Aberdeen, Washington, was mostly frustrated:

We decided to risk the 70-minute wait for Toy Story Midway Mania! because my family loves Pixar. The line is a nightmare—it took 2 hours to complete, because for every 5 regular-line people let into the ride, 40–50 FastPass+ people are let in. (Yes, I counted.) It was incredibly irritating to be in such a slow-moving line. I highly recommend riding this only if you have FastPass+.

Disney is adding a third track to Toy Story Midway Mania!, which should be completed in 2016. It will be dedicated to standby guests, while the original two tracks will serve guests with FastPass+ reservations.

MICKEY AVENUE

MICKEY AVENUE HOSTS a minor attraction on the pedestrian promenade that connects Pixar Place and Animation Courtyard.

Walt Disney: One Man's Dream ★★★

APPEAL BY AGE	PRESCHOOL ★★½	GRADE SCHOOL ★★★½	TEENS ★★★★
YOUNG ADULTS ★★★★	OVER 30 ★★★★½		SENIORS ★★★★½

What it is Tribute to Walt Disney. **Scope and scale** Minor attraction. **When to go** Anytime. **Authors' rating** Excellent; ★★★. **Duration of presentation** 25 minutes. **Preshow entertainment** Disney memorabilia. **Probable waiting time** For the film, 10 minutes.

DESCRIPTION AND COMMENTS Launched in 2001 to celebrate the 100th anniversary of Disney's birth, *One Man's Dream* consists of an exhibit area showcasing Disney memorabilia and recordings, followed by a film documenting Disney's life. On display are a replica of Walt's California office, various innovations in animation developed by Disney, and early models and working plans for Walt Disney World as well as various Disney theme parks around the world. The film provides a personal glimpse of Disney and offers insights regarding both his successes and failures.

TOURING TIPS Give yourself some time here. Every minute spent among these extraordinary artifacts will enhance your visit, taking you back to a time when the creativity and vision that created Walt Disney World were personified by one struggling entrepreneur.

ANIMATION COURTYARD

THIS AREA IS TO THE RIGHT of The Great Movie Ride in the middle of the park. It holds two large theaters used for live stage shows, plus several character-greeting locations. We think it's just a big swath of asphalt in desperate need of some landscaping or a water feature.

Disney Junior—Live on Stage! *(FastPass+)* ★★★★

APPEAL BY AGE PRESCHOOL ★★★★★ GRADE SCHOOL ★★★★ TEENS ★★½
YOUNG ADULTS ★★★ OVER 30 ★★★ SENIORS ★★★

What it is Live show for children. **Scope and scale** Minor attraction. **When to go** Per the daily entertainment schedule. **Special comments** Audience sits on the floor. **Authors' rating** A must for families with preschoolers; ★★★★. **Duration of presentation** 20 minutes. **When to arrive** 20–30 minutes before showtime.

DESCRIPTION AND COMMENTS The show features characters from the Disney Channel's *Sofia the First, Doc McStuffins,* and *Jake and the Never Land Pirates,* among others. *Disney Junior* uses elaborate puppets instead of live characters on stage. A simple plot serves as the platform for singing, dancing, puppetry, and audience participation. The characters, who ooze love and goodness, rally throngs of tots and preschoolers to sing and dance along with them. All the jumping, squirming, and high-stepping is facilitated by having the audience sit on the floor so that kids can spontaneously erupt into motion when the mood strikes. Even for adults without children, it's a treat to watch the tykes rev up.

TOURING TIPS Staged in a huge building to the right of the now-defunct Magic of Disney Animation. Get here at least 25 minutes before showtime, pick a spot on the floor, and take a breather until the action begins.

Voyage of the Little Mermaid *(FastPass+)* ★★★½

APPEAL BY AGE PRESCHOOL ★★★½ GRADE SCHOOL ★★★★ TEENS ★★★★
YOUNG ADULTS ★★★½ OVER 30 ★★★½ SENIORS ★★★★

What it is Musical stage show featuring characters from the Disney movie *The Little Mermaid*. **Scope and scale** Major attraction. **When to go** Before 9:45 a.m., just before closing, or use FastPass+. **Authors' rating** Romantic, lovable, and humorous in the best Disney tradition; ★★★½. **Duration of presentation** 15 minutes. **Preshow entertainment** Taped ramblings about the decor in the preshow holding area. **Probable waiting time** Before 9:30 a.m., 10–30 minutes; after 9:30 a.m., 35–70 minutes.

DISNEY DISH WITH JIM HILL

NEARER MY GODZILLA TO THEE Over the years, the Imagineers have come up with plenty of weird concepts for attractions at the Studios. But among the absolute weirdest had to be a proposed "Scream Actors Guild" attraction: a horror-themed spoof of award shows with an ending where the hosts present a lifetime-achievement award to . . . Godzilla. After Big G had been invited to come on down and accept his award, dimensional sound and in-theater effects would have made it feel as if Godzilla were stomping through the Studios, heading for the theater. And the end gag was supposed to have the terrible lizard literally bring the house down, as a life-size Godzilla foot stomped through the roof and splintered the stage.

DESCRIPTION AND COMMENTS *Voyage of the Little Mermaid* is a winner that appeals to every age. Sweet but not saccharine, its story is engaging, its special effects impressive, and its characters memorable.

We get a lot of mail from Europeans who complain about the "soppy sentimentality" of Americans in general and of Disney attractions in particular. These comments of a man from Bristol, England, are typical:

English cynicism made it hard for us at times to see Disney stories as anything other than gushing, namby-pamby, and full of stereotypes. Other Brits might also find the sentimentality cloying. Maybe you should prepare them for the need to rethink their wry outlook on life temporarily.

TOURING TIPS Except during the busiest holiday periods, it's unusual for anyone in line not to be admitted to the next showing of *Mermaid.* Typical waits are under 25 minutes most of the year.

When you enter the preshow lobby, stand near the doors to the theater. When they open, go inside, pick a row of seats and let 6–10 people enter the row ahead of you. The strategy is twofold: to obtain a good seat and be near the exit.

LIVE ENTERTAINMENT *at* DISNEY'S HOLLYWOOD STUDIOS

THE STUDIOS' LIVE-ENTERTAINMENT ROSTER includes theater shows; musical acts; roaming bands of street performers; and *Fantasmic!* (see page 609), a nighttime water, fireworks, and laser show that draws rave reviews. Of all of these, the theater shows, musical acts, and street performers are generally as good as or better than comparable acts at the other Disney parks. We'd be remiss if we didn't tell you to catch a show of **Mulch, Sweat & Shears** (★★★½), a group of landscaping "brothers" who make up a cover band that plays everything from AC/DC to Journey. Guests standing near the front may be invited into the act.

DISNEY CHARACTERS Donald, Daisy, Goofy, and Pluto are usually found in front of The Great Movie Ride. *Toy Story*'s Buzz and Woody are in Pixar Place in front of Toy Story Midway Mania!, while Mike and Sulley from *Monsters, Inc.,* are a little farther down the same walkway. Disney Junior stars hold court in Animation Courtyard, near *Disney Junior—Live on Stage!* Disney Channel's Phineas and Ferb, plus the cast of Pixar's *Cars* franchise, are found along the Streets of America.

Mickey, Minnie, and other characters were displaced in the July 2015 closure of The Magic of Disney Animation. Your best bet is to check the *Times Guide* for times and locations of all character appearances.

FROZEN SUMMER FUN Running from mid-June to at least September 2015, this collection of *Frozen*-themed special events is held from late morning through park closing. Here's a sample of the offerings:

Frozen Royal Welcome is a mini-parade held on Hollywood Boulevard twice a day. Anna and Elsa roll out in a horse-drawn sleigh, accompanied by Kristoff, "skaters" and "skiers," and flag twirlers.

Olaf's Summer Cool Down features the dorky snowman in his own stage show, which takes place several times a day on the event stage in front of The Great Movie Ride.

At 5:30 p.m. each day on a stage in front of the Chinese Theatre, the **Coolest Summer Ever Dance Party** features live music from Mulch, Sweat & Shears, plus *Frozen* tunes from a DJ.

Frozen Fireworks is presented nighly, usually around 9:45 p.m. *Frozen* characters join the crowd in watching fireworks set to the movie's soundtrack.

STREET ENTERTAINMENT ★★★½ The Studios has one of the best teams of roving street performers in all of Walt Disney World. Appearing primarily on Hollywood and Sunset Boulevards, the cast of characters includes stars and wannabes, agents, directors, and gossip columnists. The performers aren't shy about asking guests to join in their antics.

OSBORNE FAMILY SPECTACLE OF DANCING LIGHTS ★★★★½ What started as a traffic-snarling eyesore in Arkansas is now one of Disney's premier holiday attractions. The Streets of America are transformed with more than 5 million lights of many colors, which adorn facades that replicate New York and San Francisco. These lights periodically "dance" by blinking in sync to music that fills the area; guests are periodically dusted with suspiciously soaplike "snow" from the rooftops.

The Osborne Lights draw heavy crowds, making the Streets of America as crowded as the real streets of Manhattan during rush hour. The lights go on at dusk (normally 6 p.m.). You can loiter to be among the first to see the lights, or visit during a *Fantasmic!* show or shortly after the park has officially closed. The lights usually operate evenings from around the end of the first week of November to around the end of the first week of January.

DISNEY'S HOLLYWOOD STUDIOS TOURING PLAN

TOURING THE STUDIOS CENTERS primarily around **Toy Story Midway Mania!** and the fact that it simply cannot handle the number of guests who want to ride. It's the first choice for families with young kids.

"Not a Touring Plan" Touring Plans

For the type-B reader, these touring plans (see page 804) avoid detailed step-by-step strategies for saving every last minute in line. For DHS, these "not" touring plans include advice for adults and parents with one day in the park, for anyone with two days, and for anyone with an afternoon and a full day to tour.

BEFORE YOU GO

1. Call ☎ 407-824-4321 or visit **disneyworld.com** to verify the park's hours.

2. Buy your admission and make FastPass+ reservations before you arrive.

3. Make lunch and dinner Advance Reservations or reserve the *Fantasmic!* Dining Package (if desired) before you arrive, by calling ☎ 407-WDW-DINE (939-3463).

DISNEY'S HOLLYWOOD STUDIOS ONE-DAY TOURING PLAN *(page 818)*

TO HELP WITH FASTPASS+, we've listed the approximate FastPass+ return times for which you should attempt to make reservations. (The touring plan should work with anything close to the times shown.) We've listed in the plans the attractions most likely to need FastPass+, too. Check **touringplans.com** for the latest information.

PART THIRTEEN

UNIVERSAL ORLANDO

WHEN IT OPENED IN 1990, **Universal Studios Florida (USF)** competed directly with Disney's Hollywood Studios. Both parks offered movie- and television-themed rides and shows, while other attractions provided an educational, behind-the-scenes introduction to the cinematic arts. And both had working film- and television-production facilities.

In the summer of 1999, Universal launched its second major theme park, **Universal's Islands of Adventure (IOA)**, which competes directly with the Magic Kingdom. Universal Studios Florida; Islands of Adventure; the five Universal hotels; and the **CityWalk** dining, nightlife, and shopping complex are collectively known as **Universal Orlando** and are profiled in the next two chapters.

The parks have gone in different directions since then. Whereas Disney's Hollywood Studios essentially abandoned its production facilities long ago, at Universal there is test-marketing of television pilots to guests, along with actual filming. Then there are the attractions, the most famous being located in the groundbreaking **Wizarding World of Harry Potter–Hogsmeade** at Universal's Islands of Adventure. As if to prove this was no one-hit wonder, Universal opened the equally ambitious **Wizarding World of Harry Potter–Diagon Alley** at Universal Studios Florida in 2014.

In contrast, only one truly innovative attraction has opened at Disney's Hollywood Studios in the past decade: 2008's Toy Story Midway Mania! Not even the most ardent Disney supporter would argue that Disney is as invested in the Studios as Universal is in its parks.

Even hardcore Disney fans, such as this Moncton, Nebraska, reader, are beginning to pay attention:

> I'm a huge fan of all things Disney, so it pains me a little to say that the highlight of our most recent trip was actually Universal Orlando. Not because Disney World isn't spectacular—it always is—but because Universal's themed Harry Potter experience is by far the most immersive I've ever had. Disney has to be a little nervous. Responding to Pottermania with an Avatar land just doesn't seem like a good move—Disney on the defensive! But hey, a little competition is healthy.

_A_ UNIVERSAL PRIMER

A NEW KID ON THE BLOCK

THOUGH THIS GUIDE IS PRIMARILY about Walt Disney World, we include coverage of Universal Orlando to help you make informed decisions about how to spend your time. That said, Universal has developed into a major, world-class, multifaceted resort destination—one we can no longer adequately cover in the several dozen pages allocated here.

Therefore, we're excited to announce _The Unofficial Guide to Universal Orlando,_ by Seth Kubersky with Bob Sehlinger and Len Testa. This brand-new guide is the most comprehensive on Universal Orlando in print, with almost 400 pages devoted to the subject. Though we'll continue to cover Universal Orlando in this book, we strongly recommend the new guide for all of the tips, insights, elaborations, and attention to detail that we can't accommodate in these pages.

UNIVERSAL ON THE WEB

IF, JUDGING FROM THE PLENITUDE of independent Disney World websites, you expect a similar number of such sites for Universal, you'd be wrong. Though some of the Disney sites mentioned in Part One (see pages 37–39) cover Universal in some (usually minimal) way, independent Universal sites are practically nonexistent.

Of the independent Disney sites that deal with Universal, we recommend **mousesavers.com** for hotel and admission discounts, plus touring tips for The Wizarding World of Harry Potter. For comprehensive information and discussion, try **parkscope.net** and **orlandoparksnews.com.** For discussion boards dedicated to Universal, go to **orlandounited.com.** For crowd projections and touring tips, check our own **touringplans .com.** News and park developments are available at **orlandosentinel .com** and **orlandoweekly.com; jimhillmedia.com** offers insider information on attractions, new technologies, and updates in the parks. Finally, there's the official Universal Orlando website, **universalorlando.com.**

Universal also offers a free app for iOS and Android that displays wait times and interactive maps while you're inside the parks, using the resort's free Wi-Fi (connect to **xfinitywifi** and accept the legal terms).

COST

UNIVERSAL'S ADMISSION POLICY largely emulates Disney's Magic Your Way program (see page 59). A one-day, one-park Base Ticket is on par with those at the Disney parks; multiday single-park Base Tickets, however, are significantly less expensive at Universal. Park-hopping (or Park-to-Park, in Universal parlance) passes can be much more expensive at Disney, where, for example, a four-day Park Hopper ticket costs a little over 70% more than what you'd pay at Universal.

Be aware that you _must_ have Park-to-Park admission to ride the Hogwarts Express train between IOA and USF; single-park tickets may be upgraded at Guest Services or the train stations.

As at Disney, passes expire 14 days after the first use. Prices listed on page 628 are what you'd pay online and include tax; unlike Disney,

Continued on page 628

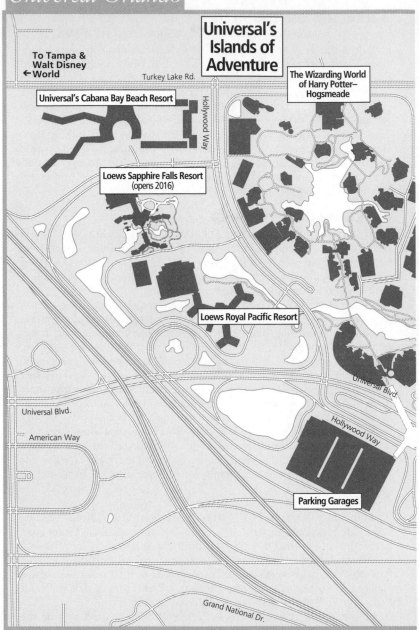

Universal Orlando

Universal's Islands of Adventure

To Tampa & Walt Disney World ←

Turkey Lake Rd.

The Wizarding World of Harry Potter–Hogsmeade

Hollywood Way

Universal's Cabana Bay Beach Resort

Loews Sapphire Falls Resort (opens 2016)

Loews Royal Pacific Resort

Universal Blvd.

Universal Blvd.

American Way

Hollywood Way

Parking Garages

Grand National Dr.

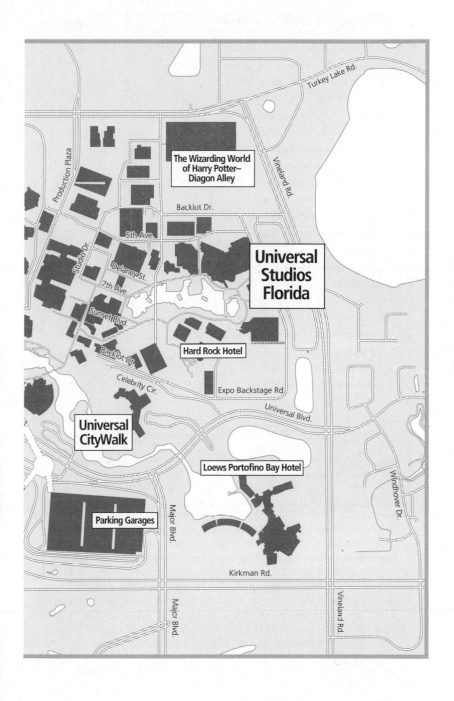

UNIVERSAL vs. WDW ADMISSIONS (prices include tax)	ADULTS	AGES 3-9
BASE TICKETS		
UNIVERSAL One-Day Base Ticket	$109	$103
WDW One-Day Base Ticket (Magic Kingdom)	$112	$105
UNIVERSAL Two-Day Base Ticket	$160	$149
WDW Two-Day Base Ticket	$204	$191
UNIVERSAL Three-Day Base Ticket	$170	$160
WDW Three-Day Base Ticket	$293	$273
UNIVERSAL Four-Day Base Ticket	$181	$170
WDW Four-Day Base Ticket	$325	$304
PARK-HOPPING		
UNIVERSAL One-Day Park-to-Park Ticket	$157	$151
WDW One-Day Park Hopper	$187	$180
UNIVERSAL Two-Day Park-to-Park Ticket	$208	$197
WDW Two-Day Park Hopper	$285	$272
UNIVERSAL Three-Day Park-to-Park Ticket	$218	$208
WDW Three-Day Park Hopper	$380	$359
UNIVERSAL Four-Day Park-to-Park Ticket	$229	$218
WDW Four-Day Park Hopper	$414	$392
ANNUAL PASSES		
UNIVERSAL Power Annual Pass (no comparable WDW pass)	$256	$256
UNIVERSAL Preferred Annual Pass	$357	$357
WDW Annual Pass	$697	$697
UNIVERSAL Premier Annual Pass	$511	$511
WDW Premium Annual Pass	$830	$830

Continued from page 625

however, Universal offers discounts when you purchase passes online at **universalorlando.com**, including $20-per-pass discounts on multiday tickets plus other time-limited specials. Passes purchased online are printable, can be used at the turnstiles, and are good for 14 days beginning with the day of first use. Though Universal discounts multiday tickets online, one-day admissions are slightly more expensive than at the gate; nevertheless, they're probably worth it for the convenience.

Undercover Tourist, a ticket discounter (**undercovertourist.com**), offers the most deeply discounted Universal tickets we're aware of to subscribers of **MouseSavers** (**mousesavers.com**). Tickets purchased through the MouseSavers newsletter include tax and free shipping.

The **Three-Park Unlimited** ticket is good for 14 consecutive days of Park-to-Park admission at both USF and IOA, plus Wet 'n Wild. Three-Park Unlimited tickets are sold by a number of third-party vendors, but not directly by Universal at this time. Only a few dollars more than the four-day Park-to-Park ticket, this ticket is poorly publicized but a great value if you like waterslides and aren't buying an Annual Pass for your extended stay.

The five-park, 14-day **Orlando Flex Ticket** allows unlimited entry to Universal Studios Florida (USF), Universal's Islands of Adventure (IOA),

SeaWorld, Aquatica, and Wet 'n Wild and costs $357.83 for adults and $350.50 for children ages 3–9, tax included. The six-park, 14-day **Orlando Flex Ticket Plus,** providing unlimited entry to USF, IOA, SeaWorld, Aquatica, Wet 'n Wild, and Busch Gardens, costs $393.23 for adults and $371.90 for children. Buy the tickets online at the websites of the participating parks, or get them at a discount at **officialticketcenter.com.** Flex Tickets are a good deal only if you visit all of the parks covered.

unofficial TIP
In order, Mondays, Sundays, and Saturdays are the best days to visit Universal Orlando.

The main Universal Orlando information number is ☎ 407-363-8000. Reach Guest Relations at ☎ 407-224-4233; order tickets by mail at ☎ 407-224-7840. The numbers for Lost and Found are ☎ 407-224-4244 (USF) and 407-224-4245 (IOA); press 2 to be connected.

A WORD ABOUT CROWDS

YOU'VE PROBABLY READ ABOUT the huge crowds that inundate the Wizarding World outposts at both Universal parks. The reports are true, but they present an unbalanced view of the crowds at the Universal parks overall. To get a quantitative grip on crowding, let's look at attendance figures compared with the size of the parks. On a day of average attendance, USF and Disney's Hollywood Studios see about the same number of guests per acre. However, USF has 26 attractions, while DHS has only 17. Therefore, the crowds are distributed among more attractions at USF, making it seem less crowded. Contrasting the Magic Kingdom with IOA, the latter averages 203 guests per day, per acre, while the Magic Kingdom—the attendance leader of all the world's theme parks—registers a whopping 495 guests per day, per acre. Depending on how you define attractions, however, the Magic Kingdom has about 42, versus 26 at Islands of Adventure. Even so, there are still one-and-a-half as many guests for each Magic Kingdom attraction as there are for each IOA attraction.

HOW MUCH TIME TO ALLOCATE

TOURING UNIVERSAL STUDIOS FLORIDA, including one meal and a visit to Diagon Alley, takes about 10–12 hours. One reader laments:

unofficial TIP
Get to the park with your admission already purchased about 45 minutes before official opening time. Arrive 60 minutes before official opening time if you need to buy admission. **Be aware that you can't do a comprehensive tour of both Universal parks in a single day.**

There's a lot of "standing" at USF, and it isn't as organized as DHS. Many of the attractions don't open until 10 a.m. We weren't able to see nearly as many attractions at Universal as we were at DHS during the same amount of time.

As the reader observes, some USF attractions don't open until 10 a.m. or later. Most theater attractions don't schedule performances until 11 a.m. or after. This means that early in the day, all park guests are concentrated among the limited number of attractions in operation.

You won't have to worry about any of this if you use our Universal Studios touring plans. We'll keep you one jump ahead of the crowd and make sure that any given attraction is running by the time you get there.

LODGING AT UNIVERSAL ORLANDO

UNIVERSAL HAS FOUR RESORT HOTELS. The 750-room **Portofino Bay Hotel** is a gorgeous property set on an artificial bay and themed like an Italian coastal town. The 650-room **Hard Rock Hotel** is an ultracool Hotel California replica, and the 1,000-room, Polynesian-themed **Royal Pacific Resort** is sumptuously decorated and richly appointed. All three are on the pricey side. The retro-style **Cabana Bay Beach Resort,** Universal's newest and largest hotel, has 1,800 moderate- and value-priced rooms, plus amenities (such as a bowling alley and lazy river) not seen at comparable Disney resorts. A fifth hotel, the Caribbean-style **Sapphire Falls Resort,** opens in 2016 with 1,000 rooms priced between those at Royal Pacific and Cabana Bay.

Like Disney, Universal offers a number of incentives for visitors to stay at its hotels. Perks available that mirror those offered by the Mouse include delivery to your on-site hotel room of purchases made in the parks, tickets and reservation information from hotel concierges, priority dining reservations at Universal restaurants, and the ability to charge purchases to your room account.

Universal charges a $20-per-night self-parking fee ($27 for valet) at its luxury resorts ($12 per night at Cabana Bay, self-parking only); day guests pay $22 for self-parking and $32 for valet. Free buses and water taxis serve Universal Studios Florida, Islands of Adventure, CityWalk, SeaWorld, Aquatica (SeaWorld's water park), and Wet 'n Wild. Hotel guests (except for those at Cabana Bay and Sapphire Falls) may use the Universal Express program without limitation all day long and are also eligible for "next available" table privileges at CityWalk restaurants and similar priority admission to Universal Orlando theme park shows. The most valuable perk to most Universal resort guests, however, is admission to The Wizarding Worlds of Harry Potter at Islands of Adventure and Universal Studios Florida 1 hour before the general public.

ARRIVING AT UNIVERSAL ORLANDO

UNIVERSAL ORLANDO CAN BE ACCESSED from eastbound I-4 by taking Exit 75A and turning left at the top of the ramp onto Universal Boulevard. If you're traveling westbound on I-4, use Exit 74B and then turn right on Hollywood Way. There are also entrances off Kirkman Road to the east, Turkey Lake Road to the north, and Vineland Road to the west. Universal Boulevard connects the International Drive area to Universal via an overpass bridging I-4. Turkey Lake and Vineland Roads are particularly good alternatives when I-4 is gridlocked.

Two multistory parking garages hold 20,000 cars; signs from all four entrances route you to the parking structures. Parking is $17 for cars and $22 for RVs, trailers, and other large rigs. Regular parking drops to $5 between 6 and 10 p.m. and is free after 10 p.m. Preferred parking is offered during the day for $25, but we've scored spaces just as good or better using the regular parking, especially when we've arrived before 10:30 a.m. An advantage of preferred parking, however, is that you'll park faster because the ratio of cars choosing preferred to regular is about 1 to 13. In addition to the garages, valet parking is available at CityWalk for $15 for a visit of up to 2 hours or $35 for longer than that. If you're a Universal hotel guest, park in the hotel lot and walk, take a free water taxi to CityWalk, or catch a shuttle bus to the parking garages' central hub.

The two rectangular garages lie along a north–south axis, with the pedestrian walkways leading to the theme parks running along the west, or long, side of each building. Because the garages are two-thirds as wide as they are long, the farther your parking place is from the west side, the worse it will be. This is why preferred parking is often not as close as regular parking—with the former, you'll be closer to the covered walkways to the parks, but if your particular space is toward the east side of the garage, you'll end up farther away than a guest who chose regular parking and was assigned a space closer to the west side of the structure.

We strongly recommend that you take a photo of the name and number of your section, level, and row. Sections are named for movies—*Jurassic Park, King Kong,* and the like. The first numeral of the number following the section name tells you what deck level you're on, and the remaining numbers specify the row. So if a sign tells you that you're on King Kong 410, you're in the King Kong section on the fourth floor in Row 10.

From the garages, moving sidewalks deliver you to CityWalk. From here, you can access the main entrances of both Universal Studios Florida and Islands of Adventure. Unlike at Disney parks, there are no trams, so depending on where in the garage your car is parked, you'll have an 8- to 20-minute hike to the theme park entrances even if you use the (sometimes) moving walkways.

If you're staying at Walt Disney World and you don't have a car, **Mears Transportation** will shuttle you from your hotel to Universal and back for $20. Pickup and return times are at your convenience. To schedule a shuttle, call ☎ 855-463-2776.

From three Denver college-aged women who tried Mears:

> *We took a Mears shuttle from Disney to Universal, and I would not recommend it. It's $20 a person and takes a very long time to get you there. It stops at SeaWorld and a couple of other places before Universal Studios. We didn't look into cab fares, but if we had a car, it would have been cheaper and easier to drive it over to Universal. We waited 45 minutes for the shuttle to pick us up from Universal.*

Taxis and ride-share services (such as **Uber** and **Lyft**) are also readily available to and from the resorts. A one-way taxi ride is $35–$45 (plus tip) depending on which Disney hotel you are leaving from, and it may be cheaper than a shuttle if you have three to five people. All transportation services drop off and pick up from the lower level of Universal's main parking hub, from which you can walk to CityWalk and the parks.

UNIVERSAL EXPRESS

SIMILAR TO DISNEY WORLD'S FASTPASS+, Universal Express is a system whereby any guest can schedule an appointment to experience an attraction later in the day with little or no waiting. Unlike FastPass+, Universal Express is not free. Two versions are available, both of which require you to cough up more money beyond your park admission:

Universal Express is free to guests at all Universal hotels except Cabana Bay Beach and Sapphire Falls Resorts; they may use the Express lines all day long simply by flashing the pass they get at check-in. This is especially valuable during peak season.

Guests staying at Cabana Bay, Sapphire Falls (opens 2016), or a non-Universal hotel can purchase Universal Express for an extra $35–$150 (depending on the season), which provides line-jumping privileges at each Universal Express attraction at a given park.

A Kansas City family of four liked the hotel Express Pass:

The Express Pass that you get "free" by staying at one of the resorts is a lifesaver. We never waited in line more than 15 minutes, and it was usually closer to 5. For my roller coaster–loving family, this was great. We didn't have a scheduled time to ride anything like Disney, so we could stray from our plan and re-ride Hulk or Rockit over and over again, which we did. The two Universal parks are close together, so park-hopping doesn't require a shuttle ride.

You can purchase Universal Express for one or both parks and for either single (one ride only on each participating attraction) or unlimited use. The number of Express Passes is limited each day, and they can sell out. Increase your chances of securing passes by buying and printing them at home off Universal's website. Speaking of participating attractions, more than 90% of rides and shows are covered by Universal Express, a much higher percentage than those covered by FastPass+ at Walt Disney World.

You can also buy Universal Express at the theme parks' ticket windows, just outside the front gates, but it's faster to do so inside the parks.

unofficial **TIP**
Universal Express is not valid at the headliner Harry Potter attractions: **Forbidden Journey**, **Escape from Gringotts**, and **Hogwarts Express**.

At Universal Studios Florida, it's available at **Super Silly Stuff**; at Islands of Adventure, you can buy Universal Express at **Jurassic Outfitters, Toon Extra,** and the **Marvel Alterniverse Store.** It's also available up to eight months in advance at **universalorlando.com.** You'll need to know when you plan on using it, though, because prices vary depending on the date.

No matter which version of Universal Express you use, it works the same: Present your pass to a greeter at each attraction entrance, get it scanned for verification, and enjoy your expedited entertainment. At shows, you can present your pass for priority seating 15 minutes before showtime, but that's less of a perk because Universal's large theaters rarely fill up.

A New York mom had a trouble-free experience but questions the value of the investment:

We bought Universal Express, but it was neither necessary nor consistently effective. By arriving at park opening, we were able to see many attractions right away without needing the passes at all. They helped on about three attractions between the two parks—a poor return for an investment of $156. On Dudley Do-Right, we still had to wait 30 minutes even with Express, whereas with Disney's free FastPass+ we never waited more than 5 minutes for an attraction. The only aspect of UE that was better than FP+ is that *touring order was unaffected: UE could be used whenever you first approached an attraction instead of your having to come back later.*

IS UNIVERSAL EXPRESS WORTH IT? The answer depends on the season you visit, hours of park operation, and crowd levels. Attendance has jumped at both parks since the opening of each Harry Potter land, especially at Universal Studios Florida since Diagon Alley opened. However, the big-ticket rides in Hogsmeade and Diagon Alley don't participate in Universal Express, so you don't get to cut in line at Universal's most in-demand attractions. Still, if you want to sleep in and arrive at a park after opening, Express is an effective, albeit expensive, way to avoid long lines at the non-Potter headliner attractions, especially during holidays and busy times.

If, however, you arrive 30 minutes before park opening and you use our touring plans (see pages 819–822), you should experience the lowest possible waits at both parks. We encourage you to try the plans first, but if waits for rides become intolerable, you can always buy Express in the parks, provided it hasn't sold out (an infrequent occurrence).

Finally, you'll want to devise a convenient way to keep track of your pass, as this Bluffton, Indiana, dad found out a little too late:

I wish I'd known ahead of time to bring a lanyard to hang our Universal Express Pass on.

UNIVERSAL EXPRESS FOR RESORT GUESTS This program allows guests at all Universal resorts except Cabana Bay and Sapphire Falls to bypass the regular line anytime and as often as desired simply by flashing a pass they get at check-in. This perk far surpasses any benefit accorded to guests of Disney resorts. Be aware that neither Harry Potter and the Forbidden Journey nor Pteranodon Flyers at IOA is a Universal Express attraction, nor is Harry Potter and the Escape from Gringotts at USF or the interpark Hogwarts Express train. Again, however, all Universal hotel guests, including those staying at Cabana Bay and Sapphire Falls, may enter one or both parks' (depending on the season) Wizarding World outposts an hour before they open to the public. Which park you may enter on any particular day, and which attractions will be operating, are at Universal's discretion and may rotate among the hotels to manage demand.

A father from Snellville, Georgia, discovered that it was cheaper for his family to stay at a Universal resort than buy Universal Express:

We got a room at the Royal Pacific Resort for $349 on a Saturday night, which allowed us to use Universal Express Saturday and Sunday. The room cost $43.63 per person per day, while an [à la carte] Express Pass this same weekend would have cost $56 per person per day, and we still would have had to pay for a hotel.

How Universal Express Affects Crowd Conditions at Attractions

This system dramatically affects crowd movement (and touring plans) in the Universal parks. A woman from Yorktown, Virginia, writes:

People in the Express line were let in at a rate of about 10 to 1 over the regular-line folks. This created bottlenecks and long waits for people who didn't have the Express privilege at the very times when it's supposed to be easier to get around!

SINGLES LINES

ANOTHER TIME-SAVING OPTION is the singles line. Several attractions have this special line for guests riding alone. As Universal employees will tell you, this line is often just as fast as the Express line. We strongly recommend using the singles line whenever possible—it will decrease your overall wait and leave more time for repeat rides or just bumming around the parks. Note, though, that some queues (particularly Forbidden Journey's and Escape from Gringotts's) are attractions in themselves and deserve to be experienced during your first ride.

U-BOT

THIS RIDE-RESERVATION SYSTEM works much like Disney's FastPass+ but incorporates the small U-Bot device. Guests can purchase access to the device at any Express kiosk (buying access online is currently not an option). Once you have your U-Bot, you can use it to reserve ride times for any Universal Express attraction, but note that you can make only one reservation at a time. The U-Bot will vibrate and display a message telling you when it's time to ride. Next, you take your U-Bot to the ride's Express entrance, where the attraction greeter will scan your device and admit you to the Express queue. U-Bot costs considerably less than an Express Pass (usually by about $10–$20).

LOCKERS

UNIVERSAL ENFORCES A MANDATORY locker system at its big thrill rides. Lockers outside these attractions are free for an amount of time that depends on the length of the standby line. So if the line is 30 minutes, for example, and the ride itself is 10 minutes, you get 40 minutes plus a small cushion of about 15 minutes. The lockers then cost $3 for each half hour after that, with a $20 maximum.

The locker banks are easy to find; each bank has a small computer in the center. When the sun is bright, the screen is almost impossible to read, so have someone block the sun or use a different computer. After selecting your language, you press your thumb onto the keypad and have your fingerprint scanned. We've seen people walk away cursing at this step, having repeated it over and over with no success. Don't press down too hard—the computer can't read your thumbprint that way. Instead, take a deep breath and lightly place your thumb on the scanner.

After you do your thumb scan, you'll receive a locker number. Write it down! When you return from your ride, go to the same kiosk machine, enter your locker number, and scan your thumb again. At Guest Relations, family-size lockers are available for $10 for the entire day, but remember that only the person who used his or her thumb to get the locker can retrieve anything from it.

UNIVERSAL, KIDS, AND SCARY STUFF

ALTHOUGH THERE'S PLENTY FOR YOUNGER CHILDREN to enjoy at the Universal parks, most major attractions can potentially make kids under age 8 wig out. At Universal Studios Florida, forget

Disaster!, Hollywood Rip Ride Rockit, Men in Black Alien Attack, Revenge of the Mummy, The Simpsons Ride, ***Terminator 2: 3-D,*** Transformers: The Ride 3-D, and ***TWISTER . . . Ride It Out.*** The first part of **E.T. Adventure** is a little dicey for a few preschoolers, but the end is all happiness and harmony. There are some scary visual effects on both the **Hogwarts Express** train that runs between the two parks and **Escape from Gringotts,** even though both are billed as family rides. **Skull Island** is visually and psychologically intense; it may be too much for little ones. Interestingly, very few families report problems with ***Beetlejuice Graveyard Revue*** or ***Universal Orlando's Horror Make-Up Show.*** Anything we haven't listed is pretty tame.

At Universal's Islands of Adventure, watch out for **The Amazing Adventures of Spider-Man, Doctor Doom's Fearfall, Dragon Challenge, Harry Potter and the Forbidden Journey, The Incredible Hulk Coaster, Jurassic Park River Adventure,** and ***Poseidon's Fury.*** Popeye & Bluto's **Bilge-Rat Barges** is wet and wild, but most younger children handle it well. **Dudley Do-Right's Ripsaw Falls** is a toss-up, to be considered only if your kids like water-flume rides. ***The Eighth Voyage of Sindbad Stunt Show*** includes some explosions and startling special effects, but again, kids tolerate it well. Nothing else should pose a problem.

CHILD SWAP "Switching off" at Universal is similar to Disney's version. The entire family goes through the whole line together before being split into riding and nonriding groups near the loading platform. The nonriding parent and child(ren) wait in a designated room, usually with some sort of entertainment (for example, Forbidden Journey at IOA shows the first 20 minutes of *Harry Potter and the Sorcerer's Stone* on a loop), a place to sit down, and sometimes restrooms with changing tables. At any theme park, the best tip we can give is to ask the greeter in front of the attraction what you're supposed to do.

BLUE MAN GROUP

NO PIECE OF ENTERTAINMENT better encapsulates the "Universal Difference" than Blue Man Group's nightly performances at CityWalk. Cirque du Soleil's *La Nouba*—the closest equivalent at Walt Disney World—is epic, opulent, and elegant, appealing to infants and grandparents alike. Blue Man Group, in comparison, is intimate, offbeat, occasionally ornery, with elements of avant-garde performance art that are as likely to provoke a loud "What the hell?" as applause. Both are phenomenal pieces of theater in their own right, and well worth every penny. But Disney doesn't provide ponchos to patrons seated in the first four rows for protection against flying paint.

The three blue men of the Blue Man Group are just that—blue—and bald and mute. Wearing black clothing and skullcaps slathered with bright-blue grease paint, they deliver a fast-paced show that uses music (mostly percussion) and multimedia effects to make light of contemporary art and life in the information age. The Universal act is just one expression of a franchise that started with three friends in New York's East Village. Now you can catch their zany, wacky, smart stuff in New York, Las Vegas, Boston, Chicago, and Berlin, among other places. The 1 hour, 45-minute Orlando production was updated and reimagined in 2012 to reflect cultural changes in the use of technology in daily life; it includes some segments similar to those seen in other cities but isn't identical.

Funny, sometimes poignant, and always compelling, Blue Man Group pounds out vital, visceral tribal rhythms on complex instruments (made of PVC pipes) that could pass for industrial intestines, and makes seemingly spontaneous eruptions of visual art rendered with marshmallows and a mysterious goo. The weekly supplies include 25½ pounds of Cap'n Crunch, 60 Twinkies, 996 marshmallows, and 9½ gallons of paint. If all this sounds silly, it is, but it's also strangely thought-provoking and deals with topics such as the value of modern art, the ubiquity and addictive nature of tablet devices, the way rock music moves you, and how we're all connected. (*Hint:* It's not the Internet.)

A live percussion band backs Blue Man Group with a relentless and totally engrossing industrial dance riff. The band resides in long, dark alcoves above the stage. At just the right moments, the lofts are lit to reveal a group of pulsating neon-colored skeletons.

Audience participation completes the Blue Man experience. The blue men often move into the audience to bring guests on stage. At the end of the show, giant glowing balloons drop from the rafters for the audience to bat around like beach balls. And a lot of folks can't help standing up to dance and laugh. Magicians for the creative spirit that resides in us all, Blue Man Group makes everyone a coconspirator in a joyous explosion of showmanship.

This show is decidedly different and requires an open mind to be appreciated. It also helps to be a little loose, because, like it or not, everybody gets sucked into the production and leaves the theater a little bit lighter in spirit. If you don't want to be pulled onstage to become a part of the improvisation, don't sit in the first half-dozen or so rows.

The Universal Box Office (☎ 888-340-5476 or 407-258-3626) is open 7 a.m.–7 p.m. EST, or you can buy tickets online at **universal orlando.com.** Advance tickets at the Universal Orlando website run $60–$110 for adults, $30–$57 for children; tickets purchased at the box office cost $10 more. The show isn't recommended for kids under age 3, but they may attend without a ticket if they sit on a lap. AAA members and Preferred and Premiere Annual Pass holders save 20% on up to six tickets, and students with school ID can buy two tickets for $34 on the day of the show, if any are left. You can also save a few dollars by bundling a Blue Man Group ticket with theme park admission or a meal at CityWalk. All Blue Man Group tickets include free CityWalk club admission after the show.

A $20 VIP upgrade option includes access to the Bluephoria private lounge 45 minutes before and after the show, two free drinks (alcoholic or soft), and a photo op with a Blue Man. The lounge is undersized, but the drinks alone are almost worth the upgrade, and the brief meet and greet is a great bonus.

The show is staged in the Sharp Aquos Theatre, which was originally the Nickelodeon soundstage. It can be accessed from CityWalk by following the path between Hard Rock Cafe and Hollywood Rip Ride Rockit, or by exiting Universal Studios Florida through the side gate near Despicable Me Minion Mayhem. Center seats in rows B, C, and D go for a premium price; we recommend center seats in rows E–L, at least nine rows back from the stage.

UNIVERSAL ORLANDO DINING PLAN

UNIVERSAL HAS REPLACED its former all-you-care-to-eat fast food Meal Deals with a **Quick Service Universal Dining Plan** that provides one quick-service meal (including an entrée and soft drink), another soft drink, and one snack. The cost is $19.99 for adults and $12.99 for kids age 9 and younger, plus tax. It's valid at most quick-service eateries in both parks (including **Three Broomsticks** at The Wizarding World of Harry Potter–Hogsmeade, the **Leaky Cauldron** in Diagon Alley, and **Fast Food Boulevard** in Springfield U.S.A.) and a smattering at Universal CityWalk, but not at any hotel eateries.

Virtually every entrée at participating venues can be purchased with a quick-service meal credit, even combo platters that include a side salad or milkshake. A few of the most expensive items, such as whole pizzas, aren't covered. For your nonalcoholic beverages, you can choose from a regular-sized fountain soda; bottled water, juice, or sports drink; or coffee, cocoa, or tea (including tall Starbucks brews). Eligible snacks include churros, pretzels, popcorn, ice cream (regular-size cup or cone, or novelty bar), funnel cakes, cookies, and pastries. Some larger items from snack vendors, such as turkey legs and hot dogs, count as a quick-service meal.

You can buy the Quick Service Dining Plan in advance, but instead, take advantage of your ability to buy into the plan on a day-by-day basis at any participating restaurant after you've already made your menu selection. If your entrée and drink add up to at least $15 before tax and you aren't eligible for any discounts, it's probably in your best interest to ask the cashier to sell you a Quick Service plan. The few extra dollars will net you another drink (worth about $3) and snack (worth $3–$6) for the afternoon, saving you $1–$4. Order a rib platter and soda with a dining plan, and your second drink and snack are essentially free. On the other hand, if you order an $8 cheese pizza and a $3 bag of chips, you'll lose about $3 on the deal. The dining-plan cards aren't tied to a particular person, so they can be traded among family members, and unused credits hold their value as long as you hold onto the card.

A **Table Service Universal Dining Plan** is also offered to on-site hotel guests buying vacation packages, but it's an even worse bargain. It costs $51.99 per adult per day ($17.99 for kids) and includes everything the Quick Service Dining Plan does, plus one table-service meal (entrée, soft drink, and select dessert, minus tip) per day. Unfortunately, fewer than a dozen restaurants on property participate, none of which are in the hotels—which is strange, because the only way to buy the Table Service Dining Plan is as part of a Universal Orlando Vacations hotel package. The Table Service Dining Plan probably wouldn't be a great deal even if Universal gave it away "free," as Disney does with its dining plan; at full price, you're basically throwing money away.

NEW AND UPCOMING AT UNIVERSAL ORLANDO

AFTER 2014'S BLOCKBUSTER PREMIERE of The Wizarding World of Harry Potter–Diagon Alley at Universal Studios Florida, the next big attraction to open at the resort will be **Skull Island: Reign of Kong,** debuting at Islands of Adventure in 2016. Located between Toon Lagoon and Jurassic Park, the new King Kong ride will send guests in safari trucks through an epic adventure that uses massive outdoor and indoor sets, animatronic figures, and gigantic 3-D screens to bring the legendary banana-breathing beast back to life. Nearby, a **Raptor Encounter** meet and greet, utilizing startlingly realistic dinosaur puppets, was installed outside the Jurassic Park Discovery Center in 2015, and the *Eighth Voyage of Sindbad* show was refreshed with new stunts.

As for Islands of Adventure, **Marvel Super Hero Island** is rumored to be ripe for an extensive makeover reflecting the *Avengers* movie series, with **The Incredible Hulk Coaster** receiving new launch mechanics as part of a major overhaul. Also, look for the 3-D visuals that were installed in Universal Studios Japan's Harry Potter and the Forbidden Journey ride to be added to IOA's original version after Universal Studios Hollywood's Hogwarts opens in 2016.

Back at USF, several older attractions are being eyed for replacement, though no official announcements have been made at press time. At press time, the **NBC Media Center** was nearing completion in the Garden of Allah area; no word yet on what that will entail, though. *Twister* is rumored to become a flight simulator starring *Tonight Show* host Jimmy Fallon, and *Disaster!* could make way for an expanded version of the Fast & Furious: Supercharged attraction added in 2015 to Universal Studios Hollywood's tram tour. And most of **Woody Woodpecker's KidZone,** comprising the Barney, Fievel, and Curious George attractions, may be closed by the time you read this, with the area becoming home to Nintendo video-game characters such as Mario and Donkey Kong. Finally, look for upgrades to the park's parades and nighttime entertainment, along with expansion of popular seasonal events such as **Halloween Horror Nights, Mardi Gras,** and **Macy's Holiday Parade.**

Just outside the theme parks, the **CityWalk** entertainment complex recently added three new table-service restaurants: **The Cowfish Sushi Burger Bar, Antojitos Authentic Mexican,** and **Vivo Italian Kitchen,** along with a number of quick-service options such as **Bread Box Handcrafted Sandwiches, Auntie Anne's** pretzels, and **Menchie's Frozen Yogurt.** They'll soon be joined by **NBC Sports Grill & Brew,** featuring Universal's first on-site microbrewery; it replaces the NASCAR Sports Grille. **NBA City** closed in August 2015, but no replacement had been announced at press time.

At the Loews-operated on-site resorts, the **Hard Rock Hotel** completed an extensive refurbishment of all its rooms in 2015, and the **Royal Pacific Resort** is currently undergoing the same. The **Sapphire Falls Resort** will open in summer 2016 as Universal's fifth on-site hotel, located (both physically and pricewise) between the deluxe Royal Pacific and the value-priced Cabana Bay Beach Resort.

Volcano Bay, Universal Orlando's first on-site themed water park, opens in 2017 adjacent to Cabana Bay. A 200-foot-tall volcano will serve as the park's centerpiece, housing a collection of innovative thrill slides and highly themed aquatic attractions. Closing at the end of 2016 is the Universal-owned **Wet 'n Wild** water park.

PART FOURTEEN

UNIVERSAL'S ISLANDS *of* ADVENTURE

WHEN UNIVERSAL'S ISLANDS OF ADVENTURE (**IOA**) opened in 1999, it provided Universal with enough critical mass to actually compete with Disney. Doubly interesting is that the second Universal park is a direct competitor to the Magic Kingdom, the most-visited theme park in the world. How direct a competitor is it? See page 642 for a comparison.

And though Universal played second fiddle to Disney for many years, times have changed: Universal's Islands of Adventure is a state-of-the-art park competing with a Disney park that is more than 35 years old and didn't add a new super-headliner attraction for many years until the Fantasyland expansion begun in 2010 launched in phases, from 2012 to 2014.

> *unofficial* **TIP**
> Roller coasters at Islands of Adventure are the real deal—not for the faint of heart or for little ones.

Incidentally, 2010 marked IOA's coming-out party. In one of the greatest seismic shifts in theme park history, Universal secured the rights to build a Harry Potter–themed area in the park. Harry P. is possibly the only fictional character extant capable of trumping Mickey Mouse, and Universal has gone all out, under J. K. Rowling's watchful and exacting eye, to create a setting and attractions designed to be the envy of the industry.

Disney and Universal officially downplay their fierce competition, pointing out that any new theme park or attraction makes Central Florida a more marketable destination. Behind closed doors, however, the two companies share a Pepsi-versus-Coke rivalry that keeps both working hard to gain a competitive edge. The good news is that all this translates into bigger and better attractions for you to enjoy.

BEWARE OF THE WET AND THE WILD

THOUGH WE'VE DESCRIBED Universal's Islands of Adventure as a direct competitor to the Magic Kingdom, know this: Whereas most Magic Kingdom attractions are designed to be enjoyed by guests of any age, attractions at Islands of Adventure are created largely for an under-40 population. The roller coasters at Universal are serious with a capital S, making Space Mountain and Big Thunder Mountain Railroad look about as frightening as Dumbo. In fact, 9 of the top 14 attractions at

Continued on page 642

Universal's Islands of Adventure

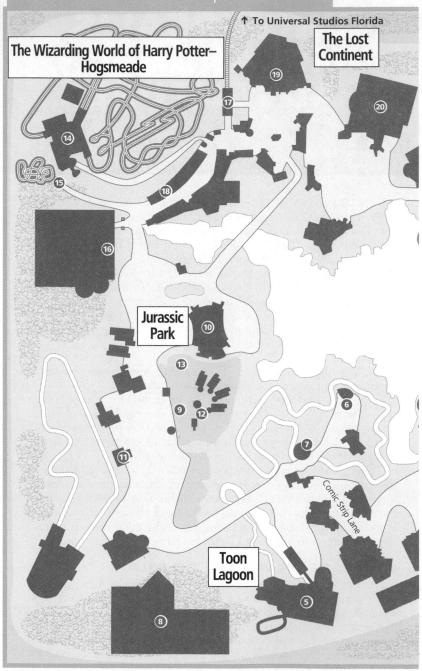

↑ To Universal Studios Florida

The Wizarding World of Harry Potter–Hogsmeade

The Lost Continent

Jurassic Park

Toon Lagoon

Comic Strip Lane

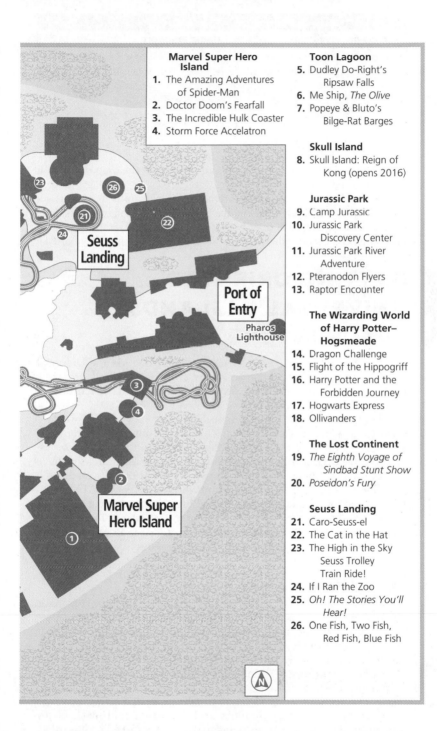

Marvel Super Hero Island
1. The Amazing Adventures of Spider-Man
2. Doctor Doom's Fearfall
3. The Incredible Hulk Coaster
4. Storm Force Accelatron

Toon Lagoon
5. Dudley Do-Right's Ripsaw Falls
6. Me Ship, *The Olive*
7. Popeye & Bluto's Bilge-Rat Barges

Skull Island
8. Skull Island: Reign of Kong (opens 2016)

Jurassic Park
9. Camp Jurassic
10. Jurassic Park Discovery Center
11. Jurassic Park River Adventure
12. Pteranodon Flyers
13. Raptor Encounter

The Wizarding World of Harry Potter–Hogsmeade
14. Dragon Challenge
15. Flight of the Hippogriff
16. Harry Potter and the Forbidden Journey
17. Hogwarts Express
18. Ollivanders

The Lost Continent
19. *The Eighth Voyage of Sindbad Stunt Show*
20. *Poseidon's Fury*

Seuss Landing
21. Caro-Seuss-el
22. The Cat in the Hat
23. The High in the Sky Seuss Trolley Train Ride!
24. If I Ran the Zoo
25. *Oh! The Stories You'll Hear!*
26. One Fish, Two Fish, Red Fish, Blue Fish

IOA AND THE MAGIC KINGDOM AT A GLANCE	
ISLANDS OF ADVENTURE	**MAGIC KINGDOM**
• Seven "islands" (includes Port of Entry)	• Six "lands" (includes Main Street)
• Two adult roller coaster attractions	• Two adult roller-coaster attractions
• A Dumbo-type ride	• Dumbo the Flying Elephant
• One flume ride	• One flume ride
• Toon Lagoon character area	• Storybook Circus character area

Continued from page 639

IOA are thrill rides; of these, 3 will not only scare the crap out of you but will also drench you with water.

For families, there are three interactive playgrounds as well as six minor attractions that young children will enjoy. Of the top rides, only the two in Toon Lagoon (described later) are marginally appropriate for little kids, and even on these rides your child needs to be fairly hardy.

GETTING ORIENTED *at* UNIVERSAL'S ISLANDS *of* ADVENTURE

BOTH UNIVERSAL THEME PARKS are accessed via the Universal CityWalk entertainment complex. After crossing CityWalk from the parking garages, bear right to Universal Studios Florida or left to Universal's Islands of Adventure.

Islands of Adventure is laid out much like Epcot's World Showcase—arranged in a large circle surrounding a lagoon—but it evinces the same thematic continuity present in the Magic Kingdom. Each "land," or "island" in this case, is self-contained and visually consistent in its theme.

You first encounter the Moroccan-style **Port of Entry,** where you'll find Guest Services, lockers, stroller and wheelchair rentals, ATM banking, lost and found, and shopping. From Port of Entry, moving clockwise around the lagoon, you access **Marvel Super Hero Island, Toon Lagoon, Jurassic Park, The Wizarding World of Harry Potter–Hogsmeade, The Lost Continent,** and **Seuss Landing.** There is no in-park transportation to move you between lands.

DECISIONS, DECISIONS

WHEN IT COMES TO TOURING IOA efficiently, you have two basic choices, and as you might expect, there are trade-offs. The Wizarding World of Harry Potter–Hogsmeade sucks up guests like a Hoover. If you're keen to experience **Harry Potter and the Forbidden Journey** without suffering 1–2 hours in line, you need to be at the turnstiles waiting to be admitted at least 30 minutes before the park opens. Once you're admitted, move as swiftly as possible to The Wizarding World and then ride Forbidden Journey and Dragon Challenge, in that order. If you can get them out of the way in about an hour, you'll find much of the remainder of the park sparsely populated. Come back to The Wizarding

NOT TO BE MISSED AT UNIVERSAL'S ISLANDS OF ADVENTURE

- The Amazing Adventures of Spider-Man • Dragon Challenge
- Harry Potter and the Forbidden Journey • Hogwarts Express
- The Incredible Hulk Coaster • Jurassic Park River Adventure
- Popeye & Bluto's Bilge-Rat Barges • Skull Island: Reign of Kong *(opens 2016)*

World later in the day to explore Hogsmeade and the shops. Hogsmeade can fill up quickly in the morning, especially on days when hotel guests are granted early entry to Islands of Adventure, but the area is often nearly empty late in the day.

If you can't be at the park when it opens, skip Potterville first thing and enjoy other attractions in IOA. The good news is that The Wizarding World usually clears out in the last hour even on busy days, so you can ride Forbidden Journey with a minimal wait if you get in the queue 10 minutes before closing.

UNIVERSAL'S ISLANDS *of* ADVENTURE ATTRACTIONS

MARVEL SUPER HERO ISLAND

THIS ISLAND, WITH ITS FUTURISTIC AND RETRO-FUTURE design and comic-book signage, offers shopping, dining, and attractions based on Marvel Comics characters.

The Amazing Adventures of Spider-Man
(Universal Express) ★★★★★

APPEAL BY AGE	PRESCHOOL ★	GRADE SCHOOL ★★★★★	TEENS ★★★★★
YOUNG ADULTS ★★★★½		OVER 30 ★★★★½	SENIORS ★★★★★

What it is Indoor adventure simulator ride based on Spider-Man. **Scope and scale** Super-headliner. **When to go** During the first 40 minutes the park is open. **Special comments** 40" minimum height requirement. **Authors' rating** One of the best attractions anywhere; not to be missed; ★★★★★. **Duration of ride** 4½ minutes. **Probable waiting time per 100 people ahead of you** 5 minutes. **Loading speed** Fast.

DESCRIPTION AND COMMENTS The Amazing Adventures of Spider-Man—covering 1½ acres and combining moving ride vehicles, 3-D film, and live action—was enhanced in 2012 with a complete high-definition digital upgrade. Thirteen reanimated 3-D scenes fuse almost seamlessly with the actual sets and props, so that in many instances guests cannot tell until the action begins whether they're looking at a movie screen or an actual brick wall. The total package is astonishing—frenetic yet fluid, and visually rich. The ride is wild yet very smooth. Though the attractions are not directly comparable, Spider-Man is technologically ahead of The Twilight Zone Tower of Terror at Disney's Hollywood Studios—which is to say that it will leave you in awe.

The storyline is that you're a reporter for the *Daily Bugle* newspaper (where Peter Parker, also known as Spider-Man, works as a mild-mannered photographer), when it's discovered that evildoers have stolen—we promise we're not making this up—the Statue of Liberty. You're drafted on the spot by your cantankerous editor to go get the story. After speeding around and being thrust into a battle between good and evil, you experience a 400-foot "sensory drop" from a skyscraper roof all the way to the pavement. Because the ride is so wild and the action so continuous, it's hard to understand the plot, but you're so thoroughly entertained that you don't really care. Plus, you'll want to ride again and again. Eventually, with repetition, the storyline will begin to make sense.

TOURING TIPS If you were on hand at park opening, ride after experiencing Harry Potter and the Forbidden Journey, Dragon Challenge, and The Incredible Hulk Coaster. If you elect to bypass all the congestion at Forbidden Journey, ride after Dragon Challenge and the Hulk. If you arrived more than 15 minutes after park opening, skip Wizarding World attractions and ride Spider-Man after the Hulk.

Doctor Doom's Fearfall (*Universal Express*) ★★★

APPEAL BY AGE	PRESCHOOL ★	GRADE SCHOOL ★★★★½	TEENS ★★★★½
YOUNG ADULTS ★★★★		OVER 30 ★★★½	SENIORS ★★

What it is Vertical ascent and free fall. **Scope and scale** Headliner. **When to go** First 40 minutes the park is open. **Special comments** 52" minimum height requirement. **Authors' rating** More bark than bite; ★★★. **Duration of ride** 40 seconds. **Probable waiting time per 100 people ahead of you** 18 minutes. **Loading speed** Slow.

DESCRIPTION AND COMMENTS Here you are (again), strapped into a seat with your feet dangling and blasted 200 feet up in the air and then allowed to partially free-fall back down. Imagine the midway game wherein a macho guy swings a sledgehammer, propelling a metal sphere up a vertical shaft to ring a bell—on this ride, you're the metal sphere.

That prospect sounds worse than it actually is—the scariest part of the ride by far is the apprehension that builds as you sit, strapped in, waiting for the ride to launch. Blasting up and falling down are actually pleasant.

TOURING TIPS We've seen glaciers that move faster than the line for Doctor Doom's Fearfall. If you want to ride without investing half a day, be one of the first to ride. If you're on hand at opening time, being among the first isn't too difficult (mainly because the nearby Wizarding World, Hulk, and Spider-Man attractions are bigger draws). Fortunately, as this reader discovered, Doctor Doom also has a singles line that's nearly always open:

If you ask a staff member for the single-rider line, they'll send you through the exit in the arcade. Then just follow the signs.

The Incredible Hulk Coaster (*Universal Express*)
★★★★½

APPEAL BY AGE	PRESCHOOL ★	GRADE SCHOOL ★★★★½	TEENS ★★★★★
YOUNG ADULTS ★★★★★		OVER 30 ★★★★½	SENIORS ★★

What it is Roller coaster. **Scope and scale** Super-headliner. **When to go** During the first 40 minutes the park is open. **Special comments** 54" minimum height requirement. **Authors' rating** A coaster-lover's coaster; not to be missed; ★★★★½. **Duration of ride** 2¼ minutes. **Probable waiting time per 100 people ahead of you** 9 minutes. **Loading speed** Moderate.

Motion Sickness

DESCRIPTION AND COMMENTS There is, as always, a storyline, but for this attraction it's of no importance whatsoever. What you need to know about this attraction is simple: You'll be shot like a cannonball from 0 to 40 mph in 2 seconds, and then you'll be flung upside down 100 feet off the ground, which will, of course, induce weightlessness. From there it's a mere six rollovers punctuated by two plunges into holes in the ground before you're allowed to get out and throw up.

Seriously, the Hulk is a great roller coaster, one of the best in Florida, providing a ride comparable to that of Montu (Busch Gardens) with the added thrill of an accelerated launch (instead of the more typical uphill crank). Plus, like Montu, this coaster has a smooth ride.

TOURING TIPS Arrive before park opening. When admitted, ride after experiencing Harry Potter and the Forbidden Journey and Dragon Challenge. If you want to steer clear of the crowds at Forbidden Journey, ride after Dragon Challenge; if you arrived more than 15 minutes after park opening, skip the Wizarding World attractions and ride the Hulk first thing. Universal provides electronic lockers near the entrance of the Hulk to deposit any items that might depart your person during the Hulk's seven inversions. Be prepared to pat down your pockets for loose change, or you'll be pulled aside for a TSA-style wanding after triggering the metal detectors.

When you reach the boarding area, note that the Hulk has a separate line for those who want to ride in the first row. A singles line is available during peak times, but you may not notice it at first, as this reader attests:

The single-rider line is kind of hard to find—ask where it is. I stood in the standby line for 20 minutes before I realized my mistake.

Storm Force Accelatron *(Universal Express)*   ★★½

APPEAL BY AGE	PRESCHOOL ★★★★★	GRADE SCHOOL ★★★½	TEENS ★★★
YOUNG ADULTS ★★★½		OVER 30 ★★½	SENIORS —

What it is Covered spinning ride. **Scope and scale** Minor attraction. **Special comments** May induce motion sickness. **When to go** During the first hour the park is open. **Authors' rating** Spiffed-up teacups; ★★½. **Duration of ride** 1½ minutes. **Probable waiting time per 100 people ahead of you** 21 minutes. **Loading speed** Slow.

Motion Sickness

DESCRIPTION AND COMMENTS Storm Force is a spiffed-up version of Disney's nausea-inducing Mad Tea Party. Here, you spin to the accompaniment of a simulated thunderstorm and swirling sound and light. A storyline loosely ties this midway-type ride to the Marvel Super Hero Island area, but it's largely irrelevant and offers no advice on keeping your lunch down.

TOURING TIPS Ride early or late to avoid long lines. If you're prone to motion sickness, keep your distance.

TOON LAGOON

THIS LAND TRANSLATES cartoon art into real buildings and settings. Whimsical and gaily colored, with rounded and exaggerated lines, Toon Lagoon is Universal's answer to the old Mickey's Toontown Fair in the Magic Kingdom—only you have about a 60% chance of drowning at Universal's version.

Comic Strip Lane

What it is Walk-through exhibit and shopping and dining venue. **Scope and scale** Diversion. **When to go** Anytime.

DESCRIPTION AND COMMENTS This is the main street of Toon Lagoon. Here you can visit the domains of such vintage Sunday-funnies favorites as *Beetle Bailey, The Family Circus,* and *Blondie*—in other words, intellectual property that Universal could get for cheap. (The characters, though classic, are probably unrecognizable to anybody younger than Generation X.) Shops and eateries tie in to the comic strip theme.

TOURING TIPS This is a great place for photo ops with cartoon characters in their own environment. It's also a great place to drop a few bucks in the diners and shops—but you probably already figured that out.

Dudley Do-Right's Ripsaw Falls
(Universal Express) ★★★½

APPEAL BY AGE	PRESCHOOL ★½	GRADE SCHOOL ★★★★½	TEENS ★★★★
YOUNG ADULTS ★★★★		OVER 30 ★★★★½	SENIORS ★★★★

What it is Flume ride. **Scope and scale** Major attraction. **When to go** Before 11 a.m. **Special comments** 44" minimum height requirement. **Authors' rating** A minimalist Splash Mountain; ★★★½. **Duration of ride** 5 minutes. **Probable waiting time per 100 people ahead of you** 9 minutes. **Loading speed** Moderate.

DESCRIPTION AND COMMENTS Inspired by the *Rocky and Bullwinkle* cartoons, this ride features Canadian Mountie Dudley Do-Right as he tries to save Nell from the evil Snidely Whiplash. Storyline aside, it's a flume ride, with the inevitable big drop at the end. Universal claims that this is the first flume ride to "send riders plummeting 15 feet below the surface of the water." Actually, though, you're just plummeting into a tunnel.

The only problem with this attraction is that everyone inevitably compares it to Splash Mountain at the Magic Kingdom. The flume is as good as Splash Mountain's, and the final drop is a whopper, but the theming and the visuals aren't even in the same league. Taken on its own terms, however, Dudley Do-Right is a darn good flume ride.

TOURING TIPS This ride will get you wet, but on average not as wet as you might expect. If you want to stay dry, however, arrive prepared with a poncho or at least a big garbage bag with holes cut out for your head and arms. After riding, take a moment to gauge the timing of the water cannons that go off along the exit walk—this is where you can really get drenched. Ride after experiencing the Marvel Super Hero rides.

Me Ship, *The Olive*   ★★★

APPEAL BY AGE	PRESCHOOL ★★★★★	GRADE SCHOOL ★★★★½	TEENS ★★
YOUNG ADULTS ★★		OVER 30 ★★½	SENIORS ★★

What it is Interactive playground. **Scope and scale** Minor attraction. **When to go** Anytime. **Authors' rating** Colorful and appealing for kids; ★★★.

DESCRIPTION AND COMMENTS *The Olive* is Popeye's three-story boat come to life as an interactive playground. Younger children can scramble around in Swee'Pea's Playpen, while older sibs shoot water cannons at riders trying to survive the adjacent Bilge-Rat Barges.

TOURING TIPS If you're into the big rides, save this for later in the day.

Popeye & Bluto's Bilge-Rat Barges
(Universal Express)   ★★★★

APPEAL BY AGE	PRESCHOOL ★½	GRADE SCHOOL ★★★★★	TEENS ★★★★½
YOUNG ADULTS ★★★★		OVER 30 ★★★★	SENIORS ★★★★

What it is Whitewater raft ride. **Scope and scale** Major attraction. **When to go** Before 11 a.m. **Special comments** 42" minimum height requirement. **Authors' rating** Bring your own soap; not to be missed; ★★★★. **Duration of ride** 4½ minutes. **Probable waiting time per 100 people ahead of you** 5 minutes. **Loading speed** Moderate.

DESCRIPTION AND COMMENTS This whitewater raft ride includes an encounter with an 18-foot tall octopus. Engineered to ensure that everyone gets drenched, the attraction even provides water cannons for nonparticipants ashore to fire at those aboard. The rapids are rougher and more interesting, and the ride longer, than Animal Kingdom's Kali River Rapids. But Bluto doesn't surpass Disney's raft ride for visuals and theming.

TOURING TIPS If you didn't drown on Dudley Do-Right, here's a second chance. You'll get a lot wetter from the knees down on this ride, so use your poncho or garbage bag and ride barefoot with your britches rolled up. This ride often opens an hour after the rest of the park. Experience the barges in the morning after the Marvel Super Hero attractions and Dudley Do-Right. If you've forgotten your wet wear, you might want to put off riding until last thing before leaving the park. Most preschoolers enjoy the barges—those who don't react more to the way the rapids look than to the roughness of the ride.

Skull Island: Reign of Kong *(opens summer 2016)*

What it is Indoor/outdoor truck safari with 3-D effects. **Scope and scale** Superheadliner. **When to go** Immediately after park opening or just before closing. **Special comments** 34" minimum height requirement. **Authors' rating** Not yet rated; not to be missed. **Duration of ride** More than 4½ minutes. **Probable waiting time per 100 people ahead of you** N/A. **Loading speed** N/A.

DESCRIPTION AND COMMENTS Skull Island: Reign of Kong is both an attraction and an entire "island" unto itself, located between Toon Lagoon's Dudley Do-Right's Ripsaw Falls and the Thunder Falls Terrace restaurant in Jurassic Park. This attraction isn't exactly based on the 2005 *King Kong* remake (though director Peter Jackson did consult on the design), nor is it directly tied to the *Kong: Skull Island* film scheduled for release in 2017. Rather, the ride is an original adventure set in the 1930s, which begins as you pass beneath a stone archway, shaped like a massive monkey skull, and start exploring the elaborate, immersive queue. Pathways wind through dense foliage and an ancient temple inhabited by a hostile indigenous tribe before leading you to your transportation: an oversize open-sided "expedition vehicle" that superficially resembles Animal Kingdom's Kilimanjaro Safari trucks.

Your ride starts with a short loop outside through the jungle (which may be bypassed in inclement weather), ending at the massive torch-framed doors in the center of Skull Island's imposing 72-foot-tall facade. The doors open, allowing you to enter a subterranean maze of corridors and caverns in which you'll be assaulted by all manner of prehistoric beasts and bugs. After barely surviving a series of multisensory near misses with various nasties, you come to an encounter with King Kong himself, brought to life through enormous 3-D screens, similar to the *King Kong 360 3-D* attraction on Universal Studios Hollywood's tram tour. Finally, just when you think it's all over, you'll have one last face-to-face with the "eighth wonder of the world," only this time in the fur-covered flesh.

TOURING TIPS Skull Island promises to be epic in every sense, from the monumental exterior to the length of the experience, said to be one of the longest in the resort. It also promises to attract queues of equally epic proportions. On the plus side, Kong should draw some guests away from The Wizarding World of Harry Potter, helping rebalance the park. You'll want to visit Skull Island first thing in the morning, or immediately following the Hogsmeade attractions if you're using Early Park Admission.

The minimum height requirement is just 34 inches—one of the lowest in the resort—and is designed to be physically accessible to most members of the family. However, on a sensory and psychological level, it's extremely intense; if you or your little one has a fear of darkness, insects, or man-eating monsters, you may want to forgo the monkey.

JURASSIC PARK

JURASSIC PARK is a Steven Spielberg film franchise about a theme park with real dinosaurs. Jurassic Park at Islands of Adventure is a real theme park (or at least a section of one) with fictitious dinosaurs.

Camp Jurassic ★★★½

APPEAL BY AGE	PRESCHOOL ★★★★★	GRADE SCHOOL ★★★★½	TEENS ★
YOUNG ADULTS ★★	OVER 30 ★★★		SENIORS ★★

What it is Interactive play area. **Scope and scale** Minor attraction. **When to go** Anytime. **Authors' rating** Creative playground, confusing layout; ★★★½.

DESCRIPTION AND COMMENTS Camp Jurassic is a great place for children to cut loose. A sort of antediluvian Tom Sawyer Island, it allows kids to explore lava pits, caves, mines, and a rainforest.

TOURING TIPS Camp Jurassic will fire the imaginations of the under-13 set—if you don't impose a time limit on the exploration, you could be here awhile. The confusing layout intersects the queuing area for Pteranodon Flyers.

Jurassic Park Discovery Center ★★½

APPEAL BY AGE	PRESCHOOL ★★★	GRADE SCHOOL ★★★★	TEENS ★★★
YOUNG ADULTS ★★★	OVER 30 ★★★		SENIORS ★★★

What it is Interactive natural-history exhibit. **Scope and scale** Minor attraction. **When to go** Anytime. **Authors' rating** Definitely worth checking out; ★★½.

DESCRIPTION AND COMMENTS This interactive educational exhibit mixes fiction from the movie *Jurassic Park,* such as using fossil DNA to bring dinosaurs to life, with skeletal remains and other paleontological displays. One exhibit lets guests watch an animatronic raptor being hatched. Another allows you to digitally "fuse" your DNA with a dinosaur's to see what the resultant creature would look like.

TOURING TIPS Cycle back after experiencing all the rides or on a second day. Most folks can digest this exhibit in 10–15 minutes.

Jurassic Park River Adventure (*Universal Express*) ★★★★

APPEAL BY AGE	PRESCHOOL ★	GRADE SCHOOL ★★★★	TEENS ★★★★
YOUNG ADULTS ★★★★	OVER 30 ★★★★½		SENIORS ★★★★★

What it is Indoor-outdoor river-raft adventure ride based on the *Jurassic Park* movies. **Scope and scale** Super-headliner. **When to go** Before 11 a.m. **Special comments** 42" minimum height requirement. **Authors' rating** Better than its Hollywood cousin; not to be missed; ★★★★. **Duration of ride** 6½ minutes. **Probable waiting time per 100 people ahead of you** 5 minutes. **Loading speed** Fast.

DESCRIPTION AND COMMENTS Guests board boats for a water tour of Jurassic Park. Everything is tranquil as the tour begins, and the boat floats among large herbivorous dinosaurs such as brontosauruses and stegosauruses. Then, as word comes in that some of the carnivores have escaped their enclosure, the tour boat is accidentally diverted into Jurassic Park's maintenance facilities. Here, the boat and its riders are menaced by an assortment of hungry meat-eaters led by the ubiquitous *T. rex.* At the climactic moment, the boat and its passengers escape by plummeting over an 85-foot drop.

TOURING TIPS Once you're under way, there's a little splashing but nothing major until the big drop at the end of the ride. Fortunately, not all that much water lands in the boat, so you don't get all that wet.

A Honolulu reader thinks Jurassic Park doesn't pass the smell test:

The Jurassic Park ride is a lot of fun—so fun, in fact, that you won't realize how truly HEINOUS the water that drenches you during the climactic splashdown is until much later. We sat in the front row for the ride and got soaked. Three hours later, my girlfriend and I realized that we reeked.

Young children must endure a double whammy on this ride. First, they're stalked by giant, salivating (sometimes spitting) reptiles; then they're sent catapulting over the falls. Unless your children are fairly hardy, wait a year or two before you spring the River Adventure on them.

Because the Jurassic Park section of IOA is situated next to The Wizarding World of Harry Potter–Hogsmeade, the boat will experience heavy crowds earlier in the day. Try to ride before 11 a.m.

Pteranodon Flyers ★★

APPEAL BY AGE	PRESCHOOL ★★★½	GRADE SCHOOL ★★★★	TEENS ★★★★
YOUNG ADULTS ★★★½	OVER 30 ★★★		SENIORS ★★★★

What it is Kiddie suspended coaster. **Scope and scale** Minor attraction. **When to go** When there's no line. **Special comments** Adults and older children must be accompanied by a child between 36" and 52" tall. **Authors' rating** All sizzle, no steak; ★★. **Duration of ride** 1¼ minutes. **Probable waiting time per 100 people ahead of you** 28 minutes. **Loading speed** More sluggish than a hog in quicksand.

DESCRIPTION AND COMMENTS This is Islands of Adventure's biggest blunder. Engineered to accommodate only 170 persons per hour, the ride dangles you on a swing below a track that passes over a small part of Jurassic Park. We recommend skipping this one. Why? Because the next ice age will probably end before you reach the front of the line! And your reward for all that waiting? A 1-minute-and-15-second ride.

TOURING TIPS Photograph the pteranodon as it flies overhead. You're probably looking at something that will someday be extinct.

Raptor Encounter ★★★½

APPEAL BY AGE	PRESCHOOL ★★	GRADE SCHOOL ★★★★	TEENS ★★★★
YOUNG ADULTS ★★★½	OVER 30 ★★★½		SENIORS ★★★

What it is Photo op with lifelike dinosaur. **Scope and scale** Minor attraction. **When to go** Check park map or attraction for appearance times. **Authors' rating** Clever girl! Sure to scare the spit out of small kids; ★★★½. **Duration of encounter** About a minute. **Probable waiting time per 100 people ahead of you** 30 minutes.

DESCRIPTION AND COMMENTS Just when everyone thinks that Disney has a lock on the meet-and-greet market, between its talking Mickeys and *Frozen* sisters, Universal does the impossible—breeds a live velociraptor and makes it pose for pictures! OK, it isn't actually a real dinosaur on display just outside the Jurassic Park Discovery Center, inside a portion of the long-closed Triceratops Encounter walk-through attraction. In fact, it's an amazingly realistic puppet, created by Michael Curry (who created designs for Disney's *Lion King* and *Finding Nemo* musicals, as well as Diagon Alley's *Tales of Beedle the Bard* show) and brought to life by talented performers.

Several times each hour, the blue siren lights around the sunken predator paddock signal the arrival of Lucy or Ethel, the park's new semi-tame stars. A game warden briefs one family at a time regarding proper safety procedures (convey calm assurance, move in slowly, and try not to smell like meat) before they step up for a photo. Don't peer too closely over the edge of the raptor enclosure; you'll spot the cleverly camouflaged legs of the puppeteer inside and spoil the illusion. A Photo Connect photographer will take your picture with his or her camera (included with Star Card packages) or your own, and selfies are also encouraged—just don't be surprised if the dino snaps when you say, "Smile!"

TOURING TIPS The Raptor Encounter has quickly become quite popular, and with limited capacity and little shade, this can become an unpleasant wait. If appearance times aren't printed on the park map, check with a team member outside the paddock entrance and arrive at least 15 minutes before a scheduled session; 20-minute appearances begin around 11 a.m. and occur about every half-hour until 6 p.m. Don't try to touch the raptor, or you may come home minus a hand—surreptitiously feeding your offspring to the dinosaurs is also discouraged by management.

THE WIZARDING WORLD OF HARRY POTTER–HOGSMEADE

IN WHAT MAY PROVE TO BE the competitive coup of all time between theme park archrivals Disney and Universal, the latter inked a deal with Warner Brothers Entertainment to create a "fully immersive" Harry Potter–themed environment based on the best-selling children's books by J. K. Rowling and the companion blockbuster movies from Warner Brothers. The books have been translated into 74 languages, with more than 450 million copies sold in more than 200 territories around the world. The movies have made more than $7.7 billion worldwide, making Harry Potter the second highest-grossing film franchise in history. The project was blessed by Rowling, who is known for tenaciously protecting the integrity of her work. In the case of the films, she demanded that Warner Brothers be true, to an almost unprecedented degree, to the books on which the films were based.

The 20-acre Wizarding World is an amalgamation of landmarks, creatures, and themes that are faithful to the films and books. You access the area through an imposing gate that opens onto **Hogsmeade,** depicted in winter and covered in snow. This is The Wizarding World's primary shopping and dining venue. Exiting Hogsmeade, you first glimpse the towering castle housing **Hogwarts School of Witchcraft and Wizardry,** flanked by the **Forbidden Forest** and **Hagrid's Hut.** The grounds and interior of the castle contain part of the queue for the super-headliner **Harry Potter and the Forbidden Journey.** Universal has gone all out on the castle, with the intention of creating an icon even more beloved and powerful than Cinderella Castle at Disney's Magic Kingdom.

"What a Long Strange Trip It's Been"

That Grateful Dead lyric is awfully appropriate when recounting the evolution of The Wizarding World–Hogsmeade. A Harry Potter theme park (or themed area) has been the chop-licking dream of the amusement industry for a decade. First, of course, there were the books, which against all odds trumped texting and TV to lure a broad age range of youth back to the printed page. Next came the movies. In securing the film rights, Warner Brothers, along with several unsuccessful suitors, learned the most important thing about exploiting the Harry Potter phenomenon: J. K. Rowling is boss.

As the Potter juggernaut took the world by storm, entertainment conglomerates began approaching Rowling about theme park rights. When she spurned a Universal Studios Florida concept for a show based on the Potter characters, industry observers were certain that she had struck a deal with Disney. In fact, Disney was in talks with Rowling about a stand-alone Harry Potter theme park. For her part, Rowling had no problem visualizing what she wanted in a theme park, but from Disney's point of view, what Rowling wanted was operationally problematic, if not altogether impossible. Never an entity to concede control, Disney walked.

Universal caught Rowling on the rebound and brought her to Orlando to tour Islands of Adventure. Among other things, they squired her around the Lost Continent section of the park, impressing her with its detailed theme execution and showing her how with a little imagination it could be rethemed. Rowling saw the potential but wasn't much more flexible with Universal than she was with Disney. From her perspective, getting a themed area right couldn't be any harder than getting a movie right, so she insisted that Stuart Craig, her trusted production designer for the films, be responsible for faithfully recreating sets from the movies. Universal, on fire to land Harry Potter, became convinced that the collaboration could work.

But theme parks and movies are two very different things. With a film, a set has to look good only for a few moments and then it's on to something else. With a theme park, a set has to look good 12–16 hours a day, in all manner of weather, and with tens of thousands of tourists rambling through it in need of food, drink, restrooms, protection from rain, and places to rest. With The Wizarding World–Hogsmeade, Rowling's insistence on authenticity occasioned conundrums not anticipated by the theme park designers, who, for example, logically assumed that guests would like to see the interior of Hagrid's Hut. No problem—a walk-through attraction will serve nicely. Of course, there's the Americans with Disabilities Act, so we'll need ramps both in and out of the hut. No way, say the movie people: Hagrid's Hut in the films had steps, so the theme park version must have them too.

Bone Up

We don't have room to explain all the Potter allusions and icons incorporated into The Wizarding World. Because they so accurately replicate scenes from the books and films, it helps immeasurably to be well versed in all things Harry. If it's been awhile since you've seen one of the movies or read one of the novels, you can brush up by watching the first four flicks in the series, in particular *Harry Potter and the Goblet of Fire* and *Harry Potter and the Sorcerer's Stone* (*Harry Potter and the Philosopher's Stone* outside India and the United States). For an easy memory jog, check out the films' trailers at **YouTube.** If you know nothing at all about Harry Potter, you'll still have fun, but to truly appreciate the nuance and detail, we suggest you hit the books.

Getting In

Crowds are certainly larger during summer and holidays, but because of The Wizarding World's overwhelming popularity, you'll encounter lines even at slower times of year. During peak periods, hotel guests may be allowed into IOA 1 hour before the general public, while all guests are usually admitted through the turnstiles into Port of Entry 30 minutes before the official opening time.

Wizarding World crowd management has been a work in progress for Universal. Now, with six years of operation under its belt, Universal has settled on a flexible system predicated on the expected level of attendance for any given day. (Similar procedures are in place at Diagon Alley; see Part Fifteen, page 682.) No matter the crowd level, if you're staying in one of Universal's on-site hotels and you have early-entry privileges for The Wizarding World, use them, arriving as early during the early-entry period as possible.

On most days of the year, from the slowest off-season through the busiest summer weeks, you can enter and depart The Wizarding World of Harry Potter–Hogsmeade as you please. The waits for the rides will still be more than an hour at times, but gaining entry to the themed area itself is not an issue.

On days when the park is busiest, such as during spring break or between December 25 and January 1, access to Hogsmeade may be limited for part of the day. Barricades are placed at both entrances to The Wizarding World–Hogsmeade once the area reaches maximum occupancy. You can then go to touch screen ticket kiosks outside the Jurassic Park Discovery Center and obtain a free return ticket (not unlike the old paper Fastpasses at Walt Disney World) to come back during your choice of designated time windows. You do not need your admission ticket to receive a timed return ticket, and one person can retrieve a time for your entire party (up to nine people). At the specified time, return to the Lost Continent entrance and present your pass to the barricade crew to gain entry.

unofficial **TIP**
If you leave The Wizarding World while the entrance barriers are in place and you wish to return, you'll either have to wait in line to get another pass (provided they haven't all been distributed) or wait until late in the day, when the barricades come down as crowds disperse.

The return time on your pass depends on crowd conditions and how many Universal resort guests are in The Wizarding World–Hogsmeade before the park opens to the general public. Depending on demand, your possible return times may be many hours in the future, and it's possible (though extremely rare) for return tickets to run out entirely. Another factor that will affect your wait is how well Harry Potter and the Forbidden Journey is operating because this is what those in line are waiting for. If the ride comes up on schedule and runs trouble-free, everything runs smoothly. If Forbidden Journey experiences problems, though, especially first thing in the morning, it gums up the works for everyone.

On these peak days, a standby queue may also be erected in the waterfront landing behind the Jurassic Park Discovery Center; because more guests can enter only as others leave, this line can be painfully slow, so a return ticket is strongly suggested. It is common for the entrance barricades to be removed during the last hour or two the park is open, thus presenting the opportunity to come and go as you please.

Once admitted to–Hogsmeade, you'll still have to wait for each ride, store, and concession, as well as for the area's one restaurant. Because Hogsmeade has less elbow room than Diagon Alley, it will reach maximum occupancy and require return tickets on days when Diagon does not, and feel more crowded once you finally get inside.

Note that guests arriving on Hogwarts Express disembark outside of Hogsmeade and must still retrieve a ticket before entering. The timed returned tickets are neither needed nor accepted for Hogwarts Express itself.

However complicated, it's all doable, as a multigenerational Grosse Pointe, Michigan, family attests:

> *Convinced of your rectitude, we went without fear to Universal. We made it to Harry Potter by 8:05, were out of the Forbidden Journey and on the Hippogriff by 8:30, and had our Butterbeer by 9.*

Ladies and Gentlemen, Start Your Broomsticks

The Wizarding World–Hogsmeade is in the northwest corner of Islands of Adventure, between The Lost Continent and Jurassic Park. From the IOA entrance, the most direct route there is through Port of Entry then right, through Seuss Landing (staying to the left of Green Eggs and Ham) and The Lost Continent, to the Hogsmeade main gate. The alternative route is to cross the bridge connecting The Lost Continent with Jurassic Park, and then turn right after entering the latter area. Note that the bridge is closed on slower days.

For the moment, though, let's begin our exploration at The Wizarding World's main entrance, on The Lost Continent side. Passing beneath a stone arch, you enter the village of **Hogsmeade.** The **Hogwarts Express** locomotive sits belching steam on your right. The village setting is rendered in exquisite detail: Stone cottages and shops have steeply pitched slate roofs; bowed multipaned windows; gables; and tall, crooked chimneys. Add cobblestone streets and gas street lamps, and Hogsmeade is as reminiscent of Sherlock Holmes as it is of Harry Potter.

Your first taste—literally—of the Harry Potter universe comes courtesy of **Honeydukes.** Specializing in Potter-themed candy such as Acid Pops (no flashbacks, guaranteed), Tooth Splintering Strong Mints, and Fizzing Whizzbees, the sweet shop offers no shortage of snacks that administer an immediate sugar high. There's also a small bakery inside; while we highly recommend the Cauldron Cakes, the big draw is the elaborately boxed Chocolate Frogs. The chocolate inside isn't anything special, but the packaging looks as if it came straight from a Harry Potter film, complete with lenticular wizard trading card.

Next door to Honeydukes and set back from the main street is **Three Broomsticks,** a rustic tavern serving English staples such as fish-and-chips, shepherd's pie, Cornish pasties, and turkey legs; kids' fare includes the obligatory mac and cheese and chicken fingers. To the rear of the tavern is the **Hog's Head** pub, which serves a nice selection of beer as well as The Wizarding World's signature nonalcoholic brew, Butterbeer (see next page). Three Broomsticks and the Hog's Head were carved out of The Lost Continent's popular Enchanted Oak Tavern, which was Potterfied pretty effectively in its reincarnation, though a good deal of seating capacity was sacrificed. To dine at Three Broomsticks anytime from its opening until roughly 8 p.m., you'll have to wait in a long queue during busier times of year. In summer 2014, waiting times for Three Broomsticks were upwards of 30 minutes much of the day (though additional capacity had been added in 2013 by replacing space-hogging booths with tables).

Roughly across the street from the pub, you'll find benches in the shade at the **Owlery,** where animatronic owls (complete with lifelike poop) ruffle and hoot from the rafters. Next to the Owlery is the **Owl Post,** where you can have mail stamped with a Hogsmeade postmark before dropping it off for delivery (an Orlando postmark will also be applied by the real USPS). The Owl Post also sells stationery, toy owls, and the like. Here, once again, a nice selection of owls preens on the timbers overhead. You access the Owl Post in either of two ways: through an interior door following the wand-choosing demonstration at Ollivanders (see below), or through **Dervish and Banges,** a magic-supplies shop that's interconnected with the Owl Post. You can't enter through the Owl Post's front door on busy days, when it serves exclusively as an exit. Because it's so difficult to get into the Owl Post, IOA sometimes stations a team member outside to stamp your postcards with The Wizarding World postmark.

unofficial **TIP**
The only restrooms in The Wizarding World at IOA, labeled PUBLIC CONVENIENCES, are in the middle of Hogsmeade. Remember where they are—especially if you're planning to ride Forbidden Journey or Dragon Challenge and you're prone to motion sickness.

Next to the Owl Post is the previously mentioned **Ollivanders** (★★★★), a musty little shop stacked to the ceiling with boxes of magic wands. Here, following a script from the Potter books, you can pick out a wand or, in an interactive experience, let it pick you. This is one of the most truly imaginative elements of The Wizarding World: A Wandkeeper sizes you up and presents a wand, inviting you to try it out; your attempted spells produce unintended, unwanted, and highly amusing consequences. Ultimately, a wand chooses you, with all the attendant special effects. It's great fun, but the tiny shop can accommodate only about 24 guests at a time. Usually just one person in each group gets to be chosen by a wand, and then the whole group is dispatched to the Owl Post and Dervish and Banges to make purchases. Wand prices range from $25 for a no-frills model to $45 for an interactive gizmo that triggers special effects hidden inside shop windows throughout Hogsmeade. The wand experience is second in popularity only to Harry Potter and the Forbidden Journey—lines build quickly after opening, and there's little to no shade. If Ollivanders is a priority, go there first thing in the morning or after 7:30 p.m. The average wait time during summer and other busy periods is 45–85 minutes between 9:30 a.m. and 7:30 p.m. If you're just looking to buy a wand without the interactive experience, a cart is usually set up between Filch's Emporium of Confiscated Goods and the Flight of the Hippogriff exit, with little to no wait.

At the far end of the village, the massive **Hogwarts** castle comes into view, set atop a rock face and towering over Hogsmeade and the entire Wizarding World. Follow the path through the castle's massive gates to the entrance of Harry Potter and the Forbidden Journey. Below the castle and to the right, at the base of the cliff, are the **Forbidden Forest, Hagrid's Hut,** and the **Flight of the Hippogriff** children's roller coaster. In the village, near the gate to Hogwarts Castle, is **Filch's Emporium of Confiscated Goods,** which offers all manner of Potter-themed gear, including Quidditch clothing, magical-creature toys, film-inspired chess sets, and, of course, Death Eater masks (breath mints extra).

In keeping with the stores depicted in the Potter films, the shopping venues in The Wizarding World–Hogsmeade are small and intimate— so intimate, in fact, that they feel congested when they're serving only 12–20 shoppers. With so many avid Potter fans, lines for the shops develop most days by 9:30 or 10 a.m., creating a phenomenon we've never seen in our 33 years of covering theme parks: The lines for the shops are longer than the lines for Dragon Challenge and Flight of the Hippogriff—at 11 a.m., there was frequently a 30- to 40-minute wait to get into the shops, but a less-than-20-minute wait to ride the coasters. Filch's Emporium is the only shop in The Wizarding World that you can enter during high season without waiting in line; the problem is that it doubles as the exit for Forbidden Journey. As throngs of riders flow out continuously, trying to enter Filch's is not unlike swimming upstream to spawn; still, it's a whole lot better than standing in lines for the other shops. Because the stores are so jammed, IOA sells some Potter merchandise, including wands, through street vendors and in Port of Entry shops.

At the end of the village and to the left is the walkway to **Jurassic Park,** the themed area contiguous to The Wizarding World.

The Butterbeer Craze

Butterbeer is a nonalcoholic, cream soda–like beverage served from a tap, with a butterscotch-y head that's added after the drink is poured. There's also a frozen version that's sort of like a slushie. Both were invented for The Wizarding World and had to meet J. K. Rowling's stringent specifications, which, among other things, required natural sugar (don't ask for Butterbeer Lite).

unofficial **TIP**
At J. K. Rowling's request, no brand-name soft drinks are available in The Wizarding World—if you want a Coke, you'll have to go to The Lost Continent or Jurassic Park.

We didn't expect to like it but were pleasantly surprised: It's tasty and refreshing, albeit *really* sweet. A 16-ounce soda in a plastic cup goes for $4.99, while the frozen version is $5.99. The same soda in a Harry Potter souvenir cup sells for an additional $8 with no discount on refills. The hot version is sold in a 12-ounce paper cup for $4.99. Finally, Diagon Alley introduced the world to soft-serve Butterbeer ice cream, which tastes almost exactly like the drinks. You can get it at Florean Fortescue's in a cup ($4.99), waffle cone ($5.99), or plastic souvenir sundae glass ($10.99). If you only want a cup of Butterbeer without toppings, the soft-serve is also served off menu at The Hopping Pot and The Fountain of Fair Fortune, both in Diagon Alley, where you'll find a much shorter wait.

It seems everyone in the park is dead-set on trying Butterbeer, as confirmed by Universal's sale of its five millionth cup in December 2012. Unfortunately, the ambrosial liquid is sold only at **Three Broomsticks,** at the **Hog's Head** pub, and by two street vendors—and that means, once again, long waits. Many guests buy from the outside vendors, waiting 30 minutes or more in line to be served. We recommend that you try your luck at the Hog's Head—the wait here is generally 10 minutes or less, and often there's nobody in line, even when the outdoor carts have lines 30 people deep only 20 feet away. Once served, you can relax with your drink at a table in the pub or out on the rear patio. Be aware that the outdoor vendors charge a few cents more and don't honor Annual Pass discounts.

Wizarding World Entertainment

Nearly every retail space sports some sort of animatronic or special-effects surprise. At **Dervish and Banges,** the fearsome Monster Book of Monsters rattles and snarls at you as Nimbus 2001 brooms strain at their tethers overhead. At the Hog's Head pub, the titular porcine part, mounted behind the bar, similarly thrashes and growls. Street entertainment at the Forbidden Journey end of Hogsmeade includes **The Frog Choir** (★★★), composed of four singers, two of whom are holding large amphibian puppets sitting on pillows. The 10-minute show is followed by a photo op. Though cute, The Frog Choir isn't much more than filler for IOA's attraction list and probably not worth going out of your way for. The 16-minute **Triwizard Spirit Rally** (★★★½) showcases dancing, martial arts, and acrobatics.

Dragon Challenge (Universal Express) ★★★★

APPEAL BY AGE	PRESCHOOL ★	GRADE SCHOOL ★★★★★	TEENS ★★★★½
YOUNG ADULTS ★★★★★		OVER 30 ★★★★½	SENIORS ★★★

What it is Roller coaster. **Scope and scale** Headliner. **When to go** Immediately after Harry Potter and the Forbidden Journey. **Special comments** 54" minimum height requirement. **Authors' rating** As good as the Hulk coaster; not to be missed; ★★★★. **Duration of ride** 2½ minutes. **Probable waiting time per 100 people ahead of you** 9 minutes. **Loading speed** Moderate.

DESCRIPTION AND COMMENTS Dragon Challenge, formerly Dueling Dragons and part of The Lost Continent, was renamed and incorporated into The Wizarding World in 2010. The storyline is that you're preparing to compete in the Triwizard Tournament from *Harry Potter and the Goblet of Fire.* As you wind through the long, long queue, you pass through tournament tents and dark passages that are supposed to be under the stadium. You'll see the Goblet of Fire on display and hear the distant roar of the crowd in the supposed stadium above you.

Riders board one of two coasters—Chinese Fireball or Hungarian Horntail—that are launched moments apart on tracks that are closely intertwined. The tracks are configured so that you get a different experience on each. The trains are dispatched sequentially instead of simultaneously, so it looks as if one train is chasing another.

Because this is an inverted coaster, your view of the action is limited unless you're sitting in the front row. Regardless of where you sit, there's plenty to keep you busy. Dragon Challenge is the highest coaster in the park and also claims the longest drop at 115 feet, plus five inversions. As on the Hulk, it's a smooth ride all the way.

Coaster fans argue about which seat on which train provides the wildest ride. We prefer the front row on either train, but coaster loonies hype the front row of Fireball and the last row of Horntail.

TOURING TIPS Use the restrooms before getting in line. The queuing area for Dragon Challenge is the longest, most convoluted affair we've ever seen, winding endlessly through a maze of faux subterranean passages. After what feels like a comprehensive tour of Mammoth Cave, you finally emerge at the loading area, where you must choose between Chinese Fireball or Hungarian Horntail. Of course, at this critical juncture, you're as blind as a mole rat from being in the dark for so long. Our advice is to follow the person in front of you until your eyes adjust to the light.

Waits for Dragon Challenge, one of the best coasters in the country, rarely exceed 30 minutes before 11 a.m. Ride after experiencing Harry Potter and the Forbidden Journey. Even if there's no line to speak of, it takes 10–12 minutes just to navigate the passages and not much less time to exit after riding. There used to be a shortcut from the exit back into the queue for re-rides, but since Universal began enforcing the mandatory locker policy with metal detectors outside the castle, everyone must be inconveniently inspected before each trip. Finally, if you don't have time to ride both coasters, the *Unofficial* crew unanimously prefers Chinese Fireball.

Flight of the Hippogriff *(Universal Express)* ★★★

APPEAL BY AGE PRESCHOOL ★★★½ GRADE SCHOOL ★★★★ TEENS ★★★
YOUNG ADULTS ★★½ OVER 30 ★★★½ SENIORS ★★★

What it is Kiddie roller coaster. **Scope and scale** Minor attraction. **When to go** First 90 minutes the park is open. **Special comments** 36" minimum height requirement. **Authors' rating** A good beginner coaster; ★★★. **Duration of ride** 1 minute. **Probable waiting time per 100 people ahead of you** 14 minutes. **Loading speed** Slow.

DESCRIPTION AND COMMENTS Below and to the right of Hogwarts Castle, next to Hagrid's Hut, the Hippogriff is short and sweet but not worth much of a wait. Fortunately, waits usually don't exceed 20 minutes, even in the non-Express line.

TOURING TIPS Have your kids ride soon after the park opens while older sibs enjoy Dragon Challenge. Check out Hogwarts Castle from the cliff bottom and Hagrid's Hut above the path for the regular line.

Hogwarts Express ★★★★½

APPEAL BY AGE PRESCHOOL ★★★★ GRADE SCHOOL ★★★★★ TEENS ★★★★
YOUNG ADULTS ★★★★½ OVER 30 ★★★★½ SENIORS ★★★★½

What it is Transportation attraction. **Scope and scale** Super-headliner. **When to go** Immediately after park opening. **Special comments** Expect lengthy waits in line; requires Park-to-Park admission. **Authors' rating** Not to be missed; ★★★★½. **Duration of ride** 4 minutes. **Probable waiting time per 100 people ahead of you** 7 minutes. **Loading speed** Moderate.

DESCRIPTION AND COMMENTS See Part Fifteen, page 688, for a full review.

TOURING TIPS Because the Hogsmeade Station doesn't include the cool Platform 9¾ effect found at the King's Cross end, expect waits for the one-way trip to be shorter here. A Park-to-Park ticket is required to board, and all guests exit at Universal Studios Florida outside of the London waterfront, so the train isn't a shortcut into Diagon Alley.

The Hogsmeade Station lies within the footprint of the Dragon Challenge roller coaster and provides pedestrian access to Hogsmeade and IOA's Lost Continent themed area. On days of low-to-average attendance, disembarking guests will be allowed directly into Hogsmeade, less than a minute's walk away. On days of heavy attendance, they'll be directed to the bridge between The Lost Continent and Jurassic Park, where they'll have to either queue to enter Hogsmeade or obtain a free timed-entry ticket to visit The Wizarding World at a specified time.

If you wish to experience the train, do so before the queue builds in midafternoon. If the line grows very long, guests wishing to ride a second time in one day may be relegated to a slower re-ride queue.

Harry Potter and the Forbidden Journey ★★★★★

APPEAL BY AGE   PRESCHOOL ★   GRADE SCHOOL ★★★★½   TEENS ★★★★★
YOUNG ADULTS ★★★★★   OVER 30 ★★★★★   SENIORS ★★★★★

Motion Sickness

What it is Motion-simulator dark ride. **Scope and scale** Super-headliner. **When to go** Immediately after park opening. **Special comments** Expect *long* waits in line; 48" minimum height requirement. **Authors' rating** Marvelous for Muggles and not to be missed; ★★★★★. **Duration of ride** 4¼ minutes. **Probable waiting time per 100 people ahead of you** 4 minutes. **Loading speed** Fast.

DESCRIPTION AND COMMENTS This ride provides the only opportunity at Universal Orlando to come in contact with Harry, Ron, Hermione, and Dumbledore as portrayed by the original actors. Half the attraction is a series of preshows, setting the stage for the main event, a dark ride. You can get on the ride in only 10–25 minutes using the singles line, but everyone should go through the main queue at least once.

From Hogsmeade you reach the attraction through the imposing Winged Boar gates and progress along a winding path. Entering the castle on a lower level, you walk through a sort of dungeon festooned with various icons and prop replicas from the Potter flicks, including the Mirror of Erised from *Harry Potter and the Sorcerer's Stone.* You later emerge back outside and into the Hogwarts greenhouses. Cleverly conceived and executed, with some strategically placed mandrakes to amuse you, the greenhouses compose the larger part of the Forbidden Journey's queuing area. If you're among the first in the park and in the queue, you'll move through this area pretty quickly. Otherwise . . . well, we hope you like plants. The greenhouses are not air-conditioned, but fans move the (hot) air around. Blessedly, there are water fountains but, alas, no restrooms.

Having finally escaped horticulture purgatory, you reenter the castle, moving along its halls and passageways. One chamber you'll probably remember from the films is a multistory gallery of portraits, many of whose subjects come alive when they take a notion. You'll see for the first time the four founders of Hogwarts: Helga Hufflepuff holding her famous cup, Godric Gryffindor and Rowena Ravenclaw nearby, and the tall, moving portrait of Salazar Slytherin straight ahead. The founders argue about Quidditch and Dumbledore's controversial decision to host an open house at Hogwarts for Muggles (garden-variety mortals). Don't rush through the gallery—the effects are very cool, and the conversation is essential to understanding the rest of the attraction.

Next up, after you've navigated some more passages, is Dumbledore's office, where the chief wizard appears on a balcony and welcomes you to Hogwarts. The headmaster's appearance is your introduction to Musion Eyeliner technology—a high-definition video-projection system that produces breathtakingly realistic, three-dimensional, life-size moving holograms. The technology uses a special foil that reflects images from HD projectors, producing holographic images of variable sizes and incredible clarity. After his welcoming remarks, Dumbledore dispatches you to the Defence Against the Dark Arts classroom to hear a presentation on the history of Hogwarts.

As you gather to await the lecture, Harry, Ron, and Hermione pop out from beneath an invisibility cloak. They suggest that you ditch the lecture in favor of joining them for a proper tour of Hogwarts, including a Quidditch match. After some repartee among the characters and a couple of special-effects surprises, it's off to the Hogwarts Official Attraction Safety Briefing and Boarding Instructions Chamber—OK, we made up the name, but you get the picture. The briefing and instructions are presented by animated portraits, including an etiquette teacher. Later on, even the famed Sorting Hat gets into the act. All this leads to the Room of Requirement, where hundreds of candles float overhead and you board the ride.

After all the high-tech stuff in your queuing odyssey, you'll naturally expect to be wowed by your ride vehicle. Surely it's a Nimbus 3000 turbo-broom, a phoenix, a hippogriff, or at least the Weasleys' flying car. But no, what you'll ride on the most technologically advanced theme park attraction in America is . . . a *bench*? Yep, a bench.

A bit anticlimactic, perhaps, but as benches go, this one's a doozy, mounted on a Kuka robotic arm. When not engaged in Quidditch matches, a Kuka arm is a computer-controlled robotic arm similar to the kind used in heavy manufacturing. If you think about pictures you've seen of automotive assembly plants, Kuka arms are like those long metal appendages that come in to complete welds, move heavy stuff around, or fasten things. With the right programming, the arms can handle just about any repetitive industrial tasks thrown at them (see **kuka-robotics.com** for more info).

Bear with us for a moment; you know how we *Unofficial*s like techno-geekery. When you put a Kuka arm on a ride platform, it provides six axes—six degrees of freedom—with synchronized motion that can be programmed to replicate all the sensations of flying, including broad swoops, steep dives, sharp turns, sudden stops, and fast acceleration. Here's where it gets really good: Up to now, when Kuka arms and similar robotic systems have been employed in theme park rides, the arm has been anchored to a stationary platform. In Forbidden Journey, the arm is mounted on a ride vehicle that moves you through a series of action scenes projected all around you. The movement of the arm is synchronized to create the motion that corresponds to what's happening in the film. When everything works right, it's mind-blowing.

When the ride was being designed, it was assumed that Kuka's robotic programming could easily produce the various movements called for in each scene. What nobody considered, however, is that the program was designed for maximum industrial efficiency. If, to correspond to the action in a given scene, the Kuka arm had to simulate 22 different motions, the software—not knowing a theme park ride from a diesel assembly line—would think, "OK, let's knock these 22 movements down to 13 and save half a minute." Because this would throw the timing of everything out of whack, Universal ended up having to create a program that would behave as it was told and not be so anal about efficiency. For you, the practical implication of all this is an extraordinary attraction with more gremlins than inhabit the dark-arts lab.

High-tech troubles aside, is the attraction itself ultimately worthy of the hype? In a word, *yes!* Your 4½-minute adventure is a headlong sprint through the most thrilling moments from the first few Potter books: You'll soar over Hogwarts Castle, narrowly evade an attacking dragon, spar with the Whomping Willow, get tossed into a Quidditch match, and fight off Dementors inside the Chamber of Secrets. Scenes alternate between enormous physical sets, complete with animatronic creatures, elaborate lighting effects, and high-definition video-projection domes that surround your field of view, similar to Soarin' or The Simpsons Ride. Those Kuka-powered benches really do "levitate" in a manner that feels remarkably like free flight, and while you don't go upside down, the sensation of floating on your back or being slung from side to side is certainly unique.

The seamless transitions between screens and sets, and the way the domes appear to remain stationary in front of you while actually moving (much like Dreamfinder's dirigible in the original Journey into Imagination at Epcot), serve to blur the boundary between actual and virtual better than any attraction before it. The greatest-hits montage plotline may be a bit muddled, but the ride is enormously effective at leaving you feeling like you just survived the scariest scrapes from the early educational career of The Boy Who Lived.

Having experienced Forbidden Journey for ourselves, we have two primary bones to pick. First, Islands of Adventure team members rush you through the queue. To understand the storyline and get the most out of the attraction, you really need to see and hear the entire presentation in each of the preshow rooms. This won't happen unless, contrary to the admonishments of the team members, you just park yourself and watch a full runthrough of each preshow. Try to find a place to stop where you can let those behind you pass and where you're as far away from any staff as possible. As long as you're not creating a logjam, the team members will leave you alone as often as not.

Another alternative is to tell the greeter at the castle entrance that you want to take the **castle-only tour.** This self-guided experience lets guests who don't want to ride view the many features of the castle via a different queue. You can pause as long as you desire in each of the various chambers and savor the preshows without being herded along. At the end, if you decide to ride, ask to be guided to the singles line—using this strategy, you'll maximize your enjoyment of the castle while minimizing your wait for the ride. Note that the castle-only tour is often unavailable on peak-attendance days.

Another gripe: The dialogue in the preshows is delivered in English accents of varying degrees of intelligibility, and at a very brisk pace. Add an echo effect owing to the cavernous nature of the preshow rooms, and it can be quite difficult for Yanks to decipher what's being said. This is especially evident in the staccato repartee between Harry, Ron, and Hermione in the Defence Against the Dark Arts classroom.

TOURING TIPS Harry Potter and the Forbidden Journey has quickly become the most popular attraction at Islands of Adventure, and one of the most in-demand theme park attractions in America. The only way to ride without a prohibitive wait is to be one of the first through the turnstiles in the morning or to visit after 7:30 or 8 p.m.

Upon entering Forbidden Journey's outside queue, you have two choices: left line or right line. They are unmarked, but the left line is for those who have bags or loose items and therefore require a locker (no charge). Our wait-time research has shown that in some cases, not needing a locker can save you as much as 30 minutes of standing in line. If you do need to stow your stuff, be aware that the Forbidden Journey locker area is small, crowded, and confusing. It may make more sense to pay the $3 to stash your things in the lockers beside Dragon Challenge.

Universal warns you to secure or leave behind loose objects, which most people interpret to mean eyeglasses, purses, ball caps, and the like. However, the ride makes a couple of moves that will empty your trousers faster than a master pickpocket—ditto and worse for shirt pockets. When these moves occur, your stuff will clatter around like quarters in a slot-machine tray. Much better to use the small compartment built into the seat back for keys, coins, phone, wallet, and pocket Bible. Be prepared, however: Team members don't give you much time to stow or retrieve your belongings.

The single-rider line is likewise unmarked, as relatively few guests use it. Whereas on most attractions the wait in the singles line is one-third the wait in the standby line, at Forbidden Journey it can be as much as one-tenth. Because the individual seating separates you from the other riders whether your party stays together or not, the singles line is a great option. To get there, enter the right (no-bags) line and keep left all the way into the castle. Past the locker area, take the first left into the singles line.

If you see a complete iteration of each preshow in the queue and then experience the ride, you'll invest 25–35 minutes even if you don't have to wait. If you elect to skip the preshows—the Gryffindor Common Room, where you receive safety and loading directions, is mandatory—and use the singles line, you can get on in about 10–25 minutes at any time of day. At a time when the posted wait in the regular line was 2 hours, we rode and were out the door in 15 minutes using the singles line.

Universal has toned down the Kuka programming to help reduce motion sickness, but we nonetheless recommend that you ride on a full stomach. If you start getting queasy, fix your gaze on your feet and try to exclude as much from your peripheral vision as possible.

If you have a child who doesn't meet the minimum height requirement of 48 inches, a child-swapping option is provided at the loading area.

The seats accommodate a wide variety of body shapes and sizes. Each bench has specially modified seats at either end. Though these allow many more people to ride, it's possible that guests of size can't fit in them. The best way to figure out whether you can fit in a regular seat or one of the modified ones is to sit in one of the test seats outside the queue or just inside the castle. After you sit down, pull down on the safety harness as far as you can. One of three safety lights will illuminate: A green light indicates that you can fit into any seat, a yellow light means that you should ask for one of the modified seats on the outside of the bench, and a red light means that the harness can't engage enough for you to ride safely.

unofficial **TIP**
Even if your child meets the height requirement, consider carefully whether Forbidden Journey is an experience he or she can handle—because the seats on the benches are compartmentalized, kids can't see or touch Mom or Dad if they get frightened.

In addition, IOA team members select guests of all sizes "at random" to plop in the test seats, but they're really looking for large people or those who have a certain body shape. Team members handle the situation as diplomatically as possible, but if they suspect you're not the right size, you'll be asked to sit down for a test. For you to be cleared to ride, the overhead restraint has to click three times; once again, it's body shape rather than weight (unless you're over 300 pounds) that's key. Most team members will let you try a second time if you don't achieve three clicks on the first go. Passing the test by inhaling sharply is not recommended unless you can also hold your breath for the entire 4½ minutes of the ride.

With The Wizarding World and especially Forbidden Journey soaking up so many guests in IOA, waits for attractions in the other themed areas are minimal up to around 11 a.m., so there's no reason to pay the big extra bucks for Universal Express.

THE LOST CONTINENT

The Eighth Voyage of Sindbad Stunt Show (Universal Express)   ★★

APPEAL BY AGE	PRESCHOOL ★★		GRADE SCHOOL ★★★½		TEENS ★★★
YOUNG ADULTS ★★★		OVER 30 ★★½			SENIORS ★★½

What it is Theater stunt show. **Scope and scale** Major attraction. **When to go** Any time on the daily entertainment schedule. **Authors' rating** Lame-o; ★★. **Duration of presentation** 17 minutes. **Probable waiting time** 15 minutes.

DESCRIPTION AND COMMENTS A story about Sindbad the Sailor is the glue that (loosely) binds this stunt show featuring water explosions, 10-foot-tall circles of flame, and various other eruptions and perturbations. Not unlike an action movie that substitutes a mind-numbing succession of explosions, crashes, and special effects for plot and character development, the production is so vacuous and redundant (not to mention silly) that it's hard to get into the spirit of the thing. A 2015 refurbishment freshened up the fisticuffs and updated some pop-culture references, while adding an inane audience-participation preshow. The "improvements" weren't enough to upgrade our opinion of the production. When our researchers went to review *Sindbad,* one team member passed, explaining that the show is like a colonoscopy—once every 10 years is enough.

TOURING TIPS See *The Eighth Voyage* after you've experienced the rides and the better-rated shows.

Poseidon's Fury (Universal Express)   ★★★½

APPEAL BY AGE	PRESCHOOL ★★		GRADE SCHOOL ★★★½		TEENS ★★½
YOUNG ADULTS ★★★		OVER 30 ★★★			SENIORS ★★★

What it is High-tech theater attraction. **Scope and scale** Headliner. **When to go** After experiencing all the rides. **Special comments** Audience stands throughout. **Authors' rating** ★★★½. **Duration of presentation** 17 minutes, including preshow. **Probable waiting time** 25 minutes.

DESCRIPTION AND COMMENTS In the first incarnation of this story, the Greek gods Poseidon and Zeus duked it out, with Poseidon as the heavy. Poseidon fought with water, and Zeus fought with fire, though both sometimes resorted to laser beams and smoke machines. In the current incarnation, the rehabilitated Poseidon now tussles with an evil wizardish guy—named Lord Darkenon, of all things—and they fight with fire, water, lasers, and smoke machines. As you might have inferred, the story is somewhat incoherent, but the special effects are still amazing, as is the theming of the preshow area. The plot unfolds in installments as you pass through a couple of antechambers and finally into the main theater. Though the production plods a bit at first, it wraps up with quite an impressive flourish. *Poseidon* is far and away the best of the Islands of Adventure theater attractions (its only competition is *Sindbad*).

TOURING TIPS If you're still wet from Dudley Do-Right, the Bilge-Rat Barges, or the Jurassic Park River Adventure, you might be tempted to cheer the evil wizard's flame jets in hopes of finally drying out. Our money, however, is on Poseidon—it's legal in Florida for theme parks to get guests wet, but setting them on fire is frowned upon.

Frequent explosions, dark, and noise may frighten younger children. Catch *Poseidon* after getting your fill of the rides.

SEUSS LANDING

THIS 10-ACRE THEMED AREA is based on Dr. Seuss's famous children's books. Buildings and attractions replicate his whimsical style, with exaggerated features, bright colors, and rounded lines. Seuss Landing has four rides; **If I Ran the Zoo,** an interactive play area populated by Seuss creatures; and *Oh, the Stories You'll Hear!,* a live musical show.

Caro-Seuss-el *(Universal Express)*   ★★★

APPEAL BY AGE	PRESCHOOL ★★★★★	GRADE SCHOOL ★★★★	TEENS ★★★
YOUNG ADULTS ★★★	OVER 30 ★★★½		SENIORS ★★★★

What it is Merry-go-round. **Scope and scale** Minor attraction. **When to go** Before 11 a.m. **Authors' rating** Wonderfully whimsical; ★★★. **Duration of ride** 2 minutes. **Probable waiting time per 100 people ahead of you** 9 minutes. **Loading speed** Slow.

DESCRIPTION AND COMMENTS Totally outrageous, this full-scale, 56-mount merry-go-round is made up entirely of Dr. Seuss characters.

TOURING TIPS Even if you're too old or you don't want to ride, Caro-Seuss-el is worth an inspection.

The Cat in the Hat *(Universal Express)*   ★★★½

APPEAL BY AGE	PRESCHOOL ★★★★½	GRADE SCHOOL ★★★★	TEENS ★★½
YOUNG ADULTS ★★½	OVER 30 ★★½		SENIORS ★★★

What it is Indoor adventure ride. **Scope and scale** Major attraction. **When to go** Before 11:30 a.m. **Special comments** 36" minimum height requirement. **Authors' rating** Dr. S. would be proud; ★★★½. **Duration of ride** 3½ minutes. **Probable waiting time per 100 people ahead of you** 5 minutes. **Loading speed** Moderate.

DESCRIPTION AND COMMENTS Guests ride on "couches" through 18 different sets inhabited by animatronic Seuss characters, including The Cat in the Hat, Thing 1 and Thing 2, and the beleaguered goldfish who tries to maintain order in the midst of bedlam.

TOURING TIPS This is fun for all ages. Try to ride early. The ride recently had its energetic spinning greatly dampened, and a new height minimum was imposed, reducing its appeal for both tykes and teens.

The High in the Sky Seuss Trolley Train Ride! *(Universal Express)*   ★★★½

APPEAL BY AGE	PRESCHOOL ★★★★★	GRADE SCHOOL ★★★½	TEENS ★★★
YOUNG ADULTS ★★★	OVER 30 ★★★		SENIORS ★★★★

What it is Elevated train. **Scope and scale** Major attraction. **When to go** Before 11:30 a.m. **Special comments** A relaxed look at the park; 34" minimum height requirement. **Authors' rating** ★★★½. **Duration of ride** 3½ minutes. **Probable waiting time per 100 people ahead of you** 9 minutes. **Loading speed** Molasses.

DESCRIPTION AND COMMENTS Trains putter along elevated tracks while a voice reads a Dr. Seuss story over the train's speakers. As each train makes its way through Seuss Landing, it passes a series of animatronic characters in scenes that are part of the story being told. Little tunnels and a few mild turns make this a charming ride.

There are two tracks at the station. As you face the platform, to your left is the Beech track, which is aquamarine; to your right is the Star track, which is purple. Each track offers a different story.

TOURING TIPS The trains are small, fitting about 20 people, and the loading speed is glacial. Ride at the end of the day or first thing in the morning.

One Fish, Two Fish, Red Fish, Blue Fish
(Universal Express) ★★★

APPEAL BY AGE	PRESCHOOL ★★★★★	GRADE SCHOOL ★★★½	TEENS ★★½
YOUNG ADULTS ★★★½	OVER 30 ★★★		SENIORS ★★★

What it is Wet version of Dumbo the Flying Elephant. **Scope and scale** Minor attraction. **When to go** Before 10 a.m. **Authors' rating** Who says you can't teach an old ride new tricks?; ★★★. **Duration of ride** 2 minutes. **Probable waiting time per 100 people ahead of you** 9 minutes. **Loading speed** Slow.

DESCRIPTION AND COMMENTS Imagine Dumbo with Seuss-style fish instead of elephants and you have half the story—the other half involves yet another opportunity to drown. Guests steer their fish up or down 15 feet in the air while traveling in circles. At the same time, they try to avoid streams of water projected from "squirt posts."

TOURING TIPS We don't know what it is about this theme park and water, but you'll get wetter than at a full-immersion baptism.

DINING *at* UNIVERSAL'S ISLANDS *of* ADVENTURE

OF IOA'S GUSTATORY OFFERINGS, we like **Three Broomsticks,** The Wizarding World of Harry Potter's counter-service restaurant, which serves Boston Market–style rotisserie chicken, plus fish-and-chips, shepherd's pie, and barbecue ribs. The **Hog's Head** pub, a short walk from Three Broomsticks, serves beer, wine, mixed drinks, and the obligatory Butterbeer. We're also fond of the gyros at **Fire Eater's Grill** and the sandwiches at **Blondie's.** Finally, we'd be remiss if we didn't tell you to skip the green eggs at the **Green Eggs and Ham Cafe.**

IOA has two sit-down restaurants: **Confisco Grille,** in Port of Entry, and **Mythos Restaurant,** in The Lost Continent. Confisco is fine for pizza and drinks. Despite its Hellenic-sounding name, Mythos isn't a Greek restaurant; rather, like a typical Applebee's or Chili's, it serves something-for-everyone fare, including Italian risotto, Asian noodles, and Mexican fish tacos, plus steaks and burgers. Nothing on the menu stands out as either very good or very bad, so stick with appetizers and drinks.

UNIVERSAL'S ISLANDS *of* ADVENTURE TOURING PLANS

DECISIONS, DECISIONS

WHEN IT COMES TO TOURING IOA efficiently in a single day, you have two basic choices, and as you might expect, there are trade-offs. The

Wizarding World of Harry Potter–Hogsmeade sucks up guests like a Hoover, and the 20-acre section of the park will be quickly overrun by crowds on days of moderately heavy attendance. Because of Harry Potter and the Forbidden Journey's several preshows, it takes about 25 minutes to experience, even if you don't have to wait, which compounds the challenge of creating an optimal touring plan.

If you're intent on experiencing Harry Potter and the Forbidden Journey first thing, be at the turnstiles waiting to be admitted at least 30 minutes before the park opens. Once you're admitted, move as swiftly as possible to The Wizarding World, then ride Forbidden Journey, followed by Flight of the Hippogriff and Dragon Challenge, in that order.

If the rides operate as designed, you're golden. You can get Hogsmeade out of the way in about an hour, and be off to other must-see attractions before the park gets crowded. Then come back to The Wizarding World late in the day to explore Hogsmeade and the shops. If, on the other hand, the ride suffers technical difficulties, you may be stuck in line a long while, during which time the crowds will have spread to other areas of IOA. By the time you exit Forbidden Journey, there will be long lines for all of the park's other popular attractions.

Unless you have Early Park Admission privileges at IOA, a much better choice (and the path we follow in our recommended touring plans) is to skip Potterville first thing. Instead, enjoy other attractions in IOA, starting at Marvel Super Hero Island. The good news is that The Wizarding World usually clears out in the afternoon and is often empty in the last hour, even on busy days. You can ride Forbidden Journey with a minimal wait if you step in the queue shortly before closing time.

UNIVERSAL'S ISLANDS OF ADVENTURE ONE-DAY TOURING PLAN *(page 819)*

THIS TOURING PLAN is for guests without Park-to-Park tickets and is appropriate for groups of all sizes and ages. It includes thrill rides that may induce motion sickness or get you wet. If the plan calls for you to experience an attraction that doesn't interest you, simply skip it and go to the next step. Be aware that the plan calls for some backtracking. If you have young children in your party, customize the plan to fit their needs and take advantage of child swap at thrill rides.

THE BEST OF UNIVERSAL STUDIOS FLORIDA AND ISLANDS OF ADVENTURE IN ONE DAY
(pages 821 and 822)

THIS TOURING PLAN is for guests with one-day Park-to-Park tickets who wish to see the highlights of Universal Studios Florida and Islands of Adventure in a single day. The plan uses Hogwarts Express to get from one park to the other and then back again; you can walk back to the first park for the return leg if the line is too long. The plan includes a table-service lunch at Mythos (make reservations online a few days before your visit) and dinner at the Leaky Cauldron; during holiday periods, you may need to substitute a quick-service snack for one or both meals to fit in all of the plan's attractions.

PART FIFTEEN

UNIVERSAL STUDIOS FLORIDA

UNIVERSAL CITY STUDIOS INC. has run a behind-the-scenes tour and movie-themed tourist attraction in Hollywood for nearly 50 years, predating all Disney parks except Disneyland. In the early 1980s, Universal announced plans to build a new theme park complex in Florida. But while Universal labored over its new project, Disney jumped into high gear and rushed its own studios and theme park into the market, beating Universal by more than a year.

Universal Studios Florida (**USF**) opened in June 1990. At the time, it was almost four times the size of Disney's Hollywood Studios (which today is the larger of the two parks), and much more of the facility was accessible to visitors. USF is spacious, beautifully landscaped, meticulously clean, and delightfully varied in its entertainment. Rides are exciting and innovative and, like many Disney attractions, focus on familiar and/or beloved movie characters or situations.

While these rides incorporate state-of-the-art technology and live up to their billing in terms of creativity and uniqueness, some lack the capacity to handle the number of guests who frequent major Florida tourist destinations. If a ride has great appeal but can accommodate only a small number of guests per ride or per hour, long lines form. (It isn't unusual for waits to exceed an hour and a quarter for E.T. Adventure, for example.) Happily, most shows and theater performances at USF take place in venues that accommodate large numbers of people. Because many shows run continuously, waits usually don't exceed twice the show's performance time (15–30 minutes).

USF is laid out in a P-configuration, with the rounded part of the *P* sticking out disproportionately from the stem. Beyond the main entrance, a wide boulevard stretches past several shows and rides to the park's New York area. Branching off this pedestrian thoroughfare to the right are four streets that access other areas of the park and intersect a promenade circling a large lake. The area of USF open to visitors is a bit smaller than Epcot.

The park is divided into seven areas: **Hollywood, New York, Production Central, San Francisco, Woody Woodpecker's KidZone, World Expo,** and **The Wizarding World of Harry Potter–Diagon Alley.** Except for Diagon Alley, where one area begins and another ends is blurry, but no matter. Guests orient themselves by the major rides, sets, and landmarks and refer, for instance, to "New York," "the waterfront," "over by E.T.," or "by Mel's Diner."

Because the majority of USF attractions really aren't thematically integrated into the areas of the park in which they reside, we present them alphabetically rather than by area.

Springfield U.S.A., part of World Expo and the setting of the long-running animated comedy *The Simpsons,* is a themed area—more like window dressing for a once-sterile part of the park—with **The Simpsons Ride** as its centerpiece. Rounding out that attraction are a spinning ride and several *Simpsons*-themed restaurants, including a real-life Moe's Tavern.

In diametric contrast, The Wizarding World of Harry Potter–Diagon Alley is an immersive themed area whose scope and scale exceed those of its older sibling at Islands of Adventure. We discuss Diagon Alley and its attractions in their own section, starting on page 683.

Services and amenities include stroller and wheelchair rental, lockers, diaper-changing and infant-nursing facilities, car assistance, and foreign-language assistance. Most of the park is accessible to disabled guests, and TDDs are available for the hearing-impaired. Almost all services are in the **Front Lot,** just inside the main entrance.

UNIVERSAL STUDIOS FLORIDA ATTRACTIONS

Animal Actors on Location (Universal Express)   ★★★½

APPEAL BY AGE	PRESCHOOL ★★★★	GRADE SCHOOL ★★★★	TEENS ★★★
YOUNG ADULTS ★★★		OVER 30 ★★★★	SENIORS ★★★★

What it is Animal-tricks and comedy show. **Scope and scale** Major attraction. **When to go** After you've experienced all rides. **Authors' rating** Cute li'l critters; ★★★½. **Duration of presentation** 20 minutes. **Probable waiting time** 25 minutes.

DESCRIPTION AND COMMENTS This show integrates video segments with live sketches, jokes, and animal tricks performed onstage. The idea is to create eco-friendly family entertainment. Several of the animal thespians are veterans of TV and movies; many were rescued from shelters. What sets *Animal Actors* apart is the use of varied and unusual kinds of animals, and the opportunity to see the animals being trained on stage. Audience members can participate as well—where else will you get the chance to hold an 8-foot albino reticulated python in your lap?

TOURING TIPS Check the daily entertainment schedule for showtimes. You shouldn't have any trouble getting in.

Continued on page 670

Universal Studios Florida

1. *Animal Actors on Location*
2. *Beetlejuice Graveyard Revue*
3. *The Blues Brothers Show*
4. Curious George Goes to Town
5. *A Day in the Park with Barney*
6. Despicable Me Minion Mayhem
7. *Disaster!*
8. E.T. Adventure
9. *Fear Factor Live*
10. Fievel's Playland
11. Harry Potter and the Escape from Gringotts
12. Hogwarts Express
13. Hollywood Rip Ride Rockit
14. Kang & Kodos' Twirl 'n' Hurl
15. *Lucy—A Tribute*
16. Men in Black Alien Attack
17. Ollivanders
18. Revenge of the Mummy
19. *Shrek 4-D*
20. The Simpsons Ride
21. *Terminator 2: 3-D*
22. Transformers: The Ride 3-D
23. *TWISTER . . . Ride It Out*
24. *Universal's Cinematic Spectacular* (seasonal)
25. *Universal Orlando's Horror Make-Up Show*
26. Woody Woodpecker's Nuthouse Coaster

Parade Route: • • • • • • • • • • • •

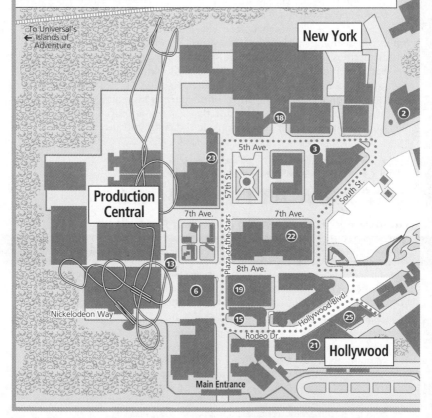

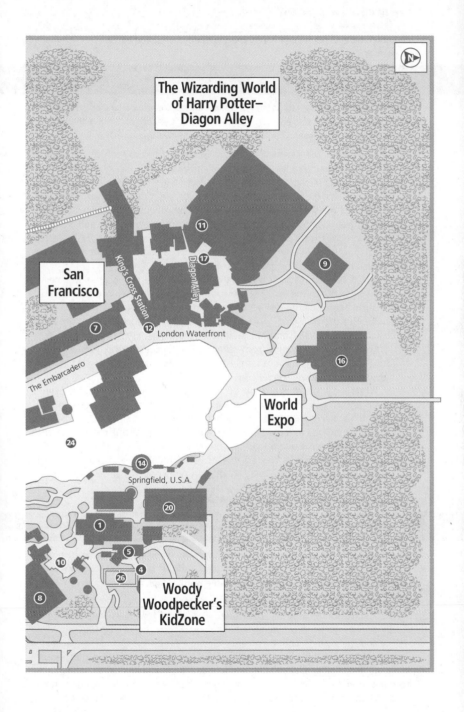

Continued from page 667

Beetlejuice Graveyard Revue (Universal Express)
★★★

APPEAL BY AGE	PRESCHOOL ★★★★		GRADE SCHOOL ★★★★	TEENS ★★★★
YOUNG ADULTS ★★★½		OVER 30 ★★★½		SENIORS ★★★

What it is Rock-and-roll stage show. **Scope and scale** Almost major attraction. **When to go** At your convenience. **Authors' rating** Capable of waking the dead; ★★★. **Duration of presentation** 18 minutes. **Probable waiting time** None.

DESCRIPTION AND COMMENTS *Beetlejuice Graveyard Revue* features Dracula, the Wolfman, and Frankenstein and his bride singing pop music from the 1980s, such as Michael Jackson and Mötley Crüe hits, with a few recent pop songs thrown in for the kids. Beetlejuice, the title character from the 1988 film of the same name, serves as the show's emcee, adding monster jokes, groan-worthy puns, and pop-culture references between songs. New characters were added when the show was updated in 2014, including Cleopatra, a female mummy; Phantasia, a female Phantom of the Opera; and a quartet of ghoulish backup dancers.

This is far from Orlando's best theme park show, though the new version is better than the last. The performers don't play any instruments, so the show seems a little like a Halloween-themed karaoke party, minus the booze. But the new cast gives its all in executing the energetic, nonstop choreography, and several of the actors have stellar vocal chops.

In response to concerns from parents, Beetlejuice's formerly risqué dialogue has been made more family-friendly; still, keep an eye on BJ in the background for some snarky sight gags.

While the show runs around 20 minutes, there is almost no break between any of the songs (or mash-ups), so sitting through a set can be something of an ordeal. The pyrotechnics are less percussive but more frequent than before, and the sound track is still cranked to 11, making for an audio assault on the audience.

TOURING TIPS The show is staged in a covered theater and participates in Universal Express. Its proximity to Diagon Alley ensures large audiences.

The Blues Brothers Show   ★★★½

APPEAL BY AGE	PRESCHOOL ★★★		GRADE SCHOOL ★★★½	TEENS ★★★½
YOUNG ADULTS ★★★½		OVER 30 ★★★★		SENIORS ★★★★

What it is Blues concert. **Scope and scale** Diversion. **When to go** Scheduled showtimes. **Special comments** A party in the street. **Authors' rating** Energetic; ★★★½. **Duration of presentation** 12 minutes. **Probable waiting time** None.

DESCRIPTION AND COMMENTS Held on the corner of the New York area, across from the lagoon, *The Blues Brothers Show* features Jake and Elwood performing a few of the hit songs from the classic 1980 movie musical, including "Soul Man" and "Sweet Home Chicago." The brothers are joined on stage by Jazz the saxophone player and his girlfriend, Mabel the waitress, who belts a cover of "Respect" to start the show.

TOURING TIPS Check the daily entertainment schedule for showtimes. The audience stands on the street during the 12-minute show, without cover or shade.

A Day in the Park with Barney *(Universal Express)*   ★★★

APPEAL BY AGE	PRESCHOOL ★★★★★	GRADE SCHOOL ★★★	TEENS ★★
YOUNG ADULTS ★★★	OVER 30 ★★★		SENIORS ★★★

What it is Live-character stage show. **Scope and scale** Major children's attraction. **When to go** Anytime. **Authors' rating** A great hit with preschoolers; ★★★. **Duration of presentation** 20 minutes, plus 5-minute preshow and character greeting after the show. **Probable waiting time** 15 minutes.

DESCRIPTION AND COMMENTS The cuddly purple dinosaur of public-TV fame leads a sing-along with the help of the audience and sidekicks Baby Bop and BJ. A short preshow gets the kids lathered up before they enter Barney's Park (the theater). Interesting theatrical effects include wind, falling leaves, clouds and stars in the simulated sky, and snow. After the show, Barney poses for photos with parents and children in the indoor playground at the theater exit.

TOURING TIPS If your child likes Barney, this show is a must. Unfortunately, we heard rumors at press time that Barney may be calling it quits at USF in the near future.

Despicable Me Minion Mayhem
(Universal Express)   ★★★★

APPEAL BY AGE	PRESCHOOL ★★★★	GRADE SCHOOL ★★★★	TEENS ★★★★
YOUNG ADULTS ★★★★	OVER 30 ★★★★		SENIORS ★★★★

What it is Motion-simulator 3-D ride. **Scope and scale** Major attraction. **When to go** The first hour after park opening or after 5 p.m. **Special comments** Expect *long* waits in line. **Authors' rating** Great fun; ★★★★. **Duration of ride** 5 minutes. **Average wait in line per 100 people ahead of you** 7 minutes; assumes all simulators in use. **Loading speed** Moderate–slow.

Motion Sickness

DESCRIPTION AND COMMENTS This motion-simulator system premiered as the Funtastic World of Hanna-Barbera when the park opened in 1990; was used again in Jimmy Neutron's Nicktoon Blast, which replaced the former in 2003; and was retained for the attraction's third and current incarnation as Despicable Me Minion Mayhem, which opened in summer 2012.

As with the former attractions, Despicable Me Minion Mayhem involves the motion simulators moving and reacting in sync with a cartoon projected on an IMAX-like screen. Though the simulators have been updated, the most significant upgrade is incorporated in the projection system, which employs high-definition 3-D digital technology.

The story combines elements from the animated movie *Despicable Me,* starring Gru, the archvillain, along with his adopted daughters and his diminutive yellow Minions. During the queue and preshow, you visit Gru's house and are then ushered into his lab, where you're turned into a Minion. The ride ends with a 3-minute dance party that you join as you exit.

TOURING TIPS The ride is just inside the USF main entrance, making crowding a problem. If you're on hand at park opening and you ride Despicable Me first, you'll have a short wait. However, you'll set yourself up for a long wait at nearby Hollywood Rip Ride Rockit. If the coaster is a priority for you, ride it first and then return to Despicable Me immediately afterward. If by that time the wait is intolerable, try again in the late afternoon. Stationary seating is available for those prone to motion sickness and for children less than 40 inches tall.

Disaster! *(Universal Express)* ★★★½

APPEAL BY AGE PRESCHOOL ★★★ GRADE SCHOOL ★★★★ TEENS ★★★★
YOUNG ADULTS ★★★★ OVER 30 ★★★★ SENIORS ★★★★

What it is Combination theater presentation and adventure ride. **Scope and scale** Major attraction. **When to go** In the morning or late afternoon. **Special comments** May frighten young children. **Authors' rating** Shaken, not stirred; not to be missed; ★★★½. **Duration of presentation** 20 minutes. **Loading speed** Moderate. **Probable waiting time** 18 minutes.

DESCRIPTION AND COMMENTS Guests are recruited for roles in a film called *Mutha Nature,* directed by the overbearing and conceited Frank Kincaid (Christopher Walken) and starring an unnamed actor you'll recognize as Dwayne "The Rock" Johnson. After the recruiting, the audience enters a soundstage, where a number of seemingly random scenes are filmed starring the guests-cum-volunteers. The filming demonstrates various techniques for integrating sets, green screens, and matte painting with live-action stunts. Next, guests board a faux subway where they experience a simulated earthquake. Following the quake, while the subway returns to the station, guests view a finished cut of *Mutha Nature* that incorporates all the soundstage shots.

TOURING TIPS Experience *Disaster!* after tackling the park's other rides.

E.T. Adventure *(Universal Express)* ★★★½

APPEAL BY AGE PRESCHOOL ★★★★ GRADE SCHOOL ★★★★ TEENS ★★★
YOUNG ADULTS ★★★ OVER 30 ★★★★ SENIORS ★★★★

What it is Indoor adventure ride based on the beloved movie. **Scope and scale** Major attraction. **When to go** During the first 90 minutes the park is open. **Special comments** 34″ minimum height requirement. **Authors' rating** A happy reunion; ★★★½. **Duration of ride** 4½ minutes. **Average wait in line per 100 people ahead of you** 5 minutes. **Loading speed** Moderate.

DESCRIPTION AND COMMENTS Guests board a bicycle-like conveyance to escape with E.T., The Extra-Terrestrial, from earthly law enforcement officials and journey to his home planet. Concerning the latter, where E.T. is reunited with family and friends, Len Testa likens it to *The Wizard of Oz*'s Technicolor scene, only reenacted with a cave full of naked mole rats. (C'mon, Len, where's the love?) The attraction is similar to Peter Pan's Flight at the Magic Kingdom, only longer and wilder.

A Baton, North Carolina, reader with perhaps too much time on his hands got to wondering:

Why do the inhabitants of E.T.'s home planet, who presumably have never visited Earth, speak better English than he does?

TOURING TIPS Most preschoolers and grade-school children love E.T. We think it's worth a 20- to 30-minute wait, but no longer than that. Lines build quickly after 10:30 a.m., and waits can be more than 2 hours on busy days. Ride in the morning or late afternoon. On peak days, a time-saving single-rider line is occasionally opened.

Fear Factor Live *(Universal Express)* ★★½

APPEAL BY AGE PRESCHOOL ★ GRADE SCHOOL ★★ TEENS ★★★★
YOUNG ADULTS ★★★ OVER 30 ★★★ SENIORS ★★

What it is Live version of the gross-out-stunt television show. **Scope and scale** Headliner. **When to go** 6–8 shows daily; crowds are smallest at the first and second-to-last shows. **Authors' rating** *Ewwww;* ★★½. **Duration of presentation** 30 minutes. **Proba-ble waiting time** 25 minutes.

DESCRIPTION AND COMMENTS *Fear Factor Live* is a stage version of the uniquely stomach-turning reality show that ran on NBC from 2001 to 2006 and again from 2011 to 2012. In the theme park iteration, six volun-teers compete for one prize; this varies but is always a package that con-tains Universal goodies ranging from park tickets to T-shirts. Contestants must be 18 years or older (with a photo ID to prove it) and weigh at least 110 pounds. Those demented enough to volunteer should arrive at least 75 minutes before showtime to sign papers and complete some obliga-tory training for the specific competitive events. Anyone who doesn't wish to compete in the stage show itself can sign up for the Critter Chal-lenge or the Food Challenge. With an adult's permission, volunteers as young as age 16 can compete in the latter.

The stage show is performed in a covered theater and consists of three different challenges. In the first, all six contestants are suspended two-and-a-half stories in the air and try to hang on to a bar as long as possible. The difficulty is compounded by heavy-duty fans blasting the contestants' faces (as you can imagine, this stunt requires exceptional upper-body strength). Only four people go on to the next round, and the person who hangs on to the bar the longest gets to choose his or her partner for the next event.

Once the first two contestants are eliminated, it's time for a brief inter-mission called the Desert Hat Ordeal. This involves a brave audience member–lunatic who has signed up for the Critter Challenge. Prepared with eye goggles and a mouthpiece, the volunteer is put in a chair with a glass case over his or her head. A wheel is spun to determine what will be crawl-ing over the volunteer's head; the creepy-crawly choices include spiders, snakes, roaches, and scorpions. The only incentive to participate is a free photo of the ordeal for contestants to take to their therapists.

Back at the main competition, the four remaining contestants are split into two teams to compete in the Eel Tank Relay. This consists of one team member grabbing beanbags out of a tank full of eels and throwing them to his or her partner to catch in a bucket. Audience members drench the contestants with high-powered water guns, further spicing up the event. The duo who buckets the most beanbags wins, going on to compete against each other in the final round for the $400 prize package.

As the stage is prepared for the finale, the folks who volunteered for the Food Challenge are split into two teams and invited to drink a mixture of curdled milk, mystery meat, and various live bugs that are all blended to-gether on stage. The team that drinks the most of the mixture within the time limit wins a glamorous plastic mug that says, "I Ate a Bug," a conve-nient euphemism for "I have the brain of a nematode."

The last event has the two remaining contestants scramble up a wall to retrieve flags, jump into a car that is lifted in the air, and then jump out of the car to retrieve more flags. When the required climbing, jumping, and flag-grabbing are accomplished, the first player to remove a rocket launcher from the backseat of the car and hit a target on the stage wall wins.

TOURING TIPS If you've ever wanted a chance to test your mettle (sanity?), *Fear Factor Live* may be your big chance. Participants for the physical stunts are chosen early in the morning and between performances out-side the theater, so head there first thing if you want to be a contestant. The contestants for the skeevier stunts, like the bug-smoothie drinking, are chosen directly from the audience. Sit close to the front and wave your hands like crazy when it comes time for selection. Finally (and seriously), this show is too intense and gross for kids age 8 and under.

Fievel's Playland ★★★

What it is Children's play area with waterslide. **Scope and scale** Minor attraction. **When to go** Anytime. **Authors' rating** A much-needed attraction for preschoolers; ★★★. **Probable waiting time** 20–30 minutes for the waterslide; otherwise, no waiting. **Loading speed** Slow for the waterslide.

DESCRIPTION AND COMMENTS This whimsical playground in Woody Woodpecker's KidZone features ordinary household items reproduced on a giant scale, as a mouse would experience them. Preschoolers and grade-schoolers can climb nets, walk through a huge boot, splash in a sardine-can fountain, seesaw on huge spoons, and climb onto a cow skull. Most of the playground is reserved for preschoolers, but a combo waterslide and raft ride is open to all ages.

TOURING TIPS Most of Fievel's Playland requires no waiting, so you can stay as long as you want. Younger children love the oversize items, and there's enough to keep teens and adults busy while little ones let off steam. The waterslide–raft ride is open to everyone but is extremely slow-loading and carries only 300 riders per hour. With an average wait of 20–30 minutes, the 16-second ride isn't worth the trouble. Also, you're highly likely to get soaked. Lack of shade is a major shortcoming of the entire attraction—the playground is scorching during the heat of the day.

Hollywood Rip Ride Rockit *(Universal Express)*   ★★★★

What it is High-tech roller coaster. **Scope and scale** Headliner. **When to go** Immediately after park opening. **Special comments** 51″ minimum height requirement; expect long waits in line. **Authors' rating** Woo-hoo! Not to be missed; ★★★★. **Duration of ride** 2½ minutes. **Average wait in line per 100 people ahead of you** 6–8 minutes. **Loading speed** Moderate.

Motion Sickness

DESCRIPTION AND COMMENTS Opened in summer 2009, Hollywood Rip Ride Rockit is USF's candidate for the most technologically advanced coaster in the world. Well, we know how long that distinction lasted, but for sure this ride has some features we've never seen before. Let's start with the basics: Rip Ride Rockit is a sit-down X-Car coaster that runs on a 3,800-foot steel track, with a maximum height of 167 feet and a top speed of 65 miles an hour. Manufactured by German coaster maker Maurer Söhne, X-Car vehicles are more maneuverable than most other kinds and use less restrictive restraints, making for an exhilarating ride.

You ascend—vertically—at 11 feet per second to crest the 17-story-tall first hill, the highest point reached by any roller coaster in Orlando, until Mako in SeaWorld opens in 2016. The drop is almost vertical, too, launching you into Double Take, a loop inversion in which you begin on the inside of the loop, twist to the outside at the top (so you're upright), and then twist back inside the loop for the descent. Double Take stands 136 feet tall, and its loop is 103 feet in diameter at its widest point. You next hurl (no, not that kind of hurl!) into a stretch of track shaped like a musical treble clef. As on Double Take, the track configuration on Treble Clef is a first. Another innovation is Jump Cut, a spiraling negative-gravity maneuver. Usually on coasters, you experience negative gravity on long, steep vertical drops; with Jump Cut you feel like you're in a corkscrew inversion, but you never actually go upside down. Other high points include a 95-degree turn, a downhill into an "underground chasm" (gotta love those Universal PR wordsmiths!), and a final incline loop banked at 150 degrees.

The ride starts in the Production Central area; weaves into the New York area near *TWISTER . . . Ride It Out,* popping out over the heads of guests in the square below; and then storms out and over the lagoon separating Universal Studios Florida from Islands of Adventure.

Each train consists of two cars, with riders arranged two across in three rows per car. Each row is outfitted with color-changing LEDs and high-end audio and video technology for each seat. Like Rock 'n' Roller Coaster at Disney's Hollywood Studios, the "Triple R" features a musical sound track, but in this case you can choose the genre of music you want to hear as you ride: classic rock, country, disco, pop, or rap. When it's over, Universal flogs a digital-video rip of your ride, complete with the sound track you chose, that you can upload to YouTube, Facebook, and the like.

From a Whalton, England, mom:

A fabulous, gut-wrenching coaster that thrilled the socks off my 8- and 9-year-olds. (Mum found it a bit too brutal to repeat.)

A perhaps-jaded Easton, Connecticut, coaster aficionado offers this:

The loud music blasting in our ears cancelled out the sound of the coaster. If only they had a "None of the Above: Silence" selection. The singles-line hint was a real time-saver.

When Hollywood Rip Ride Rockit premiered in 2009, it was pretty smooth. Alas, the wheels on the cars haven't held up well in the hot Florida sun. While perfectly safe, Rip Ride Rockit now subjects you to a lot of side-to-side jarring. To crib a phrase from Tina Turner, some folks like it easy . . . and some folks like it *rough.*

TOURING TIPS Rip Ride Rockit can put more trains on the tracks simultaneously than any other coaster in Florida, which means on paper that it should be able to handle about 1,850 riders per hour. In practice, you'll wait about 6–8 minutes for every 100 people in the queue ahead of you, indicating an hourly capacity of 1,500 riders. Because the ride is so close to the USF entrance, it's a crowd magnet, creating bottlenecks from park opening on. Your only chance to ride without a long wait is to be one of the first to enter the park when it opens.

Kang & Kodos' Twirl 'n' Hurl ★★★

APPEAL BY AGE	PRESCHOOL ★★★★	GRADE SCHOOL ★★★	TEENS ★★★
YOUNG ADULTS ★★★		OVER 30 ★★★	SENIORS ★★

What it is Spinning ride. **Scope and scale** Minor attraction. **When to go** After The Simpsons Ride. **Special comments** Rarely has a long wait. **Authors' rating** The world's wittiest spinner; ★★★. **Duration of ride** 1½ minutes. **Probable waiting time per 100 people ahead of you** 21 minutes. **Loading speed** Slow.

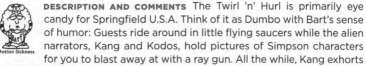
Motion Sickness

DESCRIPTION AND COMMENTS The Twirl 'n' Hurl is primarily eye candy for Springfield U.S.A. Think of it as Dumbo with Bart's sense of humor: Guests ride around in little flying saucers while the alien narrators, Kang and Kodos, hold pictures of Simpson characters for you to blast away at with a ray gun. All the while, Kang exhorts you (loudly) to destroy Springfield and makes insulting comments about humans. Preschoolers enjoy the ride, while older kids crack up over the upchuck, um, gags.

TOURING TIPS You can dig the narration from the sidelines rather than queue up for this slow-loading midway ride. If you have folks who are hot to ride, get them on whenever there are 50 or fewer guests in line.

Lucy—A Tribute ★★½

APPEAL BY AGE	PRESCHOOL ★	GRADE SCHOOL ★★	TEENS ★★
YOUNG ADULTS ★★★		OVER 30 ★★★	SENIORS ★★★

What it is Walk-through exhibit about Lucille Ball. **Scope and scale** Diversion. **When to go** Anytime. **Authors' rating** A touching remembrance; ★★½. **Probable waiting time** None.

DESCRIPTION AND COMMENTS The life and career of Lucille Ball are spotlighted, with emphasis on her role as Lucy Ricardo in *I Love Lucy.* Well designed and informative, the exhibit succeeds admirably in recalling the talent and temperament of the beloved redhead.

TOURING TIPS See *Lucy* during the hot, crowded midafternoon. By the time you read this, however, the attraction may be shuttered and converted into an interactive Hello Kitty store.

Men in Black Alien Attack *(Universal Express)* ★★★★½

APPEAL BY AGE	PRESCHOOL ★★	GRADE SCHOOL ★★★★★	TEENS ★★★★★
YOUNG ADULTS ★★★★★		OVER 30 ★★★★★	SENIORS ★★★★

What it is Interactive dark thrill ride. **Scope and scale** Super-headliner. **When to go** During the first 90 minutes the park is open. **Special comments** May induce motion sickness; 42" minimum height requirement. Switching-off option provided (see page 412). **Authors' rating** Buzz Lightyear on steroids; not to be missed; ★★★★½. **Duration of ride** 4½ minutes. **Average wait in line per 100 people ahead of you** 5 minutes. **Loading speed** Moderate–fast.

DESCRIPTION AND COMMENTS Men in Black Alien Attack brings together Will Smith and Rip Torn (as Agent J and MIB director Zed) for an interactive sequel to the hit film. The storyline has you volunteering as a Men in Black (MIB) trainee. After an introduction warning that aliens "live among us" and articulating MIB's mission to round them up, Zed expounds on the finer points of alien spotting and familiarizes you with your training vehicle and your weapon, an alien "zapper." You then load up and are dispatched on an innocuous training mission that immediately deteriorates into a situation where only you can prevent aliens from taking over the universe. If you saw the movie, you understand that the aliens are mostly giant bugs and that zapping them involves blasting them into myriad gooey body parts. Thus, the meat of the ride (pardon the pun) consists of careening around Manhattan in your MIB vehicle and shooting aliens. The technology at work is similar to that used in the Spider-Man attraction at Islands of Adventure, which is to say that it's both a wild ride and one where movies, sets, robotics, and your vehicle are all integrated into a fairly seamless package.

Men in Black is interactive in that your marksmanship and ability to blast yourself out of some tricky situations will determine how the story ends. Also, you're awarded a personal score (as at the Magic Kingdom's Buzz Lightyear's Space Ranger Spin) and a score for your car. There are about three dozen possible outcomes and literally thousands of different ride experiences determined by your pluck, performance, and, in the final challenge, your intestinal fortitude.

TOURING TIPS Each alien figure has sensors that activate special effects and respond to your zapper. Aim for the eyes and keep shooting until the aliens' eyes turn red. Also, many of the aliens shoot back, causing your vehicle to veer or spin; in the mayhem, you might fail to notice that another vehicle runs beside you on a dual track. At a certain point, you can shoot the flashing "vent" on top of this other car and make its occupants spin around. Of course, they can do the same to you.

Avoid a long wait and ride during the first 90 minutes the park is open, or try the single-rider line if you don't mind splitting your group. You can re-ride by following the signs for the child swap at the top of the exit stairs.

Revenge of the Mummy (Universal Express) ★★★★½

APPEAL BY AGE	PRESCHOOL ★★		GRADE SCHOOL ★★★★	TEENS ★★★★★
YOUNG ADULTS ★★★★½		OVER 30 ★★★★		SENIORS ★★★½

What it is Combination dark ride and roller coaster. **Scope and scale** Super-headliner. **When to go** The first hour the park is open or after 6 p.m. **Special comments** 48" minimum height requirement. Switching-off option provided (see page 412). **Authors' rating** Killer! Not to be missed; ★★★★½. **Duration of ride** 3 minutes. **Average wait in line per 100 people ahead of you** 7 minutes. **Loading speed** Moderate.

DESCRIPTION AND COMMENTS It's hard to wrap your mind around this attraction, but trust us when we say you're in for a very strange experience. Here, quoting Universal, are some of the things you can look forward to: "authentic Egyptian catacombs"; "high-velocity show-immersion system" (Huh? Quickie baptism?); "magnet-propulsion launch wave system"; "a 'Brain Fire' [!] that hovers [over guests] with temperatures soaring to 2,000°F"; and "canopic jars containing grisly remains."

When you read between the lines, Revenge of the Mummy is an indoor dark ride based on the *Mummy* flicks, where guests fight off "deadly curses and vengeful creatures" while flying through Egyptian tombs and other spooky places on a high-tech roller coaster. As far as special effects go, they're pretty good: video effects, animatronics, lighting, and enough fire-spewing gas vents to rotisserie a chicken. The endings (yes, plural) are pretty clever.

The queuing area serves to establish the storyline: You're in a group touring a set from the *Mummy* films when you enter a tomb where the fantasy world of film gives way to the real thing. Along the way, you're warned about a possible curse. The visuals are rich and compelling as the queue makes its way to the loading area, where you board a clunky, jeeplike vehicle. The ride begins as a slow, very elaborate dark ride, passing through various chambers, including one where flesh-eating scarab beetles descend on you. Suddenly your vehicle stops, then drops backward and rotates. Here's where you're shot at high speed up the first hill of the roller coaster part of the ride. We won't divulge too much, but the coaster part of the ride offers its own panoply of surprises (there are no barrel rolls or upside-down stuff, however). And though it's a wild ride by anyone's definition, the emphasis remains as much on the visuals, robotics, and special effects as on the ride itself.

TOURING TIPS Hollywood Rip Ride Rockit and Despicable Me Minion Mayhem have diminished the early-morning crowds. Nevertheless, try to ride during the first hour the park is open. If lines are long, try the singles line, which is often more expedient than Universal Express. Concerning motion sickness, if you can ride Space Mountain without ill effect, you should be fine on Revenge of the Mummy. Finally, note that the Mummy's queue contains enough scary business to frighten little kids all on its own.

Shrek 4-D (Universal Express) ★★★½

APPEAL BY AGE	PRESCHOOL ★★★★		GRADE SCHOOL ★★★★★	TEENS ★★★★★
YOUNG ADULTS ★★★★★		OVER 30 ★★★★★		SENIORS ★★★★★

What it is 3-D movie. **Scope and scale** Headliner. **When to go** The first hour the park is open or after 4 p.m. **Authors' rating** Warm, fuzzy, sometimes smelly mayhem; ★★★½. **Duration of presentation** 20 minutes. **Probable waiting time** 16 minutes.

DESCRIPTION AND COMMENTS Based on characters from the hit movie, the preshow presents the villain from the movie, Lord Farquaad, as he appears on various screens to describe his posthumous plan to reclaim his lost bride, Princess Fiona, who married Shrek. The plan is posthumous because Lord Farquaad ostensibly died in the movie, and it's his ghost making the plans, but never mind. Guests then move into the main theater, don their 3-D glasses, and recline in seats equipped with "tactile transducers" and "pneumatic air propulsion and water spray nodules capable of both vertical and horizontal motion." As the 3-D film plays, guests are also subjected to smells relevant to the on-screen action (oh, boy).

Technicalities aside, *Shrek 4-D* is a mixed bag. It's frantic, laugh-out-loud funny, and iconoclastic. Concerning the last, the film takes a good poke at Disney, with Pinocchio, the Three Little Pigs, and Tinker Bell (among others) all sucked into the mayhem. But the video quality and 3-D effects are dated by today's ultra-HD standards, the storyline is incoherently disconnected from the clever preshow, and the franchise's relevance has faded since the lackluster fourth film. On the upside, in contrast to Disney's *It's Tough to Be a Bug!*, *Shrek 4-D* doesn't generally freak out kids under age 7.

TOURING TIPS Universal claims it can move about 2,400 guests per hour through *Shrek 4-D,* but the show's location at the front of the park and directly across from Despicable Me Minion Mayhem translates to heavy traffic in the morning. If you see lines longer than 20 minutes, try visiting during mealtimes or in the last 2 hours the park is open. There's not much in the film or preshow to scare small children.

The Simpsons Ride *(Universal Express)* ★★★★

APPEAL BY AGE	PRESCHOOL ★★	GRADE SCHOOL ★★★★	TEENS ★★★★
YOUNG ADULTS ★★★★		OVER 30 ★★★★	SENIORS ★★★½

What it is Mega–simulator ride. **Scope and scale** Super-headliner. **When to go** During the first hour the park is open. **Special comments** 40" minimum height requirement; not recommended for pregnant women or people prone to motion sickness. Switching-off option provided (see page 412). **Authors' rating** Despicable Me with attitude; not to be missed; ★★★★. **Duration of ride** 4⅓ minutes, plus preshow. **Average wait in line per 100 people ahead of you** 5 minutes. **Loading speed** Moderate.

Motion Sickness

DESCRIPTION AND COMMENTS The Simpsons Ride is based on the Fox animated series that is now TV's longest-running sitcom. Featuring the voices of Dan Castellaneta (Homer), Julie Kavner (Marge), Nancy Cartwright (Bart), Yeardley Smith (Lisa), and other cast members, the attraction takes a wild, humorous poke at thrill rides, dark rides, and live shows "that make up a fantasy amusement park dreamed up by the show's cantankerous Krusty the Clown."

Two preshows involve *Simpsons* characters speaking sequentially on different video screens around the line area. Their comments help define the characters for guests who are unfamiliar with the TV show. The attraction is a simulator ride similar to Star Tours at Disney's Hollywood Studios and Despicable Me Minion Mayhem (see page 671), but with a larger screen more like that of Soarin' at Epcot. The visuals aren't as sharp as Soarin's, but they're sharp enough.

The storyline has the conniving Sideshow Bob secretly arriving at Krustyland, the aforementioned amusement park, and plotting his revenge on Krusty and Bart, who, in a past *Simpsons* episode, revealed that Sideshow

Bob had committed a crime for which he'd framed Krusty. Sideshow Bob gets even by making things go wrong with the attractions that the Simpsons (and you) are riding.

Like the show on which it's based, The Simpsons Ride definitely has an edge, and more than a few wild hairs. Like *Shrek 4-D,* it operates on several levels. There will be jokes and visuals that you'll get but will fly over your children's heads—and most assuredly vice versa.

TOURING TIPS Though not as rough and jerky as its predecessor, Back to the Future—The Ride, it's a long way from being tame. Skip it if you're an expectant mom or prone to motion sickness. Some parents may find the humor too coarse for younger kids.

Terminator 2: 3-D *(Universal Express)* ★★★★

APPEAL BY AGE	PRESCHOOL ★★★	GRADE SCHOOL ★★★★	TEENS ★★★★
YOUNG ADULTS ★★★★★		OVER 30 ★★★★★	SENIORS ★★★★

What it is 3-D thriller mixed-media presentation. **Scope and scale** Super-headliner. **When to go** After 3:30 p.m. **Special comments** One of the nation's best theme park theater attractions; very intense for some preschoolers and grade-schoolers. **Authors' rating** Furiously paced; not to be missed; ★★★★. **Duration of presentation** 20 minutes, including 8-minute preshow. **Probable waiting time** 20–40 minutes.

DESCRIPTION AND COMMENTS The evil "cop" from *Terminator 2* battles Arnold Schwarzenegger's T-100 cyborg character. In case you missed the *Terminator* flicks, here's a refresher: A bad robot arrives from the future to kill a nice boy. Another bad robot—who has been reprogrammed to be good—pops up to save the boy. The bad robot chases the boy and the good robot, menacing the audience in the process.

The attraction, like the films, is all action, and you really don't need to understand much. What's interesting is that it uses 3-D film and a theater full of sophisticated technology to integrate the real with the imaginary. Images seem to move in and out of the film, not only in the manner of traditional 3-D but also in reality: Remove your 3-D glasses a moment, and you'll see that the guy on the motorcycle is actually onstage.

TOURING TIPS The 700-seat theater changes audiences about every 19 minutes. Even so, because the show is popular, expect to wait about 30 minutes. We suggest that you save *Terminator* and other theater presentations until you've experienced all the rides. Families with young children will be relieved to know that the violence characteristic of the movie series is largely absent from the attraction—there's suspense and action, but not much blood and guts.

Transformers: The Ride 3-D ★★★★★

APPEAL BY AGE	PRESCHOOL ★★★	GRADE SCHOOL ★★★★★	TEENS ★★★★★
YOUNG ADULTS ★★★★★		OVER 30 ★★★★★	SENIORS ★★★★

What it is Multisensory 3-D dark ride. **Scope and scale** Super-headliner. **When to go** First 30 minutes the park is open or after 4 p.m. **Special comments** Must be 40″ tall to ride; single-rider line available. **Authors' rating** Not to be missed; ★★★★★. **Duration of ride** 4½ minutes. **Loading speed** Moderate–fast.

DESCRIPTION AND COMMENTS Hasbro's Transformers—those toy robots from the 1980s that you twisted into trucks and planes—have been, well, transformed into director Michael Bay's recent movie franchise. In 2013, Transformers fans at Universal Studios Florida finally received a theme park attraction befitting their pop-culture idols. Recruits to this cybertronic war enlist by entering the N.E.S.T. Base (headquarters of the heroic Auto-bots and their human allies). Inside, in the queue, video monitors catch you up on the backstory. Basically, the Decepticon baddies are after the Allspark, source of cybernetic sentience. Your job is to safeguard the shard. The highly vexing evil Megatron and his pals Starscream and Dev-astator threaten the mission, but don't worry—we have Sideswipe and Bumblebee on the bench to back us up.

Transformers harnesses the same traveling simulator system behind Is-lands of Adventure's Amazing Adventures of Spider-Man ride, and it ups the ante with photorealistic high-definition imagery, boosted by dichroic 3-D glasses that produce remarkably sharp, vivid visuals. The plot amounts to lit-tle more than a giant game of keep-away, and the uninitiated will likely be unable to tell one meteoric mass of metal from another, but you'll be too daz-zled by the debris whizzing by to notice. The ride's mix of detailed (though largely static) set pieces and video projections bring these colossi to life in one of the most intense, immersive thrill rides found in any theme park.

Two millennials had, shall we say, a visceral take on Transformers:

The illusion of being smashed through an office building is pretty convincing. If you've ever wondered what it would like to be eaten, digested, and pooped out of a giant robot, this is the ride for you.

Hopefully, it's also a ride for those who don't exactly see Transformers as a ride down the alimentary canal. Robots poop? Who knew?

TOURING TIPS This ride draws crowds—your only solace is that The Wizard-ing World of Harry Potter–Diagon Alley draws even larger throngs. Fol-low our touring plan to minimize waits. The single-rider line will get you on board faster, but as singles lines go, this is the pokiest we've seen. Finally, it's hard to focus on the fast-moving imagery from the front row; center seats in the second and third rows provide the best perspective.

TWISTER . . . Ride It Out *(Universal Express)* ★★★½

APPEAL BY AGE	PRESCHOOL ★★	GRADE SCHOOL ★★★★	TEENS ★★★★
YOUNG ADULTS ★★★★		OVER 30 ★★★★	SENIORS ★★★

What it is Theater presentation featuring special effects from the movie *Twister*. **Scope and scale** Major attraction. **When to go** Should be your first show after experiencing all rides. **Special comments** High potential for frightening young chil-dren. **Authors' rating** Gusty; ★★★½. **Duration of presentation** 15 minutes. **Proba-ble waiting time** 20 minutes.

DESCRIPTION AND COMMENTS *TWISTER* combines an elaborate set and spe-cial effects, climaxing with a five-story-tall simulated tornado created by circulating more than 2 million cubic feet of air per minute.

TOURING TIPS The wind, pounding rain, and freight-train sound of the tornado are deafening, and the entire presentation is exceptionally intense. School-children are mightily impressed; younger children are terrified. Unless you want the kids hopping in your bed whenever they hear thunder, try this attraction yourself first. Catch *TWISTER* while you can, because demolition permits have already been filed to transform the soundstage into 30 Rockefeller Center, where *The Tonight Show*'s Jimmy Fallon will reportedly take guests on an aerial tour of New York.

Universal Orlando's Horror Make-Up Show *(Universal Express)* ★★★★½

APPEAL BY AGE	PRESCHOOL ★★★	GRADE SCHOOL ★★★★	TEENS ★★★★
YOUNG ADULTS ★★★★★		OVER 30 ★★★★	SENIORS ★★★★

What it is Theater presentation on the art of makeup. **Scope and scale** Major attraction. **When to go** After you've experienced all rides. **Special comments** May frighten young children. **Authors' rating** A gory knee-slapper; not to be missed; ★★★★½. **Duration of presentation** 25 minutes. **Probable waiting time** 20 minutes.

DESCRIPTION AND COMMENTS The *Horror Make-Up Show* is a brief but humorous look at how basic monster-movie special effects are done. The show includes onstage demonstrations of effects such as blood-spurting fake knives and rubber limbs, plus how mechanical effects are combined with rubber masks to transform human heads into wolf-shaped skulls. Film clips are interspersed throughout the presentation, showing how computer-generated special effects are blended into live-action films. This may be Universal's most entertaining live show. While there's plenty of fake blood thrown around, the script is mostly funny. The hosts' running commentary about horror-film making is interspersed with plenty of pop-culture jokes for the kids.

TOURING TIPS The *Horror Make-Up Show* is the sleeper attraction at Universal. Its humor and tongue-in-cheek style transcend the gruesome effects, and most folks (including preschoolers) take the blood and guts in stride. But it's the exception that proves the rule, as this reader relates:

> *My 7- and 9-year-olds had no problem with* Terminator *but were scared by the* Horror Make-Up Show *(despite my telling them the guy was not really cutting anyone's arm off!). We ended up leaving before the show was over.*

Universal's Cinematic Spectacular: 100 Years of Movie Memories   ★★★½ (seasonal when park is open late)

APPEAL BY AGE	PRESCHOOL ★★★	GRADE SCHOOL ★★★★	TEENS ★★★½
YOUNG ADULTS ★★★★	OVER 30 ★★★★		SENIORS ★★★★

What it is Fireworks, dancing fountains, and movies. **Scope and scale** Major attraction. **When to go** 1 show a day, usually at park closing. **Special comments** Movie trailers galore. **Authors' rating** Good effort; ★★★½. **Duration of presentation** 15–20 minutes. **Probable waiting time** None.

DESCRIPTION AND COMMENTS This is USF's big nighttime event, designed to cap your day at the park. Shown on the lagoon in the middle of the park, the presentation runs through film clips and music from the first 100 years of Universal's biggest movies. The scenes are projected onto three enormous "screens" made by spraying water from the lagoon into the air (similar to *Fantasmic!* at Disney's Hollywood Studios). Fireworks and colored lights are also used to good effect throughout the presentation, which is narrated by God himself—well, actually, Morgan Freeman. It's an enjoyable way to end your day at the park.

Reviews are generally either mixed or positive. This mom of two liked it:

> *My family really enjoyed the show. It didn't have the same emotional impact as [Disney's]* Wishes, *but it was entertaining. There were so many great movies we hadn't thought about in ages!*

If you've been experiencing USF attractions throughout the day, you've already been exposed to most of the characters and memorable scenes referenced in the nighttime show. Reliving them again so soon becomes tedious after a few minutes—and the show lasts nearly 20.

TOURING TIPS The ends of the lagoon are not recommended for viewing. The best spot is directly across the lagoon from Richter's Burger Company, where the sidewalk makes a small protrusion overlooking the water. Because acquiring a spot here can be very difficult during peak season, we recommend arriving at least 45 minutes ahead of time.

Before the show begins, realize that not all of the movie clips may be suitable for young viewers. The horror montage, for example, mixes excerpts from hoary black-and-white monster movies with potentially frightenig clips from films such as *The Birds, Halloween, Psycho, The Silence of the Lambs,* and *Tales from the Crypt.*

Finally, just as Disney does with *Fantasmic!,* Universal offers a dinner package for the *Cinematic Spectacular.* As of now, the only restaurant option is Lombard's Seafood Grille; the cost is $45 for adults and $13 for kids, including tax and tip. After the meal, you'll go to a special seating area to watch the show and enjoy a dessert buffet. It's a decent option if you're in the mood for seafood and you planned to see the show anyway. Reservations are required and can be made online (**tinyurl.com/cinematicspectaculardining**) or by phone (☎ 407-224-7554, Monday–Saturday, 7:30 a.m.–10 p.m. Eastern time; until 9 p.m. on Sunday).

Woody Woodpecker's Nuthouse Coaster and Curious George Goes to Town ★★½

APPEAL BY AGE   PRESCHOOL ★★★★   GRADE SCHOOL ★★★½   TEENS —
YOUNG   ADULTS   —   OVER 30 —   SENIORS   —

What it is Interactive playground and kids' roller coaster. **Scope and scale** Minor attraction. **When to go** Anytime. **Special comments** 36" minimum height requirement for coaster. **Authors' rating** The place for rambunctious kids; ★★½. **Average wait in line per 100 people ahead of you** 5 minutes for the coaster. **Loading speed** For the coaster, *slooow.*

DESCRIPTION AND COMMENTS These two kid-friendly attractions reside, along with Fievel's Playland (see page 674), in Woody Woodpecker's KidZone. The Nuthouse Coaster is small enough for kids to enjoy but sturdy enough for adults, though its moderate speed might unnerve some smaller children. Adjacent is Curious George Goes to Town, an interactive playground that exemplifies the Universal obsession with wet stuff; in addition to innumerable spigots, pipes, and spray guns, two giant roof-mounted buckets periodically dump a thousand gallons of water on unsuspecting visitors below. Kids who want to stay dry can mess around in the foam-ball playground, also equipped with chutes, tubes, and ball-blasters.

TOURING TIPS Visit after you've experienced all the major attractions. Rumor has it that the KidZone may be closing in the near future.

THE WIZARDING WORLD OF HARRY POTTER–DIAGON ALLEY

WHEN UNIVERSAL opened The Wizarding World of Harry Potter at Islands of Adventure, it created a paradigm shift in the Disney–Universal theme park rivalry. Not only did Universal trot out some groundbreaking ride technology, but it also demonstrated that it could trump Disney's most distinctive competence: the creation of infinitely detailed and totally immersive themed areas. To say that The Wizarding World was a game changer is an understatement of the first order.

It was immediately obvious that Universal would build on its Potter franchise success—but how and where? Universal's not sitting on 27,000-plus acres like Disney, so real estate was at a premium. If Potterville was going to grow, something else had to go. Conventional wisdom suggested The Wizarding World expansion would gobble up The Lost Continent section of Islands of Adventure, and that may happen yet. But looking at the ledger, it was clear that the older Universal Studios Florida theme park could use a boost.

It just so happened that a substantial chunk of turf at USF was occupied by the aging Jaws ride and its contiguous themed area. The space would allow for substantial development; plus, its isolated location—in the most remote corner of the park—was conducive to creating a totally self-contained area where Potter themes could be executed absent any distraction from neighboring attractions. In short, it was perfect.

So how would the new Potter area tie in to the original at IOA? And what Harry Potter literary icons could be exploited? It was pretty clear that a new suburb of Hogsmeade wasn't going to cut it. Turns out that the answer was virtually shouting from the pages of the Harry Potter novels, which observe a clear dichotomy of place—plots originate in London and then unfold at distant Hogwarts.

Two London sites that figure prominently in the Potter saga brim with attraction possibilities: Diagon Alley, a secret part of London that is a sort of sorcerers' shopping mall; and the King's Cross railroad station, where wizarding students embark for the train trip to Hogwarts.

Following much deliberation and consultation with Warner Bros. and author J. K. Rowling, the final design called for a London-waterfront street scene flanking Universal Studios Lagoon. The detailed facades, anchored by the **King's Cross** railroad station on the left and including **Grimmauld Place** and **Wyndham's Theatre,** recall West London scenes from the books and movies. **Diagon Alley,** secreted behind the London street scene, is accessed through a secluded entrance in the middle of the facade. Like Hogsmeade at IOA, Diagon Alley features shops and restaurants in addition to three attractions and live entertainment.

Diagon Alley covers 20 acres—about the same area as the Hogsmeade original—but offers about two-and-a-half times the pedestrian space, since it doesn't have space- (and people-) eating outdoor roller coasters. With only one high-capacity ride (**Harry Potter and the Escape from Gringotts**), along with an enlarged version of the **Ollivanders** wand-shop experience in Hogsmeade and the **Hogwarts Express** train connecting the two Wizarding Worlds, the new area's increased elbow room is somewhat offset by a relatively reduced hourly capacity of the attractions, making Diagon Alley's maximum capacity approximately 8,000, about double Hogsmeade's occupancy limit.

In the attraction department, Universal once again came out swinging for the fences. As before with Harry Potter and the Forbidden Journey, the headliner attraction for the expansion is high-tech and cutting-edge—and once again a dark ride, but this time of the roller coaster genre. The labyrinthine passages and caverns of Gringotts Wizarding Bank, the financial institution of choice for the wizarding set, are the setting of this plot-driven 3-D dark ride–coaster.

Though Gringotts is Diagon Alley's headliner, we think that the most creative element in the two-park Potter domain is the Hogwarts Express, which recreates the train trip from London to Hogwarts and vice versa. Serving as both an attraction and transportation between USF and IOA, the Express unifies the two disparately located Wizarding Worlds.

Diagon Alley in Detail

Diagon Alley and its London waterfront are sandwiched between the San Francisco and World Expo areas of the park, about as far from Universal Studios Florida's main entrance as you can get. From the park entrance, turn right on Rodeo Drive to Mel's Diner; from here, circum-navigate the lagoon counterclockwise, keeping it to your left until you reach the entrance to the London waterfront, where wrought-iron fencing surrounds a parklike promenade. You can also access the London waterfront from the San Francisco area by walking clockwise around the lagoon and then taking a shoreline bypass along the embankment to the World Expo side of the Potter-themed area. Here you can access London through the gateway closest to the *Fear Factor Live* stadium. A third option is to take Hogwarts Express from Islands of Adventure, which exits at the London waterfront area.

Having arrived at the London area, take a moment to spot Kreacher (the house elf regularly peers from a second-story window above 12 Grimmauld Place) and chat with the Knight Bus conductor and his Caribbean-accented shrunken head. Also notable are snack and souvenir stands and a towering statue-topped fountain.

Now enter Diagon Alley next to the Leicester Square marquee in the approximate center of the building facades. As in the books and films, the unmarked portal is concealed within a magical brick wall that is ordinarily reserved for wizards and the like. (Unfortunately, the wall doesn't actually move, due to safety concerns.) However, the endless queue of Muggles (plain old humans) in shorts and flip-flops will leave little doubt where that entryway is.

Once admitted, look down the alley to the rounded facade of **Gringotts Wizarding Bank,** where a 40-foot fire-breathing Ukrainian Ironbelly dragon (as seen in *Harry Potter and the Deathly Hallows: Part 2*) perches atop the dome. To your left is the **Leaky Cauldron,** the area's flagship restaurant, serving authentically hearty British pub fare such as bangers and mash, cottage pie, and Guinness stew. You order and get your drinks at a counter; then you're seated with a candle that helps servers deliver food direct to your table. You can top off your meal with potted chocolate and sticky toffee pudding for dessert, or step around the corner to **Florean Fortescue's Ice Cream Parlour** for unusual hard-pack flavors like clotted cream, Earl Grey and lavender, and chocolate chili. Butterbeer soft-serve tastes almost exactly like the drinks, and you can get it at Florean Fortescue's in a cup ($4.99), waffle cone ($5.99), or plastic souvenir sundae glass ($10.99). If you only want a cup of Butterbeer without toppings, the soft-serve is also served off menu at The Hopping Pot and The Fountain of Fair Fortune, where you'll find a much shorter wait. If all that eating makes you thirsty, a variety of alcoholic and virgin novelty drinks are poured at **The Hopping Pot** and **Fountain of Fair Fortune.** Try the Wizard's Brew (a heavy porter) or Dragon Scale (a hoppy amber), or the Fishy Green Ale (mint boba tea with balls of blueberry juice) or Gillywater, which can be spiked with four different flavored elixirs. Of course, you can also get your Butterbeer or Pumpkin Juice fix.

Shopping is a major component of Diagon Alley in Potter lore; while Hogsmeade visitors went wild for the few wizardy shops there, Diagon Alley is the planet's wackiest mall, with a vastly expanded array of enchanted tchotchkes to declare bankruptcy over. Shops include **Weasleys' Wizard Wheezes,** a joke shop with many of the toys previously found in Hogsmeade's Zonko's, plus new gags such as Skiving

Snackboxes and Decoy Detonators. Look up through the three-story store's glass ceiling for fireworks. **Wiseacre's Wizarding Equipment,** at the exit of Escape from Gringotts, sells crystal balls, compasses, and hourglasses. **Madam Malkin's Robes for All Occasions** stocks school uniforms, Scottish wool sweaters, and dress robes for wizards and witches. Adopt a plush cat, rat, owl, or hippogriff from the **Magical Menagerie.** **Shutterbutton's** will film your family in front of a green screen and insert you into a DVD of Potter scenes (about $70); **Quality Quidditch Supplies** sells golden snitches and jerseys for your favorite teams; and **Scribbulus** carries quills, notebooks, and similar school supplies. You can pay for all this loot in Gringotts bank notes, which you can purchase inside a money exchange overseen by an imperious interactive animatronic goblin, and then spend it anywhere within Universal Orlando (think Disney Dollars). In general, Diagon Alley's stores are larger and more plentiful than the tiny shops over in Hogsmeade, with carefully planned external and internal queues to corral waiting customers.

To the right of Escape from Gringotts is **Carkitt Market,** a canopy-covered plaza where short live shows are staged every half hour or so. *Celestina Warbeck and the Banshees* (★★★★) showcases the singing sorceress swinging to jazzy tunes titled and inspired by J. K. Rowling herself, and *Tales of Beedle the Bard* (★★★½) recounts the Three Brothers fable from *Deathly Hallows* with puppets crafted by Michael Curry (*Festival of the Lion King, Finding Nemo—The Musical*).

Intersecting Diagon Alley near the Leaky Cauldron is **Knockturn Alley,** a labyrinth of twisting passageways where the Harry Potter bad guys hang out. A covered walk-through area with a projected sky creating perpetual night, it features spooky special effects in the faux shop windows (don't miss the creeping tattoos and crawling spiders) and **Borgin and Burkes,** which sells objects from the dark side of magic (watch out for the mummified hand!).

With the opening of Diagon Alley, Universal also introduced interactive wands ($45) to the parks, supplementing the nonfunctional replica wands ($35) that continue to be sold at **Ollivanders** (see page 689) and in the smaller selection at **Wands by Gregorovitch.** Medallions embedded in the ground designate a couple dozen locations split between the two Wizarding Worlds, where hidden cameras in storefront windows can detect the waving of these special wands and respond to the correct motions with special effects both projected and practical. You might use the swish and flick of Wingardium Leviosa to levitate one object or the figure-four Locomotor spell to animate another. It's a much more thematically satisfying form of interactivity than the gimmicky games found at the Magic Kingdom, but it can take some practice to get the hang of spell casting; wizards wander around the area to assist novices and demonstrate spells (though they may not loan their wands), but queues to trigger some effects can grow six deep at peak times. A map provided with each wand purchase details the location and movement for most effects, but there are some secret ones to discover on your own.

Discover is an important word in Diagon Alley—this incredibly intricate area feels like an actual place you can explore and get lost in, much like, say, Epcot's Morocco Pavilion or Disneyland's New Orleans Square. We can't overstate how seamlessly Diagon's designers have rendered the illusion of a living world, topping even Disney California Adventure's Cars Land. *Immersion* is an often-overworked buzzword in themed entertainment, but Diagon Alley exemplifies it, enveloping fans in Potter's world to a degree that far exceeds Hogsmeade's high standards. And even if you aren't a follower of the franchise, you may find yourself falling for it after experiencing Universal's incarnation.

Diagon Alley Attractions

Harry Potter and the Escape from Gringotts ★★★★★

APPEAL BY AGE	PRESCHOOL ★★	GRADE SCHOOL ★★★★	TEENS ★★★★★
YOUNG ADULTS ★★★★★		OVER 30 ★★★★★	SENIORS ★★★★

What it is Super-high-tech 3-D dark ride with roller coaster elements. **Scope and scale** Super-headliner. **When to go** Immediately after park opening or just before closing. **Special comments** Expect *looong* waits in line; 42" minimum height requirement. **Authors' rating** The ultimate realization of "Ride the Movies"; not to be missed; ★★★★★. **Duration of ride** 4½ minutes. **Probable waiting time per 100 people ahead of you** 4 minutes. **Loading speed** Moderate–fast.

DESCRIPTION AND COMMENTS Owned and operated by goblins, Gringotts is the Federal Reserve of the wizarding economy, and the scene of memorable sequences from the first and final Potter installments. It's known for its toppling column facade, chandelier-adorned lobby, and bottomless caverns (and the heart-stopping rail carts running through them). The theme park adaptation is the centerpiece of Diagon Alley, and the ultimate expression of the virtual reality rides Universal has been refining since IOA opened.

Like Forbidden Journey at IOA, Harry Potter and the Escape from Gringotts incorporates a substantial part of the overall experience into its elaborate queue, which (like Hogwarts Castle) even nonriders should experience. You enter through the bank's lobby, where you're critically appraised by glowering animatronic goblins. Your path takes you to a "security checkpoint" where your photo will be taken (to be purchased afterward as an identity lanyard in the gift shop, natch), and past animated newspapers and office windows where the scenario is set up.

Unlike Forbidden Journey, however, Gringotts doesn't rush you through its queue but rather allows you to experience two full preshows before approaching the ride vehicles. In the first, goblin banker Blordak and Bill Weasley (Ron's curse-breaking big brother) prepare you for an introductory tour of the underground vaults. Then you're off for a convincing simulated 9-mile plunge into the earth aboard an "elevator" with a bouncing floor and ceiling projections. All this is before you pick up your 3-D glasses (identical to those at Transformers: The Ride 3-D) and ascend a spiral staircase into the stalactite-festooned boarding cave where your vault cart awaits.

Also unlike Forbidden Journey, and indeed all the rest of The Wizarding World, Gringotts is not set in a nebulous "moment frozen in time" where incidents from various stories simultaneously coexist. Instead, you enter the bank at the exact moment that Harry, Ron, Hermione, and Griphook arrive to liberate the Hufflepuff Cup Horcrux from Bellatrix Lestrange's vault. But in this retelling of *Deathly Hallows: Part 2*'s iconic action scene, you (as Muggles opening new bank accounts) are ingeniously integrated into the action. Familiar film moments featuring the vaults' guardian dragon play out in the background as Bellatrix and Voldemort menace you with snakes and sinister spells, whereupon the heroic trio pauses its quest to save your hapless posteriors. The storytelling—much more coherent than Forbidden Journey's—may disorient Potter purists, but it's an intelligent way to allow fans to relive a favorite adventure without merely rehashing the plot.

Gringotts's ornately industrial ride vehicles consist of two-car trains, each holding 24 people in rows of four. The ride merges Revenge of the Mummy's indoor-coaster aspects with The Amazing Adventures of Spider-Man's seamless integration of high-resolution 3-D film (the finale dome completely surrounds your car) and massive sculptural sets (some of the rockwork inside is six stories tall), while adding a few new tricks such as independently rotating cars and motion-simulator bases built into the track.

The result is a ride that, though it doesn't break completely new ground as Forbidden Journey and Spider-Man did, combines favorite innovations from its predecessors in an exhilarating new way. It isn't quite the perfect attraction some might be anticipating. The visuals are sometimes murky and the dialogue difficult to discern. And it's slightly disappointing that no animatronic figures, moving set pieces, or actual pyrotechnics appear in the ride, though you will get spritzed with water, blasted with warm air, and sprayed with fog—this is Universal, after all. Finally, though Helena Bonham Carter and Ralph Fiennes reprised their screen roles, Daniel Radcliffe and Emma Watson did not. Harry and pals' CGI stand-ins look OK, as they're never seen up close, but Hermione's voice double is dreadful.

Nitpicks aside, whether Escape from Gringotts is *the* greatest themed thrill ride of all time or merely *one* of the greatest can be happily debated by park fans until the next great leap forward comes along.

To these New England honeymooners, there's not much to debate:

Gringotts is a terrific ride! Less intense than the Forbidden Journey but still full of surprises.

TOURING TIPS Gringotts is the pot of gold at the end of Universal's rainbow that a kazillion crazed guests are racing toward. Though the interior line is gorgeous and air-conditioned, the mostly unshaded outdoor extended queue holds 4,000 guests—you don't want to be at the end of it. If you're a Universal resort guest and you qualify for early entry, use it. Otherwise, try the attraction in the late afternoon; wait times usually peak after opening but become reasonable later in the day. Just beware that the queue may close to new arrivals 2–3 hours before the park closes, or even earlier if the ride breaks down. On most days you will need to retrieve a timed-return ticket (see page 652) before attempting to enter Diagon Alley, and then queue up again for Gringotts. As an alternative, try the attraction at the very end of the day. As long as you're inside the entrance before closing time, you should be allowed to ride as long as it hasn't broken down. But be warned that, as with any ride this advanced, Gringotts can be expected to experience some downtime almost daily.

As far as physical thrills go, Gringotts falls somewhere between Seven Dwarfs Mine Train and Space Mountain, with only one short (albeit unique) drop and no upside-down flips. It was designed to be less intense (read: less nauseating) than Forbidden Journey and therefore more appealing to families, with fewer height, weight, and size restrictions. The restraints are similar to Revenge of the Mummy's, with bars across your lap and shins, but slightly more restrictive. Use the test seat to the left of the front entrance if you're unsure, and request the third or sixth row for additional legroom.

The ride feels noticeably different depending on which row you're seated in. The front is closest to the action and has the scariest view of the drop; 3-D effects look better farther back. The sixth row gets the most coaster action, especially from the initial fall, but the screens are slightly distorted. Row three may be the sweet spot.

As is the case with most of Universal's thrill rides, you must leave your bags in a free locker. Luckily, unlike at Hogwarts Express, the lockers are separated from the attraction entrance, greatly improving guest flow. Universal Express is *not* currently accepted at this attraction. If you don't have bags and don't mind breaking up your group, the singles line will cut your wait to about a third of the posted time, but you'll skip all the preshows past the lobby.

Hogwarts Express   ★★★★½

APPEAL BY AGE   PRESCHOOL ★★★★   GRADE SCHOOL ★★★★★   TEENS ★★★★
YOUNG ADULTS ★★★★½   OVER 30 ★★★★½   SENIORS ★★★★½

What it is Transportation attraction. **Scope and scale** Super-headliner. **When to go** Immediately after park opening. **Special comments** Expect lengthy waits in line. A Park-to-Park pass is required to ride. **Authors' rating** A moving experience; not to be missed; ★★★★½. **Duration of ride** 4 minutes. **Probable waiting time per 100 people ahead of you** 7 minutes. **Loading speed** Moderate.

DESCRIPTION AND COMMENTS   Part of the genius of creating Diagon Alley at USF is that it's connected to Hogsmeade at Islands of Adventure (see Part Fourteen) by the Hogwarts Express, just as in the novels and films. The counterpart to Hogsmeade Station in IOA is Universal Studios' King's Cross station, a landmark London train depot that has been recreated a few doors down from Diagon Alley's hidden entrance. (It's important to note that King's Cross has a separate entrance and exit from Diagon Alley: You can't go directly between them without crossing through the London waterfront.)

The passage to Platform 9¾, from which Hogwarts students depart on their way to school, is concealed from Muggles by a seemingly solid brick wall, which you'll witness guests ahead of you dematerializing through. (Spoiler: The Pepper's Ghost effect creates a clever but congestion-prone photo op, but you experience only a dark corridor with whooshing sound effects when crossing over yourself.)

Once on the platform, you'll pass a pile of luggage (including an owl cage with an animatronic Hedwig) before being assigned to one of the three train cars' seven compartments. The train itself looks exactly authentic to the *n*th degree, from the billowing steam to the brass fixtures and upholstery in your eight-passenger private cabin. Along your one-way Hogwarts Express journey, you'll see moving images projected beyond the windows of the car rather than the park's backstage areas, with the streets of London and the Scottish countryside rolling past outside your window. The screen isn't 3-D, but it's slightly curved to conceal the edges and create a convincing illusion of depth. Even more impressive are the frosted-glass doors you enter through, which turn out to be amazing screens that make it seem as if someone is standing on the other side. You experience a different presentation coming and going, and in addition to pastoral scenery, there are surprise appearances by secondary characters (Fred and George Weasley, Hagrid) and threats en route (bone-chilling Dementors, licorice spiders), augmented by sound effects in the cars.

Hogwarts Express isn't an adrenaline rush in the same way that Escape from Gringotts is, but for those invested in Potter lore, it may be even more emotionally thrilling. And unlike most Potter attractions, it can be experienced by the whole family, regardless of size.

TOURING TIPS Universal was somehow surprised by a survey that showed guests considered the Hogwarts Express an attraction rather than merely a means to get back and forth between the two Wizarding Worlds. This "revelation" threw the creative team into a tizzy about how they could increase the capacity of the train—a task made all the more difficult because the stations and track were already under construction.

There's a capacity-versus-authenticity issue front and center with Hogwarts Express—and if you know J. K. Rowling's reputation for perfectionism where adaptations of her books are concerned, you know the sticky wicket this presented for Universal. The train cars from the films and novels are divided into private compartments that seat eight, but replicating those compartments means fewer seats and longer loading times (and longer queues too).

As a result, not everyone in one or the other park will be able to experience the train because its carrying capacity is relatively small and the track can accommodate only two trains, each moving in a different direction and passing one another in the middle of the journey. This leaves Universal with a few crowd-mitigating options:

First, because using the train for a one-way trip involves park-hopping, one-way passengers will need a valid two-park ticket. Disembarking passengers must enter the second park and, if desired, queue again for their return trip. You'll be allowed (nay, encouraged) to upgrade your 1-Park Base Ticket at the station entrance.

Second, Universal Express is, ironically, unavailable for Hogwarts Express, at least for the time being.

Third, if the line becomes too long, Universal may limit you to only one one-way ride per day. If you wish to take a same-day return trip, you'll be relegated to an secondary queue that promises to be exponentially slower than the already glacial standby queue.

Fourth, on days of peak attendance, Universal could close off the entry to King's Cross from outside the London waterfront and mandate a timed-return ticket for entry, as with Diagon Alley (see page 652).

Despite all these challenges, Hogwarts Express managed to move 1 million riders in its first month of operation, surprising everyone with its operational efficiency. As a result, lines rarely exceed 15 minutes in the morning and evening, though the queue may swell to an hour in midafternoon. If the wait is less than 30 minutes, it's typically quicker to take the train than walk to the other Wizarding World.

Guests exiting in Hogsmeade have a chance to take a photo with the locomotive before it backs out for its next run. Guests departing from Hogsmeade should pose with the static train outside the station before they queue up.

Ollivanders ★★★★

APPEAL BY AGE PRESCHOOL ★★★★ GRADE SCHOOL ★★★★★ TEENS ★★★★
YOUNG ADULTS ★★★★   OVER 30 ★★★½   SENIORS ★★★½

What it is Combination wizarding demonstration and shopping op. **Scope and scale** Major attraction. **When to go** After riding Harry Potter and the Escape from Gringotts. **Special comments** Audience stands. **Authors' rating** Enchanting; ★★★★. **Duration of presentation** 6 minutes. **Probable waiting time per 100 people ahead of you** 7 minutes.

DESCRIPTION AND COMMENTS Ollivanders, located in Diagon Alley in the books and films, somehow sprouted a branch location in Hogsmeade at

IOA (see page 654). Potter scholars pointed out this misplacement, but the wand shop stayed put and became one of the more popular features of The Wizarding World. It also became a horrendous bottleneck, with long lines where guests roasted in an unshaded queue. In the Diagon Alley version, Ollivanders assumes its rightful place, and with much larger digs. At IOA, only 24 guests at a time can experience the little drama where wands choose a wizard (rather than the other way around). At USF, the shop has three separate choosing chambers, turning it from a popular curiosity into an actual attraction. As for the IOA location, it continues to operate.

TOURING TIPS If your young 'un is selected to test-drive a wand, be forewarned that you'll have to buy it if you want to take it home.

Touring Strategy

The Wizarding World of Harry Potter–Diagon Alley is the queen of the hop in the theme park world in 2014 and beyond. Because of the crowds, experiencing Diagon Alley without interminable waits is a challenge—if you visited The Wizarding World of Harry Potter–Hogsmeade during its first three years at IOA, you know of what we speak. Hogsmeade opened with three rides and Ollivanders; now it has four rides plus the wand shop. As discussed earlier, Diagon Alley has another Ollivanders and only two rides, one of which, Hogwarts Express, it shares with Hogsmeade in IOA. Because only half of each day's total train passengers can board at the USF station, Diagon Alley in essence has only one-and-a-half rides, plus Ollivanders and the various shops, to entertain the expected masses. In other words, it's crazy, folks.

Unlike IOA, which currently offers early entry only during peak periods, USF admits eligible on-site resort guests 1 hour early every day, with the turnstiles opening 90 minutes before the official opening time.

As at IOA, Universal has multiple operational options for allowing guests into USF's Wizarding World. On low-attendance days, you may be able to stroll in and out of Diagon Alley without restriction. On busy days, barricades may limit access to the London waterfront in the morning (usually to be removed by lunchtime). If this happens, timed-entry return tickets specifying when you can visit may be distributed from touch screen kiosks located between Men in Black and *Fear Factor Live*. Guests are given a selection of 1-hour return windows, assuming any are still available. Once your time comes, report to the gates at the end of London near *Fear Factor Live*. On the busiest days, standby queues may snake from *Fear Factor Live* behind Men in Black toward The Simpsons Ride, but waiting in these is strongly discouraged; by late afternoon you should almost always be able to waltz right into Diagon Alley without a wait. (Gringotts, of course, is another story.)

Circling the lagoon clockwise to the waterfront is the shortest route to the Hogwarts Express, but it's also the route that about 70% of guests take. Hustling to the waterfront counterclockwise through the Simpsons area is the most direct path to the ticket kiosks.

On the upside, the rush to Diagon Alley diminishes crowds and waits at other attractions. The downside to that upside: Those who can't enter Diagon Alley right away spread to nearby attractions, particularly *Disaster!*, Men in Black Alien Attack, and to a lesser extent The Simpsons Ride and Revenge of the Mummy. Diagon Alley spillover affects wait times at these attractions all day, so experience them as early as possible.

In addition to guests flocking to Diagon Alley from the Universal Studios Florida entrance, about 168 passengers arrive from IOA's Hogsmeade Village station every 7–8 minutes on Hogwarts Express. Heading first to The Wizarding World–Hogsmeade at IOA and lining up for the Express may be the best way to experience both the train plus Gringotts in the least amount of time. Hogsmeade won't be hit with a morning inundation comparable to that of USF, and the queue there isn't slowed by a Platform 9¾ effect, so waits for the train from there should be less onerous. You'll want to grab a Diagon Alley return ticket from the opposite end of the area immediately upon arrival. If you're among the first on the train in the morning, you shouldn't be too far behind the first wave of guests who entered USF directly.

LIVE ENTERTAINMENT *at* UNIVERSAL STUDIOS FLORIDA

IN ADDITION TO THE SHOWS PROFILED PREVIOUSLY, USF offers a wide range of street entertainment. Costumed comic book and cartoon characters (Shrek, SpongeBob SquarePants, Woody Woodpecker) roam the park for photo ops supplemented by look-alikes of movie stars, both living and deceased, plus the towering, talking Transformers cyberstars, which can be said to be neither. Musical acts also pop up.

In 2012 USF introduced the Disney-like **Universal's Superstar Parade** (★★★½), featuring dancers and performers, four large and elaborate floats inspired by cartoons, and a very mixed bag of street-prowling Universal characters. The parade stops twice for a highly choreographed ensemble number. Though impressive in its scope and coordination, the performance is well-nigh impossible to take in from any given viewing spot. The same floats are trotted out individually at various times of day for mini-shows and character meet and greets.

The parade begins at the gate between Louie's Italian Restaurant, in the New York area of the park and *Beetlejuice Graveyard Revue*, in San Francisco. From there it proceeds along 5th Avenue, past Revenge of the Mummy. At the end of 5th Avenue, the parade takes a left onto Plaza of the Stars and heads toward the front of the park, where it makes another left onto Hollywood Boulevard, from whence it then disappears backstage across from Mel's Diner. The best viewing spots are along 5th Avenue, on the front steps of faux buildings in New York.

If you miss part of the parade in the New York area, you can scoot along the waterfront to Mel's Diner and catch it as it comes down Hollywood Boulevard. If after watching the parade on the New York streets you plan to leave the park, you can use the same route to access Hollywood Boulevard and the park exit before the parade arrives.

DINING *at* UNIVERSAL STUDIOS FLORIDA

USF'S FAST FOOD is utterly unremarkable: burgers, pizza, pasta, chicken fingers, sandwiches, and salads. The mediocre food is matched by the predictable theming: American diner? Check. New York Italian?

unofficial **TIP**
We advise heading to **Universal CityWalk** (see page 292) if you're looking for good-quality food.

Got it. We're a little surprised that there's not a Chinese takeout place next to a laundry in the San Francisco section. We're a *lot* surprised that the food quality isn't better, given the enormous competition coming from Disney. That said, for something quick, there's usually a **Nathan's Famous Hot Dogs** stand at Central Park in the New York area of the park, and for milkshakes made the old-fashioned way, try **Schwab's Pharmacy** on Hollywood Boulevard.

The Springfield U.S.A. themed area is home to a host of wacky *Simpsons*-inspired eateries, including **Krusty Burger, The Frying Dutchman** for seafood, **Cletus' Chicken Shack, Luigi's Pizza, Lard Lad Donuts, Lisa's Teahouse of Horror, Bumblebee Man's Taco Truck,** and **Moe's Tavern.** Serving sizes are large, and the food quality is consistent with that in the rest of the park.

An Ambler, Pennsylvania, couple sampled the offerings:

> The doughnuts at Lard Lad were fresh, flavorful, and surprisingly delicious. (Mmm . . . doughnuts . . .) The Flaming Moe is an overpriced glass of orange soda with dry ice on the bottom—for $8, it should have some alcohol in it or be larger. The queuing for Krusty Burger was frustrating during the lunch rush—they let only a few guests up to the food court area at a time—but once you go through the line and pay, an employee shows you to a table. Lunch for the four of us cost $88 with two beers and that one overpriced Flaming Moe. Duff beer was essentially a less-delicious Heineken. My husband's Krusty Burger was pretty good; my chicken-and-waffle sandwich was excellent but had too much sauce on it.

USF's two sit-down restaurants are **Finnegan's Bar and Grill,** in New York, and **Lombard's Seafood Grille,** in San Francisco. Finnegan's serves typical bar food—burgers and wings—as well as fish-and-chips and other takes on Irish cuisine. Stick to the burgers. Lombard's is the better restaurant, but it's not in the same league as Disney's Hollywood Brown Derby.

At the **Superstar Character Breakfast**, guests dine with characters from *Despicable Me, SpongeBob SquarePants, Hop,* and *Dora the Explorer.* Cost, including tax, is $27.50 for adults and $14 for kids. Call ☎ 407-224-3663 for reservations, or book at **universalorlando.com.**

There's also a weekly character breakfast at **Jake's** in the Royal Pacific Resort ($29 adults, $16 kids); reserve by calling ☎ 407-503-3463.

UNIVERSAL STUDIOS FLORIDA TOURING PLANS

BUYING ADMISSION TO UNIVERSAL STUDIOS FLORIDA

ONE OF OUR BIG GRIPES ABOUT USF is that there are never enough ticket windows open in the morning to accommodate the crowds. Therefore, we strongly recommend that you buy your admission in advance. Passes are available online or by mail from USF at ☎ 800-711-0080 and at the concierge desks or attractions box offices of many Orlando-area hotels.

Many hotels that sell Universal admissions don't issue actual passes. Instead, the purchaser gets a voucher that can be redeemed for a pass at the theme park. Fortunately, the voucher-redemption window is separate from the park's ticket-sales operation. In addition, tickets bought online can be printed at home and contain a bar code that can be read at the turnstiles.

UNIVERSAL STUDIOS FLORIDA ONE-DAY TOURING PLAN *(page 820)*

THIS PLAN IS FOR GUESTS without Park-to-Park tickets and includes every recommended attraction at USF. If a ride or show is listed that you don't want to experience, skip that step and proceed to the next. Move quickly from attraction to attraction, and if possible, hold off on lunch until after experiencing at least six rides.

THE BEST OF UNIVERSAL STUDIOS FLORIDA AND ISLANDS OF ADVENTURE IN ONE DAY *(pages 821 and 822)*

THIS TOURING PLAN is for guests with one-day Park-to-Park tickets who wish to see the highlights of Universal Studios Florida and Islands of Adventure in a single day. The plan uses Hogwarts Express to get from one park to the other and then back again; you can walk back to the first park for the return leg if the line is too long. The plan includes a table-service lunch at Mythos (make reservations online a few days before your visit) and dinner at the Leaky Cauldron; during holiday periods, you may need to substitute a quick-service snack for one or both meals to fit in all of the plan's attractions.

PART SIXTEEN

SEAWORLD ORLANDO

◼ SEAWORLD *at a* GLANCE

SEAWORLD IS A WORLD-CLASS marine-life theme park near the intersection of I-4 and the Beachline Expressway (FL 528). It's about 8 miles east of Walt Disney World. Open daily at 9 a.m. and closing between 5:30 and 11 p.m. depending on the season, SeaWorld charges about $97 for adults and $92 for children ages 3–9 at the gate (prices include tax). If you buy online at the website listed below, the same tickets will save you about $10, plus other online-only promotions are offered seasonally. Several multipark tickets are available as well, including the five-park **Orlando Flex Ticket,** which includes admission to SeaWorld, Aquatica, Universal Studios Florida, Islands of Adventure, and Wet 'n Wild. Parking is $17 per car, $22 per RV or camper; preferred parking also costs $22. For additional information, call ☎ 407-351-3600 or 888-800-5447, or visit **seaworld.com/orlando.**

unofficial **TIP**
You can't take food or drinks into SeaWorld or Aquatica.

SeaWorld offers a front-of-the-line pass called **Quick Queue Unlimited.** For $19–$34 depending on the season, you can bypass the regular lines at Manta, Kraken, Antarctica: Empire of the Penguin, Journey to Atlantis, *TurtleTrek,* Sky Tower, and Wild Arctic. The pass is good all day and can be used multiple times on any participating attraction. For an additional $14 and up, you can score reserved seats for theater and stadium shows with **SeaWorld Signature Show Seating.** Four venues are included, and you can view one performance in each.

Figure on 8–9 hours to see everything, 6 or so if you stick to the big deals. **Discovery Cove** (see page 696), another SeaWorld park, is directly across Central Florida Parkway.

SeaWorld is about the size of the Magic Kingdom and requires about the same amount of walking. In terms of size, quality, and creativity, it's unequivocally on par with Disney's major theme parks. Unlike Walt Disney World, SeaWorld primarily features stadium shows and walk-through exhibits. This means you'll spend about 80% less time waiting in line during 8 hours at SeaWorld than you would for the same-length visit at a Disney park.

Because lines, except those for Journey to Atlantis, Kraken, and Manta (see below), aren't a problem as a general rule, you can tour at almost any time of day. That said, there are always exceptions, as this mother of two correctly points out:

We went to SeaWorld on a Sunday and it was extremely crowded— so crowded that we were unable to see everything, even the major attractions. Waits were way too long for us to consider the rides.

If you visit in the morning, arrive early. Morning arrivals tend to create long waits at the ticket windows, so consider buying your admission in advance. Like those at other area theme and water parks, SeaWorld's turnstiles often open at either 8:30 or 8:45 a.m., depending on the season, which means you can enter the park before the scheduled 9 a.m. opening.

A daily entertainment schedule is printed on a place mat–sized map of the park. The featured shows are as follows:

- *Blue Horizons* (dolphin and bird show)
- *Clyde and Seamore Sea Lion High* (sea-lion, walrus, and otter show)
- *One Ocean* (Shamu and killer-whale show)
- *Pets Ahoy!* (show with performing domestic animals)

Trying to sort out a game plan for seeing the shows while you're on the run is somewhat exasperating. A better alternative is to visit **seaworld.com/orlando** and, under "Park Info," click on "Park Hours and Show Schedules." Here you can see the show roster for the day of your visit and plan your touring itinerary in advance.

Much of the year, you can get a seat for the stadium shows by showing up 10 or so minutes in advance. When the park is crowded, however, you need to be at the stadiums at least 20 minutes in advance (30 minutes in advance for a good seat). All of the stadiums have "splash zones," specified areas where you're likely to be drenched with ice-cold salt water by whales, dolphins, and sea lions. Trust us when we say you should take these seriously. You don't have to be in the tank for Shamu to douse you.

In 2013 SeaWorld introduced **Antarctica: Empire of the Penguin,** at 4 acres the largest expansion in SeaWorld history, and *TurtleTrek.* Empire of the Penguin features a trackless, high-tech ride and the largest artificial penguin habitat in the world, populated with four different species. *TurtleTrek* combines a domed 3-D theater presentation about the life of sea turtles with an outdoor tour of alligator, manatee, and turtle habitats.

Journey to Atlantis, Kraken, and **Manta** are SeaWorld's entries into the theme park super-attraction competition. Occupying the equivalent of six football fields, Journey to Atlantis is the world's first attraction to combine elements of a high-speed water ride and a roller coaster. (By the way, you'll get soaked.) Kraken is currently the second-longest roller coaster in Orlando.

Opened in 2009, Manta is a steel coaster that arranges riders four across, lying facedown and parallel to the track, beneath the expanse of a giant manta ray–shaped carriage. The coaster is said to emulate the movements of a manta ray, but if that's the case, it's a mighty frisky ray. The coaster soars and swoops through a pretzel loop, a 360-degree inline roll, and two corkscrews—not to mention a first drop of 113 feet. Manta reaches a height of 140 feet and speeds of more than 55 mph. But don't worry: Lying facedown puts you in the perfect position to throw up. Actually, the ride is very smooth. If you get sick, it'll be from the bugs you pick out of your teeth (keep your mouth closed at all times—you're supposed to be a ray, not a bat). The queuing area is a stunning underwater exhibit featuring 300 rays from five different species; several fish keep the rays company. Manta is a huge hit—roller-coaster buffs almost unanimously rank it as the top coaster in Florida. Catch all three rides just after the park opens, or prepare to wait.

SeaWorld offers quite a few guided tours. Most include the major shows; a glimpse behind the scenes; rides (without waiting) on Journey to Atlantis and Kraken; and interacting with seals, rays, penguins, or dolphins. The tour guides are a font of interesting and useful information. We learned on one tour, for example, that in the United States, more people are killed each year by vending machines than by sharks. Think about that the next time you buy a Coke.

DISCOVERY COVE

ALSO OWNED BY SEAWORLD, this intimate park is a welcome departure from the hustle and bustle of other Orlando the parks. Its more relaxed pace could be the overstimulated family's ticket back to mental health.

The main draw at Discovery Cove is the chance to swim with an **Atlantic bottlenose dolphin** from among the 45 here. The 50-minute experience (30 minutes in the water) is open to visitors age 6 and up who are comfortable in the water. The experience begins with an orientation led by trainers and an opportunity for participants to ask questions. Next, small groups wade into shallow water to get an introduction to the dolphin in its habitat. The experience culminates with two to three guests and a trainer swimming into deeper water for closer interaction with the dolphin before it tows them back to shore.

Other exhibits at Discovery Cove include the **Grand Reef,** the **Freshwater Oasis,** and the **Explorer's Aviary.** Snorkel or swim in the Grand Reef, which houses thousands of exotic fish as well as an underwater shipwreck and hidden grottoes. The Freshwater Oasis is a swimming and wading experience where you can get up close and personal with otters and marmosets. In the Explorer's Aviary, you can touch and feed gorgeous tropical birds. The park is threaded by the **Wind-Away River,** in which you can float or swim, and dotted with beaches that serve as pathways to the attractions.

All guests are required to wear flotation vests when swimming, and lifeguards are omnipresent. You'll need your swimsuit, pool shoes, and

	STAR RATINGS FOR SEAWORLD ATTRACTIONS
★★★★★	Manta (roller coaster)
★★★★½	Antarctica: Empire of the Penguin
★★★★½	One Ocean (high-tech Shamu and killer-whale show)
★★★★	Kraken (roller coaster)
★★★½	Shamu's Happy Harbor (children's play area)
★★★½	Shark Encounter
★★★½	Wild Arctic (simulation ride and Arctic-wildlife viewing)
★★★	Blue Horizons (dolphin, and bird show)
★★★	Pacific Point Preserve (sea lions and seals)
★★★	Pets Ahoy! (show with performing birds, cats, dogs, and a pig)
★★★	TurtleTrek (3-D film about sea turtles; animal habitats)
★★½	Journey to Atlantis (combination roller coaster–flume ride)
★★½	Manta Aquarium
★★	Sky Tower (400-foot-tall observation tower)
N/A	Clyde and Seamore Sea Lion High (sea-lion, walrus, and otter show; too new to rate)

a cover-up. On rare days when it's too cold to swim in Orlando, guests are provided with free wet suits. Discovery Cove also provides fish-friendly sunscreen samples; guests may not use their own sunscreen.

Discovery Cove is open 8 a.m.–5:30 p.m. daily. Admission is limited, so purchase tickets well in advance; call ☎ 877-557-7404 or visit **discoverycove.com.** Prices vary seasonally from $244 per person to $404, including tax (no children's discount). Florida residents receive a discount. Admission includes the dolphin swim; self-parking; Continental breakfast; a substantial lunch; snacks and drinks; and use of beach umbrellas, lounge chairs, towels, lockers, and swim and snorkel gear; and unlimited admission to SeaWorld and Aquatica water park (see page 714) for 14 days surrounding your visit to Discovery Cove.

For an additional $59 per person, you can experience **SeaVenture,** a 25-minute underwater stroll on the bottom of the Grand Reef aquarium. Participants wear diving helmets (large enough to accommodate eyeglasses), and no experience or scuba certification is necessary. Minimum age is 10 years.

PART SEVENTEEN

The
WATER PARKS

■ YOU'RE SOAKING *in* IT!

DISNEY HAS TWO WATER PARKS, and there are two competitive water parks in the area. At Disney World, **Typhoon Lagoon** is the more diverse splash pad, while **Blizzard Beach** takes the prize for the greater number of slides and the more bizarre theme. Outside the World are **Wet 'n Wild** and **Aquatica by SeaWorld,** both on International Drive. Wet 'n Wild, a Universal-owned water park, will permanently close on December 31, 2016, to make way for Universal Orlando's **Volcano Bay** water park, set to open in 2017.

At both Disney water parks, the following rules and prices apply: One cooler per family or group is allowed, but no glass or alcoholic beverages allowed; towels are $2; lockers are $13 small, $15 large (includes $5 refundable deposit); parking and life jackets are free. Admission, including tax, runs $62 for adults and $54 for children ages 3–9.

WATCH THE WEATHER

IF YOU BUY YOUR WALT DISNEY WORLD admission tickets before leaving home and you're considering the **Water Park Fun and More** (**WPFAM**) add-on (see page 61), you might want to wait until you arrive and have some degree of certainty about the weather during your stay. You can add the WPFAM option at any Disney resort or Guest Relations window at the theme parks. This is true regardless of whether you purchased your Base Tickets separately or as part of a package.

We get a lot of questions about the water parks during cold-weather months. Orlando-area temperatures can vary from the high 40s to the low 80s during December, January, and February. When it's warmer out, these months can serve up a dandy water-park experience, as this Batavia, Ohio, reader confirms:

> *Going to Blizzard Beach in December was the best decision ever! They told us at the entrance that if the park didn't reach 100—yes, I said 100—people by noon, they would be closing. I guess they got to 101, because it stayed open but was virtually empty. There was no wait for anything all day! In June we waited in line for an hour for Summit Plummet, but in December it was just the amount of time it*

*took to walk up the stairs. We had the enormous wave pool to our-
selves. We did everything in the entire park and ate lunch in less than 3
hours. It was perfect. The weather was slightly chilly at 71°, and over-
cast with very light rain, but the water was heated, so we were fine.*

EXTRA MAGIC HOURS

WHILE DISNEY ONCE OFFERED morning and evening Extra Magic
Hours at its water parks, it's been a couple of years since we last saw
them on the operating schedule. It's Disney's prerogative to change its
mind, however, especially during summer, so check the operating schedules a couple of days before you plan to go.

BLIZZARD BEACH

BLIZZARD BEACH IS DISNEY'S MORE EXOTIC water-adventure
park, and it arrived with its own legend. The story goes that an entrepreneur tried to open a ski resort in Florida during a particularly savage
winter. Alas, the snow melted; the palm trees grew back; and all that
remained of the ski resort was its alpine lodge, the ski lifts, and, of course,
the mountain. Plunging off the mountain are ski slopes and bobsled runs
transformed into waterslides. Visitors to Blizzard Beach catch the thaw—
icicles drip and patches of snow remain. The melting snow has formed a
lagoon (wave pool), fed by gushing mountain streams.

Both Disney water parks are distinguished by their landscaping and
the attention paid to executing their themes. As you enter Blizzard Beach,
you face the mountain. Coming off the highest
peak and bisecting the area at the mountain's base
are two long slides. To the left of the slides is the
wave pool. To the right are the children's swimming
area and the ski lift. Surrounding the layout like a
moat is a tranquil stream for floating in tubes.

unofficial **TIP**
Picnic areas are scattered
around the park, as
are pleasant places for
sunbathing.

On either side of the highest peak are tube,
raft, and body slides. Including the two slides coming off the peak,
Blizzard Beach has 19 slides. Among them is **Summit Plummet,** Disney
World's longest speed slide, which begins with a 120-foot free fall, and
the **Teamboat Springs** water-bobsled run, 1,200 feet long.

One reader reports that the Blizzard Beach slides picked her husband's pocket:

*Our family absolutely loved Summit Plummet, but it claimed all four
of our park passes/room-key cards as its victims. My husband had
the four cards in an exterior pocket of his swimsuit, secured closed
by Velcro AND a snap. But after doing Summit Plummet and Slush
Gusher twice apiece and Teamboat Springs once, he looked down,
noticed the pocket flapping open, and found all four cards missing!
So we had to cancel all the cards (they had charging privileges) and
couldn't purchase any food or drinks while we were there (we didn't
bring any cash because we planned to charge with our cards)!*

A couple from Bowie, Maryland, came away with battle scars:

*Summit Plummet gave me a bunch of bruises. Even my husband hurt
for a few days. It wasn't a fun ride. Basically, you drop until you hit*

BLIZZARD BEACH Attractions

CHAIRLIFT UP MOUNT GUSHMORE Height requirement: 32 inches. Great ride even if you go up just for the view. When the park is packed, use the singles line.

CROSS COUNTRY CREEK No height requirement. Lazy river circling the park; grab a tube.

DOWNHILL DOUBLE DIPPER Height requirement: 48 inches. Side-by-side tube-racing slides. At 25 mph, the tube zooms through water curtains and free-falls. It's a lot of fun, but rough.

MELT-AWAY BAY No height requirement. Wave pool with gentle, bobbing waves. Great for younger swimmers.

RUNOFF RAPIDS No height requirement. Three corkscrew tube slides from which to choose. The center slide is for solo raft rides; the other two slides offer one- or two-person tubes. The dark, enclosed tube makes you feel as if you were flushed down a toilet.

SKI PATROL TRAINING CAMP Height requirement: 60 inches for T-Bar. A place for preteens to train for the big rides.

SLUSH GUSHER Height requirement: 48 inches. A 90-foot double-humped slide. Ladies, cling to those tops—all others, hang on to live.

SNOW STORMERS No height requirement. Three mat-slide flumes; down you go on your belly.

SUMMIT PLUMMET Height requirement: 48 inches. A 120-foot free fall, at 60 mph. Needless to say, this ride is very intense. Make sure your child knows what to expect. Being over 48 inches tall doesn't guarantee an enjoyable experience. If you think you'd enjoy washing out of a 12th-floor window during a heavy rain, then this slide is for you.

TEAMBOAT SPRINGS No height requirement. 1,200-foot group whitewater-raft flume. Wonderful ride for the whole family.

TIKE'S PEAK 4 feet and under only. Kid-size version of Blizzard Beach. This is the place for little ones.

TOBOGGAN RACERS No height requirement. Eight-lane race course. You go down the flume on a mat. Less intense than Snow Stormers.

the slide, and that is why everyone comes off rubbing their butts. They say you go 60 mph on a 120-foot drop. I'll never do it again.

For our money, the most exciting and interesting slides are the **Slush Gusher** and Teamboat Springs on the front right of the mountain, and **Runoff Rapids** on the back side of the mountain. Slush Gusher is an undulating speed slide that we consider as exciting as the more vertical Summit Plummet without being as bone-jarring. On Teamboat Springs, you ride in a raft that looks like a children's round blow-up wading pool.

Runoff Rapids is accessible from a path that winds around the far left bottom of the mountain. The rapids consist of three corkscrew tube slides, one of which is enclosed and dark. As at Teamboat Springs, you'll go much faster on a two- or three-person tube than on a one-person tube. If you lean so that you enter curves high and come out low, you'll really fly. Because we like to steer the tube and go fast, we much prefer the open slides (where we can see) to the dark, enclosed tube. We thought crashing through the pitch-dark tube felt disturbingly like being flushed down a toilet.

The **Snow Stormers'** mat slides on the front of the mountain are fun but not as fast or as interesting as Runoff Rapids or **Downhill Double Dipper** on the far left front. **Toboggan Racers,** at the front and center of the mountain, consists of eight parallel slides where riders are dispatched in heats to race to the bottom. The ride itself is no big deal, and the time needed to get everybody lined up ensures that you'll wait extra-long to ride. A faster, more exciting race venue can be found on the side-by-side slides of the undulating Downhill Double Dipper. Competitors here can reach speeds of up to 25 miles an hour.

unofficial TIP
The more people you load into the raft, the faster it goes. If you have only a couple in it, the slide is kind of a snore.

A ski lift carries guests to the mountaintop (you can also walk up), where they can choose from Summit Plummet, Slush Gusher, or Teamboat Springs. For all other slides at Blizzard Beach, the only way to reach the top is on foot. If you're among the first in the park and don't have to wait to ride, the ski lift is fun and provides a bird's-eye view of the park. After riding once to satisfy your curiosity, however, you're better off taking the stairs to the top. The following attractions have a minimum height restriction of 48 inches: Slush Gusher, Summit Plummet, and Downhill Double Dipper.

The wave pool, called **Melt-Away Bay,** has gentle, bobbing waves. The float creek, **Cross Country Creek,** circles the park, passing through the mountain. The children's areas, **Tike's Peak** and **Ski Patrol Training Camp,** are creatively designed, nicely isolated, and, like the rest of the park, visually interesting.

Blizzard Beach (and Typhoon Lagoon, described next) is a bit convoluted in its layout. With slides on both the front and back of the mountain, it isn't always easy to find a path leading to where you want to go.

At the ski resort's now-converted base area are shops; counter-service food; restrooms; and tube, towel, and locker rentals. Blizzard Beach has its own parking lot but no lodging, though Disney's All-Star and Coronado Springs Resorts are almost within walking distance. Guests at Disney resort hotels can commute to the park aboard Disney buses.

Because it's novel and has popular slides, Blizzard Beach fills early during hotter months. To stake out a nice sunning spot and to enjoy the slides without long waits, arrive at least 35 minutes before the official opening time (check **disneyworld.com** for hours before you go).

TYPHOON LAGOON

TYPHOON LAGOON is comparable in size to Blizzard Beach. Twelve waterslides and streams, some as long as 420 feet, drop from the top of a 100-foot-tall artificial mountain. Landscaping and a typhoon-aftermath theme add interest and a sense of adventure to the wet rides.

Guests enter Typhoon Lagoon through a misty rainforest and then emerge in a ramshackle tropical town where concessions and services are situated. Special sets make every ride an odyssey as swimmers encounter bat caves, lagoons and pools, spinning rocks, formations of dinosaur bones, and many other imponderables.

Typhoon Lagoon has its own parking lot but no lodging. Disney resort guests can commute to the water park on Disney buses.

If you indulge in all features of Typhoon Lagoon, admission is a fair value. If you go primarily for the slides, you'll have only 2 early-morning hours to enjoy them before the wait becomes prohibitive.

Typhoon Lagoon provides water adventure for all ages. Activity pools for young children and families feature geysers, tame slides,

TYPHOON LAGOON ATTRACTIONS

BAY SLIDES Height requirement: 60 inches and under. A miniature two-slide version of Storm Slides, specifically designed for small children. Kids splash down into a far corner of the Surf Pool.

CASTAWAY CREEK No height requirement. Half-mile lazy river in a tropical setting. Wonderful!

CRUSH 'N' GUSHER Height requirement: 48 inches. Water roller coaster where you can choose from three slides: Banana Blaster, Coconut Crusher, and Pineapple Plunger, ranging from 410 to 420 feet long. This thriller leaves you wondering what exactly happened—if you make it down in one piece, that is; it's not for the faint of heart. If your kids are new to water-park rides, this is not the place to break them in, even if they're tall enough to ride.

GANGPLANK FALLS No height requirement. Whitewater-raft flume in a multiperson tube.

HUMUNGA KOWABUNGA Height requirement: 48 inches. Speed slides that hit 30 mph. A five-story drop in the dark rattles the most courageous rider. Women should ride this one in a one-piece swimsuit.

KEELHAUL FALLS No height requirement. Fast whitewater ride in a single-person tube.

KETCHAKIDDEE CREEK Height requirement: 48 inches and under only. Toddlers and preschoolers love this area reserved only for them. Say "splish-splash" and have lots of fun.

MAYDAY FALLS No height requirement. Wild single-person tube ride. *Hang on!*

SHARK REEF No height requirement; kids under age 10 must be accompanied by an adult. After you're equipped with fins, mask, snorkel, and a life vest, you get a brief lesson in snorkeling. Then off you go for about 60 feet to the other side of the saltwater pool, where you swim with small, colorful fish; rays; and very small leopard and hammerhead sharks. If you don't want to swim with the fish, visit the underwater-viewing chamber anytime during the day. Surface Air Snorkeling, a scubalike pursuit involving a "pony" tank, small regulator, and buoyancy vest, is also offered. Participants must be at least 5 years old. To sign up and get more information, visit the kiosk near the entrance to Shark Reef.

STORM SLIDES No height requirement. Three body slides down and through Mount Mayday.

SURF POOL No height requirement. World's largest inland surf facility, with waves up to 6 feet high. Adult supervision is required. Monday–Friday, in the early morning before the park opens or in the evening after the park closes (hours vary), surfing lessons are offered (surfboard provided). Cost is $165 for 2½ hours; minimum age is 8; class size is 12. Call ☎ 407-WDW-PLAY (939-7529). The price doesn't include park admission.

bubble jets, and fountains. For the older and more adventurous are the enclosed **Humunga Kowabunga** speed slides, the corkscrew **Storm Slides,** and three whitewater raft rides: **Gangplank Falls, Keelhaul Falls,** and **Mayday Falls.** Billed as a "water roller coaster," **Crush 'n' Gusher** consists of a series of flumes and spillways that course through an abandoned tropical fruit–processing plant. It features tubes that hold one or two people, and you can choose from three different routes: Banana Blaster, Coconut Crusher, and Pineapple Plunger, ranging between 410 and 420 feet long. Only Crush 'n' Gusher and the Humunga Kowabunga speed slides (where you can hit 30 miles an hour) have a minimum height requirement of 48 inches.

A Waterloo, Ontario, mom found Typhoon Lagoon more strenuous than she'd anticipated:

I wish I'd been prepared for the fact that we'd have to haul the tubes up the stairs of Crush 'n' Gusher. My daughter was not strong enough to carry hers, so I had to lug them up by myself. I was EXHAUSTED by the end of the day, and my arms ached for a couple of days afterward.

Had I known that was the case, I would have started lifting weights several months before our trip in preparation!

Slower metabolisms will enjoy the scenic, meandering, 2,000-foot-long **Castaway Creek,** which floats tubers through hidden grottoes and rainforests. And, of course, the sedentary will usually find plenty of sun to sleep in. Typhoon Lagoon's **Surf Pool** and **Shark Reef** are unique, the former being the world's largest inland surf facility, with waves up to 6 feet high (enough, so Disney says, to "encompass an ocean liner"). Shark Reef is a saltwater snorkeling pool with tropical fish.

SHARK REEF

FINS, MASK, SNORKEL, AND WET SUIT VEST are provided free in the wooden building beside the diving pool. After you obtain the proper equipment (no forms or money involved), you shower and then report to a snorkeling instructor. After a brief lesson, you swim about 60 feet to the other side of the pool. You're not allowed to paddle aimlessly but must traverse the pool more or less directly.

> *unofficial* **TIP**
> The Shark Reef opens 2 hours after the rest of the park; it closes 1 hour before the rest of the park, or 5 p.m., whichever is earlier.

The reef is fun if you're one of the first in line at opening. Equipment collection, showering, instruction, and the quick swim can be accomplished without much hassle. Also, when fewer guests are present, attendants are more flexible about your lingering in the pool or making minor departures from the charted course.

As crowds build, it becomes increasingly difficult and time-consuming to provide the necessary instruction. The result is platoons of would-be frogmen restlessly awaiting their snorkeling lesson. Guests are grouped in impromptu classes with the entire class briefed and then launched together. What takes 4 or 5 minutes shortly after opening can take more than an hour in the afternoon.

By far the most prevalent species in the pool is the dual-finned *Homo sapiens.* Other denizens include small, colorful tropical fish; some diminutive rays; and a few very small leopard and hammerhead sharks. In terms of numbers, it would be unusual to cross the pool and not see some fish. On the other hand, you aren't exactly bumping into them.

It's very important to fit your diving mask on your face so that it seals around the edges. Brush your hair from your forehead and sniff a couple of times once the mask is in place, to create a vacuum. Mustaches often prevent the mask from sealing properly. The first indication that your mask isn't correctly fitted will be salt water in your nose.

If you don't want to swim with fish in the morning or fight crowds later in the day, visit the underwater viewing chamber, accessible anytime without waiting, special equipment, or water in your nose.

SURF POOL

WHILE BLIZZARD BEACH and Wet 'n Wild have wave pools, Typhoon Lagoon has a Surf Pool. Most people will encounter larger waves here than they have in the ocean. The surf machine puts out a wave about every 90 seconds (just about how long it takes to get back in position if you caught the previous wave). Perfectly formed and ideal for riding, each wave is about 5–6 feet from trough to crest. Before you join the fray, watch two or three waves from shore. Because each wave breaks in almost the same spot, you can get a feel for position and timing. Observing other surfers is also helpful.

The best way to ride the waves is to swim about three-fourths of the way to the wall at the wave-machine end of the Surf Pool. When the wave comes (you'll both feel and hear it), swim vigorously toward the beach, attempting to position yourself one-half to three-fourths of a body length below the breaking crest. The waves are so perfectly engineered that they will either carry you forward or bypass you. Unlike an ocean wave, they won't slam you down.

A teenage girl from Urbana, Illinois, notes that the primary hazard in the Surf Pool is colliding with other surfers and swimmers:

The Surf Pool was nice except I kept landing on really hairy fat guys when the big waves came.

A Gate City, Virginia, mom was caught off guard by the size and power of the waves:

I had forgotten how violent the wave pool is at Typhoon Lagoon. Thinking I'd be able to hold on to two young(ish) nephews is a mistake I made only once before getting them back to shallower water.

A reader from Somerset, New Jersey, alerted us to another problem:

Typhoon Lagoon is a great family water park—our unexpected favorite. However, please tell your readers not to sit on the bottom of the wave pool—I got a horrible scratch/raspberry and saw about five others with similar injuries. The waves are stronger than they look.

Sitting on the bottom also disturbs the hippos.

The best way to avoid collisions while surfing is to paddle out far enough that you'll be at the top of the wave as it breaks. This tactic eliminates the possibility of anyone landing on you from above and assures maximum forward visibility. A corollary to this: The worst place to swim is where the wave actually breaks. You'll look up to see a 6-foot wall of water carrying eight dozen screaming surfers bearing down on you. This is the time to remember every submarine movie you've ever seen . . . Dive! Dive! Dive!

Either in the early morning before the park opens or in the evening after the park closes (hours vary), you can take surfing lessons, with an actual surfboard. Practice waves range from 3 to 6 feet tall. Most of the school's students are first-timers. Cost is $165 per person, and equipment is provided. For details, call ☎ 407-wDW-PLAY (939-7529).

TYPHOON LAGOON *versus* BLIZZARD BEACH

MANY WALT DISNEY WORLD GUESTS aren't interested in leaving the World. For them, the question is: Which is better, Typhoon Lagoon or Blizzard Beach? Our readers answer.

A mother of four from Winchester, Virginia, gives her opinion:

At Blizzard Beach, the family raft ride is great, but the kids' area is poorly designed. As a parent, when you walk your child to the top of a slide or the tube ride, they're lost to your vision as they go down because of the fake snowdrifts. There are no direct ways down to the end of the slides, so little ones are left standing unsupervised while parents scramble down from the top. The Typhoon Lagoon kids' area is far superior in design.

A couple from Woodridge, Illinois, writes:

We liked Blizzard Beach much more. It seems like they took everything from Typhoon Lagoon and made it better and faster. Summit Plummet was awesome—a total rush. Worth the half-hour wait. The toboggan and bobsled rides were really exciting—the bobsled really throws you around. The family tube ride was really good—much better and much longer than the one at Typhoon Lagoon. Tube rides were great, especially in the enclosed tube. If you have time to go to only one water park, go to Blizzard Beach.

A hungry reader from Aberdeen, New Jersey, complains:

At Blizzard Beach, there's only one main place to get food (most of the other spots are more for snacks). At lunchtime, it took almost 45 minutes to get some sandwiches and drinks.

WHEN *to* GO

unofficial TIP
During summer and holiday periods, Typhoon Lagoon and Blizzard Beach sometimes fill to capacity and close their gates before 11 a.m.

THE BEST WAY TO AVOID standing in lines is to visit the Disney World water parks when they're the least crowded. Our research, conducted over many weeks in the parks, indicates that tourists, not locals, make up the majority of visitors on any given day. And because weekends are popular travel days, the water parks tend to be less crowded then. In fact, of the weekend days we evaluated, the parks never reached full capacity; during the week, conversely, one or both parks closed every Thursday we monitored, and both closed at least once every other weekday. Therefore, we recommend going on a Monday or Friday.

A mom from Manlius, New York, describes what *crowded* means:

Because we had the all-inclusive pass, we also visited Typhoon Lagoon, arriving before opening so we could stake out a shady spot. The kids loved it until the lines got long (11 a.m.–noon), but I hated it. It made Coney Island seem like a deserted island in the Bahamas. Floating on Castaway Creek was really unpleasant. Whirling around in a chlorinated, concrete ditch with some stranger's feet in my face, periodically getting squirted by water guns, passing under cascades of cold water, and getting hung up by the crowd is not at all relaxing for me. My husband and I then decided to bob in the Surf Pool. After about 10 minutes of being tossed around like corks in boiling water, he turned a little green around the gills, and we sought the peace of our shady little territory, which, in our absence, had become much, much smaller. The kids, however, loved the body slides and the surf waves.

SOGGY TIPS FROM A WATER-PUPPY FAMILY

A BOW, NEW HAMPSHIRE, FAMILY who are evidently working on a doctorate in Disney water parks were kind enough to share their knowledge:

If you're going to the water parks, train on your StairMaster prior to going—especially if you visit Blizzard Beach. For Runoff Rapids, you climb 125 stairs (yes, I counted). Imagine doing that three times in a row, trying to keep up with kids who want to go down the slide multiple times. In addition, there are at least (and here, I'm guessing) 300 stairs if you choose the Alpine Path instead of the chairlift to get to Summit Plummet. At Typhoon Lagoon, each slide has approximately 60 steps, so at either park you have quite a bit of stairs to climb or go down.

We were at Blizzard Beach 15 minutes before park opening in late August, and we felt that this was plenty of time to beat the crowds. We noticed crowds building around 11 a.m. or so. If you are there at park opening, stash your things as quickly as possible (or send a member of your party to do so) while you take the chairlift to Summit Plummet. We were first in line for the chairlift, and we were at the top with no lines. The chairlift is definitely faster if you're one of the first in line, and you won't get winded from walking the Alpine Path. However, if you arrive later in the day, the line for the chairlift builds, and you'll be left having to climb the Alpine Path—great if you're in shape, but not so much if you're not!

Check the closing time of the water parks if you plan on arriving late afternoon. When Typhoon Lagoon closed at 8 p.m. and we arrived shortly after 2 p.m., lines tended to thin out by 4 p.m. However, when we tried that same tactic (arriving in the afternoon) when TL closed at 6 p.m., we noticed that the lines were still long, and it seemed like the crowd wasn't thinning at all. On those days, we wished that we had been there for park opening and left when crowds started to build.

We enjoyed the water parks, but we only stayed there about 3 hours max. Though the water parks are big (as in spread out), there weren't enough attractions to keep us there the entire day. Yes, they have slides, but not as many as I expected a Disney park to have. When lines started to build around late morning,

A visitor from Middletown, New York, had a somewhat better experience at Typhoon Lagoon:

On our second trip to Typhoon Lagoon, we dispensed with the locker rental (having planned to stay for only the morning when it was least crowded), and at park's opening just took right off for the Storm Slides before the masses arrived—it was perfect! We must have ridden the slides at least five times before any kind of line built up, and then we were also able to ride the tube and raft rides (Keelhaul and Mayday Falls) in a similar uncrowded, quick fashion because everyone else was busy getting their lockers! We also experienced the Shark Reef, snorkeling three times with minimal crowds that day. Shark Reef is fun and a great way to cool off because its water temp is well below the wave pool's.

unofficial **TIP**
If you're into slides, Blizzard Beach is tops among the Disney water parks.

If your schedule is flexible, a good time to visit the swimming parks is midafternoon to late in the day when the weather has cleared after a storm. The parks usually close during bad *it became less fun to wait 15-plus minutes for a slide that takes less than 2 minutes to go down. Also, the less-popular attractions, such as the lazy river, got really busy, and there were hardly any tubes to be found.*

Water shoes or water sandals are a good bet in the water parks, as the paths can get really hot in the summer, and only a few water jets are near the pathways to keep them cool. However, on some slides (such as the body slides), water shoes aren't allowed, so stash your water shoes at the base of the path where you exit and grab them on your way out.

Some slides at Blizzard Beach, such as the Downhill Double Dipper, take FOR-EVER in line because you're waiting for a tube to make it from the pool up the conveyor belt to the slide stairs. Once the tube finally arrives, you still have to wait for both parties to go down together and to exit the pool. This process takes a long time. If this slide is important to you, make it one of the first things you do. The toboggan rides can also take awhile because there is no clear system of who can take the mat when it finally arrives at the top (two mat rides are at the top of the mat conveyor belt: Toboggan Racers and Snow Stormers). Also, some slides aren't very comfortable. At TL, the Humunga Kowabunga should be called the wedgie maker. If your family is going to both water parks (like we did), I suggest skipping Gangplank Falls at Typhoon Lagoon and doing Teamboat Springs at Blizzard Beach instead. Not only is Teamboat Springs a LOT longer than Gangplank Falls, but it's also more fun.

Also, the wave pools at both parks are very different. At TL, it's "The Wave" pool. As in, there is only one, HUGE wave that you can try and bodysurf (good luck with that). At BB, it's more like "The Waves" pool, where waves are put out at a continual rate, at all times, like a gentle rocking motion, and there are tubes you can use. TL has no floatation device of any kind because, well, they'd be dangerous to everyone involved.

If you have something electronic (like a smartphone or key fob) that you need to stay dry at the water parks, purchase a waterproof container BEFORE going to the water park. The water parks only sell water-resistant containers, and even though the one we bought didn't seem to leak, it would have given us more peace of mind to have a waterproof bag/container.

weather. If the storm is prolonged, most guests leave for their hotels. When Typhoon Lagoon or Blizzard Beach reopens after inclement weather has passed, you almost have a whole park to yourself.

PLANNING YOUR DAY *at* DISNEY WATER PARKS

DISNEY WATER PARKS ARE ALMOST AS LARGE and elaborate as the major theme parks. You must be prepared for a lot of walking, exercise, sun, and jostling crowds. If your group really loves the water, schedule your visit early in your vacation. If you go at the beginning of your stay, you'll have more flexibility if you want to return.

To have a great day and beat the crowds, consider:

1. GETTING INFORMATION Call ☎ 407-WDW-MAGIC (939-6244) or check **disneyworld.com** the night before to verify when the park opens.

2. TO PICNIC OR NOT TO PICNIC Decide whether you want to carry a picnic lunch. Guests are permitted to take lunches and beverage coolers into the parks. However, alcoholic beverages and glass containers of any kind are forbidden.

3. GETTING STARTED If you're going to Blizzard Beach or Typhoon Lagoon, get up early, have breakfast, and arrive at the park 40 minutes before opening. If you have a car, drive instead of taking a Disney bus.

4. FOLLOW A GOOD TOURING PLAN We have two touring plans designed to help you avoid the crowds and bottlenecks at the Disney water parks (see pages 823 and 824). If you're attending on a day of moderate-to-heavy attendance (see the Crowd Calendar at our website), consider using one of these battle-tested plans. More are available at **touringplans.com**.

5. ATTIRE Wear your bathing suit under shorts and a T-shirt so you don't need to use lockers or dressing rooms. Regarding women's bathing suits, be advised that it's extremely common for women of all ages to part company with the top of their two-piece suit on the slides. Both the paths and beach sand get incredibly hot during the summer. Some form of food protection is a must. Your socks with do in a pinch, but sandals that strap to your feet are best. Shops in the parks sell sandals, Reef Runners, and other protective footwear that can be worn in and out of the water.

6. WHAT TO BRING You'll need a towel, sunscreen, and money. Because wallets and purses get in the way, lock them in your car's trunk or leave them at your hotel. Carry enough money for the day and your Disney resort ID (if you have one) in a plastic bag or Tupperware container, or use your MagicBand to pay for stuff. Though nowhere is completely safe, we felt very comfortable hiding our plastic money bags in our cooler. Nobody disturbed our stuff, and our cash was much easier to reach than if we'd stashed it in a locker across the park. If you're carrying a wad or you worry about money anyway, rent the locker.

A Canadian reader offers another option if you don't feel comfortable stashing your valuables:

> As our admission was from an all-inclusive ticket [not a MagicBand], I was concerned about our passes being stolen or lost, yet I didn't want the hassle of a locker. I discovered that the gift shop sells water-resistant plastic boxes (with strings to go around your neck) in two sizes for around $5, with the smallest being just big enough for passes, credit cards, and a bit of money. I would've spent nearly as much on a locker rental, so I was able to enjoy the rest of the day with peace of mind.

7. WHAT *NOT* TO BRING Personal swim gear (fins, masks, rafts, and the like) isn't allowed. Everything you need is provided or available to rent. If you forget your towel, you can rent one (cheap!). If you forget your swimsuit or lotion, they're for sale. Personal flotation devices (life jackets) are available at no cost.

8. ADMISSIONS Buy your admission in advance or about 45 minutes before official opening. If you're staying at a Disney property, you may be entitled to a discount; bring your MagicBand or hotel or campground ID. Guests staying five or more days should consider the **Water**

Park Fun and More add-on, which provides admission to both Disney swimming parks.

9. LOCKERS Rental lockers are $13 per day for a small one and $15 per day for a large, $5 of which is refunded when you return your key. Small lockers are roomy enough for one person or a couple, but a family will generally need a large locker. Though you can access your locker freely all day, not all lockers are conveniently located.

Getting a locker at Blizzard Beach or Typhoon Lagoon is truly competitive. When the gates open, guests race to the locker rental desk. Once there, the rental procedure is somewhat slow. If you aren't among the first in line, you can waste a lot of time waiting to be served. We recommend that you skip the locker. Carry a MagicBand or only as much cash as you'll need for the day in a watertight container that you can stash in your cooler. Ditto for personal items including watches and eyeglasses.

unofficial **TIP**
When lines for the slides become intolerable, head for the surf or wave pool or the tube-floating streams.

10. TUBES Tubes for bobbing on the waves, float-ing in the creeks, and riding the tube slides are available for free.

11. GETTING SETTLED Establish your base for the day. There are many beautiful sunning and lounging spots scattered throughout both Disney swimming parks. Arrive early, and you can almost have your pick. The breeze is best along the beaches of the surf pools at Blizzard Beach and Typhoon Lagoon. At Typhoon Lagoon, if there are children younger than age 6 in your party, choose an area to the left of Mount Mayday (ship on top) near the children's swimming area.

Also available are flat lounges (nonadjustable) and chairs (better for reading), shelters for guests who prefer shade, picnic tables, and a few hammocks. If you have money to burn, a handful of private covered seating areas are available at both Disney water parks for up to six guests at $345 (including tax) per day. That includes your own lounge chairs, tables, towels, private lockers, a refillable drink mug, and an attendant who'll be at your beck and call. These seating areas are avail-able by reservation at ☎ 407-WDW-PLAY (939-7529).

The best spectator sport at Typhoon Lagoon is the bodysurfing in the Surf Pool. It's second only to being out there yourself. With this in mind, position yourself to have an unobstructed view of the waves.

12. A WORD ABOUT THE SLIDES Waterslides come in many shapes and sizes. Some are steep and vertical, some long and undulating. Some resemble corkscrews; others imitate the pool-and-drop nature of white-water streams. Depending on the slide, swimmers ride mats, inner tubes, or rafts. With body slides, swimmers slosh to the bottom on the seat of their pants.

Modern traffic engineering bows to old-fashioned queuing. At the waterslides, it's just one person, one raft (or tube) at a time, and the swimmer on deck can't go until the person preceding him or her is safely out of the way. Thus, the slides' hourly capacity is limited com-pared with the continuously loading rides in the major theme parks. Because a certain interval between swimmers is required for safety, the only way to increase capacity is to increase the number of rides.

Though Typhoon Lagoon and Blizzard Beach are huge parks with many slides, they're overwhelmed almost daily by armies of guests. If your main reason for going to Typhoon Lagoon or Blizzard Beach is the slides, and you hate long lines, be among the first guests to enter the park. Go directly to the slides and ride as many times as you can before the park fills.

For maximum speed on a body slide, cross your legs at the ankles and cross your arms over your chest. When you take off, arch your back so almost all of your weight is on your shoulder blades and heels (the less contact with the surface, the less resistance). Steer by shifting most of your upper-body weight onto one shoulder blade. For top speed on turns, weight the shoulder blade on the outside of each curve. If you want to go slowly, distribute your weight equally as if you were lying on your back in bed. For curving slides, maximize speed by hitting the entrance to each curve high and exiting the curve low.

Some slides and rapids have a minimum height requirement. Riders for Humunga Kowabunga at Typhoon Lagoon and for Slush Gusher and Summit Plummet at Blizzard Beach, for example, must be 4 feet tall. Pregnant women and persons with back problems or other health difficulties shouldn't ride.

13. LAZY RIVERS Each of the water parks we cover here offer mellow lazy rivers. A great idea, the floating streams are long, tranquil inner-tube rides that give you the illusion that you're doing something while you're being sedentary.

Disney's lazy rivers flow ever so slowly around the entire park, through caves, beneath waterfalls, past gardens, and under bridges. They offer a relaxing alternative to touring a park on foot.

Lazy rivers can be reached from several put-in and takeout points. There are never lines; just wade into the creek and plop into one of the inner tubes floating by. Ride the current all the way around, or get out at any exit. It takes 30–35 minutes to float the full circuit.

unofficial **TIP**
Because Florida is so flat, approaching weather can be seen from atop the slide platforms at the swimming parks. Especially if you're dependent on Disney buses, leave the park early when you see a storm moving in.

14. LUNCH If you didn't bring a picnic, you can buy food. Quality is comparable to fast food; prices (as you might expect) are a bit high.

16. BAD WEATHER Thunderstorms are common in Florida. On summer afternoons, storms can be a daily occurrence. Water parks close during a storm. Most storms, however, are short-lived, allowing the water park to resume normal operations. If a storm is severe and prolonged, it can cause a great deal of inconvenience. In addition to the park's closing, guests compete aggressively for shelter, and Disney resort guests may have to joust for seats on a bus back to the hotel.

We recommend that you monitor the local weather forecast the day before you go, checking again in the morning before leaving for the water park. Scattered thundershowers are to be expected, but moving storm fronts are to be avoided.

17. ENDURANCE The water parks are large and require almost as much walking as one of the theme parks. Add to this wave surfing, swimming, and all the climbing required to reach the slides, and you'll be pooped by day's end. Unless you spend your hours like a lizard on a rock, don't expect to return to the hotel with much energy. Consider something low-key for the evening. You'll probably want to hit the hay early.

18. LOST CHILDREN AND LOST ADULTS It's easier to lose a child or become separated from your party at one of the water parks than it is at a major theme park. Upon arrival, pick a very specific place to meet should you get separated. If you split up on purpose, set times for checking in. Lost-children stations at the water parks are so out of the way that neither you nor your lost child will find them without help from a Disney cast member. Explain to your children how to recognize cast members (by their distinctive name tags) and how to ask for help.

WATER PARK TOURING PLANS

ONE-DAY TOURING PLANS for Blizzard Beach and Typhoon Lagoon can be found on pages 823 and 824, respectively. These plans are for parents with small children; touring plans for adults, along with our online reader survey, can be found at **touringplans.com.** We'd love to hear from families who've tried these plans.

The plans presented here include all the slides, flumes, and rides appropriate for kids in both parks. Having brought our own children to these parks, we've also included tips on which slides to try first in case this is your child's first water-park experience. For example, at Typhoon Lagoon we suggest the family whitewater-rafting ride Gangplank Falls as the first attraction. If your child enjoys that, we list Keelhaul Falls as the next step up in waterslides. If that seems a bit much, however, the touring plan recommends the Ketchakiddee Creek play area as an alternative.

WET *'n* WILD

WET 'N WILD (on International Drive in Orlando, one block east of I-4 at Exit 75A; ☎ 800-992-WILD or 407-351-1800; **wetnwildorlando .com**) is a non-Disney water-park option. Unlike Typhoon Lagoon and Blizzard Beach, in which scenic man-made mountains and integrated themes create a colorful atmosphere, Wet 'n Wild's only themes appear to be concrete, plastic, and water. Fortunately, the thrill, scope, and diversity of its rides make Wet 'n Wild an excellent alternative to the Disney swimming parks. Besides, contrary to what some Disney execs might have you believe, their water isn't any wetter.

Mears Transportation operates a shuttle to Wet 'n Wild that stops three times a day at Disney hotels. It's the same shuttle that commutes between Walt Disney World and Universal Orlando. Cost is $20 for guests age 3 and older. If you're staying outside Walt Disney World or Lake Buena Vista, or along US 192, you'll need a car. If you're staying on International Drive, you can take the **International Drive trolley** (visit **iridetrolley.com** for schedules and fees). The Wet 'n Wild parking lot charges $13 per day for cars and vans and $17 for RVs.

712 PART 17 THE WATER PARKS

Parking is ample; just be sure to hold the kids' hands when crossing the street.

You can buy your Wet 'n Wild tickets at the main gate or at **wetn wildorlando.com/tickets.** Prices are about $57 for adults and $52 for children ages 3–9, but call or check online for special deals and discounts. For $10 less than a single-day ticket (you read that right), Wet 'n Wild offers a Length of Stay pass on its website that is good for 14 consecutive days. Ticket prices are similar to those of the Disney parks, but if you attend during the summer, the park is open late (hours vary, from 9:30 a.m. until 9 p.m. at the latest; call or visit the website for details), allowing visitors to hit the slides in the morning, go back to their hotels for lunch and a nap, and then return for a dip at night. Disney water parks typically close by 7 or 8 p.m.

When you get hungry, the main food pavilions are the centrally located **Bubba's Fried Chicken and Ribs, Manny's Pizza,** and **Surf Grill,** together offering such staples as burgers, pizza, and barbecue-pork sandwiches as well as more-nutritious (and nontraditional) items such as veggie burgers and tabbouleh. Wait times are long, and prices are high but not outrageous. For guests whose budgets and impatience thresholds are less flexible, feel free to bring in a cooler of lunch fixings (remember, glass containers and alcoholic beverages are prohibited, but you can purchase beer inside).

All the slides outside the **Blastaway Beach** kids' park have a 48-inch height requirement except for multipassenger slides, for which the minimum height is 36 inches if an adult accompanies the short rider, and the Aqua Drag Racer, which has a 32-inch minimum height requirement.

BODY AND MAT SLIDES

SLIDES AT WET 'N WILD INCLUDE Aqua Drag Racer, Mach 5, The Bomb Bay, Der Stuka, and The Storm. Six stories tall, **Aqua Drag Racer** propels guests through four lanes of head-to-head competition at 15 feet per second. The **Mach 5** tower, to the left of the park entrance, consists of three mat slides. The mats increase your speed and eliminate the chafing often experienced on body slides. To go even faster, try to get a newer mat with a smoother bottom. They're easily distinguishable: The new mats have white handles, while the old mats have blue ones.

unofficial **TIP**
Though ride attendants say that all three of the Mach 5 slides are equal, the center slide appears to be the zippiest route to the bottom.

Among the body slides (those without mats or rafts) are **The Bomb Bay** and **Der Stuka,** twin speed flumes with pitches up to 79 degrees that descend from the top of a six-story tower. On The Bomb Bay you stand on a pair of doors that open, dropping you into the chute. You have to work up the nerve to launch yourself on Der Stuka. The lack of a fully enclosed tube (such as the one on the Humunga Kowabunga speed slide at Typhoon Lagoon) adds the (perhaps justifiable) fear of falling off the 250-foot slides, but their ability to float your stomach somewhere near your teeth is a pretty unforgettable thrill.

The Storm body slide, near The Bomb Bay and Der Stuka, is a hybrid ride: half slide, half toilet bowl. The steep slide creates enough momentum to launch riders into a few laps around the bowl below before they begin slipping toward the hole in the center, eventually falling into a 6-foot-deep pool. The ride is exhilarating and disorienting; when the lifeguard at the ending pool begins hollering, just stumble toward his voice and give him a thumbs-up.

RAFT AND TUBE RIDES

THE HEADLINERS AT WET 'N WILD are the raft and tube rides, including Brain Wash, Disco H2O, The Surge, The Black Hole, The Flyer, and The Blast. **Brain Wash** is an extreme six-story tube ride with a 53-foot vertical drop into a 65-foot funnel; tubes hold two or four riders. **Disco H2O** holds up to four people in one raft, ushering them down a long tube into a 1970s-era nightclub complete with lights, music, and a disco ball. The basic design of the ride is similar to that of The Storm (a long tube into a bowl), only not as frantic and disorienting; the disco theme, coupled with the fluidity of the ride, makes it a main draw.

The Surge launches from the same tower as Disco H2O and uses the same four-person rafts. Riders spin down the open-air course, drifting high onto the walls on each banked corner. To reach the top of the walls, try to go with a full raft—as with all raft rides, the more riders squeezed in, the faster you'll all go. Directly across from The Surge's splashdown pool is the entrance for The Black Hole. Bring a partner for this one; **The Black Hole** requires two riders on each raft, and honestly, who wants to embark into endless murk without some company? As impressive as the ride seems from afar, the anxiety created by the gaping entrance is the most exciting part of the ride. Yes, it's dark—a piece of green track lighting runs the length of the entire course—but besides the darkness, the ride lacks the dips and turns found on the other slides. If you're claustrophobic and scared of the dark, this isn't the ride for you; if tight spaces and inky blackness don't give you a rush, then this ride isn't for you either.

The two gentler raft rides are **The Flyer** and **The Blast,** which launch from the same tower as the Mach 5, but their entrance is accessible through the Blastaway Beach kids' area. At the base of the entrance are one- and two-person rafts; these are only for The Blast, so don't carry them up to the tower to the Flyer entrance. The Flyer is a calmer, toboggan-style ride in which riders sit one behind the other; it's suitable for families with smaller children. The Blast, a themed ride like Disco H20, is the wettest you can get without swimming. Its theme seems to be a broken waterworks, complete with spinning dials and broken pipes, all painted in comic-book red and yellow. From mist to falling water to spraying pipes, this is the best way to cool off at Wet 'n Wild.

OTHER ATTRACTIONS

THE CENTRAL FIXTURE at Wet 'n Wild, the **Surf Lagoon** wave pool, is on par with Blizzard Beach's. Unlike at Typhoon Lagoon, there's no surfing in this wave pool, but you can grab a tube or go bobbing with your body. The wave-making machine takes long breaks every day, so when you walk by and see waves, be sure to wade in.

Another any-time-of-day option is the **Lazy River.** Don't be fooled by the name, though: The circuit is short, the current fast. Don't even bother trying to walk upstream to catch a tube; it's better to swim down the river or wait patiently until one passes within reach.

Wet 'n Wild's 1-acre **Blastaway Beach** is a small-fry version of the adult menu. It's to the left of the main gate; look for the oversize sand castle capped off with a big blue bucket. The bucket actually fills with water and tips over, soaking the people in front of the castle. Blastaway Beach is the largest water-park playground in Florida. The giant sand castle alone spans two pools (upper and lower), covering more than 15,000 square feet with more than 85,000 gallons of water powering more than 100 soakers, jets, waterfalls, and water cannons; 15 slides; and the aforementioned bucket.

AQUATICA *by* SEAWORLD

AQUATICA IS ACROSS INTERNATIONAL DRIVE from the back side of SeaWorld. From Kissimmee, Walt Disney World, and Lake Buena Vista, take I-4 East, exit onto the Central Florida Parkway, and then bear left on International Drive. From Universal Studios, take I-4 West to FL 528 and from there exit onto International Drive. Admission prices are actually a little higher than those of the Disney water parks if you purchase at the gate: $61 for adults and $56 for kids. Tickets purchased online are $20 cheaper, and off-season specials online can reduce admission to as little as $17. Standard parking is $13 ($17 for RVs, $17 for preferred parking). If you don't want to wait in a queue to purchase tickets, buy them in advance at **aquaticabyseaworld.com,** or use the credit-card ticket machines to the left of Aquatica's main entrance.

Aquatica is comparable in size to the other water theme parks in the area. Attractively landscaped with palms, ferns, and tropical flowers, it's far less themed than Disney's Typhoon Lagoon and Blizzard Beach but much greener and more aesthetically appealing than Wet 'n Wild. Promotional material suggests that Aquatica is unique by virtue of combining SeaWorld's signature marine-animal exhibits with the expected water-park assortment of wave pools, slides, and creek floats. Marine exhibits, however, start and end with a float-through tank of tropical fish and a pool of black-and-white Commerson's dolphins. Print, Web, and television ads for the park show guests viewing the dolphins while descending through a see-through tube on the **Dolphin Plunge** body slide—a corkscrewing romp through a totally dark tube until you blast through the clear tube at the end. The reality, however, is that you're flushed through the clear tube so fast, and with so much water splashing around your face, that it's pretty much impossible to see anything. At Aquatica, the best option by far is to view the dolphins from the walkway surrounding the exhibit or from the subsurface viewing windows.

A Yorkshire, England, woman reacted to the Dolphin Plunge:

> The slide had the longest queue in the park. We queued for the best part of an hour and all agreed that it was a waste of time! You can barely see through the transparent part of the tube where the dolphins are (if you're lucky!), the slide is short, and the see-through bit lasts about 2 seconds!

SeaWorld's promotional hype, coupled with the location of the Plunge just inside the park entrance and the slide's low carrying capacity (about 280 persons per hour), ensures that the slide stays mobbed all day. To experience it without a long wait, ride first thing after park opening.

The first new slide at Aquatica in years, opened in 2014, **Ihu's Breakaway Falls** artfully blends hanging (without a noose) and being flushed down a really big toilet. But first you have to climb the equivalent of 10 stories of stairs. Once you haul yourself to the top of the tower and are revived, you step into one of three tubes with Plexiglas doors. At some undetermined time (Aquatica staff dither around to build your anxiety), a trapdoor opens under you, gallowslike, and down you go. Each tube offers a different ride, but all three include big vertical drops, pitched drops, and corkscrews (the toilet part). A fourth tube at the top of the tower provides a wild but less intimidating ride, with the usual sit-down-and-off-you-go launch.

Omaka Rocka is a wide-diameter, one-person enclosed tube ride. The name derives from the wave action inside the tube, which washes you alternately up one side of the tube and then the other.

Other slides include **Tassie's Twisters,** in which an enclosed tube slide spits you into an open bowl where you careen around the edge much in the manner of the ball in a roulette wheel. Close to the Dolphin Plunge, Tassie's Twisters should be your second early-morning stop. Next, head over to **Walhalla Wave** and **HooRoo Run,** both on the park's far right side. Both slides use circular rafts that can accommodate up to three people. Walhalla Wave splashes down an enclosed twisting tube, while HooRoo Run is an open-air run down a steep, straight, undulating slide. The same entrance serves both slides. Line up for Walhalla Wave (vastly more popular) on the right, for HooRoo Run on the left. Make Walhalla Wave your third slide of the day, followed by HooRoo Run.

Then pass along the right side of the children's adventure area, Walkabout Waters, to **Taumata Racer,** the park's highest-capacity slide with eight enclosed corkscrewing tubes. The remaining slide is **Whanau Way,** all the way across the park to the left of the entrance. Sporting one corkscrew and a few twists, Whanau Way employs tubes that can carry one or two people. Because it's hard to see from the park entrance, Whanau Way doesn't attract long lines until midmorning.

Taken as a whole, the slides at Aquatica aren't nearly as interesting, thrilling, or imaginative as those of its competitors, and aside from whisking you through a dolphin tank, they don't break any new ground. Also, all the slides except HooRoo Run launch you down a black hole, making every ride seem like the one before it. Dark slides are an essential part of every water-park lineup, but to have all slides dark save one makes for a very homogenized experience.

In addition to the slides, Aquatica offers side-by-side wave pools, **Cutback Cove** and **Big Surf Shores.** This arrangement allows one cove to serve up bodysurfing waves while the other puts out gently bobbing floating waves. A spacious beach arrayed around the coves is the park's primary sunning venue. Shady spots, courtesy of beach umbrellas, ring the perimeter of the area for the sun-sensitive.

Loggerhead Lane and **Roa's Rapids** are the two floating streams. The former is a slow and gentle tube journey that circumnavigates the Tassie's Twisters slide. Its claim to fame is a section of the float where a Plexiglas tunnel passes through the Fish Grotto, a tank populated by hundreds of exotic tropical fish. Unique to Aquatica, Roa's Rapids is a much longer course with a very swift current. (The other water parks have floating creeks, but most are leisurely affairs where you can fall asleep in your tube.) Buoyancy vests are available, but most adults float or swim the stream. The name notwithstanding, there are no rapids, but the flow is constricted from time to time, considerably increasing the already fast speed of the current. There's only one place to get in and out, so if you miss the takeout, you're in for another lap.

When it comes to children's water attractions, Aquatica more than equals the other area parks. In the back of the park, to the right of the wave pools, is **Kata's Kookaburra Cove,** featuring a wading pool and slides for the preschool crowd. But the real pièce de résistance is **Walkabout Waters.** If you have children under age 10, this alone may be worth the price of admission. In a calf-deep 15,000-square-foot pool, it's an immense three-story interactive playground set with slides, stairs, rope bridges, landings, and more. Water pulsates, plops, sprays, and spritzes at you from every conceivable angle. Randomly placed plastic squirting devices allow kids to take aim at unsuspecting adults, but the kids disperse quickly when either of two huge buckets dumps hundreds of gallons of water down on the entire structure. It's impossible not to get wet. It's also impossible not to have fun.

As at the other water parks, there are lockers, towels, wheelchairs, and strollers to rent and gift shops to browse. The three restaurants are **WaterStone Grill,** offering specialty sandwiches, fried fish, wraps, and salads; **Banana Beach Buffet,** an all-you-can-eat venue dishing up burgers, hot dogs, and chicken; and **Mango Market,** a diminutive eatery serving pizza, wraps, and salads. WaterStone Grill and Mango Market serve beer.

PART EIGHTEEN

BEHIND-THE-SCENES *and* VIP TOURS *at* WALT DISNEY WORLD

IF YOU'RE INTERESTED IN THE MOUSE'S INNARDS—um, make that inner workings—a number of guided tours offer a glimpse of what goes on behind the scenes. Reservations must be guaranteed with a credit card, and you need to cancel at least 48 hours in advance if you want a full refund. Many tours require that you buy park admission separately; we've noted where it isn't mandatory. Prices listed include sales tax.

unofficial **TIP**
Many tours involve lots of walking, standing, and time spent outdoors, so check the weather forecast before you head out.

Some tours are available only on certain days of the week (see the chart on the next two pages for specifics). For reservations and more information, call ☎ 407-WDW-TOUR (939-8687). Also check **blog.touringplans.com** for detailed reviews from our bloggers—just type the name of one of the tours listed here into the search box.

MULTIPARK TOURS

THE 7-HOUR **Backstage Magic** tour ($249) goes behind the scenes at all the WDW parks. Includes lunch; guests must be at least 16 years old to participate. Park admission is not required. The downside to this all-day tour is that you spend a lot of time in transit between the parks.

Disney's Holiday D-Lights (5 hours, $209) and **Disney's Yuletide Fantasy** (3 hours, $89) explore the myriad ways in which Walt Disney World transforms for the Christmas season. Neither tour requires park admission; guests must be at least age 16. Call ☎ 407-WDW-TOUR for 2016 tour dates; the holiday tours fill up quickly.

BEHIND *the* SCENES *at the* MAGIC KINGDOM

AS ITS NAME MAKES CLEAR, **Disney's Keys to the Kingdom** takes guests behind the scenes at the Magic Kingdom. This fascinating guided tour provides a detailed look at the park's logistical, technical, and operational sides. Included are the parade-assembly area, the waste-treatment plant, and the utilidor network beneath the park. The program ($79 per

Behind-the-Scenes Tours at

COST	TOUR LENGTH	COST	MINIMUM AGE
MULTIPARK TOURS			
Backstage Magic	7 hours	$249	16
Disney's Holiday D-Lights	5 hours	$209	16
Disney's Yuletide Fantasy	3 hours	$89	16
THE MAGIC KINGDOM			
Disney's Family Magic Tour	1½–2 hours	$34	None
Disney's Keys to the Kingdom	4½–5 hours	$79	16
Disney's The Magic Behind Our Steam Trains	3 hours	$54	10
Pirates and Pals Fireworks Voyage	2–3 hours	$59 age 10+, $34 ages 3–9	None
Walt Disney: Marceline to Magic Kingdom Tour	2–3 hours	$30	12
EPCOT			
Behind the Seeds at Epcot (*Unofficial* Pick: Best Value)	1 hour	$20 age 10+, $16 ages 3–9	None
Dolphins in Depth	3 hours	$199	13
Epcot DiveQuest	3 hours	$175	10
Seas Aqua Tour	2½ hours	$140	8
The UnDISCOVERed Future World	4 hours	$64	16
World Showcase DestiNations Discovered	4 hours	$109	16
DISNEY'S ANIMAL KINGDOM			
Animal Kingdom Lodge Night Safari (hotel guests only)	1 hour	$70	8
Backstage Tales	3¾ hours	$90	12
Wild Africa Trek (*Unofficial* Pick: Best Family Tour)	3 hours	$189–$249	8/48" tall
DISNEY'S BOARDWALK			
BoardWalk Ballyhoo Guided Tour	45 minutes	Free	None
FORT WILDERNESS CAMPGROUND			
Disney's Wilderness Back Trail Adventure	2 hours	$96	16/100–250 lbs
Wonders of the Wilderness Lodge	1 hour	Free	None

person) includes lunch and runs about 4½–5 hours; children must be at least 16 years old to participate.

Disney's The Magic Behind Our Steam Trains, a 3-hour tour for children ages 10 and up, takes a backstage look at the steam locomotives of the Walt Disney World Railroad. Cost is $54 per person. **Disney's Family Magic Tour** is an interactive romp through the park following clues

WALT DISNEY WORLD

FOCUS	DAYS AVAILABLE
Peeks behind the scenes at every Disney World park	M, some Th, F
Close-up look at Disney World holiday spectacles	Seasonal
Another look at holiday productions	Seasonal
Following clues in a sort of treasure hunt	Daily
Park's logistical, technical, and operational sides	Daily
Steam locomotives of the Walt Disney World Railroad	M–Sa
Cruise around Seven Seas Lagoon	F–Tu (varies seasonally)
Examination of Walt Disney's career and vision	M, W, F
Vegetable gardens in The Land	Daily
Visiting the dolphin-research facility at The Seas, plus 30 minutes of dolphin interaction	Tu–Sa
Swimming with the fish at The Seas	Tu–Sa
Swimming in the main tank at The Seas	Tu–Sa
The history of Epcot	M–F
Design of World Showcase pavilions, plus lunch	Daily at 9:30 and 10 a.m.
After-dark night-vision tour of lodge's savannas	Nightly at 10 p.m.
Observing how the animals are housed and cared for	Daily
Enhanced safari and adventure activities with meal	Daily
Tour of BoardWalk and discussion of its historical inspiration	Daily
Segway romp on campground trails and paths	Tu–Sa
Design of and inspiration for the Wilderness Lodge	W–Sa at 9 a.m.

in a sort of treasure hunt. The 1½- to 2-hour tour is offered daily for $34. **Walt Disney: Marceline to Magic Kingdom Tour** (2–3 hours, $30 age 12 and older) interprets the Magic Kingdom as a "walking time line" of Disney's life (Marceline, Missouri, was his childhood hometown).

The Contemporary Resort's **Pirates and Pals Fireworks Voyage** (2–3 hours, $59 age 10 and older; $31 ages 3–9) offers sailings with a unique view of the *Wishes* fireworks from Seven Seas Lagoon; days vary seasonally but typically include Friday–Tuesday. Your guide, Patch, sings pirate songs and delights the kids with Disney trivia. On select nights, the voyage also includes a viewing of the Floating Electrical Pageant.

Disney's Wilderness Back Trail Adventure ($95) is a 2-hour Segway romp on the trails and walking paths of Fort Wilderness Campground. Guests must be at least 16 years old and weigh 100–250 pounds.

BEHIND *the* SCENES *at* EPCOT

A TOUR CALLED **The UnDISCOVERed Future World** traces the history of Epcot, including Walt Disney's original concept. The tour takes guests to backstage areas and lasts a bit over 4 hours. The cost is $64; guests must be at least 16 years old to participate.

The hour-long **Behind the Seeds at Epcot** ($20 adults, $16 kids ages 3–9) tours the vegetable gardens and aquaculture farms in the The Land. The quality of the experience—a cross between science lecture and Willy Wonka factory tour—depends heavily on the tour guide's presentation and enthusiasm. Behind the Seeds requires same-day reservations; make them on the lower level of The Land (next to the entrance to Soarin'). We think this is the best value among Disney's behind-the-scenes tours.

The **World Showcase DestiNations Discovered** tour covers the inspiration and design of World Showcase's pavilions, including their backstage areas. The tour is for guests ages 16 and up, costs $118, and includes lunch.

EPCOT DIVEQUEST

THE SOGGIEST BEHIND-THE-SCENES experience anywhere is **Epcot DiveQuest,** in which guests who are open water scuba–certified divers (ages 10 and up; kids age 12 and younger must be accompanied by an adult) can swim around with the fish at The Seas with Nemo & Friends. Offered twice a day, Tuesday–Saturday, at 4:30 and 5:30 p.m., each tour lasts about 3 hours, including a 40-minute dive. Cost is $175 per diver and includes all gear, a souvenir drawstring bag, and a dive-log stamp. Call ☎ 407-560-5590 for recorded information. Epcot admission is not required, but proof of dive certification is.

DOLPHINS IN DEPTH

THIS TOUR (FOR GUESTS AGES 13 AND OLDER) visits the dolphin-research facility at The Seas with Nemo & Friends. There you'll witness a training session, then wade into the water for a photo (but not a swim) with a dolphin. Cost for the 3-hour experience is $199; children under age 18 must be accompanied by an adult; expectant mothers may not participate. Theme park admission is not required. Wet suits are provided. Only eight guests per day can participate; call ☎ 407-WDW-TOUR when you're ready to book.

For $229–$359 (tax included), you can visit SeaWorld's **Discovery Cove** and actually swim with a dolphin. Though the experience is only about 30 minutes long, the ticket entitles visitors to an entire day at Discovery Cove. For more information, see page 696.

SEAS AQUA TOUR

THIS IS SORT OF a watered-down (ba-dump-bump) version of Epcot DiveQuest. The 2½-hour tour lets you swim with goggles, a mini–air tank, and a flotation vest in the main tank for 30 minutes and explore backstage areas at The Seas with Nemo & Friends. It costs $140, accepts guests as young as 8 years old, and doesn't require separate park admission. Children under age 12 must be accompanied by an adult; children ages 12–17 must have a parent or guardian sign a waiver. Gear and a souvenir drawstring bag are included.

BEHIND *the* SCENES *at* DISNEY'S ANIMAL KINGDOM

IN THE 3¾-HOUR **Backstage Tales** tour, animal keepers and vets discuss conservation, animal care and behavior, and other topics. Limited to guests age 12 and older, Backstage Tales costs $90. You'll see animal enclosures, feed bins, medical facilities, and labs, but not many animals.

Our pick for best family tour at Disney World, the **Wild Africa Trek** (3 hours, $189–$249) takes groups of up to 12 onto forest hiking trails, on suspension bridges high above hippo and crocodile pools, and on a private safari complete with a gourmet meal. The experience is open to guests age 8 and older. Extensive walking is required, and guests must weigh 45–310 pounds and be at least 48" tall for the safety gear. A host of other warnings applies, so call Disney for details.

The **Night Safari** is offered only to guests of Animal Kingdom Lodge & Villas (book through the concierge).

VIP TOURS

WE CAN TELL BY THE BOOK you're reading that you're smart, and probably drop-dead gorgeous to boot. If you're also loaded and looking to avoid every possible line at Disney World while having most of your whims catered to, then a private VIP tour is what you want.

For $360–$500 per hour (depending on the season) and a 6-hour minimum, a Disney VIP host will pick you up at your resort, precheck your admission tickets, and whisk you and up to nine of your friends through a private entrance to a Disney theme park. Once in the park, your VIP guide will ensure that you wait as little as possible for whatever attractions you want to see (usually by taking you through the FastPass+ line, even if you don't have reservations) and make sure you get prime spots for viewing parades and fireworks. If you want to visit multiple parks, the VIP guide will drive you in a private car.

Unofficial Guide readers rave about the service provided by Disney's VIP tour guides, which includes everything from entertaining the kids to regaling the adults with obscure park trivia. The guides can also arrange meals if you haven't yet done so.

One of our favorite people, travel-agent whiz **Sue Pisaturo** of Small World Vacations, had this to say about her experience:

I'm usually the designated tour guide when we go to WDW. This time, I was so happy that no one asked me, "Where do we go next?" The convenience and stress-free touring were priceless. The highlight of our day was a preferred viewing location for the afternoon parade on the bridge to Liberty Square. It seemed like every character came over to hug or high-five our kids.

Tours can be booked between 3 and 90 days in advance by calling ☎ 407-560-4033. You must cancel at least 48 hours in advance to avoid a charge of 2 hours at the booked rate. To book one of the following three VIP tours, call ☎ 407-WDW-TOUR.

The **Ultimate Day for Young Families–VIP Tour Experience** and **Ultimate Day of Thrills–VIP Experience** (7 hours, $299 per person) include rides on 12 attractions in the Magic Kingdom, Hollywood Studios, and Animal Kingdom, plus lunch at a Disney full-service restaurant. The Young Families tour features rides such as Dumbo, Peter Pan's Flight, and Toy Story Midway Mania!, while the Thrills tour includes headliners like Space Mountain, Seven Dwarfs Mine Train, and Tower of Terror. Transportation between parks is included, but park admission is not—you'll need the Park Hopper feature on your Magic Your Way ticket. Annual Pass holders, Disney Vacation Club members, and Disney Visa Card holders get a 15% discount.

The **Ultimate Day VIP Tour at the Epcot International Food & Wine Festival** (6½ hours, $399 per person) takes places Thursdays and Sundays on select dates September–November (see page 49 for details on the festival). It includes Champagne and appetizers, a six-course tapas lunch, food and beverage tastings, rides on popular attractions such as Soarin' and Test Track, behind-the-scenes tours, VIP seating at one of the festival's Eat to the Beat concerts (featuring celebrity headliners such as Wilson Phillips and Chaka Khan), and reserved seating at *IllumiNations.*

PART NINETEEN

DISNEY SPRINGS, UNIVERSAL CITYWALK, SHOPPING, *and* NIGHTLIFE

VACATIONS AREN'T JUST THEME PARKS and attractions. It turns out many people actually want to shop, see some live entertainment, or just let loose in the evening. This chapter is for you.

Both Walt Disney World and Universal Orlando have built huge outdoor mall complexes with restaurants, shopping, and theaters, so their hotel and theme park guests never need to spend money outside their borders. This chapter covers both locations, known as **Disney Springs** and **Universal CityWalk,** plus the best shopping in the Orlando area and nightlife options at both Walt Disney World and Universal.

DISNEY SPRINGS

DISNEY SPRINGS IS A SHOPPING, dining, and entertainment complex strung along the banks of Village Lake, on the east side of Walt Disney World. Built in 1975 as **Lake Buena Vista Shopping Village,** it evolved over the next 25 years into **Downtown Disney,** adding nightclubs, live entertainment, and even more stores.

The nightlife and entertainment venues began to lose customers around the turn of the millennium. Most were closed by 2008, and many retail shops soon followed. Many of the closed areas stayed in limbo as Disney announced and canceled plans for various revitalization efforts. Finally, in 2013, Disney was able to move forward with a plan to double the number of shops and restaurants, redesign pedestrian walkways, and retheme the entire area.

unofficial **TIP**
To avoid parking and transportation headaches, visit Disney Springs early in the day. Shops open at 10 a.m. most of the year.

Most of the construction in Disney Springs should be finished in 2016. A number of major projects, including parking garages to address the notoriously bad traffic, have already been completed.

The best way to get to Disney Springs is by Disney transportation. Free bus service is available from every Disney resort to the stop at the Marketplace. Guests at the Old Key West, Saratoga Springs, and Port Orleans Resorts can take a water taxi to Disney Springs; the water taxi

Continued on page 726

Disney Springs

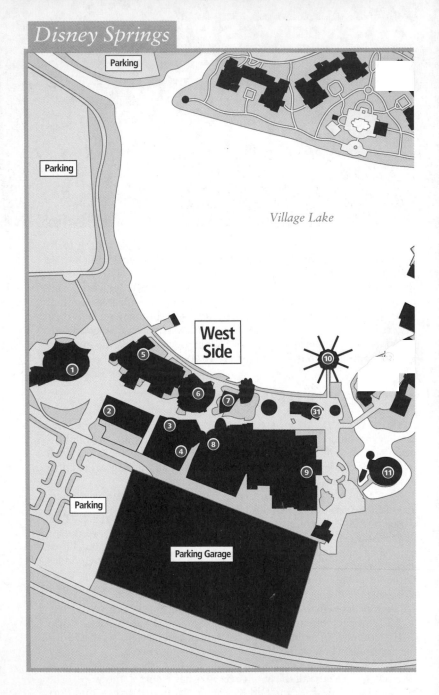

Parking

Parking

Village Lake

West
Side

Parking

Parking Garage

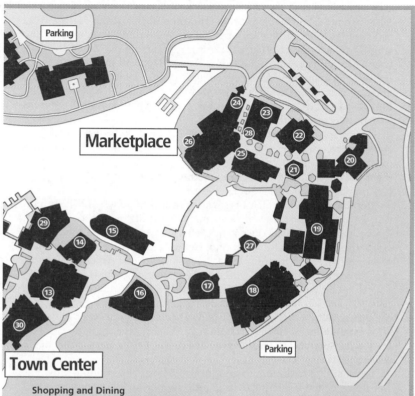

Marketplace

Town Center

Shopping and Dining

1. Cirque du Soleil *La Nouba*
2. DisneyQuest *(closes 2016)*
3. Curl by Sammy Duvall/Fit2Run
4. Splitsville
5. House of Blues
6. Wolfgang Puck Grand Cafe
7. Bongos Cuban Cafe
8. AMC Downtown Disney 24 Theatres
9. *Specialty shopping:*
   Disney's Candy Cauldron
   D-Street
   Orlando Harley-Davidson
   Pop Gallery
   Something Silver
   Sosa Family Cigars
   Sunglass Icon
   Super Hero Headquarters
10. Characters in Flight
11. Planet Hollywood
12. Paradiso 37
13. Raglan Road/Cookes of Dublin

14. Portobello
15. Fulton's Crab House
16. T-REX
17. LEGO Imagination Center
18. World of Disney/ Bibbidi Bobbidi Boutique
19. *Specialty shopping:*
    Arribas Brothers
    Basin
    Ghirardelli Soda Fountain & Chocolate Shop
    Marketplace Co-op
    Tren-D
20. Once Upon a Toy
21. Disney's Pin Traders
22. Earl of Sandwich/Mickey's Pantry/The Spice & Tea Exchange
23. Wolfgang Puck Express Cafe
24. *Specialty shopping:*
    The Art of Disney
    Disney Design-a-Tee

24. *Specialty shopping (continued):*
    Disney's Wonderful World of Memories
25. *Specialty shopping:*
    Goofy's Candy Co.
    littlemissmatched
    Marketplace Fun Finds
26. Rainforest Cafe
27. Waterside Stage
28. Disney's Days of Christmas
29. The Boathouse
30. *Specialty shopping:*
    Art of Shaving
    Apex by Sunglass Hut
    Chapel Hats
    Havaianas
    Erin McKenna's Bakery NYC
    Sanuk
    Sound Lion
    Vivoli Gelateria
31. Starbucks

Continued from page 723

ferries passengers along the Sassagoula River to the West Side dock. Allow about a half-hour for this trip, plus time waiting for the boat (10 minutes for Saratoga Springs). Guests who don't wish to walk the length of Disney Springs can take a water taxi from the West Side dock to the Marketplace dock. Saratoga Springs has walking paths to both the West Side and the Marketplace. Part of the master plan for Disney Springs includes elevated walkways from the resorts of Hotel Plaza Boulevard and direct access from I-4, which, when completed, should ease traffic considerably in the area.

Disney Springs consists of four areas, each with a distinct theme. The **Marketplace,** on the east side of the property, is where guests will find most of the Disney-owned and -operated stores, as well as the highly themed, child-pleasing restaurants **Rainforest Cafe** and **T-REX** (see profiles on pages 367 and 376 in Part Four).

The Landing, which features waterfront walkways and merchandise kiosks, has seen the most reimagining, with new shopping and dining areas. What was once a bottleneck for guests (and their strollers) trying to go from the West Side to the Marketplace is now a much more open area, with multiple pathways to alleviate pedestrian traffic, plus sweeping views of the water and Saratoga Springs Resort.

Still under construction is **Town Center,** a brand-new area situated between The Landing and the parking garage. Anchoring this area is the **Planet Hollywood** restaurant (still open during construction).

West Side has seen the least change. This is where guests can find **Cirque du Soleil** *La Nouba,* **DisneyQuest,** the **AMC** cinema, and many independent retailers.

Families will find numerous options here for entertaining kids. The Marketplace has a small carousel and mini–train rides for a nominal fee. A free fountain splash area is great for cooling down, and kid-oriented dance parties, also free, take place across from World of Disney in the amphitheater. The dance parties get your children out of the overwhelming flow of pedestrian traffic at night in the Marketplace and look like a blast.

Disney Springs shopping, entertainment, and nightlife highlights are covered later in this chapter.

DisneyQuest *(closing permanently in 2016)*

The largest building in Disney Springs besides the Cirque de Soleil arena is the five-floor DisneyQuest, on the West Side. Billed as a virtual theme park, it was supposed to be the first of many DisneyQuests throughout the country. Unfortunately, the travel industry tanked in the early 2000s, and Disney found it too expensive to update attractions that rely heavily on both technology and parts that get a lot of wear and tear from guests.

These days, most of DisneyQuest is a quaint game museum. Your smartphone probably has better graphics and more computing power than most of the games, and nostalgia is more common than cutting-edge technology.

DISNEYQUEST TICKETS Guests have multiple admission options. A DisneyQuest visit is bundled with the **Water Park Fun and More (WPFAM)**

admission add-on (see page 61) and the **Premium Annual Pass** (see page 62). Everyone else must purchase separate admission. Adult admission to DisneyQuest is $48, and kids 3–9 years old pay $42. Frankly, we don't recommend visiting DisneyQuest unless your admission is covered through your pass or ticket. The price for a one-day separate ticket is out of line with a facility that rarely sees any updates, but it can be a fun diversion if it's already part of your vacation package.

DISNEYQUEST DISCOUNTS The best discount for DisneyQuest admission for people who haven't bought the WPFAM option is to buy in advance from **Undercover Tourist** (see page 64). Regular Annual Pass holders and Disney Vacation Club members receive a gate discount; if you arrive close to closing, you may be offered a discount as well. Surprisingly, Disney doesn't offer DisneyQuest tickets for advance purchase on its website.

RECOMMENDED ATTRACTIONS Visitors arrive at the **VenturePort,** the third floor of the building, by elevator; from here, they can then take either the stairs or another elevator to the other floors. Dining options are on the fourth and fifth floors.

We enjoy the attractions that are truly interactive. **CyberSpace Mountain** (on the second floor, in the **Create Zone**) lets you design and ride your own virtual roller coaster, and while it isn't as advanced as the similar Sum of All Thrills at Epcot (see page 546), it's still pretty fun. Despite graphics that are rather primitive by today's standards, **Virtual Jungle Cruise** and **Pirates of the Caribbean—Battle for Buccaneer Gold,** both in the first floor's **Explore Zone,** score points with us for active (and sometimes exhausting) physical interaction. Kids will enjoy **Mighty Ducks Pinball Spin,** and **Buzz Lightyear's AstroBlasters** is a fun take on bumper cars, with the added bonus of shooting basketballs at your opponent's (protected by a cage) car.

Anyone who remembers changing dollar bills for quarters at the mall will enjoy the classic video games and air hockey in the **Replay Zone** (floors five and three; all games are set for free play). We've even played games we've never seen before, like fun head-to-head versions of **Pac-Man** and **Tetris,** with up to four players on a large screen. Hidden among the classics is a one-of-a-kind, real-life **Fix-It Felix Jr.,** from the Disney animated movie *Wreck-It Ralph.*

We don't recommend any of the virtual-reality games that require you to wear VR goggles, such as **Aladdin's Magic Carpet Ride.** The graphics are primitive at best; at worst, they can induce motion sickness in even the strongest of stomachs.

While nearly every game at DisneyQuest can be played at no charge, there are a few exceptions. Claw-type games where you try to retrieve a prize have a charge. Also, nearly everything in the second-floor **Create Zone** is free to play but offers a souvenir you can buy later, such as a recording or drawing—keep this in mind if you're trying to keep costs down.

CROWDS AND HOURS DisneyQuest opens for business at 11:30 a.m. and closes around 10 or 11 p.m. Rainy or exceptionally hot days will bring out guests to enjoy some indoor, air-conditioned fun, but for the most part, crowds are light and there's not much queuing for the more popular games.

*un*official **TIP**
Weekday mornings are the least crowded times to visit DisneyQuest.

Note that several major attractions at DisneyQuest have a height requirement of up to 51 inches. Smaller kids will appreciate the console games and the air hockey tables, made especially for them to be able to reach.

Reader response to DisneyQuest is very mixed, as evidenced by the following comments.

From a Pennsylvania family with kids ages 11 and 13:

Our only really big disappointment was DisneyQuest. My husband and daughters paid $48 to get in because the guy at the window told us that fee covered nearly all the experiences. Once inside, they found that at least half the stuff they wanted to do cost mega-extra-bucks. It's a truly offensive deal for people who have already spent scads in their darned parks.

But for a Cleveland family of five, DisneyQuest was a slam dunk:

If you have right-brained (creative) kids, you can't miss at DQ. Your book said 2–5 hours for the experience. We had dinner reservations that forced a cutoff at 7 hours, otherwise we could have pulled an all-nighter! The interactive stuff was fascinating. I think DQ provides parents the best chance to see their kids' brains and personalities in action.

A family from Columbia, Maryland, offers this advice to parents with babies and toddlers:

Alert your readers to bring a baby carrier–backpack to DisneyQuest. You're there for several hours, and absolutely no strollers are allowed in the entire building. [Authors' note: There is a coat check on the first floor where you can leave your stroller.]

At press time, we learned that DisneyQuest will close in 2016 to make room for **The NBA Experience,** featuring a National Basketball Association–themed restaurant, shop, and exhibits. Interactive activities, designed for guests of most ages, will focus on basketball skills as well as test agility, reflexes, and mobility.

UNIVERSAL CITYWALK

EVERY GUEST WHO DRIVES to Universal enters through CityWalk—a complex of nightlife, retail, and dining opportunities that caters to visitors and locals alike. On weekends, CityWalk draws far more locals than Disney Springs and, with its concentration of nightclubs, a much younger crowd. CityWalk also features a fantastically themed mini-golf course, **Hollywood Drive-In Golf** (see page 754 in Part Twenty, Recreation, Sports, and Spas) and a 20-screen **AMC Universal Cineplex.**

While CityWalk doesn't charge admission, visitors do need to pay for parking. If you want to visit the nightclubs, there is a cover charge in the evenings. CityWalk shopping and nightlife are discussed later in this chapter.

DINING

WE'RE WILD ABOUT many of the new dining venues that have opened at CityWalk since mid-2014. Our favorites, such as **Vivo Italian Kitchen** and **Antojitos,** serve tasty meals at a price point that would give a Disney stockholder heart palpitations. Read more about them in Part Four, Dining In and Around Walt Disney World, on pages 294 and 293, respectively.

SHOPPING *in the* THEME PARKS *and* ORLANDO

WE ALMOST TITLED THIS SECTION "Exit Through the Gift Shop," but that would have been a cliché (and Banksy beat us to it). Retail merchandise is a huge revenue source for both Walt Disney World and Universal. If you enjoy shopping, we recommend setting aside some time and money for retail therapy. And even if you don't enjoy it, you may be traveling with someone who does, so keep the tips below in mind as you exit through . . . well, you know.

TIPS FOR AVOIDING BUYER'S REMORSE

1. Know ahead of time how much things cost. Many theme park items are available at **disneystore.com**.

2. Be specific. Disney collecting can spiral out of control if you don't narrow your focus. Pick a character or movie you love and stick to that.

3. Don't buy dated merchandise. That Walt Disney World 2016 t-shirt you buy to commemorate your vacation is going to look awfully silly on January 1, 2017. There's a reason this stuff is the number-one seller at Disney outlets.

4. Speaking of the outlets, check them out if you have transportation. While we joke about the outlets being the "Island of Misfit Toys," you can sometimes find just what you're looking for at a great discount.

5. Don't fall for "limited editions." If they make 2,000 of something, is it really limited?

6. Wait. Don't make your purchases until you've been to more than one shop.

7. Consider comestibles as souvenirs. There's no buyer's remorse if you can eat the evidence.

8. Some of the best things in life are free. Consider our favorite freebies at Walt Disney World (see page 736) and skip the cash register.

WALT DISNEY WORLD SHOPPING AT A GLANCE

Disney Springs Marketplace

ARRIBAS BROTHERS There's beautiful (and expensive) glassware and crystal at every turn, including an area dedicated to sparkling Swarovski pieces. *Not* the place to take rambunctious kids.

THE ART OF DISNEY Sells pricey original Disney art, from pottery to personalized sketch art, with a few affordable souvenirs in the mix.

BASIN Browse among wooden tubs filled with soaps and lotions, then scoop your own bath salts or build your own gift basket. All the store's products are chemical-free and made with natural ingredients.

DISNEY DESIGN-A-TEE A store where guests can create custom T-shirts and personalized merchandise. Next door is **Disney's Wonderful World of Memories,** which offers stationery and scrapbook materials, as well as customizable ear hats—themes include sports, princesses, brides, grooms, and more.

DISNEY'S DAYS OF CHRISTMAS This shop is just plain fun, with hundreds of holiday decorations from ornaments to stockings to stuffed animals wearing their Christmas Day best. We especially like the station for ornament personalization. A hot seller in all the Christmas shops is the Disney monorail train (also carried at some toy stores).

DISNEY'S PIN TRADERS The spot for the largest collection of pins, with tables for trading and two Internet stations for visiting the official pin-trading website (**disneypins.com**). This location also offers a large selection of retail MagicBands and accessories.

GHIRARDELLI SODA FOUNTAIN AND CHOCOLATE SHOP You can smell the chocolate when you walk in, and most of the time a cast member is on hand to dole out free samples. Chocolate souvenirs abound, but treat yourself to a "world famous" sundae topped with the decadent hot fudge made daily at the shop. The line for ice cream often winds out the door—it's that good.

GOOFY'S CANDY CO. An interactive show kitchen with lots of sweets!

LEGO IMAGINATION CENTER This is an ideal rest stop for parents, and you don't even have to go inside the store. A hands-on outdoor play area has bins of LEGOs that the kids can go crazy with while Mom and Dad take a break. Inside is all the latest LEGO paraphernalia. Check out the "sea monster" across from the store "swimming" in Lake Buena Vista.

LITTLEMISSMATCHED Little fashion plates will have fun browsing the selection of funky printed socks, bags, and clothes. Socks are sold three to a pack in different patterns that you can mix and match.

MARKETPLACE CO-OP Six shops-within-a-shop: **Cherry Tree Lane,** for women's accessories; **D-Tech on Demand,** featuring phone cases and other electronic accessories that you can have personalized on-site; **Disney Centerpiece,** for fun home goods with that Disney touch (think *Enchanted Tiki Room* appetizer bowls and ceramic replicas of Dole Whip swirls); **The Trophy Room,** specializing in vintage-look sports apparel and collectibles; **Zoey and Pickles,** where tween girls can find the latest fashions just for them; and **Wonderground Gallery,** with original, Disney-inspired art.

MARKETPLACE FUN FINDS Disney-character merchandise organized into price points, including plush toys, clothing, and housewares.

MICKEY'S PANTRY A small shop with Disney home products, kitchen gadgets, and cookbooks. Also home to the **Spice & Tea Exchange,** which offers an assortment of one-of-a-kind teas and gourmet seasonings created and blended in Orlando.

ONCE UPON A TOY Five rooms of toys, from build-your-own Mr. Potato Heads and light sabers to a room dedicated to video games. Several favorites, including *Star Wars, Toy Story,* and *Transformers* toys, are on the shelves. Also for sale are miniature play sets of Cinderella Castle; plush animals; and plenty of pirate, princess, and fairy items.

TREN-D A fun, hip, urban-inspired boutique with fashion apparel and accessories, plus exclusive items from cutting-edge designers and Disney merchandise you won't find anywhere else.

WORLD OF DISNEY It's a superstore with 12 rooms—50,000 square feet—stacked with Disney merchandise. World of Disney is also home to one of Disney World's two **Bibbidi Bobbidi Boutiques,** sort-of salons that can turn your snot-nosed tomboy into a little princess (the second location is inside Cinderella Castle in the Magic Kingdom). At the boutique, girls can try on various princess costumes before repairing to the beauty parlor for hairstyling, makeup, a manicure, and even a princess gown, depending on which of the three packages you choose. Girls can choose between three hairstyles—Disney Diva, Pop Princess, or Fairytale Princess. At 2 p.m. daily, the newly minted princesses and divas are invited to participate in the Princess Parade. Holding onto a rope adorned with bells, the girls are walked from World of Disney to the carousel in Disney Springs and given a personalized certificate. Call the boutique at ☎ 407-WDW-STYLE for more details.

Bibbidi Bobbidi Boutique costs a bundle, but this Northport, Alabama, mother of a 4-year-old thought it was worth it:

> Yes, we spent $200, but the look on my daughter's face was priceless as she walked to the castle to eat. Everyone spoke to her, calling her "Princess." There hasn't been a day in three months since we've been home that she has not asked to go back.

If you don't have $200 in loose change lying around, there are alternatives, as a dollar-conscious Kalamazoo, Michigan, mom explains:

> The tip that tickled me the most in your book is taking little girls to the **Harmony Barber Shop** [on Main Street, U.S.A.] to get their hair done. I think I spent about $12, including tip. You don't need reservations, and in my opinion they do a better job than Bibbidi Bobbidi Boutique. They put my daughter's hair into a teased bun and used brightly colored paints and confetti to match whatever princess dress she had on. I understand that Disney doesn't want the barber shop to compete with the BBB, so I don't know if I want you telling anyone this great secret or not!

Disney Springs: The Landing and Town Center

Construction is still ongoing, but here's what's open at press time:

THE ART OF SHAVING This store sells premium grooming essentials for men and has a team of shaving specialists who offer advice on grooming techniques. Appointments suggested for a haircut or shave.

APEX BY SUNGLASS HUT Sunglasses designed with athletes and sports and outdoors enthusiasts in mind.

CHAPEL HATS Offers fashionable hats and headwear for all ages: fedoras, sun hats, floppy hats, outdoors hats, kids' hats, and more.

HAVAIANAS Sandals store offering "Make Your Own Havaianas" and "Embellish Your Own Havaianas," for women, men, and children, plus kids' rain boots.

SANUK Footwear made from nontraditional materials such as yoga mats.

SOUND LION Sells the latest technology in headphones, earbuds, speakers, and other digital sound and music products.

Several shops have committed to opening at Disney Springs but have not yet declared a home in either Town Center or The Landing:

EDWARD BEINER The Miami-based eyewear company.

LILLY PULITZER The warm-weather uniform of socialites and sorority girls everywhere, this resort-wear brand is renowned for its loud colors and splashy prints (think frogs drinking Champagne).

L'OCCITANE Here you'll find skin care, fragrances, moisturizers, soaps, and more for your beauty regimen.

PANDORA This well-known jewelry brand is known for charms, bracelets, and more.

TOMMY BAHAMA Upscale island-themed resort-casual clothing for men and women.

UGG This American company is known primarily for its boots, favored by tween and teen girls worldwide. UGG also sells clothing and home accessories.

ZARA AND UNIQLO These two fast-fashion chains interpret current trends for men, women, and children.

Disney Springs West Side

CURL BY SAMMY DUVALL Sells men's, women's, and children's summer clothing, along with watches, sunglasses, and lots of bathing suits.

DISNEY'S CANDY CAULDRON Watch as gooey treats are made in the open kitchen. You can buy everything from jelly beans to caramel apples and cotton candy—more than 200 sweets are on the shelves.

D-STREET This shop offers an eclectic mix of urban-chic apparel for men and women. It also houses the largest and most extensive collection of Vinylmation figurines, apparel, and accessories. Also available are pop-culture novelties and products from *Star Wars* and Marvel.

FIT2RUN Running gear and runDisney merchandise.

ORLANDO HARLEY-DAVIDSON Sit on a real Harley and shop for Harley outerwear, including men's and women's T-shirts and (of course) leather jackets. You can even customize your own leather vest.

POP GALLERY This gallery-like shop carries a wide variety of contemporary art, including limited-edition sculptures and paintings, high-end gift items, and even a small collection of inexpensive souvenirs such as art-instruction kits and brightly painted ceramic piggy banks.

SOSA FAMILY CIGARS They hand-roll 'em here and feature premium imports, including Arturo Fuente, Cuesta-Rey, Diamond Crown, La Gloria Cubana, Macanudo, Padrón, Partagas, Puros Indios, and Sosa. A walk-in humidor stores the top brands.

SPLITSVILLE This upscale bowling alley and eatery has a large gift shop with themed merchandise for bowling enthusiasts.

SUNGLASS ICON Designer sunglasses and eyewear.

Shopping in the Theme Parks

Each theme park has at least one major retail space, several minor ones, and space attached to most attractions. While we occasionally bemoan the homogenization of the merchandise selection, this does mean that if something catches your eye, you'll most likely see it again. Ditto for sale prices. Pricing is consistent throughout the resorts, and an item on sale in one location will be the same price at all locations.

See the next two pages for a quick-reference guide to which theme park shops carry the stuff you're looking for.

EPCOT SHOPPING Retail is a huge part of the World Showcase experience at Epcot—much more so than at the other theme parks. This is one of the few times on your vacation that you won't be able to say "well, I'll see it again later" if something catches your eye. With a selection that ranges from affordable trinkets to Mikimoto pearl-and-diamond earrings, the shops in World Showcase have something for everyone.

Walking clockwise around World Showcase, you'll find:

★ **MEXICO** The **Plaza de los Amigos** is a lovely re-creation of a charming Mexican city at dusk; here, a live mariachi band often entertains passersby. Carts and kiosks are piled with blankets, sombreros, paper flowers, animal sculptures, and tambourines. Sure, the merchandise may be cheaper south of the border, but these prices aren't bad: Piñatas are wildly popular, starting at about $10, while blankets start at about $20. Or pick up a good bottle of tequila or hot sauce to pack home. Two shops along the perimeter are **La Princesa Cristal** (a small crystal shop) and an unnamed store that sells leather handbags, wallets, and jewelry. **La Cava del Tequila** is a bar serving more than 70 varieties of tequila, plus margaritas and appetizers. For those who want to take home some spirits, tequila is sold by the bottle in the nearby kiosk, though the selection is mostly low-end.

★ **NORWAY** The **Puffin's Roost** is a series of small shopping galleries with popular imports such as trolls (from $15) and wooden Christmas ornaments ($4 and up). (May be closed at various times due to construction on the boat ride nearby.) Other hard-to-find imports include Scandinavian foods and candies, Laila perfume and body lotion, and Helly Hansen and Dale of Norway clothing, including thick woolen sweaters. You'll also find sterling-silver jewelry, butterfly pins, and classic Viking hats (with or without braids).

★ **CHINA** This pavilion features one of our favorite shops, piled with such imports as real silk kimonos, cloisonné, and thick silk rugs. **House of Good Fortune** is more like a rambling department store than a shop. You'll find everything here from silk fans to $4,000 jade sculptures to antique furniture. The silk dresses and robes are competitively priced in the $100 range. Darling handbags are $10 and up, and silk ties are around $20. We always admire the handwoven pure-silk carpets, starting around $300 for a 2-foot rug and topping out around $2,500 for a 4 x 8–foot rug. The prices are comparable to what you'd pay in a retail shop—if you could find one that imports carpets like these.

Village Traders, a shop between China and Germany, sells African woodcarvings that are as unusual as they come. Another specialty here is beautiful bead jewelry, crafted in Uganda from repurposed Disney paper products such as old handout guides.

★ **GERMANY** Shops interconnect on both sides of the cobblestoned central plaza and purvey an impressive collection of imports. Tiny **Das Kaufhaus** stocks a nice selection of Adidas sportswear. Next door is **Volkskunst,** where the walls are covered with Schneider cuckoo clocks

MAGIC KINGDOM SHOPPING SAMPLER

I WANT . . .	FIND IT AT . . .
• One-stop shopping	• **The Emporium,** Main Street
• Candy, pastries, fudge	• **The Confectionary,** Main Street; **Big Top Treats,** Fantasyland
• Disney art and collectibles	• **The Art of Disney,** Main Street
• Holiday decor	• **Olde Christmas Shoppe,** Liberty Square
• Memory cards and batteries	• **Town Square Gifts**
• Personalized mouse ears	• **The Chapeau,** Main Street; **Box Office Gifts,** Town Square
• Princess wear	• **The Emporium,** Main Street; **Castle Couture,** Fantasyland
• Tech gifts	• **Space Mountain Gift Shop,** Tomorrowland
• Women's jewelry, handbags, accessories	• **Main Street Jewelers** (has a **Pandora** shop)

EPCOT SHOPPING SAMPLER

I WANT . . .	FIND IT AT . . .
• One-stop shopping	• **MouseGear,** Future World
• Disney art and collectibles	• **The Art of Disney,** Future World
• Disney comics and books	• **ImageWorks,** Imagination! Pavilion
• Eco-friendly gifts	• **Outpost,** World Showcase
• Kitchen supplies and decor	• **Port of Entry,** World Showcase
• Memory cards and batteries	• **Camera Center,** Future World
• Personalized mouse ears	• **MouseGear,** Future World
• Princess-wear	• Norway Pavilion
• Tech gifts	• **MouseGear** and **Camera Center,** Future World

and the shelves are stocked with limited-edition steins and glassware. Next is **Der Teddybär,** featuring Engel-Puppen dolls and Steiff plush toys, among other delights for kids. Across the plaza, **Kunstarbeit in Kristall** carries a fabulous collection of Swarovski crystal, including pins, glassware, and Arribas Brothers collectibles (check out the limited-edition $37,500 replica of Cinderella Castle, blinged out with more than 20,000 Swarovski crystals). Next is the **Weinkeller,** with nearly 300 varieties of German wine. Step through the door to **Die Weihnachts Ecke,** where Christmas ornaments and handmade nutcrackers are on display year-round. Anyone with a sweet tooth will go crazy just smelling the most delicious addition to Germany's lineup, **Karamell-Küche.** Treats are made in-house with Werther's Original caramel, from caramel apples to cookies and candies made or drizzled with caramel. You'll also find an impressive selection of Werther's Original candies.

★ **ITALY II Bel Cristallo** showcases Puma sportswear, Bulgari and Emilio Pucci fragrances, Murano figurines, elaborate Venetian masks, and a small selection of Christmas decorations in the back room.

THE AMERICAN ADVENTURE Heritage Manor Gifts carries patriotic gifts with a twist, such as American-made candy, and regional souvenirs.

ANIMAL KINGDOM SHOPPING SAMPLER

I WANT . . .	FIND IT AT . . .
• One-stop shopping	• **Disney Outfitters,** Discovery Island
• African souvenirs	• **Mombasa Marketplace,** Harambe, Africa
• Dinosaur kitsch and toys	• **Chester and Hester's Dinosaur Treasures,** DinoLand U.S.A.
• Memory cards and batteries	• **Island Mercantile,** Discovery Island
• Personalized mouse ears	• **Island Mercantile,** Discovery Island

DISNEY'S HOLLYWOOD STUDIOS SHOPPING SAMPLER

I WANT . . .	FIND IT AT . . .
• One-stop shopping	• **Mickey's of Hollywood,** Hollywood Blvd.
• Candy, pastries, fudge	• **Beverly Sunset,** Hollywood and Sunset
• Holiday decor	• **It's a Wonderful Shop,** Streets of America
• Memory cards and batteries	• **The Darkroom,** Hollywood Blvd.
• Personalized mouse ears	• **Adrian and Edith's Head to Toe,** Hollywood Blvd.
• Princess wear	• **Legends of Hollywood,** Sunset Blvd.
• Tech gifts	• **Villains in Vogue,** Sunset Blvd.
• Women's jewelry, handbags, accessories	• **Keystone Clothiers,** Hollywood Blvd.

★ **JAPAN** A US branch of Japan's 300-year-old **Mitsukoshi Department Store** stretches along one entire side of the pavilion. Kid-friendly merchandise—Hello Kitty, Naruto, and Yu-Gi-Oh!—fills the front, with kimonos, slippers, handbags, and lots more at the back of the store. Mitsukoshi's expanded culinary display includes a sake-tasting bar, along with chopsticks, pretty rice bowls, a large variety of teas and teapots, and imported snacks. Pricey Mikimoto pearls (rings, necklaces, earrings, and bracelets) are showcased in a separate room. And tourists line up for an oyster guaranteed to have a pearl in its shell (pearls are polished for you by the salesperson).

★ **MOROCCO** Several shops wend through this pavilion: **Tangier Traders** sells traditional Moroccan clothing, shoes, and fezzes; **The Brass Bazaar** features brass, of course, and ceramic and wooden kitchenware (not dishwasher safe); and **Casablanca Carpets** offers a wide variety of Moroccan rugs, as well as decorative pieces such as abstract-shaped lamps, sequined pillows, and incense holders.

★ **FRANCE** We always find a few moments to browse in **Plume et Palette,** a perfume shop with more than 100 imports. You'll find scents by Dior, Chanel, Givenchy, and other top names. Famed design house **Givenchy** has a 300-square-foot cosmetics shop here—the only retail location in the United States to offer the full line of Givenchy makeup and skin-care products, as well as a large selection of fragrances. Cross over to **Les Vins de France** and **L'Esprit de la Provence,** two stores in one, with a wine room and a small selection of Provençal goods. At the back of the pavilion, **Souvenirs de France** offers T-shirts, traditional berets, *Aristocats* merchandise, and Eiffel Tower collectibles.

★ **UNITED KINGDOM** A handful of interesting imports is scattered throughout a half-dozen small shops. **The Toy Soldier** stocks costumes, books, and plush toys featuring English characters from favorite films and television shows, such as *Dr. Who* and *Downton Abbey,* as well as British rock 'n' roll–themed items, including Beatles merchandise. You'll find plenty of Alice in Wonderland, Peter Pan, and Winnie the Pooh merchandise, too. Stop in **The Crown & Crest** to look up your family name in the coat-of-arms book, and the shop will create your family's insignia in a beautiful frame of choice. At the adjacent **Sportsman's Shoppe,** you'll find plenty of football (soccer) apparel, balls, and books.

Across the street, you'll find **The Queen's Table,** a gift shop with UK-themed clothing, glassware, and more. **Lords and Ladies,** a quaint store, offers lotions, soaps, scarves, jewelry, and perfume from the United Kingdom. **The Tea Caddy** stocks Twinings tea, biscuits, and candy. The chocolate gets high marks from this Cambridge, England, reader:

> *You can buy English chocolate at [The Tea Caddy]. This is impossible to buy in America, and so I was over the moon!*

★ **CANADA** There's not much shopping here, but **Northwest Mercantile** has a wide selection of merchandise, including NHL jerseys, T-shirts, sweatshirts, aprons, and pajamas. Bottles of ice wine and maple syrup make nice souvenirs for foodies.

Our Favorite Free Souvenirs from Walt Disney World

SORCERERS OF THE MAGIC KINGDOM CARDS You can get one pack per day per player at the Magic Kingdom; special cards (also free) are given out during some events such as the Halloween and Christmas parties.

STICKERS Cast members give out so many of these, we're afraid there might be an adhesive shortage.

TRANSPORTATION TRADING CARDS Did you know that monorail and bus drivers have trading cards to give out?

SAFETY TRADING CARDS Like transportation cards, but harder to find.

PHOTOS Ask one of the Memory Maker photographers to take a photo with your camera.

TOILETRIES We may or may not have hoards of Disney resort shampoos, bath gels, and soaps in our own homes.

CELEBRATION BUTTONS Just married? Just graduated? Just happy to be nominated? There's a button for that.

KIDCOT FUN STOP CRAFTS Sometimes the best souvenir is the one you make yourself (or at least it's a good line to tell your kids).

CHOCOLATE Ghirardelli at Disney Springs gives out free samples.

More Tips for Disney Shopping

Don't want to carry your stuff around? If you're staying at a Disney hotel, you can have your packages delivered to your resort from any of the four Disney parks. Packages will be delivered to your hotel's gift shop by noon of the following day, so this service is unavailable if you're checking out of your room the same day. Same-day pickup inside the theme parks is available. For a nominal charge, you can ship items to your home.

A New Brunswick, Canada, reader spread the news:

> So often I've seen beleaguered parents loaded like Sherpas, and I can't help but wonder how well known the parks' delivery services are. In Epcot I overheard two shoppers discussing whether they should buy a large pint glass; a major point of discussion was, "How would we get it home?" I chimed in to tell them all about Disney's Package Pick-Up service.

If you remember on your flight home that you forgot to buy mouse ears for your Aunt Bertha, call **Walt Disney World Mail Order Merchandise** at ☎ 877-560-6477 Monday–Friday, e-mail **merchandise.guest .services@disneyparks.com,** or visit the Disney Catalog online at **disney parks.com/store.** Most trademarked merchandise sold at Walt Disney World is available.

SHOPPING AT UNIVERSAL ORLANDO

UNIVERSAL WASN'T ALWAYS KNOWN for souvenirs . . . but then Harry Potter happened. If your young Muggles need to gear up for their time at Hogwarts, you're in the right place. What we love about the shopping experience in The Wizarding World of Harry Potter is how integrated it is with the rest of the land—almost an attraction in itself.

Incredibly popular in The Wizarding World are the $45 interactive wands that trigger special effects throughout both Diagon Alley and Hogsmeade Village. Because of the price, you may wonder if their powers extend beyond Universal, but alas, their only magic is making money disappear from your wallet. (*Disclaimer:* We still love them.)

If Harry Potter isn't your thing, Universal Studios and Islands of Adventure still have many opportunities for you to get your spend on. Our favorites are the **Kwik-E-Mart** in Springfield U.S.A., for *Simpsons* memorabilia, and an actual **comic book shop** at Islands of Adventure in Marvel Super Hero Island.

CityWalk Shopping

CityWalk isn't as retail-heavy as Disney Springs, but you'll still find some interesting places to drop your dough.

FRESH PRODUCE Resort-casual clothing and accessories for women. They sell their own brand of clothing, as well as items from Vera Bradley and Crocs.

HART & HUNTINGTON TATTOO For guests with impulse-control issues (or really great ideas!), this outpost of the famous tattoo company offers the opportunity to make your vacation memories permanent—*really* permanent.

THE ISLAND CLOTHING STORE Shop here for upscale men's (one of the few outlets in CityWalk that caters to men) and women's clothing and accessories. You can find Tommy Bahama and Robert Graham brands. The shop shares space with **Quiet Flight Surf Shop,** which features more casual clothes and sunglasses from surf and skate brands like Quiksilver and Billabong.

P!Q Sells a variety of gifts and pop-culture collectibles at a range of price points. Its selection reminds us of a slightly more tasteful gift area at your local Urban Outfitters.

UNIVERSAL STUDIOS STORE This is the place for a variety of theme-park merchandise.

SHOPPING OUTSIDE THE THEME PARKS

ORLANDO IS NOT DESTINATION SHOPPING of the scale you see in some other Southern cities, such as Miami or Atlanta. Nor does it have the old Florida charm of Palm Beach. But, if you're looking for mall basics, outlet shopping, and big-box discount retail, you'll make out fine here.

Upscale Shopping

The **Mall at Millenia** is your best bet, anchored by **Bloomingdale's, Macy's,** and **Neiman Marcus.** You'll also find designer boutiques, such as **Burberry, Chanel, Gucci, Louis Vuitton, Yves Saint Laurent,** and **Salvatore Ferragamo.** Additionally, Millenia has the closest **Apple Store** to Universal or Walt Disney World. Millenia isn't entirely high-end, however, with fast-fashion staples such as **H&M** and **Forever 21,** as well as the usual suspects such as **Gap, Victoria's Secret, and J.Crew.** Check the mall's website at **mallatmillenia.com** for a complete directory.

Midscale Shopping

The **Florida Mall** is home to **Dillard's, JC Penney, Macy's,** and **Sears.** Apart from the anchors and high-end designer shops, Florida Mall has much the same selection as Millenia. For more information visit **simon.com /mall/the-florida-mall.**

Outlet Shopping

If you think the crowds at the parks can be overwhelming, avoid the two **Orlando Premium Outlets** (**premiumoutlets.com/orlando**) at International Drive and Vineland Avenue. Tourists arrive here by the busload, and the experience will leave you questioning everything from consumer culture to your own judgment in dropping by. For the theme park visitor, the only redeeming aspect of these two shopping malls is the **Disney Character Warehouse** (there are locations at both outlets).

ENTERTAINMENT *and* NIGHTLIFE

WALT DISNEY WORLD AND UNIVERSAL ORLANDO are often thought of as vacations for kids that adults grudgingly go on and pay for. They can be that for sure, but, if you're willing to look, you will find a few places that cater to adults after dark. First, check out your resort. Each Walt Disney World and Universal resort, from Fort Wilderness to Cabana Bay and the All-Star Resorts to the Hard Rock Hotel, has a watering hole for adults who need just a little something to take the edge off. Do we promise they'll be child-free? No, but go late, stay later, and enjoy some adult time. Even teetotalers can relax with a soda and take in the scene.

NIGHTLIFE AT WALT DISNEY WORLD RESORTS

DISNEY'S BOARDWALK OFFERS two adult-oriented venues, **Jellyrolls** and **Atlantic Dance Hall**. Jellyrolls is a dueling-piano bar that's open 7 p.m.–2 a.m. nightly (cover charge applies). Popular with locals, it's one of the few 21-and-up places you'll find at Walt Disney World. The entertainment is outstanding here. Across from Jellyrolls is **Atlantic Dance Hall**. It's often booked for private events, but on weekends it's open in the evenings (and has free admission). Atlantic Dance Hall has a DJ on hand and can be busy when large conventions are at the Swan and Dolphin or other Epcot-area resorts. Like Jellyrolls, Atlantic Dance Hall is 21-and-up.

At Coronado Springs, you'll find Disney's only true nightclub, **Rix Lounge**. This 5,000-square-foot upscale dance club and lounge is beautifully decorated, has a stellar tequila and margarita menu, features a DJ, and usually isn't busy unless there's a large convention on-site.

Other Walt Disney World resort bars with live entertainment are **Scat Cat's Lounge** at Port Orleans French Quarter and **River Roost** at Port Orleans Riverside. River Roost features **Ye Haa Bob Jackson,** an entertainer with a cult following among Disney fans. His fast-moving (and family-friendly) shows bring in locals and visitors from other resorts. Jackson's schedule is posted on his website, **yehaabob.com.** What he lacks in page-design skills, he more than makes up for with his skills at the piano and other instruments. Scat Cat's currently has karaoke and also draws a crowd.

Possibly the most anticipated opening in 2015, **Trader Sam's Grog Grotto** (inspired by the bar at the Disneyland Hotel in California) at the Polynesian Village is a delight. If you've ever found yourself in the *Enchanted Tiki Room* and thought to yourself, "booze would really make this experience better," this is the place for you. For now, this lounge is extraordinarily busy, so be prepared to wait both to enter and be served. While you're at it, pick up some souvenir tiki mugs for our collection (or start your own). See page 374 for a detailed review.

Our favorite nightspot at Walt Disney World, **Top of the World** at Bay Lake Tower, is exclusive to Disney Vacation Club members. If you're eligible, or can find a DVC member who will bring you up in return for a drink, try to stay after the Magic Kingdom fireworks when the bar clears out. The view and the setting are outstanding.

NIGHTLIFE AT DISNEY SPRINGS

THROUGHOUT DISNEY SPRINGS, you'll find live street entertainment, including singers, musicians, and performance artists. If you're looking for more-structured entertainment, though, here are a few separate-ticket venues to consider.

Cirque du Soleil *La Nouba* ★★★★★

APPEAL BY AGE   Under 21 ★★★★   21–37 ★★★★★   38–50 ★★★★   51 and up ★★★★½

Type of show Circus as theater. **Tickets and information** ☎ 407-939-7600; **cirque dusoleil.com/lanouba.** Admission cost *Golden Circle*: $159.75 adults, $133.13 children ages 3–9; *Category Front & Center:* $145.91 adults, $120.34 children; *Category 1:* $129.93 adults, $106.50 children; *Category 2:* $101.17 adults, $83.07 children; *Category 3:* $82 adults, $67.09 children; *Category 4:* $67.09 adults, $55.38 children. All prices include tax. **Cast size** 72. **Night of lowest attendance** Thursday. **Usual show-times** Tuesday–Saturday, 6 p.m. and 9 p.m. **Authors' rating** ★★★★★. **Duration of presentation** 1 hour, 45 minutes (no intermission) plus preshow.

DESCRIPTION AND COMMENTS *La Nouba* is a far cry from a traditional circus but retains all the fun and excitement of it. It is whimsical, mystical, and sophisticated, yet pleasing to all ages. The action takes place on an elaborate stage that incorporates almost every part of the theater. The original musical score is exotic, like the show.

Note: In the following paragraphs, we get into how the show *feels* and why it's special. If you don't care how it feels, or if you're not up to slogging through a boxcar of adjectives, just trust us when we tell you that *La Nouba* is great. See it.

La Nouba is a most difficult show to describe. To categorize it as a circus doesn't begin to cover its depth, though its performers could perform with distinction in any circus on earth. *La Nouba* is more, much more, than a circus. It combines elements of classical Greek theater, mime, the English morality play, Dalí surrealism, Fellini characterization, and Chaplin comedy. *La Nouba* is at once an odyssey, a symphony, and an exploration of human emotions.

The show pivots on its humor, which is sometimes black, and engages the audience with its unforgettable characters. Though light and uplifting, it is also poignant and dark. Simple in presentation, it is at the same time extraordinarily intricate, always operating on multiple levels of meaning. As you laugh and watch the amazingly talented cast, your mind enters a dimension seldom encountered in a waking state. The presentation begins to register in your consciousness more as a seamless dream than as a stage production. You're moved, lulled, and soothed as well as excited and entertained. The sensitive, the imaginative, the literate, and those who love good theater and art will find nothing in all of Disney World that compares with *La Nouba*.

Thus far, as the following comments suggest, we have not received one negative comment about *La Nouba*.

From an Exeter, England, reader:

It should be almost criminal not to see Cirque du Soleil on a visit to WDW!

The comments of a mom from Kansasville, Wisconsin, whose teens reluctantly consented to attend the show:

Even my hard-to-impress MTV-generation teens were awestruck.

Finally, from an Andover, Massachusetts, mother:

One of the true highlights of the trip was seeing Cirque du Soleil. The ticket prices were a bit steep, but I thought it might be enjoyable for my non-Disney-loving husband and decided it was no more expensive than the rest of the trip. In fact, we all loved it, and it was the best money we spent.

TOURING TIPS Be forewarned that the audience is an integral part of *La Nouba* and that at almost any time you might be plucked from your seat to participate. Our advice is to loosen up and roll with it. If you don't want to get involved, politely but firmly decline to be conscripted. Then fix a death grip on the arms of your chair. Tickets for reserved seats can be purchased in advance at the Cirque box office or over the phone, using your credit card. Don't wait until the last minute; book well in advance from home. There are often specials on *La Nouba* admission, and it is included with some Disney vacation packages. Check **cirquedusoleil.com/en /shows/lanouba/tickets/florida/offers.aspx** for offers that may coincide with your trip dates.

House of Blues

Type of show Live concerts with an emphasis on rock and blues. **Tickets and information** ☎ 407-934-BLUE (2583); **hob.com**. **Admission cost with taxes** $11 for club nights to $25 and up depending on who's performing. **Nights of lowest attendance** Monday and Tuesday. **Usual showtimes** Vary between 7 p.m. and 9:30 p.m., depending on who's performing.

DESCRIPTION AND COMMENTS Developed by original Blues Brother Dan
  Aykroyd, House of Blues comprises a restaurant and blues bar, as well as
  a concert hall. The restaurant serves Thursday–Saturday, 11:30 a.m.–11 p.m.,
  and Friday and Saturday, 11:30 a.m.–1 a.m., which makes it one of the few
  late-night-dining options in Walt Disney World. Live music cranks up every
  night at 10:30 p.m. in the restaurant–blues bar, but even before then, the
  joint is way beyond 110 decibels. The music hall next door features concerts by an eclectic array of musicians and groups. During one visit, the
  show bill listed gospel, blues, funk, ska, dance, salsa, rap, zydeco, hard rock,
  groove rock, and reggae groups over a two-week period.

TOURING TIPS Prices vary from night to night according to the fame and
  drawing power of the featured band. Tickets ranged from $11 to $50 during our visits but go higher when a really big name is scheduled.

  The music hall is set up like a nightclub, with tables and bar stools for only
  about 150 people and standing room for a whopping 1,850 people. Folks
  dance when there's room and sometimes when there isn't. The tables and
  stools are first-come, first-served, with doors opening an hour before showtime on weekdays and 90 minutes before showtime on weekends. Acoustics
  are good, and the showroom is small enough to provide a relatively intimate
  concert experience. All shows are all ages unless otherwise indicated.

NIGHTLIFE AT UNIVERSAL ORLANDO RESORTS

WITH ONLY FOUR ON-SITE HOTELS (until Sapphire Falls opens),
Universal Orlando doesn't have the variety in bars and lounges that
you'll find at Disney, but what they do have is good. We love the **Swizzle**
lobby bar at Cabana Bay, with its retro menu and great views of the
resort's public spaces. **Jake's American Bar** at the Royal Pacific has great
food and atmosphere. And **Velvet** at Hard Rock Hotel has super cocktails and unexpectedly good entertainment with its Velvet Sessions entertainment series (concert tickets cost extra). Even if there's nothing to
float your boat at your resort, all the Universal resorts are a short walk,
boat ride, or bus ride from CityWalk.

NIGHTLIFE AT UNIVERSAL CITYWALK

THE FOLLOWING NIGHTCLUB VENUES are mostly located along
the elevated curving pathway that sits behind and above CityWalk's
central plaza. At most of these venues, you must be 21 or older (passport
or photo ID required) to enter after 9 p.m. Pick up a CityWalk City
Guide brochure from the concierge stand or Guest Services for a monthly
listing of live performances and drink specials.

Bob Marley—A Tribute to Freedom

What it is Reggae restaurant and club. **Hours** Daily, 4 p.m.–2 a.m. **Cuisine** Jamai-
can-influenced appetizers and main courses. **Entertainment** Live reggae bands and
DJ in the outdoor gazebo every night. **Cover** $7 after 9 p.m. nightly (more for spe-
cial acts).

COMMENTS This club is a re-creation of Marley's home in Kingston, Jamaica, and contains a lot of interesting Marley memorabilia. The open-air courtyard is the center of action. Sunday is Ladies Night, with no cover charge for women before midnight and drink specials. Island Sounds Wednesdays also features free cover for ladies all night long, and drink specials 9 p.m.–2 a.m.

CityWalk's Rising Star

What it is Karaoke club with live band and backup singers Tuesday–Saturday (Sunday–Monday, sing to recorded tracks with live backup singers). **Hours** Nightly, 8 p.m.–2 a.m. **Cuisine** Red Oven pizza delivery. **Entertainment** Karaoke. **Cover** $7 (no extra charge to sing).

COMMENTS With live musicians backing you up, you can pretend that you've hit the big time at this opulent karaoke, which started life as CityWalk's jazz club. The song list is rather short, with only a little more than 200 options instead of the thousands you may be used to back home. Even so, this is an extremely popular spot; be sure to put your selections in as early in the evening as possible if you want to get on stage. While waiting your turn, you can get your courage up with a supersweet specialty cocktail. Guests 18 and older are welcome Sunday–Thursday, but the club is restricted to 21+ on Friday and Saturday.

The Groove

What it is High-tech disco. **Hours** Nightly, 9 p.m.–2 a.m. **Cuisine** No food. **Entertainment** DJ plays dance tunes. Sometimes there are live bands. **Cover** $7.

COMMENTS This *très chic* club designed to look like an old theater in the midst of restoration features seven bars and several themed cubbyholes (the ultramodern Blue Room, laid-back Green Room, and brothel-like Red Room) for getting away from the thundering sound system. Dancers are barraged with strobes, lasers, and heaven knows what else. VIP reserved tables with premium bottle service are available for those with money and liver cells to burn; call ☎ 407-224-2166 to book your party. Attire is casual chic with no hats or tank tops permitted for men.

Jimmy Buffett's Margaritaville

What it is Key West–themed restaurant and club. **Hours** Daily, 11 a.m.–2 a.m. **Cuisine** Caribbean, Florida fusion, and American. **Entertainment** Live rock and island-style music. **Cover** $7 after 10 p.m.

COMMENTS Jimmy's is a big place with three bars that turns into a nightclub after 10 p.m. Jimmy Buffett covers are popular (no surprise) as is island music and light rock. If you eat dinner here, you'll probably want to find another vantage point when the band cranks up on the main stage around 9 p.m. There's always an acoustic guitarist strumming on the Porch of Indecision from 5 p.m. daily. If you are already inside the restaurant eating dinner before the cover charge kicks in, you won't be kicked out when the band kicks off.

Pat O'Brien's Orlando

What it is Dueling pianos sing-along club and restaurant. **Hours** Daily, 4 p.m.–2 a.m. **Cuisine** Cajun. **Entertainment** Dueling pianos and sing-alongs. **Cover** $7 after 9 p.m. for piano bar only.

COMMENTS A clone of the famous New Orleans club of the same name. A solo pianist starts playing a little after 5 p.m., and he or she is joined by a second starting around 9 p.m. These are some of the most talented singing musicians In town and will happily handle nearly any request you throw at them (even—gasp!—Disney tunes) as long as you write it on a generous gratuity. You can dine in the courtyard or on the terrace without paying a cover.

The Red Coconut Club

What it is Modern lounge and nightclub. **Hours** Monday–Saturday, 7 p.m.–2 a.m.; Sunday, 8 p.m.–2 a.m. **Cuisine** Appetizers; Red Oven pizza delivery after 10 p.m. **Entertainment** Lounging and dancing. **Cover** $7 after 9 p.m.

COMMENTS This nightspot is billed as a nightclub and ultra-lounge, advertising talk for "hip place to be seen." The eclectic mix of decor—part 1950s, part tiki—and three bars on two levels would make it a great later-day hangout for the Rat Pack, if Frank and Dean happened to be resurrected in Orlando. There is a dance floor, and the bar serves signature martinis and mojitos. An evening here can quickly add up, with VIP bottle service starting at $100; a daily happy hour 7–9 p.m. brings the drink and appetizer prices down to more reasonable levels. Thursday is Latin Ladies Night with DJ Leony and no cover charge for women.

LIVE MUSIC AT WALT DISNEY WORLD AND UNIVERSAL ORLANDO

YOU CAN FIND NATIONALLY KNOWN musical acts at **House of Blues** at Disney Springs West Side (see profile on page 741) and **Hard Rock Cafe** in CityWalk.

Hard Rock Live at Hard Rock Cafe

Type of show Live rock/pop concerts with an emphasis on current and classic touring acts. **Tickets and information** ☎ 407-351-LIVE (5483); **hardrock.com/live /locations/orlando. Admission cost** Varies, depending on who's performing. **Usual showtimes** Vary between 7 p.m. and 9:30 p.m., depending on who's performing.

DESCRIPTION AND COMMENTS This 3,000-seat venue on the water at City-Walk draws nationally touring musicians and comics. There isn't a consistent theme to who plays here—we've seen everyone from Adam Ant to Wilco advertised, but Hard Rock definitely draws higher profile performers than House of Blues. Of course, with great renown comes great admission prices—be prepared to pay as much to see an act at Hard Rock Live as you would at a large venue in any major city.

TOURING TIPS There is security at the doors here. Plan to arrive an hour before showtime.

Free Concerts at Disney World and Universal

During slower times of year, both Walt Disney World and Universal Orlando hold special events to bring in bigger crowds and entice the locals to stop by (and purchase some food, drinks, and merchandise while they're at it).

Epcot has three concert series that are free to guests with park admission:

GARDEN ROCKS Held during the Flower and Garden Festival, this series features classic rock acts, such as the members of Jefferson Starship who are still on speaking terms with each other.

SOUNDS LIKE SUMMER Tribute bands (such as the ABBA tribute band Bjorn Again and the Bon Jovi homage Slippery When Wet) play through most of June and July.

EAT TO THE BEAT Classic and current acts accompany your trip around the World Showcase during the Food and Wine Festival . . . if you count Hanson and Big Bad Voodoo Daddy as current, that is.

As part of **Universal's Mardi Gras celebration,** you'll find free concerts from a wide variety of acts, from up-and-comers to established groups and singers with songs on the charts to classic acts who bring in the nostalgia crowd. In the past, Universal has also presented a summer concert series, but that was temporarily suspended with the opening of Diagon Alley. It's still to be seen when and if the series will resume, but we believe it will.

WALT DISNEY WORLD DINNER THEATERS

SEVERAL DINNER-THEATER SHOWS play nightly at Walt Disney World, and unlike other Disney dining venues, they take hard reservations instead of Advance Reservations, meaning you have to guarantee your reservation ahead of time with a credit card. You'll receive a confirmation number and be told to pick up your tickets at a Disney-hotel Guest Relations desk. Unless you cancel your tickets at least 48 hours before your reservation time, your credit card will still be charged the full amount. Dinner-show reservations can be made 180 days in advance; call ☎ 407-939-3463. While getting reservations for the *Spirit of Aloha Dinner Show* isn't terribly tough, booking the *Hoop-Dee-Doo Musical Revue* is a trick of the first order.

A couple from Bismarck, North Dakota, explains:

> *I'm glad we made our reservations so early (a year in advance). I was able to reserve space for us at* Spirit of Aloha *at the Polynesian Village and the* Hoop-Dee-Doo Musical Revue. *At both of these, they seat you according to when you made your reservation. At the* Hoop-Dee-Doo Musical Revue, *we had a front-center table. We were so close to the stage, we could see how many cavities the performers had!*

If you can't get reservations and want to see one of the shows:

1. Call ☎ 407-939-3463 at 9 a.m. each morning while you're at Disney World to make a same-day reservation. There are three performances each night, and for all three combined, only 3–24 people total will be admitted with same-day reservations.

2. Arrive at the show of your choice 45 minutes before showtime (early and late shows are your best bets) and put your name on the standby list. If someone with reservations fails to show, you may be admitted.

*un*official **TIP**
To make reservations for the *Hoop-Dee-Doo Musical Revue,* call as soon as you're certain of the dates of your visit. The earlier you call, the better your seats will be.

Borrowing a page from Vegas strip joints where nearsighted old coots are charged extra to sit way up front, Disney offers tiered seating for the *Hoop-Dee-Doo Musical Revue* and the *Spirit of Aloha Dinner Show*. The best seats are in Category 1. Next comes Category 2, with seats off to the side or behind Category 1. Finally, Category 3 seats are at the Orlando Greyhound station, where you watch the show on a video feed. Just making sure you're still with us—actually, they're farther still to the side or back, or on another level from the stage. For both the *Spirit of Aloha Dinner Show* and the *Hoop-Dee-Doo Musical Revue*, there's a good view from almost all seats, so you can decide if sitting closer to the action is worth the extra bucks.

Hoop-Dee-Doo Musical Revue

Pioneer Hall, Fort Wilderness Campground ☎ 407-939-3463. **Showtimes** 4, 6:15, and 8:30 p.m. nightly. **Cost** *Category 1:* $66–$70 adults, $34–$36 children ages 3–9.; *Category 2:* $59–$63 adults, $29–$31 children; *Category 3:* $55–$59 adults, $28–$30 children. Prices include tax and gratuity. **Discounts** Seasonal. **Type of seating** Tables of various sizes to fit the number in each party, set in an Old West–style dance hall. **Menu** All-you-can-eat barbecue ribs, fried chicken, corn, and strawberry shortcake. **Vegetarian alternative** On request (at least 24 hours in advance). **Beverages** Unlimited beer, wine, sangria, and soft drinks.

DESCRIPTION AND COMMENTS Six Wild West performers arrive by stagecoach (sound effects only) to entertain the crowd inside Pioneer Hall. There isn't much of a plot—just corny jokes interspersed with song or dance. The humor is of the *Hee Haw* ilk, but it's presented enthusiastically.

Audience participation includes sing-alongs, hand clapping, and a finale that uses volunteers to play parts on stage. Performers are accompanied by a banjo player and pianist who also play quietly while the food is being served. The fried chicken and corn on the cob are good, the ribs a bit tough though tasty. With the all-you-can-eat policy, at least you can get your money's worth by stuffing yourself silly.

Traveling to Fort Wilderness and absorbing the rustic atmosphere of Pioneer Hall augments the adventure. For repeat Disney World visitors, an annual visit to the revue is a tradition of sorts. Plus, warts and all, the revue is all Disney, and for some folks that's enough. The fact that performances sell out far in advance gives the experience a special aura.

Most of our readers enjoy the *Hoop-Dee-Doo Musical Revue*, but not all, as this letter from a Texas family attests:

> *What is all the hoop-dee-doo with the* Hoop-Dee-Doo Musical Revue? *The food was OK, if "gut busting" fare is your idea of a fine night out, and the entertainment was pleasant. As a dinner theater, however, our family of three found it unexceptional in every respect but its cost. Had your review of the* Revue *tempered its enthusiasm (much as you present its Polynesian counterpart), we probably would've canceled our reservation, pocketed the $100, and spent the evening joyously stunned by another glorious light-and-fireworks spectacle.*

More typical are the remarks of a Cambridge, Massachusetts, mom:

> *The kids in our group (ages 3–8) thought the* Hoop-Dee-Doo Musical Revue *was just terrific. They watched intently the whole time, laughing hysterically. With them having such a good time, how could the adults not enjoy themselves? But I wouldn't recommend the show for adults on their own. One thing we adults appreciated was the lack of commercialism: no movie tie-in, no merchandise sales. The entire experience, including its setting in the rustic Fort Wilderness campground, brought us back to simpler days and gave the kids exposure to entertainment before there were special effects.*

If you go to *Hoop-Dee-Doo,* allow plenty of driving time (about an hour) to get there. Or do as this California dad suggests:

> *To go to the* Hoop-Dee-Doo Musical Revue *at Fort Wilderness, take the boat from the Magic Kingdom rather than any bus. This is contrary to the "official" directions. The boat dock is a short walk from Pioneer Hall in Fort*

Wilderness, while the bus goes to the main Fort Wilderness parking lot, where one has to transfer to another bus to Pioneer Hall.

Disney ferry service may be suspended during thunderstorms, so if it's raining or it looks as if it's about to rain, Disney will provide bus service from the parks.

Mickey's Backyard BBQ

Fort Wilderness Campground ☎ 407-939-3463. **Showtimes** Thursday and Saturday at 5, 6:30, and 7 p.m. **Cost** $60 adults, $36 children ages 3–9. Prices include tax and gratuity. **Type of seating** Picnic tables. **Menu** Baked chicken, barbecue pork ribs, burgers, hot dogs, corn, beans, mac and cheese, salads and slaw, bread, and watermelon and ice-cream bars for dessert. **Vegetarian alternatives** On request. **Beverages** Unlimited beer, wine, lemonade, and iced tea.

DESCRIPTION AND COMMENTS Situated along Bay Lake and held in a covered pavilion next to the site of the old River Country swimming park, *Mickey's Backyard BBQ* features Mickey, Minnie, Chip 'n' Dale, and Goofy, along with a country band and line dancing. Though the pavilion gets some breeze off Bay Lake, we recommend going during the spring or fall, if possible. The food is pretty good, as is, fortunately, the insect control.

The cookout was previously offered only seasonally, from March through December, but is now year-round. Even so, dates are usually not entered into the WDW-DINE reservations system until about six months in advance. Once the dates are in the system, you can make an Advance Reservation for anytime during the dinner show's season.

The easiest way to get to the barbecue is to take a boat from the Magic Kingdom or from one of the Disney resorts on the Magic Kingdom monorail. Give yourself at least 45 minutes if you plan to arrive by boat. Ferry service may be suspended during thunderstorms, so if it's raining or it looks like it's about to rain, Disney will provide bus service from the parks.

From a Rhode Island dad:

Mickey's Backyard BBQ was a surprise hit. It was easy to get there from the Magic Kingdom, and we went back there later for Extra Magic Hours. The food at the BBQ was nice, and watching little kids line dance with the characters was about the most adorable thing I've ever seen.

Spirit of Aloha Dinner Show

Disney's Polynesian Village Resort ☎ 407-939-3463. **Showtimes** Tuesday–Saturday, 5:15 and 8 p.m. **Cost** *Category 1:* $70–$70 adults, $36–$40 children ages 3–9.; *Category 2:* $63–$67 adults, $31–$33 children; *Category 3:* $59–$63 adults, $30–$32 children. Prices include tax and gratuity. **Discounts** Seasonal. **Type of seating** Long rows of tables, with some separation between individual parties. The show is performed on an outdoor stage, but all seating is covered. Ceiling fans provide some air movement, but it can get warm, especially at the early show. **Menu** Tropical fruit, roasted chicken, island pork ribs, mixed vegetables, rice, and pineapple bread; chicken tenders, PB&J sandwiches, mac and cheese, and hot dogs are also available for children. **Vegetarian alternative** On request. **Beverages** Beer, wine, and soft drinks.

DESCRIPTION AND COMMENTS This show features South Seas–island native dancing followed by an all-you-can-eat "Polynesian-style" meal. The dancing is interesting and largely authentic, and the dancers are attractive but definitely PG-rated in the Disney tradition. We think the show has its moments and the meal is adequate, but neither is particularly special.

The show follows (tenuously) the common "girl leaves home for the big city, forgets her roots, and must rediscover them" theme. The performers are uniformly attractive ("Studmuffins!" said a female *Unofficial* researcher when asked about the men), and the dancing is very good. The story, however, never really makes sense as anything other than a slender thread between musical numbers. Our show lasted for more than 2 hours and 15 minutes.

The food does little more than illustrate how difficult it must be to prepare the same meal for hundreds of people simultaneously: The roasted chicken is better than the ribs, but neither is anything special. We conditionally recommend *Spirit of Aloha* for special occasions, when the people celebrating get to go on stage. But go to the early show and get dessert somewhere else in the World.

A well-traveled couple from Fond du Lac, Wisconsin, comments:

Spirit of Aloha was a beautiful presentation, better than some shows we have seen in Hawaii! The food, however, lacked in all areas. Better food has come out of Disney kitchens. During our visit, the fruit platter was chintzy, the honey-roasted chicken was a bit fatty, and the pineapple cake was dry.

And from a Middletown, Delaware, reader:

We booked Spirit of Aloha *using two dinner credits each. Having enjoyed the show throughout the 1980s and in 1998 with my parents and siblings, you can imagine my disappointment at how it is now. The food was decent, but the crowd noises was deafening. We still remember fondly the conversations we had around the table in the 1980s from the show. Now with the "cafeteria" so full, my husband and I couldn't even have a conversation! The show itself was overly long for all the young children in the audience. The performers were talented, but we won't go again, and I've told my extended family to skip it.*

PART TWENTY

RECREATION, SPORTS, *and* SPAS

WALT DISNEY WORLD RECREATION

MOST WALT DISNEY WORLD GUESTS never make it beyond the theme parks, the water parks, or Disney Springs. Those who do, however, will discover an extraordinary selection of recreational opportunities ranging from guided fishing adventures and water-skiing outings to hayrides, horseback riding, fitness-center workouts, and miniature golf. If you can do it at a resort, chances are good that it's available at Walt Disney World.

Boat, bike, and fishing-equipment rentals are handled on an hourly basis. Just show up at the rental office during operating hours and they'll fix you up. The same goes for various fitness centers in the resort hotels. Golf, tennis, fishing expeditions, water-ski excursions, hayrides, trail rides, and most spa services must be scheduled in advance. Though every resort features some selection of recreational options, those resorts on a navigable body of water generally offer the greatest variety. Also, the more upscale a resort, the more likely it is to have such amenities as a fitness center and spa.

RUN, DISNEY, RUN

WALT DISNEY WORLD STAGED its first long-distance road race—a 26.2-mile marathon—in January 1994. By hosting this one-day event, Disney hoped to attract a couple thousand people to Orlando during what would otherwise be the middle of a slow winter season. It was an immediate hit, drawing more than 7,000 runners and their families, most staying in a Disney hotel for longer than the one or two nights needed to run the race.

Disney added a Saturday half-marathon race to the event in 1998, just in time to catch the wave of popularity that distance running started enjoying around the turn of the millennium.

Today the **Walt Disney World Marathon Weeken**d is a four-day affair, with a 5K on Thursday and a 10K on Friday. It's not uncommon to see

25,000 runners in the big races, and a few thousand hearty souls run all four events (you get a special medal for doing so; it's appropriately of Dopey, one of Snow White's dwarfs).

Disney's race schedule has also expanded throughout the calendar and country, with no fewer than eight major races held in Disney World and Disneyland; a complete schedule and summary of events is below. Disney even has a full-time, staffed organization, **runDisney,** to coordinate and promote their events. Visit **rundisney.com** for the latest details. Prices are comparable to the big races in New York, Boston, and Chicago, but you don't get to run through Epcot in those.

As noted in Part One, *Unofficial Guide* staff and friends have run dozens of Disney races over the past decade, from simple 5Ks to the two-day, 39.3-mile half-marathon/full-marathon combo (dubbed "The Goofy" for obvious reasons). If you've never run a distance race, Disney is the perfect first event for many reasons.

BENEFITS TO RUNNING A DISNEY RACE

1. Every race runs through at least one theme park. The half-marathons go through Epcot and the Magic Kingdom, while the full marathon hits all four parks and most of the Magic Kingdom and Epcot resort areas. Even the smaller events are staged inside Epcot or the Animal Kingdom.

2. The events are efficient and organized, with thousands of volunteers, top-notch entertainment all over the course, excellent first-aid (we have experience), and great finisher medals.

3. Disney provides transportation between its hotels and the race venue, so your family can sleep in while you make your way to the start. Buses will also get you back to your hotel when you're done.

4. Everyone qualifies. Unlike, say, the Boston Marathon, where you must run a marathon in under 4 hours before even thinking about getting in, the Disney races are open to everyone who can lace up some shoes.

5. The course is flat as a pancake. The steepest uphill is probably one of the on-ramps to Epcot on World Drive. If this is your first race, a flat course is one less thing to worry about. If you're a race veteran, this is a good opportunity to set a personal record.

Here's a quick rundown of the major Disney races. For info on how they impact crowds, see "The Walt Disney World Calendar," page 48.

WALT DISNEY WORLD MARATHON WEEKEND (January 6–10, 2016) The largest Disney race of the year with upwards of 50,000 runners and their families. Races include a 5K, 10K, and half and full marathons. The big variable with the race is weather; we've run in freezing rain and we've run in 75-degree sun. Check the forecast a couple of days before you leave.

DISNEY PRINCESS HALF-MARATHON WEEKEND (February 18–21, 2016) Races include a 5K, 10K, and half-marathon, which draw upwards of 25,000 runners. As its name implies, these events are designed for women, although around 1,700 men ran it in 2015. The weather is usually a bit warmer and more predictable than January's race.

WINE & DINE HALF-MARATHON WEEKEND (early November dates TBD, 2016) Built around Epcot's fall Food & Wine Festival (see page 49), these races include a 5K and half-marathon. What makes the Wine & Dine half different from other events is that it's held at night, with a typical start time around 10 p.m. Around 13,000 people ran the 2014 event. Although it's November, the weather can be quite warm, especially if you're used to training in cooler fall temperatures up north. The finish is in Epcot, where Disney provides entertainment and keeps open many of the Food & Wine kiosks.

Disneyland offers its own set of races, too. Runners who complete a race in both Disneyland and Disney World in the same year earn a special "coast to coast" medal. In addition, Disney has staged events from 5K to 10 miles themed to attractions such as Expedition Everest and the Tower of Terror. Those events aren't on the schedule at press time, but we wouldn't be surprised to see something like these happen in 2016.

unofficial **TIP**
It cost just over $2,400 in entry fees to run every Disney race in 2014. With airfare and hotels, expect to spend around $12–$15,000.

Our blog has a number of articles on run-Disney; search for "runDisney" at **blog.tour ingplans.com** for more coverage. Also check out the Mickey Miles podcast, run by our good friends Mike and Michelle, at **mickeymilspodcast.com.**

ESPN WIDE WORLD *of* SPORTS COMPLEX

THIS 220-ACRE, STATE-OF-THE-ART competition and training center consists of a 9,500-seat ballpark; a fieldhouse; and dedicated venues for baseball, softball, tennis, track and field, beach volleyball, and 27 other sports. From Little League Baseball to rugby, the complex hosts a mind-boggling calendar of professional and amateur competitions.

In late winter and early spring, the complex is the spring-training home of the Atlanta Braves. While Disney guests are welcome at the ESPN Wide World of Sports Complex as paying spectators (prices vary according to event), none of the facilities are available for guests unless they're participants in a scheduled, organized competition. To learn which sporting events, including Major League Baseball exhibition games, are scheduled during your visit, call ☎ 407-939-GAME (4263) or check the online calendar at **disneyworldsports.com.**

The complex is also home to Orlando's Major League Soccer team, the **Orlando City Soccer Club.** Orlando City's schedule usually runs February–mid-September. Tickets start around $23.

Admission is $17 for adults, $12 children for ages 3–9 (prices include tax). Some events carry an extra charge. There's a restaurant, the **ESPN Wide World of Sports Grill,** but no on-site lodging.

Off Osceola Parkway, on Victory Way, the complex has its own parking lot and is accessible via the Disney transportation system.

WALT DISNEY WORLD GOLF

DISNEY'S **Magnolia** and **Oak Trail Golf Courses,** across Floridian Way from the Polynesian Village Resort, envelop the recreational complex of the Shades of Green military resort, and the pro shops and support facilities adjoin the hotel proper. The **Magnolia** is a challenging, 18-hole course that used to be part of the PGA tour; **Oak Trail** is a nine-hole, par-36 course for beginners.

The **Palm Golf Course,** in the same complex, underwent a major renovation by Arnold Palmer in 2013. Updates include modernized bunkers (94 of them!) and tees, and completely rebuilt greens. The Palm is 7,011 yards from the blue tees, 5,262 from the reds; it is designed for the midhandicap player.

unofficial **TIP**
Disney's golf courses are run by Arnold Palmer Golf Management. An Orlando resident, Palmer is among the most famous and well-liked athletes in the history of the sport.

It's business as usual for the **Lake Buena Vista Golf Course** at Saratoga Springs Resort & Spa, near Disney Springs.

Opened in 2014, the new **Tranquilo Golf Club at Four Seasons Orlando** sits on the site of Disney's old Osprey Ridge golf links. The course, which is also a certified Audubon wildlife sanctuary, is shared by the Four Seasons Resort Orlando (see page 262) and Golden Oak, a Disney-owned luxury residential development. Tom Fazio, who designed the original course in 1992, also supervised this redesign. Updates include new contours for the greens, plus new and renovated bunkers. A new par-3 hole (#16) features deep bunkering and sand, with a tiny green. Overall, Tranquilo is more challenging than the other Disney courses, which typically feature wide fairways and are forgiving, and is aimed more at the avid destination golfer.

Equally important at Tranquilo is the management by Four Seasons, which takes the same white-glove approach to its golf course portfolio as it does with its five-star hotels. The course is impeccably maintained, with perhaps the best conditioning of any in the Orlando area, and has a stunning practice facility, clubhouse, and staff to match. Four Seasons also added a full-blown golf academy with both hourly and multiday instruction. New club cars use GPS technology to estimate your distance to the pin. The clubhouse's Plancha restaurant serves casual Cuban-American fare next to the lake. The course is open to the public.

All Disney courses are popular, with morning tee times at a premium, especially from January through April. Expect a round to take around 5 hours. In addition to the courses, there are driving ranges and putting greens at each location.

Peak season for all courses is January–May, and off-season is May–October. Off-season and afternoon twilight rates are available. Carts, required at all courses except Oak Trail, are included in the greens fee. Tee times may be reserved 90 days in advance by Disney resort

unofficial **TIP**
To avoid the crowds, play on a Monday, Tuesday, or Wednesday, and sign up for a late-afternoon tee time.

guests (including Downtown Disney hotels and the Swan and Dolphin resorts) and 60 days in advance by day guests with a credit card. Proper golf attire, including spikeless shoes, is required. A collared shirt and Bermuda-length shorts or slacks meet the requirements.

Besides the ability to book tee times farther in advance, guests of Walt Disney World–owned resorts get other benefits that may sway a golfer's lodging decision. These include discounted greens fees, club rental, and charge privileges. The single most important, and least known, benefit is the provision of free round-trip taxi transportation between the golf courses and your hotel, which lets you avoid moving your car or dragging your clubs on Disney buses. (Cabs are paid with vouchers supplied to hotel guests.)

The following chart summarizes prices for daily play at all Disney golf courses except Oak Trail; the cost of replaying the same course on the same day (if space is available) is half the full rate.

TYPE OF ADMISSION	OPENING-3 P.M.	3-4 P.M.	4 P.M.-CLOSING
Resort guest	$120	$55	$55
Resort guest, 2-round pass	$150–$180	$150–$180	$150–$180
Day guest	$125	$55	$55
Day guest, 2-round pass	$175–$200	$175–$200	$175–$200

For more information, call ☎ 407-938-GOLF (4653); to book a tee time online, go to **golfwdw.com**.

Lake Buena Vista Golf Course ★★★

ESTABLISHED 1971 DESIGNER Joe Lee STATUS Resort

2200 Club Lake Dr., Lake Buena Vista, FL 32830; ☎ 407-938-GOLF

TEES
- **BLUE:** 6,745 yards, par 72, USGA 72.3, slope 133
- **WHITE:** 6,281 yards, par 72, USGA 70.1, slope 130
- **GOLD:** 5,910 yards, par 72, USGA 68.5, slope 125
- **RED:** 5,177 yards, par 72, USGA 69.7, slope 119

FACILITIES Pro shop, GPS, driving range, practice green, locker rooms, snack bar, food and beverage cart, and club and shoe rentals.

COMMENTS There are several memorable holes here, but this layout is the only one at Disney with housing on it—a lot of housing—which detracts from the golf experience. Nonetheless, the course itself is relatively pristine and was certified by Audubon International as a Cooperative Wildlife Sanctuary. The setting is geographically unique among the other layouts, tucked behind Saratoga Springs, and has a swampy feel reminiscent of the area's pre-Disney wetlands, with trees dripping Spanish moss. Narrow fairways and small greens emphasize accuracy over length.

Magnolia Golf Course ★★★½

ESTABLISHED 1970 DESIGNER Joe Lee STATUS Resort

1950 W. Magnolia/Palm Dr., Lake Buena Vista, FL 32830; ☎ 407-938-GOLF

TEES
- **BLACK:** 7,516 yards, par 72, USGA 76.0, slope 141
- **BLUE:** 7,073 yards, par 72, USGA 74.0, slope 137
- **WHITE:** 6,558 yards, par 72, USGA 71.6, slope 130
- **GOLD:** 6,027 yards, par 72, USGA 69.0, slope 121
- **RED:** 5,127 yards, par 72, USGA 69.6, slope 126

FACILITIES Pro shop, GPS-equipped golf carts, driving range, practice green, locker rooms, food and beverage cart, and club and shoe rentals.

COMMENTS Another fine Joe Lee creation, Magnolia is Disney's longest course and features a whopping 97 bunkers, including the famous one in the shape of Mickey Mouse's head. But the layout is slightly less challenging than the Palm's. Ten holes were lengthened and all greens resurfaced with TifEagle turf in 2005. This refurbishment added 300 yards to the already long course, and at more than 7,500 yards, it will be the longest most guests ever have the opportunity to play. Like the Palm, this course long hosted the PGA Tour (until 2012).

Oak Trail Golf Course ★★½

ESTABLISHED 1980   DESIGNER Ron Garl   STATUS Resort

1950 W. Magnolia/Palm Dr., Lake Buena Vista, FL 32830; ☎ 407-938-GOLF

TEES
- **WHITE**: 2,913 yards, par 36
- **RED**: 2,552 yards, par 36
- JUNIOR: 1,713 yards, par 36

FEES Adult, $38; junior (age 17 and under), $20. Pull carts, $6 (course is walking only). Replaying the course costs an additional $19 for adults and $10 for junior players.

FACILITIES Pro shop, driving range, practice green, locker rooms, food and beverage cart, and club and shoe rentals.

COMMENTS This Ron Garl nine-holer is a "real" course, not an executive par-3 like many nine-hole designs. Geared toward introducing children to the game, it also makes a good quick-fix or warm-up before a round, and the walking-only layout is the only such routing at Walt Disney World.

Palm Golf Course ★★★★

ESTABLISHED 1970   DESIGNER Joe Lee   STATUS Resort

1950 W. Magnolia/Palm Dr., Lake Buena Vista, FL 32830; ☎ 407-938-GOLF

TEES
- **BLUE**: 7,011 yards, par 72, USGA 73.7, slope 131
- **WHITE**: 6,479 yards, par 72, USGA 71.4, slope 125
- **GOLD**: 6,006 yards, par 72, USGA 69.2, slope 118
- **RED**: 5,262 yards, USGA 70.5, slope 126

FACILITIES Pro shop, driving range, practice green, locker rooms, food and beverage cart, and club and shoe rentals.

COMMENTS Completely renovated in 2013, with more-difficult bunkers and undulating greens. The greens play medium-fast to fast, so either go with a lot of spin and loft or try to bounce your shot in. Carts have GPS screens. Staff service is excellent. Beware the alligator in the water at #9 (not kidding).

Tranquilo Golf Club at Four Seasons Orlando

ESTABLISHED 2014   DESIGNER Tom Fazio   STATUS Resort

10100 Dream Tree Blvd., Golden Oak, FL 32830; ☎ 800-267-3046

TEES
- TALON: 7,039 yards, par 72, USGA 73.7, slope 127
- CREST: 6,629 yards, par 72, USGA 71.7, slope 124
- WINGS: 5,996 yards, par 72, USGA 68.8, slope 117
- FEATHERS (W): 5,283 yards, par 72, USGA 70.2, slope 124

FEES $105–$155 for 18 holes, including cart.

FACILITIES Pro shop, driving range, practice green, locker rooms, restaurant, and club and shoe rentals.

COMMENTS See summary on page 751.

MINIATURE GOLF

YEARS AGO, THE DISNEY INTELLIGENCE PATROL (DIP) noticed that as many as 113 guests a day were sneaking out of Walt Disney World to play Goofy Golf. The thought of those truant guests making instant millionaires of miniature-golf entrepreneurs on International Drive was enough to give a fat mouse ulcers.

The response to this assault on Disney's market share was **Fantasia Gardens Miniature Golf,** an 11-acre complex with two 18-hole dink-and-putt golf courses. One is an "adventure" course, themed after Disney's animated film *Fantasia*. The other, geared more toward older children and adults, is an innovative approach-and-putt course with sand traps and water hazards.

Fantasia Gardens is beautifully landscaped and creatively executed. It features fountains, animated statues, topiaries, flower beds, and a multitude of other imponderables that you're unlikely to find at most mini-golf courses.

Fantasia Gardens is on Epcot Resorts Boulevard, across the street from the Swan resort; it's open daily, 10 a.m.–11 p.m. To reach the course via Disney transportation, take a bus or boat to the Swan. The cost to putt, including tax, is $14 for adults and $12 for children ages 3–9. In case you arrive hungry or naked, Fantasia Gardens has a snack bar and gift shop. For more information, call ☎ 407-WDW-PLAY (939-7529).

A Texas reader highly recommends the Disney miniature golf courses:

> *Although we had a great time at every park and almost every meal, one of our best times was spent playing minigolf at Winter Summerland, outside Blizzard Beach. The theme of each course is wonderful and the golf challenging enough to be fun! Good times!*

Winter Summerland is the other miniature-golf facility, next to the Blizzard Beach water park. Winter Summerland offers two 18-hole courses—one has a "blizzard in Florida" theme, while the other sports a tropical-holiday theme. The Winter Summerland courses are much easier than the Fantasia courses, which makes them a better choice for families with preteen children. Operating hours and cost are the same as for Fantasia Gardens.

Our favorite minigolf in Orlando is **Hollywood Drive-In Golf,** in Universal CityWalk next to Universal Orlando's parking garage (just off the walkway to the parks; 6000 Universal Blvd.; ☎ 407-802-4848). One hole has the Creature from the Black Lagoon spitting water over the walkway you need to pass through; another hole has a huge alien ship that you need to walk through and for which you need to press a button so that a door opens, *Star Trek*–style, to let you out. It's a nonstop barrage of clever in-jokes, insanely well-designed holes, and unique lighting elements. There's also an iPhone app for keeping score and misting fans for keeping cool. Open daily, 9 a.m.–2 a.m.; cost is $15 for adults, $13 for children ages 3–9.

SERENITY NOW!
A Look at Disney-Area Spas

YOU'VE JUST SUGGESTED another theme park mini-marathon to your spouse, and from her barely audible murmur you realize she's debating which relative should get the kids when she stands trial for your homicide. Fortunately for you, Orlando is awash in spas ready to rub, wrap, and restore your loved one to domestic tranquility.

Note that the cost of a basic 1-hour massage is well over $100 before tip at most of these places. In an effort to get you the most inner peace for your money, we sent the *Unofficial Guide* research team to evaluate nine Walt Disney World–area spas.

At each resort, our team got a standard massage, a basic facial, and a manicure–pedicure combination. Each service was scheduled during a different week to ensure that one person's bad day didn't mar the whole evaluation. Also, we used the same researchers throughout the tests to ensure consistent comparisons of what is admittedly a somewhat subjective experience.

We rated each spa on a scale of one star (poor) to five stars (excellent) in three areas. **Customer service** includes our interactions with the spa staff on everything from scheduling appointments to the actual treatments to follow-up questions after the visit. **Facilities** rates the amenities, functionality, and decor of the locker rooms, waiting areas, and equipment used before and after the services. **Amenities** rates secondary spa offerings such as food, pools, fitness centers, and the like. In addition, **sales pressure** (rated from low to high) indicates how hard the spa staff pushes you to buy its products after your treatment. (Underlying our star system is a numerical quality scale of 0–100, so spas with the same overall star rating may have different numerical ratings.)

> **unofficial TIP**
> Check whether a gratuity has already been added to your bill before you pay. Most spas, including Disney's, tack on a tip of 18–20%.

A fabulous money-saving idea is to find out if the spa you're interested in offers a day pass. These inexpensive tickets ($10–$55 among the spas we reviewed) typically allow use of the spa's fitness center, pool, sauna, steam room, and showers for an entire day.

The Spa at Four Seasons Resort Orlando opened in late 2014 and debuts in the #2 spot of our Orlando spa ratings. Like **Senses Spa at Disney's Grand Floridian Resort,** the Four Seasons' spa has all the bells and whistles (or, if you prefer, all the candles and soft lighting) you could hope for. Our reviewers tend to prefer the Grand Floridian's warmer decor just a tiny bit more than the Four Seasons' modern marble and tile. The reviewers also mention Senses' heated stone lounges and prewarmed robes as additional benefits. Service and amenities are excellent at any of the top spas in our chart, and you won't go wrong choosing any one of them.

ORLANDO SPAS RATED & RANKED

SPA	OVERALL RATING
1. SENSES SPA at Disney's Grand Floridian Resort	★★★★½
2. THE SPA at Four Seasons Resort Orlando	★★★★½
3. THE WALDORF ASTORIA SPA	★★★★
4. SENSES SPA at Disney's Saratoga Springs Resort	★★★★
5. MANDARA SPA at Universal's Portofino Bay Hotel	★★★★
5. (TIE) RELÂCHE SPA at Gaylord Palms	★★★★
6. THE RITZ-CARLTON SPA, ORLANDO	★★★★
7. KAY CASPERSON LIFESTYLE SPA at the Buena Vista Palace	★★★½
8. MANDARA SPA at the Dolphin	★★★½
9. THE SPA at Orlando World Center Marriott Resort	★★½

SPA PROFILES

Kay Casperson Lifestyle Spa at the Buena Vista Palace
★★★½

1900 E. Buena Vista Dr., Lake Buena Vista; ☎ 407-827-3200;
buenavistapalace.com/things-to-do/spa-salon

Customer service ★★★★★. **Facilities** ★★★½. **Amenities** ★★★★. **Sales pressure** Low. **Price range** $79–$407 spa services; $35–$75 nail services; $15–$65 kids' services (ages 6–12); $25–$159 teens' services (ages 13–19); 15% discount for Florida residents Monday–Friday; 20% service charge.

COMMENTS Plush, swallow-you-whole robes are the first of the pleasures awaiting guests at Buena Vista Palace's spa, part of a chain run by beauty maven Kay Casperson. Locker rooms offer two small, private changing rooms and a posh vanity area. Treatment rooms are small and nondescript but clean. Separate waiting rooms are provided for men and women. On the downside, the facilities are older and in need of updating. Treatments were top-notch; staff encouraged the use of the sauna, steam room, and other facilities, and took time to explain the benefits of each. All of our services were administered with care and professionalism.

Water was from a cooler, and no fruit or other snacks were offered during our visits. On the upside, sales pressure after our visits was low, with no attempt to sell any of the oils, lotions, or robes applied to our bodies. A tip was included in the service, so read the receipt before adding a gratuity. Children's treatments are available, but the money's better spent on you and your sanity.

Mandara Spa at Universal's Portofino Bay Hotel ★★★★

Universal Studios, 5601 Universal Blvd., Orlando; ☎ 407-503-1244;
mandaraspa.com

Customer service ★★★★★. **Facilities** ★★★★½. **Amenities** ★★★. **Sales pressure** Medium. **Price range** $70–$595 spa services; $30–$160 hair and nail services; fitness pass, $10 hotel guests, $25 nonguests. 10–20% discount for Universal Annual Pass holders; 10% discount for Florida residents Monday–Thursday; 20% service charge.

COMMENTS The Universal Orlando Mandara was renovated in 2013, retaining its Asian ambience despite its location in an Italy-themed resort. We like the contrast, though, and find it slightly exotic. Waiting areas are decorated in comforting earth tones; treatment rooms feature silk-draped ceilings. Changing and bathroom areas are spacious and clean, but they also include less-than-subtle advertisements for products sold on premises. The remodeled treatment rooms feature additional decorative lighting and accessories.

The emphasis on tranquility extends to the stellar spa services, which included free self-heating oil for our massages. Men and women enjoy separate steam and sauna facilities; the whirlpool is unisex. The Portofino's sand-bottom pool is conveniently located near the entrance to the spa, as are nail services. The fitness center is still on the other side of the glass wall, however, so you may feel a bit like that doggy in the window.

Mandara Spa at the Dolphin   ★★★½

Walt Disney World Dolphin, 1500 Epcot Resorts Blvd., Lake Buena Vista;
☎ 407-934-4772; **mandaraspa.com**

Customer service ★★★★★. **Facilities** ★★★. **Amenities** ★★★. **Sales pressure** High. **Price range** $70–$595 spa services; $30–$160 hair and nail services; Disney Vacation Club members get 20% off; 20% service charge.

COMMENTS Although the Mandaras at the Dolphin and the Portofino Bay Hotel share an Asian theme, everything is dialed down a notch at the Dolphin spa, starting with the waiting areas, of which there are two: the Meditation room, stocked with teas, water, and fruit; and the Consultation room, which is so close to the treatment rooms that voices occasionally disrupt the clients' treatment experience.

Missing are the comfy sofas and chairs found at the Portofino Bay Mandara: At the Dolphin, it's standing-room-only. And we were surprised that both of this spa's two waiting rooms are unisex.

The treatment rooms, though pleasant, are also not on par with the Portofino Mandara's. Instead of silk-draped ceilings, an Asian-inspired wall hanging decorates one wall. Trappings aside, the Dolphin's spa also lacks a sauna, offering patrons only a coed steam room.

The one important asset that both Mandara Spas have in common is exceptional treatments delivered by skilled staff. The Dolphin's employees seemed to be the most talkative of any we encountered.

Relâche Spa at Gaylord Palms   ★★★★

Gaylord Palms Hotel & Convention Center, 6000 W. Osceola Parkway, Kissimmee;
☎ 407-586-4772; **gaylordpalms.com/spa**

Customer service ★★★★. **Facilities** ★★★★½. **Amenities** ★★★★. **Sales pressure** Low. **Price range** Price range $75–$410 spa services; $22–$100 nail services; $25–$50+ kids' services (ages 5–10); 10% discount for Florida residents Monday–Friday; fitness pass, $30 hotel guests, $55 nonguests; 20% service charge.

COMMENTS *Relâche* means "relax" in French, and the name is no exaggeration. The staff's courtesy and professionalism were apparent from our initial phone call to our reception upon arrival to the technicians and assistants who worked on us. A complete tour of the facilities is given when you arrive, and you're encouraged to show up early to enjoy everything.

After changing into a comfy robe and slippers in a spacious and clean locker room, you're ushered into either the men's or women's waiting room, where lemon water, delicious teas, and fresh and dried fruits and nuts are provided. From there you move into the coed Tea Room, with more refreshments, very comfortable seating, and soft lights and music.

The soft lights and music continue in the immaculate treatment rooms. A facial includes neck, décolleté, hand, and foot massages. Luscious, fruity creams and serums are applied and are available for purchase afterward, but sales pressure is kept low.

Our manicure was just as enjoyable, with the same refreshments available. The nail salon is clean and comfortable. As with our facial, the products used during our treatments were waiting on a tray as we checked out, but there was no sales pressure.

The Ritz-Carlton Spa, Orlando ★★★★

4012 Central Florida Parkway, Orlando; ☎ 407-393-4200; **ritzcarlton.com/en/properties/orlando/spa**

Customer service ★★★★★. Facilities ★★★★★. Amenities ★★★★★. Sales pressure Low–medium. **Price range** $145–$415 spa services; $25–$105 nail services; $49–$130 kids'/teens' services; 15% discount for Florida residents Monday–Thursday; 20% service charge.

COMMENTS The Ritz-Carlton Spa was so far ahead of anything else in Orlando when it opened almost a decade ago that it was in a class by itself. The facilities were much larger than anything in the area, and our interactions with the staff were the very definition of exemplary customer service. But while the service is still as fabulous as ever, the facilities are starting to look dated.

The spa is housed in a separate three-story building behind the main hotel. Every level is tastefully and elegantly decorated, including locker rooms, treatment rooms, and waiting rooms. Both single-sex and coed waiting areas are available. The waiting rooms and treatment rooms, while clean and functional, are showing their age, and our reviewer noted that they don't have niceties such as fresh flowers, mood lighting, or prewarmed robes—all of which the Senses Spas at the Grand Floridian and Saratoga Springs offer.

Spa-goers also have the use of a separate whirlpool tub, sauna and steam rooms, and an outside lap pool where an attendant supplies complimentary towels, water, and sunscreen. All the equipment we used and observed was in working order during our visits.

Senses Spa at Disney's Grand Floridian Resort ★★★★½

Grand Floridian Resort, 4401 N. Floridian Way, Lake Buena Vista; ☎ 407-939-7727; **disneyworld.com/spas**

Customer service ★★★★. Facilities ★★★★★. Amenities ★★★★. Sales pressure None. **Price range** $135–$495 spa services; $55–$80 nail services; $30–$45 kids' services (ages 4–12); 15–20% off for Disney Annual Pass holders and Disney Vacation Club members; 20% service charge.

COMMENTS Reopened in 2013 after a much-needed total renovation, Senses at the Grand Floridian is modeled—and named—after the spas on the *Disney Dream* and *Disney Fantasy* cruise ships. The decor features cool greens and whites, with dark furniture and marble counters. Wallpaper in the lobby depicts an unspoiled Florida–as–Garden of Eden.

Treatment rooms have glass tile, marble countertops, and mosaic-tile walls. Facials include a paraffin treatment for your hands as well as a neck, shoulder, and décolleté massage. Our reviewer says, "The treatment bed was very comfortable, and the silky-feeling sheets are divine."

The Hand and Foot Spa was created by walling off part of the entrance lobby. Treatments here are sumptuous and include hand-arm and foot-leg massages. At the end of your treatment, you also receive a goodie bag that contains all the implements used, plus bottles of nail polish.

Massage beds are heated, and the treatments are likewise soothing and invigorating. You'll even get a prewarmed robe to relax in when you're done.

Sales pressure during our visits was nonexistent—no one asked us to buy anything, ever. The one downside to Senses is the waiting area: It gets a lot of foot traffic, so it's not as relaxing as it could be.

Senses Spa at Disney's Saratoga Springs Resort ★★★★

1490-A Broadway, Lake Buena Vista; ☎ 407-827-4455; **disneyworld.com/spas**

Customer service ★★★★. **Facilities** ★★★★★. **Amenities** ★★★★. **Sales pressure** None. **Price range** $135–$495 spa services; $55–$80 nail services; $30–$45 kids' services (ages 4–12); 15–20% off for Disney Annual Pass holders and Disney Vacation Club members.

COMMENTS Saratoga Springs' spa was completely remodeled in 2013 to match the Senses Spa theming found on Disney's cruise ships and at its Grand Floridian Resort. Services, amenities, and prices at the Saratoga Springs Senses are in line with those at its Grand Floridian sibling, although the setting at Saratoga Springs is perhaps a little less formal. If you're staying at Saratoga Springs, Old Key West, or the Downtown Disney resorts, or you're coming from an off-site hotel east of Disney World, we'd recommend the shorter drive and easier commute of the Senses at Saratoga Springs.

Our reviewer enjoyed the custom-made pedicure chairs at Saratoga Springs, as well as the heated massage tables. As with many spas' mani-pedi services, you'll get to keep a bottle of the nail polish you choose, for later touch-ups. It's a nice extra.

The Spa at Four Seasons Resort Orlando ★★★★½

10100 Dream Tree Blvd., Lake Buena Vista; ☎ 407-313-7777; **fourseasons.com/orlando/spa**

Customer service ★★★★★. **Facilities** ★★★★½. **Amenities** ★★★★★. **Sales pressure** Low. **Price range** $105–$225 spa services; $35–$95 nail services; $80–$300 hair services.

COMMENTS If you've heard that you'll never have to open a door yourself at the Four Seasons, we're here to tell you it's true, at least at the Four Seasons' spa in Orlando. From parking the car (valet only, $5), to walking into the lobby, to the spa itself, we never touched a door.

The spa is located one level down from the lobby. After a quick orientation tour, we changed into luxurious robes (and less luxe rubber slippers) in our unisex locker room before heading to a coed waiting lounge. The lounge has two fireplaces, which were both roaring and welcome during our gloomy, damp fall visit. Lounge snacks included various teas, a refreshing chilled fruit juice, blanched almonds, and dried and fresh fruit. One thing we'd like to see in the lounge is an ottoman so we could put our feet up while we wait.

Treatment rooms are new, clean, and attractive, with typical spa touches, including flowers, candles, soft lighting, and soft music. Prior to our massage, we were asked to fill out a brief form asking about physical problems, ailments, or allergies. Perhaps it's a legal issue, but it's an odd point in the process to be confronted with paperwork. The massage was nice but seemed to end abruptly.

After a break and visit to the lounge, we were ready for our facial. Before that came another form to sign—again, an odd situation. That completed, the service was wonderful, and our aesthetician had a perfect touch. However, this treatment also ended abruptly; it almost seems as if the staff are on timers.

Brave spa-goers should try the Four Seasons' "Experience" showers— huge, nicely tiled, walk-in showers with a computer screen that allows you to choose lighting, music, and different water pressures and spray patterns. Be aware that there's no curtain or door, though. Wear a bathing suit as needed.

The Spa at Orlando World Center Marriott Resort ★★½

8701 World Center Dr., Orlando; ☎ 407-238-8705; **marriottworldcenter.com/spa**

Customer service ★★★★. Facilities ★★. Amenities ★★★. Sales pressure High. **Price range** $100–$450 spa services; $35–$115 nail services.

COMMENTS In a small, separate building at the back of a sprawling hotel complex, The Spa at Orlando World Center Marriott Resort requires a hike from your room, or a really good set of directions if you're coming by car.

The women's locker room has no private changing areas; however, the bathroom stalls are big enough to make do. Spa-goers have the use of steam rooms and fitness facilities. Women should know that once they're in their spa robes, they're directed to a coed quiet room to await treatments. (On our visit, the spa was rife with male bonding.)

A staffer pressured us insistently to buy expensive oils and lotions after our treatments. Worse yet, the nail-drying equipment was either broken or nonexistent when we visited for our manicure: After shelling out $35 (plus tip), we were told to sit in the quiet room and blow on our nails to dry them.

Waldorf Astoria Spa ★★★★½

Waldorf Astoria Orlando, 14200 Bonnet Creek Resort Lane, Orlando; ☎ 407-597-5360; **waldorfastoriaorlando.com/spa**

Customer service ★★★★★. Facilities ★★★½. Amenities ★★★★★. Sales pressure None. **Price range** $149–$350 facials; $149–$450 massages; $45–$90 nail services; $20 day pass; 10% discount for Florida residents; complimentary valet parking (no self-parking); 20% service charge.

COMMENTS The Waldorf Astoria Spa is just a short walk from the lobby, and our first impressions were very positive. Upon your arrival, an attendant takes you on a tour of the facilities. Once you are given your key, locker, robe, and slippers, you're free to wander the rooms before settling in the Tea Lounge. It's comfortable, but we like the lounge chairs at the Senses spas better.

The locker room and bathrooms are clean and modern. The showers are spacious and very clean, with small iridescent tiles. Beyond these is the Tea Lounge, where your treatment person meets you—which is fortunate, because the place is big enough to get lost in.

Our massage, facial, and mani–pedi were all excellent. The pedicure came with a glass of Champagne. Clearly, these are people who know what we need.

APPENDIX

READERS' QUESTIONS
to the AUTHORS

FOLLOWING ARE QUESTIONS AND COMMENTS from *Unofficial Guide* readers. Some frequently asked questions are addressed in every edition of the *Guide*.

QUESTION:

When you do your research, are you admitted to the parks for free? Do the Disney people know you're there?

ANSWER:

We pay regular admission; usually Disney doesn't know we're on-site. We pay for our own meals and lodging, both in and out of the World.

QUESTION:

How often is the Unofficial Guide *revised?*

ANSWER:

We publish a new edition once a year. The e-book (Kindle and ePub) is updated for at least six months after the print version is released.

QUESTION:

Where can I find information about what's changed at Walt Disney World in between published editions of the Unofficial Guide?

ANSWER:

We post important information online at **touringplans.com.**

QUESTION:

Do you write each new edition from scratch?

ANSWER:

Nope. When it comes to a destination the size of Walt Disney World, it's hard enough to keep up with what's new. Moreover, we put a lot of effort into communicating the most useful information in the clearest possible language. If an attraction or hotel has not changed, we're reluctant to tinker with its coverage for the sake of freshening the writing.

QUESTION:

I've never read any other Unofficial Guides. *Are they all as critical as* The Unofficial Guide to Walt Disney World?

ANSWER:

What some readers perceive as critical we see as objective and constructive. Our job is to prepare you for both the best and worst of Walt Disney World. As it happens, some folks are very passionate about what one reader calls "the inherent goodness of Disney." These readers might be more comfortable with press releases or the *Official Guide* than with the strong consumer viewpoint represented in our guide. That said, some readers take us to task for being overly *positive*.

QUESTION:

How many people have you surveyed for your age-group ratings regarding the attractions?

ANSWER:

Since the first *Unofficial Guide* was published in 1985, we've interviewed or surveyed almost 53,000 Walt Disney World patrons. Even with such a large survey population, however, we continue to find certain age groups underrepresented. Specifically, we'd love to hear more from seniors about their experiences with coasters and other thrill rides.

QUESTION:

Do you stay in Walt Disney World? If not, where?

ANSWER:

We stay at Walt Disney World lodging properties quite often. Since we began writing about Walt Disney World in 1982, we've stayed at all the Disney resorts and more than 100 different properties in various locations around Orlando, Lake Buena Vista, and Kissimmee.

QUESTION:

Bob, what's your favorite Florida attraction?

ANSWER:

What attracts me (as opposed to my favorite attraction) is **Juniper Springs,** a stunningly beautiful stream about 1½ hours north of Orlando in the Ocala National Forest. Originating in a limestone aquifer, the crystal-clear water erupts from the ground and begins a 10-mile journey to the creek's mouth at Lake George. Winding through palm, cypress, and live oak, the stream is more exotic than the Jungle Cruise, and alive with birds, turtles, and alligators. Put in at the Juniper Springs Recreation Area on FL 40, 36 miles east of Ocala. The 7-mile trip to the FL 19 bridge takes about 4½ hours. Canoe rentals and shuttle service are available at the recreation area. Call ☎ 352-625-3147 for more information.

▌ READERS' COMMENTS

OUR READERS LOVE TO SHARE TIPS. From a St. Louis mom:

When dining at Downtown Disney, it's best to arrive before 7 p.m. We ate there twice and had no problem getting seated immediately, but after 7 p.m. everywhere was packed.

And from an Ann Arbor, Michigan, mother of three:

Even though we stayed on Disney property, we stopped off on US 192 and loaded up on the local freebie visitor magazines and coupon books. We estimate they saved us over $200, mostly on food.

An Iowa City, Iowa, couple offers this observation about being in touch with your feelings:

We didn't build rest breaks into our plans but were willing to say, "OK, I'm just not having fun right now—we should leave the park," and go on to something else (like a water park, hotel pool, or shopping trip to Downtown Disney). This is a skill I would like to see more people develop. I can't count the number of people or families I saw who were obviously not having fun.

A woman from Suwanee, Georgia, offers a suggestion for the perfect Disney vacation:

Your book made our trip a much more successful one. It also frustrated our male adults, who erroneously believed this was a trip for their enjoyment. We followed your advice to get up early and see as much as possible before an early lunch. But the men refused to go back to the hotel for a nap and a meal outside the park, so we fought the crowds until 3 or 4 p.m., by which time everyone was exhausted and cranky. My mother and I decided our next trip will include your guidebook and the children—but no men!

From a Greenville, Kentucky, mom who wasn't able to take advantage of the free-admission promotion on her daughter's birthday:

We were disappointed that a birth certificate was the only acceptable ID for my daughter. We had certified shot records, and they still wouldn't accept them.

A Norwalk, Ohio, mom searched for happy feet:

*On the subject of footwear, support is just as important as comfort. On one trip I wore Keds—big mistake. My shins ached unbelievably before the end of the second day. From then on I was a die-hard tennis-shoe girl, until I discovered FitFlops [go to **fitflop.com** for stores]. You get the support of a tennis shoe with the comfort of a flip-flop.*

A reader from Crofton, Maryland, discovered that the best bargains on Disney merchandise can turn up in unexpected places:

People who want to save $$$ on Disney trinkets and aren't fussy about selection really should go to the Disney shop at Orlando Premium Outlets. I bought a talking Goofy doll for my nephew and was very pleased with the $19.99 price, which was significantly lower *than the list price. However, the VERY SAME doll was only $9.99 at (of all places!) Publix grocery store! In fact, Publix has loads of cute dolls, T-shirts, keychains, and other gifts at great prices!*

A Midwestern mom loved getting in the game, writing:

It was a thrill for me to stand behind the ropes and wait until the park officially opened—to hear the music and announcements, then hurry with the throngs to the first ride. It was so exciting! My husband wasn't so thrilled. He teased me for days about running over old ladies and little children—I didn't run! I was speed-walking!

A woman from Mount Gretna, Pennsylvania, had some questions about theme park attire:

I don't believe there was a section that addressed whether or not you could wear dresses on the rides. Quite a few amusement parks have security straps or bars that come up between one's knees, making it very difficult and immodest to wear dresses or skirts. Many women want to wear dresses for convenience, comfort, or cultural/religious convictions. I was concerned as I was packing whether this would limit any rides I could get on. I was quite pleased that it did not.

Henry Ford famously said, "You can have any color car you want, as long as it's black." A hungry (and persistent) Fairfax, Vermont, reader found that mindset alive and well at his Disney resort's food court:

The real difficulty of our stay began when I made the ill-advised decision to request a hamburger at the food court. I was first given a cheeseburger. I then informed the cast member that I requested a hamburger. She placed the burger back under the heat lamp, and I proceeded to watch the person at the grill place cheese on all 14 burgers that had just been put on the grill. Sensing my unease, another cast member asked me what I had ordered. I informed him that I was waiting for a hamburger. He then reached under the heat lamp and proceeded to give me the original cheeseburger. Had I realized that, at that very moment, fate had determined that I was not to enjoy a hamburger on this night, then I would have given up. Sadly, I did not come to this realization at that time. Instead, I chose to "spit into the wind" and insist on getting my hamburger. Thus, I watched as another 14 burgers were placed on the grill. I could almost taste the reward for my patience . . . until I saw the cast member delicately place cheese on each and every one of the new burgers. Alas, my quest for a burger ended, and my call to Pizza Hut delivery was made.

A Fenton, Missouri, woman evidently took her banker with her:

Love your book! Our last trip was with eight people total: Grandma, Grandpa, my sister and her husband and two sons (ages 4 and 12), and my finance and me.

A Widnes, England, dad knows who butters his bread:

While we didn't make the early starts, the Guide still managed to advise of enough shortcuts that enabled us to keep everyone happy. (Let's face it—I'm talking about my wife.)

A Yardley, Pennsylvania, woman of few words sums up the Walt Disney World experience thus:

Expect to wait for everything—except the bathroom!

A Nashville, Tennessee, family of three report a tough reentry:

My wife and I were so depressed when we had to adjust to reality after a week of being in Disney's alternate universe. We think Disney needs to offer some sort of debriefing or transition program to ease its visitors back into the real world. Perhaps they could send Mickey and Minnie over to make blueberry pancakes the morning after you return.

An Atlanta reader relates the story of a dirty bird and a solicitous cast member:

While riding Splash Mountain, a mother and teenage son in our boat had brought ponchos (smart move), and the son took his off before we got out of the boat . . . just in time for a bird to poop on him. He went to buy a clean shirt in the gift shop, and when the cast member found out what had happened, he gave the kid a free shirt. I thought that was very nice!

A Rockville, Maryland, woman offers a recipe for relaxation:

The true secret to our enjoyable experience was the cocktails at Planet Hollywood. I started the evening with Blazing Saddles and finished it off with Gorillas in the Mist. I didn't taste a lot of alcohol, but they sure helped me relax after a day of following a 7-year-old around a theme park. When the stress of a Disney vacation is starting to get to you and you feel like you're ready to strangle that sweet little angel by your side, this place is a must.

From a Clarksville, Maryland, family:

Your book should include a review of Legoland. We took a side trip there, and it was awesome—perfect for kids ages 4–12, with a very affordable water park for only $12 extra.

We devote an entire chapter to Legoland, including touring plans, in *Beyond Disney: The Unofficial Guide to Universal Orlando, Sea-World, and the Best of Central Florida.*

A Columbia, Missouri, woman offers advice for wives with anxious husbands:

A smartphone is the best thing in the world for keeping your husband busy in line. As long as mine had that phone, he could check e-mail, check dinner plans, and take and send pictures of the kids to family back home. He never complained about waiting in line, ever.

A Denver reader bursts our bubble (we thought we were Disney's favorites):

WDW cast members have an interesting reaction to the Guide. *In one case, with the book in hand, we got an almost vampire-vs.-holy-water reaction from one CM (who then asked if he could take a quick peek).*

A mom from Brighton, Michigan, was searching for quiet in all the wrong places:

Disney is so much flash and sparkle without a lot of time for reflection. They had to fill every quiet minute throughout the park with noise, music, talking, animation, flashing lights, etc.—as if they were afraid we'd get bored if we stopped to think. Next year we plan to go to Costa Rica instead.

There's just no pleasing some people—this London bloke, for example:

Why, oh why is Toy Story Midway Mania! rated so highly? It's like playing crummy Wii games as someone pushes you around on your sofa.

From an exhausted mother:

Make sure moms are prepared for the fact that their kids will throw tantrums . . . and so will their husbands. Disney is a magical, wonderful thing, but it was also the most exhausting thing I have ever done. It required more patience than I've needed so far as a parent.

A Scottsdale, Arizona, woman found the silver lining (and we agree):

I listen to podcasts and read various Disney websites, and the one thing I find amusing is that no one seems to spend much time on how truly beautiful the Disney resorts are. The rooms themselves are adequate, but the grounds are spectacular. If these hotels weren't affiliated with the theme parks, they would be destination resorts (provided the food was substantially improved).

All for the love of Mom, writes a woman from Haddon Heights, New Jersey:

I was traveling with my mother, who has an artificial knee, a herniated disc, and bad feet. My mantra was, "Try not to kill your mother." Without the book, I would have undoubtedly come home an orphan.

From a husband and wife from Atlanta:

My brother-in-law Pat and his wife were planning a trip to Disney for the first time with their 4-year-old daughter. My other brother-in-law Robert, who has three kids and has taken them to Disney twice, asked Pat if he had taken the Disney test: Take a $100 bill, throw it in the toilet, and flush. If you can do this without flinching, you're ready for Disney.

A mom from Flower Mound, Texas, boils our windy 850-page guide down to one paragraph, and she's pretty much right-on:

If you get just the following two things from the Guide, they're worth the cost of the entire book—especially when you put them together: (1) Get to the parks early. You won't believe what a difference it makes. The parks are wonderful in the morning. (2) The afternoon break is essential! I wouldn't even consider a WDW trip without it. If your kids are under 10 years old, turn out the lights, shut the curtains, and make them sleep. It's the difference between disaster and delight!

A Texas woman never says never:

*As I walked out of the Magic Kingdom for the last time, I promised
I wouldn't wait so long to visit again.*

This Hawaii woman either is a record-holder of some sort or forgot
to proofread before she hit SEND:

*We've used the book for more than 90 years and love it. Keep up the
good work!*

From an opinionated Georgia family of four:

*My 13-year-old son's one-word description of Space Mountain: "Awe-
some." My husband's one-word description: "Hell." My 10-year-old's
best comment: "Hey Mom, here's a Disney motto that no one talks
about: 'Bleed 'em dry.' " My 13-year-old's best comment as I was trying to get everyone to stop and pose in front of the topiaries: "Keep
movin', Mom! There's no time for memories!"*

No drugs needed for an Asheville, North Carolina, mom:

I have recommended the Guide *to everyone who has asked me about
our trip and is impressed that I made it back without a prescription
for lithium!*

A Somerville, Alabama, woman is succinct if nothing else:

Everything, other than my husband, was perfect.

Finally, a Winthrop Harbor, Illinois, reader reported a near-miss:

*I'm sorry to say this, but I didn't actually go inside Disney World.
But I did stay in Florida.*

And so it goes. . . .

ACCOMMODATIONS INDEX

Note: Page numbers of profiles are in **boldface** type.

See also the Restaurant Index on pages 774-777 and the Subject Index on pages 778-803.

See also the Restaurant Index on pages 774–777 and the Subject Index on pages 778–803.

See also the Restaurant Index on pages 774–777 and the Subject Index on pages 778–803.

See also the Restaurant Index on pages 774–777 and the Subject Index on pages 778–803.

See also the Restaurant Index on pages 774–777 and the Subject Index on pages 778–803.

RESTAURANT INDEX

Note: Page numbers of restaurant profiles are in **boldface** type.

See also the Accommodations Index on pages 768–773 and the Subject Index on pages 778–803.

See also the Accommodations Index on pages 768-773 and the Subject Index on pages 778-803.

SUBJECT INDEX

Note: Attractions at non-Disney parks are labeled; those at Disney parks are unlabeled.

See also the Accommodations Index on pages 768–773 and the Restaurant Index on pages 774–777.

See also the Accommodations Index on pages 768–773 and the Restaurant Index on pages 774–777.

See also the Accommodations Index on pages 768-773 and the Restaurant Index on pages 774-777.

Clinics, for medical care, 475–76
Club Cool, 546
Clyde and Seamore Take Pirate Island
    (SeaWorld), 695–97
Coca-Cola exhibit (Club Cool), 546
Comic book shop, *757*
Comic Strip Lane (IOA), 643–46
Complaints
    accommodations, 140
    contacting Disney staff about, 478–79
Concerts
    Blues Brothers, The, 670
    Disney Springs, 745–46
Condominiums, 248–54
Conservation Station, 576–77, 588–89
Conventions, 40, 66
Coolest Summer Ever Dance Party, 622
Corporate sponsors, admission discounts
    for, 66
Costs
    accommodations, 118–19, 125–27, 272–91
    admission, 53–59
    car rental, 454
    daily, 67
    Disney character dining, 423–24
    food/drinks, 312
    grocery items, 481
    increases in, 63
    parking, 457
    restaurants, 301, 338–41
    tolls, 448
    transportation, 449
    travel packages, 221–35
    vacation-home rental, 248–54
Costumes, of characters, 415
Counter-service restaurants, 308
    in Animal Kingdom, 332–33
    in Disney's Hollywood Studios, 333–35
    in Epcot, 329–32
    in Magic Kingdom, 326–28
Country Bear Jamboree, 484–85, 499
Couples, 431–33
Coupons, for restaurants, 300
Craig, Stuart, 651
Create Zone, DisneyQuest, 727
Credit cards, 473
Cross Country Creek, 700–701
Crowd(s). *See also* Touring plan(s); Traffic
    patterns
    Animal Kingdom, 599
    avoiding, 77–78
    children lost in, 402, 417
    DisneyQuest, 727–28
    Epcot, 566–67, 570–71
    Future World, 570–71
    live entertainment effects on, 527–28
    off-season, 39–43
    online calculator for, 42–43
    opening procedures and, 76–77, 83,
        529–31
    at parades, 527–28
    prediction, 41–43
    SeaWorld, 694–95

at shows, 103
    summer, 47–48
    time of week for, 41–43
    time of year for, 39–43, 436
    traffic patterns and, 529–31
    Universal Orlando, 629
    waiting-line strategies for, 411–13. *See
        also* FastPass+
    water parks, 700, 705–6
    Wizarding World of Harry Potter, The,
        652–53
    World Showcase, 566–67, 570–71
Crowd Calendar, 26, 41–43
Crown & Crest, The, 736
Cruise Line, Disney, 18–19
Crush 'n' Gusher, 702
Crush, Turtle Talk with, 555–56
Cub's Den, 427
Curious George Goes to Town Playground
    (USF), 668–69, 682
Curl by Sammy Duvall (store), 732
Currency exchange, 473
Customized touring plans, 80–81
Cutback Cove (Aquatica), 715
CyberSpace Mountain, 727
Cycle rides, 101–2

D Street (store), 732
Dark rides, 408
Daryl Carter Parkway, 446
Das Kaufhaus, 733–34
David's Disney Vacation Club Rentals, 123
Days of Christmas, Disney's, 730
Dehydration, 394
Dental emergencies, 476
Der Stuka (Wet 'n Wild), 712
Der Teddybär, 734
Dervish and Banges (IOA), 654, 656
Despicable Me Minion Mayhem (USF),
    668–69, 671
Diagon Alley, The Wizarding World of
    Harry Potter (USF), 20, 682–91
Diaper-changing facilities, 395–96, 490,
    544, 579, 605
Die Weihnachts Ecke (store), 734
Dietary restrictions, 307, 439
Dining. *See* Dinner theaters; Eating; Res-
    taurants; *separate Restaurant Index*
Dining plans, 225–32, 301
Dinner theaters, 744–46
    Disney's Hollywood Studios, 610–11
    Epcot, 566
    Hoop-Dee-Doo Musical Revue, 744–46
    Mickey's Backyard BBQ, 746
    reservations, 744
    Spirit of Aloha Dinner Show, 746–47
DinoLand U.S.A., attractions, 576–77,
    580–81, 595–97
    Boneyard, The, 576–77, 594–95
    for children, 406
    Dinosaur, 576–77, 580–81, 595–97
    Primeval Whirl, 576–77, 596
    Theater in the Wild, 576–77, 596–97

See also the Accommodations Index on pages 768–773 and the Restaurant Index on pages 774–777.

See also the Accommodations Index on pages 768–773 and the Restaurant Index on pages 774–777.

See also the Accommodations Index on pages 768–773 and the Restaurant Index on pages 774–777.

See also the Accommodations Index on pages 768–773 and the Restaurant Index on pages 774–777.

See also the Accommodations Index on pages 768–773 and the Restaurant Index on pages 774–777.

See also the Accommodations Index on pages 768–773 and the Restaurant Index on pages 774–777.

See also the Accommodations Index on pages 768–773 and the Restaurant Index on pages 774–777.

See also the Accommodations Index on pages 768–773 and the Restaurant Index on pages 774–777.

See also the Accommodations Index on pages 768–773 and the Restaurant Index on pages 774–777.

See also the Accommodations Index on pages 768–773 and the Restaurant Index on pages 774–777.

See also the Accommodations Index on pages 768–773 and the Restaurant Index on pages 774–777.

TOURING PLANS

"Not a Touring Plan"
TOURING PLANS

BELOW ARE THE SIMPLE RULES we use when friends ask us for touring plans that don't sound like a space-shuttle launch checklist. Use these when you don't want the regimentation of a step-by-step plan but you do want to avoid long waits in line. Skip attractions that don't suit you, and use FastPass+ if waits seem too long.

MAGIC KINGDOM

FOR PARENTS OF SMALL CHILDREN WITH ONE DAY TO TOUR, ARRIVING AT PARK OPENING *Note:* Use FastPass+ wherever you can get it. See Fantasyland first, starting with Seven Dwarfs Mine Train and Peter Pan's Flight. See Frontierland and some of Adventureland, and then take a midday break. Return to the park and complete your tour of Adventureland. Next, meet characters at the Town Square Theater and tour Tomorrowland. End on Main Street for parades and fireworks.

FOR ADULTS WITH ONE DAY TO TOUR, ARRIVING AT PARK OPENING *Note:* Use FastPass+ for attractions in the late morning and midafternoon, especially in Frontierland and Tomorrowland. See Seven Dwarfs Mine Train and Peter Pan's Flight in Fantasyland, and then head to Liberty Square. Tour Frontierland, Adventureland, and Tomorrowland next. End on Main Street for parades and fireworks.

FOR PARENTS AND ADULTS WITH TWO DAYS TO TOUR *Note:* Day One works great for Disney resort guests on Extra Magic Hours mornings. Use FastPass+ where you can. Start Day One with Seven Dwarfs Mine Train in Fantasyland; then tour Liberty Square and Frontierland before leaving the park around midday. Begin Day Two in Tomorrowland; then tour Adventureland. End on Main Street for parades and fireworks.

FOR PARENTS AND ADULTS WITH AN AFTERNOON AND A FULL DAY *Note:* The full day works great for Disney resort guests on Extra Magic Hours mornings. For the afternoon, tour Frontierland, Adventureland, and Tomorrowland (get FastPass+ reservations for Splash and Space Mountains and Big Thunder Mountain Railroad). On your full day of touring, see Fantasyland, Liberty Square, and Tomorrowland again (for any missed attractions from the previous afternoon). End on Main Street for parades and fireworks.

EPCOT

FOR PARENTS AND ADULTS WITH ONE DAY TO TOUR, ARRIVING AT PARK OPENING Ride Test Track and then Mission: Space Orange

(FastPass+ suggested start time: 9 a.m.). Next, ride Sum of All Thrills, Soarin' (FastPass+ suggested start time: 11 a.m.), and Spaceship Earth; tour other Future World East and West attractions as you come to them and as you desire. Then tour World Showcase clockwise, starting in Mexico (FastPass+ suggested start time for the Frozen Ever After boat ride or the Royal Sommerhus meet and greet in Norway, both opening in 2016: 2 p.m.). End the day with *IllumiNations*.

FOR PARENTS AND ADULTS WITH ONE DAY TO TOUR, ARRIVING LATE MORNING Tour Future World West except for Soarin'. Tour World Showcase counterclockwise, starting in Canada (FastPass+ suggested start time for the Frozen Ever After boat ride or the Royal Sommerhus meet and greet in Norway: 3 p.m.). Tour Future World East; then ride Spaceship Earth. Now ride Soarin' (FastPass+ suggested start time: 6:30 p.m.)—or, if FastPass+ is unavailable for that, try to get reservations for Test Track instead. End the day with *IllumiNations*.

FOR PARENTS AND ADULTS WITH TWO DAYS TO TOUR On Day One, start with Test Track and Mission: Space Orange (FastPass+ suggested start times: 9 a.m. and 10 a.m., respectively), and then ride Sum of All Thrills. See the rest of Future World as desired, and then tour Mexico through the United States in World Showcase (FastPass+ suggested start time for the Frozen Ever After boat ride or the Royal Sommerhus meet and greet in Norway: 2 p.m.). On Day Two, ride Soarin' (FastPass+ suggested start time: 9 a.m.), and then tour Canada through Japan in World Showcase. End the day with *IllumiNations* (use FastPass+).

DISNEY'S ANIMAL KINGDOM

FOR PARENTS AND ADULTS ARRIVING AT PARK OPENING Obtain FastPass+ reservations for Expedition Everest in Asia; then begin a land-by-land counterclockwise tour of the park, starting in DinoLand U.S.A. Work in shows as you near them, but leave *Finding Nemo—The Musical* for last. Eat dinner and end the night with *Rivers of Light* (opens 2016).

FOR PARENTS AND ADULTS ARRIVING LATE MORNING Get FastPass+ reservations for Kilimanjaro Safaris; then begin a counterclockwise tour of the park starting in Africa, saving Kali River Rapids and Expedition Everest for last. Eat dinner and end the night with *Rivers of Light* (opens 2016).

DISNEY'S HOLLYWOOD STUDIOS

FOR ADULTS ARRIVING AT PARK OPENING Obtain FastPass+ reservations for Toy Story Midway Mania! (FastPass+ suggested start time: 10 a.m.). Then begin a counterclockwise tour of the park with Rock 'n' Roller Coaster, Tower of Terror, and The Great Movie Ride. Work in shows as you near them. End the tour with *Voyage of the Little Mermaid*. End the day on Sunset Boulevard for *Fantasmic!* (If you're staying for the show, FastPass+ for Tower of Terror in the last hour the park is open would work well.)

FOR PARENTS AND ADULTS ARRIVING LATE MORNING Get FastPass+ reservations for Toy Story Midway Mania! and use those at the appropriate time; otherwise, save it for last. Start a clockwise tour of the park with the *Lights, Motors, Action! Extreme Stunt Show*, and end with Toy Story if you didn't use FastPass+. Then grab a bite to eat, and see *Fantasmic!*

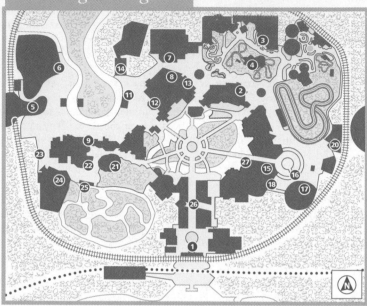

MAGIC KINGDOM ONE-DAY TOURING PLAN FOR ADULTS

1. Arrive at the Magic Kingdom entrance 50 minutes (Disney resort guests) to 70 minutes (non–Disney resort guests) before opening. Get guide maps and the *Times Guide*.

2. As soon as the park opens, head to Fantasyland and ride The Many Adventures of Winnie the Pooh.

3. Ride Under the Sea: Journey of the Little Mermaid.

4. Ride the Seven Dwarfs Mine Train.

5. In Frontierland, ride Splash Mountain.

6. Ride Big Thunder Mountain Railroad.

7. Ride It's a Small World in Fantasyland.

8. Ride Peter Pan's Flight.

9. In Frontierland, see *Country Bear Jamboree*.

10. Eat lunch.

11. In Liberty Square, ride the *Liberty Belle* Riverboat.

12. Experience *The Hall of Presidents*.

13. In Fantasyland, see *Mickey's PhilharMagic*.

14. In Liberty Square, see The Haunted Mansion.

15. See *Monsters, Inc. Laugh Floor* in Tomorrowland.

16. Ride the Tomorrowland Transit Authority PeopleMover.

17. See *Walt Disney's Carousel of Progress*.

18. Ride Buzz Lightyear's Space Ranger Spin.

19. Eat dinner.

20. Ride Space Mountain.

21. In Adventureland, explore the Swiss Family Treehouse.

22. See *Walt Disney's Enchanted Tiki Room*.

23. Play A Pirate's Adventure.

24. Ride Pirates of the Caribbean.

25. Take the Jungle Cruise.

26. See the evening parade on Main Street.

27. See the evening castle light show and fireworks on Main Street. A good viewing spot is somewhere between The Plaza Restaurant and Tomorrowland Terrace.

You can customize this touring plan and get real-time updates while you're in the park! See **touringplans.com** for details. **Suggested start times for FastPass+ reservations:** Seven Dwarfs Mine Train, 9 a.m.; Big Thunder Mountain Railroad, 10 a.m.; Peter Pan's Flight, 11 a.m.

Once you've used those three FastPass+ reservations, you'll be able to make additional FastPass+ reservations at an in-park FastPass+ kiosk. **Our recommendations for day-of FastPass+ reservations:** Around noon, make a Haunted Mansion FastPass+ reservation for around 2 p.m. Around 3 p.m., make a Space Mountain reservation for around 7 p.m. After 7 p.m., check for FastPass+ reservations for *Wishes* fireworks.

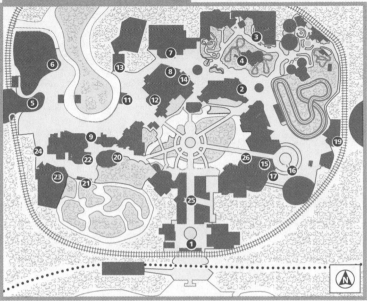

MAGIC KINGDOM AUTHORS' SELECTIVE
ONE-DAY TOURING PLAN FOR ADULTS

1. Arrive at the Magic Kingdom entrance 50 minutes (Disney resort guests) to 70 minutes (non–Disney resort guests) before opening. Get guide maps and the *Times Guide*.

2. As soon as the park opens, head to Fantasyland and ride The Many Adventures of Winnie the Pooh.

3. Ride Under the Sea: Journey of the Little Mermaid.

4. Ride the Seven Dwarfs Mine Train.

5. In Frontierland, ride Splash Mountain.

6. Ride Big Thunder Mountain Railroad.

7. Ride It's a Small World in Fantasyland.

8. Ride Peter Pan's Flight.

9. In Frontierland, see *Country Bear Jamboree*.

10. Eat lunch.

11. In Liberty Square, ride the *Liberty Belle* Riverboat.

12. Experience *The Hall of Presidents*.

13. In Liberty Square, see The Haunted Mansion.

14. In Fantasyland, see *Mickey's PhilharMagic*.

15. See *Monsters, Inc. Laugh Floor* in Tomorrowland.

16. Ride the Tomorrowland Transit Authority PeopleMover.

17. Ride Buzz Lightyear's Space Ranger Spin.

18. Eat dinner.

19. Ride Space Mountain.

20. In Adventureland, explore the Swiss Family Treehouse.

21. Take the Jungle Cruise.

22. See *Walt Disney's Enchanted Tiki Room*.

23. Ride Pirates of the Caribbean.

24. Play A Pirate's Adventure.

25. See the evening parade on Main Street.

26. See the evening castle light show and fireworks on Main Street. A good viewing spot is somewhere between The Plaza Restaurant and Tomorrowland Terrace.

You can customize this touring plan and get real-time updates while you're in the park! See **touringplans.com** for details. **Suggested start times for FastPass+ reservations:** Seven Dwarfs Mine Train, 9 a.m.; Big Thunder Mountain Railroad, 10 a.m.; Peter Pan's Flight, 11 a.m.

Once you've used those three FastPass+ reservations, you'll be able to make additional FastPass+ reservations at an in-park FastPass+ kiosk. **Our recommendations for day-of FastPass+ reservations:** Around noon, make a Haunted Mansion FastPass+ reservation for around 2 p.m. Around 3 p.m., make a Space Mountain reservation for around 7 p.m. After 7 p.m., check for FastPass+ reservations for *Wishes* fireworks.

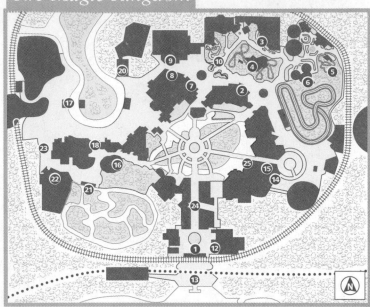

The Magic Kingdom

MAGIC KINGDOM ONE-DAY TOURING PLAN
FOR PARENTS WITH SMALL CHILDREN
(Review the Small-Child Fright-Potential Chart on pages 404–407.)

1. Arrive at the Magic Kingdom entrance 50 minutes (Disney resort guests) to 70 minutes (non–Disney resort guests) before opening. Rent strollers before the park opens. Get guide maps and the *Times Guide*.

2. As soon as the park opens, head to Fantasyland and ride The Many Adventures of Winnie the Pooh.

3. Ride Under the Sea: Journey of the Little Mermaid.

4. Ride the Seven Dwarfs Mine Train.

5. Ride The Barnstormer.

6. Ride Dumbo the Flying Elephant.

7. See *Mickey's PhilharMagic*.

8. Ride Peter Pan's Flight.

9. Ride It's a Small World.

10. See *Enchanted Tales with Belle*.

11. Eat lunch.

12. Meet Mickey Mouse at Town Square Theater on Main Street.

13. Take a midday break.

14. Ride Buzz Lightyear's Space Ranger Spin in Tomorrowland.

15. See *Monsters, Inc. Laugh Floor*.

16. Explore the Swiss Family Treehouse in Adventureland.

17. In Frontierland, take the raft over to Tom Sawyer Island. Allow at least 30 minutes to explore the island, Fort Langhorn, and the barrel bridges.

18. See *Country Bear Jamboree*.

19. Eat dinner.

20. In Liberty Square, see The Haunted Mansion.

21. In Adventureland, take the Jungle Cruise.

22. Ride Pirates of the Caribbean.

23. Play A Pirate's Adventure.

24. See the evening parade on Main Street.

25. See the evening castle light show and fireworks on Main Street. A good viewing spot is somewhere between The Plaza Restaurant and Tomorrowland Terrace.

You can customize this touring plan and get real-time updates while you're in the park! See **touringplans.com** for details. **Suggested start times for FastPass+ reservations:** Seven Dwarfs Mine Train, 9 a.m.; Peter Pan's Flight, 10 a.m.; *Enchanted Tales with Belle*, 11 a.m.

Once you've used those three FastPass+ reservations, you'll be able to make additional FastPass+ reservations at an in-park FastPass+ kiosk. **Our recommendations for day-of FastPass+ reservations:** Around lunchtime, make a Buzz Lightyear's Space Ranger Spin FastPass+ reservation for around 3:30 p.m. Make a Pirates of the Caribbean reservation for around 8 p.m. After you've used your last FastPass, check for FastPass+ reservations for *Wishes* fireworks.

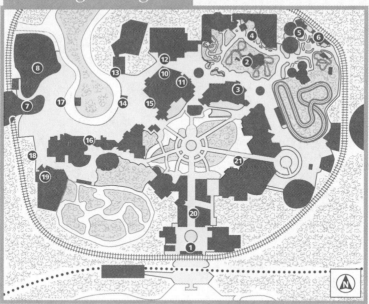

MAGIC KINGDOM TWO-DAY TOURING PLAN FOR ADULTS: DAY ONE

1. Arrive at the Magic Kingdom entrance 50 minutes (Disney resort guests) to 70 minutes (non–Disney resort guests) before opening. Get guide maps and the *Times Guide*.

2. As soon as the park opens, head to Fantasyland and ride Seven Dwarfs Mine Train.

3. Ride The Many Adventures of Winnie the Pooh.

4. Ride Under the Sea: Journey of the Little Mermaid.

5. Meet Goofy and Donald at Pete's Silly Sideshow.

6. Take the Walt Disney World Railroad from Fantasyland to Frontierland.

7. In Frontierland, ride Splash Mountain.

8. Ride Big Thunder Mountain Railroad.

9. Eat lunch.

10. Ride Peter Pan's Flight in Fantasyland.

11. See *Mickey's PhilharMagic*.

12. Ride It's a Small World.

13. In Liberty Square, see The Haunted Mansion.

14. Ride the *Liberty Belle* Riverboat.

15. Experience *The Hall of Presidents*.

16. In Frontierland, see *Country Bear Jamboree*.

17. Take the raft over to Tom Sawyer Island. Allow at least 30 minutes to explore the island, Fort Langhorn, and the barrel bridges.

18. In Adventureland, play A Pirate's Adventure.

19. Ride Pirates of the Caribbean.

20. See the evening parade on Main Street.

21. See the evening castle light show and fireworks on Main Street. A good viewing spot is somewhere between The Plaza Restaurant and Tomorrowland Terrace.

You can customize this touring plan and get real-time updates while you're in the park! See **touringplans.com** for details. **Suggested start times for FastPass+ reservations:** Big Thunder Mountain Railroad: 10:30 a.m.; Peter Pan's Flight, noon; The Haunted Mansion, 1 p.m. Check for FastPass+ reservations for *Wishes* fireworks after you've used your first three FastPasses or after 4 p.m. (whichever is later).

The Magic Kingdom

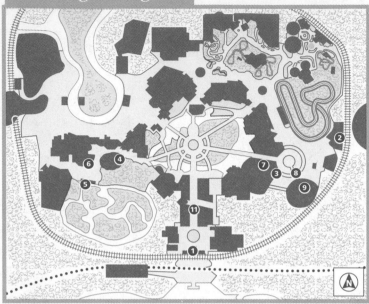

MAGIC KINGDOM TWO-DAY TOURING PLAN FOR ADULTS: DAY TWO
(Note that Day Two does not require FastPass+.)

1. Arrive at the Magic Kingdom entrance 50 minutes (Disney resort guests) to 70 minutes (non–Disney resort guests) before opening. Get guide maps and the *Times Guide*.

2. In Tomorrowland, ride Space Mountain.

3. Ride Buzz Lightyear's Space Ranger Spin.

4. In Adventureland, explore the Swiss Family Treehouse.

5. Take the Jungle Cruise. (If you want to ride Splash Mountain and/or Big Thunder Mountain Railroad again today, make FastPass+ reservations for sometime in the afternoon.)

6. See *Walt Disney's Enchanted Tiki Room.*

7. Return to Tomorrowland to see *Monsters, Inc. Laugh Floor.*

8. Ride the Tomorrowland Transit Authority PeopleMover.

9. See *Walt Disney's Carousel of Progress.*

10. Eat lunch.

11. Tour Main Street, U.S.A., and meet any characters who interest you (check the *Times Guide* for locations and times). Or shop, see live entertainment, or revisit favorite attractions.

You can customize this touring plan and get real-time updates while you're in the park! See **touringplans.com** for details.

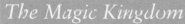

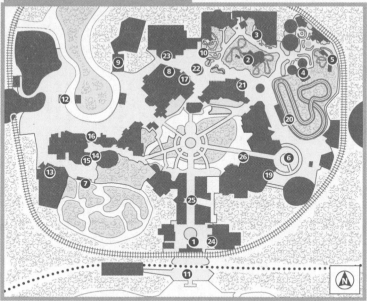

MAGIC KINGDOM DUMBO-OR-DIE-IN-A-DAY TOURING PLAN
FOR PARENTS WITH SMALL CHILDREN
(Review the Small-Child Fright-Potential Chart on pages 404–407.
Interrupt the plan for meals, rest, and a cocktail or two.)

1. Arrive at the Magic Kingdom entrance 50 minutes (Disney resort guests) to 70 minutes (non–Disney resort guests) before opening. Rent strollers before the park opens. Get guide maps and the *Times Guide*.

2. As soon as the park opens, head to Fantasyland and ride Seven Dwarfs Mine Train.

3. Ride Under the Sea: Journey of the Little Mermaid.

4. Ride Dumbo the Flying Elephant. Ride again. (*Tip:* Stand in line about 48 people behind the other parent and child. When the first parent is done riding, hand the child to the second parent in line.)

5. Ride The Barnstormer.

6. In Tomorrowland, ride the Astro Orbiter.

7. Take the Jungle Cruise in Adventureland.

8. Return to Fantasyland to ride Peter Pan's Flight.

9. In Liberty Square, see The Haunted Mansion.

10. See *Enchanted Tales with Belle.*

11. Eat lunch and take a midday break of at least 3 hours outside the park.

12. In Frontierland, take the raft over to Tom Sawyer Island. Allow at least 30 minutes to explore the island, Fort Langhorn, and the barrel bridges.

13. In Adventureland, ride Pirates of the Caribbean.

14. Ride The Magic Carpets of Aladdin.

15. See *Walt Disney's Enchanted Tiki Room.*

16. In Frontierland, see *Country Bear Jamboree.*

17. In Fantasyland, see *Mickey's PhilharMagic.*

18. Eat dinner.

19. Ride Buzz Lightyear's Space Ranger Spin in Tomorrowland.

20. Take a spin on the Tomorrowland Speedway.

21. Back in Fantasyland, ride The Many Adventures of Winnie the Pooh.

22. Ride the Prince Charming Regal Carrousel.

23. Ride It's a Small World.

24. Meet Mickey Mouse at Town Square Theater on Main Street.

25. See the evening parade on Main Street.

26. See the evening castle light show and fireworks on Main Street. A good viewing spot is somewhere between The Plaza Restaurant and Tomorrowland Terrace.

You can customize this touring plan and get real-time updates while you're in the park! See **touringplans.com** for details. **Suggested start times for FastPass+ reservations:** Seven Dwarfs Mine Train, 9 a.m.; Peter Pan's Flight, 10 a.m.; *Enchanted Tales with Belle*, 11 a.m.

    Once you've used those three FastPass+ reservations, you'll be able to make additional FastPass+ reservations at an in-park FastPass+ kiosk. **Our recommendations for day-of FastPass+ reservations:** Make a Pirates of the Caribbean FastPass+ reservation for around 3:30 p.m. Make a Haunted Mansion reservation for around 6 p.m. After you've used your last FastPass, check for FastPass+ reservations for *Wishes* fireworks.

Epcot

EPCOT ONE-DAY TOURING PLAN FOR ADULTS

1. Arrive 40 minutes before opening. Get guide maps and the *Times Guide*.

2. As soon as the park opens, ride Soarin' in The Land.

3. Ride Living with the Land.

4. In Future World East, ride Test Track.

5. Ride Sum of All Thrills.

6. Ride Mission: Space (Orange).

7. Experience *Ellen's Energy Adventure*.

8. Eat lunch (we recommend Sunshine Seasons in The Land).

9. Ride Spaceship Earth.

10. See The Seas with Nemo & Friends and *Turtle Talk with Crush*.

11. In the Imagination! Pavilion, experience Journey into Imagination with Figment.

12. Tour Mexico and ride the Gran Fiesta Tour.

13. Try the new Frozen Ever After boat ride and visit the stave church in Norway.

14. Play a game of Agent P's World Showcase Adventure. Sign up between the Mexico and Norway Pavilions.

15. Tour China and watch *Reflections of China*.

16. Tour Germany.

17. Visit Italy.

18. See *The American Adventure*.

19. Eat dinner.

20. Explore Japan.

21. Tour Morocco.

22. Visit France and see *Impressions de France*.

23. Tour the United Kingdom.

24. Tour Canada and see *O Canada!*

25. See *IllumiNations*: Prime viewing spots are along the lagoon between Canada and France. You could also try for a lagoon-side table at La Cantina de San Angel or La Hacienda de San Angel in Mexico (Advance Reservations needed at the latter), or Spice Road Table in Morocco.

You can customize this touring plan and get real-time updates while you're in the park! See **touringplans .com** for details. **Suggested start times for FastPass+ reservations:** Test Track, 9:15 a.m.; Mission: Space (Orange), 10:15 a.m.; Frozen Ever After, 3 p.m. Check for FastPass+ reservations for *IllumiNations* after you've used your first three FastPasses or after 3 p.m. (whichever is later).

EPCOT AUTHORS' SELECTIVE ONE-DAY TOURING PLAN FOR ADULTS

1. Arrive 40 minutes before opening. Get guide maps and the *Times Guide*.
2. As soon as the park opens, ride Soarin' in The Land.
3. Ride Living with the Land.
4. In Future World East, ride Test Track.
5. Ride Sum of All Thrills.
6. Ride Mission: Space (Orange).
7. Experience *Ellen's Energy Adventure*.
8. Eat lunch (we recommend Sunshine Seasons in The Land).
9. Ride Spaceship Earth.
10. See The Seas with Nemo & Friends and *Turtle Talk with Crush*.
11. Tour Mexico and ride the Gran Fiesta Tour.
12. Try the new Frozen Ever After boat ride and visit the stave church in Norway.
13. Play a game of Agent P's World Showcase Adventure. Sign up between the Mexico and Norway Pavilions.

14. Tour China and watch *Reflections of China*.
15. Tour Germany.
16. Visit Italy.
17. See *The American Adventure*.
18. Eat dinner.
19. Explore Japan.
20. Tour Morocco.
21. Visit France and see *Impressions de France*.
22. Tour the United Kingdom.
23. Tour Canada and see *O Canada!*
24. See *IllumiNations*. Prime viewing spots are along the lagoon between Canada and France. You could also try for a lagoon-side table at La Cantina de San Angel or La Hacienda de San Angel in Mexico (Advance Reservations needed at the latter), or Spice Road Table in Morocco.

You can customize this touring plan and get real-time updates while you're in the park! See **touringplans .com** for details. **Suggested start times for FastPass+ reservations:** Test Track, 9:30 a.m.; Mission: Space (Orange), 10:30 a.m.; Frozen Ever After, 2:45 p.m. Check for FastPass+ reservations for *IllumiNations* after you've used your first three three FastPasses or after 3 p.m. (whichever is later).

Epcot

Epcot

EPCOT ONE-DAY TOURING PLAN FOR PARENTS WITH SMALL CHILDREN

(Review the Small-Child Fright-Potential Chart on pages 404–407.)

1. Arrive 40 minutes before opening. Rent strollers if needed. Get guide maps and the *Times Guide*.

2. As soon as the park opens, head to the Epcot Character Spot in Innoventions West.

3. Ride Soarin' in The Land.

4. See *The Circle of Life*.

5. In the Imagination! Pavilion, experience Journey into Imagination with Figment.

6. Ride Spaceship Earth.

7. Eat lunch and take a midday break back at your hotel.

8. Experience *Ellen's Energy Adventure*.

9. See The Seas with Nemo & Friends and *Turtle Talk with Crush*.

10. Ride Living with the Land.

11. Tour Mexico and ride the Gran Fiesta Tour.

12. Try the new Frozen Ever After boat rice and visit the stave church in Norway.

13. Play a game of Agent P's World Showcase Adventure. Sign up between the Mexico and Norway Pavilions.

14. Eat dinner.

15. See *The American Adventure*.

16. Tour Canada and see *O Canada!*

17. See *IllumiNations*. Prime viewing spots are along the lagoon between Canada and France. You could also try for a lagoon-side table at La Cantina de San Angel or La Hacienda de San Angel in Mexico (Advance Reservations needed at the latter), or Spice Road Table in Morocco.

You can customize this touring plan and get real-time updates while you're in the park! See **touringplans .com** for details. **Suggested start times for FastPass+ reservations:** Soarin', 9 a.m.; Spaceship Earth, 11 a.m.; Frozen Ever After, 6 p.m. Check for FastPass+ reservations for *IllumiNations* after you've used your first three FastPasses or after 6 p.m. (whichever is later).

Epcot

EPCOT TWO–DAY EARLY–RISER TOURING PLAN: DAY ONE

*(Parents with young children should review the
Small–Child Fright–Potential Chart on pages 404–407.)*

1. Arrive 40 minutes before opening. Rent strollers if needed. Get guide maps and the *Times Guide*.

2. As soon as the park opens, see The Seas with Nemo & Friends and *Turtle Talk with Crush*.

3. In the Imagination! Pavilion, experience Journey into Imagination with Figment.

4. Ride Soarin' in The Land.

5. See *The Circle of Life*.

6. Eat lunch (we recommend Sunshine Seasons in The Land).

7. Ride Living with the Land.

8. Tour Mexico and ride the Gran Fiesta Tour.

9. Try the new Frozen Ever After boat ride and visit the stave church in Norway.

10. Watch *Reflections of China*.

11. Tour Germany.

12. Visit Italy.

13. See *The American Adventure*.

14. Explore Japan.

You can customize this touring plan and get real-time updates while you're in the park! See **touringplans .com** for details. **Suggested start times for FastPass+ reservations: Soarin'**, 10 a.m.; Living with the Land, 12:15 p.m.; Frozen Ever After, 1 p.m. If you're staying for *IllumiNations*, check for FastPass+ reservations after you've used your first three FastPasses or after 1:30 p.m. (whichever is later).

Epcot

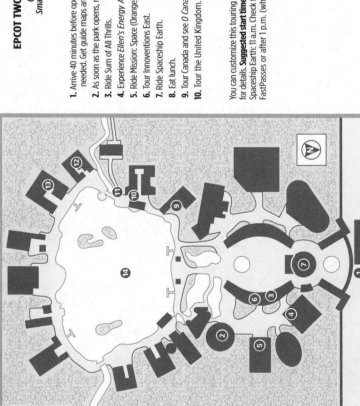

EPCOT TWO-DAY EARLY-RISER TOURING PLAN: DAY TWO

(Parents with young children should review the Small-Child Fright-Potential Chart on pages 404–407.)

1. Arrive 40 minutes before opening. Rent strollers if needed. Get guide maps and the *Times Guide.*

2. As soon as the park opens, ride Test Track.

3. Ride Sum of All Thrills.

4. Experience *Ellen's Energy Adventure.*

5. Ride Mission: Space (Orange).

6. Tour Innoventions East.

7. Ride Spaceship Earth.

8. Eat lunch.

9. Tour Canada and see *O Canada!*

10. Tour the United Kingdom.

11. Play Agent P's World Showcase Adventure. Sign up between the UK and France Pavilions.

12. Visit France and see *Impressions de France.*

13. Tour Morocco.

14. See *IllumiNations.* Prime viewing spots are along the lagoon between Canada and France. You could also try for a lagoon-side table at La Cantina de San Angel or La Hacienda de San Angel in Mexico (Advance Reservations needed at the latter), or Spice Road Table in Morocco.

You can customize this touring plan and get real-time updates while you're in the park! See **touringplans.com** for details. **Suggested start times for FastPass+ reservations:** Test Track, 9 a.m.; Mission: Space (Orange), 10 a.m.; Spaceship Earth: 11 a.m. Check for FastPass+ reservations for *IllumiNations* after you've used your first three FastPasses or after 1 p.m. (whichever is later).

Disney's Animal Kingdom

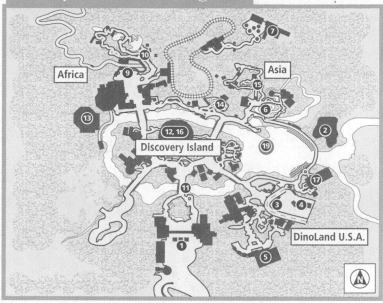

DISNEY'S ANIMAL KINGDOM ONE-DAY TOURING PLAN

1. Arrive 30–40 minutes prior to opening. Get guide maps and the *Times Guide*.

2. Experience Expedition Everest in Asia.

3. In DinoLand U.S.A., ride TriceraTop Spin if you have young children in your group.

4. Ride Primeval Whirl.

5. Follow the signs to Dinosaur and ride.

6. Ride Kali River Rapids in Asia.

7. Take the Wildlife Express Train from Africa to Conservation Station and Rafiki's Planet Watch. Tour the area and take the train back to Africa.

8. Eat lunch.

9. Ride Kilimanjaro Safaris in Africa.

10. Walk the Pangani Forest Exploration Trail.

11. Earn a couple of badges playing Wilderness Explorers.

12. Explore the trails and exhibits around The Tree of Life.

13. See *Festival of the Lion King* in Africa.

14. See *Flights of Wonder*.

15. Walk the Maharajah Jungle Trek in Asia.

16. See *It's Tough to Be a Bug!* on Discovery Island.

17. See *Finding Nemo—The Musical* in DinoLand U.S.A.

18. Eat dinner.

19. See *Rivers of Light* in Asia.

You can customize this touring plan and get real-time updates while you're in the park! See **touringplans.com** for details. **Suggested start times for FastPass+ reservations:** Dinosaur, 9 a.m.; Kali River Rapids, 10 a.m.; Kilimanjaro Safaris, 12:15 p.m.

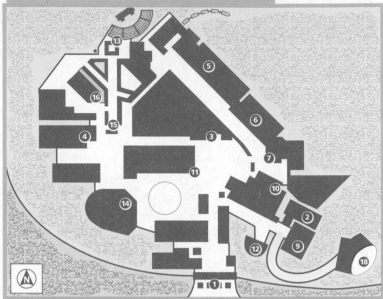

DISNEY'S HOLLYWOOD STUDIOS ONE-DAY TOURING PLAN

1. Arrive at the park 30–40 minutes before official opening time. Get guide maps and the *Times Guide*.

2. As soon as the park opens, ride Rock 'n' Roller Coaster.

3. Ride The Great Movie Ride.

4. In Echo Lake, ride Star Tours—The Adventures Continue.

5. Ride Toy Story Midway Mania! in Pixar Place.

6. See *Walt Disney: One Man's Dream*.

7. See *Voyage of the Little Mermaid*.

8. Eat lunch.

9. Ride The Twilight Zone Tower of Terror.

10. Work in *Disney Junior—Live on Stage!* if you have small children.

11. Participate in *For the First Time In Forever: A Frozen Sing-Along Celebration*.

12. See *Beauty and the Beast—Live on Stage*.

13. See the *Lights, Motors, Action! Extreme Stunt Show*.

14. See the *Indiana Jones Epic Stunt Spectacular!*

15. Explore the Streets of America on the way to *Jim Henson's Muppet-Vision 3-D*.

16. See *Muppet-Vision 3-D*.

17. Eat dinner.

18. Enjoy *Fantasmic!* Plan on arriving about 1 hour early to get good seats, or 30 minutes early for standing room only.

You can customize this touring plan and get real-time updates while you're in the park! See **touringplans.com** for details. **Suggested FastPass+ reservation times:** Star Tours, 9 a.m.; Toy Story Midway Mania!, 10 a.m.; Twilight Zone Tower of Terror, noon. Check for FastPass+ reservations for *Fantasmic!* after you've used your first three FastPasses or you've visited all attractions.

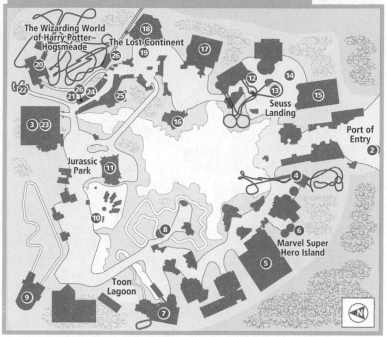

Universal's Islands of Adventure

UNIVERSAL'S ISLANDS OF ADVENTURE ONE-DAY TOURING PLAN

1. Buy your admission in advance and call ☎ 407-363-8000 the day before your visit for the official opening time.

2. Arrive at IOA 75–90 minutes before the official opening time if Early Park Admission is offered and you're eligible, or 30–45 minutes before opening for day guests. Get a park map as soon as you enter.

3. Early-entry guests should ride Harry Potter and the Forbidden Journey. Ride Flight of the Hippogriff and Dragon Challenge as well if you have time.

4. Exit Hogsmeade before early entry ends, and head to Marvel Super Hero Island to ride The Incredible Hulk Coaster. Guests without early entry should start at this step.

5. Ride The Amazing Adventures of Spider-Man.

6. Backtrack to ride Doctor Doom's Fearfall.

7. Continue clockwise and ride Dudley Do-Right's Ripsaw Falls in Toon Lagoon.

8. Ride Popeye & Bluto's Bilge-Rat Barges.

9. Take the Jurassic Park River Adventure.

10. Explore Camp Jurassic.

11. Check out the exhibits in the Jurassic Park Discovery Center.

12. Cross the bridge bypassing Hogsmeade to Lost Continent, and ride the High in the Sky Seuss Trolley Train Ride! in Seuss Landing.

13. Ride the Caro-Seuss-el.

14. Ride One Fish, Two Fish, Red Fish, Blue Fish.

15. Ride The Cat in the Hat.

16. Return to Lost Continent and eat lunch at Mythos.

17. Experience *Poseidon's Fury*.

18. See the next scheduled performance of *The Eighth Voyage of Sindbad Stunt Show*.

19. Chat with the Mystic Fountain before or after the *Sindbad* show.

20. Enter The Wizarding World of Harry Potter–Hogsmeade, and ride Dragon Challenge, or walk through the queue to see the Triwizard Tournament artifacts.

21. See the *Frog Choir* or *Triwizard Spirit Rally* perform on the small stage outside Hogwarts.

22. Ride Flight of the Hippogriff.

23. Ride Harry Potter and the Forbidden Journey. If the wait is more than 30 minutes, request a castle tour to experience the queue, and then use the single-rider line.

24. See the wand ceremony at Ollivanders and buy a wand if you wish.

25. Have dinner at Three Broomsticks.

26. See the stage show you didn't see earlier. Pose for a picture with the Hogwarts Express conductor, and explore the shops and interactive windows around Hogsmeade. Sample (or at least smell) some sweets at Honeydukes.

27. Revisit any favorite attractions, or remain in Hogsmeade until closing, enjoying the atmosphere.

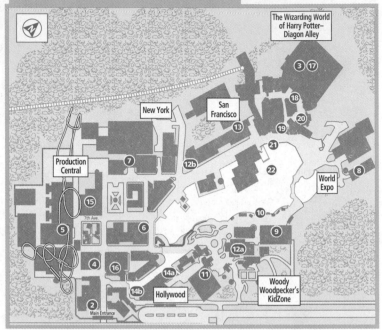

Universal Studios Florida

UNIVERSAL STUDIOS FLORIDA ONE-DAY TOURING PLAN FOR ADULTS
(Assumes: Day guest without Universal Express; 1-Day Base Ticket)

1. Buy your admission in advance and call ☎ 407-363-8000 the day before your visit for the official opening time.

2. Arrive at USF 90–120 minutes before the official opening time if Early Park Admission is offered and you're eligible, or 30–45 minutes before opening for day guests. Get a park map as soon as you enter.

3. Early-entry guests should ride Harry Potter and the Escape from Gringotts if it's operating. If it's not, enjoy the rest of Diagon Alley but don't get in line.

4. Before early entry ends, hotel guests should exit Diagon Alley and ride Despicable Me Minion Mayhem. Day guests should wait in the front lot until permitted to ride Despicable Me.

5. Ride Hollywood Rip Ride Rockit.

6. Experience Transformers: The Ride 3-D.

7. Ride Revenge of the Mummy in New York.

8. Ride Men in Black Alien Attack in World Expo.

9. Ride The Simpsons Ride.

10. Ride Kang & Kodos' Twirl 'n' Hurl if 50 or fewer people are in line.

11. Ride E.T. Adventure in Woody the Woodpecker's KidZone.

12. Work in *Animal Actors on Location* **(12a)** and *Beetlejuice Graveyard Revue* **(12b)** around lunch (we recommend Fast Food Boulevard), according to the daily entertainment schedule. If you're running behind, skip *Animal Actors*.

13. Experience *Disaster!* in San Francisco.

14. See *Universal Orlando's Horror Make-Up Show* **(14a)** and *Terminator 2: 3-D* **(14b)** according to the daily entertainment schedule.

15. See *TWISTER . . . Ride It Out* in New York.

16. See *Shrek 4-D* in Production Central.

17. By this time, you should be able to enter Diagon Alley without waiting, even on busy days. Ride Harry Potter and the Escape from Gringotts. If this is your first ride, take the standby queue. For re-rides, use the single-rider line. The Gringotts queue may close before the rest of the park if the posted wait time exceeds remaining operating hours by more than 60 minutes.

18. See the wand ceremony at Ollivanders and buy a wand if you wish.

19. Tour Diagon Alley. Browse the shops, explore the dark recesses of Knockturn Alley, and discover the interactive effects. If you're hungry, try the Leaky Cauldron or Florean Fortescue's Ice Cream Parlour.

20. See the *Celestina Warbeck* and *Tales of Beedle the Bard* shows.

21. Chat with the Knight Bus conductor and his shrunken head. Also look for Kreacher in the window of 12 Grimmauld Place, and listen to the receiver in the red phone booth.

22. If scheduled, see *Universal's Cinematic Spectacular* from Central Park (directly across the lagoon from Richter's), Duff Brewery, or the embankment in front of London.

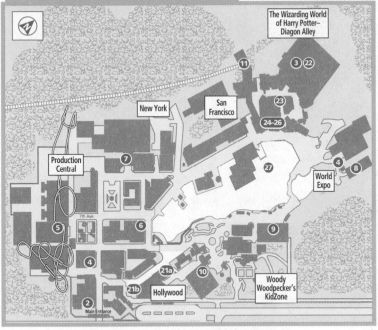

Universal Studios Florida

THE BEST OF UNIVERSAL STUDIOS FLORIDA AND ISLANDS OF ADVENTURE IN ONE DAY
(Assumes: 1-Day Park-to-Park Ticket)

1. Buy your admission in advance; call ☎ 407-363-8000 the day before your visit for the official opening time.

2. Arrive at USF 90–120 minutes before the official opening time if Early Park Admission is offered and you're eligible, or 30–45 minutes before opening for day guests. Line up at the shortest open turnstile, and get a park map as soon as you enter. **Alternative:** If only IOA is open for Early Park Admission and you're eligible, arrive at IOA's turnstiles 75–90 minutes before the official opening time. Ride Harry Potter and the Forbidden Journey. Ride Flight of the Hippogriff and Dragon Challenge as well if you have time. Take the Hogwarts Express to King's Cross Station before USF officially opens for the day, and continue at the next step.

3. Early-entry guests should ride Harry Potter and the Escape from Gringotts if it is operating. If Gringotts is not operating, enjoy the rest of Diagon Alley but don't get in line.

4. Before early entry ends, hotel guests should exit Diagon Alley and ride Despicable Me Minion Mayhem. Day guests should wait in the front lot until permitted to ride Despicable Me.

5. Ride Hollywood Rip Ride Rockit.

6. Experience Transformers: The Ride 3-D in Production Central.

7. Ride Revenge of the Mummy in New York.

8. Ride Men in Black Alien Attack in World Expo.

9. Ride The Simpsons Ride.

10. Ride E.T. Adventure in Woody Woodpecker's KidZone.

11. Ride Hogwarts Express from King's Cross Station to IOA. Have your Park-to-Park ticket ready.

(Continued on next page)

Universal's Islands of Adventure

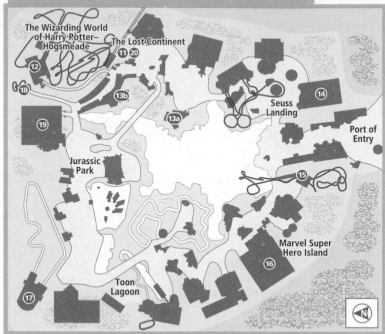

**THE BEST OF UNIVERSAL STUDIOS FLORIDA AND
ISLANDS OF ADVENTURE IN ONE DAY**
(Continued from previous page)

12. Ride Dragon Challenge in The Wizarding World of Harry Potter–Hogsmeade.

13. Eat lunch at Mythos in Lost Continent (**13a**) or Three Broomsticks in Hogsmeade (**13b**).

14. Ride The Cat in the Hat in Seuss Landing.

15. Ride The Incredible Hulk Coaster on Marvel Super Hero Island.

16. Ride The Amazing Adventures of Spider-Man.

17. Continue clockwise through Toon Lagoon, and take the Jurassic Park River Adventure.

18. Enter Hogsmeade, and ride Flight of the Hippogriff if the wait isn't too long.

19. Ride Harry Potter and the Forbidden Journey. If the wait is more than 30 minutes, request a castle tour to experience the queue, and then use the single-rider line.

20. Return to Universal Studios Florida using the Hogwarts Express from Hogsmeade Station, or walk back to the other park if the posted wait exceeds 20 minutes.

See map on previous page for the following steps.

21. See the next showing of *Universal Orlando's Horror Make-Up Show* (**21a**) upon returning to USF. If the remaining *Horror Make-Up* show-times aren't convenient, substitute with *Terminator 2: 3-D* (**21b**).

22. By this time, you should be able to enter Diagon Alley without waiting, even on busy days. Ride Harry Potter and the Escape from Gringotts. If this is your first ride, take the standby queue. For re-rides, use the single-rider line. The Gringotts queue may close before the rest of the park if the posted wait time exceeds remaining operating hours by more than 60 minutes.

23. See the wand ceremony at Ollivanders and buy a wand if you wish.

24. Tour Diagon Alley. Browse the shops, explore the dark recesses of Knockturn Alley, and discover the interactive effects. If you're hungry, try the Leaky Cauldron or Florean Fortescue's Ice Cream Parlour.

25. See the *Celestina Warbeck* and *Tales of Beedle the Bard* shows.

26. Chat with the Knight Bus conductor and his shrunken head. Also look for Kreacher in the window of 12 Grimmauld Place, and listen to the receiver in the red phone booth.

27. If scheduled, watch *Universal's Cinematic Spectacular* from Central Park (directly across the lagoon from Richter's), Duff Brewery, or the embankment in front of London.

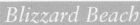

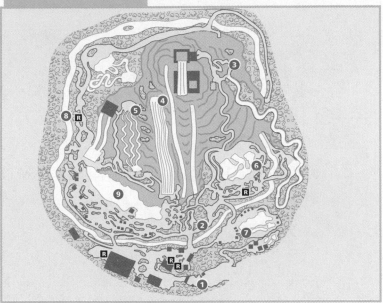

BLIZZARD BEACH ONE-DAY TOURING PLAN
FOR PARENTS WITH SMALL CHILDREN

1. Arrive at the park entrance 30 minutes before opening. Take care of locker and towel rentals at Lottawatta Lodge, to your left as you enter the park. Find a spot to stow the remainder of your gear, noting any nearby landmarks to help you find your way back.

2. Take the chairlift up Mount Gushmore to the Green Slope. *Note:* It might be faster—but more tiring—to walk to the top.

3. Raft down Teamboat Springs. Repeat as much as you like while the park is still uncrowded.

4. If your kids are up for it, try the Toboggan Racers.

5. If the kids enjoyed the Toboggan Racers, try the Snow Stormers next.

6. Visit the Ski Patrol Training Camp.

7. Ride Tike's Peak.

8. Grab some tubes and ride Cross Country Creek.

9. Swim in Melt-Away Bay's Wave Pool as long as you like.

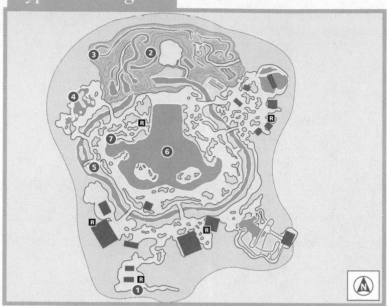

Typhoon Lagoon

TYPHOON LAGOON ONE-DAY TOURING PLAN
FOR PARENTS WITH SMALL CHILDREN

1. Arrive at the park entrance 30 minutes before opening. Take care of locker and towel rentals at Singapore Sal's, to your right after you've walked along the winding entrance path and emerged into the park. Find a spot to stow the remainder of your gear, noting any nearby landmarks to help you find your way back.

2. Ride Gangplank Falls as many times as you like.

3. If your kids enjoyed Gangplank Falls, try Keelhaul Falls if it seems appropriate.

4. Enjoy the Ketchakiddee Creek kids' play area.

5. Grab some tubes and ride Castaway Creek. A complete circuit takes 20–25 minutes.

6. Swim in the Surf Pool as long as you like.

7. Ride the Bay Slides in the Surf Pool.

8. Repeat your favorite attractions as desired.

MAGIC KINGDOM TOURING PLAN COMPANION

ATTRACTION | RECOMMENDED VISITATION TIMES | AUTHORS' RATING

Ariel's Grotto *(FastPass+)* | Before 10:30 a.m., in the 2 hours before closing, FastPass+ | ★★★

Astro Orbiter | Before 11 a.m., in the hour before closing | ★★

The Barnstormer *(FastPass+)* | Before 11 a.m., during parades, in the 2 hours before closing, FastPass+ | ★★

Big Thunder Mountain Railroad *(FastPass+)* | Before 10 a.m., in the hour before closing, FastPass+ | ★★★★
   Special comments 40" minimum height; expectant mothers should not ride

Buzz Lightyear's Space Ranger Spin *(FastPass+)* | First or last hour the park is open, FastPass+ | ★★★★

Captain Jack Sparrow's Pirate Tutorial | Check *Times Guide* for showtimes | ★★★½

Casey Jr. Splash 'N' Soak Station | Anytime | ★½

Country Bear Jamboree | Anytime | ★★★½

Dumbo the Flying Elephant *(FastPass+)* | Before 10 a.m., after 3 p.m., FastPass+ | ★★★½

Enchanted Tales with Belle *(FastPass+)* | At opening, in the 2 hours before closing, FastPass+ | ★★★★

Frontierland Shootin' Arcade | Anytime | ★½

The Hall of Presidents | Anytime | ★★★½

The Haunted Mansion | Before 11 a.m., in the 2 hours before closing | ★★★★ | *Special comment* Fright potential

It's a Small World *(FastPass+)* | Before 11 a.m., during parades, after 7 p.m., FastPass+ | ★★★½

Jungle Cruise *(FastPass+)* | Before 10:30 a.m., in the 2 hours before closing, FastPass+ | ★★★

Liberty Belle **Riverboat** | Anytime | ★★½

Mad Tea Party *(FastPass+)* | Before 11 a.m., after 5 p.m., FastPass+ | ★★ | *Special comments* Expectant mothers should not ride; motion-sickness potential

The Magic Carpets of Aladdin *(FastPass+)* | Before 11 a.m., after 7 p.m., FastPass+ | ★★½

The Many Adventures of Winnie the Pooh *(FastPass+)* | Before 10 a.m., in the hour before closing, FastPass+
   ★★★½

Meet Merida at Fairytale Gardens | Check *Times Guide* for schedule | ★★★½

Mickey's PhilharMagic *(FastPass+)* | Before 11 a.m., during parades, FastPass+ | ★★★★

Monsters, Inc. Laugh Floor *(FastPass+)* | Before 11 a.m., after 4 p.m., FastPass+ | ★★★½

Peter Pan's Flight *(FastPass+)* | First or last 30 minutes the park is open, FastPass+ | ★★★★

Pete's Silly Sideshow *(FastPass+)* | Before 11 a.m., in the 2 hours before closing, FastPass+ | ★★★½

A Pirate's Adventure: Treasure of the Seven Seas | Anytime | ★★★½

Pirates of the Caribbean *(closed through September 2015 for refurbishment)*
   Before 11 a.m., after 7 p.m. | ★★★★

Prince Charming Regal Carrousel | Before 11 a.m., after 8 p.m. | ★★★

Princess Fairytale Hall | Before 10:30 a.m., after 4 p.m. | ★★

Seven Dwarfs Mine Train *(FastPass+)* | At park opening, FastPass+ | ★★★★

Sorcerers of the Magic Kingdom | Before 11 a.m., after 8 p.m. | ★★★

Space Mountain *(FastPass+)* | At opening, FastPass+ | ★★★★ | *Special comments* 44" minimum height; expectant mothers should not ride

Splash Mountain *(FastPass+)* | At opening, during parades, just before closing, FastPass+ | ★★★★★
   Special comments 40" minimum height; expectant mothers should not ride

Stitch's Great Escape! | Before 11 a.m., during parades, after 6 p.m. | ★★★ | *Special comments* Fright potential; 40" minimum height

Swiss Family Treehouse | Anytime | ★★★ | *Special comments* Fright potential due to height

Tom Sawyer Island and Fort Langhorn | Midmorning–late afternoon | ★★★

Tomorrowland Speedway *(FastPass+)* | Before 10 a.m., in the 2 hours before closing, FastPass+ | ★★
   Special comment 54" minimum height requirement for kids to drive unassisted

Tomorrowland Transit Authority PeopleMover | Anytime, but especially during hot, crowded times of day
   (11:30 a.m.–4:30 p.m.) | ★★★½

Town Square Theater Meet and Greets *(FastPass+)* | Before 10 a.m., after 4 p.m., FastPass+ | ★★★★

Under the Sea: Journey of the Little Mermaid *(FastPass+)* | Before 10:30 a.m., in the 2 hours before closing, FastPass+ | ★★★½

Walt Disney's Carousel of Progress | Anytime | ★★★

Walt Disney's Enchanted Tiki Room | Before 11 a.m., after 3:30 p.m. | ★★★½

Walt Disney World Railroad | Anytime | ★★½

DINING INFORMATION—Counter Service
RESTAURANT | LOCATION | QUALITY | VALUE | SELECTIONS

Aloha Isle | Adventureland | Excellent | B+ | Dole Whip soft-serve, ice-cream floats, fresh pineapple spears, soft drinks

Be Our Guest Restaurant | Fantasyland | Excellent | B+ | *Breakfast:* cured meats and cheeses, open-faced bacon-and-egg sandwich with Brie, fried doughnuts. *Lunch:* Tuna niçoise salad, *croque monsieur* (grilled ham-and-cheese sandwich), carved turkey or roast beef sandwich, braised pork with bacon mashed potatoes, veggie quiche, quinoa salad

Casey's Corner | Main Street, U.S.A. | Good | B | Hot dogs, corn-dog nuggets, fries

Columbia Harbour House | Liberty Square | Good | B | Grilled salmon, fried fish and shrimp, chicken nuggets, sandwiches, clam chowder, chili, salads, kids' meals

Cosmic Ray's Starlight Cafe | Tomorrowland | Good | B | Burgers (veggie available), rotisserie chicken, hot dogs, Greek salad, chicken nuggets, barbecue-pork sandwich; some kosher

Friar's Nook | Fantasyland | Good | B | Hot dogs, specialty mac and cheese (bacon cheeseburger, beef pot roast), homemade potato chips, chicken Caesar salad, frozen drinks

Gaston's Tavern | Fantasyland | Good | C | Roast pork shank, hummus with chips, cinnamon rolls, chocolate croissants, LeFou's Brew (frozen apple-juice drink)

Golden Oak Outpost | Frontierland | Good | B+ | Waffle fries with various toppings (e.g., barbecue pork), sweet potato nuggets with powdered sugar

The Lunching Pad | Tomorrowland | Good | B– | Hot dogs, dessert pretzels, frozen sodas

Pecos Bill Tall Tale Inn & Cafe | Frontierland | Good | B | Burgers, barbecue-pork or grilled-chicken sandwich, chili, fries (plain and chili-cheese), Southwest chicken salad, kids' meals

The Pinocchio Village Haus | Fantasyland | Fair | C | Flatbread pizzas, Italian flatbread sub, chicken nuggets, salads, kids' meals

Tomorrowland Terrace Restaurant *(open seasonally)* | Tomorrowland | Fair | C | Burgers, lobster roll, chicken nuggets, pasta, salads, kids' meals

Tortuga Tavern *(open seasonally)* | Adventureland | Fair | B | Taco salad, nachos, chicken Caesar salad, burritos, kids' meals

DINING INFORMATION—Full Service
RESTAURANT | MEALS SERVED | LOCATION | PRICE | QUALITY | VALUE

Be Our Guest Restaurant | D | Fantasyland | Moderate | ★★★★ | ★★★★
Selections Pan-seared salmon, New York strip, grilled strip steak with *pommes frites*

Cinderella's Royal Table | B-L-D | Fantasyland | Expensive | ★★★ | ★★
Selections French toast, crepes (breakfast); pan-seared cod, slow-roasted pork loin, grilled swordfish (lunch and dinner); kids' menu

The Crystal Palace | B-L-D | Main Street, U.S.A. | Moderate | ★★★½ | ★★★
Selections Buffet (items change often); *best dining value in the Magic Kingdom*

Liberty Tree Tavern | L-D | Liberty Square | Moderate | ★★★ | ★★★
Selections Roasted meats, sandwiches, salads; all-you-can-eat family-style dinner

The Plaza Restaurant | L-D | Main Street, U.S.A. | Moderate | ★★ | ★★
Selections Old-fashioned diner and ice-cream shop: sandwiches, salads, sundaes, kids' menu

Tony's Town Square Restaurant | L-D | Main Street, U.S.A. | Moderate | ★★★ | ★★
Selections Sausage-and-pepper flatbread, pasta (gluten-free and whole-grain options), New York strip

Advance Reservations recommended for Magic Kingdom full-service restaurants; call
☎ *407-WDW-DINE (939-3463) or visit disneyworld.disney.go.com/reservations/dining.*

GOOD REST AREAS IN THE MAGIC KINGDOM
LOCATION | PLACE | NOTES

Back of Storybook Circus, between Big Top Treats and the train station | Fantasyland
Covered plush seating with electrical outlets and USB charging stations.

Covered porch with rocking chairs on Tom Sawyer Island | Frontierland
Across the water from the *Liberty Belle* Riverboat dock; bring refreshments from Frontierland; closes at sunset

Cul-de-sac | Main Street, U.S.A. | Between the china shop and Main Street's Starbucks on right-hand side of street as you face the castle; nearby refreshments

Picnic tables | Fantasyland | Near the *Tangled*-themed restrooms, between Peter Pan's Flight and The Haunted Mansion. Outdoors but has phone-charging stations.

Quiet seating area | Tomorrowland | Near restrooms on the right as you approach Space Mountain—look for pay phones, and there's a covered seating area farther back of that corridor; refreshments nearby

Second floor of train station | Main Street, U.S.A. | Refreshments nearby; crowded during fireworks and parades

Upstairs at Columbia Harbour House | Liberty Square | Grab a beverage and relax upstairs.
Restrooms available upstairs, too.

EPCOT **TOURING PLAN COMPANION**

ATTRACTION | LOCATION | RECOMMENDED VISITATION TIMES | AUTHORS' RATING

Agent P's World Showcase Adventure | World Showcase, various pavilions | Anytime | ★★★★

The American Adventure | United States, World Showcase | Anytime | ★★★★

Captain EO (FastPass+) | Imagination! Pavilion, Future World | Anytime | ★★★

The Circle of Life | The Land, Future World | Anytime | ★★★½

Epcot Character Spot *(FastPass+)* | Innoventions West, Future World | Before 11 a.m., FastPass+ | ★★★

Gran Fiesta Tour | Mexico, World Showcase | Before noon, after 5 p.m. | ★★½

Impressions de France | France, World Showcase | Anytime | ★★★½

Innoventions East and West | Future World | Second day or after major attractions | ★★½

Journey into Imagination with Figment *(FastPass+)* | Imagination!, Future World | Anytime | ★★½

Living with the Land *(FastPass+)* | The Land, Future World | Before 11 a.m., after 1 p.m., FastPass+ | ★★★★

Mission: Space *(FastPass+)* | Future World | First hour the park is open, FastPass+ | ★★★★
   Special comments 44" minimum height; expectant mothers should not ride; motion-sickness potential

The "Mom, I Can't Believe It's Disney!" Fountains | Future World | When it's hot | ★★★★

O Canada! | Canada, World Showcase | Anytime | ★★★½

Reflections of China | China, World Showcase | Anytime | ★★★½

The Seas Main Tank and Exhibits | The Seas with Nemo & Friends, Future World | Before 11:30 a.m., after 5 p.m. | ★★★½

The Seas with Nemo & Friends *(FastPass+)* | The Seas with Nemo & Friends, Future World Before 11 a.m., after 5 p.m.,
   FastPass+ | ★★★

Soarin' *(FastPass+)* | The Land, Future World | First 30 minutes the park is open, FastPass+ | ★★★★½
   Special comments 40" minimum height; motion-sickness potential

Spaceship Earth *(FastPass+)* | Future World | Before 10 a.m., after 4 p.m., FastPass+ | ★★★★

Sum of All Thrills | Innoventions East, Future World | Before 10:30 a.m., after 5 p.m. | ★★★★
   Special comments 48" minimum height, 54" for coaster-track designs with inversions

Test Track *(FastPass+)* | Test Track, Future World | First 30 minutes the park is open, just before closing,
   FastPass+ | ★★★★ | *Special comments* 40" minimum height; expectant mothers should not ride

Turtle Talk with Crush (FastPass+)| The Seas with Nemo & Friends, Future World | Before 11 a.m., after 5 p.m.,
   FastPass+ | ★★★★

Universe of Energy: *Ellen's Energy Adventure* | Future World | Anytime | ★★★½

DINING INFORMATION—Counter Service

RESTAURANT | LOCATION | QUALITY | VALUE | SELECTIONS

L'Artisan des Glaces | France, World Showcase | Excellent | C | Ice cream, sorbet

La Cantina de San Angel | Mexico, World Showcase | Good | B | Tacos, nachos, fried cheese empanada, margaritas,
   kids' meals

Crêpes des Chefs de France | France, World Showcase | Excellent | B+ | Dessert crepes, ice cream, beer, espresso

Electric Umbrella Restaurant | Innoventions East, Future World | Fair | B– | Burgers, chicken nuggets,
   veggie flatbread, Caesar salad with chicken, kids' meals

Fife & Drum Tavern | United States, World Showcase | Fair | C | Turkey legs, pretzels, ice cream, frozen slushes, beer

Fountain View | Future World Plaza | Fair | C | Disney-themed Starbucks with all the usual suspects: coffee drinks,
   teas, breakfast sandwiches, and pastries

Katsura Grill | Japan, World Showcase | Good | B | Beef, chicken, or salmon teriyaki; noodle bowls; sushi; miso soup;
   ice cream (green tea, azuki bean); green-tea cheesecake; beer, sake, plum wine

Kringla Bakeri og Kafe | Norway, World Showcase | Good–excellent | B | Pastries, sandwiches, vegetable torte,
   rice cream, imported beer

Les Halles Boulangerie–Pâtisserie | France, World Showcase | Good | A | Pastries, niçoise salad,
   cheese plate, sandwiches, quiches, soups

Liberty Inn | United States, World Showcase | Fair | C | Burgers, sandwiches, hot dogs, chili, chicken nuggets,
   seafood (crab cakes, shrimp and rice), New York strip steak, salads, kids' meals, some kosher

Lotus Blossom Cafe | China, World Showcase | Fair | C | Egg rolls, pot stickers, fried rice, orange chicken,
   noodle bowls

Promenade Refreshments | World Showcase Promenade | Fair | C | Hot dogs, chili dogs, frozen yogurt, beer

Refreshment Cool Post | Between Germany and China | Good | B– | Hot dogs, ice cream, the Doofenslurper
   (frozen lemonade topped with passion-fruit sorbet foam), coffee and tea, beer

Refreshment Port | Near Canada | Good | B | Croissant doughnuts, chicken nuggets, flavored coffees, hot chocolate,
   ice cream

DINING INFORMATION—Counter Service *(continued)*
RESTAURANT | LOCATION | QUALITY | VALUE | SELECTIONS

Rose & Crown Pub | United Kingdom, World Showcase | Good | C+ | Fish and chips, Scotch egg, corned beef, shepherd's pie, bangers and mash, British beers

Sommerfest | Germany, World Showcase | Good | B– | Bratwurst and frankfurter sandwiches, curried bratwurst, Reuben sandwich, baked mac and cheese, beer and wine

Sunshine Seasons | The Land, Future World | Excellent | A | Rotisserie meats; salads, sandwiches, soups; Asian noodle bowls and stir-fries; quick breakfast

Tangierine Cafe | Morocco, World Showcase | Good | B | Chicken and lamb *shawarma,* lentil and couscous salads, hummus, wraps, kids' meals, wine and beer

Yorkshire County Fish Shop | United Kingdom, World Showcase | Good | B+ | Fish and chips, shortbread, draft ale

DINING INFORMATION—Full Service
RESTAURANT | MEALS SERVED | LOCATION | PRICE | QUALITY | VALUE

Akershus Royal Banquet Hall | B-L-D | Norway, World Showcase | Expensive | ★★ | ★★★★
Selections *Koldtbord* (Norwegian buffet), pan-seared salmon, *kjottkake* (Norwegian meatballs), kids' menu

Biergarten | L-D | Germany, World Showcase | Expensive | ★★ | ★★★★
Selections Buffet with schnitzel, sausages, spaetzle, roast chicken

Le Cellier Steakhouse | L-D | Canada, World Showcase | Expensive | ★★★½ | ★★★
Selections Canadian Cheddar cheese soup, steaks, seafood

Les Chefs de France | L-D | France, World Showcase | Expensive | ★★★ | ★★★
Selections Duck breast with cherries, grilled beef tenderloin, Cabernet-braised short ribs, French onion soup

Coral Reef Restaurant | L-D | The Seas with Nemo & Friends, Future World | Expensive | ★★ | ★★
Selections Creamy lobster soup, steak and seafood, kids' menu

Garden Grill Restaurant | D | The Land, Future World | Expensive | ★★ | ★★★
Selections Beef filet, turkey with stuffing and gravy, sustainable fish of the day, kids' menu

La Hacienda de San Angel | D | Mexico, World Showcase | Expensive | ★★★½ | ★★½
Selections *Queso fundido;* corn cakes stuffed with chorizo; taco trio (pork, beef, and chicken); fried-shrimp tacos; margaritas

Monsieur Paul | D | France, World Showcase | Expensive | ★★★★½ | ★★★
Selections Black-truffle soup, red snapper in potato "scales," *pot-au-feu* of scallops, roasted duck breast

Nine Dragons Restaurant | L-D | China, World Showcase | Moderate | ★★★ | ★★
Selections Honey-sesame chicken, pot stickers, five-spiced fish, noodles, veggie stir-fry

Restaurant Marrakesh | L-D | Morocco, World Showcase | Moderate | ★★½ | ★★
Selections *Bastilla* (minced-chicken pie), shish kebabs, lemon chicken, couscous, sampler platters

Rose & Crown Dining Room | L-D | United Kingdom, World Showcase | Moderate | ★★★½ | ★★
Selections Fish and chips, bangers and mash (sausage and mashed potatoes), shepherd's pie

San Angel Inn Restaurante | L-D | Mexico, World Showcase | Expensive | ★★★ | ★★
Selections Mole poblano (chicken in chile-chocolate sauce), tacos, tostadas, quesadillas

Spice Road Table | L-D | Morocco, World Showcase | Moderate | ★★★★ | ★★★
Selections Mediterranean-style small plates; rack of lamb; beef and chicken kebabs; cocktails, wine, beer; ice cream

Teppan Edo | L-D | Japan, World Showcase | Expensive | ★★★★ | ★★★
Selections Chicken, shrimp, beef, scallops, swordfish, and veggies stir-fried on teppanyaki grill

Tokyo Dining | L-D | Japan, World Showcase | Moderate | ★★★★ | ★★★
Selections Grilled meats and seafood, tempura, sushi, and sashimi

Tutto Italia Ristorante | L-D | Italy, World Showcase | Expensive | ★★★★ | ★★★
Selections Pasta, steak, cheese polenta with braised short ribs and meatballs

Via Napoli | L-D | Italy, World Showcase | Moderate | ★★★½ | ★★★
Selections Wood-fired pizzas, pastas, salads, sandwiches; *best pizza in Walt Disney World*

Advance Reservations recommended for Epcot full-service restaurants; call ☎ 407-WDW-DINE (939-3463) or visit disneyworld.disney.go.com/reservations/dining.

GOOD REST AREAS IN EPCOT
LOCATION | PLACE | NOTES

Benches | Innoventions East and West, Future World | Air-conditioned; usually not crowded

Benches | Mexico, World Showcase | Inside the pavilion against the inside of the wall that forms the walking ramps down to the retail space; air-conditioned

Benches | The Seas with Nemo & Friends, Future World | Air-conditioned

Japan gardens =| Japan, World Showcase | To the left of Katsura Grill is a set of tables overlooking a lovely garden and koi pond. Outdoors but shaded, with refreshments nearby.

Rotunda and lobby | United States, World Showcase | Ample room; air-conditioned; refreshments nearby; usually quiet unless singers are performing

UK Rose Garden benches | United Kingdom, World Showcase | Behind the UK Pavilion is a small town square and manicured gardens; several outdoor benches are available.

DISNEY'S ANIMAL KINGDOM **TOURING PLAN COMPANION**

ATTRACTION | RECOMMENDED VISITATION TIMES | AUTHORS' RATING

The Boneyard | Anytime | ★★★

Conservation Station and Affection Section | Anytime | ★★★½

Dinosaur *(FastPass+)* | Before 10:30 a.m., after 4:30 p.m., FastPass+ | ★★★★
  Special comments Fright potential; 40" minimum height; expectant mothers should not ride

Expedition Everest *(FastPass+)* | Before 9:30 a.m., after 3 p.m. | ★★★★½
  Special comments 44" minimum height; expectant mothers should not ride

Festival of the Lion King (FastPass+) | Before 11 a.m., after 4 p.m., FastPass+ | ★★★★

Flights of Wonder | Anytime | ★★★★

Kali River Rapids *(FastPass+)* | First or last hour the park is open, FastPass+ | ★★★½
  Special comments You'll get wet; 38" minimum height; expectant mothers should note that ride is bouncy

Kilimanjaro Safaris *(FastPass+)* | At opening, in the 2 hours before closing | ★★★★★

Maharajah Jungle Trek | Anytime | ★★★★

Meet Favorite Disney Pals at Adventurers Outpost *(FastPass+)* | First thing in the morning, after 5 p.m.,
  FastPass+ | ★★★½

The Oasis | Anytime | N/A

Pangani Forest Exploration Trail | Anytime | ★★★★

Primeval Whirl *(FastPass+)* | First or last hour the park is open, FastPass+ | ★★★
  Special comments 48" minimum height; expectant mothers should not ride

Theater in the Wild/*Finding Nemo—The Musical* | Anytime | ★★★★

The Tree of Life/*It's Tough to Be a Bug! (FastPass+)* | Before noon, after 4 p.m., FastPass+ | ★★★★
  Special comment Fright potential

TriceraTop Spin | Before noon, after 3 p.m. | ★★

Wilderness Explorers | Sign up first thing in the morning and complete activities throughout the day. | ★★★★

Wildlife Express Train | Anytime | ★★

DINING INFORMATION—Counter Service

RESTAURANT | LOCATION | QUALITY | VALUE | SELECTIONS

Creature Comforts | Discovery Island near Africa | Fair | C | Disney-themed Starbucks with all the usual suspects:
  coffee drinks, teas, breakfast sandwiches, and pastries

Flame Tree Barbecue | Discovery Island | Excellent | B– | Barbecue-pork sandwich; ribs; smoked-chicken salad;
  jumbo turkey legs; fruit plate; child's plate of baked chicken drumstick, hot dog, chicken sandwich, or PB&J sandwich;
  beer and wine

Harambe Market | Africa | Good | B | Chicken and beef kebabs, curry corn dog, spice-rubbed ribs, each with a side salad;
  South African beer and wine

Kusafiri Coffee Shop and Bakery | Africa | Good | B | Pastries, bagels, hot breakfast wrap, yogurt,
  coffee, cocoa, juice

Pizzafari | Discovery Island | Fair | B | Cheese, pepperoni, and veggie pizzas; meatball sub; pasta; kids' meals

Restaurantosaurus | DinoLand U.S.A. | Good | B+ | Burgers, mac-and-cheese hot dog, chicken nuggets,
  chocolate mousse, cheesecake, kids' meals, beer

Royal Anandapur Tea Company | Asia | Good | B | Hot and iced teas, coffee, lattes, pastries

Yak & Yeti Local Food Cafes | Asia | Fair | B | Crispy honey chicken with steamed rice, Korean stir-fry barbecue
  chicken, ginger chicken salad, roasted-vegetable couscous wrap, Asian chicken sandwich. Kids' menu: chicken tenders,
  PB&J, or cheeseburger with applesauce and carrots

DINING INFORMATION—Full Service

RESTAURANT | MEALS SERVED | LOCATION | PRICE | QUALITY | VALUE

Rainforest Cafe | B-L-D | Park entrance | Moderate | ★★ | ★★ | *Selections* Pasta, turkey wraps,
  coconut shrimp, ribs, brownie cake; breakfast served at this location

Tusker House Restaurant | B-L-D | Africa | Moderate | ★★★ | ★★★
  Selections Rotisserie chicken, couscous, curry, roasted meats; character meals

Yak & Yeti Restaurant | L-D | Asia | Expensive | ★★½ | ★★ | *Selections* Seared miso salmon, glazed duck,
  tempura shrimp

Advance Reservations recommended for Animal Kingdom full-service restaurants; call ☎ 407-WDW-DINE
  (939-3463) or visit disneyworld.disney.go.com/reservations/dining.

GOOD REST AREAS IN DISNEY'S ANIMAL KINGDOM
LOCATION | PLACE | NOTES

Gazebo behind Flame Tree Barbecue | Discovery Island | Follow the path toward the water, along the left side of Flame Tree Barbecue; gazebo has ceiling fans.

Outdoor covered benches near exit from Dinosaur | DinoLand U.S.A. | Gazebo-like structure with nearby water fountain

Seating area adjacent to Dawa Bar | Africa | Refreshments nearby. Outdoors and can be noisy from street performers.

Walkway between Africa and Asia | Between Africa and Asia | Plenty of shaded rest spots, some overlooking streams; refreshments nearby; a favorite of *Unofficial Guide* researchers